CHESHIRE, FIFOOT AND FURMSTON'S

LAW OF
CONTRACT

Fifteenth Edition

M. P. FURMSTON
Bencher of Gray's Inn
Emeritus Professor of Law and Senior Research Fellow
University of Bristol

Historical Introduction
A. W. B. Simpson MA, DCL, JP
Charles and Edith Clyne Professor of Law,
University of Michigan

OXFORD
UNIVERSITY PRESS

OXFORD

UNIVERSITY PRESS

Great Clarendon Street, Oxford OX2 6DP

Oxford University Press is a department of the University of Oxford.
It furthers the University's objective of excellence in research, scholarship,
and education by publishing worldwide in

Oxford New York

Auckland Cape Town Dar es Salaam Hong Kong Karachi
Kuala Lumpur Madrid Melbourne Mexico City Nairobi
New Delhi Shanghai Taipei Toronto

With offices in

Argentina Austria Brazil Chile Czech Republic France Greece
Guatemala Hungary Italy Japan Poland Portugal Singapore
South Korea Switzerland Thailand Turkey Ukraine Vietnam

Oxford is a registered trade mark of Oxford University Press
in the UK and in certain other countries

Published in the United States
by Oxford University Press Inc., New York

© Oxford University Press 2007

British Library Cataloguing in Publication Data
Data available

Library of Congress Cataloging in Publication Data
Data available

Typeset by RefineCatch Limited, Bungay, Suffolk
Printed in Great Britain
on acid-free paper by
Ashford Colour Press Ltd., Gosport, Hants.

ISBN 978–0–19–928756–7

7 9 10 8 6

PREFACE TO THE FIFTEENTH EDITION

The first edition of this book was published in 1945, and over the following 60 years a further thirteen editions were published by Butterworths. This is the first edition of the book to be published by Oxford University Press, and all those concerned with the production of the edition have been friendly, courteous, and extremely helpful.

There have been important decisions of the House of Lords in *Actionstrength v International Glass Engineering, Shogun Finance v Hudson, HIH v Chase Manhattan Bank, Farley v Skinner,* and *Royal Bank of Scotland v Ettridge.* There have of course been many decisions of lower courts of interest, of which the decisions of the Court of Appeal in *The Great Peace* and *Baird Textile Holdings v Marks & Spencer* are perhaps particularly worthy of notice.

One of the most important developments in contract law in recent years is the increasing interest shown by contract lawyers in developments in other jurisdictions. For English lawyers, this means not only other common law systems, which have always been of interest but also developments in great civil law systems. This is reflected in the work on the UNIDROIT Principles for International Commercial Contracts and the Principles of European Contract Law. Whether these developments will be followed by the adoption of a European Contract Code remains to be seen.

In considering changes to this edition, I decided that the time had come to delete the chapter on quasi contracts. This was entirely appropriate in 1945 but now that restitution is clearly a subject in its own right, much of which falls outside the boundaries of the law of contract, it seems an anachronism. Questions along the boundary between contract and restitution continue of course to receive attention in the text.

My colleague, Professor Brenda Sufrin, has kindly revised part of Chapter 10 which deals with the modern law of competition. I am very grateful to her and also to Katrina Yates who did invaluable work in finding references on new cases and to Margaret Baillie who as usual has struggled with remarkable success with my awful handwriting and incoherent dictation, not made easier by the fact that, for much of the relevant time, we were on opposite sides of the earth. My wife, my ten children and my five grandchildren continue to provide support, encouragement, and patience as have new generations of students around the world to whom I have tried to explain the problems which are discussed in the text.

M P Furmston
Bristol
August 2006

CONTENTS

LIST OF CASES

TABLE OF STATUTES

Page references in **bold** indicate that the section is reproduced in full

1 HISTORICAL INTRODUCTION

SUMMARY

A THE MEDIAEVAL LAW[1]

English contract law as we know it today developed around a form of action known as the action of *assumpsit*, which came into prominence in the early sixteenth century as a remedy for the breach of informal agreements reached by word of mouth—by 'parol'.[2] As a coherent court-centred system the common law itself, the royal law of

---

[1] Bibliographical note: The principal secondary literature on the history of English contract law comprises: Ames *Lectures on Legal History and Miscellaneous Legal Essays* (1913); Barbour 'The History of Contract in Early English Equity' in vol IV, *Oxford Studies in Social and Legal History* (1914); Fifoot *History and Sources of the Common Law, Tort and Contract* (1949); Holdsworth *A History of English Law* (1922–66) esp vols III and VIII; Kiralfy *The Action on the Case* (1951); Simpson *A History of the Common Law of Contract: The Rise of Assumpsit* (1975); Stoljar *A History of Contract at Common Law* (1975); Atiyah *The Rise and Fall of Freedom of Contract* (1979); Cornish and Clark *Law and Society in England, 1750–1950* (1989); Ibbetson *A Historical Introduction to the Law of Obligations* (1999). There is also an extensive periodical literature, and much material is available in the publications of the Selden Society. Baker and Milsom *Sources of English Legal History* (1986) reproduce many early cases.

[2] The account given in this introduction can only pick out certain salient developments, and is kept as free from technical detail as possible. The student can also usefully start by reading Baker *An Introduction to English Legal History* (1990), esp chs 9, 10 and 16, and Milsom *Historical Foundations of the Common Law*, esp chs 10–12.

the central courts, is much older, a product of the twelfth century. The early common law was largely concerned with serious crime and land tenure, and Glanvill, writing in about 1180, tells us that in his time, 'it is not the custom of the court of the Lord King to protect private agreements'.[3] Three centuries were to pass before the common law courts acquired a general jurisdiction over both formal and informal contracts. But the limitations upon the scope of the common law of contract at any given time did not mean that there then existed no forum for contractual business, but merely that remedies had to be sought elsewhere. For the common law evolved in a society served by a bewildering diversity of courts outside the common law system, enforcing a variety of bodies of law. Thus, there were county courts, borough courts, courts of markets and fairs, courts of universities, courts of the Church, courts of manors, and courts of privileged places such as the Cinque Ports. Many such courts handled contractual business.[4] In addition the Court of Chancery in the fifteenth century developed an extensive contractual jurisdiction. The story of the growth of the common law, in contract law and elsewhere, is the story of the expansion of the common law courts' jurisdiction at the expense of other jurisdictions, and the consequential development—whether by invention or reception—of common law with which to regulate the newly acquired business.

Contracts under seal

Mediaeval law was a formulary system developed around the writs which a litigant could obtain from the chancery to initiate litigation in the royal courts, and each writ gave rise to a particular manner of proceeding or form of action, with its individual rules and procedures.[5] It is convenient, in setting out the elements of mediaeval contract law, to differentiate between formal and informal contracts;[6] not surprisingly formal contracts were absorbed into the common law first. Then, as now, important contracts were made in writing, and it was the practice to authenticate written documents by sealing them. Contracts thus entered into soon became generally actionable at common law by one of two forms of action. The action of covenant, which came into common use in the thirteenth century, originated as an action for the specific performance of agreements to do something, such as to build a house, as opposed to agreements to pay a definite sum of money; it developed into an action for damages, assessed by a jury, for the wrong of breaking a covenant. In the early fourteenth century this action came to be limited to agreements under seal, and hence the term 'covenant', originally meaning simply 'agreement', came to mean 'agreement under seal' as it still does. Where there was a formal agreement under seal to pay a definite

---

[3] Glanvill X, 18.

[4] For examples, see Fifoot *History and Sources* ch 13, and Helmholz 91 LQR 406.

[5] Though in some respects now superseded, the best introduction is still Maitland *The Forms of Action at Common Law* (1954).

[6] For a fuller account see Simpson *History* Pt I.

sum of money—that is a debt—the appropriate form of action was debt 'on an obligation'. Such agreements were looked upon as grants of debts, and the term 'obligation' or 'bond' was used to describe the sealed document which generated the duty to pay. The formality involved in sealing a document should not be over-stressed—the seal might be very elaborate, or a mere blob of wax impressed with a finger nail, but a sealed instrument was quite essential.

Penal bonds

In practice, for reasons which are not fully understood, the action of covenant was little used; instead, important agreements were commonly reduced to agreements whereby the parties entered into bonds to pay penal sums of money unless they carried out their side of the bargain. Thus if C wished to lend D £100, D would execute a bond binding himself to pay C £200 on a certain day; the bond would have a condition that it became void (a condition of defeasance) if £100 was paid before the day, and D would hand over this bond as he received the loan of £100. In, for example, a sale of land at a price of £100, the seller would execute a bond binding himself to pay a penal sum *unless* he conveyed the land as agreed, and the buyer similarly would bind himself to pay a penalty *unless* he paid the price; disputes as to whether the condition had been performed or not (and the condition contained the real agreement) were triable by jury. Such penal bonds with conditional defeasance could be adapted to cover virtually any transaction, and were widely used as con-tractual instruments; they began to pass out of use in the late seventeenth century, when the Court of Chancery began to give relief against contracts involving penal provisions.[7] Until this development the vast preponderance of the common law of contract concerned bonds and the rules which governed them.

This law was flexible though tough, sometimes to the point of harshness; it was also highly developed in a complex case law. A creditor, for example, who lost the bond, or allowed the seal to come off, was remediless; a debtor who paid but failed to have the bond defaced remained liable. The debtor who defaulted was very much at the mercy of his creditor, who could, if he wished, have him imprisoned indefinitely for default. The institution, with its topsy-turvy treatment of the underlying agree-ment, gave rise to much law on conditions, for it was in the condition to the bond that the real agreement lurked. Hence, in mediaeval law such matters as illegality and impossibility are largely dealt with in connection with conditions—is an illegal or impossible condition void? Some of this old law was later to be absorbed into the law of assumpsit, and the modern rules outlawing penal contracts originate in the seventeenth century's attack on the penal bond.[8]

---

[7] For a fuller account see Yale in 79 Selden Society, esp at 7–30. See also Henderson 18 Am J of Legal Hist, 298.

[8] See pp 786–792, below.

Informal contracts

So far as informal or parol agreements are concerned mediaeval common law was more restrictive.[9] One general limitation was financial; under the Statute of Gloucester (1278) an attempt was made to limit claims in the common law courts to those involving more than forty shillings, then a very large sum. This could be and was evaded; more serious were the restrictions developed by the courts themselves and associated with the relevant forms of action. Covenant, as we have seen, could not be used on parol agreements at all, and, hence, never grew into a general contractual remedy. Debt, and detinue, could, however, be brought: the former (known as a debt *sur contract*) for claims to specific sums owed by informal transaction, for example, the price of goods sold, or money lent; the latter to enforce claims to chattels due, for example, a horse sold or lent. These two actions covered a very considerable area of informal contract law—sale of goods, bailment, loans of money. In a money economy a debt is the normal outstanding obligation, and so an action to recover debts will cover a very large field of demand. There were, however, serious gaps in the law; in particular, there was no action for breach of an informal agreement to *do* something, for example, build a house. Thus, there was no action for failure to convey land, though the price of land sold could be recovered by debt. More generally, the method of trial in debt and detinue on informal contracts was not jury trial, but compurgation. The defendant could swear an oath that he owed nothing, and bring eleven others to support his oath, and if they carried out the ritual correctly the action was lost; perjury might imperil the soul, but no temporal remedy existed. In the sixteenth century compurgation (wager of law) came to be regarded as farcical, and oath swearers could indeed be hired for a modest fee.[10] There existed other apparent defects in the law of debt and detinue; rules developed by the mediaeval courts came to be attached to these forms of action, and were immune from frontal attack. For example, executors were not liable on informal contracts; the debt died with the debtor. Informal guarantees and promises of marriage gifts were not actionable by debt, and the latter situation, in particular, provoked controversy.

When the common law courts provided no remedy, or one inadequate in some respect, the litigant had to go elsewhere, and in many cases this may not have been an unsatisfactory alternative. But it is clear that there existed in the fifteenth century a considerable demand for the intervention of royal justice in areas not covered by the common law, in particular in the case of informal contracts, and this encouraged the fifteenth-century chancellors to develop equitable remedies to supplement the

---

[9] For a fuller account see Simpson *History*, esp pp 47–52 and 136–198; and on sale see Milsom 77 LQR 257 and Fifoot *History and Sources* ch 10.

[10] For an account see Baker [1971] CLJ at 228–230.

common law.[11] This may have been a factor which spurred the common law courts into taking action themselves to remedy the defects of their own system; although the maxim is that equity follows the law, the historical process has often been the reverse.

B THE ORIGIN OF ASSUMPSIT

The mechanism by which the old common law of informal contracts was supplemented, and eventually superseded, was an extremely curious one; it involved the use of a form of action which would not naturally appear to be concerned with contract at all. Back in the fourteenth century the common law courts developed a general jurisdiction over wrongs or torts (then called trespasses) in which the Crown had a special interest, typically those involving breach of the royal peace.[12] Actions of trespass (ie tort actions) were commenced by a writ form which was flexible, and writs could be drafted which were adapted to the special circumstances of the case—these were called writs 'on the case'. The method of trial in such actions was trial by jury, and the remedy damages, which the jury assessed. Round about 1370, it came to be settled that such tort actions on the case could be brought to remedy purely private wrongs, not involving breach of the royal peace or any special Crown interest. Among actions brought about this time there were some where the plaintiff relied in his writ on an allegation that the defendant had entered into an informal arrangement with him, and then by misconduct caused damage in a way not envisaged by the transaction. Thus, in the case of *Skyrne v Butolf* (1367),[13] the plaintiff sued a doctor to whom he had come to find a cure for the ringworm. He alleged that the defendant:

> . . . undertook (*assumpsit*), in London, in return for a certain sum of money previously paid
> into his hand, competently to cure [the plaintiff] of a certain infirmity.

Having set out these special circumstances, he went on to allege that the defendant had so negligently performed his cure as to cause damage. This form of trespass on the case has come to be called the action of assumpsit, the name being derived from the allegation in the Latin pleadings that he undertook (*assumpsit*). The early examples all involve negligent misconduct after an undertaking.[14]

---

[11] Barbour's account of this development has not been superseded, though published as long ago as 1914.

[12] Milsom's articles in 74 LQR 195, 407, 561, have superseded all earlier work on the evolution of trespass and case.

[13] YB 2 Ric 2 (Ames Series) 223. For other examples see Fifoot *History and Sources* ch 14.

[14] For a fuller account see Simpson *History* Pt II, ch 1.

Misfeasance and nonfeasance

Such trespass or tort actions could no doubt be viewed as involving a liability based upon the breach of an informal agreement, and as being (in our terms) contract actions. But as tort actions they did not, of course, require the production by the plaintiff of any formal evidence under seal, and this could be exploited by lawyers who wished to sue on informal agreements at common law. In the case of *Watton v Brinth* (1400),[15] an attempt was made to bring such an action against a builder who had undertaken to build a house, but done nothing at all to fulfil his undertaking. This amounted to an attempt to achieve by trespass action what one could not achieve by action of covenant—sue on an agreement to do something without producing an instrument under seal. The court rejected the action; as was said in 1425[16] in a similar case by Martin J: 'Verily if this action be maintainable on this matter, for every broken covenant in the world a man shall have an action of trespass'. To prevent this a curious compromise was reached: it came to be the basic doctrine of the fifteenth century that assumpsit lay for *misfeasance*, for doing something badly, but not for *nonfeasance*, doing nothing at all. Though attacked and qualified, and indeed at times rejected, the nonfeasance doctrine survived for over a century.

The action for breach of promise

The doctrine of nonfeasance was abandoned in the early sixteenth century in a series of cases[17] culminating in *Pickering v. Thoroughgood* (1533)[18]—for reasons which are still not wholly clear, but may owe something to rivalry with Chancery or to the church courts.[19] Spelman J in that case said:

> And in some books a difference has been taken between nonfeasance and malfeasance; thus on the one an action of covenant lies, and on the other an action on the case lies. This is no distinction in reason, for if a carpenter for £100 covenants with me to make me a house, and does not make it before the day assigned, so that I am deprived of lodging, I shall have an action for this nonfeasance just as well as if he had made it badly.

This was a momentous development, for the common law now had a form of action whereby in principle any undertaking could be sued upon: the action had become an action for breach of promise, and the allegation of an undertaking was indeed commonly coupled with one of a promise. The action could now remedy breach of

---

[15] YB 2 Hen 4, fo 3, pl 9, Fifoot *History and Sources* p 340.

[16] YB 3 Hen 6, fo 36, pl 33, *Fifoot* p 341.

[17] See, in particular, *Orwell v Mortoft* or *The Case of the Sale of Barley* (1505) YB 20 Hen 7, fo 8, pl 18; *Anon* Keil f 69 and 77 (*Fifoot* p 351) and the note, properly dated 1498, in YB 21 Hen 7, fo 41, pl 66 (*Fifoot* p 353).

[18] From Justice Spelman's MS Reports, 93 YB Selden Society 4 (*Pykeryng v Thurgoode*).

[19] See Helmholtz 91 LQR 406.

any informal agreement. It was triable by jury and led to the award of compensatory damages. This new departure gave rise to two problems, which preoccupied the courts in the sixteenth century. The first involved the relationship between assumpsit and the older forms of action, particularly debt *sur contract*. The second involved the evolution of a body of doctrine which would define which promises were actionable, and which not, a doctrine to define the scope of promissory liability.

C ASSUMPSIT AND DEBT

Attempts were soon made to use assumpsit not to fill gaps in the law, but to replace the action of debt *sur contract*; the primary purpose of doing so was to deprive the defendant of his right to wage his law, and force him to submit to trial by jury. *Pickering v Thoroughgood* (1533) is itself such a case, and from the 1520s onward the King's Bench allowed the plaintiff election between the older and newer remedies. By the 1570s the Court of Common Pleas took the same course, but in the late years of the sixteenth century the practice became a matter of acute disagreement between the courts of King's Bench and Common Pleas; the former court allowing assumpsit to supersede debt *sur contract*, whilst the judges of the latter court insisted that this was improper. The history of this dispute is complex[20] and to some extent still controversial; its complexity is increased by the general acceptance in sixteenth-century law of a principle, variously formulated, whereby action on the case ought not to be used simply as alternatives to older forms of actions. Great ingenuity was expended by progressives in reconciling this dogma with allowing election of remedies in practice.

Slade's Case

The dispute was settled in *Slade's Case* (1602)[21] after prolonged argument, and the view which triumphed was that of the King's Bench. The principal significance of this case was that by allowing plaintiffs to use assumpsit in place of debt *sur contract* (which in practice they would always choose to do) it produced a situation in which assumpsit became the general remedy on informal contracts, whether the plaintiff was complaining about a failure to pay a definite sum of money, or a failure to do something else—such as build a house. After *Slade's Case* the law of informal agreements was the law of a single form of action. About the same time another similar

---

[20] The development has given rise to a considerable literature. See, in particular, Ames *Lectures* pp 147 ff; Simpson 74 LQR 382; Lücke 81 LQR 422, 539, 82 LQR 81; Baker [1971] CLJ 51, 213; Simpson *History* pp 282 ff; Baker 94 Selden Society 255 ff; Ibbetson 41 Camb LJ 142, 4 OJLS 295, in the latter piece attributing to me at n 1 a view I do not hold.
[21] 4 Co Rep 91a, Yelv 21, Moore KB 433, 667; Baker gives further texts in [1971] CLJ 51.

dispute between the courts was resolved in *Pinchon's Case* (1611)[22] when it was held that liability to pay debts, now enforceable in assumpsit, passed to the executors of the debtor; this case began the process of making simple contract liability passively transmissible.

D THE DOCTRINE OF CONSIDERATION

The other principal achievement of the sixteenth and early seventeenth centuries was the evolution of a body of doctrine to define the scope of the newly recognised promissory liability. Where assumpsit was merely taking over a long-established liability, previously remedied by debt *sur contract*—such as liability to pay the price of goods sold—new doctrine was not urgently required; where innovation in the form of recognition of new contractual liabilities was involved, it was. The answer given to the problems posed was the doctrine of 'consideration', which is found in assumpsit cases around the mid-sixteenth century.[23] A consideration meant a motivating reason, and the essence of the doctrine was the idea that the actionability of a parol promise should depend upon an examination of the reason why the promise was made. The reason for the promise became the reason why it should be enforced, or not enforced. In contemporary thought a promise was a declaration of will, and the effect of the doctrine was to deprive a bare declaration of will of legal effect. Only a declaration of will supported by a good reason or motive bound the declarer to performance.

Consideration analysed

This basic idea was capable of great elaboration in two respects. First, the courts could and did develop, case by case, a vast body of learning as to which reasons were good or sufficient, and which not. Would a promise in consideration of natural love and affection to a kinsman be actionable? Would a promise to pay a debt, in consideration that a debt was owed? Would a promise in consideration of a nominal payment? Here what starts life as a list of good considerations eventually comes to be summed up in terms of a general principle, the first attempt to formulate such a principle being found in Coke's argument in *Stone v Wythipol* (1588):[24]

---

[22] 9 Co Rep 86b, 2 Brown 1 137, Cro Jac 293.

[23] The history of consideration is controversial; in addition to the works listed at p 1, n 1, above, see Holmes *The Common Law* Lect VII; Salmond *Essays in Jurisprudence and Legal History* pp 187 ff; Milsom [1954] CLJ 105; Barton 85 LQR 372; Baker 94 Seldon Society 255 ff. Baker in Arnold on the Laws and Customs of England 336. The earliest assumpsit case in the printed reports to mention consideration *eo nomine* is *Joscelin v Shelton* (1557) 3 Leon 4, Benl 57, Moo KB 51: the consideration was a future marriage, and the case concerned a promised marriage gift or dowry.

[24] Cro Eliz 126; 1 Leon 113; Owen 94; Latch 21, 78 ER 383.

. . . every consideration that doth charge the defendant in an assumpsit must be to the benefit
of the defendant or charge of the plaintiff, and no case can be put out of this rule.

The reference to a 'charge' is an echo of the passage in St Germain's *Doctor and
Student* (1530), where the author, in a critical discussion of contract law, offers the
idea of induced reliance as an alternative theory of promissory liability to an analysis
in terms of consideration.[25] But by 1588 detriment consideration had uneasily
absorbed the idea that a promise should bind if the promisee had been induced to rely
upon it.

Secondly, the courts evolved or adapted an analysis in temporal terms of the
relationship between promise and consideration, which is first found in *Hunt v Bate*
(1568).[26] A promise might be motivated by something in the past, for example, a past
favour: such a *past* (or executed) consideration was, in general, bad. A consideration
might be some continuous state of affairs—such as the existence of a marriage—and
this was a *continuous* consideration, and good. A *present* consideration meant an
act or promise contemporaneous with the promise, and a *future* (or executory) consideration—something yet to happen, such as a marriage not yet celebrated. Into
this analysis, which in part survives, was fitted the important rule that an actionable
counter-promise would rank as a good consideration.

Mutual promises

This rule was settled by 1589, when in *Strangborough v Warner*[27] it was said: 'Note,
that a promise against a promise will maintain an action on the case', and seems to
have originated in connection with bets, the earliest case being *West v Stowel* (1577);[28]
plainly unless an unperformed counter-promise is a good consideration, a bet can
never be enforced. When the plaintiff's promise was relied upon as a consideration it
had to be a present consideration—ie contemporaneous with the defendant's promise,
and as in the case of other present considerations the plaintiff did not have to perform
before he could sue; in the case of a future consideration performance had to be
shown, for without performance no consideration yet existed. Seventeenth-century
case law settled that one party to such an agreement could not withdraw without the
consent of the other, and thus it came to be law that wholly executory contracts were
both binding and actionable.

But this was a highly unsatisfactory rule, for often it was not the intention that one
party could sue without performing his side of the agreement, and a right of action
represents a bird in the bush, as compared with actual performance—a bird in the
hand. In time the courts evolved an intricate body of law whereby mutual promises
were commonly treated as mutually dependent, the obligation to perform one side

---

[25] 91 YB Selden Society 230.   [26] 3 Dyer 272a. See Simpson *History* pp 452–465.
[27] 4 Leon 3.   [28] 2 Leon 154

being treated as conditional upon performance of the other.[29] The involved old learning on dependent and independent promises was summed up in the notes to *Pordage v Cole* (1669)[30] and *Cutter v Powell* (1795).[31]

Origins of consideration

Whether the doctrine of consideration was an indigenous product, or in part derived from the doctrine of *causa promissionis* of canon or civil law, has long been a matter of controversy, and it cannot be said that its pedigree has yet been explained in a fully satisfactory way.[32] Those who have seen it as a purely homespun product have sought its origin either in a doctrine associated with debt in mediaeval case law (the doctrine of *quid pro quo*),[33] or in the acceptance by the sixteenth-century judges of a notion that only 'bargains' (ie commercial contracts of exchange) should be enforced,[34] or in a transmutation of the need to show damage in a tort action into detriment suffered as a form of consideration in a contract action.[35] The opposing view,[36] which the present writer has argued at length elsewhere, relates the early doctrine of consideration in assumpsit to the earlier doctrine of consideration in relation to uses of land (the ancestor of the modern trust) and sees its ultimate source in canon and civil law, though the precise mechanism of the reception remains problematical.

E THE SEVENTEENTH AND EIGHTEENTH CENTURIES

The structure of informal contract law established in the Elizabethan period was essentially simple; as it was said in *Golding's Case* (1586):[37]

> In every action upon the case upon a promise there are three things considerable, consideration, promise and breach of promise.

In essence this simple structure was not radically altered until the nineteenth century, when the essentially one-sided or *unilateral* concept of an actionable promise was supplanted by the more complex conception of an actionable contract, a bilateral transaction. The seventeenth and eighteenth centuries saw an extensive development

---

[29] See Stoljar *History* ch 12 and the same author in 2 Sydney L Rev 217.
[30] 1 Wms Saund 319.   [31] 6 Term Rep 320.
[32] See Simpson *History* Pt II, chs 4–7 for a full account. See also Baker in *On the Laws and Customs of England: Essays in Honor of Samuel E Thorne* (ed Morris S Arnold, 1981).
[33] Notably Holmes.
[34] Strenuously argued by Fifoot himself; see also Shatwell 1 Sydney L Rev 289.
[35] In different forms argued by Holdsworth and, recently, by Milsom.
[36] In modern times first argued by Salmond.   [37] 2 Leon 71.

of commercial law and reception of the law merchant, but in basic informal contract law what was involved was largely elaboration, rather than innovation. There were, however, certain areas of significant development, particularly in relation to the place of formality in contract law and to the enforcement of duties imposed rather by law than by the consent of the parties.

Relief against penalties

So far as the first is concerned, assumpsit began life as an action on parol, that is to say verbal, promises, and its evolution into a general promissory remedy, limited by the doctrine of consideration, left the old law of formal written contracts under seal, appropriate to commercial and social contracts of real significance, untouched. Such contracts were actionable quite irrespective of consideration, and were normally embodied in penal bonds. Though never wholly superseded, the traditional system of using formal contracts under seal for important transactions received a serious blow in the seventeenth century when the Court of Chancery began to grant relief against the penal element in such contracts. By the eighteenth century the principle had emerged that, 'Equity suffers not advantage to be taken of a penalty or forfeiture, where compensation can be made'.[38] This approach, soon adopted by the common law courts, canonised the compensatory principle in formal contracts. It had already been long accepted in assumpsit; hence the penal bond came to be less used. At the same time assumpsit, though in origin an action on verbal promises, could in principle be used where promises were *evidenced* in written documents, such as letters. Such use was no doubt encouraged by the increase in the practice of authenticating documents by signature or mark, and the general increase in the use of writing.

Statute of Frauds

Against this background was passed the Statute of Frauds (1677).[39] The unregulated character of seventeenth-century jury trial had made it, in the opinion of some, too easy for plaintiffs in assumpsit to bring actions on verbal promises inadequately proved; if the old system of wager of law had unduly favoured defendants, its supersession by *Slade's Case* unduly favoured plaintiffs. The remedy adopted was to require formality, in the new form of writing under signature, for actions on the more important agreements—for example on agreements to transfer interests in land, and contracts for the sale of goods worth more than ten pounds. The statute, an essentially reactionary measure, produced a curious list of agreements which needed writing, and was from the start supplemented by the equitable doctrine of part performance. In the eighteenth century it provoked Lord Mansfield's rational, if heretical, suggestion,

---

[38] Francis *Maxims of Equity* (1728).   [39] 29 Car 2 c 3.

that the general structure of contract law needed revision, the doctrine of consideration being confined to contracts by word of mouth (where it originated), whilst written contracts under signature ought, like contracts authenticated by the more ancient seal, to be actionable without proof of consideration. But this approach was emphatically rejected in the opinion of the judges in *Rann v Hughes* (1778):[40]

> All contracts are by the laws of England distinguished into agreements by specialty [ie under seal] and agreements by parol; nor is there any such third class as some of the counsel have endeavoured to maintain, as contracts in writing. If they be merely written and not specialties, they are parol, and a consideration must be proved.

Thus was an opportunity to rationalise the law defeated.

Quasi-contract

The seventeenth century also saw the extension of assumpsit into what came to be called quasi-contract.[41] The pleaders of the late-sixteenth century evolved a form of assumpsit which came to be known as *indebitatus assumpsit*, where the plaintiff averred that the defendant was indebted to him (*indebitatus*) in a certain sum, and had promised to pay this sum. This was appropriate when a debtor was sued in the new action, and after *Slade's Case* (1602) sanctioned this use of assumpsit it came to be settled that in *indebitatus assumpsit* the details of the transaction generating the debt need only be set out in a summary form—the defendant would be said to be indebted 'for the price of goods sold and delivered', 'for money lent', 'for work and services performed'. These were known as the common *indebitatus* counts, and the promise to pay relied upon was normally implied only, and need not be proved. *Indebitatus assumpsit* was contrasted with *special assumpsit*, a form of pleading where the details of the transaction were set out 'in detail' (specially). Now the action of debt had laid in the old law in any situation where a precise sum was due by law, whether the obligation arose from agreement, or by operation of law. In such cases the defendant was indebted, and at least from the late-seventeenth century onwards *indebitatus assumpsit* could be used, as in *London City Corpn v Goree* (1676)[42] where the action was for customary wharfage dues. This extended assumpsit to wholly fictitious promises. In addition, a standard count was evolved in *indebitatus assumpsit* to recover money 'had and received to the plaintiff's use', the earliest successful attempt being *Rooke v Rooke* (1610).[43] The evolution of *indebitatus assumpsit* provided the courts with a procedure whereby, in the guise of promissory or contractual liability, any

---

[40] 4 Bro Parl Cas 27, 7 Term Rep 350n.
[41] For fuller discussion see Jackson *The History of Quasi-Contract in English Law*, in addition to the works cited at p 1, n 1, above.
[42] Lev 174, 3 Keb 677, 1 Vent 298, Freem 433.
[43] Cro Jac 245, 1 Rolle 391, Moo KB 854.

obligation to pay money which the law was prepared to recognise might be enforced; it opened the way to the assertion by Lord Mansfield in the great case of *Moses v Macferlan* (1760)[44] that an action of *indebitatus assumpsit* on an implied promise could be brought whenever natural justice and equity required a defendant to return money. The courts also evolved a form of special assumpsit which lay on agreements to pay reasonable prices or remuneration—actions on a *quantum meruit* or *quantum valebat*. In the old law debt did not lie in the absence of any agreement for a definite sum, and this excluded *indebitatus assumpsit*, which presupposed a debt; eventually the rule changed, and either special or *indebitatus assumpsit* could be used. Such actions again tended to blur the distinction between genuine promissory liability, and liability on implied or fictional promises, and thus laid the foundation for the extensive use of the concept of an implied promise in English contract law.

F THE NINETEENTH CENTURY

The nineteenth century is usually regarded as the classical age of English contract law, and this for two reasons. The first is that the century witnessed an extensive development of the principles and structure of contract law into essentially the form which exists today, and this process appears to modern lawyers more significant when linked to the belief (which is perhaps too readily accepted) that until the Industrial Revolution contract law was somewhat crude and inadequate. The second involves a change in the attitude of thinking lawyers to contract. In previous years lawyers, in so far as they troubled themselves at all, conceived of contract law primarily as an adjunct to property law. In the nineteenth century a powerful school of thought, originating in the work of Adam Smith, saw in the extension of voluntary social cooperation through contract law, and in particular through 'freedom of contract', a principal road to social improvement and human happiness, and one distinct from the static conditions involved in the possession of private property. This line of thought, variously developed, led first to an increased and self-conscious emphasis on a policy summed up in the words of Sir George Jessel in *Printing and Numerical Registering Co v Sampson* (1875):[45]

> . . . if there is one thing more than another which public policy requires, it is that men of full age and competent understanding shall have the utmost liberty in contracting, and that their contracts, when entered into freely and voluntarily, shall be held sacred and shall be enforced by Courts of Justice.

Yet the period also saw much statutory interference in private contracts.

---

[44] 2 Burr 1005.   [45] LR 19 Eq 462.

Secondly, an increase in the moral dignity of contract encouraged thinking lawyers to feel that contract law was of central significance in the scheme of civilised legal regulation. This development lives on to this day in the presence of contract law, particularly the law governing the formation of contract, in the core of legal education.

Although many of the nineteenth-century authorities on contract are familiar as timeless living law, the period has, until recently, been relatively little studied from a historical point of view, and the doctrinal history is, indeed, still inadequately understood. It is clear, however, that the basic structure of the law of assumpsit, as established in the sixteenth and seventeenth centuries, remained generally unaltered until the nineteenth century, which saw a shift in emphasis from the essentially unilateral notion of a promise, to the conception of a contract—a bilateral conception—which generated rights and duties in the parties. This process was accompanied by a very remarkable elaboration in contractual doctrine, and the new doctrine was superimposed upon the old ideas derived from earlier case law. To a very considerable extent the initial impetus for this elaboration came from the treatise writers on contract, whose existence was a new phenomenon in the history of English contract law. In recent times there have been a number of attempts to explain the reasons for this development, but to date no consensus has emerged among historians; the increase in the sheer quality of contract law is an aspect of the history of the control over civil juries, and this too is not yet fully understood.[46]

For until 1790, when John Powell published his *Essay upon the Law of Contracts and Agreements*, there existed no systematic treatise expounding the English law of contract, and no tradition of writing such works.[47] Powell set out 'to discover the general rules and principles of natural and civil equity' on which the case law of contract was founded, and he started a tradition in which the present treatise stands. Many contract treatises appear in the nineteenth century, of which perhaps the most celebrated were Chitty (1826), Addison (1847), Leake (1867), Pollock (1875) and Anson (1879). The new literature, lacking a native tradition, leant heavily upon contractual writers in the civil (ie Roman) law tradition and in particular upon the work of R J Pothier, the great eighteenth-century French legal scholar whose work, a product of the natural law tradition, profoundly influenced the French Civil Code. Pothier's *Treatise on the Law of Obligations* was translated and published in England in 1806, after original publication in 1761–64. Appearing as it did at a critical period, the new literature led to a partial reception of ideas derived from the civil law of continental Europe, many of

---

[46] There is a major study by P S Atiyah *The Rise and Fall of Freedom of Contract* (1979); though it has not convinced all commentators, and a valuable survey by Cornish and Clark *Law and Society in England, 1750–1950* (1989) 197–226 with bibliography. See Nicholas 48 Tulane L Rev 946; Horwitz 87 Harvard L Rev 917; Simpson 91 LQR 247, 46 U Chicago L Rev 533; 1 OJLS 265; Danzig 4 J Legal Studies 249; Baker [1979] Current Legal Problems 17. See also Fifoot *Judge and Jurist in the Reign of Victoria* (1959) and the entertaining theory of Gilmore *The Death of Contract* (1974).

[47] On the evolution of the treatise see Simpson 48 U Chicago L Rev 632.

which, adapted through the case law, remain as contractual categories, as chapter heads in the books, today.

Offer and acceptance

Thus the doctrine of *offer and acceptance* first clearly emerges in the case of *Adams v Lindsell*[48] in 1818 as a mechanism for settling the moment of contracting in agreement by correspondence; it became a central doctrine, and in 1882[49] Sir William Anson was able to claim that, 'Every expression of a common intention arrived at by the parties is ultimately reducible to question and answer'. The doctrine derives ultimately from a title in *Justinian's Digest*,[50] which distinguishes between 'pollicitations' and 'promises', the former being promises made and not accepted; it first appears in English law in Powell's treatise in 1790. Eventually, the doctrine was even applied, albeit somewhat unhappily, to unilateral contracts in *Carlill v Carbolic Smoke Ball Co* (1893).[51] The relationship between the new doctrine of offer and acceptance and the old requirement of consideration, which was re-emphasised as an essential in *Eastwood v Kenyon* (1840),[52] was, and remains, difficult simply because two layers of development in contractual thought are involved.

Intention to contract

Another new development was the reception of a requirement that there must be *an intention to create legal relations* for there to be a binding contract. The earlier common law scorned such a requirement for 'of the intent inward of the heart man's law cannot judge'.[53] The doctrine, in one form or another, was commonplace in continental legal thought, and versions are found in Leake (1867) and in Pollock's influential treatise (1875), the latter version being derived from the German jurist Savigny. It was received in the case law in *Carlill v Carbolic Smoke Ball Co* (1893) and accepted by the House of Lords in *Heilbut, Symons & Co v Buckleton* (1913).[54]

The will theory

More radically, the nineteenth-century case law came to emphasise what is variously called the 'consensus' or 'will' theory of contract, exhaustively analysed in Atiyah *The Rise and Fall of Freedom of Contract*. This asserts that contractual obligations are by definition self-imposed: hence any factor showing lack of consent is fatal to the existence of a contract, and, conversely, the rules governing the formation of contract

---

[48] 1 B & Ald 681. [49] Anson *Principles of the English Law of Contract* (2nd edn) p 15.
[50] *D* 50.12.3. [51] [1892] 2 QB 484; affd [1893] 1 QB 256. See Simpson 14 JLS 345.
[52] 11 Ad & El 438. [53] St Germain *Doctor and Student* Bk III, ch VI, see s V.
[54] [1913] AC 30. See Simpson 14 Journal of Legal Studies 345 for a full illustrated discussion of this.

are all conceived of as designed to differentiate cases of true *consensus*, where two wills become one will, from cases where *consensus* is lacking. In terms of the functions of the court this theory finds expression in the idea that the exclusive task of a court in contract cases is to discover what the parties have agreed and give effect to it, except in cases of mistake, duress or illegality. This approach was not novel in English law, but it received a new emphasis from the text-writers, under the influence of foreign models; as Evans wrote in 1806:[55]

> As every contract derives its effect from the intention of the parties, that intention, as expressed, or inferred, must be the ground of every decision respecting its operation and extent, and the grand object of consideration in every question with regard to its construction.

It also conformed to the fashionable theories of the political economists.

Mistake

The ramifications of the will theory were extensive, and still influence both the law and the form in which it is expressed. Perhaps its most striking expression in nineteenth-century legal development is to be found in cases dealing with *mistake*, for, given the premise, 'Error is the greatest defect that can occur in contract . . .'[56] in consequence a doctrine of mistake follows inevitably. A good example of a case decided under the influence of a full-blown *consensus* theory is *Cundy v Lindsay* (1878),[57] the well-known case on error as to the person; a more recent conquest may be *Bell v Lever Bros*[58] (1932). A more puzzling example is *Raffles v Wichelhaus*.[59] Another branch of contract law much influenced by the will theory was the assessment of damages, where the landmark is the decision in *Hadley v Baxendale* (1854),[60] which related the damages recoverable on breach of contract to the notional foresight of the contracting party when the contract was made; contract liability was self-imposed, and the contractor's liability was to be related to what he reasonably thought he was taking on. Later nineteenth-century case law even required, in the case of unusual or special loss, a contract to bear that loss;[61] a notion close to Holmes' theory that a contract was really an agreement to pay damages in certain eventualities.[62] *Hadley v Baxendale* was itself much influenced by the French Code Civil, and by

---

55   In appendix V to his edition of Pothier's *Treatise on Obligations*, at p 35.
56   See p 152 of vol 1 of Evans' edition.
57   (1878) 3 App Cas 459. See p 312, below.
58   [1932] AC 161. See pp 291–292, below.
59   (1864) 2 H & C 906, Simpson 11 Cardozo LR 287.
60   9 Exch 341. For discussion see Washington in 48 LQR 90, Simpson in 91 LQR 273–277 and Danzig in 4 J Legal Studies 249.
61   *British Columbia Saw Mills Co v Nettleship* (1868) LR 3 CP 499.
62   See Holmes *The Common Law* Lect VIII.

Pothier, as well as by American literature on damages, and is a particularly good example of the reception of alien ideas.[63]

G IMPLIED TERMS

The basic philosophy of the will theory confines the functions of a court to enforcing the contract which the parties have made; when, however, a contractual dispute arises for which the express terms of a contract make no advance provision, the court has of necessity to employ, in resolving the dispute, material not to be found in the terms of the express contract, and in the common law system the conceptual vehicle employed is the 'implied term'. In a sense the extensive development of the use of 'implied terms' to supplement contracts, and at times to modify them, runs contrary to the credo of the will theory; in another sense it reconciles the will theory with activities of the courts which, in strict theory, ought never to be undertaken.

Implied terms in sale

The use of the concept of an implied promise has a long history in the law of assumpsit; implied promises to pay debts had, for example, been used as a basis of liability in *indebitatus assumpsit*, and there are other early examples of the implication of promises by the courts to produce just results.[64] In eighteenth- and nineteenth-century law the courts made extensive use of the notion of an implied term to read into particular contracts normal or usual incidents of that type of contract. In doing so, whilst purporting to fill out the understandings of the parties, what might in reality be involved was the imposition *ab extra* of standards derived from continental mercantile law or civil law.[65] Thus in sale of goods the original position was *caveat emptor*. On an *express* warranty, if one had been given, it was possible to sue in tort for deceit; *Stuart v Wilkins* (1778)[66] is the earliest reported case where action was brought on the contract, though the practice began rather earlier around 1750. The development of the notion of an *implied* warranty was a slow process. So far as warranty of title is concerned the law started from the position that there was no implied warranty; from the time of *Medina v Stoughton* (1700)[67] the insistence on an express warranty began to be eroded, and by the time of the decision in *Eichholz v Bannister* (1864)[68] the exception had for all practical purposes eaten up the rule; the development had

---

[63] For recent discussion of the will theory in general see Atiyah *The Rise and Fall of Freedom of Contract.*

[64] See Simpson *History* pp 491–493, 503.

[65] No full historical study of the evolution of the implied term exists.

[66] 1 Doug KB 18.   [67] 1 Salk 210, 1 Ld Raym 593.   [68] 17 CBNS 708.

taken a century and a half. So far as quality is concerned the principle of *caveat emptor* was never wholly abandoned. Although there is some slight evidence in eighteenth-century law of an implied warranty of merchantable quality where a proper price was paid,[69] or at least of the imposition of liability where the seller knew of the defect, it was held in 1802 in *Parkinson v Lee*[70] that there was no such implied warranty in the case of a sale by sample, and assumed that, in general, *caveat emptor* applied in the absence of fraud or an express warranty. But *Laing v Fidgeon* (1815)[71] held that in a sale by description the goods must be merchantable, and *Jones v Bright* (1829)[72] held that there was an implied term that goods sold for a particular purpose were suitable for it. In these and following cases the courts built up the complex structure of implied obligations codified by Chalmers in the Sale of Goods Act 1893. During the same period the courts were also using the concept of an implied term to impose a solution in cases where there had been mistake, and in cases where some drastic change of circumstances had affected a contract, as in the leading case of *Taylor v Caldwell* (1863).[73] In the implied term the courts possessed a conceptual device of great potential, but one which suffered from one major drawback—in principle an implied term could never override an express provision, however unjust its operation. Much of the development of contract law in this century has been provoked by attempts to grapple with this difficulty.

For history continues, and although the twentieth century did not perhaps witness so extensive a reformulation of the categories of contract law as the nineteenth, it has nevertheless produced a considerable body of new law. Thus the doctrine of frustration, though its roots lie back in the early nineteenth century law on charterparties, has acquired a prominence it never possessed in the nineteenth century: again the doctrine of promissory or equitable estoppel, though again based on nineteenth-century case law, has been put to new uses. In a historical system of law change has both to be fitted into the past, and if possible justified by reference to it, and the manner in which new departures are presented makes it peculiarly difficult to differentiate radical innovation from mere elaboration of existing doctrine. Perhaps the most general significant change has been an overall tendency to reject the nineteenth century's confidence in the virtues of freedom of contract and the associated will theory, without the adoption of any very clearly formulated alternative. Some writers, notably Professor Grant Gilmore and Professor P S Atiyah have argued that much of what passes as general contract law is better regarded as an outmoded relic of the past, and that the whole subject is ripe for radical revisionism. But these are matters we ought, perhaps, to leave to the judgement of future historians.

---

[69] See Horwitz 87 Harvard L Rev 926, Simpson 46 U Chicago L Rev 533.
[70] 2 East 314.   [71] 6 Taunt 108.   [72] 5 Bing 533.   [73] 32 LJQB 164.

2 SOME FACTORS AFFECTING MODERN CONTRACT LAW[1]

The English law of contract, it has been seen, was evolved and developed within the framework of assumpsit, and, so long as that framework endured, it was not necessary to pursue too fervently the search for principle. But when the forms of action were abolished this task could no longer be avoided. The lawyers of the nineteenth century, when they braced themselves to face it, were influenced by two major factors.

---

[1] See Smith, *Contract Theory*; Collins, *Regulating Contracts*.

A CONTINENTAL INFLUENCE IN THE NINETEENTH CENTURY

The first was the example of continental jurisprudence. This was felt primarily through the writings of Pothier, who drew an idealised picture of contract in eighteenth-century France. In 1806 his *Treatise on the Law of Obligations* was translated into English; in 1822 Best J declared its authority to be 'as high as can be had, next to a decision of a court of justice in this country';[2] in 1835 it was 'strenuously recommended' as a student's textbook;[3] and in 1845 Blackburn made copious references to it in his work on sale. It was not surprising, therefore, that English judges should have been tempted to accept his analysis of contract as dependent upon 'a concurrence of intention in two parties, one of whom promises something to the other, who on his part accepts such promise'.[4] More belated, and directed largely upon academic lawyers, was the influence of Savigny. The first edition of Pollock's *Treatise on the General Principles Concerning the Validity of Agreements in the Law of England* appeared in 1875, and the first edition of Anson's *Principles of the English Law of Contract* in 1879. The former was dedicated to Lord Lindley, who had first taught the writer 'to turn from the formless confusion of textbooks and the dry bones of students' manuals to the immortal work of Savigny'.[5] The latter was equally ready to acknowledge a similar debt. 'We may regard contract as a combination of the two ideas of agreement and obligation. Savigny's analysis of these two legal conceptions may, with advantage, be considered here with reference to the rules of English law.' In the result, 'agreement' was 'necessarily the outcome of consenting minds'. As Lord Cairns said in a contemporaneous and famous case, there must be 'consensus of mind' to lead to contract.[6]

---

[2] *Cox v Troy* (1822) 5 B & Ald 474 at 480.

[3] Samuel Warren *A Popular and Practical Introduction to Law Studies* (1835).

[4] *Treatise on Obligations* Pt I, s I, article I; see the English translation by Sir W D Evans, at p 4. As late as 1887, Kekewich J declared that the definitions of contract in textbooks were 'all founded' on Pothier, though he himself preferred the 'slightly different version' offered by Pollock; see *Foster v Wheeler* (1887) 36 ChD 695 at 698.

[5] In the third edition, Pollock relegated Savigny to the decent obscurity of an appendix. Lord Lindley's interest in continental legal thought was further evidenced by his translation in 1855 of Thibaut's *Jurisprudence*.

[6] *Cundy v Lindsay* (1878) 3 App Cas 459 at 465; p 312, below.

B INFLUENCE OF ECONOMIC THEORY

The weight of foreign jurisprudence was reinforced by a second factor, the pressure of economic doctrine. Sir Frederick Pollock once declared that 'the sort of men who became judges towards the middle of the century were imbued with the creed of the "philosophical Radicals" who drove the chariot of reform and for whom the authority of the orthodox economists came second only to Bentham's'. Their patron saint, he added, was Ricardo.[7] Individualism was both fashionable and successful: liberty and enterprise were taken to be the inevitable and immortal insignia of a civilised society. The state, as it were, delegated to its members the power to legislate. When, voluntarily and with a clear eye to their own interests, they entered into a contract, they made a piece of private law, binding on each other and beneficial alike to themselves and to the community at large. The freedom and the sanctity of contract were the necessary instrument of *laissez-faire*, and it was the function of the courts to foster the one and to vindicate the other. Where a man sowed, there he should be able to reap. In the words of that formidable individualist, Sir George Jessel, 'if there is one thing which more than another public policy requires it is that men of full age and competent understanding shall have the utmost liberty of contracting, and that their contracts when entered into freely and voluntarily shall be held sacred and shall be enforced by Courts of Justice'.[8] In more detached and less complacent language the sentiment was echoed by Henry Sidgwick in his *Elements of Politics*.[9] 'Suppose contracts freely made and effectively sanctioned, and the most elaborate social organisation becomes possible, at least in a society of such human beings as the individualistic theory contemplates—gifted with mature reason and governed by enlightened self-interest.'

Limits of individualistic theory

Even when they wrote them, the words of Jessel and Sidgwick could hardly have been received without reservation. To make a serious promise usually involves a moral duty to keep it: if it is part of what the law calls a contract the moral will be reinforced by a legal sanction. But the intrusion into the context of the epithet 'sacred' is at best incongruous, at worst grotesque. Moreover, when these words are examined, it will be

---

[7] 39 LQR 163 at 165. It is suggestive that the judge chosen by Pollock as typical of the general attitude was Lord Bramwell, who sought persistently to champion the cause of 'real' consent. See his judgment in *British and American Telegraph Co v Colson* (1871) LR 6 Exch 108.

[8] *Printing and Numerical Registering Co v Sampson* (1875) LR 19 Eq 462 at 465.

[9] (1879) p 82 cited in Kessler and Gilmore *Contracts, Cases and Materials* (2nd edn, 1970) p 4. See the whole of the Introduction of this book, pp 1–16. Shatwell 1 Sydney L Rev 289. An exhaustive account of the interplay of economic and social doctrines and the law of contract is to be found in Atiyah *The Rise and Fall of Freedom of Contract*. For a modern analysis of freedom of contract, see Trebilcock *The Limits of Freedom of Contract* (Harvard UP 1993); *Smith* 59 MLR 167.

seen that, despite their apparent breadth, they are hedged about with qualifications. The men to be accorded 'the utmost liberty of contracting' must be 'of full age and competent understanding'. They are to approximate as best they may to the heroes of an individualistic mythology and to be 'gifted with mature reason and governed by enlightened self-interest'. Even in the middle years of the nineteenth century the ideal was one to which few could attain. Society had long recognised the need to protect the young, the deranged, the blind, the illiterate. Common law and equity were moving in different ways and with hesitant steps to rescue the victims of misrepresentation and undue influence.[10] It was accepted that, while private enterprise was the main road to public good, freedom of contract must at times yield to the exigencies of the state and to the ethical assumptions upon which it was based. But in less obvious cases the qualifications demanded by Jessel and Sidgwick of their contracting parties were more difficult to define and to secure. How were the courts to assess the due measures of 'competent understanding' or to ensure that contracts were 'freely and voluntarily made?'

As the nineteenth century waned it became ever clearer that private enterprise predicated some degree of economic equality if it was to operate without injustice. The very freedom to contract with its corollary, the freedom to compete, was merging into the freedom to combine; and in the last resort, competition and combination were incompatible. Individualism was yielding to monopoly, where strange things might well be done in the name of liberty. The background of the law, social, political and economic, has changed. *Laissez-faire* as an ideal has been supplanted by 'social security'; and social security suggests status rather than contract.

The state may thus compel persons to make contracts, as where, by a series of Road Traffic Acts from 1930 to 1972, a motorist must insure against third-party risks; it may, as by the Rent Acts, prevent one party to a contract from enforcing his rights under it,[11] or it may empower a tribunal either to reduce or to increase the rent payable under a lease.[12] In many instances a statute prescribes the contents of the contract. The Carriage of Goods by Sea Act 1971 contains six pages of rules to be incorporated in every contract for 'the carriage of goods by sea in ships where the port of shipment is a port in the United Kingdom';[13] the Sale of Goods Act 1979 inserts into contracts of sale a number of terms which the parties are forbidden to exclude;[14] successive Landlord and Tenant Acts from 1927 to 1954 contain provisions expressed to apply 'notwithstanding any agreement to the contrary'.[15] The erosion of contract by statute continues briskly.[16]

---

[10] This is the conventional view but Atiyah ch 15 argues that during the late-eighteenth and early nineteenth centuries the move was in the opposite direction.

[11] The earliest Act was that of 1915. The law is currently to be found in the Housing Act 2004.

[12] See eg Housing Act 1988, s 14.

[13] See also the Carriage by Air Act 1961.   [14] Pp 231–252, below.

[15] See Landlord and Tenant Act 1927, s 9, Landlord and Tenant Act 1954, s 17.

[16] Eg Contracts of Employment Act 1972, Counter-Inflation Act 1973. See Kahn-Freund 30 MLR 635.

The most striking inroads into freedom of contract have been the product of statute, but common law has played its part, particularly perhaps in the regulation of exemption clauses.[17] Curiously enough there has been little analysis by English lawyers[18] of the effects of interference with freedom of contracts, perhaps because to do so might appear 'political'. It is apparent, for instance, that restrictions on freedom of contract in regard to residential tenancies have led to a dramatic reduction in the amount of residential accommodation available for rent in the private sector and in many ways have exacerbated the problems.[19] On the other hand, restrictions on freedom of contract in regard to business and agricultural tenancies do not appear to have produced the same result.[20]

The substantial inroads that have been made into freedom of contract can sometimes obscure the fact that across a broad spectrum of contract it remains a prime value because often the only way we can value goods or services is in relation to the price people are willing to pay for them. It may be foolish for a businessman to pay £100 for a bottle of claret to accompany his business lunch or for a football club to pay £20,000,000 for a player but there are no legal values which would justify refusing to enforce such contracts.

C INEQUALITY OF BARGAINING POWER

The critical analysis of freedom of contract has led to the suggestion that contracts should be treated differently where there is inequality of bargaining power. This suggestion has received formal recognition in the United States[21] and it has received not unfavourable notice in a number of English judgments, though it is not yet clearly

---

[17] See pp 202–231, below. Another example is the modern tendency to refer questions which were previously decided by reference to the intention of the parties to other tests. See pp 191–202 below.

[18] American lawyers have been much more active. See especially Posner *Economic Analysis of the Law* ch 3 and Posner and Kronman (eds) *The Economics of Contract Law*; Schwartz 49 Indiana LJ 367. Some of the American literature may perhaps be regarded as excessively 'free market' in its theoretical approach. Cf Goldberg 17 J Law and Economics 461.

[19] Theoretically, removal of restrictions would lead to the building of houses and flats for residential letting in sufficient numbers that eventually supply and demand would come into equilibrium. In practice, given the instability of the building industry, it is very doubtful whether this would be so.

[20] A possible explanation for this is that only in residential tenancies has the law interfered with the price. It is true that in economic theory restrictions as to other terms should affect the price but in practice this is often not so because parties do not in practice negotiate equally hard about all terms—although they are nearly always keenly interested in the price! The speeches in *Johnson v Moreton* [1980] AC 37, [1978] 3 All ER 37, contain much that is instructive in this area. See also Goldberg 17 J Law and Economics 461; Reiter, 1 Oxford JLS 347; Trebilcock in Studies in Contract Law 379.

[21] Uniform Commercial Code, s 2-302; Leff 115 U Pennsylvania L Rev 485; White and Summers *Uniform Commercial Code* ch 4.

the ratio of any.[22] One may, however, venture some observations. First, inequality of itself cannot be a ground of invalidity since there is usually no way for the stronger party to divest himself of the advantage and it would not be to the advantage of the weaker party to prohibit contracts between the parties altogether. Invalidity must be dependent on the stronger party taking unfair advantage of his position. Secondly, exact equality of bargaining power is unusual. Where one party is in slightly the stronger position, the process of bargaining should lead to an agreement where both parties concur equally in the result. Take the case of a potential vendor and purchaser for a private house. At any given moment the market may be favourable either to vendors or purchasers and there may be special considerations leading either vendor or purchaser to be anxious to complete a quick sale. Such factors will affect the price but no one has suggested that the subsequent contract should be invalid. Inequality of bargaining power should only be relevant where it is great in extent. Thirdly, when we talk of inequality of bargaining *power* we are often in fact thinking of inequality of bargaining *skill*. Second-hand car salesmen do not normally have greater bargaining power than their potential customers but they are usually better salesmen and better informed. Finally, we may meet cases of unequal access to relevant information. Suppose a contract is made by A and B for the sale by A to B of a painting for £50. A believes the painting to be a copy of a Constable; B 'knows' that it is an original. Our analysis of whether the resultant agreement is fair depends on whether we think that B should have shared his knowledge with A. At the intuitive level this may depend on whether A is a little old lady and B an art dealer or the other way round. It is important to bear in mind, however, that in many cases B's superior knowledge is part of his professional equipment and is the fruit of years of study and experience. In general, the acquisition of such knowledge would not be encouraged by a regime which required it to be gratuitously shared.

D THE USE OF STANDARD FORM CONTRACTS

The process of mass production and distribution, which has largely supplemented, if not supplanted, individual effort, has introduced the mass contract—uniform documents which must be accepted by all who deal with large-scale organisations. Such documents are not in themselves novelties: the classical lawyer of the mid-Victorian years found himself struggling to adjust his simple conceptions of contract to the demands of such powerful bodies as the railway companies.[23] But in the

---

[22] See Lord Diplock in *Schroeder Music Publishing Co Ltd v Macaulay* [1974] 3 All ER 616 at 624, [1974] 1 WLR 1308 at 1316 quoted below, p 25, and the cases on 'economic duress' discussed below, pp 386–390.

[23] Pp 203–212, below.

twentieth century many corporations, public and private, found it useful to adopt, as the basis of their transactions, a series of standard forms with which their customers can do little but comply.[24]

Lord Diplock pointed out that:[25]

Standard forms of contracts are of two kinds. The first, of very ancient origin, are those which set out the terms on which mercantile transactions of common occurrence are to be carried out. Examples are bills of lading, charterparties, policies of insurance, contracts of sale in the commodity markets. The standard clauses in these contracts have been settled over the years by negotiation by representatives of the commercial interests involved and have been widely adopted because experience has shown that they facilitate the conduct of trade. Contracts of these kinds affect not only the actual parties to them but also others who may have a commercial interest in the transactions to which they relate, as buyers or sellers, charterers or shipowners, insurers or bankers. If fairness or reasonableness were relevant to their enforceability the fact that they are widely used by parties whose bargaining power is fairly matched would raise a strong presumption that their terms are fair and reasonable.

The same presumption, however, does not apply to the other kind of standard form of contract. This is of comparatively modern origin. It is the result of the concentration of particular kinds of business in relatively few hands. The ticket cases in the 19th century provide what are probably the first examples. The terms of this kind of standard form of contract have not been the subject of negotiation between the parties to it, or approved by any organisation representing the interests of the weaker party. They have been dictated by that party whose bargaining power, either exercised alone or in conjunction with others providing similar goods or services, enables him to say: 'If you want these goods or services at all, these are the only terms on which they are obtainable. Take it or leave it.'

It is fair to add that even in Lord Diplock's second class there are good as well as bad reasons for the adoption of standard form contracts. In many cases the actual conclusion of the contract is in the hands of relatively junior personnel, who are not trained in contract negotiation and drafting and there are enormous economies to be effected if the company only employs one (or at most a few) standard forms of agreement.[26] As regards the first class, we should note that whole areas of English commercial practice are governed by the prevalent standard forms which

---

[24] An early standard form of contract is the Baltoon charterparty adopted in 1908 for use in the coal trade between the United Kingdom and the Baltic ports: see Rordam *Treatise on the Baltoon Charterparty* (1954). See also Sales 16 MLR 318, and the standard forms issued by the Institute of London Underwriters and reprinted in appendix II of Chalmers *Marine Insurance Act 1906.*

[25] *Schroeder Music Publishing Co Ltd v Macaulay* [1974] 3 All ER 616 at 524, [1974] 1 WLR 1308 at 1316. This case is the subject of a very illuminating analysis by Trebilcock 26 U Toronto LJ 359. For the history of standard form contracts, see Prausnitz *The Standardisation of Commercial Contracts in English and Continental Law* (1937).

[26] Macaulay 19 Vanderbilt L Rev 1051.

exist in a symbiotic relationship with the courts, so that an historical analysis of the development of a particular form would show that the clause represented a response to a decision in the past.[27]

In the complex structure of modern society the device of the standard form contract has become prevalent and pervasive. The French, though not the English, lawyers have a name for it.

> The term contract d'adhesion is employed to denote the type of contract of which the conditions are fixed by one of the parties in advance and are open to acceptance by anyone. The contract, which frequently contains many conditions is presented for acceptance en bloc and is not open to discussion.[28]

These developments emphasise that to make a contract may no longer be a purely private act. It may be controlled or even dictated by legislative or economic pressure, and it may involve the courts in feats of construction akin to or borrowed from the technique of statutory interpretation. Yet it is possible to exaggerate the effect. In daily life individually negotiated contracts exist and even abound. Moreover, as has already been said, the current law of contract is largely the creation of the nineteenth-century lawyers, and it is this law which their successors have to apply even in a new and uncongenial environment. The tools of the trade remain the same even if they are put to uses that their inventors neither envisaged nor desired.

E CONSUMER PROTECTION

Nineteenth-century contract law was dominated by disputes about commercial contracts. If litigation involved what we would now regard as a consumer transaction, it tended to involve questions like the buying of horses where a judge would naturally assume that a gentleman could look after himself.[29]

Economic theory might proclaim that in the market place the consumer was king but in the law courts he was uncrowned. The twentieth century has seen a very different approach. Increasingly sophisticated technology has meant that consumers might expend substantial sums on machines such as cars, washing-machines and

---

[27] See eg the building industry where nearly all substantial contracts are made on one or the other of the JCT forms. See Duncan Wallace *Building and Engineering Standard Forms* (reviewed Atiyah 85 LQR 564). See also Duncan Wallace 89 LQR 36 and *Gilbert-Ash (Northern) v Modern Engineering (Bristol)* [1974] AC 689, [1973] 3 All ER 195.

[28] Amos and Walton *Introduction to French Law* (2nd edn, 1963) p 152. See Kessler 43 Col L Rev 629; Friedmann *Law in a Changing Society* (2nd edn) ch 4; Atiyah *Introduction to Law of Contract* (6th edn 2005) ch 1; Lord Devlin *Samples of Law Making* ch 2; Thornely [1962] CLJ 39 at 460–449; Gluck 28 ICLQ 72.

[29] *Hopkins v Tanqueray* (1854) 15 CB 130.

televisions whose efficiency and durability they were quite unable to estimate for themselves. Consumers have responded to this trend by organising themselves as pressure groups (for example, Consumers' Association) and governments have created organisations to care for the consumer interest (Office of Fair Trading, National Consumer Council) and have appointed junior ministers with special responsibility for consumer affairs.

These developments have been reflected in changes in the law of contract whose aim has been to protect consumers. The most striking examples have perhaps been in the judicial and parliamentary attempts to deal with the problem of exemption clauses, which culminated in the Unfair Contract Terms Act 1977.[30] Other important examples are the Fair Trading Act 1973 and the Consumer Credit Act 1974.[31] It should perhaps be added that legislative attempts to protect consumers are by no means confined to the law of contract. Indeed the law of contract is in many ways an unsatisfactory instrument since enforcement depends on the consumer knowing his rights, being able to afford to enforce them and considering the cost and time involved worthwhile.

F THE RELATIONSHIP BETWEEN STANDARD FORM CONTRACTS, INEQUALITY OF BARGAINING POWER AND CONSUMER PROTECTION

Standard form contracts, inequality of bargaining power and consumer protection are three themes which underlie many developments in modern contract law. It is important to remind ourselves that there are indeed three separate themes which intertwine but remain distinct. It is easy, for instance, to think of consumers as the only class that needs protection against inequality of bargaining power but this is not so, as is shown by the enactment of the Housing Grants, Construction and Regeneration Act 1996, part II of which introduced mandatory terms in all construction contracts.

A typical construction transaction will involve a complex web of contracts. At the centre will be a contract between the person who is procuring the contract (the Employer) and the person who will organise the work (the Contractor). In practice

---

[30] See below, pp 231–254.
[31] See Borrie and Diamond *The Consumer, Society and the Law* (4th edn, 1981); Harvey and Parry *The Law of Consumer Protection and Fair Trading* (4th edn, 1992); Mickleburgh *Consumer Protection*; Cranston *Consumers and the Law* (2nd edn, 1984); Lowe and Woodroffe *Consumer Law and Practice* (6th edn, 2004); Miller and Harvey *Consumer and Trading Law Cases and Materials*; Ramsay *Consumer Protection*. See Atiyah 1 Liverpool L Rev 20.

the Contractor does little of the work himself but subcontracts it and subcontractors may in turn sub-subcontract. The contract between an Employer and a Contractor will usually employ one of family of standard form contracts produced by the Joint Contracts Tribunal (JCT). These forms are designed by the JCT to be fair as between employers and contractors as classes.[32] The JCT also produces standard forms designed to be used for the contracts between contractors and sub-contractors but in practice these contracts are often on forms drafted by the contractor's advisors to improve the position of the contractor.

In general, contractors would tend to be in a stronger position than sub-contractors, though, of course, this is not always the case. A common example of superior power is that sub-contracts drafted by contractors typically provide that the contractor need not pay the subcontractor for the work done until he has been paid by the employer, so-called '*pay when paid*' clauses. Parliament has treated this as so pervasive an abuse of the contractor's superior bargaining power that such clauses are made ineffective by section 113(1) of the 1996 Act.

G CONTRACTUAL BEHAVIOUR

Writers of contract textbooks tend to talk as if in real life agreements are effectively controlled by the law as stated in their books. A moment's reflection will show that this is not so. There is a wide range of transactions where the sums at stake are so small that litigation between the contracting parties is exceptionally unlikely.[33] Many businesses choose not to insist on their strictly legal rights. So, if a lady buys a dress and the next day decides she does not like the colour, it is clear law that she is not entitled to return it but many shops would allow her to exchange it and some would make a cash refund.

One might think that things would be different in the cold world of business but it seems that this is probably not so. In a seminal article in 1963[34] Macaulay showed that in substantial areas of business, contractual disputes were resolved by reference to norms which were significantly different from the theoretical legal position. The most important single reason for this seems to be that, in many business situations, the

---

[32] This is certainly the stated aim of the JCT. It is a matter of debate amongst specialist construction lawyers as to whether the aim is achieved.

[33] So, many contract points arise only collaterally in criminal or tax cases. See the cases on offers, pp 43–45, below, and *Esso Petroleum Co Ltd v Customs and Excise Comrs* [1976] 1 All ER 117, [1976] 1 WLR 1 discussed at p 153, below.

[34] (1963) 28 Am Sociological Rev 55. This journal may not be easily available but the article is reprinted in a number of books, for example, *Sociology of Law* (ed Aubert) p 194, Schwartz and Skolnick (eds) *Society and the Legal Order* p 161. See also Macaulay 19 Vanderbilt L Rev 1051, 11 Law and Society 507.

contract is not a discrete transaction but part of a continuing relationship between the parties and that insistence on certain strict legal rights would be disruptive of that relationship.[35] Such work as has been done in England points in the same direction.[36]

In other areas of business, strict (or even over-strict) insistence on legal rights is common.[37] It is at the moment far from clear what factors determine these differences in behaviour.[38]

H A LAW OF CONTRACT OR CONTRACTS?

An observant reader of the table of contents of this book would have noticed that it is quite different from that of a textbook on torts or criminal law, where a major part of the book would be devoted to a consideration of nominate torts or crimes. This does not mean that there are no special rules about particular contracts but in English law (unlike some other systems)[39] we start from the position that in principle the law of contract is the same for all contracts. So in *Cehave NV v Bremer Handelgesellschaft MbH* Roskill LJ said:[40]

> In principle it is not easy to see why the law relating to contracts for the sale of goods should be different from the law relating to the performance of other contractual obligations, whether charter parties or other types of contract. Sale of goods law is but one branch of the general law of contract. It is desirable that the same legal principles should apply to law of contract as a whole and that different legal principles should not apply to different branches of that law.[41]

It must be noted, however, that Parliament has consistently taken a different approach, so that most legislation with contractual implications applies only to a limited list of contracts. The Unfair Contract Terms Act 1977[42] is perhaps the most striking recent example of this tendency.

---

35 Macneil 72 Northwestern U L Rev 854. An extensive selection of Macneil's writing is contained in *The Relational Theory of Contract* (ed Campbell).

36 Beale and Dugdale 2 Brit Jo Law and Society 45; Lewis 9 Brit Jo Law and Society 153.

37 See eg *Mardorf Peach & Co v Attica Sea Carriers Corpn of Liberia, The Laconia* [1977] AC 850, [1977] 1 All ER 545.

38 It is not inconceivable that those businesses which habitually insist on strict legal rights employ more lawyers.

39 For example, classical Roman law. In his entertaining book *The Death of Contract*, Professor Grant Gilmore argues that in American law, general contract theory was an invention of the Harvard Law School. Professor Gilmore held a Chair at Yale.

40 [1976] QB 44 at 71, [1975] 3 All ER 739 at 756. For further discussion of the issues of this case see p 199, below.

41 See also *Thomas Marshall (Exports) Ltd v Guinle* [1979] Ch 227, [1978] 3 All ER 193.

42 See pp 231–253, below.

I THE INTERRELATIONSHIP OF CONTRACT AND TORT

When a plaintiff is injured and seeks compensation he may express his claim either as one in contract or in tort. Traditionally, contract lawyers and tort lawyers have taken little interest in the details of each other's subjects but this aloofness can no longer be safely practised, since over the last twenty years the area of overlap between tort and contract has significantly increased. This development has taken a number of turns. Plaintiffs have been active in exploring the possibility that they have an action against the defendant both in contract and in tort. Although a plaintiff cannot, of course, recover twice for the same injury, he may by suing in contract avoid an obstacle to an action in tort[43] or vice versa.[44]

The modern position has been authoritatively stated by the House of Lords in *Henderson v Merrett Syndicates Ltd.*[45] This case involved the consideration of preliminary points in an action brought by Names at Lloyds against their members' agents (whose principal function is to advise Names on which syndicates to join) and their managing agents (whose principal function is to underwrite contracts of insurance on behalf of the syndicates which they are managing). In some cases, the members' agents and managing agents were the same (as permitted by the relevant rules which have since been changed) and sometimes not. In general, Names would be in a contractual relationship with their members' agents but not with the managing agents, unless the managing agents were also members' agents. Among the preliminary questions considered, the House of Lords was asked to rule whether there could be a tort action against the members' agents where there was a contractual relationship between the plaintiff and the members' agent.

The principal judgment was delivered by Lord Goff. He had no doubt at all that the answer to the general question, can there be concurrent liability in contract and tort, was 'Yes' and that concurrent liability could exist on the facts of the present cases. There was a careful consideration of French law which, in general, prohibits concurrent liability in contract and tort through the doctrine of non-cumul and it was noted that the other great civil law system, the German civil code, did not have a similar doctrine. There was a careful consideration also of some Commonwealth cases, including the important decision of the Supreme Court of Canada in *Central Trust Co v Rafuse*[46] where Le Dain J said:

> A concurrent or alternative liability in tort will not be admitted if its effect would be to permit the plaintiff to circumvent or escape a contractual exclusion or limitation of liability for the act

---

[43] *Matthews v Kuwait Bechtel Corpn* [1959] 2 QB 57, [1959] 2 All ER 345.
[44] *Midland Bank Trust Co Ltd v Hett, Stubbs and Kemp* [1979] Ch 384, [1978] 3 All ER 571; see p 345.
[45] [1994] 3 All ER 506.   [46] (1986) 31 DLR (4th) 481.

or omission that would constitute the tort. Subject to this qualification, where concurrent liability in tort and contract exists the plaintiff has the right to assert the cause of action that appears to be the most advantageous to him in respect of any particular legal consequence.

Lord Goff entirely agreed with this statement and was full of praise for the judgment delivered by Oliver J in *Midland Bank Trust Co. Ltd v Hett Stubbs & Kemp.*[47]

The position now seems completely clear. The question is to be resolved by considering, in each case, whether the ingredients of a tort action and a contract action are present. The mere fact that all the ingredients for a contract are present does not prevent there being a tort duty nor, presumably, vice versa. Of course, the terms of the contract may, in particular cases, make it clear that the parties intended to exclude or limit liability in tort. This they are certainly entitled to do unless the case is one of those in which there is a statutory restriction on the ability of the parties to contract out of tort liability. A plaintiff who wants to argue that there is wider liability in tort than in contract may have greater difficulties.[48]

In other cases a plaintiff whose natural remedy lies in contract against one defendant has been successful in a tort action against a different defendant. So in *Junior Books v Veitchi Co Ltd*[49] the plaintiffs entered into a contract with A to build a warehouse. The defendants were nominated subcontractors for the flooring. It was alleged that the defendants had carelessly installed sub-standard flooring. If that were so, then the plaintiffs would normally have had an action in contract against A, and A, in turn, would have had a contract action against the defendants. However, the House of Lords held that on such facts the plaintiffs could have a tort action against the defendants even though there was no danger of physical injury or property damage to the plaintiffs.

It is unclear why in this case the plaintiffs found their normal contract action against A unsatisfactory.[50] But the possibility of an alternative tort action on such facts is clearly of great theoretical and practical significance and has led to much discussion.[51] It has been suggested that the logical result of the *Junior Books* decision is that every negligent breach of contract is a tort but the courts so far have shown no signs of accepting this position.[52] On the contrary, since 1982 subsequent decisions have confined *Junior Books v Veitchi* within the narrowest limits. Courts have consistently said that the case turns on the close commercial relationship which

---

[47] [1979] Ch 384, [1978] 3 All ER 571.

[48] This is probably what was meant by the cautionary words of Lord Scarman in *Tai Hing Cotton Mill Ltd v Liu Chong Hing Bank Ltd* [1985] 2 All ER 947 at 957.

[49] [1983] 1 AC 520, [1982] 3 All ER 201.

[50] The most plausible explanation would perhaps be that A was insolvent or that the plaintiffs had entered into a settlement with A before they realised how faulty the floor was.

[51] See *The Law of Tort: Policies and Trends in Liability for Damage to Property and Economic Loss* (ed Furmston, Duckworths 1986); Holyoak 99 LQR 591; Jaffey 5 Legal Studies 77.

[52] *Leigh and Sillivan Ltd v Aliakmon Shipping Co Ltd* [1985] QB 350, [1985] 2 All ER 44, Reynolds 11 NZULR 215.

exists between an employer in a building contract and a nominated subcontractor who is chosen by him, though he contracts with the contractor. Indeed it is common for the employer to contract direct with the nominated subcontractor as well as with the contractor and in the case most like *Junior Books v Veitchi, Greater Nottingham Co-operative Society Ltd v Cementation Piling and Foundations Ltd*[53] the Court of Appeal held that because in that case there was a direct contract between employer and nominated subcontractor, there was no room for a separate duty of care in tort between the same parties with wider limits. This case is very much in line with the insistence of the House of Lords that remorseless expansion of the tort of negligence should not be allowed to usurp the proper place of the law of contract.[54]

J GOOD FAITH IN CONTRACT LAW[55]

Do the parties owe each other a duty to negotiate in good faith? Do the parties, once the contract is concluded, owe each other a duty to perform the contract in good faith? Until recently, English lawyers would not have asked themselves these questions or, if asked, would have dismissed them with a cursory 'of course not'. On being told that the German civil code imposed a duty to perform a contract in good faith[56] or that the Italian civil code provides for a duty to negotiate in good faith,[57] a thoughtful English lawyer might have responded by suggesting that the practical problems covered by these code positions were often covered in English law but in different ways. This may still be regarded as the orthodox position but the literature of English law has begun to consider much more carefully whether there might not be merit in explicitly recognising the advantages of imposing good faith duties on negotiation and performance. This view is reinforced by the fact that other common law systems have already moved in this direction. So, the American Uniform Commercial Code, Section 1-203 provides:

---

[53] [1989] QB 71, [1988] 2 All ER 971, 17 Con LR 43.

[54] *D & F Estates Ltd v Church Comrs for England* [1988] 2 All ER 992, [1988] 3 WLR 368 and *Murphy v Brentwood District Council* [1990] 2 All ER 908, [1990] 3 WLR 414.

[55] *Good Faith and Fault in Contract Law* (ed Beatson, Friedmann, Clarendon Press 1995) (helpfully reviewed by Brownsword 15 Legal Studies 466); Adams and Brownsword, *Key Issues in Contract* (Butterworths 1995) ch 7; Peden, *Good Faith in the Performance of Contracts*; Carter and Furmston 8 Journal of Contract Law 1, 93); Carter and Peden 19 JCL 155; Peden 21 JCL 226.

[56] S 242.

[57] For general surveys see Hondius, *Pre-Contractual Liability* (Kluwer 1991) and the International Chamber of Commerce, *Formation of Contracts, Pre-Contractual Liability*. Stapleton (1999) 52 Current Legal Problems 1. For a very broad survey of what good faith might mean in contract law see Whittaker and Zimmermann, *Good Faith in European Contract Law* (2000).

> Every contract or duty within this Act imposes an obligation of good faith in its performance
> or enforcement.

In Section 205 of the American Law Institute, the Restatement of Contract (2nd) provides:

> Every contract imposes upon each party a duty of good faith and fair dealing in its perform-
> ance and its enforcement.

and in the Australian case of *Renard Constructions (ME) Pty Ltd v Minister of Public Works*[58] Priestley JA said:

> People generally, including judges and other lawyers, from all strands of the community, have
> grown used to the courts applying standards of fairness to contracts which are wholly consist-
> ent with the existence in all contracts of a duty upon the parties of good faith and fair dealing
> in its performance. In my view this is in these days the expected standard, and anything less is
> contrary to prevailing community expectations.

It is not inconceivable that on appropriate facts and with skilful argument, English law may make tentative steps in the same direction.[59]

K THE GLOBALISATION OF CONTRACT LAW

Common law contract lawyers have always taken an interest in parallel developments in other common law jurisdictions, whether the systems started to diverge in 1783 or only in the middle of the twentieth century. The last few years have seen a renaissance in the interest which the contract lawyers of the civil law and common law families have taken in each other's systems.

This interest has taken two practical forms. In 1980, the International Institute for the Unification of Private law (Unidroit) set up a working group to prepare a set of principles for international, commercial contracts. The working group reported in 1994 and its report was accepted by the Governing Council of Unidroit. A second working group, with some changes in membership, produced an enlarged edition which was approved by the Governing Council in 2004. It is believed that work will soon start on a further enlargement. At the same time another group (the Lando Commission) were at work preparing principles of European contract law.

There were both important differences and striking similarities between the two projects. In numbers Europe is predominantly a civil law area. If we regard Scotland as a civil law country, only England and Wales and Ireland come from the common law.

---

[58] (1992) 33 Con LR 72 at 112–13.
[59] *Philips Electronique Grand Public SA v British Sky Broadcasting Ltd* [1995] EMLR 472.

In the world at large, on the other hand, both its most powerful economy (the United States) and its most populous democracy (India) are members of the common law family. Both groups proceeded, however, by seeking to produce a coherent set of rules and not by counting heads. There were overlapping memberships of the two groups and there were many similarities in the final texts.[60]

Both the Unidroit Principles and the Principles of European Contract Law are examples of soft law, that is they derive their strength from the quality and persuasiveness of the text and not from any legislative fiat. In this respect, they follow in the steps of the American Restatements, which are widely treated by courts in the United States as correct statement of the law, though never approved by Congress or State Legislatures.

There has been substantial discussion as to whether the European Union should enact a European Contract Code[61] but at the moment it is unclear in which direction the debate will go. Membership of the European Union does have important effects on contract law under the existing arrangements because there are areas of central competence, such as consumer protection, which generate legislation that impacts on contract law. The Unfair Terms in Consumer Contracts Regulations is the most obvious example.

L HUMAN RIGHTS ACT 1998

The Human Rights Act 1998 which, in simple terms, incorporated the European Convention on Human Rights into English Domestic Law, was clearly a major step in public law. Less obviously the Act also has considerable potential to effect private law. This was dramatically revealed by the decision of the House of Lords in *Wilson v First County Trust Ltd.*[62]

The facts of this case were relatively simple. In January 1999, Mrs Wilson borrowed £5,000 from First County Trust Ltd (FCT). The transaction was secured on Mrs Wilson's BMW 318 Convertible. Mrs Wilson was charged a document fee of £250 and in the agreement this was added to the amount of the loan. In due course, Mrs Wilson started proceedings, claiming that the transaction was invalid under the Consumer Credit Act 1974. The Court of Appeal held that the £250 was not credit and that therefore the terms were not correctly stated in the agreement and the agreement was unenforceable. The result of this was that Mrs Wilson kept the loan and recovered the car.

---

[60] For fuller discussion see Bonell, *An International Restatement of Contract Law* (3rd edn 2005) and *A New Approach to International Commercial Contracts* (ed Bonell, Kluwer 1999).

[61] xxx. See Furmston in *Mélanges offerts à Marcel Fontaine* pp 371–378.

[62] xxxi. [2003] UKHL 40, [2003] 4 All ER 97, [2004] 1 AC 816.

The Court of Appeal thought that this result might be contrary to the Human Rights Act and proceedings were adjourned to allow the Secretary of State for Trade and Industry to be a party. In these proceedings it was assumed that the construction of the Consumer Credit Act was correct. The Court of Appeal held that s127(3) of the Consumer Credit Act was incompatible with the rights guaranteed to the creditor.

The House of Lords disagreed, principally because the events in the case had taken place before the Human Rights Act had come into force. It seems probable that the House of Lords would have reached the same conclusion if the facts had occurred after the Act had come into force but the possibility that the Human Rights Act might support a challenge of this kind was clearly recognised.

3 THE PHENOMENA OF AGREEMENT[1]

SUMMARY

1 INTRODUTION

This chapter and the three succeeding chapters on 'consideration', 'intention to create legal relations' and 'contents' of the contract are concerned with formation of the contract. They consider the rules by which English law answers two questions: Is there a contract? What are the terms of the contract? For purposes of exposition it

---

[1] A fuller discussion of many of the topics in this chapter may be found in Furmston, Norisada and Poole, *Contract Formation and Letters of Intent* (1998).

is convenient to deal with these questions separately but they are intimately connected since in the final analysis inability to say what the terms of the contract are may lead to the conclusion that there is no contract.[2] In the same fashion the rules as to agreement, consideration and intention to create legal relations are closely interlocked.[3]

This book deals only with what are usually called *simple* contracts—agreements made either by word of mouth or in writing.[4] In addition to this normal type of contract, it has long been the tradition of English lawyers to speak of 'contracts under seal', where a person undertakes an obligation by expressing his intention on paper or parchment, attaching his seal and delivering it 'as his deed'.[5] The phrase is misleading. It is true that, in the early law, the obligation engendered by the affixing of a seal was regarded as essentially 'conventional' or contractual.[6] It is also true that, in the modern law, the deed plays its part. On the one hand, it may still be necessary, in a few contracts made with corporations before 1960, that they should have been concluded by a document under seal.[7] On the other hand, if an individual wishes to bind himself by a gratuitous promise, the rule that all simple contracts require to be supported by the presence of consideration forbids him to implement his intention otherwise than by deed. If he complies with this formality, he will doubtless be made to pay damages should he break his promise. But he is thus bound, not because he has made a contract, but because he has chosen to act within the limits of a prescribed formula. The idea of bargain, fundamental to the English conception of contract, is absent. So far, indeed, is his liability removed from the normal notion of agreement that it has even been held that a deed may create a legal duty in favour of a beneficiary who is unaware of its existence.[8] The affinity of the deed is with gift, not with bargain, and it is fair to say that the so-called 'contract by deed' has little in common with agreement save its name and its history, and that it does not seem to require detailed examination in a modern book upon the law of contract. It is fair to add, however, that many

[2] See pp 54–58, below. On the other hand, mere difficulty in understanding the meaning of the contract does not make it void: *Holiday Credit Ltd v Erol* [1977] 2 All ER 696, [1977] 1 WLR 704.

[3] See, for example, the problem of revocation of offers which presents difficulties both in relation to agreement and consideration, pp 72–77, below.

[4] It has not been found easy to describe by a single epithet both the oral and the written contract, each of which has to be sharply distinguished from the so-called 'contract under seal'. In the earlier law the word 'parol' was used, see *Rann v Hughes* (1778) 7 Term Rep 350, n, p 80, below; but it is scarcely apt to designate written as well as oral agreements, and it has generally been replaced in the vocabulary of the modern English lawyer by the word 'simple', here adopted. Williston (*Contracts* s 12) and the American Law Institute Restatement of the Law of Contracts s 11, prefer 'informal'.

[5] Any requirement of a seal is removed by Law of Property (Miscellaneous Provisions) Act 1989, s 1 but the possibility of contracting by deed remains.

[6] P 22, above.

[7] P 281, below.

[8] See *Fletcher v Fletcher* (1844) 4 Hare 67; *Xenos v Wickham* (1866) LR 2 HL 296; and *Lady Naas v Westminster Bank Ltd* [1940] AC 366, [1940] 1 All ER 485.

agreements which have all the ingredients necessary for a binding simple contract are in practice made by deed. This is particularly true of buildings and engineering contracts, where all the standard forms commonly in use envisage the use of a deed. The main practical reason for this appears to be that the limitation period for contracts by deed is twelve years as opposed to the six years for simple contracts.[9] This is particularly important where, as in a building contract, the contract may easily be broken in a way which is not readily apparent to the other party.

The common law has long stressed the commercial flavour of its contract. An Englishman is liable not because he has made a promise, but because he has made a bargain.[10] Behind all forms of contract, no doubt, lies the basic idea of assent. A contracting party, unlike a tortfeasor, is bound because he has agreed to be bound. Agreement, however, is not a mental state but an act, and, as an act, is a matter of inference from conduct. The parties are to be judged not by what is in their minds, but by what they have said or written or done. While such must be, in some degree, the standpoint of every legal system, the common law, preoccupied with bargain, lays peculiar emphasis upon external appearance. As long ago as 1478 and in the context of sale, Chief Justice Brian proclaimed, 'that the intent of a man cannot be tried, for the Devil himself knows not the intent of a man',[11] and in the early years of the nineteenth century this position was reasserted by judge and jurist alike. Lord Eldon protested that his task was not 'to see that both parties really meant the same thing, but only that both gave their assent to that proposition which, be it what it may, de facto arises out of the terms of their correspondence'.[12] So, too, Austin, after saying that, 'when we speak of the intention of contracting parties, we mean the intention of the promisor or the intention of the promisee', added 'or rather, the sense in which it is to be inferred from the words used or from the transaction or from both that the one party gave and the other received it'.[13] In the common law, therefore, to speak of 'the outcome of consenting minds' or, even more mystically, of *consensus ad idem* is to mislead by adopting an alien approach to the problem of agreement. The function of an English judge is not to seek and satisfy some elusive mental element but to ensure, as far as practical experience permits, that the reasonable expectations of honest men are not disappointed. This is often compendiously expressed by saying that English law adopts an objective test of agreement.[14]

---

[9] See p 808, below.

[10] This was the firm view of the original authors but it must be confessed that there are other views. For a valuable survey see Coote 1 JCL 91, 183.

[11] *Anon* (1477) YB 17 Edw 4, fo 1, pl 2.

[12] *Kennedy v Lee* (1817) 3 Mer 441.

[13] Austin, Lect XXI, n 90.

[14] However although virtually all common lawyers agree that an objective test of agreement prevails there are significant differences as to how the objective test should be formulated and applied, see Spencer [1973] CLJ 104; Samek 52 Can Bar Rev 351; Howarth 100 LQR 265; Goddard 7 LS 263; Vorster 103 LQR 274; De Moor 106 LQR 632. See the (possibly differing) views expressed by Lord Brandon, Lord Diplock and Lord Brightman in *The Hannah Blumenthal* [1983] 1 AC 854, [1983] 1 All ER 34 and the

It is for this reason that the title of the present chapter is not 'Agreement' but 'The phenomena of agreement', concerned not with the presence of an inward and mental assent but with its outward and visible signs.

2 OFFER AND ACCEPTANCE: OFFER[15]

In order to determine whether, in any case given, it is reasonable to infer the existence of an agreement, it has long been usual to employ the language of offer and acceptance. In other words, the court examines all the circumstances to see if the one party may be assumed to have made a firm 'offer' and if the other may likewise be taken to have 'accepted' that offer. These complementary ideas present a convenient method of analysing a situation, provided that they are not applied too literally and that facts are not sacrificed to phrases.

It must be emphasised, however, that there are cases where the courts will certainly hold that there is a contract even though it is difficult or impossible to analyse the transaction in terms of offer and acceptance,[16] for as Lord Wilberforce has said:[17]

> English Law, having committed itself to a rather technical and schematic doctrine of contract, in application takes a practical approach, often at the cost of forcing the facts to fit uneasily into the marked slots of offer, acceptance and consideration.

The first task of the plaintiff is to prove the presence of a definite offer made either to a particular person or, as in advertisements of rewards for services to be rendered, to the public at large. In the famous case of *Carlill v Carbolic Smoke Ball Co*[18] it was

consideration of these views by Robert Goff LJ in *The Leonidas D* [1983] 3 All ER 737, [1984] 1 WLR 1. An illuminating discussion of whether Anglo-American law was wise so wholeheartedly to accept the objective test will be found in the opinion of Frank J in *Ricketts v Pennsylvania Rly Co* 153 F 2d 757 (1946). A classic example of objectivity is *Centrovincial Estates plc v Merchant Investors Assurance Co Ltd* [1983] Com LR 158, CA. See also Steyn LJ in *G Percy Trentham Ltd v Archital Luxfer Ltd* [1993] 1 Lloyd's Rep 25 at 27; *Cheddar Valley Engineering Ltd v Chaddlewood Homes Ltd* [1992] 4 All ER 942.

[15] Winfield 55 LQR 499; Kahn 72 SALJ 246.

[16] See eg *Clarke v Earl of Dunraven and Mount-Earl, The Satanita* [1897] AC 59, discussed at p 81, below.

[17] *New Zealand Shipping Co Ltd v A M Satterthwaite & Co Ltd* [1975] AC 154 at 167, [1974] 1 All ER 1015 at 1020.

[18] [1892] 2 QB 484; affd [1893] 1 QB 256. For a fascinating account of the setting of this case, see Simpson 14 Journal of Legal Studies 345. An example of the Smoke Ball itself may be seen at Dairyland, Tresillian Barton near Newquay, Cornwall. It should be noted that the plaintiff bought the smoke ball not from the defendants but from a chemist. In other cases English law has been reluctant to discover a contract between consumer and manufacturer where the consumer has bought from a retailer in reliance on the manufacturer's advertisements. *Lambert v Lewis* [1982] AC 225, [1981] 1 All ER 1185. Cf. *Bowerman v ABTA Ltd* [1995] NLJR 1815. See Borrie and Diamond *The Consumer, Society and the Law* (4th edn, 1981) pp 106–110. Cf Legh-Jones [1969] CLJ 54.

strenuously argued that an effective offer cannot be made to the public at large. In that case:

> The defendants, who were the proprietors of a medical preparation called 'The Carbolic Smoke Ball', issued an advertisement in which they offered to pay £100 to any person who succumbed to influenza after having used one of their smoke balls in a specified manner and for a specified period. They added that they had deposited a sum of £1,000 with their bankers 'to show their sincerity'. The plaintiff, on the faith of the advertisement, bought and used the ball as prescribed, but succeeded in catching influenza. She sued for the £100.

The defendants displayed the utmost ingenuity in their search for defences. They argued that the transaction was a bet within the meaning of the Gaming Acts, that it was an illegal policy of insurance, that the advertisement was a mere 'puff' never intended to create a binding obligation, that there was no offer to any particular person, and that, even if there were, the plaintiff had failed to notify her acceptance. The Court of Appeal found no difficulty in rejecting these various pleas. Bowen LJ effectively destroyed the argument that an offer cannot be made to the world at large.

> It was also said that the contract is made with all the world—that is, with everybody, and that you cannot contract with everybody. It is not a contract made with all the world. There is the fallacy of the argument. It is an offer made to all the world; and why should not an offer be made to all the world which is to ripen into a contract with anybody who comes forward and performs the condition? . . . Although the offer is made to the world, the contract is made with that limited portion of the public who come forward and perform the condition on the faith of the advertisement.

Offer distinguished from invitation to treat

An offer, capable of being converted into an agreement by acceptance, must consist of a definite promise to be bound, provided that certain specified terms are accepted. The offeror must have completed his share in the formation of a contract by finally declaring his readiness to undertake an obligation upon certain conditions, leaving to the offeree the option of acceptance or refusal. He must not merely have been feeling his way towards an agreement, not merely initiating negotiations from which an agreement might or might not in time result. He must be prepared to implement his promise, if such is the wish of the other party. The distinction is sometimes expressed in judicial language by the contrast of an 'offer' with that of an 'invitation to treat'. Referring to the advertisement in the *Carlill* case, Bowen LJ said:

> It is not like cases in which you offer to negotiate, or you issue advertisements that you have got a stock of books to sell, or houses to let, in which case there is no offer to be bound by any contract. Such advertisements are offers to negotiate—offers to receive offers—offers to chaffer.

The application of this distinction has long agitated the courts. It arose first in the law of auctions, where the problem may appear in at least three forms.

First, is the auctioneer's request for bids, a definite offer which will be converted into an agreement with the highest bidder, or is it only an attempt to 'set the ball rolling'? The latter view was accepted in *Payne v Cave*.[19] The bid itself constitutes the offer which the auctioneer is free to accept or to reject. In accordance with this principle the Sale of Goods Act 1979, provides that a sale by auction is complete when the auctioneer announces its completion by the fall of the hammer or in other customary manner, and that until such announcement is made any bid may be retracted.[20]

Secondly, does an advertisement that specified goods will be sold by auction on a certain day constitute a promise to potential bidders that the sale will actually be held? A negative answer was given to this question in *Harris v Nickerson*.[21] In that case the plaintiff failed to recover damages for loss suffered in travelling to the advertised place of an auction sale which was ultimately cancelled. His claim was condemned as 'an attempt to make a mere declaration of intention a binding contract'. In the words of Blackburn J:

> This is certainly a startling proposition and would be excessively inconvenient if carried out. It amounts to saying that anyone who advertises a sale by publishing an advertisement becomes responsible to everybody who attends the sale for his cab hire or travelling expenses.

Thirdly, does an advertisement that the sale will be *without reserve* constitute a definite offer to sell to the highest bidder? A Scottish court has denied that this is so, holding, in accordance with the general rule, that no agreement is complete unless and until the auctioneer acknowledges the acceptance of the bid by the fall of his hammer.[22] The point was long undecided in England, though it was the subject of *obiter dicta* in *Warlow v Harrison*.[23] The action in that case failed both in the Queen's Bench and in the Court of Exchequer Chamber because the plaintiff pleaded his claim upon an obviously incorrect ground. But three of the judges in the Exchequer Chamber were of opinion that he would succeed if he brought a fresh action pleading that the auctioneer, by his advertisement, had implicitly pledged himself to sell to the highest bidder. In the view of these judges, two separate questions must be disentangled. On the one hand, had a contract of sale been concluded, and, if so, at what moment of time? Since the advertisement was not itself an offer to sell the goods but only an 'invitation to treat', the plaintiff's bid was not an acceptance and did not constitute a sale. Was there, on the other hand, a binding promise that the sale should

---

[19] (1789) 3 Term Rep 148.
[20] Sale of Goods Act 1979, s 57(2).
[21] (1873) LR 8 QB 286.
[22] *Fenwick v Macdonald, Fraser & Co* 1904 6 F (Ct of Sess) 850.
[23] (1859) 1 E & E 309; see *Johnston v Boyes* [1899] 2 Ch 73, and *Rainbow v Howkins & Sons* [1904] 2 KB 322.

be without reserve? The majority of the Exchequer Chamber were prepared to discover such a promise. The auctioneer in his advertisement had made a definite offer to this effect, and the plaintiff, by making his bid in reliance upon it, had accepted the offer. This constituted a distinct and independent contract, and for its breach an action would lie. This view was described by Blackburn J in *Harris v Nickerson*[24] as resting upon 'very plausible grounds'. But it was not universally accepted. It is indisputable that the mere advertisement of an auction, without further qualification, is an invitation to treat and not an offer. The auction need not be held, and prospective purchasers have no legal complaint if they have wasted their time and money in coming to the sale rooms. But, if the *dicta* in *Warlow v Harrison* are correct, the addition to the advertisement of the two words 'without reserve' converts it into an offer, presumably to the public at large, that the sale will, in fact, be subject to no reserve price. If, in these circumstances, the sale is actually held and a prospective purchaser makes a bid, he accepts the offer of a sale 'without reserve', and the auctioneer, if he then puts a reserve price upon any of the lots, is liable to an action for breach of contract. But, if the auctioneer were to refuse to hold any sale at all, he would not be breaking any binding promise and could not be sued.[25]

The dispute was finally settled by the decision of the Court of Appeal in *Barry v Heathcote Ball & Co (Commercial Auctions) Ltd.*[26] The court had no doubt that an auctioneer who stated that an auction was without reserve entered into a collateral contract with the highest bidder.[27]

Similar reasoning was used in the decision of the House of Lords in relation to the analogous situation of contract by tender in *Harvela Investments Ltd v Royal Trust Co of Canada Ltd.*[28]

The first defendants held some 12% of the shares of a company as trustees of a settlement. They wished to sell the shares. The two obvious buyers were the plaintiffs who owned 43% of the shares and the second defendants who owned 40%, since if either bought the shares they would obtain control of the company. The first defendants decided to dispose of the shares by sealed competitive tender and sent identical telexes to the plaintiffs and the second defendants inviting tenders and stating, 'We confirm that if the offer made by you is the highest offer received by us we bind ourselves to accept such offer providing that such offer complies with the terms of this telex'. The plaintiffs bid $2,175,000. The second defendants bid $2,100,000 or '$100,000 in excess of any other offer which you may receive which is expressed as a

---

[24] (1873) LR 8 QB 286 at 288.

[25] See Slade 68 LQR 238, 69 LQR 21. Cf Gower 68 LQR 467. Support for the two contract analysis can be found in *Tully v Irish Land Commission* (1961) 97 ILT 174.

[26] [2001] 1 All ER 944, [2000] 1 WLR 1962; Meisel 64 MLR 468; Carter 17 JCL 69.

[27] Since it cannot be known at the time that a bid is made that it will be the highest bid, it must be possible to argue that there is a collateral contract with all who bid or even with all who attend the auction. Claimants other than the highest bidder will usually not be able to show loss however.

[28] [1986] AC 207, [1985] 2 All ER 966.

fixed monetary amount whichever is higher'. The first defendants accepted the second defendants' offer.

The House of Lords held that the first defendants were legally obliged to accept the plaintiff's offer. In coming to this conclusion their Lordships analysed the problem in a very illuminating way and adopted a two-contract approach. The telex was treated as an offer of a unilateral contract to accept the highest bid which would be followed by a bilateral contract with the highest bidder. It was further held that a referential bid such as the second defendant's was inconsistent with an obligation to accept the higher of two sealed bids.

Instances of invitation to treat

The distinction between an offer and an invitation to treat has been applied in other everyday practices. The issue, for instance, of a circular or catalogue advertising goods for sale is a mere attempt to induce offers, not an offer itself.[29] Lord Herschell has exposed the inconvenience of a contrary interpretation:

> The transmission of such a price-list does not amount to an offer to supply an unlimited quantity of the wine described at the price named, so that as soon as an order is given there is a binding contract to supply that quantity. If it were so, the merchant might find himself involved in any number of contractual obligations to supply wine of a particular description which he would be quite unable to carry out, his stock of wine of that description being necessarily limited.[30]

In *Partridge v Crittenden*[31] the appellant had inserted a notice in a periodical entitled *Cage and Aviary Birds* which read 'Bramblefinch cocks and hens, 25s each'. It appeared under the general heading of 'Classified Advertisements' and the words 'offer for sale' were not used. He was charged with unlawfully offering for sale a wild live bird contrary to the provisions of the Protection of Birds Act 1954 and was convicted. The divisional court quashed the conviction. There had been no 'offer for sale'. Lord Parker said:[32]

> I think that when one is dealing with advertisements and circulars, unless they indeed come from manufacturers, there is business sense in their being construed as invitations to treat and not offers for sale.

A not dissimilar question long remained undecided. If goods are exhibited in a shop window or inside a shop with a price attached, does this constitute an offer to sell at that price? Parke B at least felt no doubt about the matter, for, when counsel suggested that: 'If a man advertises goods at a certain price, I have a right to go into his

---

[29] Cf *Spencer v Harding* (1870) LR 5 CP 561.

[30] *Grainger & Son v Gough* [1896] AC 325 at 334. A similar rule has been applied to the notice of a scholarship: *Rooke v Dawson* [1895] 1 Ch 480.

[31] [1968] 2 All ER 421, [1968] 1 WLR 1204.

[32] Ibid at 424 and 1209, respectively.

shop and demand the article at the price marked', the learned judge peremptorily cut him short with the reply: 'No; if you do, he has a right to turn you out.'[33] This view was confirmed in *Pharmaceutical Society of Great Britain v Boots Cash Chemists (Southern) Ltd.*[34]

> The defendants adapted one of their shops to a 'self-service' system. A customer, on entering, was given a basket, and having selected from the shelves the articles he required, put them in the basket and took them to the cash desk. Near the desk was a registered pharmacist who was authorised, if necessary, to stop a customer from removing any drug from the shop.

The court had to decide whether the defendants had broken the provisions of section 18 of the Pharmacy and Poisons Act 1933, which made it unlawful to sell any listed poison 'unless the sale is effected under the supervision of a registered pharmacist'. The vital question was at what time the 'sale' took place, and this depended in turn on whether the display of the goods with prices attached was an offer or an invitation to treat. According to the plaintiffs, it was an offer, accepted when the customer put an article into his basket, and, if this article was a poison, it was therefore 'sold' before the pharmacist could intervene. According to the defendants, the display was only an invitation to treat. An offer to buy was made when the customer put an article in the basket, and this offer the defendants were free to accept or to reject. If they accepted, they did so only when the transaction was approved by the pharmacist near the cash desk. Lord Goddard, at first instance, had no hesitation in deciding that the display was only an invitation to treat so that the law had not been broken. The Court of Appeal upheld his decision and adopted his reasoning.[35]

> The transaction is in no way different from the normal transaction in a shop in which there is no self-service scheme. I am quite satisfied it would be wrong to say that the shopkeeper is making an offer to sell every article in the shop to any person who might come in and that person can insist on buying any article by saying 'I accept your offer'. I agree with the illustration put forward during the case of a person who might go into a shop where books are displayed. In most book-shops customers are invited to go in and pick up books and look at them even if they do not actually buy them. There is no contract by the shopkeeper to sell until the customer has taken the book to the shopkeeper or his assistant and said 'I want to buy this book' and the shopkeeper says 'Yes'. That would not prevent the shopkeeper, seeing the book picked up, saying: 'I am sorry I cannot let you have that book; it is the only copy I have got and I have already promised it to another customer.' Therefore, in my opinion, the mere fact that a customer picks up a bottle of medicine from the shelves in this case does not amount to an acceptance of an offer to sell. It is an offer by the customer to buy, and there is no sale effected until the buyer's offer to buy is accepted by the acceptance of the price.

---

[33] *Timothy v Simpson* (1834) 6 C & P 499 at 500.
[34] [1952] 2 QB 795, [1952] 2 All ER 456; affd [1953] 1 QB 401, [1953] 1 All ER 482.
[35] [1952] 2 QB 795 at 802, [1952] 2 All ER 456 at 458, 459.

In *Fisher v Bell*[36] Lord Parker treated the point as beyond dispute.

> It is clear that, according to the ordinary law of contract, the display of an article with a price on it in a shop window is merely an invitation to treat. It is in no sense an offer for sale the acceptance of which constitutes a contract.[37]

It is surprising that in other matters of daily life the legal position remains doubtful. If a passenger boards a bus, is he accepting an offer of carriage or is he himself making an offer in response to an invitation to treat? In *Wilkie v London Passenger Transport Board*,[38] Lord Greene thought that a contract is made when an intending passenger 'puts himself either on the platform or inside the bus'. The opinion was obiter;[39] but if it represents the law it would seem that the corporation makes an offer of carriage by running the bus and that the passenger accepts the offer when he gets properly on board. The contract would then be complete even if no fare is yet paid or ticket given.[40]

Negotiations for the sale of land present no difference of principle. But they may involve the adjustment of so many questions of detail that the courts require cogent evidence of an intention to be bound before they find the existence of an offer capable of acceptance. Thus in *Harvey v Facey*:[41]

> . . . the plaintiffs telegraphed to the defendants, 'Will you sell us Bumper Hall Pen? Telegraph lowest cash price.' The defendants telegraphed in reply, 'Lowest price for Bumper Hall Pen, £900.' The plaintiffs then telegraphed, 'We agree to buy Bumper Hall Pen for £900 asked by you. Please send us your title-deeds.' The rest was silence.

---

[36] [1961] 1 QB 394 at 399, [1960] 3 All ER 731 at 733.

[37] Although the rule is well settled, its application to self-service stores has been criticised. See Unger 16 MLR 369; cf Montrose 4 Am J Comp Law 235. Display of goods in a self-service store was held an offer in *Lasky v Economy Grocery Stores* 319 Mass 224, 65 NE 2d 305 (1946) and display of deck chairs on a beach an offer to hire in *Chapelton v Barry UDC* [1940] 1 KB 532, [1940] 1 All ER 356. In practice the question has usually arisen in the context of a criminal statute making it an offence to 'offer' goods of a prescribed description for sale. Display of goods in a shop window may well fall within the mischief of such a statute and a well-drafted statute may contain a special wider definition of 'offer'. See eg Trade Descriptions Act 1968, s 6. See further on the application of offer and acceptance to criminal offences, Smith [1972] B] CLJ 197 at 198–201, 204–208. The orthodox contract analysis of a self-service store transaction presents recurrent problems in the criminal law. See eg *Lacis v Cashmarts* [1969] 2 QB 400; *Pilgram v Rice-Smith* [1977] 2 All ER 658, [1977] 1 WLR 671; Williams [1977] CLJ 62.

[38] [1947] 1 All ER 258.

[39] The Court of Appeal held on the facts that the plaintiff had not made a contract with the Board, but was only a licensee. See also p 218, below.

[40] In practice these questions will not be governed solely by the law of contract. See Public Passenger Vehicles Act 1981 and regulations made thereunder.

[41] [1893] AC 552.

It was held by the Judicial Committee of Privy Council that there was no contract. The second telegram was not an offer, but only an indication of the minimum price if the defendants ultimately resolved to sell, and the third telegram was therefore not an acceptance. So, too, in *Clifton v Palumbo*,[42] the plaintiff and the defendant were negotiating for the sale of a large, scattered estate. The plaintiff wrote to the defendant:

> I . . . am prepared to offer you or your nominee my Lytham estate for £600,000 . . . I also agree that a reasonable and sufficient time shall be granted to you for the examination and consideration of all the data and details necessary for the preparation of the Schedule of Completion.

The Court of Appeal held that this letter was not a definite offer to sell, but a preliminary statement as to price, which—especially in a transaction of such magnitude—was but one of the many questions to be considered. In the words of Lord Greene:[43]

> There is nothing in the world to prevent an owner of an estate of this kind contracting to sell it to a purchaser, who is prepared to spend so large a sum of money, on terms written out on a half sheet of note paper of the most informal description and even, if he likes, on unfavourable conditions. But I think it is legitimate, in approaching the construction of a document of this kind, containing phrases and expressions of doubtful significance, to bear in mind that the probability of parties entering into so large a transaction, and finally binding themselves to a contract of this description couched in such terms, is remote. If they have done it, they have done it, however unwise and however unbusinesslike it may be. The question is, Have they done it?

Both *Harvey v Facey* and *Clifton v Palumbo* were distinguished in *Bigg v Boyd Gibbins Ltd*.[44] The Court of Appeal, on the facts before them, here held that the parties were not still negotiating, but had agreed on a price and made a contract. After reading the relevant letters, Russell LJ said that he could not 'escape the view that the parties would regard themselves at the end of the correspondence, quite correctly, as having struck a bargain for the sale and purchase of the property'.[45]

The distinction between offer and invitation to treat is neatly illustrated by the case of *Gibson v Manchester City Council*.[46]

---

[42] [1944] 2 All ER 497.

[43] Ibid at 499.

[44] [1971] 2 All ER 183, esp. at 185, [1971] 1 WLR 913. See also *Storer v Manchester City Council* [1974] 3 All ER 824, [1974] 1 WLR 1403.

[45] Cf Prichard 90 LQR 55.

[46] [1979] 1 All ER 972, [1979] 1 WLR 294.

In September 1970 the council adopted a policy of selling council houses to council tenants. On 16 February 1971 the City Treasurer wrote a letter to Mr Gibson stating that the council 'may be prepared to sell the house to you at the purchase price of £2,725 less 20% = £2,180 (freehold)'. The letter invited Mr Gibson to make a formal application, which he did. In the normal course, this would probably have been followed by the preparation and exchange of contracts but before that process had been completed, control of the council changed hands as a result of the local government elections of May 1971. The policy of selling council houses was reversed and the council decided only to complete those transactions where exchange of contracts had taken place. Mr Gibson claimed that a binding contract had come into existence but the House of Lords held that the Treasurer's letter of 10 February was at most an invitation to treat and that therefore Mr Gibson's application was an offer and not an acceptance.[47]

3 OFFER AND ACCEPTANCE: ACCEPTANCE

Proof of an offer to enter into legal relations upon definite terms must be followed by the production of evidence from which the courts may infer an intention by the offeree to accept that offer. It must again be emphasised that the phrase 'offer and acceptance', though hallowed by a century and a half of judicial usage,[48] is not to be applied as a talisman, revealing, by a species of esoteric art, the presence of a contract. It would be ludicrous to suppose that businessmen couch their communications in the form of a catechism or reduce their negotiations to such a species of interrogatory as was formulated in the Roman *stipulatio*. The rules which the judges have elaborated from the premise of offer and acceptance are neither the rigid deductions of logic nor the inspiration of natural justice. They are only presumptions, drawn from experience, to be applied in so far as they serve the ultimate object of establishing the phenomena of agreement, and their application may be observed under two heads: (a) the fact of acceptance, and (b) the communication of acceptance.

---

[47] The majority of the Court of Appeal had taken the opposite view [1978] 2 All ER 583, [1978] 1 WLR 520. This was partly on the basis 'that there is no need to look for a strict offer and acceptance', partly on the basis that the court was dealing with a policy decision by a local council and not with an alleged contract between private individuals, and partly that Mr Gibson had relied on the council's policy being unchanged and spent money on improving the house. The factual basis for the third ground was denied in the House of Lords. Cf *Duttons Brewery Ltd v Leeds City Council* (1982) 43 P & CR 160.

[48] See *Adams v Lindsell* (1818) 1 B & Ald 681; Simpson 91 LQR 247 at 258–262.

A The fact of acceptance

Agreement may be inferred from conduct

Whether there has been an acceptance by one party of an offer made to him by the other may be collected from the words or documents that have passed between them, or may be inferred from their conduct. The task of inferring an assent and of fixing the precise moment at which it may be said to have emerged is one of obvious difficulty, particularly when the negotiations between the parties have covered a long period of time or are contained in protracted or desultory correspondence.

This may be observed in the case of *Brogden v Metropolitan Rly Co*:[49]

> Brogden had for years supplied the defendant company with coal without a formal agreement. At length the parties decided to regularise their relations. The company's agent sent a draft form of agreement to Brogden, and the latter, having inserted the name of an arbitrator in a space which had been left blank for this purpose, signed it and returned it, marked 'approved'. The company's agent put it in his desk and nothing further was done to complete its execution. Both parties acted thereafter on the strength of its terms, supplying and paying for the coal in accordance with its clauses, until a dispute arose between them and Brogden denied that any binding contract existed.

The difficulty was to determine when, if ever, a mutual assent was to be found. It could not be argued that the return of the draft was an acceptance of the company's offer, since Brogden, by inserting the name of an arbitrator, had added a new term, which the company had had no opportunity of approving or rejecting. But assuming that the delivery of the document by Brogden to the company, with the addition of the arbitrator's name, was a final and definite offer to supply coal on the terms contained in it, when was that offer accepted? No further communication passed between the parties, and it was impossible to infer assent from the mere fact that the document remained without remark in the agent's desk. On the other hand, the subsequent conduct of the parties was explicable only on the assumption that they mutually approved the terms of the draft. The House of Lords held that a contract came into existence either when the company ordered its first load of coal from Brogden upon these terms or at least when Brogden supplied it.[50]

Counter-offer is a final rejection of original offer

Whatever the difficulties, and however elastic their rules, the judges must, either upon oral evidence or by the construction of documents, find some act from which they can infer the offeree's intention to accept, or they must refuse to admit the existence of

---

[49] (1877) 2 App Cas 666.
[50] See also *Robophone Facilities Ltd v Blank* [1966] 3 All ER 128, [1966] 1 WLR 1428.

an agreement. This intention, moreover, must be conclusive. It must not treat the negotiations between the parties as still open to the process of bargaining. The offeree must unreservedly assent to the exact terms proposed by the offeror. If, while purporting to accept the offer as a whole, he introduces a new term which the offeror has not had the chance of examining, he is, in fact, merely making a counter-offer. The effect of this in the eyes of the law is to destroy the original offer. Thus in *Hyde v Wrench*:[51]

> The defendant on 6 June offered to sell an estate to the plaintiff for £1,000. On 8 June, in reply, the plaintiff made an offer of £950, which was refused by the defendant on 27 June. Finally, on 29 June, the plaintiff wrote that he was now prepared to pay £1,000.

It was held that no contract existed. By his letter of 8 June the plaintiff had rejected the original offer and he was no longer able to revive it by changing his mind and tendering a subsequent acceptance. A counter-offer may come upon the scene not bearing its badge upon its sleeve but dressed as an 'acceptance'. In principle, to be effective an acceptance must accept all the terms contained in the offer. In practice, however, many so-called 'acceptances' while purporting to accept, also attempt to introduce new terms. Such an acceptance is in fact a counter-offer and creates no contract.[52]

Whether a communication amounts to a counter-offer or not is sometimes difficult to determine. The offeree, for example, may reply to the offer in terms which leave it uncertain, whether he is making a counter-offer or merely seeking further information before making up his mind. A mere request for information obviously does not destroy the offer. A relevant and instructive case is *Stevenson v McLean*:[53]

> The defendant offered on Saturday to sell to the plaintiffs 3,800 tons of iron 'at 40s nett cash per ton, open till Monday'. Early on Monday the plaintiffs telegraphed to the defendant: 'Please wire whether you would accept 40 for delivery over two months, or if not longest limit you would give.' No reply was received, so by a telegram sent at 1.34 pm on the same day the plaintiffs accepted the offer to sell at 40s cash. Meanwhile the defendant sold the iron to a third person and informed the plaintiffs of this in a telegram despatched at 1.25 pm. The telegrams crossed.

The plaintiffs sued to recover damages for breach of contract. They would be entitled to succeed if the original offer was still open when they sent their telegram at 1.34 pm, for, as will be seen later, an acceptance is complete and effective at the moment when a

---

[51] (1840) 3 Beav 334; and see *Brogden v Metropolitan Rly Co*, above.

[52] *Jones v Daniel* [1894] 2 Ch 332. This principle is important in relation to the 'battle of the forms', discussed, pp 209–211, below.

[53] (1880) 5 QBD 346. See also *Society of Lloyd's v Twinn* (2000) The Times 4 April

letter is posted or a telegram is handed in to the post office. But was the first telegram sent by the plaintiffs a counter-offer which destroyed the offer, or was it an innocuous request for information? It might be regarded either as the proposal of a new term or as an inquiry put forward tentatively in the hope of inducing better terms but without any intention to prejudice the position of the plaintiffs if they ultimately decided to accept the original offer. Either construction was possible. In the result Lush J held that the plaintiffs had not made a counter-offer, but had addressed to the defendant 'a mere inquiry, which should have been answered and not treated as a rejection of the offer'.[54] Another way of testing whether the first Monday telegram was a counter-offer would be to ask whether the defendant could have created a contract by accepting it. It is clear that at this stage the plaintiffs had not sufficiently shown that they agreed.

A conditional assent to an offer does not constitute acceptance. A man who, though content with the general details of a proposed transaction, feels that he requires expert guidance before committing himself to a binding obligation, often makes his acceptance conditional upon the advice of some third party, such as a solicitor. The result is that neither party is subject to an obligation. A common example of this in everyday life occurs in the case of a purchase or a lease of land. Here it is the common practice to incorporate the terms, after they have been settled, in a document which contains some such incantation as 'subject to contract', or 'subject to a formal contract to be drawn up by our solicitors'. Unless there is cogent evidence of a contrary intention, the courts construe these words so as to postpone the incidence of liability until a formal document has been drafted and signed.[55] As regards enforceability the first document is not worth the paper it is written on. It is merely a proposal to enter into a contract—a transaction which is a legal nullity—and it may be disregarded by either party with impunity. Until the completion of the formal contract both parties enjoy a *locus paenitentiae*.[56] In the case of *Branca v Cobarro*[57] the court was presented with a delicate question of construction:

> A vendor agreed to sell the lease and goodwill of a mushroom farm on the terms of a written document which was declared to be 'a provisional agreement until a fully legalised agreement, drawn up by a solicitor and embodying all the conditions herewith stated, is signed'.

[54] Ibid at 350.

[55] For an exceptional case where the court found a contract despite the use of the expression 'subject to contract'. See *Alpenstow Ltd v Regalian Properties plc* [1985] 2 All ER 545, [1985] 1 WLR 721

[56] *Winn v Bull* (1877) 7 ChD 29; *Chillingworth v Esche* [1924] 1 Ch 97; *Eccles v Bryant and Pollock* [1948] Ch 93, [1947] 2 All ER 865. *Munton v Greater London Council* [1976] 2 All ER 815, [1976] 1 WLR 649; *Derby & Co Ltd v ITC Pension Trust Ltd* [1977] 2 All ER 890. See the similar rule in Roman law, Inst iii, 23 pr.

[57] [1947] KB 854, [1947] 2 All ER 101.

The Court of Appeal held that, by using the word 'provisional', the parties had intended the document to be an agreement binding from the outset, though subsequently to be replaced by a more formal contract. It must, therefore, be in each case a question of construction whether the parties intended to undertake immediate, if temporary, obligations, or whether they were suspending all liability until the conclusion of formalities. Have they, in other words, made the operation of their contract conditional upon the execution of a further document, in which case their obligations will be suspended, or have they made an immediately binding agreement, though one which is later to be merged into a more formal contract? However the use of the formula 'subject to contract' creates a strong presumption that the parties do not intend an immediately binding contract.

The usual English practice of making agreements for the sale of land 'subject to contract' normally operates to protect the buyer since it provides time for investigation of title and survey of the premises. During the early 1970s, however, in a period of rapidly increasing house prices it came to appear unfavourable to buyers since it allowed the seller to 'gazump', that is to refuse to sign the formal contract unless the buyer would agree to an increased price. However, a Law Commission report concluded that 'gazumping' was the product of short-term factors and that any change in the law or practice would not in general benefit buyers.[58]

Agreement may be inferred from observance of written terms

Upon the particular phrase 'subject to contract' the pressure of litigation has stamped a precise significance. In other cases it is often difficult to decide if the language used justifies the inference of a complete and final agreement.[59] The task of the courts is to extract the intention of the parties both from the terms of their correspondence and from the circumstances which surround and follow it, and the question of

[58] Law Com no 65. The 'subject to contract' practice is quite independent of any legal requirement that a contract for the sale of land should be made or evidenced in writing though the two may interact; see *Tiverton Estates Ltd v Wearwell Ltd* [1975] Ch 146, [1974] 1 All ER 209, discussed at pp 271–273, below. For further discussion see Clark [1984] Conv 173, 251. Other proposals to avoid the evils of gazumping have continued to be discussed. Some would simply require changes in the practice of conveyancing solicitors. Gazumping would be less extensive if the time gap between the informal deal between buyer and seller and the formal contract were shorter as it is in many systems; other proposals such as requiring the seller to have the house surveyed before he puts it on the market would require legislation. Most proposals would not involve any change in the general law of contract as stated above.

[59] It would be a mistake to assume that the use of the words 'subject to' always indicate an inchoate agreement. So an arrangement to sell land 'subject to planning permission' may be a binding agreement, conditional on planning permission being obtained. See eg *Batten v White* (1960) 12 P & CR 66. Such a condition may impose an obligation on one or both parties to do his best to bring the condition about, eg *Martin v Macarthur* [1963] NZLR 403 ('subject to satisfactory finance'). Cf *Lee-Parker v Izzet (No 2)* [1972] 2 All ER 800, [1972] 1 WLR 775. The expression 'sub details' in an agreement for sale of a ship was held to mean that there was no contract until the details had been agreed. *Thoreson & Co (Bangkok) Ltd v Fathom Marine Co. Ltd.* [2004] EWHC 167 (Comm), [2004] 1 All ER (Comm) 935. See further pp 192–194, below.

interpretation may thus be stated. Is the preparation of a further document a condition precedent to the creation of a contract or is it an incident in the performance of an already binding obligation? As in all questions of construction, the comparison of decided cases is apt to confuse rather than to illuminate. It would appear, however, that, whenever there is evidence that the parties have acted upon the faith of a written document, the courts will prefer to assume that the document embodies a definite intention to be bound and will strive to implement its terms.[60] Such, at least, will be the instinct of a judge in a commercial transaction, where the parties are engaged in a particular trade and may be taken to have accepted its special and familiar usages as the background of their bargain. Thus in *Hillas & Co Ltd v Arcos Ltd*:[61]

> Hillas & Co had agreed to buy from Arcos Ltd, '22,000 standards of softwood goods of fair specification over the season 1930'. The written agreement contained an option to buy 100,000 in 1931, but without particulars as to the kind or size of timber or the manner of shipment. No difficulties arose on the original purchase for 1930, but, when the buyers sought to exercise the option for 1931, the sellers took the point that the failure to define these various particulars showed that the clause was not intended to bind either party, but merely to provide a basis for future agreement.

The House of Lords held that the language used, interpreted in the light of the previous course of dealing between the parties, showed a sufficient intention to be bound. Lord Tomlin said:

> The problem for a court of construction must always be so to balance matters that, without the violation of essential principle, the dealings of men may as far as possible be treated as effective, and that the law may not incur the reproach of being the destroyer of bargains.[62]

Where, on the other hand, there is no particular trade in question and no familiar business practice to clothe the skeleton of the agreement, the task of spelling out a

---

[60] *Sweet and Maxwell Ltd v Universal News Services Ltd* [1964] 2 QB 699, [1964] 3 All ER 30. *British Bank for Foreign Trade Ltd v Novinex Ltd* [1949] 1 All ER 155 suggests that once performance is complete there must be a contract and similarly *G Percy Trentham v Archital Luxfer* [1993] 1 Lloyd's Rep 25 at 27 per Steyn LJ but Cf. *British Steel Corpn v Cleveland Bridge and Engineering Co Ltd* [1984] 1 All ER 504; McKendrick (1988) 2 Oxford JLS 197.

[61] (1932) 38 Com Cas 23.

[62] Ibid at 29. The earlier decision of the House of Lords in *May and Butcher v R*, decided in 1929, but not reported until 1934, ([1934] 2 KB 17n) presents some difficulties of reconciliation. But it would appear from the judgments of the Court of Appeal in *Foley v Classique Coaches Ltd* [1934] 2 KB 1, and in *National Coal Board v Galley* [1958] 1 All ER 91, [1958] 1 WLR 16, that the view expressed by the House of Lords in *Hillas v Arcos* offer the better guide in what must always be the difficult task of discovering the intention of the parties. See also *Courtney and Fairbairn Ltd v Tolaini Bros (Hotels) Ltd* [1975] 1 All ER 716, [1975] 1 WLR 297. *Mamidoil-Jetoil Greek Petroleum Co SA v Okta Crude Oil Refinery AD* [2001] EWCA Civ 406, [2001] 2 Lloyd's Rep 76.

common intention from meagre words may prove too speculative for the court to undertake. Thus in *Scammell v Ouston*:[63]

> Ouston wished to acquire from Messrs Scammell a new motor-van on hire-purchase terms. After a considerable correspondence, Ouston gave a written order for a particular type of van, which included the words—'This order is given on the understanding that the balance of purchase price can be had on hire-purchase terms over a period of two years.' The order was accepted by Messrs Scammell in general terms, but the hire-purchase terms were never specifically determined. It later appeared in evidence that there was a wide variety of hire-purchase agreements and that there was nothing to indicate which of them the parties favoured.

Messrs Scammell later refused to provide the van, and Ouston sued for damages for non-delivery. Messrs Scammell pleaded that no contract had ever been concluded, and the House of Lords accepted this view.

Lord Wright[64] said that there were two grounds on which he must hold that no contract had been made:

> The first is that the language used was so obscure and so incapable of any definite or precise meaning that the Court is unable to attribute to the parties any particular contractual intention. The object of the Court is to do justice between the parties, and the Court will do its best, if satisfied that there was an ascertainable and determinate intention to contract, to give effect to that intention, looking at substance and not mere form. It will not be deterred by mere difficulties of interpretation. Difficulty is not synonymous with ambiguity so long as any definite meaning can be extracted. But the test of intention is to be found in the words used. If these words, considered however broadly and untechnically and with due regard to all the just implications, fail to evince any definite meaning on which the Court can safely act, the Court has no choice but to say that there is no contract. Such a position is not often found. But I think that it is found in this case.[65] My reason for so thinking is not only based on the actual vagueness and unintelligibility of the words used, but is confirmed by the startling diversity of explanations, tendered by those who think there was a bargain, of what the bargain was. I do not think it would be right to hold the appellants to any particular version. It was all left too vague. . . .
>
> But I think the other reason, which is that the parties never in intention nor even in appearance reached an agreement, is a still sounder reason against enforcing the claim. In truth, in my opinion, their agreement was inchoate and never got beyond negotiations. They did, indeed, accept the position that there should be some form of hire-purchase agreement, but they never went on to complete their agreement by settling between them what the terms of the hire-purchase agreement were to be.

---

[63] [1941] AC 251, [1941] 1 All ER 14. Contrast *Sweet and Maxwell Ltd v Universal News Services Ltd* [1964] 2 QB 699, [1964] 3 All ER 30.

[64] [1941] AC 251 at 268–269, [1941] 1 All ER 14 at 25–26.

[65] See *Jaques v Lloyd D George & Partners Ltd* [1968] 2 All ER 187, [1968] 1 WLR 625.

A comparison of these two cases is instructive. In *Hillas v Arcos*, though the document itself left a number of points undetermined, these could be settled by referring to the earlier relations of the parties and to the normal course of the trade. In *Scammell v Ouston* not only were the *lacunae* themselves more serious but there was nothing either in the previous dealings of the parties or in accepted business practice which might help to supply them. Vital questions had originally been left unanswered and no subsequent negotiations ever settled them. In these circumstances the judges, with the best will in the world, could not invent a contract which the parties had been too idle to make for themselves. At the same time, as Lord Wright pointed out, the judges will always seek to implement and not to defeat reasonable expectations. They will follow, if this is at all possible, the example of *Hillas v Arcos* rather than that of *Scammell v Ouston*.[66] In particular they will not be deterred from proclaiming the existence of a contract merely because one of the parties, after agreeing in substance to the proposals of the other, introduces a phrase or clause which, when examined, is found to be without significance. If there appears to be agreement on all essential matters, either on the face of the documents or by praying in aid commercial practice or the previous course of dealing between the parties, the court will ignore a subsidiary and meaningless addendum. The case of *Nicolene Ltd v Simmonds*[67] illustrates this anxiety of the judges to support the assumptions of sensible men if this is in any way possible.

> The plaintiffs wrote to the defendant offering to buy from him a large quantity of steel bars. The defendant replied in writing that he would be happy to supply them and thanking the plaintiffs 'for entrusting this contract to me'. He added: 'I assume that we are in agreement that the usual conditions of acceptance apply.' The plaintiffs acknowledged this letter and said that they awaited the invoice for the goods, but made no reference to the 'usual conditions of acceptance'. The defendant failed to deliver the goods and the plaintiffs sued for breach of contract.

The defendant argued that, as there had been no explicit agreement on the 'conditions of acceptance', there was no concluded contract. His own letter, at the highest, was only a counter-offer which had not been accepted. The Court of Appeal dismissed the argument and gave judgment for the plaintiffs. It appeared that there were no 'usual conditions of acceptance' to which either party could refer. The words were therefore meaningless and must be ignored.

Denning LJ said:[68]

> It would be strange indeed if a party could escape from every one of his obligations by inserting a meaningless exception from some of them ... You would find defaulters all scanning their contracts to find some meaningless clause on which to ride free.

---

[66] See *Smith v Morgan* [1971] 2 All ER 1500, [1971] 1 WLR 803; and *Brown v Gould* [1972] Ch 53, [1971] 2 All ER 1505; compare *King's Motors (Oxford) Ltd v Lax* [1969] 3 All ER 665, [1970] 1 WLR 426.

[67] [1953] 1 QB 543, [1953] 1 All ER 822.

[68] Ibid at 551–552 and 824–825, respectively.

Hodson LJ said:[69]

> I do not accept the proposition that, because some meaningless words are used in a letter which contains an unqualified acceptance of an offer, those meaningless words must, or can, be relied on by the acceptor as enabling him to obtain a judgment in his favour of the basis that there has been no acceptance at all.

Acceptance may be retrospective

The inclination of judges, whenever possible and especially in commercial transactions, to find the existence of a contract is further evident in their readiness to assume that the acceptance of an offer may have a retrospective effect. It may then serve to clothe with legal force the conduct of parties who have acted on the faith of this assumption. Few such cases, indeed, are to be found in the reports. But there seems no reason to doubt that in law, as in common sense, an acceptance may thus legitimate the past. The question was discussed by Megaw J in *Trollope and Colls Ltd v Atomic Power Constructions Ltd:*[70]

> Frequently in large transactions a written contract is expressed to have retrospective effect, sometimes lengthy retrospective effect; and this in cases where the negotiations on some of the terms have continued up to almost, if not quite, the date of the signature of the contract. The parties have meanwhile been conducting their transactions with one another, it may be for many months, on the assumption that a contract would ultimately be agreed on lines known to both the parties, though with the final form of various constituent terms of the proposed contract still under discussion. The parties have assumed that when the contract is made—when all the terms have been agreed in their final form—the contract will apply retrospectively to the preceding transactions. Often, as I say, the ultimate contract expressly so provides. I can see no reason why, if the parties so intend and agree, such a stipulation should be denied legal effect.

In the case under consideration there was no such express stipulation. But the parties had assumed that a contract would in due course be made, they had given orders and carried out work on this assumption and no other explanation of their conduct was feasible. The learned judge therefore imported into the contract, when ultimately made, a term that it should apply retrospectively to all that had been done in anticipation of it.

The requirement of certainty

The cases discussed in the preceding few pages are all examples of the tensions created by the law's demand for a minimal degree of certainty before it will classify an

---

[69] Ibid at 553 and 826, respectively. See also *Michael Richards Properties Ltd v Corpn of Wardens of St Saviour's Parish, Southwark* [1975] 3 All ER 416, where the words 'subject to contract' were struck out as being meaningless in the context.

[70] [1962] 3 All ER 1035, especially at 1040, [1963] 1 WLR 333 at 339.

agreement as a contract. Since most contracts are not negotiated by lawyers, it is all too easy for the contract makers to fail this test, particularly as legal and commercial perceptions of certainty may well diverge. So a lawyer would regard an agreement that goods are to be supplied at 'a reasonable price' as prima facie sufficiently certain but would have much more doubt about an agreement 'for a price to be agreed between us'. Many businessmen would be much happier with the second agreement rather than the first.

Although it is not possible to discover perfect consistency in this area, it is possible to identify certain commonly recurrent types of difficulty. First, the parties may have agreed to postpone the creation of the contract to some future date, which may never arise. The 'subject to contract'[71] cases are one example of this. Another is the 'letter of intent'.[72] This is a very commonly employed commercial device by which one party indicates to another that he is very likely to place a contract with him. A typical situation would involve a contractor who is proposing to tender for a large building contract and who would need to sub-contract, for example, the plumbing and electrical work. He would need to obtain estimates from the sub-contractors on which his own tender would, in part, be based but he would not wish to enter into a firm contract with them unless and until his tender was successful. Often he would send a 'letter of intent' to his chosen sub-contractors to tell them of their selection. More often than not such letters are so worded as not to create any obligation on either side but in some cases they may contain an invitation to commence preliminary work which at least creates an obligation to pay for that work.[73]

By far the most important case on letters of intent is *British Steel Corpn v Cleveland Bridge and Engineering Co Ltd*.[74]

In this case the defendants had been engaged as sub-contractors on a contract to build a bank in Saudi Arabia. The defendants were to fabricate the steelwork. The bank was of an unusual design, being suspended within a steel lattice-work frame. There were requirements for nodes at the centre of the lattice-work. Apparently, No one in the United Kingdom had made such nodes before but the plaintiffs had experience of constructing similar nodes. The defendants approached the plaintiffs with a view to engaging them to make the nodes. The negotiations both as to the technical specification of the nodes and as to the terms of the contract were complex and lengthy.

On 21 February 1979 the defendants sent a letter of intent to the plaintiffs. This stated their intention to place an order for the nodes at prices which had been quoted

---

[71] Pp 50–51, above.
[72] The legal effect of 'letters of intent' is a problem for most legal systems. An international working group led by Professor Marcel Fontaine identified as many as 26 variant forms, Fontaine *Droit des Contrats Internationaux: Analyse et Redaction de Clauses* ch 1. See Furmston, Norisada and Poole, chs 5–8.
[73] *Turriff Construction Ltd v Regalia Knitting Mills Ltd* (1971) 222 Estates Gazette 169.
[74] [1984] 1 All ER 504 Ball 99 LQR 572.

in an earlier telex from the plaintiffs. It proposed that the order be on the defendants' standard terms, which would, amongst other things, have placed unlimited liability on the plaintiffs for consequential loss in the event of delay. The plaintiffs made it clear that they were unwilling to contract on the defendants' terms. Nevertheless, they went ahead with the construction of the nodes (amidst continuing discussion both as to technical and contractual matters) and by 28 December 1979 all but one of the nodes had been delivered. The final node was not delivered until 11 April 1980 owing to a national steel strike.

The plaintiffs sued for the value of the nodes. The defendants counter-claimed for damages for late delivery. Robert Goff J held that on these facts there was no contract since it was clear that the parties had never agreed on such important questions as progress payments and liability for late delivery. It followed that there could be no damages for late delivery since there was no contract to deliver. However, he held that the plaintiffs were entitled to payment on a *quantum meruit* basis[75] since they had done the work at the defendants' request and the defendants had accepted it.

Although on the precise facts of the case, this decision seems acceptable and perhaps even inevitable, it leaves a number of questions in the air. It seems that since there was no contract either party was free at any time to abandon the project without telling the other party but this would be a commercially unacceptable result since each party was relying on the other at least to this extent. Indeed, it may be thought odd that the plaintiffs should have done over £200,000 worth of work without any right to payment, even for work already completed, in the event of the defendants changing their mind. Perhaps this was a risk that they took by doing the work, knowing that there was no contract—in the circumstances of the particular contract an acceptably small risk in commercial terms. Another difficulty concerns defects in the goods. Clearly since the buyers were not obliged to accept the goods at all, they were free to reject goods where the defect was apparent at the time of delivery. It is not clear, however, on what theory they could, if there was no contract, recover damages for goods accepted and later found to be defective.

There will be cases where what the parties describe as a letter of intent gives rise to a completed contract. A good example is *AC Controls Ltd v British Broadcasting Corporation*.[76]

In 1998 the BBC was considering the installation of a centrally controlled software access system to 57 of its premises. In January 1999 ACC submitted a tender for some £3 million, and in March 1999 they were told by the BBC that the project board had approved them as contractors. At this stage, much detail of what was to be done remained to be fixed. The BBC wished the transaction to be embodied in an elaborate formal contract but was not yet ready to complete this. On the other hand, BBC internal controls did not permit payment for work without there being a contract. As a result, a document described by both sides as a letter of intent was

---

[75] See below, p 678.   [76] (2002) 89 Com LR 52.

signed by representatives of both sides in June 1999 and this was followed by a further letter in July. Both letters instructed ACC to carry out work and provided for payment to be fixed by an independent consultant though without defining the basis of payment.

In due course the BBC abandoned the project. It was held that there was a contract to do all the survey and pre-contract work and to pay for all the work that had been done and that the provision for independent valuation necessarily meant payment of a reasonable price.

The second difficulty is that the parties may have reserved some major questions, such as price, for future decision.[77] This is dangerous but not necessarily fatal. Indeed, it is not uncommon for parties to contract on the basis that the price is to be fixed by one of them. This might appear uncertain but it is commonly assumed to be valid. So the contracts by which petrol companies agree to supply petrol to filling stations provide for the price to be that ruling at the date of delivery. Many attacks have been made on such contracts in recent years[78] but never on grounds of uncertainty. One explanation might be that the contract is to pay the *list price* at the date of delivery but in *Shell (UK) Ltd v Lostock Garage Ltd*[79] it was assumed that there was no uncertainty where the plaintiffs were delivering petrol at different prices to neighbouring garages.[80] Where the events upon which the price is to depend are themselves in the future, it is understandable that the parties will wish to settle the price by future agreement. However, in such cases it is undoubtedly prudent to provide machinery to deal with the situation where the parties prove in the event unable to agree. Courts have sometimes held agreements ineffective because of defects in such machinery but the House of Lords liberalised the law in a helpful way in *Sudbrook Trading Estate Ltd v Eggleton*.[81]

> A series of leases granted the lessee an option to purchase the freehold. The price was to be fixed by two valuers, one to be appointed by the lessor and one by the lessee, and if they were unable to agree, they were to appoint an umpire. Although the documents had clearly been prepared by lawyers they failed to deal with the situation where one of the parties refused to

[77] See cases cited p 52, n 62, above and *Loftus v Roberts* (1902) 18 TLR 532. The mere fact that the parties have reserved some non-essential terms for future negotiation does not prevent a contract from arising. *Pagnan SpA v Feed Products Ltd* [1987] 2 Lloyd's Rep 601.

[78] See especially pp 523–525, below. Since the contracts may run for up to five years, it would be commercially impossible for prices to be fixed and very difficult to operate any system of indexation of prices.

[79] [1977] 1 All ER 481.

[80] In *Lombard Tricity Finance Ltd v Paton* [1989] 1 All ER 918 it was held that a contract providing for unilateral variation of the rate of interest charged was valid. But in *Paragon Finance plc v Staunton* [2001] EWCA Civ 1466, [2002] 2 All ER 248 the Court of Appeal held that such variations should not be dishonest, capricious or arbitary.

[81] [1983] 1 AC 444, [1982] 3 All ER 1. See also *Beer v Bowden* [1981] 1 All ER 1070, [1981] 1 WLR 522n and *Corson v Rhuddlan Borough Council* (1989) 59 P & CR 185. Compare *Gillatt v Sky Television Ltd* [2000] 1 All ER (Comm) 461 where the provision for valuation 'by an independent chartered accountant' was held to be essential and not mere machinery.

appoint a valuer. The lessee sought to exercise the option, the lessor refused to appoint a valuer and argued that as a result the option was ineffective for uncertainty.

Previous decisions of the Court of Appeal had consistently upheld this view but the House of Lords (Lord Russell dissenting) held that it was wrong. The majority held that the provision for fixing of the price by valuers was a decisive indication that the price was to be a reasonable price, since valuers were professionals who would be obliged to apply professional and, therefore, reasonable standards. The option agreement was, therefore, a valid contract, albeit with defective machinery. If necessary, the court could provide its own machinery.

Finally, although the parties may have completed their negotiations, they may have expressed the result in such a form that it is not possible to say with certainty what they have agreed or what the agreement means. In *Bushwall Properties Ltd v Vortex Properties Ltd*:[82]

> The defendants agreed in writing to sell 51½ acres of land to the plaintiffs for £500,000. The purchase price was to be paid in three instalments: a first of £250,000, followed in twelve months by a second of £125,000 and then, after a further twelve months, by a final payment of £125,000. It was further provided that 'on the occasion of each completion a proportionate part of the land shall be released forthwith' to the plaintiffs. The parties provided no machinery for the allocation of the proportionate parts and the Court of Appeal held that the agreement was void for uncertainty.

Acceptance in the case of tenders

A final illustration of the difficulty experienced in deciding whether an offer has been accepted is afforded by the series of cases where a 'tender' is invited for the periodical supply of goods:

> Suppose that a corporation invites tenders for the supply of certain specific goods to be delivered over a given period. A trader puts in a tender intimating that he is prepared to supply the goods at a certain price. The corporation, to use the language of the business world, 'accepts' the tender. What is the legal result of this 'acceptance'?

There is no doubt, of course, that the tender is an offer. The question, however, is whether its 'acceptance' by the corporation is an acceptance in the legal sense so as to produce a binding contract. This can be answered only by examining the language of the original invitation to tender. There are several possible cases.

First, the corporation may have stated that it will definitely require a specified quantity of goods, no more and no less, as, for instance, where it advertises for

---

[82] [1976] 2 All ER 283, [1976] 1 WLR 591. Emery [1976] CLJ 215. So too in *Scammell v Ouston*, above. See also Samek 48 Can Bar Rev 203.

1,000 tons of coal to be supplied during the period 1 January to 31 December. Here the 'acceptance' of the tender is an acceptance in the legal sense, and it creates an obligation. The trader is bound to deliver, the corporation is bound to accept, 1,000 tons, and the fact that delivery is to be by instalments as and when demanded does not disturb the existence of the obligation.

There would also be a contract if the corporation were to state that it would take all its needs for the year from a particular supplier or take all the supplier's output for the year. In such cases, the contract is sufficiently certain to be enforced, even though at the beginning of the year one may not know the extent of the needs or output.

There is more difficulty if the corporation advertises that it *may* require articles of a specified description up to a maximum amount, as, for instance, where it invites tenders for the supply during the coming year of coal not exceeding 1,000 tons altogether, deliveries to be made *if and when* demanded, the effect of the so-called 'acceptance' of the tender is very different. The trader has made what is called a standing offer. Until revocation he stands ready and willing to deliver coal up to 1,000 tons at the agreed price when the corporation from time to time demands a precise quantity. The 'acceptance' of the tender, however, does not convert the offer into a binding contract, for a contract of sale implies that the buyer has agreed to accept the goods. In the present case the corporation has not agreed to take 1,000 tons, or indeed any quantity of coal. It has merely stated that it may require supplies up to a maximum limit.[83]

In this latter case the standing offer may be revoked at any time provided that it has not been accepted in the legal sense; and acceptance in the legal sense is complete as soon as a requisition for a definite quantity of goods is made. Each requisition by the offeree is an individual act of acceptance which creates a separate contract. If the corporation in the case given telephones for 25 tons of coal, there is an acceptance of the offer and both parties are bound to that extent and to that extent only—the one to deliver, the other to accept 25 tons. If, however, the tradesman revokes his offer, he cannot be made liable for further deliveries,[84] although he is bound by requisitions already made.[85]

The nature of a standing offer was considered in *Great Northern Rly Co v Witham*.[86] In that case:

The plaintiffs advertised for tenders for the supply of stores. The defendant made a tender in these words: 'I undertake to supply the Company for twelve months with such quantities of [specified articles] as the Company may order from time to

---

[83] Another way of analysing the difficulties here is to say that the corporation has provided no consideration until it makes a promise to buy a definite quantity of goods. Cf Adams 94 LQR 73.

[84] *Offord v Davies* (1862) 12 CBNS 748.

[85] *Great Northern Rly Co v Witham* (1873) LR 9 CP 16.

[86] Ibid. See also *Percival Ltd v LCC Asylums and Mental Deficiency Committee* (1918) 87 LJKB 677.

time.' The Company replied by letter accepting the tender, and subsequently gave various orders which were executed by the defendant. Ultimately the Company gave an order for goods within the schedule, which the defendant refused to supply.

The company succeeded in an action for breach of contract. The tender was a standing offer, to be converted into a series of contracts by the subsequent acts of the company. An order prevented *pro tanto* the possibility of revocation, and the defendant, though he might regain his liberty of action for the future, was meanwhile bound to supply the goods actually ordered.

B The communication of acceptance

Even if the offeree has made up his mind to a final acceptance, the agreement is not yet complete. There must be an external manifestation of assent, some word spoken or act done by the offeree or by his authorised agent, which the law can regard as the communication of the acceptance to the offeror.[87] What constitutes communication varies with the nature of the case and has provoked many difficult problems. A number of observations, however, may be made.

(1) Effect of silence An offeror may not arbitrarily impose contractual liability upon an offeree merely by proclaiming that silence shall be deemed consent. In *Felthouse v Bindley*:[88]

> The plaintiff, Paul Felthouse, wrote to his nephew, John, on 2 February, offering to buy his horse for £30 15s, and adding, 'If I hear no more about him, I consider the horse mine at that price'. The nephew made no reply to this letter, but intimated to the defendant, an auctioneer, who was going to sell his stock, that the horse was to be kept out of the sale. The defendant inadvertently sold the horse to a third party at an auction held on 25 February, and the plaintiff sued him in conversion.

The Court of Common Pleas held that the action must fail as there had been no acceptance of the plaintiff's offer before 25 February, and the plaintiff had therefore, at that date, no title to maintain conversion. Willes J said:

> It is clear that the uncle had no right to impose upon the nephew a sale of his horse for £30 15s unless he chose to comply with the condition of writing to repudiate the offer.

Silence is usually equivocal as to consent and the uncle's letter did not render the nephew's failure to reply unequivocal, since failure to reply to letters is a common

---

[87] See *Powell v Lee* (1908) 99 LT 284, and *Robophone Facilities Ltd v Blank* [1966] 3 All ER 128, [1966] 1 WLR 1428.
[88] (1862) 11 CBNS 869. Miller 35 MLR 489.

human weakness. It may be going too far, however, to say the silence can never be unequivocal evidence of consent.[89] The second edition of the American Restatement in section 69 provides:

> 'Acceptance by silence or exercise of dominion
>
> (1) where an offeree fails to reply to an offer, his silence and inaction operate as an acceptance in the following cases only:
>
> > (a) where an offeree takes the benefit of offered services with reasonable opportunity to reject them and reason to know that they were offered with the expectation of compensation;
> >
> > (b) where the offeror has stated or given the offeree reason to understand that assent may be manifested by silence or inaction, and the offeree in remaining silent or inactive intends to accept the offer;
> >
> > (c) where, because of previous dealings or otherwise, it is reasonable that the offeree should notify the offeror if he does not intend to accept.'

An example of (a) would arise if I see a window cleaner, who has been asked to clean the windows of my house before, approaching my front door to ask whether he should clean them today and pretend not to be in, guessing correctly that he will then go ahead and clean the windows. An example of (b) would be if the nephew in *Felthouse v Bindley* had clearly manifested his intention to accept the uncle's offer but had not communicated his acceptance to the uncle because he had been told not to bother.[90] An American example of (c) arose in *Ammons v Wilson*[91] where a seller's salesman took an order for 43,916 pounds of shortening on 23 August for prompt shipment 'subject to acceptance by seller's authorized agent at point of shipment'. The seller delayed until 4 September, while the price of shortening rose from 7½ to 9 cents a pound, and then refused to ship. The court held that on these facts it was open to the jury to find that the delay 'in view of the past history of such transactions between the parties, including the booking, constituted an implied acceptance'. There was evidence in this case that the seller's salesman had not only solicited the order but had previously taken several orders which had all been accepted. It is thought that it would be open to English courts to hold that there was a contract in each of these situations.[92]

---

[89] *Manco Ltd v Atlantic Forest Products Ltd* (1971) 24 DLR (3d) 194. *Way and Waller Ltd v Ryde* [1944] 1 All ER 9, discussed by Murdoch 91 LQR 357 and 378–379. The question has most recently arisen in a group of cases in which it has been argued that an agreement to arbitrate has been abandoned by mutual inactivity, discussed pp 708–709, below. Furmston, Norisada and Poole pp 38–49.

[90] See the discussion on p 61, above.

[91] 176 Miss 645 (1936); *Farnsworth on Contracts*, s 3.15.

[92] Suppose A makes an offer to B at a meeting and B replies that he will consult his superiors and if A hears no more within seven days he can assume the offer is accepted. It appears to be assumed in *Re Selectmove* [1995] 2 All ER 531, [1995] 1 WLR 474 that silence by B can be acceptance though the case was decided on another point. See p 122, below.

*(2) **Waiver of communication*** While an offeror may not present an offeree with
the alternatives of repudiation or liability, he may, for his own purposes, waive the
need to communicate acceptance. He may himself run the risk of incurring an
obligation, though he may not impose it upon another. Such waiver may be express
or may be inferred from the circumstances. It will normally be assumed in what are
sometimes called *unilateral* contracts. In this type of case the offer takes the form of a
promise to pay money in return for an act; and the performance of that act will usually
be deemed an adequate indication of assent.[93] In *Carlill v Carbolic Smoke Ball Co*,
the facts of which have already been given,[94] the argument that the plaintiff should
have notified her intention to put the defendants' panacea to the test was dismissed
as absurd. Bowen LJ, after stating the normal requirement of communication,
continued:[95]

> But there is this clear gloss to be made upon that doctrine, that as notification of acceptance is
> required for the benefit of the person who makes the offer, the person who makes the offer
> may dispense with notice to himself if he thinks it desirable to do so . . . and if the person
> making the offer expressly or impliedly intimates in his offer that it will be sufficient to act
> on the proposal without communicating acceptance of it to himself, performance of the
> condition is a sufficient acceptance without notification . . . In the advertisement cases it seems
> to me to follow as an inference to be drawn from the transaction itself that a person is not to
> notify his acceptance of the offer before he performs the condition . . . From the point of view
> of commonsense no other idea could be entertained. If I advertise to the world that my dog
> is lost and that anybody who brings the dog to a particular place will be paid some money, are
> all the police or other people whose business it is to find lost dogs to sit down and write me a
> note saying that they have accepted my proposal?

It should follow from this that if the nephew on the facts of *Felthouse v Bindley* had
sued the uncle, the latter would have been unable to rely on the non-communication
of acceptance.[96] It may further be argued that the true principle is that the offeror
cannot by ultimatum impose on the offeree an obligation to state his non-acceptance,
but that the contract may, nevertheless, be concluded if the offeree unequivocally

[93] See Brett J in *Great Northern Rly Co v Witham* (1873) LR 9 CP 16 and the Sixth Interim Report
of the Law Revision Committee (1937), p 23. *Unilateral* contracts are usually contrasted with *bilateral*
contracts. But in *United Dominions Trust (Commercial) Ltd v Eagle Aircraft Services Ltd* [1968] 1 All ER 104
at 108, [1968] 1 WLR 74 at 82, Diplock LJ preferred synallagmatic to bilateral because there may be more
than two parties involved.

[94] P 39, above.

[95] [1893] 1 QB 256 at 269–270.

[96] It may appear paradoxical that one party can assert that there is a contract and not the other but this
can be explained in terms of estoppel. See eg *Spiro v Lintern* [1973] 3 All ER 319, [1973] 1 WLR 1002.
Cf *Fairline Shipping Corpn v Adamson* [1975] QB 180, [1974] 2 All ER 967, where this argument was
apparently rejected by Kerr J, though on the facts there was no evidence of reliance sufficient to support an
estoppel.

manifests his acceptance.[97] This is important, for instance, in relation to the practice of 'inertia' selling, where a tradesman sends unsolicited goods to a customer, accompanied by a letter stating that if the goods are not returned within ten days, it will be assumed that they are bought. At common law it would seem clear that the customer is under no obligation to return the goods but that if he clearly shows his acceptance, eg by consuming the goods, he should be bound to pay for them. Under the Unsolicited Goods and Services Act 1971, however, a tradesman may, in such circumstances, be treated as making a gift of the goods to the customer.

(3) Mode of communication prescribed by offeror An offeror may prescribe the method of communicating acceptance. Whether some particular mode has been prescribed depends upon the inference to be drawn from the circumstances.[98] There is authority for the view that an offer by telegram is evidence of a desire for a prompt reply, so that an acceptance sent by post may be treated as nugatory.[99] The observance of the mode prescribed by the offeror obviously suffices to complete the agreement. Whether precise observance is necessary is, however, a matter of some doubt:

> Suppose, for instance, that a Burton brewer sends a note by his lorry driver to a London merchant, making an offer and asking for a reply to be sent by the lorry on its return. Is an acceptance communicated in any other manner ineffective?

If the offeree posts an acceptance in the belief that it will reach Burton before the lorry and if this is not the case, the better opinion is that the offeror may repudiate the acceptance.[100] But suppose that the acceptance is telegraphed or telephoned, so that it reaches the offeror before the return of his lorry. Is it to be regarded as ineffective merely because it was not communicated in the manner prescribed? Such a ruling, which would be repugnant to common sense, does not appear to represent English law, for, in a case where the offeree was told to 'reply by return of post', it was said by the Court of Exchequer Chamber that a reply sent by some other method equally expeditious would constitute a valid acceptance.[101] The result would, of course, be otherwise, if the offeror had insisted that a reply should be sent by the lorry *and by that*

---

[97] One difficulty with this approach is that it looks as if the nephew had indeed unequivocally accepted. Two possible escapes from this difficulty have been suggested: (a) that statements to one's own agent are not unequivocal or (b) that the true *ratio* of the case was that there was no sufficient memorandum of the contract within the Statute of Frauds.

[98] See *Kennedy v Thomassen* [1929] 1 Ch 426.

[99] *Quenerduaine v Cole* (1883) 32 WR 185.

[100] Cf the American decision in *Eliason v Henshaw* 4 Wheat 225 (1819).

[101] *Tinn v Hoffmann & Co* (1873) 29 LT 271. See also *Manchester Diocesan Council for Education v Commercial and General Investments Ltd* [1969] 3 All ER 1593, [1970] 1 WLR 241.

method only.[102] It is thought that an offeror will need to use very clear words before a means of communication will be treated as mandatory.[103]

(4) If no particular method is prescribed, the form of communication will depend upon the nature of the offer and the circumstances in which it is made. If the offeror makes an oral offer to the offeree and it is clear that an oral reply is expected, the offeree must ensure that his acceptance is understood by the offeror. Suppose that A shouts an offer to B across a river or a courtyard and that A does not hear the reply because it is drowned by an aircraft flying overhead. No contract is formed at that moment, and B must repeat his acceptance so that A can hear it.[104] This rule—that acceptance is incomplete until received by the offeror—governs conversations over the telephone no less than discussions in the physical presence of the parties, and it has now been applied to the most modern methods of communication. In *Entores Ltd v Miles Far East Corpn*:[105]

> The plaintiffs were a London company and the defendants were an American corporation with agents in Amsterdam. Both the plaintiffs in London and the defendants' agents in Amsterdam had equipment known as 'Telex Service' whereby messages could be despatched by the teleprinter operated like a typewriter in one country and almost instantaneously received and typed in another. By this instrument the plaintiffs made an offer to the defendants' agents to buy goods from them, and the latter accepted the offer. The plaintiffs now alleged that the defendants had broken their contract and wished to serve a writ upon them. This they could do, although the defendants were an American corporation with no branch in England, provided that the contract was made in England.

The defendants contended that they had accepted the offer in Holland and that the contract had therefore been made in that country. But it was held by the Court of Appeal that the parties were in the same position as if they had negotiated in each other's presence or over the telephone, that there was no binding acceptance until it had been received by the plaintiffs, that this took place in London and that a writ could therefore be issued. Parker LJ, after reciting circumstances where expediency might demand another rule,[106] said:

---

[102] Even here the offeror may waive the necessity of following the exclusive method prescribed and allow a substitute; see the difficult case of *Compagnie de Commerce et Commission SARL v Parkinson Stove Co* [1953] 2 Lloyd's Rep 487, discussed Eckersley 17 MLR 476. See also Winfield 55 LQR 499 at 515–516.

[103] See *Yates Building Co Ltd v R J Pulleyn & Sons (York) Ltd* (1975) 119 Sol Jo 370, reversing (1973) 228 Estates Gazette 1597. Cf *Wettern Electric Ltd v Welsh Development Agency* [1983] QB 796, [1983] 2 All ER 629, discussed 1983 All ER Rev 110.

[104] See the illustration given by Denning LJ in *Entores Ltd v Miles Far East Corpn* [1955] 2 QB 327 at 332, [1955] 2 All ER 493 at 495.

[105] [1955] 2 QB 327, [1955] 2 All ER 493.

[106] See below as to negotiations conducted through the post.

Where, however, the parties are in each other's presence or, though separated in space, communication between them is in effect instantaneous, there is no need for any such rule of convenience. To hold otherwise would leave no room for the operation of the general rule that notification of the acceptance must be received. An acceptor could say: 'I spoke the words of acceptance in your presence, albeit softly, and it matters not that you did not hear me'; or 'I telephoned to you and accepted, and it matters not that the telephone went dead and you did not get my message'. . . . So far as Telex messages are concerned, though the despatch and receipt of a message is not completely instantaneous, the parties are to all intents and purposes in each other's presence just as if they were in telephonic communication, and I see no reason for departing from the general rule that there is no binding contract until notice of the acceptance is received by the offeror. That being so, and since the offer—a counter offer—was made by the plaintiffs in London and notification of the acceptance was received by them in London, the contract resulting therefrom was made in London.[107]

This result was confirmed in 1982 by the House of Lords in *Brinkibon v Stahag Stahl und Stahlwarenhandelsgesellschaft GmbH*[108] where the facts were for all practical purposes identical save that the offer was made by telex in Vienna and accepted by a telex message from London to Vienna. The House of Lords held that the contract was made in Vienna.

In both these cases the telex machines were in the offices of the parties and the messages were sent during ordinary office hours. It is now common for many telex messaages to be transmitted through agencies and machines may be left on for the receipt of messages out of office hours. In *Brinkibon v Stahag Stahl* the House of Lords expressly confined their decision to the standard case and left such variants for future decision.[109]

It would seem very likely that the same rules apply to communications by fax.

Other methods of communication may present greater problems. What is the position where it is acceptable to accept by telephone if the offeree finds himself dealing with an answering machine? It is plausible to argue that one who employs such a machine invites its use but there is scope for argument as to when such an acceptance is effective. It is suggested that this should turn on what is reasonable in all the circumstances.

A much bigger practical problem arises in the field of electronic commerce.[110] In the case of two-party emails, the question is whether to apply the postal or telex

---

[107] [1955] 2 QB at 336, [1955] 2 All ER at 498.
[108] [1983] 2 AC 34, [1982] 1 All ER 293.
[109] *Mondial Shipping and Chartering BV v Astarte Shipping Ltd* [1995] CLC 1011.
[110] For a fuller discussion see Rowland and Macdonald, *Information Technology Law* (2nd edn, 2000) pp 295 et seq; Hill 17 J Contract L 151. The fullest judicial discussion is by V K Rajah JC in *Chwee Kin Keong v Digilandmall.com Ptd Ltd* [2004] SLR 594. This case is discussed more fully at p 309. Both at first instance and in the Singapore Court of Appeal [2005 15LR 502] the decision turns principally on the application of the law of unilateral mistake but the first instance judgment is helpful on the general analysis of internet sales. See Phang 21 LCL 197, (2005) 17 SAcLJ 361; Kwek Mean Luck (2005) 17 SAcLJ 411.

model. Although email is just as quick as telex or fax an email message does not signal its arrival in the way that telex or fax does. Nevertheless, it is thought that the telex analogy is more appropriate.

It is thought that similar arguments apply to full-blown electronic commerce. In this field the problems are much greater in connection with the legal requirements for writing and signature[111] than in relation to offer and acceptance.

(5) Communications through the post If no particular method of communication is prescribed and the parties are not, to all intents and purposes, in each other's presence, the rule just laid down—that an acceptance speaks only when it is received by the offeror—may be impracticable or inconvenient. Such may well be the case where the negotiations have been conducted through the post.[112] The question as to what in these circumstances is an adequate communication of acceptance arose as early as 1818 in the case of *Adams v Lindsell*.[113]

> The plaintiffs were woollen manufacturers in Bromsgrove, Worcestershire. The defendants were wool-dealers at St Ives in Huntingdon. On 2 September 1817, the defendants wrote to the plaintiffs, offering a quantity of wool on certain terms and requiring an answer 'in course of post'. The defendants misdirected their letter, which did not reach the plaintiffs until the evening of 5 September. That same night the plaintiffs posted a letter of acceptance, which was delivered to the defendants on 9 September. If the original offer had been properly addressed, a reply could have been expected by 7 September, and meanwhile, on 8 September, not having received such a reply, the defendants had sold the wool to third parties.

The trial judge directed a verdict for the plaintiffs on the ground that the delay was due to the defendants' negligence, and the defendants obtained a rule *nisi* for a new trial. The vital question was whether a contract of sale had been made between the parties before 8 September. Two cases only were cited by counsel[114] and none by the court, and it was treated virtually as a case of first impression.

As an academic problem, three possible answers were available. An offer made through the post might be regarded as accepted in the eyes of the law:

(a) as soon as the letter of acceptance is put into the post; or

(b) when the letter of acceptance is delivered to the offeror's address; or

(c) when the letter of acceptance is brought to the actual notice of the offeror.

As the law is now understood, the plaintiffs would have succeeded on any of these theories, since the defendants' offer would not be revoked by their sale to third parties

---

[111] See below, ch 7.   [112] Evans 15 ICLQ 553. Gardner 12 Oxford JLS 170.
[113] (1818) 1 B & Ald 681.
[114] *Payne v Cave* (1789) 3 Term Rep 148; and *Cooke v Oxley* (1790) 3 Term Rep 653.

on 8 September.[115] But in 1818 there were no developed rules as to revocation of offers and the court may well have thought it arguable that the sale was sufficient to revoke[116] so that an effective acceptance would need to take place before 8 September.

It is commonly said that the choice between these three possible solutions is arbitrary.[117] But the logical application of the doctrine that acceptance must be communicated would clearly point to the adoption of either (b) or (c), depending on the meaning to be given to 'communication'. In fact, the Court of King's Bench in *Adams v Lindsell* preferred the first solution and decided that the contract was concluded when the letter of acceptance was posted on 5 September. At first sight it appears strange that the requirement of communication, which is largely devoid of practical content in contracts *inter praesentes*, should not be applied to postal contracts, which provide the most important arena for its application. It is perhaps less surprising if we attend to the history of the matter. *Adams v Lindsell* was the first genuine offer and acceptance case in English law[118] and, in 1818 there was no rule that acceptance must be communicated. As so often happens in English law, the exception is historically anterior to the rule.

The decision in *Adams v Lindsell* did not at once command uncritical acceptance. Although applied by the House of Lords in 1848 in an appeal from Scotland,[119] it was distinguished in two cases[120] where the letter of acceptance did not arrive but it was applied to that situation too by the Court of Appeal in *Household Fire and Carriage Accident Insurance Co v Grant*.[121] In 1880, in *Byrne v Van Tienhoven*, Lindley J treated the question as beyond dispute:

> It may be taken as now settled that, where an offer is made and accepted by letters sent through the post, the contract is completed the moment the letter accepting the offer is posted, even though it never reaches its destination.[122]

Some notes of warning may, however, be sounded. The solution is to be applied only where no particular mode of communication is prescribed by the offeror;[123] and, as it is itself the creature of expediency, it must yield to manifest inconvenience or absurdity. As Lord Bramwell said in 1871:

> If a man proposed marriage and the woman was to consult her friends and let him know, would it be enough if she wrote and posted a letter which never reached him?[124]

---

[115] See p 73, below.
[116] This view was current as late as *Dickinson v Dodds* (1876) 2 ChD 463, discussed below.
[117] See Winfield 55 LQR 499 at 506–507. See also Nussbaum 36 Col L Rev 920.
[118] Simpson 91 LQR 247 at 260.   [119] *Dunlop v Higgins* (1848) 1 HL Cas 381.
[120] *British and American Telegraph Co v Colson* (1871) LR 6 Exch 108; *Re Imperial Land Co of Marseilles, Harris's Case* (1872) 7 Ch App 587.
[121] (1879) 4 Ex D 216.   [122] (1880) 5 CPD 344 at 348.
[123] *Holwell Securities Ltd v Hughes* [1974] 1 All ER 161, [1974] 1 WLR 155.
[124] *British and American Telegraph Co v Colson* (1871) LR 6 Exch 108.

More recently Lawton LJ has stated:[125]

> In my judgment, the factors of inconvenience and absurdity are but illustrations of a wider principle, namely, that the rule does not apply if, having regard to all the circumstances, including the nature of the subject-matter under consideration, the negotiating parties cannot have intended that there should be a binding agreement until the party accepting an offer or exercising an option had in fact communicated the acceptance or exercise to the other.[126]

It would appear further that the rule should apply only to a letter which is properly stamped and addressed.[127] A number of questions, however, remain unanswered, and some of these must now be considered.

May acceptance be recalled before it reaches offeror?

In the first place, may an offeree, perhaps by telephone or telegram, recall his acceptance after he has posted it but before it has reached the offeror? A rigorous application of the rule last laid down would forbid him to do so: the contract is complete from the moment that his letter has been put into the post. There is no English decision upon the point. The Scots case of *Dunmore (Countess) v Alexander*[128] is sometimes cited to support the view that the offeree may be allowed to withdraw. The scope of this decision, however, is not clear. It involves a question of agency, to which perhaps it is exclusively relevant; and the courts were concerned to determine the effect, not of a telegram recalling a letter, but on the simultaneous receipt of two letters. In New Zealand, Chapman J denied the possibility of altering the effect of a letter of acceptance once it has been put into the post[129] and the same view has been taken in South Africa.[130] English courts are free to choose between these opinions and their choice rests upon expediency rather than upon logic. Even upon this basis there is room for differing opinions. It may be argued, on the one hand, that to allow a letter of acceptance to be withdrawn would give the offeree the best of both worlds. By posting an acceptance he would be free either to hold the offeror to it or to recall it by telegram or telephone. On the other hand, the basic principle laid down in *Adams v Lindsell* rests, as a matter of convenience, upon the ground that it is the offeror who has chosen the post as the medium of negotiation and who must accept the hazards of

---

[125] [1974] 1 All ER 161 at 167, [1974] 1 WLR 155 at 161.

[126] A warning against the assumption that the rule in *Byrne v Van Tienhoven* is to be applied automatically was given by the court in the Australian case of *Tallerman & Co Pty Ltd v Nathan's Merchandise (Victoria) Pty Ltd* (1957) 98 CLR 93, especially at 111–112.

[127] *Re London and Northern Bank, ex p Jones* [1900] 1 Ch 220; *Getreide-Import-Gesellschaft MBH v Contimar SA Compania Industrial Commercial y Maritima* [1953] 2 All ER 223, [1953] 1 WLR 793.

[128] 1830 9 Sh (Ct of Sess) 190.

[129] *Wenkheim v Arndt* (1861) 1 JR 73.

[130] *A to Z Bazaars (Pty) Ltd v Minister of Agriculture* 1974 (4) SA 392.

his choice. If he takes 'the risks of delay and accident in the post, it would not seem to strain matters to say that he also assumes the risk of a letter being overtaken by a speedier means of communication'.[131] He may guard against any of these risks by framing his offer in appropriate terms.

Must the acceptor have knowledge of the offer?

In the second place, do contractual obligations arise if services are rendered which in fact fulfil the terms of an offer, but are performed in ignorance that the offer exists? The defendant may have offered a reward to anyone who gives information ensuring the conviction of a criminal. If the plaintiff supplies the information before he knows of the reward can he afterwards claim it? In *Neville v Kelly* in 1862,[132] though the decision rested upon another point, the Court of Common Pleas was inclined to favour such a claim, and in *Gibbons v Proctor* in 1891[133] Day and Lawrence JJ, sitting as a divisional court, apparently supported it. But they gave no reason for their opinion, which has been generally condemned by academic lawyers.[134] Agreement, it is true, has often to be inferred from the conduct of the parties although it does not exist in fact, but the inference can scarcely be drawn from the mere coincidence of two independent acts. The plaintiff, when he acted, intended not to sell his information, but to give it, and there was nothing to justify any reasonable third party in inferring the contrary.

These academic objections were received as valid in the American case of *Fitch v Snedaker*,[135] where Woodruff J, pertinently asked, 'How can there be consent or assent to that of which the party has never heard?' The position was reviewed and the ruling in *Fitch v Snedaker* taken, perhaps, a little further in the Australian case of *R v Clarke*.[136]

> The Government of Western Australia offered a reward of £1,000 'for such information as shall lead to the arrest and conviction of the murderers of two police officers, and added that, if the information should be given by an accomplice, not being himself the murderer, he should receive a free pardon. Clarke saw the offer and some time later gave the necessary information. He claimed the reward from the Crown by Petition of Right. He admitted not only that he had acted solely to save his own skin, but that, at the time when he gave the information, the question of the reward had passed out of his mind.

---

[131] Hudson 82 LQR 169 at 170.   [132] (1862) 12 CBNS 740.   [133] (1891) 64 LT 594.
[134] See the strictures of Pollock (13th edn) p 16, and of Salmond and Williams at p 72. Cf Hudson 84 LQR 503.
[135] 38 NY 248 (1868).
[136] (1927) 40 CLR 227. In *Bloom v American Swiss Watch Co* [1915] App D 100, the Appellate Division of the Supreme Court of South Africa held, disapproving *Gibbons v Proctor*, that, where information had been given without knowledge that a reward had been offered, the informer could not recover the reward.

The High Court of Australia held that his claim must fail. He was, in their opinion, in the same position as if he had never heard of the reward. In the words of Higgins J:

> Clarke had seen the offer, indeed, but it was not present to his mind—he had forgotten it and gave no consideration to it in his intense excitement as to his own danger. There cannot be assent without knowledge of the offer; and ignorance of the offer is the same thing, whether it is due to never hearing of it or to forgetting it after hearing.

Isaacs CJ reinforced his opinion with a hypothetical illustration:

> An offer of £100 to any person who should swim a hundred yards in the harbour on the first day of the year would not in my opinion be satisfied by a person who was accidentally or maliciously thrown overboard on that date and swam the distance simply to save his life, without any thought of the offer.

The position would be different if the offer of the reward had been present to the plaintiff's mind when he acted, although he may have been predominantly influenced by some other motive. In *Williams v Carwardine*,[137] where a notice had been published in terms similar to those in *R v Clarke*, the plaintiff had supplied the information with knowledge of the reward but moved rather by remorse for her own misconduct. At the assizes, Parke J gave judgment in her favour, and the defendant moved to enter a nonsuit on the ground that the suggested contract had been negatived by the finding of the jury 'that the plaintiff gave the information to ease her conscience and not for the sake of the reward'. But the judgment was upheld in the King's Bench. Motive was irrelevant, provided that the act was done with knowledge of the reward. Acceptance was then related to offer.[138]

Does agreement result from cross-offers?

What, in the third place, is the effect of two offers, identical in terms, which cross in the post?

> Suppose that A by letter offers to sell his car to B for £100 and that B, by a second letter which crosses the first in the post, offers to buy it for £100. Do these two letters create a contract?

The point was discussed by the Exchequer Chamber in *Tinn v Hoffmann & Co*,[139] where it was held by five judges against two that on the facts of that case no contract had been concluded. Of the five judges in the majority, Archibald and Keating JJ proceeded on the ground that the letters in question contained diverse terms so that the parties were not *ad idem*, while Blackburn, Brett and Grove JJ denied that

---

[137] The case was decided in 1833 and was variously reported; 5 C & P 566 is the best report and brings out clearly the fact that the plaintiff knew of the reward. Other reports are 4 B & Ad 621, 1 Nev & M KB 418, 2 LJKB 101.

[138] See also *Taylor v Allon* [1966] 1 QB 304, [1965] 1 All ER 557.

[139] (1873) 29 LT 271.

cross-offers could, in the most favourable circumstances, constitute a contract. Blackburn J said:[140]

> When a contract is made between two parties, there is a promise by one in consideration of
> the promise made by the other; there are two assenting minds, the parties agreeing in opinion
> and one having promised in consideration of the promise made by the other—there is an
> exchange of promises. But I do not think exchanging offers would, upon principle, be at all
> the same thing . . . The promise or offer being made on each side in ignorance of the promise
> or offer made on the other side, neither of them can be construed as an acceptance of the
> other.

The case, however, stands alone in the English common law and the difference of
judicial opinion makes it the less impressive. The judgments, moreover, reflect the
contemporary preoccupation with *consensus*. The American cases seem equally rare
and equally inconclusive, although the *Restatement* declares categorically that 'two
manifestations of willingness to make the same bargain do not constitute a contract
unless one is made with reference to the other'.[141] Authority, therefore, so far as it
goes, would seem to deny the efficacy of cross-offers; but it does not go very far. On
principle the issue is equally doubtful. It is certainly true that the act of neither party is
in direct relation to that of the other and that the strict requirements of offer and
acceptance are unsatisfied. But, in contrast with the situation in such cases as *Fitch v
Snedaker* and *R v Clarke*, each party does in truth contemplate legal relations upon an
identical basis, and each is prepared to offer his own promise as consideration for the
promise of the other. There is not only a coincidence of acts, but, if this is thought to
be relevant, a unanimity of mind.

4 TERMINATION OF OFFER

It is now necessary to consider the circumstances in which an offer may be terminated
or negatived. It may be revoked, it may lapse, it may be subject to a condition that fails
to be satisfied or it may be affected by the death of one of the parties.

A Revocation

It has been established ever since the case of *Payne v Cave* in 1789[142] that revocation is
possible and effective at any time before acceptance: up to this moment *ex hypothesi* no

---

[140] Ibid at 279.
[141] *Restatement of the Law of Contracts* (American Law Institute) s 23. For the American cases, see
Corbin on Contracts § 59.
[142] (1789) 3 Term Rep 148.

legal obligation exists. Nor, as the law stands, is it relevant that the offeror has declared himself ready to keep the offer open for a given period. Such an intimation is but part and parcel of the original offer, which must stand or fall as a whole. The offeror may, of course, bind himself, by a separate and specific contract, to keep the offer open; but the offeree, if such is his allegation, must provide all the elements of a valid contract, including assent and consideration.[143] In *Routledge v Grant*[144] the defendant offered on 18 March to buy the plaintiff's house for a certain sum, 'a definite answer to be given within six weeks from the date'. Best CJ held that the defendant could withdraw at any moment before acceptance, even though the time limit had not expired. The plaintiff could only have held the defendant to his offer throughout the period if he had bought the option by a separate and binding contract.

Revocation of offer must be communicated

The revocation of an offer is ineffective unless it has been communicated to the offeree. It is not enough for the offeror to change his mind. For some years, it is true, obsessed with the theory of *consensus*, the judges were content with the mere alteration of intention.[145] But business necessity, in this instance no less than in the definition of acceptance, overbore deductions from a priori conception of contract and required some overt act from which the intention might be inferred. Convenience, indeed, demanded a more stringent rule for revocation than for acceptance. To post a letter was a sufficient act of acceptance, since the offeree was entitled to assume that he thereby satisfied the expectations of the offeror. The offeror, when he decided to revoke, could rely on no such assumption. Thus in *Byrne v Van Tienhoven*:[146]

---

[143] It was recommended by the Law Revision Committee in 1937 that the law be altered so as to make binding an agreement to keep an offer open for a definite period of time or until the occurrence of some specified event, even if there is no consideration for the agreement. See Sixth Interim Report (1937), p 31. The Law Commission has made a similar recommendation but limited to firm offers made in the 'course of business': Working Paper 60 (1975). See Lewis 9 Journal of Law and Society 153. The English rule appears particularly inconvenient in principle where A's offer will be used by B as the basis of an offer which B is going to make to C. This is typically the case in the construction industry where A is a potential sub-contractor and B a potential main contractor who makes a tender to C, a potential employer incorporating the prices which his potential sub-contractors have quoted to him. In this situation B is exposed to the risk that A will revoke his offer to B at the same moment that C accepts B's offer to C. Canadian courts in this situation have held A the sub-contractor bound: *Northern Construction Co v Glage Heating and Plumbing* [1986] 2 WWR 649; *Calgary v Northern Construction Co* (1985) 3 Const LJ 179. Lewis's article op cit suggests that this problem is perceived to be less difficult in practice than in theory in the construction industry. This is presumably because the sub-contractor's price is usually a good indication of what other sub-contractors would charge. The most obvious example of a case where this would not be so is where the sub-contractor's price is based on a mistake in his calculations. This is also the case where the sub-contractor is most likely to wish to withdraw his offer as the facts of the Canadian cases show.

[144] (1828) 4 Bing 653.

[145] See *Cooke v Oxley* (1790) 3 Term Rep 653, and *Head v Diggon* (1828) 3 Man & Ry KB 97.

[146] (1880) 5 CPD 344. See also *Stevenson v McLean* (1880) 5 QBD 346 and *Henthorn v Fraser* [1892] 2 Ch 27.

The defendants posted a letter in Cardiff on 1 October, addressed to the plaintiffs in New York, offering to sell 1,000 boxes of tin-plates. On 8 October they posted a letter revoking the offer. On 11 October the plaintiffs telegraphed their acceptance and confirmed it in a letter posted on 15 October. On 20 October the letter of revocation reached the plaintiffs.

It was held that the revocation was inoperative until 20 October, that the offer, therefore, continued open up to that date, and that it had been accepted by the plaintiffs in the interim. Lindley J, giving judgment for the plaintiffs, pointed out 'the extreme injustice and inconvenience which any other conclusion would produce'. The decision leaves undefined the precise moment at which communication takes place but it seems reasonable to argue that, at least in the case of a business, a letter which arrives on a normal working day should be treated as a communication even if unopened.[147]

The offeror, therefore, if he relies on a revocation, must prove, not only that he has done some act which manifests his intention, but that the offeree has knowledge of that act. But it would seem that he need not himself have furnished this information. In *Dickinson v Dodds*:[148]

The defendant, on 10 June, gave the plaintiff a written offer to sell a house for £800, 'to be left over until Friday 12 June, 9 am'. On Thursday 11 June, the defendant sold the house to a third party, Allan, for £800, and that evening the plaintiff was told of the sale by a fourth man, Berry. Before 9 am on 12 June, the plaintiff handed to the defendant a formal letter of acceptance.

The Court of Appeal held that the plaintiff, before attempting to accept, 'knew that Dodds was no longer minded to sell the property to him as plainly and clearly as if Dodds had told him in so many words', that the defendant had validly withdrawn his offer and that the plaintiff's purported acceptance was too late. The decision was followed in *Cartwright v Hoogstoel*[149] in 1911, where Eve J rested his judgment on the ground that 'the defendant had, by conduct brought to the knowledge of the plaintiff, effectually withdrawn the offer before acceptance'.

The language of the judgments in *Dickinson v Dodds* reflects the persistence of the *consensus* theory and is not free from practical difficulty. Is the offeree bound by any hint or gossip that he may hear, or must he winnow the truth from the chaff? All that can be said is that it is a question of fact in each case. Was the information such that a reasonable man should have been persuaded of its accuracy?

---

[147] Cf Cairns LJ in *The Brimnes* [1974] 3 All ER 88 at 115, [1974] 3 WLR 613 at 642. In *Shuey v United States* 92 US 73 (1875) it was held that an offer made by advertisement in a newspaper could be revoked by a similar advertisements even though the second advertisement were not read by some offerees.

[148] (1876) 2 ChD 463.   [149] (1911) 105 LT 628.

Nearly all systems of contract law, both common law and civilian, make extensive use of the techniques of offer and acceptance in order to decide whether there is agreement. The handling of revocation is one of the most important areas of difference. In general, common law systems are much more willing to permit revocation of offers than are civilian systems. Article 2.1.4 of the Unidroit Principles represents a compromise between these approaches. It provides:

(1) Until a contract is concluded an offer may be revoked if the revocation reaches the offeree before it has dispatched an acceptance.

(2) However, an offer cannot be revoked

(a) if it indicates, whether by stating a fixed time for acceptance or otherwise, that it is irrevocable; or

(b) if it was reasonable for the offeree to rely on the offer as being irrevocable and the offeree has acted in reliance on the offer.

Is a promise in return for an act revocable?

A further difficulty is suggested by the nature of 'unilateral' contracts.[150] If the offeror contemplates, not the creation of mutual promises, but the dependence of his own promise upon the offeree's performance of an act, may he revoke his offer at any time before the completion of this act? A reward may have been advertised for the return of a lost dog to a given address, a sum of money may have been promised if, at the end of five years, the offeree can prove that he has abstained from strong drink throughout the period, or, as in the illustration put by Brett J in *Great Northern Rly Co v Witham*,[151] the defendant may have said to the plaintiff 'If you will go to York, I will give you £100'. May the offeror, by giving notice, revoke his offer when he sees his dog being led through the streets towards his house, or when the offeree has endured three years of abstinence, or when, after a laborious journey, he has succeeded in reaching Doncaster? The application of the ordinary rules of revocation would suggest an affirmative answer. An offer may be revoked at any moment before it matures by acceptance into a contract, and it has generally been assumed that, when a promise is offered in return for an act, there is no acceptance until the act has been completely performed.[152]

This solution has been felt to be hard, and methods of evasion have been sought.[153] It has been suggested in the United States that two separate offers are inherent in the offeror's statement: an express offer to pay on the performance of the act, and an

---

[150] See p 65, above.

[151] (1873) LR 9 CP 16. See also *Rogers v Snow* (1572) Dalison 94; Simpson *History* pp 426–427.

[152] See p 65, above. An allied but logically distinct difficulty is that in a unilateral contract the consideration for the promise is the promisee's performance of the stipulated act. See p 97, below.

[153] It has, however, been argued that too much can be made of the hardship. Both parties retain their freedom of volition before acceptance; and if, in the hypothetical case suggested above, the abstainer refused to continue his course of temperance after two years, he could not be sued. See Wormser 26 Yale LJ 136.

implied offer not to revoke if the offeree begins his task within a reasonable time.[154] On this assumption, the beginning of the task not only constitutes the acceptance of the implied offer, but also supplies the consideration which the law requires for its validity, as for that of every contract not under seal.[155] If the offeror attempts thereafter to revoke, he may be sued for the breach of this secondary promise. This American suggestion was, indeed, anticipated by the Supreme Court of New South Wales which, as early as 1860, decided that in the case of a unilateral contract the original offer may not be withdrawn after the offeree has started to act.[156] In England Sir Frederick Pollock suggested that a distinction should be drawn between the acceptance of the offer and the consideration necessary to support it. The latter, no doubt, is the completion of the act, and, until this takes place, the offeror need pay no money. The former may be assumed as soon as the offeree 'has made an unequivocal beginning of the performance requested', and proof of this fact makes revocation impossible.[157] The suggestion was adopted in 1937 by the Law Revision Committee.[158]

It may be suggested that neither reason nor justice compels a choice between the stark alternatives of making such offers revocable until performance is complete or irrevocable once performance is commenced.[159] Much must depend on the nature of the offer and it is perhaps unfortunate that discussion has centred upon an apparently frivolous and unexplained walk to York. In some cases the parties may well understand that the offeror reserves a right to revoke at any time until performance is complete, while in others it may be proper to hold that he cannot revoke once the promisee has started performance. There may well be intermediate cases where the promisor can revoke after performance has started but is obliged to compensate the offeree for his trouble.[160]

Two instructive cases are *Luxor (Eastbourne) Ltd v Cooper*[161] and *Errington v Errington and Woods*.[162] In the former case an owner of land promised to pay an estate agent a commission of £10,000 if he effected a sale of the land at a price of £175,000. The House of Lords held that the owner could revoke his promise at any time before completion of the sale. At first sight this might appear to support the view that offers of unilateral contracts are freely revocable until performance. But the House of Lords

---

[154] See McGovney 27 Harvard L Rev 644.

[155] See Ch 4, below.

[156] *Abbott v Lance* (1860) Legge's New South Wales Reports 1283. It will be seen that this two-contract analysis is similar to that propounded in *Warlow v Harrison*, discussed at p 41, above.

[157] *Pollock on Contract* (13th edn) p 19.

[158] Sixth Interim Report (1937), pp 23–24, 31. A similar solution is adopted in the *Restatement* s 45, *Farnsworth on Contracts* 3.24.

[159] See Atiyah *Essays in Contract* pp 199–206; Murdoch 91 LQR 357 at 369–375.

[160] See Viscount Haldane LC in *Morrison Shipping Co Ltd v R* (1924) 20 Ll L Rep 283 at 287.

[161] [1941] AC 108, [1941] 1 All ER 33, discussed pp 636 ff, below. See also the somewhat elusive discussion, *arguendo*, in *Offord v Davies* (1862) 12 CBNS 748.

[162] [1952] 1 KB 290, [1952] 1 All ER 149.

did not rely on any such principle which would have provided a complete and simple answer to the plaintiff's claim. Instead, they held that, *in the circumstances of the case*, it would not be proper to imply an undertaking by the owner not to revoke his promise once performance had begun. Clearly this argument assumed that if such an undertaking could be implied, it would be binding.

Errington v Errington appears to be just such a case. A father bought a house for his son and daughter-in-law to live in. He paid one third of the purchase price in cash and borrowed the balance on a building society mortgage. He told the son and daughter-in-law that if they paid the weekly instalments, he would convey the house to them when all the instalments were paid. They duly paid the instalments though they never contracted to do so. The Court of Appeal had no doubt that so long as they were paying the instalments, the father's promise was irrevocable. It is easy to see why a promise not to revoke should be implied and binding on such facts.[163]

In *Daulia Ltd v Four Millbank Nominees Ltd*[164] the Court of Appeal stated unequivocally that once the offeree had embarked on performance it was too late for the offeror to revoke his offer. Unfortunately, this statement was clearly obiter since the Court also held that the offeree had completed his performance before the purported revocation.[165]

Bankers' commercial credits

Perhaps the most important practical example of the problem is that of bankers' commercial credits. These are a device developed to facilitate international trade. Exporters and importers may find themselves dealing with merchants in other countries whose credit worthiness is unknown to them and may in any event be unable to finance the transaction themselves, the buyer being unable to pay for the goods until he has subsold them and the seller unable to obtain or manufacture the goods without a completely reliable assurance of payment.[166]

From the lawyer's point of view, and reduced to its simplest terms, the device involves three separate transactions.

(1) A clause is inserted in the initial contract of sale, whereby the seller requires payment in a particular manner. The buyer is to ask his bank to open a credit in the seller's favour, which shall remain irrevocable for a given time.

---

[163] It is true that this case has been doubted by property lawyers but these doubts relate to the proper analysis of the son and daughter-in-law's interest in the land and not to the contractual position. See Cheshire and Burn's *Modern Law of Real Property* (16th edn 2000) pp 642–646. Megarry and Wade *Law of Real Property* (6th edn, 2000) pp 1055–1056.

[164] [1978] Ch 231, [1978] 2 All ER 557; Harpum and Lloyd Jones [1979] CLJ 31.

[165] Further, the difficulties discussed in the text were not explored in the judgment.

[166] Davis *Law Relating to Commercial Letters of Credit* (3rd edn, 1963); Gutteridge and Megrah *The Law of Bankers' Commercial Credits* (7th edn 1984); Ellinger *Documentary Letters of Credit* (1970).

(2) The buyer makes an agreement with his bank, whereby the bank undertakes to open such a credit in return for the buyer's promise to reimburse the bank, to pay a small commission, and to give the bank a lien over the shipping documents.

(3) The buyer's bank notifies the seller that it has opened an irrevocable credit in his favour, to be drawn on as soon as the seller presents the shipping documents.

It is upon the third of these transactions that doubts have arisen. What is the legal position of the seller should the bank refuse to honour its promise? He could sue the buyer on the original contract of sale, but this would be to abandon the credit scheme.

In earlier editions of this work we have treated this as a problem in privity of contract, that is, as to whether the seller derives rights under the undoubted contract between buyer and bank.[167] In practice, however, the seller does not seek to enforce the contract between buyer and bank but a direct contract between the banker and himself. Litigation on credits is by no means infrequent but no bank has yet argued that there is no contract between it and the seller. Several dicta support the existence of such a contract[168] and it seems safe to assume that any court would be reluctant to cast doubt on the efficacy of such a valuable commercial tool. Writers on the subject have devoted much care to analysing the theoretical obstacles to such a solution.[169] One such obstacle is the supposed revocability of offers of unilateral contracts. The bank's letter of credit could easily be treated as an offer to pay if the seller presents the prescribed documents but commercial practice treats the bank's offer (where the credit is described as irrevocable) as irrevocable as soon as it is received by the seller.

B Lapse of time

If an offer states that it is open for acceptance until a certain day, a later acceptance will clearly be ineffective. Even if there is no express time limit an offer is normally open only for a reasonable time. So in *Ramsgate Victoria Hotel Co v Montefiore*:[170]

> The defendant had applied in June for shares in the plaintiff company and had paid a deposit into the company's bank. He heard nothing more until the end of November, when he was informed that the shares had been allotted to him and that he should pay the balance due upon them.

---

[167] See eg 8th edn, pp 432–434.

[168] See especially *Hamzeh Malas & Sons v British Imex Industries Ltd* [1958] 2 QB 127, [1958] 1 All ER 262; *Urquhart Lindsay & Co Ltd v Eastern Bank Ltd* [1922] 1 KB 318.

[169] *Davis* ch 7; *Gutteridge and Megrah* ch 3; *Ellinger* pp 39 ff.

[170] (1866) LR 1 Exch 109. See also *Hare v Nicoll* [1966] 2 QB 130, [1966] 1 All ER 285; and *Manchester Diocesan Council for Education v Commercial and General Investments Ltd* [1969] 3 All ER 1593, [1970] 1 WLR 241 which contains an instructive examination by Buckley J of the rationale of the rule.

The Court of Exchequer held that his refusal to take them up was justified. His offer should have been accepted, if at all, within a reasonable time, and the interval between June and November was excessive. The American case of *Loring v City of Boston*[171] offers a further illustration:

> A reward was offered in May 1837, for the 'apprehension and conviction' of incendiaries. The advertisement continued in the papers for a week, but was never followed by any notice of revocation. In January 1841, the plaintiff secured an arrest and conviction for arson, and sued for the reward.

The offer was held to have lapsed by the passage of time, and the plaintiff failed.

C Failure of a condition subject to which the offer was made

An offer, no less than an acceptance, may be conditional and not absolute; and if the condition fails to be satisfied, the offer will not be capable of acceptance. The condition may be implied as well as expressed. A striking illustration is afforded by the case of *Financings Ltd v Stimson*:[172]

> On 16 March the defendant saw at the premises of X, a dealer, a motor car advertised for £350. He wished to obtain it on hire purchase and signed a form provided by X. The form was that of the plaintiffs, a finance company, and stated: 'This "agreement" shall be binding on [the plaintiffs] only upon signature on behalf of the plaintiffs.' On 18 March the defendant paid the first instalment of £70 and took away the car. On 20 March, dissatisfied with it, the defendant returned it to X, saying that he was ready to forfeit his £70. On 24 March the car was stolen from X's premises, but was recovered badly damaged. On 25 March, in ignorance of these facts, the plaintiffs signed the 'agreement'.

When the plaintiffs subsequently discovered what had happened, they sold the car for £240 and sued the defendant for breach of the hire-purchase contract. The Court of Appeal gave judgment for the defendant. The so-called 'agreement' was in truth an offer by the defendant to make a contract with the plaintiffs. But it was subject to the implied condition that the car remained, until the moment of acceptance, in substantially the same state as at the moment of offer. As Donovan LJ asked:[173]

> Who would offer to purchase a car on terms that, if it were severely damaged before the offer was accepted, he, the offeror, would pay the bill? . . . The county court judge held that there

---

[171] 7 Metcalf 409 (1884).   [172] [1962] 3 All ER 386, [1962] 1 WLR 1184.
[173] Ibid at 390. Lord Denning MR and Donovan LJ (Pearson LJ dissenting) were also prepared to find for the defendant on the ground that, when he returned the car to the dealer, he revoked his offer and that the dealer had ostensible authority to accept the revocation of the plaintiffs' behalf.

must be implied a term that, until acceptance, the goods would remain in substantially the same state as at the date of the offer; and I think that this is both good sense and good law.

As the implied condition had been broken before the plaintiffs purported to accept, the offer had ceased to be capable of acceptance and no contract had been concluded.

D Death

The effect of death upon the continuity of an offer is more doubtful. It is clear that the offeree cannot accept after he has had notice of the offeror's death.[174] But is the offeror's estate bound if the offeree performs an act of acceptance in ignorance of the death? In *Dickinson v Dodds*[175] Mellish LJ, in an obiter dictum, expressed the opinion 'that, if a man who makes an offer dies, the offer cannot be accepted after he is dead'. The case of *Bradbury v Morgan*,[176] however, suggests that, in principle at least, this opinion does not represent the law:

> X had written to the plaintiffs, requesting them to give credit to Y and guaranteeing payment up to £100. The plaintiffs gave credit to Y. X then died, and the plaintiffs, in ignorance of this fact, continued the credit to Y. The plaintiffs now sued X's executors on the guarantee.

It was held that the defendants were liable. In the words of Pollock CB:

> This is a contract, and the question is whether it is put an end to by death of the guarantor. There is no direct authority to that effect; and I think that all reason and authority, such as there is, are against that proposition.

Channell B was equally emphatic:

> In the case of a contract death does not in general operate as revocation, but only in exceptional cases, and this is not within them.

The truth would seem to be that the effect of death varies according to the nature of the particular contract. If, as in the case of a guarantee, the offer is of a promise which is independent of the offeror's personality and which can be satisfied out of his estate, death does not, until notified, prevent acceptance. If, as in the case of agency[177] or in an offer to write a book or to perform at a concert, some element personal to the offeror is involved, his death automatically terminates the negotiations.[178]

---

174 See *Re Whelan* [1897] 1 IR 575, and *Coulthart v Clementson* (1879) 5 QBD 42.
175 (1876) 2 ChD 463 at 475. See also *Pollock on Contract* (13th edn) p 30.
176 (1862) 1 H & C 249.
177 P 640, below.   178 See Ferson 10 Minn LJ 373.

Effect of death of offeree

Upon the converse case of the offeree's death there appears to be no English authority. The question was, indeed, considered obiter by Warrington LJ in *Reynolds v Atherton*.[179] He was of opinion that an offer ceases, by operation of law, on the death of the offeree, though he regarded the language of revocation in this context as inappropriate:

> I think it would be more accurate to say that, the offer having been made to a living person who ceases to be a living person before the offer is accepted, there is no longer an offer at all. The offer is not intended to be made to a dead person or to his executors, and the offer ceases to be an offer capable of acceptance.

The dictum, indeed, was coloured by an anachronistic reference to the *consensus* theory, and the point was expressly reserved by Lord Dunedin when the case reached the House of Lords.[180] But it is not unreasonable to suggest that an offer, unless made to the public at large, assumes the continued existence of a particular offeree, and that the destruction of this assumption frustrates the intention to contract. This view has been taken in Canada. In *Re Irvine* it was held by the Appellate Division of the Supreme Court of Ontario that an acceptance handed by an offeree to his son for posting, but not in fact posted until after the offeree's death, was invalid.[181]

5 CONSTRUCTING A CONTRACT

The rules thus developed by the common law as to the making, acceptance and revocation of offers illustrate the almost self-evident truth that while contract is ultimately based upon the assumption of agreement, the courts, like all human tribunals, cannot peer into the minds of the parties and must be content with external phenomena. The existence of a contract, in many cases, is to be inferred only from conduct. To do justice, however, the courts may have to go beyond the immediate inferences to be drawn from words and acts and may be tempted or driven to construct a contract between persons who would seem, at first sight, not to be in contractual relationship with each other at all.

A classic example of this process is the case of *Clarke v Dunraven*:[182]

---

[179] (1921) 125 LT 690 at 695–696.
[180] (1922) 127 LT 189 at 191.   [181] [1928] 3 DLR 268.
[182] [1897] AC 59, affirming the decision of the Court of Appeal, reported *sub nom The Satanita* [1895] P 248. See also *Rayfield v Hands* [1960] Ch 1, [1958] 2 All ER 194, *Modahl v British Athletic Federation Ltd* [2002] 1 WLR 1192.

The owners of two yachts entered them for the Mudhook Yacht Club Regatta. The rules of the Club, which each owner undertook in a letter to the Club Secretary to obey, included an obligation to pay 'all damages' caused by fouling. While manoeuvring for the start, the *Satanita* fouled the *Valkyrie* and sank her. The owner of the latter sued the owner of the former for damages.

The defendant argued that his only liability was under a statute whereby his responsibility was limited to £8 per ton on the registered tonnage of his yacht.[183] The plaintiff replied that the fact of entering a competition in accordance with the rules of the Club, created a contract between the respective competitors and that by these rules the defendant had bound himself to pay 'all damages'. The vital question, therefore, was whether any contract had been made between the two owners: their immediate relations were not with each other but with the Yacht Club. It was held, both by the Court of Appeal and by the House of Lords, that a contract was created between them either when they entered their yachts for the race or, at latest, when they actually sailed.[184] The competitors had accepted the rules as binding upon each other.

The rôle of the judges in thus constructing a contract was accepted and explained in 1913 by Lord Moulton.[185]

> It is evident, both on principle and on authority, that there may be a contract the consideration for which is the making of some other contract. 'If you will make such and such a contract I will give you one hundred pounds,' is in every sense of the word a complete legal contract. It is collateral to the main contract, but each has an independent existence, and they do not differ in respect of their possessing to the full the character and status of a contract.

The use of the title 'collateral contracts' to designate such creatures is thus sanctioned by high authority and, indeed, had been known to the law for the previous fifty years.[186]

The name is not, perhaps, altogether fortunate. The word 'collateral' suggests something that stands side by side with the main contract, springing out of it and fortifying it. But, as will be seen from the examples that follow, the purpose of the device is usually to enforce a promise given prior to the main contract and but

---

[183] Merchant Shipping Act, Amendment Act 1862, s 54(1).

[184] See the judgments of Lord Esher [1895] P at 255, and of Lord Herschell [1897] AC at 63.

[185] *Heilbut, Symons & Co v Buckleton* [1913] AC 30 at 47. See Greig 87 LQR 179 at 185–190.

[186] *Lindley v Lacey* (1864) 17 CBNS 578; and *Erskine v Adeane* (1873) 8 Ch App 756. See Wedderburn [1959] CLJ 58. It may be added that the case of *Collen v Wright* (1857) 8 E & B 647, seems to offer an early example of a 'collateral contract': p 633, below. *Carlill v Carbolic Smoke Ball Co* [1892] 2 QB 484; on appeal [1893] 1 QB 256, p 34, above is another example of a collateral contract between manufacturer and consumer where the consumer bought the goods from a retailer relying upon the manufacturer's advertisements. In that area such a finding is unusual: *Lambert v Lewis* [1982] AC 225, [1980] 1 All ER 978. See also *Esso Petroleum Ltd v Customs and Excise Comrs* [1976] 1 All ER 117, [1976] 1 WLR 1, discussed more fully at p 153, below.

for which this main contract would not have been made. It is often, though not always, rather a preliminary than a collateral contract. But it would be pedantic to quarrel with the name if the invention itself is salutary and successful. Its value has been attested by a number of cases. Thus in *Shanklin Pier Ltd v Detel Products Ltd:*[187]

> The plaintiffs had made a contract with X and Co to repair and repaint their pier. Under this contract the plaintiffs had the right to specify the materials to be used. The defendants induced them to specify the use of a particular paint made by the defendants by giving them assurances as to its quality. The paint was applied by X and Co with sad effect, and the plaintiffs had to spend £4,000 to put matters right.

The plaintiffs sued the defendants for breach of their undertaking. The defendants argued that there was no contract between the plaintiffs and themselves, because the paint had been bought from the defendants by X and Co. But it was held that in addition to the contract for the sale of the paint, there was a collateral contract between plaintiffs and defendants by which, in return for the plaintiffs specifying that the defendants' paint should be used, the defendants guaranteed its suitability.

A series of hire-purchase cases is especially instructive.

In *Webster v Higgin:*[188]

> The defendant was considering the hire purchase of a car owned by the plaintiff, a garage proprietor. The plaintiff's agent said to the defendant: 'If you buy the Hillman we will guarantee that it is in good condition.' The defendant then signed a hire-purchase agreement containing a clause that 'no warranty, condition, description or representation as to the state or quality of the vehicle is given or implied'. The car, in the words of Lord Greene, 'was nothing but a mass of second-hand and dilapidated ironmongery'.

The plaintiff sued for the return of the car and for the balance of the instalments still due. Had the hire-purchase agreement stood alone, the clause quoted might have precluded the defendant from pleading the state of the car.[189] But the Court of Appeal held that not one but two contracts had been made by the parties. The hire-purchase agreement itself had been preceded by a separate contract effected by an exchange of promises. The plaintiff, through his agent, had offered to guarantee the condition of the car in return for the promise to take it on hire-purchase terms. The plaintiff had broken this separate contract. In the result the parties gave mutual undertakings to the court, the defendant to return the car and the plaintiff to treat the hire-purchase

---

[187] [1951] 2 KB 854, [1951] 2 All ER 471.   [188] [1948] 2 All ER 127.
[189] The plaintiff, however, might have been guilty of a fundamental breach: see pp 223–230, below.

contract as at an end; and the court ordered the plaintiff to refund the deposit and the instalments which the defendant had already paid.

In *Brown v Sheen and Richmond Car Sales Ltd*:[190]

> The plaintiff wanted to obtain a car. The defendants showed him one, saying that it was 'in perfect condition and good for thousands of trouble-free miles'. The plaintiff, relying on this statement, decided to take it, but could not pay cash. It was therefore agreed that the transaction should be financed through X and Co, a finance company. In accordance with the usual course of such business, the defendants sold the car to X and Co, and X and Co made a hire-purchase contract with the plaintiff. When the car was delivered to the plaintiff, he found that it was not in good condition and had to spend money in putting it in order.

He sued the defendants for breach of their undertaking that the car was 'in perfect condition', and the defendants were held liable.

In *Andrews v Hopkinson*:[191]

> The plaintiff wanted to obtain a second-hand car. The defendant, a car dealer, recommended one, saying: 'It's a good little bus. I would stake my life on it.' Hire-purchase arrangements were then made. The plaintiff paid a deposit of £50 to the defendant; the defendant sold the car to X and Co, a finance company; and X and Co made a hire-purchase contract with the plaintiff. X and Co then delivered the car to the plaintiff, who signed a delivery note stating that he was 'satisfied as to its condition'. Up to this moment the plaintiff had not examined the car. A week later, when the plaintiff was driving it, it suddenly swerved into a lorry. The car was wrecked and the plaintiff was seriously injured. On examination it became clear that, when the car was delivered, the steering mechanism was badly at fault.

The plaintiff might have been precluded by the delivery note from suing X and Co on the hire-purchase contract. But he recovered damages from the defendant for breach of the undertaking given by the latter before the hire-purchase contract had been made.

In each of these cases the defendant had given an undertaking to the plaintiff which induced the plaintiff to make an independent contract. In each of them the court was able to construct a preliminary or 'collateral' contract, 'the consideration for which', in Lord Moulton's words, was 'the making of some other contract', and for whose breach an action would lie. Reciprocal promises could be spelt out of the dealings between the parties. 'If you will promise to specify my paint to be used on your pier or to enter into a contract for the hire purchase of a car, I will promise

---

[190] [1950] 1 All ER 1102.   [191] [1957] 1 QB 229, [1956] 3 All ER 422.

that the paint is of good quality, or the car in good condition.'[192] The device, like other judicial inventions, must not be abused. In 1965, in the case of *Hill v Harris*, Diplock LJ said:

> When parties have entered into a lease which has been the subject of negotiations between them over a period of something like six months, [a court] is unlikely to find the terms on which the premises are to be held, or the relevant covenants in relation to the premises, outside the terms of the negotiated lease itself.[193]

On the facts of this particular case the Court of Appeal was not prepared to discover the existence of any agreement other than that contained in the lease. But, there is good authority for saying that, where the facts justify the conclusion, a court may properly 'construct a collateral contract' from things said or done during the preliminary negotiations.[194] Used with discretion, an instrument has thus been forged which, without offending orthodox views of contract, may enable substantial justice to be done.

6 INCHOATE CONTRACTS

The account of contract formation given in this chapter reflects the rather rigid and formalistic stance which English law has taken on this question. It often looks as if English courts have committed themselves to the view that until there is a contract, the parties are under no obligation. This is not, however, the way that parties negotiate in practice. Except in the simplest cases, the parties do not move at once from total non-agreement to complete agreement; they proceed by agreeing on differing matters in turn and in general it would be regarded as disreputable for a party to go back on something which has already been agreed just because there are other matters not yet agreed. So it is perfectly possible, while accepting the decision of the House of Lords in *Gibson v Manchester City Council*[195] as entirely correct as a technical

---

[192] Readers of the judgments in these three cases will observe that the word 'warranty' is used to describe the undertakings given by the defendants. As will be seen (p 196, below), this word, in modern legal language, is used to denote a term of comparatively minor importance included in a contract. It would therefore seem inappropriate in the present context, where the task of the court was to construct an entirely independent contract, one side of which was the undertaking in question. But, though the language employed may be unhappy, the result of the cases is in line with previous developments, as described by Lord Moulton. See Diamond 21 MLR 177.

[193] [1965] 2 All ER 358 at 362, [1965] 2 WLR at 1336.

[194] *City and Westminster Properties (1934) Ltd v Mudd* [1959] Ch 129, [1958] 2 All ER 733. See p 144, below.

[195] [1979] 1 All ER 972, [1979] 1 WLR 294, see p 46, above.

application of private law contract principles, to have sympathy with the view of Lord Denning that this is not the way in which a public body should negotiate.

The English approach clearly has important messages for contract negotiators. It is clearly risky to leave terms to be agreed later and so on and very desirable that, if this is done, some objectively operable machinery should be provided which the courts can take as a basis for finding a concluded agreement.[196] It is inevitable, however, that the parties will from time to time wish to leave questions to be resolved at a later date. With careful drafting this can sometimes be done by the use of conditional contracts.[197] The trick here is to make sure that the condition is sufficiently certain that the court can hold it to have been satisfied. Sometimes Letters of Intent will pass this test though in the majority of cases they will not.[198]

Some legal systems handle this problem by imposing a duty to negotiate in good faith.[199] This is expressly provided by the Italian civil code and other civil law systems have developed a doctrine of *culpa in contrahendo* though in some systems this is regarded as tortious rather than contractual. There are signs of similar movement in American law. *Hughes Aircraft Systems International v Airservices Australia*[200] suggests that Australian law may develop in the same way. There is no explicit recognition of such a notion in English law though some of the cases discussed in this and the previous section could be regarded as examples of an undeveloped doctrine of this kind.

An important question is whether the parties can, by agreement, impose on themselves a duty to negotiate in good faith. A negative answer was given to this question by the House of Lords in *Walford v Miles*.[201]

In this case the defendants, who were husband and wife, owned a photographic processing business which they were interested in selling. In 1985 there had been abortive negotiations with a company in which their accountants had a substantial interest. In late 1986 the plaintiffs, who were brothers, one of whom was a solicitor and the other an accountant, heard that the business might be for sale at about £2 million and the plaintiffs were very anxious to buy at this price which they regarded as a bargain. In March 1987 the plaintiffs agreed 'subject to contract' to buy the business.

On 18 March 1987 there was an oral agreement between one of the plaintiffs and Mr Miles that if the plaintiffs obtained a comfort letter from their bankers, confirming that they were prepared to provide the finance of £2 million, the defendants would terminate negotiations with any third party. The comfort letter from the bank was provided, but on 30 March the defendants' solicitors wrote to the plaintiffs stating

---

[196] See *Sudbrook Trading Estate Ltd v Eggleton* [1983] 1 AC 444, [1982] 3 All ER 1, discussed p 58, above.

[197] See p 192, below.   [198] See p 57, above.

[199] Carter and Furmston, 8 JCL 1, 93. Furmston, Norisada and Poole ch 10.

[200] (1997) 146 ALR 1; Furmston 114 LQR 362.

[201] [1992] 1 All ER 453.

that the defendants had decided to sell the business to the company in which their accountants were interested.

The plaintiffs claimed that, although there was no binding contract for the sale of the business, there was a binding preliminary contract. The argument was that in return for the provision of the comfort letter the defendants had bound themselves to a 'lock-out' agreement, that is, an agreement which would give the plaintiffs an exclusive opportunity to come to terms with the defendants. The House of Lords did not doubt that it was in principle possible to make a binding lock-out agreement. However, in order to make any commercial sense, such an agreement would have to have an express or implied time limit. If all that A does is to promise not to negotiate with anyone other than B, that in itself does not impose a legal obligation to negotiate with B; still less to reach an agreement with B. But, of course, if A has agreed not to negotiate with anyone but B for 6 months, this would put A under some commercial pressure, which may in some cases be very great, to make a serious attempt to reach agreement with B.

The agreement in this case had no express time limit. The plaintiffs argued that it was subject to an implied term that the defendants 'would continue to negotiate in good faith with the plaintiffs'. One answer to this claim would be that no such term would be implied. However, the answer given by the House of Lords was that even if such a term was implied it would not help the plaintiffs because a duty to negotiate in good faith was meaningless and without content.

This decision has not escaped criticism.[202] Other systems reveal that there is no necessary antipathy between the freedom to reach a concluded contract or not and a duty to negotiate in good faith. This is most obviously displayed in the case of a party who enters negotiations with no intention of reaching a result but simply to waste the other party's time. Of course, the fact that a duty to negotiate in good faith does not impose a duty to reach a concluded contract is important as to the remedy. The plaintiffs in this case claimed the amount of profit they would have made if a contract had been concluded. It is respectfully submitted that this contention was misconceived. The plaintiffs' loss, if there was a breach of an obligation to negotiate in good faith, was in the money they had wasted on the negotiations. In fact, a sum had been awarded in respect of this loss by the trial judge and was not the subject of an appeal.

The statement by the House of Lords that it was possible in principle to make a binding 'lock-out' agreement was applied by the Court of Appeal in *Pitt v PHH Asset Management*.[203] In this case, the defendant placed a property on the market through a firm of estate agents at £205,000. Both the plaintiff and a Miss Buckle were interested in buying the property. Miss Buckle made a written offer of £185,000. The plaintiff offered £190,000, which was accepted subject to contract. Miss Buckle increased her

---

[202] Carter and Furmston above and Neill 108 LQR 405. See Unidroit Principles Article 2.1.15 (Negotiations in Bad Faith).
[203] [1993] 4 All ER 961.

offer to £195,000 and the acceptance of the plaintiff's offer was then withdrawn. The plaintiff increased his offer to £200,000 and Miss Buckle made an offer of the same amount but the plaintiff's offer was accepted, subject to contract. Miss Buckle then increased her offer again to £210,000 and the acceptance of the plaintiff's latest offer was again withdrawn. The plaintiff threatened to seek an injunction to prevent the sale to Miss Buckle and also to tell Miss Buckle that he was withdrawing so that she should lower her offer.

It is quite clear legally that whatever one might think of the behaviour of all the parties, nobody was at this stage contractually bound to anyone else. However, the plaintiff and the selling agent acting on behalf of the defendant then reached an oral agreement that the defendant would sell the property to the plaintiff for £200,000 and would not consider any further offers, provided the plaintiff exchanged contracts within two weeks of receipt of a draft contract. That agreement was recorded in a letter from the plaintiff to the selling agent and the agreement was confirmed by the defendant in a letter of the same date to the selling agent, a copy of which was sent to the plaintiff.

The defendant sent a draft contract to the plaintiff and eight days later the plaintiff indicated that he was ready to exchange contracts. However, on the same day, the plaintiff received a letter saying that it had been decided to go ahead with the sale to Miss Buckle at £210,000 unless the plaintiff was prepared to exchange contracts on the same day at that price. This the plaintiff refused to do.

It is clear that on these facts there was no binding contract between the plaintiff and the defendant for the sale of the property but the plaintiff argued that the defendant was in breach of an agreement not to consider any further offers within the 14-day period. The trial judge and the Court of Appeal held that the plaintiff's claim succeeded.

Of course, the defendant could have waited for 14 days and then have reopened negotiations with other potential buyers but this would be commercially risky for the defendant since it would very likely lose the chance of selling to the plaintiff. In this situation, it is the possibility of playing two or more potential purchasers off against each other which provides the best chance of maximising the price received. What the case shows is that there are steps which potential purchasers may take to defend themselves against such behaviour.

The all or nothing approach is not in fact adopted by the courts in all cases. Sometimes the court will hold that although the main contract has not been concluded, nevertheless there is a collateral contract which gives rise to some rights during the negotiating process. A good example is *Blackpool & Fylde Aero Club Ltd v Blackpool Borough Council.*[204] In this case the defendant Council which owned and managed an airport invited the plaintiffs, together with six other parties, to tender for

---

[204] [1990] 3 All ER 25, [1990] 1 WLR 1195; Phang 4 JCL 46.

the concession for operating pleasure flights from the airport. The invitation to tender required tenders to be submitted in an envelope which was provided and stated that the envelope was not to bear any identifying mark and that tenders received after 12 noon on 17 March 1983 would not be considered. The plaintiffs had successfully tendered for this concession on a number of previous occasions and delivered by hand to the letter box in the Town Hall at 11 am on 17 March a tender which would have been the highest. Unfortunately, the letter box was not in fact cleared until the following day and the Tender Committee therefore assumed that the plaintiffs' tender had not been delivered in time, put it on one side and awarded the concession to another tenderer. The plaintiffs were naturally much aggrieved but they appeared to have a major problem since it was clear that the Council had never agreed to accept the highest tender or indeed to accept any tender at all. Nevertheless, the Court of Appeal held that it was implicit in the adoption of a formal and elaborate tendering machinery of this kind that the Council implicitly undertook to operate it according to its terms. The Council should therefore have considered the plaintiffs' tender and had only failed to do so because of the inefficiency of their own servants, which was clearly no excuse. It followed that the plaintiffs were entitled to damages.[205]

Two later cases suggest that the *Blackpool* case is the origin of a general principle that, at least in the public sector, one who invites tenders, implicitly promises to adhere strictly to the rules of the game. In *Hughes Aircraft Systems International v Airservices Australia*[206] Finn J held that the defendant was under a contractual obligation scrupulously to apply the published criteria in regard to tendering for the Australian advanced air-traffic system.

In *Harmon CFEM Facades (UK) Ltd v Corporate Officer of the House of Commons*[207] the claimant, a subsidiary of an American company, was the unsuccessful tenderer for the fenestration contract for the new parliamentary building in Bridge Street, Westminster. The trial judge held that the claimant was in fact the lowest bidder but that the bids had been manipulated so as to prefer another bidder, which was a consortium that included a British partner. This was held to be a breach of contract.[208] His Honour Judge Humphrey Lloyd QC said:

> In the public sector where competitive tenders are sought and responded to, a contract comes into existence whereby the prospective employer impliedly agrees to consider all tenders fairly.[209]

---

[205] Obviously there would be a problem about the amount of damage which the plaintiff could recover though he was certainly deprived of a substantial chance of being awarded the contract. In fact the amount of damages was not before the Court of Appeal.

[206] (1997) 146 ALR 1.

[207] (1999) 67 Con LR 1.

[208] As well as of European procurement law.

[209] In later proceedings the judge held that the claimant could recover as damages the costs of tendering and a substantial part of the profit it would have made on the contract

Even though there is no contract, a party may be entitled to restitutionary relief on the grounds that the other party has derived benefit from the transaction for which he should compensate the plaintiff even though no contract has arisen. One example we have already met is *British Steel Corpn v Cleveland Bridge and Engineering Co Ltd*.[210] Another example is *Marston Construction Co Ltd v Kigass Ltd*.[211] In this case the plaintiffs were invited, amongst others, to tender for the building of a replacement factory for the defendants. The plaintiffs were the only tenderers who were invited to discuss their tender further with the defendants. The defendants at all times made it clear that they would not go ahead with the project unless they received enough money from their insurance claim but asked the plaintiffs to go ahead with preparatory work. The plaintiffs did some £25,000 worth of preparatory work before it became clear that the defendants would not proceed with the building. It was held that in the circumstance the plaintiffs were entitled to a reasonable payment for the work which they had done at the defendants' request.[212]

A different view was taken by Rattee J in *Regalian Properties plc v London Dockland Development Corpn*.[213] In this case, the plaintiffs in 1986 entered into negotiations with the defendant corporation for a residential development in the former London docks area. The plaintiffs offered £18.5 million for a licence to build the development. This was accepted 'subject to contract'. There followed long delays which were caused partly by the requirement of the Development Corporation for further designs of what was to be a high-profile and high-prestige project and partly by the need for the defendants to obtain vacant possession of all of the land which was to form part of the project. By October 1988, land prices had collapsed to such an extent that it became clear that the project was not viable and it was abandoned. The plaintiffs brought an action claiming some £3 million, representing fees which they had paid to various professional firms in respect of the proposed development. Rattee J rejected the plaintiff's case. The dealings had all been 'subject to contract' and the Development Corporation had done nothing to encourage the plaintiffs to think that they would be paid for this work.[214]

Finally, it is possible in some cases that what is said and done in the course of negotiations may give rise to a claim in tort. It would certainly seem that someone who entered into negotiations for a contract fraudulently, never intending to bring them to a conclusion, should be liable for the loss which this inflicted on the other

---

[210] [1984] 1 All ER 504, p 48, above Jones 18 U of Western Ontario LR 447.

[211] (1989) 15 Con LR 116. See also *William Lacey (Hounslow) Ltd v Davies* [1957] 2 All ER 712, [1957] 1 WLR 932.

[212] One might perhaps explain this case on an implied contract basis but the judge's reasoning is entirely in terms of restitution. In the interesting case of *A-G of Hong Kong v Humphreys Estate (Queen's Gardens) Ltd* [1987] AC 114 [1987] 2 All ER 387, no claim on a restitutionary basis was made.

[213] [1995] 1 All ER 1005. Mannolini 59 MLR 111.

[214] Rattee J was critical of both the result and the reasoning in *Marston v Kigass*, above. He was critical of the reasoning in *William Lacy v Davies* n 211, above, but not the result.

party. It has certainly been held that what has been said in the negotiations may give rise to liability for negligent misrepresentation.[215]

7 LONG-TERM RELATIONSHIPS

Most of the contracts discussed in this book call for relatively immediate performance: a contract to sell goods to be delivered today, tomorrow or next week; a contract to travel by train today or by airplane next month; but this is clearly not true of all contracts. A time charterparty may well run for five years, a contract for life insurance or a pension may envisage performance in 30 years' time; a lease, which is a contract as well as a transfer of property, may run for 99 or even 999 years.

In such contracts the draughtsman, who will often be a lawyer, will try to provide for the most likely long-term contingencies. In some cases this will be very difficult. A good example would be a contract to explore for oil, where the timespan will be long, the risks great and difficult accurately to foresee, and the sums involved very large.[216]

There are also long-term relationships where there are undoubtedly many contractually binding transactions but it is debatable whether there is a binding overarching contract. At a trivial level, I may buy my morning paper from the same newsagent every day for fifty years. Each purchase is a contract but I do not promise to buy a paper tomorrow and the newsagent does not promise to be open to sell a paper to me.

A situation somewhat like this was before the court in *Baird Textile Holdings Ltd v Marks and Spencer plc*.[217] The claimant had been one of the principal suppliers of garments to the defendant retailers for some 30 years. Very substantial orders were placed, predominantly twice a year for the summer and winter seasons. Obviously the orders gave rise to contracts but nothing had ever been written down about the long-term position. In October 1999 the defendants told the claimants that the relationship would come to an end at the end of the current production season without any previous notice.

Baird claimed that they were entitled to reasonable notice and that in the circumstances three years would be reasonable notice. Marks and Spencer moved to strike out on the ground that Baird's claim had no reasonable prospect of success. This meant that the allegations in Baird's statement of claim had to be assumed to be true but it also meant that if the motion were successful there would be no disclosure of Marks & Spencer's papers. If the case had gone to trial it might have been

---

[215] *Esso Petroleum Co Ltd v Mardon* [1976] QB 801, [1976] 2 All ER 5. See p 346, below.

[216] The problems for contract law of dealing with long-term contracts of this kind has been the subject of extensive discussion by Ian McNeil. This work is most conveniently found in *The Relational Theory of Contract: Selected Works of Ian McNeil* (ed. Campbell).

[217] [2001] EWCA Civ 274 [2002] 1 All ER (Comm) 737.

revealed what Marks & Spencer (and indeed Baird) had thought the relationship was.[218]

Baird argued that either there was a contract or, alternatively, Marks & Spencer were estopped from termination without notice. Granted Baird's own evidence that it was Marks & Spencer's policy to manage the relationship with the suppliers without putting anything in writing, it is not surprising that the Court of Appeal held that there was no contract.

It appears more arguable that there was a case fit for trial that Marks & Spencer had led Baird to believe that they would be given some notice and should be estopped. Both the Australian and American version of the doctrine of promissory estoppel approach this position.[219] The Court of Appeal recognised that if the leading Australian case of *Waltons Stores (Interstate) v Maher*[220] were English law, the case would have to go to trial but that this would require a decision of the House of Lords.

---

[218] There is substantial evidence about the relationship between car manufacturers and suppliers in the American car industry. See *International Encyclopaedia of Comparative Law* Vol VII ch 3, pp 18–23.

[219] *Waltons Store (Interstate) Ltd v Maher* (1998) 164 CLR 387; *Hoffmann v Red Owl Stores Inc* 133 NW 2d 267 (1965).

[220] (1998) 164 CLR 387.

4 CONSIDERATION

1 FUNCTION AND DEFINITION

In the previous chapter we saw that agreement, or at least the outward appearance of agreement, was an essential ingredient of a contract. But it is likely that few legal systems treat all agreements as enforceable contracts. In early systems the distinction between unenforceable and enforceable agreements is often one of form, and signs of that can be found in English law in the survival of the rule that a promise by deed is legally binding.

In developed English law, that is since the sixteenth century, the crucial factor is the presence or the absence of 'consideration'. It is natural to assume that the adoption of this test is related to some underlying theory about why agreements are enforced.[1]

---

[1] The literature on why contracts are legally enforced is extensive. See eg Hughes Parry *The Sanctity of Contracts in English Law;* Cohen and Cohen *Readings in Jurisprudence and Legal Philosophy* pp 100–195;

It has therefore been forcefully argued that 'consideration' is a word long rooted in the language of English law and denotes its fundamental attitude to contract and that when, in the middle of the sixteenth century, the lawyers evolved, through the action of assumpsit, a general contractual remedy, they decided at the same time that it would not avail to redress the breach of any and every promise, whatever its nature. In particular, it has been said that it was decided that assumpsit was not to be used to enforce a gratuitous promise so that the plaintiff must show that the defendant's promise, upon which he was suing, was part of a bargain to which he himself had contributed.[2] So it has been persuasively argued that the doctrine of considerations represents the adoption by English law of the notion that only bargains should be enforced.[3]

This view has not gone unchallenged. The history of consideration is still not completely clear but it seems inherently unlikely that sixteenth-century English judges would ever have asked themselves a highly abstract question such as 'Should we enforce bargains or promises?' The pragmatic habits of the English and the absence of institutional writing make it probable that in the sixteenth and seventeenth centuries there was no single *doctrine* of consideration, but a number of considerations which were recognised as adequate to support an action for breach of a promise.[4] So consideration probably meant at this stage the reason for the promise being binding, fulfilling something like the role of *causa* or *cause* in continental systems.[5]

Lord Mansfield's attack on consideration

The doctrine of consideration was accepted throughout the seventeenth and in the first half of the eighteenth century as an integral part of the new law of contract. But when Lord Mansfield became Chief Justice of the King's Bench in 1756 its pride of place was challenged. At first, Lord Mansfield refused to recognise it as the vital criterion of a contract and treated it merely as evidence of the parties' intention to be bound. If such an intention could be ascertained by other means, such as the presence of writing, consideration was unnecessary.[6] This direct assault was repelled with ease. In *Rann v Hughes* in 1778[7] it was proclaimed that:

Atiyah *Promises, Morals and Law* (usefully reviewed by Raz 95 Harvard LR 916 and Simpson 98 LQR 470); Fried *Contract as Promise A Theory Of Contractual Obligations* (reviewed Atiyah 95 Harvard LR 509); Atiyah *Essays on Contract* especially essays 6 and 7; Coote 1 JCL 91, 183.

[2] Fifoot *History and Sources of the Common Law* pp 395 ff.

[3] See eg Hamson 54 LQR 233; Shatwell 1 Sydney L Rev 289.   [4] See Simpson *History* chs IV–VII.

[5] Simpson 91 LQR 247 at 267. On the relationship between consideration and cause see Windeyer J in *Smith v Jenkins* (1969) 44 ALJR 78 at 83. Von Mehren 72 Harvard L Rev 1009; Markesinis [1978] CLJ 53. Atiyah has argued that this is still the function of consideration, *Essays on Contract* essay 8. Cf Treitel 50 ALJ 439. The equation of consideration and bargain is also criticised by Pound 33 Tulane L Rev 455. See also Chloros 17 ICLQ 137. On the other hand in the history of ideas what is believed is often more important than what is true. Whatever its historical validity, the equation between consideration and bargain has had a powerful influence on twentieth-century writing.

[6] *Pillans v Van Mierop* (1765) 3 Burr 1664. For the varied fortunes of the doctrine of consideration between 1765 and 1840, see Fifoot *History and Sources of the Common Law* pp 406–411.

[7] (1778) 7 Term Rep 350, n.

... all contracts are, by the laws of England, distinguished into agreements by specialty, and agreements by parol; nor is there any such third class . . . as contracts in writing. If they be merely written and not specialties, they are parol, and a consideration must be proved.

Lord Mansfield's second approach was more insinuating. Accepting the concept of consideration as essential to English contract, he defined it in terms of moral obligation.

Where a man is under a moral obligation, which no Court of law or equity can enforce, and promises, the honesty and rectitude of the thing is a consideration . . . The ties of conscience upon an upright mind are a sufficient consideration.[8]

According to this view, whenever a man is under a moral duty to pay money and subsequently promises to pay, the pre-existing moral duty furnishes consideration for the promise. The equation of consideration and moral obligation was accepted, though with increasing distrust, for nearly sixty years, and was finally repudiated only in 1840. In *Eastwood v Kenyon*:[9]

On the death of John Sutcliffe, his infant daughter, Sarah, was left as his sole heiress. The plaintiff, as the girl's guardian, spent money on her education and for the benefit of the estate, and the girl, when she came of age, promised to reimburse him. She then married the defendant, who also promised to pay. The plaintiff sued the defendant on this promise.

Lord Denman dismissed the action and condemned the whole principle of moral obligation upon which it was founded. Such a principle was an innovation of Lord Mansfield, and to extirpate it would be to restore the pure and original doctrine of the common law. Moreover, as he pointed out, the logical inference from the acceptance of moral duty as the sole test of an actionable promise was the virtual annihilation of consideration. The law required some factor additional to the defendant's promise, whereby the promise became legally binding; but, if no more was needed than the pressure of conscience, this would operate as soon as the defendant voluntarily assumed an undertaking. To give a promise was to accept a moral obligation to perform it.[10]

---

[8] *Hawkes v Saunders* (1782) 1 Cowp 289 at 290.

[9] (1840) 11 Ad & El 438. Extra-judicial criticism had been offered by the reporters Bosanquet and Puller in 1802 (see the note to *Wennall v Adney* (1802) 3 Bos & P 247), and Lord Tenterden had expressed some doubts in 1831 (*Littlefield v Shee* (1831) 2 B & Ad 811). But no decisive rejection occurred until 1840.

[10] Simpson *History* p 323, argues that far from being an aberration of Lord Mansfield, the 'moral obligation' consideration lies at the heart of the early history of the doctrine. Some exceptional cases survived *Eastwood v Kenyon*. See eg *Flight v Reed* (1863) 1 H & C 703, where the plaintiff advanced money to the defendant against promissory notes void under the usury statutes. After the repeal of the statutes and without any further advances, the defendant executed new promissory notes which were held binding, the only consideration being the moral obligation to repay the void loans. This case was not followed in *Sharp v Ellis* [1972] VR 137. See also the cases of past consideration discussed below.

Attempts to define consideration

As a result of *Eastwood v Kenyon* it was clear that consideration was neither a mere rule of evidence nor a synonym for moral obligation. How then was it to be defined? In the course of the nineteenth century it was frequently said that a plaintiff could establish the presence of consideration in one of two ways. He might prove either that he had conferred a benefit upon the defendant in return for which the defendant's promise was given, or that he himself had incurred a detriment for which the promise was to compensate.[11]

The antithesis of benefit and detriment, though reiterated in the courts, is not altogether happy. The use of the word 'detriment', in particular, obscures the vital transformation of assumpsit from a species of action on the case to a general remedy in contract. So long as it remained tortious in character, it was necessary to prove that the plaintiff had suffered damage in reliance upon the defendant's undertaking. When it became contractual, the courts concentrated, not on the consequences of the defendant's default, but on the facts present at the time of the agreement and in return for which the defendant's promise was given. 'Detriment' is clearly a more appropriate description of the former than of the latter situation. Nor is this criticism of merely antiquarian interest. The typical modern contract is the bargain struck by the exchange of promises. If A orders goods on credit from B, both A and B are bound from the moment of agreement, and, if the one subsequently refuses to execute his part of it, the other may sue at once. The consideration for each party's promise is the other party's promise. It is difficult to see that at this stage either party has suffered benefit or detriment unless each party is said to have received the benefit of the other's promise and suffered the detriment of making his own. But such benefit and detriment assumes that the promises are binding, which is precisely what it is sought to prove.[12] A further disadvantage to the use of the word 'detriment' is that it has to be understood in a highly technical sense. So a promise to give up smoking is capable of being a detriment in the law of consideration even though smoking is bad for the promisor. This is technically sound but likely to confuse.

A different approach to the problem of consideration may be made through the language of purchase and sale. The plaintiff must show that he has bought the

---

[11] 'A consideration of loss or inconvenience sustained by one party at the request of another is as good a consideration in law for a promise by such other as a consideration of profit or convenience to himself': Lord Ellenborough in *Bunn v Guy* (1803) 4 East 190. 'Consideration means something which is of value in the eye of the law, moving from the plaintiff: it may be some detriment to the plaintiff or some benefit to the defendant': Patteson J in *Thomas v Thomas* (1842) 2 QB 851. 'A valuable consideration in the sense of the law, may consist either in some right, interest, profit or benefit accruing to one party, or some fore bearance, detriment, loss or responsibility given, suffered or undertaken by the other': *Currie v Misa* (1875) LR 10 Exch 153. 'The general rule is that an executory agreement, by which the plaintiff agrees to do something on the terms that the defendant agrees to do something else, may be enforced, if what the plaintiff has agreed to do is either for the benefit of the defendant or to the trouble or prejudice of the plaintiff': per Lord Blackburn in *Bolton v Madden* (1873) LR 9 QB 55.

[12] *Harrison v Cage* (1698) 5 Mod Rep 411.

defendant's promise either by doing some act in return for it or by offering a counter-promise. Sir Frederick Pollock summarised the position in words adopted by the House of Lords in 1915:

> An act or forbearance of one party, or the promise thereof, is the price for which the promise of the other is bought, and the promise thus given for value is enforceable.[13]

This definition of consideration as the price paid by the plaintiff for the defendant's promise is preferable to the nineteenth-century terminology of benefit and detriment. It is easier to understand, it corresponds more happily to the normal exchange of promises and it emphasises the commercial character of the English contract.

2 CONSIDERATION—EXECUTORY, EXECUTED AND PAST

Here and in the next two sections the technical rules which the judges have evolved for the application of their doctrine of consideration will be examined.

The accepted classification of consideration is into the two categories, *executory* and *executed.* The classification reflects the two different ways in which the plaintiff may buy the defendant's promise. Consideration is called *executory* when the defendant's promise is made in return for a counter-promise from the plaintiff, *executed* when it is made in return for the performance of an act. An agreement between seller and buyer for the sale of goods for further delivery on credit is an example of the former. At the time when the agreement is made, nothing has yet been done to fulfil the mutual promises of which the bargain is composed. The whole transaction remains *in futuro*. Of the latter, the best example is the offer of a reward for an act. If A offers £5 to anyone who shall return his lost dog, the return of the dog by B is at once the acceptance of the offer and the performance of the act constituting the required consideration. B has earned the reward by his services, and only the offeror's promise remains outstanding. But whether the plaintiff relies upon an executory or on an executed consideration, he must be able to prove that his promise or act, together with the defendant's promise, constitute one single transaction and are causally related the one to the other.[14]

---

[13] *Pollock on Contracts* (13th edn) p 133; *Dunlop v Selfridge* [1915] AC 847 at 855. See also Law Revision Committee, Sixth Interim Report, para 17. The conception of consideration as the price of the promise is similarly stressed by the *American Restatement of Contracts* 2nd para 71. See *Farnsworth on Contracts* 2.2. See also Salmond and Williams' *Law of Contract* p 101, and Denning 15 MLR 1.

[14] *Wigan v English and Scottish Law Life Insurance Association* [1909] 1 Ch 291.

If the defendant makes a further promise, subsequent to and independent of the transaction, it must be regarded as a mere expression of gratitude for past favours or as a designated gift, and no contract will arise. It is irrelevant that he may have been induced to give the new promise because of the previous bargain. In such a case the promise is declared, in traditional language, to be made upon *past* consideration; or, more accurately, to be made without consideration at all. Two illustrations may be offered, one from a classical and one from a modern case. In *Roscorla v Thomas*:[15]

> The declaration stated that, 'in consideration that the plaintiff at the request of the defendant, *had* bought of the defendant a certain horse, at and for a certain price, the defendant promised the plaintiff that the said horse was sound and free from vice'. The plaintiff sued for breach of this promise.

The court held (1) that the fact of the sale did not itself imply a warranty that the horse was sound and free from vice, and (2) that the express promise was made after the sale was over and was unsupported by fresh consideration. The plaintiff could show nothing but a 'past' consideration and must fail. In *Re McArdle*:[16]

> A number of children, by their father's will, were entitled to a house after their mother's death. During the mother's life, one of the children and his wife lived with her in the house. The wife made various improvements to the house, and at a later date all the children signed a document addressed to her, stating that 'in consideration of your carrying out certain alterations and improvements to the property, we hereby agree that the executors shall repay to you from the estate, when distributed, the sum of £488 in settlement of the amount spent on such improvements'.

The Court of Appeal held that, as all the work on the house had in fact been completed before the document was signed, this was a case of past consideration and that the document could not be supported as a binding contract.

The distinction between executed and past consideration, while comparatively easy to state in the abstract, is often difficult to apply in practice, and a long and subtle line of cases has marked its interpretation in the courts. Both the distinction and the difficulty were appreciated by the judges before the close of the sixteenth century. They were required to consider the position where the plaintiff had performed services for the defendant without any agreement for remuneration and the defendant had subsequently promised to pay for them. They decided that assumpsit would lie if, but only if, the services were originally performed at the

---

[15] (1842) 3 QB 234.
[16] [1951] Ch 669, [1951] 1 All ER 905.

defendant's request.[17] The law was settled in this sense in 1615 in the case of *Lampleigh v Brathwait*.[18]

> Thomas Brathwait had killed Patrick Mahume and had then asked Anthony Lampleigh to do all he could to get a pardon for him from the King. Lampleigh exerted himself to this end, 'riding and journeying to and from London and Newmarket' at his own expense, and Brathwait afterwards promised him £100 for his trouble. He failed to pay it and Lampleigh sued in assumpsit.

It was argued, inter alia, that the consideration was past, but the court gave judgment for the plaintiff on the ground that his services had been procured by the previous request of the defendant.

> It was agreed that a mere voluntary courtesy will not have a consideration to uphold an assumpsit. But if that courtesy were moved by a suit or request of the party that gives the assumpsit, it will bind; for the promise, though it follows, yet it is not naked, but couples itself with the suit before.

The previous request and subsequent promise were thus to be treated as part of the same transaction.

This extended definition was applied at the end of the seventeenth century to cases where the defendant promised to pay a debt which was not enforceable at the time of his promise owing to some technical rule of law. Thus in *Ball v Hesketh*[19] the defendant, when an infant, had borrowed money from the plaintiff and, after coming of age, had promised to repay it. In accordance with the general immunity conferred by the law upon infants, he could not have been made liable on the original loan. But it was held that his subsequent promise entitled the plaintiff to sue him in assumpsit. So, too, in *Hyleing v Hastings*[20] it was held that a debt, the recovery of which was barred by the Statute of Limitations, was revived by a subsequent promise of payment. At the same time, the influence of commercial practice, felt with increasing urgency, familiarised the courts with the idea that a plaintiff, who sued on a negotiable instrument, need only show that value had once been given for it by some previous holder and was himself absolved from the necessity of proving fresh consideration. All these developments threatened to obliterate the distinction between executed and past consideration. It is not surprising, therefore, that they should have been used by Lord Mansfield to support his doctrine of moral obligation.[21]

But when, in the nineteenth century, this doctrine was rejected it became necessary to delimit afresh the boundaries of past and executed consideration. This was achieved

---

[17] See *Hunt v Bate* (1568) 3 Dyer 272a, and *Sidenham and Workington's Case* (1584) 2 Leon 224. See also Simpson *History* pp 452–458.

[18] (1615) Hob 105.   [19] (1697) Comb 381.   [20] (1699) 1 Ld Raym 389.

[21] See pp 94–95, above.

by accepting the test of *Lampleigh v Brathwait* that the plaintiff's services must have been rendered at the defendant's request, but emphasising the further fact that both parties must have assumed throughout their negotiations that the services were ultimately to be paid for.[22] They must have been performed in the way of business, not as an office of friendship. This 'revised version' was adopted by the court in *Re Casey's Patents, Stewart v Casey*.[23]

> A and B, the joint owners of certain patent rights, wrote to C as follows: 'In consideration of your services as the practical manager in working our patents, we hereby agree to give you one-third share of the patents.'

In an action which turned upon the effect of this agreement it was argued for A and B that their promise was made only in return for C's past services as manager and that there was therefore no consideration to support it. Bowen LJ refused to accept this argument.

The rule was succinctly stated by Lord Scarman:[24]

> An act done before the giving of a promise to make a payment or to confer some other benefit can sometimes be consideration for the promise. The act must have been done at the promisor's request, the parties must have understood that the act was to be remunerated further by a payment or the conferment of some other benefit, and payment, or the conferment of a benefit must have been legally enforceable had it been promised in advance.

The other exceptional cases discussed above have been removed or confirmed by statute. By section 2 of the Infants Relief Act 1874, no action is allowed upon any promise made after full age to pay a debt contracted during infancy.[25] By the Limitation Act 1980, if the debtor, after the debt has been barred, acknowledges the creditor's claim, the plaintiff may sue on this acknowledgment. No promise, express or implied, is necessary, and no consideration need be sought.[26] The third class of case, where the defendant is sued upon a negotiable instrument, survives as a genuine exception to the ban upon past consideration. It is to be explained as a concession to long-standing commercial custom, and it has been confirmed by section 27 of the Bills of Exchange Act 1882. By this section, 'valuable consideration for a bill may be constituted by (a) any consideration sufficient to support a simple contract, (b) an antecedent debt or liability'.[27]

---

[22] This further fact, though it was not expressed by the court in *Lampleigh v Brathwait*, seems on the whole to be implicit in the language of the judgment.

[23] [1892] 1 Ch 104. See also *Kennedy v Broun* (1863) 13 CBNS 677.

[24] *Pao On v Lau Yiu Long* [1980] AC 614 at 629, [1979] 3 All ER 65 at 74.

[25] See pp 548–565, below.   [26] See pp 811–814, below.

[27] It has been ruled that the 'antecedent debt or liability' must be that of the maker or negotiator of the instrument and not of a stranger: *Oliver v Davis* [1949] 2 KB 727, [1949] 2 All ER 353.

3 CONSIDERATION MUST MOVE FROM THE PROMISEE

As long as consideration, under Lord Mansfield's influence, could be identified with moral duty, it was possible to support an action by a person for whose benefit a promise had been given even if the consideration had been supplied by someone else.[28] But once this identification was repudiated, the judges insisted that only he could sue on a promise who had paid the price of it. How otherwise could the plaintiff prove his share in the bargain upon which his action was based? Thus in *Price v Easton*[29] the defendant promised X that if X did certain work for him he would pay a sum of money to the plaintiff. X did the work, but the defendant did not pay the money. The court of Queen's Bench held that the plaintiff could not sue the defendant and explained their decision in two different ways. Lord Denman said that the plaintiff could not 'show any consideration for the promise moving from him to the defendant'. Littledale J said that 'no privity is shown between the plaintiff and the defendant'. In *Tweddle v Atkinson* in 1861[30] the judges, while endorsing the decision in *Price v Easton*, preferred the first of these reasons. 'It is now established', said Wightman J 'that no stranger to the consideration can take advantage of a contract, although made for his benefit.'

Relation of consideration to the doctrine of privity
It has long been a controversial question whether the rule that consideration must move from the promisee and the doctrine of privity of contract are fundamentally distinct or whether they are merely variations on a common theme. Two different factual situations may indeed arise. The plaintiff may be a party to an agreement without furnishing any consideration.

> A, B and C may all be signatories to an agreement whereby C promises A and B to pay A £100 if B will carry out work desired by C.

On the other hand, the person anxious to enforce the promise may not be a party to the agreement at all.

> B and C may make an agreement whereby B promises to write a book for C and C promises to pay £100 to A.

Historically A could not sue C in either case. But must he be said to fail in the first situation because consideration has not moved from him, and in the second because

---

[28] See *Dutton v Poole* (1677) 2 Lev 210. See Simpson *History* pp 475–485.
[29] (1833) 4 B & Ad 433.
[30] (1861) 1 B & S 393.

he is not privy to the contract? The nineteenth-century judges distinguished the two situations in law as well as in fact. So, too, in 1915[31] Viscount Haldane declared two principles to be 'fundamental in the law of England'. The first was that 'only a person who is a party to a contract can sue on it', and the second that 'only a person who has given consideration may enforce a contract not under seal'. The distinction was endorsed by the Law Revision Committee in 1937.[32]

This view, however, has been questioned.[33] It has been persuasively argued that there is no basic distinction between the two principles stated by Lord Haldane: they are but different ways of saying the same thing. The underlying assumption of English law is that a contract is a bargain. If a person furnishes no consideration, he takes no part in a bargain: if he takes no part in a bargain, he takes no part in a contract. In the second of the hypothetical cases stated above, it is obvious that A is a stranger to the contract. But he is equally a stranger in the first: he is a party to an agreement, but he is not a party to a contract. It is true that, if the doctrine of consideration were abolished, the problem of privity would remain, as it still remains in other legal systems.

The question was discussed by the High Court of Australia in 1967 in *Coulls v Bagot's Executor and Trustee Co Ltd*.[34]

> C agreed to grant to the O'Neil Construction Co Ltd the exclusive right to quarry on his land in return for a minimum royalty of £12 a week for a period of ten years. C also 'authorised the company' to pay all money arising from this agreement to himself and his wife jointly. The agreement was in writing (not under seal) and was signed by C, by his wife and by O'Neil. Eighteen months later, C died. The O'Neil company in fact paid the royalty to C's wife; and the High Court was now asked, in an action between the wife and C's executors, to decide whether the company was bound or entitled to make such payment to her.

The High Court was divided upon the construction of the agreement.[35] But four of the judges were of opinion that if, on its true interpretation, the wife was a party to the agreement, she was entitled to receive the royalties payable after her husband's death even though she personally had given no consideration for the company's promise.

The High Court did not define with precision the relationship of privity of contract

[31] *Dunlop v Selfridge* [1915] AC 847 at 853: see p 573, below.
[32] Sixth Interim Report, p 22.
[33] See Smith and Thomas *A Casebook on Contract* (11th edn) pp 279–283; Salmond and Williams *The Law of Contracts* pp 99–100; Furmston 23 MLR 373 at 382–384.
[34] [1967] ALR 385.
[35] Three judges held that the clause 'authorising the company' to pay C's wife was merely a revocable mandate which had been revoked by C's death.

to the rule that consideration must move from the promisee. Barwick CJ seems to have treated the two rules as separate requirements:[36]

> It must be accepted that, according to our law, a person not a party to a contract may not himself sue upon it so as directly to enforce its obligations. For my part I find no difficulty or embarrassment in this conclusion. Indeed, I would find it odd that a person to whom no promise was made could himself enforce a promise made by another.

Windeyer J, on the other hand, asked if there were any 'useful distinction between denying a right of action to a person because no promise was made to him, and denying a right of action to a person to whom a promise was made because no consideration for it moved from him'.[37]

In the present case, the wife was a party to the agreement; but had consideration moved from her? At first sight it would seem that her husband was the only person who had given consideration for the company's promise. Nevertheless, Barwick CJ and Windeyer J found a way round the difficulty. Husband and wife were joint promisees.

Windeyer J said:[38]

> The promise is made to them collectively. It must, of course, be supported by consideration, but that does not mean by consideration furnished by them separately. It means a consideration given on behalf of them both, and therefore moving from both of them. In such a case the promise of the promisor is not gratuitous; and, as between him and the joint promisees, it matters not how they were able to provide the price of his promise to them.

The solution is neat and would simply require the rule to be restated so as to insist that consideration must move either from a single promisee or from one of a number of joint promisees.

The point was raised in *McEvoy v Belfast Banking Co Ltd*:[39]

> A father, who had £10,000 on deposit with the Belfast Bank, transferred it to a deposit account in the names of himself and of his infant son. Soon afterwards he died. The executors were allowed by the bank to withdraw the money and put it into an account in their own names. The money was in fact lost in attempts to keep the family business alive; and the son sued the bank.

The Bank argued, inter alia, that no rights accrued to the son over the deposit account because he had furnished no consideration. The argument was rejected by Lord Atkin:

---

[36] [1967] ALR at 394–395.

[37] Ibid at 405. See also the discussion in *Trident General Insurance Co Ltd v McNiece Bros Pty Ltd* (1988) 62 ALJR 508 at 511 per Mason CJ and Wilson J.

[38] Ibid.

[39] [1935] AC 24.

The contract on the face of it purports to be made with A and B, and I think with them jointly and severally. A purports to make the contract on behalf of B as well as himself, and the consideration supports such a contract.[40]

The doctrine of consideration has not been abolished but the doctrine of privity has been subjected to major change by the Contract (Rights of Third Parties) Act 1999. This Act is discussed in chapter 14. The Act does not specifically refer to the rule that consideration must move from the promisee but it is clear that whenever a third party acquires rights under the Act, it will not be open to the defendant to argue that consideration has not moved from the third party.

4 SUFFICIENCY OF CONSIDERATION

Consideration has been defined as the act or promise offered by the one party and accepted by the other as the price of that other's promise. The question now arises whether any act and any promise, regardless of their content, will satisfy this definition. Ames, indeed, argued that, with obvious reservations in the interests of morality and public policy, the question must be answered in the affirmative.[41] A survey of decided cases, however, will show that his argument, whatever its logical merits, does not represent the actual position. Certain acts and promises, it will be seen, are deemed incapable in law of supporting an action for breach of contract by the person who has supplied them. But, while most jurists have been forced by the results of litigation to accept this conclusion, there has been great divergence of opinion as to the test of such capacity. Two main lines of divergence may be observed.

There is doubt, in the first place, as to whether the criterion, whatever it may be, is equally applicable to acts and to promises. That such is the case was asserted by Chief Justice Holt three centuries ago[42] and reasserted by Leake in his book on Contracts in the middle of the nineteenth century:

It may be observed that whatever matter, if executed, is sufficient to form a good executed consideration, if promised, is sufficient to form a good executory consideration.[43]

---

[40] Ibid at 43. Lord Thankerton (at 52) said that he would have agreed with this statement if he had thought that the father had designed to make the son a contracting party. See Cullity 85 LQR 530, especially at 531–534 and *New Zealand Shipping Co Ltd v A M Satterthwaite & Co Ltd* [1975] AC 154 at 180, [1974] 1 All ER 1015 at 1030, per Lord Simon of Glaisdale. On the other hand, there are formidable arguments the other way, as is shown by Coote [1978] CLJ 301.

[41] See Ames *Lectures on Legal History* pp 323 ff.

[42] 'Where the doing a thing will be a good consideration, a promise to do that thing will be so too': *Thorpe v Thorpe* (1701) 12 Mod Rep 455.

[43] *Leake on Contracts* (1st edn) p 314.

The adoption of a single test would clearly simplify the problem: once determine its character in the case of an act and it could be applied automatically in the case of a promise. Sir Frederick Pollock, however, denied the possibility of a single test and declared that, in certain cases, a promise may, while an actual performance may not, afford a consideration to support a counter-promise.[44]

In the second place, whether the test be single or double, little success has attended the efforts of jurists to express it in language at once definite and comprehensive. Williston, who has devoted particular care to the problem, can only state it in terms of the formula of benefit and detriment current in the nineteenth century, which has already been shown to be unsatisfactory. Executed consideration, according to his view, consists of 'a detriment incurred by the promisee or a benefit received by the promisor at the request of the promisor': executory consideration consists of 'mutual promises in each of which the promisor undertakes some act or forbearance that will be, *or apparently may be*, detrimental to the promisor or beneficial to the promisee'.[45] This language, it is suggested, restates the problem rather than solves it, and, as will be seen, is to be applied to actual cases only with difficulty and with a certain sense of strain.

It is, indeed, not without significance that these controversies are, for the most part, carried on outside the courts. The judges have been content to deny the name of consideration to certain acts or promises without attempting to generalise the grounds of their prohibition; and it may well be that the process of judicial thought is purely empirical and does not lend itself to *ex post facto* rationalisation. It will be well, at least, to discuss in turn the individual rules applied by the courts and then to ask if any comprehensive test can be adopted.

These rules may, for the sake of exposition, be grouped into two classes:

(a) those rules which forbid the courts to upset a bargain merely because the act or promise supplied by the plaintiff is an inadequate recompense for the defendant's promise;

(b) those rules which expressly declare that certain acts or promises do not constitute consideration.

Here, as in other aspects of contract, the choice of appropriate terminology to describe a particular legal position is a matter of difficulty. The word 'adequacy' has long been associated with the reluctance of the courts lightly to interfere with an agreement which the parties themselves have deemed fair and reasonable, and some other word must be chosen to indicate the cases in which, perhaps as an exceptional measure, the courts reserve the right of interference. For this latter purpose the epithet 'sufficient'

---

[44] *Pollock on Contracts* (13th edn) pp 147–150; and see pp 137–141, below. Williston seems to take a middle view: *Williston on Contracts* (3rd edn) para 103.

[45] *Williston on Contracts* (3rd edn) paras 102 and 103. The italics are ours. Williston uses the terms 'unilateral' and 'bilateral' to express the antithesis 'executed' and 'executory'. But the latter words have been adopted here as more in consonance with English usage.

has been sanctioned, if not hallowed, by more than three centuries of judicial usage. It was adopted by the Elizabethan judges when they established the doctrine of consideration and repeated by their successors in the seventeenth century. It was assumed to be appropriate both by Lord Mansfield and by his opponents, and it was accepted by Lord Denman in *Eastwood v Kenyon*.[46] In the present chapter, therefore, though there is a conscious artificiality in contrasting such words as 'adequacy' and 'sufficiency' which in popular use are regarded as synonyms, consideration will be described as 'sufficient' or 'insufficient' according to whether the judges allow or disallow the validity of particular acts or promises.

A Adequacy of consideration

It has been settled for well over three hundred years that the courts will not inquire into the 'adequacy of consideration'. By this is meant that they will not seek to measure the comparative value of the defendant's promise and of the act or promise given by the plaintiff in exchange for it, nor will they denounce an agreement merely because it seems to be unfair. The promise must, indeed, have been procured by the offer of some return capable of expression in terms of value. A parent, who makes a promise 'in consideration of natural love and affection' or to induce his son to refrain from boring him with complaints, cannot be sued upon it, since the essential elements of a bargain are lacking.[47] But if these elements be present the courts will not balance the one side against the other. The parties are presumed to be capable of appreciating their own interests and of reaching their own equilibrium. In 1587 it was said that, 'when a thing is to be done by the plaintiff, be it never so small, this is a sufficient consideration to ground an action';[48] and this rejection of a quantitative test has been constantly reiterated. In *Thomas v Thomas*:[49]

> The plaintiff's husband had expressed the wish that the plaintiff, if she survived him, should have the use of his house. After his death the defendant, his executor, agreed to allow her to occupy the house (a) because of the husband's wishes, (b) on the payment by her of £1 a year.

The court declined to be influenced by the husband's wishes: motive was 'not the same thing with consideration'. But they accepted the plaintiff's promise to pay the £1 a year as affording consideration for the defendant's promise, and

---

[46] From examples too numerous for citation in a footnote the following cases may be selected: *Richards' and Bartlet's Case* (1584) 1 Leon 19; *Knight v Rushworth* (1596) Cro Eliz 469; *Bret v JS* (1600) Cro Eliz 756; *Grisley v Lother* (1613) Hob 10; *Davis v Reyner* (1671) 2 Lev 3; *Rann v Hughes* (1778) 7 Term Rep 350n; *Hawkes v Saunders* (1782) 1 Cowp 289; *Eastwood v Kenyon* (1840) 11 Ad & El 438. It may also be observed that the phrase 'sufficient consideration' is used in this sense by *Williston on Contracts* (3rd edn) para 101; and see American *Restatement of the Law of Contracts* paras 76 ff.

[47] See *Bret v JS* (1600) Cro Eliz 756; and *White v Bluett* (1853) 23 LJ Ex 36.

[48] *Sturlyn v Albany* (1587) Cro Eliz 67.   [49] (1842) 2 QB 851.

defendant's counsel admitted that he could not rest any argument upon its manifest inadequacy.[50]

The principle may be studied in its application to cases where a person seeks to stay the prosecution of a legal claim with which he is threatened. Such agreements may take a variety of forms. The person against whom the claim is made may admit the claim but ask the claimant to give him more time to pay. Such an agreement is often described as a forbearance. Alternatively, he may dispute the claim (or while accepting that there is a claim, dispute the amount) but offer to settle the dispute for less than the amount claimed.[51] Such an agreement is usually described as a compromise. It would appear, however, that all these situations are subject to the same principles. They will here be discussed as examples of a single category.

It was originally held that a promise not to pursue a claim which in truth was without legal basis could not be good consideration. If it had been submitted to the arbitrament of the courts the promisor must have failed, and it could not be a 'detriment' to be saved from a losing hazard.[52] But in the nineteenth century this position was abandoned, and the compromise of a doubtful claim was upheld by the courts. The change was justified on grounds of convenience. In the words of Bowen LJ:

> The reality of the claim which is given up must be measured, not by the state of the law as it is ultimately discovered to be, but by the state of the knowledge of the person who at the time has to judge and make the concession. Otherwise you would have to try the whole cause to know if the man had a right to compromise it.[53]

In the modern law, the consideration in such cases is said to be the surrender, not of a legal right, which may or may not exist and whose existence, at the time of the compromise, remains untested, but of the *claim* to such a right.

This attitude is sensible. It is true that if the claim is baseless, the claimant may appear to have got something for nothing or that, contrariwise, if a claimant settles a good claim for less than its true value he may appear to have given up something for nothing but this is to ignore the cost, both monetary and psychic, of litigation. It is in the public interest to encourage reasonable settlements,[54] indeed the legal system could not operate at all if the vast majority of civil disputes were not settled out of

---

[50] A modern illustration is afforded by the case of *Alexander v Rayson* [1936] 1 KB 169. See also the analysis of the arrangements in *Burdis v Livsey* [2003] QB 36. These problems were not before the House of Lords when it heard the appeal sub nom *Lagden v O'Connor* [2004] 1 AC 1067.

[51] If A claims £100 from B and B says that only £50 is owed and pays £50 there is no consideration when A accepts the £50. The position would be different if B admitted that £50 was owed and offered £51 *Ferguson v Davies* [1997] 1 All ER 315.

[52] *Stone v Wythipol* (1588) Cro Eliz 126; *Jones v Ashburnham* (1804) 4 East 455. See the useful historical discussion by Beatson [1974] CLJ 97 at 100–103.

[53] *Miles v New Zealand Alford Estate Co* (1886) 32 ChD 266 at 291. See also *Callisher v Bischoffsheim* (1870) LR 5 QB 449.

[54] *D v NSPCC* [1978] AC 171 at 232, [1977] 1 All ER 589 at 606, per Lord Simon of Glaisdale.

court. The rule has however to be surrounded by certain safeguards. A plaintiff who relies upon the surrender of a claim to support a contract must prove:

(a) that the claim is reasonable in itself, and not 'vexatious or frivolous';

(b) that he himself has an honest belief in the chance of its success and;

(c) that he has concealed from the other party no fact which, to his knowledge, might affect its validity.[55]

In *Horton v Horton (No 2)*:[56]

The parties were husband and wife. In March 1954, by a separation agreement under seal, the husband agreed to pay the wife £30 a month. On the true construction of the deed the husband should have deducted income tax before payment, but for nine months he paid the money without deduction. In January 1955 he signed a document, not under seal, agreeing that, instead of 'the monthly sum of £30', he would pay such a monthly sum as 'after the deduction of income tax should amount to the clear sum of £30'. For over three years he paid this clear sum, but then stopped payment. To an action by his wife he pleaded that the later agreement was unsupported by consideration and that the wife could sue only on the earlier deed.

The Court of Appeal held that there was consideration to support the later agreement. It was clear that the original deed did not implement the intention of the parties. The wife, therefore, might have sued to rectify the deed, and the later agreement represented a compromise of this possible action. Whether such an action would have succeeded was irrelevant:[57] it sufficed that it had some prospect of success and that the wife believed in it.

Upon this principle and subject to these safeguards, a compromise of a claim and a forbearance to sue will each be upheld, and, as how been suggested above, there is no intrinsic difference of principle between them. In the latter case, however, it is irrelevant whether the time of forbearance be long or short or even whether it is for any specified time at all. Nor need there be any actual promise to forbear, if such an understanding can be inferred from the circumstances and is followed by a forbearance in fact.[58]

---

[55] Such would seem to be the conclusions to be drawn from the language of the judgments in *Callisher v Bischoffsheim* and *Miles v New Zealand Alford Estate Co* (above). See also *Owners of Portofino Tan Steamer v Berlin Derunaptha* (1934) 39 Com Cas 330. In *Miles v New Zealand Alford Estate Co* (above) at 291, Bowen LJ said: 'It seems to me that if an intending litigant *bona fide* forbears a right to litigate a question of law or fact which it is not vexatious or frivolous to litigate, he does give up something of value.' In an interesting article, in which these words are cited, Kelly points out that the surrender of a defence may furnish consideration no less than the surrender of a claim: 27 MLR 540.

[56] [1961] 1 QB 215, [1960] 3 All ER 649.

[57] Cf *Whiteside v Whiteside* [1950] Ch 65, [1949] 2 All ER 913.

[58] *Alliance Bank Ltd v Broom* (1864) 2 Drew & Sm 289. *Mousaka Inc v Golden Seagull Maritime Inc* [2002] 1 Lloyd's Rep 797.

It is possible that there remain some cases where although the parties believe in good faith that they are compromising a doubtful claim, the court will hold that the claim was manifestly bad and the compromise therefore ineffectual. This can hardly happen where the facts are doubtful, since the court would scarcely investigate the facts in order to strike down a compromise but it might happen where there was ignorance or misapprehension of the law. Even with questions of law, however, it would usually be possible to discover sufficient doubt to support the agreement.[59] In *Magee v Pennine Insurance Co Ltd*[60] the majority of the Court of Appeal held that a compromise though valid at common law could be set aside in equity because it was based on a common mistake, since it was clear that the defendants had a complete answer to the plaintiff's claim.

The boundaries of these principles were tested in the important and difficult case of the *Bank of Credit & Commerce International SA v Ali*.[61]

In 1990 the respondent was made redundant by the appellant bank. The redundancy notice stated that he would receive his statutory redundancy payment and an *ex gratia* payment. In addition, the respondant was offered and accepted a payment of a further month's gross salary if he would sign a document stating that this payment:

> . . . was in full and final settlement of all or any claim whether under statute, common law or in equity of whatsoever nature that exists or may exist. . . .

At this time the respondent did not know, though the higher management of the bank knew, that the bank was in fact a fraudulent and insolvent shell. Neither the respondent nor the bank could have known in 1990 that in 1997 the House of Lords would hold in *Malik v Bank of Credit and Commerce International SA*[62] that other BCCI employees could have a claim for damages on the basis that there had been a breach of an implied term of mutual confidence between the bank and its employees and that in principle employees could recover damages for the damage that having been employed by the bank had done to their careers (so-called stigma damages).[63]

The respondent brought an action claiming stigma damages. The bank argued that the claim was barred by the agreement made in 1990.

The document signed in 1990 has all the appearance of having being drafted by a lawyer and it looks as if the draftsmen intended to exclude any claims which might turn up. Indeed, Lightman J and Lord Hoffmann dissenting in the House of Lords held that this was indeed its effect. However the majority of the House of Lords held that although:

---

[59] See *Haigh v Brooks* (1839) 10 Ad & El 309, discussed more fully in the 8th edn of this work, pp 72–73.
[60] [1969] 2 QB 507, [1969] 2 All ER 891, discussed at p 299, below.
[61] [2001] UKHL 8, [2002] 1 AC 251, [2001] 1 All ER 961.
[62] [1998] AC 20, [1997] 3 All ER 1.   [63] For further discussion see p 771, below.

A party may at any rate in a compromise agreement supported by valuable consideration, agree
to release claims or rights of which he was unaware and of which he could not be aware . . . the
court will be very slow to infer that a party intended to surrender rights and claims of which he
was unaware and could not have been aware.[64]

A modern illustration of the premise that it is for the parties to make their own
bargain is afforded by the current practice of manufacturers to recommend the sale of
their goods by offering, as an inducement to buy, something more than the goods
themselves. In *Chappell & Co Ltd v Nestlé Co Ltd*:[65]

The plaintiffs owned the copyright in a dance tune called 'Rockin' Shoes'. The
Hardy Co made records of the tune which they sold to the Nestlé Co for 4d each,
and the Nestlé Co offered them to the public for 1s 6d each, but required, in
addition to the money, three wrappers of their sixpenny bars of chocolate. When
they received the wrappers, they threw them away. Their main object was to
advertise their chocolate, but they also made a profit on the sale of the records.

The plaintiffs sued the defendants for infringement of copyright, and the defendants
were admittedly liable unless they could rely on section 8 of the Copyright Act 1956.
Under this section a person may make a record of a musical work provided that this is
designed for retail sale and provided that he pays to the copyright owner a royalty of
6¼ per cent 'of the ordinary retail selling price'. The defendants offered the statutory
royalty based on the price of 1s 6d per record. The plaintiffs refused the offer, contending that the money price was only part of the consideration for the record and
that the balance was represented by the three rappers. The House of Lords by a
majority gave judgment for the plaintiffs. It was unrealistic to hold that the wrappers
were not part of the consideration. The offer was to supply a record in return, not
simply for money, but for the wrappers as well.

Lord Somervell said:

The question[66] is whether the three wrappers were part of the consideration . . . I think that
they are part of the consideration. They are so described in the offer. 'They', the wrappers, 'will
help you to get smash hit recordings.' . . . It is said that, when received, the wrappers are of no
value to the respondents, the Nestlé Co Ltd. This I would have thought to be irrelevant. A
contracting party can stipulate for what consideration he chooses. A peppercorn does not cease
to be good consideration if it is established that the promisee does not like pepper and will
throw away the corn.

---

[64] [2001] 1 All ER 965, 966 per Lord Bingham.
[65] [1960] AC 87, [1959] 2 All ER 701.
[66] Ibid at 87 and 701, respectively. Analogous problems arise where a tradesman gives trading stamps.
See *Bulpitt & Sons Ltd v S Bellman* (1962) LR 3 RP 62. Another example is to be found in *Esso Petroleum
Ltd v Customs and Excise Comrs* [1976] 1 All ER 117, [1976] 1 WLR 1, discussed more fully at p 153,
below.

Consideration in relation to bailments

The necessity, sometimes assumed, of discovering a consideration to support a bailment presents another aspect of the search for a bargain. A bailment is a delivery of goods on condition that the recipient shall ultimately restore them to the bailor: they may thus be hired or lent or pledged or deposited for safe custody. So natural a transaction must be recognised at an early date by every system of law. In English law it was protected by the writ of detinue long before the evolution of a general contractual remedy, and it was only the pressure of procedural convenience which led to the supersession of this writ by *indebitatus assumpsit*. But, once the rights of the bailor were secured by a form of action normally identified with contract, there was an inevitable temptation to discuss the problems of bailment in terms of contract and to demand the presence of consideration. Thus in *Bainbridge v Firmstone* in 1838:[67]

> The plaintiff, at the defendant's request, had consented to allow the defendant to remove and weigh two boilers, and the defendant had, at the same time, promised to return them in their original sound condition. The plaintiff sued for breach of this promise, and the defendant pleaded lack of consideration.

The Court of Queen's Bench rejected the plea. Patteson J thought that, whether there was a benefit to the defendant or not, there was 'at any rate a detriment to the plaintiff from his parting with the possession for even so short a time'.

Lord Denman avoided the language of benefit and detriment.

> The defendant had some reason for wishing to weigh the boilers; and he could do so only by obtaining permission from the plaintiff, which he did obtain by promising to return them in good condition.

By one or other of these lines of argument it is, of course, possible to find a consideration, though the description of the transaction as a bargain struck by the exchange of a promise on the one side and a permission on the other wears a somewhat artificial appearance. But it is not difficult to suggest cases where such language is wholly inappropriate. If B gratuitously accepts goods which A deposits with him for safe custody, B may undoubtedly be liable if he injures or fails to return them. But there is no benefit to B, and, as the delivery was to secure A's advantage, no detriment to A: nor is there any price paid for B's promise, express or implied, to take care of the goods.

The leading case of *Coggs v Bernard*, decided in 1703,[68] illustrates at once the unique conception of bailment and the misleading inferences drawn from its fortuitous association with the writ of assumpsit.

---

[67] (1838) 8 Ad & El 743. See also *Hart v Miles* (1858) 4 CBNS 371.
[68] (1703) 2 Ld Raym 909.

The plaintiff declared that the defendant had undertaken to remove several hogsheads of brandy from one cellar to another, and that he had done the work so carelessly that one of the casks was staved and a quantity of brandy was spilt. The defendant argued that the declaration was bad as disclosing no consideration for the undertaking.

Chief Justice Holt, rejecting the argument, was, indeed, at pains to find a consideration. 'The owner's trusting him with the goods is a sufficient consideration to oblige him to a careful management.'[69] But that this tribute to the doctrine was mere lip-service is shown by the ensuing passages in his judgment:

> If the agreement had been executory, to carry these brandies from the one place to the other such a day, the defendant had not been bound to carry them. But this is a different case, for assumpsit does not only signify a future agreement, but in such a case as this, it signifies an actual entry upon the thing and taking the trust upon himself. And if a man will do that, and miscarries in the performance of his trust, an action will lie against him for that, though nobody could have compelled him to do the thing.

The defendant was liable, not because he had agreed to carry the casks, but only because he had actually started to move them. The case was not one of contract at all, but turned upon the peculiar status of the bailee.

At the present day, no doubt, in most instances where goods are lent or hired or deposited for safe custody or as security for a debt, the delivery will be the result of a contract. But this ingredient, though usual, is not essential. An infant may be liable as a bailee, whereas, had the transaction to be based on contract, the Infants Relief Act 1874 would have protected him:[70] a railway company owes a duty, independently of contract, to an owner whose goods it has accepted for carriage.[71] Confusion will be avoided only if it is remembered that bailment is a relationship *sui generis* and that, unless it is sought to increase or diminish the burdens imposed upon the bailee by the very fact of the bailment, it is not necessary to incorporate it into the law of contract and to prove a consideration.

This was clearly stated by Lord Denning MR in *Building and Civil Engineering Holidays Scheme Management Ltd v Post Office*.[72]

> At common law, bailment is often associated with a contract, but this is not always the case . . . An action against a bailee can often be put, not as an action in contract, nor in tort, but as an action on its own, *sui generis*, arising out of the possession had by the bailee of the goods.

---

[69] Such 'trusting' is clearly not in truth a good consideration. It is not the price of any promise; it is not a benefit to the defendant; and, as it was designed to effectuate the plaintiff's sole purposes, it was no detriment to him.

[70] See p 563, below.

[71] See *R v McDonald* (1885) 15 QBD 323; and *Meux v Great Eastern Rly Co* [1895] 2 QB 387.

[72] [1966] 1 QB 247 at 260–261, [1965] 1 All ER 163 at 167. See also per Diplock LJ in *Morris v C W Martin & Sons* [1966] 1 QB 716 at 731, [1965] 2 All ER 725 at 734; and *Chesworth v Farrar* [1967] 1 QB 407, [1966] 2 All ER 107. Palmer *Bailment* (2nd edn) pp 26–31.

Liability for improper performance of gratuitous service

A somewhat similar position may arise where loss has been caused in the performance of a gratuitous service. The legal consequences of such a situation were discussed in the case of *De La Bere v Pearson*.[73]

> The defendants advertised in their paper that their city editor would answer inquiries from readers desiring financial advice. The plaintiff wrote, asking for the name of a good stockbroker. The editor recommended an 'outside broker', who was in fact an undischarged bankrupt. This circumstance was not known to the editor, but could have been discovered by him without difficulty. Relying on the recommendation, the plaintiff sent sums of money to the broker for investment and the broker misappropriated them. The Court of Appeal held the defendants liable in contract.

It is not at first sight easy to see how the facts of this case can be made to satisfy the doctrine of consideration. The plaintiff doubtless paid money for a copy of the paper, but did he pay for the recommendation? The mere act of inquiring the name of a stockbroker can hardly be described with any sense of reality as the price of the editor's reply. It may indeed be urged that the plaintiff paid not only for the physical fact of the paper but for all its contents—news, articles, advertisements and financial advice; and that the payment might thus be regarded as consideration for the whole service offered by the defendants. Colour is lent to this interpretation by the fact that the plaintiff had long been a reader of the paper and knew that one of its features was the provision of financial advice. The case was not, however, argued on this basis nor was the point taken by the Court of Appeal, whose members were content substantially to assume the existence of a contract. While, therefore, it is possible to support the decision on the ground of contract, it is not surprising that Sir Frederick Pollock should have suggested that the cause of action might be better regarded 'as arising from default in the performance of a voluntary undertaking independent of contract'.[74] The question, in other words, should be approached as a problem in tort, and, viewed from this angle, it would turn upon the scope of the duty of care. To discuss this duty in any detail is outside the ambit of the present book; but, in view of the judgments of the House of Lords in *Hedley Byrne & Co Ltd v Heller & Partners Ltd*,[75] it is at least possible that, if the facts of *De la Bere v Pearson* were to recur, the plaintiff might succeed in an action of negligence.

---

[73] [1908] 1 KB 280. See also *Elsee v Gatward* (1793) 5 Term Rep 143, and *Skelton v London North Western Rly Co* (1867) LR 2 CP 631.

[74] See *Pollock on Contracts* (13th edn) p 140.

[75] [1964] AC 465, [1963] 2 All ER 575. See especially per Lord Devlin at 527–528 and 610, respectively. See pp 343–347, below.

Distinction between gift and sale not always obvious

The refusal of the courts to discuss the adequacy of consideration may make it difficult, on occasion, to distinguish a gift and a sale. If A promises B to give him his new Rolls-Royce car for nothing, there is obviously no consideration and no contract. If A promises B to give him his new Rolls-Royce car, if B will fetch it from the garage, there is still no consideration and no contract. The requirement that B is to fetch the car is not the price of the promise, but the condition precedent to the operation of A's generosity. The transaction is not a sale, but a conditional gift.[76] But, if A promises B to give him his new Rolls-Royce car if B will give him one shilling, there is consideration and there is a contract. Such a conclusion has inspired the comment that the doctrine of consideration corresponds as little with reality and is as much a formality as the rule that a gratuitous promise becomes binding by the mere affixing of a seal.[77] But this view is surely an over-bold generalisation upon extreme cases. The fact that the courts will enforce such a transaction as that envisaged in the third hypothesis stated above or in the actual case of *Thomas v Thomas*,[78] though it may appear a legal quibble, is a logical inference from two assumptions, neither of which is unreasonable: that in every parol contract the plaintiff must show that he has bought the defendant's promise, and that the courts will not negative as disproportionate the price which the parties themselves have fixed. If a mere token payment is named, a transaction virtually gratuitous may well be invested with the insignia of contract, but, in the absence of dishonesty, there is no reason why persons should not take advantage of existing legal rules and adapt them to their own requirements. Such adaptations are the commonplace of legal history.[79]

B Insufficiency of consideration

It is now necessary to discuss cases where, though a bargain has been struck, the consideration may yet be deemed, in the technical sense already indicated, 'insufficient'. The judges, when they exercise this power of interference, are applying an extrinsic test which frustrates the expectations of the parties. It does not follow, however, that such a test is necessarily harsh, still less that it is illogical. In some of the cases the law is settled, others are shrouded in controversy; but in all of them the grounds of interference seem to be the same. The plaintiff has procured the defendant's promise by discharging or by promising to discharge a duty already imposed upon him for

[76] For a case where the judges experienced great difficulty in deciding whether they had to deal with a contract or a conditional gift, see *Wyatt v Kreglinger* [1933] 1 KB 793. A more recent example is *Dickinson v Abel* [1969] 1 All ER 484, [1969] 1 WLR 295.

[77] See Holmes *The Common Law* p 273; Markby *Elements of Law* ch XV; Buckland and McNair *Roman Law and Common Law* (2nd edn) p 276.

[78] P 106, above.

[79] It is worth observing that the Roman law, untrammelled by a doctrine of consideration, found a similar difficulty in distinguishing gifts and sales. See *Digest* 18.1.36, 18.1.38.

other reasons. Now consideration need not be adequate and may, on occasion, be extremely tenuous, but it must comprise some element which can be regarded as the price of the defendant's promise; and merely to repeat an existing obligation may well seem to offer nothing at all. The cases in which this argument has been urged may be grouped into four classes. In each of them the essential question is whether the courts can discover the promise or performance of something more than the plaintiff is already bound to do.

1 Where a public duty is imposed upon the plaintiff by law

It may be appreciated that a person, who by his official status or through the operation of the law is under a public duty to act in a certain way, is not regarded as furnishing consideration merely by promising to discharge that duty. No one, for example, would expect a policeman to bargain with a citizen for the price of his protection. The position was stated in 1831 in *Collins v Godefroy*.[80] The plaintiff had attended on *subpoena* to give evidence on the defendant's behalf in a case in which the defendant was a litigant, and he alleged that the defendant had promised to pay him six guineas for his trouble. Lord Tenterden held that there was no consideration for this promise.

> If it be a duty imposed by law upon a party regularly *subpoenaed*, to attend from time to time to give his evidence, then a promise to give him any remuneration for loss of time incurred in such attendance is a promise without consideration.

In spite or, perhaps, because of the obvious character of the argument, the cases in which it has been raised are few; and some of them at least disclose a tendency to uphold the agreement by assuming that something more was undertaken than the bare discharge of the duty. Thus in *England v Davidson*,[81] the defendant offered a reward to anyone who should give information leading to the conviction of a felon. The plaintiff, a police constable, gave such evidence. The defendant pleaded, not only that the plaintiff had merely done his duty, but that the contract was against public policy. Lord Denman's judgment, rejecting these pleas, consists of two sentences.

> I think there may be services which the constable is not bound to render, and which he may therefore make the ground of a contract. We should not hold a contract to be against the policy of the law, unless the grounds for so deciding were very clear.

Similar arguments were considered and again rejected in the more modern case of *Glasbrook Bros v Glamorgan County Council*.[82] The question had arisen as to how

---

[80] (1831) 1 B & Ad 950. See also *Morris v Burdett* (1808) 1 Camp 218, where it was held that, in so far as a high bailiff or a sheriff is required by law to do certain acts and incur certain expense in the course of a parliamentary election, there is no consideration for a promise by the successful candidate to reimburse him.

[81] (1840) 11 Ad & El 856.   [82] [1925] AC 270.

best to protect a coal mine during a strike. The police authorities thought it enough to provide a mobile force, the colliery manager wanted a stationary guard. It was ultimately agreed to provide the latter at a rate of payment which involved the sum of £2,200. The company refused to pay and, when sued, pleaded the absence of consideration. The House of Lords gave judgments for the plaintiffs. The police were bound to afford protection, but they had a discretion as to the form it should take, and an undertaking to provide more protection than in their discretion they deemed necessary was consideration for the promise of reward. Viscount Cave LC said:

> If in the judgment of the police authorities, formed reasonably and in good faith, the garrison was necessary for the protection of life and property, then they were not entitled to make a charge for it.

In *Harris v Sheffield United Football Club Ltd*[83] the defendants argued that this meant that they were not obliged to pay for the large number of policemen who attended their ground at home matches because, in present conditions of crowd behaviour, a major police presence at the ground was necessary to preserve law and order. The Court of Appeal thought that there was a fundamental difference on the facts. In the *Glasbrook* case the threat to law and order was external to the parties since neither could call off the strike. In the present case, the defendants had voluntarily chosen to put on their matches at times, typically Saturday afternoons, when large attendances and therefore large possibilities of disorder were likely, and when a substantial police presence could only be achieved by calling policemen off their rest days and paying large sums of overtime. The police authority were, therefore, entitled to be paid.

The readiness of the judges thus to find a consideration if this be humanly possible is illustrated by the case of *Ward v Byham.*[84]

> A man and a woman, though not married, lived together from 1949 to 1954. In 1950 a child was born to them. In 1954 the man, the defendant in the case, turned the woman out of his house but kept and looked after the child. Some months later the woman, the plaintiff in the case, asked for the child. The defendant wrote offering to let her have the child and to pay £1 a week for its maintenance provided (a) the plaintiff could 'prove that she will be well looked after and happy', and (b) 'that she is allowed to decide for herself whether or not she wishes to live with you'. The plaintiff then took the child. For seven months the defendant paid the weekly sum as agreed, but the plaintiff then married another man and the defendant stopped payment.

---

[83] [1988] QB 77, [1987] 2 All ER 838. The action was in form a claim under the Police Act 1964 for payment for 'special police services' but the test applied by the court was exactly the same as that applied under the general law of contract.

[84] [1956] 2 All ER 318, [1956] 1 WLR 496. Cf *Horrocks v Forray* [1976] 1 All ER 737, [1976] 1 WLR 230.

The plaintiff sued for breach of contract and the defendant pleaded the absence of consideration. By section 42 of the National Assistance Act 1948, the mother of an illegitimate child was bound to maintain it; and it was, therefore, argued that the mother had done no more than promise to fulfil her statutory duty. But the Court of Appeal gave judgment for the plaintiff. The majority of the court (Morris and Parker LJJ) held that she had exceeded the duty cast upon her by the Act by promising, in accordance with the terms of the defendant's letter, both to 'look after the child well' and satisfy the defendant that it was 'happy', and to allow the child to decide which home it preferred. There was thus 'sufficient' consideration for the defendant's promise to pay. Denning LJ was prepared to go further and hold that the father's promise was binding even if the mother had done no more than she was already bound to do, since 'a promise to perform an existing duty, or the performance of it, should be regarded as good consideration, because it is a benefit to the person to whom it is given'.[85]

2 Where the plaintiff is bound by an existing contractual duty to the defendant[86]

The somewhat obvious rule—that there is no consideration if all that the plaintiff does is to perform, or to promise the performance of, an obligation already imposed upon him by a previous contract between him and the defendant—is illustrated by a group of cases in the first half of the nineteenth century. In *Stilk v Myrick*[87] a seaman sued for wages alleged to have been earned on a voyage from London to the Baltic and back. In the course of the voyage two sailors had deserted, and, as the captain could not find any substitutes, he promised the rest of the crew extra wages if they would work the ship home short-handed. In the earlier case of *Harris v Watson*[88] Lord Kenyon had rejected a similar claim because it savoured of blackmail; but Lord Ellenborough in *Stilk v Myrick*, though he agreed that the action would not lie, preferred to base his decision on the absence of consideration. The crew were already bound by their contract to meet the normal emergencies of the voyage and were doing no more than their duty in working the ship home. Had they exceeded their duty, or if the course of events, by making the ship unseaworthy, had relieved them from its performance, the case would have been different. Thus in *Hartley v Ponsonby*[89] the shortage of labour was so great as to make the further prosecution of the voyage exceptionally hazardous, and, by discharging the surviving members of the crew from their original obligation, left them free to enter into a new contract. Both the general

---

[85] Ibid at 319, 498, respectively. See also *Williams v Williams* [1957] 1 All ER 305, [1957] 1 WLR 148, where Denning LJ repeated this statement but added the qualification, 'so long as there is nothing in the transaction which is contrary to the public interest'.

[86] Reynolds and Treitel 7 Malaya L Rev 1.

[87] (1809) 2 Camp 317.

[88] (1791) Peake 102.

[89] (1857) 7 E & B 872.

rule and the qualification to it were regarded as still good law by Mocatta J in *North Ocean Shipping Co Ltd v Hyundai Construction Co Ltd.*[90] *Stilk v Myrick* was reconsidered by the Court of Appeal in *Williams v Roffey Bros & Nicholls (Contractors) Ltd.*[91] In this case the defendants were a firm of building contractors who entered into a contract for the refurbishment of a block of 27 flats. They sub-contracted the carpentry work to the plaintiff for £20,000. Although there was no formal arrangement to this effect, the plaintiff was paid money on account. After the contract had been running for some months and the plaintiff had finished the carpentry at nine of the flats and done some preliminary work in all the rest, for which he had received some £16,200 on account, he found that he was in financial difficulties. These difficulties arose partly because the plaintiff had underestimated the cost of doing the work in the first place and partly because of faulty supervision of his workmen. The plaintiff and the defendants had a meeting at which the defendants agreed to pay the plaintiff a further £10,300 at a rate of £575 per flat to be paid as each flat was completed. The plaintiff carried on work and finished some eight further flats but only one further payment of £1,500 was made.

The plaintiff stopped work and brought an action for damages. The defendants argued that they were not liable as they had simply promised to pay the plaintiff extra for doing what he was in any case obliged to do, that is to finish the contract. The Court of Appeal might perhaps have found consideration in what Russell LJ described as the replacement of 'a haphazard method of payment by a more formalised scheme involving the payment of the specified sum on the completion of each flat' since it was clear that under the original contract there was no express agreement for stage payments. However, all three members of the Court of Appeal appear to have concurred in the leading judgment which was delivered by Glidewell LJ who said:

> The present state of the law on this subject can be expressed in the following proposition:
>
> (i) if A has entered into a contract with B to do work for, or to supply goods or services to, B in return for payment by B, and
>
> (ii) at some stage before A has completely performed his obligations under the contract B has reason to doubt whether A will, or will be able to, complete his side of the bargain, and
>
> (iii) B thereupon promises A an additional payment in return for A's promise to perform his contractual obligations on time, and
>
> (iv) as a result of giving his promise B obtains in practice a benefit, or obviates a disbenefit, and

---

[90] [1979] QB 705, [1978] 3 All ER 1170. This case is discussed more fully at p 389, below. See also *The Proodos C* [1981] 3 All ER 189.

[91] [1990] 1 All ER 512. Halson 106 LQR 183; Phang 107 LQR 21; Adams & Brownsword 53 MLR 536.

(v)   B's promise is not given as a result of economic duress or fraud on the part of A, then

(vi)   the benefit of B is capable of being consideration for B's promise, so that the promise will be legally binding.[92]

It is clear that where one party to a contract refuses to go on unless he is paid more, this will often be improper and in modern cases has been characterised as economic duress. This topic is discussed in a later chapter.[93] In the present case, however, there was no suggestion that the plaintiff had ever made any improper threat. Glidewell LJ thought that in the circumstances the critical question was whether the defendants had received a benefit. It is clear that in cases of this kind there are often good commercial reasons why a promisor would choose to promise more to ensure the performance. If the promisee were to go out of business or become insolvent it would almost inevitably cost a good deal more to engage somebody to complete the work. Good and reliable trading partners are hard to find and it may be sensible to help them keep afloat rather than look for a new partner.

This decision has been forcefully criticised by Coote as 'remote from received learning'.[94] Alternatively, it may be regarded as no more than the realistic acceptance that the true rationale of *Stilk v Myrick* is that the promise to pay extra was procured by threats. However, the situation cannot be quite so simple. Presumably, if the promisor, without any solicitation or discussion with the promisee, simply writes to the promisee to say that he has spontaneously decided to pay a bonus at the end of the contract, that is a gratuitous promise and not enforceable since he receives no benefit for it. On the other hand, if the promisee goes so far as to suggest that he will not perform unless he is paid extra then the matter goes off to be considered as one of economic duress. This leaves a rather narrow track in which he brings his difficulties to the attention of the promisor and enables the promisor to realise that he may not complete performance unless he is paid more but without coming anywhere near threatening not to perform. It is not clear that this would prove an easy distinction to apply in practice.

A very similar problem which has given rise to very extensive litigation is this:

> If A owes B a debt and pays or promises to pay part of it in return for B's promise to forgo the balance, can A hold B to this promise?

The problem differs slightly from that propounded in *Stilk v Myrick*. There, a person sought fresh remuneration for the performance of an existing contractual duty:

---

[92] This proposition was considered and reworded by Santow J in *Musumeci v Winadell Pty Ltd* (1994) 34 NSWLR 723 at 747.

[93] See pp 386–390, below.

[94] 3 JCL 23 at 24. See also *Anangel Atlas v IHI Co Ltd (No 2)* [1990] 2 Lloyd's Rep 526 at 545. The correctness of the reasoning in *Williams v Roffey* was seriously doubted by Colman J in *South Caribbean Trading Ltd v Trafigura Beheer* [2005] 1 Lloyd's Rep 128.

here he seeks to avoid the duty.[95] The problem was familiar to the common lawyers before the development of assumpsit as a contractual remedy and, therefore, before the doctrine of consideration had been envisaged. Its implications were examined within the sphere of debt in 1455 and again in 1495.[96] In the latter year Chief Justice Brian stated a rule which, if set in an archaic environment, has still a modern connotation.

> The action is brought for £20, and the concord is that he shall pay only £10, which appears to be no satisfaction for the £20; for payment of £10 cannot be payment of £20. But if it was of a horse which was to be paid according to the concord, this would be good satisfaction, for it does not appear that the horse be worth more or less than the sum in demand.

The writ of debt rested on the idea not of promise but of duty, and a partial performance could not be received as a discharge of that duty. Even to allow a substituted performance might seem to offend against the principle upon which the writ was based, and was, at any rate, the utmost relaxation which the law could permit.

The rule enunciated by Chief Justice Brian was adopted in 1602 in *Pinnel's Case*.[97]

> Pinnel sued Cole in debt for £8 10s due on a bond on 11 November 1600. Cole's defence was that, at Pinnel's request, he had paid him £5 2s 6d on 1 October, and that Pinnel had accepted this payment in full satisfaction of the original debt.

Judgment was given for the plaintiff on a point of pleading, but the court made it clear that, had it not been for a technical flaw, they would have found for the defendant, on the ground that the part payment had been made on an earlier day than that appointed in the bond. The debt could be discharged, not by a merely partial performance of the original obligation, but only through the introduction, at the creditor's request, of some new element—the tender of a different chattel or part payment at a fresh place or on an earlier date.

> Payment of a lesser sum on the day in satisfaction of a greater cannot be any satisfaction for the whole, because it appears to the Judges that by no possibility a lesser sum can be a satisfaction to the plaintiff for a greater sum. But the gift of a horse, hawk or robe, etc. in satisfaction is good. For it shall be intended that a horse, hawk or robe, etc. might be more beneficial to the plaintiff than the money in respect of some circumstance, or otherwise the plaintiff would not have accepted it in satisfaction . . . The payment and acceptance of parcel before the day in satisfaction of the whole would be a good satisfaction in regard of circumstance of time; for peradventure parcel of it before the day would be more beneficial to him than the whole at the day, and the value of the satisfaction is not material. So if I am bound in £20 to pay you £10

---

[95] The agreement to discharge a previous debt is often discussed under the title of *accord and satisfaction*. The *accord* is the agreement to discharge the existing obligation, the *satisfaction* is the consideration required to support it. See p 709, below.

[96] *Anon* (1455) YB 33 Hy 6, fo 48, pl 32; *Anon* (1495) YB 10 HY 7, fo 4, pl 4.

[97] (1602) 5 Co Rep 117a. Simpson *History* pp 103–107.

at Westminster, and you request me to pay you £5 at the day at York, and you will accept it in full satisfaction of the whole £10, it is a good satisfaction for the whole: for the expenses to pay it at York is sufficient satisfaction.

It will be observed that the plaintiff sued in *Pinnel's Case* not in assumpsit but in debt, so that no question of consideration arose. But the problem had already been discussed in the new contractual environment in *Richards v Bartlet* in 1584.[98] A buyer, sued in assumpsit for the price of goods, pleaded a promise by the seller to accept 3s 4d in the pound. The plea was held bad on the ground that there was no consideration for this promise. 'For no profit but damage comes to the plaintiff by this new agreement, and the defendant is not put to any labour or charge by it.' The decision was followed in subsequent cases, and a rule, originating in the peculiar requirements of debt, was thus acclimatised in the alien soil of assumpsit. This trans-ference of thought has been severely criticised.[99] A plaintiff who sued in assumpsit was required to prove consideration for the defendant's undertaking, but there was no logical need to lay a similar burden upon a party who sought to use a promise only by way of defence. The presence of consideration was vital to the formation of a contract, but irrelevant to its discharge. The decision in *Richards v Bartlet*, however, while by no means inevitable and certainly unfortunate in its results, was not unintelligible. Assumpsit rested on promise as conspicuously as debt on duty, and the judges not unnaturally reacted by treating the promise, on which the defendant relied, as binding only on the same conditions as the original promise on which the plaintiff sued. But if this argument were once accepted, the defendant must prove a consideration for the plaintiff's promise to discharge the contract, and he could hardly satisfy this requirement by performing or promising to perform no more than a part of what he was already bound to do.

Whatever the merits of these rival arguments, the rule laid down in *Richards v Bartlet* or, as it is generally if less appropriately called, the rule in *Pinnel's Case*, was accepted and applied by the courts. Not, indeed, until 1884 was it challenged in the House of Lords in the case of *Foakes v Beer*.[100]

Mrs Beer had obtained a judgment against Dr Foakes for £2,090. Dr Foakes asked for time to pay. The parties agreed in writing that, if Dr Foakes paid £500 at once and the balance by instalments, Mrs Beer would not 'take any proceedings what-ever on the judgment'. A judgment debt bears interest as from the date of the judgment. The agreement made no reference to the question of interest. Dr Foakes ultimately paid the whole amount of the judgment debt itself, and Mrs Beer then claimed the interest. Dr Foakes refused to pay it and Mrs Beer applied 'to be

---

[98] (1584) 1 Leon 19. Simpson *History* pp 447–448, 470–475.

[99] See Pollock *Principles of Contract* (13th edn) p 150); Ames *Lectures on Legal History* pp 329 ff; Corbin 27 Yale LJ 535. *Contra, Williston on Contracts* (3rd edn) para 120.

[100] (1884) 9 App Cas 605.

allowed to issue execution or otherwise proceed on the judgment in respect of the interest'. Dr Foakes pleaded the agreement and Mrs Beer replied that it was unsupported by consideration.

The House of Lords gave judgment in favour of Mrs Beer for the amount of the interest. The question, 'nakedly raised by the appeal', was whether the so-called rule in *Pinnel's Case* should be rejected.
Lord Selborne said:

> The doctrine itself . . . may have been criticised, as questionable in principle, by some persons whose opinions are entitled to respect, but it has never been judicially over-ruled; on the contrary I think it has always, since the sixteenth century, been accepted as law. If so, I cannot think that your Lordships would do right if you were now to reverse, as erroneous, a judgment of the Court of Appeal, proceeding upon a doctrine which has been accepted as part of the law of England for 280 years.

The decision by the House of Lords may be criticised. Lord Blackburn, indeed, had prepared a dissenting judgment, and it was with reluctance that he ultimately acquiesced in the views of his colleagues. 'All men of business', he pointed out, 'every day recognise and act on the ground that prompt payment of a part of their demand may be more beneficial to them than it would be to insist on their rights and enforce payment of the whole.'[101] There is, however, something to be said on the other side. It is tempting to think of a creditor as like a villain in a Victorian melodrama, twiddling his wax moustache at the thought of foreclosing the mortgage on the heroine's ancestral home. This vision tends to obscure the fact that in real life, it is often the debtor who behaves badly, fobbing off the creditor with excuses and using every device to avoid repayment so that in the end the creditor is driven to accept less than is due. The real criticism of *Foakes v Beer* is perhaps that it provides no means by which such cases can be treated differently from genuine bargains.

In *Re Selectmove Ltd*[102] the taxpayer company owed the Revenue substantial amounts of income tax and national insurance contributions and the company's managing director at a meeting in July 1991 with the collector of taxes suggested that the company should pay the tax and national insurance contributions as they fell due and repay the arrears at the rate of £1,000 per month from 1 February 1992. The collector said that the proposal went further than he would have liked and that he would seek the approval of his superiors and revert to the company if it was unacceptable. The company heard nothing further until 9 October 1991 when the Revenue demanded payment of the arrears in full. In due course, the Revenue served a statutory demand and presented a winding-up petition. The company sought to resist this on the grounds that the debt was disputed by the company in good faith and on substantial grounds.

---

[101] Ibid at 622.   [102] [1995] 2 All ER 531, Peel 110 LQR 353

It is clear that by October 1991 the company had failed to keep up with the payments which it had itself proposed. Even if the meeting in July had therefore given rise to a binding agreement, it would have been very doubtful whether the company could hold the Revenue to the bargain since they had not kept their own side of it.

The Court of Appeal, however, considered whether the July arrangement did give rise to a binding agreement in the first place. This obviously presented a number of problems such as, for instance, whether the collector had done enough to indicate a concluded agreement[103] and whether he had actual or apparent authority to bind the Revenue to such an agreement. The central question which was discussed, however, was whether or not, assuming all these difficulties could be overcome, an arrangement of this kind would be binding or whether it would fail for lack of consideration. Counsel for the taxpayer argued that the decision of the Court of Appeal in *Williams v Roffey Bros*[104] provided authority for the proposition that a promise to perform an existing obligation can amount to good consideration provided there are practical benefits to the promisee. The Court of Appeal rejected this argument. Peter Gibson LJ said:

> I see the force of the argument, but the difficulty that I feel with it is that if the principle of *Williams'* case is to be extended to an obligation to make payment, it would in effect leave the principle in *Foakes v Beer* without any application. When a creditor and a debtor who are at arm's length reach agreement on the payment of the debt by instalments to accommodate the debtor, the creditor will no doubt always see a practical benefit to himself in so doing. In the absence of authority there would be much to be said for the enforceability of such a contract. But that was a matter expressly considered in *Foakes v Beer* yet held not to constitute good consideration in law. *Foakes v Beer* was not even referred to in *Williams'* case, and it is in my judgment impossible, consistently with the doctrine of precedent, for this court to extend the principle of *Williams'* case to any circumstances governed by the principle of *Foakes v Beer*.

Exceptions to the rule

The decision in *Foakes v Beer* has been criticised but not yet abrogated.[105] There are, however, important qualifications to it. The first is as old as the rule itself. The rule does not apply where the debtor does something different, for example, where, with the creditor's consent, he delivers a horse in full settlement of the debt. Just as where A sells a horse to B for £100, the court will not inquire whether the horse is worth more or less than £100, so if A delivers a horse to B in discharge of a debt of £100, the court will again not inquire as to its value. So an agreed payment of a peppercorn

---

[103] See p 117, above.

[104] [1990] 1 All ER 512.

[105] The Law Revision Committee proposed such abrogation in 1937, but the proposal has not so far been implemented.

will do and, a *fortiori*, £50 plus a peppercorn will do. So too early payment of a smaller sum or payment at a different place will do.[106]

If any new element in the debtor's promise was regarded as constituting consideration for the discharge of the original debt, it would be tempting to urge that the tender of a promissory note would be a sufficient novelty for the purpose. By accepting the peculiar obligation inherent in a negotiable security, the debtor would be doing something which he was not already bound to do. The point was taken in 1846 in *Sibree v Tripp*.[107]

> The defendant owed the plaintiff £1,000 and was sued for this sum. The action was settled on the terms that the defendant would give the plaintiff promissory notes for £300 in full satisfaction. One of the notes was not met, and the plaintiff then sued (inter alia) for the original £1,000.

The Court of Exchequer gave judgment for the defendant. Baron Alderson re-examined the whole position.

> It is undoubtedly true, that payment of a portion of a liquidated demand, in the same manner as the whole liquidated demand ought to be paid, is payment only in part; because it is not one bargain, but two; namely, payment of part and an agreement, without consideration, to give up the residue. The Courts might very well have held the contrary and have left the matter to the agreement of the parties; but undoubtedly the law is so settled. But if you substitute a piece of paper or a stick of sealing-wax, it is different, and the bargain may be carried out in its full integrity. A man may give, in satisfaction of a debt of £100, a horse of the value of £5, but not £5. Again, if the time or place of payment be different, the one sum may be a satisfaction of the other. Let us, then, apply these principles to the present case. If for money you give a negotiable security, you pay it in a different way. The security may be worth more or less: it is of uncertain value. That is a case falling within the rule of law I have referred to.

The decision in *Sibree v Tripp* was applied by the divisional court in *Goddard v O'Brien*[108] in 1882 to a payment by cheque, and its rationale was accepted in an obiter dictum by Lord Selborne in *Foakes v Beer*.[109] To give negotiable paper was to furnish fresh consideration.

A layman would no doubt be surprised to find that a promissory note for £300 would discharge a debt of £1,000, whereas payment of £300 in cash would not do. Granted the premises, however, the rule was logical enough, since negotiable instruments do have some advantages over cash (eg greater ease of portability and transferability) for which a creditor might be willing to pay. The extension to payment by

---

[106] Early payment is always of some value to the creditor. Payment at another place may be simply for the convenience of the debtor, in which case, it would not amount to consideration: *Vanbergen v St Edmund's Properties Ltd* [1933] 2 KB 223.

[107] (1846) 15 M & W 23, having been previously rejected in *Cumber v Wane* (1721) 1 Stra 426.

[108] (1882) 9 QBD 37.

[109] (1884) 9 App Cas 605.

cheque was another matter since creditors do not usually accept payment by cheque in order to obtain the advantages of a negotiable instrument. Normally payment by cheque, even of the full sum, affects only a conditional discharge of the debt so that the debt is extinguished only when the cheque is honoured and it would be inconsistent with normal business practice to have different rules for payment by cheque and by cash. In 1965 in *D & C Builders Ltd v Rees*[110] the Court of Appeal refused to recognise the distinction.

> The plaintiffs were a small firm. They did work for the defendant, for which the defendant owed them £482. For months they pressed for payment. At length the defendant's wife, acting for her husband and knowing that the plaintiffs were in financial difficulties, offered them £300 in settlement. If they refused this offer, she said, they would get nothing. The plaintiffs reluctantly agreed. They were given a cheque for £300, which was duly honoured. Then they sued for the balance of the original debt.

The Court of Appeal gave judgment for the plaintiffs. The position was stated in forceful terms by Lord Denning.[111]

> It is a daily occurrence that a merchant or tradesman, who is owed a sum of money, is asked to take less. The debtor says he is in difficulties. He offers a lesser sum in settlement, cash down. He says he cannot pay more. The creditor is considerate. He accepts the proffered sum and forgives him the rest of the debt. The question arises: is the settlement binding on the creditor? The answer is that, in point of law, the creditor is not bound by the settlement. He can the next day sue the debtor for the balance, and get judgment ... Now suppose that the debtor, instead of paying the lesser sum in cash, pays it by cheque. He makes out a cheque for the amount. The creditor accepts the cheque and cashes it. Is the position any different? I think not. No sensible distinction can be taken between payment of a lesser sum by cash and payment of it by cheque. The cheque, when given, is conditional payment. When honoured, it is actual payment. It is then just the same as cash. If a creditor is not bound when he receives a payment by cash, he should not be bound when he receives payment by cheque.

The Court of Appeal thus overruled the decision of the divisional court in *Goddard v O'Brien*. *Sibree v Tripp*, as it had been decided by a tribunal of equal standing with themselves, could not be rejected but was distinguished. In *Sibree v Tripp* the promissory notes were taken not as conditional payment but in absolute discharge of the original debt. Clearly if the notes had been given only as conditional payment, the plaintiff's claim would have succeeded in any event, since one of the notes had not been honoured.[112]

A second exception was suggested by Denning J as he then was, in *Central London Property Trust Ltd v High Trees House Ltd*.[113]

---

[110] [1966] 2 QB 617, [1965] 3 All ER 837.   [111] Ibid at 623 and 839–840, respectively.
[112] See Chorley 29 MLR 317 and his *Gilbart Lectures on Banking* (1967).   [113] [1947] KB 130.

In September 1939, the plaintiffs leased a block of flats to the defendants at a ground rent of £2,500 per annum. In January 1940, the plaintiffs agreed in writing to reduce the rent to £1,250, plainly because of war conditions, which had caused many vacancies in the flats. No express time limit was set for the operation of this reduction. From 1940 to 1945 the defendants paid the reduced rent. In 1945 the flats were again full, and the receiver of the plaintiff company then claimed the full rent both retrospectively and for the future. He tested his claim by suing for rent at the original rate for the last two quarters of 1945.

Denning J was of opinion that the agreement of January 1940 was intended as a temporary expedient only and had ceased to operate early in 1945. The rent originally fixed by the contract was therefore payable, and the plaintiffs were entitled to judgment. But he was also of opinion that, had the plaintiffs sued for arrears for the period 1940 to 1945, the agreement made in 1940 would have operated to defeat their claim.

The reasoning of the learned judge is interesting. He agreed that there was no consideration for the plaintiff's promise to reduce the rent. If, therefore, the defendants had themselves sued upon that promise, they must have failed. Their claim would have depended upon a contract of which one of the essential elements was missing. But where the promise was used merely as a defence, why should the presence or absence of consideration be relevant? The defendants were not seeking to enforce a contract and need not prove one. Was there, then, any technical rule of English law whereby the plaintiffs could be prevented from ignoring their promise and insisting upon the full measure of their original rights? At first sight, the doctrine of estoppel would seem to supply the answer. By this doctrine, if one person makes to another a clear and unambiguous representation of fact intending that other to act on it, if the representation turns out to be untrue, and if that other does act upon it to his prejudice, the representor is prevented or 'estopped' from denying its truth. He cannot, as it were, give himself the lie and leave the other party to take the consequences. The doctrine would meet admirably the situation in the *High Trees* case but for one difficulty. In 1854 in *Jorden v Money*,[114] a majority of the House of Lords held that estoppel could operate only on a misrepresentation of existing fact. Upon this basis it was improper to apply it where, as in the *High Trees* case, a party sought to rely on a promise of future conduct.[115]

---

[114] (1854) 5 HL Cas 185.

[115] Professor Atiyah subjected *Jorden v Money* to a searching analysis in *Essays on Contracts* pp 231–239. He suggests that, had the judgments in that case been properly interpreted and applied, there would have been no need for the later development of a distinct doctrine of 'promissory estoppel'. He reluctantly concedes, however, that the doctrine 'has now itself grown so strong and vigorous that it may be too late for the courts to recognise what they have actually done'. Certainly *Jorden v Money* has been treated in many later cases as authority for the proposition in the text. See eg *Citizens' Bank of Louisiana v First National Bank of New Orleans* (1873) LR 6 HL 352; *Maddison v Alderson* (1883) 8 App Cas 467; Spencer Bower and Turner *Estoppel by Representation* (3rd edn, 1977) pp 31–35.

To avoid this difficulty, Denning J sought to tap a slender stream of authority which had flowed in equity since the judgment of Lord Cairns in 1877 in *Hughes v Metropolitan Rly Co.*[116]

> In October 1874, a landlord gave his tenant six months' notice to repair the premises. If the tenant failed to comply with it, the lease could be forfeited. In November the landlord started negotiations with the tenant for the sale of the reversion, but these were broken off on 31 December. Meanwhile the tenant had done nothing to repair the premises. On the expiry of six months from the date of the original notice the landlord claimed to treat the lease as forfeited and brought an action of ejectment.

The House of Lords held that the opening of negotiations amounted to a promise by the landlord that, as long as they continued, he would not enforce the notice, and it was in reliance upon this promise that the tenant had remained quiescent. The six months allowed for repairs were to run, therefore, only from the failure of the negotiations and the consequent withdrawal of the promise, and the tenant was entitled in equity to be relieved against the forfeiture. Lord Cairns said:[117]

> It is the first principle upon which all Courts of Equity proceed, that if parties who have entered into definite and distinct terms involving certain legal results—certain penalties or legal forfeiture—afterwards by their own act or with their own consent enter upon a course of negotiations which has the effect of leading one of the parties to suppose that the strict rights arising under the contract will not be enforced or will be kept in suspense, or held in abeyance, the person who otherwise might have enforced those rights will not be allowed to enforce them where it would be inequitable having regard to the dealings which have thus taken place between the parties.

Taken at their full width and without regard to the facts of the case, these observations might appear in conflict with the decision in *Jorden v Money* but that case was not cited and no mention of estoppel was made in the judgments. It seems unlikely that the House of Lords had forgotten *Jorden v Money* which had been followed with approval only four years before.[118] It is much more probable that the decision was recognised as entirely consistent with *Jorden v Money*. Two additional factors, at least, were present. The first was that the landlord sought to enforce a right, that to forfeit the lease, which only arose because the tenant, relying on the landlord, had not repaired. If the decision had gone the other way the landlord's right to have the premises repaired would have been transmuted into a much more

---

[116] (1877) 2 App Cas 439. This case was followed and applied in *Birmingham and District Land Co v London and North Western Rly Co* (1888) 40 ChD 268; *Salisbury v Gilmore* [1942] 2 KB 38, [1942] 1 All ER 457.

[117] (1877) 2 App Cas 439 at 448.

[118] *Citizens' Bank of Louisiana v First National Bank of New Orleans* (1873) LR 6 HL 352.

valuable right to forfeit the lease. It is easy to see that this would be grossly unfair. The second distinction was that the decision of the House of Lords simply suspended and did not extinguish the landlord's right to have the premises repaired. The tenant was given extra time to repair but not relieved of his obligation to do so.

If we apply the principle of *Hughes v Metropolitan Rly Co* to the facts of the *High Trees* case it can readily be seen that the landlords, having accepted part of the rent in full settlement one quarter day, could not next day purport to distrain for the balance and that if they decided to claim the balance, they must at least give extra time for payment. But Denning J stated that he would have been prepared to hold the landlord's right to the balance of the rent extinguished and was clearly therefore seeking to take the principle a stage further.

Since 1947 the precise status of the doctrine has been a subject of much speculation[119] and Lord Hailsham LC has stated[120] that:

> The time may soon come when the whole sequence of cases based on promissory estoppel since the war, beginning with *Central London Property Trust Ltd v High Trees House Ltd*, may need to be reviewed and reduced to a coherent body of doctrine by the courts. I do not mean to say that any are to be regarded with suspicion. But as is common with an expanding doctrine they do raise problems of coherent exposition which have never been systematically explored.

A major difficulty in stating the law in this area is that many of the leading cases can be explained as involving either the present doctrine or a consensual variation supported by consideration[121] or as examples of waiver.[122] In most cases this does no more than cause inconvenience to writers of textbooks but exceptional situations do occur where doctrinal purity produces practical results. In principle one ought first to consider whether the transaction is contractually binding for 'even if an estoppel may give rise to a contractual obligation, it does not follow, and it would be a strange doctrine, that a contract gives rise to an estoppel'.[123]

---

[119] Spencer Bower and Turner *Estoppel by Representation* (3rd edn) ch XIV; Denning 15 MLR 1, 5 JSPTL 77; Sheridan 15 MLR 325; Bennion 16 MLR 441; Wilson 67 LQR 330, [1965] CLJ 93; Gordon [1963] CLJ 222; Jackson 81 LQR 84, 223; Clarke [1974] CLJ 260; Seddon 24 ICLQ 438; Stoljar 3 JCL 1. Lord Denning's own extra-judicial account of the doctrine is contained in *The Discipline of Law* Pt 5. Wilken and Villiers, *The Law of Waiver Variation, and Estoppel* ch 8.

[120] *Woodhouse A C Israel Cocoa Ltd SA v Nigerian Produce Marketing Co Ltd* [1972] AC 741 at 758, [1972] 2 All ER 271 at 282.

[121] See p 709, below; Stoljar 35 Can Bar Rev 485; Dugdale and Yates 39 MLR 680; Adams 36 Conv 245; Reiter 27 U Toronto LJ 439.

[122] See p 713, below. Lord Denning MR has suggested in a number of judgments and in his book that estoppel and waiver are the same doctrine but this seems very doubtful. *Brikom Investments Ltd v Carr* [1979] QB 467, [1979] 2 All ER 753. See also *Motor Oil Hellas (Corinth) Refineries SA v Shipping Corpn of India, The Kanchenjunga* [1990] 1 Lloyd's Rep 391.

[123] *Secretary of State for Employment v Globe Elastic Thread Co Ltd* [1979] 2 All ER 1077 at 1082, [1979] ICR 706 at 711.

We will consider first those aspects of the doctrine which appear well settled and then discuss the areas of uncertainty.

(1) There is now substantial judicial support for describing the doctrine, whatever its precise content, as one of 'promissory estoppel'.[124] In some earlier discussions the title 'equitable estoppel' was employed but as Megarry J has pointed out[125] equitable estoppel includes both proprietary estoppel[126] and promissory estoppel.[127]

(2) The doctrine operates only by way of defence and not as a cause of action. This was made clear by the judgments of the Court of Appeal in *Combe v Combe*.[128]

A wife started proceedings for divorce and obtained a decree *nisi* against her husband. The husband then promised to allow her £100 per annum free of tax as permanent maintenance. The wife did not in fact apply to the Divorce Court for maintenance, but this forbearance was not at the husband's request. The decree was made absolute. The annual payments were never made and ultimately the wife sued the husband on his promise to make them.

Byrne J gave judgment for the wife. He held, indeed, that there was no consideration for the husband's promise. It had not been induced by any undertaking on the wife's part to forgo maintenance; and, in any case, since it was settled law that maintenance was exclusively a matter for the court's discretion, no such undertaking would have been valid or binding.[129] But he thought that the principle enunciated in the *High Trees* case enabled the wife to succeed, since the husband had made an unequivocal promise to pay the annuity, intending the wife to act upon it, and she had in fact so acted.

---

[124] See eg Lord Hailsham LC, above, n 14; per Buckley J in *Beesly v Hallwood Estates Ltd* [1960] 2 All ER 314 at 324, [1960] 1 WLR 549 at 560; per Lord Hodson in *Emmanuel Ajayi v RT Briscoe (Nigeria) Ltd* [1964] 3 All ER 556 at 559, [1964] 1 WLR 1326 at 1330; per Megarry J in *Slough Estates Ltd v Slough Borough Council* (1967) 19 P & CR 326 at 362.

[125] *Re Vandervell's Trusts, White v Vandervell Trustees Ltd (No 2)* [1974] Ch 269 at 300–301, [1974] 1 All ER 47 at 74–75; reversed on other grounds [1974] Ch 269, [1974] 3 All ER 205.

[126] That is the line of cases running from *Dillwyn v Llewelyn* (1862) 4 De GF & J 517 to *E R Ives Investments Ltd v High* [1967] 2 QB 379, [1967] 1 All ER 504. See Spencer Bower and Turner *Estoppel by Representation* (3rd edn) ch XII.

[127] A different objection is that the name equitable estoppel may obscure the fact that the rule in *Jorden v Money* was in itself an equitable one, the case going on appeal to the House of Lords from the Court of Chancery. Yet a third objection is that it is no longer appropriate to try to distinguish between the rules of common law and equity in this area: per Lord Simon of Glaisdale in *United Scientific Holdings Ltd v Burnley Borough Council* [1978] AC 904 at 945, [1977] 2 All ER 62 at 84. In *Crabb v Arun District Council* [1976] Ch 179 at 193, [1975] 3 All ER 865 at 875, Scarman LJ did not find the distinction between proprietary and promissory estoppel valuable.

[128] [1951] 2 KB 215, [1951] 1 All ER 767. See also *The Proodos C* [1981] 3 All ER 189.

[129] See *Hyman v Hyman* [1929] AC 601. The common law position is now modified by statute so that a wife, despite her promise not to sue for maintenance in return for her husband's promise of an allowance, may sue for that allowance, though the husband may not enforce her promise. See Cretney *Principles of Family Law* (7th edn) pp 324–329. This does not overturn the principle in *Hyman v Hyman*. See p 514, below.

This decision was clearly an illegitimate extension of a principle which, if it is to be reconciled with orthodox doctrine, must be used only as a defence and not as a cause of action. To allow a plaintiff to sue upon such a promise is simply to ignore the necessity of consideration. The Court of Appeal therefore reversed the decision; and Denning LJ took the opportunity to restate the position.

> The principle stated in the *High Trees* case . . . does not create new causes of action where none existed before. It only prevents a party from insisting upon his strict legal rights, when it would be unjust to allow him to enforce them, having regard to the dealings which have taken place between the parties.

The other two judges in the Court of Appeal, Birkett and Asquith LJJ, were clear that the principle must be 'used as a shield and not as a sword'.[130] This striking metaphor should not be sloppily mistranslated into a notion that only defendants can rely on the principle. There is no reason why a plaintiff should not rely on it, provided that he has an independent cause of action. So, if upon the facts of *Hughes v Metropolitan Rly Co* the landlord had gone into possession, putting the tenant into the position of plaintiff, the result would surely be the same. On such facts the tenant's cause of action would be the lease and the doctrine would operate to negative a possible defence by the landlord that he was entitled to forfeit. As Spencer Bower says 'Estoppel may be used either as a minesweeper or a minelayer, but never as a capital ship.'[131]

(3) Finally it is settled that there must be a promise, either by words or by conduct, and that its effect must be clear and unambiguous.[132] An interesting example of this principle in operation is the decision of the Supreme Court of Canada in *John Burrows Ltd v Subsurface Surveys Ltd.*[133]

[130] Cf Jackson 81 LQR 84, 223; *Re Wyvern Developments Ltd* [1974] 2 All ER 535, [1974] 1 WLR 1097; Atiyah 38 MLR 65 at 67. Cf *Argy Trading Development Co Ltd v Lapid Developments Ltd* [1977] 3 All ER 785, [1977] 1 WLR 444. Promissory estoppel can be a cause of action in the United States: *Restatement of Contracts* article 90. Henderson 78 Yale LJ 343. In the important case of *Waltons Stores (Interstate) Ltd v Maher* (1988) 76 ALR 513, the High Court of Australia has allowed promissory estoppel to be used as a cause of action. Bagot 62 ALJ 926. See also *Austotel Ltd v Franklins Selfserve Pty Ltd* (1989) 16 NSWLR 582; Parkinson 3 JCL 50, Mescher 64 ALJ 536, Duthie 104 LQR 362. In *Baird Textiles Holdings Ltd v Marks and Spencer plc* [2001] EWCA Civ 274, [2002] 1 All ER (Comm) 737, discussed at pp 91–92, the Court of Appeal thought that *Waltons v Maher* could only become English law via a decision of the House of Lords. *Waltons v Maher* and a number of other Australian authorities were cited to the House of Lords in *Actionstrength Ltd v International Glass Engineering* [2003] 2 All ER 615, discussed at p 268 but they were not discussed in the speeches.

[131] See per Luckhoo JA in *Jamaica Telephone Co Ltd v Robinson* (1970) 16 WIR 174 at 179. It seems that proprietary as opposed to promissory estoppel may in some cases support a cause of action. See *Crabb v Arun District Council* [1976] Ch 179, [1975] 3 All ER 865. The reasoning of the Court of Appeal in this case is criticised by Atiyah 92 LQR 174 on the basis that the facts would have supported a finding of contract but this is convincingly refuted by Millett 92 LQR 342.

[132] *Woodhouse A C Israel Cocoa Ltd SA v Nigerian Produce Marketing Co Ltd* [1972] AC 741, [1972] 2 All ER 271.

[133] (1968) 68 DLR (2d) 354. See also *Legione v Hateley* (1983) 152 CLR 406; Sutton 1 JCL 205.

A contract of loan provided for monthly repayments and gave the creditor a right to demand repayment of the whole sum if any instalment were paid more than ten days late. Of the first eighteen payments, eleven were more than ten days late without objection. It was held that this did not disentitle the creditor from exercising his right of acceleration when the nineteenth instalment was late.[134]

We now turn to consider those aspects of the doctrine which remain unsettled.

(1) We have already seen that in *Hughes v Metropolitan Rly Co* the House of Lords held that the landlord's right to have the premises repaired was suspended and not extinguished. It has been widely thought that the distinction between suspension and extinction is an essential aspect of the doctrine. It is certainly factually present in many of the leading cases including the decision of the House of Lords in *Tool Metal Manufacturing Co Ltd v Tungsten Electric Co Ltd.*[135]

The appellants were the registered proprietors of British letters patent. In April 1938, they made a contract with the respondents whereby they gave the latter a licence to manufacture 'hard metal alloys' in accordance with the inventions which were the subject of the patents. By the contract the respondents agreed to pay 'compensation' to the appellants if in any one month they sold more than a stated quantity of the alloys.

Compensation was duly paid by the respondents until the outbreak of war in 1939, but thereafter none was paid. The appellants agreed to suspend the enforcement of compensation payments pending the making of a new contract. In 1944 negotiations for such new contract were begun but broke down. In 1945 the respondents sued the appellants inter alia for breach of contract and the appellants counter-claimed for payment of compensation as from 1 June 1945. The respondents' action was substantially dismissed, and all the arguments then centred on the counter-claim. The Court of Appeal held in the first action[136] that the agreement operated in equity to prevent the appellants demanding compensation until they had given reasonable notice to the respondents of their intention to resume their strict legal rights and that such notice had not been given.

In September 1950, the appellants themselves started a second action[137] against the respondents claiming compensation as from 1 January 1947. The only question in this section action was whether the appellants' counter-claim in the first action amounted to reasonable notice of their intention to resume their strict legal rights.

---

134 Cf *Garlick v Phillips* 1949 (1) SA 121 at 133, per Watermeyer CJ.
135 [1955] 2 All ER 657, [1955] 1 WLR 761.
136 (1950) 69 Restrictive Practices Court 108.
137 Obviously everything decided by the Court of Appeal in the first action was *res judicata* in the second action.

At first instance, Pearson J held that the counter-claim in the first action in 1945 amounted to such notice. The Court of Appeal reversed this decision but the House of Lords disagreed with the Court of Appeal and restored the judgment of Pearson J.[138]

It seems to have been regarded as an essential ingredient by the Privy Council in *Emmanuel Ayodeji Ajayi v R T Briscoe (Nigeria) Ltd.*[139]

> The defendant had contracted with the plaintiffs for the hire purchase of eleven lorries. The plaintiffs sued to recover instalments due under the contract and obtained judgment. The defendant appealed to the Federal Supreme Court of Nigeria and for the first time pleaded a promissory estoppel. He alleged that the plaintiffs had voluntarily promised to suspend the payment of the instalments until certain conditions had been fulfilled and that this promise had not been kept.

The Privy Council dismissed the appeal on the ground that the appellant had not proved failure to fulfil the conditions. But Lord Hodson, in giving the advice of the Judicial Committee stated that the doctrine of promissory estoppel was subject to the following qualifications.[140]

> (a) that the other party has altered his position, (b) that the promisor can resile from his promise on giving reasonable notice, which need not be a formal notice, giving the promisee a reasonable opportunity of resuming his position, (c) the promise only becomes final and irrevocable if the promisee cannot resume his position.

The view that promissory estoppel is only suspensory in operation (except in cases where it is no longer possible to restore the promisee to his original position) is attractive because it provides a ready means of reconciling the decisions in *Jorden v Money*, *Hughes v Metropolitan Rly Co* and *Foakes v Beer*. On the other hand, Denning J in the *High Trees* case thought the doctrine operated to extinguish the landlord's right to the balance of the rent[141] and he repeated the view that promissory estoppel can operate to extinguish a debt after part payment in *D & C Builders Ltd v Rees*.[142] On the face of it, this view can only be reconciled with *Foakes v Beer* by arguing that that case was decided on purely common-law grounds and that the House had overlooked

---

[138] In his judgment, Lord Simonds expressed the view that the principle to be found in *Combe v Combe* 'may well be far too widely stated': [1955] 2 All ER at 660, [1955] 1 WLR at 764.

[139] [1964] 3 All ER 556, [1964] 1 WLR 1326. See also *Brickwoods Ltd v Butler and Walters* (1969) 21 P & CR 256; *Offredy Developments Ltd v Steinbock* (1971) 221 Estates Gazette 963.

[140] Ibid at 559 and 1330, respectively.

[141] In the case the landlord's right to the rent after the war was revived but in Denning J's analysis this was because the promise was only to last while the flats were not fully occupied. He does not discuss the question of whether the landlord might have changed his mind in, say 1943, and claimed the full rent thenceforth.

[142] [1966] 2 QB 617, [1965] 3 All ER 837.

its own decision in *Hughes v Metropolitan Rly Co*, decided only seven years earlier.[143] The notion of suspension has to be applied with particular care if we are dealing with a situation of continuing obligations, such as that to pay rent under a lease. At any particular moment we may have to consider the position with regard to past rent, presently due rent and rent which is due in the future. If we consider the facts of the *High Trees* case, the following alternatives appear logically possible:

(1) that as each underpayment was made, the right to the balance was lost for ever; or

(2) that underpayment with consent did not give rise to the legal consequences normally attached to non-payment of rent but that the appropriate steps could be taken to revive the right to receive payment by reasonable notice.

The second alternative is clearly suspensory but the first appears not to be. It is perfectly consistent, however, with a further rule that the right to *future* rent can be revived by reasonable notice. Suppose that on the first quarter day of 1942, the landlords had intimated that they would require the full rent to be paid from the second quarter day of 1942, would they have been entitled to do so? The tenor of Denning J's judgment suggests not, but on the whole the reasoning of the authorities suggests the contrary.

(2) It is still not clear what conduct by the promisee must follow the promise before it becomes binding. In the doctrine of estoppel by representation of fact, the representor is only estopped if the representee has acted on the representation to his detriment.[144] It is not surprising that by analogy it has been argued that a similar requirement applies to promissory estoppel.

Such detrimental reliance was factually present in *Hughes v Metropolitan Rly Co*; indeed the tenant had not only acted to his detriment but acted to his detriment vis-à-vis the promisor (the landlord) by omitting to repair. Such action vis-à-vis the promisor is present in many of the other cases where the doctrine has been applied.[145] It is perhaps no coincidence that these are also cases where the doctrine has operated suspensively, since it will usually be much easier to restore the promisee to his original position where he has altered it vis-à-vis the promisor than where he has altered it vis-à-vis a third party.

Action by the promisee to his detriment was regarded as essential by McVeigh J in *Morrow v Carty*.[146] In *Emmanuel Ayodeji Ajayi v R T Briscoe (Nigeria) Ltd*,[147] the Privy

---

[143] It is not clear that even such an oversight would render the decision in *Foakes v Beer per incuriam*. See *Cassell & Co v Broome* [1972] AC 1027, [1972] 1 All ER 801.

[144] Spencer Bower and Turner *Estoppel by Representation* (3rd edn) pp 101–111.

[145] Eg *Birmingham and District Land Co v London and North Western Rly Co* (1888) 40 ChD 268; *Salisbury v Gilmore* [1942] 2 KB 38, [1942] 1 All ER 457; *Tool Metal Manufacturing Co Ltd v Tungsten Electric Co Ltd* [1955] 2 All ER 657, [1955] 1 WLR 761.

[146] [1957] NI 174.

[147] P 132, above. See also *Jamaica Telephone Co Ltd v Robinson* (1970) 16 WIR 174.

Council stated that the promisee must have altered his position and it has been commonly assumed that this means altered *for the worse*. On the other hand, this has been consistently denied by Lord Denning MR, who restated his views in *W J Alan & Co Ltd v El Nasr Export and Import Co*[148] where he said:[149]

> I know that it has been suggested in some quarters that there must be detriment. But I can find no support for it in the authorities cited by the judge. The nearest approach to it is the statement of Viscount Simonds in the *Tool Metal* case, that the other must have been led to alter his position, which was adopted by Lord Hodson in *Emmanuel Ayodeji Ajayi v R T Briscoe (Nigeria) Ltd*. But that only means that he must have been led to act differently from what he otherwise would have done.

However, in that case the other two members of the Court of Appeal left the question open, Stephenson LJ because he held the promisee had acted to his detriment[150] and Megaw LJ because he held that there had been a consensual variation of the contract for consideration.[151] Lord Denning MR repeated his views in *Brikom Investments Ltd v Carr*[152] but again the other members of the court decided the case on other grounds.[153]

Another approach was adopted in the New Zealand case of *P v P*.[154]

> A husband and wife had separated, and by the deed of separation the husband agreed to pay a monthly sum to the wife. Later the parties were divorced and the court ordered the husband to pay to the wife one shilling a year as maintenance. The wife was insane; and her administrator, the Public Trustee, told the husband (a) that the court order cancelled the provisions of the separation deed, (b) that if he paid the arrears due under the deed he would be under no further liability. The husband accordingly paid the arrears but paid no more instalments. More than four years later the Public Trustee found that he had wrongly interpreted the effect of the court order and sued for the monthly instalments. The husband pleaded the principle set out in the *High Trees* case and in *Combe v Combe*.

McGregor J gave judgment for the defendant. The latter had been induced by the statement of the Public Trustee not to proceed, as he might have done, to take steps under an Act of 1928 to set aside the separation deed. The Public Trustee, therefore, should not be allowed to enforce his legal claim.

---

[148] [1972] 2 QB 189, [1972] 2 All ER 127.
[149] Ibid at 213 and 140, respectively.
[150] Ibid at 221 and 147, respectively.
[151] Ibid at 217–218 and 143, respectively. Stephenson LJ agreed that there was a consensual variation. Clarke [1974] CLJ 260 at 278–280, doubts whether there was consideration for such a variation but for present purposes the important point is that two members of the court thought it necessary to find it.
[152] [1979] QB 467 at 482, [1979] 2 All ER 753 at 758, 759.
[153] See discussion at p 716, below.
[154] [1957] NZLR 854; Sheridan 21 MLR 185. For other New Zealand cases, see the 8th New Zealand edition of this work, pp 127–129.

McGregor J thought that the governing test was 'whether it would be inequitable to allow the party seeking so to do to enforce the strict rights which he had induced the other party to believe will not be enforced'. Clearly on the facts of this case the husband had acted to his detriment and it seems likely that the tests of inequity and detrimental reliance would in practice substantially overlap.

This approach was followed by Robert Goff J in *The Post Chaser*[155] who said:

> The fundamental principle is that stated by Lord Cairns LC, viz that the representor will not be allowed to enforce his rights where it would be inequitable having regard to the dealings which have thus taken place between the parties. To establish such inequity, it is not necessary to show detriment; indeed, the representee may have benefited from the representation, and yet it may be inequitable, at least without reasonable notice, for the representor to enforce his legal rights . . . But it does not follow that in every case in which the representee had acted, or failed to act, in reliance on the representation, it will be inequitable for the representor to enforce his rights for the nature of the action or inaction may be insufficient to give rise to the equity.

(3) A final doubt is whether the promisee must have acted equitably if he is to rely on the doctrine. Such a requirement was stated by Lord Denning MR in *D & C Builders Ltd v Rees*,[156] the facts of which have already been discussed.[157] This is a case which illustrated perfectly our earlier suggestion that the rule in *Foakes v Beer* was not devoid of virtue since the merits were clearly on the side of the plaintiff creditors.[158] Winn LJ simply applied the principle of *Foakes v Beer* and did not consider the application of promissory estoppel but Lord Denning MR had in earlier cases stated the principle in a form sufficiently wide to cover the defendants. He did not resile from the width of his earlier statements but qualified them by a rider that a promise can only be relied on when it has been given with full consent and not if it has been extracted by threats. If the courts do eventually hold that the doctrine of promissory estoppel has outflanked *Foakes v Beer*, it would appear necessary to have some such saving clause. This will clearly involve the gradual working out of what conduct by the promisee should be regarded as inequitable in this context.[159] In *Adams v R Hanna & Son Ltd*[160] it was suggested that a debtor who seeks to persuade a creditor to accept less than is owed, only acts equitably when he makes full and frank disclosure of his financial position.

---

[155] [1982] 1 All ER 19 at 27. See also the observation of the same judge in *Amalgamated Investments and Property Co Ltd v Texas Commerce International Bank Ltd* [1982] QB 84, [1981] 1 All ER 923 approved on different grounds by Court of Appeal [1982] QB 84, [1981] 3 All ER 577. For further discussion of the *Texas* case and estoppel by convention see *Kenneth Allison Ltd v A E Limehouse & Co* [1991] 4 All ER 500 at 514 per Lord Goff. See too *Taylor Fashions Ltd v Liverpool Victoria Trustees Co Ltd* [1982] QB 133n, [1981] 1 All ER 897.

[156] [1966] 2 QB 617, [1965] 3 All ER 837.

[157] P 125, above.   [158] P 122, above.

[159] Winder 82 LQR 165; Cornish 29 MLR 428.   [160] (1967) 11 WIR 245.

3 Compositions with creditors

It has long been a common practice for the creditors of an impecunious debtor to make an arrangement with him whereby each agrees to accept a stated percentage of his debt in full satisfaction. The search for a sufficient consideration to support so reasonable an agreement has caused the courts much embarrassment. It would appear at first sight to fall under the ban in *Pinnel's Case*, and such was the view adopted in 1804 by Lord Ellenborough. 'It is impossible to contend that acceptance of £17 10s is an extinguishment of a debt of £50.'[161] But the inconvenience of such a conclusion was so manifest that it could not be accepted.

Two alternative suggestions have been proffered. The first was the second thought of Lord Ellenborough himself. There was consideration for the composition, he suggested in 1812, in the fact that each individual creditor agreed to forgo part of his debt on the hypothesis that all the other creditors would do the same.[162] A moment's reflection will expose the weakness of this argument. Such a consideration would, no doubt, suffice to support the agreement as between the creditors themselves. But, if the debtor sought to rely upon it, he would be met by the immediate objection that he himself had furnished no return for the creditors' promises to him, and, as already observed, it is a cardinal rule of the law that the consideration must move from the promisee.[163] A second solution is to say that no creditor will be allowed to go behind the composition agreement, to the prejudice either of the other creditors or of the debtor himself, because this would be a fraud upon all the parties concerned. The solution was suggested by Lord Tenterden in 1818 and supported by Willes J in 1863, and it has since won general approbation.[164] But it is frankly an argument *ab inconvenienti* and evades rather than meets the difficulty.

Similar difficulties arise with a second situation.

> Suppose that A owes B £100 and that C promises B £50 on condition that B will discharge A. If the £50 is paid and B still sues A for the balance, how is A to resist the action?

No promise of discharge was given to him, nor, if it had been, would he have supplied any consideration for it. The question arose in 1825 in *Welby v Drake*.[165]

---

[161] *Fitch v Sutton* (1804) 5 East 230.

[162] *Boothbey v Sowden* (1812) 3 Camp 175. The argument was adopted, though obiter, by the court in *Good v Cheesman* (1831) 2 B & Ad 328.

[163] See p 101, above.

[164] See *Wood v Robarts* (1818) 1 Stark 417; and *Cook v Lister* (1863) 13 CBNS 543 at 595. See also *Couldery v Bartrum* (1881) 19 ChD 394, where Sir George Jessel, amid a sustained invective against the rule in *Pinnel's Case*, can say no more than the law 'imports' a consideration to support the composition agreement; and *Hirachand Punamchand v Temple* [1911] 2 KB 330.

[165] (1825) 1 C & P 557.

The defendant had drawn a bill for £18, which had been returned unaccepted and which had come into the hands of the plaintiff. The defendant's father then made an agreement with the plaintiff, whereby he promised to pay him £9 in return for the plaintiff's promise to receive it in full satisfaction of his claim. The money was duly paid, but the plaintiff still sued the defendant.

Lord Tenterden directed judgment for the defendant.

> If the father did pay the smaller sum in satisfaction of this debt, it is a bar to the plaintiff's now recovering against the son; because, by suing the son, he commits a fraud on the father, whom he induced to advance his money on the faith of such advance being a discharge of his son from further liability.

The plea of fraud was approved by Willes J in *Cook v Lister*[166] and applied by the Court of Appeal in *Hirachand Punamchand v Temple*,[167] and reliance was placed upon the analogy of composition agreements. Both classes of cases, therefore, may be said to rest upon this basis, and should be treated as exceptions to the general requirement of consideration.

4 Where the plaintiff is bound by an existing contractual duty to a third party

The next type of case is where the plaintiff performs, or promises to perform, an obligation already imposed upon him by a contract previously made, not between him and the defendant, but between himself and a third party. The question whether such a promise or performance affords sufficient consideration has provoked a voluminous literature—more generous, indeed, than the practical implications would seem to warrant.[168]

The problems involved may thus be stated. If A and B have made a contract under which an obligation remains to be performed by A, and A now makes this obligation the basis of a new agreement with C, there are two possibilities. C's promise may have been induced either by A's promise to perform his outstanding obligation under the contract with B, or by A's actual performance of it. In other words, A may seek to support the validity of his agreement with C by reliance either on executory or on executed consideration. There is, as has already been remarked, divergence of juristic

---

[166] (1863) 13 CBNS 543 at 595.

[167] [1911] 2 KB 330. See also *Re L G Clarke, ex p Debtor v Ashton & Son* [1967] Ch 1121, [1966] 3 All ER 622. This assumes that the creditor has made an agreement with the third party. Cf *IRC v Fry* [2001] STC 1715. The courts have usually shown greater reluctance to allow A to use a contract between B and C as a defence to an action by B. See pp 214–223, below. See also Gold 19 Can Bar Rev 165. In *Welby v Drake* the creditor sued for the full amount of the original debt; in *Hirachand Punamchand v Temple* only for the balance.

[168] Davis [1937] CLJ 203; Ballantine 11 Mich L Rev 423; Pollock *Principles of Contract* (13th edn) pp 147–150; Holdsworth *HEL* vol VIII, pp 40–41; *Williston On Contracts* (3rd edn) paras 131, 131A.

opinion as to the identity of the test applicable to determine the sufficiency of the one type of consideration and of the other.[169]

How far is this distinction between executory and executed consideration to be regarded as relevant? Sir Frederick Pollock thought that, in principle at least, it should be decisive.[170] In his opinion the *promise* might be good consideration, for it involved the promisor in two possible actions for breach of contract instead of one, and thus was a detriment within the meaning of the law.[171] The *performance* should not be accepted as good consideration, since, as it discharged the previous contract, it was not a detriment at all. This theory, however, is not altogether convincing. The validity of the promise may be accepted: the insufficiency of the performance is open to criticism. In the first place, it assumes that the only test of consideration is a detriment to the promisee. The assumption may be historically sound: the idea of detriment at least recalls the early association of assumpsit and case. But the complementary idea of benefit was soon introduced into the language of the courts, and has been constantly emphasised by the judges. While, therefore, the performance may not be a detriment to the promisee, it is certainly a benefit to the promisor.[172] In the second place, the distinction involves a practical absurdity. If the mere promise of an act is sufficient consideration to induce a counter-promise, surely the complete performance of that act should be accepted. To hold the contrary, it has been well said, seems to assert 'that a bird in the hand is worth less than the same bird in the bush'.[173] Once more, the conflict between principle and technicality comes to the surface, and once more the difficulties inherent in the use of the terms 'detriment' and 'benefit' would be avoided if the element of bargain were stressed and the language of sale adopted. Promise and performance may equally be regarded as the price of a counter-promise.

Although the question has often been said to be an open one, the cases have with one exception uniformly upheld either promise or performance as sufficient consideration. This seems to be the effect of some seventeenth-century cases, though no doubt the court did not there see the problem in modern terms.[174]

The one discordant case is *Jones v Waite*.[175]

In this case the defendant agreed to pay money to the plaintiff in return for the plaintiff's promise (a) to execute a separation deed and (b) to pay his (the

---

[169] See p 104, above.

[170] *Principles of Contract* (13th edn) pp 147–150. Holdsworth appears to agree: *HEL* vol VIII, pp 40–41.

[171] To this argument it has sometimes been objected that it assumes what it seems to prove. The promisor exposes himself to two suits only if he can be sued by the new party. But the new party can sue only if the promisor has given consideration. It seems, however, that Pollock meets the objection fairly by pointing out that this assumption must necessarily be made in the case of all mutual promises.

[172] See *Williston on Contracts* (3rd edn) paras 131 and 131A.

[173] See Ballantine 11 Mich L Rev 423 at 427.

[174] Eg *Bagge v Slade* (1616) 3 Bulst 162; Simpson *History* pp 451–452.

[175] (1839) 5 Bing NC 341.

plaintiff's) debts to a third party. The promise to execute the separation deed raised questions of public policy[176] but was held good consideration. The Court of Exchequer Chamber held, however, that the plaintiff's promise to pay his own debts was no consideration.

Lord Abinger CB said:[177]

> A man is under a moral and legal obligation to pay his just debts. It cannot therefore be stated as an abstract proposition, that he suffers any detriment from the discharge of that duty; and the declaration does not show in what way the defendant could have derived any advantage from the plaintiff paying his own debts. The plea therefore shows the insufficiency of that part of the consideration.

This is no doubt a strong authority but it should be noted that the plaintiff's failure on this point was due, at least in part, to his failure to allege any benefit to the defendant. This leaves open the possibility of upholding the contract where a benefit to the promisor can be shown. In fact the case was not as influential as might have been expected since it was lost sight of for over a hundred years, no doubt because when the case was taken to the House of Lords only the separation agreement point was taken.[178]

Jones v Waite was not therefore cited or discussed in a trilogy of cases in the 1860s, of which the first is *Shadwell v Shadwell*.[179]

The plaintiff, who was engaged to marry Ellen Nicholl, received the following letter from his uncle:

> '11th August, 1838, Gray's Inn.
> My dear Lancey—I am glad to hear of your intended marriage with Ellen Nicholl; and, as I promised to assist you at starting, I am happy to tell you that I will pay to you one hundred and fifty pounds yearly during my life, and until your annual income derived from your profession of a chancery barrister shall amount to six hundred guineas, of which your own admission shall be the only evidence that I shall receive or require.
> Your ever affectionate uncle,
> Charles Shadwell.'

The plaintiff married Ellen Nicholl and never earned as much as six hundred guineas a year as a barrister. The instalments promised by the uncle were not all paid during his life, and after his death, the plaintiff brought an action to recover the arrears from the personal representatives.

The defendants pleaded that, as the plaintiff was already bound to marry Ellen Nicholl before the uncle wrote his letter, there was no consideration for his promise.

---

[176] See p 516, below.   [177] Ibid at 356.
[178] (1842) 9 Cl & Fin 101.   [179] (1860) 9 CBNS 159, 30 LJCP 145.

On these facts it might well have been held that there was no more than a conditional promise of a gift by the uncle and indeed that was the dissenting view of Byles J.[180] The majority of the court held that the letter was intended contractually and that there was consideration for it.

Erle CJ, giving the opinion of Keating J, and himself, thought that there was both a detriment to the plaintiff and a benefit to the uncle: a detriment because 'the plaintiff may have made the most material changes in his position and have incurred pecuniary liabilities resulting in embarrassment, which would be in every sense a loss if the income which had been promised should be withheld', and a benefit, because the marriage was 'an object of interest with a near relative'.

The facts and the decision in *Chichester v Cobb*[181] were for practical purposes identical and we need only note that Blackburn J experienced no difficulty in discovering consideration on such facts.

The third case is *Scotson v Pegg*.[182]

> The plaintiffs had contracted with a third party, X, to deliver a cargo of coal to X or *to the order of* X. X sold this cargo to the defendant and directed the plaintiffs, in pursuance of their contract, to deliver it to the defendant. The defendant then made an agreement with the plaintiffs in which, 'in consideration that the plaintiffs, at the request of the defendant, would deliver to the defendant' the cargo of coal, the defendant promised to unload it at a stated rate.

For breach of this promise the plaintiffs sued, and the defendant once more pleaded lack of consideration. If, it was argued, the plaintiffs were already bound by the contract with X to deliver the coal to the defendant in accordance with X's order, what were they now giving in return for the defendant's promise to unload at a certain rate? However, the two judges present at the hearing, Martin and Wilde BB both gave judgment for the plaintiffs. Martin B was content to say that the delivery of the coal was a benefit to the defendant. Wilde B thought there was also a detriment to the plaintiffs. It might have suited them, as against X, to break their contract and pay damages, and the delivery to the defendant had prevented this possible course of conduct.[183]

Although these three cases are not entirely satisfactory, they at least all point in the same way and one further along which principle directs us. All doubts on the matter may now be regarded as resolved by the decision of the Privy Council in *New Zealand Shipping Co v A M Satterthwaite & Co, The Eurymedon*.[184] The facts and issues of this

---

[180] Cf *Jones v Padavatton* [1969] 2 All ER 616, [1969] 1 WLR 328, discussed pp 146–147, below. Though logically it should make no difference, the court is perhaps more likely to strain to discover a contract where the action lies against the executors than against the promisor.

[181] (1866) 14 LT 433.

[182] (1861) 6 H & N 295, 3 LT 753.   [183] This argument is only found in 3 LT.

[184] [1975] AC 154, [1974] 1 All ER 1015. Reynolds 90 LQR 301. Followed on this point *Pao On v Lau Yiu Long* [1979] 3 All ER 65, [1979] 3 WLR 435.

case are complex and are discussed more fully later.[185] For present purposes we may say that the essential facts were that the plaintiff made an offer to the defendant that if the defendant would unload the plaintiff's goods from a ship (which the defendant was already bound to do by a contract with a third party), the plaintiff would treat the defendant as exempt from any liability for damage to the goods. The majority of the judicial committee of the Privy Council had no doubt[186] that the defendant's act of unloading the ship was good consideration.[187]

---

[185] See pp 214–223, below.

[186] The minority expressed no concluded view for they did not think the transaction could be construed as an offer of this kind.

[187] Ibid at 168 and 1021, respectively.

5 INTENTION TO CREATE LEGAL RELATIONS

SUMMARY

The question now to be discussed is whether a contract necessarily results once the court has ruled that the parties must be taken to have made an agreement and that it is supported by consideration.[1] This conclusion is commonly denied. The law, it is said, does not proclaim the existence of a contract merely because of the presence of mutual promises. Agreements are made every day in domestic and in social life, where the parties do not intend to invoke the assistance of the courts should the engagement not be honoured. To offer a friend a meal is not to invite litigation. Contracts, in the words of Lord Stowell,

> . . . must not be the sports of an idle hour, mere matters of pleasantry and badinage, never intended by the parties to have any serious effect whatever.[2]

It is therefore contended that, in addition to the phenomena of agreement and the presence of consideration, a third contractual element is required—the intention of the parties to create legal relations.

This view, commonly held in England,[3] has not passed unchallenged; and the criticism of it made by Professor Williston demands attention, not only as emanating from a distinguished American jurist, but as illuminating the whole subject now under discussion. In his opinion, the separate element of intention is foreign to the common law, imported from the Continent by academic influences in the nineteenth

---

[1] It is assumed here that the contract cannot be challenged on the ground that it violates public policy or is avoided by statute. Such flaws are discussed in Ch 11, below.

[2] *Dalrymple v Dalrymple* (1811) 2 Hag Con 54 at 105.

[3] Eg *Pollock on Contract* (13th edn) p 3; Law Revision Committee, Sixth Interim Report, p 15.

century[4] and useful only in systems which lack the test of consideration to enable them to determine the boundaries of contract:

> The common law does not require any positive intention to create a legal obligation as an element of contract ... A deliberate promise seriously made is enforced irrespective of the promisor's views regarding his legal liability.[5]

His own views may be reduced to three propositions:

(1) If reasonable people would assume that there was no intention in the parties to be bound, there is no contract.

(2) If the parties expressly declare or clearly indicate their rejection of contractual obligations, the law accepts and implements their intention.

(3) Mere social engagements, if accompanied by the requisite technicalities, such as consideration, may be enforced as contracts.

English lawyers may well be prepared to accept the first two of these propositions: decided cases refute the third.[6] But their acceptance does not necessarily justify the complete rejection of intention to create legal relations as an independent element in the formation of contract. It is certainly true, and of great significance, that the very presence of consideration normally implies the existence of such an intention. To make a bargain is to assume liability and to invite the sanction of the courts. Professor Williston performed a valuable service by insisting that the emphasis laid by foreign systems on this element of intention is out of place in the common law, where it follows naturally from the very nature of contract. Consideration, bargain, legal consequences—these are interrelated concepts. But it is possible for this presumption to be rebutted. If A and B agree to lunch together and A promises to pay for the food if B will pay for the drink, it is difficult to deny the presence of consideration and yet equally clear that no legal ties are contemplated or created.[7] It seems necessary, therefore, to regard the intention to create legal relations as a separate element in the English law of contract, though, by the preoccupation of that law with the idea of bargain, one which does not normally obtrude upon the courts.

The cases in which a contract is denied on the ground that there is no intention to involve legal liability may be divided into two classes. On the one hand, there are social, family or other domestic agreements, where the presence or absence of an

---

[4] Historically this would appear correct. Simpson 91 LQR 263–265.

[5] *Williston on Contracts* (3rd edn) s 21. Williston has not lacked support: see Tuck 21 Can Bar Rev 123; Hamson 54 LQR 233; Shatwell 1 Sydney L Rev 289; Unger 19 MLR 96; Hepple [1970] CLJ 122; Hedley 5 Oxford LJS 391. Cf Chloros 33 Tulane L Rev 607.

[6] Eg *Balfour v Balfour* [1919] 2 KB 571; p 123, below. See also *Lens v Devonshire Club* (1914) Times, 4 December, discussed by Scrutton LJ in *Rose and Frank Co v J R Crompton & Bros Ltd* [1923] 2 KB 261.

[7] It may be objected that there is only consideration if the promises are given in exchange for each other but some test of intention is needed to discover whether this is so.

intention to create legal relations depends upon the inference to be drawn by the court from the language used by the parties and the circumstances in which they use it.[8] On the other hand, there are commercial agreements where this intention is presumed and must be rebutted by the party seeking to deny it. In either case, of course, intention is to be objectively ascertained.

A DOMESTIC AGREEMENTS

Agreements between husband and wife

In the course of family life many agreements are made, which could never be supposed to be the subject of litigation. If a husband arranges to make a monthly allowance to his wife for her personal enjoyment, neither would normally be taken to contemplate legal relations. On the other hand, the relation of husband and wife by no means precludes the formation of a contract, and the context may indicate a clear intention on either side to be bound. Whether any given agreement between husband and wife falls on the one side of the borderline or the other is not always easy to determine. Two contrasting cases may illustrate the position.

In *Merritt v Merritt*:[9]

> The husband left the matrimonial home, which was in the joint names of husband and wife and subject to a building society mortgage, to live with another woman. The husband and wife met and had a discussion in the husband's car during which the husband agreed to pay the wife £40 a month out of which she must pay the outstanding mortgage payments on the house. The wife refused to leave the car until the husband recorded the agreement in writing and the husband wrote and signed a piece of paper which stated 'in consideration of the fact that you will pay all charges in connection with the house . . . until such time as the mortgage repayments has been completed I will agree to transfer the property in to your sole ownership'. After the wife had paid off the mortgage the husband refused to transfer the house to her.

It was held by the Court of Appeal that the parties had intended to affect their legal relations and that an action for breach of contract could be sustained.

---

[8] It is not irrelevant to notice that by s 1(1) of the Law Reform (Miscellaneous Provisions) Act 1970, 'an agreement between two persons to marry one another shall not under the law of England and Wales have effect as a contract giving rise to legal rights, and no action shall lie in England or Wales for breach of such an agreement, whatever the law applicable to the agreement'.

[9] [1970] 2 All ER 760, [1970] 1 WLR 1211. See also *McGregor v McGregor* (1888) 21 QBD 424; *Pearce v Merriman* [1904] 1 KB 80. *Re Windle* [1975] 3 All ER 987, [1975] 1 WLR 1628.

In *Balfour v Balfour*:[10]

The defendant was a civil servant stationed in Ceylon. His wife alleged that, while they were both in England on leave and when it had become clear that she could not again accompany him abroad because of her health, he had promised to pay her £30 a month as maintenance during the time that they were thus forced to live apart. She sued for breach of this agreement.

The Court of Appeal held that no legal relations had been contemplated and that the wife's action must fail.[11]

Atkin LJ had no doubt that, while consideration was present, the evidence showed that the parties had not designed a binding contract.[12]

> It is necessary to remember that there are agreements between parties which do not result in contracts within the meaning of that term in our law. The ordinary example is where two parties agree to take a walk together or where there is an offer and an acceptance of hospitality. Nobody would suggest in ordinary circumstances that those agreements result in what we know as a contract, and one of the most usual forms of agreement which does not constitute a contract appears to me to be the arrangements which are made between husband and wife . . . To my mind those agreements, or many of them, do not result in contracts at all . . . even though there may be what as between other parties would constitute consideration . . . They are not contracts because the parties did not intend that they should be attended by legal consequences.

In *Pettitt v Pettitt*,[13] several members of the House of Lords, though accepting the principle enunciated in *Balfour v Balfour*, thought the decision on the facts very close to the line.[14] It was also observed that though many agreements between husband and wife are not intended to be legally binding, performance of such agreements may well give rise to legal consequences.

So Lord Diplock said:[15]

> Many of the ordinary domestic arrangements between man and wife do not possess the legal characteristics of a contract. So long as they are executory they do not give rise to any chose in

---

[10] [1919] 2 KB 571.

[11] Tuck 21 Can Bar Rev 97, rests the decision in this case on the absence of consideration. Duke LJ certainly took this view: but the whole tenor both of counsel's arguments and of the judgments of Warrington and Atkin LJJ shows that the decision turned on the lack of intention to contract.

[12] Ibid at 578–579.

[13] [1970] AC 777, [1969] 2 All ER 385.

[14] Per Lord Hodson, ibid at 806 and 400, respectively; per Lord Upjohn, ibid at 816 and 408, respectively.

[15] Ibid at 822 and 413–414, respectively. See also per Lord Reid, ibid at 796 and 391, respectively: see Lesser 23 U of Toronto LJ 148 at 162–164. That it is easy to lose sight of the distinction between contract and property is shown by the decision in *Spellman v Spellman* [1961] 2 All ER 498, [1961] 1 WLR 921, discussed by Diamond 24 MLR 789.

action, for neither party intended that non-performance of their mutual promises should be the subject of sanctions in any court (see *Balfour v Balfour*). But this is relevant to non-performance only. If spouses do perform their mutual promises the fact that they could not have been compelled to do so while the promises were executory cannot deprive the acts done by them of all legal consequences upon proprietary rights; for these are within the field of the law of property rather than of the law of contract. It would, in my view, be erroneous to extend the presumption accepted in *Balfour v Balfour* that mutual promises between man and wife in relation to their domestic arrangements are prima facie not intended by either to be legally enforceable to a presumption of a common intention of both spouses that *no* legal consequences should flow from acts done by them in performance of mutual promises with respect to the acquisition, improvement or addition to real or personal property . . . for this would be to intend what is impossible in law.

Agreements between parent and child

Agreements between parent and child may present problems similar to those of husband and wife. An illustration is afforded by the case of *Jones v Padavatton*:[16]

> Mrs Jones lived in Trinidad. Her daughter had a post in the Indian Embassy in Washington. She had been married and had a young son, but was now divorced. Mrs Jones wished her to go to England and become a barrister, and offered to make her a monthly allowance while she read for the Bar. The daughter reluctantly accepted the offer and went to England in 1962. In 1964 Mrs Jones bought a house in London. The daughter lived with her child in part of it, and the rest was let to tenants, whose rent covered expenses and the daughter's maintenance. In 1967, Mrs Jones and her daughter quarrelled, and Mrs Jones issued a summons claiming possession of the house. At the time of the hearing, the daughter had passed only a portion of Part I of the Bar examinations.

Two agreements fell to be considered. By the first the daughter agreed to leave Washington and read for the Bar in London, and her mother agreed to pay her a fixed monthly sum. By the second the mother allowed the daughter to live in the house which the mother had bought, and the rent received from the tenants provided for the daughter's maintenance. In each agreement there was an exchange of promises, but in neither were the terms put into writing, nor was the duration of the agreement precisely defined. The question was whether in either case the parties had intended to create legal relations.

At the hearing in the county court, the judge dismissed the mother's claim for possession of the house, but his decision was reversed by the Court of Appeal. Danckwerts and Fenton Atkinson LJJ thought that neither agreement was intended to

---

[16] [1969] 2 All ER 616, [1969] 1 WLR 328.

create legal relations. 'The present case is one of those family arrangements which depend on the good faith of the promises which are made and are not intended to be rigid, binding arrangements.'[17] Salmon LJ agreed that the appeal should be allowed, but on different grounds. In his opinion the first agreement was a contract designed to last for a period reasonably sufficient to enable the daughter to pass the Bar examinations. For this purpose the five years which had elapsed since the date of the agreement was a reasonable time, and the contract had therefore come to an end. The second agreement, involving the possession of the house, was so imprecise and left so many details unsettled that it was impossible to construe it as a contract. Nothing in the agreement nor in the available evidence suggested that the mother had intended to renounce her right to dispose of her house as and when she pleased. The daughter was a mere licensee.[18]

Other domestic arrangements

A further group of cases involve domestic agreements which are made neither between husband and wife nor between parent and child. In *Simpkins v Pays*:[19]

> The defendant owned a house in which she lived with X, her granddaughter, and the plaintiff, a paying boarder. The three took part together each week in a competition organised by a Sunday newspaper. The entries were made in the defendant's name, but there was no regular rule as to the payment of postage and other expenses. One week the entry was successful and the defendant obtained a prize of £750. The plaintiff claimed a third of this sum, but the defendant refused to pay on the ground that there was no intention to create legal relations but only a friendly adventure.

Sellers J gave judgment for the plaintiff. He agreed that 'there are many family associations where some sort of rough and ready statement is made which would not establish a contract'. But on the present facts he thought that there was a 'mutuality in the arrangement between the parties'. It was a joint enterprise to which each contributed in the expectation of sharing any prize that was won.

---

[17] Ibid at 620 and 332. Both Danckwerts and Fenton Atkinson LJJ cited and applied *Balfour v Balfour*.

[18] Ibid at 623 and 335, respectively. Cf *Hardwick v Johnson* [1978] 2 All ER 935, [1978] 1 WLR 683.

[19] [1955] 3 All ER 10, [1955] 1 WLR 975. For a simple case where there was no intention to create legal relations, see *Buckpitt v Oates* [1968] 1 All ER 1145. See also *Parker v Clark* [1960] 1 All ER 93, [1960] 1 WLR 286. Cf *Osorio v Cardona* (1984) 15 DLR (4th) 619. *Grocutt v Khan* [2003] Lloyd's Rep IR464.

B COMMERCIAL AGREEMENTS[20]

In commercial agreements it will be presumed that the parties intended to create legal relations and made a contract. But the presumption may be rebutted.

(1) It is common enough to advertise goods by flamboyant reports of their efficacy and to support these by promises of a more or less vague character if they should fail of their purpose. If a plaintiff, induced to buy on the faith of such reports and promises, finds that they are not borne out by the facts and sues for breach of contract, the defendant may attempt to plead that there was no intention to create legal relations and that only the most gullible customer would think otherwise.

The point arose in the case of *Carlill v Carbolic Smoke Ball Co*,[21] where the defendants advertised their preparation by offering to pay £100 to any purchaser who used it and yet caught influenza within a given period, and by declaring that they had deposited £1,000 with their bankers 'to show their sincerity'. The plaintiff bought the preparation, used it and caught influenza. Among the many ingenious defences raised to her action was the plea that no legal relations were ever contemplated. The advertisement, it was said, was 'a mere puff', 'a mere statement by the defendants of the confidence they reposed in their remedy', 'a promise in honour'. The Court of Appeal rejected this plea. The fact of the deposit was cogent evidence that the defendants had contemplated legal liability when they issued their advertisement. What would have been the view of the court in the absence of any such deposit is a matter of speculation, and it is not to be concluded that all advertisements are to be treated as serious offers.[22]

In *Carlill v Carbolic Smoke Ball Co* the plaintiff did not buy the smoke ball from the defendant but from a retailer. The question before the court was therefore whether there was a contract with the defendant. A more modern example is *Bowerman v Association of British Travel Agents Ltd*.[23]

> The claimant booked a holiday with a tour operator who was member of the Defendant Association (ABTA). The tour operator displayed on its wall an ABTA notice which stated that in the event of the financial failure of an ABTA member before a holiday:
>
> > ABTA arranges for you to be reimbursed the money you have paid in respect of your holiday arrangement.
>
> The tour operator became insolvent shortly before the claimant's holiday. The claimant made a claim against ABTA who argued that the notice was not intended

---

[20] There can of course be commercial agreements between members of a family, eg *Snelling v John G Snelling Ltd* [1973] QB 87, [1972] 1 All ER 79.

[21] [1893] 1 QB 256.

[22] Cf p 39 n 18, above.   [23] [1996] CLC 451, [1995] NLJR 1815, McMeel 113 LQR 47.

to give rise to a contract with the claimant. The majority of the Court of Appeal rejected this contention.

Hobhouse LJ said:

> This document is intended to be read and would reasonably be read by a member of the public as containing an offer of a promise which the customer is entitled to accept by choosing to do business with an ABTA member.

A more common factual situation arises where there is undoubtedly a contract but there is dispute as to whether a statement made by one of the parties before the contract forms part of the contract. This question is discussed more fully later[24] and it will suffice for the moment to say that here, too, the governing test is the parties' intention.[25]

(2) The parties may make an agreement on a matter of business or of some other transaction normally the subject of contract, but may expressly declare that it is not to be binding in law. If such a declaration is made, it will, like other unambiguous expressions of intention, be accepted by the courts.[26]

Perhaps the most remarkable instance of a clause expressly outlawing an agreement is to be found in the case of *Rose and Frank v Crompton*.[27] The plaintiffs were a New York firm which dealt in tissues for carbonising papers. The defendants manufactured such tissues in England. In July 1913, the parties made a written agreement whereby the defendants gave the plaintiffs certain rights of selling their tissues in the United States and in Canada for a period of three years with an option to extend the time. The agreement contained the following clause, described as 'the Honourable Pledge Clause':

> This arrangement is not entered into nor is this memorandum written, as a formal or legal agreement, and shall not be subject to legal jurisdiction in the law courts either of the United States or England, but it is only a definite expression and record of the purpose and intention of the parties concerned, to which they each honourably pledge themselves.

The agreement was subsequently extended so as to last until March 1920; but in 1919 the defendants terminated it without giving the appropriate notice specified in the agreement, and they further refused to execute orders which had been received and accepted by them before the termination. The plaintiffs sued for damages for breach of the agreement and for non-delivery of the goods comprised in these orders. To appreciate the decision reached by the courts, it is necessary to separate these two claims.

---

[24] See pp 165–172, below.

[25] See eg *Heilbut Symons & C v Buckleton* [1913] AC 30, *J Evans & Son (Portsmouth) Ltd v Andrea Merzario* [1976] 2 All ER 930 [1976] 1 WLR 1078; *Independent Broadcasting Authority v EMI Electronics Ltd and BICC Construction Ltd* (1980) 14 BLR 1.

[26] *Jones v Vernon's Pools Ltd* [1938] 2 All ER 626; *Appleson v H Littlewood Ltd* [1939] 1 All ER 464.

[27] [1923] 2 KB 261; revsd [1925] AC 445.

The first was for breach of the agreement contained in the written document of July 1913, whereby the defendants granted selling rights to the plaintiffs. Here the plaintiffs failed. The document doubtless contemplated that orders for goods were from time to time to be given by the plaintiffs and fulfilled by the defendants. But, as the parties had specifically declared that the document was not to impose legal consequences, there was no obligation to give orders or to accept them or to stand by any clause in the agreement. Scrutton LJ said in the Court of Appeal:[28]

> It is quite possible for parties to come to an agreement by accepting a proposal with the result that the agreement does not give rise to legal relations. The reason of this is that the parties do not intend that their agreement shall give rise to legal relations. This intention may be implied from the subject-matter of the agreement, but it may also be expressed by the parties. In social and family relations such an intention is readily implied, while in business matters the opposite result would ordinarily follow. But I can see no reason why, even in business matters, the parties should not intend to rely on each other's good faith and honour, and to exclude all idea of settling disputes by any outside intervention, with the accompanying necessity of expressing themselves so precisely that outsiders may have no difficulty in understanding what they mean.

The second claim, on the other hand, was based, not on the promises comprised in the original document, but on the specific orders actually accepted by the defendants before they terminated the agreement. Here the plaintiffs succeeded. As each individual order was given and accepted, this constituted a new and separate contract, inferred by the courts from the conduct of the parties and enforceable without reference to the original memorandum. In the words of Lord Phillimore:[29]

> According to the course of business between the parties which is narrated in the unenforceable agreement, goods were ordered from time to time, shipped, received and paid for, under an established system; but, the agreement being unenforceable, there was no obligation on the American company to order goods or upon the English companies to accept an order. Any actual transaction between the parties, however, gave rise to the ordinary legal rights; for the fact that it was not of obligation to do the transaction did not divest the transaction where done of its ordinary legal significance.

Words inserted by one party in an agreement and devised, or subsequently used, to exclude legal relations may be ambiguous. In such a case the onus of proving this intention lies heavily upon the party who asserts it. A helpful example is to be found in *Edwards v Skyways Ltd*.[30]

The plaintiff was employed by the defendants as an aircraft pilot. In January 1962, the defendants told him that they must reduce their staff and gave him three months' notice to terminate his employment. By his contract he was a member of

---

[28] [1923] 2 KB at 288.   [29] [1925] AC at 455.
[30] [1964] 1 All ER 494, [1964] 1 WLR 349.

the defendants' contributory pension fund and was thereby entitled, on leaving their service, to choose one of two options: (a) to withdraw his own total contributions to the fund, (b) to take the right to a paid-up pension payable at the age of fifty. He was a member of the British Air Line Pilots Association. Their officials had a meeting with the defendants, and it was agreed that, if the plaintiff chose option (a), the defendants would make him an 'ex gratia' payment equivalent or approximating to the defendants' contributions to the pension fund. The plaintiff, relying on this agreement, chose option (a). The defendants paid him the amount of his own contributions but refused to make the 'ex gratia' payment.

The plaintiff sued the defendants for breach of contract. It was admitted that the Association had acted as the plaintiff's agents and that there was consideration for the defendants' promise. But the defendants argued that the use of the words 'ex gratia' showed that there was no intention to create legal relations. Megaw J gave judgment for the plaintiff. As this was a business and not a domestic agreement, the burden of rebutting the presumption of legal relations lay upon the defendants: it was a heavy burden and they had not discharged it.[31]

There is an overlap here between arguments that the agreement is or is not intended to create legal relations and arguments that the agreement is or is not sufficiently certain to be enforced. This is illustrated by the decision in *Kleinwort Benson Ltd v Malaysia Mining Corpn Bhd.*[32]

The plaintiff's bank had agreed to make a loan facility of up to £10,000,000 available to the defendants wholly owned subsidiary, MMC Metals Ltd, which was trading in tin on the London Metal Exchange. The bank was not willing to lend the money simply on the basis of the subsidiary's credit worthiness. The defendants, however, were not willing to enter into a full guarantee of the subsidiary's engagements. After lengthy negotiations the defendants agreed to issue a 'Letter of Comfort' which stated amongst other things that 'it is our policy to ensure that the business of [MMC] is at all times in a position to meet its liabilities to you [under the loan facility agreement]'. During the negotiations the plaintiffs indicated that they were willing to accept this Letter of Comfort rather than a guarantee but that they would charge a somewhat higher rate of interest as a result. In due course the subsidiary became insolvent owing to the collapse of the World Tin Market and the plaintiffs claimed that the defendants should reimburse them for the subsidiary's outstanding indebtedness.

---

[31] Ibid at 500 and 357, respectively. Cf the use of the word 'understanding' in *J H Milner & Son v Percy Bilton Ltd* [1966] 2 All ER 894, [1966] 1 WLR 1582; and of the phrase 'without prejudice' in *Tomlin v Standard Telephones and Cables Ltd* [1969] 3 All ER 201, [1969] 1 WLR 1378. The Court of Appeal appear to have gone very far in discovering a contract in *Gore v Van Der Lann* [1967] 2 QB 31, [1967] 1 All ER 360, discussed p 217, below, and cogently criticised by Odgers 86 LQR 69 and Harris 30 MLR 584.

[32] [1989] 1 All ER 785, [1989] 1 WLR 379.

At first instance, Hirst J treated the question as one of intention to create legal relations and held that since the transaction was clearly highly commercial there was nothing to rebut the presumption that it was intended to be legally binding.[33] The Court of Appeal disagreed. They thought that the question turned on the legal meaning to be attached to the precise form of words used. There were other clauses in the Letter of Comfort which probably did impose a promissory obligation but the relevant words were carefully drafted so as simply to be a statement of the defendant's existing intention. If it had been an untrue statement of the defendant's intention at the time it was made it would, in principle, have given rise to liability in misrepresentation[34] but it did not amount to a promise that the defendants would not change their policy. On this view, the legal effect of a Letter of Comfort depends on the precise wording used and not on some preconceived notion of the legal effects of Letters of Comfort.[35]

The decision of the Court of Appeal was vigorously criticised as commercially unrealistic by Rogers CJ sitting in the Commercial Division of the Supreme Court of New South Wales in *Banque Brussels Lambert v Australian National Industries Ltd.*[36]

> Spedley Securities wished to obtain a loan facility of US $5,000,000 from the plaintiff. Spedley Securities was a wholly owned subsidiary of Spedley Holdings Ltd, 45% of the shares of which were held by the defendant. There were elaborate negotiations as to what form of assurance the defendants would give to the bank in return for the bank advancing credit to Spedley Securities. Eventually a letter was issued by the defendants in which they undertook, amongst other things, to give the plaintiffs 90 days' notice of any decision to dispose of or reduce their shareholding and giving the bank a right to give 30 days' notice for repayment of loans if they received such a notice.

The practical thrust of this undertaking was that, in practice, it would be extremely difficult for the defendants to dispose of their shareholding if it was known to a potential buyer that the loans of the subsidiary company were being called up by its bankers. In fact some years later the defendants did dispose of their shareholding without giving notice to the bank and Rogers CJ held that this amounted to a breach of contract. These decisions appear clearly reconcilable on the facts since the undertaking to give notice of the potential disposal of the shares was much more naturally characterised as promissory than the statement about policy in the *Kleinwort Benson* case. It is clear, however, that Rogers CJ was not content simply to distinguish the two cases. He said:

> There should be no room in the proper flow of commerce for some purgatory where statements made by a businessman, after hard bargaining and made to induce another business

---

[33] [1988] 1 All ER 714, [1988] 1 WLR 799.   [34] See pp 332–337, below.
[35] See also *Chemco Leasing Spa v Rediffusion* [1987] 1 FTLR 201.
[36] (1989) 21 NSWLR 502. Tyree 2 JCL 279.

person to enter into a business transaction would, without any express statement to that effect, reside in a twilight zone of merely honourable engagement. The whole thrust of the law today is to attempt to give proper effect to commercial transactions. It is for this reason that uncertainty, a concept so much loved by lawyers, has fallen into disfavour as a tool for striking down commercial bargains.

Of course it is often the case that parties entering into agreements do not expect to encounter legal difficulties and if they thought about the matter would often think that it would be too expensive to resolve any legal difficulties that did arise in the courts. It by no means follows that they lack the intention to create legal relations. The point was neatly tested in *Esso Petroleum Ltd v Customs and Excise Comrs.*[37]

The appellants devised a sales promotion scheme linked to the 1970 World Cup, which involved the production of many millions of 'coins' bearing the likenesses of various members of the England squad. The intention was that the coins would be distributed to Esso retailers and that an elaborate marketing scheme would be mounted to encourage members of the public to buy Esso petrol in order to collect sets of the coins. The scheme was advertised in the press and on television and posters were displayed at Esso filling stations stating 'one coin given with every four gallons of petrol'. The technical question before the House of Lords was whether the coins were chargeable to purchase tax as having been 'produced in quantity for general sale' and this turned on the correct analysis of the transaction that took place at the petrol pump. Esso argued that the advertisement of the coins was not intended to create legal relations. It was no doubt true that the coins were of little intrinsic value and that it was unlikely that any motorist who bought four gallons of petrol and was then refused a coin would resort to litigation but the majority of the House of Lords (Viscount Dilhorne and Lord Russell of Killowen dissenting) had no doubt that this was irrelevant.[38]

An instructive case is *Emonds v Lawson.*[39] The claimant accepted an offer from a set of chambers of an unfunded pupillage. No money was to change hands but the Court of Appeal had no doubt that there was intention to create legal relations and indeed consideration. The transaction was for the benefit of both sides. The pupil barrister had a prospect of being offered a tenancy if the pupillage went well; the chambers had an interest in attracting good quality applicants.[40]

---

[37] [1976] 1 All ER 117, [1976] 1 WLR 1; Atiyah 39 MLR 335.
[38] Esso succeeded on a second argument since of the three Lords of Appeal who thought that the coins were supplied under a contract only one (Lord Fraser of Tullybelton) thought that they were supplied under a contract of sale. Lord Wilberforce and Lord Simon of Glaisdale thought that there were two contracts; a contract to sell petrol and a collateral contract to transfer one coin for every four gallons of petrol.
[39] [2000] QB 501
[40] The nature of the contract did not, however, make the pupil a 'worker' entitled to the minimum wage.

Agreements between industrial corporations and trade unions have raised the question of intention to create legal relations. Thus in *Ford Motor Co Ltd v Amalgamated Union of Engineering and Foundry Workers:*[41]

> An agreement was made in 1955 between the Ford Motor Co on the one side and nineteen trade unions on the other side. The agreement was in writing and was drafted with careful precision. It contained a term providing that 'at each stage of the procedure set out in this agreement every attempt will be made to resolve issues raised, and until such procedure has been carried through there shall be no stoppage of work or other unconstitutional action'. In 1969, despite this provision, some unions which were parties to the agreement issued notices declaring a strike. The Ford Motor Co applied for interlocutory injunctions to restrain the calling of such a strike.

Offer, acceptance and consideration were present. Was there also an intention to create legal relations? Geoffrey Lane J thought that there was not. He relied mainly on 'the climate of opinion voiced and evidenced by the extra-judicial authorities'.

> Agreements such as these, composed largely of optimistic aspirations, presenting grave practical problems of enforcement and reached against a background of opinion adverse to enforceability, are in my judgment not contracts in the legal sense and are not enforceable at law. Without clear and express provisions making them amenable to legal action, they remain in the realm of undertakings binding in honour.[42]

This decision was obviously of great importance in labour law, where, however, it has been overtaken by statute. The Industrial Relations Act 1971, section 34(1) (introduced by the Conservative government) provided that collective agreements in writing should be presumed to have been intended to be legally enforceable. It is believed that this provision had little practical effect, since the vast majority of collective agreements were expressly stated not to be intended to be legally enforceable, and it was in its turn reversed by the Trade Union and Labour Relations Act 1974, section 18, which enacted a contrary presumption.

The decision remains of interest to contract lawyers since at first sight collective agreements fall into the category of commercial agreements[43] and one might expect them to be legally binding. Further it is agreed that provisions of collective agreements may be incorporated into individual contracts of employment where they will be legally binding.[44] Geoffrey Lane J relied substantially on evidence

---

[41] [1969] 2 All ER 481, [1969] 1 WLR 339.   [42] Ibid at 496 and 356, respectively.

[43] Isadore Katz described a collective agreement as 'at once a business compact, a code of relations and a treaty of peace', quoted by Wedderburn *The Worker and the Law* (2nd edn, 1971) p 177.

[44] Eg *National Coal Board v Galley* [1958] 1 All ER 91, [1958] 1 WLR 16; Wedderburn *The Worker and the Law* (3rd edn) pp 329–343.

that experts in industrial relations regarded collective agreements as not intended to create legal relations.[45] This view has been criticised[46] but on balance it appears correct[47] and substantially validated by practical experience between 1971 and 1974.[48]

---

[45] See especially Kahn-Freund in *The System of Industrial Relations in Great Britain* (ed Flanders and Clegg, 1954) and Report of the Royal Commission on Trade Unions (the Donovan Report) (1968, Cmnd 3623), ch VII, especially paras 465–474. Cf McCartney in *Labour Relations and the Law* (ed Kahn-Freund, 1965).

[46] Selwyn 32 MLR 377; Hepple [1970] CLJ 122.

[47] See Wedderburn *The Worker and the Law* (3rd edn) ch 4; Clark 33 MLR 117.

[48] See Weekes, Mellish, Dickson and Lloyd *Industrial Relations and the Limits of Law*, especially ch 6.
CFF15/ch 5

6 THE CONTENTS OF THE CONTRACT

Scope of this chapter

Although it may be clear that a valid contract has been made, it will still be necessary to determine the extent of the obligations that it creates. Its map must be drawn, its features delineated and its boundaries ascertained. It must first be discovered what terms the parties have expressly included in their contract.

The contents of the contract are not necessarily confined to those that appear on its face. The parties may have negotiated against a background of commercial or local usage whose implications they have tacitly assumed, and to concentrate solely upon their express language may be to minimise or to distort the extent of their liabilities. Evidence of custom may thus have to be admitted. Additional consequences, moreover, may have been annexed by statute to particular contracts, which will operate despite the parties' ignorance or even contrary to their intention. The courts may also read into a contract some further term which alone makes it effective and which the parties must be taken to have omitted by pure inadvertence. All these implications, customary, statutory or judicial, may be as important as the terms expressly adopted by the parties.

Even when the terms have been established, it does not follow that they are all of equal importance. One undertaking may be regarded as of major importance, the breach of it entitling the injured party to end the contract; the breach of another, though demanding compensation, may leave the contract intact. Rules of valuation have therefore to be elaborated.

Finally, it will be necessary to consider the important and difficult problems which arise when the contract contains provisions which purport to exclude or limit the liability of one of the parties in certain events.

1 EXPRESS TERMS

A What did the parties say or write?

If the extent of the agreement is in dispute, the court must first decide what statements were in fact made by the parties either orally or in writing. In exceptional circumstances English law demands a degree of formality either as a substantive or as a procedural requirement of contract. As a general rule, however, no formality is needed.[1] A contract may be made wholly by word of mouth, or wholly in writing, or partly by word of mouth and partly in writing.

If the contract is wholly by word of mouth, its contents are a matter of evidence normally submitted to a judge sitting as a jury. It must be found as a fact exactly what it was that the parties said, as, for example, in *Smith v Hughes*[2] where the question was whether the subject matter of a contract of sale was described by the vendor as 'good oats' or as 'good old oats'.

If the contract is wholly in writing, the discovery of what was written normally presents no difficulty, and its interpretation is a matter exclusively within the jurisdiction of the judge.[3] But on this hypothesis the courts have long insisted that the parties are to be confined within the four corners of the document in which they have chosen to enshrine their agreement. Neither of them may adduce evidence to show that his intention has been misstated in the document.

> It is firmly established as a rule of law that parol evidence cannot be admitted to add to, vary or contradict a deed or other written instrument. Accordingly, it has been held that . . . parol evidence will not be admitted to prove that some particular term, which had been verbally agreed upon, had been omitted (by design or otherwise) from a written instrument constituting a valid and operative contract between the parties.[4]

So in *Hawrish v Bank of Montreal*:[5]

> A solicitor, acting for a company, signed a form proffered by the company's bank, by which he personally gave a 'continuing guarantee' up to $6,000 'of all present and future debts' of the company. He wished to give evidence that the guarantee was intended to be only of a then current overdraft of $6,000.

The Supreme Court of Canada held that such evidence was inadmissible.

This rule, which is often called the 'parol evidence' rule (though the evidence excluded by it is not merely oral), is a general rule applicable to all written instruments and not merely to contracts, but it can, within its proper limitations, be regarded as an expression of the objective theory of contract, that is, that the court is usually concerned not with the parties' actual intentions but with their manifested intention.

---

[1] Ch 7, below.

[2] (1871) LR 6 QB 597.

[3] See Bowen LJ in *Bentsen v Taylor, Sons & Co (No 2)* [1893] 2 QB 274. So the court is not bound by concessions made by a party as to the meaning of the contract: *Bahamas International Trust Co Ltd v Threadgold* [1974] 3 All ER 881, [1974] 1 WLR 1514.

[4] *Jacobs v Batavia and General Plantations Trust* [1924] 1 Ch 287, per P O Lawrence J at 295. See *Cross & Tapper on Evidence* (8th edn, 1995) pp 765–774.

[5] (1969) 2 DLR (3d) 600.

In a complex commercial situation, it will often happen that the documents to which the parties eventually put their hands will not fully realise the hopes and aspirations of either party but that should not make the contract any less binding. So evidence of the parties' negotiations before the contract is excluded[6] and similarly evidence of the parties' post-contractual behaviour is not admissible to show their intention,[7] though it might be to show a variation of the contract or to found an estoppel.

Of course there may be no effective dispute as to what was said but still a fundamental disagreement as to what it meant. In principle the meaning of what was said has to be solved by applying the objective test[8] Both this rule and the difficulties of applying it are well illustrated by *Thake v Maurice.*[9] In this case Mr and Mrs Thake had five children and did not wish to have any more. The defendant carried out a vasectomy on Mr Thake. In due course Mrs Thake became pregnant but because she did not suspect that she might be pregnant no question of her having an abortion arose until it was too late to have one safely. It was agreed that it was an implied term of the contract between the plaintiff and defendant that the sterilisation would be carried out with reasonable professional care and skill and that indeed reasonable professional care and skill had been exercised. The Thakes argued that the defendant had undertaken not merely to use reasonable care and skill but to guarantee that the operation would be successful in permanently sterilising Mr Thake.[10] This argument was based on what had been said by the defendant in the consultations with Mr and Mrs Thake. It was accepted that the defendant had emphasised the irreversible nature of the operation, that is that the Thakes would not be able to change their minds after the operation had been carried out with any significant chance of success. The Thakes understood this conversation as stating that there was no chance of the operation falling to make Mr Thake sterile if it was carried out with reasonable care and skill. In fact the defendant well knew that there was a not insignificant possibility of spontaneous recanalisation which, as happened in the case, would make Mr Thake fertile once more without his knowing it. The trial judge and one of the members of the Court of Appeal thought the effect of this conversation, objectively construed, was that the defendant had warranted that the operation would make Mr Thake sterile:

---

6   *Prenn v Simmonds* [1971] 3 All ER 237, [1971] 1 WLR 1381. Cf *LCC v Henry Boot & Sons* [1959] 3 All ER 636, [1959] 1 WLR 1069. In some circumstances it may be permissible to show that the parties have struck out part of a standard form of contract. See eg *Louis Dreyfus et Cie v Parnaso Cia Naviera SA* [1960] 2 QB 49, [1960] 1 All ER 759; *Mottram Consultants Ltd v Bernard Sunley & Sons Ltd* [1975] 2 Lloyd's Rep 197. *Punjab National Bank v De Boinville* [1992] 3 All ER 104.

7   *Schuler AG v Wickman Machine Tool Sales* [1974] AC 235, [1973] 2 All ER 39.

8   See Lord Steyn in *Deutsche Genossenschaftsbank v Burnhope* [1996] 1 Lloyd's Rep 113 at 122 and Staughton LJ in *Charter Reinsurance Co Ltd v Fagan* [1996] 1 Lloyd's Rep 261 at 265. Lewison, *The Interpretation of Contracts* (2nd edn 1997).

9   [1986] QB 644, [1986] 1 All ER 497; see also *Eyre v Measday* [1986] 1 All ER 488.

10   In fact the plaintiff succeeded on the alternative theory that the defendant was negligent in having failed to warn the Thakes of the possibility of spontaneous recanalisation.

the majority of the Court of Appeal thought that objectively construed, the conversation did not have this effect since 'in medical science all things, or nearly all things, are uncertain [since] that knowledge is part of the general experience of mankind'.

In practice much of the time of the courts is taken up with the process of deciding what the words used by the parties mean. Although the question of what a contract in writing means is undoubtedly technically a legal question, it is today clear that the process is no different from that by which the meaning of words is discovered in other contexts.

The leading modern explanation is that by Lord Hoffmann in *Investors Compensation Scheme Ltd v West Bromwich Building Society*[11] where he said:

> My Lords, I will say at once that I prefer the approach of the learned judge. But I should preface my explanation of my reasons with some general remarks about the principles by which contractual documents are nowadays construed. I do not think that the fundamental change which has overtaken this branch of the law, particularly as a result of the speeches of Lord Wilberforce in *Prenn v Simmonds* [1971] 3 All ER 237 at 240–242, [1971] 1 WLR 1381 at 1384–1386 and *Reardon Smith Line Ltd v Hansen-Tagen, Hansen Tangen v Sanko Steamship Co* [1976] 3 All ER 570, [1976] 1 WLR 989, is always sufficiently appreciated. The result has been, subject to one important exception, to assimilate the way in which such documents are interpreted by judges to the common sense principles by which any serious utterance would be interpreted in ordinary life. Almost all the intellectual baggage of 'legal' interpretation has been discarded. The principles may be summarised as follows:
>
> 1. Interpretation is the ascertainment of the meaning which the document would convey to a reasonable person having all the background knowledge which would reasonably have been available to the parties in the situation in which they were at the time of the contract.
>
> 2. The background was famously referred by Lord Wilberforce as the 'matrix of fact', but this phrase is, if anything, an understated description of what the background may include. Subject to the requirement that it should have been reasonably available to the parties and to the exception to be mentioned next, it includes absolutely anything which would have affected the way in which the language of the document would have been understood by a reasonable man.
>
> 3. The law excludes from the admissible background the previous negotiations of the parties and their declarations of subjective intent. They are admissible only in an action for rectification. The law makes this distinction for reasons of practical policy and, in this respect only, legal interpretation defers from the way we would interpret utterances in ordinary life. The boundaries of this exception are in some respects unclear. But this is not the occasion on which to explore them.

---

[11] [1998] 1 All ER 98 at 114–115. Staughton [1999] CLJ 303. Kramer 23 OJLS 173; Carter and Stewart 18 JCL 182; Carter and Yates 20 JCL 233; Carter and Peden 21 JCL 172; Carter and Peden 21 JCL 277.

4. The meaning which a document (or any other utterance) would convey to a reasonable man is not the same thing as the meaning of its words. The meaning of the words is a matter of dictionaries and grammars; the meaning of the document is what the parties using those words against the relevant background would reasonably have been understood to mean. The background may not merely enable the reasonable man to choose between the possible meanings of words which are ambiguous but even (as occasionally happens in ordinary life) to conclude that the parties must, for whatever reason, have used the wrong words or syntax (see *Mannai Investment Co Ltd v Eagle Star Life Assurance Co Ltd* [1997] 2 WLR 945.

5. The 'rule' that words should be given their 'natural and ordinary meaning' reflects the commonsense proposition that we do not easily accept that people have made linguistic mistakes, particularly in the formal documents. On the other hand, if one would nevertheless conclude from the background that something must have gone wrong with the language, the law does not require judges to attribute to the parties an intention which they plainly could not have had.

The process was very clearly described by Lord Steyn in *Sirius International Insurance Co (Publ) v FAI General Insurance Ltd*[12] when he said[13]

> The settlement contained in the Tomlin order must be construed as a commercial instrument. The aim of the inquiry is not to probe the real intentions of the parties but to ascertain the contextual meaning of the relevant contractual language. The inquiry is objective: the question is what a reasonable person, circumstanced as the actual parties were, would have understood the parties to have meant by the use of specific language. The answer to that question is to be gathered from the text under consideration and its relevant contextual scene.

It is clear that contextualism is now king and is to be preferred to literalism. But what is literalism? Lord Steyn offered an answer in the same speech when he said[14]

> The tendency should therefore generally speaking be against literalism. What is literalism? It will depend on the context. But an example is given in *The Works of William Paley* (1838 edn) vol III, p 60. The moral philosophy of Paley influenced thinking on contract in the nineteenth century. The example is as follows. The tyrant Temures promised the garrison of Sebastia that no blood would be shed if they surrendered to him. They surrendered. He shed no blood. He buried them all alive. This is literalism. If possible it should be resisted in the interpretative process.

It will often happen that the contract which requires construction is one in common use by many different parties. Good examples are building contracts, nearly all of which are made on one of the family of contracts produced by the JCT. In such cases it must usually be the case that the contract will have the same meaning and that the

---

[12] [2005] 1 All ER 191.   [13] [2005] 1 All ER 191 at 200.   [14] [2005] 1 All ER 191 at 200.

context will have little effect. This was clearly stated by Lord Millett in *AIB Group (UK) plc v Martin*:[15]

> My Lords, your Lordships are concerned with the application of an interpretation clause contained in a standard form. Both features are significant. A standard form is designed for use in a wide variety of different circumstances. It is not context-specific. Its value would be much diminished if it could not be relied upon as having the same meaning on all occasions. Accordingly the relevance of the factual background of a particular case to its interpretation is necessarily limited. The danger, of course, is that a standard form may be employed in circumstances for which it was not designed. Unless the context in a particular case shows that this has happened, however, the interpretation of the form ought not to be affected by the factual background.[16]

Another important question relating to the construction of standard form contracts was considered by the House of Lords in *Homburg Houtimport BV v Agrosin Private Ltd, The Starsin*:[17]

> In this case it was necessary to decide for the purposes of claims by the goods owner under a bill of lading whether the contract was with the shipowner or with the time charterer. The bill of lading was of a standard kind with many densely printed standard clauses on the back and spaces on the front which were filled in to reflect the particular transaction. The bill of lading was signed by the charterer's port agent as agent for the charterer, which was described on the face of the bill of lading as the carrier. The clauses on the back stated that the owner was the carrier. The House of Lords, reversing the Court of Appeal, held that the charterer was the carrier on the ground that in the circumstances the front of the bill of lading carried much more weight than the back.

Lord Steyn said:

> How is the problem to be addressed? For my part there is only one principled answer. It must be approached objectively in the way in which a reasonable person, versed in the shipping trade, would read the bill. The reasonable expectations of such a person must be decisive. In my view he would give greater weight to words specially chosen, such as the words which appear above the signature, rather than standard form printed conditions. Moreover, I have no doubt that in any event he would, as between provisions on the face of the bill and those on the reverse side of the bill, give predominant effect to those on the face of the bill. Given the speed at which international trade is transacted, there is little time for examining the impact of barely legible printed conditions at the time of the issue of the bill of lading. In order to find

---

[15] [2001] UKHL 63, [2002] 1 All ER 353.

[16] It is noteworthy that although in the most recent cases there is almost complete agreement on how the process of construction should be described, there are widespread differences in the results. See especially *BCCI v Ali* discussed p 109, above.

[17] [2003] UKHL 12, [2004] 1 AC 715, [2003] 2 All ER 785.

out who the carrier is, it makes business common sense for a shipper to turn to the face of the bill, and in particular to the signature box, rather than clauses at the bottom of column two of the reverse side of the bill.

The exclusion of oral evidence to 'add to, vary or contradict' a written document has often been pronounced in peremptory language but in practice its operation is subject to a number of exceptions. In the first place, the evidence may be admitted to prove a custom or trade usage and thus to 'add' terms which do not appear on the face of the document and which alone give it the meaning which the parties wished it to possess.[18] In the second place, there is no reason why oral evidence should not be offered to show that, while on its face the document purports to record a valid and immediately enforceable contract, it had been previously agreed to suspend its operation until the occurrence of some event, such as the approval of a third party, and that this event had not yet taken place. The effect of such evidence is not to 'add to, vary or contradict' the terms of a written contract, but to make it clear that no contract has yet become effective.[19] Thirdly, there is a limited equitable jurisdiction to rectify a written document where it can be shown that it was executed by both parties under a common mistake. This will be discussed more fully later.[20]

Finally, the exclusion of oral evidence is clearly inappropriate where the document is designed to contain only part of the terms—where, in other words, the parties have made their contract partly in writing and partly by word of mouth. This situation is so comparatively frequent as in effect to deprive the ban on oral evidence of the strict character of a 'rule of law' which has been attributed to it. It will be presumed, 'that a document which *looks* like a contract is to be treated as the *whole* contract'.[21] But this presumption, though strong, is not irrebuttable. In each case the court must decide whether the parties have or have not reduced their agreement to the precise terms of an all-embracing written formula. If they have, oral evidence will not be admitted to vary or to contradict it; if they have not, the writing is but part of the contract and must be set side by side with the complementary oral terms. The question is at bottom one of intention and, like all such questions, elusive and conjectural. It would seem,

---

[18] P 172, below.   [19] *Pym v Campbell* (1856) 6 E & B 370.   [20] Pp 321–328, below.

[21] Wedderburn [1959] CLJ 58, esp at 59–64, citing Lord Russell of Killowen CJ in *Gillespie Bros v Cheney, Eggar & Co* [1896] 2 QB 59 at 62. Written contracts quite often contain clauses stating that the written contract is the whole of the agreement between the parties. It seems that at least between two parties who have had legal advice such a clause will be treated as meaning what it says. See *Deepak Fertilisers and Petrohemicals v Davy McKee (London) Ltd* (1998) 62 Con LR 86; *Inntrepeneur Pub Co Ltd v East Crown Ltd* [2000] Lloyd's Rep 611; *Watford Electronics Ltd v Sanderson CFL Ltd* [2001] 1 All ER (Comm) 696; *McGrath v Shah* (1987) 57 P & CR 452; *Leyland Motor Corpn of Australia v Wauer* [1981] 104 LSJS 460 (South Australia); *Thomas Witter Ltd v TBP Industries Ltd* [1996] 2 All ER 573 at 595–597. For a useful discussion of the impact of entire contract clauses on implied terms see *ExxonMobil Sales and Supply Corp v Texaco Ltd* [2003] EWHC 1964, [2004] 1 All ER (Comm) 435. No doubt in the final analysis, everything must turn on the precise words used and the context. However where one party to the contract is a consumer, the Director-General of Fair Trading in exercising his powers under the Unfair Terms in Consumer Contracts Regulations (see below p 257) has objected vigorously to such clauses.

however, that the more recent tendency is to infer, if the inference is at all possible, that the parties did not intend the writing to be exclusive but wished it to be read in conjunction with their oral statements.[22]

Thus in *Walker Property Investments (Brighton) Ltd v Walker*:[23]

The defendant in 1938, then in treaty for the lease of a flat in a house belonging to the plaintiffs, stipulated that, if he took the flat, he was to have the use of two basement rooms for the storage of his surplus furniture and also the use of the garden. Subsequently, a written agreement was drawn up for the lease of the flat, which made no reference either to the storage rooms or to the garden.

The Court of Appeal held that the oral agreements should be read with the written instrument so as to form one comprehensive contract.

So, too, in *Couchman v Hill*:[24]

The defendant's heifer was put up for auction. The sale catalogue described it as 'unserved', but added that the sale was 'subject to the auctioneers' usual conditions' and that the auctioneers would not be responsible for any error in the catalogue. The 'usual conditions' were exhibited at the auction and contained a clause that 'the lots were sold with all faults, imperfections and errors of description'. The plaintiff, before he bid, asked both the auctioneer and the defendant if they could confirm that the heifer was 'unserved', and they both said 'Yes'. On this under-standing he bid for and secured the heifer. It was later found that the heifer was in calf, and it died as a result of carrying its calf at too young an age.

On these facts the Court of Appeal held that the plaintiff was entitled to recover damages for breach of contract. The documents in the case, in their opinion, formed not the whole but part only of the contract, and the oral assurance could be laid side by side with them so as to constitute a single and binding transaction.

Yet another illustration is offered by the case of the *SS Ardennes (Cargo Owners) v Ardennes (Owners)*.[25]

The plaintiffs were growers of oranges in Spain and the defendants were ship-owners. The plaintiffs wished to export their oranges to England and shipped them on the defendants' vessel on the faith of an oral promise by the defendants' agent that the vessel would sail straight to London. In fact she went first to Antwerp, so that the oranges arrived late in London and the plaintiffs lost a favourable market. When the plaintiffs claimed damages for breach of contract, the defendants relied on the bill of lading which expressly allowed them to proceed 'by any route and whether directly or indirectly' to London.

[22] But see *Hutton v Watling* [1948] Ch 398, [1948] 1 All ER 803.
[23] (1947) 177 LT 204. Cf *Henderson v Arthur* [1907] 1 KB 10.
[24] [1947] KB 554, [1947] 1 All ER 103.
[25] [1951] 1 KB 55, [1950] 2 All ER 517.

Judgment was given for the plaintiffs. The bill of lading, while it was evidence of the contract between shipper and shipowner,[26] was not in the present case exclusive evidence. The oral promise made on behalf of the defendants was equally part of the contract and was binding upon them.

The practical effect of decisions such as this is to emasculate the parol evidence rule, since a party can always get such evidence before the court by pleading that the contract is not wholly in writing and modern courts are reluctant to limit the contract to a written document where to do so would cause injustice. There remain only the restrictions on the kinds of evidence which can be led to explain the *meaning* of contract. These are very important but are perhaps better regarded as a distinct doctrine since they apply equally to an oral contract.[27]

B Are the statements of the parties terms of the contract?

What the parties said or wrote may be clearly established; but it does not necessarily follow that all their words have become part of the contract. Their statements may be classified either as terms of the contract or as 'mere representation'. The distinction was long of great practical importance, but new developments have reduced its effect without lessening its conceptual significance.

If a statement is a term of the contract, it creates a legal obligation for whose breach an appropriate action lies at common law. If it is a 'mere representation', the position is more complicated.[28] It is clear that, if a party has been induced to make a contract by a fraudulent misrepresentation, he may sue in tort for deceit and may also treat the contract as voidable. But it was long believed to be a principle of the common law that there should be 'no damages for innocent misrepresentation', and that, in this context, 'innocent' meant any misrepresentation which was not fraudulent.[29] In the nineteenth century, equity indeed allowed the right of rescission to a party who had been induced to make a contract by such an 'innocent' misrepresentation, but this remedy was limited in a number of ways.[30] In 1963 in *Hedley Byrne & Co Ltd v Heller & Partners Ltd*,[31] the House of Lords held that in some circumstances damages could be obtained for negligent misstatement. The precise effect of this decision on the law of contract is not clear;[32] but, by the Misrepresentation Act 1967, representees acquired a remedy which in most cases will be preferable to an action of negligence. Section 2(1) of this

---

[26] It should be noted that situations such as this can be analysed either as one contract, partly oral, partly in writing, or as two contracts, one in writing, the second an oral collateral contract. Both analyses are to be found in the cases. See pp 170–172, below.

[27] The Law Commission considered whether the parol evidence rule should be amended or abolished and decided that no change was necessary (Law Com No 154, 1986) Carter 1 JCL 33.

[28] The effect of misrepresentation is discussed fully in Ch 9, below.

[29] See per Lord Moulton in *Heilbut Symons & Co v Buckleton* [1913] AC 30 at 48.

[30] Pp 315–319, below.

[31] [1964] AC 465, [1963] 2 All ER 575.   [32] Pp 343–347, below.

Act in effect gives a right to damages to anyone induced to enter a contract by a negligent misrepresentation, and casts upon the representor the burden of disproving negligence.[33] But, where a statement is made neither fraudulently nor negligently, the injured party can still obtain damages only by showing that it forms part of his contract. Contractual cartography thus remains important.

To draw the map of the contract, at least where it is not wholly committed to writing, has proved as difficult as it is important. In the copious litigation which the problem has provoked, three subsidiary tests have been suggested as possible aids to its solution.

(a) *At what stage of the transaction was the crucial statement made?* It must, in the opinion of the court, have been designed as a term of the contract and not merely be an incident in the preliminary negotiations. Two cases may be contrasted.

In *Bannerman v White*:[34]

> A prospective buyer, in the course of negotiating for the purchase of hops, asked the seller if any sulphur had been used in their treatment, adding that, if it had, he would not even trouble to ask the price. The seller answered that no sulphur had been used. The negotiations thereupon proceeded and resulted in a contract of sale. It was later discovered that sulphur had been used in the cultivation of a portion of the hops—5 acres out of 300—and the buyer, when sued for the price, claimed that he was justified in refusing to observe the contract.

The buyer's claim could not be upheld unless the statement as to the absence of sulphur was intended to be part of the contract, for the jury found that there was no fraud on the part of the seller. The buyer contended that the whole interview was one transaction, that he had declared the importance he attached to his inquiry, and that the seller must have known that if sulphur had been used there could be no further question of a purchase of the hops. The seller, on the other hand, contended that the conversation was merely preliminary to, and in no sense a part of, the contract. The jury found that the seller's statement was understood and intended by both parties to be part of the contract, and their finding was unanimously confirmed by the Court of Common Pleas.

In *Routledge v McKay*:[35]

> The plaintiff and defendant were discussing the possible purchase and sale of the defendant's motorcycle. Both parties were private persons. The defendant, taking the information from the registration book, said on 23 October that the cycle was a 1942 model. On 30 October a written contract of sale was made, which did not refer to the date of the model. The actual date was later found to be 1930. The buyer's claim for damages failed in the Court of Appeal.

---

[33] Pp 347–350, below.   [34] (1861) 10 CBNS 844.
[35] [1954] 1 All ER 855, [1954] 1 WLR 615.

In this case, the interval between the negotiations and the contract was well marked. But the facts are not always so accommodating; and the courts, in their anxiety to reach a result which may reasonably reflect the presumed intention of the parties, have more than once treated the making of the contract as a protracted process. An instance is offered by *Schawel v Reade*, an Irish case which came on appeal to the House of Lords in 1913.[36]

> The plaintiff, who wanted a stallion for stud purposes, started to examine a horse advertised for sale by the defendant. The defendant interrupted him, saying 'You need not look for anything: the horse is perfectly sound'. The plaintiff therefore stopped his examination. A few days later the price was agreed, and three weeks later the sale was concluded. The horse in fact was unfit for stud purposes.

The trial judge asked the jury two questions: (1) 'Did the defendant, at the time of the sale, represent to the plaintiff that it was fit for stud purposes?' (2) 'Did the plaintiff act on that representation in the purchase of the horse?' The vital factor was whether the representation had been made 'at the time of the sale'. The jury found that it had, and the House of Lords held that the defendant's statement was a term of the contract.

(b) *Was the oral statement followed by a reduction of the terms to writing?* If it was so followed, the court must decide whether it was the intention of the parties that the contract should be comprised wholly in their document or whether the contract was to be partly written and partly oral.[37] The exclusion of an oral statement from the document may suggest that it was not intended to be a contractual term. The facts of *Routledge v McKay* tend to support such a construction.[38] But in other cases the courts have not shrunk from reading together an earlier oral statement and a later document so as to unite them in a single comprehensive contract. In *Birch v Paramount Estates Ltd*:[39]

> The defendants, who were developing an estate, offered a house they were then building to the plaintiff, saying 'it would be as good as the show house'. The plaintiff later agreed to buy the house, and the written contract of sale contained no reference to this particular representation. The house was not as good as the show house.

The Court of Appeal treated the defendants' statement as part of the concluded contract and allowed the plaintiff's claim for damages.

---

[36] [1913] 2 IR 81. Cf *Hopkins v Tanqueray* (1854) 15 CB 130.
[37] P 163, above.
[38] P 166, above.
[39] (1956) 167 Estates Gazette 396, cited in *Oscar Chess Ltd v Williams* [1957] 1 All ER 325 at 329. Cf *Heilbut Symons & Co v Buckleton* [1913] AC 30, critically analysed by Greig in 87 LQR 179 at 185–190.

(c) *Had the person who made the statement special knowledge or skill as compared with the other party?* If this is the case, the court may be more willing to infer an intention to make the statement a term of the contract. Such was the position in *Birch v Paramount Estates Ltd* and in *Schawel v Reade*,[40] and such was at least a contributory factor in the decision of the Court of Appeal in *Harling v Eddy*.[41]

> The defendant offered his heifer for sale by auction. The auction catalogue contained a clause that 'no animal is . . . sold with a warranty unless specially mentioned at the time of offering, and no warranty so given shall have any legal force or effect unless the terms thereof appear on the purchaser's account'. The heifer had an 'unpromising appearance' and buyers held aloof until the defendant said that there was 'nothing wrong with her' and that he would 'absolutely guarantee her in every respect'. The plaintiff then bid for her and bought her. She was in fact tubercular and she died.

The defendant's guarantee was, in the language of the catalogue, 'specially mentioned at the time of offering', but it did not 'appear on the purchaser's account'. But the defendant had exclusive means of knowing the heifer's condition, and the Court of Appeal allowed the plaintiff to recover damages.

The third test may perhaps offer a less dubious guide to the intention of the parties than either of the two previous tests. But none of them is to be regarded as decisive. In the words of Lord Moulton:

> [they] may be criteria of value in guiding a jury in coming to a decision whether or not a warranty was intended; but they cannot be said to furnish decisive tests, because it cannot be said as a matter of law that the presence or absence of those features is conclusive of the intention of the parties. [This] can only be deduced from the totality of the evidence, and no secondary principles of such a kind can be universally true.[42]

These three criteria must therefore be received only as possible aids to the interpretation of the facts. Their impact upon the members of a court is vividly illustrated by the case of *Oscar Chess Ltd v Williams*.[43]

> The plaintiffs were car dealers, and the defendant wished to obtain from them on hire purchase a new Hillman Minx and to offer a second-hand Morris car in part exchange. The sum available for the Morris depended on its age. According to the registration book its date was 1948; the defendant in good faith confirmed this, and the plaintiffs believed him. On this assumption the sum to be allowed for it was £290. The parties then orally agreed that the plaintiffs would arrange for the hire purchase of the new Hillman, would take the Morris and allow £290 for it.

[40] N 36, above.
[41] [1951] 2 KB 739, [1951] 2 All ER 212. See also *Coffey v Dickson* [1960] NZLR 1135.
[42] *Heilbut Symons & Co v Buckleton* [1913] AC 30 at 50–51.
[43] [1957] 1 All ER 325, [1957] 1 WLR 370.

This agreement was carried out. Eight months later the plaintiffs found that the date of the Morris was not 1948 but 1939, the trade-in price for which year was only £175. The registration book had presumably been altered by a previous holder before reaching the defendant's hands. The plaintiffs now sued the defendant for the difference between the two allowances ie £115.

The county court judge held that the statement as to the age of the car was a term in the contract and gave judgment for the plaintiffs. This decision was reversed by a majority in the Court of Appeal (Denning and Hodson LJJ). Morris LJ dissented. It is instructive to apply each of the suggested tests to the facts. There was no apparent or substantial interval between the statement as to the age of the car and the agreement of hire purchase. The first and chronological test should therefore have helped the plaintiffs. As Morris LJ said, 'there was a statement made at the time of the transaction'. The second test was also in the plaintiff's favour. Nothing had been reduced to writing and no point could therefore have been made of the superior claims of a document over mere word of mouth. Hodson LJ was driven to say that 'the distinction is a fine one, and one which I shall be reluctant to draw unless compelled to do so'; and Denning LJ emphasised the undoubted truth that there is no basic difference between a written and an oral contract. The third test, on the other hand, so far as it was applicable to the facts, told in the defendant's favour. It was not he, the maker of the statement, but the plaintiffs, as car dealers, who possessed special knowledge and skill and who, if anyone, could have discovered in time the true age of the car.

In this case it may seem unfortunate that a serious statement of manifest importance to the parties was not held to be a term of the contract. Some such impression is left by many of the decisions; and the anxiety of the judges to escape from a perennial dilemma may be illustrated by the subsequent case of *Dick Bentley Productions Ltd v Harold Smith (Motors) Ltd*.[44]

> The plaintiffs told the defendants that they were looking for a 'well-vetted' Bentley car. The defendants said that they had such a car. One morning Mr Bentley went to see it, and the defendants told him that it had done only 20,000 miles since fitted with a replacement engine and gearbox. In the afternoon Mr Bentley took the car for a short run and bought it. The plaintiffs later found that the car was unsatisfactory and that the statement as to mileage was untrue. They sued for damages.

---

[44] [1965] 2 All ER 65, [1965] 1 WLR 623. Sealy [1965] CLJ 178. See also *Beale v Taylor* [1967] 3 All ER 253, [1967] 1 WLR 1193, where the vintage of the car was held to be part of its description within s 13 of Sale of Goods Act 1893. On the other hand in *Harlingdon and Leinster Enterprises Ltd v Christopher Hull Fine Art Ltd* [1991] QB 564, [1990] 1 All ER 737 a statement as to the attribution of a painting was treated as not part of the description because the seller knew less about the alleged painter than the buyer even though the seller charged a price appropriate to a genuine article. It is an odd feature of the overlap between general contract law and the law of sale of goods that it is possible to argue that such statements are either express terms or implied terms or representations.

The Court of Appeal held that the defendants' statement was a term of the contract and that the plaintiffs were entitled to damages. This decision may readily be accepted; but it was necessary to distinguish *Oscar Chess Ltd v Williams*. Lord Denning, who was a member of the court in both cases, found the distinction in the presence or absence of negligence. In *Oscar Chess Ltd v Williams* the defendant had not been negligent. In *Dick Bentley Productions Ltd v Harold Smith (Motors) Ltd* negligence was present: the defendants 'ought to have known better'.

It is difficult to understand why a statement should be a term of the contract if it is negligent and a 'mere representation' if it is not.[45] It might have been safer to have based the decision upon the existence of a 'collateral' contract. This approach seems to have been envisaged by Salmon LJ.

> In effect, Mr Smith said: 'If you will enter into a contract to buy this motor car from me for £1,850, I undertake that you will be getting a motor car which has done no more than twenty thousand miles since it was fitted with a new engine and a new gearbox.'[46]

There is ample authority for the use of a 'collateral' contract to avoid the dilemma of 'term' or 'representation'. A significant case is that of *City and Westminster Properties (1934) Ltd v Mudd.*[47]

> The defendant had been for six years the tenant of the plaintiffs' shop, to which a small room was annexed and in which, as they knew, he was accustomed to sleep. In 1947 he was negotiating for a new lease, and the plaintiffs inserted a clause restricting the use of the premises to 'showrooms, workrooms and offices only'. The plaintiffs' agent orally assured the defendant that, if he accepted the lease with this clause intact, he would still be allowed to sleep on the premises. On this understanding he signed the lease. The plaintiffs now brought an action against him for forfeiture of the lease on the ground that he had broken the covenant restricting the use of the premises.

Harman J held that the defendant had indeed broken this covenant but that, in answer to the breach, he could plead the collateral contract made before the lease was signed. This, he said, is:

> . . . a case of a promise made to him before the execution of the lease that, if he would execute it in the form put before him, the landlord would not seek to enforce against him personally the covenant about using the property as a shop only. The defendant says that it was in reliance on this promise the he executed the lease and entered on the onerous obligations contained in it. He says, moreover, that but for the promise made he would not have executed the lease, but

---

[45] The presence of negligence may, of course, be significant both in opening the possibility of an action in tort and in proceedings under the Misrepresentation Act 1967; p 166, above and pp 347–350, below.

[46] [1965] 2 All ER 65 at 68, [1965] 1 WLR at 629. See also *Esso Petroleum Co Ltd v Mardon* [1976] QB 801, [1976] 2 All ER 5.

[47] [1959] Ch 129, [1958] 2 All ER 733. For collateral contracts, see p 81, above.

would have moved to other premises available to him at the time. If these be the facts, there was a clear contract acted on by the tenant to his detriment and from which the landlords cannot be allowed to resile.[48]

The contract protecting the defendant was clearly separate from the tenancy agreement and may thus be stated: 'if you will promise me not to enforce this particular clause in the lease I will promise to execute it'.

It will be seen that where parties enter into a written contract after one party has made oral assurances there are at least three possibilities:

(1) the contract is contained wholly in the written document;[49]

(2) the contract is partly written and partly oral;[50] or

(3) there are two contracts, there being an oral collateral contract as well as the written contract.[51]

In the first case, it is possible that the assurances will give rise to liability under the law relating to misrepresentation, where they amount to a statement of fact.[52]

In many cases, the second and third alternatives appear to be treated as interchangeable. So in *Evans (J) & Sons (Portsmouth) Ltd v Andrea Merzario Ltd*:[53]

The plaintiffs were in the habit of importing machines from Italy and for this purpose they used the services of the defendants forwarding agents, business being conducted on the standard conditions of the forwarding trade. Prior to 1967 it had always been arranged that the goods would be carried below deck because of the risk of corrosion. In 1967 the defendants decided to change over to transportation in containers and there were discussions with the plaintiffs, who were orally assured that the goods would be carried below deck.[54] On this basis the plaintiffs continued to employ the defendants under printed standard conditions which permitted the defendants to arrange for the goods to be carried on deck. On one voyage goods belonging to the plaintiffs were carried on deck and lost when they slid into the sea. The Court of Appeal held that the defendants could not rely on the printed conditions. Lord Denning MR analysed the oral assurance as amounting to a collateral contract. Roskill and Geoffrey Lane LJJ held that there was a single contract, partly written and partly oral.

The differences in analysis often, as here, produce no difference in result but there are cases where the difference appears significant. One is where the contract is required to

---

[48] Ibid at 145–146 and 742–743, respectively.

[49] Eg *Routledge v McKay* [1954] 1 All ER 855, [1954] 1 WLR 615.

[50] Eg *Couchman v Hill* [1947] KB 554, [1947] 1 All ER 103.

[51] Eg *City and Westminster Properties (1934) Ltd v Mudd* [1959] Ch 129, [1958] 2 All ER 733.

[52] See pp 332–337, below.   [53] [1976] 2 All ER 930, [1976] 1 WLR 1078.

[54] Far more cargo is carried above deck in container ships than in ships designed for conventional carrying.

be in writing as in a lease. Another is where the rights under the written contract are likely to be transferred as in leases or bills of lading. If there are two contracts, it is possible to argue that the rights under the written contract have been transferred and that those under the oral collateral contract have not.

2 IMPLIED TERMS[55]

The normal contract is not an isolated act, but an incident in the conduct of business or in the framework of some more general relation such as that of landlord and tenant. It will frequently be set against a background of usage, familiar to all who engage in similar negotiations and which may be supposed to govern the language of a particular agreement. In addition, therefore, to the terms which the parties have expressly adopted, there may be others imported into the contract from its context. These implications may be derived from custom or they may rest upon statute or they may be inferred by the judges to reinforce the language of the parties and realise their manifest intention.

A Terms implied by custom

It is a well-established rule that a contract may be subject to terms that are sanctioned by custom, whether commercial or otherwise, although they have not been expressly mentioned by the parties. In *Hutton v Warren* in 1836[56] it was proved that, by a local custom, a tenant was bound to farm according to a certain course of husbandry and that, at quitting his tenancy, he was entitled to a fair allowance for seed and labour on the arable land. The Court of Exchequer held that the lease made by the parties must be construed in the light of this custom. The judgment of Baron Parke is illuminating both on the possibility of importing terms into a contract and on the underlying rationale.

> It has long been settled, that, in commercial transactions, extrinsic evidence of custom and usage is admissible to annex incidents to written contracts, in matters with respect to which they are silent. The same rule has also been applied to contracts in other transactions of life, in which known usages have been established and prevailed; and this has been done upon the principle of presumption that, in such transactions, the parties did not mean to express in writing the whole of the contract by which they intended to be bound, but a contract with reference to those known usages. Whether such a relaxation of the strictness of the common law was wisely applied, where formal instruments have been entered into, and particularly leases under seal, may well be doubted; but the contrary has been established by

---

[55] Phang [1993] JBL 242.   [56] (1836) 1 M & W 466.

such authority, and the relation between landlord and tenant have been so long regulated upon the supposition that all customary obligations, not altered by the contract, are to remain in force, that it is too late to pursue a contrary course; and it would be productive of much inconvenience, if this practice were now to be disturbed.

The common law, indeed, does so little to prescribe the relative duties of landlord and tenant, since it leaves the latter at liberty to pursue any course of management he pleases, provided he is not guilty of waste, that it is by no means surprising that the Courts should have been favourably inclined to the introduction of those regulations in the mode of cultivation which custom and usage have established in each district to be the most beneficial to all parties.[57]

A later illustration of the place of custom in contracts is offered by *Produce Brokers Co Ltd v Olympia Oil and Cake Co Ltd* in 1916.[58]

A written agreement for the sale of goods provided that 'all disputes *arising out of this contract* shall be referred to arbitration'. A dispute was submitted to arbitrators who in their award insisted on taking into consideration a particular custom of the trade.

The House of Lords held that they were right to do so. Lord Sumner said:[59]

The real question . . . is the definition of the limits as expressed in the submission [to arbitration]. If 'this contract' in the arbitration clause means the real bargain between the parties, expressed in the written and printed terms, though, where trade customs exist and apply, not entirely so expressed, then the jurisdiction [of the arbitrators] is complete. The custom, if any, was part of the bargain . . . If the bargain is partly expressed in ink and partly implied by the tacit incorporation of trade customs, the first function submitted to the arbitrators is to find out what it is: to read the language, to ascertain the custom, to interpret them both, and to give effect to the whole . . . The dispute, which arose in fact and which raised a question of custom, did not arise out of the contract *and* something else; it arose *out of the contract itself,* and involved the contract by raising the custom, and so was within the submission.

The importation of usage, as it rests on the assumption that it represents the wishes of the parties, must be excluded if the express language of the contract discloses a contrary intention. The parties must then be supposed, while appreciating the general practice, to have chosen to depart from it. *Expressum facit cessare tacitum.* The position, which, indeed, might be considered self-evident, was vigorously stated by Lord Birkenhead in *Les Affréteurs Réunis Société Anonyme v Walford.*[60]

---

[57] (1836) 1 M & W 466 at 475–476.

[58] [1916] 1 AC 314. See also *Cunliffe-Owen v Teather and Greenwood* [1967] 3 All ER 561, [1967] 1 WLR 1421.

[59] Ibid at 330–331.

[60] [1919] AC 801; affirming [1918] 2 KB 498. See p 578, below, as to the right of the broker to sue upon a contract to which he was not a party.

Walford, as broker, had negotiated a charterparty between the owners of the SS 'Flore' and the Lubricating and Fuel Oils Co Ltd. By a clause in the charterparty the owners promised the charterers to pay Walford, *on signing the charter*, a commission of 3 per cent on the estimated gross amount of hire. The owners, defending an action brought by Walford for this commission, pleaded, into alia, a custom of the trade that commission was payable only when hire had actually been earned. The 'Flore' had been requisitioned by the French Government before the charterparty could be operated and no hire had in fact been earned.

Despite the incompatibility of any such custom with the clause in the contract requiring payment as soon as the parties signed, Bailhache J accepted the plea and gave judgment for the defendants. Lord Birkenhead, reversing the decision, castigated an unhappy error.[61]

> The learned judge . . . has in effect declared that a custom may be given effect to in commercial matters which is entirely inconsistent with the plain words of an agreement into which commercial men, certainly acquainted with so well-known a custom, have nevertheless thought proper to enter.

Custom thus comes not to destroy but to fulfil the law. It must not contradict the express terms of a contract but must serve rather to reinforce them and assist their general purpose and policy. Lord Jenkins has emphasised both the negative and the positive test to be applied before it is to be admitted.

> An alleged custom can be incorporated into a contract only if there is nothing in the express or necessarily implied terms of the contract to prevent such inclusion and, further, that a custom will only be imported into a contract where it can be so imported consistently with the tenor of the document as a whole.[62]

If, however, a custom satisfies these tests, its operation may be far-reaching. This has certainly been the case in the past. It is not too much to say that the greater part of modern commercial law, and, as Baron Parke stated in *Hutton v Warren*, no small portion of the law governing landlord and tenant, have been constructed upon its basis. The development of the law exhibits a fairly constant process. A particular practice is shown to exist and the parties to a contract are proved to have relied upon it. In course of time it is assumed by the courts to be so prevalent in a trade or locality as to form the foundation of all contracts made within that trade or locality, unless expressly excluded. Finally, it is often adopted by the legislature as the standard rule for the conduct of the business in question. The law in such cases is not so much

---

[61] [1919] AC at 809.
[62] *London Export Corpn Ltd v Jubilee Coffee Roasting Co* [1958] 2 All ER 411 at 420, [1958] 1 WLR 661 at 675. See also *Kum v Wah Tat Bank Ltd* [1971] 1 Lloyd's Rep 439.

imposed *ab extra* by judges or Parliament as developed by the pressure of commercial convenience or local idiosyncrasy.

This process of development can be traced in many branches of the commercial law. As soon as the common law courts busied themselves with the problems of marine insurance, they accepted the necessity of construing the words of a policy in the light of the surrounding circumstances. In *Pelly v Royal Exchange Assurance*[63] in 1757:

> The plaintiff had insured his ship and tackle during the whole voyage from London to China and back again to London. On arrival in the River Canton, the tackle, according to the usage of the ship-masters, was removed and put into a warehouse where it was accidentally burnt.

To claim on the policy it was objected that, as the loss had occurred on shore at the end of the outward journey, it was not within the compass of the voyage and fell outside the insured risks. Lord Mansfield refused the contention.

> What is usually done by such a ship, with such a cargo and in such a voyage, is understood to be referred to by every policy; and to make a part of it, as much as it was expressed.

Various terms came to be implied as a matter of course in all policies, some vital and some subsidiary; though, with the inveterate tendency, both of businessmen and of lawyers, to confuse the issues by careless phraseology, the word 'warranty' was obstinately established in the law of marine insurance where, at least in modern speech, 'condition' was more appropriate. Thus, to give only one example, it was regarded as vital that an insured ship should be seaworthy, and the courts therefore implied a 'warranty' to this effect in every policy. In the words of Baron Parke:[64]

> In the case of an insurance for a certain voyage, it is clearly established that there is an implied warranty that the vessel shall be sea-worthy, by which it is meant that she shall be in a fit state as to repairs, equipment and crew, and in all other respects, to encounter the ordinary perils of the voyage insured at the time of sailing upon it.

This and other terms are now implied in policies by sections 33 to 41 of the Marine Insurance Act 1906, which incidentally perpetuates the terminological confusion by providing that 'a warranty is a condition which must be exactly complied with, whether it be material to the risk or not', and that its breach discharges the insurer as from the moment of its occurrence.[65] The contractual basis of the liability is sustained by the proviso that the 'warranty' shall be excluded by an express term, if the two are inconsistent.[66]

---

[63] 1 Burr 341; and see *Salvador v Hopkins* (1765) 3 Burr 1707.
[64] In *Dixon v Sadler* (1839) 5 M & W 405 at 414.
[65] Marine Insurance Act 1906, s 33 (3).
[66] Ibid, s 35(3).

B Terms implied by statute

The provisions of the Marine Insurance Act offer an obvious example of terms implied by statute as the culmination of a long process of development. But the translation of usage into agreement and of agreement into statutory language is most evident in the history of contracts for the sale of goods. Buyers and sellers frequently fail to express themselves with regard to matters that may later provoke a dispute. Two illustrations may be given.

Suppose that the seller is in fact not the owner of the goods which he has purported to sell. Must he be taken to have tacitly guaranteed the fact of his ownership?

Suppose that the goods are useless for the purpose for which the buyer requires them. Is it a tacit term of the contract that they shall be suitable for that purpose?

At first the common law judges refused to recognise any term which had not been expressly inserted in the contract. Thus, in the second hypothesis propounded above, the foundation of the common law, as of Roman law,[67] was the maxim *caveat emptor*. In the absence of fraud, and provided that the goods were open to inspection, the buyer could not complain of defects in the article bought. He should have used his own judgement and not have expected the seller to depreciate his own wares, for he was always free to protect himself by exacting an express warranty.

The original rule, however, was gradually modified by the usage of the market, which recognised that there were several cases in which a contract of sale was subject to a tacit undertaking by the seller; and, during the first half of the nineteenth century, these modifications were recognised by the courts and adopted as normal implications in such contracts. Thus, in a sale *by sample* it was an implied term of the contract that the bulk should correspond with the sample and that the buyer should, by examination, be able to satisfy himself of such correspondence.[68] In a sale *by description*, the goods must not only answer the description but must be of 'merchantable quality'.[69] If, moreover, a buyer explained that he required goods for a particular purpose and that he relied on the seller's skill and judgement to provide such goods, then the seller, unless he expressly guarded himself, was taken to have accepted this additional responsibility.[70] There was more hesitation in deciding whether, upon the sale of goods, the seller impliedly undertook to transfer a good title. The implication was denied by Baron Parke as late as 1849,[71] but in 1864 Erle CJ asserted its existence, and his view prevailed.[72]

By 1868, when Benjamin published the first edition of his *Treatise on the Sale of Personal Property*, he was able to assume that the courts had completed their

---

[67] Mackintosh *Roman Law of Sale*, note D.
[68] *Parker v Palmer* (1821) 4 B & Ald 387; *Lorymer v Smith* (1822) 1 B & C 1.
[69] *Gardiner v Gray* (1815) 4 Camp 144.   [70] *Jones v Bright* (1829) 5 Bing 533.
[71] *Morley v Attenborough* (1849) 3 Exch 500.   [72] *Eichholz v Bannister* (1864) 17 CBNS 708.

absorption of commercial practice. By that date the list of tacit undertakings to be read into a contract for the sale of goods was virtually closed. The time was ripe for codification, and the various implications which the judges had gradually accepted were ultimately adopted as normal terms of the contract by the Sale of Goods Act 1893, wherever the parties had not evinced a contrary intention.

The Sale of Goods Act 1893, was substantially a codification of the common law of sale as the draftsman, Sir Mackenzie Chalmers, perceived it.[73] It consists for a large part, of rules which are to be applied unless the parties provide otherwise. As far as the seller's obligations as to title and as to the quality of the goods are concerned, the relevant sections are sections 12–15,[74] which operate by implying terms into the contract. These terms could however be excluded by contrary intention[75] and it became not unusual for sellers to seek to exclude the undertakings which would otherwise be implied.[76] The example provided by the Sale of Goods Act 1893 was developed by legislation dealing with the related contract of hire purchase.

It is over a hundred years since manufacturers and traders first sought to reach potential customers who could not afford at once to pay the price of their goods.[77] They began to make contracts whereby the price was payable in instalments and the possession of the goods passed at once to the customer, but the supplier retained the ownership until the last instalment had been paid. By this means they hoped to protect themselves even if the customer, before completing payment, improperly sold the goods to an honest buyer. But by section 9 of the Factors Act 1889, substantially reproduced in section 25(2) of the Sale of Goods Act 1979, a person who has agreed to buy goods and who has obtained possession of them with the seller's consent may, by delivering them to a *bona fide* purchaser or pledgee, pass a good title. In *Lee v Butler*.[78]

---

[73] Later writers have sometimes doubted whether his perception of the common law was correct. See eg the difficulties over s 6, discussed below. The Act is by no means identical with Chalmers' draft bill: see the first (1890) and the second (1894) editions of Chalmers *Sale of Goods*.

[74] Earlier editions of this work contained a much fuller account of this topic but although of great interest and importance, it is more appropriately discussed in works on sale. See *Benjamin's Sale of Goods* (4th edn, 1992) ch 11; Atiyah *The Sale of Goods* (9th edn, 1995) chs 8–12; Furmston, *Sale and Supply of Goods* (3rd edn, 2000).

[75] There was a dispute as to whether the seller could exclude his implied undertakings as to title under s 12, but this is now of purely historical interest.

[76] Such attempts were perhaps less frequent than sometimes suggested. A seller would be most likely to seek to exclude his implied obligations in a consumer transaction. But most consumer sales are made without a written contract, the usual vehicle for exclusion clauses. For this reason exclusion clauses were much more common in hire-purchase transactions, where there is always a written contract.

[77] See Thornely [1962] CLJ 39. The major works are Goode *Hire Purchase Law and Practice* (2nd edn, 1970) and Guest *The Law of Hire Purchase* (1966). A valuable introduction is Diamond *Commercial and Consumer Credit* (3rd edn, 1985).

[78] [1893] 2 QB 318.

> The plaintiff let furniture on a 'hire and purchase agreement' to X. X was to pay £1 at once and the balance of £96 in monthly instalments from May to August. The furniture was to become X's property only when the last instalment was paid. Before this condition was satisfied X sold and delivered the furniture to the defendant.

The Court of Appeal held that, on the proper construction of the agreement, X was under an absolute obligation to pay all the instalments and that he had therefore 'agreed to buy' the furniture. He had accordingly passed a good title to the defendant, who could not be sued by the plaintiff.

To avoid this result a new device was adopted and was tested in *Helby v Matthews (Olivetti)*.[79]

> The plaintiff, a dealer, agreed to hire a piano to X at a monthly rent. If the rent was duly paid for 36 months the ownership would pass to X; but X was entitled to terminate the hiring whenever he pleased. After paying four instalments X improperly pledged the piano to the defendant.

The House of Lords held that, as X could determine the hiring at any time, he was not under any obligation to buy the piano but had only an option of purchase. He had therefore not 'agreed to buy it', neither section 9 of the Factors Act nor section 25(2) of the Sale of Goods Act applied, and no title passed to the defendant. Henceforth manufacturers and dealers preferred to adopt not the first but the second form of contract—a bailment coupled with an option to purchase. 'Hire purchase' was not yet a term of art, but it was a potent commercial instrument.

The twentieth century saw an enormous extension of this type of business, covering an ever-widening range of goods. The diversity of transactions has demanded a corresponding diversity of legal machinery; and, with the growth not only of the total volume of hire purchase but of the cost of the individual articles involved, the monetary resources of dealers have had to be reinforced by the formation of finance companies. In addition to the earlier and simpler 'hire-purchase contract' between supplier and customer there has been evolved a complex arrangement between supplier, customer and finance company. Thus, if a customer wishes to obtain a car from a dealer on hire-purchase terms, the dealer will not as a rule make the hire-purchase contract directly with the customer. He will sell the car to a finance company, and the finance company will let it on hire purchase to the customer. Three contracts may thus be involved: a 'collateral' or 'preliminary' contract between dealer and the customer, a contract of sale between the dealer and the finance company, and a contract of hire purchase between the finance company and the customer. The extent to which economic reality has thus been divorced from legal mechanics has more than once been exposed by the courts. In *Yeoman Credit Ltd v Apps* Lord Justice Harman said:[80]

---

[79] [1895] AC 471.   [80] [1962] 2 QB 508 at 522, [1961] 2 All ER 281 at 291.

The difficulty and the artificiality about hire-purchase cases arise from the fact that the member of the public involved imagines himself to be buying the article by instalments from the dealer, whereas he is in law the hirer of the article from a finance company with whom he has been brought willy-nilly into contact, of whom he knows nothing and which, on its part has never seen the goods which are the subject-matter of the hire.

In *Bridge v Campbell Discount Co Ltd*, Lord Denning[81] translated the facts into legal forms or fictions.

> If you were able to strip off the legal trappings in which [the present transaction] has been dressed and see it in its native simplicity, you would discover that [the appellant] agreed to buy a car from a dealer for £405, but could only find £105 towards it. So he borrowed the other £300 from a finance house and got them to pay it to the dealer, and he gave the finance house a charge on the car as security for repayment. But if you tried to express the transaction in those simple terms, you would soon fall into troubles of all sorts under the Bills of Sale Acts, the Sale of Goods Act and the Moneylenders Acts. In order to avoid these legal obstacles, the finance house has to discard the rôle of a lender of money on security and it has to become an owner of goods who let them out on hire . . . So it buys the goods from the dealer and lets them out on hire to [the appellant]. [The appellant] has to discard the rôle of a man who has agreed to buy goods and he has to become a man who takes them on hire with only an option of purchase . . . And when these new rôles have been assumed, the finance house is not a moneylender but a hire-purchase company free of the trammels of the Moneylenders Acts.

The dominant party in this transaction is the finance company; and the comparative weakness of the customer, combined with the insidious temptation to improvidence, has forced Parliament to come to the customer's aid. The first Hire Purchase Act was passed in 1938.

It was followed by further Acts in 1954, 1964, and 1965. None of these Acts applied to all contracts of hire purchase but only to those where the 'hire-purchase price'[82] was below a certain figure. There were therefore two sets of rules applicable to contracts of hire purchase; a statutory set for those within the financial ambit of the relevant statute and a common law set for those falling outside. The relative importance of common law and statute varied as inflation eroded the real value of the current limit. In particular many hire-purchase transactions concerning cars fell outside the statute during the 1950s and early 1960s when the limit was still the £300 settled in 1938.

---

[81] [1962] AC 600 at 627, [1962] 1 All ER 385 at 398.

[82] Ie 'the total sum payable by the hirer under a hire-purchase agreement in order to complete the purchase of goods to which the agreement relates, exclusive of any sum payable as a penalty or as compensation or damages for a breach of the agreement': Hire Purchase Act 1965, s 58(1).

Whether a hire-purchase contract fell under statute or common law, terms would normally be implied in it. The courts in implying terms into common law hire-purchase transactions relied on the helpful analogies provided by the Sale of Goods Act 1893 while the draftsman of the various Hire Purchase Acts also built upon the models provided by the earlier Act. The terms implied at common law or under the statute were therefore similar but not identical. So for instance both followed section 12 of the Sale of Goods Act in holding that the owner (seller) had implied obligations as to title but while under the Hire Purchase Act 1965[83] the term implied was that the owner shall have 'a right to sell the goods *at the time when property is to pass*', at common law the courts implied a term that the owner should have a right to sell the goods both at the time when the hiring commences and at the time when the property is to pass.[84]

There was however a most important difference between the position at common law and under the Hire Purchase Acts. At common law the implied terms, like those in the Sale of Goods Act 1893, could in principle be excluded by contrary agreement[85] but under the Hire Purchase Acts the owner was either prohibited from contracting out of his implied obligations[86] or allowed to do so only in certain strictly defined conditions.[87]

The position in regard to both sale and hire purchase was carried a stage further by the Supply of Goods (Implied Terms) Act 1973.[88] This Act made a number of very important changes. First, it amended the implied terms contained in sections 12, 13, 14 of the Sale of Goods Act 1893. The new implied terms are very much in historical prolongation of the old, but the opportunity was taken to fill gaps and remedy deficiencies which eighty years of experience had revealed.

Secondly, the new implied terms (and also section 15 of the Sale of Goods Act 1893, dealing with sales by sample which was not amended by the 1973 Act) have been extended to all contracts of hire-purchase, irrespective of the ambit of the Hire Purchase Act.

Finally, the Act contained comprehensive provisions, prohibiting or limiting the power of the seller (owner) to exclude these implied obligations. These will be discussed more fully later.[89]

The Sale of Goods Act 1893 together with its later amendments has now been consolidated in the Sale of Goods Act 1979. The statutory regime for sale of goods coexisted with a common law regime for similar contracts for the supply of goods.

---

[83] S 17(1).   [84] *Karflex Ltd v Poole* [1933] 2 KB 251.

[85] Subject to the various common law rules as to such exclusions. Discussed pp 202–230, below.

[86] Eg Hire Purchase Act 1965, 17(1), 18(3), 19(2) and 29(3) (implied terms as to title and description).

[87] Eg Hire Purchase Act 1965, ss 17(2), (3), (4), 18(1), (2), (3) (implied terms as to merchantability and fitness for purchase).

[88] This gives effect, subject to some modifications, to the first report of the Law Commission on exemption clauses in contracts (Law Com No 24, 1969). See Carr 36 MLR 519; Turpin [1973] CLJ 203.

[89] Pp 231–257, below.

Thus in *Samuels v Davis*:[90]

The plaintiff was a dentist who agreed with the defendant to make a set of false teeth for the defendant's wife. The teeth were made and delivered, but the defendant refused to pay for them on the ground that they were so unsatisfactory that his wife could not use them.

There was controversy as to whether the contract was for the sale of goods or for work and materials, but the Court of Appeal held that, in the circumstances of the case, the question was irrelevant. If it were the former, the provisions of the Sale of Goods Act applied; if the latter, they would import into the contract, on the analogy of the Act, a term that the teeth should be reasonably fit for their purpose. The implied terms for such contracts as work and materials, exchange and hire are now laid down by the Supply of Goods and Services Act 1982 in terms which follow very closely those of the Sale of Goods Act 1979. Further amendments have been made by the Sale and Supply of Goods Act 1994 to the formulation of the implied terms both in contracts for the sale of goods and other contracts for the supply of goods.

C Terms implied by the courts[91]

Other terms have been judicially implied in a number of transactions. For well over a hundred years there has thus been imported into a contract for the lease of a furnished house a term that it shall be reasonably fit for habitation at the date fixed for the beginning of the tenancy. So if the house is infested with bugs or if the drainage is defective or if a recent occupant suffered from tuberculosis, the tenant will be entitled to repudiate the contract and to recover damages.[92] A similar term is implied if a person contracts to sell land and to build, or to complete the building of, a house upon the land.[93] But the term may be excluded, in accordance with the general principle of the common law, either by clear and unambiguous language or if its implication would be inconsistent with an express term of the contract. Thus in *Lynch v Thorne*:[94]

---

[90] [1943] KB 526, [1943] 2 All ER 3. The House of Lords discussed the extent and nature of the terms which may be implied in contracts for work and materials in *Young & Marten Ltd v McManus Childs Ltd* [1969] 1 AC 454, [1968] 2 All ER 1169; and *Gloucestershire County Council v Richardson* [1969] 1 AC 480, [1968] 2 All ER 1181.

[91] Burrows 31 MLR 390.

[92] *Smith v Marrable* (1843) 11 M & W 5; *Wilson v Finch Hatton* (1877) 2 Ex D 336; *Collins v Hopkins* [1923] 2 KB 617.

[93] *Perry v Sharon Development Co Ltd* [1937] 4 All ER 390; see also *Hancock v B W Brazier (Anerley) Ltd* [1966] 2 All ER 901, [1966] 1 WLR 1317. There is no such implication on the sale of a completed house: *Hoskins v Woodham* [1938] 1 All ER 692. But see now Defective Premises Act 1972, discussed Spencer [1974] CLJ 307, [1975] CLJ 48.

[94] [1956] 1 All 744, [1956] 1 WLR 303. Later cases suggest that in appropriate cases a builder may be under a duty to warn his customer that the design of the house is defective. *Brunswick Construction Ltd v Nowlan* (1974) 21 BLR 27, *Equitable Debenture Assets Corpn Ltd v William Moss* (1984) 2 Con LR 1.

The defendant contracted to sell the plaintiff a plot of land on which was a partially erected house and to complete its construction. The contract provided that the walls were to be of nine-inch brick. The defendant built the house in accordance with this specification, but it was in fact unfit for human habitation because the walls would not keep out the rain.

The Court of Appeal gave judgment for the defendant. They could not imply a term which would 'create an inconsistency with the express language of the bargain'.

A fruitful source of controversy is to be found in the relationship of master and servant, where express contractual terms are often absent or prescribe inadequately the reciprocal rights and duties of the parties. The position here was examined by the House of Lords in *Lister v Romford Ice and Cold Storage Co Ltd.*[95]

The appellant Lister was employed by the respondents as a lorry driver. His father was his mate. While backing his lorry, he drove negligently and injured his father. The father sued the respondents, who were held vicariously liable for the son's negligence. The respondents now sued the son, inter alia, for breach of contract.

They urged the implication in his contract of service of a term that he would use reasonable care and skill in driving the lorry. The son replied with a battery of implications: that the respondents, as employers, should not require him to do anything unlawful, that they should insure him against any personal liability he might incur in the course of his employment, that they should indemnify him 'against all claims or proceedings brought against him for any act done in the course of employment'.

The House of Lords, by a majority, gave judgment for the respondents. There was authority for implying in the master's favour that the servant would 'serve him with good faith and fidelity'[96] and that he would use reasonable care and skill in the performance of his duties.[97]

This latter undertaking the son in the present case had clearly broken. There were certainly reciprocal terms to be implied in the servant's favour. The master for his part must use due care in respect of the premises where the work was to be done, the way in which it should be done and the plant involved; and he must not require the servant to do an unlawful act.[98] But the respondents had not broken any of these terms, and the further obligations suggested by the appellant were not warranted.

[95] [1957] AC 555, [1957] 1 All ER 125.
[96] *Robb v Green* [1895] 2 QB 315; *Hivac Ltd v Park Royal Scientific Instruments Ltd* [1946] Ch 169, [1946] 1 All ER 350.
[97] *Harmer v Cornelius* (1858) 5 CBNS 236.
[98] See *Matthews v Kuwait Bechtel Corpn* [1959] 2 QB 57, [1959] 2 All ER 345, and *Gregory v Ford* [1951] 1 All ER 121. In the latter case it was held that the master had committed an unlawful act in requiring the servant to drive an uninsured vehicle contrary to s 35(1) of the Road Traffic Act 1930. In *Lister v Romford Ice and Cold Storage Co Ltd*, the appellant argued that the respondents had again broken this section; but the House of Lords held that there had been no such breach.

In all these cases the court is really deciding what should be the content of a paradigm contract of hire, of employment, etc. The process of decision is quite independent of the intention of the parties except that they are normally free, by using express words, to exclude the term which would otherwise be implied. So the court is in effect imposing on the parties a term which is reasonable in the circumstances.[99] This process received a most instructive application in *Liverpool City Council v Irwin*.[100]

> The defendants were the tenants of a maisonette on the ninth floor of a fifteen floor tower block owned by the plaintiffs. There was no formal tenancy agreement. There was a list of tenants' obligations prepared by the landlord and signed by the tenant but there were no express undertakings of any kind by the landlord. Owing to vandalism the amenities of the block were seriously impaired so that the lifts were regularly out of action, the stairs were unlit and the rubbish shutes did not work. The defendants withheld payment of rent, alleging that the council were in breach of implied terms of the contract of tenancy. The council argued that there were no implied terms[101] but the House of Lords rejected this argument. It was necessary to consider what obligations 'the nature of the contract itself implicitly requires'[102] and since it was not possible to live in such a building without access to the stairs and the provision of a lift service it was necessary to imply some term as to these matters. On the other hand it was not proper to imply an absolute obligation on the landlords to maintain these services. It was sufficient to imply an obligation on the landlord to take reasonable care to maintain the common parts in a state of reasonable repair. It was not shown that the landlords were in breach of that implied term.[103]

Another important example is *Scally v Southern Health and Social Services Board*.[104]

> The plaintiffs were medical practitioners employed in Northern Ireland by the defendants. The terms of employment included a contributory pension scheme and an employee had, in principle, to complete 40 years of service to qualify for full pension. In 1974 a change in regulations gave employees the right to buy extra

---

[99] Per Lord Denning MR, in *Greaves & Co (Contractors) Ltd v Baynham Meikle & Partners* [1975] 3 All ER 99 at 103.

[100] [1977] AC 239, [1976] 2 All ER 39. Peden 117 LQR 459. Ayres and Gertner (1989) 94 Yale LJ 97.

[101] This argument was accepted by the majority of the Court of Appeal [1976] QB 319, [1975] 3 All ER 658 where the case was fought rather on the *Moorcock* doctrine, discussed p 185, below. Compare the interesting judgment of Lord Denning MR expressly disapproved of in the House of Lords.

[102] Per Lord Wilberforce [1977] AC 239 at 254, [1976] 2 All ER 39 at 44. See also Lord Cross [1977] AC 239 at 257, [1976] 2 All ER 39 at 46. Cf *Mears v Safecar Security Ltd* [1983] QB 54, [1982] 2 All ER 865.

[103] See further *Shell (UK) Ltd v Lostock Garage Ltd* [1977] 1 All ER 481; *Bremer Vulkan Schiffbau and Maschinenfabrik v South India Shipping Corpn* [1981] AC 909, [1981] 1 All ER 289; *Sim v Rotherham Metropolitan Borough Council* [1987] Ch 216, [1986] 3 All ER 387.

[104] [1991] 4 All ER 563.

years on very favourable terms but this right had to be exercised within 12 months from 10 February 1975 by persons already employed and within 12 months from first taking up of employment by those employed thereafter. There was a discretion to extend this 12-month time limit and to vary the terms of purchase where the time was so extended. The plaintiffs did not exercise their rights because they did not know of them. They claimed that their employer was under a duty to inform them of this change in the terms of their employment and that a term should be implied into the contract of employment.

Lord Bridge, in delivering the only reasoned speech in the House, said:[105]

> The problem is a novel one which could not arise in the classical contractual situation in which all the contractual terms, having been agreed between the parties, must, ex hypothesi, have been known to both parties. But in the modern world it is increasingly common for individuals to enter into contracts, particularly contracts of employment, on complex terms which have been settled in the course of negotiations between representative bodies or organisations and many details of which the individual employee cannot be expected to know unless they are drawn to his attention.

Lord Bridge had no hesitation in holding that it was necessary to imply such a term where 'the following circumstances obtain'.[106]

> (1) The terms of the contract of employment have not been negotiated with the individual employee but result from negotiation with a representative body or are otherwise incorporated by reference; (2) A particular term of the contract makes available to the employee a valuable right contingent upon action being taken by him to avail himself of its benefit; (3) The employee cannot, in all the circumstances, reasonably be expected to be aware of the term unless it is drawn to his attention.[107]

Another interesting development of implied terms in contracts of employment occurred in *Malik v Bank of Credit and Commerce International*.[108] The bank appeared on the surface to be an ordinary high street bank. Unknown to customers and to most of its staff, including the claimants, it was a complete fraud dedicated to cheating customers and third parties. The bank eventually became insolvent and the claimants were made redundant. They argued that the bank was in breach of an implied term of the contract of employment that neither party should 'engage in conduct likely to undermine the trust and confidence required if the employment relationship is to

---

[105] Ibid at 569.
[106] Ibid at 571. See also *Spring v Guardian Assurance plc* [1994] 3 All ER 129; *Wilson v Best Travel Ltd* [1993] 1 All ER 353; *Wong Mee Wan v Kwan Kin Travel Services Ltd* [1995] 4 All ER 745. *Crossley v Faithful & Gould Holdings Ltd* [2004] EWCA Civ 293, [2004] 4 All ER 447.
[107] Ibid at 571–572.
[108] [1997] 3 All ER 1. The case also raised important questions about what damages could be recovered for breach of such an implied term. See below p 771.

continue'. The bank accepted that the authorities supported the implication of a term of this kind but argued that it should not apply:

(a) where the dishonest behaviour of the bank was aimed at customers and not employees; or

(b) where the employee only became aware of the dishonest conduct after he had ceased to be employed; or

(c) unless the conduct was such as to destroy or seriously damage the relationship between employee and employer.

The House of Lords rejected all three of these suggested limitations.[109]

In addition to terms thus imported into particular types of contract, the courts may, in any class of contract, imply a term in order to repair an intrinsic failure of expression. The document which the parties have prepared may leave no doubt as to the general ambit of their obligations; but they may have omitted, through inadvertence or clumsy draftsmanship, to cover an incidental contingency, and this omission, unless remedied, may negative their design. In such a case the judge may himself supply a further term, which will implement their presumed intention and, in a hallowed phrase, give 'business efficacy' to the contract. In doing this he purports at least to do merely what the parties would have done themselves had they thought of the matter. The existence of this judicial power was asserted and justified in the case of *The Moorcock*.[110]

> The defendants were wharfingers who had agreed, in consideration of charges for landing and stowing the cargo, to allow the plaintiff, a shipowner, to discharge his vessel at their jetty. The jetty extended into the Thames, and, as both parties realised, the vessel must ground at low water. While she was unloading, the tide ebbed and she settled on a ridge of hard ground beneath the mud. The plaintiff sued for the resultant damage.

The defendants had not guaranteed the safety of the anchorage, nor was the bed of the river adjoining the jetty vested in them but in the Thames Conservators. But the Court of Appeal implied an undertaking by the defendants that the river bottom was, so far as reasonable care could provide, in such a condition as not to endanger the vessel. Bowen LJ explained the nature of the implication.[111]

> I believe if one were to take all the cases, and there are many, of implied warranties or covenants in law, it will be found that in all of them the law is raising an implication from the presumed intention of the parties, with the object of giving to the transaction such efficacy

---

[109] For further proceedings see [1999] 4 All ER 83, [2002] 3 All ER 750. For the same implied term in a different context see *University of Nottingham v Eyett* [1999] 2 All ER 437.

[110] (1889) 14 PD 64.

[111] Ibid at 68, 70.

as both parties must have intended that at all events it should have. In business transactions such as this, what the law desires to effect by the implication is to give such business efficacy to the transaction as must have been intended at all events by both parties who are businessmen . . . The question is what inference is to be drawn where the parties are dealing with each other on the assumption that the negotiations are to have some fruit, and where they say nothing about the burden of this unseen peril, leaving the law to raise such inferences as are reasonable from the very nature of the transaction.

Since this case was decided in 1889, its authority has often been invoked; and the principle upon which it rests has been amplified. Scrutton LJ said in 1918:

A term can only be implied if it is necessary in the business sense to give efficacy to the contract, ie if it is such a term that it can confidently be said that if at the time the contract was being negotiated someone had said to the parties: 'What will happen in such a case?' they would both have replied: 'Of course so and so will happen; we did not trouble to say that; it is too clear.'[112]

MacKinnon LJ said in 1939:

Prima facie that which in a contract is left to be implied and need not be expressed is something so obvious that it goes without saying; so that, if while the parties were making their bargain an officious bystander were to suggest some express provision for it in their agreement, they would testily suppress him with a common, 'Oh, of course.'[113]

Lord Pearson said in 1973:

An unexpressed term can be implied if and only if the court finds that the parties must have intended that term to form part of their contract: it is not enough for the court to find that such a term would have been adopted by the parties as reasonable men if it had been suggested to them: it must have been a term that went without saying, a term *necessary* to give business efficacy to the contract, a term which, although tacit, formed part of the contract which the parties made for themselves.[114]

Thus explained, *the Moorcock* is still full of life. In *Gardner v Coutts & Co*:[115]

X, in 1948, sold freehold property to Y. By a written contract with Y made on the day following the sale, X agreed that Y and her successors should have the option of buying the adjoining property, which X retained, if X at any time during his life wished to sell it. In 1958 the plaintiff was the successor in title to Y. In 1963 X conveyed the adjoining property to his sister by way of gift without giving the

---

[112] *Reigate v Union Manufacturing Co (Ramsbottom)* [1918] 1 KB 592 at 605.

[113] *Shirlaw v Southern Foundries (1926) Ltd* [1939] 2 KB 206 at 227, [1939] 2 All ER 113 at 124.

[114] *Trollope and Colls Ltd v North West Metropolitan Regional Hospital Board* [1973] 2 All ER 260 at 268, [1973] 1 WLR 601 at 609.

[115] [1967] 3 All ER 1064, [1968] 1 WLR 173. See also *Finchbourne Ltd v Rodrigues* [1976] 3 All ER 581; *Essoldo v Ladbroke Group* [1976] CLY 337.

plaintiff the option of purchase. In 1965 X died; and the plaintiff now sued his executors for breach of contract.

The written contract between X and Y contained no term providing expressly for the event of X giving, as opposed to selling, the property to a third party. Cross J implied in the contract a term that X's promise should cover a gift as well as a sale.

> If I apply the test laid down by Scrutton LJ and MacKinnon LJ I am confident that at the time, whatever views [X] may have formed later, if somebody had said to him, 'You have not expressly catered for the possibility of your wanting to give away the property', he would have said, as undoubtedly [Y] would have said, 'Oh, of course that is implied. What goes for a contemplated sale must go for a contemplated gift.'[116]

This power of judicial implication is a convenient means of repairing an obvious oversight. But it may easily be overworked, and it has more than once received the doubtful compliment of citation by counsel as a last desperate expedient in a tenuous case. In a passage immediately preceding the words of Lord Justice MacKinnon, quoted above, the learned judge gave a warning against the abuse of the power, and especially against the temptation to invoke indiscriminately the relevant sentences of Bowen LJ in *The Moorcock*.

> They are sentences from an *extempore* judgment as sound and sensible as all the utterances of that great judge; but I fancy that he would have been rather surprised if he could have foreseen that these general remarks of his would come to be a favourite citation of a supposed principle of law, and I even think that he might sympathize with the occasional impatience of his successors when *The Moorcock* is so often flushed for them in that guise.[117]

That this warning was needed is shown by two cases decided since it was given. In *Spring v National Amalgamated Stevedores and Dockers Society*.[118]

> The defendants and the Transport and General Workers Union agreed at the Trade Union Congress at Bridlington in 1939 certain rules for the transfer of members from one union to another. This was called the 'Bridlington Agreement'. In 1955 the defendants, in breach of this agreement, admitted the plaintiff to their Society. He knew nothing of the agreement nor was it expressly included in the defendants' rules. The breach of the agreement was submitted to the Disputes Committee of the Trade Union Congress which ordered the defendants to expel the plaintiff from their Society. When the defendants sought to do so, the plaintiff sued them

---

[116] Ibid at 1069 and 179, respectively. For an application of *The Moorcock* see *British School of Motoring Ltd v Simms* [1971] 1 All ER 317, where Talbot J, was ready to imply a term that any car provided by the school for driving lessons would be covered by insurance. See also per Megarry J in *Coco v A N Clark (Engineers) Ltd* [1968] FSR 415 at 424.

[117] *Shirlaw v Southern Foundries (1926) Ltd* [1939] 2 KB 206 at 227, [1939] 2 All ER 113 at 124.

[118] [1956] 2 All ER 221, [1956] 1 WLR 585. See also *Gallagher v Post Office* [1970] 3 All ER 712.

for breach of contract, claimed a declaration that the expulsion was *ultra vires* and asked for an injunction to prevent it.

The defendants suggested that a term should be implied in their contract with the plaintiff that they should comply with the 'Bridlington Agreement' and take any appropriate steps to fulfil it. But the Vice-Chancellor of the County Palatine Court of Lancaster rejected the suggestion and granted to declaration and injunction for which the plaintiff had asked. He referred to the test suggested by MacKinnon LJ and said:

> If that test were to be applied to the facts of this case and the bystander had asked the plaintiff, at the time when the plaintiff paid his 5s and signed the acceptance form, 'Won't you put into it some reference to the Bridlington Agreement?' I think (indeed I have no doubt) that the plaintiff would have answered, 'What's that?'[119]

In *Sethia (1944) Ltd v Partabmull Rameshwar*:[120]

The plaintiffs carried on business in London and the defendants were Calcutta merchants. In 1947 the plaintiffs bought from the defendants certain quantities of jute which the defendants were to ship to Genoa. As both parties knew, no jute could be exported from India save by licence of the Government of India, and in 1947 the Government adopted a 'quota system' whereby a shipper must choose as his 'basic year' any one year from 1937 to 1946 and was allotted a quota in regard to the countries to which he had made shipments in that year. The defendants chose 1946 as their basic year, but, as in that year they had shipped nothing to Italy, they were not entitled to any licence for Genoa. Subsequently, however, they were allowed to ship rather less than a third of the contract quantity of jute. The plaintiffs sued for breach of contract. The defendants admitted that the contract did not expressly provide that shipments should be 'subject to quota', but argued that such a term must be implied to give it 'business efficacy'.

The Court of Appeal refused to imply the term. In the first place, it was proved that in the jute trade contracts were sometimes made expressly 'subject to quota' and sometimes with no such phrase. The defendants, therefore, by omitting the phrase, must be supposed to have accepted an absolute obligation to deliver the jute. In the second place, to imply the term would be to commit the buyers to consequences dependent upon facts exclusively within the sellers' knowledge. The buyers certainly knew of the quota system; but the sellers chose the basic year and they alone knew to what countries they had previously exported in that year.

[119] [1956] 2 All ER 221 at 231.
[120] [1950] 1 All ER 51. See also *Western Bank Ltd v Schindler* [1977] Ch 1, [1976] 2 All ER 393; *Federal Commerce and Navigation Co Ltd v Tradax Export SA, The Maratha Envoy* [1978] AC 1, [1977] 2 All ER 849; *Frobisher (Second Investments) Ltd v Kiloran Trust Co Ltd* [1980] 1 All ER 488. *Ashmore v Corpn of Lloyd's (No 2)* [1992] 2 Lloyd's Rep 620.

The 'business efficacy' and 'officious bystander' tests are usually treated as if they are alternative ways of stating a single test. However, it is clear that there might be an implied term which was necessary to give business efficacy to the contract but which, because of their conflicting interests, the parties would not have agreed, if questioned by the officious bystander, as to its obviousness. In *Codelfa Construction Pty Ltd v State Railway Authority of New South Wales*[121] Mason CJ treated the tests as cumulative but it is not clear whether this is the law in England.[122]

A dramatic example of the potential scope of such 'implied in fact' terms was provided by the decision of the House of Lords in *Equitable Life Assurance Society v Hyman*.[123] In this case the appellant had issued large numbers of with profits pension policies. Under these contracts the policyholders invested money with the appellant which would produce a capital sum on the policyholder's retirement. The amount of the capital sum would depend partly on the amount invested and partly on the success of the investment policies followed by the appellant. The directors of the society were given a wide discretion by Article 65 of the Rules which provided that they should 'apportion the amount of [the] declared surplus by way of bonus among the holders of the participating policies on such principles, and by such methods, as they may from time to time determine'.

In practice the directors would be unlikely to pay out all of the profit in a given year as a bonus because they would want to keep money in hand for less successful years. Bonuses would be declared during the running of the policy (and once declared could not be revoked) and a 'terminal' bonus (usually larger) would be paid at the end of the policy.

Because of the Inland Revenue rules which make pensions attractive to taxpayers, the policyholder could not take the whole of the capital sum in cash and had to convert a substantial part into an annuity. Pension providers do not necessarily offer the best rates for conversion to annuities and policyholders are normally free to get the best annuity which is available on the market.

Some of the policies offered by the appellant had an unusual feature in that they contained a provision to convert the capital sum into an annuity at a guaranteed annual rate (GAR). The dispute concerned these policies. When the policies were sold the GAR was well below the market rate but during the 1980s and 1990s annuity rates fell steadily so that the GAR was significantly above the market rate. The reaction of the directors was to propose to pay a lower terminal bonus to policyholders who held GAR contracts. The House of Lords held that a term should be implied to prevent this.

Lord Steyn said

---

[121] [1982] 149 CLR 337.
[122] Steyn J in *Mosvolds Rederi A/S v Food Corpn of India* [1986] 2 Lloyd's Rep 68.
[123] [2002] 1 AC 408, [2000] 3 All ER 961.

> The directors of the society resolved upon a differential policy which was designed to deprive the relevant guarantees of any substantial value. In my judgment an implication precluding the use of the directors' discretion in this way is strictly necessary. The implication is essential to give effect to the reasonable expectations of the parties.

In New South Wales today, this result would probably be explained on the basis of an implied term that the contract be performed in good faith.[124] Good faith and reasonable expectations are implicit in much of the process of implying terms even when they are not explicitly referred to. English courts will certainly imply duties of co-operation where the contract cannot be performed without it;[125] in *CEL Group Ltd v Ned Lloyd Lines UK Ltd*[126] the Court of Appeal held that a company which had contracted to give a carrier exclusive rights to provide its road haulage and transportation services had implicitly undertaken that it would do nothing of its own motion to bring to an end its own requirement for road haulage services.

In general, the parties are entitled to provide for the exclusion of terms which would otherwise be implied. In some important cases, Parliament has provided that the implied terms cannot be excluded and such implied terms, therefore, become mandatory.[127] In such cases, Parliament is in effect laying down a rule of law but it is doing so by using the technique of implying a term into the contract. The effect of this is to give the party thus protected the basic contractual remedies. Where exclusion of the normal implied terms is permitted there will be questions of interpretation. No problem arises if the contract says expressly that no terms are to be implied, or words to that effect. Difficult questions can arise, however, where it is argued that the express terms impliedly exclude normal implied terms. There must be cases where the express term covers the ground so closely that there is no room for an implied term but there will also be cases in which it is possible that the express and normal implied terms can co-exist.

Johnstone v Bloomsbury Health Authority[128] is a very instructive case in this context:

> The plaintiff was employed by the defendant health authority as a junior hospital doctor under a contract which required him to work 40 hours per week and to 'be available' for overtime of a further 48 hours per week on average. The plaintiff alleged that he had been required to work so many hours a week, with so little sleep, that he was physically sick, that his health was damaged and that the safety of patients was put at risk. He argued that the authority was therefore in breach of its duties as his employer to take reasonable care for his safety and well-being. He sought declarations that he could not lawfully be required to work so many hours

---

[124] See eg *Renard Constructions (ME) Pty Ltd v Minister of Public Works* (1992) 26 NSWLR 234; Peden *Good Faith in the Performance of Contracts*.

[125] *London Borough of Merton v Stanley Hugh Leach* (1995) 32 Building LR 51.

[126] [2003] EWCA Civ 1716, [2004] 1 All ER (Comm) 689.

[127] See p 235, below.

[128] [1991] 2 All ER 293.

as would foreseeably injure his health.[129] The authority argued on a preliminary point that the terms of the plaintiff's employment excluded any duty in relation to safe system of work so far as concerned the hours of work.[130]

Leggatt LJ accepted the argument of the authority. The majority disagreed and thought the case should go to trial but the reasons given were not identical. Both Stuart-Smith LJ and Browne-Wilkinson thought that (subject perhaps to the provisions of the Unfair Contract Terms Act 1977) it was open to the authority by clear words to exclude the normal implied duty to provide a reasonably safe system of work but they did not think that the provision as to hours of work had produced this effect. Both thought that the provisions as to the hours of work had to be read together with the normal implied term. Taken literally, the provision as to hours of work would have permitted the authority to require the plaintiff to work 168 hours in one week if, over a period (not specified in the contract terms), his average had been brought down to 88 hours a week. Few, if any, people can work with adequate respect for their health or the safety of others for such a long period. It was reasonable, therefore, to treat the implied term as to a reasonably safe system of work as cutting back, to some extent, the more extreme forms of overtime working which the authority might apparently, looking only at the express terms, have required. Stuart-Smith LJ would have required the authority when doing this to have regard to the personal stamina and physical strength of the individual doctor. Browne-Wilkinson VC would not have gone so far and would not have permitted the authority to impose hours of work which would impair the health of a reasonably robust young doctor. So, if the evidence at trial showed that a reasonably robust young doctor could work 100 hours a week, provided he had at least five hours' sleep each night, the express and implied term could live together.[131]

3 THE RELATIVE IMPORTANCE OF CONTRACTUAL TERMS

Common sense suggests and the law has long recognised that the obligations created by a contract are not all of equal importance. It is primarily for the parties to set their own value on the terms that they impose upon each other. But it is rare for them to

---

[129] He also argued that the contract was contrary to s 2(1) of the Unfair Contract Terms Act 1977 and void on the ground of public policy.

[130] If successful, this argument would have avoided the need for any factual investigation of the effect of the long hours worked either on the plaintiff personally or on junior doctors in general.

[131] Of course, if the evidence showed that no reasonably robust doctor could work more than 88 hours a week, there would be a conflict between the express and implied terms.

express with any precision what, if anything, they have in their minds; and the resultant task of inferring and interpreting their intention is, as always, a matter of great difficulty. In the present context it has been further complicated by the phraseology adopted by the judges both to limit the operation of a contract and to value its component parts. Two words in particular, *conditions* and *warranties*, have been employed with such persistence and with so little discrimination that some preliminary attempt must be made to fix their meaning.

To lawyers familiar with the Roman jurisprudence and trained in modern Continental systems the use of the word *condition* in this context must appear a solecism. By them a condition is sharply distinguished from the actual terms of a contract, and is taken to mean, not part of the obligation itself, but an external fact upon which the existence of the obligation depends.[132] The operation of a contract may thus be postponed until some event takes place, or the occurrence of this event may cancel a contract which has already started to function. A purchaser may agree to buy a car only if it satisfies a certain test, or he may conclude the sale, reserving the right in certain circumstances to re-open the whole transaction.

The orthodox application of the word is by no means unknown to English lawyers.[133] Agreements are often made which are expressed to be 'subject to' some future event, performance or the like. Such agreements may produce a variety of different effects.

First, there may be no contract at all. This may be either, as in agreements 'subject to contract', because the parties have agreed not to be bound until some future event (eg the execution of a formal contract) which cannot take place without the concurrence of both parties or because the condition is uncertain. So in *Lee-Parker v Izzet (No 2)*[134] it was held that an agreement 'subject to the purchaser obtaining a satisfactory mortgage' was void for uncertainty.[135]

Secondly, the whole existence of the contract may be suspended until the happening of a stated event, or as it is said in the common law, be subject to a *condition precedent*. In *Pym v Campbell*:[136]

The defendants agreed in writing to buy from the plaintiff a share in an invention.

---

[132] See Buckland and McNair *Roman Law and Common Law* (2nd edn) pp 247–256. For French law, see the Code Civil, Art 1168. Scots law has substantially adopted the Continental position, though some complaints have been made of confusion arising from a flirtation with the English terminology: see Gow *The Mercantile and Industrial Law of Scotland* pp 201–214.

[133] See Montrose 15 Can Bar Rev 309; Stoljar 15 MLR 425, 16 MLR 174.

[134] [1972] 2 All ER 800, [1972] 1 WLR 775.

[135] Similar conditions had been held sufficiently certain in a number of New Zealand cases and Australian cases, eg *Barber v Crickett* [1958] NZLR 1057; *Martin v Macarthur* [1963] NZLR 403; *Scott v Rania* [1966] NZLR 527. *Meehan v Jones* (1982) 56 ALJR 813; Coote 40 Conv 37; Swanton 58 ALJ 633, 690; Furmston 3 Oxford JLS 438. See also *Janmohamed v Hassam* [1976] CLY 2851. Much of the learning on uncertain conditions is to be found in cases on conditional gifts. No doubt similar principles may apply to contracts but probably the threshold of uncertainty should be higher in a commercial setting.

[136] (1956) 6 E & B 370.

When the plaintiff sued for a breach of this agreement, the defendants were allowed to give oral evidence that it was not to operate until a third party had approved the invention and that this approval had never been expressed.

'The evidence showed', said Erle J, 'that in fact there was never any agreement at all.' A more recent example is offered by the case of *Aberfoyle Plantations Ltd v Cheng*,[137] which came before the Judicial Committee of the Privy Council from Malaya.

> In 1955 the parties agreed to sell and to buy a plantation part of which consisted of 182 acres comprised in seven leases that had expired in 1950. In the intervening years the vendor had tried but failed to obtain a renewal of the leases. Clause 4 of the agreement therefore provided that 'the purchase is conditional on the vendor obtaining a renewal' of the leases. If he proved 'unable to fulfil this condition this agreement shall become null and void'.

The vendor failed to obtain the renewal, and the Judicial Committee held that the purchaser could recover the deposit that he had paid. Lord Jenkins said:

> At the very outset of the agreement the vendor's obligation to sell, and the purchaser's obligation to buy, were by clause 1 expressed to be subject to the condition contained in clause 4. It was thus made plain beyond argument that the condition was a condition precedent on the fulfilment of which the formation of a binding contract of sale between the parties was made to depend.[138]

Thirdly, a condition may operate, not to negative the very existence of a contract, but to suspend, until it is satisfied, some right or duty or consequence which would otherwise spring from the contract. Thus in *Marten v Whale*:[139]

> The plaintiff agreed with X to buy a plot of land from him subject to the approval by the plaintiff's solicitor 'of title and restrictions'. At the same time the plaintiff agreed to sell his motorcar to X—this second agreement to be in consideration of the first agreement and to be completed simultaneously with it. The plaintiff allowed X to take possession of the car, and X sold it at once to the defendant who took it without notice of the plaintiff's rights. The plaintiff's solicitor then refused to approve the restrictions binding the land. The plaintiff sued the defendant to recover the car and for damages.

The Court of Appeal held that he must fail. The solicitor's approval was a condition precedent, not to the creation of the contract for sale of the car, but only to the passing of property under it. It was—though not a sale—an agreement to sell, and the defendant obtained a title under section 25(2) of the Sale of Goods Act.

It will not always be easy to decide whether the failure of a condition precedent prevents the formation of a contract or only suspends the obligations created by it.

---

[137] [1960] AC 115, [1959] 3 All ER 910.
[138] Ibid at 128 and 916, respectively.   [139] [1917] 2 KB 480.

Particular difficulties seem to be raised by the case of *Bentworth Finance Ltd v Lubert.*[140]

> The plaintiffs, under a hire-purchase agreement, let a second-hand car to the defendant, who was to pay 24 monthly instalments. The car was delivered to the defendant but without a log-book. The defendant neither licensed nor used it and refused to pay the instalments. The plaintiffs retook possession of the car and sued for the instalments.

The Court of Appeal held that the plaintiffs could not sue the defendant. The delivery of the log-book was a condition precedent upon which the liability to pay the instalments depended. The decision itself may readily be supported. But it is hard to accept the court's view that, until the log-book was supplied, there was no contract at all.[141]

Where there is a contract but the obligations of one or both parties are subject to conditions a number of subsidiary problems arise. So there may be a question of whether one of the parties has undertaken to bring the condition about. In *Bentworth Finance Ltd v Lubert* it could have been plausibly argued that the plaintiff had promised to deliver the log-book. There is a clear distinction between a promise, for breach of which an action lies and a condition, upon which an obligation is dependent. But the same event may be both promised and conditional, when it may be called a promissory condition.[142] A common form of contract is one where land is sold 'subject to planning permission'. In such a contract one could hardly imply a promise to obtain planning permission, since this would be outwith the control of the parties but the courts have frequently implied a promise by the purchaser to use his best endeavours to obtain planning permission.[143] Another question is whether the condition may be waived. It would appear that where the condition is solely for the benefit of one party, he can waive the condition and make the contract unconditional.[144]

[140] [1968] 1 QB 680, [1967] 2 All ER 810. See Carnegie 31 MLR 78.

[141] Similarly it would appear wrong to hold as Goulding J did in *Myton Ltd v Schwab-Morris* [1974] 1 All ER 326, [1974] 1 WLR 331 that payment of a deposit by a purchaser was a condition precedent to the coming into existence of a contract of sale. Payment of the deposit is rather part of the buyer's obligations and a condition precedent to the seller's obligation to convey; *Millichamp v Jones* [1983] 1 All ER 267 [1982] 1 WLR 1422; *Damon Cia Naviera SA v Hapag-Lloyd International SA* [1985] 1 All ER 475 [1985] 1 WLR 435, CA.

[142] See *Bashir v Comr of Lands* [1960] AC 44, [1960] 1 All ER 117, Montrose 23 MLR 350. See also per Sachs LJ in *Property and Bloodstock Ltd v Emerton* [1968] Ch 94 at 120–121, [1967] 3 All ER 321 at 330–331.

[143] See *Re Longlands Farm, Long Common, Botley, Hants, Alford v Superior Developments* [1968] 3 All ER 552; *Hargreaves Transport Ltd v Lynch* [1969] 1 All ER 455, [1969] 1 WLR 215. See also *Smallman v Smallman* [1972] Fam 25, [1971] 3 All ER 717 ('subject to the approval of the court' imposes an obligation to apply to the court for approval). Wilkinson 38 Conv 77.

[144] See *Wood Preservation v Prior* [1969] 1 All ER 364, [1969] 1 WLR 1077. The judgment of Goff J [1968] 2 All ER 849 also repays careful study. Cf *Heron Garage Properties Ltd v Moss* [1974] 1 All ER 421, [1974] 1 WLR 148, discussed Smith [1974] CLJ 211. See also *IRC v Ufitec Group Ltd* [1977] 3 All ER 924.

There is yet a fourth possibility, that one party may be able unilaterally to bring a contract into existence. The most common example is an option to buy land. The holder of the option is under no obligation to exercise it but if he does, a bilateral contract of sale between him and the owner will come into existence. In a unilateral contract, the obligation of the promisor may be conditional. So in *Carlill v Carbolic Smoke Ball Co*,[145] there was a binding contract once the plaintiff had bought the smoke ball and used it as prescribed, but the defendant's obligation to pay was conditional on the plaintiff catching influenza. It appears that where one party has the power unilaterally to bring a contract into existence on certain conditions, strict compliance with those conditions will be required.[146]

If a contract has come into existence but is to terminate upon the occurrence of some event, it is said to be subject to a *condition subsequent*. An example often cited is the case of *Head v Tattersall*.[147]

> The plaintiff bought from the defendant a horse, guaranteed 'to have been hunted with the Bicester hounds', with the understanding that he could return it up to the following Wednesday, if it did not answer the description. While in the plaintiff's possession, but without fault on his part, the horse was injured, and was then found never in fact to have been hunted with the Bicester hounds. The plaintiff returned it within the time limit and sued for the price he had paid.

It was held that a contract of sale had come into existence, but that the option to return the horse operated as a condition subsequent of which the plaintiff could take advantage. He was entitled to cancel the contract, return the horse despite the injuries it had suffered, and recover the price.

But, while familiar with its orthodox meaning, English lawyers have more often used *condition* with less propriety to denote, not an external event by which the obligation is suspended or cancelled, but a term in the contract which may be enforced against one or other of the parties. The distinction insisted upon by the civilians is thus obliterated. Confusion is worse confounded by the fact that *warranty* is also used to indicate a term in the contract and by the failure over many years to define either word with precision. Buller J thus said in 1789:[148]

> It was rightly held by Holt CJ and has been uniformly adopted ever since, that an affirmation at the time of a sale is a warranty, provided it appear on evidence to have been so intended.

---

[145] [1892] 2 QB 484, discussed, p 39, above.

[146] See eg *Hare v Nicoll* [1966] 2 QB 130, [1966] 1 All ER 285. See also the difficult but important case of *United Dominions Trust (Commercial) Ltd v Eagle Aircraft Services Ltd* [1968] 1 All ER 104, [1968] 1 WLR 74; criticised Atiyah 31 MLR 332.

[147] (1871) LR 7 Exch 7. Cf Stoljar 69 LQR 485 at 506–511; Sealy [1972B] CLJ 225. Another example is *Thompson v Asda-MFI Group plc* [1988] Ch 241 [1988] 2 All ER 722.

[148] *Pasley v Freeman* (1789) 3 Term Rep 51.

It was by the Sale of Goods Act 1893 that some measure of order was imposed upon the language of the law. By section 11(1)(b) a condition is defined as a stipulation in a contract of sale, 'the breach of which may give rise to a right to treat the contract as repudiated', and a warranty as a stipulation 'the breach of which may give rise to a claim for damages but not to a right to reject the goods and treat the contract as repudiated'. By section 62 it is added that a warranty is 'collateral to the main purpose of the contract', but no further light is shed upon the nature of a condition.

The Sale of Goods Act was treated by many lawyers as containing not only a definition of the words 'condition' and 'warranty' but also an implicit assertion that all contractual terms were either conditions or warranties. This dichotomy enjoyed widespread acceptance between 1893 and 1962 as a means of resolving the practical question of identifying the breaches which entitled the injured party to terminate the contract.[149]

This approach was shown to be over simplistic by the decision of the Court of Appeal in *Hong Kong Fir Shipping Co Ltd v Kawasaki Kisen Kaisha Ltd*:[150]

> The plaintiffs owned a ship which they chartered to the defendants for a period of 24 months from her delivery at Liverpool in February 1957. When delivered, her engine-room staff were too few and too incompetent to cope with her antiquated machinery. It was admitted that the plaintiffs had thus broken a term in the contract to provide a ship 'in every way fitted for ordinary cargo service' and that the ship was unseaworthy. On her voyage to Osaka she was delayed for 5 weeks owing to engine trouble, and at Osaka 15 more weeks were lost because, through the incompetence of the staff, the engines had become even more dilapidated. Not until September was the ship made seaworthy. In June the defendants had repudiated the charter. The plaintiffs sued for breach of contract and claimed damages for wrongful repudiation.

It was held both by Salmon J and by the Court of Appeal that the breach of contract of which the plaintiffs had admittedly been guilty did not entitle the defendants to treat the contract as discharged but only to claim damages, and the plaintiffs won their action. In orthodox language the plaintiffs had broken a warranty and not a condition. The Court of Appeal, however, was reluctant to perpetuate a dichotomy which required each term of a contract to be pressed, at whatever cost, into one of two categories. Diplock LJ acknowledged that it was apposite to simple contractual undertakings. But there were he thought, other clauses too complicated to respond to such

---

[149] That this question, however approached, has always presented difficult questions of drawing the line can be seen by contrasting *Poussard v Spiers and Pond* (1876) 1 QBD 410 and *Bettini v Gye* (1876) 1 QBD 183. See Beck 38 MLR 413.
[150] [1962] 2 QB 26, [1962] 1 All ER 474.

treatment.[151] Thus, in the case before the court, the obligation of seaworthiness was embodied in a clause, adopted in many charterparties, which—partly through judicial interpretation—had become one of formidable complexity. It comprised, as Upjohn LJ pointed out, a variety of undertakings, some serious and some trivial.

> If a nail is missing from one of the timbers of a wooden vessel, or if proper medical supplies or two anchors are not on board at the time of sailing, the owners are in breach of the seaworthi- ness stipulation. It is contrary to common sense to suppose that, in such circumstances, the parties contemplated that the charterer should at once be entitled to treat the contract as at an end for such trifling breaches.[152]

To so heterogeneous a clause the dichotomy of condition and warranty was, in the opinion of the court, inapplicable. It might perhaps have been helpful to regard the undertaking of 'seaworthiness', not as a single term, but as a bundle of obligations of varying importance. But even on this construction the task of the court, as envisaged in the *Hong Kong Fir* case, was not to evaluate the term as it stood in the contract, but to wait and see what happened as a result of the breach. Thus if the breach of a term, itself of apparently minor significance, caused severe loss or damage, the injured party might be able to treat the contract as discharged.

The decision in the *Hong Kong Fir* case led some to believe that classification of terms was no longer necessary but this would clearly have been to depart too far from history. That a distinction must be made between major and minor terms, rather than between the more or less serious effect of a breach, was certainly assumed by some judges in the second half of the nineteenth century. They also said that, to draw this distinction, they must place themselves at the date of the contract and not await the chances of the future. In 1863 in *Behn v Burness*, the court had to evaluate a statement in a charterparty that a ship was 'now in the port of Amsterdam'. The statement was inaccurate: the ship only arrived at Amsterdam four days after the date of the charter. Williams J said:

> The court must be influenced in the construction [of the contract], not only by the language of the instrument, but also by the circumstances under which and the purposes for which, the charter-party was entered into . . . A statement is more or less important in proportion as the object of the contract more or less depends upon it. For most charters . . . the time of a ship's arrival to load is an essential fact, for the interest of the charterer. In the ordinary course of charters it would be so: the evidence of the defendant shows it to be actually so in this case. Then, if the statement of the place of the ship is a substantive part of the contract, it seems to us that we ought to hold it to be a condition.[153]

---

[151] Ibid at 70, and 487, respectively. So, too, Upjohn LJ, ibid at 64 and 484, respectively. Upjohn LJ repeated his views in *Astley Industrial Trust Ltd v Grimley* [1963] 2 All ER 33 at 46–47, [1963] 1 WLR 584 at 598–599. See Reynolds 79 LQR 534; Furmston 25 MLR 584.

[152] Ibid at 62–63 and 483, respectively.

[153] *Behn v Burness* (1863) 3 B & S 751 at 757, 759.

In *Bettini v Gye*, Blackburn J declared that the classification of a term as major or minor 'depends on the true construction of the contract taken as a whole'. He cited Parke B in *Graves v Legg*:

> The court must ascertain the intention of the parties, to be collected from the instrument and the circumstances legally admissible in evidence with reference to which it is to be construed.[154]

In these cases the court insisted that the test is to be found, not in the greater or less degree of loss or damage caused by the breach of contract, but in examination of the contract itself at the time and in the circumstances in which it was made.

In 1970 the Court of Appeal had to reconsider the whole question in *the Mihalis Angelos*.[155]

> On 25 May 1965, the owners of a vessel let it to charterers for a voyage from Haiphong in North Vietnam to Hamburg. In clause 1 of the charter the owners said that the vessel was 'expected ready to load under this charter about 1 July 1965'. On the date of the charter she was in the Pacific on her way to Hong Kong, where she had to discharge the cargo which she was then carrying and have a special survey lasting two days. It would take her a further two days to reach Haiphong. She did not in fact complete discharge at Hong Kong until 23 July. It was found as a fact that the owners, when the contract was made, had no reasonable ground for expecting that she would be ready to load under the charter 'about 1 July'.

The members of the Court of Appeal were not unnaturally pressed with the arguments adopted in the *Hong Kong Fir* case. But they were of opinion that the distinction between 'condition' and 'warranties', though not of universal application, was still valuable, apart from statute, in many classes of contract and notably in charter-parties.[156] On the facts before them, the court held that the 'expected readiness' clause was a condition.[157] In reaching this conclusion, the court had to choose between the aims of certainty and elasticity, each of which has its part to play in the administration and development of the law. The relative importance of these aims depends upon the type of transaction involved. In a charterparty, where shipowner and charterer meet on equal terms, they, or their lawyers, seek a firm foundation of principle and authority on which they may build and yet make such variations as the law allows and the particular requirements demand. Edmund Davies LJ said:

---

[154] *Bettini v Gye* (1876) 1 QBD 183; *Graves v Legg* (1854) 9 Exch 709. See also *Bentsen v Taylor, Sons & Co (No 2)* [1893] 2 QB 274 at 281.

[155] [1971] 1 QB 164, [1970] 3 All ER 125. Greig 89 LQR 93.

[156] See *Behn v Burness*, p 197, above.

[157] All three members of the court agreed on this ruling. Lord Denning dissented on other questions before the court but not in the result.

Notwithstanding the observations in the *Hong Kong Fir Shipping Co* case, if the fact is that a provision in a charter-party such as that contained in clause 1 in the present case has generally been regarded as a condition, giving the charterer the option to cancel on proof that the representation was made either untruthfully or without reasonable grounds, it would be regrettable at this stage to disturb an established interpretation. The standard text-books unequivocally state that such a clause as we are here concerned with is to be regarded as a condition.[158]

Megaw LJ said:[159]

> One of the important elements of the law is predictability. At any rate in commercial law there are obvious and substantial advantages in having, where possible, a firm and definite rule for a particular class of legal relationships . . . It is surely much better both for shipowners and charterers (and incidentally for their advisers) when a contractual obligation of this nature is under consideration—and still more when they are faced with the necessity of an urgent decision as to the effects of a suspected breach of it—to be able to say categorically: 'If a breach is proved, then the charterer can put an end to the contract.'

The alternative was to leave the parties to speculate on the ultimate reaction of the courts if litigation ensued.

In the *Hong Kong Fir* case it was clear that if the obligation as to seaworthiness had to be forced into one of the two slots marked condition or warranty, it must go into the latter. The practical thrust of the argument therefore was that there might be some breaches of undertakings which were not conditions, which might entitle the injured party to terminate.[160] The argument is at least as likely to be presented in reverse, so that the contract breaker argues that the practical results of breach do not justify allowing the innocent party to bring the contract to an end. So in *Cehave NV v Bremer Handelsgesellschaft mbH, The Hansa Nord:*[161]

> The sellers had sold a cargo of citrus pulp pellets to the buyers cif Rotterdam. One of the terms of the contract was 'shipment to be made in good condition'. Some part of the cargo was not so shipped and on arrival at Rotterdam the whole cargo was rejected by the buyers. The defects do not appear to have been very serious as the goods were sold by order of the Rotterdam Court and eventually found their way back into the hands of the buyers[162] who used them for their originally intended purpose as cattle feed. However the buyers argued that there was no room for the application of the *Hong Kong Fir* approach in sale cases on the grounds that the scheme of the Sale of Goods Act envisaged that all terms in a contract of sale should be either conditions or warranties. If this argument had succeeded it would have been necessary for the Court of Appeal to decide whether this term was a

---

[158] Ibid at 199 and 133–134, respectively.   [159] Ibid at 205 and 138, respectively.
[160] There is no doubt that there are some breaches of the seaworthiness obligation which have this result. See *Stanton v Richardson* (1872) LR 7 CP 421; affd LR 9 CP 390.
[161] [1976] QB 44, [1975] 3 All ER 739.   [162] At a greatly reduced price.

condition or warranty but the Court was clear that this was the wrong approach. Although the Sale of Goods Act had classified some terms as conditions or warranties, it did not follow that all terms had to be so classified. Accordingly it was possible to apply general principles and consider the effect of the breach. Since this was not serious the buyers had not been entitled to reject.

This reasoning was endorsed by the House of Lords in *Reardon Smith Line v Hansen-Tangen.*[163]

In this case the respondents had agreed to charter a tanker as yet unbuilt from a Japanese steamship company and later sub-chartered it to the appellants. The contract described the specification of the ship in detail and identified it as Osaka No 354.[164] In fact Osaka had so many orders that the work was sub-contracted to the Oshima yard where it was built as Oshima 004. The completed vessel was in all respects up to specification but, the tanker market having meanwhile collapsed, the appellants sought to reject the vessel as not complying with its contract description. The argument clearly had little merit but it had some support in the cases on contractual description in sale of goods.[165] The House of Lords were clear that these cases were ripe for review, but should not in any case be allowed to infect the rest of the law of contract and that since the breach here was of a technical nature, the appellants were not entitled to reject.

It is now perhaps possible to summarise these developments as follows:

(1) It is certainly open to the parties to indicate expressly the consequences to be attached to any particular breach. It will not necessarily be sufficient for this purpose to describe the term as 'a condition', for as we have seen, the word condition has many meanings and the court may decide that in a given contract it does not mean that the term is one any breach of which entitles the injured party to treat the contract as at an end.[166]

(2) What the parties may do expressly, may be done for them by implication or imputation. So the Sale of Goods Act 1979 provides that certain of the seller's implied obligations are conditions and clearly custom might produce the same result. Simi-

---

[163] [1976] 3 All ER 570, [1976] 1 WLR 989.

[164] Meaning apparently that it was to be built by the Osaka Shipping Co and that its yard number was 354.

[165] See eg *Re Moore & Co and Landauer & Co* [1921] 2 KB 519.

[166] *Schuler AG v Wickman Machine Tool Sales Ltd* [1974] AC 235, [1973] 2 All ER 39. The judgments of the Court of Appeal in this case [1972] 2 All ER 1173, [1972] 1 WLR 840 also contain much interesting learning on the use of the word 'condition'. Nevertheless the use of the word condition' in a contract drafted by a lawyer ought usually to be construed in this sense. The parties, at least in commercial contracts, are entitled to say that some matter usually unimportant is important to them and 'condition' is the obvious technical term to use for this purpose. See Lord Wilberforce's dissenting speech in *Schuler v Wickman* and his observations in *Reardon Smith v Hansen Tangen* [1976] 3 All ER 570 at 574, [1976] 1 WLR 989 at 996. See also the useful discussion in *George Hunt Cranes Ltd v Scottish Boiler and General Insurance Co Ltd* [2001] EWCA Civ 1964, [2002] 1 All ER (Comm) 366.

larly, if a term is commonly found in contracts of a particular class and such a term has in the past been held to be a condition, this provides strong support for a finding that the parties intended it to be a condition.[167]

(3) In the above situations it is possible, with some confidence, to say at the time of the contract that a term is a condition. In most other situations the question only assumes any significance when the contract is broken. Then as Lord Devlin has observed[168] 'both term and breach can be considered together . . . It is . . . by considering the nature of the term in the light of the breach alleged that the judge will have to make up his mind.' Nevertheless there may well be contractual situations where the court may be clear that a term is a condition even though it is possible to envisage breaches of it which would not be serious. A good example is *Bunge Corpn v Tradax Export SA.*[169]

> In this case the sellers sold 5,000 tons of US soya bean meal fob one US gulf port at sellers' option for shipment in June 1975. The buyers were required to 'give at least 15 consecutive days' notice of probable readiness of vessel' but did not give notice until 17 June. Obviously there did not remain fifteen days before the end of June but it did not necessarily follow that the sellers could not have completed their obligation to ship in June since in many cases this obligation could be completed in thirteen days rather than fifteen.

The House of Lords held that as the sellers' obligation to ship during June was certainly a condition, the buyers' obligation to give timely notice of readiness should equally be treated as a condition, without enquiry in particular cases as to whether delay had caused any serious consequences. Lord Wilberforce observed:[170]

> In suitable cases the courts should not be reluctant, if the intentions of the parties as shown by the contract so indicate, to hold that an obligation has the force of a condition, and that indeed they should usually do so in the case of time clauses in mercantile contracts. To such cases the 'gravity of the breach' approach of *Hong Kong Fir* would be unsuitable.[171]

(4) In making his decision the judge will sometimes find it helpful to concentrate primarily on the broken term, in others primarily on the extent of the breach.[172] In

---

[167] *The Mihalis Angelos*, p 168, above.   [168] [1966] CLJ 192 at 199–200.

[169] [1981] 2 All ER 513, [1981] 1 WLR 711.   [170] Ibid at 542 and 716, respectively.

[171] The question of timely performance has historically been approached through the question of whether 'time is of the essence'. But this appears to be an alternative formulation of the same issues. See *United Scientific Holdings Ltd v Burnley Borough Council* [1978] AC 904, [1977] 2 All ER 62 and discussion at pp 702–705, below. See also *Gill and Duffus SA v Société pour l'Exportation des Sucres SA* [1985] 1 Lloyd's Rep 621. The difficulties of deciding whether the structure of the contract makes a time provision a condition are well illustrated by *CIE Commerciale Sucrés et Denrés v C Czarnikow Ltd, The Naxos* [1990] 3 All ER 641, [1990] 1 WLR 1137.

[172] The words 'extent of the breach' themselves conceal an ambiguity since they may refer either to the extent to which the contract is broken or to the effects of that breach. It is not impossible for a small breach to have devastating consequences.

some contracts, such as sale, it has historically been normal to use the first approach, while, in others, such as building contracts, it has been common to use the second[173] but even in a contract of sale it is open to a court to hold that an obligation which has not been stamped either by statute or previous decisions as a 'condition', is an intermediate obligation, the effect of whose breach depends on whether it goes to the root of the contract.

4 EXCLUDING AND LIMITING TERMS

The common law has long been familiar with the attempt of one party to a contract to insert terms excluding or limiting liabilities which would otherwise be his. The situation frequently arises where a document purporting to express the terms of the contract is delivered to one of the parties and is not read by him. A passenger receives a ticket, stating the terms, or referring to terms set out elsewhere, on which a railway are prepared to carry him or take charge of his luggage. A buyer or hirer signs a document, containing clauses designed for the seller's or owner's protection. Are these terms or clauses part of the contract so as to bind the passenger, the buyer or the hirer, despite his ignorance of their character or even of their existence.[174]

The problems caused by exclusion clauses overlap with those caused by two other emergent themes of modern contract law, the increased use of standard forms contracts[175] and the development of special rules for the protection of consumers.[176] Exclusion clauses are usually, though not necessarily, contained in standard form contracts but they are by no means the only problem which such contracts present for the courts.

The common law has found it very difficult to develop doctrines that can be applied equally appropriately to both commercial and consumer transactions. This failure (in what may well be an impossible task) is responsible for much of the complexity in the account which follows.[177]

Before we turn to consider the particular rules which English law has developed, we should notice that there are divergent views as to what exclusion clauses do.[178] One view is that such clauses go to define the promisor's obligation. According to this view one should read the contract as a whole and decide what it is that the promisor has

---

[173] See pp 680–688, below.

[174] The theoretical problems raised by the operation of exception clauses are considered by Coote *Exception Clauses* (1964), an invaluable work. See also Macdonald *Exemption Clauses and Unfair Terms* (2nd edn, 2006).

[175] See pp 24–26, above.   [176] See p 26, above.   [177] See *Coote*.

[178] See per Lord Reid in *Suisse Atlantique d'Armement Maritime SA v NV Rotterdamsche Kolen Centrale* [1967] 1 AC 361 at 406, [1966] 2 All ER 61 at 76.

agreed to do. There is no doubt that this is what the courts sometimes do. So in *G H Renton & Co Ltd v Palmyra Trading Corpn of Panama*:[179]

> The respondent issued bills of lading, subject to the Hague Rules, covering the shipment of timber from ports in British Columbia to London. The bills of lading contained a clause permitting the master, in the event of industrial disputes at the port of delivery, to discharge at the port of loading or any other convenient port. In the event a strike broke out among dock workers in the Port of London and the master discharged the cargo at Hamburg. The appellant argued that the discharge at Hamburg was a breach of contract and that the strike clause did not provide an effective defence since it sought to provide a relief of liability contrary to the Hague Rules.[180] The House of Lords held that the respondents had not broken the contract since the strike clause did not provide a defence in the event of misperformance but went to define what it was that the carrier had agreed to do.[181]

However, in other cases, exclusion clauses have been regarded as mere defences. According to this view one should first construe the contract without regard to the exemption clauses in order to discover the promisor's obligation and only then consider whether the clauses provide a defence to breach of those obligations.[182]

It is clear that this difference is not merely theoretical but likely to provide significantly different results in many cases. Both approaches are to be found in the cases though the second is probably the more common. It is possible that both approaches are correct and that the real question is to choose which to apply to a particular clause. Certainly some clauses, eg clauses limiting the amount of damages that can be recovered, look like defences[183] while others are more naturally regarded as defining the obligation.

The problems raised by the attempt of one party to a contract to exclude or to limit the liability which would otherwise be his has produced prolific and persistent litigation as a result of which it is possible to hazard certain conclusions.

(1) At the outset of its inquiry the court must be satisfied that the particular document relied on as containing notice of the excluding or limiting term is in truth

---

[179] [1957] AC 149, [1956] 3 All ER 957. The House of Lords discussed this case in *Jindal Iron & Steel Co Ltd v Islamic Solidarity Shipping Company Jordan Inc* [2005] 1 All ER 175 and decided not to reconsider it.

[180] Art III, r 8.

[181] See also *East Ham Corpn v Bernard Sunley & Sons* [1966] AC 406, [1965] 3 All ER 619. Cf the construction given to a different strike clause by Russell LJ in *Torquay Hotel Co v Cousins* [1969] 2 Ch 106 at 143, [1969] 1 All ER 522 at 534.

[182] See eg Denning LJ in *Karsales (Harrow) Ltd v Wallis* [1956] 2 All ER 866 at 869, [1956] 1 WLR 936 at 940.

[183] Though this is denied by Barwick CJ in *State Government Insurance Office of Queensland v Brisbane Stevedoring Pty Ltd* (1969) 43 ALJR 456 at 461.

an integral part of the contract.[184] It must have been intended as a contractual document and not as a mere acknowledgment of payment. To hold a party bound by the terms of a document which reasonable persons would assume to be no more than a receipt is an affront to common sense. An illustration of the point is afforded by the case of *Chapelton v Barry UDC*.[185]

> The plaintiff wished to hire two deck-chairs from a pile kept by the defendant council on their beach. The chairs were stacked near a notice which read . . . 'Hire of Chairs 2d per session of 3 hours', and which requested the public to obtain tickets from the chair attendant and retain them for inspection. The plaintiff took the chairs and obtained two tickets from the attendant, which he put in his pocket without reading. When he sat on one of the chairs, it collapsed and he was injured. He sued the council, who relied on a provision printed on the tickets excluding liability for any damage arising from the hire of a chair.

The Court of Appeal held the defendants liable. No reasonable man would assume that the ticket was anything but a receipt for the money. The notice on the beach constituted the offer, which the plaintiff accepted when he took the chair, and the notice contained no statement limiting the liability of the council. The defendants had failed to satisfy the preliminary requirement of identifying the ticket as a contractual document, and it was superfluous, therefore, to ask if it contained a due announcement of any conditions.

The case of *McCutcheon v David MacBrayne Ltd*[186] affords a second illustration.

> The defendants owned steamers operating between the Scottish mainland and the islands. The plaintiff asked a Mr McSporran to arrange for the plaintiff's car to be shipped to the mainland. Mr McSporran called at the defendants' office and made an oral contract on the plaintiff's behalf for the carriage of the car. On the voyage, through the defendants' negligence, both ship and car were sunk. The plaintiff sued the defendants for the value of the car.

The defendants pleaded terms, excluding liability for negligence, contained in 27 paragraphs of small print displayed both outside and inside their office. The terms were also printed on a 'risk note' which customers were usually asked to sign. On this occasion the defendants omitted to ask Mr McSporran to sign the risk note. All they did was to give him, when he had paid in advance the cost of carriage, a receipt stating that 'all goods were carried subject to the conditions set out in the notices'. The House of Lords gave judgment for the plaintiff. Neither he nor Mr McSporran had read the

---

[184] Approved by Lord Denning MR in *White v Blackmore* [1972] 2 QB 651 at 666, [1972] 3 All ER 158 at 167. Clarke [1976] CLJ 51; *The Eagle* [1977] 2 Lloyd's Rep 70; Clarke [1978] CLJ 21.

[185] [1940] 1 KB 532, [1940] 1 All ER 356. See also *Henson v London North Eastern Rly Co and Coote and Warren Ltd* [1946] 1 All ER 653.

[186] [1964] 1 All ER 430, [1964] 1 WLR 125. See also *Burnett v Westminster Bank Ltd*, p 206, below.

words on the notices or on the receipt; and there was in truth no contractual document at all. The risk note was not presented to Mr McSporran, and the receipt was given only after the oral contract had been concluded.

(2) If the document is to be regarded as an integral part of the contract, it must next be seen if it has, or has not, been signed by the party against whom the excluding or limiting term is pleaded. If it is unsigned, the question will be whether reasonable notice of the term has been given. That this was the crucial test was pronounced by Mellish LJ in 1877 in the case of *Parker v South Eastern Rly Co*, where the defendants claimed that a passenger was bound by terms stated on a cloakroom ticket of which he was ignorant.[187] Had the defendants done what was sufficient to give notice of the term to the person or class of person to which the plaintiff belonged? The question is one of fact, and the court must examine the circumstances of each case.[188]

The time when the notice is alleged to have been given is of great importance. No excluding or limiting term will avail the party seeking its protection unless it has been brought adequately to the attention of the other party before the contract is made. A belated notice is valueless. Thus in *Olley v Marlborough Court Ltd*:[189]

> A husband and wife arrived at a hotel as guests and paid for a week's board and residence in advance. They went up to the bedroom allotted to them, and on one of its walls was a notice that 'the proprietors will not hold themselves responsible for articles lost or stolen unless handed to the manageress for safe custody'. The wife then closed the self-locking door of the bedroom, went downstairs and hung the key on the board in the reception office. In her absence the key was wrongfully taken by a third party, who opened the bedroom door and stole her furs.

The defendants sought to incorporate the notice in the contract. The Court of Appeal thought that even if incorporated in the contract, the term was not sufficiently clear to cover the defendant's negligence but Singleton and Denning LJJ considered that in any case the contract was completed before the guests went to their room.[190]

---

[187] (1877) 2 CPD 416, especially at 422–423. The test was approved by the House of Lords in *Richardson v Rowntree* [1894] AC 217. See also *Thornton v Shoe Lane Parking Ltd* [1971] 2 QB 163, [1971] 1 All ER 686; p 207, below.

[188] There are a vast number of nineteenth- and early twentieth-century cases on railway and steamship tickets. These 'ticket cases' are more fully discussed in the 4th edition of this work at pp 104–107. English judges have tended to take a restricted view of what need be done to give reasonable notice. See eg *Thompson v London Midland and Scottish Rly Co* [1930] 1 KB 41. American judges starting from the same test have been more demanding, eg rejecting tickets in very small print which is difficult to read, eg *Lisi v Alitalia Lines Aerea Italiane SpA* [1968] 1 Lloyd's Rep 505, affirming [1967] 1 Lloyd's Rep 140; *Silvestri v Italia Societa per Azioni di Navigazione* [1968] 1 Lloyd's Rep 263.

[189] [1949] 1 KB 532, [1949] 1 All ER 127. In *Chapelton v Barry UDC* (p 173, above), the ticket, even had it been a contractual document, was given to the plaintiff after he had accepted the offer to hire a chair. In *BCT Software Solutions Ltd v Arnold Laver & Co Ltd* [2002] EWHC 1298 (Ch), [2002] 2 All ER Comm 85, the claimant's standard conditions were held inconsistent with the parties' express agreement.

[190] If the plaintiffs had stayed at the hotel before it might be argued that there was a course of dealing between the parties. See p 206, below.

A striking if unusual illustration of the time factor is offered by *Burnett v Westminster Bank Ltd.*[191]

> The plaintiff had for some years accounts at two of the defendants' branches—branch A and branch B. A new cheque book was issued to him by branch A, on the front cover of which was a notice that 'the cheques in this book will be applied to the account for which they have been prepared'. These cheques were in fact designed for use in a computer system, operated by branch A, and 'magnetised ink' was used which the computer could 'read'. The plaintiff knew that there were words on the cover of the cheque book, but had not read them. He drew a cheque for £2,300, but crossed out branch A and substituted branch B. The computer could not 'read' the plaintiff's ink. He later wished to stop the cheque and told branch B. Meanwhile the computer had debited his account at branch A. He sued the defendants for breach of contract, and they pleaded the limiting words on the cover of the cheque book.

Mocatta J gave judgment for the plaintiff. The cheque book was not a document which could reasonably be assumed to contain terms of the contract; and the defendants had not in fact given adequate notice of the restriction to the plaintiff. They were, in effect, seeking, without his assent, to alter the terms of the contract.

A further point must be made. The court may infer notice from previous dealings between the parties. This possibility was demonstrated in the case of *Spurling v Bradshaw.*[192]

> The defendant had dealt for many years with the plaintiffs, who were warehousemen. He delivered to them for storage eight barrels of orange juice. A few days later he received from them a document acknowledging the receipt of the barrels and referring on its face to clauses printed on the back. One such clause exempted the plaintiffs 'from any loss or damage occasioned by the negligence, wrongful act or default' of themselves or their servants. When ultimately the defendant came to collect the barrels, they were found to be empty.

The defendant refused to pay the storage charges, and the plaintiffs sued him. He counter-claimed for negligence and, in answer to this counter-claim, the plaintiffs pleaded the exempting clause. The defendant sought to argue that, as the document containing it was sent to him only after the conclusion of the contract, it was too late to affect his rights. But he admitted that in previous dealings he had often received a similar document, though he had never bothered to read it, and he was now held to be bound by it.

The phrase 'course of dealing', on which the inference of notice may rest, is not easily defined. But it is clear that it must be a consistent course. In *McCutcheon v*

---

[191] [1966] 1 QB 742, [1965] 3 All ER 81.
[192] [1956] 2 All ER 121, [1956] 1 WLR 461. See Hoggett 33 MLR 518.

David MacBrayne Ltd[193] the plaintiff's agent had dealt with the defendants on a number of occasions. Sometimes he had signed a 'risk note' and sometimes he had not. Lord Pearce said:[194]

> The respondents rely on the course of dealing. But they are seeking to establish an oral contract by a course of dealing which always insisted on a written contract. It is the consistency of a course of conduct which gives rise to the implication that in similar circumstances a similar contractual result will follow. When the conduct is *not* consistent, there is no reason why it should still produce an invariable contractual result. The respondents having previously offered a written contract, on this occasion offered an oral one. The appellant's agent duly paid the freight for which he was asked and accepted the oral contract thus offered. This raises no implication that the condition of the oral contract must be the same as the conditions of the written contract would have been had the respondent proffered one.

A discussion of familiar problems in a novel setting is to be found in *Thornton v Shoe Lane Parking Ltd.*[195]

> The plaintiff wished to park his car in the defendants' automatic car park. He had not been there before. Outside the park was a notice, stating the charges and adding the words 'All cars parked at owners' risk'. As the plaintiff drove into the park a light turned from red to green, and a ticket was pushed out from a machine. Nobody was in attendance. The plaintiff took the ticket and saw the time on it. He also saw that it contained other words, but put it into his pocket without reading them. The words in fact stated that the ticket was issued subject to conditions displayed on the premises. To find these conditions the plaintiff would have had to walk round the park until he reached a panel on which they were displayed. The plaintiff never thought to look for them. One condition purported to exempt the defendants from liability not only for damage to the cars parked but also for injury to customers, however caused. When the plaintiff returned to collect his car, there

---

[193] See p 205, above, for the facts of this case. In this case Lord Devlin suggested that a term could be introduced by a course of dealings only if there was actual knowledge of its content (as opposed to its existence). This statement was unnecessary for the decision and clearly goes too far in view of *Henry Kendall & Sons v William Lillico & Sons* [1969] 2 AC 31, [1968] 2 All ER 444. It appears relatively easy to show that terms are included in a contract by a course of dealings in a commercial context. See *British Crane Hire Corpn Ltd v Ipswich Plant Hire Ltd* [1975] QB 303, [1974] 1 All ER 1059, where an oral contract was treated as subject to the conditions of a trade association which both parties commonly employed. This case appears not to depend on a course of dealings between the parties but on the court's perception of the shared assumptions of the parties. It is more difficult in consumer transactions: see *Mendelssohn v Normand Ltd* [1970] 1 QB 177, [1969] 2 All ER 1215; *Hollier v Rambler Motors (AMC) Ltd* [1972] 2 QB 71, [1972] 1 All ER 399, though these cases can also be explained on the ground that there was not sufficient consistency or continuity of dealing. See also *PLM Trading Co (International) Ltd v Georgiou* [1987] CLY 430; Swanton 1 JCL 223, Macdonald 8 LS 48.

[194] [1964] 1 All ER 430 at 439–440, [1964] 1 WLR 125 at 138.

[195] [1971] 2 QB 163, [1971] 1 All ER 686.

was an accident in which he was injured. The defendants pleaded the exempting term.

The Court of Appeal gave judgment for the plaintiff. The first question raised was the moment at which the contract was made.[196] It was not easy to apply the long line of 'ticket cases', reaching back for a hundred years, to the mechanism of an automatic machine. Lord Denning said:[197]

> The customer pays his money and gets a ticket. He cannot refuse it. He cannot get his money back. He may protest to the machine, even swear at it. But it will remain unmoved. He is committed beyond recall. He was committed at the very moment when he put his money into the machine. The contract was concluded at that time. It can be translated into offer and acceptance in this way: the offer is made when the proprietor of the machine holds it out as being ready to receive the money. The acceptance takes place when the customer puts his money into the slot. The terms of the offer are contained in the notice placed on or near the machine stating what is offered for the money. The customer is bound by these terms as long as they are sufficiently brought to his notice before-hand, but not otherwise. He is not bound by the terms printed on the ticket if they differ from the notice, because the ticket comes too late. The contract has already been made.

Even if the automatic machine was regarded as a booking clerk in disguise and the older ticket cases applied, the plaintiff would still succeed. In the leading case of *Parker v South Eastern Rly Co*,[198] three questions were posed. (a) Did the plaintiff know that there was printing on the ticket? In the instant case he did. (b) Did he know that the ticket contained or referred to conditions? In the instant case he did not know. (c) Had the defendants done what was sufficient to draw the plaintiff's attention to the relevant conditions? In the instant case the condition was designed to exempt the defendants from liability for personal injury caused to the customer. So wide an exception was, in the context, unusual and required an unusually explicit warning. Such warning the defendants had not given, and they could not escape liability for the plaintiff's injury. In this case the requirement of explicit warning about unusual terms was applied in the context of an exemption of liability. However, it appears that this doctrine is not limited to exempting clauses but is of general application. This was the view of the Court of Appeal in *Interfoto Picture Library Ltd v Stiletto Visual Programmes Ltd*.[199]

> In this case the defendants were an advertising agency who needed to obtain some photographs of the 1950s for a presentation which they were preparing. For this purpose they rang the plaintiffs who ran a library of photographs and asked if they had any suitable photographs of the period. The plaintiffs sent a bag containing 47

---

[196] Megaw LJ, while he concurred in the decision, reserved his opinion as to the precise moment when the contract was made.

[197] Ibid at 169 and 689, respectively.

[198] (1877) 2 CPD 416: see p 205, above.   [199] [1989] QB 433, [1988] 1 All ER 348.

transparencies with a delivery note clearly stating that the transparencies were to be returned by 19 March (14 days after the enquiry) and setting out a number of printed conditions. The Court of Appeal had no doubt that in principle the contract was on the terms contained in the delivery note. One of the conditions provided that for every day after 14 days that the transparencies were kept there would be a holding fee per transparency of £5 plus VAT per day. In fact, the defendants did not return the transparencies until 2 April and were faced with a bill for £3,783.50.

The Court of Appeal held that the defendants were not obliged to pay this sum because the plaintiffs had failed to give adequate notice of such a surprising term. It was not sufficient to incorporate the term into the standard printed conditions. More vigorous steps should be taken such as printing the term in bold type or sending a covering note drawing specific attention to it.

In applying the principle that surprising terms require extra notice, it will obviously be essential to know what terms are surprising. In some cases, common sense will provide an answer but this will not always be the case. It may be necessary to enquire and therefore for the relevant party to lead evidence as to what the normal practice is in a particular trade, profession or locality. In fact, the relevant trade association, the British Association of Picture Libraries and Agencies (BAPLA) does produce a guide as to what terms are normal which is based on consultation with representative bodies of typical customers such as the Publishers Association, the Society of Authors and so on. This guide does in fact state that a free period of loan, followed by a provision for payment for holding over, is to be expected. This is of course a common feature of similar arrangements such as borrowing books from a library. If the term in this case was surprising therefore, it was not so much because there was provision for payments after the 14th day but because of the rate of payment. Much would turn here on the effect of the evidence as to what the normal rate was.[200]

A problem which has not so far received much attention from the courts is the so-called 'battle of the forms'.[201] This occurs where one party sends a form stating that the contract is on his terms and the other party responds by returning a form stating

---

[200] If the failure to return the photographs was a breach of contract then it would be arguable that some levels of charge would be invalid as being penalties. See below, pp 786–792. In *AEG (UK) Ltd v Logic Resource Ltd* [1996] CLC 265, Hobhouse LJ delivered an important dissenting judgment expressing some reserve as to the width of the *Interfoto* principle. He took the position that the clause before the Court of Appeal (which put the cost of returning defective goods on to the buyer) was not unusual and that the real objection of the majority to it was that it was unreasonable. He would have wished to restrict the use of tests based on unreasonableness. Cf Brooke LJ in *Lacey's Footwear Ltd v Bowler International Freight Ltd* [1997] 2 Lloyd's Rep 369 at 385. See Macdonald [1999] CLJ 413, Bradgate 60 MLR 582. So far courts do not appear to apply the *Stiletto* reasoning where the contract has been signed.

[201] See Furmston, Norisada and Poole *Contract Formstion and Letters of Intent, Chapter 4.* Hoggett 33 MLR 518, Adams [1983] JBL 297, Jacobs 34 ICLQ 297, MacKendrick 8 OJLS 197.

that the contract is on his terms! At least five solutions seem possible, viz that there is a contract on the first party's terms, a contract on the second party's terms, a contract on the terms that common law would normally imply in such circumstances, a contract on some amalgam of the parties' terms or no contract at all. In theory there is much to be said for the last solution since there is neither agreement nor apparent agreement on the terms of the contract. In practice however it may be that the courts will try to give effect to the intention of the parties to make some contract. It has been suggested that each succeeding form should be treated as a counter-offer so that the last form should be regarded as accepted by the receiver's silence. This is a possible view but not perhaps easy to reconcile with the conventional view of *Felthouse v Bindley*.[202]

The leading decision in *Butler Machine Tool Co v Ex-Cell-O Corpn*[203] is interesting but, unfortunately, indecisive.

> The sellers offered to sell a machine tool to the buyers for £75,535, delivery in ten months and the buyers replied placing an order. The offer and order were on the sellers' and buyers' standard printed stationery, respectively. Each document contained various terms and there were of course differences between the terms. In particular the sellers' terms included a price variation clause, which if incorporated into the contract, would have entitled them to charge the price ruling at the day of delivery, whereas the buyers' terms contained no provision for price variation. The buyers' conditions had a tear off slip, which the sellers were invited to and did return, containing the words 'we accept your order on the terms and conditions thereon'. The slip was accompanied by a letter from the sellers, stating that the buyers' order had been entered into in accordance with the original offer. When the machine tool was delivered, the sellers claimed to be entitled to another £2,892 under their terms.

The Court of Appeal held that on the facts the sellers had contracted on the buyers' terms, since the return of the acknowledgment slip amounted to an acceptance of the buyers' counter-offer. The accompanying letter did not qualify this acceptance but simply confirmed the price and description of the machine.[204] This decision makes the result turn entirely on the sellers' tactical error in returning the acknowledgement slip. In future well-trained warriors in the battle of the forms will take care not to return documents originating from the other side.

---

[202] Pp 61–62, above. See also *British Road Services Ltd v Arthur Crutchley & Co Ltd* [1968] 1 All ER 811; *Transmotors Ltd v Robertson, Buckley & Co Ltd* [1970] 1 Lloyd's Rep 224; *OTM Ltd v Hydranautics* [1981] 2 Lloyd's Rep 211; *Nissan UK Ltd v Nissan Motor Manufacturing Ltd* (1994) unreported, CA.

[203] [1979] 1 All ER 965, [1979] 1 WLR 401; Rawlings 42 MLR 715.

[204] This decision has been criticised on the facts, since it seems very unlikely in practice that the sellers intended to accept the buyer's standard conditions rather than to maintain adherence to their own. If the decision is correct, it is presumably on the basis of a rather stringent application of the objective test of agreement.

The Court of Appeal also considered what the position would have been if the seller had not returned the slip. Lawton and Bridge LJJ thought the solution lay in applying the traditional rules of offer and counter-offer. This would mean that in many cases there was no contract, at least until the goods were delivered and accepted by the buyer.[205] Lord Denning MR on the other hand thought that one should first of all look to see if the parties thought they had contracted and if they had one should look at the documents as a whole to discover the content of their agreement.[206] The majority view is certainly more consistent with orthodox theory. On the other hand it may be thought unsatisfactory to employ a rule which would leave so many agreements in the air. The problem is one that is common to most developed legal systems and there have been a number of attempts at statutory reform, though none seems to have found a wholly satisfactory solution.[207]

(3) If the document is signed it will normally be impossible or at least difficult, to deny its contractual character, and evidence of notice, actual or constructive, is irrelevant. In the absence of fraud or misrepresentation, a person is bound by a writing to which he has put his signature, whether he has read its contents or has chosen to leave them unread.[208] The distinction between the signed and the unsigned document was taken by Lord Justice Mellish in *Parker v South East Rly Co*, and was emphasised and illustrated in *L'Estrange v Graucob*.[209] The plaintiff bought an automatic machine from the defendants on terms contained in a document, described as a 'Sales Agreement', and including a number of clauses in 'legible, but regrettably small print', which she signed but did not read. The Divisional Court held that she was bound by these terms and that no question of notice arose. In the words of Scrutton LJ:[210]

> In cases in which the contract is contained in a railway ticket or other unsigned document, it is necessary to prove that an alleged party was aware, or ought to have been aware, of its terms and conditions. These cases have no application when the document has been signed. When a document containing contractual terms is signed, then, in the absence of fraud, or, I will add, misrepresentation, the party signing it is bound, and it is wholly immaterial whether he has read the document or not.

---

[205] See *Sauter Automation v H C Goodman (Mechanicez Services)* (1986) 34 BLR 81; *Chichester Joinery Ltd v John Mowlem Co Ltd* (1987) 42 BLR 100.

[206] Lord Denning's views here are reminiscent of his views in *Gibson v Manchester City Council* [1978] 2 All ER 583, [1978] 1 WLR 520 which were emphatically disapproved of by the House of Lords [1979] 1 All ER 972, [1979] 1 WLR 294. See p 47, above. Of course the *Gibson* case did not involve a battle of the forms.

[207] Uniform Commercial Code, s 2-207; *Farnsworth on Contract 3.21*; Uniform Laws on International Sales Act 1967, Sch 2, Art 7; Unidroit-Principles of International Commercial Contracts, Art 2.22.

[208] For the possibility of pleading mistake, see pp 284–289, below. But even here there are no decided cases where the plea of mistake has availed in the absence of fraud.

[209] [1934] 2 KB 394. For the dictum of Mellish LJ, see (1877) 2 CPD 416 at 421. See Spencer [1973] CLJ 104.

[210] [1934] 2 KB 394 at 403.

The qualification imposed upon the absolute character of signed documents by the last sentence quoted from this judgment will be readily understood. It was applied in the case of *Curtis v Chemical Cleaning and Dyeing Co.*[211]

> The plaintiff took to the defendants' shop for cleaning a white satin wedding dress trimmed with beads and sequins. The shop assistant gave her a document headed 'Receipt' and requested her to sign it. With unusual prudence, the plaintiff asked its purport, and the assistant replied that it exempted the defendants from certain risks and, in the present instance, from the risk of damage to the beads and sequins on the dress. The plaintiff then signed the document, which in fact contained a clause 'that the company is not liable for any damage, however caused'. When the dress was returned, it was stained and, in an action by the plaintiff for damages, the defendants relied on this clause.

The Court of Appeal held that the defence must fail. The assistant, however innocently, had misrepresented the effect of the document, and the defendants were thus prevented from insisting upon the drastic terms of the exemption. The plaintiff was entitled to assume, as the assistant had assured her, that she was running the risk only of damage to the beads and sequins.

(4) The courts have developed a number of rules which they employ as a means of controlling improper use of exemption and limiting clauses. So the courts have held that clear words must be used if they are designed to excuse one party from a serious breach of the contract.[212] Similarly, clear words must be used if one party is to be excused from the results of his negligence. A particular problem, which has given rise to a good deal of litigation, arises where a party is potentially liable both on the basis of negligence and on the basis of strict liability. A good example is the common carrier of goods, who holds himself out as prepared to carry goods to any person whatever. In addition to his liability for negligence such a person, by virtue of his calling, is strictly responsible for the safety of the goods entrusted to him, save for damage caused by an act of God, the Queen's enemies, an inherent defect in the goods themselves, or the fault of the consignor. In such a situation general words excluding liability have often been taken to exclude the strict liability but not to exclude negligence based liability. Similarly, in *White v John Warrick & Co Ltd*,[213] the plaintiff hired a cycle from the defendants under a contract which provided that 'nothing in this agreement shall render the owners liable for any personal injury'. The saddle tilted forward while the plaintiff was riding the bicycle and he was injured. The court held that the words

---

[211] [1951] 1 KB 805, [1951] 1 All ER 631. See *Jaques v Lloyd D George & Partners Ltd* [1968] 2 All ER 187. It may also, in any future case, be necessary to consider the effect of the Misrepresentation Act 1967, s 3: pp 369–372, below.

[212] Discussed more fully p 223 below. Howarth 36 NILQ 101.

[213] [1953] 2 All ER 1021, [1953] 1 WLR 1285.

used were sufficient to exclude the defendants' strict liability in contract for hiring a defective cycle but not their tort liability, if any, for negligence.[214]

Courts have sometimes come close to saying that in order to exclude liability for negligence one has to say in terms that liability for negligence is excluded. This clearly goes too far as appears from the decision of the House of Lords in *HIH Casualty and General Insurance v Chase Manhattan Bank*[215]

In this case the bank was lending money against the receipts of movies to be made in the future. The bank wished to lay off a substantial part of the risk and entered into a contract of insurance with the appellant. The detailed negotiations were in the hands of intermediaries who were much better informed than either of the principals. The insurance contract contained extensive disclaimers. The House of Lords held that the bank could and had excluded liability for the negligence of its agents.[216] This case can usefully be regarded as a reconsideration of the principles stated by Lord Morton in *Canada Steamship Lines Ltd v R*[217] in the light of modern principles of construction.

Another principle which can overlap with the previous two is the so-called *contra proferentum* rule which says that if there is any doubt as to the meaning and scope of the excluding or limiting term, the ambiguity should be resolved against the party who inserted it and seeks to rely on it.[218] Courts have sometimes gone very far in using this approach. So in *Hollier v Rambler Motors (AMC) Ltd*:[219]

> The plaintiff agreed with the manager of the defendants' garage that his car should be towed to the garage for repair. While at the garage the car was substantially damaged by fire as a result of the defendants' negligence. The defendants argued that the transaction was subject to their usual terms which included 'The company is not responsible for damage caused by fire to customer's cars on the premises'.

The Court of Appeal held that even if this provision was incorporated into the contract, it would not operate to provide a defence. The defendants argued that in

---

[214] See also Lord Greene MR in *Alderslade v Hendon Laundry Ltd* [1945] KB 189, [1945] 1 All ER 244.

[215] [2003] 1 All ER (Comm) 349, [2003] 2 Lloyd's Rep 61; Bennett (2003) 19 J Contract L 205.

[216] But had not excluded liability for the agent's fraud if they were indeed fraudulent. See p 371, below.

[217] [1952] AC 192.

[218] It is not completely clear whether the proferens is the person responsible for the drafting of the clause or the person who seeks to rely on it. In the reported cases the defendant has been both.

[219] [1972] 2 QB 71 [1972] 1 All ER 399. See also *Akerib v Booth Ltd* [1961] 1 All ER 380, [1961] 1 WLR 367; *Morris v C W Martin & Sons Ltd* [1966] 1 QB 716, [1965] 2 All ER 725; *Hawkes Bay and East Coast Aero Club Ltd v Macleod* [1972] NZLR 289; Coote [1972A] CLJ 53; cf *Arthur White (Contractors) Ltd v Tarmac Civil Engineering Ltd* [1967] 3 All ER 586, [1967] 1 WLR 1508; *Adams v Richardson & Starling Ltd* [1969] 2 All ER 1221, [1969] 1 WLR 1645; *Lamport and Holt Lines Ltd v Coubro & Scutton (M and I) Ltd and Coubro and Scrutton (Ruggers and Shipwrights) Ltd, The Raphael* [1982] 2 Lloyd's Rep 42. The same principles apply to clauses in which one party undertakes to indemnify another against the consequences of the latter's negligence; *Smith v South Wales Switchgear Ltd* [1978] 1 WLR 165. Adams and Brownsword [1982] JBL 200; [1988] JBL 146.

the circumstances the only way in which they could be liable for damage by fire was if they were negligent and that the words were therefore appropriate to exclude liability for negligence. The court held that the clause could be read by a reasonable customer as a warning that the defendants would not be responsible for a fire caused without negligence. It was not therefore sufficiently unambiguous to exclude liability for negligence.[220]

It is arguable that this case has crossed the line between legitimate strict construction and illegitimate hostile construction. It is certain that in later cases the House of Lords has warned against the excesses of hostile construction. In *Ailsa Craig Fishing Co Ltd v Malvern Fishing Co Ltd*[221] Lord Wilberforce said of clauses of limitation that 'one must not strive to create ambiguities by strained construction . . . The relevant words must be given, if possible, their natural plain meaning.'[222] In *George Mitchell (Chesterhall) Ltd v Finney Lock Seeds Ltd*[223] Lord Diplock agreed with Lord Denning in the Court of Appeal that recent legislation[224] had 'removed from judges the temptation to resort to the device of ascribing to the words appearing in exemption clauses a tortured meaning so as to avoid giving effect to an exclusion or limitation of liability when a judge thought that in the circumstances to do so would be unfair'.[225]

(5) Even if the excluding or limiting term is an integral part of the contract and even if its language is apt to meet the situation that has in fact occurred, questions may arise as to whether the term can operate to protect a person who is not a party to the contract.[226] This often happens, for example, under contracts of carriage where the carrier has excluded or limited his own liability and an injured passenger or consignor of goods seeks to sue the servant or agent whose negligence has caused him damage. Thus in *Adler v Dickson*:[227]

> The plaintiff was a passenger in the Peninsular and Oriental Steam Navigation Co's vessel *Himalaya*, and was travelling on a first-class ticket. The 'ticket' was a lengthy printed document containing terms exempting the company from liability. There was a general clause that 'passengers are carried at passengers' entire risk' and a particular clause that 'the company will not be responsible for any injury whatsoever to the person of any passenger arising from or occasioned by the negligence of the company's servants'. While the plaintiff was mounting a gangway, it moved and fell and she was thrown onto the wharf from a height of 16 feet and sustained

---

[220] The case is criticised by Barendt 35 MLR 644. Cf Coote [1973] CLJ 14.

[221] [1983] 1 All ER 101, [1983] 1 WLR 964. [222] [1983] 1 All ER 101 at 104.

[223] [1983] 2 AC 803, [1983] 2 All ER 737. [224] See p 230, below.

[225] Ibid at 810 and 739, respectively. In *Macey v Qazi* [1987] CLY 425 it was stated that the *contra proferentum* principle should only be used as a last resort. The Court of Appeal stressed the importance of a fully contextual approach in *McGeown v Direct Travel Insurance* [2003] EWCACiv 1606, [2004] 1 All ER (Comm) 609.

[226] See Coote *Exception Clauses* ch 9; Treitel 18 MLR 172; Furmston 23 MLR 373 at 385–397; Atiyah 46 ALJ 212; Rose 4 Anglo-American L Rev 7.

[227] [1955] 1 QB 158, [1954] 3 All ER 397.

serious injuries. She brought an action for negligence, not against the company, but against the master and boatswain of the ship.

The Court of Appeal held that, while the clauses protected the company from liability, they could avail no one else. The *ratio decidendi* of the court was that the ticket did not, on its true construction, purport to exempt the master or boatswain. The Court of Appeal also considered, obiter, what the position would have been if the ticket had said that the master and boatswain were not to be liable. On this question there were divergent views. Jenkins LJ said,

> . . . even if these provisions had contained words purporting to exclude the liability of the company's servants, *non constat* that the company's servants could successfully rely on that exclusion . . . for the company's servants are not parties to the contract.[228]

Morris LJ agreed but Denning LJ took the opposite view.

In *Scruttons Ltd v Midland Silicones Ltd*:[229]

> A drum containing chemicals was shipped in New York by X on a ship owned by the United States Lines and consigned to the order of the plaintiffs. The bill of lading contained a clause limiting the liability of the shipowners, as carriers, to 500 dollars (£179). The defendants were stevedores who had contracted with the United States Lines to act for them in London on the terms that the defendants were to have the benefit of the limiting clause in the bill of lading. The plaintiffs were ignorant of the contract between the defendants and the United States Lines. Owing to the defendants' negligence the drum of chemicals was damaged to the extent of £593. The plaintiffs sued the defendants in negligence and the defendants pleaded the limiting clause in the bill of lading.

Diplock J found for the plaintiffs, and his judgment was upheld both by the Court of Appeal and by the House of Lords.[230] Their Lordships (Lord Denning dissenting) took the view that privity of contract was a fatal objection to the defendant's claim. The defendants were not parties to the bill of lading and could derive no rights under it. This rule appears simple but it is not without difficulties.

(a) The House of Lords relied on the fact that the United States Supreme Court had recently reached the same decision in *Krawill Machinery Corpn v R C Herd & Co Inc*[231] but that decision owed nothing to the doctrine of privity on contract which does not exist in its English form in the United States. It was rested simply, as *Scuttons v Midland Silicones* could have been, on the basis that nothing in the bill of lading expressly or impliedly excluded the liability of the stevedore. Later American cases have shown that a suitably worded clause can extend immunity to non-parties.[232]

---

[228] Ibid at 186 and 403, respectively. [229] [1962] AC 446, [1962] 2 All ER 1.
[230] Ibid. [231] [1959] 1 Lloyd's Rep 305, 359 US 297.
[232] Eg *Carle and Montanari Inc v American Export Isbrandtsen Lines Inc* [1968] 1 Lloyd's Rep 260; affd 386 F 2d 839: cert denied 390 US 1013 (1968).

(b) The House of Lords also relied on the decision of the High Court of Australia in *Wilson v Darling Island Stevedoring Co Ltd*.[233] Stevedores here pleaded an exemption clause in a contract evidenced by a bill of lading and made between the owner of goods and a carrier. The plea failed. It is true that Fullagar J said,

> The obvious answer . . . is that the defendant is not a party to the contract, evidenced by the bill of lading, that it can neither sue nor be sued on that contract, and that nothing in a contract between two other parties can relieve it from the consequences of a tortious act committed by it against the plaintiff.[234]

Dixon CJ agreed with Fullagar J, but the remainder of the court took different views and it is clear that the result would have been different if the bill of lading had stated clearly that the stevedores were not to be liable.

(c) The decision of the House is not easy to reconcile with its earlier decision in *Elder Dempster & Co v Patterson Zochonis & Co*.[235] In that case, Scrutton LJ and a unanimous House of Lords including Lord Sumner had assumed that a non-party could in some circumstances shelter behind an exemption clause contained in a contract between two other parties. In *Scruttons v Midland Silicones* the House of Lords put the *Elder Dempster* case on one side on the ground that its precise ratio was obscure.[236] It may perhaps be thought that in commercial matters what Lord Sumner and Scrutton LJ thought self-evidently correct is not often self-evidently wrong.[237]

(d) The house appeared to assume that only a contract between plaintiff and defendant would do to exclude the defendant's liability. But it is very doubtful whether this is the law. Thus we have seen that a debt owed by A to B may be rendered unenforceable by B's acceptance of part-payment by C.[238] Further, the liability of the stevedores was tortious and not contractual and tortious liability may be excluded by consent, which need not be contractual.[239]

An interesting, if inconclusive case is that of *Morris v C W Martin & Sons Ltd*.[240]

> The plaintiff sent her mink stole to a furrier to be cleaned. The furrier told her that he himself did no cleaning but that he could arrange for this to be done by the defendants. The plaintiff approved this proposal. The furrier accordingly, acting as principal and not as agent, made a contract with the defendants, a well-known firm, to clean the plaintiff's fur. While in the possession of the defendants, the fur

---

[233] [1956] 1 Lloyd's Rep 346, 95 CLR 43.

[234] [1956] 1 Lloyd's Rep 346 at 357.

[235] [1924] AC 522. For fuller discussion of this difficult case see p 214 n 225, above.

[236] On the relevance of this case to the doctrine of precedent, see Dworkin 25 MLR 163 at 171–174.

[237] It appears that the *Elder Dempster* case should be explained on the basis of a bailment on terms. See *The Pioneer Container* [1994] 2 All ER 250, discussed p 220, below.

[238] See p 137, above.

[239] See Kitto J in *Wilson v Darling Island Stevedoring Co Ltd* (1955) 95 CLR 43 at 81 and the advice of the Privy Council in *The Pioneer Container* [1994] 2 All ER 250, discussed p 220, below.

[240] [1966] 1 QB 716, [1965] 2 All ER 725.

was stolen by their servant. The plaintiff sued the defendants, who pleaded exemption clauses contained in their contract with the furrier.

The Court of Appeal held the defendants liable. The three members of the court agreed (a) that, when the defendants received the fur in order to clean it, they became bailees for reward; (b) that, as such bailees, they owed a common law duty to the plaintiff; (c) that the clauses on which they relied were not adequate to meet the facts of the case.[241] It was unnecessary, therefore, to answer the question whether, if the clauses had been unambiguous and comprehensive, they would have protected the defendants as against the plaintiff, who was not a party to the contract. Lord Denning thought that the plaintiff might have been bound by these clauses because she had impliedly agreed that the furrier should contract for the cleaning of the fur on terms usual in the trade. Diplock and Salmon LJJ preferred to keep the question open.

(e) It seems possible that the House of Lords may have taken a somewhat simplistic view of the merits, viz that exemption clauses are bad and their operation accordingly to be confined as narrowly as possible. This is understandable if applied to the carriage of passengers as in *Adler v Dickson* but it makes less sense in relation to carriage of goods.[242] Here the exemption clauses—the Hague rules—have been approved by Parliament and are in many circumstances mandatory. The parties will (or at least should) have insured on the basis that liability is as laid down by the rules. It certainly makes no sense to allow their loss to be transferred on to the carrier's servants, who are the least likely to be insured or financially equipped to bear it. (Stevedores are perhaps in a different position since they are normally persons of substance and/or likely to carry insurance though even here it is not clear why loss should be transferred from the cargo owner's insurer to the stevedore's.) These arguments have been substantially accepted by the revised Hague Rules. The Carriage of Goods by Sea Act 1971 gives the benefit of limiting terms in the carrier's contract to his servants or agents, but not to independent contractors. Similar provisions are to be found in a number of international transport conventions.[243]

In view of these difficulties, it is perhaps not surprising that ways have been sought to avoid the effect of *Scruttons v Midland Silicones*. One possible course is for the contracting party to intervene in the action and apply to stay it. This possibility was inconclusively tested in *Gore v Van der Lann (Liverpool Corporation intervening)*.[244]

The plaintiff was an old-age pensioner who applied for and received a free pass on the Liverpool Corporation's buses. The pass purported to be a licence to travel

[241] See pp 213–214, above. See also the helpful judgment of Lord Hobhouse in *Homburg Houtimport BV v Agrosin Private Ltd, The Starsin* [2003] UKHL 12, [2003] 2 All ER 785.

[242] See per Lord Denning MR in *Gillespie Bros & Co Ltd v Roy Bowles Transport Ltd* [1973] QB 400 at 412, [1973] 1 All ER 193 at 197–198.

[243] See Giles 24 ICLQ 379 at 390.

[244] [1967] 2 QB 31, [1967] 1 All ER 360; Odgers 86 LQR 69. See also *Genys v Mathews* [1965] 3 All ER 24, [1966] 1 WLR 758.

on the corporation's buses on condition that neither the corporation nor its servants would be liable for injury, etc. however caused. The plaintiff was injured and brought an action against the driver alleging negligence.

In the event the Court of Appeal held that the pass constituted not a licence but a contract,[245] and that the exclusion of liability was therefore void under section 151 of the Road Traffic Act 1960. The court considered the application for a stay, obiter, and suggested that a stay might be obtained either if there were an express promise not to sue the servant or if the employer were under a legal (and not simply a moral) obligation to reimburse the servant for any damages he might be held liable to pay. The former possibility was applied, in a different setting, by Ormrod J in *Snelling v John G Snelling Ltd.*[246]

A second possibility is to seek to create a direct contract between potential plaintiff and potential defendant. An elaborate attempt to do this was upheld by the majority of the Judicial Committee of the Privy Council in *New Zealand Shipping Co Ltd v A M Satterthwaite & Co Ltd, The Eurymedon:*[247]

> The consignor loaded goods on a ship for carriage to the plaintiff consignee in New Zealand. The carriage was subject to a bill of lading issued by the carrier's agent, which contained the following clause: 'it is hereby expressly agreed that no servant or Agent of the carrier (including every independent contractor from time to time employed by the carrier) shall in any circumstances whatsoever be under any liability whatsoever to the shipper, consignee or owner of the goods or to any holder of the bill of lading for any loss or damage or delay of whatsoever kind arising or resulting directly or indirectly from any neglect or default on his part while acting in the course of or in connection with his employment and, without prejudice to the generality of the foregoing provisions in this clause, every exemption, limitation, condition and liberty herein contained, and every right, exemption from liability, defence and immunity of whatsoever nature applicable to the carrier or to which the carrier is entitled hereunder shall also be available and shall extend to protect every such servant or agent of the carrier acting as aforesaid and for the purpose of all the foregoing provisions of this clause the carrier is or shall be deemed to be acting as Agent or Trustee on behalf of and for the benefit of all persons who are or might be his servants or Agents from time to time (including independent contractors as aforesaid) and all such persons shall to this extent be or be deemed to be parties to the contract in or evidenced by this bill of lading'.[248]

---

[245] This decision has been forcefully criticised by Odgers, above, on the ground that it is difficult to reconcile with *Wilkie v London Passenger Transport Board* [1947] 1 All ER 258. See p 45, above.

[246] [1973] QB 87, [1972] 1 All ER 79. See p 582, below.

[247] [1975] AC 154, [1974] 1 All ER 1015. Coote 37 MLR 453; Reynolds 90 LQR 301.

[248] This clause is popularly known as the 'Himalaya clause', being named after the ship in *Adler v Dickson*, p 214, above. That the clause was not revised after *Scruttons Ltd v Midland Silicones Ltd* is perhaps evidence of the conservatism of both the legal and shipping professions.

After the plaintiff had become the holder of the bill of lading, the cargo was damaged as a result of the negligence of the defendant, the stevedores, employed by the carriers to unload the cargo in New Zealand. The plaintiff sued for damages and the defendant relied on the clause above.

The majority of the Judicial Committee of the Privy Council (Viscount Dilhorne and Lord Simon of Glaisdale dissenting) held for the defendant. They held that the clause, although it looked like an attempt to make the stevedores (and others) parties to the contract of carriage could be treated as an offer by the consignor of a unilateral contract, viz that if those involved in performance of the main contract would play their part (eg in the case of the stevedore, unload the goods) the consignor would hold them free from liability. The stevedore was held to have accepted the offer by unloading the goods and the plaintiff consignee by presenting the bill of lading to have contracted on bill of lading terms.[249]

Both the correctness and the ambit of this decision have been the subject of debate. Critics have plausibly argued that the clause was not aptly worded to produce this result and that it might have been more beneficial to reject the clause and compel the draftsman to try again. They have also pointed to technical difficulties presented by the majority analysis, eg would the result have been different if the stevedore had injured the goods before they had unloaded them or before the consignees took up the bill of lading.[250] Defenders of the decision have replied with force that it shows a robust awareness of the commercial realities of the situation.

Since 1974 *The Eurymedon* has been considered in a number of Commonwealth decisions,[251] on the whole with some lack of enthusiasm. The most important decision is *Salmond and Spraggon (Australia) Pty Ltd v Port Jackson Stevedoring Pty Ltd, The New York Star*.[252] In this case the relevant contractual provisions were identical to those of *The Eurymedon*. The appellant stevedores had safely unloaded the goods into their warehouse, whence they were stolen owing to their negligence. The High Court of Australia gave judgment for the consignees (Barwick CJ dissenting) but on a variety of grounds. Mason and Jacobs JJ accepted *The Eurymedon* but distinguished it on the ground that the stevedores' immunity only applied while they were doing work that the carrier was employed to do and that once the goods had been discharged into

---

[249] Cf *Brandt v Liverpool, Brazil and River Plate Steam Navigation Co* [1924] 1 KB 575.

[250] It is assumed that the burden of an exemption clause cannot be imposed on a non-party without his consent. This seems correct in principle, though there are three decisions at first instance which can be read to the contrary: *Fosbroke-Hobbes v Airwork Ltd and British American Air Services Ltd* [1937] 1 All ER 108; *Pyrene Co v Scindia Navigation Co* [1954] 2 QB 402, [1954] 2 All ER 158; *Cockerton v Naviera Aznar SA* [1960] 2 Lloyd's Rep 450.

[251] See Clarke 29 ICLQ 132; Palmer *Bailment* (2nd edn, 1991), pp 1610–1625.

[252] [1979] 1 Lloyd's Rep 298, 52 ALJR 337 (High Court of Australia); Reynolds 95 LQR 183; Palmer and Davies 41 MLR 745; [1980] 3 All ER 257 [1981] 1 WLR 138 (Privy Council); Reynolds 96 LQR 506.

the warehouse,[253] the stevedores were acting on their own behalf and not as agents for the carriers. Stephen and Murphy JJ both in effect rejected *The Eurymedon*.[254] The Privy Council in a brief judgment allowed the stevedores' appeal. They assumed without much elaboration the correctness of *The Eurymedon* and rejected the suggested distinction on the ground that where the consignee does not collect direct from the ship, the carrier still acts as carrier when he discharges into a warehouse and that the stevedores were therefore acting for the carriers when they did likewise.

An important step towards clarity is provided by the decision of the Privy Council in *The Pioneer Container, KH Enterprise (cargo owners) v Pioneer Container (owners)*.[255] In this case, goods were being carried under bills of lading, clause 26 of which provided:

> This Bill of Lading contract shall be governed by Chinese Law. Any claim or other dispute arising thereunder shall be determined at Taipei in Taiwan unless the carrier otherwise agrees in writing.

In some cases the bills of lading had been issued to the goods' owners[256] but many of the goods' owners had not entered into bill of lading contracts with the defendants but had received bills of lading from other shipowners which contained provisions such as:

> 6. The Carrier shall be entitled to sub-contract on any terms the whole or any part of the handling, storage or carriage of the Goods and any and all duties whatsoever undertaken by the Carrier in relation to the Goods . . .

These plaintiffs wished to argue that the exclusive jurisdiction clause was not as a matter of contract binding on them because they had never entered into a contract with the defendants. Of course, the contract which they had entered into might have contained a Himalaya clause which extended protection to agents and sub-contractors but the present dispute was not concerned with such a clause. The defendants' argument was that although they had no contract with the plaintiffs, they were bailees of the plaintiff's goods on the basis of the terms of their own bill of lading. The advice of the Privy Council was delivered by Lord Goff who approved the statement by *Pollock and Wright on Possession*[257] as follows:[258]

---

[253] It appears that this point was not argued before the High Court having been rejected as unarguable by Glass JA in the Court of Appeal.

[254] It appears also that there was no argument as to the correctness of *The Eurymedon* before the High Court.

[255] [1994] 2 All ER 250. See also *The Mahkutai* [1996] 2 Lloyd's Rep 1.

[256] In respect of those owners, the disputes before the Privy Council on appeal from the Hong Kong Court of Appeal were concerned with familiar conflict of law questions as to whether the court should in its discretion allow an action to start in Hong Kong despite the exclusive jurisdiction clause.

[257] P 169.

[258] [1994] 2 All ER 250 at 257.

If the bailee of a thing sub-bails it by authority, there may be a difference according as it is intended that the bailee's bailment is to determine and the third person is to hold as the immediate bailee of the owner, in which case the third person really becomes a first bailee directly from the owner and the case passes back into a simple case of bailment, or that the first bailee is to retain (so to speak) a reversionary interest and there is no direct privity of contract between the third person and the owner, in which case it would seem that both the owner and the first bailee have concurrently the rights of a bailor against the third person according to the nature of the sub-bailment.

So, where, as in the present case, the sub-bailment was with the consent of the owner, its effect was to create a direct bailment between owner and sub-bailee.

On what terms does the new bailee hold? Lord Goff held that the owner is bound by the sub-bailee's conditions if he has consented to them. Consent can, for this purpose, be express or implied, or indeed, in some circumstances, the original bailee may have apparent authority to consent on behalf of the owner. So the relationship between owner and sub-bailee may be governed by what the owner has agreed to, even though that agreement is not embodied in a contract between owner and sub-bailee.[259]

A further masterly consideration of the problems in this field is to be found in the advice of the Judicial Committee of the Privy Council delivered by Lord Goff in *The Mahkutai*[260] where he made it clear that there were overwhelming policy reasons for having a uniform allocation of risk between shipowner, time charterer, stevedores and cargo owners which might, in an appropriate case, justify and require the creation of a common law exception to privity of contract.[261]

An interesting decision on the same problem in a different context is *Southern Water Authority v Carey*.[262] In this case main contractors entered into a contract with the plaintiffs for the construction of a sewage scheme. The defendants were sub-contractors. The main contract was on the I Mech E/IEE Model Form A which contained a clause 30(vi) which provided:

> The contractor's liability under this clause shall be in lieu of any condition or warranty applied by law as to the quality or fitness for any particular purpose of any portion of the works taken over under clause 28 (taking over) and save as in this clause expressed neither the contractor nor his sub-contractors, servants or agents shall be liable, whether in contract, tort or otherwise in respect of defects in or damage to such portions, or for any injury, damage

---

[259] It follows that the decision of Donaldson J in *Johnson Matthey & Co Ltd v Constantine Terminals Ltd* [1976] 2 Lloyd's Rep 215, that the terms of the sub-bailee's conditions may prevail even where the owner has not agreed to them, is to that extent wrong.

[260] [1996] 3 All ER 502.

[261] *The Mahkutai* was not such a case because the primary issue was the applicability of an exclusive jurisdiction clause which raised different questions.

[262] [1985] 2 All ER 1077, 1 Con LR 40. See also *Twins Transport v Patrick and Brocklehurst* (1983) 25 BLR 65.

or loss of whatsoever kind attributable to such defects or damage. For the purposes of this sub-clause the contractor contracts on his own behalf and on behalf of and as trustee for his sub-contractors, servants and agents.

The plaintiffs sued the defendants in tort. His Honour Judge David Smout, QC, Official Referee, held that although prima facie carelessness by a sub-contractor which was likely to and did cause damage to the building owner would give rise to liability, any duty of care should be limited by relevant surrounding circumstances and that the contractual setting was decisive in defining the area of risk which the plaintiffs and defendant had respectively accepted. It would appear material for this purpose that the contract between the plaintiffs and the main contractors was on a well-known standard form, the terms of which would be very familiar to plaintiffs, main contractors and defendants alike.

The logic of this reasoning was carried a stage further in *Norwich City Council v Harvey*.[263] In this case the plaintiff engaged a firm of contractors to build an extension to a swimming pool complex under JCT 1963 (1977 revision). Clause 20 of this contract places the risk of loss or damage by fire during the course of the works on the employer and requires him to maintain adequate insurance against loss or damage by fire. This clause has been held to put the risk of damage by fire on the employer even when the damage is caused by the negligence of the contractor.[264] In the present case both the existing works and the extension were damaged by fire owing to the negligence of an employee of the sub-contractor who had been engaged by the contractor to do certain roofing work. The plaintiffs sued the sub-contractors and their employee. In this case there was of course no contract between the plaintiffs and the sub-contractors. Normally, one would expect the sub-contractors to be under a duty of care in respect of any personal injury or property damage which might be caused by their careless performance of their duties under the contractual arrangements. The Court of Appeal held that in the present case the defendants were not under such a duty of care. This carries the reasoning of the *Carey* case a step further because there was no express provision in the present case as to the liability of the sub-contractors. The Court of Appeal reached the conclusion that the sub-contractors should be free from liability on the basis that the employers had assumed the risk of damage by fire as against the sub-contractors as well as against the contractors. In considering this conclusion it is important to bear in mind that the parties were operating under an extremely well-known and well-established form so that everyone concerned knew or at least ought to have known the allocation of risk; that a very large proportion of the actual work under a modern construction contract is done by sub-contractors and that the same allocation of risk provision is contained in the sub-contract as in the main contract, the sub-contract itself being of the same provenance as the main contract.

---

[263] [1989] 1 All ER 1180, [1989] 1 WLR 828.
[264] *Scottish Special Housing Association v Wimpey Construction UK Ltd* [1986] 2 All ER 957, [1986] 1 WLR 995.

This decision makes excellent commercial sense since it encourages the taking out of a single insurance policy to cover all the interests which may be affected by damage to the works while they are in progress which must be the most economic arrangement for everyone except the insurance companies.

Cases of this kind now fall to be considered in the light of developments in the law of tort. The question is now whether it is fair, just and reasonable to impose a duty of care on a sub-contractor in relation to the property of the employer. In doing this, it will be appropriate to look at the contractual setting but, as the House of Lords emphasised in *British Telecommunications plc v James Thomson & Sons (Engineers) Ltd*,[265] in doing so, it will be necessary to look at the whole of that setting.[266]

In so far as the difficulties in this field arise from privity of contract they will have been largely removed by the passing of the Contract (Rights of Third Parties) Act 1999. This is discussed more fully in Chapter 14 but it should be noted here that section 1(6) makes it clear that the Act applies to the situation in which a third party seeks to take advantage of the exclusions or limitations of liability contained in a contract between other parties.

(6) If a person contracts to deliver or do one thing and he delivers or does another, he has failed to perform his contractual duty. The proposition is self-evident. As long ago as 1838, Lord Abinger sought to contrast the breach of a term in a contract for the sale goods with the complete non-performance of the contract.

> If a man offers to buy peas of another, and he sends him beans, he does not perform his contract. But that is not a warranty; there is no warranty that he should sell him peas; the contract is to sell peas, and if he sends him anything else in their stead, it is a non-performance of it.[267]

So, too, in *Nichol v Godts*:[268]

> A seller contracted to sell to a buyer 'foreign refined rape oil, warranted only equal to sample'. The oil delivered corresponded with the sample, but was found not to be 'foreign refined rape oil' at all.

The seller was held not to be protected by the term he had inserted; and Pollock CB remarked that 'if a man contracts to buy a thing, he ought not to have something else delivered to him'.

Looking back in 1966 upon these and similar cases, Lord Wilberforce said:[269]

---

[265] (1998) 61 Con LR 1.
[266] In that case, careful reading of the contract meant that nominated sub-contractors did not owe a duty of care but that domestic sub-contractors did.
[267] *Chanter v Hopkins* (1838) 4 M & W 399 at 404.
[268] (1854) 10 Exch 191. See also *Wieler v Schilizzi* (1856) 17 CB 619.
[269] *Suisse Atlantique Société d'Armement Maritime SA v NV Rotterdamsche Kolen Centrale* [1967] 1 AC 361 at 433, [1966] 2 All ER 61 at 92–93.

Since the contracting parties could hardly have been supposed to contemplate such a mis-performance, or to have provided against it without destroying the whole contractual substratum, there is no difficulty here in holding exception clauses to be inapplicable.

In the present century the reasoning thus adopted in contracts for the sale of goods has been applied to contracts of hire purchase. In *Karsales (Harrow) Ltd v Wallis:*[270]

> The defendant inspected a car owned by X, found it in good order and wished to take it on hire purchase. X therefore sold it to the plaintiffs, and they re-sold it to a hire-purchase company. The defendant made a contract with this company. The contract contained a term that 'no condition or warranty that the vehicle is road-worthy or as to its condition or fitness for any purpose is given by the owner or implied therein'. One night a 'car' was left outside the defendant's premises. It looked like the car in question. But it was a mere shell; the cylinder head was broken; all the valves were burnt; two pistons were broken, and it was incapable of self-propulsion.

The defendant refused to accept it or to pay the hire-purchase instalments; and, when sued for these, pleaded the state of the so-called car. In reply to this plea, the plaintiffs relied on the excluding term. The Court of Appeal held that the thing delivered was not the thing contracted for. The excluding term therefore did not avail the plaintiffs, and judgment was given for the defendant.[271]

A parallel but distinct development has long been a feature of the law governing the carriage of goods by sea. It is implied in every voyage charterparty and in all bills of lading that the ship will not depart from the route laid down in the contract, or, if none is there prescribed, from the normal trade route. If, without lawful excuse, she does so depart, she is guilty of a deviation. In *Joseph Thorley Ltd v Orchis Steamship Co:*[272]

> A cargo was shipped on a vessel described as 'now lying in the port of Limassol and bound for London'. Instead of proceeding direct to London, the ship went first to a port in Asia Minor, then to a port in Palestine and then to Malta. When she reached London, the cargo was damaged through the negligence of the stevedores. The shipowners pleaded a term in the bill of lading exempting them from such liability.

---

[270] [1956] 2 All ER 866, [1956] 1 WLR 936.

[271] In this case the car was spectacularly defective since (a) it was in very different condition when delivered than it had been when inspected and (b) in some Platonic sense it was not a 'car' at all, since it was incapable of self-propulsion. But the principle was quickly extended to a situation where neither of these factors were present but simply a congeries of defects: *Yeoman Credit v Apps* [1962] 2 QB 508, [1961] 2 All ER 281. See also *Astley Industrial Trust v Grimley* [1963] 2 All ER 33, [1963] 1 WLR 584 and *Charterhouse Credit Co v Tolly* [1963] 2 QB 683, [1963] 2 All ER 432.

[272] [1907] 1 KB 660. 'Lawful excuse' covers eg saving life or the ship itself. Livermore 2 JCL 241.

It was held that the deviation, though it was not the direct cause of the damage, precluded the shipowners from relying on this term. Fletcher Moulton LJ said:[273]

> The cases show that, for a long series of years, the Courts have held that a deviation is such a serious matter, and changes the character of the contemplated voyage so essentially, that a shipowner who has been guilty of a deviation cannot be considered as having performed his part of the bill of lading contract, but something fundamentally different, and therefore he cannot claim the benefit of stipulations in his favour contained in the bill of lading.

The result of the 'deviation' cases has been summarised by Lord Wilberforce.[274]

> A shipowner, who deviates from an agreed voyage, steps out of the contract, so that clauses in the contract (such as exception or limitation clauses) which are designed to apply to the contracted voyage are held to have no application to the deviating voyage.

From the carriage of goods by sea the courts turned to the carriage of goods by land, and thence to bailment in general. In *Lilley v Doubleday*,[275] the defendant agreed to store in his repository, goods owned by the plaintiff. In fact he stored some of them in another warehouse. These latter goods were destroyed by fire, though without the defendant's negligence. The plaintiff was held to be entitled to recover their value. By depositing them elsewhere than in his repository the defendant, had 'stepped out of his contract', and he thus lost the benefit of any exemption clauses. Such cases, based on the analogy of carriage of goods by sea and attended by similar consequences, are often described as instances of 'quasi-deviation'.

A later example of such quasi-deviation is given by *Alexander v Railway Executive*.[276]

> The plaintiff was a stage performer. Together with an assistant, X, he had been on tour and he now deposited in the parcels office at Launceston railway station three trunks containing properties for what he called an 'escape illusion'. He paid 5d for each trunk, obtained for each a ticket and promised to send instructions for their despatch. Some weeks later, and before such instructions were sent, X persuaded the parcels clerk by telling a series of lies to allow him to open the trunks and remove several articles. X was subsequently convicted of larceny. The plaintiff now sued the defendants for breach of contract and the defendants pleaded the following term: 'Not liable for loss, misdelivery or damage to any articles which exceed the value of £5 unless at the time of deposit the true value and nature thereof have been declared by the depositor [and an extra charge paid].' There had been no such declaration or payment.

Devlin J gave judgment for the plaintiff. Sufficient notice, it is true, had been given of the term, but it did not cover the facts of the case: the word 'misdelivery' was not apt

273 [1907] 1 KB at 669.
274 *Suisse Atlantique etc v NV Rotterdamsche etc* [1967] 1 AC 361 at 433–434, [1966] 2 All ER 61 at 93.
275 (1881) 7 QBD 510. See also *Gibaud v Great Eastern Rly Co* [1921] 2 KB 426 at 435.
276 [1951] 2 KB 882, [1951] 2 All ER 442.

to describe a deliberate delivery to the wrong person. Nor, if it did meet the facts, could it avail the defendants. They had been guilty of a 'fundamental breach of contract' in allowing X to open the trunks and remove their contents.

The phrase 'fundamental breach of contract', used in this case by Devlin J had been adopted fifteen years earlier by Lord Wright, when he analysed the nature and effect of a contract for the carriage of goods by sea.

> An unjustified deviation is a fundamental breach of a contract of affreightment . . . The adventure has been changed. A contract, entered into on the basis of the original adventure, is inapplicable to the new adventure.[277]

Whether a party has been guilty of such a fundamental breach is not an easy question to answer: each case must be examined in its context.[278] In borderline cases, much may turn upon the onus of proof. If the defendant pleads an excluding or limiting term and the plaintiff in reply alleges a fundamental breach, is it for the plaintiff to prove such a breach or for the defendant to disprove it?

The question was discussed in *Hunt and Winterbotham (West of England) Ltd v BRS (Parcels) Ltd.*[279]

> The defendants contracted with the plaintiffs to carry 15 parcels of woollen goods to Manchester. Only 12 parcels arrived. The plaintiffs sued the defendants for damages equal to the value of the 3 lost parcels, and the defendants pleaded a term of the contract limiting the amount which might be claimed for any such loss 'however sustained'. The plaintiffs alleged negligence but did not in their pleadings allege a fundamental breach. The defendants offered no evidence to explain why or where the parcels had been lost.

The Court of Appeal gave judgment for the defendants. On the assumption that the defendants had in fact been guilty of negligence, the term protected them unless they had committed a fundamental breach of contract. The vital question was to determine the onus of proof. The court held that the burden lay upon the plaintiffs and that they had not discharged it. Lord Evershed admitted that this conclusion was severe: the plaintiffs had no means of knowing how their goods had been lost, and the defendants could not or would not offer any explanation. But, hard as it may seem, it is not illogical. He who makes an allegation must prove it. It is for the plaintiff to make out a prima facie case against the defendant. If he succeeds in this task, it is for the

---

[277] *Hain Steamship Co v Tate and Lyle Ltd* [1936] 2 All ER 597 at 607–608.

[278] Compare *Hollins v J Davy Ltd* [1963] 1 QB 844. [1963] 1 All ER 370, and *Mendelssohn v Normand Ltd* [1970] 1 QB 177, [1969] 2 All ER 1215. The criteria for deciding what is 'fundamental' may very well vary between different types of contract. So courts have tended to regard the distinction between deliberate and careless breaches as relevant in bailment cases, but this seems to play no part in sale or hire purchase. See *A F Colverd & Co Ltd v Anglo Overseas Transport Co Ltd* [1961] 2 Lloyd's Rep 352, and *John Carter v Hanson Haulage (Leeds) Ltd* [1965] 2 QB 495, [1965] 1 All ER 113.

[279] [1962] 1 QB 617, [1962] 1 All ER 111. See Wedderburn [1962] CLJ 17; Aikin 26 MLR 98.

defendant to plead and to prove some special plea such as an excluding or limiting term. The burden must then pass back to the plaintiff who must show some reason why the term is to be disregarded.

On the other hand a different result was reached in *Levison v Patent Steam Carpet Cleaning Co Ltd*.[280] In this case the plaintiffs entrusted a carpet worth £900 to the defendants for cleaning under a contract which purported to limit the defendant's liability to £40. The carpet disappeared in circumstances which could not be explained by the defendants. It was possible therefore that it had been lost by fundamental breach and the Court of Appeal held that the defendants could only limit their liability if they could show that the loss arose from some cause which did not constitute fundamental breach. It is not too easy to see the distinction between this case and *Hunt and Winterbotham (West of England) Ltd v BRS (Parcels) Ltd*.[281] One suggested explanation is that fundamental breach was not specifically pleaded in the *Hunt* case and another possibility would be a different rule for contracts of carriage and other bailments. Perhaps the least unsatisfactory explanation is that *Levison* was a consumer.[282]

The courts have thus developed over a period of years two sets of rules. The failure to distinguish them has helped to blur the choice between two propositions: (1) that by a rule of law no excluding or limiting term may operate to protect a party who is in fundamental breach of his contract; and (2) that the question is not one of substantive law but depends upon the interpretation of the individual contract before the court. This distinction between a rule of law and a rule of construction permeates English law as a whole and in its long life has generated many curious subtleties and provoked many petty quarrels.[283] A rule of law is to be applied whether or not it defeats the intention of the parties. A rule of construction exists to give effect to the intention. Within the sphere of contract the doctrine of public policy operates as a rule of law: a contract which offends it is void despite the wishes of the parties. The effect of mutual mistake, on the other hand, is assessed by applying a rule of construction: it must be asked what, if anything, a reasonable person would think was 'the sense of the promise'.[284]

If there were a rule of law that no exemption clause however clear could exclude liability for fundamental breach, the nature of the exemption clause would be of vital significance. Where the clause went to define the extent of the promisor's obligation, the possibility of fundamental breach would be *pro tanto* excluded since nothing can

---

[280] [1978] QB 69, [1977] 3 All ER 498. Males [1978] CLJ 24; Stone 41 MLR 748; Palmer *Bailment* (2nd edn, 1991) pp 1552–1557.

[281] [1962] 1 QB 617, [1962] 1 All ER 111.

[282] The case would now fall within Unfair Contract Terms Act 1977, s 3.

[283] The rule in *Shelley's Case*, abrogated in 1925 after three centuries of controversy, is the classical example of this dichotomy. Its memory is happily embalmed in a judgment of sustained irony delivered by Lord MacNaughten in *Van Grutten v Foxwell* [1897] AC 658 at 670–676.

[284] P 306, below.

be a fundamental breach which is not first a breach.[285] There was much academic discussion of the nature of the doctrine[286] and puzzlement as to its content. Were there two distinct doctrines—breach of a fundamental term and fundamental breach or were they simply alternative formulations of the same doctrine? What was the relationship between fundamental terms and conditions? Could the doctrine be side-stepped by 'shrinking the core of the contract', ie by the promisor accepting a small obligation from the beginning instead of accepting a larger obligation and trying to cut it down by exemption clauses?[287]

Before 1964 the tendency of the courts was to prefer the first of these alternatives and to rely upon a rule of law.[288] But in that year, Pearson LJ chose the second alternative.

> As to the question of fundamental breach, I think there is a rule of construction that normally an exception or exclusive clause or similar provision in a contract should be construed as not applying to a situation created by a fundamental breach of contract. This is not an independent rule of law imposed by the court on the parties willy-nilly in disregard of their contractual intention. On the contrary it is a rule of construction based on the presumed intention of the parties.[289]

Two years later the House of Lords was given the opportunity to indicate its preference in the case of *Suisse Atlantique Société d'Armement Maritime SA v NV Rotterdamsche Kolen Centrale.*[290]

The plaintiffs owned a ship which in December 1956 they chartered to the defendants for the carriage of coal from the United States to Europe. The charter was to remain in force for two years' consecutive voyages. The defendants agreed to load and discharge cargoes at specified rates; and, if there was any delay, they were to pay a thousand dollars a day as demurrage. In September 1957, the plaintiffs claimed that they were entitled to treat the contract as repudiated by the defendants' delays in loading and discharging cargoes. The defendants rejected this contention. In October 1957, the parties agreed (without prejudice to their

---

[285] *The Angelia* [1973] 2 All ER 144, [1973] 1 WLR 210.

[286] See eg Montrose 15 Can Bar Rev 760; Unger 4 Business L Rev 30; Melville 19 MLR 26; Guest 77 LQR 98; Reynolds 79 LQR 534; Montrose [1964] CLJ 60, 254; Devlin [1966] CLJ 192.

[287] See Wedderburn [1957] CLJ 12, [1960] CLJ 11. No doubt a shrunken core would be less attractive to a potential promisee than an apparently whole apple. See also Barton 87 LQR 20 on possible use of a deed as a method of exemption.

[288] See *Alexander v Railway Executive* [1951] 2 KB 882, [1951] 2 All ER 442, p 179; *Karsales (Harrow) Ltd v Wallis* [1956] 2 All ER 866, [1956] 1 WLR 936, p 224, above; *Yeoman Credit Ltd v Apps* [1962] 2 QB 508, [1961] 2 All ER 281.

[289] *UGS Finance Ltd National Mortgage Bank of Greece SA* [1964] 1 Lloyd's Rep 446 at 453. See also the valuable judgments of the High Court of Australia in *Sydney City Council v West* (1965) 114 CLR 481 and *Thomas National Transport (Melbourne) Pty Ltd v May and Baker (Australia) Pty Ltd* [1966] 2 Lloyd's Rep 347.

[290] [1967] 1 AC 361, [1966] 2 All ER 61. Treitel 29 MLR 546; Drake 30 MLR 531; Jenkins [1969] CLJ 257.

dispute) to continue with the contract. The defendants subsequently made eight round voyages. The plaintiffs then claimed all the money which they had lost through the delays. The defendants argued that the claim must be limited to the agreed demurrage for the actual days in question. The plaintiffs replied that the delays were such as to entitle them to treat the contract as repudiated: the demurrage clause therefore did not apply, and they could recover their full loss.

Mr Justice Mocatta, the Court of Appeal and the House of Lords all held that the plaintiffs must fail. They had elected to affirm the contract, and the demurrage clause applied. But in the House of Lords, and for the first time, the plaintiffs argued that the defendants had been guilty of a fundamental breach of contract which prevented them from relying on a 'limiting term'. The House of Lords rejected this argument. There was, on the facts, no fundamental breach, nor was the provision for demurrage a 'limiting term': it was a statement of agreed damages in the event of delay. In the result it was unnecessary for the House of Lords to discuss the meaning and effect of fundamental breach. But the arguments offered to them by the plaintiffs raised issues of general contractual importance which they felt they must examine. Their opinions, though not technically binding on the courts, represent views which cannot be disregarded.

The five members of the House of Lords who heard the *Suisse Atlantique* case approved, with some doubts but no dissent, the approach to the problem of fundamental breach which Pearson LJ had preferred in 1964. The rules to be applied should be regarded as rules of construction and not as rules of law.[291]

It was unfortunate that the first modern consideration of the topic by the House of Lords should have involved atypical facts and arguably not presented a fundamental breach situation at all. A further difficulty was that their Lordships attached considerable significance to the fact that the plaintiffs had affirmed the contract. This led some to think that exemption clauses might be disregarded in deciding whether there had been a sufficient breach to entitle the injured party to terminate the contract and that if he did so the excluding or limiting clauses could be treated as ineffective.

This lack of total clarity in the speeches in the House of Lords was followed by a series of decisions in the Court of Appeal, which behaved as if the House of Lords had never spoken at all[292] and continued to treat fundamental breach as a rule of law.

---

[291] It is noteworthy however that their Lordships did not think any of the earlier cases in which the rule was treated as one of law were incorrect in the result. Both Lord Reid and Lord Wilberforce appeared to reserve the possibility that there might be super-fundamental breaches liability for which could not be excluded.

[292] *Harbutt's Plasticine Ltd v Wayne Tank and Pump Co Ltd* [1970] 1 QB 447, [1970] 1 All ER 225; *Farnworth Finance Facilities Ltd v Attryde* [1970] 2 All ER 774, [1970] 1 WLR 1053; *Wathes (Western) Ltd v Austins (Menswear) Ltd* [1976] 1 Lloyd's Rep 14. These cases, especially the first, were subject to powerful criticism. See Weir [1970] CLJ 189; Baker 33 MLR 441; Legh-Jones and Pickering 86 LQR 513, 87 LQR 515; Dawson 91 LQR 380; Fridman 7 Alberta L Rev 281; Reynolds 92 LQR 172. For a valiant attempt to reconcile House of Lords and Court of Appeal, see *Kenyon Son & Craven Ltd v Baxter Hoare & Co Ltd* [1971] 2 All ER 708, [1971] 1 WLR 519.

This indiscipline was firmly corrected in *Photo Production Ltd v Securicor Transport Ltd*.[293]

> The plaintiffs, the owners of a factory, entered into a contract with the defendants, a security organisation, under which the defendants were to arrange for periodic visits to the factory during the night. On one such visit, an employee of the defendants started a small fire which got out of hand and destroyed the entire factory and contents, worth about £615,000. The plaintiffs brought an action and the defendants relied on exemption clauses, including one which provided that 'under no circumstances' were they 'to be responsible for any injuries act or default by any employee . . . unless such act or default could have been foreseen and avoided by the exercise of due diligence' by the defendants. (It was not alleged that the defendants had been negligent in engaging this employee.)

In the Court of Appeal it was held that this exemption could not avail the defendants because they had been guilty of a fundamental breach but the House of Lords unanimously reversed this decision. Lord Wilberforce said:[294]

> I have no second thoughts as to the main proposition that the question whether, and to what extent, an exclusion clause is to be applied to a fundamental breach, or a breach of a fundamental term, or indeed to any breach of contract, is a matter of construction of the contract.

Furthermore, he thought the clause completely clear and adequate to cover the defendant's position. The plaintiff's action therefore failed. It is instructive to note that the House of Lords thought this result not only technically correct but also fair and reasonable.[295] This may seem surprising since the plaintiffs had suffered such an enormous loss but the key to understanding lies in the insurance position. In a commercial contract of this kind, many of the contractual provisions operate to allocate risks and in practice therefore to decide who should insure against the risk. Any prudent factory owner will insure his factory against damage or destruction by fire and he is much the best person to fix the value of the premises. It is doubtful if *Photo Production's* fire insurance premiums would have been significantly reduced if Securicor had accepted a higher degree of responsibility[296] but very likely that if Securicor had not excluded liability, they would have had to charge a considerably higher fee. It follows that the arrangements adopted were probably the most economically efficient and there was certainly no adequate reasons why the court should interfere with the parties' negotiated allocation of the risk.

---

[293] [1980] AC 827, [1980] 1 All ER 556; Nicol and Rawlings 43 MLR 567.

[294] And the other Lords agreed. The speeches appear deliberately brief as if to ensure that they cannot be misunderstood.

[295] Thereby providing clues as to the application of the reasonableness test under the Unfair Contract Terms Act 1977.

[296] Because the risk of a fire being started by a Securicor employee was such a small part of the total risk covered.

5 STATUTORY PROVISIONS: UNFAIR CONTRACT TERMS ACT 1977

Over the years Parliament has come to intervene more and more extensively in this area. This intervention has so far been piecemeal, that is, it has operated by the prohibition or regulation of exemption clauses in particular types of contract rather than by the enactment of rules applicable to all contracts. The intervention has been largely but by no means exclusively in the field of consumer protection. Part II of the Fair Trading Act 1973 gave the Secretary of State a discretion to make orders, on the recommendation of the Consumer Protection Advisory Committee, regulating unfair consumer trade practices.[297] Such an order might forbid the use of particular types of exemption clause in particular situations and it would then be a criminal offence to insert such a term in such a contract. This is a radical new departure from the usual legislative technique of declaring the clause void.[298]

We cannot give an exhaustive list of such provisions here but a number of examples may be given.[299]

(1) The Road Traffic Act 1960, section 151, provides that:

A contract for the conveyance of a passenger in a public service vehicle shall, so far as it purports to negative or to restrict the liability of a person in respect of a claim which may be made against him in respect of the death of, or bodily injury to, the passenger while being carried in, entering or alighting from the vehicle, or purports to impose any conditions with respect to the enforcement of any such liability, be void.[300]

(2) A similar, but not identical, provision is contained in the Transport Act 1962. By section 43(7) it is enacted that:

The Boards[301] shall not carry passengers by rail on terms or conditions which (a) purport, whether directly or indirectly, to exclude or limit their liability in respect of the death of, or bodily injury to, any passenger other than a passenger travelling on a free pass, or (b) purport,

---

[297] For a full account, see Cunningham *the Fair Trading Act 1973: Consumer Protection and Competition Law* ch 3, pp 30–41.

[298] Where a clause is simply declared void, a tradesman may continue to insert it in his contracts and it will give him effective protection against those who do not know the law or do not take legal advice—a very large proportion of the population! Such an order is made by the Consumer Transactions (Restrictions on Statements) Order 1976 SI 1976/1813 as amended by SI 1978/27.

[299] See also Grunfeld 24 MLR 62 at 64–65; Patents Act 1949, s 57.

[300] This section was discussed by the Court of Appeal in *Gore v Van der Lann* (*Liverpool Corpn intervening*) [1967] 2 QB 31, [1967] 1 All ER 360. See p 217, above. See also Motor Vehicles (Passenger Insurance) Act 1971.

[301] Four Boards were created by the Transport Act 1962, including the British Railways Board. The Transport Act 1968 drastically changed the organisation which has been changed again by the process of privatisation.

whether directly or indirectly, to prescribe the time within which or the manner in which any such liability may be enforced.

Any such terms or conditions 'shall be void and of no effect'.

(3) The most important legislative provisions are the Unfair Contract Terms Act 1977[302] and the Unfair Terms in Consumer Contracts Regulations 1999. Between them the Act and the Regulations would now govern the result of the majority of cases which we have discussed in this section and arguably we should have started our discussion with them. However the Act presupposes the existing law, does not oust it altogether and cannot easily be understood without reference to it. The Act and the Regulations overlap and fit together awkwardly. It will be simplest, therefore, to consider them separately.

1 The scope of the Act

The title of the Act is grossly misleading. It does not deal in principle with all unfair contract terms but only with unfair exemption clauses. It does not, in general, deal with unfair imposition of liability.[303] Even in the context of exemption clauses, it does not introduce a test of fairness. Some clauses are declared ineffective per se; others are subjected to a test of reasonableness.

The Act is divided into three parts. Part I applies to England, Wales and Northern Ireland; Part II to Scotland and Part III to the whole of the United Kingdom.[304] We shall confine our discussion to Part I and III.

The Act applies widely but it does not apply to all contracts. The provisions as to which contracts fall within the purview of the Act are complex:

(1) Sections 2 to 7 (the main enacting provisions of Part I) apply only to business liability.[305] Business liability is defined as 'liability for breach of obligations or duties arising—(a) from things done or to be done by a person in the course of a business (whether his own business or another's); and (b) from the occupation of premises used for business purposes by the occupier'. There is no definition of 'business' but section 14 provides that 'business' includes 'a profession and the activities of any Government department or local or public authority'. This still leaves a number of unclear areas, for example, state schools

---

[302] Coote 41 MLR 312; Adams 41 MLR 703; Mann 27 ICLQ 661; Sealy [1978] CLJ 15. Palmer and Yates [1981] CLJ 108; Adams and Brownsword 104 LQR 94; Palmer 7 BLR 57; Macdonald [1994] JBL 441.

[303] To some small extent, this may not be true of s 3 (see p 237, below) or s 4 (see p 246, below) Nicol [1979] CLJ 273.

[304] It is believed that the objectives of Part I and Part II are to a considerable extent the same but the language used is very different and the results may well not be the same.

[305] S 1(3). S 6(4) is the one exception but this is relatively unimportant since exemption clauses are relatively unusual in non-business sales and fewer terms are implied into a sale where the seller is not a merchant.

are clearly within the Act; public schools may not be but it is thought that a purposive interpretation would include them.

(2) Schedule 1 contains a list of contracts to which the whole or part of sections 2, 3, 4 and 7 do not apply. These include:

(a) contracts of insurance (including contracts of annuity);

(b) contracts relating to the creation, transfer or termination of interests in land;[306]

(c) contracts relating to the creation, transfer or termination of rights or interests in intellectual property such as patents, trade marks, copyrights etc.;

(d) contracts relating to the formation or dissolution of a company or the constitution or rights or obligations of its members;

(e) contracts relating to the creation or transfer of securities or of any right or interest therein;

(f) contracts of marine salvage or towage; or charterparty of ships or hovercraft or of carriage of goods by sea, by ship or hovercraft (except in relation to section 2(1) or in favour of a person dealing as consumer).

It will be seen that a number of extremely common and important contracts are thereby excluded.

(3) International supply contracts are outside the scope of the Act. International supply contracts are defined by section 26. There are three requirements:

(a) the contract is one for the sale of goods or under which either the ownership or possession of goods will pass; and

(b) the places of business (or if none, habitual residences) of the parties are in the territories of different states (the Channel Islands and the Isle of Man being treated for this purpose as different states from the United Kingdom); and

(c) Either—

   (i) at the time the contract is concluded the goods are in the course of carriage or will be carried from the territory of one state to the territory of another; or

   (ii) the acts constituting the offer and acceptance have been done in the territories of different states; or

   (iii) the contract provides for the goods to be delivered to the territory of a state other than that within which the acts of offer and acceptance were done.

---

[306] Wilkinson [1984] Conv 12. See *Electricity Supply Nominees Ltd v IAF Group plc* [1993] 3 All ER 372.

The precise scope of this provision was examined in *Amiri Flight Authority v BAE Systems plc.*[307] The claimant, an entity established under the law of the United Arab Emirates to provide aircraft for flights by local VIPs, bought a BAE 146–100 aircraft from the defendants. In due course defects were alleged in the plane, the defendant relied on exemption clauses in the contract and one of the questions was whether the contract was an international sale contract. Requirement (i) was not met because the airplane was both manufactured and delivered in England; similarly requirement (ii) was not met because the offer and acceptance both took place in the UAE. Tomlinson J held that the words 'delivered to the territory' in (iii) should be read as if they were 'delivered in the territory'. His principal reason for doing so was that the definition was very largely taken from article 1.1 of the Uniform Law on International Sales Act 1967 which used the word 'in' instead of the word 'to'. The Court of Appeal disagreed. They considered the legislative history of the section and concluded that the change in the wording was deliberate. This seems clearly correct as a matter of statutory construction but it does mean that which side of the line the facts fall will not necessarily be related to any clear policy objective.

(4) Where English law is the proper law of the contract 'only by choice of the parties' sections 2 to 7 shall not operate as part of the proper law. Both (3) and (4) are concerned with the problem of international contracts, that is contracts having a close connection with more than one country. Historically English courts and arbitrators have enjoyed a wide jurisdiction in respect of disputes over such contracts. It would appear that these provisions are designed not to frighten away foreign businessmen by subjecting their contracts to the control imposed by the Act.

2 The arrangement of the act

The main enacting provisions of Part I are sections 2, 3, 6 and 7. These sections interrelate in a curious way. Section 6 applies only to contracts of sale and hire purchase.[308] Section 7 applies to contracts other than contracts of sale or hire purchase under which possession or ownership of goods passes, for example, contracts of hire, exchange or for work and materials.[309] These two sections are therefore mutually exclusive, applying as they do only to specific types of contract. Sections 2 and 3, on the other hand, are of general application and are potentially applicable to any contract within the scope of the Act, including those covered by section 6 or 7. It is

---

[307] [2003] 1 All ER (Comm) 1 (Tomlinson J); [2004] 1 All ER (Comm) 385.
[308] It is largely a re-enactment of the relevant parts of the Supply of Goods (Implied Terms) Act 1973.
[309] This last category is a very important one in practice, embracing most contracts where goods are being manufactured especially to the customer's requirements instead of being supplied from stock.

possible, therefore, for different provisions in, for example, a contract of sale to be subject to sections 2, 3 and 6.

Section 2 deals with liability for negligence. Negligence is defined under section 1 to mean the breach either of a contractual obligation, 'to take reasonable care or to exercise reasonable skill in the performance of the contract' or of 'any common law duty to take reasonable care or exercise reasonable skill' or 'of the common duty of care imposed by the Occupiers' Liability Act 1957'. It will be seen, therefore, that this section is dealing with liability for negligence both in contract and tort.

Section 3 deals with two quite distinct though overlapping types of contract. One is where the contract is between two parties, one of whom deals as consumer;[310] the other is where it is between two parties, one of whom deals on the 'other's written standard terms of business'. Obviously many consumer contracts are on the supplier's written standard terms of business but equally many business contracts are too. Unfortunately, the Act is completely silent as to the meaning of the expression.[311] It clearly covers the case of a business which has its own custom-built terms but what of a business which uses standard trade association terms. It seems natural to say that, say, a road haulier who always carries goods on the terms of the Road Haulage Association standard conditions falls within the policy of the section. But what of two commodity traders who have regular dealings on the basis of their trade association terms. Is either dealing on the other's written standard terms of business? Another unclear example would be a builder who habitually enters into building contracts under the JCT Contract Form. Arguably these are his standard terms of business since he regularly employs them; on the other hand he has no direct voice in the drafting of the conditions.[312] It is also questionable at what stage standard terms of business, which are amended in negotiation, cease to be standard terms.[313]

3 Contract terms made totally ineffective by the Act

The Act applies in two ways, either to make a term totally ineffective or to subject it to a test of reasonableness. The following terms are made ineffective:

(a) *Personal injury or death* Under section 2(1) it is no longer possible to exclude or restrict liability in negligence for personal injury or death 'by reference to any contract terms or to a notice given to persons generally or to particular persons'. The reference to notices embraces wide areas of tort liability, where there was

---

[310] Who is a consumer is discussed, p 238, below.

[311] The corresponding provision in Part II, s 17 uses the formula 'standard form contract' which is easier to apply.

[312] In practice these difficulties may not matter too much, since the section applies the test of reasonableness and in many cases terms caught by a wide construction of 'written standard terms of business' would survive a test of reasonableness.

[313] See *St Albans City and District Council v International Computers Ltd* [1996] 4 All ER 481.

no contractual relationship between the parties, for example, where visitors are allowed on to premises without payment.[314]

(b) In contracts of sale or hire purchase, the implied undertakings as to title of the seller or owner cannot be excluded or restricted.[315]

(c) In consumer[316] contracts of sale or hire purchase, the seller or owner's implied undertakings as to conformity of goods with description or sample, or as to their quality or fitness for a particular purpose cannot be excluded or restricted.[317]

(d) The same rule applies to contracts within section 7 when the goods are supplied to a consumer.[318]

4 Terms subjected to a test of reasonableness[319]

(a) *Loss or damage arising from negligence other than personal injury or death.*[320] This provision, like section 2(1), is primarily aimed at attempts to exclude or limit tort based liability for negligently inflicted injury though it no doubt also includes attempts to exclude contractual duties of care. It is necessary to say a little more about tort based liability here. It is of course fundamental that in English tort law liability in negligence depends on the existence of a duty of care. As we have already seen in the discussion of exemption clauses and third parties[321] the contractual set up may be relevant to the existence of the duty of care. So an exclusion clause may be argued to negative the existence of a duty of care rather than to provide a defence for a negligent breach of a duty of care. An argument along these lines was rejected by the House of Lords in the twin appeal in *Smith v Eric S Bush* and *Harris v Wyre Forest District Council.*[322] In both cases the plaintiffs had bought houses with the help of mortgages, which had been granted after a professional valuation of the house carried out on behalf of the mortgagee. In both cases the valuer was careless and failed to notice major defects in the house which in effect made both houses valueless. When the plaintiffs discovered the defects they sought to sue the valuers in tort. Shortly, their argument was that the valuer knew that if he gave a favourable report the lenders were likely to make an offer of a mortgage and that the plaintiffs would know that this must be based on a favourable report on the premises (at least that they were good for the money which was being lent, though not necessarily for the price which was being paid) and that they could therefore safely buy the property without having to worry

---

[314] Note that both s 2(1) and s 2(2) are subject to a cryptic provision that 'a person's agreement to or awareness of [the contract term or notice] is not of itself to be taken as indicating his voluntary acceptance of any risk': s 2(3).

[315] S 6(1).   [316] See p 238, below.   [317] S 6(2).

[318] S 7(2). the implied terms in these contracts are now defined by the Supply of Goods and Services Act 1982.

[319] As to the content of the reasonableness test, see p 240, below.

[320] S 2(2). And see n 314, above.

[321] See p 214, above.   [322] [1990] 1 AC 831, [1989] 2 All ER 514.

about the existence of major defects. The House of Lords approved an earlier decision in *Yianni v Edwin Evans and Sons*[323] that in principle liability could lie on such facts.

After the earlier decision most mortgage lenders had altered their practice. In particular many lenders of money including the two mortgagees in the present cases had adopted the practice of saying that the valuation constituted no kind of guarantee as to the value or condition of the property. In the Court of Appeal in *Harris* an argument was accepted that the effect of the disclaimer was not to provide a defence for breach of a duty of care but to prevent a duty of care arising in the first place. This argument was based on a number of statements in the leading decision of the House of Lords in *Hedley Byrne & Co Ltd v Heller & Partners Ltd*[324] in which it had been said that liability for careless statements depends on the maker of the statement assuming liability for it. This argument was robustly rejected by the House of Lords. It appears to follow that since 1977 at least it is no use someone giving advice in a situation where liability would normally attach because the transaction was a serious one and hoping to escape liability by the deployment of a standard form disclaimer. It is important to emphasise that in this particular kind of transaction although there was no formal contractual relationship between the borrower and the valuer it was the borrower who paid for the valuation since it is the normal practice of lenders to charge a valuation fee which is not returnable if the valuation proves too low. Also many lenders are legally required to have valuations which are professionally carried out so the situation is not one in which it can be argued with any plausibility that everybody knew that the answer was being given off the cuff. It does not follow from this that there cannot be other situations of a non-standard kind where it can be successfully argued that there is no assumption of liability.

(b) *Contracts falling within section 3* This section contains a complex set of provisions, which are far from easy to understand or interpret. It provides that the person who deals with the consumer or on his own written standard terms of business:

cannot by reference to any contract term—

 (a) when himself in breach of contract, exclude or restrict any liability of his in respect of the breach; or

 (b) Claim to be entitled—

  (i) to render a contractual performance substantially different from that which was reasonably expected of him, or

  (ii) in respect of the whole or any part of his contractual obligation, to render no performance at all

unless the term satisfies the reasonableness test.

The principal difficulty is the relationship between (a) and (b) above. It is clear that many cases of rendering a substantially different performance and most cases of

---

[323] [1982] QB 438, [1981] 3 All ER 592.   [324] [1964] AC 465, [1963] 2 All ER 575.

rendering no performance will be breaches but those that are will fall within (a) and the draftsman must therefore have intended (b) to apply to such acts which were not breaches of contract at all. Presumably, this was an attempt to block a hole which draftsmen of standard form contracts might otherwise exploit by converting breaches into non-breaches. Unfortunately the Act does not appear to be based on, still less to state, any coherent theory as to the relationship between exemption clauses and clauses defining liability. This means that, as worded, (b) appears to catch not only ingeniously drafted exemption clauses but also provisions that have never previously been thought of as at all like exemption clauses. Suppose for instance a supplier of machine tools provided in his standard printed conditions that payment terms are 25 per cent with order and 75 per cent on delivery and that he should be under no obligation to start manufacture until the initial payment is made. Such a provision may now have to pass the test for reasonableness under section 3(2)(b)(ii). Of course it would very likely pass with flying colours but it is not a good argument for putting hurdles on a motorway that most cars will drive through them.

Another puzzle, more easily explicable, is the double test of reasonableness under section 3(2)(b)(i). It might be thought that delivery of a contractual performance substantially different from that which was reasonably expected could not be reasonable but this is probably not so, as where the substitute performance was better than what was contractually required, for instance, if an airline reserves the right to move tourist-class passengers to first-class seats at no extra cost.

(c) In non-consumer contracts of sale or hire purchase, the seller or owner's implied undertakings as to conformity of goods with description or sample or as to their quality or fitness for a particular purpose.[325]

(d) Similarly with the supplier's implied undertakings as to these matters in non-consumer contracts under section 7.[326]

(e) The liability of the supplier in all contracts under section 7 'in respect of (a) the right to transfer ownership of the goods, or give possession; (b) the assurance of quiet possession to a person taking goods in pursuance of the contract'.[327]

5 The concept of consumer

The Act follows and extends the approach of the Supply of Goods (Implied Terms) Act 1973 in providing special rules for consumers and indeed it should be regarded as the greatest success of the consumer protection movements to date, so far as the law of contract is concerned. The definition of 'deals as consumer' is contained in section 12(1). This introduces a threefold test for the purposes of section 6 and 7, viz: the consumer

---

[325] S 6(3).   [326] S 7(3).

[327] S 7(4). Note that this was the one difference in approach between s 6 and s 7. Cf s 6(1). However, this difference was substantially removed by the new s 3(A) introduced by the Supply of Goods and Services Act 1982.

(a) . . . neither makes the contract in the course of a business nor holds himself out as doing so; and

(b) the other party does make the contract in the course of a business; and

(c) . . . the goods passing under or in pursuance of the contract are of a type ordinarily supplied for private use or consumption.

Outside sections 6 or 7, requirement (c) does not apply—no doubt because it is much more difficult to distinguish consumer services than consumer goods. It should be noted that transactions between consumers are not consumer transactions for the purpose of the Act because of the combined requirements (a) and (b). There will be a number of cases where deciding whether the transaction is a consumer transaction may require some investigation. An obvious example would be where a businessman buys a car to be used partly for business and partly for private use. It is thought that whether he deals as consumer should turn on whether he buys it through his business account or his private account. A different view was taken however by the Court of Appeal in *R & B Customs Brokers Co Ltd v United Dominions Trust Ltd (Saunders Abbott (1980) Ltd, third party)*.[328] In this case the plaintiffs acquired a second-hand Colt Shogun from the defendants on conditional sale terms. The plaintiffs were a company owned and controlled by Mr and Mrs Bell, which ran a business as shipping brokers and freight forwarding agents. The car was to be used by Mr and Mrs Bell partly for the business and partly for private use. At first sight it would seem clear that the transaction was a business sale since the company was the customer and the company only existed for the purpose of conducting the business. However, the Court of Appeal were persuaded that the company was in fact a consumer since it was not in the business of buying cars (the company apparently had only one car at a time and had only bought one or two previously). This decision has strong claims to be regarded as wrong, whatever style of statutory interpretation one adopts. On a literal interpretation, the transaction must be a business one because that was the purpose of the company. One might depart from a literal interpretation and adopt a purposive interpretation but this would require consideration of the purpose of the act. The reason for making a distinction between consumers and non-consumers must be that consumers are presumed as a class to be less able to protect themselves. It has to be remembered in this context that business buyers are not deprived of all protection because an unreasonable exemption will still be ineffective as against them. The Court of Appeal was greatly influenced by decisions on the meaning of 'course of a business' in relation to the Trade Descriptions Act 1968. It was argued that it would be inelegant to have different meanings of this expression in different statutes. But there are many other statutes which use the concept of business and it is hard to believe that such a common word does not derive shades of meaning from its context and from

---

[328] [1988] 1 All ER 847, [1988] 1 WLR 321; Jones and Harland 2 JCL 266.

the purpose of the statute in which it is found. Furthermore, the question which arises under the Trade Descriptions Act is usually whether a seller is acting in the course of a business, whereas under the Unfair Contract Terms Act the question will more commonly be whether a buyer is acting in the course of a business. The notion of regularity to which the Court of Appeal attached importance is much easier to apply to a seller than to a buyer. Many organisations which are undoubtedly businesses may buy particular kinds of article very infrequently. It is difficult to believe that this is the right test to apply since the regularity with which the plaintiffs had been buying cars had little or nothing to do with their need for protection.

It is very hard to reconcile the decision of the Court of Appeal in the *R&B* case with its later decision in *Stevenson v Rogers*[329] where a fisherman sold his fishing boat to the claimants who sought to bring an action under the implied terms of the Sale of Goods Act 1979. The defendant argued that he was in business as a fisherman and not as a seller of fishing boats. The Court held that the sale was in the course of business. The Court were much pressed with the *R&B* case. Formally they distinguished it as turning on the meaning of 'business' in a different statute but careful reading of the judgments does not support the view that both cases can be correctly decided.

It may appear odd that anyone should deprive himself of his protected consumer status by holding himself out as buying in the course of business, where he is not doing so, but a common example would be a consumer who obtains a trade card to enable him to buy at discount terms from the wholesaler.[330]

6 The reasonableness test[331]

The reasonableness test stands at the centre of the strategy of the Act. By its adoption Parliament appears to accept the modern orthodoxy that it is sensible and practicable to refer difficult questions to a standard of reasonableness and to share the lawyer's assumption that he is an expert in what is reasonable. It is questionable whether these assumptions are well founded. A more far-reaching criticism would be that the courts are often quite unable to tell what is reasonable without a detailed knowledge of the business background, which it would be oppressive to compel the parties to establish on a case by case basis.[332]

The Act offers some limited guidance on the application of the test. This is contained partly in section 11 and partly in Schedule 2.

---

[329] [1999] QB 1028.

[330] Under s 12(2) a buyer at a sale by auction or competitive tender is not to be regarded as dealing as consumer. Under s 12(3) the burden of proof rests on those who allege that a party does not deal as consumer.

[331] Brown & Chandler, 109 LQR 41.

[332] Consider, for instance, the elaborate statements of relevant commercial background to be found in the judgments of the Restrictive Practices Court and the reports of the Monopolies Commission. See Ch 10, below.

a Time for application of tests In relation to contract terms the question is whether the term 'shall have been a fair and reasonable one to be included having regard to the circumstances which were, or ought reasonably to have been, known to or in the contemplation of the parties *when the contract was made*'.[333] This provision resolves a dispute between the English and Scottish Law Commissions as to whether to adopt this date or to consider rather reasonableness at the date the defendant seeks to rely on the term. Since decisions are actually made at this later date, it may not prove easy to exclude facts which become known between the date of the contract and the date of the dispute. This is perhaps particularly important in relation to the way the contract is broken, which obviously cannot be known at the time the contract is made. Suppose a clause imposes a requirement that the plaintiff report a breach within a short period, a common requirement particularly in relation to contracts of carriage. This might be a reasonable requirement in relation to some breaches and not in relation to others. If the reasonableness requirement is to be considered in the light of events at the time of contract, the court will have to decide the question of reasonableness in relation to all possible breaches, without considering the actual breach.[334]

In relation to a notice not having contractual effect the test is to be applied 'having regard to all the circumstances obtaining when the liability arose or (but for the notice) would have arisen'.[335] It will be noted that nothing is said here about the parties' knowledge of the circumstances.

b Burden of proof It is for the person alleging that a term or notice is reasonable to show that it is.[336]

c Factors to be taken into account Section 11 (2) provides that in considering the requirement of reasonableness in relation to sections 6 and 7, the court is to have regard to the matters specified in Schedule 2. There is no such requirement in regard to the application of reasonableness in relation to other sections. The reason for this curious position is that guidelines were provided under the Supply of Goods (Implied Terms) Act 1973—the precursor of section 6 and have been extended to section 7 but that between 1973 and 1977 the views of the Law Commission as to the wisdom of providing guidelines changed.[337] In practice it has not proved possible to prevent reasonableness notions developed in relation to one section from infecting the consideration of reasonableness in relation to other sections.[338]

---

[333] S 11(1).

[334] See *Stewart Gill Ltd v Horatio Myer & Co Ltd* [1992] 2 All ER 257. Effective draftmanship may therefore require breaking the exempting clause down into a number of less comprehensive provisions.

[335] S 11(3).

[336] S 11(5).

[337] See the First and Second Reports of the Law Commission on Exemption Clauses (1969 and 1975).

[338] This was accepted as inevitable by Potter J in *The Flamar Pride* [1990] 1 Lloyd's Rep 434.

Five 'guidelines' are set out in Schedule 2. The court is adjured to consider them 'in particular'[339] so that it is clear that even when they apply they are not the only factors to be considered:

(a) the strength of the bargaining positions of the parties relative to each other, taking into account (among other things) alternative means by which the customer's requirements could have been met;

(b) whether the customer received an inducement to agree to the term, or in accepting it had an opportunity of entering into a similar contract with other persons, but without having to accept a similar term;

(c) whether the customer knew or ought reasonably to have known of the existence and extent of the term (having regard, among other things, to any custom of the trade and any previous course of dealing between the parties);

(d) where the term excludes or restricts any relevant liability if some condition is not complied with, whether it was reasonable at the time of the contract to expect that compliance with that condition would be practicable;

(e) whether the goods were manufactured, processed or adapted to the special order of the customer.

In relation to guidelines (a) and (d) it appears clear in which direction the guideline leads; it will be easier to show that the term is reasonable if the parties' bargaining position is equal or if the customer received an inducement to agree or knew or ought to have known of the term or could readily have complied with the condition. In relation to (e) however, it is not clear whether the fact that the goods are made to special order makes it more or less reasonable to exclude or limit liability. Perhaps the answer is that either is possible, depending on the rest of the circumstances.

Guideline (b) is an important and interesting one. When the courts had to decide the application of a 'just and reasonable' requirement under section 7 of the Railway and Canal Traffic Act 1854 they held it reasonable for a carrier to offer two tariffs, a lower one at the owner's risk and a higher one at the carrier's risk. It would seem possible that contracting parties subject to a reasonableness test might well adopt this practice, though whether it is reasonable in any particular case, must also turn on the reasonableness of the differential between the two rates.[340]

Guideline (c) at first sight appears puzzling, since for the term to be part of the contract at all, the rules as to incorporation will have to be satisfied. Presumably, however, this guideline contemplates that a higher degree of awareness of the term may make it more reasonable to uphold it.

---

[339] See also s 11(2).

[340] The failure by a film processor to offer a two-tier service was treated as strong evidence of unreasonableness by Judge Clarke in *Woodman v Photo Trade Processing* (1981) 131 NLJ 933.

In relation to the application of these guidelines it is helpful to consider first the case of *R W Green Ltd v Cade Bros Farm.*[341] This was a case involving the application of the reasonableness test under the Supply of Goods (Implied Terms) Act 1973. Although that test was not formulated in exactly the same language as under the present Act, the differences are not significant for present purposes.

> The plaintiffs were seed potato merchants who had had regular dealings for several years with the defendants who were brothers running a farm in partnership. The contracts were for the sale of seed potatoes and were on the standard conditions of the National Association of Seed Potato Merchants. These conditions provided *inter alia* that 'notification of rejection, claim or complaint must be made to the seller . . . within three days . . . after the arrival of the seed at its destination' and that any claim to compensation should not amount to more than the contract price of the potatoes. In respect of one contract for the sale of 20 tons of King Edward potatoes, it later appeared that they were affected by potato virus Y, which could not be detected by inspection of the seed potatoes at the time of delivery. As a result the defendants claimed that they had suffered loss of profits. The plaintiffs sued for the price of the potatoes and the defendants counter-claimed for the loss of profits.

In considering the reasonableness of the exempting provisions Griffiths J observed that although it would probably have been difficult for the buyers to obtain seed potatoes otherwise than on these conditions, the conditions had been in operation for many years and had been the subject of discussion between the Association and the National Farmers' Union. Guidelines (a) and (c) therefore pointed in favour of reasonableness. The sellers sought to justify the requirement to complain within three days on the grounds that potatoes are a very perishable commodity and may deteriorate badly after delivery, particularly if badly stored. He thought this a very reasonable argument in relation to defects discoverable by reason of inspection but not in relation to a defect like virus Y, which was not discoverable by inspection. Griffiths J therefore held that the purported exclusion of liability for lack of timely complaint was unreasonable but that the limitation of liability to the price of the potatoes was reasonable.

The House of Lords has delivered two leading decisions on unreasonableness. The first is that in *George Mitchell (Chesterhall) Ltd v Finney Lock Seeds Ltd.*[342] Curiously this was also a case involving seeds. The appellants, a firm of seed merchants, contracted to sell to the respondents, 30 lbs of Dutch winter cabbage seed for £201.60. The respondents planted 63 acres with the seeds. The resultant crop was worthless, partly because the seed delivered was autumn seed and partly because even as autumn seed it was of inferior quality. The respondents sued for damages for loss of the crop

---

[341] [1978] 1 Lloyd's Rep 602.

[342] [1983] 2 AC 803, [1983] 2 All ER 737. This action concerned the wording of the modified s 55 of the Sale of Goods Act 1979 but for most purposes this makes no difference to the guidance given by the House of Lords.

and the appellants argued that they were protected by a clause in their standard conditions of sale limiting liability to replacing defective seeds or refunding payment.

The House of Lords, differing in this respect from the majority of the Court of Appeal, held that the clause was sufficiently clear and unambiguous to be effective at common law but that it did not pass the reasonableness test.

Perhaps the most important feature of the leading speech by Lord Bridge was his insistence that although the question of reasonableness was not strictly a matter of judicial discretion an appellate court should treat the decision of the trial judge with great respect and only interfere with it if it proceeded on some erroneous principle or was plainly and obviously wrong. This statement was clearly designed to discourage a flow of appeals on reasonableness.

In concluding that the instant clause was unreasonable, the House attached considerable weight to evidence, paradoxically led by the sellers, that they commonly made *ex gratia* payments in the case of complaints which they regarded as 'justified'. This was treated as showing that the sellers did not themselves regard their terms as reasonable though it might perhaps be regarded as showing no more than that the sellers did not always think it good business to stand rigidly on their rights. This point is perhaps of purely passing importance since it is hardly likely that sellers will lead such evidence again.

Other factors which were thought to point towards unreasonableness were that the seller's breach was the result of gross negligence and that the evidence was that sellers could insure against delivering the wrong seed without a significant increase in price. This last factor must often be an important one.[343] The second case was the twin appeals in *Smith v Eric S Bush* and *Harris v Wyre Forest District Council*.[344] In this case, having held that the valuer's disclaimer was subject to the test of reasonableness, the House of Lords went on to hold that it did not pass the test. In a very helpful passage in his speech, Lord Griffiths drew attention to a number of matters which should always be considered. These were:

(1) 'Were the parties of equal bargaining power?'

(2) 'In the case of advice, would it have been reasonably practicable to obtain the advice from an alternative source taking into account considerations of costs and time?' On the facts of the particular case the House of Lords thought it unrealistic to expect a first time buyer whose financial resources were stretched to the limit in order to find the deposit and probably to furnish the house, to find extra money for an independent full structural survey. It is clear that this argument applies with diminishing force as the house increases in value and the resources of its purchaser are proportionately increased.

(3) 'How difficult is the task being undertaken for which liability is being excluded?' It was clear that in the present case it did not impose an excessive

---

[343] See p 245, below.   [344] [1990] 1 AC 831, [1989] 2 All ER 514.

burden on valuers since they were only being required to reach that degree of reasonable care and skill which the law in general demands of valuers and which the valuer has in any case to achieve in order to discharge his duty to the mortgage lender.

(4) 'What are the practical consequences of the decision on the question of reasonableness?' In the present case, the risk was one which the valuer could easily cover by professional indemnity insurance at a relatively modest cost, whereas the house purchasers were exposed to an enormous potential loss against which they were unlikely in practice to insure or even to be able to afford to insure.

The process of deciding whether a clause is reasonable will often involve balancing a collection of factors, some of which point towards reasonableness and some against. It has been suggested that the fact that the terms are in very small print or are very difficult to understand is an argument against their reasonableness.[345] On the other hand it is easier to justify reasonableness in relation to limitation of liability or to the exclusion of particular types of loss than to total exclusion of liability.[346] Presumably the fact that the clauses are well known and that the parties are represented by solicitors are factors pointing towards reasonableness but they were outweighed by contrary indications in *Walker v Boyle*.[347]

d The relevance of insurance The guidelines do not suggest that the court should take into account the availability of insurance or the question of who can most efficiently insure the risk. However it seems clear from the reasoning above[348] that questions of the most economic insurance arrangement are intimately connected with the reasonableness test. Where a clause is designed to limit liability rather than to exclude it altogether, section 11(4) requires the court to have regard to:

---

[345] Per Staughton J *obiter in Stag Line Ltd v Tyne Ship Repair Group Ltd* [1984] 2 Lloyd's Rep 211 at 222.

[346] Ibid.

[347] [1982] 1 All ER 634 [1982] 1 WLR 495 (actually a case on s 3 of Misrepresentation Act 1967). See also *Rees-Hough Ltd v Redland Reinforced Plastics Ltd* (1983) 2 Con LR 109.

[348] See also *Photo Production Ltd v Securicor Transport Ltd* [1980] AC 827, [1980] 1 All ER 556 and Lord Denning MR in *Lamb v London Borough of Camden* [1981] QB 625 at 638, [1981] 2 All ER 408 at 415. In *The Flamar Pride* [1990] 1 Lloyd's Rep 434, Potter J thought the actual insurance position was irrelevant. In *St Albans City and District Council v International Computers Ltd* [1996] 4 All ER 481 the defendant's standard conditions limited liability to £100,000. The Court of Appeal held the recoverable damages to be about £685,000 and that their limitation was unreasonable. This seems to turn at least in part on the fact that the defendants had insurance cover far in excess of the amount of liability and in part on a not wholly articulated notion that the defendants were better able to carry the substantial risks of defective software. Other useful cases on reasonableness include *Britvic Soft Drinks v Messer UK Ltd* [2002] 2 All ER (Comm) 321; *Bacardi-Martini Beverages Ltd v Thomas Hardy Packaging Ltd* [2002] 2 All ER (Comm) 335; *Granville Oil and Chemicals Ltd v Davies Turner & Co Ltd* [2003] 1 All ER (Comm) 819; *Sam Business Systems v Hedley & Co* [2003] 1 All ER (Comm) 465; *Frans Maas (UK) Ltd v Samsung Electronics (UK) Ltd* [2005] 2 All ER (Comm) 783; *Watford Electronics Ltd v Sanderson CFL Ltd* [2001] 1 All ER (Comm) 696.

(a) the resources which he could expect to be available to him for the purpose of meeting the liability should it arise; and

(b) how far it was open to him to cover himself by insurance.

It would seem clear that under(a) there must be a reasonable relationship between the resources and the limitation which it is sought to justify. More difficulty surrounds the construction of (b). It might be read to apply only to those cases where insurance was not obtainable at all, but it is suggested that this is too narrow and that the words should also cover the much more common case where the premium for insurance in excess of the stipulated limits would in all the circumstances be unacceptably high.

7 Other provisions

a Anti-evasion clauses The Act contains a number of clauses, whose purpose appears to be to render ineffective devices, to which ingenious draftsmen might otherwise resort, to escape or minimise the effect of the Act.

i Unreasonable indemnity clauses
Section 4 provides:

(1) A person dealing as consumer cannot by reference to any contract term be made to indemnify another person (whether a party to the contract or not) in respect of liability that may be incurred by the other for negligence or breach of contract, except in so far as the contract term satisfies the requirement of reasonableness.

(2) This section applies whether the liability in question—

(a) is directly that of the person to be indemnified or is incurred by him vicariously;

(b) is to the person dealing as consumer or to someone else.

A contract of indemnity is one in which a person A (the indemnifier) agrees to make good any legal liability which another person B (the indemnifiee) is held to be under. The liability may be one which B is under to a third party C or which B is under to A. In the latter case the result will be that A has a claim against B but that B is then entitled to call on A to indemnify him and thereby in effect to nullify A's claim. This obviously produces a result very like that of an exemption clause. Even where three parties are involved, this may in fact still be the case since it is not uncommon to find that A has agreed to indemnify B in respect of B's liability to C under a contract in which B agrees to indemnify C against C's liability to A.[349]

Indemnity clauses are common in both consumer and commercial contracts and section 4 is obviously designed to curb their misuse. It does appear however to have

---

[349] See eg *Gillespie Bros & Co Ltd v Roy Bowles Transport Ltd* [1973] QB 400, [1973] 1 All ER 193. The same clause may function as an exemption clause or an indemnity clause depending on the circumstances in which it is sought to apply it. See *Phillips Products Ltd v Hyland* [1987] 2 All ER 620, [1987] 1 WLR 659n. *Thompson v Lohan (Plant Hire) Ltd (J W Hurdiss Ltd, third party)* [1987] 2 All ER 631, [1987] 1 WLR 649.

gaps. First it does not apply at all outside consumer transactions. This means that in those cases where in a commercial contract between A and B a term purporting to exclude or restrict B's liability to A would be subject to a test of reasonableness, B may nevertheless stipulate that A is to indemnify him against such liability. Secondly in a consumer context it only applies a test of reasonableness, whereas in many cases the liability in question will be one which cannot be excluded at all. However, it seems probable that a court will not easily be persuaded that it is reasonable for B to seek to shift back to A, by an indemnity clause, a risk which has been firmly placed on him.

ii Secondary contracts
Section 10 provides:

> A person is not bound by any contract term prejudicing or taking away rights of his which arise under, or in connection with the performance of, another contract, so far as those rights extend to the enforcement of another's liability which this Part of this Act prevents that other from excluding or restricting.

This provision is not a masterpiece of lucidity but its general thrust appears clear. It is aimed at situations where there are two related contracts and it seeks to prevent a party doing indirectly in the second what he could not have done directly in the first. A common example would be a consumer contract to buy a television set with an associated contract for its maintenance. The sale contract would clearly fall within section 6 so that the seller's implied obligations could not be excluded or restricted. An attempt to exclude or restrict obliquely in the maintenance contract would also fall within the present section. It would seem that the same result would not follow if the contract were a non-consumer sale since then the Act does not *prevent* the seller from excluding or restricting his liability but only subjects his attempts to do so to a test of reasonableness.

iii Choice of law
Section 27(2) provides:

> This Act has effect notwithstanding any contract term which applies or purports to apply the law of some country outside the United Kingdom, where (either or both)—
>
> (a) the term appears to the court, or arbitrator or arbiter to have been imposed wholly or mainly for the purpose of enabling the party imposing it to evade the operation of this Act; or
>
> (b) in the making of the contract one of the parties dealt as consumer, and he was then habitually resident in the United Kingdom, and the essential steps necessary for the making of the contract were taken there, whether by him or by others on his behalf.

Where a contract has connections with more than one country, the court will have to decide which law to apply. The rules for this purpose are part of the conflict of laws[350] and a detailed discussion would be out of place here. However, it is clear that as a rule where the parties have made an express choice of governing law, considerable, and in many cases decisive, weight will be given to this choice. On the other hand it is very doubtful whether the parties can in respect of an otherwise entirely English contract, make a choice of a foreign governing law. The present provision clearly envisages some departure from the ordinary rules though of a rather curiously drafted kind. It will be noted that the section does not make the choice invalid but that the Act applies notwithstanding, so that the choice of a foreign law may otherwise be effective. As far as section 27(2)(a) is concerned, the Act will apply only if the term choosing a foreign law is *imposed* (a very strong word) and only if it is wholly or mainly for the purpose of evasion. This latter requirement would appear to involve an inquiry into motive, which will usually not be apparent from the face of the contract. There are, after all, many reasons, good or bad, why another system of law might be chosen especially once we pass outside the purely English domestic contract, which was probably dealt with by the common law. Under section 27(2)(b) the crucial question is the meaning of 'essential steps'. Does this mean *all* the essential steps, ie offer, acceptance and communication of acceptance? It is thought that it probably does, since if it were only the final essential step which was required to take place in the United Kingdom, Parliament might more conveniently have adopted the familiar test of where the contract was made.[351] Even so, the provision may have a very wide reach. Suppose an English consumer makes a contract in England with an agent of the Japanese National Railways for personal effects to be carried by rail from Tokyo to Osaka on a standard contract form which provides that the contract is governed by Japanese law. This appears to fall within the literal words of the section but this would produce a very odd result since on such facts, it is very probable that Japanese law would be held to be the governing law even where there was no express choice of law.

b Provisions for the avoidance of doubt The Act contains a number of provisions which appear to have been inserted because of doubts as to the precise state of the common law and consequently as to its possible interrelation with the Act.

(i) Section 1(4) provides:

> In relation to any breach of duty or obligation, it is immaterial for any purpose of this Part of this Act whether the breach was inadvertent or intentional, or whether liability for it arises directly or vicariously.

In some cases of fundamental breach it has been suggested that a deliberate breach may be more easily held fundamental[352] but it is clear that the distinction

---

[350] For further discussion see Dicey and Morris on the *Conflict of Laws* (12th edn, 1993) pp 1187–1284, and Cheshire and North *Private International Law* (12th edn, 1992) pp 447–471.
[351] See eg *Entores Ltd v Miles Far East Corpn* [1955] 2 QB 327, [1955] 2 All ER 493, p 65, above.
[352] See p 226, above.

between inadvertent and deliberate breaches is not relevant for the purposes of Part I of the Act.

(ii) Section 9 provides:

(1) Where for reliance upon it a contract term has to satisfy the requirement of reasonableness, it may be found to do so and be given effect accordingly notwithstanding that the contract has been terminated either by breach or by a party electing to treat it as repudiated.

(2) Where on a breach the contract is nevertheless affirmed by a party entitled to treat it as repudiated, this does not of itself exclude the requirement of reasonableness in relation to any contract term.

Section 9(1) assumes that a substantive doctrine of fundamental breach may exist and appears to be aimed in particular at a case such as *Harbutt's Plasticine Ltd v Wayne Tank and Pump Co Ltd*[353] where the exemption clause in question might well, if subjected to a test of reasonableness, have been held reasonable but the reasoning of the Court of Appeal would have denied it effect. Now that that doctrine has been given its quietus by the decision of the House of Lords in *Photo Production Ltd v Securicor Transport Ltd*,[354] this subsection will have little if any scope. In the same way, subsection (2) deals with the possibility, to which some credibility was given by some of the speeches in *Suisse Atlantique Société d'Armement Maritime SA v NV Rotterdamsche Kolen Centrale*[355] that the effect of the exemption clause might differ according to whether the injured party claimed to treat the contract as at an end or to affirm it.[356] Again, this possibility now seems less important but, in any case, section 9(2) does not prevent an injured party who has affirmed from contending that an exempting term is unreasonable.

(iii) The side note to section 13 states that it is concerned with 'Varieties of exemption clause'. It provides:

(1) To the extent that this Part of this Act prevents the exclusion or restriction of any liability it also prevents—

(a) making the liability or its enforcement subject to restrictive or onerous conditions;

(b) excluding or restricting any right or remedy in respect of the liability, or subjecting a person to any prejudice in consequence of his pursuing any such right or remedy;

(c) excluding or restricting rules of evidence or procedure; and (to that extent) sections 2 and 5 to 7 also prevent excluding or restricting liability by reference to terms and notices which exclude or restrict the relevant obligation or duty.

(2) But an agreement in writing to submit present or future differences to arbitration is not to be treated under this Part of this Act as excluding or restricting any liability.

---

[353] [1970] 1 QB 447, [1970] 1 All ER 225.   [354] [1980] 1 All ER 556. See p 230, above.
[355] [1967] 1 AC 361, [1966] 2 All ER 61.   [356] See 9th edition of this work at p 165.

This is a curious provision. One might expect a statute dealing with exemption clauses to place a definition of exemption clauses at its centre but the Act fails to state any clear conceptual basis. The present section does not offer a definition but rather a statement that whatever the central thrust of the Act, certain marginal matters are also included. It would embrace clauses which require claims to be brought within a short time; which restrict particular remedies such as the right of rejection or which purport to reverse the burden of proof. It includes clauses excluding the usual provisions as to set-off[357] but does not include a compromise of an existing claim.[358]

c Other provisions

i Misrepresentation

Section 8 provides an amended version of section 3 of the Misrepresentation Act 1967 and is discussed in detail elsewhere.[359] An important point which should be emphasised, however, is that since the section operates within the context of the 1967 Act, it is free from the restrictions of the present Act as to the contracts to which it applies and is therefore of general application. So, for instance, although the Unfair Contract Terms Act does not apply to contracts for sale of land, the Misrepresentation Act 1967 does. If a vendor of land makes a pre-contractual statement, which might be classified as either a misrepresentation or a contractual term, and the contract of sale contains a clause limiting liability to £10, the clause will be subject to a test of reasonableness in so far as it limits liability for a misrepresentation but only to common law controls so far as it limits liability for breach of a contractual term. So, paradoxically, the vendor might be in a better position by making it clear that the statement was a contractual undertaking.

ii Manufacturer's guarantees

Section 5 provides:

(1) In the case of goods of a type ordinarily supplied for private use or consumption, where loss or damage—

   (a) arises from the goods proving defective while in consumer use; and

   (b) results from the negligence of a person concerned in the manufacture or distribution of the goods,

   liability for the loss or damage cannot be excluded or restricted by reference to any contract term or notice contained in or operating by reference to a guarantee of the goods.

(2) For these purposes—

   (a) goods are to be regarded as 'in consumer use' when a person is using them, or has them in his possession for use, otherwise than exclusively for the purposes of a business; and

---

[357] *Stewart Gill Ltd v Horatio Myer & Co Ltd* [1992] 2 All ER 257.
[358] *Tudor Grange Holdings Ltd v Citibank NA* [1991] 4 All ER 1.   [359] See p 369, below.

    (b) anything in writing is a guarantee if it contains or purports to contain some promise or assurance (however worded or presented) that defects will be made good by complete or partial replacement, or by repair, monetary compensation or otherwise.

  (3) This section does not apply as between the parties to a contract under or in pursuance of which possession or ownership of the goods passed.

This is an important provision but its effect requires some explanation. Manufacturers do not as a rule sell direct to consumers and where they do section 6 will apply.[360] The present section deals with the common case where the goods pass from manufacturer to customer through a chain of wholesalers and retailers but the manufacturer nevertheless 'guarantees' the goods. This is particularly common in relation to consumer durables. The legal effect of such guarantees is murky. In some cases a consumer might argue that he had bought, relying on the manufacturer's guarantee,[361] but usually this would not be a plausible argument. In some cases the manufacturer attaches to the 'guarantee' a returnable card and it might perhaps be argued that the return of the card was consideration for the manufacturer's promise. In practice, there would be no great advantage in most cases to the consumer in the 'guarantee' being legally binding since most manufacturers will most of the time honour the guarantee whether it is legally binding or not and, usually, the amounts at stake would not justify the consumer in resorting to litigation. Indeed, paradoxically, the consumer may be better off if the 'guarantee' is not binding, since in practice many manufacturers have so worded their 'guarantees' as to offer a small service, for example, replacement of defective parts within a year of purchase, in return for the consumer abandoning his common law right of action in tort. This would often be a bad bargain from the consumer' viewpoint. If my negligently manufactured colour television explodes and burns down my house, it will be a small consolation that I am entitled to a new tube! It seems likely that this feature of 'guarantees' was often not understood by consumers, particularly as the 'guarantees' often give pride of place to their positive aspects. Be that as it may, section 5 ensures that where the 'guarantee' does constitute a contract between manufacturer and consumer, these exempting provisions will be ineffective. It should be emphasised, however, that it says nothing as to the preliminary question of whether the 'guarantee' does constitute a contract. It should be noted that 'consumer' as used here has rather a different sense than in the rest of the Act. If we take the case of the businessman who buys a car partly for private and partly for business use, we have seen[362] that under the test laid down in section 12 the question should be whether he *buys* through his business or his private account; for the purposes of the present section, however, it is sufficient that he *uses* the car partly for private purposes, even if he is using the car for business purposes at the time of the accident.

---

[360] S 5(3) makes it clear that ss 6 and 7 cannot overlap with s 5.
[361] Adopting reasoning such as that in *Carlill v Carbolic Smoke Ball Co* [1893] 1 QB 256.
[362] P 238, above.

iii Saving for other relevant legislation
Section 29 provides:

(1) Nothing in this Act removes or restricts the effect of, or prevents reliance upon, any contractual provision which—

(a) is authorised or required by the express terms or necessary implication of an enactment; or

(b) being made with a view to compliance with an international agreement to which the United Kingdom is a party, does not operate more restrictively than is contemplated by the agreement.

(2) A contract term is to be taken—

(a) for the purposes of Part I of this Act, as satisfying the requirement of reasonableness; and

(b) for those of Part II, to have been fair and reasonable to incorporate, if it is incorporated or approved by, or incorporated pursuant to a decision or ruling of, a competent authority acting in the exercise of any statutory jurisdiction or function and is not a term in a contract to which the competent authority is itself a party.

(3) In this section—

'competent authority' means any court, arbitrator or arbiter, government department or public authority;

'enactment' means any legislation (including subordinate legislation) of the United Kingdom or Northern Ireland and any instrument having effect by virtue of such legislation; and

'statutory' means conferred by an enactment.

This is an important provision since it is increasingly common for statutes, often as the result of international convention, to lay down mandatory contractual terms and thereby to provide a statutory solution to the allocation of risks in relation to certain contracts, for example, that a carrier may not exclude his liability for certain events but may limit it to a prescribed amount.

8 Evaluation of the Act

The Unfair Contract Terms Act does not stand alone; indeed it forms part of a worldwide pattern. In the past thirty years many countries have sought to tackle the problems of standard form contracts, inequality of bargaining power and exemption clauses by legislation.[363] Some of these Acts appear more comprehensive in

---

[363] The first example seems to be the Israeli Standard Contracts Law 1964. Other countries which have followed suit include Sweden (1971); Denmark (1974); Federal Germany (1976); France (1978) and Finland (1978). See Berg 28 ICLQ 560. See also in the United States the Uniform Commercial Code, s 2-302. Deutch *Unfair Contracts.* Hellner 1 Oxford JLS 13. See also the United States Magnusson–Moss Warranty Act.

scope[364] but the Unfair Contract Terms Act is clearly a major work, the most important statute in the English contract law since the Statute of Frauds. It is perhaps inauspicious that it should come exactly three hundred years after its great predecessor and one may wonder whether it will make as much difficulty for litigants and as much money for lawyers.

Certainly the Act is not immune from criticism. It makes a negative contribution to simplicity in two ways; first, it does not render any of the previous law redundant, so that it is still necessary to master the whole of the common law before considering the statute[365] and secondly, as those who have read so far may agree, the Act is not internally simple. Its scope cannot be concisely stated, its main sections overlap confusingly, key concepts such as 'reasonableness' and 'consumer' are not consistently used and it has a yawning conceptual void at its centre. It is certainly not a masterpiece of the draftsman's art.

Perhaps these inelegancies are outweighed by the substantive improvements which are made in the law. Certainly in so far as the law of contract can help the consumer, he appears significantly better off.[366] Ironically, the most important change may have come in the law of tort, with the outlawing of notices purporting to exclude liability for negligently inflicted death or personal injury.

It should perhaps be mentioned in conclusion that Parliament may not only invalidate or regulate exemption clauses but may also impose them. The classic example is the Hague Rules, which by the Carriage of Goods by Sea Act 1924,[367] are mandatory in bills of lading covering cargo carrying voyages from UK ports.[368] These rules provide for the limitation of the carrier's liability. Such rules are commonly to be found in international conventions on carriage.[369]

6 THE UNFAIR TERMS IN CONSUMER CONTRACTS REGULATIONS 1999[370]

The Directive on Unfair Terms in Consumer Contracts was adopted by the Council of Ministers on 5 April 1993. Member States were required to implement its pro-

---

[364] Particularly that in Federal Germany.

[365] Though many of the leading authorities upon which the common law is based would, on their facts, now fall under the statutory tests.

[366] Though it has been argued that this improvement has only been achieved by imposing extra costs on the supplier, which will in the long run be passed on to the consumer.

[367] As amended by the Carriage of Goods by Sea Act 1971.

[368] The rules are incorporated by agreement or imposed by the legislation of other countries in many other cases.

[369] See eg the Warsaw Convention on carriage by air incorporated into English law by the Carriage by Air Act 1932.

[370] Collins 14 Oxford LJS 229; Macdonald [1994] JBL 441; Dean 56 MLR 581; Bright and Bright 111 LQR 655.

visions by 31 December 1994. The Directive was not mandatory as to its precise terms; it laid down a minimum standard which Member States must reach for protection of consumers against unfair terms in consumer contracts. Most Member States of the European Union already had legislation in place which deals with this area. In the case of the United Kingdom, the relevant legislation is the Unfair Contract Terms Act 1977. The Act is both wider and narrower than the Directive. It would have been possible for the Government to identify those areas at which the Directive is aimed, which the Act has not reached and to legislate to expand consumer protection to these areas. The Government decided not to do this and instead to introduce secondary legislation under section 2(2) of the European Communities Act 1972.

The Unfair Terms in Consumer Contracts Regulations were laid before Parliament on 14 December 1994 and came into force on 1 July 1995. They were replaced with effect from 1 October 1999 by the Unfair Terms in Consumer Contracts Regulations 1999. It would appear that the purpose of the 1999 Regulations was to conform more closely than the 1994 Regulations had done to the Directive.[371]

A To what contracts do the Regulations apply?

The Regulations apply only to consumer contracts and only to standard forms of contract.

The European Court of Justice held in *Oceano Grupo Editorial SA v Quintero*[372] that a court can raise the question of unfairness of its own motion. This is undoubtedly important in principle though if the consumer is unaware of the regulation and is not legally represented the facts raising issues of fairness may not be before the court.

The Regulations define a consumer as 'a natural person who in making a contract to which these Regulations apply, is acting for purposes which are outside his business'. The courts have held that a company can be a consumer for the purposes of the Act[373] but this possibility is expressly excluded by the Regulations.

The Regulations do not apply to contracts which have been individually negotiated. They are limited to contracts which have been 'drafted in advance'. Of course, it is extremely common in consumer contracts, if there is a written document, for the document to have been drafted in advance by the businesses' advisers. Nevertheless, even in such contracts there may be some negotiation, particularly about the price. The Regulations say that 'the fact that a specific term or certain aspects of it have been individually negotiated' does not exclude the application of the Regulations if an overall assessment of the contract indicates that it is nevertheless a pre-formulated standard contract.

---

[371] C-240/98 [2000] ECR I-4941.
[372] For instance by extending the scope to contracts involving land.
[373] See p 239, above.

The limitation to consumer contracts would exclude most international sales and charter party transactions. Perhaps the most important and obvious area which is covered by the Regulations but not by the Act is contracts for insurance. The Regulations do not apply to terms in a contract of insurance which define the insured risk or the liability of the insurer if they are in plain intelligible language but they will apply to other provisions. For instance, many insurance contracts have elaborate and demanding requirements for reporting losses and making claims. It seems certain that consumers will argue that some of these clauses are unfair.

The 1994 Regulations applied only to contracts for the supply of goods and services. The provision producing this limitation does not appear in the 1999 Regulations. It is probable therefore that the Regulations apply to transactions involving land.[374] This appears more in accord with the wording of the Directive (especially the French version).

B The effect of the Regulations

Under the Regulations, terms classified as unfair are struck out and in principle the rest of the contract would be left in being unless the effect of striking out the offending term is to leave a contract which makes no sense. There are two important differences between the Act and the Regulations here. The first is that, despite its name, the Act is not concerned with unfair terms. Whether a term is unfair is never a test of its validity under the Act. Some terms are simply struck out. Other terms are valid if reasonable. Invalidity does not depend on fairness or unfairness.

The other is that, in principle, the Regulations can be used to attack any term which can be argued to be unfair.

C Unfairness under the Regulations

Clause 8(1) of the Regulations provides that 'an unfair term in a contract concluded with a consumer by a seller or supplier shall not be binding on the consumer' and 8(2) 'the contract shall continue to bind the parties if it is capable of continuing in existence without the unfair term'. Unfairness is defined by Clause 5(1) of the Regulations which provides ' "Unfair term" means any term which, contrary to the requirement of good faith, causes a significant imbalance in the parties' rights and obligations arising under the contract to the detriment of the consumer'. So the possible scope of arguments about unfairness is very wide. However, there is one very important limitation which is contained in Clause 6(2) which provides 'In so far as it is in plain intelligible language the assessment of fairness of a term shall not relate (a) to the definition of the main subject matter of the contract or (b) to the adequacy of the price or remuneration as against the goods or services sold or supplied'. This

---

[374] *London Borough of Newham v Khatun* [2004] 3 WLR 417.

means that it will not be open to a consumer to argue that a contract is unfair because he or she has been charged too much. This provision represents a vital decision as to a central part of the application of the unfairness concept. It is perfectly easy to understand why it was thought not expedient to leave judges with the task of deciding whether the price was fair. This would be the sort of question which could often not be answered without hearing complex economic evidence of a kind which many lawyers and judges are not trained to evaluate. On the other hand, questions of price must often be an important ingredient in questions of fairness and unfairness. Supposing I sell you a car which has been badly damaged in an accident, requires extensive repair work and is totally unroadworthy as it stands. If I sell you the car at a price which reflects all these defects, it is hard to say that the contract is unfair. If I sell you the car at a price which would be appropriate for the same car in perfect second hand condition but seek to conceal the defects and to exclude liability by the words in the small print, it is much more plausible to regard the contract as unfair.

The second schedule to the 1994 Regulations required particular regard to be had to 'the strength of the bargaining positions of the parties; whether the consumer has an inducement to agree to the terms; whether the goods or services were sold or supplied to the special order of the consumer; and the extent to which the seller or supplier has dealt fairly and equitably with the consumer'. It will be seen that the first three of these conditions are also relevant to reasonableness under the Act. This schedule does not appear in the 1999 Regulations. However very much the same language appears in recital 16 of the Directive and a judge could properly look at this in interpreting the Regulations.

Section 7 of the Regulations provides 'A seller or supplier shall ensure that any written term of a contract is expressed in plain intelligible language'. Where 'there is doubt about the meaning of a term, the interpretation most favourable to the consumer shall prevail'. The second sentence is simply a statement in statutory form of a rule which the English courts have always applied and which indeed is to be found in virtually all legal systems. Although there were suggestions in *Stag Line v Tyne Shiprepair*[375] that putting a clause in very small print or very difficult language might make it unreasonable, there are no cases in which this suggestion has been implemented. The wording of the first sentence of Section 7 is therefore of great practical importance. Many businesses operate at the moment by making a glowing statement in their marketing and trying to weasel out of them in the small print by obscure and complex jargon. Section 7 will make this ineffective and certainly therefore requires consumer contracts to be carefully re-read and in many cases extensively re-written.

Finally, it should be noted that Section 5(5) provides that Schedule 2 contains 'an indicative and non-exhaustive list of the terms which may be regarded as unfair'. It should be noted that the list is not a black list in that the Regulations does not say in terms that inclusion on the list means that the clause is unfair. It is rather a grey

---

[375] [1984] 2 Lloyd's Rep 211 at 222; see p 245, above.

list in the sense that inclusion on the list raises a strong inference that in most circumstances a clause of this kind should be treated as unfair.

D Powers of the Director-General of Fair Trading

Under the 1994 Regulations, the Director-General was given powers to try to prevent the continued use of unfair terms, including in particular the power to seek an injunction to prevent a trader using unfair terms. In practice many traders agree to abandon the use of offending terms without any application to court.[376] The Office of Fair Trading (OFT) issues regular bulletin to report progress on these questions.[377] The 1999 Regulations extended these powers to statutory regulators and trading standards departments. They also extended to the Consumers Association the power to seek injunctions.

The decision of the House of Lords in *Director-General of Fair Trading v First National Bank plc*[378] is of great interest because in this case the defendant challenged the view of the Director-General. The subject matter of dispute was a clause in the defendant's standard conditions for consumer loans. If valid, the effect of this clause was that if the debtor defaulted and the bank obtained a judgment, interest would continue to accrue at the contractual rate if, as would usually be the case, the contractual rate was higher than the judgment debt rate.

The House of Lords held that the clause was open to review since it did not relate to part of the core obligation but, reversing the Court of Appeal, that the clause was fair. On balance the speeches in the House of Lords support the view that the scope of the 'core' should be restrictively construed.

---

[376] For an application see *Director General of Fair Trading v First National Bank plc* [2000] 1 All ER 240; [2000] 2 All ER 759 Mitchell 116 LQR 557, Beresford [2000] CLJ 242.

[377] [2000] 1 WLR 98.

[378] See MacDonald *Exemption Clauses and Unfair Terms*, ch 4.

7 UNENFORCEABLE CONTRACTS

The elements required to form a contract have now been considered. Where they are all present, the parties are entitled to assume that the expectations reasonably raised by their conduct will be sanctioned by the courts. It will be necessary hereafter to examine the circumstances in which this assumption may be defeated in greater or in lesser degree by the presence of other factors—by mistake, for example, which at common law may make the contract 'void', or by misrepresentation, which may make it 'voidable'. But the English law has not been content to classify contracts as 'valid' on the one hand and as 'void' or 'voidable' on the other. It has allowed an intermediate position, where a contract, though valid, may yet be 'unenforceable' by an action at law unless and until certain technical requirements are satisfied. The 'unenforceable contract' is clearly a creature of procedural rather than of substantive law; and the origin of so peculiar a position is to be found in the passage, as long ago as 1677, of the Statute of Frauds. It is necessary, therefore, to examine the history of this statute and to observe its surviving effects in the modern law.

1 HISTORY AND POLICY OF THE STATUTE OF FRAUDS

Of the twenty-five sections of this Statute, two have been important in the history of contract, section 4 and section 17.

Section 4:

> No action shall be brought whereby to charge any executor or administrator upon any special promise to answer damages out of his own estate; or whereby to charge the defendant upon any special promise to answer for the debt, default or miscarriage of another person; or to charge any person upon any agreement made upon consideration of marriage; or upon any contract or sale of lands, tenements or hereditaments, or any interest in or concerning them; or upon any agreement that is not to be performed within the space of one year from the making thereof; unless the agreement upon which such action shall be brought, or some memorandum or note thereof, shall be in writing and signed by the party to be charged therewith or some other person thereunto by him lawfully authorised.

Section 17:

> No contract for the sale of goods, wares or merchandises for the price of £10 sterling or upwards shall be allowed to be good except the buyer shall accept part of the goods so sold and actually receive the same, or give something in earnest to bind the bargain or in part payment, or that some note or memorandum in writing of the said bargain be made and signed by the parties to be charged by such contract or their agents thereunto lawfully authorised.

The *raison d'être* of the statute is to be found partly in the condition of seventeenth-century litigation and partly in the background of social and political uncertainty against which it must be focused. On the one hand, the difficulty of finding the facts in a common law action was considerable. Not only were juries entitled to decide from their own knowledge and apart from the evidence, but no proper control could be exercised over their verdicts. Moreover, until the middle of the nineteenth century, a ludicrous rule of the common law forbade a person to testify in any proceedings in which he was interested, and the parties to a contract might have to suffer in silence the ignorant or wanton misconstruction of facts which they alone could have set in a proper light.[1] The mischief had been aggravated by the acceptance in the sixteenth century of the validity of mutual promises unaccompanied by formality or by the proof of a *quid pro quo*, or, in other words, by the adoption of the principle of purely consensual contracts. On the other hand, the confusion attending the rapid succession of Civil War, Cromwellian dictatorship and Restoration had encouraged unscrupulous litigants to pursue false or groundless claims with the help of manufactured evidence. The statute, therefore, avowed as its object 'prevention of many fraudulent practices which are commonly endeavoured to be upheld by perjury and subornation of perjury'.

Contemporary conditions, while they suggest the necessity for some Parliamentary intervention, do not explain the particular form which it took. To modern eyes the choice of contracts in sections 4 and 17 appears quite arbitrary. It has to be remembered, however, that these form but a small part of the statute, the bulk of which is devoted to the protection of proprietary interests in general. Writing was thus required to support the conveyance of land, the creation of leases, the proof of wills and declaration of trust;[2] and, in 1677, the adolescent law of contract was itself regarded as but a species of the law of property.[3] On this assumption it might be supposed that all contracts would have been included within the scope of the statute, and such, indeed, was apparently the original intention.[4] The reasons for the rejection of this draft and the substitution of specified types of contract remain a matter of speculation. Of the six selected, the close association with the conveyance of property doubtless explains the presence of contracts for the sale of goods, for the sale of interests in land, and, perhaps, with the growing importance of settlements, of agreements in consideration of marriage. A naive reluctance to rely upon belated recollection apparently prompted the inclusion of agreements not to be performed within a year. Of guarantees and promises by representatives to meet debts out of their own pockets it is only possible to say that, as the language of the section suggests, they were regarded by contemporary lawyers as of a 'special' character, either because they appeared strangely disinterested or offered peculiar opportunities to the perjurer. It is interesting, and perhaps significant, that these insular reasons for legislative intervention found a counterpart in parallel action on the Continent, where the acceptance of liability based on promise raised similar difficulties. It has, indeed, been suggested that a French Ordonnance of 1566, and possibly a later Ordonnance of 1667, offered the model or supplied the impetus to the English Statute of 1677.[5]

---

[1] Readers of *Pickwick Papers* will remember that, in the case of *Bardell v Pickwick*, neither the plaintiff nor the defendant entered the witness-box (ch 34). On the history of the Statute, see Holdsworth *History of English Law* vol VI, pp 379–397; Simpson *History* ch XIII.

[2] Ss 1–3, 5–9.

[3] Thus Blackstone described the Statute as 'a great and necessary security to private property': Comm iv, p 432.

[4] See the original draft set out in Holdsworth *History of English Law* vol VI, appendix I.

[5] See Rabel 63 LQR 174.

Upon the foundations thus darkly laid a vast structure of case law has been erected. Its extent may be gauged from the space accorded to it in standard textbooks, not only in England but in America, where the provisions of the Statute have been generally accepted.[6] Through this maze of litigation it is difficult to trace any guiding principle. But it is possible to suggest some clues to the underlying, and sometimes unconscious, aspirations of the judges. In the first place, the language of the statute was more than usually obscure. This fault has been judicially emphasised for at least two hundred years and is not confined to any one section. Of sections 5 and 6, relating to wills, Lord Mansfield declared the draftsmanship to be 'very bad'. He could not believe Lord Hale to be its author 'any further than perhaps leaving some loose notes behind him which were afterwards unskilfully digested'.[7] Sir James Stephen, in his analysis of section 17, concluded that the draftsman failed to understand the words he used and had but an imperfect appreciation of his own intentions.[8] Lord Wright in 1939 summarised the cases on sections 4 and 17 as 'all devoted to construing badly-drawn and ill-planned sections of a statute, which was an extemporaneous excrescence on the common law'.[9]

In the second place, the literal application of so imperfect a statute was likely to defeat its cardinal aim and to convert it into a potent instrument of fraud. The honest man disdained, the rogue coveted, its assistance. Lord Mansfield said that 'the very title and the ground on which the statute was made have been the reason of many exceptions against its letter',[10] and his colleague, Wilmot J, declared that, 'had it always been carried into execution according to the letter, it would have done ten times more mischief than it has done good, by protecting, rather than preventing, frauds'.[11] A hundred years later Sir James Stephen expressed himself even more strongly. 'The special peculiarity of the 17th section of the Statute of Frauds is that it is in the nature of things impossible that it ever should have any operation, except that of enabling a man to escape from the discussion of the question whether he has or has not been guilty of a deliberate fraud in breaking his word.'[12] In the third place, the statute, it has been seen, was the product of a particular social and professional environment, and, when conditions changed, the statute itself lost its *raison d'être*.

---

[6] Thus, of the 344 pages which comprise the first edition of *Blackburn on Sale*, published in 1845, 117 are devoted to the interpretation of s 17, and even in the eighth edition of *Benjamin on Sale* (1950), 140 pages are required to deal with the same section. In *Williston on Contracts* 3rd edn, the discussion of ss 4 and 17 occupies six chapters and over 800 pages.

[7] *Wyndham v Chetwynd* (1757) 1 Wm Bl 95.

[8] 1 LQR 1 (1885).

[9] *Legal Essays and Addresses* at p 226. The uniform tenor of judicial criticism is interrupted by the lone voice of Lord Kenyon, who declared the Statute to be 'very beneficial' and to be 'one of the wisest laws in our Statute Book'. See *Chater v Beckett* (1797) 7 Term Rep 201 at 204, and *Chaplin v Rogers* (1800) 1 East 192 at 194. The approval of Lord Nottingham, as a part-author of the Statute, may be dismissed as ex parte.

[10] *Anon* (1773) Lofft 330.

[11] *Simon v Metivier (or Motivis)* (1766) 1 Wm Bl 599 at 601.

[12] 1 LQR 1.

After the Evidence Act 1851 had permitted litigants to offer oral evidence in courts of common law, it became a conspicuous anachronism. Once more to quote Sir James Stephen, 'it is a relic of times when the best evidence on such subjects was excluded on a principle now exploded'.[13]

It is not surprising that the judges, impelled by these considerations, should have attempted to avoid the worst effects of the statute by a strained construction of its language. But the process, while often serving justice, more often made confusion worse confounded; and, by the end of the nineteenth century, practitioner and student alike had to pick their way through a tangle of case law behind which the original words of the statute were barely perceptible. In 1893, section 17 was repealed and replaced by section 4 of the Sale of Goods Act. Sir M D Chalmers, when he drafted this section, did so with obvious reluctance, observing wistfully that the Statute of Frauds had 'never applied to Scotland and Scotsmen never appear to have felt the want of it';[14] but it could not well have been omitted in an Act designed as a measure of codification. In 1925 the provisions in section 4 of the Statute of Frauds governing contracts for the sale of interests in land was repealed and re-enacted with slight modifications by section 40 of the Law of Property Act 1925; and this re-enactment may be justified by the relative complexity of the land law and the consequent need to secure ample time for investigation and reflection.

While these portions of the Statute of Frauds were being reproduced in modern legislation, criticism of the statute itself became ever more prevalent and ever more vocal. It was condemned by Sir Frederick Pollock in 1913[15] and by Sir William Holdsworth in 1924,[16] and in 1932 Professor Williams ended his study of section 4 with the words 'the case for the repeal of the Statute seems unanswerable'.[17] The Law Revision Committee recommended in 1937 that both section 4 of the Statute of Frauds and section 4 of the Sale of Goods Act should be repealed. But their report was not accepted, and in 1952 the question was remitted to the Law Reform Committee. They also recommended repeal, but with one modification. Contracts of guarantee, in their opinion, were traps for the unwary and required special treatment. 'inexperienced people might be led into undertaking obligations which they did not fully understand', and unscrupulous persons might 'assert that credit had been given on the faith of a guarantee which in fact the alleged surety had no intention of giving'.[18] They thought, therefore, that this particular class of contract should retain the protection which it had long enjoyed. The proposals of the Committee were this time accepted. By the Law Reform (Enforcement of Contracts) Act 1954, section 4 of the Sale of Goods Act was repealed and all section 4 of the Statute of Frauds save in so

---

[13] Ibid. [14] See Chalmers *Sale of Goods Act* (12th edn, 1945) p 26.
[15] 29 LQR 247. [16] Holdsworth *History of English Law*, vol VI, p 396.
[17] Williams *The Statute of Frauds, Section IV*, p 283.
[18] See Law Reform Committee First Report, Cmd 8809. A minority of the earlier Committee in 1937 had felt an equal solicitude for the victims of spurious guarantees, but had suggested a different remedy.

far as it concerned 'any special promise to answer for the debt, default or miscarriage of another person'. The Statute has been an unconscionable time dying and even now is not quite dead. To the surviving aspects of its long and dismal story it is now necessary to turn.

2 STATUTE OF FRAUDS, SECTION 4, AND LAW OF PROPERTY ACT 1925, SECTION 40

It is necessary to discuss in turn the two types of contract which may still be unenforceable under these Acts and their interpretation by the courts, the manner in which their technical requirements may be satisfied, and the effect of non-compliance. Section 40 of the Law of Property Act 1925 was repealed by section 2 of the Law of Property (Miscellaneous Provisions) Act 1989. This Act came into force on 27 September 1989 but its provisions are not retrospective. For the moment therefore both the 1925 and 1989 Act need to be understood. The Act of 1989 is discussed in section 3.

A The two types of contract and their interpretation

1 Special promise to answer for the debt, default or miscarriage of another person

When the Law Revision Committee first reported in 1937, a minority thought that contracts of guarantee should be *void* unless the terms were embodied in a written document. The later Committee, while sharing the view that such contracts offered peculiar perils to the unsophisticated, preferred to retain the old, if scarcely hallowed, language familiar to generations of lawyers, and with it the special quality of 'unenforceability'. The words quoted above were therefore saved from the general wreck of section 4 of the Statute of Frauds, and they have still to be applied, encrusted as they are with nearly three centuries of judicial interpretations.

It seems tolerably clear that the Parliament of 1677 designed by these words to cover promises by one person to guarantee the liability of another. But the determination of their exact scope has proved an arduous and complicated task. An obvious difficulty is the significance of the three terms, 'debt, default or miscarriage', unless, indeed, they are synonymous. The question was raised in 1819 in *Kirkham v Marter*.[19]

The defendant's son had, without the plaintiff's permission, ridden the plaintiff's horse and killed him, and he was therefore guilty of a tort against the plaintiff. The plaintiff threatened to sue him, and, in consequence of this threat, the defendant

---

[19] (1819) 2 B & Ald 613.

orally promised the plaintiff to pay to him the agreed value of the horse if the plaintiff would forbear his suit.

The defendant, when sued on this promise, pleaded the Statute of Frauds, and the plaintiff argued that the statute applied only where the liability guaranteed arose out of a pre-existent debt. The argument was rejected. Chief Justice Abbott said:

> The word 'miscarriage' has not the same meaning as the word 'debt' or 'default'; it seems to me to comprehend that species of wrongful act, for the consequences of which the law would make the party civilly responsible.[20]

The words of the statute were not confined to cases of contract; and, as the son had been guilty of a tort for which he might be sued, the father's undertaking was a 'promise to answer for the miscarriage of another person'. It would seem, therefore, that the guarantee in the case of a contractual liability is covered by the word 'debt' and, perhaps, by that of 'default', and the guarantee of a tortious liability by the word 'miscarriage'.

This conclusion may be accepted as a reasonable interpretation of terms which had no precise legal meaning. It is more difficult to justify the construction placed by the judges on the requirement that the liability guaranteed must be that 'of another person'. They decided that the legislature intended by these words to confine the statute to cases where the defendant had made a direct promise to the plaintiff to guarantee him against the default of some third party. It was thus held in *Eastwood v Kenyon*[21] that, if the promise was made, not to the creditor, but to the debtor himself, the statute did not apply.

Lord Denman said:

> The facts were that the plaintiff was liable to a Mr Blackburn on a promissory note; and the defendant, for a consideration, . . . promised the plaintiff to pay and discharge the note to Blackburn. If the promise had been made to Blackburn, doubtless the statute would have applied: it would then have been strictly a promise to answer for the debt of another; and the argument on the part of the defendant is, that it is not less the debt of another, because the promise is made to that other, viz. the debtor, and not to the creditor, the statute not having in terms stated to whom the promise, contemplated by it, is to be made. But upon consideration we are of opinion that the statute applies only to promises made to the person to whom another is answerable.

By a more comprehensive process of interpretation it has also been ruled that the use of the words 'of another person' assumes the continued existence of some primary liability owed by a third party to the plaintiff, to which the defendant's guarantee is subsidiary and collateral. A distinction has thus been taken between an arrangement whereby the original debtor continues liable and one in which he is discharged. In other words, a contract is not a guarantee within the statute unless there are three parties—the creditor, the principal debtor and the secondary debtor or guarantor. The

---

[20] Ibid at 616.   [21] (1840) 11 Ad & El 438 at 445.

essence of the contract is that the guarantor agrees, not to discharge the liability in any event, but to do so only if the principal debtor fails in this duty. There are thus two cases in which a contract is excluded from the statute on the ground that the promisor is not in fact answering 'for another person'.

The first case is where the result of a contract is to eliminate a former debtor and to substitute a new debtor in his place. Here it is idle to speak of guaranteeing the debt of another since that other has been released from all liability. As was said in an early case, if two come to a shop and one buys, and the other says to the seller:

> 'Let him have the goods, I will be your paymaster', or 'I will see you paid', this is an undertaking as for himself, and he shall be intended to be the very buyer and the other to act but as his servant.[22]

These words, though striking and often quoted, must be taken, not as an infallible test for the operation of the statute, but as an indication of the parties' intention. Whatever the language used, the question must be whether they intended that the promisor should assume sole or subsidiary liability. Even the stark phrase, 'Let him have the goods, I will see you paid', when thus read in the light of the context, may mean no more than, 'If he does not pay, I will'.

Again, suppose that a seller is unwilling to accept further orders from a buyer unless payment is made or security given for goods already supplied. If there is an oral agreement by which the creditor agrees to supply further goods to the debtor in consideration that X will assume sole responsibility for the existing debt, the statute does not apply. X's undertaking releases the original debtor from the liabilities so far incurred, and it is thus absolute and not in any way conditional upon non-payment by a third party.[23]

Secondly, a contract is not within the statute if there has never at any time been another person who can properly be described as the principal debtor. This is well illustrated by *Mountstephen v Lakeman*.[24]

> The defendant was chairman of the Brixham Local Board of Health. The surveyor to the board proposed to the plaintiff, a builder, that he should construct the connection between the drains of certain houses and the main sewer. The plaintiff desired to know how he was to be paid, and following conversation took place:
>
> Defendant: 'What objection have you to making the connection?'
> Plaintiff: 'I have none, if you or the board will order the work or become responsible for the payment.'
> Defendant: 'Go on, Mountstephen, and do the work, and I will see you paid.'

The plaintiff did the work and debited the board, which disclaimed liability on the ground that they had never directly or indirectly made any agreement with him. The plaintiff then sued the defendant, who pleaded the statute.

---

[22] *Birkmyr v Darnell* (1704) 1 Salk 27.
[23] *Goodman v Chase* (1818) 1 B & Ald 297.   [24] (1871) LR 7 QB 196; affd LR 7 HL 17.

The court had to consider the purpose and effect of the conversation between the parties. Did it mean that the defendant guaranteed a liability that primarily rested upon the board, or that he himself assumed an original and sole liability? Only in the former case could there be a contract to answer for the debt 'of another person'. Since the board had not ordered the work to be done and therefore was not a debtor in any sense of the word, it was held that the defendant was himself the only debtor and that his promise was outside the statute.

The court in this case sought to emphasise the distinction by suggesting appropriate nomenclature. If the undertaking was collateral and within the statute, it was to be described as a 'guarantee', if original and outside it, as an 'indemnity'.[25] Such terminology is doubtless of service in clarifying the issues to be faced. But contracting parties cannot be expected to use words as legal terms of art, and it remains for the court to interpret the sense of their agreement rather than to accept their language at its face value. If its purpose is to support the primary liability of a third party, it is caught by the statute, whatever the words by which this intention is expressed. If there is no third party primarily liable, the statute does not apply.[26]

These variations upon the theme 'of another person', if somewhat artificial, may be allowed to rest upon the inherent ambiguity of the language. A further distinction can be regarded only as a deliberate evasion of the statute.[27] Even though the defendant's promise is undoubtedly a 'guarantee' and not an 'indemnity', it will still be outside the statute, if it is merely an incident in a larger transaction. To come within the statute the guarantee must be the main object of the transaction of which it forms a part. The courts have adopted this argument in two types of case.

The first is where the defendant has given a guarantee in his capacity as a *del credere* agent. A *del credere* agent is one who, for an extra commission, undertakes responsibility for the due performance of their contracts by persons whom he introduces to his principal. Thus in *Couturier v Hastie*[28] the plaintiffs orally employed the defendants as *del credere* agents to sell a cargo of corn. The defendants sold it to a Mr Callender in ignorance of the fact that, at the time of the sale, it had ceased to exist as a commercial entity. Mr Callander, when he learned the truth, repudiated liability and the plaintiffs

---

[25] See Blair 29 MLR 522; Steyn 90 LQR 246.

[26] See *Guild & Co v Conrad* [1894] 2 QB 885, and compare the language of Vaughan Williams LJ in *Harburg India Rubber Comb Co v Martin* [1902] 1 KB 778 at 784–785. The distinction between guarantee and indemnity has passed from the Statute of Frauds into the general conceptual equipment of the English lawyer. See its application in the field of infants' contracts in *Yeoman Credit Ltd v Latter* [1961] 2 All ER 294, [1961] 1 WLR 828; Furmston 24 MLR 648; *Stadium Finance Co Ltd v Helm* (1965) 109 Sol Jo 471; Steyn 90 LQR 246 at 251–254; and in the field of recourse agreement between finance companies and dealers *Unity Finance Ltd v Woodcock* [1963] 2 All ER 270, [1963] 1 WLR 455; *Goulston Discount Co Ltd v Clark* [1967] 2 QB 493, [1967] 1 All ER 61. See also *Western Credit Ltd v Alberry* [1964] 2 All ER 938, [1964] 1 WLR 945.

[27] See the remarks of Lord Wright in *Legal Essays and Addresses* at pp 226–230.

[28] (1852) 8 Exch 40.

sued the defendants on their implied guarantee. The defendants pleaded, inter alia,[29] the Statute of Frauds, and the court rejected the plea. A higher reward had been paid to them, said Parke B,[30] in consideration

> of their assuming a greater share of responsibility than ordinary agents, namely, responsibility for the solvency and performance of their contracts by their vendees. This is the main object of the reward being given to them; and, though it may terminate in a liability to pay the debt of another, that is not the immediate object for which the consideration is given.

This language was adopted and applied by the Court of Appeal in *Sutton & Co v Grey*.[31] The defendants had undertaken to introduce clients to a firm of stockbrokers. It was orally agreed that the defendants should receive half the commission earned from the resulting transactions and that they should be liable for half the losses caused by the default of the clients. It was held that this last liability, though in essence a guarantee, was but part of a wider agreement and outside the statute.

The second type of case is where the defendant enjoys legal rights over property which is subject to an outstanding liability due to a third party. If, in order to relieve the property from the incumbrance, he guarantees the discharge of the liability, his promise is excluded from the statute and is binding even though made orally. In *Fitzgerald v Dressler*:[32]

> A sold linseed to B, who resold it at a higher price to C. A, as the seller, was entitled to a lien over the goods; he was free, that is to say, to keep them in his possession until he had received payment from B. C was anxious to obtain immediate possession, and A agreed to make delivery to C before he had been paid by B, in return for C's oral promise to accept liability for this payment.

It was argued that this promise was a guarantee within the meaning of the statute on the ground that, since B remained liable to A, C had in effect promised to discharge B's liability only if B himself failed to do so. The court rejected the argument and held C bound by his promise.

> At the time the promise was made, the defendant was substantially the owner of the linseed in question, which was subject to the lien of the original vendors for the contract price. The effect of the promise was neither more nor less than this, to get rid of the incumbrance, or, in other words, to buy off the plaintiff's lien. That being so, it seems to me that the authorities clearly establish that such a case is not within the statute.[33]

The result of such cases, however convenient, is so manifest a gloss upon the statute as, in more recent years, to disturb the judicial conscience. It has therefore been ruled that their reasoning will apply only where the defendant was the substantial owner of the property for the protection of which the guarantee was given. If he has no more than a

---

[29] The case also raised vital questions upon the effect of mistake. See p 286, below.
[30] 8 Exch 40 at 55.   [31] [1894] 1 QB 285.
[32] (1859) 7 CBNS 374.   [33] Ibid at 394. See also *Williams v Leper* (1766) 3 Burr 1886.

personal interest in its security, he will be within the ambit of the statute. Thus in *Harburg India Rubber Comb Co v Martin*:[34]

> The defendant was the director of and a shareholder in the Crowdus Accumulator Syndicate Ltd which he had in fact financed. The plaintiffs were judgment creditors of the syndicate and had sought by a writ of *fieri facias* to levy execution upon its property. The defendant orally promised the plaintiffs that he would indorse bills for the amount of the debt, if they would withdraw their writ.

The Court of Appeal held that the promise was a guarantee, not an indemnity, and that it did not fall within either of the exceptions discussed above. The defendant was not a debenture-holder but a shareholder, and he had no property in the goods upon which the plaintiffs sought to levy execution. His interest, therefore, was personal rather than proprietary. Vaughan Williams LJ sought to rationalise and to delimit the scope of the exceptions.

> Whether you look at the 'property cases' or at the '*del credere* cases', it seems to me that in each of them the conclusion arrived at really was that the contract in question did not fall within the section because of the object of the contract. In each of these cases there was in truth a main contract—a larger contract—and the obligation to pay the debt of another was merely an incident of the larger contract. If the subject-matter of the contract was the purchase of property, the relief of property from a liability, the getting rid of incumbrances, the securing greater diligence in the performance of the duty of a factor, or the introduction of business into a stock-broker's office—in all those cases there was a larger matter which was the object of the contract. That being the object of the contract, the mere fact that as an incident to it—not as the immediate object, but indirectly—the debt of another to a third person will be paid, does not bring the case within the section. This definition or rule for ascertaining the kind of cases outside the section covers both 'property cases' and '*del credere* cases'.

The courts, in applying this part of the section, may thus be confronted with two separate questions. Is the contract a guarantee or an indemnity, and, even if an undoubted guarantee, was it the main object of the parties' solicitude or a mere incident in a larger transaction? The answers given by generations of judges to these questions produce a result which would have astonished the draftsmen of the statute. It also suggests serious doubts as to the wisdom of retaining the old language and its unwieldy accumulation of case law. If it must be assumed that contracts of guarantee require special treatment, it would surely have been better to adopt the minority view of 1937 and declare such contracts void unless their terms were embodied in a written document. The slate would at least have been wiped clean and the judges enabled to approach their problems afresh unhampered by the subtleties and evasions of the past.

The difficulties presented by the guarantee rule were well illustrated by *Action-strength Ltd v International Glass Engineering*.[35] In this case the second defendant

---

[34] [1902] 1 KB 778. See also *Davys v Buswell* [1913] 2 KB 47.
[35] [2003] UKHL 17, [2003] 2 AC 541, [2003] 2 All ER 615.

(Saint-Gobain Glass) wished to build a new factory in Yorkshire and the first defendant (Inglen) was the main contractor. The claimant entered into a contract with Inglen to provide construction workers at the site. Actionstrength was paying the workers itself and looking to be reimbursed by Inglen. Inglen fell behind with these payments and Actionstrength was threatening to pull the men off the site. Action-strength alleged that at a meeting on site, representatives of Saint-Gobain had said that if Actionstrength carried on they would see that Actionstrength were paid.

Actionstrength kept the workers on site for another month during which time the indebtedness of Inglen grew greatly. It then sued Inglen and Saint-Gobain. It obtained summary judgment against Inglen which went into liquidation.

Saint-Gobain argued that even if Actionstrength's account was true, its promise was an oral guarantee and not enforceable.

In the Court of Appeal Actionstrength argued that Saint-Gobain's promise was not a guarantee. The Court of Appeal held that it was[36] and on appeal this was accepted by Actionstrength who argued that Saint-Gobain was estopped from relying on the guarantee argument. This argument was rejected by the House of Lords.

Lord Bingham said[37]

'. . . in seeking to show inducement or encouragement Actionstrength can rely on nothing beyond the oral agreement of Saint-Gobain which in the absence of writing is rendered unenforceable by section 4. There was no representation by Saint-Gobain that it would honour the agreement despite the absence of writing, or that it was not a contract of guarantee, or that it would confirm the agreement in writing.'

One can see that if Actionstrength's argument had succeeded, some (but not all) oral guarantees would become enforceable but the representations listed by Lord Bingham would have had no meaning unless Actionstrength were familiar with section 4 of the Statute of Frauds. We do not know whether they were. If they were, their behaviour would on any view have been incautious but many people know nothing of section 4 and would simply have relied on Saint-Gobain's promise. As Lord Hoffman N said[38]

'If one assumes that a judge would find that Actionstrength's version of events was right, to hold the promise unenforceable would certainly appear unfair . . . morally, there would be no excuse for Saint-Gobain not keeping its promise.'

It must be said that Saint-Gobain do not look much like the inexperienced person that the Law Reform Committee wished to protect in 1952. They had a clear commercial interest in encouraging Actionstrength not to withdraw since financial problems for Inglen could easily translate into extra costs for them.[39]

---

[36] [2002] EWCA Civ 1477, [2002] 4 All ER 468.   [37] [2003] 2 All ER 615 at 620.

[38] [2003] 2 All ER 615 at 621.

[39] It seems strongly arguable that an Australian Court would have reached a different result on these facts. Robertson 19 JCL 173. Several of the leading Australian estoppel cases were cited to the House of Lords but none were discussed in the speeches.

2 Any contract for the sale or other disposition of land or any interest in land

These words, now to be found in section 40(1) of the Law of Property Act 1925, replace the old wording of section 4 of the Statute of Frauds, 'any contract or sale of lands, tenements or hereditaments or any interest in or concerning them'. The differences are purely linguistic: no substantial alteration in the law seems to have been intended or effected, and the old decisions still apply.

The words 'any interest in land' are comprehensive and cover leases as well as sales. They have thus been held to comprise agreements to take or let furnished lodgings or to shoot over land or to take water from a well.[40] A contract will fall within section 40(1) if it has as one term a sale or other disposition of land, even though there are many other terms.[41] A unilateral contract in which the owner of land agrees to enter into a bilateral contract of sale if a potential purchaser does certain acts is within the section.[42]

Section 40 of the Law of Property Act 1925 was repealed by section 2 of the Law of Property (Miscellaneous Provisions) Act 1989 but the repeal was not retrospective. This means that if a dispute relating to a contract made before 27 September 1989 came before the courts today the 1925 Act would still apply. Transactions involving land have such long-running consequences that this is still possible but is now sufficiently unlikely to justify referring the reader to earlier editions of this work.

B The statutory requirements

> The agreement upon which such action shall be brought, or some memorandum or note thereof, shall be in writing and signed by the party to be charged therewith or some other person thereunto by him lawfully authorised.

Such was the language applied by section 4 of the Statute of Frauds to all the contracts within its scope and which still applies to the 'special promise to answer for the debt, default or miscarriage of another person'. The efforts of the courts to interpret these words have provoked a wilderness of cases through which it is possible only to indicate the hazardous and inconsequent paths trodden by the unwilling feet of litigants.[43]

---

[40] *Inman v Stamp* (1815) 1 Stark 12; *Webber v Lee* (1882) 9 QBD 315; *Tyler v Bennett* (1836) 5 Ad & El 377. See also *Lavery v Pursell* (1888) 39 ChD 508, where it was held that the sale of a house which provided that the house was to be demolished and the materials removed was the sale of an interest in land. For a more comprehensive discussion, see Farrand *Contract and Conveyance* (3rd edn) pp 32–35.

[41] *Steadman v Steadman* [1974] QB 161, [1973] 3 All ER 977, CA. This point was not argued in the House of Lords [1976] AC 536, [1974] 2 All ER 977.

[42] *Daulia Ltd v Four Millbank Nominees Ltd* [1978] Ch 231, [1978] 2 All ER 557; Harpum and Lloyd Jones [1979] CLJ 31.

[43] Many problems were necessarily worked out on the parts of the Statute now repealed; but these cases will still apply, *pari passu*, to the surviving fragments.

1 The contents of the 'note or memorandum'

The agreement itself need not be in writing. A 'note or memorandum' of it is sufficient, provided that it contains all the material terms of the contract. Such facts as the names or adequate identification of the parties,[44] the description of the subject matter,[45] the nature of the consideration,[46] comprise what may be called the minimum requirements. But the circumstances of each case need to be examined to discover if any individual term has been deemed material by the parties; and, if so, it must be included in the memorandum.[47]

There are however a number of qualifications to this principle. First, it appears that a term which will in any case be implied need not be expressed. Secondly, if the omitted term is entirely for his favour, a plaintiff may enforce the contract as evidenced by the memorandum and waive the benefit of the omitted term.[48] Conversely, it has been argued that if an omitted term is entirely for the defendant's benefit, a plaintiff should be entitled to submit to the term, that is, to enforce the contract as evidenced in the memorandum plus the omitted term. This exception was applied in *Martin v Pycroft*,[49] denied in *Burgess v Cox*[50] and is now apparently reinstated by *Scott v Bradley*.[51]

Provided, however, that the document relied on by the plaintiff does contain all the material terms, it need not have been deliberately prepared as a memorandum. The courts have accepted as sufficient a telegram, recital in a will, a letter written to a third party,[52] a written offer,[53] and even a letter written by the defendant with the object of repudiating his liabilities.[54] All that is required is that the 'memorandum' should have come into existence before the commencement of the action brought to enforce the contract. Thus in *Farr, Smith & Co v Messers Ltd*[55] an action was started against the defendants in the name of certain plaintiffs, and a statement of defence was filed which set out the terms of the agreement in question. Leave was then given to

---

[44] Compare *Potter v Duffield* (1874) LR 18 Eq 4, and *Rossiter v Miller* (1878) 3 App Cas 1124, per Lord Cairns at 1140–1141.

[45] Compare *Caddick v Skidmore* (1857) 2 De G & J 52, and *Plant v Bourne* [1897] 2 Ch 281.

[46] As a special statutory exception, the consideration need not be stated in a document offered in support of an agreement 'to answer for the debt, default or miscarriage of another person': Mercantile Law Amendment Act 1856, s 3.

[47] *Tweddell v Henderson* [1975] 2 All ER 1096, [1975] 1 WLR 1496.

[48] *North v Loomes* [1919] 1 Ch 378. In *Hawkins v Price* [1947] Ch 645, [1947] 1 All ER 689, Evershed J said obiter that a plaintiff could not waive a 'material' term but it is not clear why not if it is entirely for his benefit. No doubt most 'material' terms will usually be for the benefit of both parties and therefore outside the exception.

[49] (1852) 2 De GM & G 785.

[50] [1951] Ch 383, [1950] 2 All ER 1212, criticised Megarry 67 LQR 299.

[51] [1971] Ch 850, [1971] 1 All ER 583.

[52] See *Godwin v Francis* (1870) LR 5 CP 295; *Re Hoyle, Hoyle v Hoyle* [1893] 1 Ch 84; *Gibson v Holland* (1865) LR 1 CP 1.

[53] *Parker v Clark* [1960] 1 All ER 93, [1960] 1 WLR 286.

[54] *Buxton v Rust* (1872) LR 7 Exch 279.

[55] [1928] 1 KB 397. See also *Grindell v Bass* [1920] 2 Ch 487.

amend the writ and statement of claim by striking out the original plaintiffs and substituting the plaintiff company. It was held that this new step was in effect the commencement of a new action, and that the original statement of defence, signed by counsel as the defendant's agent, could therefore be regarded as a sufficient memorandum to satisfy the statute.

A document which denies that there is a contract cannot in general be a sufficient memorandum.[56] There is one clear exception to this rule. A written offer will suffice even though it shows on its face that at the time it was written there was no contract.[57] In a more recent group of cases the Court of Appeal has been concerned with a second possible exception. In *Griffiths v Young*[58] the agreement was originally 'subject to contract' and the memorandum so stated.[59] Subsequently the parties agreed that the agreement should become binding at once. It was held that the memorandum was sufficient even though it appeared to state that there was no contract on the ground that the phrase 'subject to contract' was a suspensive condition, which had been lifted. In *Law v Jones*[60] the Court of Appeal (Russell LJ dissenting) took this decision a stage further. In this case the parties made an unconditional oral contract for the sale of land but the solicitors' letters which constituted the only possible memorandum were all marked 'subject to contract'. The majority accepted that a document which denied the existence of a contract would not do but thought that a document marked 'subject to contract' did not so much deny the existence of a contract as contemplate that a contract would in the future come into existence. The validity of this distinction was denied by a differently constituted Court of Appeal in *Tiverton Estates Ltd v Wearwell Ltd*[61] where on substantially similar facts it was held that there was no sufficient memorandum. This decision was generally welcomed since it had been widely thought that the decision in *Law v Jones* would inhibit the progression of normal 'subject to contract' correspondence between conveyancing solicitors.[62] However in yet a fourth Court of Appeal decision *Daulia Ltd v Four Millbank Nominees Ltd*,[63] Buckley and Orr LJJ, who had constituted the majority in *Law v Jones*,[64] suggested that that decision had been misunderstood in *Tiverton Estates Ltd v Wearwell Ltd*[65] and that *Law v Jones* turned on a new unconditional oral contract coming into

---

[56] *Thirkell v Cambi* [1919] 2 KB 590.

[57] *Warner v Willington* (1856) 3 Drew 523 at 532; *Reuss v Picksley* (1866) LR 1 Exch 342 at 350.

[58] [1970] Ch 675, [1970] 3 All ER 601. The many difficulties in this case are exposed by Prichard 90 LQR 55.

[59] Made up by the combination of letters exchanged by the parties' solicitors, joined together under the rules discussed; pp 274–276, below.

[60] [1974] Ch 112, [1973] 2 All ER 437.

[61] [1975] Ch 146, [1974] 1 All ER 209. The Court of Appeal held that it was not bound by the decision in *Law v Jones* since that decision was inconsistent with the earlier decision of the Court of Appeal in *Thirkell v Cambi* [1919] 2 KB 590. Cf Emery [1974] CLJ 42. The Court of Appeal also thought the *ratio decidendi* of *Griffiths v Young* incorrect, though the case might be correctly decided because of further facts not set out in the text above.

[62] Since it would open the door to allegations that there was an oral contract.

[63] [1978] Ch 231, [1978] 2 All ER 557.   [64] N 60, above.   [65] N 61, above.

existence *after* the exchange of the 'subject to contract' correspondence, of which the correspondence might in appropriate cases constitute a memorandum.[66]

2 The signature

Only the person whom it is sought to hold liable on the agreement, or his agent, need sign the memorandum. A plaintiff who has not signed can sue a defendant who has.[67]

The word 'signature' has been very loosely interpreted. In the first place, it need not be a subscription; that is to say, it need not be at the foot of the memorandum, but may appear in any part of it, from the beginning to the end. In the second place, it need not, in the popular sense of the word, be a 'signature' at all. A printed slip may suffice, if it contains the name of the defendant. This relaxation of the statutory language was well established a hundred years ago and offers a striking instance of the way in which legislation may be overlaid by judicial precedent. Blackburn J said in 1862:[68]

> If the matter were *res integra* I should doubt whether a name printed or written at the head of a bill of parcels was such a signature as the statute contemplated; but it is now too late to discuss that question. If the name of the party to be charged is printed or written on a document intended to be a memorandum of the contract, either by himself or his authorised agent, it is his signature, whether it is at the beginning or middle or foot of the document.

A more modern example of generous interpretation is offered by the case of *Leeman v Stocks*.[69]

> The defendant instructed an auctioneer to offer his house for sale. Before the sale the auctioneer partially filled in a printed form of agreement of sale by inserting the defendant's name as vendor and the date fixed for completion. The plaintiff was the highest bidder, and after the sale the auctioneer inserted in the form the plaintiff's name as purchaser, the price and a description of the premises. The plaintiff signed the form. The defendant then refused to carry out the contract, and the plaintiff sued for specific performance. The defendant pleaded failure to satisfy section 40 (1) of the Law of Property Act 1925, and in particular that he had never signed any document.

It was held that there was a sufficient memorandum to satisfy the statute and that the defendant was liable. It was true that he had not 'signed' it in the ordinary sense of the word. But his agent, acting with his authority, had inserted his name as vendor into the printed form, and this form was clearly designed to constitute the final written record of the contract made between the parties.[70]

---

[66] It is not easy to reconcile these decisions with each other but for a valiant attempt see Wilkinson 95 LQR 6. See also *Cohen v Nessdale Ltd* [1982] 2 All ER 97.

[67] *Laythoarp v Bryant* (1836) 2 Bing NC 735.

[68] *Durrell v Evans* (1862) 1 H & C 174 at 191.   [69] [1951] Ch 941, [1951] 1 All ER 1043.

[70] Perhaps illogically a more stringent test has been adopted where a signed memorandum has been altered after signature: *New Hart Builders Ltd v Brindley* [1975] Ch 342, [1975] 1 All ER 1007.

In whatever position the 'signature' is found, however, it must be intended to authenticate the whole of the document. If it refers only to certain parties or is a mere incidental or isolated phenomenon, it cannot be relied on by the plaintiff. So in *Caton v Caton:*[71]

> Mr Caton proposed to marry Mrs Henley. He wrote out a document, beginning: 'in the event of a marriage between the under-mentioned parties, the following conditions as a basis for a marriage settlement are mutually agreed on.' Then followed several sentences, each in this fashion: 'Caton to do so and so, Henley to have so and so.' Neither party signed the paper, either personally or through agents, nor was a settlement ever executed.

It was held that the mere fact that the names appeared in various parts of the document did not make them signatures within the meaning of the statute, for in no single instance did it appear that they were intended to cover the whole of the document.

Where the memorandum is alleged to be signed by an agent, it must be shown that the agent has actual or ostensible authority to sign a memorandum. So, for instance, an estate agent, although undoubtedly for some purposes an agent of the vendor, does not necessarily have authority to sign a memorandum on his behalf.[72] However, if the document has been signed by an agent, it does not matter whether he intends to sign as agent or on his own behalf.[73]

3 The joinder of several documents

The framers of the Statute of Frauds clearly contemplated the inclusion of all the contractual terms in a single document. But here again the judges, in their anxiety to protect honest intentions from the undue pressure of technicality, have departed widely from the original severity of the statute. The reports reveal a progressive laxity of interpretation.

It was already settled by the beginning of the nineteenth century that the plaintiff might rely on two or more documents to prove his case. But at this period it was still necessary that the one document should specifically, and on its face, refer to the other. To introduce oral evidence so as to form a connecting link between them would be to permit the very process which the statute sought to exclude. Thus in *Boydell v Drummond*[74] the defendant had agreed to take a number of Shakespearian engravings, to be published over a course of years. The terms of the agreement were contained in a prospectus which was exhibited in the plaintiff's shop and which the defendant had seen. The defendant, however, had signed only a book, entitled

---

[71] (1867) LR 2 HL 127.

[72] *Gavaghan v Edwards* [1961] 2 QB 220, [1961] 2 All ER 477 (criticised Albery 78 LQR 178); *Davis v Sweet* [1962] 2 QB 300, [1962] 1 All ER 92. See as to a solicitor stakeholder *Elias v George Sahely & Co (Barbados) Ltd* [1983] 1 AC 646, [1982] 3 All ER 801.

[73] *Elpis Maritime Co Ltd v Marti Chartering Co Ltd, The Maria D* [1991] 3 All ER 758.

[74] (1809) 11 East 142.

'Shakespeare Subscribers, their Signatures', which did not refer to the prospectus and which contained no terms at all. The court refused to allow the plaintiff to prove by oral evidence that the book was intended to be read with the prospectus and so to satisfy the statute. Le Blanc J said:[75]

> If there had been anything in that book which had referred to the particular prospectus, that would have been sufficient. If the title to the book had been the same with that of the prospectus, it might perhaps have done. But as the signature now stands, without reference of any sort to the prospectus, there was nothing to prevent the plaintiff from substituting any prospectus and saying that it was the prospectus exhibited in his shop at the time, to which the signature related. The case therefore falls directly within this branch of the Statute of Frauds.

By insisting upon an internal and express reference in one document to the other, the courts, while abandoning the letter, might claim to be promoting the spirit of the statute. But in the latter half of the nineteenth century they took a more uncompromising step. They still excluded oral evidence designed to introduce a second document to which no reference at all was made in the first. But if, without any express reference, the language or form of the document signed by the defendant indicated another document as relevant to the contract, oral evidence was allowed to identify that other. Thus in *Pearce v Gardner*[76] an envelope and a letter, shown by oral evidence to have been enclosed in it, were allowed to form a joint memorandum within the meaning of the statute. So, too, in *Long v Millar*[77] the plaintiff was allowed to couple a written agreement to buy land, which he had signed, with a receipt for the deposit, which the defendant had signed. The present state of the law is illustrated by the case of *Timmins v Moreland Street Property Ltd.*[78]

> At a meeting between the parties the defendants agreed to buy the plaintiff's freehold property for £39,000. At this meeting the defendants gave to the plaintiff a cheque for £3,900 as deposit on the price. The cheque was made out to X and Co, the plaintiff's solicitors. The plaintiff then gave to the defendants a receipt, which he signed, in which he described the sum of £3,900 as 'deposit for the purchase of [named premises] which I agree to sell at £39,000'. Later the defendants stopped the cheque and repudiated the contract. The plaintiff sued for breach of contract. The defendants pleaded section 40 of the Law of Property Act 1925. The plaintiff sought to read together the cheque which the defendants had signed and the receipt which he himself had signed so as to form a complete memorandum.

The Court of Appeal, with some reluctance, gave judgment for the defendants. The law was thus stated by Jenkins LJ:[79]

---

[75] Ibid at 158.   [76] [1897] 1 QB 688.

[77] (1879) 4 CPD 450. See also *Stokes v Whicher* [1920] 1 Ch 411.   [78] Ibid at 120 and 276.

[79] [1958] Ch 110, [1957] 3 All ER 265. See also *Elias v George Sahely & Co (Barbados) Ltd* [1983] 1 AC 646, [1982] 3 All ER 801.

It is still indispensably necessary, in order to justify the reading of documents together for this purpose, that there should be a document signed by the party to be charged, which while not containing in itself all the necessary ingredients of the required memorandum, does contain some reference, express or implied, to some other document or transaction. Where any such reference can be spelt out of a document so signed, then parol evidence may be given to identify the other document referred to, or, as the case may be, to explain the other transaction, and to identify any document relating to it. If by this process a document is brought to light which contains in writing all the terms of the bargain so far as not contained in the document signed by the party to be charged, then the two documents can be read together so as to constitute a sufficient memorandum for the purposes of section 40.

A plaintiff, therefore, who wishes to use this means of escape from the strict letter of the statute, must prove:

(1) the existence of a document signed by the defendant;

(2) a sufficient reference, express or implied, in that document to a second document;

(3) a sufficiently complete memorandum formed by the two when read together.

In the present case there was a cheque signed by the defendants, and, if this could be read with the receipt, the two documents might have furnished the required memorandum. But the cheque was made payable, not to the plaintiff, but to a firm of solicitors, and there was nothing on it which served to connect it with the property in question. The plaintiff accordingly failed to satisfy the second of the three conditions stated above, and could not overcome the statutory defence.

C The effect of non-compliance with the statutory requirements

Both section 4 of the Statute of Frauds and section 40(1) of the Law of Property Act 1925 state that 'no action shall be brought' upon the agreements involved unless the necessary memorandum is forthcoming. In *Leroux v Brown*[80] it was held that the requirement was procedural. It did not mean that the contract was void but simply that no action could be brought upon it. It is for this reason that this chapter is entitled Unenforceable Contracts.

This distinction was important in *Leroux v Brown* because the contract was made in France and was valid under French law but was of a kind which required written evidence in England. The Court held that if the plaintiff chose to sue in England, English procedural rules applied.

Jervis CJ said:[81]

I am of opinion that the fourth section applies, not to the solemnities of the contract, but to the procedure, and therefore that the contract in question cannot be sued upon here. The

---

[80] (1852) 12 CB 801.   [81] (1852) 12 CB 801 at 824.

contract may be capable of being enforced in the country where it was made, but not in England. . . . The statute, in this part of it, does not say that, unless those requirements are complied with, the contract shall be void, but merely that no action shall be brought upon it. . . . This may be a very good agreement, though, for want of a compliance with the requisites of the statute, not enforceable in an English court of justice.

The principle of *Leroux v Brown* was affirmed by the House of Lords in *Maddison v Alderson* in 1883.[82] Lord Blackburn said:

> It is now finally settled that the true construction of the Statute of Frauds, both the 4th and the 17th sections, is not to render the contracts within them void, still less illegal, but is to render the kind of evidence required indispensable when it is sought to enforce the contract.

Other consequences were held to flow from the fact that the contract was not void but merely unenforceable. In particular in transactions involving land the courts of equity developed a doctrine of 'part performance' under which the contract might become enforceable as a result of some behaviour after the contract. The doctrine was far from wholly clear and its limits were still in dispute as late as the leading case of *Steadman v Steadman*[83] but the replacement of the 1925 Act by the 1989 Act means that the reader can now be referred to the 14th edition of this book.

3 LAW OF PROPERTY (MISCELLANEOUS PROVISIONS) ACT 1989, SECTION 2

A fundamental change in the rules for the making of contracts for the sale of interests in land was made by section 2 of the Law of Property (Miscellaneous Provisions) Act 1989. Whereas section 40 of the Law of Property Act required contracts for the sale of interests in land to be *evidenced* in writing, the 1989 Act requires contracts for the sales of interests in land to be *made* in writing.

Section 2 provides as follows:

(1) A contract for the sale or other disposition of an interest in land can only be made in writing and only by incorporating all the terms which the parties have expressly agreed in one document or, where contracts are exchanged, in each.

(2) The terms may be incorporated in a document either by being set out in it or by reference to some other document.

(3) The document incorporating the terms or, where contracts are exchanged, one of the documents incorporating them (but not necessarily the same one) must be signed by or on behalf of each party to the contract.

---

[82] Ibid at 488.   [83] [1976] AC 536, [1974] 2 All ER 977.

(4) Where a contract for the sale or other disposition of an interest in land satisfies the conditions of this section by reason only of the rectification of one or more documents in pursuance of an order of a court, the contract shall come into being, or be deemed to have come into being, at such time as may be specified in the order.

(5) This section does not apply in relation to–

    (a) A contract to grant such a lease as is mentioned in section 54(2) of the Law of Property Act 1925 (short leases);

    (b) a contract made in the course of a public auction; or

    (c) a contract regulated under the Financial Services Act 1986; and nothing in this section affects the creation or operation of resulting, implied or constructive trusts.

(6) In this section—

    'disposition' has the same meaning as in the Law of Property Act 1925;

    'interest in land' means any estate, interest or charge in or over land or in or over the proceeds of sale of land.

(7) Nothing in this section shall apply in relation to contracts made before this section comes into force.

(8) Section 40 of the Law of Property Act 1925 (which is superseded by this section) shall cease to have effect.

It will be seen that this section replaces section 40 of the Law of Property Act but that it is not retrospective. It applies to contracts made on or after 27 September 1989. This section was based on the recommendation of the Law Commission.[84] The Law Commission thought the existing position under section 40 to be unsatisfactory. There was a case for simply abolishing section 40 and leaving it to the parties to decide whether to put the contract in writing, as no doubt the great majority of them would do. However, the Law Commission thought that the overriding consideration was that no change in the law should increase the chances of parties entering into a binding contract for the sale or purchase of land without first taking legal advice. This is a clear cut and understandable policy but it obviously has a price. From time to time, courts will be confronted with an oral agreement for the sale of an interest in land accompanied by other conduct which makes the case for giving one of the parties a remedy very attractive. The doctrine of part performance could come to the rescue here under section 40 but that doctrine is clearly gone. However, there will be cases in which a court can help by deploying some doctrine such as collateral contract or estoppel.[85] A good example of a case where estoppel arguments might have been raised is *McCausland v Duncan Lawrie Ltd*.[86]

---

[84] Law Com No 164 (1987); Annand 105 LQR 553.
[85] As happened in *Record v Bell* [1991] 4 All ER 471. Bently and Coughlan 10 LS 325.
[86] [1996] 4 All ER 995.

The parties had made a written agreement dated 26 January 1995 under which the vendors agreed to sell and the purchasers agreed to buy a property for £210,000. The purchasers agreed to pay a deposit of £1,000 and the balance of £209,000 on completion. The contractual date for completion was 26 March 1995.

26 March was a Sunday and the vendor's solicitors wrote to the purchasers solicitors suggesting that completion should take place on Friday 24 March. This proposal was accepted by a letter from the purchaser's solicitors but there was no document signed by or on behalf of both parties.

In due course the purchasers failed to complete on 24 March and on the same day the vendor's solicitors sent a completion notice to the purchaser's solicitors. The Court of Appeal held that there had been no effective variation of the original contract. This meant that the trial judge had been wrong to strike out the purchaser's claim for specific performance. This did not exclude arguments based on estoppel being considered at the trial but this would require a careful analysis of the evidence.

It will be seen that the signatures of both parties (or an authorised agent) are required. In the common case of exchange of contracts however, section 2(3) will mean that the contract can become binding as soon as each party has signed his copy. Presumably, however, where the parties have arranged for exchange, the contract will not usually come into existence until the exchange has taken place. Exchange of contracts is to be construed in a technical sense. An exchange of letters each signed by one party will not do.[87]

Section 2(2) contemplates that the necessary documentation may consist in adding documents together. Commentators took different views as to whether the rules developed in relation to section 40 should be applied here or not[88] but the Court of Appeal held in *First Post Homes Ltd v Johnson*[89] that they should not.

The requirement that the contract is signed by both parties has already given rise to a lively dispute in relation to the creation of options. In *Spiro v Glencrown Properties Ltd*[90] the plaintiff granted an option to the first defendant to buy a property in Finchley for £745,000. The purchaser gave a notice exercising the option within the stipulated time limit but in due course failed to complete. The second defendant was the guarantor of the first defendant. Both defendants argued that although the option was granted in writing and signed by both parties the requirements of the statute had not been met because the notice exercising the option had only been signed by one party. Of course, at a common sense level, this argument has no appeal since it would defeat the whole purpose of an option if the option grantor was required to sign the document exercising the option as well as the option grantee. Nevertheless, counsel for the defendants put forward a not unpersuasive argument based on many statements by judges which characterised an option as an irrevocable offer, so that there

---

[87] *Commission for the New Towns v Cooper* [1995] 2 All ER 929, cf *Hooper v Sherman* [1994] Court of Appeal Transcript 1428.

[88] See above, nn 84, 85.   [89] [1995] 4 All ER 355.   [90] [1991] 1 All ER 600.

would be no contract until the offer was accepted. However Hoffmann J held that the irrevocable offer analysis was metaphorical and not to be taken literally. Accordingly, he held that the requirements of the section were satisfied.

4 OTHER RULES ABOUT FORM

It may well be that the most widely held lay misapprehension about English law is that a contract needs to be in writing and signed. In fact since the sixteenth century the common law has been signally free of any rules requiring contracts to be made or evidenced in a particular way. The only common law exception was that contracts made by corporations had to be made under seal but that rule was first eroded by exceptions and finally abolished by the Corporate Bodies' Contracts Act 1960.[91]

There are however a considerable number of statutory rules about particular types of contract, requiring them to be made or evidenced in a particular way. A detailed account would be out of place here but we may notice that these cases fell into a number of groups.

(1) *The contract must be under seal.* All leases for three years or more must be under seal.[92] A contract to grant such a lease, however, need only be evidenced in writing[93] and will for many purposes create the same rights between the parties.

(2) *The contract must be in writing.* A bill of exchange must be in writing[94] but this is perhaps not a true case since an oral agreement to the same effect would still be a contract but would not be a bill of exchange. In recent years Parliament has come to regard prescription of formal requirements as a useful tool for consumer protection.[95] The most important example is now the Consumer Credit Act 1974. Under section 61(1) a regulated consumer credit agreement must be in the prescribed form and under section 60 the Secretary of State is required to make regulations as to the form and content of documents.[96] Under section 65 an improperly executed regulated agreement can be enforced against the debtor only on the order of the court but the court is given a wide discretion under section 127 as to enforcement.

---

[91] The common law rules continue to apply to contracts made before 29 July 1960. A statement of them may be found in the 8th edn of this work at pp 414–417.

[92] Law of Property Act 1925, ss 52, 54(2).

[93] Under the Law of Property Act 1925, s 40(1) discussed above.

[94] Bills of Exchange Act 1882, s 3(1). As to whether it should be written on paper see *Board of Inland Revenue v Haddock*: Herbert *Uncommon Law* (2nd edn, 1936) p 201.

[95] Particularly under the Hire Purchase Acts of 1938, 1964 and 1965.

[96] Similar powers under the Hire Purchase Acts have been used to require particularly important information to be put in prominent boxes or special colours. Under the Consumer Credit Act a regulated consumer credit agreement (not exempted by s 74) must not only be in writing but also in prescribed form and signed.

(3) *The contract must be evidenced in writing.* The provisions deriving from the Statute of Frauds are the main examples but another is provided by contracts of marine insurance. Here a written policy is normally issued and the Marine Insurance Act 1906[97] renders a policy 'inadmissible in evidence' unless it is embodied in a policy signed by the insurer but the policy is not normally the contract, which is completed when the slip which the broker presents to the insurer is initialled by the latter.[98]

(4) *There are fiscal or criminal sanctions if the contract is not put into writing.* All policies of life insurance are in practice in writing but there is no legal requirement that they should be. However, any insurer who does not issue a stamped policy within a month of receiving the first premium is liable to a fine.[99]

5 WRITING, SIGNATURE AND ELECTRONIC COMMERCE

As we have already said general English contract law does not normally require writing or signature. However English commercial practice has historically relied heavily on the transfer of written (and usually signed) documents. So bills of lading stand at the centre of international sales transactions and millions of cheques are being issued each day to move money between accounts.

Undoubtably the advent of computers and the development of electronic communication represents a major challenge and opportunity in this respect. In the UK the passing of the Electronic Communications Act 2000 gives the 'appropriate minister' wide powers to make orders carrying this process forward.[100]

---

[97] See ss 21, 22, 23 and 24.

[98] See per Blackburn J in *Ionides v Pacific Fire and Marine Insurance Co* (1871) LR 6 QB 674 at 685.

[99] Stamp Act 1891, as amended by Finance Act 1970, s 32.

[100] See Electronic Signatures Regulations 2002, SI 2002/318; Electronic Commerce: Formal Requirements in Commercial Transactions, Advice from Law Commission, December 2001. For a fuller account see Rowland and MacDonald, *Information Technology Law* (2nd edn) pp 308–326.

8 MISTAKE

SUMMARY

1 INTRODUCTION[1]

The first fact to appreciate in this somewhat elusive branch of the law is that the word 'mistake' bears a more restricted meaning in professional than in popular speech. A

---

[1] The literature on mistakes is extensive. See eg Stoljar *Mistake and Misrepresentation: A Study in Contractual Principles* (1968); Slade 70 LQR 385; Atiyah 73 LQR 340; Wilson 17 MLR 515; Unger 18 MLR 259; Smith and Thomas 20 MLR 38; Atiyah and Bennion 24 MLR 421; Shatwell 33 Can Bar

layman might well believe that no force whatever should be allowed to an agreement based on an obvious misunderstanding. The law, however, does not take the simple line of ruling that a contract is void merely because one or both of the parties would not have made it had the true facts been realised. Many examples might be given of situations where a mistake in the popular sense is denied legal significance and where a remedy, if available at all, is granted upon some other ground. If, for instance, A agrees to buy from B a roadside garage abutting on a public highway and, unknown to A but known to B, a bypass road is about to be constructed which will divert the traffic from the garage, A cannot escape from the contract on the ground of mistake.[2] If he has been misled by the statement of B, he may be able to obtain the rescission of the contract, but this will be on the ground, not of mistake, but of a false representation. In the popular sense of the term, indeed, all cases of misrepresentation involve a misunderstanding; but they by no means all raise the legal doctrine of mistake.

The narrow scope allowed to mistake in the English legal system is a fact to be not only noticed but welcomed. In the few cases in which it operates the effect, at least at common law, is said to be that the whole transaction is void from the very beginning. This drastic result may be unobjectionable as far as the parties themselves are concerned, but the reaction upon third parties may be deplorable. From a complete nullity no rights can be derived. Goods may have been sold and delivered on credit by A to B under an apparent contract, and may then be *bona fide* bought and paid for by C. If the original contract between A and B is now declared void for mistake, B has obtained no title to the goods and can pass none. C, though he has acted innocently and in the ordinary course of business, will in principle be liable to A for the full value of the goods.[3] If, indeed, the case can be dealt with not at common law but in equity, so unfortunate a result may be averted. The courts, in the exercise of their equitable jurisdiction to grant a decree *in personam*, may grant specific relief against the consequences of mistake without declaring the contract a nullity. In this way they may protect not only the innocent stranger who has become involved in the sequence of events, but also one of the original parties if the demands of substantial justice are to be satisfied. It follows, therefore, that in any discussion of mistake it will often be found necessary to distinguish its treatment at common law and in equity, with the hope that the jurisdiction of the latter will develop at the expense of the former. In *United Scientific Holdings Ltd v Burnley Borough Council*[4] the House of Lords were strongly of the opinion that common law and equity should no longer be regarded as distinct systems. These observations were not made in the context of contractual mistake, but they were clearly wide enough to embrace that topic. Although their

---

Rev 164; Atiyah 2 Ottawa L Rev 337. Goldberg and Thomson [1978] JBL 30, 147; Cartwright 103 LQR 594; Phang 9 LS 291; Smith 110 LQR 400.

[2] Example given by Lord Atkin in *Bell v Lever Bros* [1932] AC 161 at 224.

[3] There are, of course, exceptions to the applications of the doctrine *nemo dat quod non habet*; see *Benjamin's Sale of Goods* (4th edn, 1992) paras 7-001–7-113.

[4] [1978] AC 904, [1977] 2 All ER 62.

Lordships' observations received a less than ecstatic welcome from distinguished equity lawyers,[5] there may well be much to be said for consolidation of law and equity in this area. Unfortunately, in the complete absence of any relevant authority, it is for the moment quite impossible to say with precision what form this consolidation would take. It seems necessary, therefore, to continue, for the moment, to expound common law and equity separately.

The classification adopted in this chapter must now be explained. If attention is fixed merely on the factual situations, there are three possible types of mistake; common, mutual and unilateral.

In common mistake, both parties make the same mistake. Each knows the intention of the other and accepts it, but each is mistaken about some underlying and fundamental fact. The parties, for example, are unaware that the subject matter of their contract has already perished.

In mutual mistake, the parties misunderstand each other and are at cross purposes. A, for example, intends to offer his Ford Sierra car for sale, but B believes that the offer relates to the Ford Granada also owned by A.[6]

In unilateral mistake, only one of the parties is mistaken. The other knows, or must be taken to know, of his mistake. Suppose, for instance, that A agrees to buy from B a specific picture which A believes to be a genuine Constable but which in fact is a copy. If B is ignorant of A's erroneous belief, the case is one of mutual mistake, but, if he knows of it, of unilateral mistake.

When, however, the cases provoked by these factual situations are analysed, they will be seen to fall, not into three, but only into two distinct legal categories. Has an agreement been reached or not? Where common mistake is pleaded, the presence of agreement is admitted. The rules of offer and acceptance are satisfied and the parties are of one mind. What is urged is that, owing to a common error as to some fundamental fact, the agreement is robbed of all efficacy. Where either mutual or unilateral mistake is pleaded, the very existence of the agreement is denied. The argument is that, despite appearances, there is no real correspondence of offer and acceptance and that therefore the transaction must necessarily be void.[7]

---

[5] Baker 93 LQR 529; Pettit *Equity and the Law of Trusts* (6th edn) pp 9–10.

[6] The distinction between the epithets 'common' and 'mutual', though surprisingly often confused both in and out of the reports, is clearly stated in the *Oxford English Dictionary*. 'Common' is there defined as 'possessed or shared alike by both or all the persons or things in question'. 'Mutual' was, indeed, at one period used as a synonym for 'common'; but according to the *OED*, this is 'now regarded as incorrect' and properly means 'possessed or entertained by each of two persons towards or with regard to the other'. See the more caustic words of Fowler in *Modern English Usage* under 'mutual'.

[7] Although the two problems are different in principle, the difference has often been forgotten, especially by those pioneer English writers on contract, Pollock and Anson, who strove to include all types of mistake under the general rubric of *consensus*. It will be seen that the word 'mistake' is being used in two different senses. In common mistake and unilateral mistake, mistake means error, but in mutual mistake, mistake means 'misunderstanding'. the parties are at cross-purposes but there is not necessarily an error which can be corrected.

One type of problem is thus presented by common mistake, and a second by mutual or unilateral mistake. But the distinction between these two latter forms of mistake is still important. Though the problem they pose is the same, the method of approach to it differs. If mutual mistake is pleaded, the judicial approach, as is normally the case in contractual problems, is objective; the court, looking at the evidence from the standpoint of a reasonable third party, will decide whether any, and if so what, agreement must be taken to have been reached. If unilateral mistake is pleaded, the approach is subjective; the innocent party is allowed to show the effect upon *his* mind of the error in the hope of avoiding its consequences.

It is important to note that to have any effect at all, the mistake must be one which exists at the moment the contract is concluded. This is dramatically illustrated by the facts of *Amalgamated Investment and Property Co Ltd v John Walker & Sons Ltd.*[8]

> In this case the plaintiffs were negotiating to buy a commercial property from the defendants. The defendants knew that the plaintiffs intended to redevelop the property and both parties knew that planning permission was needed for this purpose. In their pre-contract enquiries, the plaintiffs specifically asked the defendants whether the property was designated as a building of special architectural or historic interest. On 14 August 1973 the defendants replied in the negative. At that date, the answer was both truthful and accurate but, unknown to the parties (and, because of strange government procedures, without the possibility of their knowledge) the Department of the Environment had it in mind to list the building. On 25 September 1973 the parties signed a contract in which the defendants agreed to sell the building to the plaintiffs for £1,710,000. On 26 September 1973 the Department of the Environment informed the defendants that the building had been included on the statutory list of buildings of special architectural or historic interest, and the list was given legal effect on the following day when signed by the Minister. The evidence was that so listed the building was only worth £210,000.

The plaintiffs claimed that the contract should be rescinded for common mistake.[9] The Court of Appeal rejected this argument on the ground that, for this purpose, the critical date was the date of the contract. At that date, both parties believed the building not to be listed and that was in fact the case.

---

[8] [1976] 3 All ER 509, [1977] 1 WLR 164; Brownsword 40 MLR 467.
[9] There was an alternative plea based on the doctrine of frustration which also failed.

2 THE TWO CATEGORIES OF CASES

A Where agreement has been reached, but upon the basis of a common mistake

In this category there is no question of lack of agreement. The exact offer made by A has been accepted by B. It is clear, for instance, that B has accepted A's offer to sell a specific picture for £1,000. It is admitted, however, that both parties wrongly believed the artist to have been Constable. B now contends that owing to this common mistake the agreement cannot be allowed to stand, since the fundamental assumption upon which its very being is based has proved to be false.

The task here is to ascertain what attitude the courts have adopted towards an agreement that neither party would have made had they realised the untruth of what they both honestly believed to be true, and not only true but essential to the making of the bargain. It is also necessary to consider whether there are different rules at common law and in equity.

1 Agreements that are void both at common law and in equity

The exact significance of the principle laid down at common law and shared by equity is no doubt somewhat controversial, but if what the judges have said is interpreted in the light of what they have done it would appear that a common mistake has no effect whatsoever at common law unless it is such as to eliminate the very subject matter of the agreement; in other words, unless it empties the agreement of all content.

This principle has clearly been applied in a number of decisions dealing with what may conveniently and shortly be called cases of *res extincta*. It is well established that if, unknown to the parties, the specific subject matter of the agreement is in fact non-existent, no contract whatever ensues. In the leading case of *Couturier v Hastie*,[10] the question concerned the sale of a cargo of corn supposed at the time of the contract to be in transit from Salonica to the United Kingdom, but which unknown to the parties had become fermented and had already been sold by the master of the ship to a purchaser at Tunis. It was held that the buyer was not liable for the price of the cargo. The case was heard by the Court of Exchequer, the Court of Exchequer Chamber and finally, after a consultation with nine of the judges, by the House of Lords. It was the unanimous view of each court that everything depended upon the construction of the contract. Had the purchaser agreed to buy specific goods or had he agreed to buy an adventure—namely the benefit of the insurance that had been effected to cover the possible failure of the goods to arrive? The former construction was ultimately preferred. Once this had been decided, it followed as a matter of course that the

---

[10] (1852) 8 Exch 40; reversed (1853) 9 Exch 102; reversal affirmed (1856) 5 HL Cas 673. See Nicholas 48 Tulane L Rev 946 at 966–972.

contract was void, for in the nature of things a contract to sell and deliver specific goods presupposes the existence of goods capable of delivery. Both parties contemplated an existing something to be bought and sold. It was not the mistake *per se* that prevented the formation of a contract in *Couturier v Hastie*, and, indeed, the word 'mistake' was never mentioned in any of the judgments. The crucial fact was the absence of the contemplated subject matter, which necessarily emptied the contract of all content. Lord Cranworth said:

> Looking to the contract itself alone, it appears to me clearly that what the parties contemplated, those who bought and those who sold, was that there was an existing something to be sold and bought . . . The contract plainly imports that there was something which was to be sold at the time of the contract, and something to be purchased. No such thing existing . . . there must be judgment . . . for the defendants.[11]

The view adopted in *Couturier v Hastie* had already been taken in the earlier case of *Strickland v Turner*,[12] where:

> X had bought and paid for an annuity upon the life of a person who, unknown to the buyer and seller, was already dead.

It was held that X had got nothing for his money and that the total failure of consideration entitled him to recovery in full.

Six years after *Couturier v Hastie*, the court in *Pritchard v Merchants' and Tradesman's Mutual Life Assurance Society*,[13] again dealt with the case of *res extincta*.

> The beneficiary of a life insurance policy, which had lapsed owing to the non-payment of the premium, paid to the insurers a renewal premium which was sufficient to revive the policy. The parties, however, were ignorant that the assured had died before the payment was made.

The beneficiary failed to recover the amount due under the policy, since

> . . . the premium was paid and accepted upon an implied understanding on both sides that the party insured was then alive. Both parties were labouring under a mistake, and consequently the transaction was altogether void.[14]

It is true that the presence of a mistake was mentioned in the judgment, but it was the special character of that mistake—the erroneous assumption of the assured's continued existence—that enabled the court to pronounce the contract void.

In *Galloway v Galloway*[15] a separation deed between a man and woman was declared a nullity, because it was made on the mistaken and common assumption that

---

[11] (1856) 5 HL Cas 673 at 681–682.

[12] (1852) 7 Exch 208. See also the somewhat analogous case of *Scott v Coulson* [1903] 2 Ch 249.

[13] (1858) 3 CBNS 622.

[14] Ibid at 640, per Williams J. As Byles J pointed out at 645, the premium could have been recovered as having been paid and received under a mistake of fact.

[15] (1914) 30 TLR 531; followed in *Law v Harragin* (1917) 33 TLR 381.

they were in fact married to each other. The supposition upon which the parties had proceeded was that the subject matter of the contract, the marriage, was in existence.

Equity was approaching the problem of *res extincta* in much the same way and at the same time as the common law. In one case where A had bought a remainder in fee expectant upon an estate tail and had given a bond for the money, both parties being ignorant that the entail had been barred and the remainder destroyed, Richards CB said:

> If contracting parties have treated while under a mistake, that will be sufficient ground for the interference of a Court of Equity: but in this case there is much more. Suppose I sell an estate innocently, which at the time is actually swept away by a flood, without my knowledge of the fact; am I to be allowed to receive £5,000 and interest, because the conveyance is executed, and a bond given for that sum as the purchase money, when, in point of fact, I had not an inch of that land, so sold, to sell?[16]

The Chief Baron ordered the refunding of all interest paid and the cancellation and re-delivery of the bond.

The principle applicable to the *res extincta* has been extended, at any rate in equity, to the analogous case of what may be called the *res sua*, ie if A agrees to buy or take a lease from B of property which both parties believe to belong to B but which in fact belongs to A.[17] The contract is of necessity a nullity, since B has nothing to sell or convey.[18] As Knight Bruce LJ said in one of the cases: 'It would be contrary to all the rules of equity and common law to give effect to such an agreement.'[19] This is so however only when the *res sua* comprises the whole of the land sold or let.[20]

If we pause here for a moment, it seems clear that the reason why a contract relating to a *res extincta* or to a *res sua* cannot be recognised is not so much the fact of the common mistake as the absence of any contractual subject matter. If a contract may be discharged by subsequent impossibility of performance,[21] then *a fortiori* its very genesis is precluded by a present impossibility. In the case both of the *res sua* and the *res extincta*,

> . . . the parties intended to effectuate a transfer of ownership: such a transfer is impossible: the stipulation is *naturali ratione inutilis*.[22]

A different view of *res extincta* was taken by the High Court of Australia in *McRae v Commonwealth Disposals Commission*[23] upon the following facts.

---

[16] *Hitchcock v Giddings* (1817) 4 Price 135 at 141.
[17] *Bingham v Bingham* (1748) 1 Ves Sen 126; *Cochrane v Willis* (1865) 1 Ch App 58.
[18] *Debenham v Sawbridge* [1901] 2 Ch 98 at 109, per Byrne J.
[19] *Cochrane v Willis* (1865) 1 Ch App 58 at 63.
[20] *Bligh v Martin* [1968] 1 All ER 1157, [1968] 1 WLR 804.
[21] Ch 20, below.
[22] *Bell v Lever Bros Ltd* [1932] AC 161 at 218, per Lord Atkin.
[23] (1951) 84 CLR 377; Cowen 68 LQR 30; Fleming 15 MLR 229.

The Commission invited tenders 'for the purchase of an oil tanker lying on Jourmaund Reef, which is approximately 100 miles north of Samarai'. The plaintiff
submitted a tender which was accepted. In fact there was no tanker lying anywhere
near the latitude or longitude stated by the Commission and no place known as
Jourmaund Reef, but the plaintiff did not discover this until he had incurred
considerable expense in fitting out a salvage expedition. Though not fraudulent,
the employees of the Commission were clearly careless and had no adequate reason
for believing that the tanker existed.

The High Court of Australia awarded damages to the plaintiff on the ground that the
Commission had implicitly warranted the existence of the tanker.

The first question that arises is whether this decision, though it certainly meets the
needs of justice, can be supported on the ground stated by the court. The criticism has
been made that it conflicts with the principle derived from a line of cases, of which
Couturier v Hastie[24] is the most important, that there can be no contract about a non-
existent subject matter. The court met this argument by denying that *Couturier v
Hastie* established any such principle. It is true that in that case the plaintiff was the
seller, and therefore there was no need to rely on the concept of *res extincta* or on the
doctrine of mistake to reach the conclusion that a seller who fails to deliver the goods
cannot recover the price. The plaintiff could have recovered the price only by showing
that the contract was not an ordinary contract of sale of goods, but the sale either of
the shipping documents or of the chance that the goods still existed. This he failed to
do. It does not necessarily follow that the buyer could not have sued for non-delivery.

On the other hand it would seem that the legislature accepted the conventional
view of *Couturier v Hastie* when it enacted that:

> Where there is a contract for the sale of specific goods and the goods without the knowledge of
> the seller have perished at the time when the contract is made, the contract is void.[25]

It has, indeed, been argued that this section enacts no rigid rule, but only a rule of
construction which can be excluded by evidence of a contrary intention,[26] but there
are no words in the section to show that it can be displaced in this way. Even if it be
assumed that the section lays down a rigid rule of law, it is still possible to suggest that
it is not a complete statement of the common law, and that its scope must therefore be
limited to goods which, in its own words, 'have perished at the time when the contract
was made'. On this assumption, *McRae's* case[27] is outside the language of the section.
It seems, however, to be a manifest inelegance to distinguish goods which were once *in
esse* but have since perished, and goods which have never existed at all; though the
inelegance is not altogether surprising in a statutory provision which in terms applies
only to part of a problem. But at least the section, on its literal interpretation, contains

[24] P 286, above. [25] Sale of Goods Act 1979, s 6.
[26] Atiyah 73 LQR 340. [27] *McRae v Commonwealth Disposals Commission* (1951) 84 CLR 377.

nothing to prevent a court from holding that it applies only to 'perished goods'. It is still open to argument that in all other cases it is a question of construction whether (a) the contract is void, or (b) the seller has contracted that the goods are in existence, or (c) the buyer has bought a chance.[28] On the whole, however, it would seem more likely that an English court would regard section 6 of the Sale of Goods Act as a correct statement of the common law and hold that a contract for the sale of non-existent goods is void.

The second question is whether the decision in *McRae's* case can be supported on other grounds according to the law as administered in England.

In a previous edition of this book, it was suggested that the plaintiff could recover on a collateral contract.[29] The defendants, when they invited tenders from the public, promised that the ship existed, and in reliance on that promise the plaintiff offered to buy it. In effect, what the defendants said in their advertisement to the public was: 'In return for any offer you may make we promise that the tanker exists.' The difficulty with this suggestion, however, is that the consideration for a collateral contract is usually the entering into the main contract. If the main contract is void, it might be ruled that the consideration is illusory. As against this, however, a collateral contract was discovered in *Strongman (1945) Ltd v Sincock*,[30] where the main contract was illegal and therefore void.

There are two further grounds upon which the plaintiff might succeed. He might be able to maintain an action for damages either under the Misrepresentation Act 1967, or under the doctrine laid down by the House of Lords in *Hedley Byrne & Co Ltd v Heller & Partners Ltd*. These two possibilities are canvassed at a later stage in this book.[31]

If the problems that have arisen in practice were confined to cases of *res extincta* and *res sua*, it would be superfluous to suggest the existence of an independent doctrine of common mistake. It would be unnecessary to attribute the failure of the contract to the mistake *per se*. The supposed contract would be a nullity in English, as it was in Roman law, simply because there was nothing to contract about. It has, however, been suggested that these cases of *res extincta* and *res sua* are only examples of a wider class based upon a wider principle—that, whenever the parties are both mistaken about some fundamental fact, their mistake will be fatal to the existence of the contract. If this view is supported by authority, then it must be admitted that the common law recognises an independent doctrine of common mistake.

Some judicial statements certainly incline to this view. For instance, Lord Wright, after remarking that in general the test of intention in the formation of contracts is objective, said:

---

[28] Atiyah 73 LQR 340; Atiyah and Bennion 24 MLR 421; and Atiyah 2 Ottawa L Rev 337, where he relies heavily on deductions from the decision in *Financings Ltd v Stimson* [1962] 3 All ER 386, [1962] 1 WLR 1184.

[29] For collateral contracts, see pp 81–84, above.

[30] [1955] 2 QB 525, [1955] 3 All ER 90; p 509, below. [31] Pp 343–350, below.

> But proof of mistake affirmatively excludes intention. It is, however, essential that the mistake relied on should be of such a nature that it can be properly described as a mistake in respect of the underlying assumption of the contract or transaction or as being fundamental or basic.[32]

This statement, however, was made obiter, and it is necessary to see if it is supported by actual authority.

The problem was exhaustively discussed by the House of Lords in *Bell v Lever Bros Ltd*,[33] where the facts were these:

> Lever Brothers, who had a controlling interest in the Niger Company, appointed Bell managing director of the latter company for five years at an annual salary of £8,000. After three years the services of Bell became redundant owing to the amalgamation of the Niger Company with a third company, and Lever Brothers agreed to pay him £30,000 as compensation for the loss of his employment. After they had paid this money, they discovered for the first time that Bell had committed several breaches of duty during his directorship which would have justified his dismissal without compensation. They therefore sued for the recovery of £30,000 on the ground inter alia of common mistake, but failed.

The facts did not raise a case of unilateral mistake, for the jury found that Bell's mind was not directed to his breaches of duty at the time when he made the compensation agreement. According to the argument of Lever Brothers, that agreement was based upon the underlying and fundamental assumption that the parties were bargaining about a service contract which could only be terminated with compensation; but the truth, unknown to both of them at the time, was that the contract might in fact have been terminated without compensation. The parties were dealing with a terminable contract, but they thought that they were dealing with one that was non-terminable. Was this sufficient to annul the contract? The Law Lords assumed that some species of common mistake is capable of making a contract void. The difficulty, however, is to ascertain from their speeches what the character of the mistake must be in order to have this nullifying effect. The language of their Lordships is open to two interpretations.

First, there are certain passages which suggest that a contract is void if the parties have proceeded on a false and fundamental assumption, irrespective of the character of the fact assumed to be true. Lord Warrington, for example, referred to the judgment of Wright J in the court below in these words:

> The learned judge thus describes the mistake invoked in this case as sufficient to justify a Court in saying that there was no true consent—namely, 'Some mistake or misapprehension as to some facts which by the common intention of the parties, whether expressed or more generally implied, constitute the underlying assumption without which the parties would not

---

[32] *Norwich Union Fire Insurance Society Ltd v Price* [1934] AC 455 at 463.
[33] [1932] AC 161.

have made the contract they did'. That a mistake of this nature common to both parties is, if proved, sufficient to render a contract void is, I think, established law.[34]

Lord Warrington then cited *Strickland v Turner*[35] and *Scott v Coulson*[36] in support of the proposition.

Lord Thankerton was more precise and cautious in describing the expression 'underlying assumption', but his description was wide enough to embrace cases other than the non-existence of the subject matter. He said:

> In my opinion it can only properly relate to something which both [parties] must necessarily have accepted in their minds as an essential and integral element of the subject-matter.[37]

He, too, illustrated the proposition by *Strickland v Turner* and *Scott v Coulson* with the addition of *Couturier v Hastie*.

Lord Atkin, after referring to the cases of *res extincta*, continued as follows:

> Mistake as to quality of the thing contracted for raises more difficult questions. In such a case a mistake will not affect assent unless it is the mistake of both parties, and is as to the existence of some quality which makes the thing without the quality essentially different from the thing as it was believed to be.[38]

The second possible interpretation of the speeches, or at least of the decision, is that the only false assumption sufficiently fundamental to rank as operative mistake is the assumption that the very subject matter of the contract is in existence. Thus Lord Atkin, having expressed himself, as we have just seen, in wide terms, offered in a later passage a more restricted view of the case. The test, he now declared, was merely this:

> Does the state of the new facts destroy the identity of the subject-matter as it was in the original state of facts?[39]

It will also be recalled that Lord Warrington and Lord Thankerton, in illustrating what they had in mind by a fundamental assumption sufficient, if untrue, to nullify a contract, cited only the decisions concerned with *res extincta*.

How then is *Bell v Lever Bros Ltd* to be interpreted? Despite the wide language of the speeches, the decision, it is submitted, is no authority for any general doctrine of common mistake, and the second of the two possible interpretations is to be preferred. This submission is supported by the significant fact that, by a majority of three to two, the House of Lords held that the circumstances of the case itself disclosed no operative mistake. If, however, a false and fundamental assumption by the two parties excludes consent, and if an assumption bears this character when, to quote Lord Atkin, 'the new state of facts makes the contract something different in kind

---

[34] Ibid at 206.   [35] P 287, above.

[36] [1903] 2 Ch 249; where a contract for the sale of a life policy was made under the mistaken belief shared by both parties that the assured was alive. The contract was set aside by the court.

[37] [1932] AC 161 at 235.   [38] Ibid at 218.   [39] Ibid at 227.

from the contract in the original state of facts',[40] or again when 'it relates to the existence of some quality which makes the thing without the quality essentially different from the thing as it was believed to be',[41] how can it reasonably be denied that the test was satisfied in *Bell v Lever Bros Ltd*? If not satisfied there, it is difficult to see how it can ever be satisfied.[42] The contemplated subject matter of the bargain was a service contract of great value to Bell, the actual subject matter was worthless. It was extravagantly different in kind from what the parties originally contemplated, unless the words 'in kind' are to be construed in the narrowest sense.[43]

This submission is fortified by later decisions. *Solle v Butcher*,[44] for instance, shows that, in the view of the Court of Appeal, a common mistake, though clearly funda-mental, does not as a general principle nullify a contract at common law, and it therefore favours the narrow interpretation of *Bell v Lever Bros Ltd*. The facts were these:

> A had agreed to let a flat to X at a yearly rental of £250. Both parties had acted on the assumption that the flat, having been so drastically reconstructed as to be virtually a new flat, was no longer controlled by the Rent Restriction Acts. They were mistaken in this respect. The maximum permissible rent was therefore only £140, for after the execution of the lease it was too late for A to serve the statutory notice under which the sum might have been increased to about £250. The tenant, X, after being in possession for some two years, sought to recover the rent he had overpaid.

Presuming that the mistake was one of fact, not of law,[45] this was surely a case where the parties had wrongly assumed a fact of fundamental importance. To recall Lord Thankerton's statement in *Bell v Lever Bros Ltd*,[46] their assumption related 'to some-thing which both must necessarily have accepted in their minds as an essential and integral element of the subject matter'. There are few things more essential in modern

---

[40] Ibid at 226.

[41] Ibid at 218.

[42] The decision of the Privy Council in *Sheikh Bros Ltd v Ochsner* [1957] AC 136, turned solely upon the interpretation of the Indian Contract Act 1872.

[43] Of course on facts such as *Bell v Lever Bros Ltd* there will often be *some* remedy. The defendants could have been compelled to account for any profit they had made by their breach of duty (no doubt these profits were significantly less than the very generous severance payments which the defendants received). The majority view was that Bell was not under a duty to report his own breaches of duty; in the similar case of *Sybron Corpn v Rochem* [1984] Ch 112, [1983] 2 All ER 707 it was held that each of a number of dishonest senior employees was under a duty to report breaches of duty by other employees engaged in a conspiracy to defraud the employer. See also *Horcal Ltd v Gatland* [1984] IRLR 288.

[44] [1950] 1 KB 671, [1949] 2 All ER 1107.

[45] Jenkins LJ took the view that it was a mistake of law and was therefore to be disregarded. In 1950 the distinction between mistake of fact and mistake of law was regarded as fundamental but it was swept aside by the House of Lords in *Kleinwort Benson v Lincoln City Council* [1998] 4 All ER 513. See also *Brennan v Bolt Burden* [2005] QB 303 discussed below p 296.

[46] [1932] AC 161 at 235; p 291, above.

conditions than the applicability or non-applicability of the Rent Restriction Acts. A controlled flat carrying a rent of £140 is an essentially different thing from a flat that commands the highest rent procurable in the open market. If, therefore, *Bell v Lever Bros Ltd* is interpreted as deciding that a contract based on a false and fundamental assumption common to the parties is void, the tenant in *Solle v Butcher* should have been entitled at common law to recover the overpaid rent and, indeed, had he so claimed, the whole rent paid, as being money paid without consideration. Yet it was held that the contract was not void *ab initio*. The same conclusion was reached by Goff J in *Grist v Bailey*.[47]

Another significant pointer in the same direction is *Leaf v International Galleries*,[48] where the plaintiff bought from the defendants a picture which they both mistakenly believed had been painted by Constable. Thus the picture without this quality was essentially different from what the parties believed it to be. The plaintiff rested his claim for the recovery of the purchase price not upon mistake but upon misrepresentation, and the Court of Appeal, as a whole, agreed that it could not have been based upon mistake. The mistake, though 'in one sense essential or fundamental',[49] did not avoid the contract.

The views expressed in *Solle v Butcher* and *Leaf v International Galleries* were repeated in two later cases.

In *Harrison and Jones Ltd v Bunten and Lancaster Ltd*,[50]

> The buyers agreed in writing to buy from the sellers '100 bales of Calcutta kapok, Sree brand', equal to standard sample. The seller delivered goods which in all respects answered this description and which were equal to sample. It appeared, however, that both parties had made the contract in the belief that 'Calcutta kapok, Sree brand' was pure kapok and consisted of tree cotton, though the truth was that it contained a mixture of bush cotton and was commercially a quite different and inferior category of goods.

The buyers contended that this common mistake made the contract void, but the contention was rejected by Pilcher J.

> When goods, whether specific or unascertained, are sold under a known trade description without misrepresentation, innocent or guilty, and without breach of warranty, the fact that

---

[47] [1967] Ch 532, [1966] 2 All ER 875; p 298, below.

[48] [1950] 2 KB 86, [1950] 1 All ER 693.

[49] Ibid at 89 and 694. So too in *Harlington and Leinster Enterprises Ltd v Christopher Hill Fine Art Ltd* [1990] 1 All ER 737, [1990] 3 WLR 13 where both parties wrongly believed the subject matter of the contract to be a painting by Gabriele Munter, a German expressionist. This was in fact a stronger case than *Leaf* since the buyer paid a genuine Munter price whereas the buyer in *Leaf* does not appear to have paid a genuine Constable price.

[50] [1953] 1 QB 646, [1963] 1 All ER 903. See also *Diamond v British Columbia Thoroughbred Breeders' Society and Boyd* (1965) 52 DLR (2d) 146 and cf *Naughton v O'Callaguan (Rogers, third parties)* [1990] 3 All ER 191.

both parties are unaware that goods of that known trade description lack any particular quality is, in my view, completely irrelevant; the parties are bound by their contract, and there is no room for the doctrine that the contract can be treated as a nullity on the ground of mutual[51] mistake, even though the mistake from the point of view of the purchaser may turn out to be of a fundamental character.

In *Frederick E Rose (London) Ltd v William H Pim Jnr & Co Ltd:*[52]

The plaintiffs in London received an order from their house in Egypt for 'Moroccan horsebeans described here as *feveroles*'. The plaintiffs, not knowing what 'feveroles' were, enquired of the defendants, who said that the word was a mere synonym for horsebeans, which they were in a position to supply. The plaintiffs thereupon made an oral contract with the defendants for the purchase of 'horse-beans' and the contract, in these terms, was later put into writing. The defendants delivered the horsebeans to the plaintiffs, who in turn sold and delivered them to an Egyptian firm. When they reached Egypt, the Egyptian buyers found that, though horsebeans, they were not 'feveroles' and claimed damages as on a breach of warranty.

The plaintiffs wished in turn to claim damages from the defendants, but were faced with the initial difficulty that their written contract spoke only of 'horsebeans' and these had been duly supplied. They therefore asked for rectification of the contract so as to make it read 'feveroles', and intended, if successful, to claim damages for the defendants' failure to supply this mysterious article. Here it is to be observed that one of the arguments raised by the defendants' counsel was that the contract was void for mistake. That the parties made their contract under the influence of a common mistake was clear: they thought the 'feveroles' was just another name for 'horsebeans'. But the Court of Appeal refused to hold the contract void. Lord Denning LJ asked:

What is the effect in law of this common mistake on the contract between the plaintiffs and defendants? . . . I am clearly of opinion that the contract was not a nullity. It is true that both parties were under a mistake and that the mistake was of a fundamental character with regard to the subject-matter. The goods contracted for—horsebeans—were essentially different from what they were believed to be—'feveroles'. Nevertheless, the parties to all outward appearances were agreed. They had agreed with quite sufficient certainty on a contract for the sale of goods by description, namely, horsebeans. Once they had done that, nothing in their minds could make the contract a nullity from the beginning, though it might, to be sure, be a ground in some circumstances for setting the contract aside in equity.[53]

So in successive editions of this work the authors and the present editor have argued that at common law there was no doctrine of common mistake as such and that a

---

[51] The facts disclosed what in this chapter is denominated common mistake.
[52] [1953] 2 QB 450, [1953] 2 All ER 739.
[53] [1953] 2 QB 450 at 459–460. On this, see pp 297–301, below.

contract would be void only if there was nothing to contract about, either because the subject matter does not exist at the time of the agreement or because the object of a purported sale already belongs to the buyer. This view, however, was rejected by Steyn J in *Associated Japanese Bank (International) Ltd v Credit du Nord.*[54] In this case a high-class fraudster, Jack Bennett, approached the plaintiff bank with a scheme to raise money by the sale and lease back of precision engineering machines. The bank agreed to buy the machines from Bennett for a little over £1 million and to lease them back to him. The plaintiff bank insisted the transaction be guaranteed and the defendant bank became the guarantor. In fact the machines did not exist and Mr Bennett having obtained £1 million disappeared without keeping up the payments on the lease. The plaintiff sought to enforce the guarantee against the defendant, neither bank having bothered to verify the existence of the machines. Steyn J held that the action failed. His principal ground of decision was that, as a matter of construction of the guarantee, it was either an express or implied condition that the machines existed. Alternatively, and of much more interest for present purposes, he would have been prepared to hold that the contract of guarantee was void for common mistake. At first sight this might look like a case of *res extincta* since the machines did not exist but, of course, the subject matter of the contract of guarantee was not the machines but Bennett's obligations to the plaintiff bank. Those obligations certainly existed since Bennett knew very well that the machines did not exist and there was, therefore, no common mistake as between the plaintiffs and Bennett. It is clear that both the plaintiff and the defendant bank believed that the machines existed and that they would not have entered into the transaction if they had not been deceived as to this. On the other hand, even if there is a doctrine of common mistake, as Steyn J certainly thought, it must be narrower than this since parties often enter into undoubtedly binding transactions which they would not have entered into if they had known the true state of the facts. In the present case, the parties presumably would not have entered into the transaction if it had been the case that the machines were of little value and they had realised this, but that would surely on no view be a case of operative common mistake.[55]

In *Brennan v Bolt Burdon*[56] the claimant had issued a claim form relating to a claim to damages for personal injury on 7 June 2001. The form was valid for four months. On Saturday 6 October 2001, the form was delivered to the three defendants. The first and third defendants filed applications that although actually delivered on 6 October, the claim forms should be treated by virtue of CPR r6.7 as having been delivered on Monday, 8 October and should therefore be set aside. These applications

---

[54] [1988] 3 All ER 902, [1989] 1 WLR 255; Treitel 104 LQR 501; Cartwright [1988] LCMLQ 300; Carter 3 JCL 237; Smith 110 LQR 400.

[55] It should also be noted that the learned judge thought that in order for the doctrine of common mistake to operate the party relying on it must show that his mistake was reasonably based.

[56] [2005] 1 QB 303.

were successful, the judge following the judgment of McCombe J in *Anderton v Clwyd County Council.*[57] No application was made by the second defendant at this stage. On 13 February 2002, in a conversation between the claimant's then solicitor and a solicitor employed by Islington, the second defendants, it was agreed that the claimant would discontinue the first action if Islington did not apply for costs.

On 3 July 2002, the Court of Appeal reversed the decision of McCombe J in *Anderton v Clwyd County Council.*[58]

> The claimant sought to continue the action against Islington. Islington argued that the action was the subject of a binding compromise. The claimant argued that the compromise agreement was vitiated by mistake of law.

The Court of Appeal held that although a compromise agreement might be vitiated by a mistake of law, the facts of the case did not justify this conclusion in the present case. Maurice Kay LJ said[59]

> For a common mistake of fact or law to vitiate a contract of any kind, it must render the performance of the contract impossible: see *Great Peace Shipping Co Ltd v Tsavliris Salvage Ltd.*[60]

2 Agreements in respect of which equity may give relief

In the days when the courts of common law and equity were separate, cases involving common mistake might come before either set of courts. In principle, if the contract were void at common law it would be equally void in equity but the converse was not necessarily true. A mistake which did not make the contract void at common law might affect the relief available in equity. Most obviously it might lead the court to exercise its discretion to refuse specific performance.[61] A much more difficult question is whether there is a jurisdiction in equity to set aside contracts which are not void at common law. We shall consider this question first and then consider the undoubted equitable jurisdiction to rectify a written contract or deed that does not accurately record the agreement made by the parties.

a Agreements that may be set aside In general, equity follows the law in the case of the *res extincta* and the *res sua* and regards the contract as a nullity. It either refuses specific performance or sets the contract aside notwithstanding that it has been executed.[62]

Thus, in *Cooper v Phibbs:*[63]

> X agreed to take a lease of a fishery from Y, although, unknown to both parties, it already belonged to X himself. X filed a petition in Chancery for delivery up of the

---

[57] (unreported) 25 July 2001.   [58] [2002] 1 WLR 3174.   [59] [2005] 1QB 303 at 314.
[60] [2003] QB 679.   [61] See pp 300–301, below.
[62] *Colyer v Clay* (1843) 7 Beav 188; *Cochrane v Willis* (1865) 1 Ch App 58.
[63] (1867) LR 2 HL 149; followed in *Jones v Clifford* (1876) 3 ChD 779; *Allcard v Walker* [1896] 2 Ch 369.

agreement and for such relief 'as the nature of the case would admit of and to the court might seem fit'.

The House of Lords set the agreement aside, but only on the terms that Y should have a lien on the fishery for such money as he had expended on its improvement. Lord Westbury stated the principle in these words:

> If parties contract under a mutual [sic], mistake and misapprehension as to their relative and respective rights, the result is that the agreement is liable to be set aside as having proceeded upon a common mistake.[64]

The Court of Appeal went further in *Solle v Butcher*,[65] where having held that the mistake was not sufficient to make the contract void at common law, it held that it could be set aside in equity. To set it aside *simpliciter* would have been inequitable to the tenant since this would require his immediate dispossession, and therefore he was put on terms. He was given the choice of surrendering the lease entirely or of remaining in possession at the full rent that would have been permissible under the Acts had the landlord served the statutory notice upon him within the proper time limit.

In the later case of *Grist v Bailey*:[66]

> The plaintiff agreed to buy the defendant's house subject to an existing tenancy. The value of the house with vacant possession was about £2,250, but the purchase price was fixed at £850 since both parties believed that the tenancy was protected by the Rent Acts. This belief was wrong. In fact, the tenant left without claiming protection.
>
> In an action for specific performance brought by the plaintiff, the defendant counterclaimed that the contract be set aside on the ground of common mistake.

Goff J held that, though the mistake did not suffice to nullify the contract at law, it was material enough to attract the intervention of equity. In the circumstances, however, the learned judge felt that it would be improper merely to refuse a decree of specific performance. Instead, he dismissed the plaintiff's action, but only on the

---

[64] *Cooper v Phibbs* (1867) LR 2 HL 149 at 170. In the next sentence, however, he said that the agreement 'cannot stand'. It was pointed out in *Bell v Lever Bros Ltd* that in the passage cited in the text, the word 'void' should be substituted for 'liable to be set aside': [1931] 1 KB 557 at 585, per Scrutton LJ and 591, per Lawrence LJ; [1932] AC at 218, per Lord Atkin. There is perhaps some logical difficulty in seeing how a court of equity could set aside on terms a contract which was already void at common law. What exactly the court was doing in *Cooper v Phibbs* is helpfully considered by Matthews 105 LQR 599. See also *Huddersfield Banking Co Ltd v Henry Lister & Son Ltd* [1895] 2 Ch 273.

[65] [1950] 1 KB at 693. See also critical notes by ALG 66 LQR 169; and by Atiyah and Bennion, 24 MLR 421 at 440–442.

[66] [1967] Ch 532, [1966] 2 All ER 875. See also *Laurence v Lexcourt Holdings Ltd* [1978] 2 All ER 810, [1978] 1 WLR 1128.

terms that the defendant would enter into a fresh contract to sell the house at its appropriate vacant possession price.

In *Magee v Pennine Insurance Co Ltd*,[67] the Court of Appeal followed these authorities, but imposed no terms upon the mistaken party. The facts were as follows:

> The plaintiff acquired a car on hire-purchase terms through a garage and signed a proposal form for its insurance by the defendants for an amount not exceeding £600. The form, which was filled in by the salesman at the garage, contained several innocent misrepresentations. The defendants accepted the proposal and issued a policy which was later renewed for another car acquired by the plaintiff. This car was seriously damaged in an accident. In reply to the plaintiff's claim for £600, the defendants offered by way of compromise to pay him £375. The plaintiff accepted this offer, but the defendants then discovered the existence of the misrepresentations.

In an action brought to recover the £375, the Court of Appeal by a majority held that the compromise agreement, though not void at law, was founded on a common mistake.

It is clear that both parties were mistaken in the sense that, as a result of the misrepresentations, they considered the plaintiff's rights under the policy to be more valuable than they were in fact. On the other hand there was no mistake as to the subject matter of the compromise. Each party correctly understood that the purpose of their agreement was to settle the amount to which the plaintiff was entitled. It would, therefore, seem that on the authority of *Bell v Lever Bros Ltd*, the compromise was not void at common law. But the majority of the Court of Appeal held that the mistake under which the parties laboured was sufficiently fundamental to enable the agreement to be set aside in equity. Winn LJ dissented. He found it impossible to distinguish the facts from those in *Bell v Lever Bros Ltd*.

There is much force in this dissenting judgment unless it can be said that in *Bell v Lever Bros Ltd* the House of Lords confined their attention to the doctrines of the common law.[68] This was certainly not the view of Lord Blanesburgh who expressed his satisfaction that it had been possible to take a view of 'equity and procedure' which shielded the appellants from liability to repay the money received under the compensation agreements.[69] Several equity authorities had been cited by counsel, and Lord Warrington in his dissenting speech stated that the rules on the matter were identical both at law and in equity.[70]

Although many observers in 1950 thought that Denning LJ had hit a good length ball outside the off stump through midwicket, most thought it had reached the

---

[67] [1969] 2 QB 507, [1969] 2 All ER 891. Harris 32 MLR 688.
[68] Atiyah and Bennion 24 MLR 421 at 439–442, 85 LQR 454–456. See also the discussion of compromises of worthless claims, pp 107–110, above.
[69] [1932] AC at 200.   [70] Ibid at 210.

boundary. The case has been followed or assumed to be correct in other Court of Appeal decisions.[71]

The position has been radically altered by the decision of the Court of Appeal in *Great Peace Shipping Ltd v Tsavliris Salvage (International) Ltd, The Great Peace.*[72]

In September 1999, the *Cape Providence* was on her way from Brazil to China when she suffered severe structural damage in the South Indian Ocean. The appellants offered their salvage services which were accepted on the Lloyd's open form of salvage agreements. A tug was found in Singapore which would take five or six days to reach the *Cape Providence*. It was thought prudent to see if there was a merchant vessel which was nearer so as to provide if necessary for rescuing the crew. A respected and normally competent organisation told the agents of the appellants that the *Great Peace* was about 12 hours away and a deal was done for the short-term hire of the *Great Peace* at $US 16,500 a day for 5 days. At the moment of the contract the ships were about 410 miles apart though neither knew this. About two hours later the agents of the *Cape Providence* discovered the true position. They then sought to find a nearer ship and two hours later, having done so, purported to cancel. The owners of the *Cape Providence* argued that the contract was void and that they were not bound to pay the owners of the *Great Peace* anything.

The Court of Appeal held that the contract was not void at common law. This seems clearly correct. At the time of the contract the ships were about 39 hours apart and the *Great Peace* would therefore offer cover for some three days before the tug arrived. This was well worth having as was shown by the decision to wait two hours before purporting to cancel.

One may suspect that Lord Denning would not have thought it appropriate to set aside the contract in equity but the Court of Appeal did not ask themselves that question. Instead, they roundly rejected Lord Denning's account of the law. *Bell v Lever Brothers* was not a decision at common law alone; the equity cases and particularly *Cooper v Phibbs* were before the House of Lords and *Cooper v Phibbs* did not turn on any special equitable rule. It followed that *Solle v Butcher* could only be right if *Bell v Lever Brothers* was wrong and the Court of Appeal had no power in *Solle v Butcher* to say that *Bell v Lever Brothers* was wrong.

How does this leave the law? If the judgment in the *Great Peace* had been that of the House of Lords it would be clear that *Solle v Butcher* was no more but it was not. It is not clear that the *Great Peace* fits any of the categories enunciated in *Young v Bristol Aeroplane* where the Court of Appeal was not bound by its earlier decisions. If this is so it would be at least arguable that a later Court of Appeal could choose between the decisions. In any such choice it seems clear that the *Great Peace* presents a more

---

[71] Lord Denning's description of the equitable rule is subjected to a characteristically penetrating analysis in Meagher, Gummow and Lehane *Equity: Doctrine and Remedies* (4th edn, 2002) pp 492–498.

[72] [2002] EWCA CW 1407, [2003] QB 679, [2002] 4 All ER 689. Chandler, Devenney and Poole [2004] JBL 34.

scholarly argument but there may be fact situations where *Solle v Butcher* continues to offer an attractive solution.

b Rectification of written agreements Equity, in the exercise of its exclusive juris-diction, has satisfactorily dealt with cases where, though the consent is undoubted and real, it has by mistake been inaccurately expressed in a later instrument. Suppose that A orally agrees to sell a house, exclusive of its adjoining yard, to B. Owing to a mistake the later formal and written instrument includes the yard as part of the property to be sold, and, what is worse, the subsequent conveyance actually conveys the yard to B.[73] Can A have the written agreement and the deed rectified, or will he be successfully met by the plea that what has been written and signed must stand?

It may be answered at once that in cases of this type, where it is proved that owing to a mistake the written contract does not substantially represent the real intention of the parties, the court has jurisdiction, not only to rectify the written agreement, but also to order specific performance of it as rectified.[74]

> The essence of rectification is to bring the document which was expressed and intended to be in pursuance of a prior agreement into harmony with that prior agreement.[75]

It is, however, not the contract itself which is rectified, but the incorrect manner in which the common intention of the parties has been expressed in a later document.

> What you have got to find out is what intention was communicated by one side to the other and with what common intention and common agreement they made their bargain.[76]

It has long been settled that oral evidence is admissible to prove that the intention of the parties expressed in the antecedent agreement, whether written or not, does not represent their true intention. Thus, rectification forms an exception, but a justifiable exception, to the cardinal principle that parol evidence cannot be received to con-tradict or to vary a written agreement. The basis of that principle is that the writing affords better evidence of the intention of the parties than any parol proof can supply; but to allow it to operate in a case of genuine mistake would, as Story has said,

> . . . be to allow an act originating in innocence to operate ultimately as a fraud, by enabling the party who receives the benefit of the mistake to resist the claims of justice under the shelter of a rule framed to promote it. In a practical view, there would be as much mischief done by refusing relief in such cases, as there would be introduced by allowing parol evidence in all cases to vary written contracts.[77]

---

[73] *Craddock Bros Ltd v Hunt* [1923] 2 Ch 136. See also *United States v Motor Trucks Ltd* [1924] AC 196.
[74] *United States v Motor Trucks Ltd* [1924] AC 196. *Shipley UDC v Bradford Corpn* [1936] Ch 375 at 394–395. The jurisdiction is discretionary but it is not a ground for refusing to exercise the discretion that the application is to correct an error which would otherwise lead to the payment of more tax than necessary. *Re Slocock's Will Trusts* [1979] 1 All ER 358.
[75] *Lovell and Christmas Ltd v Wall* (1911) 104 LT 85, per Cozens-Hardy MR.
[76] Ibid at 93, per Buckley LJ.   [77] Story *Equity Jurisprudence* s 155.

A question that has long agitated the courts and upon which conflicting dicta are to be found is whether the common intention of the parties must have crystallised into a legally enforceable contract prior to the written document whose rectification is sought. The controversy was not resolved until the decision of the Court of Appeal in *Joscelyne v Nissen*[78] where the facts were these:

> The plaintiff, who shared a house with the defendant, his daughter, proposed to her that she should take over his car-hire business. At an early stage in the ensuing conversations, it was made clear that if the proposal were accepted, she should pay all the household expenses, including the electricity, gas and coal bills due in respect of the part of the house occupied by her father. This oral bargain no doubt disclosed the common intention of the parties, but it could not be described as a finally binding contract. The discussion culminated in a written contract which, on its true construction, placed no liability upon the daughter to pay the household expenses. After honouring the bargain for a time, she ultimately refused to pay the electricity, gas and coal bills, though she continued to take the profits of the business.

In an action brought by the father, it was ordered that the written document be rectified so as specifically to include the daughter's liability for these bills. Her argument that the liability had not been imposed upon her by an antecedent contract was rejected. The court endorsed the view of Simonds J expressed in *Crane v Hegeman-Harris Co Inc*,[79] that

> ... it is sufficient to find a common continuing intention in regard to a particular provision or aspect of the agreement. If one finds that, in regard to a particular point, the parties were in agreement up to the moment when they executed their formal instrument, and the formal instrument does not conform with that common agreement, then this court has jurisdiction to rectify, although it may be that there was, until the formal instrument was executed, no concluded and binding contract between the parties.[80]

An antecedent agreement, for instance, is rectifiable notwithstanding that it is unenforceable because of its failure to comply with some statutory provision requiring it to be in writing or to be supported by written evidence.[81] Thus, the result is that 'you do not need a prior contract, but a prior common intention'.

---

[78] [1970] 2 QB 86. Baker 86 LQR 303; Bromley 87 LQR 532.

[79] [1971] 1 WLR 1390n at 1391, adopting the view of Clauson J in *Shipley UDC v Bradford Corpn* [1936] Ch 375. *Crane v Hegeman-Harris Co Inc* was decided in 1939 and reported in [1939] 1 All ER 662, but this report omits several pages of the judgment.

[80] [1939] 1 All ER at 664. For inconsistent dicta, see *Mackenzie v Coulson* (1869) LR 8 Eq 368 at 375, per James V-C; *Faraday v Tamworth Union* (1916) 86 LJ Ch 436 at 438, per Younger J; *Lovell and Christmas Ltd v Wall* (1911) 104 LT 85 at 88, per Cozens-Hardy MR; *W Higgins Ltd v Northampton Corpn* [1927] 1 Ch 128 at 136, per Romer J; *Frederick E Rose v Wm H Pim Ltd* [1953] 2 QB 450 at 461, per Denning LJ.

[81] *United States v Motor Trucks Ltd* [1924] AC 196. A decision dealing with the now repealed s 4 of the Sale of Goods Act 1893.

The burden of proving this common and continuing intention lies upon the party who claims that the written contract should be rectified.[82] As regards the standard of proof required, all that can be said is that the claim will fail unless the common intention upon which it is based is proved by *convincing* evidence. It is not necessary that the evidence should be 'irrefragable' as Lord Thurlow once suggested, or that it should settle the question 'beyond all reasonable doubt' as is demanded by the criminal law.[83] If the negotiations leading up to the execution of the written instrument were vague and inconclusive, so that it is impossible to ascertain what the parties really meant, then the writing represents the only agreement that has been concluded, and there is no antecedent and common intention upon which notification can be based.[84]

Moreover, it must be shown that the alleged common intention, though once undoubtedly reached, continued unchanged down to the time when the instrument was reached. Proof that the parties varied their original intention and that the instrument represents what they finally agreed is fatal to a suit for rectification.[85]

Finally, it must be emphasised that the issue relates not to the individual intention of the parties, but to their common intention. If the defendant can satisfy the court that he understood the agreement to be exactly what was stated in the written instrument, rectification will be excluded.[86] There are some old cases in which a mistake by one party has by itself been relied on by the court to justify offering the other party the choice between submitting to rectification or having the whole contract rescinded but these were overruled by the Court of Appeal in *Riverlate Properties Ltd v Paul*.[87] A mistake by one party, which is known to the other party, will suffice to justify rectification however, at least where the knowledge of the other party is tantamount to sharp practice. Even the need for sharp practice was denied in *Thomas Bates & Son Ltd v Wyndham's (Lingerie) Ltd*[88] provided that it would be inequitable to allow one party to take advantage of the other's mistake. It was said to be essential that the one party's mistake is known to the other in *Agip SpA v Navigazione Alta Italia SpA*[89] but this was denied by the Court of Appeal in *Commission for the New Towns v Cooper (GB) Ltd*[90] where Stuart-Smith LJ said:

> I would hold that where A intends B to be mistaken as to the construction of the agreement, so conducts himself that he diverts B's attention from discovering the mistake by making false and misleading statements, and B in fact makes the very mistake that A intends, then notwith-

---

[82] *Tucker v Bennett* (1887) 38 ChD 1 at 9, per Cotton LJ.

[83] *Joscelyne v Nissen* [1970] 2 QB 86 at 98, *per curiam*. For Lord Thurlow's remark, see *Shelburne v Inchiquin* (1784) 1 Bro CC 338 at 341; *Thomas Bates & Son Ltd v Wyndham's (Lingerie) Ltd* [1981] 1 All ER 1077, [1981] 1 WLR 505.

[84] *C H Pearce Ltd v Stonechester Ltd* [1983] CLY 451.

[85] *Marquess of Breadalbane v Marquess of Chandos* (1837) 2 My & Cr 711 (rectification of a marriage settlement).

[86] *Lloyd v Stanbury* [1971] 2 All ER 267, [1971] 1 WLR 535.

[87] [1975] Ch 133, [1974] 2 All ER 656.   [88] [1981] 1 All ER 1077, [1981] 1 WLR 505.

[89] [1984] 1 Lloyd's Rep 353.   [90] [1995] 2 All ER 929 at 946.

standing that A does not actually know, but merely suspects that B is mistaken, and it cannot be shown that the mistake was induced by any misrepresentation, rectification may be granted. A's conduct is unconscionable and he cannot insist on performance in accordance to the strict letter of the contract; that is sufficient for rescission. But it may also not be unjust or inequitable to insist that the contract be performed according to B's understanding, where that was the meaning that A intended that B should put upon it.

A good modern example of a case where rectification was refused is *George Wimpey UK Ltd v VI Construction Ltd.*[91] In this case the claimant sought rectification of an agreement by which they bought land from the defendants. It was always intended that the claimants would build flats on the land and there were long and complex negotiations in which experienced solicitors were involved on both sides. It was envisaged that Wimpey would pay a price which consisted of a basic element plus a figure that reflected the excess of actual sale prices of the flats over estimated prices. There were many drafts of a possible contract and, in these drafts, enhancement of the value of a flat, such as possession of a river view, were showed by the notation '+E'. In the later stages of the negotiations the notation '+E' was omitted but this was not noticed by the person negotiating on behalf of Wimpey. In due course contracts were exchanged. Wimpey sought rectification. The Court of Appeal denied rectification for two reasons. The first was that Wimpey had failed to provide convincing evidence that VIC had shut its eyes to the obvious. Perhaps more important was the second reason. The decision to enter into the contract had been taken by the Board of Wimpey. The Director who had negotiated on behalf of Wimpey had not had authority to bind Wimpey. No evidence had been led by Wimpey as to the state of mind of the Board. Accordingly, it was not possible to avoid the inference that the Board intended to approve the contract in the form in which it was put to it.

Of course, if the document is unilateral, as in a voluntary settlement, it is the intention of the settlor which is important: *Re Butlin's Settlement Trusts.*[92]

B Where an apparent agreement is alleged to be vitiated by mutual or unilateral mistake

The second category of case is where to outward appearances a contract has been concluded, but one of the parties alleges that his mind was affected by a fundamental mistake of fact and that he never intended to make that precise contract. Here, unlike the case of common mistake, the question of consent is directly raised. It is alleged that despite appearances there is no genuine agreement since there is no corresponding offer and acceptance. X, who admittedly accepted Y's offer to sell certain pearls, now alleges that he thought that he was being offered real pearls, not imitation as in fact they are.

---

[91] (2005) 103 Con LR 67.   [92] [1976] Ch 251, [1976] 2 All ER 483.

Before considering the manner in which the law deals with such an allegation it is
necessary to emphasise that at common law only fundamental mistake is material.
This principle was stated by Blackburn J in a passage that has always been regarded as
an authoritative statement of the law.[93] A mistake is wholly immaterial at common
law unless it results in a complete difference in substance between what the mistaken
party bargained for and what in fact he will obtain if the contract is fulfilled; as for
example where the buyer intends to buy real pearls and the seller intends to sell
imitation pearls. Translated into the familiar rubric of offer and acceptance, this
means that the only type of mistake which is ever capable of excluding offer and
acceptance is one that prevents the mistaken party from appreciating the fundamental
character of the offer or the acceptance. The formation of agreement depends upon
the correspondence of offer and acceptance, and if the offer is made in one sense but
accepted in another, as in the example of the real and imitation pearls, there is at least
ground for arguing that there is no consent and therefore no genuine agreement. The
mistaken party can at any rate say—for what it is worth—that he personally did not
intend to make the contract which he appears to have made.

But once it is admitted that he accepted and intended to accept the precise offer
made to him, he obviously cannot deny the existence of the resulting agreement
merely by proving that his acceptance was due to a mistake. The evidence may show,
for instance, that in a contract for the sale of land the purchaser intended to purchase
that land from *that* vendor at *that* price, but that his reason for doing so was his
mistaken idea that the land was rich in minerals. In other words, he would not have
concluded the bargain had he appreciated the true position. Nevertheless, there was
no fundamental mistake. He understood the true character of the offer, he intended
to accept the exact terms proposed by the vendor and therefore it is vain for him to
deny the existence of a common intention. This is so even though his inflated view
of the value of the land was known to the vendor. In this case, equitable relief may
conceivably be available to him[94] but he may not plead that the contract is a nullity.
No doubt the motive or reason that persuaded him to conclude the agreement was
utterly false, but an agreement intentionally made does not cease to be an agreement
merely because it has been actuated by a mistaken motive. This truism was copiously
illustrated by Lord Atkin in the following passage.

> A buys B's horse; he thinks the horse is sound and he pays the price of a sound
> horse; he would certainly not have bought the horse if he had known as the fact is
> that the horse is unsound. If B has made no representation as to soundness and has
> not contracted that the horse is sound, A is bound and cannot recover back the
> price . . . A agrees to take on lease or to buy from B an unfurnished dwelling house.
> The house is in fact uninhabitable. A would never have entered into the bargain if
> he had known the fact. A has no remedy, and the position is the same whether B

[93] *Kennedy v Panama Royal Mail Co* (1867) LR 2 QB 580 at 587.   [94] Pp 317–321, below.

knew the facts or not, so long as he made no representation or gave no warranty. A buys a roadside garage business from B abutting on a public thoroughfare; unknown to A but known to B, it has already been decided to construct a bypass road which will divert substantially the whole of the traffic from passing A's garage. Again A has no remedy. All these cases involve hardship on A and benefit to B, as most people would say, unjustly. They can be supported on the ground that it is of paramount importance that contracts should be observed, and that if parties honestly comply with the essentials of the formation of contracts—ie, *agree in the same term on the same subject-matter*—they are bound, and must rely on the stipulations of the contract for protection from the effect of facts unknown to them.[95]

It should also be emphasised that the burden of persuading the court to disturb what to outward appearances is a binding contract falls on the party who alleges the mistake. Moreover, the burden is not light, for the result of holding that there is no contract may seriously prejudice a third party who has in good faith made a bargain relating to the subject matter of the apparent agreement.

1 Effect of mutual and unilateral mistake at common law

a Mutual mistake Let us first examine the case of mutual mistake, where each party is mistaken as to the other's intention, though neither realises that the respective promises have been misunderstood. This situation would arise, for instance, if B were to offer to sell his Ford Sierra car to A and A were to accept in the belief that the offer related to a Ford Granada. In such a case, no doubt, if the minds of the parties could be probed, genuine consent would be found wanting. But, the question is not what the parties had in their minds, but what reasonable third parties would infer from their words or conduct.

Applying itself to that task, the court has to determine what Austin called 'the sense of the promise'.[96] In other words, it decides whether a sensible third party would take the agreement to mean what A understood it to mean or what B understood it to mean, or whether indeed any meaning can be attributed to it at all. The promisor may have made his promise in one sense, the promisee may have accepted it in another. There may have been mistake of a fundamental character which caused the one to put a wrong interpretation upon the promise of the other. But it is for the court to decide what, if any, is the interpretation to be put on what the parties have said or done.

---

[95] *Bell v Lever Bros Ltd* [1932] AC 161 at 224, per Lord Atkin. The case of *Smith v Hughes* (1871) LR 6 QB 597, illustrates how difficult it may be to decide whether the parties agreed in the same terms on the same subject matter. In *Dip Kaur v Chief Constable for Hampshire* [1981] 2 All ER 430, [1981] 1 WLR 578 a customer approached a supermarket checkout bearing a pair of shoes one with a £6.99 price tag and the other a £4.99 price tag. The customer intended to pay whatever price the cashier rang up but hoped that, as happened, the cashier would ring up £4.99. It was held that the customer has committed no criminal offence as there was a valid contract. *Quaere* whether a court would reason in the same way in a civil case.

[96] *Lectures on Jurisprudence* Lect 21, note 89.

In a leading case, Blackburn J explained the attitude of the law. He said:

> If whatever a man's real intention may be, he so conducts himself that a reasonable man would believe that he was assenting to the terms proposed by the other party, and that other party upon that belief enters into the contract with him, the man thus conducting himself would be equally bound as if he had intended to agree to the other party's terms.[97]

Again in another case, Pollock CB said:

> If any person, by a course of conduct or by actual expressions, so conducts himself that another may reasonably infer the existence of an agreement . . . whether the party intends that he should do so or not, it has the effect that the party using that language or who has so conducted himself, cannot afterwards gainsay the reasonable inference to be drawn from his words or conduct.[98]

The result is that if, from the whole of the evidence, a reasonable man would infer the existence of a contract in a given sense, the court, notwithstanding a material mistake, will hold that a contract in that sense is binding upon both parties. The apparent contract will stand. Two decisions may be cited by way of illustrations.

In *Wood v Scarth*:[99]

> The defendant offered in writing to let a public house to the plaintiff for £63 a year, and the plaintiff, after an interview with the defendant's clerk, accepted the offer by letter. The defendant intended that a premium of £500 should be payable in addition to the rent and he believed that the clerk had made this clear to the plaintiff. The latter, however, believed that his only financial obligation was the payment of rent.

It was held at *nisi prius* that the apparent contract must stand. The mistake of the defendant could not at law gainsay what would obviously be inferred from the acceptance of his exact offer.

In *Scott v Littledale*:[100]

> The defendants sold by sample to the plaintiff a hundred chests of tea then lying in bond '*ex* the ship *Star of the East*' but later discovered that they had submitted a sample of a totally different tea lower in quality than that contained in the chests.

In an action for non-delivery of the hundred chests, the common law court, though it conceded that the sellers might be entitled to partial relief in equity, refused to declare the contract void. The sellers had no doubt submitted a wrong sample by mistake, but they were precluded by their own conduct from disputing the natural inference that would be drawn from the facts.

---

[97] *Smith v Hughes* (1871) LR 6 QB 597 at 607.

[98] *Cornish v Abington* (1859) 4 H & N 549 at 556.

[99] (1858) 1 F & F 293. The full facts cannot be appreciated unless the earlier case in equity between the same parties (1855) 2 K & J 33, is also considered.

[100] (1858) 8 E & B 815.

Cases may occur, of course, in which it is impossible to impute any definite agreement to the parties. If the evidence is so conflicting that there is nothing sufficiently solid from which to infer a contract in any final form without indulging in mere speculation, the court must of necessity declare that no contract whatsoever has been created.

An illustration of this situation is *Scriven Bros & Co v Hindley & Co*:[101]

> This was an action to recover the price of some Russian tow alleged to have been sold at an auction by the plaintiffs to the defendants. The auctioneer was employed to sell both hemp and tow, and his catalogue specified two separate lots, one comprising 47, the other 176 bales. The catalogue failed to state that the latter contained tow, not hemp. The same shipping mark, indicating what ship had brought the goods to England, was entered against each lot. Samples of each lot were on view, but the defendants did not inspect these as they had already seen samples of the hemp at the plaintiff's show rooms. The defendants, believing that both lots contained hemp, successfully bid an extravagant price for the 176 bales of tow. Witnesses from both sides admitted that in their experience Russian tow and Russian hemp had never been landed from the same ship under the same shipping mark.

Here the plaintiffs intended to sell tow, the defendants intended to buy hemp. The plaintiffs were unaware of the intention to bid for hemp only, for though the auctioneer realised that the defendants had shown a lack of judgment he thought that this merely reflected their ignorance of the market value of tow. Though clearly there was no genuine agreement between the parties, the question was whether the judge should presume the existence of a contract for the sale of tow. This he declined to do. The sense of the promise could not be determined. Owing to the ambiguity of the circumstances it could not be affirmed with reasonable certitude which commodity was the subject of the contract. There was therefore no binding contract.

In the leading case of *Raffles v Wichelhaus*[102] the facts were these:

> A agreed to buy and B agreed to sell a consignment of cotton which was to arrive '*ex Peerless* from Bombay'. In actual fact two ships called *Peerless* sailed from Bombay, one in October, the other in December. It was held that the buyer was not liable for refusal to accept cotton despatched by the December ship.

For procedural reasons the court never decided whether there was a contract or not. All that was actually decided was that it was open to the defendant to show that the contract was ambiguous and that he intended the October ship. If the case had gone to trial it would then have been open to the jury to hold either that there was no

---

[101] [1913] 3 KB 564. Cf *Tamplin v James*, p 318, below; *contra*, Jaffey 10 Bracton LJ 109 at 110.
[102] (1864) 2 H & C 906. See Simpson 91 LQR 247 at 268, Simpson 11 Cardozo LR 287.

contract or to hold that there was a contract either for the October ship or the December ship. In modern terms this would turn on whether a reasonable man would deduce an agreement from the behaviour of the parties though in 1864 it might well have been thought to turn on whether the parties actually intended the same ship.

b Unilateral mistake We must now consider the attitude of common law to uni-lateral mistake, the distinguishing feature of which, as we have seen, is that the mistake of X is known to the other party, Y. It must be stressed that, in this context, a man is taken to have known what would have been obvious to a reasonable person in the light of the surrounding circumstances. Thus in *Hartog v Colin and Shields*:[103]

> An offer was accepted to sell certain Argentine hareskins at a certain price per pound. The preliminary negotiations, however, had proceeded on the clear under-standing that the skins would be sold at so much per piece, not per pound, and at the trial expert evidence proved the existence of a trade custom to fix the price by reference to a piece. The value of a piece was approximately one-third of that of a pound.

It was held that the buyer must be taken to have known the mistake made by the sellers in the formulation of their offer.

An instructive modern example is the Singapore case of *Chwee Kin Keong v Digilandmall Com Pte Ltd*.[104] In this case, the defendants mistakenly advertised colour laser printers on the internet at S $66 (Singapore). The real price was S $3,854. The plaintiffs placed orders for 1,606 over the internet and the defendants' computer went through the appropriate motions to complete the contract. These transactions were carried out in the early hours of a Singapore day. When the defendants woke up they immediately repudiated the transactions. The Court of Appeal had no doubt that there was no contract. On the facts there could be no doubt that the plaintiffs knew very well that Digilandmall did not intend to sell the printers for S $66.[105]

The majority of cases in which the question of unilateral mistake has arisen have been cases of mistaken identity, and their examination will serve to show the way in which the courts approach the problem.[106]

Suppose that A, pretending to be X, makes an offer to B which B accepts in the belief that A is in fact X. In subsequent proceedings arising out of this transaction, B alleges that he would have withheld his acceptance had he not mistaken A's identity. If this allegation is proved and if B's intention was known to A at the time of the acceptance, there is, as a matter of pure logic, no correspondence between offer and

[103] [1939] 3 All ER 566.
[104] [2005] 1 SLR 502. See Phang 21 JCL 197, (2005) 17 S Ac LJ 361; Kwek Mean Luck (2005) 17 SALJ 411.
[105] At first instance [2004] SLR 594 VK Rajah JC had considered the position if the plaintiffs only had constructive knowledge.
[106] See Williams 23 Can Bar Rev 271, 380.

acceptance and therefore there should be no contract. Nevertheless, outward appearances cannot be neglected, and the prima facie presumption applicable to this type of case is that, despite the mistake, a contract has been concluded between the parties. The onus of rebutting this presumption lies upon the party who pleads mistake.[107]

To discharge this burden, he must prove (i) that he intended to deal with some person other than the person with whom he has apparently made a contract; (ii) that the latter was aware of this intention; (iii) that at the time of negotiating the agreement, he regarded the identity of the other contracting party as a matter of crucial importance; and (iv) that he took reasonable steps to verify the identity of that party.

(i) The first of these requirements presupposes a confusion between two distinct entities. If this is not the case there is no operative mistake. Two cases illustrate this point. In *Sowler v Potter*:[108]

> In May 1938, the defendant, who was then known as Ann Robinson, was convicted of permitting disorderly conduct at a café in Great Swan Alley, EC. In July of the same year she assumed the name of Ann Potter and negotiating under that name obtained a lease of Mrs Sowler's premises in Coleman St, EC. The agent who had conducted the negotiations on behalf of Mrs Sowler stated in evidence that he remembered the conviction of Ann Robinson. 'Therefore', said the trial judge, 'he thought when he entered into this contract with the defendant that he was entering into a contract with some person other than the Mrs Ann Robinson who had been convicted.'

On this interpretation of the facts Tucker J held the lease to be void *ab initio*, since the plaintiff was mistaken with regard to the identity of the tenant.

It may be questioned, with respect, whether this decision was correct. At the time when the agent concluded the bargain, the possibility that the defendant might be Ann Robinson was not within his contemplation, and therefore he could scarcely deny that he intended to grant the lease to the person with whom he had dealt. It is no doubt true that he would not have formed this intention had he appreciated what manner of person the tenant was, but once it was clear that he had that intention in fact the mistaken reason or motive that induced it was not enough to nullify the lease. To apply the words of A L Smith LJ in an earlier case, there was only one entity—the woman known at one moment as Ann Robinson, at another as Ann Potter—and it was with this one entity that the landlord intended to contract.[109] On the other hand the lease was clearly voidable on the ground of fraudulent misrepresentation, for in answer to a request for a reference, the defendant submitted the name of a

---

[107] Ie upon the offeree in the hypothetical case given above but if the offeror is the mistaken person the onus lies upon him.

[108] [1940] 1 KB 271. For a fuller report, see [1939] 4 All ER 478. For a criticism of the decision, see Goodhart 57 LQR 228.

[109] *King's Norton Metal Co Ltd v Edridge, Merrett & Co Ltd* (1897) 14 TLR 98 at 99.

certain Mr Hopfenkopf, an obvious accomplice in her crafty scheme. This gentleman, according to the finding of the judge, 'deliberately wrote what he knew perfectly well to be untrue for the purpose of deceiving the plaintiff'.[110] The lease was therefore voidable and there was no reason to invoke the law of mistake.[111]

In *King's Norton Metal Co Ltd v Edridge, Merrett & Co Ltd*:[112]

> A man named Wallis, for the purpose of cheating, set up in business as Hallam & Co. He prepared writing paper at the head of which was a faked illustration of a large factory and a statement that Hallam & Co had depots at Belfast, Lille and Ghent. Writing on this paper, he ordered and obtained goods from the plaintiffs which were later bought from him in good faith by the defendants. The plaintiffs had previously sold goods to Wallis and had been paid by a cheque signed 'Hallam & Co'. In an action against the defendants for the value of the goods, the plaintiffs contended that their apparent contract with Hallam & Co was void, since they mistakenly believed that such a firm existed, and that therefore the property in the goods still resided in them.

The contention failed. The plaintiffs, since they could not have relied on the credit of a non-existent person, must have intended to contract with the writer of the letter, though of course they would not have formed this intention had they known that he was masquerading under an *alias*. They were unable to show that they meant to contract with Hallam & Co, not with Wallis, for there was no other entity in question. The contract was no doubt voidable for fraud, but as it had not been avoided at the time of the sale by Wallis to the defendants, the title of the latter prevailed over that of the plaintiffs.

(ii) To satisfy the second requirement, the mistaken party must prove that the other party was aware of the mistake. This requirement seldom causes difficulty, since in the majority of cases the mistake has been induced by the fraud of that party. In *Boulton v Jones*,[113] however, the matter was by no means clear.

> Jones, who had been accustomed to deal with Brocklehurst, sent him a written order for 50 feet of leather hose on the very day that Brocklehurst had transferred his business to his foreman, the plaintiff. The plaintiff executed the order, but Jones accepted and used the goods in the belief that they had been supplied by Brocklehurst. He refused to pay the price, alleging that he had intended to contract with Brocklehurst personally, since he had a set-off which he wished to enforce against him.

[110] This aspect of the case is reported only in [1939] 4 All ER 478.

[111] Disapproval of the decision was expressed by the Court of Appeal in *Gallie v Lee* [1969] 2 Ch 17 at 33, per Lord Denning; at 41, per Russell LJ; at 45, per Salmon LJ.

[112] N 109, above. See also *Porter v Latec Finance (Queensland) Pty Ltd* (1964) 111 CLR 177.

[113] (1857) 2 H & N 564, 27 LJ Ex 117. It should be noted that the report of this case given in Hurlstone and Norman is incomplete, and that for a proper understanding of the judgment, reference should be made to the other reports, especially to the Law Journal.

It was held that Jones was not liable for the price, but it is not clear whether the mistake was regarded by the court as unilateral or mutual. If the court was convinced that the plaintiff knew of the set-off and therefore that the order was not intended for him, the contract was clearly vitiated by unilateral mistake and was rightly held void.[114] But on the facts as a whole it is perhaps more reasonable to treat the mistake as mutual. On this interpretation the sense of the promise fell to be determined, and the decision is more difficult to support. A disinterested spectator, knowing nothing of the set-off and looking at the circumstances objectively, would naturally assume the identity of the supplier to be a matter of indifference to the purchaser of such an ordinary commodity as hose piping.

Most of the identity cases, however, have been obvious examples of unilateral mistake and in most the mistake has been due to the fraud of one of the parties. A clear instance is *Hardman v Booth*[115] where the facts were these:

> X, one of the plaintiffs, called at the place of business of Gandell & Co. This firm consisted of Thomas Gandell only, though the business was managed by a clerk called Edward Gandell. X, being fraudulently persuaded by Edward that the latter was a member of the firm, sold and delivered goods to the place of business of Gandell & Co but invoiced them to 'Edward Gandell & Co'. Edward, who carried on a separate business with one Todd, pledged the goods with the defendant for advances *bona fide* made to Gandell & Todd. The plaintiffs now sued the defendant for conversion.

Here no contract of sale ever came into existence, since X's offer was made to Thomas only, and Edward, though he knew this fact, purported to accept it for himself. Edward thus acquired no title to the goods capable of transfer to the innocent defendant, and the latter was liable for conversion.

(iii) Controversy is most frequently provoked by the need to satisfy the third of the requirements—that, at the time of negotiating the agreement, the person labouring under the mistake regarded the identity of the other contracting party as a matter of crucial importance, and that this was apparent from his conduct during the negotiations. The problem arose in an acute form in the case of *Cundy v Lindsay*.[116]

> A fraudulent person named Blenkarn, writing from '37 Wood St, Cheapside', offered to buy goods from the plaintiffs, and he signed his letter in such a way that his name appeared to be 'Blenkiron & Co'. The latter were a respectable firm carrying on business at 123 Wood St. Blenkarn occupied a room which he called 37 Wood St, but in fact its entrance was from an adjoining street. The plaintiffs,

---

[114] Bramwell B seems to have taken this view of the facts, for he said: 'It is an admitted fact that the defendant supposed he was dealing with Brocklehurst, and the plaintiff misled him by executing the order unknown to him': (1857) 27 LJ Ex at 119.

[115] (1863) 1 H & C 803.

[116] (1878) 3 App Cas 459.

who were aware of the high reputation of Blenkiron & Co, though they neither knew nor troubled to ascertain the number of the street where they did business, purported to accept the offer and despatched the goods to 'Messrs Blenkiron & Co, 37 Wood St, Cheapside'. These were received by the rogue Blenkarn, and he in turn sold them to the defendants, who took them in all good faith. The plaintiffs now sued the defendants for conversion.

The case is difficult, for the facts admitted of two different inferences.

First, it might be inferred that, just as in *Hardman v Booth*, the plaintiffs intended to sell to Blenkiron & Co, but that Blenkarn fraudulently assumed the position of buyer. If this represented the true position, an offer to sell to Blenkiron & Co was knowingly 'accepted' by Blenkarn and therefore no contract would ensue.

Secondly, unlike *Hardman v Booth*, it might be inferred that the plaintiffs, though deceived by the fraud of Blenkarn, intended or were at least content to sell to the person who traded at 37 Wood St, from which address the offer to buy had come and to which the goods were sent. If this were the true position, there was a contract with Blenkarn of 37 Wood St, though one that was voidable against him for his fraud.

The second inference was drawn unanimously by three judges in the Queen's Bench Division,[117] but the Court of Appeal and the House of Lords, with equal unanimity, preferred the first view.

Such a conclusion prejudices third parties who later deal in good faith with the fraudulent person. On the view of the facts taken by the House of Lords, the defendants in *Cundy v Lindsay* were of course liable, for there had never been a contract of sale between the plaintiffs and Blenkarn, and Blenkarn therefore possessed no title which he could pass to a third person. On the other hand, had the view of the facts taken by the Queen's Bench Division prevailed, while the contract between the plaintiffs and Blenkarn would have been voidable for the latter's fraud, the defendants would nevertheless have been secure, since they had innocently acquired this voidable title to the goods before it had in fact been avoided by the plaintiffs.

The problem whether this third requirement has been satisfied has proved even more troublesome where the contract has been made *inter praesentes*, not through the post as in *Cundy v Lindsay*. Three cases concerned with this aspect of the problem invite comparison: *Phillips v Brooks Ltd, Ingram v Little* and *Lewis v Averay*.

The facts of *Phillips v Brooks, Ltd*[118] were as follows:

A man called North entered the plaintiff's shop and selected pearls of the value of £2,550 and a ring worth £450. He then wrote out a cheque for £3,000 saying, as he did so, 'You see who I am, I am Sir George Bullough', and then gave an address

---

[117] *Cundy v Lindsay* (1876) 1 QBD 348, per Blackburn, Mellor and Lush JJ.

[118] [1919] 2 KB 243. The only case concerning mistake *inter praesentes* to reach the House of Lords is *Lake v Simmons* [1927] AC 487 but that case can be regarded as doing no more than decide the meaning of the word 'customer' in an insurance policy. See also *Dennant v Skinner and Collom* [1948] 2 KB 164, [1948] 2 All ER 29; *Citibank Bank plc v Brown Shipley & Co Ltd* [1991] 2 All ER 690.

in St James's Square. The plaintiff had heard of Bullough and upon consulting a directory found that he lived at the address given. He then said: 'Would you like to take the articles with you?' North replied: 'You had better have the cheque cleared first, but I should like to take the ring, as it is my wife's birthday tomorrow.' The plaintiff let him do so. North pledged the ring for £350 to the defendant, who had no notice of the fraud.

These facts, as in *Cundy v Lindsay*, admitted of two possible answers. The plaintiff either intended to sell the ring to the person present in the shop, whoever he was, or he intended to sell to Bullough and to nobody else. If the first solution was correct, then a contract of sale had been concluded, though one that was voidable for the fraudulent representation of North that the means of payment would be furnished by Bullough. Being voidable, ie, valid until disaffirmed, a good title to the ring would be acquired by the defendant. If, however, the second solution was correct, then the plaintiff's mistake prevented a contract from arising. Not even a voidable title would pass to North, and the defendant could acquire no right of property whatsoever.

Horridge J adopted the first solution. He drew the inference that the jeweller, doubtless gratified that he had secured Bullough as a customer, intended, come what might, to sell to the person present in the shop. It is submitted, with respect, that this was the correct inference. The jeweller could succeed only upon proof that he intended to contract with Bullough and with nobody else, but in fact the evidence that he tendered scarcely supported this view. Beyond looking up Bullough's address in a directory, he had taken no steps to verify his customer's story and it would seem that he deliberately took the risk of the story being true.

The facts in *Ingram v Little*[119] were these:

A swindler, falsely calling himself Hutchinson, went to the residence of the plaintiffs and negotiated for the purchase of their car. They agreed to sell it to him for £717, but, on hearing his proposal to pay by cheque, called the bargain off. He therefore told them that he was P G M Hutchinson having business interests in Guildford and that he lived at Stanstead House, Caterham. Upon hearing this, one of the plaintiffs slipped out of the room, consulted the telephone directory at a nearby post office and verified that P G M Hutchinson lived at the Caterham address. Feeling reassured, the plaintiffs, though they had never previously heard of P G M Hutchinson, agreed to sell the car to the swindler. He later sold it to the defendant who acted in good faith.

These facts raised similar problems to those which confronted Horridge J in *Phillips v Brooks Ltd*[120] but, unlike that learned judge, the majority of the Court of Appeal held that the offer of the plaintiffs to sell the car was to be interpreted as made solely

---

[119] [1961] 1 QB 31, [1960] 3 All ER 332. See Hall [1961] CLJ 86.
[120] [1919] 2 KB 243.

to P G M Hutchinson and that the swindler was incapable of accepting it. The plaintiffs therefore succeeded in their claim against the defendant for the return of the car or alternatively for damages.

The facts of *Lewis v Averay*,[121] the most recent decision on the subject, were these:

A rogue, posing as Richard Greene the well-known film actor, called upon the plaintiff and offered to buy his car which was advertised for sale at £450. The plaintiff accepted the offer, and was given a cheque, signed R A Green, for £450. Afraid that the cheque might be worthless, he resisted a proposal that the car should be removed at once. The rogue, by way of showing that he was Richard Greene, produced a special pass of admission to Pinewood Studios bearing an official stamp. Satisfied with this, the plaintiff handed over the log book and allowed the car to be taken away. The cheque had been stolen and was worthless. The rogue, now passing as Lewis, sold the car to the defendant and handed over the log book to him.

The action of conversion by the plaintiff for the recovery of the car or its value failed. The Court of Appeal followed *Phillips v Brooks Ltd*, expressed disagreement with *Ingram v Little*, and held that despite his mistake, the plaintiff had concluded a contract with the rogue. He had failed to rebut the prima facie presumption that he had made a contract with the rogue when he allowed the car to be taken away. The contract was no doubt voidable for fraud, but it could not be avoided now that the car had come into the hands of an innocent purchaser for value.

Between these three cases it is not easy to differentiate; and the task has been complicated by the suggestion now current in judicial and academic circles, though vigorously rejected by Lord Denning MR,[122] that a distinction must be drawn between the identity and the attributes of a person. It is said that a mistake as to attributes, as opposed to identity, will not suffice to enable the contract to be treated as void *ab initio*. The distinction reflects, as in a glass darkly, the views of Aristotle,[123] but whatever its significance in philosophy it is not a safe guide through the crude problems of litigation. If A seeks to escape from his apparent contract with B, he must satisfy the court that he mistakenly identified B with X. He will fail unless he shows that by his behaviour during the process of negotiating the contract he made it abundantly clear that such identification was a matter of crucial importance to him. This he will usually seek to do by showing that his mind was directed to some particular attribute possessed by X but wanting in B. This attribute will vary with the circumstances. In one case it may be credit-worthiness or social standing; in another it may be skill in some vocation. A hypothetical example of the latter was suggested by Pearce LJ in *Ingram v Little*.

---

[121] [1972] 1 QB 198, [1971] 3 All ER 907.

[122] *Lewis v Averay* [1972] 1 QB 198 at 206, [1971] 3 All ER 907 at 911.

[123] See Bertrand Russell *History of Western Philosophy* (2nd impression, 1947) p 185.

> If a man orally commissions a portrait from some unknown artist who had deliberately passed himself off, whether by disguise or merely by verbal cosmetics, as a famous painter, the imposter could not accept the offer. For though the offer was made to him physically, it is obviously, as he knows, addressed to the famous painter. The mistake in identity on such facts is clear and the nature of the contract makes it obvious that the identity was of vital importance to the offeror.[124]

In short, it is submitted that for legal purposes, 'identity' is not opposed to 'attributes'. Rather, it is made manifest by them. It is tempting, indeed, to suggest that a person's identity is but an amalgam of his various attributes.

(iv) It is not enough for the plaintiff to show that he had made known the importance which he attached to the identity of the other party. In all cases, whether the contract is made *inter praesentes* or *inter absentes*, he must go further and establish that he took all reasonable steps to verify the identity of the person with whom he was invited to deal. This, perhaps, is the heart of the matter. In *Phillips v Brooks Ltd* and *Lewis v Averay* the respective plaintiffs failed because their attempts to test the truth of what they had been told were inadequate. What is surprising is that the same conclusion was not reached in *Ingram v Little*.

It is sometimes said that the distinction between a contract made *inter praesentes* and one made *inter absentes* is one of law. The distinction, however, is merely one of fact. It may, no doubt, be more difficult to rebut the prima facie presumption in favour of the contract where the offer is made to, and accepted by, the person to whom it is orally addressed. But the task of the person labouring under the mistake is different not in kind, but in degree. If in *Cundy v Lindsay* the rogue had appeared in person armed with forged references purporting to come from the respectable Blenkiron & Co the decision would scarcely have gone against the plaintiffs.

The three cases—*Phillips v Brooks Ltd, Ingram v Little* and *Lewis v Averay*—are substantially indistinguishable on the facts.[125] In *Lewis v Averay*, the Court of Appeal applied *Phillips v Brooks Ltd*. They doubted the decision in *Ingram v Little* and it would now be dangerous to rely upon it. *Cundy v Lindsay*, as a decision of the House of Lords, is, at common law, unassailable, though it is permissible to regret the inference which their Lordships drew from the facts. The cases as a whole pose the familiar dilemma: which of two innocent parties is to bear a loss caused by the fraud of a third. The common law does not countenance the idea of apportionment. But this idea has already been accepted and applied by the legislature in the doctrine of frustration. By the Law Reform (Frustrated Contracts) Act 1943, the courts are given, within stated limits, the discretion to divide the loss between two innocent parties.[126]

---

[124] [1961] 1 QB 31 at 57.

[125] In *Phillips v Brooks Ltd*, the shopkeeper knew of the existence of Sir George Bullough: in *Ingram v Little*, the plaintiffs had never heard of Mr P G M Hutchinson. But if this difference is one of importance, it would seem to tell against the plaintiffs and to throw doubt on the decision.

[126] Pp 741–748, below.

This example might well be followed in a further statute and applied to cases of unilateral mistake.[127]

Both the *inter praesentes* and *inter absentes* cases were reviewed by the House of Lords in *Shogun Finance Ltd v Hudson*.[128]

> A man went to a dealers and negotiated to acquire a Mitsubishi Shogun on hire-purchase terms. He was allowed to take the car away and soon afterwards sold it to Mr Hudson. In general, someone who acquires goods on hire-purchase does not become the owner and is, therefore, not able to transfer ownership to a sub-buyer until he has paid all the instalments, but there is a special exception to this rule for motor cars under s 27 of the Hire-Purchase Act 1964. Under this section a non-trade buyer who buys in good faith from a hirer under a hire-purchase agreement becomes the owner.

Mr Hudson argued that he could take the benefit of this section but the finance company argued that it did not apply because there had been no hire-purchase agreement. When the man had been at the dealers he had said that his name was Patel and had produced Mr Patel's driving licence. The hire-purchase forms had been completed at the dealers and faxed to the finance company. The finance company conducted a credit search on Mr Patel but took no steps to check the identity of the person they were dealing with.

Clearly, if the car had been bought from the dealer this would have been an *inter praesentes* case. All the Law Lords considered the *inter praesentes* cases and at least four thought that *Phillips v Brooks* and *Lewis v Averay* were correctly decided. This usefully clarifies this area of law. Lord Nicholls and Lord Millett thought that the case should be treated as if it were an *inter praesentes* case but the majority disagreed. In substance they followed *Cundy v Lindsay*[129]. The hire-purchase document was drafted as an offer by the customer. Mr Patel was named as the customer and there could be no hire-purchase contract with anyone else. Obviously, there could be no contract with Mr Patel since he knew nothing about the transaction and, therefore, there was no hire-purchase contract and the Hire-Purchase Act 1964 did not apply.

2 Effect of mutual and unilateral mistake in equity

a Mutual mistake Equity follows the law in holding that a mutual mistake does not as a matter of principle nullify a contract.[130] In the nature of things, indeed, there is no

---

[127] This suggestion was made by Lawson in *the Rational Strength of English Law* (1951), pp 69–70. It was supported by Devlin LJ in *Ingram v Little* but rejected by the Law Reform Committee in its Twelfth Report (Cmnd 2958, 1966). The suggestions which were made by the Law Reform Committee were not implemented.

[128] [2003] UKHL 62, [2004] 1 AC 919, [2004] 1 All ER 215; McLauchlan 21 JCL 1.

[129] [1878] 3 App Cas 459.

[130] *Preston v Luck* (1884) 27 ChD 497.

room for equitable relief, since the court, after considering the mistake and every other relevant fact, itself determines the sense of the promise. In general, therefore, a party is not allowed to obtain rectification or rescission of a contract or to resist its specific performance on the ground that he understood it in a sense different from that determined by the court.

The position is illustrated by the case of *Tamplin v James*.[131]

> James who had been the highest bidder at an auction sale of a public house, resisted a suit for specific performance on the ground that he had made a mistake. At the time when he made his bid he believed that a certain field, which had long been occupied by the publican, was part of the lot offered for sale, though in fact it was held under a separate lease from a third party. There was no misdescription or ambiguity in the particulars of sale.

On these facts specific performance of the contract in the sense understood by the auctioneer was decreed. Baggalay LJ said:[132]

> Where there has been no misrepresentation and where there is no ambiguity in the terms of the contract, the defendant cannot be allowed to evade the performance of it by the simple statement that he has made a mistake. Were such to be the law, the performance of a contract could seldom be enforced upon an unwilling party who was also unscrupulous.

Again, where a lessor's agent had agreed to grant a lease for seven or fourteen years, which the lessor mistakenly understood to mean a lease determinable at *his* option at the end of seven years instead of at the tenant's option, it was held that specific performance must be decreed against the lessor according to the ordinary and accepted meaning of the words used.[133]

Nevertheless, the particular remedy of specific performance, since it is exceptional in nature, is one that lies very much within the discretion of the courts, and there certainly are cases in which it has not been forced upon a party who has mistaken the admitted sense of a contract. The remedy will not, indeed, be withheld 'merely upon a vague idea as to the true effect of the contract not having been known',[134] but as Bacon VC said in one case:

> It cannot be disputed that Courts of Equity have at all times relieved against honest mistakes in contracts, when the literal effect and the specific performance of them would be to impose a burden not contemplated, and which it would be against all reason and justice to fix, upon the person who, without the imputation of fraud, has inadvertently committed an accidental

---

[131] (1880) 15 ChD 215; followed in *Van Praagh v Everidge* [1902] 2 Ch 266.

[132] *Tamplin v James* (1880) 15 ChD 215 at 217–218.

[133] *Powell v Smith* (1872) LR 14 Eq 85.

[134] *Watson v Marston* (1853) 4 De GM & G 230, 238, per Turner LJ.

mistake; and also where not to correct the mistake would be to give an unconscionable advantage to either party.[135]

In the case of mutual mistake, therefore, while equity generally follows the law, it may be prepared, if the occasion warrants, to refuse to grant a decree of specific performance of the contract against the mistaken party.[136] It is not possible, however, to specify the cases in which this remedy will be withheld, for the exercise of any discretionary jurisdiction must inevitably be governed by the particular circumstances of each case. But the guiding principle was stated by Lord Romilly in an instructive case where a freehold estate that was subject to an existing tenancy had been bought by the defendant at an auction under the honest, but mistaken, belief that the rent stated in the particulars of sale referred not to the whole, but only to half of the land. Had he read the particulars carefully he could have discovered the truth.[137] Lord Romilly MR said:

> If it appears upon the evidence that there was, in the description of the property, a matter on which a person might *bona fide* make a mistake, and he swears positively that he did make such mistake, and his evidence is not disproved, this court cannot enforce specific performance against him. If there appear on the particulars no ground for the mistake, if no man with his senses about him could have misapprehended the character of the parcels, then I do not think it is sufficient for the purchaser to swear that he made a mistake or that he did not understand what he was about.[138]

In the result, the Master of the Rolls dismissed the bill for specific performance.

In *Paget v Marshall*[139] Bacon VC went further and held that in some circumstances a plaintiff's uncommunicated mistake as to the sense of the contract might be so serious that the defendant could properly be put to his election either to submit to rectification or allow rescission of the whole contract. This case has long been considered of doubtful authority,[140] and since the decision of the Court of Appeal in *Riverlate Properties Ltd v Paul*[141] such a course can only be supported on the ground that the defendant knew the plaintiff's mistake.[142]

b Unilateral mistake In the case of unilateral mistake it is clear that if one party to the knowledge of the other is mistaken as to the fundamental character of the offer—if he did not intend, as the other well knew, to make the apparent contract— the apparent contract is a nullity and there is no need, indeed no room, for any equitable relief. However, although equity follows the law in this respect and admits

---

[135] *Barrow v Scammell* (1881) 19 ChD 175 at 182.

[136] Compare, for instance, the treatment of *Wood v Scarth*, p 307, above, by a common law court: (1858) 1 F & F 293 and by the Court of Chancery: (1855) 2 K & J 33. For a discussion of equitable relief, see Stoljar 28 MLR 265 at 269–272.

[137] *Swaisland v Dearsley* (1861) 29 Beav 430.   [138] Ibid at 433–434.

[139] (1884) 28 ChD 255.   [140] See *May v Platt* [1900] 1 Ch 616 at 623, per Farwell J.

[141] [1975] Ch 133, [1974] 2 All ER 656.   [142] See pp 301–304, above.

that the contract is a nullity, it is prepared to clinch the matter by formally setting the contract aside or by refusing a decree for its specific performance.[143] In *Webster v Cecil*,[144] for instance:

> Cecil, who had already refused to sell his land to Webster for £2,000, wrote a letter to him in which he offered to sell for £1,250. Webster accepted by return of post, whereupon Cecil, realising that he had mistakenly written £1,250 for £2,250, immediately gave notice to Webster of the error.

This was operative mistake at common law. Knowledge of the mistake was clearly to be imputed to Webster and in the result Lord Romilly refused a decree of specific performance.[145]

A contract may also be rectified on the ground of unilateral mistake, if the plaintiff proves that it was intended to contain a certain term beneficial to himself, but that the defendant allowed it to be concluded without that term, knowing that the plaintiff was ignorant of its omission. For instance:

> A tender by the plaintiffs for the erection of a school for the defendants provided that the work should be completed in 18 months. The defendants, however, prepared a contract which provided for completion in 30 months, and the plaintiffs executed this contract without noticing the alteration. Before execution by the defendants, one of their officers discovered that the plaintiffs were ignorant of the alteration but they took no steps to disabuse them. The price for the work would have been higher had the tender been based on a period of 30 months.[146]

On these facts, rectification on the ground of common mistake was ruled out, since the parties held different views of what was intended to be inserted in the contract. Nevertheless, the court ordered the contract to be rectified on the ground of unilateral mistake by the substitution of the shorter for the longer period.[147]

In the interesting case of *Taylor v Johnson*[148] the respondent had granted the appellant an option to buy a piece of land of approximately ten acres. In due course the option was exercised and a contract was drawn up. In both the option and the contract the purchase price was stated to be $15,000. The respondent gave evidence that she had mistakenly believed that the purchase price was $15,000 per acre. The evidence suggested that the land was worth $50,000 but that if a proposed rezoning

---

[143] *Wilding v Sanderson* [1897] 2 Ch 534; *Re International Society of Auctioneers and Valuers, Baillie's Case* [1898] 1 Ch 110.

[144] (1861) 30 Beav 62.

[145] In *Garrard v Frankel* (1862) 30 Beav 445 and *Harris v Pepperell* (1867) LR 5 Eq 1, the party aware of the mistake was given the option of having the contract set aside or of submitting to it with the mistake rectified.

[146] *A Roberts & Co Ltd v Leicestershire County Council* [1961] Ch 555, [1961] 2 All ER 545.

[147] See Megarry 77 LQR 313. See further cases discussed above, p 319.

[148] (1983) 151 CLR 422, (1983) 45 ALR 265.

of the land went through, the value would be about $195,000. There was evidence from which the court inferred that the appellant knew of the respondent's mistake and deliberately set out to make it difficult for the respondent to discover the mistake. The majority of the High Court of Australia thought that on these facts the contract was valid at common law but was liable to be set aside in equity. In their joint judgment Mason ACJ, Murphy and Deane JJ said:

> A party who has entered into a written contract under a serious mistake about its contents in relation to a fundamental term will be entitled in equity to an order rescinding the contract if the other party is aware that circumstances exist which indicate the first party's entering the contract under some serious mistake or misapprehension about either the content or subject matter of that term and deliberately sets out to ensure that the first party does not become aware of the existence of his mistake or misapprehension.

3 DOCUMENTS MISTAKENLY SIGNED

A group of cases must now be considered which have long been treated as forming a separate category at common law and which may be regarded as an appendix to the general discussion of mistake. These cases occur where a person is induced by the false statement[149] of another, to sign a written document containing a contract that is fundamentally different in character from that which he contemplated. The fraudulent person may be the other party to the apparent contract but more often he is a stranger. The following is a typical illustration of the situation:

> Lord William Neville produces to Clay some documents entirely covered with blotting paper except for four blank spaces that have been cut in it. He says that the hidden documents concern a private family matter and that his own signature requires a witness. Thereupon Clay signs his name in the blank spaces. The truth is that the documents are promissory notes to the value of £11,113 signed by Clay in favour of Lewis. On the faith of these notes Lewis advances money to Lord William Neville.[150]

Such a case as this is affected by mistake in the sense that the first victim of the fraud, the person who signs the document, appears to have made a contract or a disposition of property, though his intention was to append his signature to a transaction of an entirely different character. The category of document actually signed is not what he thought it was. But nevertheless can he rely upon this fact as a defence if he is later sued upon the apparent contract by the second victim of the fraud, as for instance by the man who has given value in good faith for a promissory note?

---

[149] *Hasham v Zenab* [1960] AC 316 at 335.　　[150] *Lewis v Clay* (1897) 67 LJQB 224.

The rule applicable to such a case has come to be that the mistaken party will escape liability if he satisfies the court that the signed instrument is radically different from that which he intended to sign and that his mistake was not due to his carelessness.

The origin of this rule is to be found in the mediaeval common law relating to deeds.[151] At least as early as the thirteenth century, a deed was regarded as being of so solemn a nature that it remained binding upon the obligor until it had been cancelled and returned to him. It was immaterial that this might cause injustice. In one case, for instance, in 1313, an absolute deed by which the defendant granted £100 to the plaintiffs was accompanied by a contemporaneous deed which relieved him of this obligation if he satisfied a certain condition. The condition was satisfied, but the absolute deed survived, and upon its production the payment of the £100 was enforced.[152] The only defence open to the defendant in such circumstances was to plead that the deed as executed was not his deed in the sense that it did not represent his intention and was not what he had in mind to do. He did not in truth consent to what he had done. In the language of the age, *scriptum predictum non est factum suum*.

In the course of its development, this plea of *non est factum* was made available to a defendant who could not read, whether owing to illiteracy or blindness, so as to enable him to escape liability upon proof that the written terms of the deed did not correspond with its effect as explained to him before he put his seal to it. In 1582, for instance, in *Thoroughgood's Case*.[153]

> William Chicken, being in arrears with his rent, tendered to his landlord, Thoroughgood, a deed by which he was relieved from 'all demands whatsoever' which Thoroughgood had against him. Thus the dispensation on its face comprised not only arrears of rent, but also the right to recover the land. Thoroughgood was illiterate, but a bystander, affecting to be helpful, seized the deed and said: 'The effect of it is this, that you do release to William Chicken all the arrears of rent that he doth owe you and no otherwise, and thus you shall have your land back again.' After replying, 'If it be no otherwise, I am content,' Thoroughgood sealed the deed. Chicken subsequently sold the land to an innocent purchaser.

Thoroughgood sued in trespass *quare clausum fregit* and recovered his land. It was said by the Court of Common Pleas to be 'the usual course of pleading' that the defendant was a layman and without learning, and that he had been deceived by a distorted recital of the contents of the deed.

The plea, as its language showed, was confined to cases where the defendant was sued on a deed, and at a time when illiteracy was frequent enough to demand special protection, it was unexceptionable. It might have been wiser, therefore, to have

---

[151] Fifoot *History and Sources of the Common Law* pp 231–233, 248–249.
[152] *Fifoot* pp 232, 244–246, *Esthalle v Esthalle* (1613) YB 6 & 7 Ed 2 Eyre of Kent, vol II (27 Selden Society 21).
[153] (1582) 2 Co Rep 9a.

discarded it altogether when society became more sophisticated; but in the course of the nineteenth century the courts extended it with little reflection and without warrant to cases of simple contracts, and abandoned the requirement of illiteracy. The justification for these extensions was now said to be want of consent. On this view the contract was a complete nullity. Thus in 1869, in *Foster v Mackinnon*,[154] the following passage occurs in the judgment of a strong court delivered by Byles J:

> It seems plain, on principle and on authority, that if a blind man, or a man who cannot read, or who for some reason (not implying negligence) forbears to read, has a written contract falsely read over to him, the reader misreading to such a degree that the written contract is of a nature altogether different from the contract pretended to be read from the paper which the blind or illiterate man afterwards signs; then, at least if there be no negligence, the signature so obtained is of no force. And it is invalid not merely on the ground of fraud, where fraud exists, but on the ground that the mind of the signer did not accompany the signature; in other words that he never intended to sign, and therefore in contemplation of law never did sign, the contract to which his name is appended.[155]

Thus the intention of the mistaken party is the vital factor. In the words of Lord Wilberforce: 'It is the lack of consent that matters, not the means by which this result was brought about.'[156] The document is a nullity just as if a rogue had forged the signer's signature.[157] But fraud that does not induce lack of consent merely renders the contract voidable.[158]

It will be observed that the judgment of Byles J, which was approved by the House of Lords in *Saunders v Anglia Building Society*[159] (known in the lower courts as *Gallie v Lee*), expanded the scope of the plea *non est factum* in two respects; it extended it to unsealed contracts and to the situation where an educated man, to whom no negligence is attributable, has failed to scrutinise what he has signed.[160] Nevertheless, the judiciary is now agreed that, if the confidence of third parties who normally rely upon the authenticity of signatures is not to be eroded, the plea must be confined within narrow limits. A heavy burden of proof lies upon the party by whom it is invoked. The main difficulty is to define the degree of difference that must exist between the signed contract and that which the mistaken party intended to sign before it can be said that the consent of the signatory was totally lacking. A definitive formula of universal application is scarcely possible. Everything depends upon the circumstances of each case. It will be recalled that the court in *Foster v Mackinnon*

---

[154] (1869) LR 4 CP 704. Present, Bovill CJ, Byles, Keeting and Montague Smith JJ. For the facts, see p 326, below.

[155] Ibid at 711.

[156] *Saunders v Anglia Building Society* [1971] AC 1004 at 1026, [1970] 3 All ER 961 at 972.

[157] Ibid affirming, *sub nom Gallie v Lee* [1969] 2 Ch 17 at 30, [1969] 1 All ER 1062 at 1066, CA, per Lord Denning MR.

[158] See, for example, *Norwich and Peterborough Building Society v Steed (No 2)* [1993] 1 All ER 330.

[159] [1971] AC 1004.

[160] As to the meaning of negligence in this context, see pp 326–328, below.

required the written contract to be 'of a nature altogether different' from that which the mistaken party believed it to be. In *Saunders v Anglia Building Society* the Law Lords suggested a variety of alternative expressions, such as 'radically', 'fundamentally', 'basically', 'totally' or 'essentially' different in character or substance from the contract intended; but it is doubtful whether these add much to what was said by Byles J. In the comparatively few cases in which the plea has succeeded, the degree of difference between the intention and the act of the signatory has been wide enough to satisfy the most exacting of arbiters. The contract, for instance, has been held void where the signatory's intention was directed to a power of attorney, not to a mortgage:[161] to a guarantee, not to a bill of exchange;[162] to a testification to the fraudulent person's signature, not to a promissory note for £11,113;[163] to a proposal for insurance, not to a guarantee of the fraudulent person's overdraft.[164]

The difficulty that confronts a party who pleads that a contract signed by him is altogether different from what was in his mind is well illustrated by *Saunders v Anglia Building Society*[165] where the facts were as follows:

> The plaintiff, a widow 78 years of age, gave the deeds of her leasehold house to her nephew in order that he might raise money on it. She made it a condition that she should remain in occupation of it until she died. She knew that the defendant, a friend of her nephew, would help him to arrange a loan.
>
> A document was prepared by a dishonest managing clerk which assigned the leasehold not by way of gift to the nephew, but by way of sale to the equally dishonest defendant. Some days later the defendant took this document to the plaintiff and asked her to sign it. She had broken her glasses and was unable to read, but in reply to her request the defendant told her that the document was a deed of gift to her nephew. She therefore executed it. The defendant, who paid no money either to the plaintiff or to her nephew, mortgaged the house to a building society for £2,000, but failed to pay the instalments due under the transaction.

The plaintiff, at the instigation of her nephew, sued the defendant and the building society for a declaration that the assignment was void. She invoked the doctrine *non est factum*, claiming that what she had intended was a gift of the property to her nephew, not its outright sale to the defendant.

The House of Lords, affirming the decision of the Court of Appeal, rejected this claim. The distinction stressed by the plaintiff was no doubt impressive at first

---

[161] *Bagot v Chapman* [1907] 2 Ch 222.
[162] *Foster v Mackinnon* (1869) LR 4 CP 704. But the bill was not to be void if, at a new trial, the signatory was found to have been negligent; p 326, below.
[163] *Lewis v Clay* (1897) 67 LJQB 224.
[164] *Carlisle and Cumberland Banking Co v Bragg* [1911] 1 KB 489, p 327, below. In *Muskham Finance Co v Howard* [1963] 1 QB 904, [1963] 1 All ER 81, the difference between the intention and the act of the signatory was far less pronounced than in the three cases cited above.
[165] [1971] AC 1004, [1970] 3 All ER 961. Stone 88 LQR 190.

sight, but when considered in the light of the evidence it did not establish that the assignment to the defendant was totally different in character and nature from what she had in mind. Three of the Law Lords adopted the view of Russell LJ in the Court of Appeal that the paramount consideration was the 'object of the exercise'.[166] According to the evidence, the object of the plaintiff was to enable the assignee to raise a loan on the security of the property for the benefit of her nephew—an object that would have been attained under the signed document, had the defendant acted in an honest manner.[167]

A question that was canvassed by the House of Lords in this case was whether the distinction between the character and the contents of a document, which had gradually won the recognition of the courts, should be discarded. The effect of this distinction was that if a party appreciated the character and nature of the contract that he had signed, he could not escape liability merely because he was mistaken as to its details or its contents. In *Howatson v Webb*,[168] for instance:

> The defendant held certain property at Edmonton as the trustee and nominee of a solicitor by whom he was employed as managing clerk. After obtaining new employment, he executed certain deeds which, in answer to his request, were described by the solicitor as being 'just deeds transferring that property'. In fact one of the deeds was a mortgage by the solicitor to X as security for a loan of £1,000. The mortgage was transferred by X to the plaintiff, who now sued the defendant under the personal covenant in the deed for the repayment of the sum together with interest.

The defendant pleaded *non est factum*. What he had in mind was an absolute conveyance to a new nominee, not a conveyance to a third party under which he assumed personal obligations. Warrington J, however, held that the mistake affected only the contents of the deed and that therefore the plea failed. 'He was told that they were deeds relating to the property to which they did in fact relate. His mind was therefore applied to the question of dealing with that property. The deeds did deal with that property . . . He knew he was dealing with the class of deed with which in fact he was dealing, but did not ascertain its contents.'[169] A Court of Appeal later explained this

---

[166] [1969] 2 Ch at 40–41, adopted by Viscount Dilhorne, Lord Wilberforce and Lord Pearson. See also, *Mercantile Credit Co Ltd v Hamblin* [1965] 2 QB 242, [1964] 3 All ER 592.

[167] This approach, however, ignored the overriding condition that nothing was to interfere with the plaintiff's right to remain in occupation of the house.

[168] [1907] 1 Ch 537; affd [1908] 1 Ch 1.

[169] [1907] 1 Ch at 549. See also *Bagot v Chapman* [1907] 2 Ch 222 at 227, per Swinfen Eady J. In affirming the decision of Warrington J, in *Howatson v Webb* [1908] 1 Ch 1, the Court of Appeal regarded it as so obviously correct as not to merit considered judgments, and Cozens-Hardy MR remarked that 'it would be a waste of time if I were to do more than say that I accept and approve of every word of his judgment'.

decision on the ground that 'the character and class of document was that of a conveyance of property, and Webb knew this'.[170]

In *Gallie v Lee*, Lord Denning MR rejected this distinction in forcible and convincing terms. Among other objections he found it irrational; a mistake as to contents may be no less fundamental or radical than one relating to the character of a contract. The distinction would mean, for instance, that the plea of *non est factum* will not avail a man who signs a bill of exchange for £10,000 having been told that it is for £100, since he fully appreciates the character of the document. Why should the result be different if he believes the document to be a bill of exchange for £1,000, though in truth it is a guarantee for the same sum?[171] Salmon LJ agreed that the liability of a signatory should not be allowed to turn upon 'a relatively academic distinction', but he was content to retain it as affording at least some restraint upon a plea that had become 'a dangerous anachronism in modern times'.[172] In the House of Lords, Lord Reid expressed his dissatisfaction with the distinction,[173] Lord Wilberforce described it as 'terminologically confusing and in substance illogical',[174] while Viscount Dilhorne accepted the criticisms of Lord Denning.[175] The inference is that it has received its quietus.

The final question is whether the plea of *non est factum* will be withheld from a party if the mistake was due to his own negligence. In *Foster v Mackinnon*,[176] the Court of Common Pleas stated in unambiguous terms that a signatory is barred by his negligence from pleading his mistake against an innocent third party who has acted to his loss upon the faith of the document.

> The action before the court was against the defendant, described as 'a gentleman far advanced in years', as indorser of a bill of exchange. It appeared that one Callow took the bill to him and asked him to sign it, telling him that it was a guarantee. The defendant, in the belief that he was signing a guarantee similar to one which he had given before, signed the bill on the back. He looked only at the back of the paper, but it was in the ordinary shape of a bill of exchange, and it bore a stamp the impress of which was visible through the paper. The bill was later negotiated to the plaintiff who took it without notice of the fraud.

The action was first tried by the Lord Chief Justice, who told the jury that if the defendant signed the paper without knowing that it was a bill and under the belief that it was a guarantee, and if he was not guilty of any negligence in so signing the paper, then he was entitled to their verdict. The jury found that the defendant had not been negligent and returned a verdict in his favour. On appeal, the Court of Common

---

[170] *Muskham Finance Ltd v Howard* [1963] 1 QB 904 at 912, [1963] 1 All ER 81 at 83, *per curiam*.
[171] [1969] 2 Ch at 31–32, [1969] 1 All ER at 1066. See also Salmon LJ at 43–44 and 1078, respectively.
[172] Ibid at 44 and 1078, respectively.   [173] [1971] AC at 1017, [1970] 3 All ER 961 at 964.
[174] Ibid at 1034–1035 and 971, respectively.
[175] Ibid at 1022 and 967, respectively.   [176] (1869) LR 4 CP 704.

Pleas endorsed the direction given by the trial judge, but ordered a fresh trial on the ground that the issue of negligence had not been fully and satisfactorily considered. In the result, therefore, the right of the defendant to sustain the plea of *non est factum* was to depend upon whether he was eventually found to have been guilty of negligence.

Unfortunately, this ruling that negligence is material was thrown into confusion by the decision of a later Court of Appeal in *Carlisle and Cumberland Banking Co v Bragg*[177] on the following facts:

> A man called Rigg produced a document to Bragg and told him that it was a copy of a paper concerning an insurance matter which Bragg had signed some days previously and which had since got wet and blurred in the rain. Bragg signed without reading the paper. The document was in fact a continuing guarantee of Rigg's current account with the plaintiff bank. The jury found that Bragg had been negligent.

Despite this finding, the Court of Appeal affirmed the decision of Pickford J and held that Bragg was not estopped by his negligence from pleading *non est factum* since *Foster v Mackinnon* was inapplicable in the instant circumstances. This departure from the principle laid down by Byles J in *Foster v Mackinnon* was based upon at least two erroneous grounds.

First, the construction put upon the judgment of Byles J, was that negligence is material only where the signed document is a negotiable instrument. What in fact the learned judge clearly indicated was that the signer of a negotiable instrument would be liable, negligence or no negligence; and that negligence was relevant in relation to documents other than negotiable instruments: for example (as in the actual case before him) to a guarantee.

Secondly, it was said that, even if negligence were relevant, it would not be material unless the defendant owed a duty of care to the plaintiff. This reasoning was demolished by the House of Lords in *Saunders v Anglia Building Society*. No doubt a duty of care is an essential element in a plaintiff's cause of action when he sues in tort for negligence, but it has no place where a defendant is sued on a contract. In that context it has no technical significance, and it just means carelessness. In *Foster v Mackinnon*, for instance, the trial judge rejected the plea of *non est factum* not because the defendant had violated a duty of care owed to his neighbour, but on the simple ground that he had failed to act as a reasonable man. In the words of Lord Wilberforce:

> In my opinion, the correct rule, and that which prevailed until *Bragg's* case, is that, leaving aside negotiable instruments to which special rules may apply, a person who signs a document, and parts with it so that it may come into other hands, has a responsibility, that of the normal man of prudence, to take care what he signs. . . . I would add that the onus of proof in this matter rests on him, ie to prove that he acted carefully, and not in the third party to prove the

---

[177] [1911] 1 KB 489.

contrary. I consider, therefore, that *Carlisle and Cumberland Banking Co v Bragg* . . . was wrong, both in the principle it states and in its decision, and that it should no longer be cited for any purpose.[178]

The same principles apply where a person signs a document, knowing that it contains blanks which the other party will fill in.[179]

[178] [1971] AC 1004 at 1027, [1970] 3 All ER at 972–973. Similar statements were made by the other Law Lords. Thus Lord Reid said: 'The plea [of *non est factum*] cannot be available to anyone who was content to sign without taking the trouble to find out at least the general effect of the document . . . It is for the person who seeks the remedy to show that he should have it.' Ibid at 1016 and 963–964, respectively.
[179] *United Dominions Trust v Western* [1976] QB 513, [1975] 3 All ER 1017; Marston [1976] CLJ 218.

9 MISREPRESENTATION, DURESS AND UNDUE INFLUENCE

1 MISREPRESENTATION[1]

A Introduction

Misrepresentation straddles many legal boundaries. More than other topics in the law of contract, it is an amalgam of common law and equity. Equity has, for instance, acted to fill *lacunae* created by the narrow common law definition of fraud and to supplement the inadequate common law remedies for misrepresentation. Again misrepresentation has roots both in contract and in tort, and it is impossible to give a coherent account of the subject without discussing both contract and tort together, though the present account will naturally concentrate on the contractual aspect.

Even within the law of contract, the rules relating to misrepresentation cannot be viewed in isolation. They are part of a web of rules (which includes also the rules as to terms of a contract[2] and as to mistake)[3] affecting the nature and extent of contractual undertakings. Although it is convenient for purposes of exposition to discuss these topics in isolation, practical problems often require their simultaneous application.

The basic problem in misrepresentation is the effect of pre-contractual statements. Suppose that A agrees to sell a secondhand car to B for £5000 and in the course of the pre-contractual negotiations he states that it is a 1999 model which has run for only

---

[1] Stoljar *Mistake and Misrepresentation* (1968); Spencer Bower, Turner and Handley *The Law of Actionable Misrepresentation* (4th edn, 2000); Greig 87 LQR 179.

[2] Pp 157–165, above.

[3] Ch 8, above.

20,000 miles. After B has bought the car, he discovers that these statements are untrue. What remedies, if any, are available? The initial common law approach to this problem is based on the principle that promissory statements should be ineffective unless they form part of the contract. So the first question to be asked in our hypothetical case is whether A has not merely stated that the car is a 1999 model and has covered only 20,000 miles, but has *contracted* that this is so.[4]

To approach the matter in this way is logical enough, but the result has not been satisfactory. Dissatisfaction might properly have been directed either at the rules determining when a statement is to be treated as forming part of the contract[5] or at the sometimes strange reluctance of the courts to hold apparently serious undertakings to be terms of the contract.[6] But in practice, it has been felt that the solution should take the form of devising remedies, which do not depend on holding such statements to be terms of the contract.

Hence arose the concept of a 'mere representation'—a statement of fact which had induced the representee to enter into the contract but which did not form part of the contract. The common law came to give rescission for fraudulent misrepresentation and to grant damages in the tortious action of deceit. During the nineteenth century, equity also developed a general remedy of rescission for all misrepresentations inducing contracts. The right to rescind, however, was subject to the operation of certain 'bars',[7] and equity could not grant financial compensation for consequential loss except in the restricted form of an 'indemnity'.

Until 1963, however, it was held to be a fundamental principle that there could be 'no damages' for innocent misrepresentation'.[8] It was well established that an action for damages based on a pre-contractual statement must show either that the statement was fraudulent or that it was a term of the contract. In 1963, it was decided by the House of Lords in *Hedley Byrne & Co Ltd v Heller & Partners Ltd*[9] that the principle 'no damages for innocent misrepresentation' had never been fundamental or, at least, was no longer fundamental. In law, however, it is impossible to expunge the heresies (or outworn orthodoxies) of the past and all cases decided before 1963 have to be re-examined in the light thus shed on them.

---

[4] This approach can be seen to fit in with the rules about consideration (see eg *Roscorla v Thomas* (1842) 3 QB 234, p 98, above) and indeed with the view that the English law of contract is concerned with the enforcement of bargains, since clearly it is more expensive to sell warranted cars than unwarranted cars. See Hepple [1970] CLJ 122 at 131–132.

[5] Pp 165–172, above. Both because the rules make results unpredictable and because some of them, especially the parol evidence rule, hinder decisions that an oral statement forms part of the contract.

[6] Eg *Oscar Chess v Williams* [1957] 1 All ER 325, [1957] 1 WLR 370. Cf *Dick Bentley Productions Ltd v Harold Smith (Motors) Ltd* [1965] 2 All ER 65, [1965] 1 WLR 623, and *Beale v Taylor* [1967] 3 All ER 253, [1967] 1 WLR 1193.

[7] Pp 351–361, below.

[8] *Heilbut, Symons & Co v Buckleton* [1913] AC 30 at 49, per Lord Moulton. Innocent at this stage meant simply non-fraudulent.

[9] [1964] AC 465, [1963] 2 All ER 575.

The decision of the House of Lords in *Hedley Byrne & Co Ltd v Heller & Partners Ltd*[10] was a decision in tort and its impact on the law of contract was not easy to assess. Before the courts had had time to solve the problems thus created, Parliament intervened by passing the Misrepresentation Act 1967. This Act did not attempt a radical restatement of the law. It made important changes in the law but at all points it assumes a knowledge of the existing law. This is a dangerous assumption since, in some respects, the pre-Act law was far from clear. The draftsman did not avoid the hazards thus created but compounded them by curious drafting. In the result, though the Misrepresentation Act undoubtedly improves the position of representees as a class, it makes the exposition of the law even more complex.

We shall start our discussion by examining more fully precisely what is meant by misrepresentation and considering the types of misrepresentation. This will be followed by an account of the remedies for misrepresentation and a summary of the effects of the Misrepresentation Act 1967. Finally we shall examine those exceptional cases where the law imposes liability for non-disclosure, and the relationship between misrepresentation and estoppel.

B The nature of misrepresentation

A representation is a statement of fact made by one party to the contract (the representor) to the other (the representee) which, while not forming a term of the contract, is yet one of the reasons that induces the representee to enter into the contract. A misrepresentation is simply a representation that is untrue. The representor's state of mind and degree of carefulness are not relevant to classifying a representation as a misrepresentation but only to determining the type of misrepresentation, if any.[11]

It has already been observed[12] that while terms of a contract may be of a promissory nature, the concept of a representation is limited to statements of facts. But precedent has given a sophisticated meaning to the notion of a statement of fact and it is therefore necessary to consider in some detail the meaning of representation and also of inducement.

1 The meaning of representation

A representation means a statement of *fact* not a statement of intention or of opinion.

A representation, as we have seen, relates to some existing fact or some past event. Since it contains no element of futurity it must be distinguished from a statement of intention. An affirmation of the truth of a fact is different from a promise to do something in the future, and produces different legal consequences.[13] This distinction is of practical importance. If a person alters his position on the faith of a

---

[10] Ibid.   [11] See pp 341–350, below.   [12] See p 331, above.
[13] *Beattie v Lord Ebury* (1872) 7 Ch App 777 at 804, per Mellish LJ.

representation, the mere fact of its falsehood entitles him to certain remedies.[14] If, on the other hand, he sues upon what is in truth a promise, he must show that this promise forms part of a valid contract. The distinction is well illustrated by *Maddison v Alderson*,[15] where the plaintiff, who was prevented by the Statute of Frauds from enforcing an oral promise to devise a house, contended that the promise to make a will in her favour should be treated as a representation which would operate by way of estoppel. The contention, however, was dismissed, for:

> The doctrine of estoppel by representation is applicable only to representations as to some state of facts alleged to be at the time actually in existence, and not to promises *de futuro*, which, if binding at all, must be binding as contracts.[16]

Despite the antithesis, however, between a representation of fact which is untrue and an unfulfilled promise to do something *in futuro*, it by no means follows that a statement of intention can never be a representation of fact. It at least implies that the alleged intention does indeed exist, and if this is not true there is a clear misrepresentation of an existing fact. The state of mind is not what it is represented to be, and as Bowen LJ observed in *Edgington v Fitzmaurice*:

> The state of a man's mind is as much a fact as the state of his digestion. It is true that it is very difficult to prove what the state of a man's mind at a particular time is, but if it can be ascertained it is as much a fact as anything else. A misrepresentation as to the state of a man's mind is, therefore, a misstatement of fact.[17]

In this case, a company issued a prospectus which invited a loan from the public and stated that the money would be employed in the improvement of the buildings and the extension of the business. This was untrue, since the intention from the first had been to expend the loan upon the discharge of certain existing liabilities. It was held that the prospectus was a fraudulent misrepresentation of a fact. The company had not made a promise which they might or might not be able to fulfil; they had simply told a lie. It will be perceived that both the requirement that the representation be a statement of fact and its qualification in *Edgington v Fitzmaurice* owe much to an origin in fraud. It is difficult to misrepresent the state of one's mind other than dishonestly.

The expression of an opinion properly so called, ie the statement of a belief based on grounds incapable of actual proof, as where the vendor of a business estimates the prospective profits at so much a year, is not a representation of fact, and, in the

---

[14] Pp 356–367, below.

[15] (1883) 8 App Cas 467.

[16] Ibid at 473. The judgment of Stephen J in the court of first instance ((1879) 5 ExD 293) should be closely studied.

[17] (1885) 29 ChD 459 at 483; and see *Angus v Clifford* [1891] 2 Ch 449 a: 470, per Bowen LJ and the observations of Lord Wilberforce in *British Airways Board v Taylor* [1976] 1 All ER 65 at 68, [1976] 1 WLR 13 at 17.

absence of fraud, its falsity does not afford a title to relief. Thus in *Bisset v Wilkinson*,[18] the vendor of a holding in New Zealand, which had not previously been used as a sheep farm, told a prospective purchaser that in his judgement the carrying capacity of the land was two thousand sheep. It was held that this was an honest statement of opinion of the capacity of the farm, not a representation of its actual capacity.

It has never been doubted, however, that an expression of opinion may in certain circumstances constitute a representation of fact, as for instance where it is proved that the opinion was not actually held, or that it was expressed upon a matter upon which the speaker was entirely ignorant.

> It is often fallaciously assumed that a statement of opinion cannot involve the statement of a fact. In a case where the facts are equally well known to both parties, what one of them says to the other is frequently nothing but an expression of opinion . . . But if the facts are not equally well known to both sides, then a statement of opinion by the one who knows the facts best involves very often a statement of a material fact, for he impliedly states that he knows facts which justify his opinion.[19]

Thus, if it can be proved that the speaker did not hold the opinion or that a reasonable man possessing his knowledge could not honestly have held it, or that he alone was in a position to know the facts upon which the opinion must have been based[20] there is a misrepresentation of fact for which a remedy lies. In *Smith v Land and House Property Corpn*,[21] a vendor described his property in August as being 'let to Mr Frederick Fleck (a most desirable tenant) at a rental of £400 a year (clear of rates, taxes, insurance, etc) for an unexpired term of 27½ years, thus offering a first-class investment'. In fact the Lady Day rent had been paid by instalments under pressure and no part of the Midsummer rent had been paid. It was held that the description of Fleck as 'a most desirable tenant' was not a mere expression of opinion. It was an untrue assertion that nothing had occurred which could be regarded as rendering him an undesirable tenant.

Again, if what is really an opinion is stated as a fact, as for instance where company promoters, desiring to magnify the future earning capacity of a mine, publish the forecasts of experts as if they were positive facts,[22] there is a representation in the true sense of the term.

Somewhat akin to the distinction between opinion and fact is the general rule that *simplex commendatio non obligat*. Eulogistic commendation of the *res vendita* is the age-old device of the successful salesman. Thus to describe land as 'uncommonly rich water meadow'[23] or as 'fertile and improvable',[24] is not to make a representation of fact. This principle has in the past been applied in a fashion rather indulgent to

---

[18] [1927] AC 177.
[19] *Smith v Land and House Property Corpn* (1884) 28 ChD 7 at 15, per Bowen LJ.
[20] *Brown v Raphael* [1958] Ch 636, [1958] 2 All ER 79.　　[21] (1884) 28 ChD 7.
[22] *Reese River Silver Mining Co Ltd v Smith* (1869) LR 4 HL 64.
[23] *Scott v Hanson* (1829) 1 Russ & M 128.　　[24] *Dimmock v Hallett* (1866) 2 Ch App 21.

salesmen and there is much to be said for applying more demanding standards.[25] Certainly a statement which purports to be supported by facts and figures, as for instance that timber trees are 'of an average size approaching a given number of feet,[26] does not cease to be a representation of fact merely because it is expressed in a laudatory vein. The Trade Descriptions Act 1968 extends the criminal liability for false descriptions; but, by section 35, a contract for the supply of goods is not to be 'unenforceable' by reason only of a contravention of the Act.

In previous editions of this work it was said that a representation of law cannot found an action merely because it is wrong. At the time this was a statement of the orthodox view that there was a fundamental distinction between mistakes of law and mistakes of fact. This view has now been abandoned[27] but there are still problems. A representation of law is basically a statement of the representor's opinion as to what the law is and it follows that if the representor does not in fact hold this opinion he misrepresents his state of mind and liability should accrue under the principle in *Edgington v Fitzmaurice*.[28] It might further be argued that, as with other statements of opinion, there will be cases where the representor implicitly represents that he has reasonable grounds for his belief. In any case it is difficult to distinguish between representations of fact and law. A representation, for instance, that the drains of a house are sanitary is obviously a statement of fact. It is equally obvious that to state an abstract proposition of law, as for instance that an oral contract of guarantee is not enforceable by action, is a representation of law.[29] The distinction, however, becomes intractable when a statement of fact is coupled, expressly or implicitly, with a proposition of law. It is evident that in practice contracts are much more likely to be induced by mixed statements of this kind than by abstract propositions of law, as in *Solle v Butcher*,[30] where a man states that a flat is not an old but a new flat and is therefore outside the Rent Restrictions Act.

Can silence constitute misrepresentation?
A representation, whether expressed as a positive assertion of fact or inferred from conduct, normally assumes an active form, but an important question is whether it can ever be implied from silence. To put the enquiry in another form: when, if ever, is it the duty of a contracting party to disclose facts that are within his own knowledge?

---

[25] See the observations of Lord Diplock in *Erven Warnink BV v J Townend & Sons (Hull) Ltd* [1979] AC 731 at 743, [1979] 2 All ER 927 at 933.

[26] *Lord Brooke v Rounthwaite* (1846) 5 Hare 298..

[27] This view was rejected by the House of Lords in *Kleinwort Benson v Lincon City Council* [1998] 4 All ER 513.

[28] (1885) 29 ChD 459; Hudson (1958) SLT 16. A misrepresentation as to foreign law is a misrepresentation of fact: *André & Cie SA v Ets Michel Blanc & Fils* [1979] 2 Lloyd's Rep 427.

[29] *Beattie v Lord Ebury* (1872) 7 Ch App 777 at 802; *Beesly v Hallwood Estates Ltd* [1960] 2 All ER 314 at 323, [1960] 1 WLR 549 at 560.

[30] [1950] 1 KB 671, [1949] 2 All ER 1107, p 244, above. See also *Laurence v Lexcourt Holdings Ltd* [1978] 2 All ER 810, [1978] 1 WLR 1128.

The general rule is that mere silence is not misrepresentation.[31] 'The failure to disclose a material fact which might influence the mind of a prudent contractor does not give the right to avoid the contract'[32] even though it is obvious that the contractor has a wrong impression that would be removed by disclosure.[33] Tacit acquiescence in the self-deception of another creates no legal liability, unless it is due to active misrepresentation or to misleading conduct. Thus, to take one important example, there is no general duty of disclosure in the case of a contract of sale, whether of goods or of land.

> There being no fiduciary relation between vendor and purchaser in the negotiation, the purchaser is not bound to disclose any fact exclusively within his knowledge which might reasonably be expected to influence the price of the subject to be sold. Simple reticence does not amount to legal fraud, however, it may be viewed by moralists. But a single word, or (I may add) a nod or a wink, or a shake of the head, or smile from the purchaser intended to induce the vendor to believe the existence of a non-existing fact, which might influence the price of the subject to be sold, would be sufficient ground for a Court of Equity to refuse a decree for a specific performance of the agreement.[34]

This general rule, of course, is not confined to contracts of sale. In *Turner v Green*,[35] for instance:

> Shortly before two solicitors effected a compromise on behalf of their respective clients, the plaintiff's solicitor was informed of certain legal proceedings which made the compromise a prejudicial transaction for the defendant. He kept the information to himself.

It was held that the solicitor's silence was not sufficient ground for withholding a decree of specific performance.

Silence constitutes misrepresentation in three cases

There are, however, at least three sets of circumstances in which silence or non-disclosure affords a ground for relief. These are, firstly, where the silence distorts positive representation; secondly, where the contract requires *uberrima fides*; thirdly, where a fiduciary relation exists between the contracting parties. Only the first of these will be discussed at this stage.[36]

Silence upon some of the relevant factors may obviously distort a positive assertion. A party to a contract may be legally justified in remaining silent about some material fact, but if he ventures to make a representation upon the matter it must be a full and

---

[31] *Fox v Mackreth* (1788) 2 Cox Eq Cas 320 at 320 and 321, per Lord Thurlow.
[32] *Bell v Lever Bros Ltd* [1932] AC 161 at 227, per Lord Atkin.
[33] *Smith v Hughes* (1871) LR 6 QB 597.
[34] *Walters v Morgan* (1861) 3 De GF & J 718 at 723–24, per Lord Campbell.
[35] [1895] 2 Ch 205.   [36] See pp 372–381, below.

frank statement, and not such a partial and fragmentary account that what is withheld makes that which is said absolutely false.[37] A half truth may be in fact false because of what it leaves unsaid, and, although what a man actually says may be true in every detail, he is guilty of misrepresentation unless he tells the whole truth. If a vendor of land states that the farms are let, he must not omit the further fact that the tenants have given notice to quit.[38] If a tradesman accepts a dress for cleaning and asks the client to sign a document, telling him that it exempts him from liability, for damage to beads and sequins, though in fact the exemption extends to 'any damage howsoever arising', he has conveyed a false impression which amounts to a misrepresentation.[39]

Moreover, a party who makes a false statement in the belief that it is true comes under an obligation to disclose the truth should he subsequently discover that he was mistaken.[40] Similarly if he makes a statement which is true at the time, but which is found to be untrue in the course of the subsequent negotiations, he is equally under an obligation to disclose the change of circumstances. This latter issue was raised in *Davies v London and Provincial Marine Insurance Co.*[41]

> A company ordered the arrest of their agent in the belief that he had committed a felony under the Larceny Act 1861. Certain friends of the agent, in order to prevent his arrest, offered to deposit a sum of money as security for any deficiency for which he might be liable. While this offer was under consideration the company, having been advised by counsel that no felony had been committed, withdrew the instructions for arrest. Later in the same day the offer was renewed and it was accepted by the company without disclosing that there could no longer be any question of arrest.

It was held that the contract must be rescinded.

2 The meaning of inducement

A representation does not render a contract voidable unless it was intended to cause and has in fact caused the representee to make the contract. It must have produced a

---

[37] *Oakes v Turquand and Harding* (1867) LR 2 HL 325 at 242–343. In *Jaques v Lloyd D George & Partners Ltd* [1968] 2 All ER 187 at 190–191, [1968] 1 WLR 625 at 630, Lord Denning MR suggested that an estate agent who tendered a contract to a client for signature, impliedly represented that it contained the usual provision for payment, viz on completion of the sale only, and that failure to reveal that the contract contained a provision for payment more favourable to the estate agent might, without more, amount to a misrepresentation. These remarks were obiter and should be treated with some reserve. Wilkinson 31 MLR 700.

[38] *Dimmock v Hallett* (1866) 2 Ch App 21.

[39] *Curtis v Chemical Cleaning and Dyeing Co* [1951] 1 KB 805, [1951] 1 All ER 631, p 212, above. See also *Ames v Milward* (1818) 8 Taunt 637.

[40] *Davies v London and Provincial Marine Insurance Co* (1878) 8 ChD 469 at 475, per Fry J; *With v O'Flanagan* [1936] Ch 575, [1936] 1 All ER 727.

[41] (1878) 8 ChD 469. Cf *Wales v Wadham* [1977] 2 All ER 125, [1977] 1 WLR 199, criticised Phillips 40 MLR 599 and *Argy Trading Development Co v Lapid Developments Ltd* [1977] 3 All ER 785, [1977] 1 WLR 444.

misunderstanding in his mind, and that misunderstanding must have been one of the reasons which induced him to make the contract. A false statement, whether innocent or fraudulent, does not *per se* give rise to a cause of action.

It follows from this that a misrepresentation is legally harmless if the plaintiff:

(a) never knew of its existence; or

(b) did not allow it to affect his judgement; or

(c) was aware of its untruth.

Let us take these hypotheses *seriatim.*

·(a) A plaintiff must always be prepared to prove that an alleged misrepresentation had an effect upon his mind, a task which he certainly cannot fulfil if he was never aware that it had been made. Thus in one case a shareholder who pleaded that he had been induced to acquire shares by a misrepresentation, failed in his action for rescission, since, though false reports concerning the financial state of the company had previously been published, he was unable to prove that he had read one syllable of the reports or that anyone had told him of their contents.[42] Perhaps the most remarkable case on the subject is *Horsfall v Thomas*,[43] where the facts were these:

A gun containing a defect was delivered to a buyer, and after being fired for six rounds, flew to pieces. It is not quite clear what exact form the defect took, for the case was withdrawn from the jury. The buyer alleged that 'the breach end of the chamber was all soft and spongy, and that a metal plug had been driven into the breach over this soft part'.[44] Bramwell B said that the seller or his workmen 'had done something to the gun which concealed the defect in it'. But one fact which was quite clear was that the buyer had never examined the gun.

To an action brought upon a bill of exchange which the buyer had accepted by way of payment, it was pleaded that the acceptance had been induced by the fraud and misrepresentation of the seller. The Court of Exchequer Chamber unanimously held, however, that even if all the allegations of the buyer could be proved, his plea could not succeed, for since he had never examined the gun, the attempt to conceal the defect had produced no effect upon his mind.[45]

[42] *Re Northumberland and Durham District Banking Co, ex p Bigge* (1858) 28 LJ Ch 50.

[43] (1862) 1 H & C 90.

[44] Ibid at 94–95.

[45] This decision, although a simple illustration of the doctrine that an intention to mislead must be followed by success in order to justify rescission, is not altogether satisfactory on other grounds. Bramwell B, in delivering the judgment of the court, indicated that the manufacturing seller of an article is bound to disclose any latent defect of which he is aware, but if this is the rule, it is a little difficult to see why the facts alleged by the buyer, presuming them to be true, did not make it applicable. It is doubtful, however, whether any such duty is imposed on the seller; see the remarks of Cockburn CJ in *Smith v Hughes* (1871) LR 6 QB 597 at 605, where he dissented from *Horsfall v Thomas*.

(b) A representee who does not allow the representation to affect his judgement, although it was designed to that end, cannot make it a ground for relief. He may, for instance, have regarded it as unimportant, as in *Smith v Chadwick*,[46] where:

> A prospectus contained a false statement that a certain important person was on the board of directors, but the plaintiff frankly admitted in cross-examination that he had been in no degree influenced by this fact.

He may on the other hand have preferred to rely upon his own acumen or business sense or upon an independent report which he specially obtained. Thus in *Attwood v Small*:[47]

> A vendor accompanied an offer to sell a mine with statements as to its earning capacities which were exaggerated and unreliable. The buyers agreed to accept the offer if the vendor could verify his statements and they appointed experienced agents to investigate the matter. The agents, who visited the mine and were given every facility for forming a judgment, reported that the statements were true, and ultimately the contract was completed.

It was held by the House of Lords that an action to rescind the contract for misrepresentation must fail, since the purchasers did not rely on the vendor's statements, but tested their accuracy by independent investigations and declared themselves satisfied with the result.

It is clear, however, that the right to relief would be endangered if a defendant were free to evade liability by proof that there were contributory causes, other than his misrepresentation, which induced the plaintiff to make the contract, and that his representation was not the decisive cause.

Cranworth LJ asked:

> Who can say that the untrue statement may not have been precisely that which turned the scale in the mind of the party to whom it was addressed?[48]

The courts, therefore, although denying relief to a plaintiff who entirely disregards the misrepresentation, have consistently held that the misrepresentation need not be his sole reason for making the contract. If it was clearly one inducing cause it is immaterial that it was not the only inducing cause.[49] In *Edgington v Fitzmaurice*,[50] for instance:

> The plaintiff was induced to take debentures in a company, partly because of a misstatement in the prospectus and partly because of his own erroneous belief that debenture holders would have a charge upon the property of the company.

---

[46] (1884) 9 App Cas 187 at 194.
[47] (1838) 6 Cl & Fin 232.
[48] *Reynell v Sprye* (1852) 1 De GM & G 660 at 708.
[49] Approved in *Barton v Armstrong* [1976] AC 104 at 119, [1975] 2 All ER 465 at 475.
[50] (1885) 29 ChD 459.

Thus he had two inducements, one the false representation, the other his own mistake, and on this ground it was pleaded, but unsuccessfully pleaded, that he was disentitled to rescission.

In addition to having induced the representee to enter the contract, it is said that the representation must be material.[51] There does not appear to be any 20th century misrepresentation case where the result turns on the precise meaning to be given to this requirement.[52] However, the matter was very fully considered in the leading House of Lords decision in *Pan Atlantic Co Ltd v Pinetop Insurance Co Ltd*[53] In his exhaustive review of the law of misrepresentation and non disclosure, Lord Mustill said that the basic principles were the same and that in both misrepresentation and non disclosure a party who seeks to have a contract set aside must show both actual inducement and materiality, that is, that the subject matter of misrepresentation or non disclosure related to a matter which would have influenced the judgement of a reasonable man.[54]

(c) Knowledge of the untruth of a representation is a complete bar to relief, since the plaintiff cannot assert that he has been misled by the statement,[55] even if the misstatement was made fraudulently. In such a case, 'the misrepresentation and the concealment go for just absolutely nothing, because it is not *dolus qui dat locum contractui*'.[56]

It must be carefully noticed, however, that relief will not be withheld on this ground except upon clear proof that the plaintiff possessed actual and complete knowledge of the true facts—actual not constructive, complete not fragmentary. The onus is on the defendant to prove that the plaintiff had unequivocal notice of the truth. In particular, the mere fact that a party has been afforded an opportunity to investigate and verify a representation does not deprive him of his right to resist specific performance or to sue for rescission.[57] As Lord Dunedin once said:

> No one is entitled to make a statement which on the face of it conveys a false impression and then excuse himself on the ground that the person to whom he made it had available the means of correction.[58]

---

[51] *Smith v Chadwick* (1882) 20 ChD 27 at 44–45, per Jessel MR.

[52] But see *Museprime Properties Ltd v Adhill Properties Ltd* [1990] 36 EG 114

[53] [1994] 3 All ER 581; Birds and Hird 59 MLR 285.

[54] Many lawyers had not seen this as clearly as Lord Mustill. So, in practice, most reported cases show parties concentrating on actual inducement in misrepresentation cases and on materiality in non disclosure cases. There may be a question whether proof of materiality raises a presumption of actual inducement. In practice this is likely to be much more important in non-disclosure than in misrepresentation cases. See *County NatWest Ltd v Barton* [2002] 4 All ER 494; *Huyton SA v Distribuidora Internacional de Productos Agricolas* [2003] EWCA Civ 1104, [2004] 1 All ER (Comm) 402. See p 374, below.

[55] *Jennings v Broughton* (1854) 5 De GM & G 126; *Begbie v Phosphate Sewage Co* (1875) LR 10 QB 491.

[56] *Irvine v Kirkpatrick* 1850 7 Bell App 186 at 237, per Lord Brougham.

[57] *Redgrave v Hurd* (1881) 20 ChD 1.

[58] *Nocton v Lord Ashburton* [1914] AC 932 at 962.

If, for instance,

> a prospectus misdescribes the contracts made by the promoters on behalf of the company; or
> a vendor of land makes a false statement about the contents of a certain lease; or
> a vendor of a law partnership misstates the average earnings of the business during the last three years,

it is no answer to a suit for relief to say that inspection of the contracts or of the lease or of the bills of costs was expressly invited but was not accepted.[59]

C Types of misrepresentation

1 Fraudulent misrepresentation

'Fraud', in common parlance, is a somewhat comprehensive word that embraces a multitude of delinquencies differing widely in turpitude, but the types of conduct that give rise to an action of deceit at common law have been narrowed down to rigid limits. In the view of the common law, 'a charge of fraud is such a terrible thing to bring against a man that it cannot be maintained in any court unless it is shown that he had a wicked mind'.[60] Influenced by this consideration, the House of Lords has established in the leading case of *Derry v Peek*[61] that an absence of honest belief is essential to constitute fraud. If a representor honestly believes his statement to be true, he cannot be liable in deceit, no matter how ill-advised, stupid, credulous or even negligent he may have been. Lord Herschell, indeed, gave a more elaborate definition of fraud in *Derry v Peek*,[62] saying that it means a false statement 'made (1) knowingly, or (2) without belief in its truth, or (3) recklessly, careless whether it be true or false', but, as the learned judge himself admitted, the rule is accurately and comprehensively contained in the short formula that a fraudulent misrepresentation is a false statement which, when made, the representor did not honestly believe to be true.

The important feature of this decision is the insistence of the House of Lords that the distinction between negligence and fraud must never be blurred. Fraud is dishonesty, and it is not necessarily dishonest, though it may be negligent, to express a belief upon grounds that would not convince a reasonable man.

The facts of *Derry v Peek* were these:

---

[59] The first two instances are given by Jessel MR in *Redgrave v Hurd*, above, at 14; the last represents the facts in the case itself. See also *Central Rly Co of Venezuela (Directors etc) v Kisch* (1867) LR 2 HL 99 at 120. It would seem that it would not normally be contributory negligence to rely on such statements without checking them. *Gran Gelato Ltd v Richcliff (Group) Ltd* [1992] 1 All ER 865. Contributory negligence is not available at all as a defence to deceit. *Alliance and Leicester Building Society v Edgestop Ltd* [1994] 2 All ER 38.

[60] *Le Lievre v Gould* [1893] 1 QB 491 at 498, per Lord Esher.

[61] (1889) 14 App Cas 337; Lobban 112 LQR 287.   [62] Ibid at 374.

A company, after submitting its plans to the Board of Trade, applied for a special Act of Parliament authorising it to run trams in Plymouth by steam power. The Act which was ultimately passed provided that the trams might be moved by animal power, or, if the consent of the Board of Trade were obtained, by steam or mechanical power. The directors, believing that this consent would be given as a matter of course, since the plans had already been submitted to the Board of Trade without encountering objection, thereupon issued a prospectus saying that the company had the right to use steam power instead of horses. The respondent took shares upon the faith of this statement. The Board of Trade refused their consent, and the company was ultimately wound up.

It was held by the House of Lords, reversing the decision of the Court of Appeal, that an action of deceit against the directors claiming damages for fraudulent misrepresentation must fail. Lord Herschell said:

> The prospectus was . . . inaccurate. But that is not the question. If they [the directors] believed that the consent of the Board of Trade was practically concluded by the passing of the Act, has the plaintiff made out, which it was for him to do, that they have been guilty of a fraudulent misrepresentation? I think not. I cannot hold it proved as to any one of them that he knowingly made a false statement, or one which he did not believe to be true, or was careless whether what he stated was true or false. In short, I think they honestly believed that what they asserted was true.[63]

In testing the honesty of the representor's belief, his statement must not be considered according to its ordinary meaning, but according to its meaning as understood by him.[64] Carelessness is not dishonesty; but, of course, if a man is reckless, a court may well be justified in concluding that he could not have been honest. 'There may be such an absence of reasonable ground for his belief as, in spite of his assertion, to carry conviction to the mind that he had not really the belief which he alleges.'[65]

Again, if a representor deliberately shuts his eyes to the facts or purposely abstains from their investigation, his belief is not honest and he is just as liable as if he had knowingly stated a falsehood.[66]

Motive is irrelevant in an action of deceit. Once it has been proved that the plaintiff has acted upon a false representation which the defendant did not believe to be true, liability ensues, although the defendant may not have been actuated by any bad

---

[63] Ibid at 379. It should be noted that the decision of the House of Lords was based on the trial judge's finding that the defendants believed their statements to be true. He might well have held that they merely hoped and believed that they would soon become true. Such a finding would have led to judgment for the plaintiffs. See Pollock 5 LQR 410; Anson 6 LQR 72.

[64] *Akerhielm v De Mare* [1959] AC 789, [1959] 3 All ER 485; *Gross v Lewis Hillman Ltd* [1970] Ch 445, [1969] 3 All ER 1476; *McGrath Motors (Canberra) Pty Ltd v Applebee* (1964) 110 CLR 656.

[65] *Derry v Peek* (1889) 14 App Cas 337 at 369, per Lord Herschell.

[66] Ibid at 376, per Lord Herschell.

motive.[67] The representor is not liable, however, until the representee has acted on the representation and thereby suffered loss.[68]

2 Negligent misstatement at common law

The plaintiffs in *Derry v Peek*[69] formulated their claim as an action in the tort of deceit. But it was assumed at the time, and for seventy years afterwards,[70] that the House of Lords in this case decided that no action would lie for negligent words, at least where reliance on them produced purely financial loss, as opposed to physical damage. All non-fraudulent misrepresentations should be classed together as innocent misrepresentations.

There was, however, an important equitable exception in that by an application of the general doctrine of 'constructive fraud', which is discussed below,[71] an action would lie for negligent misrepresentation if there was a fiduciary relationship between the parties. So in *Nocton v Lord Ashburton*[72] this principle was applied by the House of Lords to negligent advice given by a solicitor to his client.[73]

In 1963 the House of Lords delivered its famous judgment in *Hedley Byrne & Co Ltd v Heller & Partners Ltd*[74] in which it held that in some circumstances an action would lie in tort for negligent misstatement. In this case the plaintiffs entered into advertising contracts on behalf of Easipower on terms under which they would themselves be liable if Easipower defaulted. Wishing to check on Easipower's credit, they asked their bank to inquire of the defendants, who were Easipower's bankers. Relying on the replies, they continued to place orders and suffered substantial loss when Easipower went into liquidation. The House of Lords held that the plaintiffs' action failed since the defendants' replies had been given 'without responsibility'; but they also stated that, but for this disclaimer, an action for negligence could lie in such circumstances. Their Lordships did not however attempt to define with precision the circumstances in which such an action would lie. Detailed consideration of the

---

[67] *Foster v Charles* (1830) 6 Bing 396; affd 7 Bing 105.
[68] *Briess v Woolley* [1954] AC 333, [1954] 1 All ER 909; *Diamond v Bank of London and Montreal Ltd* [1979] QB 333, [1979] 1 All ER 561.
[69] (1889) 14 App Cas 337.
[70] *Le Lievre v Gould* [1893] 1 QB 491; *Candler v Crane, Christmas & Co* [1951] 2 KB 164, [1951] 1 All ER 426.
[71] See pp 379–381, below.
[72] [1914] AC 932. On the difficult question of the relationship between fraud at common law and fraud in equity, see Sheridan *Fraud in Equity* pp 12–37.
[73] Negligent advice given by a solicitor to his client would normally amount to a breach of an implied term of the contract between them. In *Nocton v Lord Ashburton* the plaintiff did not formulate his claim in contract because of problems of limitation. Before 1873, a plaintiff could not have recovered damages for a claim of this kind but only specifically equitable remedies such as account. Damages were awarded in *Woods v Martins Bank* [1959] 1 QB 55, [1958] 3 All ER 166.
[74] [1964] AC 465, [1963] 2 All ER 575.

resultant problems must be left to works on the law of torts[75] but a few observations must be made since it is now possible to argue that a negligent precontractual misrepresentation made by one party to the contract to the other may give rise to an action for damages in tort.

It is clear that the House of Lords did not simply assimilate negligent statements to negligent acts. Liability for negligent statements depends upon the existence of a 'special relationship' between plaintiff and defendant. Such a relationship does not necessarily involve direct contact between the parties. In *Hedley Byrne & Co Ltd v Heller & Partners Ltd* itself, the advice was passed through the plaintiff's bank and neither party knew the identity of the other. The defendant knew, however, that the information would be passed to a customer of the inquiring bank and that it was required so that the customer could decide whether to extend credit to Easipower. It would seem probable that the adviser must know in general terms the purpose for which the advice is sought. But where advice is given before entering into a contract between the person giving advice and the person receiving it, this is not likely to be a practical difficulty.

It has been suggested that the duty to take care in giving advice is imposed only on professional men and perhaps only on those professional men whose profession it is to give advice. If such a limitation exists, it would gravely restrict the application of this rule to pre-contractual statements. Though the possibility was extensively canvassed by the Privy Council in *Mutual Life and Citizens' Assurance Co Ltd v Evatt*,[76] later English cases suggest that this difficult case, whatever it decided, is not law in England.[77]

It is important to note that there is nothing in the judgment in *Hedley Byrne & Co Ltd v Heller & Partners Ltd* to suggest that liability can attach only to statements of fact as defined above.[78] It can extend beyond this to other forms of negligent advice, such as the expression of an opinion about the law.

Early decisions after 1963 did little to clarify whether, and if so when, the doctrine in *Hedley Byrne & Co Ltd v Heller & Partners Ltd* might be used to impose liability for negligent pre-contractual statements. It was held that actions would not lie in tort

[75] There are many articles discussing the effect of the case on the law both of tort and of contract. These include Honoré 8 JSPTL 284; Stevens 27 MLR 121; Weir [1963] CLJ 216; Gordon 38 ALJ 39, 79; Coote 2 NZULR 263.

[76] [1971] AC 793, [1971] 1 All ER 150; Rickford 34 MLR 328. The decision should probably be regarded as turning primarily on what a plaintiff must allege in his pleadings under the unreformed New South Wales procedure. Note that of the three Lords who sat in both *Hedley Byrne & Co v Heller* and *Mutual Life v Evatt*, two were in the minority in the latter case. In *W B Anderson & Sons Ltd v Rhodes (Liverpool) Ltd* [1967] 2 All ER 850, liability was imposed in a purely commercial context.

[77] See eg *Esso Petroleum Co Ltd v Mardon* [1976] QB 801, [1976] 2 All ER 5; *Batty v Metropolitan Property Realisations Ltd* [1978] QB 554, [1978] 2 All ER 445.

[78] Pp 332–337, above.

against an architect[79] or a solicitor[80] for negligent advice which was in breach of contract on the theory that a single duty cannot give rise to actions both in contract and tort. This theory was criticised,[81] and was hard to reconcile with numerous decisions allowing actions by servants against masters or by passengers against carriers to be brought indifferently in contract or tort.[82]

It appears now to have been abandoned. More recently cases have held that if a plaintiff can show that all the ingredients of a tortious claim are present, he is not disentitled from pursuing it because he also has a claim in contract. The matter was examined in an exceptionally full and careful judgment by Oliver J in *Midland Bank Trust Co Ltd v Hett, Stubbs and Kemp*.[83]

> In this case a father owned a farm, which he let to his son. In 1961 the father agreed to give the son an option to buy the freehold reversion within the next ten years. The defendant solicitors acted for both father and son in the transaction and drew up a formal agreement embodying the terms of the option. They omitted however to register it as an estate contract. In August 1967 the father sold the farm to his wife. In October 1967 the son attempted to exercise the option and discovered for the first time that the property had been sold and the option never registered. In due course the son decided to sue the defendants for professional negligence and issued a writ in July 1972.[84] On the face of it, there was a clear breach of contract but equally this appeared to be well outside the limitation period since the contract had been broken in 1961 when the option had not been registered. The plaintiffs sought to overcome this difficulty in two ways. As regards the claim in contract, they argued that there was a continuing breach until the father's sale in August 1967, when it became impossible to register. Alternatively they argued that there was a claim in tort, arising out of the solicitors' negligence. A tort action if it existed could not have been brought before damage had been inflicted, that is by the father's sale to his wife in 1967, and so a tort action would be still within the limitation period.

Oliver J held for the plaintiffs on both grounds.[85] As regards the claim based on *Hedley*

---

[79] *Bagot v Stevens, Scanlan & Co* [1966] 1 QB 197, [1964] 3 All ER 577.

[80] *Clark v Kirby-Smith* [1964] Ch 506, [1964] 2 All ER 835.

[81] Poulton 82 LQR 346, and see *Reid v Traders General Insurance Co, Dares Motors and Myers* (1963) 41 DLR (2d) 148 at 154, per Ilsley CJ. Symmons 21 McGill LJ 79.

[82] See eg *Matthews v Kuwait Bechtel Corpn* [1959] 2 QB 57, [1959] 2 All ER 345.

[83] [1979] Ch 384, [1978] 3 All ER 571; Stanton 42 MLR 207; Jolowicz [1979] CLJ 54.

[84] He shortly afterwards died and the action was taken over by the plaintiffs as executors.

[85] He found this principle to be logically implicit in *Esso Petroleum Co Ltd v Mardon* [1976] QB 801, [1976] 2 All ER 5. See also *Batty v Metropolitan Property Realisations Ltd* [1978] QB 554, [1978] 2 All ER 445, cited at a late stage to Oliver J but not fully considered by him. Oliver's J judgment was approved by Lord Denning MR in *Photo Production Ltd v Securicor Transport Ltd* [1978] 3 All ER 146 at 150–151, [1978] 1 WLR 856–862, in a passage not criticised by the House of Lords when reversing the Court of Appeal. See also the decision of the Supreme Court of Canada in *Central Trust Co v Rafuse* (1986) 31 DLR (4th) 481 (Can SC) Hayek 1 JCL 43.

Byrne & Co Ltd v Heller & Partners Ltd he saw no difficulty in this existing alongside a contractual claim. The key question was whether there was a 'special relationship' between plaintiff and defendant and not how that relationship arose. The reasoning of Oliver J was enthusiastically approved by Lord Goff delivering the principal speech in the House of Lords in *Henderson v Merrett Syndicates.*[86]

These cases all concern negligence in the course of performing a contractual duty to take care, but if tortious and contractual obligations can coexist after the contract is concluded, it would seem that they can also coexist before the contract is concluded.[87] This view is confirmed by *Esso Petroleum Co Ltd v Mardon.*[88]

> In this case the plaintiffs had let a petrol filling station to the defendant for three years. The station was on a newly developed site and during the negotiations for the lease one L, a dealer sales representative employed by the plaintiff, with over 40 years' experience, had told the defendant that he thought the potential 'throughput' of the station in the third year would be of the order of 200,000 gallons. The defendant suggested that 100,000 gallons might be a more realistic figure but his doubts were quelled by L's expertise and great experience. In the event the throughput in the third year was only 86,502 gallons. At this level the station was uneconomic and the defendant gave up the tenancy. The plaintiffs sued for arrears of rent and the defendant counterclaimed for damages for negligence.

The Court of Appeal held for the defendant.[89] In making statements about the station's prospects during the pre-contractual negotiations, the plaintiffs owed the defendant a duty of care since they had a financial interest in the advice they were giving and knew that the defendant was relying on their knowledge and expertise. Further they were in breach of the duty of care, since L's forecast, although honestly made, failed to take into account the actual configuration of the site as developed.

It does not of course follow from this decision that parties in pre-contractual negotiations always owe each other a duty of care, but it appears that we can now confidently state that if all the ingredients of a duty of care are present, the duty is not excluded by the fact that the parties are in a pre-contractual situation.

Another interesting and difficult problem, which has not yet been before the English courts, concerns the effect of a negligent pre-contractual statement, which is

---

[86] [1994] 3 All ER 506; [1994] 3 WLR 761.

[87] This is how *Woods v Martins Bank* [1959] 1 QB 55, [1958] 3 All ER 166, should now be explained. The possibility might have been raised in *Dick Bentley Productions v Harold Smith (Motors)* [1965] 2 All ER 65, [1965] 1 WLR 623, but the case went on other grounds.

[88] [1976] QB 801, [1976] 2 All ER 5; Sealy [1976] CLJ 221. The Court of Appeal also held that Esso had given a contractual warranty that their opinion was carefully formed. See also *Dillingham Construction Pty Ltd v Downs* [1972] 2 NSWLR 49; *Sealand of the Pacific Ltd v Ocean Cement Ltd* (1973) 33 DLR (3d) 625; *Capital Motors Ltd v Beecham* [1975] 1 NZLR 576; *Gran Gelato Ltd v Richcliff (Group) Ltd* [1992] 1 All ER 865.

[89] The facts took place before 1967 and there was therefore no claim under the Misrepresentation Act 1967 See pp 347–350, below.

not eventually followed by a contract. As a rule there will be no question of liability since no damage will have resulted but this is not necessarily so. Suppose for instance X, a main contractor who is preparing a tender for building a new office block asked Y, a central heating sub-contractor, for an estimate and that Y carelessly quotes a figure which is too low. Suppose further that relying on Y's figures, X puts in a tender, which again is too low and that one morning X receives in the post two letters, one accepting his tender for the building and the other from Y revoking his quotation. As a matter of offer and acceptance, it is clear that X has made a binding main contract and has no contractual action against Y. It is arguable, however, that he now has a tortious action. It is true that this may be said to be evading the rules of offer and acceptance,[90] but it is thought that this is not so. X's loss does not follow from Y's revocation but from Y's carelessness in fixing the offer figure. If the figure had been carefully calculated, X would usually have been able to go out into the market to engage another central heating contractor at much the same price but if the figure is too low he will not be able to do this. So it is not implausible to argue that the situation is one where Y knew that X would rely on his figure and would suffer loss if it were unreliable and that therefore y owed x a duty of care.

3 Negligent misrepresentation under the Misrepresentation Act 1967

In 1962 the Law Reform Committee in its 10th Report recommended that damages should be given for negligent misrepresentation.[91] This recommendation was, of course, based on the law as it was assumed to be before *Hedley Byrne & Co Ltd v Heller & Partners Ltd*, and it may well be that it would have been wise to reconsider it in the light of that decision. Instead it was enacted by the Misrepresentation Act 1967,[92] section 2(1) of which provides that:

> Where a person has entered into a contract after a misrepresentation has been made to him by another party thereto and as a result thereof he has suffered loss, then, if the person making the misrepresentation would be liable to damages in respect thereof had the misrepresentation been made fraudulently, that person shall be so liable notwithstanding that the misrepresentation was not made fraudulently, unless he proves that he had reasonable ground to believe and did believe up to the time the contract was made that the facts represented were true.

It is clear that the object of this subsection is to impose liability in damages for negligent misrepresentation and to reverse the normal burden of proof by requiring the representor to disprove his negligence, but a singularly oblique technique was adopted for this purpose[93] since the draftsman elected to proceed by reference to the common law rules on fraud. This has led some commentators to talk of a 'fiction of

---

[90] *Holman Construction Ltd v Delta Timber Co Ltd* [1972] NZLR 1081.
[91] Cmnd 1762, paras 17 and 18.
[92] 1967, s 7.   [93] Atiyah and Treitel 30 MLR 369 at 375; Fairest [1967] CLJ 239 at 244–245.

fraud'.[94] Though it would be quixotic to defend the drafting of the section, it is suggested that there is no such 'fiction of fraud' since the section does not say that a negligent misrepresentor shall be treated for all purposes as if he were fraudulent. No doubt the wording seeks to incorporate by reference some of the rules relating to fraud but it does not follow that it has incorporated all of them.[95]

Since in an action based on the Act the representor will have to bear the burden of disproving his negligence, it would seem that a plaintiff will usually formulate his claim under the Act rather than sue at common law for fraud or negligence. But in some cases an action at common law may still be preferred.

Firstly, a plaintiff who relies upon the doctrine in *Hedley Byrne & Co Ltd v Heller & Partners Ltd*, need not establish that a misrepresentation *stricto sensu* has been made.[96]

Secondly, it may well be that different rules as to remoteness and measure of damages apply to the three forms of action open to the plaintiff.[97] The prospect of recovering heavier damages might spur him to assume the greater burden of proving fraud or negligence.

Thirdly, the statutory action only applies 'where a person has entered into a contract'. If, as will sometimes happen, the effect of the representor's statements is to make the contract void *ab initio* for mistake, it would seem that there would be no action under the statute for there would be no contract. This may be illustrated by considering the case of *McRae v Commonwealth Disposals Commission*.[98] It will be remembered that in this case the defendants sold the plaintiffs a non-existent ship and later argued that they were not liable for loss incurred by the plaintiffs in searching for the ship since there was no contract for lack of subject matter. We have already suggested[99] that an English court might prove unwilling to follow the High Court of Australia's view that there was a contract that the ship existed. If an English court were to hold the contract void in such a situation, it would seem that no action could be brought under the Act. But the plaintiff could still recover in tort at common law by proving that the defendant was either fraudulent or negligent in stating that the ship existed, since it is not a requirement of these actions that the representee shall have entered into a contract but simply that he shall have suffered loss in reliance on the statement. Since the defendants in *McRae v Commonwealth Disposals Commission* were clearly negligent it would seem that the decision in that case can now best be explained by reliance on *Hedley Byrne & Co Ltd v Heller & Partners Ltd*.

---

[94] Atiyah and Treitel, above.

[95] See the illuminating discussion by Mummery J in *Alliance and Leicester Building Society v Edgestop Ltd* [1994] 2 All ER 38 as to the availability of contributory negligence as a defence to claims in deceit and under Misrepresentation Act 1967, s 2(1). The subsection does not impose liability on an agent who makes a misrepresentation. *Resolute Maritime Inc v Nippon Kaiji Kyokai* [1983] 2 All ER 1, [1983] 1 WLR 857. The House of Lords held in *Standard Chartered Bank v Pakistan National Shipping Corp* (No 2) [2002] UKHL 43, [2003] 1 All ER 173 that contributory negligence was not available as a defence to fraudulent misrepresentation.

[96] See pp 343–347, above.

[97] See pp 362–368, below.   [98] (1951) 84 CLR 377.   [99] Pp 288–290, above.

The complexities of the interrelationships between these rules are well illustrated by *Howard Marine and Dredging Co Ltd v A Ogden & Sons (Excavations) Ltd.*[100]

> The defendants were engaged by the Northumbrian Water Authority for a substantial excavation contract. This involved carrying the spoil to sea in seagoing barges and dumping it there. The defendants, although very experienced at excavation work, had no experience of dumping at sea. In order to carry out the contract they needed to charter two seagoing barges and in order to calculate their tender for the contract they needed to know the cost of chartering the barges. One factor in this cost would be the soil carrying capacity of the barges, since this would have an important input on the speed at which the earth could be removed and thereby on the length of the contract. Negotiations took place between the defendants and the plaintiffs, who were the owners of two suitable barges in the course of which the plaintiff's marine manager stated that the payload was 1600 tonnes.[101] This figure was based on his recollection of the deadweight figure of 1800 tonnes given by Lloyds Register. Very exceptionally however, the Lloyds Register was wrong. The true deadweight figure given by the barge's German shipping document (which the marine manager had seen) was 1195 tonnes, giving a payload of 1055 tonnes. In due course the defendants chartered the barges from the plaintiffs, but the written contract contained no mention of these figures.

Finding that because of the shortfall in capacity, they were not able to proceed with the work as quickly as they had planned, the defendants ceased to pay the charter hire. The plaintiffs withdrew the barges and sued for outstanding payments and the defendants counter-claimed for damages both under Misrepresentation Act 1967, section 2(1) and at common law.[102]

All the ingredients of liability under section 2(1) were present unless the plaintiffs could prove that 'they had reasonable ground to believe . . . that the facts represented were true'. There was no doubt that the marine manager had made the statement honestly and Lord Denning MR thought it was reasonable for him to rely on the Lloyds Register figure. The majority of the Court of Appeal held that it was not reasonable not to refer to the shipping documents on such an important matter. The Court was also divided in its views as to negligence at common law. Lord Denning MR thought that the situation was not one calling for care in the making of the

---

[100] [1978] QB 574, [1978] 2 All ER 1134; Sealy [1978] CLJ 229; Brownsword 41 MLR 735; Sills 96 LQR 15.

[101] This statement was made after the defendant had tendered for the excavation contract and had their tender accepted. This would appear very relevant to the quantum of any claim since much of the defendants' loss flowed from tendering at the wrong figure. The decision of the Court of Appeal was concerned only with liability and not with quantum.

[102] They also argued unsuccessfully that the statements as to payload were warranties.

statement and that in any event the marine manager had not been careless. Shaw LJ took the opposite view on both points and Bridge LJ did not reach a concluded view on either.

The case confirms that the statutory action has the advantage that there is no need to establish a duty of care. The majority view also suggests, what had not been clearly perceived before, that is, that the representor may not escape liability, simply by disproving negligence but must affirmatively prove reasonable grounds of belief.[103]

4 Innocent misrepresentation

Before 1963, the phrase 'innocent misrepresentation' was used to describe all misrepresentations which were not fraudulent. Now that two classes of negligent misrepresentation have appeared, the appellation 'innocent' should clearly be restricted to misrepresentations that are made without fault.

D Remedies for misrepresentation

1 Relationship between remedies for breach of contract and remedies for misrepresentation

As we have already seen,[104] classical doctrine drew a firm distinction between those statements which formed terms of a contract and those which constituted mere representations. The practical effect of this distinction has been diminished by the Misrepresentation Act 1967 but it remains conceptually significant. Before the Act, however, it was not clear whether the same statement could simultaneously be both a term of the contract and a mere representation.

In discussing this possibility we must consider two separate types of case. The first is where a statement is made during pre-contractual negotiations and the same statement later appears as a term of the (written) contract. In this case one might think that the representee could exercise his remedies for misrepresentation in respect of the first statement and his remedies for breach of contract in respect of the second, but there was some authority for the view that the representation 'merged' with the term so that no remedies would be available for the misrepresentation.[105] All doubts on this question are now resolved by section 1 of the Misrepresentation Act 1967, which provides:

> Where a person has entered into a contract after a misrepresentation has been made to him and—

---

[103] Exactly what this means is far from clear. See the helpful analysis by Brownsword 41 MLR 735 at 737.

[104] P 330, above.

[105] *Pennsylvania Shipping Co v Compagnie Nationale de Navigation* [1936] 2 All ER 1167. Cf *Compagnie Française des Chemins de Fer Paris-Orleans v Leeston Shipping Co* (1919) 1 Ll L Rep 235. Fairest [1967] CLJ 239 at 241–242.

(a) the misrepresentation has become a term of the contract; . . . then, if otherwise he would be entitled to rescind the contract without alleging fraud, he shall be so entitled . . . notwithstanding the matters mentioned in paragraph (a) . . . [of this section].

This obscurely worded provision means that a misrepresentee may rescind for a misrepresentation, even though the same undertaking has later become a term of the contract.

The second type of case arises where it is possible to argue that a statement, which occurs only once in the history of a transaction may be classified either as a term of the contract or as a representation. If it is classified as a representation, there would be no question of granting the remedies appropriate to a contractual term and if it is classified as a term, there would be no question of granting the remedies for 'mere representations'. In practice, the classification has always been made where the plaintiff claims damages on the ground that the statement is a term of the contract. But in the converse case where the plaintiff claims rescission for misrepresentation, it does not appear ever to have been argued that the remedy should be refused because the statement was properly classified as a term.

A good example is *Leaf v International Galleries*[106] where the plaintiff bought a picture from the defendant, which the latter stated incorrectly to have been painted by Constable. Clearly this statement might well have been held to be a term of the contract if the plaintiff had sought damages, but he wished to return the picture, and therefore sued for rescission for innocent misrepresentation. Though the Court of Appeal was clearly somewhat embarrassed at the possibility of a plaintiff being able to rescind for innocent misrepresentation when the right to reject for breach of condition was lost,[107] the case was decided on the basis that the defendant's statement was a 'mere' representation but that the right to rescind was lost by lapse of time.[108] In other cases, also, the same assumption has been allowed to go unchallenged.[109] Nevertheless it is suggested that in principle the categories of terms and representations are mutually exclusive and that a plaintiff cannot elect to treat a term as a representation. If this is so, it would follow that section 1 of the Misrepresentation Act 1967 had no application to such a case, since it is not one in which a misrepresentation has become a term, but one in which a statement has always been a term.[110]

---

[106] [1950] 2 KB 86, [1950] 1 All ER 693; p 294, above.
[107] [1950] 2 KB at 91, [1950] 1 All ER at 695.
[108] See p 357, below.
[109] Eg *Long v Lloyd* [1958] 2 All ER 402, [1958] 1 WLR 753. See Atiyah 22 MLR 76, where the argument in the text is forcefully put. See also *Naughton v O'Callaghan (Rogers, third parties)* [1990] 3 All ER 191.
[110] The thesis in this section is also important in connection with the provisions of the Misrepresentation Act as to exemption clauses—see pp 369–372, below.

2 Rescission

It is a fundamental principle that the effect of a misrepresentation is to make the contract voidable and not void.[111] This means that the contract is valid unless and until it is set aside by the representee.[112] On discovering the misrepresentation the representee may elect to affirm or to rescind the contract.

A contract is affirmed if the representee declares his intention to proceed with the contract or does some act from which such an intention may reasonably be inferred.[113]

A contract is rescinded if the representee makes it clear that he refuses to be bound by its provisions. The effect then is that the contract is terminated *ab initio* as if it had never existed. In the words of Lord Atkinson:

> Where one party to a contract expresses by word or act in an unequivocal manner that by reason of fraud or essential error of a material kind inducing him to enter into the contract he has resolved to rescind it, and refuses to be bound by it, the expression of his election, if justified by the facts, terminates the contract, puts the parties *in statu quo ante* and restores things, as between them, to the position in which they stood before the contract was entered into.[114]

An election, once it has been unequivocally made, whether in favour of affirmation or of rescission, is determined for ever.[115] It cannot be revived. If the representee elects to rescind the contract, the general rule is that within a reasonable time he must communicate his decision to the representor, for the latter is entitled to treat the contractual *nexus* as continuing until he is informed of its termination.[116] This general rule, however, is subject to two exceptions.

First, if the result of the misrepresentation is that possession of property is delivered to the representor, the recaption of the property by the representee is itself a communication of the rescission.[117]

---

[111] In exceptional cases, as in that of mistaken identity a misrepresentee may cause a mistake which may entitle the misrepresentee to treat the contract as void. But this is the result of the mistake and not of the misrepresentation.

[112] *Newbigging v Adam* (1886) 34 ChD 582 at 592.

[113] See p 357, below.

[114] *Abram Steamship Co v Westville Shipping Co Ltd* [1923] AC 773 at 781. Unfortunately the word 'rescission' is also often used to describe the position where a party elects to treat a contact as discharged because of a breach of one of the essential terms. But there the contract is not rendered void *ab initio: Mussen v Van Diemen's Land Co* [1938] Ch 253 at 260, [1938] 1 All ER 210 at 215, per Farwell LJ. The *further* liability of either party to perform the outstanding contractual obligations is terminated, but causes of action that have already arisen by virtue of the breach remain remediable by an action for damages. See *R V Ward v Bignall* [1967] 1 QB 534 at 548, [1967] 2 All ER 449 at 455, per Diplock LJ. It would clearly add greatly to clarity if the word rescission were confined to the present remedy. This has been emphasised in a number of recent decisions pp 691–692, below.

[115] *Clough v London and North Western Rly Co* (1871) LR 7 Exch 26 at 35, *per curiam.*

[116] *Car and Universal Finance Co Ltd v Caldwell* [1965] 1 QB 525, [1964] 1 All ER 290.

[117] Ibid.

Secondly, if the representor disappears so effectively that it is impossible to find him, the requirement of communication will be satisfied if the representee records his intention to rescind the contract by some overt act that is reasonable in the circumstances. This was recognised for the first time in *Car and Universal Finance Co Ltd v Caldwell*[118] on the following facts:

> The defendant sold and delivered a car to X in return for a cheque that was dishonoured the next day, by which time both the car and X had disappeared. The defendant immediately notified the police and the Automobile Association and requested them to find the car. While the search was proceeding, X sold the car to M Ltd motor dealers, who had notice of X's defective title. Ultimately, M Ltd sold the car to the plaintiffs who bought it in good faith.

It was held that the defendant, by setting the police and the Automobile Association in motion, had sufficiently evinced his intention to rescind the contract. As soon as he made this clear, the ownership of the car reverted to him, and therefore the later sale by M Ltd vested no title in the plaintiffs, the innocent purchasers.[119]

Rescission, even though enforced by a court, is always the act of the defrauded party in the sense that it is his election which effectively destroys the contractual *nexus* between him and the other party.[120] It follows that rescission is effective from the date it is communicated to the representor and not from the date of any judgment in subsequent litigation. Nevertheless, the representee may fortify his position by bringing an action for rescission in equity, a step that is desirable if the fraudulent

---

[118] N 116, above.

[119] In this case the car was not sold by the rogue X directly to the innocent purchaser. It was first sold by him to M Ltd who had notice of his defective title, and later sold to the innocent purchaser. In *Newtons of Wembley Ltd v Williams* [1965] 1 QB 560, [1964] 3 All ER 532, the facts were similar except that there was a direct sale by the rogue to the innocent buyer, and it was held that the latter acquired a good title by virtue of the Factors Act 1889, s 9.

This distinction between the effect of a direct and an indirect sale after the contract between the rogue and the true owner has been rescinded is a reproach to the law (see Cornish 27 MLR 472 at 477). The Law Reform Committee, however, has recommended in its 12th Report that until notice of rescission of a contract is communicated to the other contracting party (ie in the instant example, to the rogue) an innocent purchaser from the latter shall be able to acquire a good title (Cmnd 2958 (1966)). If statutory effect is given to this recommendation, the distinction between a direct and an indirect sale will virtually disappear, for it will usually be impossible for the true owner to communicate with the rogue before the sale to the innocent purchaser.

It would seem that the exception to the general rule recognised in *Caldwell's* case concerning communication of rescission, applies equally to a case of innocent misrepresentation, though it is difficult to envisage circumstances in which the problem would arise, since an innocent person, unlike the rogue in *Caldwell's* case, would have no occasion to abscond: [1965] 1 QB at 551–552, per Sellers LJ. Upjohn LJ left the question open: ibid at 555. In *MacLeod v Kerr* 1965 SC 253, the Court of Session took the opposite view to *Car and Universal Finance Co Ltd v Caldwell.*

[120] *Abram Steamship Co v Westville Shipping Co* [1923] AC 773 at 781.

party ignores the cancellation of the contract and if there is a possibility that innocent third parties may act on the assumption that it still exists.

As we have seen, the effect of rescission is to nullify the contract *ab initio*. An essential requirement of this remedy, where the contract has been partly or wholly performed, is therefore the restoration of the parties to their original positions. In the language of the law, *restitutio in integrum* is essential.[121]

Common law, unlike equity, provides no action for rescission. But it has always recognised that a contract is automatically terminated if the representee elects to rescind rather than to affirm it, provided that the restoration of the *status quo ante* is feasible. In this latter respect, however, common law is at a disadvantage as compared with equity. The remedial procedure at its command is not sufficiently flexible and comprehensive to enable the process of restoration to be effected according to the exigencies of each particular case. The court is restricted to saying that there can be no rescission unless the parties can be restored to the exact positions that they formerly occupied.[122]

The courts of equity, however, soon developed a suit for rescission, and since their remedial procedure was far more elastic than that of the common law, they were able to take a more realistic view of *restitutio in integrum*. In the words of Lord Blackburn, the court, in the exercise of its equitable jurisdiction, 'can take account of profits and make allowance for deterioration. And I think the practice has always been for a court of equity to give this relief whenever, by the exercise of its powers, it can do what is practically just, though it cannot restore the parties precisely to the state they were in before the contract.'[123] Therefore, if satisfied that the misrepresentation has been made, it annuls the contract and then makes such consequential orders as may be necessary in the particular circumstances to restore as far as possible the *status quo ante* of both parties.

At one time equity followed the common law in limiting relief to cases of fraudulent misrepresentation but this was seen to be too harsh a view. The rule gradually established was that where a party was induced to enter into a contract by the innocent misrepresentation of the other party, he was entitled to escape from his obligations by electing to rescind the contract. To render this election effective, he must make his intention clear by word or act to the other party, or institute a suit for rescission, or plead the misrepresentation as a defence to a suit for a specific performance.[124] It was early decided that an innocent misrepresentation was a good ground for refusal of specific performance, but for a considerable period the view prevailed that a greater degree of misrepresentation, in fact fraudulent misrepresentation, was

---

[121] See p 358, below.

[122] *Clarke v Dickson* (1858) EB & E 148 at 155. *Erlanger v New Sombrero Phosphate Co* (1878) 3 App Cas 1218 at 1278.

[123] 3 App Cas at 1278–1279. See also *Spence v Crawford* [1939] 3 All ER 271.

[124] *Rawlins v Wickham* (1858) 3 De G & J 304; *Torrance v Bolton* (1872) 8 Ch App 118.

necessary to justify a suit for rescission.[125] This illogical distinction was later abandoned, and it was established by the middle of the nineteenth century that, whether the misrepresentation was fraudulent or not, the representee was entitled to rescind the contract, and if it was written to have it delivered up for cancellation.[126]

The result of this development was that, by the middle of the nineteenth century, rescission has become a general remedy for misrepresentation though damages were available only for fraudulent misrepresentation. Rescission might often be a completely effective remedy, but this would not always be the case. If a farmer bought a cow, represented, incorrectly, to be free from tuberculin, and it infected the rest of his herd, it would comfort him little to be able to return the cow. If the representation was fraudulent there was no problem since an action for damages could be brought. If it were not fraudulent, the question arose whether the right to rescind could be manipulated so as to restore the representee entirely to the *status quo ante*. It was held that to do this *in toto* would be to give damages; but the courts drew a subtle distinction between an award of damages and the grant of an indemnity and held that the representee must be indemnified against obligations incurred as a result of the representation.

To what obligations, then, does the indemnity relate? The answer is that the plaintiff must be indemnified, not against all obligations even though they may be correctly described as having arisen under, or out of or as a result of the contract but only against those necessarily *created by* the contract.[127] The burden must be one that has passed to the representee as a necessary and inevitable result of the position which he assumed upon completion of the contract.

If, for example, A procures the dissolution of his partnership with B and C on the ground of innocent misrepresentation, he nevertheless remains personally liable for partnership debts contracted while he was a member of the firm. His position as partner was created by the contract and it is the inevitable and automatic result of having occupied this position that he is now burdened with liability for debts. Hence they are a proper subject for indemnity.

The distinction between what is true indemnity and what is equivalent to damages is neatly illustrated by *Whittington v Seale-Hayne.*[128]

The plaintiffs, who were breeders of prize poultry, were induced to take a lease of certain property belonging to the defendants by an oral representation that the premises were in a thoroughly sanitary condition. This representation was not contained in the lease that was later executed, and so was not a term of the contract.

---

[125] *Cooper v Joel* (1859) 1 De GF & J 240; *Re Liverpool Borough, Bank Duranty's Case* (1858) 26 Beav 268; *Torrance v Bolton* (1872) 8 Ch App 118; *Wauton v Coppard* [1899] 1 Ch 92.

[126] *Cadman v Horner* (1810) 18 Ves 10.

[127] *Newbigging v Adam* (1886) 34 ChD 582 at 594 per Bowen LJ; the other judges, Cotton and Fry LJJ, gave a wider scope to indemnity, but it is believed that the narrower test stated by Bowen LJ is correct. Such was the view of Farwell J in *Whittington v Seal-Hayne* (1990) 82 LT 49.

[128] (1900) 82 LT 49.

The premises were in fact insanitary. The water supply was poisoned, and in consequence the manager of the poultry farm became seriously ill, and the poultry either died or became valueless. Moreover the Urban District Council declared that the house and premises were unfit for habitation and required the plaintiffs to renew the drains.

In their action for rescission the plaintiffs, while admitting that owing to the absence of fraud they could not recover damages, contended that they were entitled to an indemnity against the consequences of having entered into the contract. These consequences were serious, since they included the following losses: value of stock lost, £750; loss of profit on sales, £100; loss of breeding season, £500; rent and removal of stores, £75; medical expense, £100. It was held that the claim for the plaintiffs in respect of these losses was in effect a claim for damages, and that their right to an indemnity was limited to what they had expended upon rates and to the cost of effecting the repairs ordered by the Council. The obligation to pay rates and to effect the repairs were obligations which the plaintiffs were required to assume by the contract; but the contract created no obligation to erect sheds, to appoint a manager or to stock the premises with poultry.

The practical importance of the distinction between indemnity and damages has been reduced by recent developments which have extended the right to damages,[129] Further, as we shall see,[130] the Misrepresentation Act 1967, section 2(2), gives the court a general power to grant damages in lieu of rescission. But there will remain cases in which the representee has no *right* to damages and in which the court will decide not to use its *power* to grant damages. In such cases the distinction will still be operative.

The orthodox view is that partial rescission is not possible[131] though the High Court of Australia has taken the opposite view[132] and powerful arguments have been advanced against the orthodox view.[133]

3 Limits to the right of recission

It is a paradoxical result of the history of this branch of the law that rescission should be regarded as the second best alternative to damages. In fact, it is in many ways a much more drastic remedy and it is natural therefore that restrictions have been placed upon its availability. The right to rescind is lost (i) if the representee has affirmed the contract; (ii) in certain circumstances by lapse of time; (iii) if *restitutio in integrum* is no longer possible, or (iv) if rescission would deprive a third party of a right in the

---

[129] Under *Hedley Byrne & Co Ltd v Heller & Partners Ltd* and Misrepresentation Act 1967, s 2(1).

[130] P 362, below.

[131] *De Molestina v Ponton* [2002] EWHC 2413 (Comm), [2002] 1 All ER (Comm) 587; *TSB Bank plc v Camfield* [1995] 1 All ER 951.

[132] *Vardasz v Pioneer Concrete (SA) Pty Ltd* (1995) 184 CLR 102

[133] Poole and Keyser, 121 LQR 273.

subject matter of the contract which he has acquired in good faith and for value. We shall now consider these limits *seriatim* and then discuss the changes made by the Misrepresentation Act 1967.

a Affirmation of the contract Affirmation is complete and binding when the representee, with full knowledge of the facts and of the misrepresentation, either declares his intention to proceed with the contract or does some act from which such an intention may reasonably be inferred.[134] The Reports contain many examples of implicit affirmation by shareholders. A person who applies for and obtains shares upon the faith of a prospectus containing misrepresentation is entitled to rescind the allotment and to recover the price paid; but if after learning of the misrepresentation he attempts to sell the shares or pays money due upon the allotment or retains dividends paid to him, he loses his right of rescission, since these acts show an intention to treat the contract as subsisting.[135] They are acts of ownership over the shares wholly inconsistent with an intention to repudiate the allotment.

b Lapse of time Lapse of time without any step towards repudiation being taken does not in itself constitute affirmation, but it may be treated as evidence of affirmation, and it was said in a leading case that when the lapse of time is great 'it probably would in practice be treated as conclusive evidence' of an election to recognise the contract.[136] Everything depends upon the facts of the case and the nature of the contract. In particular it is material to consider whether the representor has altered his position in the reasonable belief that rescission will not be enforced, or whether third parties have been misled by the inactivity of the representee.[137]

In principle, lapse of time can only be evidence of affirmation if it comes after the representee has discovered that he is entitled to rescind. But in *Leaf v International Galleries*,[138] it was held that a contract for the sale of goods could not be rescinded on the basis of a non-fraudulent misrepresentation when five years had elapsed between the sale and discovery of the truth. It was said that 'it behoves the purchaser either to '

[134] *Clough v London and North Western Rly Co* (1871) LR 7 Exch 26 at 34, *Seddon v North Eastern Salt Co Ltd* [1905] 1 Ch 326 at 334; *Car and Universal Finance Co Ltd v Caldwell* [1965] 1 QB 525 at 550, [1964] 1 All ER 290 at 293. The difficult case of *Long v Lloyd* [1958] 2 All ER 402, [1958] 1 WLR 753, would seem to have been decided on the ground that the plaintiff's conduct amounted to an affirmation of the contract: see especially [1958] 1 WLR 761. The *ratio decidendi*, however, is not clear; see Atiyah 22 MLR 76; Odgers [1958] CLJ 166. It appears that the representee must know not only of facts entitling him to rescind but also of his right to rescind *Peyman v Lanjani* [1985] Ch 457, [1984] 3 All ER 703. Affirmation may bar the right to rescind but leave intact any right to damages, *Production Technology Consultants v Bartlett* [1988] 1 EGLR 182, 25 EG 121.
[135] *Re Hop and Malt Exchange and Warehouse Co, ex p Briggs* (1866) LR 1 Eq 483; *Scholey v Central Rly Co of Venezuela* (1868) LR 9 Eq 266, n.
[136] *Clough v London and North Western Rly Co* (1871) LR 7 Exch 26 at 35.
[137] *Lindsay Petroleum Co v Hurd* (1874) LR 5 PC 221 at 240; *Aaron's Reef v Twiss* [1896] AC 273 at 294.
[138] [1950] 2 KB 86, [1950] 1 All ER 693.

verify or, as the case may be, to disprove the representation within a reasonable time, or else stand or fall by it'.[139] It may be doubted whether this reasoning would apply to a fraudulent representation.

c Restitutio in integrum **impossible** Part of the consequential relief to which a representee is entitled upon rescission is the recovery of anything that he may have paid or delivered under the contract. It is, however, a necessary corollary of this right that he should make a similar restoration of anything obtained by him under the contract. Otherwise the main object of rescission, which is that the parties should both be remitted to their former position, would not be attained. A buyer, for instance, who avoided a contract for misrepresentation, would not be able to recover the price in full while retaining the goods. This would be inequitable as well as inconsistent with the object of rescission.

> Though the defendant has been fraudulent, he must not be robbed, nor must the plaintiff be unjustly enriched, as he would be if he both got back what he had parted with and kept what he had received in return. The purpose of relief is not punishment, but compensation.[140]

The rule is, therefore, that rescission cannot be enforced if events which have occurred since the contract and in which the representee has participated make it impossible to restore the parties substantially to their original position. The representee must be, not only willing, but also able, to make *restitutio in integrum*.

This doctrine finds its most common application when the things delivered to the representee under the contract have been radically changed in extent or character by him or with his consent. Thus if a partnership in which the representee was induced to take shares is converted into a limited liability company, rescission is excluded, since the existing shares are wholly different in nature and status from those originally received.[141] Rescission is equally impossible if the subject matter of the contract is a mine that has been worked out[142] or operated for a substantial time,[143] or if it comprises goods that have been consumed or altered by the buyer.[144]

The rule requiring restoration is not, however, enforced to the letter if the result will be unfair. Thus property transferred by the defendant may have deteriorated in the hands of the plaintiff, so that it cannot be restored in its original state. Nevertheless, provided that its substantial identity remains, its restoration will be ordered on the terms that the plaintiff pay compensation for its deterioration. It is considered fairer

---

[139] Ibid at 92 and 696, respectively, per Jenkins LJ.

[140] *Spence v Crawford* [1939] 3 All ER 271 at 288–289, per Lord Wright.

[141] *Clark v Dickson* (1858) EB & E 148; *Western Bank of Scotland v Addie* (1867) LR 1 Sc & Div 145.

[142] *Vigers v Pike* (1842) 8 Cl & Fin 562.

[143] *Attwood v Small* (1838) 6 Cl & Fin 232; *Clarke v Dickson*, n 141 above.

[144] *Clarke v Dickson*, (1858) EB & E 148 at 155, per Crompton J.

on equitable principles that the defendant should be compelled to accept compensation than to keep the full profit of his wrongdoing.[145]

d Injury to third parties The right of the representee to elect whether he will affirm or disaffirm a contract procured by misrepresentation is subject to this limitation, that, if before he reaches a decision an innocent third party acquires for value an interest in the subject matter of the contract, the right of rescission is defeated.[146]

The most frequent instance of this limitation is where goods have been obtained from their owner by fraud. If the fraud makes the contract void at common law on the grounds already discussed in the chapter on Mistake,[147] no title passes to the fraudulent person and the latter can pass none to any third party, however innocent this third party may be. If, however, the contract is voidable only, then the title so obtained by the fraudulent person is valid until it has been avoided, and any transfer of it made before avoidance to an innocent third party for valuable consideration cannot be defeated by the owner.[148] An apt illustration of the rule is *White v Garden*[149] where the facts were these:

> Parker bought fifty tons of iron from Garden by persuading him to take in payment a bill of exchange which had apparently been accepted by one Thomas of Rochester. Parker resold the iron to White, who acted in good faith, and Garden made delivery in one of his barges at White's wharf. Garden, upon discovering that the bill of exchange was worthless since there was no such person as Thomas of Rochester, seized and removed part of the iron that was still in the barge.

Garden was held liable in trover. The title to the iron had passed to Parker under a contract that was temporarily valid and, while still undisturbed, had been passed to an innocent purchaser. It was not a case of operative mistake, since Garden intended to contract with Parker. It must be added that a third party, if he is to acquire an indefeasible title under a voidable contract, must not only act *bona fide*, but also give consideration.[150] In one case for instance:

> A debtor and his surety persuaded the creditor to accept from the debtor a transfer of a mortgage which the debtor knew to be imaginary but which the surety believed to be valid. Later, at the solicitation of the surety and in reliance on the transfer which he believed to be genuine, the creditor released the surety from further obligation.[151]

---

[145] *Lagunas Nitrate Co v Lagunas Syndicate* [1899] 2 Ch 392 at 457, pre Rigby LJ; adopted in *Spence v Crawford* [1939] 3 All ER 271 at 279–280. See also *Newbigging v Adam* (1886) 34 ChD 582; *Adam v Newbigging* (1888) 13 App Cas 308.

[146] *Clough v London and North Western Rly Co* (1871) LR 7 Exch 26 at 35.   [147] Ch 8, above.

[148] *White v Garden* (1851) 10 CB 919; *Babcock v Lawson* (1879) 4 QBD 394, affd (1880) 5 QBD 284; *Phillips v Brooks Ltd* [1919] 2 KB 243; *Stevenson v Newnham* (1853) 13 CB 285 at 302, per Parke B.

[149] (1851) 10 CB 919.

[150] *Scholefield v Templer* (1859) 4 De G & J 429 at 433–443, per Lord Campbell.

[151] Ibid.

It was held that the creditor was entitled to rescind the release and to be restored to his rights against the surety, since the latter, though honest, had given no consideration for his release.

Another type of case where the remedy of rescission is affected by the existence of third party rights, concerns the winding-up of companies. A person who is induced to become a shareholder by reason of a false representation is entitled to rescind the contract as against the company, which means that he can divest himself of the shares and recover what he has paid. But this right is lost if its exercise will prejudice the creditors of the company. The established rule is, therefore, that the commencement of winding-up proceedings completely bars the right of a shareholder to avoid the contract under which he obtained his shares.[152]

e Effect of Misrepresentation Act 1967 The law relating to limits to the right of rescission was substantially amended by section 1 of the Misrepresentation Act 1967 which provides:

> Where a person has entered into a contract after a misrepresentation has been made to him, and—
>
> (a) the misrepresentation has become a term of the contract; or
>
> (b) the contract has been performed;
>
> or both, then, if otherwise he would be entitled to rescind the contract without alleging fraud, he shall be so entitled, subject to the provisions of this Act, notwithstanding the matters mentioned in paragraphs (a) and (b) of this section.

The effect of this provision is that the only limits to the right of rescission are now the four already mentioned. The purpose of the section can only be understood by examining the pre-existing law. We have already discussed paragraph (a).[153] Paragraph (b) was designed to abolish two previous rules, or perhaps more accurately, one rule and one supposed rule, viz: the rule in *Wilde v Gibson* and the rule in *Seddon v North Eastern Salt Co Ltd.*

In *Wilde v Gibson*,[154] the House of Lords held that a conveyance of land could not be avoided after completion on the basis of an innocent misrepresentation by the vendor about a defect in title, viz the existence of a right of way. Lord Campbell said that 'where the conveyance has been executed . . . a court of equity will set aside the conveyance only on the ground of actual fraud'.[155] It can be seen that there is much to be said for this rule, since it is the normal practice of purchasers to employ solicitors who carry out a full investigation of title. These considerations would not apply so strongly to physical defects in the property though the employment of surveyors is becoming more common and would have little weight in the case of sale of goods or shares or the performance of other contracts.

---

[152] *Oakes v Turquand and Harding* (1867) LR 2 HL 325.
[153] Pp 350–351, above.   [154] (1848) 1 HL Cas 605.   [155] Ibid at 632–633.

Despite these considerations, Joyce J in *Seddon v North-Eastern Salt Co Ltd*[156] treating Lord Campbell's statement in *Wilde v Gibson* as one of general application, purported to lay down a rule that 'the court will not grant rescission of an executed contract for the sale of a chattel or chose in action on the ground of an innocent misrepresentation'.[157] This rule was clearly based on a misunderstanding of the rationale of *Wilde v Gibson*; it ignored contrary earlier authority[158] and it was not even necessary for the decision in *Seddon's* case itself, since the representee had affirmed the contract. Yet it succeeded in muddying the waters for the next sixty years. It was applied in *Angel v Jay*[159] to an executed lease induced by an innocent misrepresentation that the drains were not defective and it was restated by McCardie J in *Armstrong v Jackson*.[160] In three cases in the 1950s[161] the Court of Appeal had an opportunity to confirm or overrule *Seddon's* case but in each case the opportunity was spurned and the decision went on other grounds, though in the first two of the cases Denning LJ declared that the rule did not exist.

If the authority of the rule in *Seddon's* case was doubted, its injustice was almost universally accepted. In its 10th Report,[162] the Law Reform Committee agreed with this verdict and recommended the abolition of the rule in *Seddon's* case. The Committee thought however that the rule in *Wilde v Gibson* should be retained in the interests of finality and that it should apply both to defects in title and to physical defects and to sales and long leases of land.[163]

It will be seen that Parliament has abolished both rules so that it is now possible for a representee to seek rescission of any type of contract including one for the sale of land even though it has been performed. It would seem that this change has created the possibility of considerable hardship to an owner-occupier who sells his house and uses the purchase money to buy another. Such a vendor will normally only be able to repay the purchase price by selling his new house and rearranging a mortgage on his old house. It is clear that justice does not always require these heavy burdens to be imposed on an innocent representor-vendor and it is important therefore in considering the practical effect of section 1(b) of the Act to bear in mind that under section 2(2) the court now has a general power to give damages in lieu of rescission.[164] It would seem that this type of case might well be one where the court would choose to exercise this power.

---

[156] [1905] 1 Ch 326.   [157] Reporter's headnote. See [1905] 1 Ch 332–333.

[158] See Hammelmann 55 LQR 90. But cf Howard 26 MLR 272.

[159] [1911] 1 KB 666.   [160] [1917] 2 KB 822 at 825.

[161] *Solle v Butcher* [1950] 1 KB 671, [1949] 2 All ER 1107; *Leaf v International Galleries* [1950] 2 KB 86, [1950] 1 All ER 693; *Long v Lloyd* [1958] 2 All ER 402, [1958] 1 WLR 753.

[162] Cmnd 1782, paras 3 to 13 (1962).

[163] The committee recommended drawing a line between long and short leases by using the test provided by s 54(2) of the Law of Property Act 1925.

[164] See p 356, above.

4 Damages

We have seen that as the law has finally developed, any misrepresentation gives rise to a right in the representee to rescind. The right to damages, on the other hand, is not universal but depends on showing that the representor's statement is either fraudulent or negligent in the senses set out above. However the Misrepresentation Act 1967 made a further important change by conferring on the court a general power to grant damages in lieu of rescission. By section 2(2) of the Act it is provided that:

> Where a person has entered into a contract after a misrepresentation has been made to him otherwise than fraudulently, and he would be entitled by reason of the misrepresentation to rescind the contract, then, if it is claimed in any of the proceedings arising out of the contract that the contract ought to be or has been rescinded, the court or arbitrator may declare the contract subsisting and award damages in lieu of rescission, if of the opinion that it would be equitable to do so, having regard to the nature of the misrepresentation and the loss that would be caused by it if the contract were upheld, as well as to the loss that rescission would cause the other party.

Thus, the victim of an innocent misrepresentation may be awarded damages instead of, but not in addition to, rescission if the court in its discretion considers it equitable to do so. It is clear that either the claimant or the defendant may seek to persuade the court that it would be equitable to award damages in lieu of rescission.[165]

For subsection 2(2) of the Act to operate, the facts must be such that the representee 'would be entitled by reason of the misrepresentation, to rescind the contract'. In previous editions of this work, it was argued that these words meant that the remedy of rescission must still be available for the plaintiff at the time of the action and that if he had lost the right of rescission, for instance because *restitutio in integrum* was no longer possible or because an innocent third party had acquired an interest in the subject matter of the contract then the exercise of the judicial discretion to give damages under section 2(2) of the Act was at an end. However, this reasoning was rejected by Jacob J in *Thomas Witter Ltd v TBP Industries Ltd.*[166] In this case, Jacob J held that it was not necessary that the right to rescind should be available at the time the court gave judgment. He thought that judicial discretion would exist if the right to rescind had ever existed or at the least that the right to rescind existed when the representee first sought to rescind. On the facts of the case, it was not necessary to choose between these alternatives. Jacob J relied on his interpretation of the legislative history of this part of the Misrepresentation Act but

---

[165] *UCB Corporate Services Ltd v Thomason* [2005] 1 All ER (Comm) 601.
[166] [1996] 2 All ER 573.

other interpretations of the Parliamentary discussions do not point so clearly to his conclusion.[167]

Under section 2(2) of the Act, rescission and damages are alternatives; but if the representee has a right to damages because of the representor's fraud or negligence, he may sue for damages either instead of or as well as rescinding. In these cases rescission and damages are in no sense mutually exclusive though clearly the amount of damages to which the representee will be entitled will be effected by whether or not he has successfully rescinded. In some cases rescission will repair all the loss the representee has suffered but in other cases he will have suffered consequential loss.[168]

In any case, whenever the representee seeks damages, it will be necessary to decide upon what principles damages are to be assessed. It appears not improbable that different rules apply to each of the possible heads of claim and it is therefore necessary to consider them *seriatim*. But before doing so a basic distinction must be drawn between damages in contract and damages in tort. This distinction is important for two reasons. First, the purpose of damages is different in contract and in tort. In contract the object of damages is to put the injured party as nearly as may be in the position he would have enjoyed if the contract had been performed; in tort it is to restore the injured party to the position he occupied before the tort was committed. This difference in approach will mean that sometimes a greater sum can be obtained in contract than in tort and sometimes a greater sum in tort than in contract though in other cases it may make no difference.[169] Secondly, the test of remoteness of damage in tort is generally foreseeability at the moment of breach of duty; in contract it appears that some higher degree of probability than is embraced by the word 'foreseeable' is required and it is clear that the relevant moment is that of the making of the contract.[170]

We will now consider each of the possible claims for damages in turn.

---

[167] See Beale 111 LQR 385 and His Honour Judge Jack QC in *Zanzibar v British Aerospace (Lancaster House) Ltd* [2000] CLC 735. The Court of Appeal appear to have taken the opposite view in *Sindall v Cambridgeshire County Council* [1994] 3 All ER 932 which had not been reported when *Thomas Witter Ltd v TBP Industries Ltd* was decided in 1994 and was not cited to Jacob J. See also *The Lucy* [1983] 1 Lloyds Rep 188.

[168] See eg the example of the infected cow, p 355, above. In these cases the plaintiff is rescinding the contract and pursuing a claim in tort. A plaintiff cannot normally rescind the contract for initial invalidity and at the same time seek damages for breach of that contract. See Albery 91 LQR 337.

[169] Suppose for instance that X buys and pays for a set of dining-room chairs represented incorrectly to be Chippendale and that he is unable to rescind. Then if A is the actual price, B the value of a genuine set of Chippendale chairs of this type and C the actual value of the chairs bought then prima facie the amount recoverable in contract would be B–C and in tort A–C. Only if A and B are the same will the amount recoverable in tort and contract be the same. If A is greater than B, the plaintiff should try to formulate his claim in tort. If B is greater than A he should try to formulate it in contract. In either case there may also be claims for consequential loss, which will be governed by the rules of remoteness stated in the text.

[170] For fuller discussion of these problems in contract, see pp 751–797, below, and for tort, see Salmond and Heuston *The Law of Torts* (20th edn) pp 515–540; Winfield and Jolowicz *Tort* (14th edn) pp 147–188 and 632–675; Street *The Law of Torts* (9th edn) pp 249–264.

a For fraudulent misrepresentation It is clear that the claim for damages for fraudulent misrepresentation is a claim in tort. So the general governing rule is that the
plaintiff should be restored to the position he would have been in if the representation
had not been made.[171] It is sometimes deduced from this that a plaintiff in an action
for deceit cannot recover damages for loss of profit. That this is too simple a view is
shown by the decision of the Court of Appeal in *East v Maurer*.[172] In this case, the first
defendant owned two ladies hairdressing salons. In 1979 the plaintiffs bought one of
them for £20,000. During the negotiations, the first defendant said that he did not
intend to work at the second salon except in emergencies and intended to open a salon
abroad. In fact, he continued to work at the second salon and this was extremely
damaging to the business since many of his customers in the first salon moved to the
second salon. Since the first defendant had not contracted that he would not work in
the second salon, the plaintiffs could not recover the profits they would have made
if they had not had to face his competition. However, the Court of Appeal held that if
the plaintiffs had not bought the business at all, they would have invested money in
another hairdressing business which would have been profitable. However, the
appropriate sum to compensate for this loss was based on an assessment of what profit
the plaintiffs would have made in another business, granted their relative lack of
experience, rather than on an assessment of the profits which the first defendant had
been making in the old business. There is authority moreover for the view that in
considering what consequential loss can be recovered, the test of remoteness is not the
normal one of foreseeability. In *Doyle v Olby (Ironmongers)*,[173] the Court of Appeal
held that 'the defendant is bound to make reparation for all the actual damages
directly flowing from the fraudulent inducement . . . it does not lie in the mouth
of the fraudulent person to say that [the damage] could not reasonably have been
foreseen'.[174]

---

[171] *McGregor Damages* (15th edn) paras 1718–1722. Winfield and Jolowicz *Tort* (14th edn) p 289.
[172] [1991] 2 All ER 733.
[173] [1969] 2 QB 158 [1969] 2 All ER 119.
[174] Ibid at 167 and 122, respectively. The Court of Appeal relied on the discussion in Mayne and
McGregor *Damages* (12th edn) paras 955–957. Cf the critical discussion by Treitel 32 MLR 556. At
one time it was not clear whether exemplary damages might be recovered in deceit, *Mafo v Adams* [1970]
1 QB 548, [1969] 3 All ER 1404; *Denison v Fawcett* (1958) 12 DLR (2d) 537, but there were clear
statements that they could not in *Cassell & Co Ltd v Broome* [1972] AC 1027, [1972] 1 All ER 801, per
Lord Hailsham LC at 1076, 828, respectively, and per Lord Diplock at 1131, 874, respectively. See also
Archer v Brown [1985] QB 401, [1984] 2 All ER 267. The topic of exemplary damages was considered by
the Law Commission in its Report *Aggravated, Exemplary and Restitutionary Damages* (Law Com No
247) (1997) which recommended the retention of exemplary damages and indeed some extension of the
possibility. The Government (Hansard (H C Debates) 9 November 1999 Col 502) indicated that it was
right to defer a decision on further legislation. The whole question should now be reconsidered in the light
of the decision of the House of Lords in *Kuddus v Chief Constable of Leicestershire Constabulary* [2001]
UKHL 29, [2001] 3 All ER 193 that exemplary damages might be available for the tort of misfeasance in
public office. The reasoning of at least some of the speeches in this case supports the view that there may be
circumstances in which exemplary damages may be recovered in deceit.

An interesting question arose in *Smith New Court Securities Ltd v Scrimgeour Vickers*.[175] In this case, the plaintiffs had been induced to buy a parcel of shares in Ferranti at 82.25p per share by a fraudulent misrepresentation made by an employee of the defendants. At the time of the contract, the shares were trading in the market at about 78p per share. However, unknown to both parties and by reason of a wholly unconnected fraud, the shares were grossly overvalued. Ferranti had been the victims of a major fraud by an American confidence trickster who had sold a worthless business to them. On discovering the fraud, the plaintiffs might have elected to rescind the contract but instead they chose to dispose of the shares through the market at prices ranging from 49p to 30p per share. If the plaintiffs had elected to rescind, they would have avoided the whole of the loss but the Court of Appeal held that, in an action for damages, the plaintiffs could only recover the difference between the contract price and the market price at the date of the contract, that is 4.25p per share, and not the difference between the contract price and what the shares were actually worth at the date of the contract (in the Court's valuation 44p per share). The House of Lords disagreed and held that the plaintiffs could recover the whole of their loss.[176] In the words of Lord Steyn

> The legal measure is to compare the position of the plaintiff as it was before the fraudulent statement was made to him with his position as it became as a result of his reliance on the fraudulent statement.[177]

b For negligent misstatement at common law Here again it is clear that the claim is one in tort and so the tortious rules apply. Furthermore, since the action lies in negligence, there can be no doubt that any problems of remoteness are to be resolved by applying the foreseeability test. In *Esso Petroleum Co Ltd v Mardon*,[178] the Court of Appeal applied the same test to damages for breach of warranty and for negligence but this was because the warranty was that the forecast was carefully made and not that it was correct.

In *South Australia Asset Management Corpn v York Montague Ltd*[179] a number of cases were considered in which the claimants had lent money to enable property developers to buy commercial properties at the height of a property boom. The borrowers were unable to repay the loans when the boom collapsed and the claimants sought to argue that they had only lent the money relying on negligent valuations of the property by defendant valuers. In those cases where negligence was established, the

---

[175] [1994] 4 All ER 225.   [176] [1996] 4 All ER 769.

[177] In *Clef Aquitaine SARL v Laporte Materials (Barrow) Ltd* [2000] 3 All ER 493 the claimant as a result of the defendant's fraud entered into two long-term distribution agreements. The agreements were profitable but not as profitable as they would have been if the truth had been revealed at the time the contract was made. The Court of Appeal held that the claimant could recover damages to compensate for the loss of this extra profit.

[178] [1976] QB 801, [1976] 2 All ER 5. Discussed pp 346–347, above.

[179] [1996] 3 All ER 365

claimants argued that they would not have entered into the transaction at all but for the negligent valuation and that they should therefore recover all the loss that they had suffered. This argument was accepted by the Court of Appeal but rejected by the House of Lords which held that the claimants could only recover that part of the loss which foreseeably followed from the careless valuation and not that part which flowed from collapse of the property market.[180]

c Under the Misrepresentation Act 1967 Neither section 2(1) nor section 2(2) of the Misrepresentation Act 1967 contains any statement of the test to be applied in assessing damages under them. The only dim clue is provided by section 2(3) which states:

> Damages may be awarded against a person under subsection (2) of this section whether or not he is liable to damages under subsection (1) therefore, but where he is so liable any award under the said subsection (2) shall be taken into account in assessing his liability under the said subsection (1).

This perhaps suggests that less may be recovered under section 2(2) than under section 2(1) and this would not be irrational since the defendant needs to be at fault for the action to succeed under section 2(1) but not under section 2(2). It still leaves unresolved the tests to be applied.

It has been suggested[181] that damages under section 2(1) should be calculated on the same principles as govern the tort of deceit. This suggestion is based on a theory that section 2(1) is based on a 'fiction of fraud'. We have already suggested that this theory is misconceived.[182] On the other hand the action created by section 2(1) does look much more like an action in tort than one in contract and it is suggested that the rules for negligence are the natural ones to apply.[183]

However, although it is thought that this approach is correct in principle the earliest cases to arise were against it. In *Jarvis v Swans Tours Ltd*[184] Lord Denning MR said[185] 'it is not necessary to decide whether they were representations or warranties; because, since the Misrepresentation Act 1967, there is a remedy in damages for misrepresentation as well as of breach of warranty', and in *Watts v Spence*[186] Graham J gave damages for loss of bargain under section 2(1) of the Misrepresentation Act

---

[180] It will be seen that this rule is considerably less favourable to the claimant than that laid down for deceit above p 364. A further complication in these valuation cases is that the valuer may plausibly argue that the claimant's lending policy was partly to blame and that this amounts to contributory negligence. See *Platform Home Loans Ltd v Oyston Shipways Ltd* [1999] 1 All ER 833.

[181] Atiyah and Treitel 30 MLR 369 at 373–374. But cf Treitel *The Law of Contract* (10th edn) pp 335–337.

[182] P 347, above.

[183] Taylor 45 MLR 139; Cartwright [1987] Conv 423; Wadsley 54 MLR 698.

[184] [1973] QB 233, [1973] 1 All ER 71. See also *Gosling v Anderson* (1972) 223 Estates Gazette 1743.

[185] Ibid at 237 and 73, respectively.

[186] [1976] Ch 165, [1975] 2 All ER 528, criticised Baker 91 LQR 307.

1967. In neither case however does the difference between damages in contract and in tort appear to have been in the forefront of the argument.

More recently Ackner J in *André & Cie SA v Ets Michel Blanc & Fils*[187] considered the matter more fully and held that the tortious measure was the correct one to apply. In *Naughton v O'Callaghan (Rogers, third parties)*[188] the plaintiff bought a thorough-bred yearling colt at the Newmarket sales in September 1981. It was described in the catalogue at 'Lot 200. A chestnut colt named Fondu' and as having a sire called Nomalco whose dam was Habanna whose sire in turn was Habitat. Habitat was establishing a good reputation as a sire of winners and class horses and Habanna was a good class horse which had won two races. The plaintiff paid 26,000 guineas for the horse. Some two years later, after Fondu had unsuccessfully taken part in six races, it was discovered that Fondu was not the son of Habanna at all but of Moon Min. On these facts the plaintiff might plausibly have argued that it was a term of the contract that Fondu's dam was Habanna. However, although it was clear by the time of the action that the horse was worth much less than the 26,000 guineas paid for it in 1981, the evidence was that in 1981 Fondu would have reached a figure near to 26,000 guineas even if the pedigree had been correctly stated in the catalogue. The plaintiff therefore formulated his claim as one for misrepresentation. On this basis, he recovered the training fees and the cost of keeping the horse between the date of the purchase and the date when he discovered its true pedigree.

In the most recent decision of the Court of Appeal in *Royscot Trust Ltd v Rogerson*,[189] the Court enthusiastically embraced the fiction of fraud and purported to grant damages based on a deceit measure on the grounds that the words were clear. Of course, in construing the terms of a statute, words are clear if the interpreter has no doubt even though other people may think the words bear a different meaning. Of course, anyone who thought the words were not clear would want to consider whether it was sensible to have the same rule for fraudulent and non fraudulent misrepresenta-tion or, indeed, whether the draftsman in 1967 would have been clear about a rule whose principal authority was a decision of the Court of Appeal in 1969. In fact, in appears very doubtful whether the decision of the Court of Appeal would have been different if they had applied the negligence rule, since they held the critical event to be reasonably foreseeable.[190]

As far as section 2(2) is concerned, it is pertinent to stress that damages under this subsection are given in lieu of rescission. It seems probable, therefore, that in the case

---

[187] [1977] 2 Lloyd's Rep 166 at 181. Ackner J's judgment was affirmed by the Court of Appeal [1979] 2 Lloyd's Rep 427 but this point was not considered. See also *McNally v Welltrade International* [1978] IRLR 497. *Chesneau v Interhome Ltd* [1983] CLY 988.

[188] [1990] 3 All ER 191.

[189] [1991] 3 All ER 294.

[190] In *Smith New Court Securities Ltd v Scrimgeour Vickers (Asset Management) Ltd* [1996] 4 All ER 769, p 322, above both Lord Browne-Wilkinson and Lord Steyn went out of their way to say that they were expressing no view about the correctness of *Royscot*.

of innocent misrepresentation, the Act does not disturb the rule that financial relief for consequential loss should be limited to an indemnity. It is suggested therefore that in assessing damages under section 2(2), the guiding rule is to produce, as nearly as maybe, the same effect as could be obtained by rescission plus indemnity and not to recoup consequential loss which would fall outside this limited relief. Thus on facts such as those in *Whittington v Seale-Hayne*[191] it would seem that a plaintiff whose claim to damages rested solely on section 2(2) would not be compensated for such items as the value of stock lost. This was in substance the view taken by Jacob J in *Thomas Witter Ltd v TBP Industries Ltd.*[192] The matter was also discussed by the Court of Appeal in *William Sindall plc v Cambridgeshire County Council*[193] though *obiter* since the Court was agreed that there had in fact been no misrepresentation. The Court were agreed that, if there had been a misrepresentation, it would have been an appropriate case to give damages in lieu of rescission since to rescind would have been to transfer back to the representor not only the loss flowing from the subject matter of the misrepresentation (the absence of a sewer) but also the whole loss caused by a quite independent collapse in the property market. Both Hoffmann and Evans LJJ agreed that damages under section 2(2) were different from damages under section 2(1). Hoffmann LJ said:

> Damages under section 2(2) should never exceed the sum which would have been awarded if the representation had been a warranty. It is not necessary for present purposes to discuss the circumstances in which they may be less.[194]

E Review of effects of Misrepresentation Act 1967[195]

Our discussion has involved very frequent references to the Misrepresentation Act 1967 but it is perhaps worthwhile now to attempt to look at the Act as a whole.

Although there can be little doubt that the general effect of the Act will be to improve the lot of representees as a class, this has been achieved at the cost of making an already complex branch of the law still more complicated. At least three factors have contributed to this. The first was the general policy decision to proceed by a limited number of statutory amendments to the common law. This means that the Act can only be understood if the previous law has been mastered and since the previous law was often far from clear the Act has been erected on an uncertain base. Secondly, the Act was based on the view of the common law taken by the Law Reform Committee in 1962, which was overtaken by the decision in *Hedley Bryne & Co Ltd v Heller & Partners.*[196] This has meant the creation of two different kinds of negligent misrepresentation with different rules and an uncertain relationship. Thirdly, these

[191] (1900) 82 LT 49. See p 355, above.
[192] [1996] 2 All ER 573.   [193] [1994] 3 All ER 932   [194] [1994] 3 All ER 932 at 955.
[195] Atiyah and Treitel 30 MLR 369; Fairest [1967] CLJ 239.
[196] [1964] AC 465, [1963] 2 All ER 575.

defects in approach were compounded by drafting which is frequently obscure and sometimes defective.[197]

An important example of the type of problem created by the Act is the meaning of the phrases 'after a misrepresentation has been made to him' (which occurs three times in sections 1 and 2) and 'any misrepresentation made by him' (which occurs in section 3). The Act does not define 'misrepresentation' and the question has been raised whether these words are apt to extend to situations where the law imposes a duty of disclosure.[198] It would seem reasonably clear that the Act extends to those cases where silence is treated as assertive conduct, as where it distorts a positive assertion made by the representor or where the representor fails to reveal that an earlier statement made by him is no longer true.[199] It is much more debatable whether the word 'misrepresentation' is wide enough to cover cases of non-disclosure *stricto sensu*,[200] such as contracts *uberrimae fidei*, but even here it might be argued that failure to disclose the existence of a material fact is equivalent to affirmation of its non-existence. Similar difficulties may arise from the failure to define the meaning of 'rescission' in the Act.[201]

We have already dealt at length with the effects of sections 1 and 2 of the Act. Both are concerned to improve the representee's remedies for misrepresentation, section 1 by removing possible limits to the right of rescission and section 2 by widening the possibility of obtaining damages. Apart from section 5, which deals with problems of retrospectivity, the other enacting sections of the Act are sections 3 and 4. Section 4 made some changes in the Sale of Goods Act designed to render the buyer's right to reject for breach of condition less liable to defeasance. Section 3 calls for further discussion.

Misrepresentation and exemption clauses

In its original form section 3 provided:

> If any agreement (whether made before or after the commencement of this Act) contains a provision which would exclude or restrict—
>
> > (a) any liability to which a party to a contract may be subject by reason of any misrepresentation made by him before the contract was made; or
> >
> > (b) any remedy available to another party to the contract by reason of such a misrepresentation;
>
> that provision shall be of no effect except to the extent (if any) that, in any proceeding arising out of the contract, the court or arbitrator may allow reliance on it as being fair and reasonable in the circumstances of the case.

---

[197] See Atiyah and Treitel, above, and the critical remarks of the New Zealand Contracts and Commercial Law Reform Committee in their Report on Misrepresentation and Breach of Contract (1967). See now Contractual Remedies Act 1979 (New Zealand).

[198] Atiyah and Treitel 30 MLR 369–370; Hudson 85 LQR 524.   [199] Pp 335–337, above.

[200] See pp 372–379, below.   [201] Atiyah and Treitel 30 MLR 370–371.

In 1977, section 8 of the Unfair Contract Terms Act provided for an amended version, which now reads:

> 3. If a contract contains a term which would exclude or restrict—
>
> > (a) any liability to which a party to a contract may be subject by reason of any misrepresentation made by him before the contract was made; or
> >
> > (b) any remedy available to another party to the contract by reason of such a misrepresentation;
>
> that term shall be of no effect except in so far as it satisfies the requirement of reasonableness as stated in section 11(1) of the Unfair Contract Terms Act 1977; and it is for those claiming that the term satisfies that requirement to show that it does.

It will be seen that the major change has occurred in the final portion of the section where the requirement of reasonableness under section 11(1) of the Unfair Contract Terms Act 1977[202] has been substituted for the wider phrasing adopted in the original. This might have, but in fact did not, make a difference in *Howard Marine and Dredging Co Ltd v A Ogden & Sons (Excavations) Ltd*,[203] the facts of which have already been discussed. In that case the plaintiffs, in addition to arguing that they were not liable either for negligence at common law or under section 2(1) of the Misrepresentation Act 1967, contended that their liability was in any case excluded by a provision in the charterparty that 'the charterer's acceptance of handing over the vessel shall be conclusive evidence that they have examined the vessel and found her to be in all respects . . . fit for the intended and contemplated use by the charterers and in every other way satisfactory to them'. The crucial question then was to what extent was it reasonable to allow reliance on it, and this permitted consideration of post-contract events;[204] today the question would be whether such a term was a reasonable term to insert in the contract.

In either form the section goes beyond the Law Reform Committee's recommendations which would simply have barred the exclusion of liability for fraudulent and negligent misrepresentation.[205] The section does not go well with the rules relating to clauses excluding liability for breach of contractual terms.[206]

Although since 1977, the court may have power to treat such a clause either as totally ineffective or as subject to the reasonableness test, it will only do so where the contract is of a kind which falls within the scope of the Act.[207] The Misrepresentation Act however is quite general in scope so that its provisions will apply even to misrepresentations, which induce a contract, which is itself outside the scope of the Unfair Contract Terms Act. Furthermore it is often arguable whether a statement is

---

[202] See p 240, above. [203] [1978] QB 574, [1978] 2 All ER 1134.
[204] The Court of Appeal held (Lord Denning MR dissenting) that it was not.
[205] Cmnd 1782, paras 23–24. [206] Pp 202–257, above.
[207] See pp 231–233, above.

properly classified as a term or a representation and, as we have seen,[208] there is no clear decision as to whether it is open to a plaintiff to treat a contractual term as a representation. If this is permissible, a plaintiff may by formulating his claim in misrepresentation, deprive of effect a clause which would have excluded liability for breach of contract.[209]

Although section 3 is clearly aimed both at clauses which exclude liability and at those which restrict remedies, it contains no definition of its ambit in either area. Yet it is well known that the line between clauses excluding and defining liability is very fine and such common commercial occurrences as non-cancellation or arbitration clauses would seem to fall within the literal scope of (b). These difficulties are well illustrated by *Overbrooke Estate Ltd v Glencombe Properties Ltd*.[210]

> The plaintiffs instructed auctioneers to sell a property. The particulars of sale stated that 'neither the auctioneers nor any person in the employment of the auctioneers has any authority to make or give any representation or warranty'. The defendants, who were the highest bidders at the auction, alleged that three days before the auction, they had asked the auctioneers questions about the development plans of the local authorities, to which they had received inaccurate answers.

Brightman J held that even if the defendants could prove these allegations, they would constitute no defence. It was clear that the defendants had the particulars of sale and therefore knew or ought to have known that nothing told them by the auctioneers could bind the plaintiffs. Section 3 of the Misrepresentation Act 1967 was irrelevant since the provision in the particulars of sale did not constitute an exemption clause, but was a limitation on the apparent authority of the auctioneers. This decision appears impeccable but one may suspect that if the draftsman had foreseen it, he would have proceeded differently.[211]

On the other hand the Court of Appeal in *Cremdean Properties Ltd v Nash*[212] held that what was to be treated as a representation for the purposes of the section was to be approached in a broad and reasonable way, so that it would not do to make what would ordinarily be classified as a representation accompanied by a statement that it was not to be treated as a representation.

Apart from the Misrepresentation Act there are common law controls. In *HIH Casualty and General Insurance Ltd v Chase Manhattan Bank*[213] the House of Lords held that it was not possible for a contracting party to stipulate to exclude liability for

---

[208] Pp 350–352, above.

[209] As to reasonableness see pp 240–246, above and *Walker v Boyle* [1982] 1 All ER 634, [1982] 1 WLR 495 and *South Western General Property Co v Marton* [1983] CLY 1736, 263 Estates Gazette 1090.

[210] [1974] 3 All ER 511, [1974] 1 WLR 1335. Coote [1975] CLJ 17.

[211] Cf Consumer Credit Act 1974, s 56(3).

[212] (1977) 244 Estates Gazette 547.

[213] [2003] 1 All ER (Comm) 349; [2003] 2 Lloyd's Rep 61. See above p 213.

its own fraud. In this case if anybody had been fraudulent[214] it was the defendant's agent. Some members of the House of Lords thought that it might be possible by appropriate drafting to exclude liability for the fraud of one's agent though there was a clear majority for the view that the words used did not have this effect. In this case the bank were lending money, secured against the receipts from as yet unmade movies. This was a highly speculative transaction and the intermediaries who were negotiating it had no particular connection with either the bank or the insurance company. In the circumstances it would seem that the bank might validly have stipulated if they could get the insurers to agree that the intermediaries were not their agents.

F Non-disclosure

We have already seen that English law draws a clear distinction between misrepresentation and non-disclosure.[215] Apart from exceptional cases where silence amounts to assertive conduct,[216] there is no general duty to disclose information that would be likely to affect the other party's decision to conclude the contract. To this rule there are two important exceptions.

1 Contracts *uberrimae fidei*

In certain contracts where, from the very necessity of the case, one party alone possesses full knowledge of all the material facts, the law requires him to show *uberrima fides*. He must make full disclosure of all the material facts known to him, otherwise the contract may be rescinded.[217] It is impracticable to give an exact list of these contracts, nor can it be said that the extent of the duty of disclosure is constant in each case. We will deal somewhat fully with the contract of insurance and then more briefly with contracts for the purchase of shares and with family arrangements.

Contracts of insurance provide the outstanding example.[218] These are generally sub-divided into two classes according as they are designed to meet a marine or a non-marine risk, for the law with regard to the former has been codified by the Marine Insurance Act 1906. It has been established, however, since at least the eighteenth century, that every contract of insurance, irrespective of its subject matter, involves *uberrima fides* and requires full disclosure of such material facts as are known to the assured. As Lord Mansfield demonstrated in *Carter v Boehm*,[219] insurance is a contract

---

[214] The question was decided as a preliminary point.   [215] P 335, above.

[216] Pp 336–337, above.

[217] Where there is a duty to disclose, non-disclosure makes the contract voidable and not void. *Mackender v Feldia AG* [1967] 2 QB 590, [1966] 3 All ER 847.

[218] Hasson 32 MLR 615; Achampong 36 NILQ 329.

[219] (1766) 3 Burr 1905 at 1909. Exceptionally a contract of guarantee, eg a fidelity guarantee, may rank as a contract of insurance: *London General Omnibus Ltd v Holloway* [1912] 2 KB 72. Blair 29 MLR 522 at 524–536.

upon speculation where the special facts upon which the contingent chance is to be computed lie generally in the knowledge of the assured only, so that good faith requires that he should not keep back anything which might influence the insurer in deciding whether to accept or reject the risk. A fact is material if it is one that would affect the mind of a prudent insurer even though its materiality is not appreciated by the assured.[220] In the words of Bayley J:

> I think that in all cases of insurance, whether on ships, houses, or lives, the underwriter should be informed of every material circumstance within the knowledge of the assured; and that the proper question is, whether any particular circumstance was in fact material? and not whether the party believed it to be so. The contrary doctrine would lead to frequent suppression of information, and it would often be extremely difficult to shew that the party neglecting to give the information thought it material. But if it be held that all material facts must be disclosed, it will be in the interest of the assured to make a full and fair disclosure of all the information within their reach.[221]

The duty of disclosure in the case of marine insurance is prescribed as follows in the Marine Insurance Act:

> Subject to the provisions of this section, the assured must disclose to the insurer, before the contract is concluded, every material circumstance which is known to the assured, and the assured is deemed to know every circumstance which, in the ordinary course of business, ought to be known by him. If the assured fails to make such disclosure, the insurer may avoid the contract.[222]

Every circumstance is material which would influence the judgment of a prudent insurer in fixing the premium, or determining whether he will take the risk.[223]

Thus, for example, the assured must inform the underwriter that the ship is over-due[224] or has put into an intermediate port for repair;[225] that the insured goods are to be carried on deck, a place where it is not usual to stack them;[226] or that the cargo is to be taken on board at a particular port where loading is a hazardous operation.[227]

The question in each case is whether the fact would have been material in influencing the mind of a prudent insurer, not whether loss has resulted from the undisclosed fact. Thus, where the assured concealed a report that the ship when last seen was in a position of danger, though as a matter of fact she survived on this

---

[220] *London Assurance v Mansel* (1879) 11 Ch D 363. *Lambert v Co-operative Insurance Society* [1975] 2 Lloyd's Rep 485.

[221] *Lindenau v Desborough* (1828) 8 B & C 586 at 592.

[222] Marine Insurance Act 1906, s 18(1).

[223] Ibid, s 18(1).

[224] *Kirby v Smith* (1818) 1 B & Ald 672.

[225] *Uzielli v Commercial Union Insurance Co* (1865) 12 LT 399.

[226] *Hood v West End Motor Car Packing Co* [1917] 2 KB 38.

[227] *Harrower v Hutchinson* (1870) LR 5 QB 584.

occasion only to be captured later by the Spaniards it was held that the policy could be avoided for non-disclosure.[228]

A difficult question which has arisen in a number of recent cases is whether the insured should reveal that allegations have been made against him of a serious nature (and which would be material if true) but of which he denies the truth. It appears that in some cases at least the existence of the allegations is a material fact which should be disclosed.[229]

The duty of good faith continues after the contract of insurance has been concluded. The most important example relates to fraudulent claims. It is well established that if the insured has a valid claim but seeks to attach to it additional bogus claims, the effect is that not only the bogus but also the well founded claims fail.[230]

There has been much discussion as to what exactly is meant by 'influencing the mind of a prudent insurer'. Clearly, this test is satisfied if it is shown that the prudent insurer would have refused the proposal or would only have accepted it at a higher premium or subject to an excess. However, the Court of Appeal, in *Container Transport International Inc v Oceanus Mutual Underwriting Association (Bermuda) Ltd*[231] went further and held that a fact was material if a prudent insurer would like to have known it though the evidence showed that the prudent insurer would in fact have accepted the proposal on standard terms. This view was much criticised but it was accepted as correct by the majority of the House of Lords in *Pan Atlantic Insurance Co Ltd v Pinetop Insurance Co Ltd.*[232] There was a powerful dissenting judgment by Lord Lloyd with whom Lord Templeman agreed. The House of Lords went on, however, to say that the insurer must show not only that the information not disclosed was material in this sense, but also that it was in fact so induced to enter into the contract. This restates what had certainly been lost sight of for the best part of 100 years in

---

[228] *Seaman v Fonereau* (1743) 2 Stra 1183. In its 5th Report, the Law Reform Committee suggested that it would be practicable to frame a new statutory definition of 'material' on the following lines: 'For the purposes of any contract of insurance no fact shall be deemed material unless it would have been considered material by a reasonable insured'; Cmnd 62 (1957), p 7. See now the more comprehensive proposals for reforming contracts in the Law Commission's Report of October 1980 (Law Com No 104). It now appears likely that there will not be legislation to implement this report. In *Drake Insurance plc v Provident Insurance plc* [2004] 2 All ER (Comm) 65 the insured fail to tell the insurer about a speeding conviction (a material fact) but also failed to tell them that the driver of another car involved in a rear-end collision with his wife had paid in full, a circumstance which under the insurer's system would have cancelled out his conviction. The Court of Appeal thought the insurer not entitled to avoid. See also *Assicurazioni General v Arab Insurance Group* [2002] EWCA Civ 1642, [2003] 1 All ER (Comm) 140.

[229] *Brotherton v Aseguradora Colseguros* [2003] EWHC 335 (Comm), [2003] 1 All ER (Comm) 774; [2003] EWCA Civ 705, [2003] 2 All ER 298. *Strive Shipping Corp v Hellenic Mutual War Risks Association (Bermuda) Ltd, The Grecia Express* [2002] 2 All ER (Comm) 213.

[230] *Manifest Shipping Co Ltd v Uni-Polaris Shipping Co Ltd, The Star Sea* [2001] UKHL 1, [2001] 1 All ER 743; *Agapitos v Agnew* [2002] EWCA Civ 247, [2002] 1 All ER 714; *Axa General Insurance Ltd v Gottlieb* [2005] 1 All ER (Comm) 445.

[231] [1984] 1 Lloyd's Rep 476.

[232] [1994] 3 All ER 581.

relation both to misrepresentation and to non disclosure: there are two separate tests of materiality and actual inducement. In practice, decisions on misrepresentation have concentrated on actual inducement and decisions on non disclosure on materiality. In practice, once materiality is established, the significance of the requirement of inducement will turn largely upon whether there is a presumption and, if so, of what strength, that actual inducement can be deduced from materiality. This is because the insured will have little or no information as to what may or may not have induced the insurer. If the insurer has actually to give evidence as to inducement, a skilful cross-examination by the counsel for the insured may leave the court unconvinced. If there is a presumption, the insured may be able to avoid giving evidence and thereby denying the insured the chance of cross-examination. In the *Pan Atlantic* case, Lord Mustill thought there was a presumption but Lord Lloyd did not agree.[233]

A similar duty of disclosure exists in the case of non-marine insurances. Whether the policy is taken out of life, fire, burglary, fidelity or accidental risk, it is the duty of the assured to give full information of every material fact; and it has been held by the Court of Appeal that the definition of 'material' contained in the Marine Insurance Act 1906, namely every circumstance 'which would influence the judgment of a prudent insurer in fixing the premium, or determining whether he will take the risk', is applicable to all forms of insurance.[234] It has thus been held in each of the following cases that the policy was vitiated for non-disclosure:

> In a proposal for fire insurance, the assured stated that no proposal by him had previously been declined by any other company; in fact, another company had previously refused to issue a policy in respect of his motor vehicle.[235]

> In applying for a fire insurance policy, the proposer omitted to mention that a fire had broken out next door upon the day of the proposal.[236]

> In a proposal for a policy insuring the repayment of a loan, the proposer failed to divulge that, owing to the financial debility of the borrower, the interest had been fixed at 40 per cent.[237]

The duty of disclosure thus imposed by law is confined to facts which the assured knows or ought to know. 'The duty', said Fletcher-Moulton LJ, 'is a duty to disclose, and you cannot disclose what you do not know.'[238] Thus if the question—'Have you

---

233 See also *St Paul Fire & Marine Insurance Co (UK) Ltd v McConnell Dowell Constructors Ltd* [1996] 1 All ER 96; Birds and Hird 59 MLR 285.

234 *Locker and Woolf Ltd v Western Australian Insurance Co Ltd* [1936] 1 KB 408. As to the burden of proof, see *Slattery v Mance* [1962] 1 QB 676, [1962] 1 All ER 525.

235 *Locker and Woolf Ltd v Western Australian Insurance Co Ltd,* above.

236 *Bufe v Turner* (1815) 6 Taunt 338.

237 *Seaton v Heath* [1899] 1 QB 782. See also *Woolcott v Sun Alliance and London Insurance Ltd* [1978] 1 All ER 1253, [1978] 1 WLR 493.

238 *Joel v Law Union and Crown Insurance Co* [1908] 2 KB 863 at 884, per Fletcher-Moulton LJ.

any disease?'—is put to an applicant for a life assurance policy, and he answers in the negative, fully believing his health to be sound, the resulting contract cannot be rescinded upon proof that at the time of his answer he was suffering from malignant cancer. The duty, however, may be enlarged by the express terms of the contract, and in fact insurers have taken extensive, perhaps indeed unfair, advantage of this contractual freedom. In practice they almost invariably require the assured to agree that the *accuracy* of the information provided by him shall be a condition of the validity of the policy. To this end it is common to insert a term in the proposal form providing that the declarations of the assured shall form the basis of the contract. The legal effect of this term is that if his answer to a direct question is inaccurate, or if he fails to disclose some material fact long forgotten or even some fact that was never within his knowledge, the contract may be avoided despite his integrity and honesty of purpose. Nay more, his incorrect statement about a matter that is nothing more than a matter of opinion is sufficient to avoid the policy. Thus, for instance, one of the commonest questions put to a person who applies for a life insurance is 'Have you any disease?', a matter which, even for a doctor, is often a subject of mere speculation or opinion.

> But the policies issued by many companies are framed so as to be invalid unless this and many other like questions are correctly—not merely truthfully—answered, though the insurers are well aware that it is impossible for anyone to arrive at anything more certain than an opinion about them. I wish I could adequately warn the public against such practices on the part of insurance offices.[239]

The courts view this practice with distaste and they do what they can to mitigate its severity by imposing a strict burden of proof upon insurers.[240]

The above account has talked of disclosure by the insured. It is natural to talk in this way since it is usually the insured who will know facts which would have affected the judgement of the insurer if they had been disclosed. However, it is clear that in principle, the duty of disclosure lies equally on the insurer. This was one of the important questions which arose in *Banque Financière de la Cité SA v Westgate Insurance Co Ltd.*[241] In this case a Mr Ballestero persuaded syndicates of banks to lend his companies many millions of Swiss francs. The loans were secured partly by gemstones (which later turned out to be virtually valueless) and partly by credit insurance policies covering failure by the borrowing companies to repay the loans. Insurance policies were issued by the defendant insurers and contained clauses which excluded liability in the event of fraud. Mr Ballestero disappeared with the money and the plaintiff

---

[239] Ibid at 885, per Fletcher-Moulton LJ. See Hasson 34 MLR 29 and the Report of the Law Commission (Law Com no 104) and also the statement of practice of the British Insurance Association (discussed Birds 40 MLR 677).

[240] *Bond Air Services Ltd v Hill* [1955] 2 QB 417, [1955] 2 All ER 476; *West v National Motor and Accident Insurance Union Ltd* [1955] 1 All ER 800. For other respects in which the scales are weighted against the insured, see the 5th Report of the Law Reform Committee (1957), Cmnd 62.

[241] [1990] 1 QB 665, [1987] 2 All ER 923, per Steyn J (*Banque Keyser Ullmann SA v Skandia (UK) Insurance Co Ltd)* [1989] 2 All ER 952, CA; affd [1990] 2 All ER 947, [1990] 3 WLR 364, HL.

lenders sought to recover it from the defendant insurers. On the face of it they could not do so because the policies excluded recovery in the event of Mr Ballestero's fraud. But the plaintiffs argued that they would not have entered into the transaction if the defendant insurers had made, as they should have done, a full disclosure of a material fact. This was that the insurers knew that the insurance policies had been procured by an employee of the insurance broker falsely representing that the full amount of the loan was insured when he only held a cover note valid for 14 days.

These facts raised a series of issues. The first issue was whether the insurers were in general under a duty of disclosure to the plaintiffs. All the courts which considered the question held that the duty of disclosure between insurer and insured was reciprocal. The next question was whether the particular information about the dishonest behaviour of the employee of the insurance broker should have been revealed by the insurers to the insured. It is clear that the duty is not to reveal all information but to reveal material information. When considering disclosure by the insured, it is well established that the test of materiality relates to what would affect the judgment of a reasonable insurer either to refuse the policy or to accept it only on special terms (such as charging a higher premium or requiring the insured to pay the first part of any loss himself). In disputed cases this can be resolved by expert evidence as to the behaviour of reasonable insurers. It is difficult, if not impossible, to see how expert evidence could be given as to the behaviour of the reasonable insured. Both Steyn J and the Court of Appeal thought that there had been a failure to disclose material facts in the present case though they applied a somewhat different test. Steyn J thought that the insurer should reveal facts which would affect the judgement of the reasonable insured so far as good faith and fair dealing required. The Court of Appeal took a somewhat narrower view. In particular they did not think that an insurer need reveal to the insured that other reputable insurers would cover the risk at lower premiums. They thought that 'the duty falling on the insurer must at least extend to disclosing all facts known to him which are material either to the nature of the risks sought to be covered or to the recoverability of a claim under the policy which a prudent insured would take into account in deciding whether or not to place the risk for which he seeks cover with that insurer'. The House of Lords took a completely different line on this issue. They thought that the plaintiffs' loss did not arise from the insurer's non-disclosure but from the fraud of Mr Ballestero, which was wholly independent of that. They thought that even if the agent of the insurance brokers had behaved entirely properly and honestly the banks would still not have been protected since then they would have had insurance policies subject to a fraud exception, which is exactly what they ended up with in any case.[242] In the result, therefore, the House of Lords did not have to

---

[242] At first instance it appears to have been accepted that if the lenders had known of the dishonesty of the insurance broker's employee, they would not have gone through with the loan transactions. See also *Bank of Nova Scotia v Hellenic Mutual War Risks Association (Bermuda) Ltd, The Good Luck* [1991] 3 All ER 1 as to the legal effect of a promissory warranty given by the insured that a ship will not enter a high risk area without notice.

express a view on how the materiality test should be expressed. Nor did they have to consider a third question on which Steyn J and the Court of Appeal took different views. This was as to the nature of the remedy which would be available to the plaintiffs. It is well settled that in general the remedy for non-disclosure is to set the contract aside. But it would have helped the plaintiff bankers not at all to set the contract of insurance aside (or rather it would only have helped them to recover their premiums) since setting the contract aside would simply mean that they were not protected. There is an obvious lack of reciprocity in practice here between insurer and insured. Steyn J would have been willing to give the insured a remedy in damages arising from non-disclosure by the insurer but the Court of Appeal rejected this, partly on the grounds that voidability as the only remedy was well established by authority and partly on the grounds that it would be to impose a liability in damages for behaviour which might be totally without fault, since the duty of disclosure was strict and not negligence based.

Contracts to take shares in companies
A contract to take shares in a company is often made on the faith of the prospectus issued by the promoters. It has long been recognised that the document is a fruitful source of deception, for persons who desire to foist an undertaking upon the public are not usually remarkable either for the accuracy of their representations or for the industry with which they search for facts that might usefully be disclosed. There are a number of statutes which have provisions affecting liability in this respect[243] and the Companies Act 1985, section 56, contains a list of matters that every prospectus must contain. The result of the statutory provisions, especially when taken together with the extra legal controls operated by the Stock Exchange, is that a contract to take shares has become closely akin to one which is *uberrimae fidei.*[244]

Family arrangements
The expression 'family arrangements' covers a multitude of agreements made between relatives and designed to preserve the harmony, to protect the property or to save the honour of the family.[245] It comprises such diverse transactions as the following: a resettlement of land made between the father as tenant for life and the son as tenant in tail in remainder; an agreement to abide by the terms of a will that has not been properly executed, or to vary the terms of a valid will; the release of devised property from a condition subsequently imposed by the testator; or an agreement by a younger legitimate son to transfer family property to an illegitimate elder son.

---

[243] Companies Act 1985, especially ss 56, 57, 66, 67, 68, 69; Prevention of Fraud (Investments) Act 1958; Protection of Depositors Act 1963; Financial Services Act 1986; Gower *Modern Company Law* (4th edn) pp 366–393.

[244] There was authority for a duty of disclosure at common law. *Central Rly Co of Venezuela (Directors etc) v Kisch* (1867) LR 2 HL 99 at 113. Cf *Aaron's Reefs Ltd v Twiss* [1896] AC 273 at 287.

[245] See generally, White and Tudor's *Leading Cases in Equity* vol 1, pp 198 ff.

Equity, though always anxious to sustain family arrangements, insists that there should be the fullest disclosure of all material facts known to each party, even though no inquiry about them may have been made. The parties must be on an equal footing.

Thus, in *Gordon v Gordon*,[246] a division of property, based upon the probability that the elder son was illegitimate, was set aside nineteen years afterwards upon proof that the younger son had concealed his knowledge of a private ceremony of marriage solemnised between his parents before the birth of his brother; and in *Greenwood v Greenwood*[247] an agreement to divide the property of a deceased relative was avoided on the ground that one of the parties failed to disclose information which he alone possessed concerning the amount of the estate.

2 Constructive fraud

In cases where the representor had no honest belief in the truth of his statement, equity has long had a concurrent jurisdiction with the common law. The court to which a plaintiff would resort before the Judicature Act would depend upon whether the remedy he sought was on the one hand the recovery of damages for deceit or on the other rescission and an account of profits. Equity, however, in the exercise of its exclusive jurisdiction has from early days given a more extended meaning to the word 'fraud' than has the common law, and has developed a doctrine of *constructive fraud*. Lord Haldane said in a leading case:

> But in addition to this concurrent jurisdiction, the Court of Chancery exercised an exclusive jurisdiction in cases which, although classified in that Court as cases of fraud, yet did not necessarily import the element of *dolus malus*. The Court took upon itself to prevent a man from acting against the dictates of conscience as defined by the Court, and to grant injunctions in anticipation of injury, as well as relief where injury had been done.[248]

It is not unnatural that a principle of jurisdiction defined in such expansive terms should have been gradually applied to a wide field of human activities and to what at first sight appear to be a welter of unrelated items;[249] but one important example pertinent to the present discussion is where, owing to the special relationship between the parties, a transaction may be voidable in equity for non-disclosure. 'Under certain circumstances a duty may arise to disclose a material fact, and its non-disclosure may have the same effect as a representation of its non-existence.'[250] Whenever the relation between the parties to a contract is of a confidential or fiduciary nature, the person in whom the confidence is reposed and who thus possesses influence over the other cannot hold that other to the contract unless he satisfies the court that it is advanta-

---

[246] (1821) 3 Swan 400.   [247] (1863) 2 De GJ & Sm 28.
[248] *Nocton v Lord Ashburton* [1914] AC 932 at 952.
[249] See eg the extended meaning of fraud given by Lord Hardwicke in *Earl of Chesterfield v Janssen* (1751) 2 Ves Sen 125 at 155.
[250] Ashburner *Principles of Equity* (2nd edn) 283. For a classification of relationships, see Sealy [1962] CLJ 69, [1963] CLJ 119.

geous to the other party and that he has disclosed all material facts within his knowledge.[251]

Such a confidential relationship is deemed to exist between persons connected by certain recognised ties, such as parent and child, principal and agent,[252] solicitor and client, religious superior and inferior, and trustee and beneficiary. But the courts have always refused to confine this equitable jurisdiction to such familiar relations. They are prepared to interfere in a contract wherever one party deliberately and voluntarily places himself in such a position that it becomes his duty to act fairly and to have due regard to the interests of the other party. In a leading case, Lord Chelmsford stated the general principle in these words:

> Wherever two persons stand in such a relation that, while it continues, confidence is necessarily reposed by one, and the influence which naturally grows out of that confidence is possessed by the other, and this confidence is abused, or the influence is exerted to obtain an advantage at the expense of the confiding party, the person so availing himself of his position will not be permitted to retain the advantage, although the transaction could not have been impeached if no such confidential relation had existed.[253]

These words were spoken in a case where X, an extravagant undergraduate much pressed by his Oxford creditors and anxious to extricate himself from his financial embarrassment, sought the advice of Y. Having recommended the sale of the undergraduate's Staffordshire estate, Y offered to buy it himself for £7,000 without disclosing that, owing to the existence of subjacent minerals, X's interest was worth at least double that amount. The offer was accepted and the conveyance executed, but some years later the sale was set aside by the court at the insistence of X's heir. Y was constructively fraudulent in the sense that he wrongfully exploited to his own advantage the commanding position in which he stood.

This principle is well illustrated by *Hilton v Barker Booth and Eastwood (a firm).*[254] In this case, the claimant was a developer in a modest way and in 1990 put up a sign on a piece of land in Blackpool which he had acquired carrying the words 'Hilton Homes' and his telephone number. In June or July 1990 he received a phone call from a Mr Bromage who expressed an interest in buying flats on the site once they had been built. The defendant solicitors acted for both Mr Hilton and Mr Bromage. The defendants knew that at the time Mr Bromage had recently come out of prison where he had spent some 9 months having been convicted of a number of offences relating to fraudulent trading while an undischarged bankrupt and so on. This history was well known to the defendants but they did not reveal it to Mr Hilton. In 1990 plans were reached to develop a different site. Mr Hilton agreed to buy the site from its

---

[251] *Moody v Cox and Hatt* [1917] 2 Ch 71 at 88, per Scrutton LJ.
[252] *Regal (Hastings) Ltd v Gulliver* [1967] 2 AC 134n, [1942] 1 All ER 378.
[253] *Tate v Williamson* (1866) 2 Ch App 55 at 61.
[254] [2005] 1 All ER 651

owners for £85,000; to develop it by erecting six flats and to sell the developed property to Mr Bromage for £351,000. There was another contract by which Mr Bromage, unknown to Mr Hilton, agreed to sell on the flats to a sub purchaser for £390,000. All three contracts were exchanged on 10 September 1990 and the defendants acted for both Mr Bromage and Mr Hilton. It was clearly professionally improper for the defendants to act on both sides in a case of this kind, where there was a conflict of interest. The defendants went further because they privately advanced to Mr Bromage £25,000 which was paid by way of a deposit, as they did in respect of a further development transaction on the Watson Road site. By November 1991 the flats on the first development were ready for completion but Mr Bromage failed to complete. In January 1992 the defendants finally revealed that they could not act for both parties and told Mr Hilton that he should get another solicitor. In due course, Mr Hilton started proceedings against the defendants. The trial judge held that the defendants had been in breach of their professional duty to Mr Hilton and went on to hold that this had not caused Mr Hilton any loss since, if he had gone to another independent solicitor, that solicitor would not have known of Mr Bromage's conviction and would not therefore have told Mr Hilton about it. The Court of Appeal affirmed this decision though on not quite the same grounds. They held that it was an implied term of the contract between the defendants and Mr Hilton that they were released from any duty of disclosure in relation to matters which they were legally obliged to treat as confidential.

The House of Lords thought these decisions clearly wrong. They were inconsistent with the leading case of *Moody v Cox*.[255] As Lord Walker of Gestingthorpe in the principal reasoned speech said, this case establishes that if a solicitor puts himself in a position of having two irreconcilable duties, it is his own fault. 'In this case BBE were in the position (through their own fault) of having two irreconcilable duties, to Mr Bromage and to Mr Hilton, and of also having a personal interest (because of the undisclosed £25,000 loan, which was likely to be recoverable only if Mr Bromage did well in his transaction with Mr Hilton). On the face of it their position was significantly worse than that of the solicitor in *Moody v Cox*.

> Mr Gibson submitted that a solicitor who has conflicting duties to two clients may not prefer one to another. That is, I think, correct as a general rule, and it distinguishes the case of two irreconcilable duties from a conflict of duty and personal interest (where the solicitor is bound to prefer his duty to his own interest). Since he may not prefer one duty to another, he must perform both as best he can. This may involve performing one duty to the letter of the obligation, and paying compensation for his failure to perform the other. But in any case the fact that he has chosen to put himself in an impossible position does not exonerate him from liability.

---

[255] [1917] 2 Ch 71

G Relationship between misrepresentation and estoppel[256]

It not infrequently happens that A enters into a contract with B on the faith of a misrepresentation made by X. Here, unless X is the agent of B, there can be no question of a remedy against B and since there will normally be no contract between A and X,[257] many of the remedies discussed in this chapter will be unobtainable. One cannot rescind a contract that does not exist and actions under the Misrepresentation Act 1967 only lie where the representation 'has been made . . . by another party' to the contract. X can certainly be sued in tort if he is fraudulent and in some cases an action may now lie for negligence under *Hedley Byrne & Co Ltd v Heller & Partners.*[258]

In some such cases, assistance may be obtained from the doctrine of estoppel by representation. This was stated by Lord Macnaghten as follows:

> It is . . . a principle of universal application, that if a person makes a false representation to another and that other acts upon that false representation the person who has made it shall not afterwards be allowed to set up that what he said was false and to assert the real truth in place of the falsehood which has so misled the other.[259]

It would appear that the constituents of a representation for estoppel by misrepresentation are the same as for actionable misrepresentation.[260] The main obstacle to a wide use of this principle is that it is said that estoppel is not in itself a cause of action.[261] If this is right, it follows that the plaintiff who wishes to employ the principle of estoppel must formulate some independent cause of action which would have succeeded had the estoppel statement been true. He may then rely on estoppel to defeat a defence which would otherwise be available to the defendant, since evidence to prove the untruth of the statement will be inadmissible.

This possibility is neatly illustrated by *Burrows v Lock.*[262] The facts were these:

> X was entitled to a sum of £288 held on his behalf by a trustee. A. He assigned part of this to Y by way of security, notice of the assignment being given to A. Ten years later he purported to assign the whole of the £288 to Z in return for valuable consideration. Before completing this transaction, Z consulted A, who having forgotten the previous assignment to Y, represented that X was still entitled to the full sum of £288.

---

[256] Spencer Bower and Turner *The Law Relating to Estoppel by Representation* (3rd edn, 1977); Ewart on *Estoppel*; Atiyah *Essays on Contract*, Essay 10; Jackson 81 LQR 84, 223.

[257] Unless the court discovers a 'collateral' contact with X.

[258] [1964] AC 465, [1963] 2 All ER 575.

[259] *Balkis Consolidated Co v Tomkinson* [1893] AC 396 at 410, citing Lord Cranworth in *Jorden v Money* (1854) 5 HL Cas 185 at 210, 212.

[260] Spencer Bower and Turner *The Law Relating to Estoppel by Representation* (3rd edn, 1977) pp 29 ff.

[261] This is certainly the orthodox view. See especially *Law v Bouverie* [1891] 3 Ch 82. Cf the views of Atiyah and Jackson, n 257, above.

[262] (1805) 10 Ves 470. Sheridan *Fraud in Equity* pp 31–36. Cf *United Overseas Bank v Jiwani* [1977] 1 All ER 733.

Z later filed a bill against A, who was held liable for so much of the trust fund as had previously been assigned to Y. Here Z had an independent cause of action, for had the representation of the trustee been correct he would have been entitled to the whole sum of £288 against the trustee, for the effect of the assignment would have been that the trustee held the £288 on behalf of Z. In fact the trustee held part of the fund on trust for Y, but he was estopped from setting this up to defeat the claim of Z.

The possibility of formulating an action for damages for negligent misstatement will have reduced but not removed the importance of this more devious route to damages. In addition it should be noted that cases may arise where estoppel will operate as a defence and here of course there will be no need to formulate an independent cause of action.

2 DURESS AND UNDUE INFLUENCE[263]

Since agreement depends on consent, it should follow that agreement obtained by threats or undue persuasion is insufficient. Both common law with a limited doctrine of duress and equity with a much wider doctrine of undue influence have acted in this area. It is clear that in equity the effect of undue influence is to make the contract voidable, but it is disputed whether the effect of duress at common law is to make the contract void or voidable. The question would be important if questions of affirmation or third party rights were involved but there is no satisfactory modern authority. The majority of writers state that duress makes the contract voidable[264] but this has been vigorously controverted.[265] There are a number of modern cases which discuss whether duress renders a marriage void or voidable and it is sometimes assumed that the rule is the same for marriage and for contract.[266] But even if this assumption is correct, it does not provide a clear answer since the cases do not agree[267] and in none of them was it necessary to decide the question.

[263] Winder 56 LQR 97, 3 MLR 97, 4 Conv (NS) 274; Winfield 60 LQR 341.

[264] See eg Pollock *Principles of Contract* (13th edn) p 179, citing the second rule in *Whelpdale's Case* (1604) 5 Co Rep 119a, 77 ER 239.

[265] Lanham 29 MLR 615.

[266] *Parojcic v Parojcic* [1958] 1 WLR 1280 at 1283.

[267] See eg *Parojcic v Parojcic*, above; *Buckland v Buckland* [1968] P 296, [1967] 2 All ER 300. Manchester 29 MLR 622; *Singh v Singh* [1971] 2 All ER 828 at 830. An elaborate historical survey by Tolstoy 27 MLR 385, shows that the rule was originally that the marriage was void. For marriage the question was resolved by the Nullity of Marriage Act 1971, s 2 (c) (now Matrimonial Causes Act 1973, s 12(c)) whereby the effect of duress is to render the marriage voidable. In *DPP for Northern Ireland v Lynch* [1975] 1 All ER 913 at 938, [1975] AC 653 at 695, Lord Simon of Glaisdale stated that duress made contracts voidable though this was clearly obiter. The whole of this case repays study for its analysis of the operation of duress. See further the debate Atiyah 98 LQR 197; Tiplady 99 LQR 198 Atiyah 99 LQR 353. As a matter of criminal law *Lynch* was overruled in *R v Howe* [1987] AC 417, [1987] 1 All ER 771, a case which has received a less than ecstatic welcome from commentators, see eg Milgate [1988] CLJ 61.

Both common law and equity agree that a party cannot be held to a contract unless he is a free agent, but the contribution made by common law to this part of the subject has been scanty. It is confined to the avoidance of contracts obtained by duress, a word to which a very limited meaning has been attached. Duress at common law, or what is sometimes called *legal duress*, means actual violence or threats of violence to the person, ie threats calculated to produce fear of loss of life or bodily harm.[268] It is a part of the law which nowadays seldom raises an issue.

That a contract should be procured by actual violence is difficult to conceive, and a more probable means of inducement is a threat of violence. The rule here is that the threat must be illegal in the sense that it must be a threat to commit a crime or a tort.[269] Thus to threaten an imprisonment that would be unlawful if enforced constitutes duress, but not if the imprisonment would be lawful.[270] Again a contract procured by a threat to prosecute for a crime that has actually been committed,[271] or to sue for a civil wrong,[272] or to put the member of a trade association on a stop-list,[273] is not as a general rule voidable for duress. But it may be void as being contrary to public policy, as for example where it is in effect an agreement tending to pervert the course of justice.[274] It must be established that the threats were a reason for entering into the contract but it need not be shown that they were the only or even the main reason. Once it has been proved that unlawful threats were made, it is for the threatener to show that they were not a reason for the other party contracting.[275]

For duress to afford a ground of relief, it must be duress of a man's person, not of his goods.[276] In *Skeate v Beale*,[277] for instance, a tenant agreed that if his landlord would withdraw a distress for £19 10s in respect of rent, he would pay £3 7s 6d immediately and the remainder, £16 2s 6d, within one month. To an action to recover £16 2s 6d the tenant pleaded that the distress was wrongful, since only £3 7s 6d was due, and that the landlord threatened to sell the goods at once unless agreement was made. This plea was disallowed. But it has been held that money paid under duress of goods may be recovered.[278] Clearly these two rules are difficult to reconcile.[279]

Equity had concurrent jurisdiction with the courts of common law with regard to

---

[268] Co Litt 253b. For a modern example see *Friedeberg-Seeley v Klass* [1957] CLY 1482, 101 Sol Jo 275.

[269] Cf *Ware and De Freville Ltd v Motor Trade Association* [1921] 3 KB 40.

[270] *Cumming v Ince* (1847) 11 QB 112; *Biffin v Bignell* (1862) 7 H & N 877; *Smith v Monteith* (1844) 13 M & W 427.

[271] *Fisher & Co v Appolinaris Co* (1875) 10 Ch App 297.

[272] *Powell v Hoyland* (1851) 6 Exch 67.

[273] *Thorne v Motor Trade Association* [1937] AC 797, [1937] 3 All ER 157.

[274] Pp 480–484, below.   [275] *Barton v Armstrong* [1976] AC 104, [1975] 2 All ER 465.

[276] *Atlee v Backhouse* (1838) 3 M & W 633 at 650, per Parke B.

[277] (1840) 11 Ad & El 983.

[278] *Astley v Reynolds* (1731) 2 Stra 915; *T D Keegan Ltd v Palmer* [1961] 2 Lloyd's Rep 449.

[279] Goff and Jones *The Law of Restitution* (3rd edn) pp 206–222. Beatson [1974] CLJ 97, shows that the duress of goods doctrine owes its existence to a factual overlap with the rule that a compromise of a doubtful claim is valid.

duress, but by an application of its comprehensive doctrine of constructive fraud,[280] it exercised a separate and wider jurisdiction over contracts made without free consent. It developed a doctrine of undue influence.[281] This doctrine is accurately stated by Ashburner:

> In a court of equity if A obtains any benefit from B, whether under a contract or as a gift, by exerting an influence over B which, in the opinion of the court, prevents B from exercising an independent judgment in the matter in question, B can set aside the contract or recover the gift. Moreover in certain cases the relation between A and B may be such that A has peculiar opportunities of exercising influence over B. If under such circumstances A enters into a contract with B, or receives a gift from B, a court of equity imposes upon A the burden, if he wishes to maintain the contract or gift, of proving that in fact he exerted no influence for the purpose of obtaining it.[282]

The only rider to make to this statement is that an intention by A to benefit himself personally is not essential to justify rescission of a contract. It is enough that in the exercise of his influence he has not made the welfare of B, to the exclusion of all other persons, his paramount consideration.[283]

Unconscionable bargains

Historically this area of equity has embraced not only the present doctrine of undue influence and the special rules about disclosure, discussed above,[284] but also rules about unconscionable bargains.[285] As is often the case however, the term 'unconscionable bargains' bears a much narrower meaning in equity than in lay usage. The typical transaction, assumed by the older authorities, involved an improvident arrangement by an expectant heir to anticipate his inheritance—a situation unlikely to occur often today with the virtual disappearance of strict settlements. Though there are old cases under this rubric which turn on the infirmity of one of the parties,[286] it has been doubted whether an English court would now set aside a transaction merely because one of the parties were poor, ignorant or weak-minded.[287] A Northern Ireland court did so however in *Buckley v Irwin*[288] and there are several Canadian decisions to the same effect.[289]

---

[280] P 379, above.

[281] See especially White and Tudor *Leading Cases in Equity* vol 1, pp 203 ff; Hanbury and Maudsley *Modern Equity* (13th edn, 1989) pp 788–794. Sheridan *Fraud in Equity* pp 87–106.

[282] *Ashburner on Equity* (2nd edn) p 299; see also *Allcard v Skinner* (1887) 36 ChD 145 at 181 and 183, per Lindley LJ.

[283] *Bullock v Lloyds Bank Ltd* [1955] Ch 317, [1954] 3 All ER 726.

[284] Pp 379–381, above.

[285] See Sheridan *Fraud in Equity* pp 125–145; Goff and Jones *The Law of Restitution* (3rd edn) pp 257–267. The special statutory rules about money lending contained in the Money-Lenders Acts 1900 and 1927 were substantially a strengthening of equitable doctrine in a particularly vulnerable area. They have now been replaced and extended by the Consumer Credit Act 1974, ss 137–140.

[286] Eg *Evans v Llewellin* (1787) 1 Cox Eq Cas 333.

[287] Treitel *Law of Contract* (3rd edn) p 351. Cf 10th edn, pp 383.   [288] [1960] NI 98.

[289] See eg *Knupp v Bell* (1968) 67 DLR (2d) 256; *Marshall v Canada Permanent Trust Co* (1968) 69 DLR (2d) 260; *Mundinger v Mundinger* (1968) 3 DLR (3d) 338; Enman 16 Anglo-American LR 191.

Unconscionability has been much more vigorously developed in the law of Australia.[290] Perhaps the most striking example is *Commercial Bank of Australia Ltd v Amadio*.[291] In this case, Amadio Builders had an overdraft account with the Commercial Bank of Australia. Vincenzio Amadio was the managing director of the company. Vincenzio's parents, though neither poor nor illiterate, were relatively old and not very fluent in written English. They greatly admired Vincenzio whom they thought of as a very successful businessman. In fact, the company was insolvent and heavily in debt to the bank. The bank, in cooperation with Vincenzio, helped to conceal the company's difficulties from the public by selective dishonour of the company's cheques. In due course, the bank proposed to close the company's account unless security was provided by way of a mortgage on property owned by Vincenzio's parents. The parents were persuaded to sign the appropriate papers by the manager at a visit to their house. Vincenzio told his parents that the guarantee would be for six months only and have an upper limit of $50,000. Both these statements were, to his knowledge, untrue. The branch manager did tell the parents that the guarantee was not limited to six months. The parents received no independent advice. In due course, the company went insolvent, owing the bank nearly £240,000 and the bank sought to enforce the mortgage. In the High Court, it was held that the transaction should be set aside on the grounds that the bank's behaviour was unconscionable. An English court might well have reached the same conclusion on these facts by the application of the rules of undue influence.[292]

In *Portman Building Society v Dusangh*[293] a father borrowed money on mortgage from the claimants so as to fund a loan to his son who was planning to buy a supermarket. The father was 72, retired, illiterate in English and spoke it poorly. No fraud or undue influence on the part of the son was alleged and the son was not in financial difficulties at the time of the loan. The father, the son and the building society were all represented by the same solicitor. In due course, the supermarket failed, the building society sought to enforce the mortgage and the father argued that the transaction was unconsionable. The possibility of attacking such a transaction as unconsionable was not excluded but on the facts the transaction was held not to be unconsionable.

Economic duress

In the past English law, unlike American law,[294] has not used these fertile doctrines to deal with the general problem of inequality of bargaining power. This battle has been fought on other fronts.[295] A prophetic exception however may be found in the

---

[290] Carter and Harland, *Contract Law in Australia* Ch 15.
[291] (1983) 151 CLR 447.
[292] Se pp 392–402, below.
[293] [2000] 2 All ER (Comm) 221
[294] See the masterly survey by J P Dawson 45 Michigan L Rev 253; McKeand (2001) 17 J Contract L 1.
[295] See pp 202–257, above. English law has been in some danger of treating exemption clauses as the only manifestation of unequal bargaining power.

judgment of Lord Denning MR in *D & C Builders Ltd v Rees*,[296] where he held that the plaintiffs' consent to acceptance of part payment in full satisfaction of a debt 'was no true accord. The debtor's wife held the creditor to ransom. The creditor was in need of money to meet his own commitments and she knew it.'[297] This case involved not the creation of a contract through improper pressure, but its discharge.[298]

In the eighth edition of this work we suggested that it was possible that one day a bold court might use this statement as a springboard for a new development. This prophecy was fulfilled, with perhaps surprising speed, by the judgment of Lord Denning MR in *Lloyds Bank Ltd v Bundy*.[299]

> The defendant was an elderly farmer, whose home and only asset was a farmhouse, which had belonged to the family for generations. The defendant, his son and a company of which the son was in control all banked at the same branch of the plaintiff bank. The company ran into difficulties and the defendant guaranteed its overdraft up to £1,500 and charged his house to the bank for that sum. Later he executed a further guarantee for £5,000 and a further charge for £6,000. As the farmhouse was worth only £10,000 he was advised by his solicitor that that was the most he should commit to the son's business. However the company's difficulties persisted and in December 1969 a newly appointed assistant manager of the branch told the son that further steps must be taken. The son said that his father would help. The assistant manager went to see the father at his farmhouse taking with him completed forms for a further guarantee and charge up to a figure of £11,000. He told the father that the bank could only continue to support the company if he executed the guarantee and charge and the father did so. In May 1970 a Receiver was appointed of the company and the bank took steps to enforce the guarantee and charge.

The Court of Appeal set aside the guarantee and charge. The father looked to the bank for financial advice and placed confidence in it. Since it was in the bank's interest that the father should execute the new guarantee, the bank could not discharge the burden of giving independent advice itself. It was incumbent on the bank therefore to

---

[296] [1966] 2 QB 617, [1965] 3 All ER 837. Discussed p 125, above. See Winder 82 LQR 165; Cornish 29 MLR 428.

[297] Ibid at 625 and 841, respectively. See also *Arrale v Costain Civil Engineering Ltd* [1976] 1 Lloyd's Rep 98.

[298] See Reynolds and Treitel 7 Malaya L Rev 1 at 21–23.

[299] [1975] QB 326, [1974] 3 All ER 757. See also per Lord Diplock in *Schroeder Music Publishing Co Ltd v Macaulay* [1974] 3 All ER 616 at 623, [1974] 1 WLR 1308 at 1315; *Clifford Davis Management Ltd v WEA Records Ltd* [1975] 1 All ER 237, [1975] 1 WLR 61. Though these two latter cases concern the application of the restraint of trade doctrine (pp 517–537 ff, below) they contain observations of general application. See too the dictum of Brightman J in *Mountford v Scott* [1974] 1 All ER 248 at 252 (not reported in [1975] Ch 258); affd on other grounds [1975] Ch 258, [1975] 1 All ER 198. 'The Court would not permit [an] educated person to take advantage of the illiteracy of the other.'

see that the father received independent advice on the transaction and in particular on the affairs of the company. This they had failed to do.

This reasoning was well within the scope of the traditional statements of the doctrine and Cairns LJ and Sir Eric Sachs so decided the case. Lord Denning MR, however, conducted a broad review of the existing law and concluded:

> Gathering all together, I would suggest that through all these instances there runs a single thread. They rest on 'inequality of bargaining power'. By virtue of it, the English law gives relief to one who, without independent advice, enters into a contract upon terms which are very unfair or transfers property for a consideration which is grossly inadequate, when his bargaining power is grievously impaired by reason of his own needs or desires, or by his own ignorance or infirmity, coupled with undue influences or pressures brought to bear on him by or for the benefit of the other. When I use the word 'undue' I do not mean to suggest that the principle depends on proof of any wrongdoing. The one who stipulates for an unfair advantage may be moved solely by his own self-interest, unconscious of the distress he is bringing to the other. I have also avoided any reference to the will of the one being 'dominated' or 'overcome' by the other. One who is in extreme need may knowingly consent to a most improvident bargain, solely to relieve the straits in which he finds himself. Again, I do not mean to suggest that every transaction is saved by independent advice. But the absence of it may be fatal. With these explanations, I hope this principle will be found to reconcile the cases.[300]

This statement was neither approved nor disapproved by the other members of the Court and therefore does not technically form part of the *ratio decidendi* of the case. The same could no doubt be said of many historic pronouncements in English law, such as Lord Atkin's speech in *Donoghue v Stevenson*.[301] Although a general reception of notions of inequality of bargaining power into English law would probably generate a need for sub-rules and qualifications, it is submitted that it would on balance be a fruitful source for future development of the law.[302]

It is now clear that in his judgments in *D & C Builders Ltd v Rees* and *Lloyd's Bank Ltd v Bundy* Lord Denning was suggesting the introduction into English law of not one but two new doctrines, economic duress and inequality of bargaining power. So far the former suggestion has fallen on much more fertile ground than the latter. In delivering the advice of the Privy Council in *Pao On v Lau Yiu Long*[303] Lord Scarman observed that 'there is nothing contrary to principle in recognising economic duress as a factor which may render a contract voidable, provided always that the basis of such recognition is that it must always amount to a coercion of will, which vitiates consent'.[304]

---

[300] Ibid at 339 and 765, respectively.
[301] [1932] AC 562. See Pollock's *Law of Torts* (15th edn) pp 326–333.
[302] Cf Sealy [1975] CLJ 21; Carr 38 MLR 463. Tiplady 46 MLR 601.
[303] [1979] 3 All ER 65 at 79, [1979] 3 WLR 435 at 451.
[304] See also Lord Scarman's observations in *Burmah Oil Co Ltd v Bank of England* [1979] 3 All ER 700 at 729–730, [1979] 3 WLR 722 at 754–755.

Since the Privy Council was quite clear that there had in fact been no coercion of the will, this statement was not surprisingly of the most guarded kind and more weight should perhaps be attached to the judgment of Mocatta J in *North Ocean Shipping Co Ltd v Hyundai Construction Co Ltd.*[305]

The defendants, a firm of shipbuilders, had agreed to build a tanker for the plaintiffs, who were shipowners. The price was agreed at US $30,950,000 payable in five instalments. After the plaintiffs had paid the first instalment the international value of the dollar suffered a sharp decline and the defendants demanded an increase of 10 per cent in the price and threatened not to complete the ship if this was not forthcoming. Unknown to the defendants, this threat was particularly powerful as the plaintiffs had made a profitable contract to charter the ship on completion. The plaintiffs although advised that the defendants had no legal claim therefore agreed to pay the extra money demanded, and paid the remaining four instalments plus 10 per cent and in due course received delivery of the tanker. Some eight months later they claimed repayment of the excess over the originally agreed price. Mocatta J held[306] that in principle this was a case of economic duress, since the threat not to build the ship was both wrongful and highly coercive of the plaintiffs' will but he also held that the plaintiffs had lost their right to set the contract aside by affirmation. The House of Lords in *Universe Tankships of Monrovia v International Transport Workers Federation*,[307] a difficult labour law case, clearly assumed that there was a doctrine of economic duress which would render the contract voidable because one party had entered into it as a result of economic pressure which the law regards as illegitimate.

CTN Cash and Carry Ltd v Gallaher Ltd[308] contains an interesting discussion of the proper limits of economic duress.

In this case, the defendants were distributors of cigarettes and the plaintiffs ran a cash and carry business from six warehouses in towns in the north of England. The plaintiffs were accustomed to buying cigarettes from the defendants. There was no long running contract and each purchase was a separate transaction. Further, the defendants from time to time gave credit and they had given credit on previous occasions to the plaintiffs, but had never undertaken to do so on a regular basis, so that they had absolute discretion to withdraw credit facilities at any time.

In November 1986 the manager of one of the plaintiff's warehouses placed an order for cigarettes with the defendants. Unfortunately, owing to a mistake, the cigarettes were delivered to the wrong warehouse. When the mistake was

---

[305] [1979] QB 705, [1978] 3 All ER 1170; Adams 42 MLR 557; Coote [1980] CLJ 40. See also *The Siboen and The Sibotre* [1976] 1 Lloyd's Rep 293.

[306] He also held that there was technical consideration for the contract in the provision by the defendants of an increased letter of credit to guarantee repayments of the price if the ship was not completed.

[307] [1983] 1 AC 366, [1982] 2 All ER 67. See also *B & S Contracts and Design Ltd v Victor Green Publications Ltd* [1982] ICR 654; affd [1984] ICR 419; *Atlas Express Ltd v Kafco (Importers and Distribution) Ltd* [1989] QB 833, [1989] 1 All ER 641.

[308] [1994] 4 All ER 714.

discovered, it was agreed that the defendants would move the cigarettes to the right warehouse but, unfortunately, before this was done, the whole of the cigarettes, worth some £17,000, were stolen from the first warehouse. The parties disagreed about the results of this. Each party thought that the theft was at the risk of the other party. By the time the case reached the Court of Appeal, it was clear that the plaintiffs were right and that the goods were still at the risk of the defendants while they were in the wrong warehouse awaiting transport to the right warehouse. However, this was not clear in 1986, nor in 1988 when the parties' negotiations for settlement went a stage further. Sometime in 1988 or 1989 a representative of the defendants made it clear to the plaintiffs that if they did not pay the £17,000 for the stolen cigarettes all credit facilities would be withdrawn. The plaintiffs decided that paying for the cigarettes was the lesser of two evils and accordingly did so. In the present action, the plaintiffs sought to get the money back on the grounds that they had only paid it as a result of economic duress.

The Court of Appeal held that the plaintiffs' claim failed. It was accepted that the plaintiffs had only paid the money, which was not owing, because of the threat to remove credit facilities and that this was a threat which was in the circumstances highly coercive. The Court of Appeal, however, thought that the threat was not in the circumstances improper.

One view would be that one can make any threats one likes as long as carrying them out would be lawful. On this view, the only question would be whether the defendants were entitled to withdraw the credit facilities. There was no doubt that they were and this analysis would have provided a very simple answer. However, it is important to underline that the Court of Appeal did not answer the question in this way. They accepted that there could be circumstances in which a threat to do something which one was actually entitled to do was improperly coercive. They thought that the line between improper and proper threats, where the threat was to do something which could lawfully be done, was difficult to draw but that the present case was clearly on the proper side of the line. The primary reason for this was that, at the time when the defendants made the threat, they thought that the £17,000 was in fact due to them. In other words, they were using the threat as a means of getting money which they believed to be due to them and not as a means of extorting money which they knew not to be due to them. Accordingly, the plaintiffs' claim failed.

It is important to note that in the present case the plaintiffs claimed only on the ground of economic duress. It is conceivable that there is some other ground on which the plaintiffs were entitled to have the money repaid; for instance, that it was money paid under a mistake. It is impossible to be sure of this because such a claim was not pleaded and therefore the facts which could have been relevant to deciding whether it could succeed were not examined.

The notion of inequality of bargaining power is clearly much wider since it does not necessarily depend on improper conduct by the stronger party. So far it has been approached by English courts with considerable caution.[309] In a number of cases where counsel have sought to rely on this the court has concluded on the facts that there was nothing more than hard but fair bargaining.[310]

The most important case is *National Westminster Bank plc v Morgan*.[311] In this case the Morgan's family home, which was owned jointly by Mr and Mrs Morgan, was mortgaged to a building society. The husband, an optimistic but unsuccessful businessman, was unable to meet the mortgage repayments and the building society had started proceedings for possession. The bank were approached to help and agreed to refinance the mortgage. The bank manager visited the Morgans in their home with the relevant papers. Mrs Morgan made it clear to the bank manager that she had no confidence in her husband's business schemes. The bank's standard documents did, in fact, cover bank lending to the husband for his business but the bank manager assured Mrs Morgan that this was not the case. Mrs Morgan signed the documents but later sought to set the charge aside on the ground of undue influence. She failed at first instance, succeeded in the Court of Appeal and failed in the House of Lords.

The case presents a number of difficulties. First, it is clear that Mrs Morgan's signature was obtained by the bank manager's misrepresentation as to the effect of the documents but no reliance was placed on this because by the trial no money was outstanding on business borrowing by Mr Morgan who was now dead.[312] Secondly, the differences between the Court of Appeal and the House of Lords seem to rest as much on their analysis of the facts as on their view of the law. The Court of Appeal had relied not on the judgment of Lord Denning MR in *Lloyds Bank Ltd v Bundy* but on the judgment of Sir Eric Sachs in the same case. Lord Scarman in delivering the leading judgment in the House of Lords described the views of Sir Eric Sachs[313] as 'good sense and good law'. For him the decisive consideration was that the transaction carefully analysed was not disadvantageous to the Morgans since it enabled them to stay in their home on terms not inferior to those that they had enjoyed under their building society mortgage.

If, as Lord Scarman emphasised, each case turns on a meticulous examination of its own facts, the decision does not prevent another court on another day from deciding that the stronger party has 'crossed the line' but it does discourage expansive

---

[309] It has been much more enthusiastically received in Canada, see eg *Morrison v Coast Finance* (1965) 55 DLR (2d) 710; *Black v Wilcox* (1976) 70 DLR (3d) 192; *Davidson v Three Spruces Realty Ltd* (1977) 79 DLR (3d) 481; *Harry v Kreutziger* (1978) 95 DLR (3d) 231; *A & K Lick-A-Check Franchises Ltd v Cordiv Enterprises Ltd* (1981) 119 DLR (3d) 440 and in Australia, see eg *Commercial Bank of Australia v Amadio* (1983) 57 ALJR 358 (Hardingham 4 Oxford JLS 273).

[310] *Multiservice Book Binding Ltd v Marden* [1979] Ch 84, [1978] 2 All ER 489; *Burmah Oil Co Ltd v Bank of England* (1981) unreported (Hannigan [1982] JBL 104); *Alec Lobb (Garages) Ltd v Total Oil (GB) Ltd* [1985] 1 All ER 303, [1985] 1 WLR 173.

[311] [1985] AC 686, [1985] 1 All ER 821.

[312] For a case where a mortgagor succeeded on misrepresentation but failed on undue influence, see *Cornish v Midland Bank plc* [1985] 3 All ER 513.

[313] [1975] QB 326 and 347, [1974] 3 All ER 757 and 772.

statements of broad principle in this area.[314] What we can say is that there is no case in English law in which a court has explicitly found that the parties were in a relationship of unequal bargaining power; that the stronger party unfairly took advantage of his superior bargaining power but that nevertheless the contract should stand. It may be asserted with modest confidence that it will be a long time before such a case appears. If this is correct, one may perhaps ask why Lord Denning's judgment in *Lloyds Bank v Bundy* excited so much suspicion. One answer would be a characteristically English suspicion of broad general principles. Another would be misunderstanding. What Lord Denning said might have been significantly more acceptable if he had rather said that 'the categories of unfairness are never closed'. It is not an essential part of the approach in the *Bundy* case that all existing categories should be swept away. An alternative would be to recognise the continued usefulness of the existing categories but to postulate the possibility of a residuary category where the court might intervene even though what had transpired could not readily be slotted in to any of the existing categories.

Historically, courts have divided contracts which may be rescinded[315] for undue influence into two categories: those where there is no special relationship between the parties and those where a special relationship exists. A refinement of this classification was approved by the House of Lords in *Barclays Bank plc v O'Brien*.[316] In this case, the following classification was approved:

> *Class 1: actual undue influence.* In these cases it is necessary for the claimant to prove affirmatively that the wrongdoer exerted undue influence on the complainant to enter into the particular transaction which is impugned.
>
> *Class 2: presumed undue influence.* In these cases the complainant only has to show, in the first instance, that there was a relationship of trust and confidence between the complainant and the wrongdoer of such a nature that it is fair to presume that the wrongdoer abused that relationship in procuring the complainant to enter into the impugned transaction. In class 2 cases therefore there is no need to produce evidence that actual undue influence was exerted in relation to the particular transaction impugned: once a confidential relationship has been proved, the burden then shifts to the wrongdoer to prove that the complainant entered into the impugned transaction freely, for example by showing that the complainant had independent advice. Such a confidential relationship can be established in two ways, viz:
>
> *Class 2A.* Certain relationships (for example solicitor and client, medical advisor and patient) as a matter of law raise the presumption that undue influence has been exercised.
>
> *Class 2B.* Even if there is no relationship falling within class 2A, if the complainant proves the de facto existence of a relationship under which the complainant generally reposed trust and confidence in the wrongdoer, the existence of such relationship raises the presumption of

---

[314] Cf *Avon Finance Co Ltd v Bridger* [1985] 2 All ER 281.

[315] Rescission is the usual but not necessarily the only remedy. See *Mahoney v Purnell* [1996] 3 All ER 61

[316] [1993] 4 All ER 417.

undue influence. In a class 2B case therefore, in the absence of evidence disproving undue influence, the complainant will succeed in setting aside the impugned transaction merely by proof that the complainant reposed trust and confidence in the wrongdoer without having to prove that the wrongdoer exerted actual undue influence or otherwise abused such trust and confidence in relation to the particular transaction impugned.[317]

In both categories 1 and 2B, someone who seeks to set the transaction aside cannot rely simply on the relationship with the other party being one where equity presumes undue influence. The difference is that in category 1 undue influence is being shown with respect to the particular transaction whereas in category 2B undue influence is being deduced from the fact that the relationship, although raising no presumption of undue influence, can be shown in fact to be one where one party was accustomed to giving way to the other. This can perhaps be best understood by taking as an example a relationship of husband and wife. It is clear that there is no presumption of undue influence between husband and wife and therefore the relationship will never fall within category 2A. However, it is certainly the case that in some marriages one partner always does what the other party wants. If this can be shown, then we are in category 2B. Alternatively, it may be shown that in relation to the particular transaction one partner has been overborne by the other. It is easy to see that in such a situation the disadvantaged party may well argue in the alternative that the situation is in category 2B, or category 1. There is no reason why both allegations might not be successful.[318]

a No special relationship between the contracting parties Here it must be affirmatively proved that one party in fact exerted influence over the other and thus procured a contract that would otherwise not have been made. The courts have never attempted to define undue influence with precision, but it has been described as 'some unfair and improper conduct, some coercion from outside, some overreaching, some form of cheating and generally, though not always, some personal advantage obtained by'[319] the guilty party. Examples are: coercing the mind of a person of weak intellect by a claim to possess supernatural powers;[320] taking advantage of a lady who suffers from religious delusions[321] or who is convinced of the truth of messages from the dead transmitted through a spiritualistic medium,[322] playing on the fears of a son concerning the state of his father's health.[323]

A leading case on the subject is *Williams v Bayley*[324] where the facts were these:

A son gave to his bank several promissory notes upon which he had forged the endorsement of his father. At a meeting between the three parties, the banker made

---

[317] Ibid at 423.   [318] *Re Craig, Meneces v Middleton* [1971] Ch 95, [1970] 2 All ER 390.
[319] *Allcard v Skinner* (1887) 36 ChD 145 at 181, per Lindley LJ.
[320] *Nottidge v Prince* (1860) 2 Giff 246.
[321] *Norton v Relly* (1764) 2 Eden 286.   [322] *Lyon v Home* (1868) LR 6 Eq 655.
[323] *Mutual Finance Ltd v John Wetton & Sons Ltd* [1937] 2 KB 389, [1937] 2 All ER 657.
[324] (1866) LR 1 HL 200.

it reasonably evident that if some arrangement were not reached the son would be prosecuted. This impression was conveyed in such expressions as: 'We have only one course to pursue; we cannot be parties to compounding a felony': 'This is a serious matter, a case of transportation for life.' The effect of these expressions upon the father is shown by his somewhat despairing words: 'What be I to do? How can I help myself? You see these men will have their money.' In the result the father agreed in writing to make an equitable mortgage to the bank in consideration of the return of the promissory notes.

This agreement was held to be invalid on the ground that undue pressure had been exerted. The bankers had clearly exploited the fears of the father for the safety of his son, and had thus brought themselves within the equitable principle that, where there is inequality between parties and one of them by taking an unfair advantage of the situation of the other forces an agreement upon him, the transaction will be set aside.[325]

b Where a confidential relationship exists between the parties Here, the equitable view is that undue influence must be presumed, for the fact that confidence is reposed in one party either endows him with exceptional authority over the other or imposes upon him the duty to give disinterested advice. The possibility that he may put his own interest uppermost is so obvious that he comes under a duty to prove that he has not abused his position.[326] Whether a confidential relationship exists or not, the question is always the same—was undue influence used to procure the contract or gift? But the burden of proof is different. If B seeks to avoid a contract with A, then in the absence of any confidential relationship, the entire onus is on B to prove undue influence, but if he proves the existence of such a relationship, the onus is on A to prove that undue influence was not used. A must rebut the presumption of undue pressure.

The special relationships that raise a presumption in favour of undue influence include those of solicitor and client,[327] doctor and patient,[328] trustee and *cestui que trust*,[329] guardian and ward,[330] parent and child,[331] religious adviser and disciple;[332] but do not include husband and wife.[333] Whether they include parties engaged to be married does not admit of a simple answer since the decision of the Court of Appeal in

---

[325] Ibid, at 216, per Lord Chelmsford.

[326] *Allcard v Skinner* (1887) 36 ChD 145 at 181.

[327] See White and Tudor's *Leading Cases in Equity* vol 1, pp 232–234.

[328] *Radcliffe v Price* (1902) 18 TLR 466; *Re CMG* [1970] Ch 574, [1970] 2 All ER 740.

[329] *Ellis v Barker* (1871) 7 Ch App 104.

[330] *Hylton v Hylton* (1754) 2 Ves Sen 547.

[331] *Lancashire Loans Ltd v Black* [1934] 1 KB 380.

[332] Pp 395–396, below. See the instructive judgment of the Supreme Court of Ghana in *Rita Read v Ramsome Divine Attitsogbe* (2006) Commonwealth Law Reports.

[333] *Bank of Montreal v Stuart* [1911] AC 120 at 126. *Domenco v Domenco and Ignat* (1963) 41 DLR (2d) 267. But see *Backhouse v Backhouse* [1978] 1 All ER 1158, [1978] 1 WLR 243.

Zamet v Hyman.[334] The *ratio decidendi* of that case is far from clear, but perhaps a fair interpretation of the judgments is that the presumption will not arise unless the transaction is patently and strikingly unfavourable to the party who seeks its avoidance.[335] We will now illustrate the operation of the principle by considering the case of religious adviser and disciple.

It may well be that the origin of the strict law relating to undue influence is the hostility which the courts have always shown towards spiritual tyranny, for as Lindley LJ said in a leading case: 'The influence of one mind over another is very subtle, and of all influences religious influence is the most dangerous and the most powerful, and to counteract it courts of equity have gone very far.'[336] The facts of *Allcard v Skinner*, the case from which these words are taken, bear this out.

> In 1868 the plaintiff, a woman about 35 years of age, was introduced by her spiritual adviser, one Nihill, to the defendant, who was the lady superior of a Protestant institution known as 'The Sisters of the Poor'. Nihill was the spiritual director and confessor of this sisterhood. Three years later the plaintiff became a sister and took the vows of poverty, chastity and obedience. The vow of poverty was strict, since it required the absolute surrender for ever of all individual property. The plaintiff remained a sister for eight years until 1879 during which time she gave property to the value of about £7,000 to the defendant. She left the sisterhood in 1879 by which time all but £1,671 of the money given had been spent by the defendant upon the purposes of the institution. The plaintiff took no action until 1885, but in that year she sued for the recovery of the £1,671 on the ground that it had been procured by the undue influence of the defendant.

The Court of Appeal found as a fact that no personal pressure had been exerted on the plaintiff and no unfair advantage taken of her position, but that the sole explanation of the gift was her own willing submission to the vow of poverty. Notwithstanding this, however, the court held that her gifts were in fact made under a pressure that she could not resist and that, so far as they had not been spent with her consent on the purposes of the institution, they were recoverable in principle when the pressure was removed by her resignation from the sisterhood.[337] Not only had there been no independent advice, but there was no opportunity of obtaining it, for one of the rules of the sisterhood said: 'Let no Sister seek advice of any extern without the Superior's leave.'

Nevertheless the plaintiff did not recover, for it was held that her claim was barred by her laches[338] and her acquiescence after she had left the sisterhood. Admittedly the claim was not one to which the Statutes of Limitation applied, and no doubt the

---

[334] [1961] 3 All ER 933, [1961] 1 WLR 1442. See Megarry 78 LQR 24.

[335] The court did not appear to agree with the stricter view of Maugham J in *Re Lloyd's Bank Ltd* [1931] 1 Ch 289.

[336] *Allcard v Skinner* (1887) 36 ChD 145 at 183.   [337] Ibid at 186.

[338] Laches is the neglect of a person to assert his rights.

general principle of equity is that delay alone is not a bar to relief. Nevertheless it has always been held that for a person to remain inactive for a long period with a full appreciation of what his rights are, materially affects the question whether he ought to obtain relief. Moreover in the present case there was evidence of acquiescence of the plaintiff. She had been surrounded by advisers for the last five years, she had taken care to revoke a will previously made in favour of the sisterhood, she had ceased to be a Protestant and had joined the Church of Rome, and the reasonable inference was that having considered the question of claiming relief she had determined not to challenge the validity of her gifts.

In contrast with *Allcard v Skinner* may be mentioned *Morley v Loughnan*,[339] where an action, brought six months after the donor's death to recover £140,000 extorted from an epileptic by a Plymouth Brother, was successful.

A contract procured by undue influence cannot be rescinded after affirmation, express or implied, as is seen from *Allcard v Skinner*, nor against persons who acquire rights under it for value and without notice of the facts,[340] but it may be avoided against purchasers for value with notice[341] and also against volunteers, ie persons who give no consideration, though they may be unaware of the undue influence. In the lofty words of Wilmot CJ:

> Whoever received . . . [the gift]. must take it tainted and infected with the undue influence and imposition of the person procuring the gift; his partitioning and cantoning it out amongst his relations and friends, will not purify the gift, and protect it against the equity of the person imposed upon. Let the hand receiving it be ever so chaste, yet if it comes through a corrupt polluted channel, the obligation of restitution will follow it.[342]

The onus is on the party in whom confidence is reposed to show that the party to whom he owed the duty in fact acted voluntarily, in the sense that he was free to make an independent and informed estimate of the expediency of the contract or other transaction.[343] It has been said in several cases that the only way in which the presumption can be rebutted is proof that the person to whom the duty of confidence was owed received independent advice before completion of the contract, and one judge at least has stated that the giving of advice does not suffice unless it has actually been followed.[344] On the other hand, the Privy Council has emphasised that if evidence is given of circumstances sufficient to show that the contract was the act of a free and independent mind, the transaction will be valid even though no external advice was given.[345]

339 [1893] 1 Ch 736. 340 *Bainbrigge v Brown* (1881) 18 ChD 188.
341 *Maitland v Irving* (1846) 15 Sim 437; *Lancashire Loans Ltd v Black* [1934] 1 KB 380.
342 *Bridgeman v Green* (1755) Wilm 58 at 65.
343 *Allcard v Skinner* (1887) 36 ChD 145 at 171.
344 *Powell v Powell* [1900] 1 Ch 243 at 246, per Farwell J.
345 *Inche Noriah v Shaik Allie Bin Omar* [1929] AC 127; approved by Lawrence LJ in *Lancashire Loans Ltd v Black* [1934] 1 KB 380 at 413.

Their Lordships are not prepared to accept the view that independent legal advice is the only way in which the presumption can be rebutted; nor are they prepared to affirm that independent legal advice, when given, does not rebut the presumption, unless it be shown that the advice was taken. It is necessary for the donee to prove that the gift was the result of the free exercise of independent will. The most obvious way to prove this is by establishing that the gift was made after the nature and effect of the transaction had been fully explained to the donor by some independent and qualified person so completely as to satisfy the Court that the donor was acting independently of any influence from the donee and with the full appreciation of what he was doing; and in cases where there are no other circumstances this may be the only means by which the donee can rebut the presumption.[346]

Their Lordships then added, however, that facts which indicate that the donor was a free agent cannot be disregarded 'merely because they do not include independent advice from a lawyer'.

It is not every fiduciary relation that raises the equitable presumption of undue influence. As Fletcher-Moulton LJ once observed, fiduciary relations are many and various, including even the case of an errand boy who is bound to bring back change to his master, and to say that every kind of fiduciary relation justifies the interference of equity is absurd. 'The nature of the fiduciary relation must be such that it justifies the interference.'[347] On the other hand equity has not closed the list of persons against whom the presumption is raised. There are certain special relations where undue influence is invariably presumed, but they do not cover all the possible cases, for the basis of the doctrine is that 'the relief stands upon a general principle, applying to all the variety of relations in which dominion may be exercised by one person over another'.[348]

In his speech in *National Westminster Bank plc v Morgan* [1985] AC 686, [1985] 1 All ER 821, Lord Scarman not only rejected a general doctrine of inequality of bargaining power but also reformulated the test of undue influence. The method and terms of this reformulation are puzzling since it relied principally on a previously little known Indian appeal to the Privy Council and appeared to require as an element of undue influence, at least where there is no special relationship between the contracting parties, that the contract should be manifestly disadvantageous to one party and that one party should be under the domination of the other. Such a strong formulation was

---

[346] [1929] AC 127 at 135. The case concerned a gift, which in the present connection is on the same footing as a contract. An aged and wholly illiterate woman made a gift of land to her nephew who managed her affairs. A lawyer gave her independent and honest advice prior to the execution of the deed, but he did not know that the gift included practically all her property and he did not explain that a will would be a wiser method of benefiting the nephew. The gift was set aside. Cf *Re Brocklehurst's Estate, Hall v Roberts* [1978] Ch 14, [1978] 1 All ER 767.

[347] *Re Coomber, Coomber v Coomber* [1911] 1 Ch 723 at 728–729.

[348] *Huguenin v Baseley* (1807) 14 Ves 273 at 286, per Sir S Romilly, *arguendo*, adopted by Lord Cottenham; *Dent v Bennett* (1839) 4 My & Cr 269 at 277. Examples are: *Tate v Williamson* (1866) 2 Ch App 55; *Inche Noriah v Shaik Allie Bin Omar* [1929] AC 127; *Tufton v Sperni* [1952] 2 TLR 516.

quite unnecessary for the decision of the *Morgan* case since in effect the House of Lords was saying that it was a perfectly straightforward case of lender and borrower with no special features. It is extremely difficult to find the tests of manifest disadvantage or domination in the previous 300 years of history of the undue influence doctrine.[349] In *CIBC Mortgages v Pitt*[350] the House of Lords clearly rejected any requirement of manifest disadvantage as far as a category 1 case is concerned. Lord Browne-Wilkinson said that actual undue influence was a species of fraud and that it had never been suggested that victims of fraud must prove that the transaction was manifestly disadvantageous.[351] Lord Browne-Wilkinson expressed his views about category 1 in words which were in effect an open invitation to Counsel to reargue the correctness of the manifest disadvantage requirement in regard to categories 2A and 2B.[352]

The questions of the classification of undue influence and the requirement of manifest disadvantage were fully reconsidered in the extensive speeches in the House of Lords in *Royal Bank of Scotland plc v Etridge (No.2)* 353 Lord Nicholls in a speech, which Lord Bingham presiding said commanded the unqualified support of the whole House, rejected proposals to remove the requirement but at the same time deprecated the expression 'manifest disadvantage' and thought its use should be dropped. Several of the speeches express doubts about the division of cases of presumed undue influence into two sub-categories.

There have been a series of cases in recent years in which there have been plausible arguments that undue influence (or fraud or misrepresentation or duress) have been practised in connection with a borrowing transaction but it has been disputable whether the undue influence should be attributed to the lender. A useful starting point is *Avon Finance Co Ltd v Bridger*.[353] Here the defendants were an elderly couple who had bought a house for their retirement for £9,275. The arrangements for buying the house had been entirely in the hands of their son, who was a chartered accountant, in whom they placed total but misplaced confidence. The purchase price was provided by a mortgage for £5,000, by a loan of £1,775 from the defendants and by £2,500 provided by the son. In order to provide this £2,500, the son had borrowed £3,500 from Avon Finance on the security of his parents' house. In order to do this, he had obtained his parents' signature to the documents by telling them that they were in connection with the building society mortgage of £5,000. The son failed

---

[349] This is clearly stated in the decision of the Court of Appeal in *Goldsworthy v Brickel* [1987] Ch 378, [1987] 1 All ER 853. The Court of Appeal thought that it was not 'necessary for the party to whom the trust and confidence is reposed to dominate the other party in any sense in which that word is generally understood'.

[350] [1993] 4 All ER 433.

[351] The same might be said of common law duress. See *Barton v Armstrong* [1976] AC 104.

[352] [2001] UKHL 44, [2001] 4 All ER 449

[353] [1985] 2 All ER 281 (actually decided in 1979).

to keep up his payments to the finance company who thereupon sought to enforce their security against the defendants. Clearly in this case there was fraud as between the son and his parents, but did this affect the rights of the plaintiffs? The Court of Appeal held that it did. A number of different reasons were given in the judgments. Perhaps the most important reason is that the plaintiff had appointed the son as their agent to get his parents to sign the loan documents. As a result, the son's fraud (and undue influence) were to be attributed to the finance company. In the circumstances, the finance company ought at least to have dealt directly with the parents and perhaps also to have taken steps to see that the parents had independent advice. This analysis based on asking whether the lenders had made the person who exercised the undue influence or fraud, misrepresentation or duress, their agent for the purpose of the transaction, was followed in a whole series of Court of Appeal decisions.[354]

This analysis was rejected by the House of Lords in *Barclays Bank v O'Brien*.[355] In this case the husband, who was a shareholder in a manufacturing company, wanted to increase the overdraft which the company had with the plaintiff bank. It was agreed that the overdraft would be increased to £135,000 reducing to £120,000 after three weeks. The husband offered as security a personal guarantee to be secured by a second charge over the matrimonial home which was jointly owned by himself and his wife. The manager quite properly gave instructions for the preparation of the necessary documents and for the bank's staff to explain the documents to both husband and wife and to explain the need for independent legal advice if there was any doubt. However, these instructions were not followed by the bank's staff and both the husband and the wife signed the documents without reading them. The wife alleged that the husband had put her under undue pressure to sign and that she had succumbed to that pressure and also that her husband had misrepresented to her the effect of the legal charge. She said that although she knew she was signing the mortgage she believed that security was limited to £60,000 and would only last three weeks. The trial judge had refused to set the transaction aside but the Court of Appeal unanimously allowed the appeal. Scott LJ thought it was wholly artificial to enquire whether the husband was the agent of the bank, since any such agency was wholly fictional. On the other hand, he thought that as a matter of policy married women who provided security for their husband's debts and others in an analogous position, such as elderly parents on whom pressure might be brought to bear by adult children, would be treated as a specially protected class so that the transaction might be set aside under general equitable principles.

---

[354] *Kingsnorth Trust Ltd v Bell* [1986] 1 All ER 423; [1986] 1 WLR 119. *Coldunell Ltd v Gallon* [1986] QB 1184, [1986] 1 All ER 429. *Midland Bank plc v Shephard* [1988] 3 All ER 17; *Bank of Baroda v Shah* [1988] 3 All ER 24; *Bank of Credit and Commerce International SA v Aboody* [1990] 1 QB 923, [1992] 4 All ER 955, [1989] 2 WLR 759.

[355] [1993] 4 All ER 417.

The House of Lords agreed with Scott LJ that the analysis in terms of agency was artificial and misleading. Lord Browne-Wilkinson rejected the notion that there was a special equity in favour of wives. He thought that the key to the problem was the doctrine of notice so that:

> ... where a wife has agreed to stand surety for her husband's debts as a result of undue influence or misrepresentation, the creditor will take subject to the wife's equity to set aside the transaction if the circumstances are such as to put the creditor on enquiry as to the circumstances in which she agreed to stand surety.

In applying this principle, it is clearly relevant that the surety is the spouse of the debtor, since husbands and wives behave in financial matters in ways which are different from those which parties acting at arm's length would do. A lender who finds a wife standing surety to a husband's business borrowing should therefore have very much in mind the serious possibility that the wife has been misled or over persuaded and ought to take reasonable steps to satisfy himself that the wife's agreement has been properly obtained. If he does not do so, he can be treated as having constructive notice of the wife's rights.

A second decision of the House of Lords in *CIBC Mortgages v Pitt*[356] needs to be read together with *Barclays Bank v O'Brien*. The two cases were heard by the same five Lords of Appeal and in each case the single reasoned speech was that of Lord Browne-Wilkinson. Nevertheless, the facts are significantly different and some important additional issues not addressed in *O'Brien* are considered.

> Mr and Mrs Pitt owned in 1986 the family home in Willesden which was then valued at some £270,000, subject to a building society mortgage for £16,700. In 1986 Mr Pitt told Mrs Pitt that he wished to raise money on the house to buy shares on the stock market. Mrs Pitt was not convinced that this would be a good idea but she was then subjected by Mr Pitt to what the trial judge held to be actual undue influence, as a result of which she agreed to the suggestion.
>
> Mr Pitt got in touch with the plaintiffs and told them that he wished to raise a mortgage on the house for the purpose of buying a holiday home. He raised a loan for £150,000 for repayment over 19 years. The money was said to be available for paying off the existing mortgage and the balance 'to be used to purchase a second property without the applicants resorting to any additional borrowing'. Clearly, this involved Mr Pitt misleading the plaintiffs but Mrs Pitt signed all the papers without reading them. The plaintiffs' solicitors acted for Mr and Mrs Pitt as well as for the plaintiffs in respect of the transaction. Mrs Pitt signed all the mortgage documents without reading them. No-one suggested that she should get independent advice and she did not do so.
>
> In fact, Mr Pitt not only did not intend to spend the balance of the mortgage

356 [1993] 4 All ER 433.

money on a holiday home; he did not intend simply to buy shares on the Stock Exchange. What he did was to buy shares and then use the shares as collateral for further loans to buy further shares and so on. He thereby acquired a vast number of shares and very substantial indebtedness. Apparently, at one stage, he was indeed a paper millionaire but he never realised any of the gains on the shares. When, in October 1987, the stock market crashed, he was left in a hopelessly exposed position. The banks, who had advanced money against the shares, sold them. Mr Pitt was unable to keep up the payments due on the charge on the family home. At the time of trial in July 1992, the total sum outstanding on the charge was nearly £209,000 which, by this time, was said to be greater than the value of the house.

The trial judge held that there had been no misrepresentation by Mr Pitt to Mrs Pitt; that Mr Pitt had been guilty of actual undue influence; that the transaction was manifestly disadvantageous to Mrs Pitt and that Mr Pitt had not acted as the agent of the plaintiffs. The Court of Appeal reversed the judge's decision that the transaction was manifestly disadvantageous to Mrs Pitt. As stated above, the House of Lords held that manifest disadvantage was not a requirement in a case of actual undue influence.

Mrs Pitt could certainly set aside the transaction as against Mr Pitt. However, of course, the practical question is whether she could set aside the transaction as against the plaintiffs. In this respect, the House of Lords thought the situation substantially different from *O'Brien*. For a wife to mortgage her share of the family home in order to underwrite borrowings by the husband alone in respect of his business was of itself a sufficiently suspect transaction to require the lender to warn of the desirability of independent advice. For a husband and wife to jointly borrow money on the home for a joint purpose like buying a holiday home was not a transaction which in itself in any way aroused suspicion. So, someone in the position of Mrs Pitt could only overturn the transaction if they could show either actual notice or some event putting the lender on enquiry.

This raises very interesting questions which were not discussed in detail as to what would be required to put the lender on enquiry. Presumably, if Mr Pitt had told the lender of his intention to pursue a speculative programme on the Stock Exchange, the risks to the wife would have been sufficiently obvious to require the lender to urge her to take independent advice. Suppose he had told the lenders what he is alleged to have told Mrs Pitt, that is that he intended to use the money to buy shares. Although Mr Pitt had told Mrs Pitt that this proposal would lead to an increase in her standard of living, it is difficult to see how this could in fact have been true since there would only have been a net increase in the family income if the dividends from the shares exceeded the sums necessary to service the mortgage. Taking into account the mortgage interest rates at the time of the transaction, such results could only have been obtained by investing in extremely risky shares. Would this be sufficient to require the bank to suggest the desirability of independent advice?

These two decisions of the House of Lords were followed by an extensive chain of Court of Appeal decisions[357] and eventually by a third House of Lords decision in *Royal Bank of Scotland plc v Etridge* (No. 2).[358] Although the speeches in the House of Lords contain numerous tributes to the classical nature of Lord Browne-Wilkinson's analysis there is in practice a significant edging away. The most important modification is to go over to a rule that in all normal circumstances the lending bank should take steps to see that the wife is advised by a solicitor. Lord Nicholls sets out what the solicitor should do in a meeting with the wife in the following passage.

> When an instruction to this effect is forthcoming, the content of the advice required from a solicitor before giving the confirmation sought by the bank will, inevitably, depend upon the circumstances of the case. Typically, the advice a solicitor can be expected to give should cover the following matters as the core minimum. (1) He will need to explain the nature of the documents and the practical consequences these will have for the wife if she signs them. She could lose her home if her husband's business does not prosper. Her home may be her only substantial asset, as well as the family's home. She could be made bankrupt. (2) He will need to point out the seriousness of the risk involved. The wife should be told the purpose of the proposed new facility, the amount and principal terms of the new facility, and that the bank might increase the amount of the facility, or change its terms, or grant a new facility without reference to her. She should be told the amount of her liability under her guarantee. The solicitor should discuss the wife's financial means including her understanding of the value of the property being charged. The solicitor should discuss whether the wife or her husband has any other assets out of which repayment could be made if the husband's business should fail. These matters are relevant to the seriousness of the risks involved. (3) The solicitor will need to state clearly that the wife has a choice. The decision is hers and hers alone. Explanation of the choice facing the wife will call for some discussion of the present financial position, including the amount of the husband's present indebtedness, and the amount of his current overdraft facility. (4) The solicitor should check whether the wife wishes to proceed. She should be asked whether she is content that the solicitor should write to the bank confirming he has explained to her the nature of the documents and the practical implications they may have for her, or whether, for instance, she would prefer him to negotiate with the bank on the terms of the transaction. Matters for negotiation could include the sequence in which the various securities will be called upon or a specific or lower limit to her liabilities. The solicitor should not give any confirmation to the bank without the wife's authority.

It should be noted that the House of Lords did not require that the wife should be advised by an independent solicitor.

There may however be cases where it is clear that no competent solicitor could possibly have advised the transaction. In *Crédit Lyonnais Bank Nederland NV v*

---

[357] See *Massey v Midland Bank plc* [1995] 1 All ER 929; *Banco Exterior Internacionale v Mann* [1995] 1 All ER 936; *Barclays Bank plc v Thomson* [1997] 4 All ER 816 *Yorkshire Bank plc v Tinsley* [2004] EWCA Civ 816, [2004] 3 All ER 463.

[358] [2001] UKHL 44, [2001] 4 All ER 449; Scott (2002) 18 J Contract L 236.

Burch[359] the defendant was employed in a relatively junior position by a tour operating company dominated by a Mr Pelosi, on whom the defendant relied heavily though there was no sexual or emotional relationship between them. The company wished to increase its overdraft from £250,000 to £270,000 and the bank required security. The defendant had an equity of some £70,000 in her flat and she was persuaded by Mr Pelosi to agree to granting a second charge over the flat to secure all company borrowing both past and future. The Court of Appeal thought the transaction so spectacularly disadvantageous that it should be struck down. Millett LJ said that independent advice 'is neither always necessary nor always sufficient'.

---

[359] [1997] 1 All ER 144.

10 CONTRACTS RENDERED VOID BY STATUTE

Of the various contracts rendered void by statute, there are only two which seem to require discussion in a general book upon contract. These are, first, wagering contracts and, secondly, agreements prohibited by competition law.

A WAGERING CONTRACTS

At common law, bets were enforceable. By a complex series of statutes from 1710 to 1892 wagering contracts were rendered void. These statutes were repealed by sections 334 and 356 of the Gambling Act 2005. Most of this Act came into force in November 2005 but these sections had not come into force at the time of writing. The repeal was not retrospective and the law as stated in this chapter will apply to transactions before the Act comes into force.

1 The definition of a wagering contract

The primary meaning of 'wagering' is staking something of value upon the result of some future uncertain event, such as a horse race, or upon the ascertainment of the truth concerning some past or present event, such as the population of London, with regard to which the wagering parties express opposite views. In *Carlill v Carbolic Smoke Ball Co*,[1] Hawkins J gave the following definition of a wagering contract which later received the unqualified approval of the Court of Appeal:[2]

> A wagering contract is one by which two persons, professing to hold opposite views touching the issue of a future uncertain event, mutually agree that, dependent upon the determination of that event, one shall win from the other, and that other shall pay or hand over to him, a sum of money or other stake; neither of the contracting parties having any other interest in that contract than the sum or stake he will so win or lose, there being no other real consideration for the making of such contract by either of the parties.[3]

There are several aspects of this definition which require to be considered.

In the first place, its limitation to a future uncertain event is incorrect, for a wager is none the less a wager though it concerns a past or present fact or event.

Secondly, an essential feature of a wagering contract is that one party is to win and the other to lose upon the determination of the event.[4] Each party must stand either to win or lose under the terms of the contract. It is not a wagering contract if one party may win but cannot lose, or if he may lose but cannot win, or if he can neither win nor lose. For instance, in *Ellesmere v Wallace*:[5]

> Edgar Wallace nominated a horse for a race, the advertised conditions of which were that £5 or £2 had to be paid to the Jockey Club according as a nominated horse started or did not start in the race. Another condition was that the owner of the winning horse should receive £200 provided by the Jockey Club and also the entrance moneys paid by the various nominators less a sum of £30. Wallace's horse did not run, and when sued for the recovery of he pleaded that the contract between him and the Jockey Club was void as being a wagering contract.

The Court of Appeal held that the money was recoverable. The argument that the contract was a wager, since if the horse was successful Wallace would win £200 plus a further amount and if it failed he would lose £5, was fallacious, for the Jockey Club did not stand to win or lose anything as a result of the nomination. They did not lose under the contract merely because that particular horse succeeded, for their liability was to pay £200 to the successful owner no matter who he might be. Their liability would be no greater or less whether Wallace nominated or did not nominate a horse. Moreover they did not win anything if Wallace's horse failed in the

---

[1] [1892] 2 QB 484.   [2] *Ellesmere v Wallace* [1929] 2 Ch 1 at 24, 36, 48–49.
[3] [1892] 2 QB 484 at 490–91.
[4] *Thacker v Hardy* (1878) 4 QBD 685; *Lockwood v Cooper* [1903] 2 KB 428.   [5] [1929] 2 Ch 1.

race, since the nomination fee did not accrue to them but was earmarked for the successful owner.

Thus, a bet placed with the Horseracing Totalisator Board is not a wagering contract within the meaning of the Gaming Act 1845, since the board can neither win nor lose on the transaction. Its function is merely to divide the aggregate amount received, less expenses, among the successful contributors.[6] The same is true of the 'treble chance' on the football pools. It will be seen therefore that many betting transactions are not legally wagers.

Thirdly, if an essential feature of a wager is that there must be two persons either of whom is capable of winning or losing, it follows that there must be no more than two parties or two groups of parties to the contract. It was argued, for instance, in *Ellesmere v Wallace* that there was a multipartite wagering contract between Wallace and each of the other nominators, but, as Russell LJ demonstrated, it was impossible to express in terms of wagers the effect of several persons nominating horses for the race. It could not be shown that Wallace made a bet with each nominator. If his horse lost the race then he himself would lose the alleged bet, ie what he had paid as entrance fee, but the other party to the supposed wager would not necessarily win anything. He would win only if his horse won the race.[7]

> The truth is that you cannot have more than two parties or two sides to a bet. You may have a multipartite agreement to contribute to a sweepstakes (which may be illegal as a lottery if the winner is determined by chance, but not if the winner is determined by skill), but you cannot have a multipartite agreement for a bet unless the numerous parties are divided into two sides, of which one wins or the other wins, according to whether an uncertain event does or does not happen.[8]

The last essential feature of a wager is that the stake must be the only interest which the parties have in the contract.[9] If A lays B ten to one in sovereigns against a particular horse for the St Leger, B stands to win £10, A stands to win £1, but neither of them has any other interest whatsoever in the contract. On the other hand if either party to a contract, under which money is payable upon the determination of an uncertain event, possesses an interest in the subject matter of the contract that will be affected in value according to the determination of the event, the contract is not void as being a wager. Thus in one sense every contract of insurance is a bet on the outcome of a future uncertain event and therefore literally speaking a wager. A wife, for instance, who insures her husband's life for £10,000 in return for an annual premium of £200, stands to gain or lose according to the eventual length of the life assured. To apply this rigorous reasoning, however, would not be practical politics and it has long

---

[6] *Tote Investors Ltd v Smoker* [1968] 1 QB 509, [1967] 3 All ER 242; *Osorio v Cardona* (1984) 15 DLR (4th) 619.
[7] [1929] 2 Ch 1 at 50–51.
[8] Ibid at 52, per Russell LJ. See also *Tote Investors Ltd v Smoker*, above.
[9] *Carlill v Carbolic Smoke Ball Co* [1892] 2 QB 484.

been established that whether a contract of insurance is a wager depends upon whether the assured has what is called an insurable interest in the event upon which the insurance money becomes payable. If A ships cargo on B's vessel bound for a foreign port, the contract by which he insures the safe arrival of the ship is not a wager since his own property is at risk during the voyage, though in effect it means that the insurer will pay £x in one event but nothing in another. But if A has no cargo on board, the contract by which he insures the safe arrival of the vessel is a wager, for his only interest in the fate of the vessel is that if she is lost he recovers £x, while if she reaches her destination he loses the amount of his premium.[10] The modern practice of insuring against bad weather provides another example. If a cricketer insures against the fall of more than one-eighth of an inch of rain during the first three days of the Canterbury cricket week, the contract is valid if he is financially interested in the match, as for instance if it is being played for his benefit, but void if he has no such interest.

The question whether the parties are interested in something more than the mere winning or losing of a stake depends upon the substance of the agreement, not upon its outward form.

> In construing a contract with a view to determining whether it is a wagering one or not, the Court will receive evidence in order to arrive at the substance of it, and will not confine its attention to the mere words in which it is expressed, for a wagering contract may be sometimes concealed under the guise of language which, on the face of it, if words were only to be considered, might constitute a legally enforceable contract.[11]

Thus in *Brogden v Marriott*,[12] A agreed to buy a horse from B, the price to be £200 if it trotted within a month at eighteen miles an hour, but a shilling if it failed to attain this speed. The horse having failed in its attempt, A claimed it at the nominal price of a shilling, but the agreement was held to be a wager, not a *bona fide* conditional contract. A rather more subtle case is *Rourke v Short*[13] where the facts were these:

> The parties to a proposed contract for the sale of rags disagreed about the price that had been paid upon the occasion of a former sale. They ultimately agreed that if the seller's memory proved to be accurate the price of the present sale should be six shillings per cwt, otherwise it should be three shillings per cwt. The seller proved to be correct.

The buyer refused to accept the rags, and an action by the seller to recover the price failed. Lord Campbell expressed the view that:

---

[10] Cf *Kent v Bird* (1777) 2 Cowp 583.

[11] *Carlill v Carbolic Smoke Ball Co* [1892] 2 QB 484 at 491–492, per Hawkins J. Cf *Universal Stock Exchange v Strachan* [1896] AC 166 at 173.

[12] (1836) 3 Bing NC 88.

[13] (1856) 5 E & B 904.

The previous price was the point on which the wager was to turn, and the stake was the difference of the price to be now paid . . . It makes no difference that there was a real intention to part with the goods.[14]

Another type of case in which it becomes necessary to ascertain the real nature of an agreement is where a client instructs a stockbroker to buy or sell shares. A contract of this nature may be a wager, and it is so where it takes the form of what is called a contract for differences, ie where the parties agree merely to pay or receive the difference between the price of certain shares on one day and their price on another day.[15] For instance:

A instructs B, a stockbroker, to procure a thousand ordinary shares in a certain company at £80 a share, the transaction to be completed at the next Stock Exchange settling day, a fortnight hence.

If in this case it is found as a fact that neither party contemplated the delivery of shares, but intended that if the market price rose above £80 at the next settling day, B should pay the difference between that price and £80 to A, while if it fell A should pay the difference to B, then the contract is void as a wager. If on the other hand the intention is that the shares shall actually be purchased by B, the contract is not a wager. This is so even though A, to the knowledge of B, is not prepared to take the shares up but intends to resell them before the settling day and thus to gain or lose according as the price since the day of their purchase rises or falls.[16] Where such is the intention of the parties, B is clearly authorised to enter into contracts for the purchase of shares from jobbers, and is entitled to be indemnified by A against the obligations that he thereby incurs.[17] Thus contracts for the purchase of shares are not wagers unless the agreement is that the purchaser has no right to claim delivery and the seller has no right to insist upon it.[18] As Cave J said in his direction to the jury in *Universal Stock Exchange Ltd v Strachan*:[19]

In order to be a gambling transaction such as the law points at it must be a gambling transaction in the intention of both the parties to it.

Exactly the same principles apply to other potentially speculative transactions, such as dealing in commodity futures.[20]

An interesting modern example is *Morgan Grenfell v Welwyn Hatfield District Council*.[21] In this case, the defendant local authority entered into pairs of contracts in one of

---

[14] Ibid at 910.   [15] *Grizewood v Blane* (1852) 11 CB 538.

[16] *Thacker v Hardy* (1878) 4 QBD 685; *Weddle, Beck & Co v Hackett* [1929] 1 KB 321; *Woodward v Wolfe* [1936] 3 All ER 529.

[17] *Thacker v Hardy*, above.

[18] *Ironmonger & Co v Dyne* (1928) 44 TLR 497 at 499, per Scrutton LJ.

[19] [1896] AC 166 at 167–168.

[20] *Wilson, Smithett and Cope Ltd v Terruzzi* [1976] QB 683, [1976] 1 All ER 817.

[21] [1995] 1 All ER 1.

which, with the plaintiff, it was a floating interest rate payer and the plaintiff was a fixed interest rate payer and in the second of which the roles were reversed between it and another local authority (Islington). In due course, these transactions were held to be *ultra vires* local authorities.[22] The plaintiff brought an action in restitution and the defendants made a similar claim against Islington. Islington raised a preliminary issue that such transactions partook of the nature of gaming and wagering and were therefore contrary to section 18 of the Gaming Act 1845 and/or section 1 of the Gaming Act 1892.

The judgment of Hobhouse J provides a useful restatement of classic discussions of the line between gaming and wagering contracts and valid contracts. Some transactions, such as betting on which horse will come first in a race, are necessarily wagers. Other contracts may, on their face, appear to have nothing to do with wagering but it may be possible to show in particular circumstances that the transaction is in substance a wager. Interest rate swap contracts are of such a kind. They may in particular cases be gaming contracts but they are not necessarily so. One feature of the present case was clearly that Welwyn were not entering into any speculation since, whatever the movement in interest rates, their element of profit would remain the same. However, this fact is not in itself decisive since a bookmaker who laid off all bets and relied entirely on arbitraging movements of odds might reduce or eliminate his risk but the transactions would still be wagering. A further distinction between Welwyn and the bookmaker was in its purpose which was clearly non-speculative. The purpose of Islington was not the same since it was not entering into back to back transactions. Islington's primary purpose was not to speculate on the movement of interest rates but to raise money in advance which could be treated as a revenue receipt by incurring revenue liabilities spread over a period of years. It was therefore not a wager.

Many speculative financial transactions of this kind have been taken out of the law of gaming by the Financial Services Act 1986, section 63 of which provides:

(1) No contract to which this section applies shall be void or unenforceable by reason of—(a) section 18 of the Gaming Act 1845, section 1 of the Gaming Act 1892 or any corresponding provisions in force in Northern Ireland . . .

(2) This section applies to any contract entered into by either or each party by way of business and the making or performing of which for either party constitutes an activity which falls within paragraph 12 of Schedule 1 to this Act or would do so apart from Parts III and IV of that Schedule.

Para 12 of Schedule 1 provides

Buying, selling, subscribing for or underwriting investments or offering or agreeing to do so, either as principal or as an agent.

---

[22] *Hazell v Hammersmith and Fulham London Borough Council* [1991] 1 All ER 545.

In *City Index Ltd v Leslie*[23] the plaintiffs were a company specialising in offering gambling in relation to financial indices such as the FT30. For instance they would offer a forecast of what the FT30 index would be at close of business of the day and a client who thought the forecast too conservative could make a 'buy' bet on the basis that he would win the amount bet per point above the forecast index at the end of the day, although he would lose a similar amount for each point for which the index failed to reach the forecast figure. Contrariwise, if he thought the forecast was too high he could place a 'sell' bet which would have the reverse effect. Such bets have long been regarded as invalid and unenforceable under the Gaming Acts but the Court of Appeal agreed that the 1986 Act had validated and made enforceable this transaction.

2 The effect of a wagering contract

a The effect as between the parties

The Gaming Act 1845 in the following section renders all wagering contracts void.

> All contracts or agreements, whether by parole or in writing, by way of gaming or wagering, shall be null and void; and no suit shall be brought or maintained in any court of law or equity for recovering any sum of money or valuable thing alleged to be won upon any wager, or which shall have been deposited in the hands of any person to abide the event on which any wager shall have been made.
>
> Provided always that this enactment shall not be deemed to apply to any subscription or contribution or agreement to subscribe or contribute for or towards any plate, prize or sum of money to be awarded to the winner or winners of any lawful game, sport, pastime or exercise.[24]

It is convenient for purposes of exposition to deal separately with the four branches of this section.

The first is as follows:

> All contracts or agreements, whether by parole or in writing, by way of gaming or wagering shall be null and void.

The effect of these words is that a wagering contract is 'struck with invalidity at the outset, ie before the event contemplated by the wager has occurred'.[25] It is void, though not illegal. It confers no rights upon either party. If the loser fails to pay, recovery cannot be enforced by action, whether brought for the amount of the bet or on an account stated.[26] If he stops a cheque which he has given for the amount, he cannot be sued. If he pays the winner in cash or gives him a cheque which is

---

[23] [1991] 3 All ER 180.   [24] S 18.
[25] *Hill v William Hill (Park Lane) Ltd* [1949] AC 530 at 552, [1949] 2 All ER 452 at 464, per Lord Greene.
[26] *Alberg v Chandler* (1948) 64 TLR 394.

honoured, it might be expected that, as the contract is void and the payments therefore made without consideration, he should be entitled to recover the money. The law does not take this view. The Act is apparently treated as conferring a privilege which the loser may waive if he pleases, and payment constitutes waiver. In the words of Bowen LJ the loser merely 'waives a benefit which the statute has given to him and confers a good title to the money upon the person to whom he pays it'.[27]

The second branch is as follows:

> No suit shall be brought or maintained in any court of law or equity for recovering any sum of money or valuable thing alleged to be won upon any wager.

The interpretation put upon these words by the House of Lords in *Hill v William Hill (Park Lane) Ltd*,[28] is that they do not merely repeat what is enacted in the first branch, but that they strike at fresh agreements made by the parties subsequently to the original wagering contract itself.

The result of this interpretation is to overrule a number of decisions dating back at least to 1870. These had distinguished the original wager from a later and distinct contract under which the loser, for a fresh consideration, promises to pay the amount of the bet. In several cases of this type the courts had enforced the later contract. What generally happens is that the winner puts pressure upon the loser by a threat to do something to his detriment if he continues to be recalcitrant. He may thus threaten to expose the loser's dishonourable conduct to his club[29] or to his bank manager[30] or, if he happens to be a bookmaker or an owner of a race horse, to report him to Tattersalls[31] or to the Jockey Club.[32] The loser then makes a fresh promise to pay in consideration that the winner will forbear to implement his threat. Thus, in *Hyams v Stuart King*:[33]

> Two bookmakers, A and B, had betting transactions which resulted in a sum becoming due from A to B. A failed to pay, but ultimately agreed to do so in consideration that B would refrain from declaring him a defaulter to the injury of his business with his customers.

Although the agreement was in substance no more than a repetition of the void wagering contract, the majority of the Court of Appeal held it to be enforceable. They took the view that it was free from vice. In the opinion of Farwell LJ, it was unaffected by the Act of 1845 since it was not a wager but merely a contract designed to avoid the consequences of having made a wager. Again, it was not illegal *per se*, since it is not illegal to tell the members of the betting fraternity that a bookmaker is prone to

---

[27] *Bridger v Savage* (1885) 15 QBD 363 at 367.   [28] [1949] AC 530, [1949] 2 All ER 452.

[29] *Re Browne, ex p Martingell* [1904] 2 KB 133.

[30] *Poteliakhoff v Teakle* [1938] 2 KB 816, [1938] 3 All ER 686.

[31] *Goodson v Baker* (1908) 98 LT 415. Such a threat does not constitute blackmail: *Burden v Harris* [1937] 4 All ER 559.

[32] *Bubb v Yelverton* (1870) LR 9 Eq 471.   [33] [1908] 2 KB 696.

default; nor was it tainted with illegality merely because it sprang from a wager, for a wager, though void, is not illegal. Fletcher Moulton LJ dissented. He could not regard the contract as other than a contract to pay money alleged to have been won upon a wager and therefore directly within the language of the second limb of the statute. The sole object of this colourable agreement was that the bet should be paid.

The controversy aroused by this decision was finally laid to rest forty years later by the decision of the House of Lords in *Hill v William Hill (Park Lane) Ltd.*[34] The facts were these:

> On 22 July 1946, the committee of Tattersalls made an order that the appellant, an owner of race horses, should discharge the amount of his unpaid bets of £3,635 12s 6d due to the respondents by paying £635 12s 6d within fourteen days and thereafter by paying monthly instalments of £100.
>
> In August 1946, the appellant, having failed to comply with the order, gave the respondents a cheque for £635 12s 6d post-dated to 10 October and promised to begin the monthly instalments in November in consideration that the respondents would refrain from enforcing the order. Enforcement of the order would involve his being posted as a defaulter and warned off Newmarket Heath. The appellant failed to pay the instalments and the respondents sued to recover their amount.

By a majority of four to three, the House of Lords held that this contract, though unaffected by the first branch of the section since it was clearly not a contract 'by way of gaming or wagering', was nevertheless void under the second branch.

The minority were of opinion that the second branch was neither intended nor apt to invalidate a contract that was not itself a wager. In their view, it was a mere procedural provision designed to fortify the preceding words. 'The second or procedural part', said Lord Radcliffe, 'is introduced by the word *and*; the words *alleged to be won* are used to describe the sum of money of which recovery by legal action is forbidden.'[35] Lord Greene expressed his disagreement with this argument in the following words:

> The language of the first branch is entirely different from the language of the second branch. Under the first branch the agreement is a nullity before the race is run. The second branch assumes the race to have been run and the bet to have been lost. It is true that the language of the second branch would prohibit the bringing of an action upon a wager which had been won. To that extent I agree that it covers ground already adequately covered by the first branch. But this is no justification for limiting the words of the second branch as suggested. They are quite general and when read in their ordinary meaning they extend to any action to recover money alleged to be won on a wager.[36]

---

[34] [1949] AC 530, [1949] 2 All ER 452.

[35] [1949] AC at 579; and see 541, per Lord Jowitt.

[36] *Hill v William Hill (Park Lane) Ltd* [1949] AC 530 at 552, [1949] 2 All ER 452 at 465; see also Lord MacDermott at 577 and 480, respectively.

The same conclusion was reached by the majority of the Law Lords. The respondents; action was brought to 'recover a sum of money alleged to be won upon a wager' and was therefore rendered void by the statute.

The single question of fact, therefore, that always falls to be determined in this type of case is not whether there was a fresh bargain but whether, according to the true nature and substance of the contract, the money sought to be recovered is money alleged, either by plaintiff or defendant, to be won upon a wager.[37] This question is, in essence, one of intention. In each case 'the court must look to the reality of the transaction and come to a finding as to what the true intention was'.[38] Thus in *Hill v William Hill (Park Lane) Ltd*, there could be no doubt that the subject matter of the fresh contract was the very sum of money won on the wager. The contract referred specifically and solely to the sum fixed in the order of Tattersall's committee, and this sum was identical in amount and character with the wagering debt.[39] Again, if, as in *Coral v Kleyman*,[40] A fails to pay a lost bet to B and his father promises to pay the amount due in consideration that B will not report the failure to Tattersalls, an action brought on this promise must fail; the transaction is but a transparent device to avoid the second branch of the statute. The position, however, may be more doubtful. Suppose, for instance, that the loser promises to transfer his motor car to the winner in return for the latter's promise that the non-payment of the wager shall be concealed from the loser's friends. Is the subject matter of this promise 'a valuable thing alleged to be won on a wager' within the meaning of the statute? If the words of the statute are to be read literally, the promise is not caught by them; it cannot be said that the motor car was 'alleged to be won on the wager'. But the courts are hardly likely to suffer so obvious an evasion. The view emphasised in *Hill v William Hill (Park Lane) Ltd* is that one object of the second branch of section 18 is 'to preclude resort to an obvious way round the earlier provision',[41] and a promise by the loser to transfer to the winner a car substantially equal to the amount of the bet is only a slightly less transparent device to avoid the statute than a new promise to pay the money itself. But the loser's promise may wear, at least on the surface, a more innocent aspect. Suppose he agrees to sell to the winner for £2,000 a horse worth £3,000, and, when sued for breach of contract, pleads that the agreement was made in consideration that his failure to pay the lost bet should not be published by the winner. Such a case may well provoke prolonged argument, and human ingenuity may yet devise more subtle methods of evasion. The principle, however, remains the same however difficult to apply. No fresh contract is

---

37 Ibid at 578 and 481, respectively, per Lord MacDermott.

38 Ibid at 574 and 478, respectively, per Lord MacDermott. At 559 and 468 respectively, Lord Greene says: 'I must not be understood as suggesting that there can never be a case where a promise by a defaulting backer given in consideration of a promise by the winner of a bet not to report the defaulter may be enforced.'

39 Ibid at 564 and 472, respectively, per Lord Normand; at 546 and 461, respectively, per Lord Simon.

40 [1951] 1 All ER 518.

41 [1949] AC 530, [1949] 2 All ER 452 at 577 and 480, respectively, per Lord MacDermott.

valid if, in the opinion of the court, it discloses in substance an intention that the wager shall be paid.[42]

The third branch of section 18 may be rendered as follows:

> No suit shall be brought or maintained in any court of law or equity for recovering any sum of money or valuable thing which shall have been deposited in the hands of any person to abide the event on which any wager shall have been made.

The construction put upon these words is that they merely prevent recovery by the winner of the money deposited with the stakeholder by his opponent.[43] They do not prevent either party from recovering his own stake before it has been paid away by the stakeholder.[44]

The last branch of the section consists of the proviso and is expressed in these words:

> Provided always that the enactment shall not be deemed to apply to any subscription or contribution or agreement to subscribe or contribute for or towards any plate, prize or sum of money to be awarded to the winner or winners of any lawful game, sport, pastime or exercise.

The object of this is that lawful prizes shall be recoverable. It does not, however, save any transaction which is substantially a wager. If the so-called prize is in truth nothing more than a stake put up by wagering parties and merely masquerading as a prize, it is not recoverable.[45] This was the position in *Diggle v Higgs*,[46] where:

> A and B agreed to walk a match for £200 a side and each deposited this amount with X to be paid to the winner.

It was held that the winner was not entitled to recover the loser's deposit from X, since the money was deposited by way of wager. It was held in *Ellesmere v Wallace*,[47] as we have already seen,[48] that there cannot be a multipartite wagering contract. It would seem to follow, therefore, that the winner of a lawful game in which there are several competitors can recover the agreed prize, even though it consists wholly of money deposited by the competitors themselves, always presuming, of course, that they are not divided into two sides.

At common law games of mere skill, ie those in which the element of chance is negligible, such as football, cricket, billiards, horse and foot racing, are lawful. For-

---

[42] The attitude of the courts is indicated by the case of *R v Weisz* [1951] 2 KB 611, [1951] 2 All ER 408. A client alleged that a firm of bookmakers owed him £373 upon bets placed with them, and, to induce them to pay, he instructed his solicitors to issue a writ. The writ was endorsed as a claim for money due on an account stated, though the endorsement was completely fictitious. It was held that an attempt to deceive the court by disguising the true nature of the claim and putting forward a feigned issue was a contempt of court and could be punished as such.

[43] *Varney v Hickman* (1847) 5 CB 271; *Diggle v Higgs* (1877) 2 Ex D 422.   [44] P 416, below.

[45] *Diggle v Higgs* (1877) 2 Ex D 422; *Trimble v Hill* (1879) 5 App Cas 342.

[46] (1877) 2 Ex D 422.   [47] [1929] 2 Ch 1.   [48] Pp 405–406, above.

merly, certain games in which success depended upon chance, such as pharaoh, passage, roulette and all games played with dice, except backgammon, were declared illegal by statute.[49] Now no game is *per se* illegal, but 'gaming' will be illegal if it contravenes the Gaming Act 1968. To attempt any detailed analysis of this Act in the present book would be out of place, but two points may be made.

First, 'gaming' for the purposes of the Act is defined by section 52 as:

> the playing of a game of chance for winnings in money or money's worth, whether any person playing the game is at risk of losing any money or money's worth or not.[50]

By the same section 'game of chance' excludes any 'athletic game or sport', but with that exception includes 'a game of chance and skill combined and a pretended game of chance and skill combined'.

Secondly, Part I of the Act deals with gaming elsewhere than on premises licensed or registered under Part II; Part II deals with gaming on premises which are so licensed or registered; and Part III deals with gaming by means of machines. Under Part I, which is alone relevant to this book, gaming is prohibited if:

(a) the game involves playing or staking against a bank, whether the bank is held by one of the players or not: (or)

(b) the nature of the game is such that the chances in the game are not equally favourable to all the players; (or)

(c) the nature of the game is such that the chances in it lie between the player and some other person, or (if there are two or more players) lie wholly or partly between the players and some other person, and those chances are not as favourable to the player or players as they are to that other person.[51]

Moreover, no charge, whether in money or money's worth, may be made 'in respect of the gaming', and no levy may be charged, directly or indirectly, on any of the stakes or winnings of the players.[52] In streets and public places gaming, subject to an exception for certain games played on licensed premises, is completely prohibited.[53] The Act lays down penalties for contraventions of any of these prohibitions.[54]

---

[49] Gaming Act 1738, s 2; Gaming Acts 1739 and 1744. These statutes were repealed by the Betting and Gaming Act 1960, Sch 6.

[50] Contrast the definition of a 'wagering contract' given above at p 405. If one party is not at risk, there is no wagering contract within the meaning of that definition; but the statutory definition of 'gaming' is satisfied.

[51] Gaming Act 1968, s 2(1). By s 2(2), this prohibition does not apply to gaming on a domestic occasion in a private dwelling, or to gaming in a hostel, hall of residence, etc, by the residents or inmates thereof. As to gaming at entertainments not held for private gain, see s 41.

[52] Sections 3 and 4. See however s 40 as to special charges for playing at certain clubs and institutes.

[53] Ss 5 and 6. See also s 7 for special provisions as to persons under 18 years of age.

[54] S 8. See also s 46 as to forfeiture of anything relating to the offence.

b The effect as between principal and agent

The relationship of principal and agent may arise under a wagering contract in two distinct cases.

First, where the stakes are deposited with an agent as a stake-holder.

Secondly, where a principal instructs an agent to effect wagering transactions on his behalf.

Where the two wagering parties, A and B, each deposit a stake with X to abide the event, the legal position of X is that he is the agent of A with regard to A's stake and the agent of B with regard to B's stake. In each case his authority is the same, namely, to pay the money to the winner. The rule of agency law relevant to this case is that if an agent acts within the scope and during the continuance of his lawful authority the principal is bound, but that if he exercises the authority after it has been revoked he is liable to his principal for the consequences.

The effect of this upon a wagering contract in which stakes are deposited is that, notwithstanding the determination of the event upon which the wager turns, either party may require the repayment of his stake before it has been paid away in accordance with his former instructions. If the loser makes no demand until his stake has been paid to the winner, his right of recovery is gone, for the stakeholder has merely exercised the authority actually conferred upon him.[55] If, on the other hand, the loser demands the return of his money before it has been paid to the winner, the stakeholder is personally liable if he disregards the revocation of his authority and hands the stake to the winner.[56] In *Diggle v Higgs*, the facts of which have already been given,[57] the stakeholder paid both stakes to the winner in spite of a written order to the contrary from the loser, and he resisted an action for its recovery by relying upon the words of the Gaming Act 1845 that 'no suit shall be brought to recover any sum of money . . . deposited in the hands of any person to abide the event'.[58] But, as we have seen, the meaning attributed to these words by the Court of Appeal was that the winner cannot recover his *opponent's* stake from the stakeholder, not that a depositor is disentitled to recover his own stake.[59]

Where an agent is instructed to effect a wagering transaction on behalf of his principal, litigation may arise in two ways: the agent may claim relief against the consequences of having acted within the scope of his authority, or the principal may sue the agent for failure to carry out the authority.

In considering the first of these problems it is necessary to notice the general rule of law that an agent is entitled to be indemnified by his principal against

---

[55] *Varney v Hickman* (1847) 5 CB 271.

[56] *Hampden v Walsh* (1876) 1 QBD 189.

[57] P 414, above.

[58] P 413, above.

[59] It has also been decided that the recovery of a party's own stake is not prevented by the Gaming Act 1892 (p 345, below), since the word 'paid' there means 'paid out and out': *O'Sullivan v Thomas* [1895] 1 QB 698.

liability incurred by him in executing his instructions, unless the instructions are unlawful.[60] The rule has been neatly summarised by Hawkins J in these words:

> If one man employs another to do a legal act, which in the ordinary course of things will involve the agent in obligations pecuniary or otherwise, a contract on the part of the employer to indemnify his agent is implied by law.[61]

The question whether this doctrine applies where an agent is employed to effect a wager arose in *Read v Anderson:*[62]

> The defendant instructed the plaintiff, a turf commission agent and a member of Tattersalls, to back certain horses at the Ascot meeting. The plaintiff did so, and in the result a sum of £175 became due to him from the defendant in respect of the bets that had been lost. A turf commission agent always backs a horse in his own name and becomes solely responsible to the person with whom the bet is made. If he is declared a 'defaulter' owing to his failure to pay a lost bet, he becomes subject to certain disqualifications which have a serious effect upon his business.

It was held that the plaintiff, having paid £175 out of his own pocket to the person with whom he had made the bet, was entitled to recover the amount from the defendant.

The decision in *Read v Anderson* provoked so many actions of a similar nature that eight years later the legislature intervened and stopped the practice by the Gaming Act 1892. This provides as follows:

> Any promise, express or implied, to pay any person any sum of money paid by him under or in respect of any contract or agreement rendered null and void by the . . . (Gaming Act 1845), or to pay any sum of money by way of commission, fee, reward, or otherwise in respect of any such contract, or of any services in relation thereto or in connexion therewith, shall be null and void, and no action shall be brought or maintained to recover any such sum of money.[63]

In short, any promise, express or implied, to pay to X any money which has been *paid by him under or in respect of* a wagering contract is void. Thus, although the rule that a principal must indemnify his agent against the consequences of exercising a lawful authority is still a leading doctrine of English law, it has no application where the consequences result from steps taken in furtherance of a wagering contract. The agent has no cause of action either on an account stated[64] or for money paid at the request of his principal.

With regard to the other aspect of agency, ie to claims made by the principal against the agent, two rules have been established.

---

[60] *Thacker v Hardy* (1878) 4 QBD 685 at 687, per Lindley J.
[61] *Read v Anderson* (1882) 10 QBD 100 at 108.   [62] (1882) 10 QBD 100; affd 13 QBD 779.
[63] S 1.   [64] *Law v Dearnley* [1950] 1 KB 400, [1950] 1 All ER 124.

First, the principal cannot sue the agent for a failure to carry out instructions. In *Cohen v Kittell*[65] the defendant, who had been employed by the plaintiff to bet on commission, failed to place bets upon certain horses which he had been instructed to back. The plaintiff therefore sued him for breach of the contract of agency, and claimed as damages the money that he would have received had the bets been made.

It was held that the action failed, since an agent can incur no legal liability for failure to make a contract which, even if it had been made, would have been void.

In *A R Dennis & Co Ltd v Campbell*[66] the defendant was employed as the manager of one of the plaintiffs' betting shops. Betting was on a cash basis only and credit was not allowed, but in breach of his instructions the defendant allowed one customer to bet on credit terms. The customer made bets totalling £1,000, lost, and failed to pay up. The plaintiffs sued the defendant for the £1,000. The Court of Appeal held that the action failed since the £1,000 was 'a sum of money . . . alleged to be won upon a wager' within section 18 of the Gaming Act 1845. In addition, it was not shown that the plaintiffs had suffered any loss by the defendant's breach of his instructions since if he had refused the customer credit, the transaction would probably have not taken place at all.

Secondly, it is well established as a general rule of law that where a person has received money on behalf of another he cannot resist an action for its recovery by the plea that he received it in respect of a void transaction.[67] In accordance with this rule it has been held that a principal can successfully maintain an action for money had and received against an agent who has made bets on his behalf and who refuses to hand over winnings received from the loser.[68]

> If one agrees to receive money for the use of another upon consideration executed, however frivolous or void the consideration might have been in respect of the person paying the money, if indeed it were not absolutely immoral or illegal, the person so receiving it cannot be permitted to gainsay his having received it for the use of that other.[69]

The result is that if A backs a horse with B and wins, the Gaming Act 1845 prevents him from recovering his winnings from B. But if he employs C to make the bet with B, he can recover any winnings that are actually paid by B to C. In this last case C, if he is unscrupulous, may plead that he did not in fact place the bet as agent but accepted it himself as a principal. If, however, C holds himself out as a betting agent he may, at any rate in the absence of clear evidence to the contrary, be estopped from denying that he acted as agent.[70]

---

[65] (1889) 22 QBD 680.   [66] [1978] QB 365, [1978] 1 All ER 1215.

[67] *Cheshire & Co v Vaughan Bros & Co* [1920] 3 KB 240 at 255, per Scrutton LJ.

[68] *Bridger v Savage* (1885) 15 QBD 363; *De Mattos v Benjamin* (1894) 63 LJQB 248.

[69] *Griffith v Young* (1810) 12 East 513 at 514–515, per Lord Ellenborough.

[70] *Moore v Peachey* (1891) 7 TLR 748; *Potter v Codrington* (1892) 9 TLR 54; *Grimerd v Wiltshire* (1894) 10 TLR 505.

c Securities given in respect of wagering contracts

The type of question that requires consideration here is this: suppose that a cheque or other security, given by A to B in payment of money due under a wagering contract, is transferred by B to X, is it enforceable in the hands of X or some subsequent transferee from him? In order to answer this question it is necessary to distinguish two classes of wagers, namely those on games and those on events other than games, for the Gaming Acts of 1710 and 1835 have dealt specially with securities given for gaming wagers.

The first section of the Gaming Act 1710, may be summarised as follows:

> All securities given for money won by playing at any game whatsoever, or by betting on games, or for the repayment of money knowingly lent for the purpose of gaming or betting as aforesaid shall be utterly void, frustrate and of no effect.

This stringent enactment might well cause disaster to an innocent person, for a cheque or other negotiable instrument given in any of the circumstances specified by the statute would be worthless in the hands of a subsequent transferee, notwithstanding that he had given value for it in ignorance of its origin. This injustice was therefore nullified by section one of the Gaming Act 1835, which provides that every security rendered void by the Act of 1710 shall no longer be void but shall be deemed to have been given for an illegal consideration.

To illustrate the operation of this section, let us suppose that A, having lost a bet to B on a horse race, gives B a cheque for the amount. Let us suppose further that the cheque in the ordinary course of business passes through several hands and that the present holder, X, sues A to recover the amount for which it is drawn.

Now here X holds a cheque which at the time when it was given suffered from two defects: firstly, it was unsupported by consideration, since it was given in respect of a void wagering contract; secondly, it was tainted by illegality, since it came within the terms of the Act of 1835. X, however, can cure these defects by proof that he is a 'holder in due course', an expression which describes the holder of a bill of exchange, cheque or promissory note, complete and regular on the face of it, who takes it in good faith and for value without notice of any defect of title in the person who negotiated it to him.[71] Normally every holder is presumed to be a holder in due course; but where the instrument is tainted in its origin by illegality, as it is in the hypothetical case under discussion, the burden is on the holder to prove affirmatively that 'subsequent to the . . . illegality value has in good faith been given'.[72]

The result, therefore, is that X can recover on the cheque provided that he proves two facts, namely, that he or some previous holder gave value for it and that he had no notice of the illegal consideration. When the action is heard, the defendant, A, will give evidence that the cheque was drawn in payment of a gaming debt, and then X must prove that when he took the cheque he was unaware of the circumstances in

---

[71] Bills of Exchange Act 1882, s 29(1)(a) and (b).   [72] Ibid, s 30.

which it was given.[73] In short, the effect of the Act of 1835 is to throw the burden of proving value and good faith upon the holder of the bill or note.

The position with regard to a cheque which is drawn to enable a person to game on licensed premises is considered later.[74]

A cheque or other security given for money lost under a non-gaming wager is given without consideration, since the wager itself is void, but there is no rule either at common law or by statute which taints it with illegality. Its one defect is want of consideration, and this is cured by its subsequent transfer for value. If, for instance, a cheque is given by A to B in payment of a bet on the date of the next war, and is later indorsed by B to X in settlement of an account for goods delivered, it is enforceable at the suit of X. It is quite immaterial that at the time of taking the cheque he was aware of the circumstances in which it was given by A to B.

Further, in a case such as this, where the consideration for the original drawing of the cheque is void but not illegal, there is a presumption that the holder, ie X in the above example, has given consideration. In other words the burden is on the defendant to prove that consideration has not been given.[75] Thus in *Fitch v Jones*:[76]

> Jones made a bet with B concerning the amount of the hop duty in 1854. Having lost, he gave B a promissory note for £40 in payment. B indorsed the note to Fitch. When sued on the note, Jones pleaded that a duty lay on Fitch to prove that consideration had been given.

The plea failed and judgment was given for the plaintiff.

What has been said in this section applies only to subsequent transfers of a security. An original party to a wagering contract cannot sue upon a security given in respect of the wager, no matter whether it is given for a void or for an illegal consideration.[77]

d The effect as between lender and borrower

The law which regulates the right of a lender to recover loans made for wagering purposes is both confused and illogical, and precludes a scientific analysis. It may be considered under five heads.

It was held in 1838 that money lent for playing at or betting on an illegal game is irrecoverable.[78] Now no game is *per se* illegal, but the right of recovery will still be excluded if the gaming is conducted illegally, ie in contravention of the provisions of the Gaming Act 1968.[79]

---

[73] *Hay v Ayling* (1851) 16 QB 423; *Woolf v Hamilton* [1898] 2 QB 337.   [74] P 422, below.

[75] *Fitch v Jones* (1855) 5 E & B 238; *Lilley v Rankin* (1886) 56 LJQB 248.

[76] (1855) 5 E & B 238.   [77] *William Hill (Park Lane) Ltd v Hofman* [1950] 1 All ER 1013.

[78] *M'Kinnell v Robinson* (1838) 3 M & W 434.

[79] Certain games were declared illegal by various statutes, but these have now been repealed; p 414, above.

The second question is whether a loan is recoverable if made for the purpose of gaming that will be lawfully conducted. In *Carlton Hall Club v Laurence*,[80] the divisional court invoked the Gaming Acts of 1710 and 1835[81] and denied any right of recovery. The first of these statutes, as we have seen, provided that all securities given for the repayment of money knowingly lent for the purpose of playing at or betting upon any game whatsoever should be utterly void. The second enacted that such a security should not be void but should be deemed to have been given for an illegal consideration. Neither statute, it will be noticed, provided in terms that a loan for gaming as distinct from a security given by the borrower should be void, and the question was whether the contract of loan itself was also statutorily affected. The facts were these:

> The plaintiffs, proprietors of a club in Maida Vale, were accustomed to sell chips representing a money value to members who wished to play games for money. They supplied the defendant with chips to the value of £28 7s 3d for the express purpose of playing poker and snooker, and accepted his cheque for this amount. The cheque was dishonoured.

It was clear that the plaintiffs could not recover on the cheque, since it constituted a security within the meaning of the statutes. Instead, they sued on the contract of loan, arguing that the statutes did not invalidate the contract and its consideration but only the cheque, and they were able to cite several authorities prior to 1835 in which it had been held that a loan of money for the purpose of gaming, as distinct from a security given in respect of the loan, was valid and enforceable. There is considerable force in this argument. Neither statute deals with the loan itself, but only with the right of a person to enforce a security given in respect of the loan. Moreover, the later statute, so far from prejudicing the rights of lenders, is merely designed to afford some measure of protection to third parties. The court, however, followed a dictum of the Court of Exchequer in 1842,[82] and found for the defendant, holding that the combined effect of the Acts of 1719 and 1835 is to avoid all loans where the contractual undertaking is that the money shall be used in playing at or betting upon games.

In *CHT Ltd v Ward*,[83] the Court of Appeal doubted *Carlton Hall Club v Laurence* and expressed the view obiter that a loan for lawful gaming is recoverable, but found that in the instant circumstances the lender was precluded from recovery by the Gaming Act 1892.[84]

---

[80] [1929] 2 KB 153.
[81] P 419, above.
[82] *Applegarth v Colley* (1842) 10 M & W 723 at 732.
[83] [1965] 2 QB 63 at 86, [1963] 3 All ER 835 at 842–843, *per curiam*. See also *MacDonald v Green* [1951] 1 KB 594 at 600, per Cohen LJ.
[84] P 417, above.

The plaintiffs, proprietors of a club, issued chips on credit to the defendant which she used for the purpose of gaming. They sued her to recover the amount by which her losses had exceeded her winnings.

The plaintiffs contended that the issue of chips was equivalent to a loan for lawful gaming and as such recoverable; but the fatal flaw in this argument was that they had in fact paid the gaming losses of the defendant, since their practice was to pay cash to the winners at the end of each session. Therefore the promise of the defendant was rendered void by the Gaming Act 1892, as being a promise to pay a sum paid by the club in respect of her gaming contracts.

Special provision, however, has now been made for loans connected with gaming that is lawfully conducted on licensed premises. The Gaming Act 1968 provides that where gaming takes place upon premises licensed for this purpose, neither the licensee nor his agent shall make any loan or allow any credit (a) for enabling any person to take part in the game, or (b) in respect of any losses incurred by any person in the gaming.[85] To contravene this provision is an offence under the Act.[86]

But a cheque drawn to enable a person to take part in gaming on licensed premises is enforceable if it satisfies certain conditions. It is enacted that neither the licensee nor his agent shall accept such a cheque and give in exchange cash or tokens, unless:

(a) it is not a post-dated cheque;

(b) it is exchanged for the equivalent amount of cash or tokens;

(c) it is delivered to a bank within two 'banking days' for payment or collection.[87]

It is expressly provided that nothing in the Gaming Acts of 1710, 1835, 1845 or 1892 shall affect the validity of, or any remedy in respect of, any cheque which is accepted in exchange for cash or tokens to be used by a player on premises licensed or registered under Part II of the Act of 1968.[88]

The third proposition concerns loans made for the purpose of gaming in foreign countries and later sued upon in England. It is now well established that money lent for the purpose of play abroad can be recovered in England provided that it is recoverable in the country where the gaming takes place.[89] Moreover, a lender who accepts an English cheque or other security in payment of the amount, though he is precluded by the Acts of 1710 and 1835 from enforcing the security, may disregard the cheque and successfully maintain an action in England upon the original contract of loan.[90]

---

[85] Gaming Act 1968, s 16(1).

[86] Ibid, s 23.

[87] Ibid, s 16(2) and (3). The expression 'banking days' means a day which is a business day under s 92 of the Bills of Exchange Act 1882; Gaming Act 1968, s 16(5).

[88] Gaming Act 1968, s 16(4), in conjunction with s 9.

[89] *Quarrier v Colston* (1842) 1 Ph 147; *Saxby v Fulton* [1909] 2 KB 208.

[90] *Société Anonyme des Grands Etablissements du Touquet Paris-Plage v Baumgart* (1927) 96 LJKB 789.

Fourthly, a lender who pays the amount of the loan, not to the borrower, but directly to the person to whom the borrower has lost money under a wagering contract, whether it be a wager upon a game or some other event, has no right of recovery.[91] Further it was held in *MacDonald v Green*[92] that there is no right of recovery if the money is paid directly to the borrower, provided that it is lent subject to an undertaking that it shall be passed to the winner in discharge of the bet. The reason in these cases is that the money has been paid 'under or in respect of' a wagering contract, and is therefore rendered irrecoverable by the Gaming Act 1892. For the same reason the amount of a loan is irrecoverable if, at the request of the borrower, it is paid to a stakeholder to abide the event of a wager made by the borrower with a third party.[93]

Fifthly, money lent to a borrower and used by him to pay bets which he has already lost is recoverable,[94] provided that it does not impose any obligation upon him to employ the money in this particular manner. The contract of loan in this case is unobjectionable. It is not void under the Gaming Act 1845 since it is not a wagering contract; it is not caught by the Gaming Acts 1710 and 1835 which, so far as regards loans, are confined to money lent for the purpose of gaming or betting on games, and do not extend to loans in respect of games or bets already completed; and it is not void under the Gaming Act 1892 for the money is at the free disposal of the borrower and therefore, in the view of the Court of Appeal, it has not been paid to him 'under or in respect of' a wagering contract.

> The distinction is clear enough: a loan which leaves the borrower at liberty to apply the money as he wishes, is not invalidated by the Gaming Act 1892, even though it is contemplated by both parties that he will probably pay betting debts with it; but when a loan is hampered by a stipulation that the money *is* to be used for payment of a betting debt, then no matter whether the stipulation is express or implied or to be inferred from the circumstances, the loan is a payment in respect of the betting debt and is hit by the Act.[95]

The Court of Appeal construed a contract in the first of these two senses, in the case of *Re O'Shea*,[96] where one Lancaster guaranteed the overdraft of a debtor to the extent of £500 which in fact enabled him to pay lost bets. The debt that thus became due to Lancaster was held to be valid and enforceable. Kennedy LJ described the position in these words:

> What was done here was that the debtor went to Lancaster and said 'I have incurred a debt, will you increase the guarantee to the bank in order to enable me to pay it?' I cannot without

---

[91] *Tatam v Reeve* [1893] 1 QB 44; *Woolf v Freeman* [1937] 1 All ER 178; *Saffery v Mayer* [1901] 1 KB 11. *CHT Ltd v Ward* [1965] 2 QB 63, [1963] 3 All ER 835.

[92] [1951] 1 KB 594, [1950] 2 All ER 1240; *Hill v Fox* (1859) 4 H & N 359.

[93] *Carney v Plimmer* [1897] 1 QB 634.   [94] *Re O'Shea, ex p Lancaster* [1911] 2 KB 981.

[95] *Macdonald v Green* [1951] 1 KB 594 at 605–660, [1950] 2 All ER 1240 at 1244–1245, per Denning LJ.

[96] [1911] 2 KB 981.

forcing the words treat that as a transaction in which there was a payment by Lancaster to the creditor. There has been no payment by him 'in respect of any contract or agreement', and unless there has been such a payment the statute does not apply.[97]

Thus what should be observed with some care is that a loan is not irrecoverable under the Gaming Act 1892 unless there is a definite agreement, express or implied, that the money is to be used for gaming or for paying lost bets. The mere probability that it will be so used is no bar to recovery. In the *Carlton Hall* case there was perhaps some justification for inferring an agreement in that sense, since apparently the poker chips were useless for any other purpose; in *MacDonald v Green* the Court of Appeal was satisfied that the understanding to apply the money to the payment of betting losses was a true term of the contract; but in *Re O'Shea* the evidence disclosed no obligation binding the borrower to employ the money for any particular purpose.

Lastly, the question whether money lent for the purpose of making a bet, or paying a lost bet, on a non-gaming wager, which has not yet called for a judicial decision, presumably depends upon the same considerations. The money will be recoverable unless it is lent subject to a binding obligation, express or implied, that it is to be used solely for the purpose of betting.

B AGREEMENTS PROHIBITED BY COMPETITION LAW

EC and UK Competition Rules

The validity of contracts may be affected by both EC and UK competition laws. UK competition law underwent fundamental reform in 1998 with the passing of the Competition Act 1998 and UK domestic law is now largely based upon the EC provisions. For this reason it is necessary to look at the EC competition rules before turning to the UK provisions. The EC rules apply where there is an effect on inter-Member State trade and the UK rules apply where the effect is in the United Kingdom. It is possible for both sets of rules to apply concurrently.[98]

---

[97] Ibid at 988.

[98] The position on this is now laid down in Council Regulation 1/2003, Article 3. If there is an effect on inter-Member State trade, national competition authorities cannot apply national rules without also applying EC rules. They cannot apply stricter national rules to agreements but may to the unilateral conduct of dominant firms. They can apply provisions of national law that 'predominantly pursue an objective different from' that pursued by the EC competition rules (Art 3(3)). Art 3(3) may prove problematic, eg in its relation to UK restraint of trade law.

1 The EC Competition Rules

The EC competition rules are contained in Articles 81–89 (ex Articles 85–94) of the Treaty of Rome.[99] The principal substantive provisions which affect transactions between private parties are Article 81(ex Article 85) and Article 82 (ex Article 86).[100] Of these, Article 81, which deals with agreements between undertakings, has the greatest impact on the enforceability of contracts. However, Article 82 deals with abuses by firms in a dominant position and can, in some situations, affect the enforceability of contractual arrangements entered into by such firms.

Regulation 17,[101] the first regulation implementing the EC competition rules, came into force in 1962 and from then until 1 May 2004 EC competition law was primarily enforced by the EC Commission.[102] On 1 May 2004, Council Regulation 1/2003 came into force.[103] This regulation brought about the 'modernisation' of the application and enforcement of EC competition law. Enforcement is now decentralised so that the national competition authorities[104] of the Member States, as well as the Commission, enforce the EC rules.[105] Furthermore, enforcement of the competition rules by the national courts in actions between private parties had always been possible because of the direct effect of Article 81(1) and (2) and of Article 82. Despite this, private enforcement was not common anywhere in the Community, although cases in which competition law was used as a defence were more numerous than offensive actions. The 'modernisation' of enforcement was supposed to increase private actions and the Commission particularly wishes to encourage damages claims. In December 2005, the Commission published a Green Paper to inaugurate a consultation on how actions for damages for breach of the competition rules could be facilitated.[106]

It is important to note that the policy objectives behind the EC competition rules encompass both competition goals and the promotion of the single European market.

---

[99] The Articles of the Treaty of Rome were renumbered by the Treaty of Amsterdam. The renumbering took effect on 1 May 1999. In this chapter, the new Article numbers are used even when referring to matters taking place before 1 May 1999.

[100] Arts 83–85 (ex-Arts 87–89) concern matters of procedure and enforcement; Art 86 (ex-Art 90) concerns the application of the competition rules to public undertakings and undertakings given special or exclusive rights by the State; and Arts 87–89 concern State Aids.

[101] Council Regulation 17 OJ Spec Ed [1959–62] 87.

[102] The Competition Directorate-General (DG Comp) deals with competition law (including State Aids). Until 1999 DG Comp was known as DG IV.

[103] Council Regulation 1/2003 OJ [2003] L1/1.

[104] The NCA in the UK is the Office of Fair Trading (OFT) but the sector regulators also have power to enforce the EC rules in their sector.

[105] See Commission Notice on cooperation within the Network of Competition Authorities, OJ [2004] C 101/43.

[106] Commission Green Paper of 19 December 2005, COM(2005) 672 final. The problem is that the detailed rules governing damages actions in national courts vary between Member States and the differences are deeply embedded in both substantive and procedural national laws.

The Commission's current thinking is to see both objectives as serving the same end, which is '. . . to protect competition on the market as a means of enhancing consumer welfare and of ensuring an efficient allocation of resources. Competition and market integration serve these ends since the creation and preservation of an open single market promotes an efficient allocation of resources throughout the Community for the benefit of consumers'.[107] EC competition law is, therefore, concerned to prevent undertakings hindering inter-Member State trade and this means that contractual terms which hinder the free flow of goods and services between Member States will normally be prohibited.

Article 81

Article 81 contains three paragraphs. Article 81(1) prohibits agreements, concerted practices and decisions of associations of undertakings which have as their object or effect the prevention, restriction or distortion of competition within the common market and which may affect trade between Member States. It then gives a non-exhaustive list of five particular examples. Article 81(2) says that agreements or decisions prohibited by Article 81(1) are void. Article 81(3), however, provides that Article 81(1) may be declared inapplicable to agreements, decisions and concerted practices which fulfil certain criteria. The burden of proving an infringement of Article 81(1) rests on the party or authority alleging the infringement. Once that is proved, the burden of proving that Article 81(3) is satisfied shifts to the undertaking(s) claiming the benefit of that paragraph.[108]

Article 81(1)—the prohibition of anti-competitive agreements
Article 81(1) provides:

> The following shall be prohibited as incompatible with the common market: all agreements between undertakings, decisions by associations of undertakings and concerted practices which may affect trade between Member States and which have as their object or effect the prevention, restriction or distortion of competition within the common market, and in particular those which:
>
> (a) directly or indirectly fix purchase or selling prices or any other trading conditions;
>
> (b) limit or control production, markets, technical development, or investment;
>
> (c) share markets or sources of supply;
>
> (d) apply dissimilar conditions to equivalent transactions with other trading parties, thereby placing them at a competitive disadvantage;
>
> (e) make the conclusion of contracts subject to acceptance by the other parties of supplementary obligations which, by their nature or according to commercial usage, have no connection with the subject of such contracts.

---

[107] See Commission Notice on the application of Art 81(3) of the Treaty, OJ [2004] C101/97; DG Competition Discussion Paper on the application of Art 82 of the Treaty to exclusionary abuses, December 2005.

[108] Council Regulation 1/ 2003, Art 2.

Article 81 and its supporting structure has produced a complex body of law into which it would be inappropriate to venture here,[109] but the following major points should be noted. The Treaty of Rome contains no definition clause, so the meaning of the terms used in Article 81 has been clarified by judgments of the Community Courts (the European Court of Justice and the Court of First Instance), the decisional practice of the Commission, and 'soft law' Notices and other documents issued by the Commission:[110]

(a) 'Agreement' is interpreted very widely and encompasses any kind of understanding between the parties, whether or not intended to be legally binding. The concept of an agreement within the meaning of Article 81(1) centres around the existence of a concurrence of wills between at least two parties, the form in which it is manifested being unimportant so long as it constitutes the faithful expression of the parties' intentions.[111] It is therefore wider than the concept of a contract in UK law as discussed elsewhere in this book. It covers written agreements', oral agreements, informal understandings, 'gentlemen's agreements, standard conditions of sale, and trade association rules, but not a collective agreement between trade unions and employers.[112] For an agreement to exist it is 'sufficient that the undertakings in question should have expressed their joint intention to conduct themselves on the market in a specific way'.[113] An agreement may be spelt out of a course of dealings between the parties where one party may be taken as having tacitly acquiesced in terms imposed by the other,[114] and out of decisions taken by a supplier in the context of a selective distribution network.[115] However, genuinely unilateral conduct on the part of one party, where the other party has not acquiesced, is not an agreement because it does not involve the concurrence of wills which is the hallmark of an

---

[109] See Whish *Competition Law* (5th edn, Butterworths, 2003); Jones and Sufrin *EC Competition Law: Text, Cases and Materials* (2nd edn, OUP, 2004); Bellamy and Child *European Community Law of Competition* (5th edn, Sweet & Maxwell, 2001 and supplements); *Butterworths Competition Law* (looseleaf); Korah *An Introductory Guide to EC Competition Law and Practice* (8th edn, Hart Publishing, 2004), Furse *Competition Law of the UK and* EC (6th edn, OUP, 2006); Faull and Nikpay *The EC Law of Competition* (2nd edn, OUP, 2006).

[110] These Notices include the Commission Notice on Agreements of Minor Importance OJ [2001] C 368/13; Guidelines on vertical restraints OJ [2000] OJ C 291/1; Guidelines on Horizontal Restraints OJ [2001] OJ C 3/2; Guidelines on technology transfer agreements OJ [2004] C 101/2; Commission Notice on the application of Art 81(3) of the Treaty OJ [2004] C101/97; Commission Notice on the effect on trade concept contained in Art 81 and 82 of the Treaty OJ [2004] C 101/81.

[111] Case T-41/96 *Bayer AG v EC Commission* [2001] ECR II-3383, [2001] 4 CMLR 126, para 69, aff'd by the European Court of Justice Cases 2 and 3/01P, *Bundesverband der Arzneimittel-Importeure EV and Commission v Bayer AG* [2004] ECR I-23, [2004] 4 CMLR 653.

[112] Case C-67/96 *Albany International BV v Stichting Bedrijfspensioenfonds Textielindustrie* [1999] ECR I-5751, [2000] 4 CMLR 446.

[113] Case T-41/96 *Bayer AG v EC Commission* [2001] ECR II-3383, [2001] 4 CMLR 126, para 67; Case T-7/89 *SA Hercules Chemicals NV v Commission* [1991] ECR II-711, para 2.

[114] Case C-277/87 *Sandoz Prodotti v Commission* [1990] ECR I-45.

[115] Case 107/82 *AEG-Telefunken v Commission* [1983] ECR 3151, [1984] 3 CMLR 325.

agreement.[116] In *Bayer*[117] there was held to be no agreement where a pharmaceutical firm refused to supply its distributors in some Member States with more than certain amounts of its products. The refusal was motivated by the firm's desire to prevent the distributors exporting to other Member States where prices were higher. As the distributors had never acquiesced in the limitation on their supplies—and indeed complained about it—the firm's conduct could not amount to an agreement within Article 81(1), despite the fact that it was such as to affect inter-Member State trade. This principle was applied in *Unipart v O2 (UK) Ltd*[118] where the English Court of Appeal held that the adoption of an alleged 'margin-squeeze' level price by a firm that was not in a dominant position could not be considered as an agreement within Article 81(1). The court held that the customer's obligation to pay the supplier's prices as set from time to time was not an agreement that could found a claim under Article 81(1), but a unilateral act.

Undertakings are taken as having entered into agreements prohibited by Article 81(1) through the activities of their employees, despite the ignorance of the senior management.[119]

There is no 'intra-enterprise conspiracy' in EC competition law. Under the so-called 'single economic entity doctrine' two or more legally separate entities may be regarded as one party for the purposes of Article 81(1), so that arrangements between parent and subsidiary companies, or between different subsidiaries of the same parent, will not be regarded as 'agreements'. This is so however anti-competitive the arrangements seem to be.[120] The same applies to the application of the concept of a 'concerted practice'. For the purposes of competition law the notion of the parties to the agreement includes the parties' connected companies.

(b) 'Concerted practice' is a problematic concept covering behaviour which amounts to collusion between parties falling short of an agreement (even given the wide interpretation of 'agreement' under Article 81(1)). The European Court of Justice has described a concerted practice as 'any form of coordination by undertakings which, without having reached the stage where an agreement properly so called has been concluded, knowingly substitutes practical cooperation between them for the risks of competition'.[121] Nothing turns on whether the conduct of parties is

---

[116] Case T-41/96 *Bayer AG v EC Commission* [2001] ECR II-3383, [2001] 4 CMLR 126, aff'd by the European Court of Justice Cases 2 and 3/01P *Bundesverband der Arzneimittel-Importeure EV and Commission v Bayer AG* [2004] ECR I-23.

[117] Ibid.   [118] [2004] EWCA Civ 1034, [2004] UKCLR 1453.

[119] Cases 100–103/80 *Musique Diffusion Française SA v Commission* (*Pioneer*) [1983] ECR 1825 [1983] 3 CMLR 221.

[120] Eg Case C-73/95P *Viho Europe BV v Commission* [1996] ECR I-5457, [1997] 4 CMLR 419 (dividing the common market by export bans).

[121] Case 48/69 *ICI v Commission (Dyestuffs)* [1972] ECR 619, [1972] CMLR 557, para 64; Case C-49/92P *EC Commission v Anic Partecipazioni SpA* [2001] 4 CMLR 602, para 115; see also Case 40/73 *Suiker Unie v EC Commission* [1975] ECR 1663, [1976] 1 CMLR 295; Cases C-89/85 etc *A Ahlstrom Oy v Commission* [1993] ECR I-1307, [1993] 4 CMLR 407.

categorised as an agreement or as a concerted practice: all that matters is that they have colluded. Where undertakings have been engaged in a cartel, proof that they have entered into concerted practices may be difficult to find, and the Commission is not able to rely on parallel behaviour, such as similar price increases, as evidence that they have infringed Article 81(1), unless there is no other plausible explanation for the parallel behaviour.[122] A concerted practice requires the parties to it to actually behave collusively on the market, rather than merely to plot to behave anti-competitively. However, once parties have been proved to have engaged in concertation, their subsequent behaviour on the market is presumed to have been influenced by the concertation, and the burden of proof therefore shifts to the undertakings to disprove the concerted practice.[123]

(c) 'Decisions by associations of undertakings' means that collusion between undertakings within the context of trade associations or similar bodies[124] is caught by the Article 81(1) prohibition. The rules and constitution of the association will count as a 'decision'. A non-binding recommendation by the association will count as a decision if its object or effect is to influence the members' commercial behaviour.[125]

(d) An 'undertaking' is 'any entity engaged in an economic activity, regardless of its legal status and the way in which it is financed'.[126] An economic activity is any activity consisting in offering goods and services on a given market.[127] 'Undertaking' is therefore a wide concept embracing everything from a multi-national company to an individual person[128] and the entity does not have to take a legally recognised form. The greatest problem is in the area of public bodies, bodies acting in some way under the aegis of the state, and those providing some type of 'public service'. The European Court of Justice has said that the distinction is between 'a situation where the state acts in the exercise of official authority and that where it carries on economic activities of an industrial or commercial nature by offering goods and services on the market'.[129] The crucial factor is the nature of the activity rather than the nature of the body

---

[122] Cases C-89/85 etc *A Ahlstrom Oy v Commission* [1993] ECR I-1307, [1993] 4 CMLR 407. This creates particular difficulties where oligopolistic industries are concerned as the economic theory of oligopolistic interdependence predicts that oligopolies can indulge in parallel behaviour without colluding, see Bishop and Walker *The Economics of EC Competition Law* (2nd edn, Sweet & Maxwell, 2002), paras 2.28–2.42.

[123] Case C–199/92P *Hüls AG v Commission* [1999] ECR I-4287, [1999] 5 CMLR 1016.

[124] Such as agricultural cooperatives, see eg *MELDOC* [1986] OJ L348/50.

[125] Cases 96–102, 104, 105, 108 and 110/82 *NV IAZ International Belgium SA v Commission* [1983] ECR 3369, [1984] 3 CMLR 276.

[126] Case C-41/90 *Höfner v Macroton* [1991] ECR I-1979, [1993] 4 CMLR 306, para 21.

[127] Case 118/85 *Commission v Italy* [1987] ECR 2599, para 7.

[128] Although it does not include employees, Case 40/73 *Suiker Unie v EC Commission* [1975] ECR 1663, [1976] 1 CMLR 295, para 539.

[129] Case C-343/95 *Diego Cali v SEPG* [1997] ECR I-1547, [1997] 5 CMLR 484, para 16.

performing it.[130] The characteristics of an economic activity, apart from the offer of goods or services, appear from the jurisprudence of the Court to be the bearing of economic risk and the potential to make a profit.[131] It should be noted that the *purchase* of goods and services does not necessarily constitute an economic activity, as it will depend on what the buyer does with them. In *FENIN*[132] the bodies constituting the Spanish Health Service were held not to be undertaking in respect of their purchases of medical goods and equipment, as the subsequent use to which the bodies put the goods was not resale but the provision of medical services free of charge to patients.

(e) In order to be caught by Article 81(1) the agreement, concerted practice or decision[133] must have as its 'object or effect' the 'prevention, restriction or distortion of competition'. The terms 'prevention', 'restriction' and 'distortion' are generally used interchangeably, and although one or the other may be more suitable in a particular context 'restriction' is commonly used to cover them all, and will be so used in this chapter. The competition to which Article 81(1) refers may be that between the parties to the agreement or that between one or more of them and a third party, which means that both horizontal agreements (agreements between parties at the same level of the market, such as two manufacturers) and vertical agreements (agreements between parties at a different level of the market, such as a supplier and its distributors)—or to put it another way, agreements between both competitors and non-competitors—can be caught.[134] Some agreements are prohibited by Article 81(1) because their object is anti-competitive, which does not necessarily mean that the parties had a subjective intention to behave anti-competitively, but that the agreement restricts competition by its very nature. Examples of this are agreements between competitors to fix prices or divide up markets between them, and export bans in vertical agreements. If the object of the agreement is not the restriction of competition, then its effect on the market has to be examined.[135]

---

[130] See Case C-41/90 *Höfner v Macroton* [1991] ECR I-1979, [1993] 4 CMLR 306; Case C-244/94 *Fédération Française des Sociétés d'Assurance v Ministère de l'Agriculture* [1995] ECR I-4013 [1996] 4 CMLR 536); Case 364/92 *SAT Fluggesellschaft v Eurocontrol* [1994] ECR I-43, [1994] 5 CMLR 208); Case C-159/91 *Poucet v Assurances Générales de France* [1993] ECR I-637; Case C-343/95 *Diego Cali v SEPG* [1997] ECR I-1547, [1997] 5 CMLR 484; Cases C-264, 306, 354 and 355/01 *AOK Bundesverband and others v Ichtyol-Gesellschaft Cordes and others* [2004] ECR I-2493, [2004] 4 CMLR 1261.

[131] See Odudu *The Boundaries of EC Competition Law: The Scope of Article 81* (OUP, 2006).

[132] Case C-205/03P *Federación Nacional de Empresas de Instrumentación Científica, Médica, Técnica y Dental (FENIN) v Commission*, 13 July 2006; the case concerned Art 82 rather than Art 81, but the concept of 'undertaking' is the same in both Articles.

[133] In this chapter 'agreement' is used as shorthand for all three, unless the context otherwise requires.

[134] Cases 56 and 58/64 *Etablissements Consten SA & Grundig-Verkaufs-GmbH v Commission* [1966] ECR 299, [1966] CMLR 418.

[135] Case 56/65 *Société Technique Minière v Maschinebau Ulm GmbH* [1966] ECR 235, [1966] 1 CMLR 357; Commission Guidelines on the application of Art 81(3) OJ [2004] C 101/97, paras 21–24.

The 'prevention, restriction or distortion of competition' test is an economic one, which means that the agreement should be looked at in its economic context in order to assess the impact that it really has on competition.[136] There have been decades of controversy about whether the test is applied too broadly, particularly by the Commission, to catch agreements which are not really anti-competitive. The question is to what extent the pro- and anti-competitive aspects of an agreement should be weighed up under Article 81(1)—the so-called 'rule of reason' approach—rather than under Article 81(3). In *Métropole Télévision v Commission*,[137] the Court of First Instance said that the existing case law did not establish the existence of a rule of reason under Article 81(1) and that the pro- and anti-competitive aspects of a restriction should be weighed under Article 81(3), rather than Article 81(1). Article 81(1), said the Court of First Instance, should not be applied 'wholly abstractly and without distinction to all agreements whose effect is to restrict the freedom of action of one or more of the parties'.[138] The current approach of the Commission is to take a more economic approach to the application of Article 81(1) than it has done in the past, thus catching fewer agreements within the prohibition. The Commission now says that negative effects on competition are likely to occur when the parties to an agreement individually or jointly have or obtain some degree of market power and the agreement contributes to the creation, maintenance or strengthening of the market power, or allows its exploitation.[139]

(f) The Article 81(1) prohibition applies only if there is an appreciable effect on inter-Member State trade. This effect may be direct or indirect, actual or potential[140] and, again, this test has been widely interpreted by the Commission and the Community Courts and an agreement will be caught by Article 81(1) if it is merely capable of having such an effect. There may be an effect on inter-Member State trade if there is likely to be an impact on the competitive structure in the EC.[141] The

---

[136] Cases 56 and 58/64 *Etablissements Consten SA & Grundig-Verkaufs-GmbH v Commission* [1966] ECR 299, [1966] CMLR 418; Case C-234/89 *Stergios Delimitis v Henninger Bräu* [1991] ECR I-935, [1992] 5 CMLR 210; Case C-250/92 *Gøttrup Klim v KLG* [1994] ECR I-5641, [1996] 4 CMLR 191.

[137] Case T-112/99 *Métropole Télévision v Commission* [2001] ECR II-2459, [2001] 5 CMLR 1236, paras 72–78.

[138] Case T-112/99 *Métropole Télévision*, para 77.

[139] Commission Guidelines on the application of Art 81(3) OJ [2004] C 101/97, para 25. See also Commission Guidelines on horizontal restraints OJ [2001] C 3/2; Commission Guidelines on vertical restraints OJ [2000] C 291/1; Commission Guidelines on technology transfer agreements OJ [2004] C 101/2.

[140] Case 56/65 *Société Technique Minière v Maschinebau Ulm GmbH* [1966] ECR 234, [1966] 1 CMLR 357.

[141] This form of the test is usually used in Art 82 rather than Art 81 cases. See Cases 6,7/73 *Istituto Chemioterapico Italiano Spa and Commercial Solvents Corpn v EC Commission* [1974] ECR 223 [1974] 1 CMLR 309. In cases concerning maritime transport on shipping routes between the EC and third countries there has been held to be an effect on inter-Member State trade because of the effect on the competition between ports in different Member States, see eg *CEWAL* OJ [1993] L34/20, [1995] 5 CMLR 198 (affirmed in Cases C-395 and 396P *Compagnie Maritime Belge v Commission* [2000] ECR I-1365, [2000] 4 CMLR 1076), concerning shipping between the North Sea ports and West Africa.

application of the 'effect on inter-Member State trade' criteria, and the meaning of 'appreciable' in this context is dealt with in the Commission Notice on the effect on trade concept.[142] The general principle laid down by the Commission in the Notice is that there is a negative rebuttable presumption;[143] in that agreements are not capable of appreciably affecting trade between Member States where the aggregate market share of the parties on any relevant market in the EU affected by the agreement does not exceed 5 per cent; and (in the case of horizontal agreements) that the aggregate annual EU turnover of the undertakings in the products covered by the agreement does not exceed €40 million; or (in the case of vertical agreements) that the supplier's aggregate EU turnover in the products covered by the agreement does not exceed €40 million.[144] The Commission calls this the NAAT (no appreciable effect on trade) rule.[145] However, where an agreement is capable of affecting inter-Member State trade by its very nature, for example an agreement about imports and exports or one that covers several Member States, there is a rebuttable positive presumption that where the turnover of the parties in the contract products exceeds €40 million the effects on inter-Member State trade *are* appreciable.[146]

(g) The restriction of competition also has to be 'appreciable' before Article 81(1) applies.[147] The Commission periodically publishes a Notice as to the thresholds below which it considers that Article 81 does not normally apply because the agreement is *de minimis*. The current Notice[148] sets the thresholds in terms of the parties' market shares: if the parties are actual or potential competitors, the agreement will not be caught by Article 81(1) if the aggregate market share of all the parties does not exceed 10%, and if they are not actual or potential competitors, the agreement is not caught by Article 81(1) if the market share held by each of the parties does not exceed 15%.[149] Crucially, however, the Notice does not apply if the agreement contains any 'hard-core' restrictions. In agreements between competitors these are fixing prices when selling to third parties, limiting sales or output, and the allocation of markets and customers.[150] In agreements between non-competitors they are minimum resale

---

[142] Commission Guidelines on the effect on trade concept contained in Art 81 and 82 of the Treaty OJ [2004] C 101/81.

[143] Ibid, para 50.

[144] Ibid, para 52. As far as undertakings classified as 'small and medium-sized undertakings' (SMEs) by the EU (the current definition of an SME is laid down in the Annex to Commission Recommendation 2003/361 OJ [2003] L124/36) are concerned, para 50 of the Notice refers back to the Commission Notice on Agreements of Minor Importance OJ [2001] C 368/1, para 3, which states that agreements between such undertakings are not normally capable of affecting trade between Member States.

[145] Commission Guidelines on the effect on trade concept, para 50.

[146] Ibid, para 53.

[147] Case 5/69 *Völk v Vervaecke* [1969] ECR 295.

[148] Commission Notice on agreements of minor importance OJ [2001] C 368/13.

[149] Ibid, para 7.   [150] Ibid, para 11(1).

price fixing and certain territorial protection clauses.[151] If an agreement is on a market where there is a foreclosure effect due to parallel networks of similar agreements entered into by different suppliers, the thresholds in agreements between both competitors and non-competitors are reduced to 5 per cent.[152]

(h) EC competition law has extra-territorial effect. The European Court of Justice has held that agreements wholly between undertakings outside the EU may be caught by Article 81(1) if they are 'implemented' inside the EU.[153] Also, the single economic entity doctrine[154] may bring foreign parent companies into the jurisdiction of the EU through the activities of their subsidiaries.[155]

(i) As explained above Article 81(1) applies to both horizontal and vertical agreements.[156] Horizontal agreements between competitors may attempt to rig the market by means of price-fixing, market sharing, production quotas, bid-rigging, etc, in order to reduce competition between them and maintain prices above the competitive level. Such arrangements are known as 'cartels' and the agreements and concerted prices comprising them invariably fall within the Article 81(1) prohibition and will not satisfy the exception provision in Article 81(3). Consequently, these arrangements are normally made clandestinely, in the knowledge that they are not legally enforceable and that if discovered the participating undertakings may incur heavy fines.[157] Other types of horizontal agreements, however, may be beneficial in that they bring undertakings together to cooperate in joint ventures and research and development arrangements, for example. These agreements may be between actual or potential competitors, but may not be, as some horizontal cooperation is between parties who have 'complementary' rather than competing technologies.[158] Such horizontal agreements will be the outcome of careful negotiation and the parties will be striving to

---

[151] Ibid, para 11(2). These restrictions are the same as those 'black-listed' in the block exemption Verticals Regulation OJ [1999] L336/21, Article. 4.

[152] Commission Notice on agreements of minor importance, para 8. The Notice says that individual suppliers with a market share not exceeding 5% are generally not considered to contribute significantly to a culmulative foreclosure effect, and that such an effect is unlikely if less than 30% of the market is covered by parallel networks.

[153] Cases 89, 104, 114, 116, 117 and 125–129/85 *A Ahlström Oy v Commission* [1988] ECR 5193, [1988] 4 CMLR 901. In a case concerning the EC Merger Regulation the Court of First Instance has held that the EC Commission has jurisdiction over mergers between non-EU companies where 'it was foreseeable that a proposed concentration would have an immediate and substantial effect within the Community', Case T-102/96 *Gencor Ltd v Commission* [1999] ECR II-753, [1999] 4 CMLR 971. The concept of 'having effects' may be wider than that of 'implementation'. For the position under the UK Competition Act 1998, below pp 445 ff.

[154] See above p 428.

[155] Case 48/69 *ICI v Commission (Dyestuffs)* [1972] ECR 619, [1972] CMLR 557.

[156] Cases 56 & 58/64 *Etablissements Consten SA & Grundig-Verkaufs-GmbH v Commission* [1966] ECR 299, [1966] CMLR 418: see p 430.

[157] For the consequences of infringing Art 81, see below p 438.

[158] For example, *Optical Fibres* OJ [1986] L 236/30 concerned a joint venture between an undertaking with cable technology and one with glass technology.

ensure that their agreements comply with the competition rules and are valid. The application of Article 81 to horizontal cooperation agreements is the subject of a set of Commission Guidelines.[159]

Vertical agreements are those between parties that operate for the purposes of the agreement at a different level of the production or distribution chain,[160] such as agreements between suppliers and distributors or suppliers and commercial customers.[161] Vertical agreements may affect both inter-brand competition (between different producers) and intra-brand competition (between different distributors of the same brand). Apart from resale price maintenance, vertical agreements are generally considered, in the absence of market power, to be less potentially problematic for the competitive process than horizontal agreements.[162] In EC competition law, however, distribution and other vertical agreements have been seen as a threat to the single market because of their tendency to divide markets on geographical lines and hinder the free flow of goods between Member States. The Commission 'modernised' its approach to vertical agreements in 1999 when it produced a set of Guidelines on vertical agreements[163] and a new block exemption.[164]

Another category of agreements concerns the licensing of intellectual property rights. These may be made between competitors or non-competitors. The Commission has issued Guidelines on technology transfer agreements and a block exemption.[165]

Article 81(3)—inapplicability of Article 81(1) to certain agreements
Article 81(3) provides:

> The provisions of paragraph 1 may, however, be declared inapplicable in the case of:
>
> – any agreement or category of agreements between undertakings;
>
> – any decision or category of decisions by associations of undertakings;
>
> – any concerted practice or category of concerted practices,
>
> which contributes to improving the production or distribution of goods or to promoting technical or economic progress, while allowing consumers a fair share of the resulting benefit, and which does not:
>
> (a) impose on the undertakings concerned restrictions which are not indispensable to the attainment of these objectives;

---

[159] Guidelines on horizontal restraints OJ [2001] OJ C 3/2.

[160] The definition in Regulation 2790/1999 OJ [1999] L336/21 (the Verticals Regulation), Article 2(1).

[161] Agreements between suppliers and private end-users who are not buying for resale or to use in their own business are not within Art 81(1) because the buyers is not acting as an 'undertaking': see above p 429.

[162] See Jones and Sufrin *EC Competition Law: Text, Cases and Materials* (2nd edn, OUP, 2004) ch 9.

[163] Guidelines on Vertical Restraints, OJ [2000] C 43/1.

[164] Regulation 2790/1999, the 'Verticals Regulation', OJ [1999] L336/21; see below pp 436–443.

[165] Guidelines on technology transfer agreements OJ [2004] C 101/2 and Regulation 772/2004 [2004] OJ L 123/11.

(b) afford such undertakings the possibility of eliminating competition in respect of a substantial part of the products in question.

Thus Article 81(3) sets out the criteria which agreements caught by Article 81(1) must meet if they are to escape from the prohibition. Two are positive (first, improving production or distribution, or promoting technical or economic progress and secondly, allowing consumers a fair share of these benefits) and two negative (no indispensable restrictions and no substantial elimination of competition). In fact, there is only one substantive criterion, improving production or distribution or promoting technical or economic progress. The other three are conditions or limitations on the first.

Until 1 May 2004 only the EC Commission had the power to apply Article 81(3) and declare Article 81(1) inapplicable because the criteria had been met.[166] Neither national competition authorities, national courts or the Community Courts had any power to do so. Article 81(3) was not directly applicable. The Commission exercised its power by granting individual exemptions to agreements which were notified to it[167] and by issuing block exemptions.[168]

Individual exemptions took the form of a decision, one of the forms of EC legislation provided for by Article 249 (ex Article 189) of the EC Treaty. In practice the Commission issued very few individual exemptions.[169] In the great majority of cases the Commission settled the case informally by sending the parties a 'comfort letter' telling them that it considered that the agreement did meet the criteria for exemption but that it did not intend to proceed to a formal decision.[170] This left the parties without legal security as comfort letters could not be treated by national courts as equivalent to a decision.[171]

---

[166] Council Regulation 17 OJ Spec Ed [1959–62]. 87, Art 9(1). Regulation 17 was the main regulation implementing the competition rules until 1 May 2004. There were provisions analogous to Art 9(1) in the regulations implementing the competition rules in the special sectors, eg Council Regulation 1017/68 OJ Spec Ed [1968] 302, applying the competition rules to rail, road and inland waterway transport.

[167] Regulation 17, Art 4(1). Art 4(2) provided for a limited category of 'non-notifiable agreements'.

[168] Art 81(3), it will be noted, provides for Art 81(1) to be declared inapplicable in respect of 'categories' of agreements etc. The Council conferred on the Commission the power to do this by way of block exemptions in respect of vertical agreements and bilateral intellectual property licences (Council Regulation 19/65 OJ [1965–1966] 35 as amended by Council Regulation 1215/99) and in respect of horizontal cooperation agreements (Council Regulation 2821/71 OJ [1971] 1032). The Council has also authorised the Commission to issue block exemptions in parts of the transport sector, and in certain cases, the Council has itself issued block exemptions (for instance, Council Regulation 4056/86 OJ [1986] L378/4 on maritime transport).

[169] See the Commission's Annual Reports on Competition Policy.

[170] Or, in some cases, that it considered that the agreement did not infringe Art 81(1) in the first place.

[171] For the position of national courts in applying the EC competition rules before Regulation 1/2003, see Case C-234/89 *Stergios Delimitis v Henninger Bräu* [1991] ECR I-935, [1992] 5 CMLR 210; Commission Notice on Co-operation between National Courts and the Commission OJ 1993 C39/5.

The notification and individual exemption system was abolished as from 1 May 2004 when Regulation 1/2003 came into force. Under the 'modernised' enforcement system, Regulation 1/2003, Article 1 has rendered Article 81(3) a 'directly applicable legal exception', which can be invoked by parties in any national court or before the Commission or any national competition authority. Agreements which are prohibited by Article 81(1) but meet the Article 81(3) criteria are lawful from the time of their conclusion without any need for a prior constitutive decision, as was previously the case. The whole of Article 81 is directly applicable, and can be applied by national courts and national competition authorities as well as the Commission if and when the matter of the lawfulness of an agreement becomes an issue before them.[172]

Block exemptions are regulations which provide that agreements which comply with their terms satisfy the Article 81(3) criteria and are therefore not prohibited by Article 81. Under Regulation 17 they were, therefore, automatically exempted without notification to the Commission. Older block exemptions[173] contained lists of both 'black' clauses—provisions which an agreement could not include if it was to come within the block exemption—and 'white' clauses—provisions which the agreement *could* contain. However, the most recent block exemptions—such as those on vertical restraints,[174] research and development agreements,[175] specialisation agreements,[176] and technology transfer agreements[177]—contain only black clauses. As block exemptions are regulations and therefore directly applicable,[178] national courts have always been able to apply them and declare an agreement which complies with a block exemption to be exempted from Article 81(1) by virtue of Article 81(3).

The legal position of block exemptions, therefore, was not changed by Regulation 1/2003. However, they became even more important to parties entering into agreements. The abolition of the notification and individual exemption procedure means that if an agreement is not within a block exemption there is usually no way the parties

---

[172] The reform was first proposed by the Commission in its White Paper on modernisation of the rules implementing Arts 85 and 86 (now Arts 81 and 82) of the EC Treaty OJ [1999] C 132/1. The reasons behind it were largely concerned with the effect of the forthcoming enlargement of the EU to 25 Member States on the already over-burdened DG Comp. The Commission wished to concentrate its resources on combating cartels, serious abuses of market power and dealing with competition problems in the new Member States. The centralised exemption system by which the Commission had a monopoly on the application of Art 81(3) was seen as a waste of resources, and a barrier to the full participation of the national competition authorities in the enforcement of competition law and to the bringing of actions in national courts. See further, Whish and Sufrin 'Community Competition Law: Notification and Exemption—Goodbye to All That' in Hayton (ed) *Law's Future(s)* (Hart Publishing, 2000); Wesseling *The Modernisation Of EC Antitrust Law* (Hart Publishing, 2000).

[173] Eg, Commission Regulation 1983/83 on exclusive distribution agreements; Commission Regulation 1984/83 on exclusive purchasing agreements; Commission Regulation 240/96 on technology transfer agreements.

[174] Commission Regulation 2790/1999, OJ [1999] L336/21 on vertical restraints.

[175] Commission Regulation 2659/2000 on research & development agreements [200] OJ L 304/7.

[176] Commission Regulation 2658/2000 on specialisation agreements [2000] OJ L304/3.

[177] Commission Regulation 772/2004 [2004] OJ L 123/11.   [178] Art 249EC.

can be absolutely certain that the agreement complies with the Article 81.[179] There are two exceptional procedures under the new system, but neither is likely to be often available. First, under Regulation 1/2003, Article 10, the Commission can, acting on its own initiative, take a decision that Article 81 is not applicable to a particular agreement.[180] It can only do this 'where the Community public interest . . . so requires'. Secondly, the Commission has issued a Notice stating that it will issue 'guidance letters' where a matter raises novel points of fact or law.[181]

It is important to note that the ability of the parties to an agreement to take advantage of a block exemption is limited by the fact that most block exemptions now contain thresholds whereby the block exemption only applies if the parties have less than a certain share of the market. An agreement may at its inception be within a block exemption, but if the relevant market share[182] increases above the threshold during the lifetime of the agreement the exemption will cease to apply, with the consequences for the validity of the agreement discussed below.[183] The block exemptions contain transitional provisions, so that the parties have a certain period[184] in which to adjust their agreements. A major problem over this is that the calculation of market share runs into the notorious problems of market definition.[185]

There has been long-standing controversy over the application of Article 81(3), centred on whether or not the first condition (improving production or distribution or promoting technical or economic progress) can encompass 'socio-political' goals (such as the environment or employment) as well as 'competition' goals. This, in turn, is part of a wider debate over the objectives of competition law. The question has been given added urgency as far as Article 81(3) is concerned by Regulation 1/2003 rendering the provision directly applicable, as the national courts and national competition authorities, as well as the Commission, now have to grapple with it. The Commission's sets of Guidelines on different types of agreement address the individual application of Article 81(3)[186] but in 2004 the Commission produced a general

---

[179] They are of course heavily reliant on their lawyers, both in-house and external, to give them advice based on the case law, decisional practice, legislation and soft law.

[180] Or decision of association of undertakings or concerted practice.

[181] Comission Notice on informal guidance relating to novel questions concerning Arts 81 and 82 of the EC Treaty that arise in individual cases (guidance letters) [2004] OJ C 101/78.

[182] The market share may be an aggregate of the market share of the parties (eg under Regulation 2659/2000 on research and development agreements the threshold in agreements between competitors is 25% of the parties' combined market share); but may be of just one party (in Regulation 2790 on vertical agreements the market share which matters is usually that of the supplier, and the threshold is 30%).

[183] See pp 438 ff below.

[184] Up to two years under some block exemptions in certain circumstances.

[185] The Commission's current approach to market definition is set out in its Notice on the definition of the relevant market for the purposes of Community competition law [1997] OJ C372/5.

[186] Commission Guidelines on the application of Art 81(3) OJ [2004] C 101/97, para 25. See also Commission Guidelines on horizontal restraints OJ [2001] C 3/2; Commission Guidelines on vertical restraints OJ [2000] C 291/1; Commission Guidelines on technology transfer agreements OJ [2004] C 101/2.

Notice on Article 81(3).[187] This Notice reduces the first condition of Article 81(3) to a matter of efficiency gains: the question to be asked is whether the agreement will produce specific, verifiable and measurable cost or qualitative efficiencies.[188] The scope for socio-political factors is limited, the Notice states that 'goals pursued by other Treaty provisions can be taken into account to the extent that they can be subsumed under the four conditions of Article 81(3)'.[189]

Voidness under Article 81(2) and the other consequences of entering into a prohibited agreement

There are a number of consequences of parties entering into an agreement prohibited by Article 81(1) which does not individually satisfy Article 81(3) and is not block-exempted. Under the implementing regulations the Commission may fine the parties[190] and/or adopt a decision ordering them to bring the infringement of the competition rules to an end.[191] As Article 81(1) is directly applicable, parties may rely on it as a defence (a shield) or as a cause of action (a sword).[192]

Article 81 expressly provides for the sanction of voidness. Article 81(2) says:

> Any agreements or decisions prohibited pursuant to this Article shall be automatically void.

Despite this plain wording, the European Court of Justice has held that only the elements of an agreement which infringe Article 81 are void, not the whole agreement.[193] Whether the non-infringing provisions of the agreement can stand depends on the test for severability in the law applied by the national court before which the status of the agreement has arisen in litigation.[194] There is no Community law doctrine of severance. This means that the outcome of litigation can vary depending on the applicable law of the contract, a problem which could be mitigated by harmonisation of the Member States rules on severance. In UK law the leading case on sever-

---

[187] Commission Guidelines on the application of Art 81(3) OJ [2004] C 101/97.

[188] Ibid, paras 48–72.

[189] Ibid, para 42. See Lugard and Hancher, *Honey, I Shrunk the Article! A Critical Assessment of the Commission's Notice on Article 81(3) of the EC Treaty* [2004] ECLR 410; G Monti, *Article 81 and Public Policy* (2002) 39 CMLRev 1057.

[190] Regulation 1/2003, Art 23 (2). See Commission Guidelines on the method of setting fines, 28.6.06. The fine may be as much as 10% of the undertaking's turnover in the previous year. In theory this relates to all products (or services), worldwide, see Cases 100–103/80 *Musique Diffusion Française SA v Commission (Pioneer)* [1983] ECR 1825 [1983] 3 CMLR 221, and the turnover concerned is that of the group of connected companies to which the infringing undertaking belongs. In practice, the turnover accounted for by the product to which the infringement relates will be relevant, see eg Case T-77/92 *Parker Pen v Commission* [1994] ECR II-549.

[191] Regulation 1/2003, Art 7(1).

[192] *Unipart v O2* [2004] EWCA Civ 1034, [2004] UKCLR 1453, see p 428 above, was an attempt to do this.

[193] Case 56/65 *Société Technique Minière v Maschinenbau Ulm GmbH* [1966] ECR 235, [1966] 1 CMLR 357, 376.

[194] Case 319/82 *Société de Vente de Ciments et Bétons de L'Est SA v Kerpen and Kerpen GmbH* [1983] ECR 4173, [1985] 1 CMLR 511.

ability in competition cases is *Chemidus Wavin*[195] in which Buckley LJ said that the question was whether, after excising the prohibited provisions, the contract could be said to fail for consideration or any other ground, or would be so changed in its character as not to be the sort of contract that the parties intended to enter into at all.[196] This was applied in *Inntrepreneur Estates Ltd v Mason*[197] in which a Deputy High Court judge said that in the lease of a public house it would be possible to sever a beer tie obligation from the obligation to pay rent.[198]

A question which arose before the English High Court in *Passmore v Morland plc*[199] was whether an agreement which is void for infringing the competition rules is void for ever or can be void or valid depending on its economic effects from time to time.[200] In that case:

> Passmore took a lease of a pub from Inntrepreneur in February 1992. The tenancy agreement contained a beer-tie, an exclusive purchasing agreement whereby Passmore contracted to buy all its beer from Inntrepreneur, its assigns and nominees. Five months later Inntrepreneur transferred the reversion of the lease, and it was eventually acquired by the defendant, Morland. The terms of the lease did not fall within the relevant block exemption,[201] and a notification to the Commission for individual exemption made in July 1992 was later withdrawn, apparently because the Commission informed Inntrepreneur that the terms did not qualify for exemption. In 1997, Passmore informed Morland that he considered the beer-tie was unenforceable for infringing Article 81(1) and that he reserved the right to buy beer products from other brewers with immediate effect.

The crucial fact was that Inntrepreneur owned approximately 4,500 on-licensed premises in 1992, all let on terms which included a beer-tie similar to that in Passmore's lease, whereas Morland was a small brewer whose tied estate amounted to only 0.19% of licensed outlets in the UK. The Court of Appeal held that even if the cumulative effect of Inntrepreneur's agreements was to restrict competition because it foreclosed the market to other producers—so that according to the judgment of the European Court of Justice in *Delimitis*[202] the agreement with Passmore infringed Article 81(1) and was void under Article 81(2)—the infringement and, therefore, the voidness came to an end when Morland acquired the lease. Morland's share of the

---

[195] *Chemidus Wavin v Société pour la Transformation* [1978] 3 CMLR 514, CA.

[196] Ibid, at 520.

[197] [1993] 2 CMLR 293, QB.

[198] See also *Inntrepreneur Estates (GL) Ltd v Boyes* [1993] 2 EGLR 112.

[199] [1998] 4 All ER 468; affd [1999] 3 All ER 1005, [1999] 1 CMLR 1129, CA.

[200] Passmore's action was for a declaration that the beer-tie was unenforceable. He had originally claimed damages and restitution as well, but the claims were not pursued because of the Court of Appeal judgment in *Gibbs Mew v Gemmell*, discussed below p 441 which had been delivered in the meantime.

[201] Commission Regulation 1984/83 on exclusive purchasing agreements.

[202] Case C-234/89 *Stergios Delimitis v Henninger Bräu* [1991] ECR I-935, [1992] 5 CMLR 210.

market was so insignificant that the arrangement with Passmore was *de minimis* and not brought within Article 81(1) by the network effect. The Court of Appeal held that in such a situation an agreement which is void at its inception can spring to life when its economic effects change, *in casu* by a change in the parties, and become valid. The reverse can also occur, so that a previously valid agreement may become void. As Chadwick LJ said:

> Agreements are prohibited when and while they are incompatible with competition in the common market and not otherwise.

In coming to this decision Chadwick LJ distinguished the case before him from *Shell UK Ltd v Lostock Garage Ltd*[203] in which the Court of Appeal held that a petrol-tie agreement valid at the time that it was entered into did not become unenforceable for restraint of trade because it subsequently became unreasonable or unfair. That rule could not apply in the context of EC competition law.[204] As explained above, it is also possible for the status of agreements to change by moving in and out of the protection of a block exemption because the parties' market shares have changed.[205]

The greatest problem for national courts in applying Article 81(2) used to be the Commission's monopoly over individual exemptions, which meant that the courts could decide that an agreement was caught by Article 81(1) but not that it satisfied Article 81(3).[206] These difficulties have now been swept away by Regulation 1/2003. The problems that remain now are, simply, those of applying the provisions. One of the Notices issued by the Commission to accompany Regulation 1/2003 was a replacement for its previous Notice on cooperation between the Commission and the national courts.[207] The courts have had to grapple with the issue of what are the consequences as between the parties of entering into a prohibited agreement. We have seen above in *Passmore v Morland* a situation where one party attempted to escape its contractual obligations by pleading that the contract infringed Article 81(1). The UK courts have not always shown themselves sympathetic to this tactic, the so-called 'Euro-defence' popularly known as the 'last refuge of the damned', but attitudes appear to be changing as the ordinary courts become more familiar with competition law arguments.[208] Article 81 has been used as a sword as well as a

---

[203] [1977] 1 All ER 481, [1977] 1 WLR 1187.

[204] And will not apply in the context of domestic competition law under the Competition Act 1998, see pp 445 ff, below.

[205] See p 437, above.

[206] See p 435, above.

[207] Commission Notice on the cooperation between the Comission and the courts of the EU member states in the application of Arts 81 and 82 of the EC Treaty [2004] OJ C 101/65, replacing Commission Notice on cooperation between national courts and the Commission [1993] OJ C39/5.

[208] See D Beard in Ward and Smith *Competition Litigation in the UK* (Sweet & Maxwell, 2005) 7-082. In England and Wales Civil Procedure Rules Practice Direction B12, Rule 2.1 stipulates that any party whose statement of case raises or deals with an issue relating to the application of Arts 81 or 82 must commence proceedings in the Chancery Division of the High Court or apply for their transfer there

shield.[209] Many of the cases where parties have pleaded Article 81 in the UK courts have involved tied house agreements, because for a long time the Commission, fearing the foreclosure effect on the beer market of networks of tying agreements, applied Article 81(1) very widely to such agreements and was very restrictive as to the terms to which it would grant exemption.[210] More recently, the Commission has been readier to hold that beer-ties are either not caught by Article 81(1),[211] or satisfy Article 81(3),[212] and the current block exemption on vertical restraints takes a broader brush approach and does not contain special provisions for beer ties.[213]

One major question which has arisen is whether a party to a contract which is void for infringing the competition rules can not only avoid its enforcement but also claim restitution of benefits it has paid to the other party under the contract and/or damages for the harm it suffered from the contract's operation. In *Gibbs Mew plc v Gemmell*,[214] another tied house case, the Court of Appeal said *obiter* that such recovery was impossible since an agreement prohibited by Article 81(1) is not only void but illegal: being illegal the principle *in pari delicto* applied and in English law neither party can claim from the other party for loss caused to him by being party to an illegal contract.[215] The categorisation of an infringing agreement as illegal therefore bars

---

[209] In *Panayiòtou v Sony Music Entertainment (UK) Ltd* [1994] ECC 395, for example, the singer George Michael asked for a declaration that his recording contract with Sony was void on the basis that it infringed Art 81(1) as well as arguing that it was void as being in restraint of trade at common law. Parker J held that Art 81(1) was not infringed as the recording contract did not have an appreciable effect on inter-Member State trade. The conclusion about the lack of effect on inter-member state trade was rather doubtful but the case did not go to appeal as it was settled.

[210] The inter-Member State trade effect arises in these cases from the difficulties of importers trying to penetrate a market networked with tying agreements. Commission Regulation 1983/84, the block exemption on exclusive purchasing agreements, contained special provisions on beer-ties. Case C-234/89 *Stergios Delimitis v Henninger Bräu* [1991] ECR I-935, [1992] 5 CMLR 210, a seminal judgment of the European Court of Justice on the application of Art 81(1), concerned a beer-tie which was outside the block exemption because of specific clauses which did not comply with the detailed requirements of the block exemption.

[211] An approach approved by the Court of First Instance in Case T-25/99 *Roberts v Commission* [2001] ECR II-1881 following the test laid down by the European Court of Justice in *Delimitis* (see note 205, above) for ascertaining whether a beer-tie is caught by Art 81(1).

[212] Eg *Whitbread* OJ [1999] L88/26, [1999] 5 CMLR 118; *Bass* OJ [1999] L 186/1, [1999] 5 CMLR 782; *Scottish and Newcastle* OJ [1999] L186/28, [1999] 5 CMLR 831.

[213] Regulation 2790/1999 on vertical restraints, OJ [1999] L336/21.

[214] [1999] ECC 97, [1998] Eu LR 588.

[215] This rule is discussed below, pp 494 ff. In general English contract law it would make a difference whether the contract is classified as illegal or as void (see Chs 11 and 12); whether the doctrine of severance applies (see p 541) and whether the parties are treated as equally at fault (see pp 487 ff). This firm statement by the Court of Appeal was in line with a number of unreported High Court decisions where claims by a party to an agreement infringing Art 81 for restitution or damages had been rejected: eg *Inntrepreneur Estates v Milne*, 30 July 1993; *Inntrepreneur Estates plc v Smythe*, 14 October 1993; *Trent Taverns v Sykes* [1998] Eu LR 571; *Parkes v Esso Petroleum Co Ltd* [1998] Eu LR 550 (concerning a petrol rather than a beer-tie).

any restitutionary or damages claim by either party. Peter Gibson LJ rejected the argument that the parties were not *in pari delicto* because the publican was much the weaker party, and said that Article 81(1) was concerned not with inequality of bargaining power between the parties to the illegal agreement but with the effect of that agreement on competition.

The point in *Gibbs Mew*, however, was referred by a later Court of Appeal to the European Court of Appeal under the Article 234 reference procedure in *Courage v Crehan*.[216] The Court of Appeal asked the European Court of Justice, in effect, whether a party to a prohibited tied house agreement was entitled to claim from the other party damages arising from his adherence to the prohibited agreement and whether, or in what circumstances, a rule of national law which prevented him doing so (ie as enunciated in *Gibbs Mew*) was inconsistent with Community law. The case was of great importance because the Community Courts had never previously definitively ruled that competition damages were available in *any* situation.[217] In *Crehan* the European Court of Justice said that the effectiveness of Article 81 would be put at risk if individuals were unable to claim damages.[218] It therefore established the existence of a Community right to damages, albeit one that has to be exercised in the national courts of the Member States. The European Court of Justice said that Community law did preclude an absolute rule in national law which prevented any party to an agreement which infringed Community law from recovering damages; Community law did not, however, preclude a rule to the effect that a party who bore significant responsibility for the distortion of competition could not recover.[219] The question is whether one party found himself in a markedly weaker position than the other, such as seriously to compromise or even eliminate his freedom of negotiation and his capacity to avoid or reduce loss.[220] In other words, the European Court of Justice—unlike the Court of Appeal—was prepared to recognise inequality of bargaining power in this context.

When Mr Crehan's claim for damages was actually heard in the English courts he was treated as one who was in an unequal bargaining position with no significant responsibility for the breach of the competition rules.[221] The Court of Appeal appeared to treat the claim as one arising from a breach of statutory duty, but not subject to the usual constraints of statutory duty damages actions. The Court of Appeal was overturned by the House of Lords, not on the damages issue but on the grounds that the trial judge had been right in holding himself not bound by findings of fact by the Commission in previous decisions relating to the state of the UK beer market. The trial judge had disagreed with the Commission's assessment of the

---

[216] Case C-453/99 *Courage v Crehan* [2001] ECR I-6297, [2001] 5 CMLR 28.

[217] Lord Diplock had indicated that third party damages were available in the UK in *Garden Cottage Foods Ltd v Milk Marketing Board* [1984] AC 130, [1983] 2 All ER 770.

[218] *Courage v Crehan*, paras 26–27.   [219] Ibid, para 36   [220] Ibid, para 33.

[221] *Crehan v Inntrepeneur* [2004] EWCA Civ 637.

market and held that Article 81(1) was not infringed. So Mr Crehan's claim collapsed.[222]

The EC Commission is keen to encourage the private enforcement of the competition rules in the national courts, particularly claims for damages. There are numerous problems in respect of bringing such claims, partly stemming from the differences existing between both the substantive and procedural laws across the Member States. The Commission has published a Green Paper initiating a public debate as to whether, or how, these could be addressed.[223] UK law contains special provisions for damages actions arising from breaches of EC or UK competition law. The Competition Act 1998 section 47A provides that claims for damages may be brought before the Competition Appeal Tribunal where there has already been a decision by the EC Commission that Article 81[224] has been infringed or by the Office of Fair Trading (or the Competition Appeal Tribunal on appeal) that the Chapter I prohibition of the Competition Act 1998[225] or Article 81[226] has been infringed.[227] The Competition Appeal Tribunal is bound by the decision that the relevant prohibition has been infringed.

Article 82

Article 82 prohibits an undertaking in a dominant position in the common market or a substantial part of it from abusing that position. It provides:

> Any abuse by one or more undertakings of a dominant position within the common market or in a substantial part of it shall be prohibited as incompatible with the common market in so far as it may affect trade between Member States.

Such abuse may, in particular, consist in:

(a) directly or indirectly imposing unfair purchase or selling prices or other unfair trading conditions;

(b) limiting production, markets or technical development to the prejudice of consumers;

(c) applying dissimilar conditions to equivalent transactions with other trading parties, thereby placing them at a competitive disadvantage;

(d) making the conclusion of contracts subject to acceptance by the other parties of supplementary obligations which, by their nature or according to commercial usage, have no connection with the subject of such contracts.

The question of whether or not an undertaking is in a dominant position in a substantial part of the common market is a complex one on which there are over 40

---

[222] [2006] UKHL 38. For the details of the Court of Appeal judgment, see Holmes and Lennon, The Crehan Judgment [2004] *ECLR* 676.

[223] Commission Green Paper on Damages Actions for Breach of EC Antitrust Rules, 19 December 2005 COM(2005) 672 final, and Annex. See http://www.europa.eu.int/comm/competition/antitrust/others/actions_for_damages/gp.html

[224] Or Art 82.   [225] See pp 447 ff, below.

[226] Or Art 82 or the Chapter II prohibition.   [227] So-called 'follow-on' actions.

years of cases and decisions by the Community Courts and the EC Commission, and the reader is referred to the specialist works on the subject.[228] The terms 'undertaking' and 'may affect trade between Member States' are given the same interpretation as they are for the purposes of Article 81.[229]

As with 'dominant position' the concept of an 'abuse' is complex. The list in paragraphs (a) to (d) of the Article is non-exhaustive, and 'exclusionary' ('anti-competitive') as well as 'exploitative' conduct is caught by Article 82.[230] In particular the European Court of Justice has held that it can be an abuse for a dominant firm to enter into some kinds of contractual arrangements. This may be because they are unfair to the other party[231] or because they have the effect of foreclosing the market to competitors. So, for example, agreements by which a dominant firm enters into requirements contracts, exclusive purchasing arrangements, contracts providing for loyalty rebates (whereby the buyer gets a discount if it buys solely from the dominant firm) or tying arrangements, may amount to an abuse.[232]

The underlying idea behind Article 82 is that a firm in a dominant position can distort competition by its unilateral conduct. Although Article 82 does not expressly say that the abusive provisions of the agreement are void, it is assumed that that is the consequence of the Article 82 prohibition and that the other party can treat them as unenforceable (the same issue of severability arises as in respect of Article 81[233]).[234] As far as the other party claiming restitution or damages is concerned, the ruling in *Crehan*[235] means that it must be possible to claim damages in a national court. The question of whether one party bears significant responsibility for the infringement of the competition rules would not arise as the bases of Articles 81 and 82 are different. Whereas Article 81(1) prohibits *agreements*, Article 82 prohibits *abuses of a dominant position*, so a non-dominant undertaking cannot infringe Article 82

---

[228] See fn 112, p 427, above.

[229] See pp 429 and 431, above.

[230] Case 6/72 *Europemballage Corpn & Continental Can Co Inc v EC Commission* [1973] ECR 215 [1973] CMLR 199.

[231] As is contemplated in Article 82(a) itself.

[232] See Case 85/76 *Hoffmann-La Roche v Commission* [1979] ECR 461 [1979] 3 CMLR 211; Case 322/81 *Nederlandsche Banden-Industrie Michelin v Commission* [1983] ECR 3461 [1985] 1 CMLR 282; Case T-203/01 *Manufacture Française Pneumatiques Michelin v Commission* (*Michelin II*) [2004] 4 CMLR 923. The idea that some types of contractual arrangement entered into by undertakings in a dominant position are more or less *per se* abusive without an examination of their actual effects on the market is a deeply controversial one. Despite the jurisprudence of the Community Courts, the Commission would now prefer a different approach: see Commission Discussion Paper on the application of Art 82 of the Treaty to exclusionary abuses, 19 December 2005, http://www.europa.eu.int/comm/competition/antitrust/others/discpaper2005.pdf.

[233] See pp 438–439, above.

[234] See R Whish *The Enforceability of Agreements under EC and UK Competition Law* in F D Rose (ed) *Lex Mercatoria: Essays in International Commercial Law in Honour of Francis Reynolds* (LLP, 2000) 297–319 at 317.

[235] Case C-453/99 *Courage v Crehan* [2001] ECR I-6297, [2001] 5 CMLR 28, see p 442, above.

2 The UK Competition Rules

The position before 1 March 2000

United Kingdom legislation for the regulation of restrictive trading agreements was consolidated by the Restrictive Trade Practices Act 1976.[236] Minimum resale price maintenance was dealt with by specific legislation. It was prohibited by the Resale Prices Act 1964, and then by the Resale Prices Act 1976. Procedures under the Fair Trading Act 1973, which provided for industry-wide investigations in situations of scale and complex monopoly, and under the Competition Act 1980, which provided for investigations into anti-competitive practices by particular firms,[237] could result in firms being prohibited from entering into certain types of agreement.

The position after the coming into force of the Competition Act 1998

The Restrictive Trade Practices Act 1976 and the Resale Prices Act 1976 were repealed by the Competition Act 1998, which came into force on 1 March 2000.[238] There were transitional provisions for agreements which were made before 1 March 2000 (the 'starting date'). The Competition Act 1998 applies to all agreements made on or after the starting date to the exclusion of the two 1976 Acts. The anti-competitive practices provisions of the Competition Act 1980 were repealed[239] but the monopoly provisions of the Fair Trading Act remained in force until replaced by the market investigation reference provisions of the Enterprise Act 2002, which came into force on 1 June 2003.[240]

The Competition Act 1998

UK competition law was fundamentally reformed by the Competition Act 1998. The reasons for the reform were the unsatisfactory and inadequate nature of the previous

---

[236] For some twenty years before that, restrictive agreements relating to goods had been subject to statutory regulation by virtue of Part I of the Restrictive Trade Practices Act 1956 (from 1948 to 1956 such agreements had been subject to statutory regulation by virtue of the Monopolies and Restrictive Practices (Inquiry and Control) Act 1948). During that period Part I of the 1956 Act was amended by the Restrictive Trade Practices Act 1968 and further amended five years later by the Fair Trading Act 1973. In particular, provision was made by the Acts of 1968 and 1973 for the extension of the scope of Part I of the 1956 Act by statutory order. Part I was applied in 1969 to information agreements relating to goods (Restrictive Trade Practices (Information Agreements) Order 1969 (SI 1969/1842) and in 1976 to restrictive agreements relating to services. No order was ever made by the Secretary of State under s 12 of the 1976 Act for regulating information agreements relating to services (this point is relevant to the proceedings by the Office of Fair Trading against independent schools in 2005, see p 452, below).

[237] Market-share and turnover thresholds below which businesses were excluded from the provisions of the 1980 Act were set by Order. The relevant figures were 25% of the market and £10 million (after 1994) annual turnover: Anti-Competitive Practices (Exclusions) Order 1994, SI 1994/1557 amending Anti-Competitive Practices (Exclusions) Order 1980, SI 1980/979.

[238] Competition Act 1998, s 74 and Sch 14.

[239] Competition Act 1998, s 17.

[240] Enterprise Act 2002, ss 131–184. The reform of the investigatory procedure resulted from the White Paper *A World Class Competition Regime* Cm 5233 (2001).

law,[241] the need for more stringent provisions, including more effective enforcement measures and more effective sanctions, and the desirability of harmonising UK law with EC competition law.[242]

The Competition Act 1998 brought into domestic competition law provisions analogous to Article 81 and Article 82 EC, but without the 'effect on trade between Member States' criteria. The 'Chapter I prohibition', contained in section 2 of the Act, is equivalent to Article 81 and the 'Chapter II prohibition', contained in section 18, is equivalent to Article 82. The whole essence of the UK provisions is that they broadly replicate EC law. The key to the Act is section 60, the 'governing principles' clause. It provides that so far as is possible, and 'having regard to any relevant differences between the provisions concerned', the authorities and courts in the UK are to maintain consistency with EC law. This is to be done by following the decisions of the European Court of Justice and 'having regard to' decisions or statements of the Commission. The scope and significance of section 60 is considered further below[243] but the basic position is that the concepts in the Act, such as 'agreement', 'undertaking', and 'object or effect the prevention, restriction or distortion of competition' must be given the same meaning in UK law as they have in EC law.

Primary responsibility for enforcing the Competition Act 1998 lies with the Office of Fair Trading.[244] The Office of Fair Trading publishes a series of Guidelines explaining the provisions of the Competition Act and its policy in applying them.[245] The Guidelines include explanations of the relevant EC law. Appeals from decisions

---

[241] For an account of the 1976 Acts, see Ch 10 of the 13th edn of this book.

[242] See the Secretary of State (Margaret Beckett) during the Second Reading of the Bill, Hansard, HC, 11 May 1998, col 25. The genesis of the reform of UK law was the Liesner reports of the late 1970s, *A Review of Monopolies and Mergers Policy* Cm 7198 (1978) and *A Review of Restrictive Trade Practices Policy* Cm 7512 (1979). Under the Conservative government there were two Green Papers *Review of Restrictive Trade Practices Policy: A Consultative Document*, Cm 331 (1988) and *Abuse of Market Power: A Consultative Document on Possible Legislative Options*, Cm 2100 (1992), a White Paper *Opening Markets: New Policy on Restrictive Trade Practices* Cm 727 (1989), and a further consultation document and a draft Bill in 1996. The incoming Labour government announced its intention to reform competition law in the Queen's Speech in May 1997 and introduced the Competition Bill into the House of Lords in October 1997. It received the Royal Assent on 9 November 1998.

[243] See pp 453–457, below.

[244] Prior to the coming into force of the relevant provisions of the Enterprise Act 2002 on 1 April 2003 competition law was enforced by the Director General of Fair Trading who headed the Office of Fair Trading, which was then a non-minsterial government department. The Enterprise Act 2002 established the Office of Fair Trading as a body corporate carrying out functions on behalf of the Crown (Enterprise Act 2002, s 1).

[245] As required by Competition Act 1998, s 52. New sets of Guidelines were issued in 2004 to take account of the 'modernisation' programme in EC law which occasioned changes to the UK regime: see p 448, below.

of the Office of Fair Trading lie to the Competition Appeal Tribunal[246] on the merits and thence on a point of law to the Court of Appeal.[247]

The Chapter I Prohibition

The Competition Act 1998 section 2(1)–(3) provides:

(1) Subject to section 3, agreements between undertakings, decisions by associations of undertakings or concerted practices which—

   (a) may affect trade within the United Kingdom, and

   (b) have as their object or effect the prevention, restriction or distortion of competition within the United Kingdom, are prohibited unless they are exempt in accordance with the provisions of this Part.

(2) Subsection (1) applies, in particular, to agreements, decisions or practices which:

   (a) directly or indirectly fix purchase or selling prices or any other trading conditions;

   (b) limit or control production, markets, technical development or investment;

   (c) share markets or sources of supply;

   (d) apply dissimilar conditions to equivalent transactions with other trading parties, thereby placing them at a competitive disadvantage;

   (e) make the conclusion of contracts subject to acceptance by the other parties of supplementary obligations which, by their nature or according to commercial usage, have no connection with the subject of such contracts.

(3) Subsection (1) applies only if the agreement, decision or practice is, or is intended to be, implemented in the United Kingdom.

The wording of subsection (2) is identical to the corresponding paragraph of Article 81(1). The wording of subsection (1) is almost identical, except that competition must be distorted *in the United Kingdom* and trade affected *in the United Kingdom*. Section 2(7) provides that 'the United Kingdom' means—in relation to an agreement which operates or is intended to operate only in a part of the United Kingdom—that part. It does not provide, however, that the part has to be substantial or significant, and this means that the Act can catch agreements which have only a very localised effect. Subsection 2(3) addresses the question of extra-territorial effect which is not expressly provided for in Article 81(1) but has been dealt with by the European Court of Justice.[248] Subsection 2(3) uses the wording used by the European Court of Justice in the *Wood Pulp* judgment, ie that the agreement be 'implemented in' the

---

[246] Previously, until 2003, the Competition Commission Appeal Tribunal (CCAT).
[247] Competition Act 1998, ss 46–49.   [248] See p 433, above.

territory.[249] By making express provision for this, Parliament intended to exclude the possibility of a full-scale 'effects doctrine'[250] becoming applicable under the Act in the future as a result of developments in European jurisprudence being imported into domestic competition law via section 60.[251]

As with Article 81, there is provision for agreements which fall within the Chapter I prohibition to be excepted from the prohibition. The criteria for this are laid down in section 9(1) and are identical to those in Article 81(3).[252] As under Article 81(3), the burden of proving that section 9(1) is satisfied rests on the party claiming it.[253]

The scheme of the Chapter I prohibition was deliberately modelled on Article 81(1). When the Act came into force it therefore provided for the Secretary of State, on the Office of Fair Trading's recommendation, to issue block exemptions, and for the Office of Fair Trading to operate a notification and individual exemption system like that then pertaining under Regulation 17 in respect of EC law.[254] The Act also provided for 'parallel exemptions' whereby agreements benefiting from an EC exemption—block[255] or individual—were automatically exempted in addition from the Chapter I prohibition.

Individual notification and exemption were swept away by statutory instrument in 2004 in order to bring UK law into line with the 'modernised' EC regime.[256] As with EC law, an agreement which falls within the Chapter I prohibition and is not within a block exemption will be judged *ex post* by the Office of Fair Trading or a UK court in the light of section 9(1) if and when the compatibility of the agreement with the competition rules becomes an issue.

The provisions of the Competition Act 1998 relating to block exemptions remain. The Secretary of State can issue them on the advice of the Office of Fair Trading.[257] The concept of 'parallel exemptions' applied to block exemptions has also survived the

---

[249] Cases 89, 104, 114, 116, 117 and 125–129/85 *A Ahlström Oy v Commission* [1988] ECR 5193, [1988] 4 CMLR 901.

[250] For the effects doctrine in US antitrust law, see *Butterworths Competition Law*, Division XII; Jones and Sufrin, n 112, 427, above, Ch 16.

[251] Lord Simon, Hansard, HL, 13 November 1997, col 261. The Court of First Instance has used the word 'effect' in a merger case, Case T-102/96 *Gencor Ltd v Commission* [1999] ECR II-753, [1999] 4 CMLR 971.

[252] The policy of the Office of Fair Trading in applying the Chapter I prohibition is set out in the Guideline *Agreements and Concerted Practices*, Office of Fair Trading 414. Para 5.5 refers to the Commission Guidelines on the application of Art 81(3) and says that 'the Office of Fair Trading will have regard to this Notice in considering the application of Art 81(3) and s 9(1).

[253] Competition Act 1998 s 9(2).

[254] Ibid, ss 4, 7, and 12–16 (s 7 concerned notification under block exemption 'opposition procedures').

[255] Or rather, would have benefited had there been an effect on inter-member state trade.

[256] See the Competition Act 1998 and Other Enactments (Amendment) Regulations 2004, SI 2004/1261; Office of Fair Trading Guideline *Modernisation*, Office of Fair Trading 442.

[257] Competition Act 1998, s 6.

2004 reforms, and means that agreements which do not infringe Article 81(1) because they do not affect inter-Member State trade, but which would come within a block exemption if they did, are automatically exempted from the Chapter I prohibition.[258] The parallel exemption provision is of great importance because it means that apart from one instance[259] it has not been necessary for the Secretary of State to make Orders providing for block exemptions, as it has been considered sufficient to rely on the EC exemptions.

One way in which the Chapter I prohibition differs from Article 81(1) is that the Act provides for certain types of agreement to be *excluded* (rather than exempted) from the prohibition.[260] This means that such agreements are not caught by section 2(1) in the first place. The exclusions are: mergers and concentrations; compliance with planning requirements; the rules of 'European Economic Area regulated financial markets'; undertakings entrusted with services of general economic interest;[261] agreements made to comply with a legal requirement; agreements made to avoid conflict with the UK's international obligations (to be excluded by Order of the Secretary of State); agreements needed to be excluded for exceptional and compelling reasons of public policy (to be excluded by Order of the Secretary of State); coal and steel agreements where the EC Commission has exclusive jurisdiction; and agreements relating to certain agricultural products. It is provided that the Secretary of State may add to these exclusions, or make deletions.[262] In addition the Competition Act 1998, section 50 provides that the Secretary of State may exclude vertical agreements and land agreements, or modify the way in which the Act applies to them. The Secretary of State has exercised the section 50 power, currently in respect of land agreements only.[263]

As discussed above[264] the European Court of Justice has read a *de minimis* requirement into Article 81(1) by which the prohibition does not apply unless the restriction of competition or the effect on inter-Member State trade is appreciable. Although the appreciability requirement does not appear in the Act, it was Parliament's intention that it should apply, and it is imported into the Chapter I prohibition by section 60.[265] The Office of Fair Trading Guideline on the Chapter I prohibition states that the Office of Fair Trading will have regard to the Commission's approach as set out in the Notice on agreements of minor importance and that as a matter of practice the

[258] Ibid, s 10.
[259] Ibid, (Public Transport Ticketing Schemes Block Exemption) Order 2001, SI 2001/319, which allows bus and train operators to offer travel cards and through-tickets. See Office of Fair Trading Guideline 439.
[260] Competition Act 1998, s 3 and Schs 1–3.
[261] This exclusion corresponds to Art 86EC.
[262] Competition Act 1998, s 3(2) and (3).
[263] Ibid, (Land and Vertical Agreements Exclusion) Order 2000, SI 2000/310, see pp 450–451, below.
[264] Pp 432 ff.
[265] Lord Simon, Hansard, HL, 9 February 1998, col 887.

Office of Fair Trading is likely to consider that an agreement will not fall within either Article 81 or the Chapter I prohibition when it is covered by the Notice.[266]

Vertical Agreements and Resale Price Maintenance under the Chapter I Prohibition
Historically, UK competition law was not much concerned with vertical agreements. The Restrictive Trade Practices Acts were directed towards the suppression of anti-competitive horizontal agreements. Vertical agreements such as distribution arrange-ments normally escaped the Restrictive Trade Practices Act 1976 by virtue of section 9(3) and Schedule 3(2).[267] Minimum resale price maintenance was, however, pro-hibited, first by the Resale Prices Act 1964 and then by the Resale Prices Act 1976. The 1964 Act accomplished the dismantling of individual resale price maintenance agreements which had begun some thirty years before in the grocery trade in response to normal market forces. The effect of the Acts was to prohibit suppliers of goods which did not qualify for exemption granted by the Restrictive Practices Court from establishing minimum prices at which those goods could be resold or from seeking to compel dealers to observe those prices, whether by discriminatory action or the withholding of supplies. Only two exemption orders were made by the Restrictive Practices Court. These were in respect of books[268] and medicaments.[269] The Net Book Agreement exemption was challenged as being incompatible with EC law,[270] but before the matter was finally determined, resale price maintenance on books was abandoned in the UK by various leading publishers in the mid-1990s, and given the collapse of the agreement the Restrictive Practices Court discharged the exemption order on the application of the Director General of Fair Trading.[271] Upon the repeal of the Resale Prices Act by the Competition Act 1998, special transitional provisions provided for the continuance of the exemption granted by the Restrictive Practices Court to medicaments (over-the-counter medicines).[272] However, in 1998 the Director General of Fair Trading had begun the process of applying to the Restrictive Practices Court to remove the exemption and when the pharmaceutical manufacturers abandoned their opposition to this on 15 May 2001 the Restrictive Practices Court immediately made an order removing the exemption.

---

[266] Office of Fair Trading 414 *Agreements and Concerted Practices* paras 2.18–2.19. This is a change from the position pre-2004, when the relevant Office of Fair Trading Guideline contained a higher *de minimis* threshold.

[267] And by the fact that under the Act agreements were caught only if at least two parties accepted restrictions. A distribution agreement which imposed obligations on only one party was therefore outside the Act.

[268] *Re Net Book Agreement 1957* [1962] 3 All ER 751, LR 3 RP 246. The Net Book Agreement involved both collective and individual resale price maintenance.

[269] *Re Medicaments Reference (No 2)* [1971] 1 All ER 12, LR 7 RP 267.

[270] Case C-360/92P *Re the Net Book Agreement: Publishers Association v Commission* [1995] ECR I-23, [1995] 5 CMLR 33.

[271] *Re Net Book Agreement 1957 (M and N)* [1997] 16 LS Gaz R 29.

[272] Competition Act 1998, Sch 13, para 23.

Except for resale price maintenance, UK law never shared the EC law's preoccupation with vertical restraints because the fear that vertical restraints impede the single market is not relevant in the domestic sphere. The Competition Act 1998 continued that UK policy, by providing for the Secretary of State to exclude vertical restraints from the Chapter I prohibition.[273] This was done when the Competition Act 1998 first came into force.[274] The exclusion did not apply to *minimum* resale price maintenance[275]

The exclusion of vertical agreements other than resale price maintenance from the Chapter I prohibition was abolished by Order in 2004.[276] EC law on vertical restraints therefore now applies in respect of vertical agreements by reason of the Competition Act 1998, section 60 in the same way as to other types of agreement. The Office of Fair Trading has issued a Guideline on vertical restraints[277] and the Verticals Regulation 2790/1999 applies by virtue of section 10 on parallel exemptions. Vertical agreements can also fall under the Chapter II prohibition (below) in the same way that that they can fall within Article 82.[278] Furthermore, vertical agreements in particular markets can be scrutinised under the market investigation reference procedure in the Enterprise Act 2002.

The Application of the Chapter I Prohibition
Most of the application of the Chapter I prohibition has concerned its enforcement against cartels[279] and against the illegal fixing of resale prices.[280] However, the first decision by the Office of Fair Trading[281] was in the *General Insurance Standards Council,*[282] where the General Insurance Standards Council notified its rules and the Office of Fair Trading held that they did not infringe the Chapter I prohibition. A third party appealed against this to the Competition Commission Appeal Tribunal (as the Competition Appeal Tribunal then was) which withdrew the decision and remitted it to the Office of Fair Trading for reconsideration.[283] The General Insurance

---

[273] Competition Act 1998, s 50.

[274] Ibid, (Land and Vertical Agreements Exclusion) Order 2000 SI 2000/310.

[275] See Case 161/84 *Pronuptia de Paris GmbH v Pronuptia de Paris Irmgard Schillgallis* [1986] ECR 353, [1986] 1 CMLR 414; Guidelines on Vertical Restraints, OJ [2000] C 43/1 paras 225–228 for EC law on minimum RPM.

[276] The Competition Act 1998 (Land Agreements, Exclusion and Revocation) Order 2004, SI 2004/1260. The Order retained the exclusion of land agreements. Land agreements are those which deal with the creation, alteration transfer or termination of an interest in land, and certain obligations and restrictions in relation thereto. The exclusion is explained in Guideline Office of Fair Trading 434, *Land Agreements.*

[277] Office of Fair Trading Guideline 419, *Vertical Restraints.*   [278] See p 444, above.

[279] Such as *Arriva/FirstGroup plc* Case CA/98/9/2002, [2002] UKCLR 322 (market-sharing between bus companies around Leeds).

[280] Such as *Hasbro/Argos/Littlewoods* CA98/2/2003, [2003] UKCLR 553; *Price Fixing of Replica Football Kit* CA98/06/2003, [2003] UKCLR 6, upheld by the Competition Appeal Tribunal, see *JJB Sports v Office of Fair Trading* [2004] Competition Appeal Tribunal 17 (appeal to the Court of Appeal pending).

[281] In fact by the Director General of Fair Trading as it was pre-2003.

[282] CA98/1/2001.

[283] *Institute of Independent Insurance Brokers v Director General of Fair Trading* [2001] Competition Appeal Tribunal 4, [2001] CompAR 62.

Standards Council removed the provisions which had caused the Competition Commission Appeal Tribunal's concern, and the Office of Fair Trading held that as amended they did not infringe. In *LINK Interchange Network Ltd*[284] an exemption was given to the multilateral agreement setting the interbank payment for cash withdrawals. However, in September 2005 the Office of Fair Trading found that a collective agreement between members of MasterCard UK Members Forum, setting the multilateral interchange fee paid on virtually all purchases in the UK made using UK-issued MasterCard credit and charge cards between 1 March 2000 and 18 November 2004, restricted competition and infringed Article 81 of the EC Treaty and the Chapter I prohibition.[285] On 2 February 2006, the Office of Fair Trading launched an investigation into MasterCard's new arrangements.[286] The decision of September 2005 was ultimately set aside by the Competition Appeal Tribunal after the OFT submitted a defence to Mastercard's appeal in which it changed in major respects the grounds upon which it had reached its decision. The OFT had offered to withdraw it but the Competition Appeal Tribunal rejected that procedure in favour of setting it aside.[287]

However, perhaps the most striking application of the Chapter I prohibition at the time of writing has been the Office of Fair Trading's action against fifty independent schools, against whom it issued a statement of objections on 9 November 2005.[288] The schools were charged with exchanging detailed information on the fees they intended to charge between 1 March 2001[289] and June 2003. The schools are considered to be 'undertakings' for the purposes of the Chapter I prohibition, pursuant to EC case law as they are engaged in the economic activity of supplying services.[290] The fact that they are (or were at the relevant time) charities under UK law and that they are not 'not for profit' organisations is irrelevant to their classification as undertakings.[291]

The Chapter II Prohibition
The Chapter II prohibition mirrors Article 82EC. Section 18(1) provides:

> Subject to section 19,[292] any conduct on the part of one or more undertakings which amounts to the abuse of a dominant position in a market is prohibited if it may affect trade within the United Kingdom.

---

[284] CA98/7/2001, [2002] UKCLR 59.   [285] CA98/05/05.

[286] Office of Fair Trading Press Release 20/06.   [287] [2006] CAT 14, 10.7.06.

[288] Office of Fair Trading Press Release 214/05.

[289] The Competition Act 1998 came into force on 1 March 2000 but because of the transitional arrangements the Chapter 1 prohibition did not apply to this agreement until 1 March 2001. Previously, such exchanges of information pertaining to the provision of services had not been caught by the Restrictive Trade Practices Act 176; see p 445, above.

[290] See pp 429–430, above and p 456, below.

[291] For the possible remedy in this case, see p 458, below.

[292] S 19 provides that the Chapter II prohibition does not apply to the matters excluded by Sch 1 and Sch 3 or to such other exclusions as the Secretary of State shall provide. These are similar to, but less extensive than, the exclusions from the Chapter I prohibition listed p 449, above.

The section then goes on to give a list of particular abuses which is identical to the list in Article 82. Section 18(3) says that a 'dominant position' means a dominant position within the United Kingdom and that the 'United Kingdom' means the United Kingdom or any part of it. As with the Chapter I prohibition, therefore, the Chapter II prohibition can apply to very localised situations: the 'any part' does not have to be a substantial part.

Since as a result of section 60 the Chapter II prohibition is to be interpreted in the same way as Article 82, agreements which are entered into by dominant firms are capable of constituting an abuse.[293] An agreement may infringe both prohibitions, and an agreement covered by a block exemption may nevertheless constitute an abuse.

Section 60
As already noted, section 60 sets out principles designed to ensure consistency between domestic and EC law. Subsections (1) to (3) provide:

(1) The purpose of this section is to ensure that so far as is possible (having regard to any relevant differences between the provisions concerned), questions arising under this Part in relation to competition within the United Kingdom are dealt with in a manner which is consistent with the treatment of corresponding questions arising in Community law in relation to competition within the Community.

(2) At any time when the court determines a question arising under this Part, it must act (so far as is compatible with the provisions of this Part and whether or not it would otherwise be required to do so) with a view to securing that there is no inconsistency between—

(a) the principles applied, and decision reached, by the court in determining that question; and

(b) the principles laid down by the Treaty and the European Court, and any relevant decision of that Court, as applicable at that time in determining any corresponding question arising in Community law.

(3) The court must, in addition, have regard to any relevant decision or statement of the Commission.

'Court' includes tribunals, the Office of Fair Trading and the sector regulators.[294] Whereas the courts must ensure so far as is possible, having regard to any relevant differences between the provisions concerned, that there is no inconsistency with the principles laid down by the Treaty of Rome and the European Court or with any relevant decision of the European Court, they must only 'have regard to' any relevant decision or statement of the Commission. Examples of statements include notices, decisions, the Annual Reports on Competition Policy, comfort letters which have

---

[293] See the discussion of Art 82, p 444, above.
[294] The sector regulators have concurrent powers under the Act, s 54 and Sch 10.

been the subject of a notice in the Official Journal (but not individual statements of opinion by individual Commission officials). Part I of the Act covers both the substantive rules and matters of procedure but the Office of Fair Trading's view, based on statements made by the Government during the Bill's passage, is that UK law may diverge from EC procedures. To some extent there are procedural differences written into the Act itself, so those matters are covered by the proviso about relevant differences, but the Office of Fair Trading's detailed procedural rules are made under the enabling provision in section 51. Nevertheless, the Office of Fair Trading considered at one time that section 60 does not apply to procedural matters other than the 'high level principles' of EC law.[295] The 'high level principles' are the general principles of law and fundamental human rights jurisprudence developed by the European Court of Justice, such as the principles of proportionality, legal certainty and the right against self-incrimination. In fact, to a large extent these would have to be recognised in the application of the Competition Act 1998 regardless of section 60 because of the jurisprudence of the European Court of Human Rights and the Human Rights Act 1998. However, in *Pernod-Ricard SA and Campbell Competition Appeal Tribunal v Office of Fair Trading*[296] the Competition Appeal Tribunal held that the EC provisions on the procedural rights of complainants should be applied in Competition Act 1998 proceedings, saying

'. . . we are of the view that, by virtue of section 60 of the 1998 Act, we should resolve the questions before us in the same way as they would be resolved under Community law in an equivalent situation.'[297]

Differences between the EC and UK rules include the fact that the Competition Appeal Tribunal hears appeals on the merits, while challenges to Commission decisions before the Court of First Instance are by way of judicial review.[298] Other procedural variations include different rules on legal professional privilege;[299] the possibility of forcible entry by Office of Fair Trading inspectors conducting investigations;[300] slight differences in the 'leniency' provisions whereby favourable treatment is

---

[295] See eg the Denning Lecture 1999 *The Competition Act 1998 and EC Jurisprudence: Some Questions Answered* given by the then Director General of Fair Trading, John Bridgeman, on 12 October 1999.

[296] [2004] Competition Appeal Tribunal 10, [2004] CompAR 776.

[297] Ibid, para 234.

[298] Under Art 230EC, although note that the Court of First Instance takes a rigorous view of what constitutes 'judicial review'; see for example its overturning of the Commission decision in the *Bayer* case, Case T-41/96 *Bayer AG v EC Commission* [2001] ECR II-3383, [2001] 4 CMLR 126, discussed p 428, above. Appeal to the European Court of Justice is only on a point of law.

[299] Competition Act 1998, s 30. The EC rules which were laid down in Case 155/79 *AM&S Ltd v Commission* [1982] ECR 1575, [1982] 2 CMLR 264 are more restrictive than the UK rules.

[300] Competition Act 1998, s 28(2). Such entry can only be affected under a warrant issued by a High Court judge and force ('such force as is reasonably necessary for the purpose') can only be used against the premises, not against persons.

offered to cartel participants who 'whistleblow';[301] and that there is an immunity from penalties for 'small agreements' and 'conduct of minor significance' under the Act.[302] It was anticipated at the time that the Competition Act 1998 was passed that the interpretation and application of section 60 would give rise to much argument. It was thought that there were difficult issues to be resolved as to what amounts to a 'corresponding question arising in Community law' in subsection (1) for example, or what 'have regard to' means in subsection (3). The greatest problem is the meaning of the proviso 'having regard to any relevant differences between the provisions concerned' in respect of differences which are not expressed in the Act. As mentioned above,[303] a major objective of EC competition law is the attainment and maintenance of the single market. Much EC competition law has been driven by single market rather than competition imperatives, and Community case law which concerns single market issues cannot be seen as 'corresponding' to questions arising under the Act. During the passage of the Bill, government ministers made it quite clear that this difference in objectives did constitute a 'relevant difference' for the purpose of the proviso.[304] Single market concerns have had the most profound effect on the development of the EC rules of vertical agreements[305] but they have arisen in many other cases, and it was difficult to see how UK courts could to go about unpicking European Court of Justice judgments to ascertain which parts section 60 is instructing them to follow. Furthermore, while the objective of the Competition Act 1998 was purely to promote competition as part of the 'enterprise culture',[306] EC competition law has at times appeared to be protecting competitors rather than competition, protecting the weaker parties to agreements, or taking social (such as employment or environmental) considerations into account.

However, the last two factors may prove less important in future. As discussed above,[307] the EC Commission currently explains the objective of single market integration as being an aspect of ensuring the enhancement of consumer welfare and ensuring an efficient allocation of resources. As far as 'competitors or competition' is

---

[301] Office of Fair Trading Guideline 423 (Office of Fair Trading's Guidance as to the appropriate amount of a penalty) and Commission Notice on the immunity from fines and reduction of fines in cartel cases [2002] OJ C 45/3.

[302] 'Small agreements' and 'conduct of minor significance' are defined by Order, currently the Competition Act 1998 (Small Agreements and Conduct of Minor Significance) Regulations 2000, SI 2000/262, in terms of the annual turnover of the parties involved (an aggregate of £20 million in the case of agreements and £50 million in the case of conduct). The immunity does not affect the voidness of agreements, see p 457, below.

[303] See p 426, above.

[304] Lord Simon, Hansard, HL, 25 November 1997, col 961 and Hansard, HL, 5 March 1998, col 1363.

[305] See p 434, above.

[306] See the statement of the Secretary of State, Margaret Beckett, moving the Second Reading of the Competition Bill in the House of Commons, Hansard, HC, 11 May 1998, col 23.

[307] P 426.

concerned, the Commission is now firmly of the view that competition law is to protect the competitive process and not to protect competitors.

A good illustration of the way in which the UK authorities have applied section 60 was the *Bettercare* case.[308] The Competition Appeal Tribunal (Competition Commission Appeal Tribunal as it then was) scrupulously examined the Community case law on the circumstances in which bodies with some type of 'public' function are 'undertakings' for the purposes of Article 81 or Article 82.[309] The Competition Appeal Tribunal was faced with the question of whether a Health and Social Services Trust in Northern Ireland was acting as an undertaking when it purchased nursing home and residential care services from a private company. The company, Bettercare, had complained to the Office of Fair Trading that the relevant Trust was in a dominant position as a purchaser of such services and that it abused that position by agreeing to contract only at excessively low prices. The Office of Fair Trading, having considered the European authorities, concluded that the purchase of these services was not of an economic or commercial nature and that the Trust was therefore not acting as an 'undertaking' within the Chapter II prohibition. The Competition Appeal Tribunal set aside the Office of Fair Trading's decision on the grounds that the European Court of Justice's definition of an 'economic activity' as 'the offering of goods or services on the market'[310] could not be applied to the purchasing activities of public bodies and that the contracts between the Trust and Bettercare were commercial transactions in which the Trust was indeed acting as an undertaking engaged in economic activity. The Competition Appeal Tribunal's judgment had crucial implications for a range of public bodies in the UK who increasingly operate in a market environment and where private bodies are increasingly providing what was once the sole domain of public providers. However, a subsequent judgment of the Court of First Instance, *FENIN*,[311] cast doubt on *BetterCare*. FENIN, a trade association of medical goods' suppliers to Spanish National Health Service bodies, complained to the Commission that these bodies' practice of paying bills very late amounted to an abuse of the Spanish national health service organisations' dominant position. The Commission rejected the complaint on the ground that the health service organisations were not acting as

---

[308] *BetterCare Group Ltd v Director General of Fair Trading*, [2002] Competition Appeal Tribunal 7, [2002] CompAR 299.

[309] Such as Case C-67/96 *Albany International BV v Stichting Bedrijfspensioenfonds Textielindustrie* [1999] ECR I-5751, [2000] CMLR 446; Case C-41/90 *Höfner v Macroton* [1991] ECR I-1979; Case C-244/94 *Fédération Française des Sociétés d'Assurance v Ministère de l'Agriculture* [1995] ECR I-4013, [1996] 4 CMLR 536; Case 364/92 *SAT Fluggesellschaft v Eurocontrol* [1994] ECR I-43, [1994] 5 CMLR 208; Case C-159/91 *Poucet v Assurances Générales de France* [1993] ECR I-637; Case C-343/95 *Diego Cali v SEPG* [1997] ECR I-1547, [1997] 5 CMLR 484; Case C-35/96 *Commission v Italy* [1998] ECR I-3851; Case C-475/99 *Firma Ambulanz Glöckner v Landkreis Südwestppalz* [2001] ECR I-8089.

[310] Case C-35/96 *Commission v Italy* [1998] ECR I-3851, para 36.

[311] Case T-319/99 *Federación Nacional de Empresas de Instrumentación Cientifica, Médica, Técnica y Dental (FENIN) v Commission* [2003] ECR II-357, [2003] 5 CMLR 1, aff'd by the ECJ C-205/03 (Fenin v Commission, 11 July 2006).

'undertakings' when they made the purchases from FENIN. The Court of First Instance upheld this, citing their previous case law and stating that '. . . it is the activity consisting of offering goods and services on a given market that is the characteristic feature of an economic activity . . ., not the business of purchasing as such'. Whether purchasing was an economic activity had to be determined by the subsequent use to which the goods are put: '[t]he nature of the purchasing activity must therefore be determined according to whether or not the subsequent use of the purchased goods amounts to an economic activity'.[312] On the basis that the goods were bought from FENIN in order to treat patients free under the NHS the Court of First Instance held that Spanish national health service's purchasing was not an economic activity. The Office of Fair Trading subsequently decided that the Trust's conduct was not abusive in any event.[313] The Office of Fair Trading, recognising the dissonance between *Bettercare* and *FENIN*, issued a Policy Note in August 2004[314] setting out its approach to the matter of the application of the Chapter 1 and Chapter II prohibitions to public bodies in the light of *FENIN* and a later case, *AOK*.[315]

Voidness and other consequences of breaching the prohibitions in the Competition Act 1998
The Competition Act 1998, section 2(4) provides that 'any agreement or decision which is prohibited by subsection (1) is void'. This mirrors Article 81(2) which is considered above.[316] As explained there, under Article 81(2) it is the infringing provisions, rather than the whole agreement, which is void. The original draft bill, which was published in August 1997, was worded to try to make clear that the voidness extended only to the infringing provisions but this was later changed, apparently in order not to depart from the wording in Article 81(2). Given that the matter is governed by the consistency requirement in section 60 it seems right to conclude that section 2(4) renders void only the parts of the agreement which are prohibited and that the European Court of Justice case law on the effect of Article 81(2) will apply equally to section 2(4). What is said above[317] about severance therefore applies equally in respect of the Chapter I prohibition.

Where the Chapter II prohibition is concerned, the same considerations as pertain to agreements which amount to an abuse of a dominant position under Article 82 will apply.[318]

It would appear that the judgments of the Court of Appeal in *Passmore v Morland*[319] about the possibility of the transient voidness of prohibited agreements, and in *Gibbs Mew v Gemmell*,[320] holding that a prohibited agreement is not just void

---

[312] Ibid, para 36.
[313] *Bettercare Group Ltd/North and North & West Belfast Health and Social Services Trust*, Office of Fair Trading Decision CA98/09/2003.
[314] Policy Note 1/2004, Office of Fair Trading 443.
[315] Cases C-264,306,354 & 355/01, *AOK Bundesverband and others v Ichtyol-Gesellschaft Cordes* [2004] ECR I-2493.
[316] See p 438.   [317] See p 439.   [318] See p 444, above.
[319] [1999] 3 All ER 1005, [1999] 1 CMLR 1129.   [320] [1999] ECC 97, [1998] Eu LR 588.

but illegal, apply equally in respect of agreements prohibited by the Competition Act 1998.

The Competition Act 1998 originally said nothing about parties who infringe the Chapter I or Chapter II prohibitions being liable to third parties, although there were a number of places in the provisions where such a possibility seemed to be assumed. The position now is that the insertion of section 47A by the Enterprise Act 2002 expressly provides 'follow-on' damages actions to be brought in the Competition Appeal Tribunal, and the availability of damages actions in the ordinary courts is not doubted. It will, however, be interesting to see whether the UK courts follow the European Court of Justice judgment in *Crehan v Courage*[321] and allow the weaker party to an agreement infringing the Chapter I prohibition to obtain damages or restitution from the other party. The better view is that *Crehan* will be applied, notwithstanding the fact that the EC judgment was partly based on the EC law principle of 'effectiveness'. This is particularly in view of the openness of the Competition Appeal Tribunal to following EC procedures in *Pernod-Ricard*.[322]

The Competition Act 1998 provides that undertakings may be fined for entering into prohibited agreements.[323] The Office of Fair Trading may also give the parties 'such directions as it considers appropriate' for bringing the infringement to an end'.[324] The width of the Office of Fair Trading's discretion to come to a settlement with the parties was demonstrated in February 2006 when it announced that it had agreed a settlement with the independent schools alleged to have exchanged fee-pricing information.[325] Under this arrangement the schools would make a £3 million ex gratia payment into a charitable trust to benefit pupils who attended the schools between 2001 and 2004. This is the first time that the Office of Fair Trading negotiated an agreed resolution to an infringement decision case.[326]

Criminal Sanctions for entering into Prohibited Agreements
The Enterprise Act 2002 introduced into UK the 'cartel offence' which criminalises certain forms of anti-competitive activity.[327] Individuals 'dishonestly'[328] engaging in

---

[321] Case C-453/99, see p 385, above.

[322] See p 454, above. This is the view taken by D. Beard in Ward and Smith *Competition Litigation in the UK* (Sweet & Maxwell, 2005), 7-019.

[323] See Competition Act 1998, s 36 and Office of Fair Trading 423 *OFT's Guidance as to the appropriate amount of a penalty*. The limits laid down there are as in Regulation 1/2003 ie no more than 10% of the undertakings turnover in the preceeding year. Under s 39 no penalties can be imposed in respect of 'small agreements' ie non-price fixing agreements where the parties' combined annual turnover does not exceed £20 million: Competition Act 1998 (Small Agreements and Conduct of Minor Significance) Regulations 2000, SI 2000/62.

[324] Competition Act 1998, s 32.   [325] See p 452, above.

[326] The terms of the settlement appeared in a statement put on to the Office of Fair Trading website on 27 February 2006.

[327] Enterprise Act 2002, ss 188–204. The offence is not tied to an infringement of Article 81 or the Chapter I prohibition but to certain specified activities.

[328] The standard is the normal criminal standard laid down in *R v Ghosh* [1982] 2 All ER 689.

price-fixing, market-sharing and bid-rigging arrangements are liable to a sentence of up to five years imprisonment and/or a substantial fine.

The first criminal prosecution mounted by the Serious Fraud Office against a cartel did not, however, charge the individuals concerned with the cartel offence but with conspiracy at common law. This means that individuals can be charged with conduct which took place before 1 June 2003 when the Enterprise Act 2002 came into force. The charges were brought in respect of alleged price-fixing of certain drugs sold to the NHS between January 1996 and December 2000.[329]

---

[329] SFO Press Release 5 April 2006, http://www.sfo.gov.uk/news/prout/pr_455.asp?id=455

11 CONTRACTS ILLEGAL BY STATUTE OR AT COMMON LAW

SUMMARY

1 CONTRACTS PROHIBITED BY STATUTE

A contract that is expressly or implicitly prohibited by statute is illegal. In this context, 'statute' includes the orders, rules and regulations that ministers of the Crown and other officials are so frequently authorised by Parliament to make.

If the contract in fact made by the parties is expressly forbidden by the statute, its illegality is undoubted. Express statutory prohibition of contracts is by no means uncommon. So Parliament may provide in pursuance of a policy of controlling credit, that no contract of hire purchase shall be entered into, unless at least 25 per cent of the cash price is paid by way of an initial payment.[1] Where it is alleged that the prohibition is implied, the court is presented with a problem the solution of which depends upon the construction of the statute. What must be ascertained is whether the object of the legislature is to forbid the contract. In pursuing this enquiry a variety of tests have been applied. For instance, if the sole object of the statute is to increase the national revenue, as for instance by requiring a trader to take out a licence; or to punish a contracting party who fails to furnish or furnishes incorrectly certain particulars, the contract that he may have made is not itself prohibited.[2] On the other hand, if even one of the objects is the protection of the public or the furtherance of some other aspect of public policy, a contract that fails to comply with the statute may be implicitly prohibited.[3] But no one test is decisive, for in every case the purpose of the legislature must be considered in the light of all the relevant facts and circumstances.[4]

It has been persuasively argued that an important question ought to be whether the statute necessarily contemplates that the prohibited acts will be done in performance

[1] See eg *Stoneleigh Finance Ltd v Phillips* [1965] 2 QB 537, [1965] 1 All ER 513; *Kingsley v Sterling Industrial Securities Ltd* [1967] 2 QB 747, [1966] 2 All ER 414. Of course there may still be problems of construction involved in discovering exactly which contracts are prohibited. See eg *Wilson, Smithett and Cope Ltd v Terruzzi* [1976] QB 683, [1976] 1 All ER 817.

[2] *Learoyd v Bracken* [1894] 1 QB 114. *London and Harrogate Securities Ltd v Pitts* [1976] 3 All ER 809, [1976] 1 WLR 1063.

[3] *Victorian Daylesford Syndicate v Dott* [1905] 2 Ch 624 at 630.

[4] *St John Shipping Corpn v Joseph Rank Ltd* [1957] 1 QB 267 at 285–287, [1956] 3 All ER 683 at 690, per Devlin J; p 466, below. In some cases a statute while prohibiting an act may expressly provide that contractual liability is not affected, eg Banking Act 1979, s 1(8). See *SCF Finance Co Ltd v Masri (No 2)* [1987] QB 1002, [1987] 1 All ER 175.

of a contract.[5] This distinction can be simply illustrated. Let us suppose that a Road Traffic Act makes it an offence (a) to sell a car in unroadworthy condition and (b) to drive on certain roads at more than 30 mph.[6] It can readily be seen that breach of provision (a) will always involve the making of a contract, while breach of provision (b) will only in exceptional circumstances do so. It is plausible therefore to argue that the statute impliedly prohibits contracts to sell unroadworthy cars but does not impliedly prohibit contracts to drive cars in excess of the speed limit.[7]

An example of a revenue statute is afforded by *Smith v Mawhood*,[8] where a tobacconist was allowed to recover the price of tobacco delivered, notwithstanding his failure to take out a licence and to have his name painted on his place of business as he was statutorily required to do under a penalty of £200. Parke B said:

> I think the object of the legislature was not to prohibit a contract of sale by dealers who have not taken out a licence pursuant to the act of Parliament. If it was, they certainly could not recover, although the prohibition were merely for the purpose of revenue. But, looking at the act of Parliament, I think its object was not to vitiate the contract itself, but only to impose a penalty upon the party offending, for the purpose of the revenue.[9]

Again, a stockbroker who has bought or sold shares for his principal is not prevented from recovering his commission by his failure in breach of the Stamp Act 1891, to issue a stamped contract note containing details of the transaction.[10] The more numerous statutes, however, are those directed either to the protection of the public or to the fulfilment of some object of general policy. This is especially true at the present day when State intervention in individual activity is more pronounced than formerly and where even revenue statutes are used in part at least as instruments of policy.

The approach of the courts to this problem of implied prohibition may be illustrated by contrasting the two cases of *Cope v Rowlands*[11] and *Archbolds (Freightage) Ltd v S Spanglett Ltd.*[12]

In the former, a statute provided that any person who acted as broker in the City of London without first obtaining a licence should forfeit and pay to the City the sum of £25 for every such offence. The plaintiff, who was unlicensed, sued the defendant for work that he had done in buying and selling stock. In delivering judgment for the defendant, Parke B said:

> The legislature had in view, as one object, the benefit and security of the public in those important transactions which are negotiated by brokers. The clause, therefore, which imposes

---

[5] Buckley 38 MLR 535.

[6] See Road Traffic Act 1934, s 8(1), reversed Road Traffic Act 1972, s 60(5) and *Vinall v Howard* [1953] 2 All ER 515, [1953] 1 WLR 987; reversed on other grounds [1954] 1 QB 375, [1954] 1 All ER 458.

[7] Such a contract may still be illegal on common law principles, as being a contract to commit a crime. See p 473, below.

[8] (1845) 14 M & W 452.   [9] Ibid at 463.   [10] *Learoyd v Bracken* [1894] 1 QB 114.

[11] (1836) 2 M & W 149.   [12] [1961] 1 QB 374, [1961] 1 All ER 417.

a penalty, must be taken . . . to imply a prohibition of all unadmitted persons to act as brokers, and consequently to prohibit, by necessary inference, all contracts which such persons make for compensation to themselves for so acting.[13]

The facts of *Archbolds (Freightage) Ltd v S Spanglett Ltd*[14]

The Road and Rail Traffic Act 1933 provided that no person should *use* a vehicle for the carriage of goods unless he held a 'A' or a 'C' licence. The former entitled him to carry the goods of others for reward; the latter to carry his own goods but not the goods of others.

The defendants, who held a 'C' licence, agreed with the plaintiffs to carry 200 crates of whisky belonging to third parties from Leeds to London. The plaintiffs were unaware that the defendants held no 'A' licence. The whisky was stolen *en route* and the plaintiffs claimed damages for its loss.

One question that arose in the action,[15] was whether the contract for carriage was prohibited by the Act, either expressly or implicitly.

It was not expressly prohibited, for the Act did not in terms strike at a contract to carry goods, but at the use of an unlicensed vehicle on the road. It was not as if the plaintiffs had contracted for the use of an unlicensed vehicle and had used it themselves. It was argued, however, that contracts for the carriage of goods made with unlicensed carriers were implicitly forbidden by the Act. This depended upon the construction of the Act. What was its fundamental purpose?[16] The Court of Appeal was satisfied that the instant contract did not fall within the ambit of the legislation and that there was no implied prohibition. In the words of Pearce LJ:

The object of the Road and Rail Traffic Act, 1933, was not (in this connection) to interfere with the owner of goods or his facilities for transport, but to control those who provided the transport, with a view to promoting its efficiency. Transport of goods was not made illegal but the various licence holders were prohibited from encroaching on one another's territory, the intention of the Act being to provide an orderly and comprehensive service.[17]

If it is alleged that a contract has been impliedly prohibited, then it clearly is important to look at the policy of the relevant statute and to consider whether that policy is served by holding that the particular contract has been impliedly prohibited. On the other hand, if the argument is that the contract has been expressly prohibited there is, in principle, no room for such considerations since of course Parliament is entitled to

---

[13] (1836) 2 M & W 149 at 159.   [14] See Furmston 24 MLR 394.
[15] For the further question, see p 466, below.
[16] See *St John Shipping Corpn v Joseph Rank* [1957] 1 QB 267 at 285–287, [1956] 3 All ER 683 at 688–690; *Hughes v Asset Management* [1995] 3 All ER 669; *Fuji Finance Inc v Aetna Insurance Co Ltd* [1994] 4 All ER 1025.
[17] [1961] 1 QB at 386, [1961] 1 All ER at 423.

prohibit contracts even when it makes no sense to do so. Of course, one would not expect Parliament to make foolish decisions but so wide is the scope of statutory interference with ordinary life and so complex the process of parliamentary drafting that it is certain that from time to time statutes will prohibit contracts where the results of doing so look extremely odd.

This is well brought out in a series of cases arising out of the Insurance Companies Act 1974. This Act was a major piece of public regulation of the insurance industry. In broad terms the Act involved dividing insurance business up into a large number of categories requiring those who wished to conduct insurance business to obtain authorisation to do so. What was to happen where someone carried on insurance business when they were not authorised? The leading case is now *Phoenix General Insurance Co of Greece SA v Administratia Asigurarilor de Stat.*[18] The plaintiffs had been authorised under the original scheme of the 1974 Act to write the insurance business which they were in fact writing. In 1977 regulations issued under the 1974 Act substituted a new set of categories which were complex and difficult to understand. The plaintiffs went on writing the same categories of insurance. The trial judge, Hobhouse J, held that the policies which they were writing were now unauthorised. The Court of Appeal reversed this decision and held that in fact what the plaintiffs had done was authorised under the transitional provisions contained in the 1977 regulations but the Court of Appeal went on to consider very fully what the legal position was where the insurer was writing business of a kind which he was not entitled to write. This question could arise in at least three different contexts. One is an attempt by the insurer to enforce the policy directly; the second is an attempt by the insurer, having paid out on the policy, to recover under a reinsurance contract; the third is an attempt by an insured to recover on the policy. It is clear that, at least in regard to the third situation, one ought to hold that the insured can recover if it is at all possible to do so since the whole purpose of the Insurance Companies Act is to protect the insured against the activities of unauthorised insurers and in the nature of things an insured will seldom if ever know whether the insurer is authorised or not. The Court of Appeal entirely accepted the force of these considerations but held that effect could not be given to them because it was clear that the wording of the Act expressly forbad recovery. This was because the Act did not merely prohibit unauthorised insurers from 'effecting contracts of insurance' but also from 'carrying out contracts of insurance'. The Court of Appeal held that this could not be read otherwise than as prohibiting not only the entry into contracts of insurance but also their performance by paying when the risk occurred. This is clearly a deeply

---

[18] [1988] QB 216, [1987] 2 All ER 152. See also the same case at first instance [1986] 1 All ER 908, [1987] 2 WLR 512 and the earlier first instance decisions in *Bedford Insurance Co Ltd v Instituto de Resseguros do Brasil* [1985] QB 966, [1984] 3 All ER 766 and *Stewart v Oriental Fire and Marine Insurance Co Ltd* [1985] QB 988, [1984] 3 All ER 777.

unsatisfactory result but one for which Parliament and not the Court of Appeal must take the blame.[19]

Illegality may infect either formation or performance of contract
A distinction which has an important bearing upon the consequences of illegality is that the disregard of a statutory prohibition may render the contract either illegal as formed or illegal as performed.[20]

A contract is illegal as formed if its very creation is prohibited, as for example where one of the parties has neglected to take out a licence as required by statute.[21] In such a case it is void *ab initio*. It is a complete nullity under which neither party can acquire rights whether there is an intention to break the law or not.

A contract is illegal as performed if, though lawful in its formation, it is performed by one of the parties in a manner prohibited by statute. In *Anderson Ltd v Daniel*,[22] for instance:

> A statute required that every seller of artificial fertilizers should give to the buyer an invoice stating the percentages of certain chemical substances contained in the goods. In the instant case, the sellers had delivered ten tons of artificial manure without complying with the statutory requirement. The sellers brought an action for the price of the goods.

In such circumstances as these, where the contract is lawful in its inception but is executed illegally, the position of the party responsible for the infraction of the statute is clear. All contractual rights and remedies are withheld from him. Thus the sellers in *Anderson Ltd v Daniel* lost their action. They had failed to perform the contract in the only way in which the statute allowed it to be performed. On the other hand, as will be seen later,[23] the appropriate remedies are available to the other party provided that he can establish his innocence. If, however, he has been privy to or has condoned the illegality, he will be in the same position as if the contract had been illegal in its formation and he will therefore be remediless.[24]

But it must be emphasised that a contract is not automatically rendered illegal as performed merely because some statutory requirement has been violated in the course of its completion.[25] Whether this is the result raises a question of construction similar

---

[19] As far as enforcement of such policies by the insured against the insurer was concerned, Parliament acted quickly to remedy the situation by the Financial Services Act 1986, s 132, as to the interpretation of which see *Deutsche Ruckversicherung AG v Walbrook Insurance Co Ltd* [1996] 1 All ER 791.

[20] See especially the judgment of Devlin J in *St John Shipping Corpn v Joseph Rank Ltd* [1957] 1 QB 267 at 283–287.

[21] *Cope v Rowlands* (1836) 2 M & W 149; *Re Mahmoud and Ispahani* [1921] 2 KB 716; *Bostel Bros Ltd v Hurlock* [1949] 1 KB 74, [1948] 2 All ER 312.

[22] [1924] 1 KB 138.   [23] P 487, below.

[24] *B & B Viennese Fashions v Losane* [1952] 1 All ER 909; *Ashmore Benson, Pease & Co Ltd v Dawson Ltd* [1973] 2 All ER 856, [1973] 1 WLR 828; criticised Hamson [1973] CLJ 199. Cf Buckley 25 NILQ 421.

[25] See the rhetorical question of Sachs LJ in *Shaw v Groom* [1970] 2 QB 504 at 522.

to that which was considered in *Archbolds (Freightage) Ltd v S Spanglett Ltd.*[26] What has to be determined here is whether it was the express or implied intention of the legislature that such a violation as that which the guilty party has committed should deprive him of all remedies. Was the observance of the particular enactment regarded as a necessary prerequisite of his right to enforce the contract? That such is the intention, though clear enough in *Anderson Ltd v Daniel,* is not lightly to be implied. Commercial life is nowadays hedged in by so many statutory regulations, that it would scarcely promote the interests of justice to drive a plaintiff from the seat of judgment merely because he has committed a minor transgression.[27]

If the contract as performed is not expressly prohibited by statute, its alleged illegality must be based upon public policy, and in a passage that has frequently been approved, Lord Wright once remarked that public policy is often 'better served by refusing to nullify a bargain save on serious and sufficient grounds'.[28] The attitude of the courts where some statutory requirement has been infringed during the performance of a contract may be illustrated by two leading cases.

In *St John Shipping Corpn v Joseph Rank Ltd,*[29] the facts were as follows:

> The Merchant Shipping Act 1932 forbids the loading of a ship to such an extent that the loadline becomes submerged. A penalty is imposed for breach of the statute.
>
> The master of the plaintiff's ship, which had been chartered to an English firm for the carriage of grain from a port in Alabama to England, put into a port in the course of the voyage and took on bunkers, the effect of which was to submerge the loadline contrary to the Act. The master was prosecuted in England for the offence and was fined £1,200.
>
> The defendants, to whom the ownership of part of the goods had passed, withheld part of the freight due, contending that the plaintiffs could not enforce a contract which they had performed in an illegal manner.

Devlin J rejected the contention. The illegal loading was merely an incident in the course of performance that did not affect the core of the contact.

> In the statutes to which the principle has been applied, what was prohibited was a contract which had at its centre—indeed often filling the whole space within its circumference—the prohibited act; contracts for the sale of prohibited goods, contracts for the sale of goods without accompanying documents when the statute specifically said there must be accompanying documents; contracts for work and labour done by persons who were prohibited from doing the whole of the work and labour for which they demanded recompense.[30]

---

[26] P 463, above.

[27] *St John Shipping Corpn v Joseph Rank Ltd* [1957] 1 QB 267 at 522, per Devlin J; approved by Sachs LJ in *Shaw v Groom* [1970] 2 QB 504 at 522.

[28] *Vita Food Products v Unus Shipping Co Ltd* [1939] AC 277 at 293, [1939] 1 All ER 513 at 523.

[29] [1957] 1 QB 267, [1956] 3 All ER 683.   [30] Ibid at 289 and 691, respectively.

Again, in *Shaw v Groom*.[31]

> A landlord sued his tenant for arrears of rent amounting to £103 due in respect of a weekly tenancy. The tenant contended that the action must fail, since the rent book issued to him by the plaintiff did not contain all the information required by the Landlord and Tenant Act 1962. Such a default was punishable by a fine not exceeding £50.

The Court of Appeal dismissed this contention. The contract was not to be stigmatised as illegal in its performance. The intention of the legislature was that non-compliance with the statutory requirement should render the landlord liable to a fine, not that it should deny him access to the courts. Unless this limited construction was placed upon the Act, the result might well be that the landlord would forfeit a sum far in excess of the maximum fine. In the words of Sachs LJ:

> It seems to me appropriate, accordingly, to allow this appeal on the broad basis that, even if the provision of a rent book is an essential act as between landlords and weekly tenants, yet the legislature did not by . . . the Act of 1962 intend to preclude the landlord from recovering any rent due or impose any forfeiture on him beyond the prescribed penalty.[32]

2 CONTRACTS ILLEGAL AT COMMON LAW ON GROUNDS OF PUBLIC POLICY

A Introduction

Certain types of contract are forbidden at common law and are therefore prima facie illegal. The first essential to an understanding of this head of the law, which has been clouded by much confusion of thought, is to discover if possible the principle upon which the stigma of illegality is based. The present law is the result of a development that stretches back to at least Elizabethan times,[33] but its foundations were not effectively laid until the eighteenth century. What the judges of that period were at pains to emphasise was that they would not tolerate any contract that in their view was injurious to society.[34] Injury to society, however, is incapable of precise definition, and it is not surprising that the particular contracts found distasteful on this ground were described in somewhat vague and indeterminate language. To give a few examples,

---

[31] [1970] 2 QB 504, [1970] 1 All ER 702.
[32] Ibid at 526 and 714, respectively. Harman LJ also found for the plaintiff, but based his decision on the ground that the provision of a correctly completed rent book was not an essential part of the lawful performance of the contract; ibid at 516.
[33] Pollock *Principles of Contract* (13th edn) p 291, note by Winfield.
[34] Fifoot *Lord Mansfield* pp 122–125.

nobody would be allowed 'to stipulate for iniquity',[35] no contract would be enforced that was 'contrary to the general policy of the law',[36] or 'against the public good',[37] or *contra bonos mores*[38] or which had arisen *ex turpi causa*.[39]

It seems justifiable to infer from such expressions as these that the judges were determined to establish and sustain a concept of public policy. Contractual freedom must be fostered, but any contract that tended to prejudice the social or economic interest of the community must be forbidden.

Not unnaturally, a principle stated in such sweeping terms as these has its disadvantages. It is imprecise, since judicial views will inevitably differ upon whether a particular contract is immoral or subversive of the common good; there is no necessary continuity in the general policy of the law, for what is anathema to one generation seems harmless to another; and the public good affects so many walks of life that the causes of action that can be said to arise *ex turpi causa* must in the nature of things vary greatly in their degree of harm to the community.

It is this variation in the degree of harm done that requires emphasis, for the word 'illegal' has been, and still is, used to cover a multitude of sins and even cases where little, if any, sin can be discovered. The list of 'illegal' contracts includes inter alia agreements to commit a crime or a tort, to defraud the revenue, to lend money to an alien enemy, to import liquor into a country where prohibition is in force, to procure a wife for X in return for a reward, to provide for a wife if she should ever separate from her husband and finally an agreement in restraint of trade between master and servant or between the seller and buyer of a business, such as that by which a servant promises not to work in the future for a trade rival of his present employer. If these contracts are scrutinised in the order given, it will be seen that the improbity which they reveal is a constantly diminishing factor and that it is entirely absent from the agreement in restraint of trade. There is nothing disgraceful in a master and servant coming to such an agreement, and the only complaint that their conduct invokes is the possible economic inexpedience of allowing a workman to restrict his freedom to exploit his skill as and where he will.

Common sense suggests that the consequences at law of entering into one of these so-called illegal contracts should vary in severity according to the degree of impropriety that the conduct of the parties discloses. It is obvious that an agreement to commit a crime cannot be put on the same footing as an undertaking by a servant that he will not later enter the employment of a rival trader. The former is so transparently reprehensible judged by any standard of morals that it must be dismissed as illegal, with the result that both parties must be excluded from access to the courts and denied all remedies; but the latter should certainly not attract the full rigour of the

---

[35] *Collins v Blantern* (1767) 2 Wils 341 at 350, per Wilmot LCJ.

[36] *Lowe v Peers* (1768) 4 Burr 2225 at 2233, per Aston J.   [37] *Collins v Blantern*, above.

[38] *Girardy v Richardson* (1793) 1 Esp 13, per Lord Kenyon.

[39] *Holman v Johnson* (1775) 1 Cowp 341 at 343, per Lord Mansfield.

maxim *ex turpi causa non oritur actio*, with its implication that it can originate no rights or liabilities whatsoever. The parties have done nothing disgraceful, they have not conspired against the proprieties and, although they cannot be allowed to enforce such part of the contract as is tainted, it would be unjustifiable to regard them as outcasts of the law unable to enforce even the innocent part of their bargain. To describe their contract as illegal as a whole is an abuse of language. Speaking of the contract in restraint of trade, for instance, Farwell LJ said, 'it is not unlawful in the sense that it is criminal or would give any cause of action to a third person injured by its operation, but it is unlawful in the sense that the law will not enforce it'.[40] In the eighteenth century, when the principle of public policy was taking root and the instances of unsavoury bargains were comparatively simple, it was perhaps not strange that the judges should have used somewhat exaggerated language in rejecting contracts that revealed wickedness, but in the complex conditions of today the indiscriminate use of the term 'illegal' is, to say the least, confusing.

Modern judges have in fact taken a more realistic view of this part of the law and have concluded that the so-called illegal contracts fall into two separate groups according to the degree of mischief that they involve.[41] Some agreements are so obviously inimical to the interest of the community that they offend almost any concept of public policy; others violate no basic feelings of morality, but run counter only to social or economic expedience. The significance of their separation into two classes, as we shall see, lies in the different consequences that they involve.

That the various contracts traditionally called illegal do not involve similar consequences was stressed by Somervell LJ, in the following passage:[42]

> In *Bennett v Bennett*, it was pointed out that there are two kinds of illegality of differing effect. The first is where the illegality is criminal, or *contra bonos mores*, and in those cases, which I will not attempt to enumerate or further classify, such a provision [*sic*], if an ingredient in the contract, will invalidate the whole, although there may be many other provisions in it. There is a second kind of illegality which has no such taint; the other terms in the contract stand if the illegal portion can be severed, the illegal portion being a provision which the court, on grounds of public policy, will not enforce. The simplest and most common example of the latter class of illegality is a contract for the sale of a business which contains a provision restricting the vendor from competing in or engaging in trade for a certain period or within a certain area.

---

[40] *North-Western Salt Co v Electrolytic Alkali Co* (1912) 107 LT 439 at 444. See also *Mogul Steamship Co v McGregor, Gow & Co* [1892] AC 25 at 39, per Lord Halsbury. In the court below (1889) 23 QBD 598 at 619, Lindley LJ said, 'The term "illegal" here is a misleading one. Contracts . . . in restraint of trade are not in my opinion illegal in any sense, except that the law will not enforce them.' See also *A-G Commonwealth of Australia v Adelaide Steamship Co Ltd* [1913] AC 781 at 797, per Lord Parker.

[41] *Bennett v Bennett* [1952] 1 KB 249, [1952] 1 All ER 413. The actual decision in *Bennett v Bennett* was reversed by the Maintenance Agreements Act 1957 (now the Matrimonial Causes Act 1973, s 34).

[42] *Goodinson v Goodinson* [1954] 2 QB 118 at 120–121, [1954] 2 All ER 255 at 256. It should be noticed that the concluding sentence of this citation refers to two forms of severance that are in fact distinguishable; see pp 541–546 ff, below.

> There are many cases in the books where, without in any way impugning the contract of sale, some provision restricting competition has been regarded as in restraint of trade and contrary to public policy. There are many cases where not only has the main contract to purchase been left standing but part of the clause restricting competition has been allowed to stand.

Assuming, then, that contracts vitiated by some improper element must be divided into two classes, how are the more serious examples of 'illegality' at common law to be distinguished from the less serious? Which of the contracts that have been frowned upon by the courts are so patently reprehensible—so obviously contrary to public policy—that they must be peremptorily styled illegal? Judicial authority is lacking, but it is submitted that the epithet 'illegal' may aptly and correctly be applied to the following six types of contract:

A contract to commit a crime, a tort or a fraud on a third party.
A contract that is sexually immoral.
A contract to the prejudice of the public safety.
A contract prejudicial to the administration of justice.
A contract that tends to corruption in public life.
A contract to defraud the revenue.

There remain three types of contract which offend 'public policy', but which are inexpedient rather than unprincipled.

A contract to oust the jurisdiction of the court.
A contract that tends to prejudice the status of marriage.
A contract in restraint of trade.

If the word 'illegal' is to be reserved for the more reprehensible type of contract another title must be chosen to designate those which fall within the second degree of public policy, and which for that reason have been treated with comparative leniency by the courts. The most appropriate title seems to be 'void', since these contracts are in practice treated by the courts as void either as a whole or at least in part. In *Bennett v Bennett* Denning LJ described covenants in restraint of trade as 'void not illegal'.

> They are not 'illegal', in the sense that a contract to do a prohibited or immoral act is illegal. They are not 'unenforceable', in the sense that a contract within the Statute of Frauds is unenforceable for want of writing. These covenants lie somewhere in between. They are invalid and unenforceable.[43]

The word 'void' used as a descriptive title certainly has its disadvantages. It is already applied to a number of disparate contracts and is not applied to them in any uniform sense or with uniform results. At common law it has long been used to indicate the consequences of mistake; by statute it has been used with dubious results in wagering

---

[43] [1952] 1 KB 249 at 260, [1952] 1 All ER 413 at 421.

transactions and in contracts made by infants. But linguistic precision cannot survive the complexity of life. A continental jurist has said that, unlike the physical sciences where there is no interim stage between effect and no-effect, in legal science the effects of disobeying a legal rule may be graded to suit the individual situation.

> Thus, the difference between an act that is valid and an act that is void is unlike the difference between 'yes' and 'no', between effect and no-effect. It is a difference of grade and quantity. Some effects are produced, while others are not.[44]

For better or for worse, then, it has been decided for the purposes of this book to describe the three less serious types of 'illegal' contracts as *contracts void at common law on grounds of public policy.*

Some general observations must be added upon the doctrine of public policy in the current law.[45]

Since public policy reflects the mores and fundamental assumptions of the community, the content of the rules should vary from country to country and from era to era. There is high authority for the view that in matters of public policy the courts should adopt a broader approach than they usually do to the use of precedents.[46]

Such flexibility may manifest itself in two ways: by the closing down of existing heads of public policy and by the opening of new heads. There is no doubt that an existing head of public policy may be declared redundant. So in the nineteenth century it was stated that Christianity was part of the law of England and that accordingly a contract to hire a hall for a meeting to promote atheism was contrary to public policy[47] but fifty years later this view was decisively rejected.[48]

More controversy surrounds the question of whether the courts still retain freedom to recognise new heads of public policy. It has been denied that any such freedom exists[49] and Lord Thankerton said that the task of the judge in this area was 'to expound and not to expand', the law.[50] It may be thought surprising however that in this of all areas, the courts should abrogate their function of developing the common law. To some extent the discussion is artificial since much development may take place within the existing heads but it is difficult to assert that new circumstances cannot arise which do not fall readily into any of the recognised heads. Courts have responded

---

[44] Baumgarten, cited by Cohn, 64 LQR 326.

[45] See Lloyd *Public Policy* (1953); Winfield 42 Harvard L Rev 76; Gellhorn 35 Columbia L Rev 679; Shand [1972A] CLJ 144.

[46] See *Nordenfelt v Maxim Nordenfelt Guns and Ammunition Co* [1894] AC 535, per Lord Watson at 553.

[47] *Cowan v Milbourn* (1867) LR 2 Exch 230.

[48] *Bowman v Secular Society Ltd* [1917] AC 406.

[49] See *Janson v Driefontein Consolidated Mines* [1902] AC 484 at 491. *Geismar v Sun Alliance and London Insurance Ltd* [1978] QB 383 at 389, [1977] 3 All ER 570 at 575.

[50] *Fender v St John-Mildmay* [1938] AC 1 at 23, [1937] 3 All ER 402 at 407. Cf the illuminating judgment of Windeyer J in *Brooks v Burns Philp Trustee Co Ltd* [1969] ALR 321 at 331–349.

to this challenge in the past by the development of new heads[51] and it is thought that they will, in exceptional circumstances, do so again.

This question would be relevant, for instance, if it were argued that contracts involving racial, religious or sexual discrimination were contrary to public policy. It is arguable that the Court of Appeal's decision in *Nagle v Feilden*[52] represents recognition of such a possibility and there is some Australian authority too.[53] Undoubtedly any such argument would raise important questions, in particular whether the existence of legislation in this area[54] should be regarded as relevant either as (a) delimiting precisely the area of reprehensible discriminatory conduct or (b) (preferably) as a legislative signal that discrimination is against the public interest.[55] It is thought however that the least satisfactory answer would be that the law is totally petrified. Another recently canvassed head of public policy has involved the validity of contractual provisions, which attempt to allocate some of the risks of inflation by tying repayment of debts to foreign currencies. In *Treseder-Griffin v Co-operative Insurance Society Ltd*,[56] Denning LJ expressed the opinion, obiter, that such provisions were contrary to public policy but this view was not followed by Browne-Wilkinson J in *Multiservice Bookbinding Ltd v Marden*,[57] a decision approved in its turn by Lord Denning MR in *Staffordshire Area Health Authority v South Staffordshire Waterworks Co*.[58] In none of these cases was any weight attached to any argument based on novelty.

Similarly, in *Lancashire County Council v Municipal Mutual Insurance Ltd*[59] the plaintiff County Council had an insurance policy with the defendant insurers in respect of claims made against it. The defendants repudiated liability in respect of two claims where exemplary damages had been awarded against the plaintiffs. The defendants argued that it was against public policy to allow insurance against the payment of exemplary damages. This was a question entirely free from English authority although research showed that this was the rule in some but not all

[51] See eg *Neville v Dominion of Canada News Co Ltd* [1915] 3 KB 556; Furmston 16 U of Toronto LJ 267 at 293–297. This case, involving, as it did, the balancing of conflicting public interests in the preservation of confidentiality and the free availability of information was the precursor of many important modern cases. Many, but not all, of these cases have been litigated outside the contractual context but the underlying policies involved must be constant although how they are to be applied must depend on the context. See in particular *D v NSPCC* [1978] AC 171, [1977] 1 All ER 589; *Riddick v Thames Board Mills Ltd* [1977] QB 881, [1977] 3 All ER 677; *Initial Services Ltd v Putterill* [1968] 1 QB 396, [1967] 3 All ER 145.
[52] [1966] 2 QB 633, [1966] 1 All ER 689.
[53] *Newcastle Diocese (Church Property Trustees) v Ebbeck* (1960) 34 ALJR 413.
[54] Eg Race Relations Act 1968; Equal Pay Act 1970.
[55] See further Lester and Bindman *Race and Law*; Hepple *Race: Jobs and the Law in Britain*; Garner 34 MLR 478. It is thought that the view in the text is substantially the same as that stated by Lord Wilberforce in *Blathwayt v Baron Cawley* [1976] AC 397 at 425–426, [1975] 3 All ER 625 at 636. See also *Ahmad v Inner London Education Authority* [1978] QB 36, [1978] 1 All ER 574; Race Relations Act 1976, s 72.
[56] [1956] 2 QB 127, [1956] 2 All ER 33.
[57] [1979] Ch 84, [1978] 2 All ER 489; Bishop and Hindley 42 MLR 338.
[58] [1978] 3 All ER 769, [1978] 1 WLR 1387.   [59] [1996] 3 All ER 545

American States (where awards of exemplary damages are much more common and in general much larger in amount). If novelty had been of itself decisive there would have been no need for further discussion. Although Simon Brown LJ said that 'The Courts should be wary of minting new rules of public policy when the legislature had not done so' the Court of Appeal's rejection of the defendants' argument turns on a careful analysis of the relevant policy considerations.

A final observation may be made as to the way in which the courts determine the content of public policy. Apart from reliance on previous precedents, this is done by a priori deduction from broad general principles. It is not the practice in English courts for the parties to lead sociological or economic evidence as to whether particular practices are harmful and it is doubtful to what extent such evidence would be regarded as relevant if it were adduced.[60]

B The contracts described [61]

It is now necessary to describe and discuss the six contracts that are properly to be termed illegal at common law on the ground of public policy.

a A contract to commit a crime, a tort or a fraud on a third party

There is no need to stress the obvious fact that an agreement is illegal and void if its object, direct or indirect, is the commission of a crime or a tort. The rule has been applied to many cases, as for instance where the design was to obtain goods by false pretences;[62] to defraud prospective shareholders;[63] to disseminate obscene prints;[64] to publish a libel;[65] to assault a third party;[66] or to rig the market, ie artificially to enhance the true value of shares by entering into a contract to purchase them at a fictitious premium.[67]

An agreement made with the object of defrauding or deceiving[68] a third party is illegal, and a familiar illustration of this is where A agrees to recommend B for a post, whether public or private, in consideration that B, if appointed, will pay part of the emoluments or a secret commission to A.[69]

---

[60] See eg *Texaco Ltd v Mulberry Filling Station* [1972] 1 All ER 513, [1972] 1 WLR 814. Cf the use of Monopolies Commission Report in *Esso Petroleum Co Ltd v Harpers Garage (Stourport) Ltd* [1968] AC 269, [1967] 1 All ER 699. Cf the use of the 'Brandeis Brief' in American law: *Muller v Oregon* 208 US 412 (1908).

[61] See Furmston 16 U of Toronto LJ 267.

[62] *Berg v Sadler and Moore* [1937] 2 KB 158, [1937] 1 All ER 637. But for a criticism of this difficult case, see Furmston 16 U of Toronto LJ 267 at 290–291. See Theft Act 1968, ss 15 and 16.

[63] *Begbie v Phosphate Sewage Co* (1875) LR 10 QB 491.

[64] *Fores v Johnes* (1802) 4 Esp 97.   [65] *Apthorp v Neville & Co* (1907) 23 TLR 575.

[66] *Allen v Rescous* (1676) 2 Lev 174.   [67] *Scott v Brown, Doering, McNab & Co* [1892] 2 QB 724.

[68] *Brown Jenkinson & Co Ltd v Percy Dalton (London) Ltd* [1957] 2 QB 621, [1957] 2 All ER 844.

[69] *Waldo v Martin* (1825) 4 B & C 319. See also *Harrington v Victoria Graving Dock Co* (1878) 3 QBD 549.

In this context it is appropriate to remember the ambit of the crime of conspiracy[70] and that any agreement which amounts to a criminal conspiracy will also be an illegal contract.

An allied rule of public policy is that no person shall be allowed to benefit from his own crime.[71] This is a doctrine of general application. So it is important not only in the law of contract but also, for example, in the law of succession. In one case, for instance, a wife, who had killed her husband by a single blow with a domestic chamber pot, was convicted of manslaughter by reason of her diminished responsibility and was sentenced to be detained without limit of time in Broadmoor hospital. Such a 'hospital order' is remedial in nature, and it implies that the convicted person is not deserving of punishment. It was therefore, argued that the wife was not precluded from taking a benefit under her deceased husband's will. The argument was rejected. Having been justly convicted of a crime, the degree of her moral guilt was irrelevant.[72]

The rule that the court will not assist a person to recover the fruits of his crime applies equally to his representatives. This is well illustrated by *Beresford v Royal Insurance Co Ltd*.[73]

> X, who had insured his life with the defendant company for £50,000, shot himself two or three minutes before the policy would have been invalidated by non-payment of the premium. He was sane at the time of his death. As the law then stood, suicide was a crime.[74] On the true construction of the contract, the company had agreed to pay the money to X's representatives even though he should die by his own hand and whether he should then be sane or insane.

An action in which X's executor claimed payment of the £50,000 failed. In the words of Lord Macmillan:

> To enforce payment in favour of the assured's representative would be to give him a benefit, albeit in a sense a post-mortem benefit, the benefit, namely, of having by his last and criminal act provided for his relatives or creditors.[75] Neither the House of Lords nor the Court of Appeal stigmatised the contract of insurance itself as illegal. It was not void *in toto*. Lord Atkin and Lord Thankerton were therefore of opinion that if, for example, X had assigned his policy

---

[70] Which is not as wide as it once was. Criminal Law Act 1977.

[71] *Cleaver v Mutual Reserve Fund Life Association* [1892] 1 QB 147 at 156, per Fry LJ; *Re Crippen's Estate* [1911] P 108 at 112, per Sir Samuel Evans P; Youdan 89 LQR 235; Goval and Smith [1973] CLJ 81.

[72] *Re Giles, Giles v Giles* [1972] Ch 544, [1971] 3 All ER 1141. But see now Forfeiture Act 1982. *Re DWS (decd)* [2001] 1 All ER 97.

[73] [1937] 2 KB 197, [1937] 2 All ER 243; aff'd [1938] AC 586, [1938] 2 All ER 602.

[74] This is no longer so; Suicide Act 1961, s 1. It can therefore be argued that if the facts of *Beresford* recurred the result would now be different. See *Dunbar v Plant* [1997] 4 All ER 289.

[75] [1938] AC at 605.

as security for a loan, the lender would have been entitled to recover the amount of the loan from the insurance company.[76]

In *Gray v Barr*,[77] this rule was applied again.

The defendant involuntarily killed X in the course of making an unlawful and violent attack upon him with a loaded gun. This amounted to manslaughter. Judgment was given against him in a civil action for the payment of £6,668 by way of compensation to X's widow. He admitted liability, but claimed an indemnity against this sum under an insurance policy which indemnified him against all sums that he might become liable to pay as damages in respect of bodily injury caused by an accident.

His claimed failed. Having intentionally attacked the deceased in a violent and unlawful manner, it was contrary to public policy that he should be indemnified against the consequences, however unintentional the killing of his victim might have been. At first sight this decision appears inevitable but it has been forcefully criticised.[78] It has been pointed out that since the policy was one of liability insurance, the defendant would have no claim against the insurance company unless he were liable to the plaintiff and it would be the plaintiff who suffered from the decision unless the defendant were sufficiently wealthy to pay the damages from his own resources.[79]

Such considerations, though not adopted in *Gray v Barr* have prevailed in the case of motor car insurance. A motorist, who is insured against liability for damages payable to third persons injured as a result of his negligent driving, is entitled to an indemnity under the policy even though the negligence has been so gross as to amount to manslaughter. This right, however, does not avail him if the injury has been deliberately caused in cold blood. Even in this case, however, the victim of the assault, if he receives no compensation from the guilty party, has a right of recovery against the assurers in accordance with the compulsory insurance regulations laid down by modern legislation.[80]

[76] Ibid at 600, per Lord Atkin, with whom Lord Thankerton agreed. Lord Macmillan reserved his opinion on the question: ibid at 605; *Hardy v Motor Insurers' Bureau* [1964] 2 QB 745 at 760, per Lord Denning MR; *Davitt v Titcumb* [1990] Ch 110, [1989] 3 All ER 417. For further illustrations, see Furmston 16 U of Toronto LJ 267 at 269–272.

[77] [1970] 2 QB 626, [1970] 2 All ER 702; affd [1971] 2 QB 554, [1971] 2 All ER 949.

[78] Fleming 34 MLR 176. Cf *Fire and All Risks v Powell* [1966] VR 513.

[79] There is no evidence in the report as to the defendant's wealth nor is it easy to see how a rule could apply which involved a means test on the defendant. It is clear however that in most tort actions defendants are not worth suing unless they carry liability insurance: Atiyah *Accidents, Compensation and The Law* (5th edn, 1993) chs 9 and 10.

[80] *Tinline v White Cross Insurance Association Ltd* [1921] 3 KB 327; *James v British General Insurance Co Ltd* [1927] 2 KB 311. *Hardy v Motor Insurers' Bureau* [1964] 2 QB 745 at 761, per Lord Denning MR citing Road Traffic Act 1960, s 207. *Gardner v Moore* [1984] AC 548, [1984] 1 All ER 1100.

The principle that no benefit can accrue to a criminal from his crime, however, must obviously not be pushed too far.[81] Nowadays there are many statutory offences, some of them involving no great degree of turpitude, which rank as crimes, and it has several times been doubted whether they are all indiscriminately affected by the rule of which *Beresford*'s case is an example.[82]

b A contract that is sexually immoral

Although Lord Mansfield laid it down that a contract *contra bonos mores* is illegal,[83] the law in this connection appears to concern itself only with what is sexually reprehensible. The precise ambit of this head of public policy is, however, very far from clear. It has been plausibly argued that sexual mores have changed radically and that public policy should reflect this,[84] but it is not easy to state how far the changes have gone. It seems very unlikely that prostitutes can sue for their fees. Equally, if a landlord lets a room to a prostitute for ten times the normal rent, knowing that she will use it to receive clients, the contract is surely illegal. On the other hand, in the older cases, it is stated that an agreement intended to bring about or facilitate illicit cohabitation is illegal,[85] though it has also been held that an agreement to pay for such cohabitation after the event is bad only for lack of consideration and therefore enforceable if under seal.[86]

These latter cases must now require reconsideration. It is extremely common for landlords to let accommodation, knowing or reasonably suspecting that the occupants are living together but are not married. The courts have shown no disposition to resolve landlord–tenant disputes in such cases by invoking public policy.[87] Similarly, it is common for such unmarried couples to enter into arrangements for the pooling of their incomes and the acquisition of assets, including houses or flats. Several such cases have been before the courts, when the relationship has broken down

---

[81] *Howard v Shirlstar Container Transport Ltd* [1990] 3 All ER 366, [1990] 1 WLR 1292.

[82] *Beresford v Royal Insurance Co Ltd* [1937] 2 KB 197 at 220, per Lord Wright MR; *Marles v Philip Trant & Sons Ltd (No 2)* [1954] 1 QB 29 at 37, per Denning LJ; *St John Shipping Corpn v Joseph Rank Ltd* [1957] 1 QB 267 at 292, [1956] 3 All ER 683 at 687, per Devlin J; *Osman v J Ralph Moss Ltd* [1970] 1 Lloyd's Rep 313.

[83] *Jones v Randall* (1774) 1 Cowp 37.

[84] Dwyer 93 LQR 386; Devlin 39 MLR 1 at 12; Honoré *Sex Law* pp 44–51, 131–132.

[85] *Benyon v Nettlefold* (1850) 3 Mac & G 94; *Ayerst v Jenkins* (1873) LR 16 Eq 275.

[86] *R v Bernhard* [1938] 2 KB 264, [1938] 2 All ER 140; *Nye v Moseley* (1826) 6 B & C 133. Although this distinction, as stated, sounds very odd, it produces a comprehensible result, since the practical purpose of the agreement in the last cited case was to provide for a discarded mistress, a not dishonourable course of conduct.

[87] In most cases the point has gone by default. See eg *Somma v Hazelhurst* [1978] 2 All ER 1011, [1978] 1 WLR 1014; *Dyson Holdings Ltd v Fox* [1976] QB 503, [1975] 3 All ER 1030 (but note that the court is bound to take public policy points of its own motion, see p 428, below). It was however expressly taken and rejected in *Heglibiston Establishment v Heyman* (1977) 246 Estates Gazette 567, 36 P & CR 351 (not following *Upfill v Wright* [1911] 1 KB 506).

and it has been assumed that in principle such arrangements are capable of being binding contracts.[88]

It is plausible to argue that in such relationships the agreement is enforceable because there is other consideration to support it[89] or that, in modern times, it is not to be assumed that one party rather than the other is providing sexual services.

c A contract prejudicial to the public safety

In an early case Lord Alvanley said:

> We are all of opinion that . . . it is not competent to any subject to enter into a contract to do any thing which may be detrimental to the interests of his own country; and that such a contract is as much prohibited as if it had been expressly forbidden by act of parliament.[90]

Detrimental contracts within the meaning of this statement are those which tend either to benefit an enemy country or to disturb the good relations of England with a friendly country.

Contracts made in time of war afford the outstanding example of the first class. A state of war between Great Britain and another country must clearly react upon a contract made with an alien enemy by a British subject or a person owing obedience to the Crown, since it may result in injury to the Commonwealth or advantage to the enemy.[91]

The expression 'alien enemy' is not necessarily restricted to its popular meaning. It denotes a status that depends not upon the nationality of the contracting party, but upon whether he is voluntarily resident in or carrying on a business in the enemy's country or in a country within the effective control of the enemy.[92] Thus a British subject or a neutral who is resident in enemy territory is treated as an alien enemy in the present context. An enemy national who happens to be present in England during the war may be sued in the Queen's courts, but he cannot himself bring any action.[93] On the other hand, if he is resident here with the licence of the Crown, as for instance where he is registered under the Aliens Restriction Acts, the courts are open to him and a contract may be enforced by him even during the continuance of

---

[88] Clearly in practice many such arrangements like those made between husband and wife fall short of being contractually binding for other reasons. See eg *Tanner v Tanner* [1975] 3 All ER 776, [1975] 1 WLR 1346; *Eves v Eves* [1975] 3 All ER 768, [1975] 1 WLR 1338; *Horrocks v Forray* [1976] 1 All ER 737, [1976] 1 WLR 230; *Chandler v Kerley* [1978] 2 All ER 942, [1978] 1 WLR 693.

[89] Barton 92 LQR 168.

[90] *Furtado v Rogers* (1802) 3 Bos & P 191 at 198. See in general McNair and Watts *Legal Effects of War*, especially ch 4.

[91] The following account is confined to the position at common law. In time of war, many of the matters that arise are governed by special legislation.

[92] *Porter v Freudenberg* [1915] 1 KB 857; *Sovracht (V/O) v Van Udens Scheepvart en Agentuur Maatschappij (NV Gebr)* [1943] AC 203, [1943] 1 All ER 76. For the purposes of the Trading with the Enemy Act 1939, which penalises persons having intercourse with the enemy, de facto residence, though not voluntary, is sufficient; *Vamvakas v Custodian of Enemy Property* [1952] 2 QB 183, [1952] 1 All ER 629.

[93] *Porter v Freudenberg* [1915] 1 KB 857; *Halsey v Lowenfeld* [1916] 2 KB 707.

hostilities.[94] It goes without saying that a contract made during war with an alien enemy is illegal. If it is made during peace with a person who later becomes an alien enemy owing to the outbreak of war and if it involves intercourse with the enemy country or is in other respects obnoxious from the standpoint of public policy, then it is immediately abrogated *in so far as it is still executory*.[95] It is not merely suspended during hostilities, but is cut short *eo instanti* upon the commencement of the war. It can give rise to no further rights and obligations for the object of the law is to provide certainty at a time when everything else is uncertain and to enable the parties to engage in another adventure without waiting to see whether hostilities cease soon enough to render fulfilment of the contract possible.[96] If, for instance, an Englishman agrees to charter a ship to a German company for a period of ten years, the effect of an outbreak of war between Great Britain and Germany is to absolve the parties at once from their future obligations, notwithstanding that peace may be restored before the expiration of ten years. This rule applies not only to contracts with an enemy alien, but also to those made between British subjects and neutrals or even between British subjects themselves if benefit may thereby accrue to the enemy country.[97]

The doctrine of abrogation, then, affects the contract so far as it is still executory. It does not affect it so far as performance has already been completed.[98] Accrued rights, though not immediately enforceable, are not destroyed. Common law, it must be stressed, does not countenance the confiscation of enemy property and, subject to what may be arranged in the ultimate peace treaty and to any statutory provisions for the administration of enemy property found in this country, it is well established that contractual rights already accrued in favour of an alien enemy at the outbreak of war remain intact, though of course the right to enforce them is suspended until hostilities cease.[99]

No attempt has ever been made to give an exhaustive definition of 'accrued rights', but it is clear that the right to the payment of a liquidated sum of money already due under a contract falls within this category and therefore survives the outbreak of war.[100] Such a sum is regarded as a debt incurred before the creditor was infected with enemy status, and since nothing remains outstanding except its payment and since confiscation of his property is ruled out, he is entitled to enforce a payment when hostilities cease. Thus he may ultimately recover the bank balance that was standing to

---

[94] *Schaffenius v Goldberg* [1916] 1 KB 284.

[95] *Ertel Bieber & Co v Rio Tinto Co* [1918] AC 260 at 267–268, 274, per Lord Dunedin.

[96] *Esposito v Bowden* (1857) 7 E & B 763 at 792, per Willes J.

[97] *Schering Ltd v Stockholms Enskilda Bank Aktiebolag* [1946] AC 219 at 257, [1946] 1 All ER 36 at 40; *Kuenigl v Donnersmarck* [1955] 1 QB 515, [1955] 1 All ER 46.

[98] *Ottoman Bank v Jebara* [1928] AC 269 at 276; *Schering Ltd v Stockholms Enskilda Bank Aktiebolag*, above, at 241, 258 and 41, and 55, respectively.

[99] *Daimler Co Ltd v Continental Tyre and Rubber Co (Gt Britain) Ltd* [1916] 2 AC 307 at 347, per Lord Parker.

[100] McNair and Watts *Legal Effects of War* (4th edn) pp 137–138, approved in *Schering Ltd v Stockholms Enskilda Bank Aktiebolag* [1946] AC 219 at 240, [1946] 1 All ER 36 at 40, per Lord Thankerton; and in *Arab Bank Ltd v Barclays Bank Ltd* [1954] AC 495 at 537, [1954] 2 All ER 226 at 239, per Lord Asquith.

his credit at the outbreak of war.[101] Even future instalments of a debt that have fallen due after the outbreak of war are regarded as liquidated sums within the meaning of the rule, so that the right to recover them is merely postponed.[102]

A further exception to the principle of abrogation, as described by Lord Dunedin, is that those contracts 'which are really the concomitants of property' are suspended, not destroyed, even though they are still executory.[103] These, as in the case of accrued rights, have never been precisely defined, but they are generally taken to mean contracts connected with land such as restrictive covenants and covenants running with the land at common law or by statute.[104]

There is, therefore, no general rule that all executory contracts with an alien enemy are abrogated. 'The executory contract which is abrogated must either involve intercourse, or its continued existence must be in some other way against public policy as that has been laid down in decided cases.[105] The judges have refused to formulate what contracts escape abrogation as being innocuous from the point of view of public policy, but one example at least is a separation agreement under which a husband has agreed to make periodic payments to his wife. If in such a case the wife becomes an alien enemy, the husband none the less remains liable to pay the sums falling due under the contract.[106]

A contract which contemplates the performance in a foreign and friendly country of some act which is inimical to the public welfare of that country is a breach of international comity, and is regarded as illegal by the English courts.[107] Thus it is unlawful to make an agreement in England to raise money in support of a revolt against a friendly Government,[108] to enter into a partnership for the purpose of importing liquor into a country contrary to its prohibition laws,[109] or to do something in a foreign country which will violate the local law.[110] In *Lemenda Trading Co Ltd v African Middle-East Petroleum Co Ltd*[111] the defendants, a London company, entered into a contract with the plaintiffs, a company registered in Nassau, under which the

---

[101] *Arab Bank Ltd v Barclays Bank* [1954] AC 495, [1954] 2 All ER 226.

[102] *Schering Ltd v Stockholms Enskilda Bank Aktiebolag* [1946] AC 219, [1946] 1 All ER 36. Though well established, this rule is in fact illogical, since the creditor might, for instance, assign the debt for immediate payment and thus increase the resources of the enemy, per Lord Goddard at 269 and 57, respectively.

[103] *Ertel Bieber & Co v Rio Tinto Co Ltd* [1918] AC 260 at 269.

[104] *Schering Ltd v Stockholms Enskilda Bank Aktiebolag* [1946] AC 219 at 252, [1946] 1 All ER 36 at 47, per Lord Russell of Killowen.

[105] *Ertel Bieber & Co v Rio Tinto Co Ltd* [1918] AC 260 at 269, per Lord Dunedin.

[106] *Bevan v Bevan* [1955] 2 QB 227, [1955] 2 All ER 206.

[107] *Foster v Driscoll* [1929] 1 KB 470 at 510, 520–522.

[108] *De Wütz v Hendricks* (1824) 2 Bing 314.   [109] *Foster v Driscoll* [1929] 1 KB 470.

[110] *Regazzoni v K C Sethia (1944) Ltd* [1958] AC 301, [1957] 3 All ER 286. This is a principle of considerable width. See Mann 21 MLR 130, cf A L G 73 LQR 32. See also *Fielding and Platt v Selim Najjar* [1969] 2 All ER 150, [1969] 1 WLR 357; *National Westminster Bank Ltd v Barclays Bank International Ltd* [1975] QB 654, [1974] 3 All ER 834.

[111] [1988] QB 448, [1988] 1 All ER 513.

plaintiffs agreed to assist the defendants in procuring the renewal of a supply contract with the Qatar National Oil Company for the supply of crude oil. The understanding was that the plaintiff would use its influence with the Chairman or Managing Director of the Qatar National Oil Company and would be paid, if successful, on a commission basis. This contract was subject to English law. The defendants had also entered into a contract with the Qatar National Oil Company and had executed a side letter to that contract agreeing that the contract had been negotiated without the assistance of agents or brokers paid on a commission basis. Under Qatar law a commission contract for the supply of oil was void and unenforceable. The defendants obtained the renewal of the supply contract and the plaintiff claimed commission. The defendant argued that even if the plaintiff had been instrumental in helping them get the supply contract renewed, any agreement to pay him commission was contrary to English public policy. This view was accepted by Phillips J who said:

> In my judgment, the English courts should not enforce an English law contract which falls to be performed abroad where
>
> (i) it relates to an adventure which is contrary to a head of English public policy which is founded on general principles of morality and
>
> (ii) the same public policy applies in the country of performance so that the agreement would not be enforceable under the law of that country. In such a situation international comity combines with English domestic public policy to militate against enforcement.

d A contract prejudicial to the administration of justice

'It is admitted that any contract or engagement having a tendency, however slight, to affect the administration of justice, is illegal and void.[112] There are many examples of this rule, as for instance, an agreement not to appear at the public examination of a bankrupt nor to oppose his discharge,[113] an agreement not to plead the Gaming Acts as a defence to an action on a cheque given for lost bets,[114] and an agreement to withdraw divorce proceedings;[115] an agreement by a witness not to give evidence or only to give evidence for one side,[116] but perhaps the most familiar example is an agreement to stifle a prosecution.

It is in the interests of the public that the suppression of a prosecution should not be made the matter of a private bargain.[117] Whether a man ought to be prosecuted or not depends upon considerations that vary in each case, but the person with whom the decision rests is under a social duty in the discharge of which he must be free from the influence of indirect motives.[118] It is therefore well established that the courts will

---

[112] *Egerton v Brownlow* (1853) 4 HL Cas 1 at 163, per Lord Lyndhurst.
[113] *Kearley v Thomson* (1890) 24 QBD 742.
[114] *Cooper v Willis* (1906) 22 TLR 582.   [115] *Gipps v Hume* (1861) 2 John & H 517.
[116] *Harmony Shipping Co S A v Davis* [1979] 3 All ER 177, [1979] 1 WLR 1380.
[117] *Clubb v Hutson* (1865) 18 CBNS 414 at 417, per Erle CJ.
[118] *Jones v Merionethshire Permanent Benefit Building Society* [1892] 1 Ch 173 at 183, per Bowen LJ.

neither enforce nor recognise any agreement which has the effect of withdrawing from the ordinary course of justice a prosecution for a public offence.[119] An agreement to stifle a prosecution, ie to prevent proceedings already instituted from running their normal course, or to compromise a prosecution, is illegal and void, even though the prosecutor derives no gain, financial or otherwise, and even though the agreement secures the very object for which the proceedings were taken.[120]

This rule, however, applies only where the offence for which the defendant is prosecuted is a matter of public concern, ie one which pre-eminently affects the interests of the public. If the offence is not of this nature, but is one in which the injured person has a choice between a civil and a criminal remedy, as for instance in the case of a libel or an assault, a compromise is lawful and enforceable. The question whether the offence was of public concern arose in the leading case of *Keir v Leeman*.[121]

> A commenced a prosecution for riot and assault against seven defendants who had assaulted and ejected a sheriff's officer and his assistants while they were levying an execution in respect of a judgment debt due to A. Before the trial began. X and Y agreed to pay to A the amount of the debt, together with costs, in consideration that A would not proceed with the prosecution. A accordingly gave no evidence against the defendants and he consented with the leave of the judge to a verdict of 'not guilty' being entered. X and Y, when sued upon the agreement, pleaded that it was an unlawful compromise and therefore void. This plea prevailed.

Denman CJ after remarking that some indictments for misdemeanour might be compromised, said:

> We shall probably be safe in laying it down that the law will permit a compromise of all offences, though made the subject of criminal prosecution, for which the injured party might sue and recover damages in an action. It is often the only manner in which he can obtain redress. But if the offence is of a public nature, no agreement can be valid that is founded on the consideration of stifling a prosecution for it . . . In the present instance the offence is not confined to personal injury, but is accompanied with riot and obstruction of a public officer in the execution of his duty. These are matters of public concern and therefore not legally the subject of a compromise.

Other instances of public offences in respect of which no compromise is permitted are perjury,[122] obtaining money or credit by false pretences,[123] forgery,[124] interference with and obstruction of a public highway.[125]

---

[119] *Windhill Local Board of Health v Vint* (1890) 45 ChD 351 at 363, per Cotton LJ.
[120] *Keir v Leeman* (1846) 9 QB 371; *Windhill Local Board of Health v Vint*, above.   [121] Above.
[122] *Collins v Blantern* (1767) 2 Wils 341.
[123] *Clubb v Hutson* (1865) 18 CBNS 414; *Jones v Merionethshire Permanent Benefit Building Society* [1892] 1 Ch 173. See Theft Act 1968, ss 15 and 16.
[124] *Brook v Hook* (1871) LR 6 Exch 89.
[125] *Windhill Local Board of Health v Vint* (1890) 45 ChD 351.

An example of the rule, that an offence for which either a civil or a criminal remedy is available may be the subject of a lawful compromise, is *Fisher & Co v Apollinaris Co*[126] where the facts were these:

> The Apollinaris Co prosecuted Fisher under the Trade Marks Act for selling his mineral water in bottles that bore their trade mark. It was then agreed that, in consideration of the abandonment of the prosecution, Fisher would give a letter of apology to the company and would authorise them to make what use of it they considered appropriate. After the abandonment, the company proceeded to publish continuously the letter of apology in the daily press. Fisher sued to restrain this publication on the ground that the apology had been obtained by an improper use of criminal proceedings.

It was held that the agreement was valid, since there was nothing unlawful in the withdrawal of a prosecution for an offence of that particular kind.

The account given above is based on the law as it was before the Criminal Law Act 1967. That act made a number of changes in the criminal law. Section 1 abolished the distinction between felonies and misdemeanours and section 5(1) introduced a new offence of concealing an arrestable offence, which replaced the wider offences of misprision of felony and compounding a felony. The act makes no mention of the law of contract but it is arguable that it alters it indirectly.[127] Before the act any agreement to conceal a felony was itself a criminal offence and therefore necessarily an illegal contract. So the public–private dichotomy which previously applied only to misdemeanours might in theory be applied to all offences. In the same way since an agreement to conceal an arrestable offence is no longer a criminal offence if the only consideration for it is the making good of the loss or injury caused by the offence, it can be argued that such an agreement should now be enforceable. On balance, however, it is thought that to take an agreement out of the ambit of the criminal law does not by itself indicate that it should be enforced.

Maintenance and champerty

A further example of contracts that tend to pervert the due course of justice are those which savour of maintenance or champerty. 'Maintenance may nowadays be defined as improperly stirring up litigation and strife by giving aid to one party to bring or defend a claim without just cause or excuse.'[128] Champerty is where there is a further agreement that the person who gives the aid shall receive a share of what may be recovered in the action.

Formerly, maintenance was a misdemeanour, and also a tort for which damages were recoverable by the other party in the action. This is no longer the case. The Criminal Law Act 1967 provides that maintenance, including champerty, shall

---

[126] (1875) 10 Ch App 297.
[127] For a fuller account, see Buckley 3 Anglo-American L Rev 472; Hudson 43 MLR 532.
[128] *Re Trepca Mines Ltd (No 2)* [1963] Ch 199 at 219, [1962] 3 All ER 351 at 355E per Lord Denning.

no longer be punishable as a crime or actionable as a tort.[129] It is further provided, however, that this abolition of criminal and civil liability 'shall not affect any such rule of law as to the cases in which a contract is to be treated as contrary to public policy or otherwise illegal'.[130] Therefore, the long established rule still stands that an agreement tainted by maintenance or champerty is void as being contrary to public policy.

The Act did not therefore reverse the long established rule that agreements tainted by maintenance or champerty were void as being contrary to public policy.[131] However, recent developments have shown that apparently well settled policies in this area are now open to debate and reconsideration.

For centuries it has been taken for granted that it was professionally improper as well as illegal for lawyers to agree with claimant clients to conduct litigation on the basis that payment would be related to results. (It was not improper or illegal for lawyers to do work for no payment nor was it improper or illegal to take on as a client someone who in practice was unlikely to be able to pay the fees if the claim was not successful.) For certain kinds of litigation this rule has now been reversed by the Courts and Legal Services Act 1990, section 58. The most obvious example is personal injuries where in practice a very high percentage of claims are successful. The details of this change are outside the scope of this book but this development has raised the question whether there might be a parallel change in the common law.

In *Thai Trading v Taylor*[132] the second defendant was a lawyer who had acted for the first defendant, his wife, in a contract dispute with the plaintiffs on the basis that he would charge his usual fees if the defence was successful and make no charge if it were not. The Court of Appeal held this agreement lawful. This decision has however since been held wrong[133] on the basis that it contravened the Solicitors Practice Rules which had been held by the House of Lords in *Swain v Law Society*[134] to have the force of a statute.

In *Bevan Ashford v Geoff Yeadle (Contractors) Ltd*[135] the plaintiff solicitors entered into an arrangement with the defendant company to conduct an arbitration on the basis that they would receive their normal fees if successful. Counsel were engaged on the basis that he would receive no fee if the defendants claim in the arbitration failed

---

[129] Ss 13(1) and 14(1).

[130] S 14(2).

[131] *Rees v De Bernardy* [1896] 2 Ch 437. As to whether an arrangement is champertous see *Giles v Thompson* [1993] 3 All ER 321. As to whether any exceptions may exist to this rule, see now the differing views in *Wallersteiner v Moir (No 2)* [1975] QB 373, [1975] 1 All ER 849. It was agreed in *Trendtex Trading Corpn v Crédit Suisse* [1982] AC 679, [1981] 3 All ER 520 that the modern tendency was for the scope of maintenance to diminish.

[132] [1998] 3 All ER 65 not following *Aratra Potato Co Ltd v Taylor Johnson Garrett* [1995] 4 All ER 695.

[133] *Hughes v Kingston upon Hull City Council* [1999] 2 All ER 49; *Awwad v Geraghty & Co* (a firm) [2000] 1 All ER 608.

[134] [1982] 2 All ER 827. [135] [1998] 3 All ER 238.

and an uplift of 50 per cent above his normal fee if the claim succeeded. Sir Richard Scott V-C held that these arrangements were outside section 58 of the Courts and Legal Services Act 1990 but that they were lawful at common law by virtue of a change in public policy.

In *Mohamed v Alaga & Co*[136] the claimant was a leading member of the Somali community in the United Kingdom. He alleged that he had made a deal with the defendant solicitors under which he would introduce Somali refugees to the defendant with a view to the refugees applying for legal aid and the defendant representing them on their asylum applications. He further alleged that he had agreed to give help in preparing and presenting the applications and that the defendants had agreed to pay commission equivalent to one half of any fees received by them on legal aid. It was accepted that such an agreement would be contrary to section 7 of the Solicitors Practice Rules 1990.

The Court of Appeal held that any such contract would be illegal even if, as he alleged, the claimant was ignorant of the prohibition. However, it was held that the claimant could recover on a *quantum meruit* basis for the value of any work he had done for the defendant.

The position of other professionals involved in litigation was considered in *Factortame Ltd v Secretary of State for the Environment, Transport and the Regions (No.2).*[137] As the result of complex and important earlier litigation it had been held that the claimants were entitled to compensatory damages from the government as the result of what was held to be an unlawful prohibition on their fishing in United Kingdom territorial waters. The computation of the damages was complicated and the claimants were very short of money. The Court of Appeal held that an agreement between the claimants and a firm of accountants who were to work on the figures that the accountants would receive 8 per cent of the amount recovered was valid. The accountants were doing work which could have been done by solicitors but in which neither solicitors nor accountants had a monopoly. The accountants were not themselves to give evidence. The Court would clearly have been reluctant to approve a similar arrangement for an expert witness.

An allied problem arises where a company is in financial difficulties and has as its main asset a cause of action which if successfully pursued would generate funds which would resolve or at least reduce the difficulties. In this situation it may be attractive to sell the cause of action to an individual since individuals, unlike companies, may be eligible for legal aid and less likely to be subject to orders to provide security for costs. In *Norglen Ltd v Reeds Rains Prudential Ltd*[138] the House of Lords held that an assignment by a company to an individual would not be invalid for this reason.[139]

---

[136] [1999] 3 All ER 699   [137] [2003] QB 381, [2002] 4 All ER 97.

[138] [1998] 1 All ER 218. A liquidator has special powers to deal in causes of action under s 214 of Insolvency Act 1986. See *Re Oasis Merchandising Services Ltd* [1997] 1 All ER 1009.

[139] For further consideration of circumstances in which funding another's cause of action is an abuse of process see *Stocznia Gdanska SA v Latvian Shipping Co (No 2)* [1998] 1 All ER 883.

e A contract liable to corrupt public life

It has long been the rule that any contract is illegal which tends to corruption in the administration of the affairs of the nation. A familiar example of a transaction offensive to this principle is a contract for the buying, selling or procuring of public offices.[140] Story says:

> It is obvious that all such contracts must have a material influence to diminish the respectability, responsibility and purity of public officers, and to introduce a system of official patronage, corruption and deceit wholly at war with the public interest.[141]

Thus in one case:

> A agreed that if by the influence of B he were appointed Customs Officer of a port, he would appoint such deputies as B should nominate and would hold the profits of the office in trust for B. It was held, after A had secured the post, that no action lay against him for breach of this agreement.[142]

Similarly a contract to procure a title for a man in consideration of a money payment is illegal at common law.[143]

On the same principle an agreement to assign or mortgage future instalments of the salary of a public office is void, since the law presumes that the object of the salary is to maintain the dignity of the office and to enable the holder to perform his duties in a proper manner.[144] This restriction was applied in the eighteenth century to officers in the army,[145] and the common assumption is that it extends to judges[146] and to civil servants generally, such as clerks of the peace[147] and parliamentary counsel to the Treasury,[148] but whether the extension is justified either by the authorities themselves or by the change that has gradually occurred in the status of the civil service is doubtful.[149]

To attract the doctrine the office must be public in the strict sense of that word, and the holder of an office whose emoluments do not derive from national funds, such as a clergyman of the Church of England, is not subject to the restriction.[150]

---

[140] *Blachford v Preston* (1799) 8 Term Rep 89.   [141] *Equity Jurisdiction* s 295.

[142] *Garforth v Fearon* (1787) 1 Hy Bl 328.

[143] *Parkinson v College of Ambulance Ltd and Harrison* [1925] 2 KB 1. See now the Honours (Prevention of Abuses) Act 1925, which makes the parties to such a contract guilty of a misdemeanour.

[144] *Liverpool Corpn v Wright* (1859) John 359.

[145] *Flarty v Odlum* (1790) 3 Term Rep 681; *Barwick v Reade* (1791) 1 Hy Bl 627.

[146] *Arbuthnot v Norton* (1846) 5 Moo PCC 219.

[147] *Palmer v Bate* (1821) 2 Brod & Bing 673.

[148] *Cooper v Reilly* (1829) 2 Sim 560. For the view that this decision and those cited in the two preceding notes are not conclusive, see Logan 61 LQR 241 at 247–248.

[149] The authorities are closely and critically reviewed by Logan 61 LQR 241.

[150] *Re Mirams* [1891] 1 QB 594.

f A contract to defraud the revenue

There is a clear infringement of the doctrine of public policy if it is apparent, either directly from the terms of the contract or indirectly from other circumstances, that the design of one or both of the parties is to defraud the revenue, whether national[151] or local.[152] In *Miller v Karlinski*, for instance.[153]

> The terms of a contract of employment were that the employee should receive a salary of £10 weekly and repayment of his expenses, but that he should be entitled to include in his expenses account the amount of income tax due in respect of his weekly salary.

In an action brought by him to recover ten weeks' arrears of salary and £21 2s 8d for expenses it was divulged that about £17 of this latter sum represented his liability for income tax. It was held that the contract was illegal, since it constituted a fraud upon the revenue. No action lay to recover even arrears of salary, for in such a case the illegal stipulation is not severable from the lawful agreement to pay the salary.[154]

It is doubtful whether the well-known case of *Alexander v Rayson*[155] exemplifies this principle. The facts were these:

> The plaintiff agreed to let a service flat to the defendant at an annual rent of £1,200. This transaction was expressed in two documents, one a lease of the premises at a rent of £450 a year, the other an agreement by the plaintiff to render certain specified services for an annual sum of £750. It was alleged that his object was to produce only the lease to the Westminster Assessment Committee, and by persuading this body that the premises were worth only £450 a year, to obtain a reduction of their rateable value. The defendant was ignorant of this alleged purpose. The plaintiff ultimately failed to accomplish his fraudulent object. He sued the defendant for the recovery of £300, being a quarter's instalment due under both documents.

The Court of Appeal held that, if the alleged fraud was not disproved by the plaintiff when the trial was resumed in the court of first instance, he could recover neither on the lease nor on the contract.

---

[151] *Miller v Karlinski* (1945) 62 TLR 85; *Napier v National Business Agency Ltd* [1951] 2 All ER 264, 67 LQR 449–451.

[152] *Alexander v Rayson* [1936] 1 KB 169; applied in *Edler v Auerbach* [1950] 1 KB 359, [1949] 2 All ER 692.

[153] Above.

[154] *Napier v National Business Agency Ltd*, above; *Warburton v Birkenhead & Co Ltd* (1951) 102 L Jo 52. It seems that the position may be different where the tax irregularity arises entirely on the initiative of the employer, *Hall v Woolston Hall Leisure Ltd* [2000] 4 All ER 787, though this case can also be explained on the basis that the right not to be discriminated against on the ground of sex is independent of the validity of the contract.

[155] [1936] 1 KB 169.

It is clear that both the agreement and the lease were harmless in themselves and might well have been performed without any fraud on the part of the lessor. In the words of one critic:

> The contract was not one to do an act contrary to the policy of the law (defrauding the revenue); but one to do an act in itself legal but intended by one of the parties to provide a setting for an act contrary to the policy of the law (defrauding the revenue).[156] The case exemplifies the general principle that a contract *ex facie* lawful will be unenforceable by the plaintiff if his intention is to exploit it for an illegal purpose.[157]

This reasoning was approved and applied by Field J in *21st Century Logistic Solutions Ltd v Madysen Ltd.*[158]

3 THE CONSEQUENCE OF ILLEGALITY

A Introduction: the relevance of the state of mind of the parties

Whether the parties are influenced by a guilty intention is inevitably material in estimating the consequences of an illegal contract. Its materiality may be stated in three propositions.

First, if the contract is illegal in its inception, neither party can assert that he did not intend to break the law. Both parties have expressly and clearly agreed to do something that in fact is prohibited at common law, as for example, where a British subject agrees to insure an alien enemy against certain risks. The position is the same if the parties have agreed to do something that is expressly or implicitly forbidden by statute.[159] In both these cases, the contract is intrinsically and inevitably illegal, and, so far as consequences are concerned, no allowance is made for innocence. The British subject, for instance, may well be ignorant that it is unlawful to contract with an alien enemy, but none the less he will be precluded by the maxim *ignorantia juris haud excusat* from relying upon his ignorance.[160] The very contract is unlawful in its formation.

Secondly, if the contract is *ex facie* lawful, but both parties intend to exploit it for an illegal purpose, it is illegal in its inception despite its innocuous appearance. Both parties intend to accomplish an unlawful end and both are remediless. This is true, for instance, of an agreement to let a flat if there is a common intention to use it for immoral purposes.

Thirdly, if the contract is lawful in its formation, but one party alone intends to exploit it for an illegal purpose, the law not unnaturally takes the view that the

---

[156] Furmston 16 U of Toronto LJ 267 at 287. [157] Pp 506 ff, below.
[158] [2004] 2 Lloyd's Rep 92. [159] *Re Mahmoud and Ispahani* [1921] 2 KB 716.
[160] *Waugh v Morris* (1873) LR 8 QB 202 at 208, *per curiam*, as explained in *J M Allan (Merchandising) v Cloke* [1963] 2 QB 340, [1963] 2 All ER 258.

innocent party need not be adversely affected by the guilty intention of the other.[161] This has been frequently stressed by the judges. In one case in 1810, for instance, the plaintiffs, acting on behalf of a Russian owner, had insured goods on a vessel already en route from St Petersburg and had paid the premium. The contract was made after war had broken out between Russia and England, but the fact was not known, and could not have been known to the plaintiffs. The ship was seized by the Russians and taken back to St Petersburg. The plaintiffs succeeded in an action for the recovery of the premium.[162] Lord Ellenborough, after remarking that the insurance would have been illegal in its inception had the plaintiffs known of the outbreak of war, said:

> But here the plaintiffs had no knowledge of the commencement of hostilities by Russia, when they effected this insurance; and, therefore no fault is imputable to them for entering into the contract; and there is no reason why they should not recover back the premiums which they have paid for an insurance from which, without any fault imputable to themselves, they could never have derived any benefit.[163]

Whether a party is innocent or guilty in this respect depends upon whether 'he is himself implicated in the illegality',[164] or more precisely whether he has participated in the furtherance of the illegal intention.[165] If, for instance, A lets a flat to B, a woman whom he knows to be a prostitute, the very contract will be unlawful if he knows that B's object is to use the premises for immoral purposes,[166] but this will not be the case if all that he is aware of is B's mode of life, for a reasonable person might not necessarily infer that the purpose of the letting was to further immorality.[167] Even a prostitute must have a home.

Perhaps the best known case on this subject so far as illegality at common law is concerned, is *Pearce v Brooks*,[168] where the facts were as follows:

> The plaintiffs agreed to supply the defendant with a new miniature brougham on hire until the purchase money should be paid by instalments during a period that was not to exceed twelve months. The defendant was a prostitute and she undoubtedly intended to use the carriage, which was of a somewhat intriguing

---

[161] See, eg, *Oom v Bruce* (1810) 12 East 225; *Clay v Yates* (1856) 1 H & N 73 at 80; *Pearce v Brooks* (1866) LR 1 Exch 213 at 217, 221; *Alexander v Rayson* [1936] 1 KB 169 at 182; *Re Trepca Mines Ltd (No 2)* [1963] Ch 199 at 220–221, [1962] 3 All ER 351 at 356. If the agreement is legal in its inception, the mere fact that it *could* be illegally performed is no ground of invalidity: *Laurence v Lexcourt Holding Ltd* [1978] 2 All ER 810, [1978] 1 WLR 1128.

[162] *Oom v Bruce* (1810) 12 East 225.   [163] Ibid at 226.

[164] *Scott v Brown, Doering, McNab & Co Ltd* [1892] 2 QB 724 at 728, per Lindley LJ.

[165] *Re Trepca Mines Ltd (No 2)* [1963] Ch 199, [1962] 3 All ER 351; *J M Allan (Merchandising) Ltd v Cloke* [1963] 2 QB 340 at 348. *Belmont Finance Corpn Ltd v Williams Furniture Ltd* [1979] Ch 250, [1979] 1 All ER 118.

[166] *Girardy v Richardson* (1793) 1 Esp 13. See p 476, above.

[167] *Crisp v Churchill* (1794) cited in 1 Bos & P at 340. In practice the size of the rent may be a very good guide to the landlord's state of mind.

[168] (1866) LR 1 Exch 213.

nature, as a lure to hesitant clients. One of the two plaintiffs was aware of her mode of life, but there was no direct evidence that either of them knew of the use to which she intended to put the carriage. The jury, however, found that the purpose of the woman was to use the carriage as part of her display to attract men and that the plaintiffs were aware of her design. On this finding, Bramwell B gave judgment for the defendant in an action brought against her to recover a sum due under the contract.

It was held on appeal that there was sufficient evidence to support the finding of the jury. The Court of Exchequer Chamber was satisfied on the evidence that the plaintiffs were not only aware of the defendant's intention, but were even guilty of some complicity in her provocative scheme.

In order to emphasise the distinction between innocence and guilt that affects this branch of the law, the precise consequences of an illegal contract will now be detailed under two separate heads, namely: the consequence where a contract is illegal in its inception; the consequence where a contract lawful in its inception is later exploited illegally or is illegally performed.

B The consequence where the contract is illegal in its inception

The general principle, founded on public policy, is that any transaction that is tainted by illegality in which both parties are equally involved is beyond the pale of the law. No person can claim any right or remedy whatsoever under an illegal transaction in which he has participated.[169] *Ex turpi causa non oritur actio.* The court is bound to veto the enforcement of a contract once it knows that it is illegal, whether the knowledge comes from the statement of the guilty party or from outside sources.[170] Even the defendant can successfully plead the *turpis causa*, and though his 'defence is very dishonest'[171] and 'seems only worthy of the Pharisee who shook himself free of his natural obligations by saying Corban,[172] it is allowed for the reasons given by Lord Mansfield in *Holman v Johnson*:

> The objection, that a contract is immoral or illegal as between plaintiff and defendant, sounds at all times very ill in the mouth of the defendant. It is not for his sake, however, that the objection is ever allowed; but it is found in general principles of policy, which the defendant has the advantage of, contrary to the real justice, as between him and the plaintiff, by accident, if I may say so. The principle of public policy is this: *ex dolo malo non oritur actio.* No Court will lend its aid to a man who founds his cause of action upon an immoral or an illegal act. If, from the plaintiff's own stating or otherwise, the cause of action appear to arise *ex turpi causa,*

---

[169] *Gordon v Metropolitan Police Chief Comr* [1910] 2 KB 1080 at 1098, per Buckley LJ.

[170] *Re Mahmoud and Ispahani* [1921] 2 KB 716 at 729, per Scrutton LJ.

[171] *Thomson v Thomson* (1802) 7 Ves 470 at 473, per Sir William Grant MR.

[172] The words of Lord Dunedin in *Sinclair v Brougham* [1914] AC 398 at 436, adapted to the present context by Street *Law of Gaming* 464.

or the transgression of a positive law of this country, then the Court says he has no right to be assisted. It is upon that ground the Court goes; not for the sake of the defendant, but because they will not lend their aid to such a plaintiff. So if the plaintiff and defendant were to change sides, and the defendant was to bring his action against the plaintiff, the latter would then have the advantage of it; for where both are equally in fault *potior est conditio defendentis.*[173]

The practical application of this general principle must now be stated in some detail.

a The contract is void

A contract that is illegal as formed and is therefore void *ab initio* is treated by the law as if it had not been made at all.[174] It is totally void, and no remedy is available to either party. No action lies for damages, for an account of profits or for a share of expenses. Thus, in the case of an illegal contract for the sale of goods, the buyer, even though he has paid the price, cannot sue for non-delivery; the seller who has made delivery cannot recover the price. A servant cannot recover arrears of salary under an illegal contract of employment.[175] In the case of an illegal lease, the landlord cannot recover the rent or damages for the breach of any other covenant.[176] The position is the same not only where a contract is prohibited at common law on grounds of public policy, but also where its very formation is prohibited by statute. An apt illustration is afforded by *Re Mahmoud and Ispahani*[177] where the facts were these:

> The plaintiff agreed to sell linseed oil to the defendant, who refused to take delivery and was sued for non-acceptance of the goods. A statutory order provided that no person should buy or sell certain specified articles, including linseed, unless he was licensed to do so. Before the conclusion of the contract, the defendant untruthfully alleged that he held a licence and the plaintiff, who himself was licensed, believed the allegation.

Once it was established that each party was forbidden by statute to enter into the contract, the court had no option but to enforce the prohibition even though the defendant relied upon his own illegality. The honest belief of the plaintiff that the defendant held a licence was irrelevant.[178]

Again, an award made by an arbitrator in respect of a prohibited contract will be set aside by the court.[179] A builder who does work at a cost exceeding the sum authorised by statute cannot recover the excess,[180] and if, having done both authorised and

---

[173] (1775) 1 Cowp 341 at 343.
[174] *Mogul Steamship Co v McGregor, Gow & Co* [1892] AC 25 at 39, per Lord Halsbury.
[175] *Miller v Karlinski* (1945) 62 TLR 85.
[176] *Alexander v Rayson* [1936] 1 KB 169.   [177] [1921] 2 KB 716.
[178] Distinguish the case when a contract *lawful* in its formation is performed in an illegal manner by one of the parties; pp 506 ff, below.
[179] *David Taylor & Son Ltd v Barnett Trading Co* [1953] 1 All ER 843, [1953] 1 WLR 562.
[180] *Bostel Bros Ltd v Hurlock* [1949] 1 KB 74, [1948] 2 All ER 312; *Dennis & Co Ltd v Munn* [1949] 2 KB 327, [1949] 1 All ER 616.

unauthorised work, he receives payment under the contract generally, he cannot appropriate the sum to the unlawful work.[181] In all cases where a contract is illegal in its formation, neither party can circumvent the rule—*ex turpi causa non oritur actio*— by pleading ignorance of the law.[182]

Although a contract is illegal in its formation and therefore void, the Court of Appeal has now held that the ownership of goods may pass to the buyer under an illegal contract of sale even if both parties are *in pari delicto*.[183] This decision requires to be examined with some particularity.

Since an illegal contract is totally void, the inescapable conclusion would seem to be that the ownership of movables cannot pass by virtue of the contract itself if this arises *ex turpi causa* and if both parties to it are *in pari delicto*. *Nil posse creari de nilo*.[184]

If, therefore, the ownership is to pass at all, this must be affected by some independent rule of law extraneous to the so-called but abortive contract. It is true that in the case of a gift the ownership of goods may be transferred by delivery, provided that this is what the parties intend. But since this intention is one of the decisive elements of the transaction, it would seem logical to insist that it must be disregarded if it is tainted by illegality.[185] In 1960, however, Lord Denning, giving the opinion of the Privy Council in *Singh v Ali*[186] expressed a view which it is respectfully suggested goes beyond previous statements of the law.

> There are many cases which show that when two persons agree together in a conspiracy to effect a fraudulent or illegal purpose—and one of them transfers property to the other in pursuance of the conspiracy—then, so soon as the contract is executed and the fraudulent or illegal purpose is achieved, the property (be it absolute or special) which has been transferred by the one to the other remains vested in the transferee, notwithstanding its illegal origin . . . The reason is because the transferor, having fully achieved his unworthy end, cannot be allowed to turn round and repudiate the means by which he did it—he cannot throw over the transfer.[187]

This statement invites three comments.

Firstly, the transfer of ownership is here said to depend not upon delivery, but upon the execution of the contract. A contract is executed as soon as one party has fully performed his side of the bargain, even if it still remains in whole or in part to be performed by the other party. A contract of sale, therefore, is executed by the seller

---

[181] *A Smith & Son (Bognor Regis) Ltd v Walker* [1952] 2 QB 319, [1952] 1 All ER 1007.

[182] *J M Allan (Merchandise) Ltd v Cloke* [1963] 2 QB 340, [1963] 2 All ER 258. See also Higgins 25 MLR 149.

[183] *Belvoir Finance Co Ltd v Stapleton* [1971] 1 QB 210, [1970] 3 All ER 664.

[184] Lucretius *De Rerum Natura* i 155.

[185] See, however, an obiter dictum by Parke B in *Simpson v Nicholls* (1838) 3 M & W 240, as revised (1839) 5 M & W 702, where he was commenting upon the earlier case of *Williams v Paul* (1830) 6 Bing 653.

[186] [1960] AC 167, [1960] 1 All ER 269.

[187] [1960] AC at 176, [1960] 1 All ER at 272.

when he delivers the goods to the buyer; and in this context at least delivery and execution are synonymous.

Secondly, Lord Denning cited, as authority for his statement, an obiter dictum of Parke B in *Scarfe v Morgan*.[188] In that case the court was concerned with the validity of a bailee's lien which, it had been argued, was illegal and void. The lien was in fact held to be untainted by illegality. But Parke B said that even if it had been illegal, it would still exist 'because the contract was executed and the special property[189] had passed by the delivery of the chattel to the defendant. The maxim would apply— *in pari delicto potior est conditio possidents.*' It will be seen that this dictum of Baron Parke was confined to the case of a 'special property' in the chattel, but that in *Singh v Ali* it was extended to include the 'general property'. Thus the vital distinction between ownership and the limited interest which a bailee might enjoy in the chattel was obscured.

Thirdly, as between the parties themselves, the question whether the property has passed is academic, for if the contract is illegal and if the parties are *in pari delicto* neither can establish a cause of action against the other without disclosing his own wrongdoing. So if, in an illegal contract of sale, the seller has delivered the goods he cannot recover them and for this purpose it matters not whether the seller or the buyer is the owner of the goods. Conversely, if the seller has not delivered the goods, the buyer cannot demand them whether he is the owner or not. But if an innocent third party becomes involved in the cycle of events, it is vital to determine which of the original parties is the owner of the contractual subject matter. This is well illustrated by *Belvoir Finance Co Ltd v Stapleton*,[190] the facts of which were as follows:

> The plaintiffs bought three cars from dealers, paid for them and let them on hire-purchase terms to the Belgravia Car Co, who kept a fleet of cars for letting out on hire to the public. The plaintiffs never took delivery of the three cars in question, which went directly from the dealers to the Belgravia Car Co. Both the contract of sale between the dealers and the plaintiffs and the hire-purchase contracts between the plaintiffs and the Belgravia Car Co were illegal to the knowledge of all three parties as contravening statutory regulations. The Belgravia Car Co, fraudulently and in breach of the hire-purchase contracts, sold the three cars to innocent purchasers. One of these sales was effected by the defendant, the assistant manager of the Belgravia Car Co, and the plaintiffs now sued him personally in conversion.

To succeed in this action the plaintiffs had to show that the ownership of the car was vested in them at the time of the conversion. They had therefore to prove that despite the illegality of the original contract of sale, they had acquired and still enjoyed the 'general property' in the car. The Court of Appeal decided this issue in their favour. Lord Denning MR cited his statement in *Singh v Ali*[191] and continued:

---

[188] (1838) 4 M & W 270.   [189] That is, possession.
[190] [1971] 1 QB 210, [1970] 3 All ER 664.
[191] P 491, above.

> Although the plaintiffs obtained the car under a contract which was illegal, nevertheless, inasmuch as the contract was executed and the property passed, the car belonged to the finance company and they can claim it.[192]

It is submitted with respect that this decision is contrary to the established principles which determine the effect of illegality. It will be observed, moreover, that in the instant case the car had never been delivered to the plaintiffs. The court endeavoured to counter this formidable objection by falling back upon the rules for the passing of property contained in sections 17 and 18 of the Sale of Goods Act 1893. These rules are based essentially upon the intention of the parties as disclosed by their conduct, the terms of the contract and the circumstances of the case. But they clearly envisage the existence of a valid contract and can scarcely operate where the parties have deliberately sought to implement an agreement that is vitiated by illegality.

The Lords Justices expressed the opinion that, were the finance company to be precluded by the illegality of the contract from maintaining the action, any stranger would be free to seize the car with impunity since there would be nobody able to establish a legal title against him. This would be to recognise a right of confiscation. It is submitted with respect, however, that the suggestion is not well founded. The person who happens to be in possession of the car after and as a result of the illegal contract (as in the instant case the Belgravia Car Co or the ultimate purchaser), would be able to maintain trespass against a wrongful intruder. In an action of trespass, the existing possession of the plaintiff, even though held without title, is conclusive evidence of his right to possession against a wrongdoer. The latter cannot set up the better title of a third person, unless he shows that he acted with the authority of that third person.[193] The position is the same in conversion, unless the wrongdoer shows that he acted with the authority of a third person who has a better right to possession than the plaintiff.[194]

In *Saunders v Edwards*[195] the defendant entered into a contract to sell the lease of a flat to the plaintiffs. In the course of the negotiations he fraudulently represented that the flat included a roof terrace. In fact, he had improperly created an access onto a flat roof outside the flat over which he had no rights. The plaintiffs agreed to take the flat and it is clear that if these had been the only facts, the plaintiffs would have had an action for fraud when they discovered the true state of affairs. However, when the conveyance was completed, it was agreed between the plaintiffs and the defendant that the purchase price of £45,000 should be apportioned as to £40,000 for the flat and as to £5,000 for some chattels which were being thrown in. Both parties knew that the chattels were not worth anything like £5,000. When sued for his fraud, the defendant argued that the plaintiffs' action was barred because of their participation in this conveyancing scheme so as to minimise their liability to stamp duty. The Court

[192] [1971] 1 QB 210 at 218, [1970] 3 All ER 664 at 667.
[193] *Jeffries v Great Western Rly Co* (1856) 5 E & B 802.
[194] Ibid. [195] [1987] 2 All ER 651, [1987] 1 WLR 1116.

of Appeal agreed that the plaintiffs' behaviour in regard to the apportionment of the price of the flat and the chattels was improper and that they would not have been entitled to enforce the contract for the sale of the flat. The court took the view however that the plaintiffs' action in respect of the fraud was wholly separate from the contract and should therefore succeed.

Similarly, in *Euro-Diam Ltd v Bathurst*[196] the plaintiffs had agreed to sell diamonds to German buyers which they had insured with the defendant. While the diamonds were still at the plaintiffs' risk they were stolen and they claimed on the insurance policy. There was no impropriety in connection with the policy but it appeared that in order to oblige the German buyers the plaintiffs had supplied an invoice stating the value of the diamonds to be significantly less than the true value so as to enable the German buyers to reduce or exclude payment of German customs duty. The insurers argued that this prevented the plaintiffs from enforcing their rights under the insurance contract. The Court of Appeal rejected this conclusion. There had been no deception of the insurers; there was no causal connection between the policy of insurance and the undervaluation of the diamonds in the sale contract and the plaintiffs themselves had made no profit from the transaction.

Both these cases can be said to turn on the plaintiffs' course of action being independent of the contract which was illegal. They can also be seen to exemplify a robust attitude by the courts to arguments of this kind. In both cases the defendants were devoid of merits and the delinquencies of the plaintiffs were relatively small compared to the loss they would suffer if the defendants' argument had been allowed to succeed.

b Money paid and chattels or land transferred are irrecoverable

Neither party can recover what he has given to the other under an illegal contract if in order to substantiate his claim he is driven to disclose the illegality.[197] The maxim *in pari delicto potior est conditio defendentis* applies and the defendant may keep what he has been given. If, for instance, a seller sues for the recovery of goods sold and delivered under an illegal contract he will fail, for to justify his claim he must necessarily disclose his own iniquity. Thus in *Taylor v Chester*:[198]

> The plaintiff deposited with the defendant the half of a £50 note as a pledge to secure the payment of money due for a debauch held by the plaintiff and divers prostitutes at the defendant's brothel.

An action of detinue, based upon a refusal by the defendant to redeliver the note, was dismissed, for the plaintiff could not impugn the validity of the pledge without revealing the immoral character of the contract.

---

[196] [1990] 1 QB 1, [1988] 2 All ER 23. See also *Thackwell v Barclays Bank plc* [1986] 1 All ER 676.
[197] *Scott v Brown, Doering, McNab & Co* [1892] 2 QB 724 at 734, per A L Smith LJ; *Chettiar v Chettiar* [1962] AC 294, [1962] All ER 494.
[198] (1869) LR 4 QB 309.

The result is that gains and losses remain where they have accrued or fallen. If, for instance, a scheme to defraud X, concocted by A and B, succeeds, and the money is obtained by B, no action for an account or recovery lies at the suit of A,[199] as was once solemnly adjudged in a case where one highwayman sued another for an account of their plunder.[200] The general position is well illustrated by *Parkinson v College of Ambulance Ltd and Harrison*,[201] where the facts were these:

> The secretary of the defendant charity fraudulently represented to the plaintiff that the charity was in a position to divert the foundation of honour in his direction and to procure him at least a knighthood, if he would make an adequate donation. After a certain amount of bargaining, the plaintiff paid £3,000 to the charity and undertook to do more when the knighthood was forthcoming. He did not, however, receive any honour and he sued for the return of the money as had and received to his use.

It was held by Lush J that the action must fail. The transaction was manifestly illegal to the knowledge of the plaintiff. He could sue neither for money had and received for the recovery of damages, nor could he repudiate the contract and regain his money on the plea that the transaction was executory.

Property recoverable if disclosure of illegality not essential to cause of action
A plaintiff, however, may recover money, chattels or land transferred under an illegal contract to the defendant, if he can frame a cause of action entirely independent of the contract, for in these circumstances he is not compelled to disclose the illegality. 'Any rights which he may have irrespective of his illegal interest will, of course, be recognised and enforced.'[202]

Suppose, for instance, that a lease for ten years is made by A to B for a purpose known by both parties to be illegal. A cannot sue for the recovery of rent, since to substantiate his claim he must necessarily rely upon the illegal transaction.[203] Nor, it is apprehended, can he recover possession of the land before expiry of the agreed term. If he attempted to do so, B would allege possession by virtue of the lease, the illegality of which would preclude A from enforcing the covenant for the payment of rent.[204] But once the term of ten years has expired, A has an independent cause of action by virtue of his ownership. Though he cannot be allowed to recover what he has transferred in pursuance of the illegal transaction, yet he cannot be denied the right of ownership

---

[199] *Sykes v Beadon* (1879) 11 ChD 170; *Berg v Sadler and Moore* [1937] 2 KB 158.

[200] *Everet v Williams* (1725) cited in Lindley *The Law of Partnership* (13th edn) p 130n; *Sykes v Beadon*, above, at 195–196, per Jessel MR; 9 LQR 197.

[201] [1925] 2 KB 1.

[202] *Scott v Brown, Doering, McNab & Co* [1892] 2 QB 724 at 729, per Lindley LJ. Gooderson [1958] CLJ 199. *Iraqi Ministry of Defence v Arcepey Shipping Co SA* [1981] QB 65, [1980] 1 All ER 480.

[203] *Gas Light and Coke Co v Turner* (1840) 6 Bing NC 324.

[204] *Alexander v Rayson* [1936] 1 KB 169 at 196–197, [1935] All ER 185 at 193, *per curiam*. See Salmond and Williams *Principles of the Law of Contracts* p 347, nd.

which he has not transferred.[205] Once the illegal, but temporary, title has ceased, he can rely upon his prior and lawful title.

The principle, that a plaintiff can recover what he has transferred under an illegal contract if he can found his action upon some independent and lawful ground, was applied by the Privy Council in *Amar Singh v Kulubya*[206] on the following facts:

> A statutory ordinance in Uganda prohibited the sale or lease of 'Mailo' land by an African to a non-African except with the written consent of the Governor. Without obtaining this consent, the plaintiff, an African, agreed to lease such land of which he was the registered owner to the defendant, an Indian, for one year and thereafter on a yearly basis. The agreement, therefore, was void for illegality, and no leasehold interest vested in the defendant. After the defendant had been in possession for several years, the plaintiff gave him seven weeks' notice to quit and ultimately sued him for recovery of the land.

He succeeded. His claim to possession was based not upon the agreement, to the illegality of which on his own admission he had been a party, but on the independent and untainted ground of his registered ownership. He was not forced to have recourse to the agreement.[207]

This decision illustrated the familiar statement of du Parcq LJ in an earlier case when delivering the judgment of the court:

> Prima facie, a man is entitled to his own property, and it is not a general principle of our law (as was suggested) that when one man's goods have got into another's possession in consequence of some unlawful dealings between them, the true owner can never be allowed to recover those goods by an action. The necessity of such a principle to the interests and advancement of public policy is certainly not obvious.[208]

In *Tinsley v Milligan*[209]

> The parties, who were lovers, jointly purchased a house which was registered in the name of Tinsley as the sole legal owner. The house was used by the parties as a lodging house which was run jointly by them and which provided most of their income. The parties had registered the house in the sole name of Tinsley so as to enable Milligan to make fraudulent claims for benefit to the Department of Social Security. The money obtained from these deceptions formed part of the parties' shared income. After this practice had gone on for some time, Milligan made a clean breast of it to the Department of Social Security and the matter was resolved

---

[205] *Jajbhay v Cassim* [1939] App D 537 at 557.

[206] [1964] AC 142, [1963] 3 All ER 499; criticised Cornish 27 MLR 225.

[207] The Privy Council considered that the notice of seven weeks to quit the land, which was insufficient to determine a yearly tenancy was not referable to the illegal agreements: [1964] AC 142 at 150.

[208] *Bowmakers Ltd v Barnet Instruments Ltd* [1945] KB 65 at 70.

[209] [1993] 3 All ER 65.

to the satisfaction of the Department without prosecution. Thereafter, Milligan only claimed benefit to which she was properly entitled. In due course, the parties quarrelled and Tinsley moved out. Tinsley then started an action for possession on the basis that the house was solely hers. Milligan counterclaimed for an order for sale and a declaration that the house was held by Tinsley on trust for the parties in equal shares.

On these facts it would, but for the deception practised on the Department of Social Security, have been clear that Milligan was entitled to the relief which she sought. Tinsley argued that Milligan should be denied relief either on the basis of the maxim *ex turpi causa oritur non actio* or on the equitable principle that he who comes to equity must come with clean hands. In both cases, the thrust of the argument was that by choosing to put the house in Tinsley's name in order to obtain benefits to which she was not legally entitled, Milligan had debarred herself from asserting the equitable rights which she would otherwise have had to the property. The Court of Appeal had held that Milligan's claim should succeed on the basis that the improper conduct by Milligan was not sufficiently serious to merit the severe penalty which would be inflicted by depriving her of her interest in the house. The House of Lords were agreed that the test used by the Court of Appeal was not correct and that the result of the case could not depend on a balancing exercise between the impropriety of Milligan and the severity of the penalty imposed or whether any result which arose out of the balancing exercise would shock the public conscience.

Nevertheless, the House of Lords was divided as to the result in the present case. The majority view of Lord Jauncey, Lord Lowry and Lord Browne-Wilkinson was most fully expressed by the latter. He stated the general principles as follows:

(1) Property in chattels and land can pass under a contract which is illegal and therefore would have been unenforceable as a contract.

(2) A plaintiff can at law enforce property rights so acquired provided that he does not need to rely on the illegal contract for any purpose other than providing the basis of his claim to a property right.

(3) It is irrelevant that the illegality of the underlying agreement was either pleaded or emerged in evidence: if the plaintiff has acquired legal title under the illegal contract that is enough.[210]

He went on to deny that there was any significant difference in the general principles between common law and equity. It was clear that Milligan was putting forward an equitable claim since the sole legal title was in Tinsley. However, Milligan's equitable claim did not depend in any way on the fraud practised on the Department of Social Security. It depended only on the presumption of resulting trust which arose from

---

[210] Ibid at 86.

the fact that Milligan had put up half of the purchase price of the house and that the relationship between Tinsley and Milligan was not such as to give rise to a presumption of advancement. Of course, it follows on this line of reasoning that if the relationship between Tinsley and Milligan had been such as to give rise to a presumption of advancement then the result would have been different since Milligan would then have needed to rely on the fraudulent purpose to explain why the presumption of advancement should be negated. The minority view was that the matter should still be governed by the principle stated by Lord Eldon in *Muckleston v Brown*[211] where he said:

> The Plaintiff stating, he had been guilty of a fraud upon the law, to evade, to disappoint, the provision of the Legislature, to which he is bound to submit, and coming to equity to be relieved against his own act, and the defence being dishonest, between the two species of dishonesty the Court would not act; but would say 'Let the estate lie, where it falls'.

In *Tribe v Tribe*[212] the Court of Appeal had to consider the effect of *Tinsley v Milligan* in a situation where there was a presumption of resulting trust.

> The plaintiff owned 459 out of 500 shares in a family company and was the tenant of two leasehold premises which were occupied by the company as licensee. In 1987 the landlords of those premises served schedules of dilapidations on the plaintiff requiring him to carry out substantial repairs. The plaintiff was advised by his solicitor that he was facing the possibility of heavy payments. In an effort to put resources outside the reach of the landlords, the plaintiff transferred his shares to the defendant, who was one of his sons. The transfer was expressed to be for a consideration of £78,030 but this sum was never paid nor was it ever intended to be paid. In fact, the payments to the landlords never eventuated because one of the landlords accepted the surrender of the lease and the other landlord sold the reversion. The plaintiff asked for the shares back but his son refused to redeliver them. When the father brought an action, the son argued that there was a presumption of advancement in his favour and that the father could not rebut the presumption of advancement without revealing his illegal purpose in making the transfer in the first place.

This reasoning was rejected by the Court of Appeal. The Court held that one of the major exceptions to the *in pari delicto* rule arose where the transferor had repented of the transaction before it was carried into effect—the so called *locus poenitentiae*. In this case the illegal purpose was to defraud creditors but no creditors had ever been defrauded. Accordingly, it was not too late for the father to change his mind and recover the shares from his son.

---

[211] (1801) 6 Ves 52 at 68 and 69, [1775–1802] All ER Rep 501 at 506.
[212] [1995] 4 All ER 236; [1996] CLJ 23.

A similar, though perhaps more dubious decision was given in *Bowmakers Ltd v Barnet Instruments Ltd* upon the following facts:[213]

> S sold machine tools to the plaintiffs. This sale was illegal, since it contravened an Order made by the Minister of Supply under the Defence of the Realm Regulations. The plaintiffs delivered the tools to the defendants under three separate hire-purchase agreements which were assumed by the Court of Appeal to be themselves illegal. The defendants, after paying only a few of the instalments due under the contracts, sold the tools delivered under the first and third agreements and refused the demand of the plaintiffs to redeliver those that were the subject matter of the second agreement.

Judgment was given for the plaintiffs in their action to recover damages for the conversion of the tools.

In considering this decision it is necessary to distinguish the first and third agreements—where the defendants had wrongfully sold the goods—from the second—where they had retained them contrary to the demand of the plaintiffs.

The significant feature of the wrongful sales was that they constituted an act of conversion which *ipso facto* terminated the bailment.[214] The plaintiffs might therefore argue that there was no longer any existing contract upon which the defendants could found a possessory right. The right to immediate possession had automatically revested in the plaintiffs. Could it not thus be said that owing to the termination of the bailment the plaintiffs had an independent cause of action in virtue of their admitted ownership? The defendants, on the other hand, might argue that they had acquired effective possession under the bailment and that the plaintiffs were driven to rely upon that illegal transaction in order to show that the sale was a breach of the contractual terms, just as a lessor who alleged the termination of a lease for condition broken would be required to prove the existence of a proviso for re-entry.

The Court of Appeal preferred the first line of reasoning. It was completely irrelevant that the chattels had originally come into the possession of the defendants by virtue of the illegal contract. That contract was now defunct. It formed no part of the cause of action. Thus, with the disappearance of the only transaction that could restrict their rights, the plaintiffs could base their claim to possession solely upon their ownership of the chattels.

While few would dispute this conclusion and the limitation thus put upon the application of the maxim *ex turpi causa non oritur actio*, it is a little difficult to agree that the second agreement was susceptible of the same *ratio decidendi*. In the case of this agreement the cause of action was the refusal of the defendants to comply with the demand for the return of the goods. Since the effective possession had passed to them

---

[213] [1945] KB 65, [1944] 2 All ER 579. See Hamson 10 CLJ 249; Coote 35 MLR 38; Teh 26 NILQ 1; Stewart 1 JCL 134.

[214] *North Central Wagon and Finance Co Ltd v Graham* [1950] 2 KB 7, [1950] 1 All ER 780.

by virtue of its delivery, the sole justification for this demand was their failure to pay the agreed instalments. The plaintiffs, therefore, were inevitably driven back to the contract in order to prove the amounts of the instalments, the dates at which they were due and the agreed effect of their non-payment. This part of the decision, therefore, seems open to question.

Two exceptions to the ban on recoverability

There are two exceptions to the general rule that a party cannot recover what he had given to the other party under an illegal contract. These are (a) where the parties are not *in pari delicto*, and (b) where the plaintiff repents before the contract has been performed.

(a) Where the parties are not in pari delicto If the parties to an illegal contract are not *in pari delicto*, the court in certain circumstances will allow the less blameworthy to recover what he may have transferred to the other. This relief is granted to the plaintiff upon proof that he has been the victim of fraud, duress or oppression at the hands of the defendant, or that the latter stood in a fiduciary position towards him and abused it.[215] Where, for instance, the plaintiff has effected an insurance which in fact is illegal but which was represented to him by the insurer as lawful, he will be entitled to recover the premiums which he has paid if the representation was fraudulent,[216] but not if it was not.[217] A common illustration of want of delictual parity is oppression. 'It can never be predicated as *par delictum* where one holds the rod and the other bows to it.'[218] For instance, in *Smith v Cuff*,[219] the defendant, a creditor of the plaintiff, agreed with the other creditors to accept a composition of ten shillings in the pound, but he consented to this only after he had secretly arranged that the plaintiff should give him a promissory note for the remainder of his debt. The note was given, negotiated to a third party and its amount paid by the plaintiff. It was held that, since there had been oppression on one side and submission on the other, the plaintiff was entitled to recover the amount from the defendant. In a later case where the facts were similar, Cockburn CJ said: 'It is true that both are *in delicto*, because the act is a fraud upon the other creditors, but it is not *par delictum*, because the one has the power to dictate, the other no alternative but to submit.'[220]

Another type of case where the parties are not regarded as equally delictual is where the contract is rendered illegal by a statute, the object of which is to protect one class of persons from the machinations of another class, as for example where it forbids a landlord to take a premium from a prospective tenant. Here, the duty of observing the law is placed squarely upon the shoulders of the landlord, and the protected person,

---

[215] *Harse v Pearl Life Assurance Co* [1904] 1 KB 558 at 564. *Shelley v Paddock* [1980] QB 348, [1980] 1 All ER 1009; Buckley 94 LQR 484.

[216] *Hughes v Liverpool Victoria Legal Friendly Society* [1916] 2 KB 482.

[217] *Harse v Pearl Life Assurance Co*, above.

[218] *Smith v Cuff* (1817) 6 M & S 160 at 165, per Lord Ellenborough.   [219] (1817) 6 M & S 160.

[220] *Atkinson v Denby* (1862) 7 H & N 934 at 936.

the tenant, may recover an illegal premium in an action for money had and received, even if the statute omits to afford him this remedy either expressly or by implication.[221] In the words of Lord Mansfield:

> Where contracts or transactions are prohibited by positive statutes, for the sake of protecting one set of men from another set of men; the one, from their situation and condition being liable to be oppressed and imposed upon by the other; there, the parties are not *in pari delicto*; and in furtherance of these statutes, the person injured after the transaction is finished and completed, may bring his action and defeat the contract.[222]

(b) Where party to executory contract repents before performance.[223] The second exception to the ban on restitution recognises the virtue of repentance in the case of a contract which is still executory. A party to such a contract, despite its illegality, is allowed a *locus poenitentiae*, and he may recover what he has transferred to his co-contractor, provided that he takes proceedings before the illegal purpose has been substantially performed. If he repents in time, he will be assisted by the court, but in the present state of the authorities it is not clear at what point his repentance is to be regarded as overdue.

The leading case on the subject is *Kearley v Thomson*,[224] where the defendants, who were the solicitors of the petitioning creditor in certain bankruptcy proceedings, agreed neither to appear at the public examination of the bankrupt nor to oppose his discharge in consideration of a sum of money paid to them by the plaintiff. They did not appear at the examination, and before any application had been made for the discharge of the bankrupt they were sued by the plaintiff for the return of the money. The contract was illegal as tending to pervert the course of justice, and it was held that the non-appearance at the examination was a sufficient execution of the illegal purpose to defeat the plaintiff's right to recovery. Fry LJ said:

> I hold, therefore, that where there has been a partial carrying into effect of an illegal purpose in a substantial manner, it is impossible, though there remains something not performed, that the money paid under that illegal contract can be recovered back.[225]

The word 'partial' in this statement must be regarded as qualified by the later word 'substantial', for otherwise it is difficult to reconcile the earlier case of *Taylor v Bowers*.[226] In that case:

---

[221] *Kiriri Cotton Co Ltd v Dewani* [1960] AC 192, [1960] 1 All ER 177, where there was no express provision in the statute that the premium should be recoverable. If there is such a provision, as in *Gray v Southouse* [1949] 2 All ER 1019, the fact that the tenant is *particeps criminis* does not affect his right of recovery. See also *Nash v Halifax Building Society* [1979] Ch 584, [1979] 2 All ER 19.

[222] *Browning v Morris* (1778) 2 Cowp 790 at 792. See *Barclay v Pearson* [1893] 2 Ch 154 at 166–168.

[223] Merkin 97 LQR 420.

[224] (1890) 24 QBD 742. See *Re National Benefit Assurance Co Ltd* [1931] 1 Ch 46; *Harry Parker Ltd v Mason* [1940] 2 KB 590, [1940] 4 All ER 199; *Ouston v Zurowski and Zurowski* [1985] 5 WWR 169. Beatson 91 LQR 313.

[225] Ibid at 747.   [226] (1876) 1 QBD 291.

T, being financially embarrassed and desiring to avoid the seizure of his stock by his creditors, made a fictitious assignment of it to A, and received sham bills of exchange in return. The stock, having been removed, was later mortgaged by A to the defendant without the knowledge of T. The defendant was aware of the unlawful assignment.

It was held that T was entitled to recover his goods. It is clear that the illegal purpose had been *partially* effected, for the creditors, realising that the greater part of T's visible wealth had disappeared with the removal of his stock, would probably abandon any attempt to exact payment by process of law. In the unanimous opinion of seven judges, however, nothing had been done to carry out the illegal purpose beyond the removal of the stock and this was insufficient to defeat the plaintiff. In *Kearley v Thomson*, on the other hand, the fraudulent injury to the creditors had been *substantially* accomplished, for the general body of creditors would be influenced by the abstention of the petitioning creditor from the cross-examination of the debtor.[227]

In *Taylor v Bowers*, Mellish LJ made a statement that is transparently too wide if it is divorced from the facts. He said:

> If money is paid or goods delivered for an illegal purpose, the person who has so paid the money or delivered the goods may recover them back before the illegal purpose is carried out.[228]

If this were correct, it would frequently happen that the mere frustration of his illegal scheme owing to circumstances beyond his control would entitle such a person to recover his property. *Bigos v Bousted*,[229] concerned with statutory illegality, is a case in point.

> A, in contravention of the Exchange Control Act 1947, agreed to supply B with the equivalent of £150 in Italian currency. B, as security for his promise to repay the loan, deposited a share certificate with A. A failed to supply any Italian currency and B sued him for recovery of the certificate.

The statement of Mellish LJ literally construed, would justify recovery, since the illegal purpose had not been carried out. B had in fact received no more Italian money than was permissible by law. He therefore pleaded that he had repented in time. His so-called repentance, however, was 'but want of power to sin', for it is clear that he would gladly have accepted the promised lire had his illegal design not been foiled by A's breach of faith. Pritchard J therefore held that the case was on all fours wit *Alexander v Rayson*[230] and that B's change of heart after his scheme had failed did not bring him within the exception.

---

[227] In *George v Greater Adelaide Land Development Co Ltd* (1929) 43 CLR 91, a decision of the High Court of Australia, Knox CJ, at 100, regarded *Taylor v Bowers* as a case of property deposited with a stakeholder, as to which see n 231, below.

[228] (1876) 1 QBD 291 at 300.

[229] [1951] 1 All ER 92.   [230] [1936] 1 KB 169, [1935] All ER 185; p 486, above.

Another type of case in which recovery can be had despite a partial performance of the illegal purpose is where money has been deposited with a stakeholder under an illegal contract, as for example where competitors in a lottery, such as a missing-word competition, pay entrance fees to the organiser. Here the money is recoverable, not merely before the result has been ascertained, but even after this event, provided that payment has not been made to the winner.[231] In such a case the illegal purpose has obviously been performed by the holding of the lottery, yet it is said that 'the contract is not completely executed until the money has been paid over, and therefore the party may retract at any time before that has been done'.[232]

The truth is that it is difficult to extract from these authorities the precise meaning in the present context of an 'executory' contract. Over a hundred years ago, Fry LJ observed that the principle which forbids the recovery of property delivered under an illegal contract requires reconsideration by the House of Lords.[233] Such reconsideration is still awaited.

c A subsequent or collateral contract, which is founded on or springs from an illegal transaction, is illegal and void [234]

It would be singular if the law were otherwise.[235] It is irrelevant that the new contract is in itself innocuous, or that it formed no part of the original bargain, or that it is executed under seal,[236] or that the illegal transaction out of which it springs has been completed. If money is due from A to B under an illegal transaction and A gives B a bond[237] or a promissory note[238] for the amount owing, neither of these instruments is enforceable by B.

The leading authority is *Fisher v Bridges*,[239] where A agreed to sell to B certain land which was to be used for the purposes of a lottery that was illegal because forbidden by statute. The land was conveyed to B and the price except for £630 was paid. Later, B executed a deed by which he covenanted to pay £630 to A. In an action to enforce this covenant, it was pleaded that the action must fail, since the agreement to sell was made 'to the intent and in order, and for the purpose, as the defendant well knew', that the land when conveyed should be sold by way of an illegal lottery.[240] The Exchequer Chamber, reversing the Court of Queen's Bench, held the plea to be good and dismissed the action.

---

[231] *Barclay v Pearson* [1893] 2 Ch 154; *Greenberg v Cooperstein* [1926] Ch 657 at 665.

[232] *Hastelow v Jackson* (1828) 8 B & C 221 at 226–227, per Littledale J.

[233] *Kearley v Thomson* (1890) 24 QBD 742 at 746. For a critical appraisal of the present state of the law, see Grodecki 74 LQR 254.

[234] *Simpson v Bloss* (1816) 7 Taunt 246; *Redmond v Smith* (1844) 7 Man & G 457; *Geere v Mare* (1863) 2 H & C 339; *Clay v Ray* (1864) 17 CBNS 188.

[235] *Redmond v Smith*, above, at 494, per Tindal J.   [236] *Fisher v Bridges* (1854) 3 E & B 642.

[237] Ibid.   [238] *Jennings v Hammond* (1882) 9 QBD 225.   [239] (1854) 3 E & B 642.

[240] See the report of the case in the court of first instance: (1853) 2 E & B 118.

It is clear that the covenant was given for the payment of the purchase money. It springs from, and is the creature of, the illegal agreement; and, as the law would not enforce the original illegal contract, so neither will it allow the parties to enforce a security for the purchase money, which by the original bargain was tainted with illegality.[241]

In *Fisher v Bridges* the parties to the illegal transaction and to the subsequent contract were the same persons. The question arises, therefore, whether a contract made by a third party in furtherance of the illegal purpose is itself tainted. This was the issue in *Cannan v Bryce*[242] where the court made the solution of this problem turn upon the knowledge of the third party. Did he know that the original contract was illegal?

X had entered into a stock-jobbing contract by which he agreed to pay differences according to the rise and fall of the stock.[243] A statute of 1733 prohibited the practice of stock-jobbing.[244] He borrowed money from Y in order to pay the losses that he ultimately incurred, and by way of security he assigned to Y the proceeds of certain cargoes which he had shipped abroad. X then became bankrupt and his trustee claimed that the cargoes still formed part of the bankrupt estate, since the assignment to Y was illegal.

It was held that the trustee was entitled to judgment. In the words of Abbott CJ 'if it be unlawful for one man to pay, how can it be lawful for another to furnish him with the means of payment?' But the Chief Justice was careful to emphasise that his statement was confined to a case where the third party had full knowledge of the object to which the loan was to be applied.[245]

A similar question arose in *Spector v Ageda*[246] on the following facts.

A memorandum dated 8 September 1967, stated that a Mrs Maxwell, a money-lender, had lent £1,040 to the borrower, to be paid on 8 November with interest at 2% a month. In fact only £1,000 was lent, since interest for two months, amounting to £40, had been added to the principal sum. Such a provision for the payment of compound interest is illegal under the Moneylenders Act 1927.[247] The illegal loan was not repaid on 8 November and Mrs Maxwell sued the borrower in the following February for the recovery of £1,180, the amount then due.

---

[241] (1854) 3 E & B 642, *per curiam* at 649. It is respectfully submitted that in *Belvoir Finance Co Ltd v Cole Ltd* [1969] 2 All ER 904, [1969] 1 WLR 1877, Donaldson J was scarcely justified in holding that the original purchase of the two Triumph cars was not tainted by the illegality of the subsequent hire-purchase transaction. As in *Fisher v Bridges*, the contract of sale was made to the intent and in order that the cars should be bailed by way of hire-purchase transactions which both parties knew were to be effected in a manner contrary to a statutory order. It is a little difficult to subscribe to the view of the learned judge that the two pairs of contracts, though commercially connected, were not legally connected.

[242] (1819) 3 B & Ald 179.   [243] As to contracts for differences, see p 408, above.

[244] 7 Geo 2 c 8; repealed by the Gaming Act 1845.   [245] Ibid at 185.

[246] [1973] Ch 30, [1971] 3 All ER 417. See also *Portland Holdings Ltd v Cameo Motors Ltd* [1966] NZLR 571.

[247] S 7.

At that point the plaintiff entered upon the scene. She was the sister and the solicitor of Mrs Maxwell, but she was now also acting as the solicitor of the borrower. She agreed to advance to the latter £1,180 with interest at 12% per annum. She honoured this agreement and the Maxwell loan was repaid.

In the present action, the question was whether the plaintiff could recover from the borrower £1,180 with interest at 12 per cent. In the view of Megarry J, *Cannan v Bryce* did not wholly support the contention that the agreement to make the advance was illegal, but he had no doubt that it was warranted by *Fisher v Bridges*. 'In that case, the subsequent contract was between the original parties: but a third party who takes part in the subsequent transaction with knowledge of the prior illegality can, in general, be in no better position.'[248] In the instant case, it was clear that the plaintiff had concurred in the making of the Maxwell loan and had been fully aware of the illegal provision for the payment of compound interest. Therefore her action failed.

d A foreign contract, if contrary to English public policy, is unenforceable

An action is frequently brought in England upon a foreign contract. By a foreign contract is meant one which is more closely connected with a foreign country than with England, as, for instance, when it is made in France by an Englishman and a Frenchman and is performable only in France. In such a case the rule is that the substance of the obligation—the essential validity of the contract—must be governed by what is called the 'proper law', ie in effect the law of the country with which the transaction is most closely connected. The English doctrine of consideration, for instance, could not be invoked in an action for breach of the contract given above. Nevertheless, the rights of the parties as fixed by the proper law, if put in suit in England, are subject in general to the English doctrine of public policy. If the contract, though valid by the foreign law, is repugnant to what has been called the 'stringent domestic policy' of England,[249] it cannot be enforced in England. This, however, does not mean that each individual rule comprised in the comprehensive doctrine of public policy applies to a foreign contract. That doctrine strikes at acts which vary greatly in their degree of turpitude. Certain of its prohibitory rules exemplify principles which in the English view it is of paramount importance to maintain in English courts; others, such as that directed against a fraud on the revenue, are presumably designed to protect purely English interests. It is the former rules only, those upon which there can be no compromise, that apply to an action on a foreign contract.

Which of the rules are sufficiently important to be applied without exception is a somewhat controversial question that cannot be adequately discussed in a book on the elements of contract.[250] The decisions, however, at least warrant the statement that

---

[248] [1973] Ch 30 at 43, [1971] 3 All ER 417 at 427.

[249] Westlake *Private International Law* (7th edn) p 51.

[250] See eg Dicey and Morris *The Conflict of Laws* (11th edn) pp 1215–1232; Cheshire and North's *Private International Law* (11th edn) pp 482–489; Kahn-Freund 39 Grotius Society 39.

most of the contracts already described in this chapter as being repugnant to public policy and illegal, would not be enforced in an English action, whatever view might be taken of their validity by their proper law.[251] This is clearly so, for instance, in the case of a French contract to commit a crime or a tort, or to promote sexual immorality, or to prejudice the public safety of England. It might be thought that an agreement to stifle a foreign prosecution would scarcely arouse the moral indignation of an English court, but no such indifference to what is normal in certain countries was shown by the Court of Appeal in *Kaufman v Gerson*.[252] In that case:

> A Frenchman coerced a Frenchwoman into signing a contract in France by the threat that if she refused to sign he would prosecute her husband for a crime of which he was accused.

The contract was valid by French law, but an action brought for its breach in England was dismissed on the ground that to enforce it 'would contravene what by the law of this country is deemed an essential moral interest'.[253] It is to be noted that the objection of the Court of Appeal was at least as much to the coercive nature of the plaintiff's behaviour as to any stifling of the prosecution. Presumably, therefore, an English court would apply the rule that has been laid down in the United States of America and would refuse to enforce any contract which tended to promote corruption in the public affairs of a foreign country, however irreproachable such conduct might be in the view of the foreign law.[254]

C The consequence where a contract lawful in its inception is later illegally exploited or performed

The situation envisaged here is that a contract is lawful *ex facie* and is not disfigured by a common intention to break the law, but that one of the parties, without the knowledge of the other, in fact exploits it for some unlawful purpose. In these circumstances, the guilty party suffers the full impact of the maxim *ex turpi causa non oritur actio* and all remedies are denied to him.[255] 'Any party to the agreement who had the unlawful intention is precluded from suing upon it . . . The action does not lie because the court will not lend its help to such a plaintiff.'[256]

---

[251] *Robinson v Bland* (1760) 2 Burr 1077 at 1084; *Dynamite Act v Rio Tinto Co* [1918] AC 260.
[252] [1904] 1 KB 591.
[253] Ibid at 599–600.
[254] *Oscanyan v Arms Co* 103 US 261 at 277 (1881). See also *Lemenda Trading Co Ltd v African Middle East Petroleum Co Ltd* [1988] QB 448, [1988] 1 All ER 513. Discussed above p 479. Cf *Westacre Investments Inc v Jugo Import—SDPR Holding Co Ltd* [1999] 3 All ER 864; *Royal Boskalis Westminster NV v Mountain* [1997] 2 All ER 929.
[255] *Cowan v Milburn* (1867) LR 2 Exch 230; *Alexander v Rayson* [1936] 1 KB 169.
[256] *Alexander v Rayson* [1936] 1 KB 169 at 182, *per curiam*.

On the other hand, the rights of the innocent party are unaffected, except in respect of anything done by him after he has learned of the illegal purpose. In *Cowan v Milbourn*,[257] for instance, the defendant agreed to let a room to the plaintiff on 20 January, but chancing to hear that the premises were to be used for an unlawful purpose, he notified the plaintiff that the agreement would not be fulfilled. An action brought against him for breach of contract failed. But if, after the intended purpose had come to his knowledge, he had let the defendant into possession in accordance with the contract, Bramwell B observed that he could not have recovered the agreed price.[258]

Apart from this exceptional case of acquired knowledge, however, all the normal contractual remedies are available to the innocent party. He may enforce the contract;[259] he may sue on a *quantum meruit* or *quantum valebant* for the value of work or goods supplied before discovery of the unlawful intention;[260] and he may recover property that he has transferred to the guilty party.[261]

It must be noticed that this right to recover property does not conflict with the decision of the Exchequer Chamber in *Feret v Hill*, where:[262]

> The plaintiff induced the defendant to grant him a lease of premises in Jermyn Street by falsely representing that he intended to carry on therein the business of a perfumier. His intention, however, was to use them for immoral purposes, and, having obtained possession he converted them into a common brothel. He refused to quit and was forcibly ejected by the defendant. He brought an action of ejectment to recover possession and was successful.

This decision of a common law court must not be misunderstood. The elemental facts are simple: the lease had been executed, the tenant had been let into possession, and therefore in the eyes of the law a legal estate, together with the right to possession, had become vested in him. The court did not decide that the landlord was precluded from recovering possession. It merely decided that the tenant was not prevented by his antecedent fraud from acquiring a right to possession and that his right was not automatically forfeited either by his fraud or by his subsequent immoral use of the premises.[263] The landlord was ill-advised. He was not entitled to take the law into his own hands, to treat the lease as a nullity and to extrude the tenant from a possession recognised, at any rate for the time being, as lawful. But he would have been entitled,

---

[257] Above.

[258] This had been made clear in *Jennings v Throgmorton* (1825) Ry & M 251.

[259] *Lloyd v Johnson* (1798) 1 Bos & P 340; *Mason v Clarke* [1955] AC 778 at 793, 805, [1955] 1 All ER 914 at 920, 927; *Fielding and Platt Ltd v Najjar* [1969] 2 All ER 150, [1969] 1 WLR.

[260] *Clay v Yates* (1856) 1 H & N 73; *Bowry v Bennett* (1808) 1 Camp 348.

[261] *Oom v Bruce* (1810) 12 East 225.

[262] (1854) 15 CB 207.

[263] See the remarks of Maule J (one of the judges in *Feret v Hill*) in *Canham v Barry* (1855) 15 CB 597 at 611–612.

as indeed was assumed by the members of the court,[264] to take proceedings in equity for the rescission of the lease.

The rule is that if X transfers an interest in land or goods to Y, being induced to do so by a fraudulent misrepresentation similar to that made in *Feret v Hill*, he can, subject to any rights that may have been obtained for value by innocent third parties, take proceedings in any division of the High Court to secure the rescission of the contract and the recovery of his property.[265]

The superior position of the innocent party is equally apparent where a contract, though lawful as formed, is performed by his co-contractor in a manner prohibited by statute. In such a case, the party responsible for the illegal performance is remediless. So far as he alone is concerned, he is in exactly the same position as if the contract had been illegal and void *ab initio*.[266] But the innocent party is little affected, for in the words of Pollock:

> The fact that unlawful means are used in performing an agreement which is *prima facie* lawful and capable of being lawfully performed does not of itself make an agreement unlawful.[267]

If, indeed, the innocent party knows or ought to know that the contract can only be performed illegally or that the party responsible intends to perform it illegally, he is precluded from enforcing it either directly or indirectly.[268] Otherwise the normal remedies are open to him.

Thus he may recover damages for breach of contract.[269] It is not open to the defendant to plead that, because he himself adopted an illegal mode of performance, the apparent contract is no contract.

> Suppose that B has agreed to sell goods to A and that upon making delivery he is required by statute to furnish A with an invoice stating certain prescribed particulars. B in fact delivers goods that fall short of the standard fixed by the contract, and also fails to furnish the statutory invoice.

A, as the innocent party, must surely be able to sue B for breach of contract. Otherwise the absurd result would follow that if B delivered no goods at all he would be liable in damages, since there would have been no performance and no illegality; but that if he broke his contract by delivering inferior goods without the requisite invoice, this illegal mode of performance would free him from liability. Escape from a lawful obligation can scarcely be gained by a self-induced act of illegality.

---

264 *Feret v Hill*, above, at 226, per Maule J.

265 *Alexander v Rayson* [1936] 1 KB 169 at 192, *per curiam*.

266 *Anderson Ltd v Daniel* [1924] 1 KB 138 at 145, per Parker LJ.

267 *Principles of Contract* (13th edn) p 346.

268 *Archbolds (Freightage) Ltd v S Spanglett Ltd* [1961] 1 QB 374 at 374, [1961] 1 All ER 417 at 422, per Pearce LJ.

269 *Neilson v James* (1882) 9 QBD 546.

That the sensible is also the judicial solution was adumbrated in 1924 in *Anderson v Daniel*,[270] where the Court of Appeal stressed that in such a case as that supposed above it is only the guilty party who is remediless, a conclusion which was confirmed by *Marles v Philip Trant & Sons Ltd (No 2)*:[271]

> X agreed to sell to the defendants seed described as spring wheat. He delivered winter wheat and thereby broke his contract, but no illegality had as yet been committed either in the formation or the performance of the contract. The defendants innocently resold the wheat as spring wheat to the plaintiff, a farmer. This contract was still lawful as formed. It was, however, illegal as performed, since the defendants failed to comply with a statute which required an invoice to be delivered with the goods.

The farmer, upon discovering the seed to be winter wheat, sued the defendants for breach of contract. Despite the illegality of performance, he was allowed, as the innocent party, to recover damages. It was also held that the defendant's illegal performance of his contract with the plaintiff did not debar him from recovery against X for X's breach of their contract.

It is also reasonably clear in principle that the innocent party is entitled to take legal action to recover money or other property transferred by him under the contract.[272] Since he has taken no part in the unlawful performance, he can be in no worse position than a party to a contract illegal in its formation, who is allowed at common law to recover what he has parted with if he is not *in pari delicto* with the other party.[273]

Where a contract will become illegal unless performed in the manner required by statute, one party, as a condition of entering into it, may exact a promise from the other agreeing to keep performance free from the taint of illegality. If so, this exchange of promises creates a distinct promise separate from the main contract and in the event of its breach the guilty party is liable in damages. Such a case was *Strongman (1945) Ltd v Sincock*.[274]

> The plaintiffs, a building firm, agreed to modernise certain houses belonging to the defendant, an architect. In view of certain statutory regulations, it was illegal to carry out the work without the licence of the Ministry of Works. Before the contract was made, the defendant orally promised that he would make himself responsible for obtaining the necessary licences. The plaintiffs did work to the value of £6,359, but since licences for only £2,150 had been obtained, the defendant, who had paid them £2,900, refused to pay the balance of £3,459 on the ground that the work had been illegally performed.

---

270 [1924] 1 KB 138 at 145, per Bankes LJ; at 147, per Scrutton LJ; at 149, per Atkin LJ.
271 [1954] 1 QB 29, [1953] 1 All ER 651.
272 *Siffken v Allnutt* (1813) 1 M & S 39.
273 P 500, above.   274 [1955] 2 QB 525, [1955] 3 All ER 90.

The plaintiffs' claim to enforce the main contract for the recovery of the balance failed. They could not evade the consequences of the contravention of the law by passing to the defendant the responsibility for legalising the work. But in the sense that they had trusted him to take the necessary steps, the Court of Appeal were prepared to regard them as so far 'innocent' as to allow them an independent cause of action based on the defendant's promise to obtain the requisite licences. This promise was given before the work started and in consideration of the undertaking by the plaintiffs to do the work. There was thus constituted a 'collateral' or 'preliminary' contract valid in itself and distinct from the main contract.

It was stressed by the Court of Appeal, however, that only exceptionally will a collateral contract relieve the promisee from his obligation to observe a statutory regulation.[275] The circumstances must justify his belief that the obligation is no longer his. There was adequate justification in the instant circumstances, for the defendant said in evidence: 'I agree that where there is an architect it is the universal practice for the architect and not the builder to get licences.'

4 PROOF OF ILLEGALITY

The rules of evidence that govern the proof of illegality, whether the contract is illegal by statute or at common law, may be summarised as follows:

First, where the contract is *ex facie* illegal, the court takes judicial notice of the fact and refuses to enforce the contract, even though its illegality has not been pleaded by the defendant.

Secondly, where the contract is *ex facie* lawful, evidence of external circumstances showing that it is in fact illegal will not be admitted, unless those circumstances have been pleaded.

Thirdly, when the contract is *ex facie* lawful, but facts come to light in the course of the trial tending to show that it has an illegal purpose, the court takes judicial notice of the illegality notwithstanding that these facts have not been pleaded. But it must be clear that all the relevant circumstances are before the court.[276]

---

[275] See especially per Birkett LJ at 540. In a case where the defendant represented that he already held a licence, the Supreme Court of New South Wales held that the plaintiff, upon learning the truth and upon disaffirming the contract, could sue the defendant in fraud for damages to the amount of the work done and materials supplied; *Hatcher v White* (1953) 53 SRNSW 285.

[276] *North Western Salt Co Ltd v Electrolytic Alkali Co Ltd* [1914] AC 461; *Edler v Auerbach* [1950] 1 KB 359, especially at 371, [1949] 2 All ER 692; *Chettiar v Chettiar* [1962] AC 294, [1962] 1 All ER 494; *Snell v Unity Finance Co Ltd* [1964] 2 QB 203, [1963] 3 All ER 50. Cf *Peffer v Rigg* [1978] 3 All ER 745, [1977] 1 WLR 285; *Ferguson v John Dawson & Partners (Contractors) Ltd* [1976] 3 All ER 817, [1976] 1 WLR 346.

5 REFORM

It is clear that the rules relating to the effects of an illegal contract are complex, difficult to state accurately and lead to decisions which are not obviously fair as between the parties or effectively promote the underlying policy objectives.

In 1998 the Law Commission produced a Consultation Paper (No 154) which criticised the existing law and provisionally proposed that it should be replaced by a structured discretion. This Paper has not so far been followed by a report containing definitive proposals for legislation.

12 CONTRACTS VOID AT COMMON LAW ON GROUNDS OF PUBLIC POLICY

SUMMARY

It is now necessary to describe the three types of contract which, though they offend public policy, are treated by the courts not as illegal but as void, and to discuss their consequences.

1 THE CONTRACTS DESCRIBED

A Contracts to oust the jurisdiction of the courts

It has long been established that a contract which purports to destroy the right of one or both of the parties to submit questions of law to the courts is contrary to public policy and is *pro tanto* void.[1] Speaking of the common practice of referring disputes to domestic tribunals, Lord Denning said:

> Parties cannot by contract oust the ordinary courts from their jurisdiction . . . They can, of course, agree to leave questions of law, as well as questions of fact, to the decision of the domestic tribunal. They can, indeed, make the tribunal the final arbiter on questions of fact, but they cannot make it the final arbiter on questions of law. They cannot prevent its decisions being examined by the courts. If parties should seek, by agreement, to take the law out of the hands of the courts and put it into the hands of a private tribunal, without any recourse at all to the courts in cases of error of law, then the agreement is to that extent contrary to public policy and void.[2]

In *Baker v Jones*,[3] for instance, an association was formed to promote the sport of weightlifting in the United Kingdom, and control of its affairs was vested in a central council. It was provided that this council should be the sole interpreter of the rules of the association and that its decisions should in all cases and in all circumstances be final. It was held that to give the council the sole right of interpretation was void and that the court had jurisdiction to consider whether the interpretation adopted by the council in a given case was correct in law.

It should be observed, however, that an arbitration agreement, by which contracting parties provide that, before legal proceedings are taken, questions of law and fact shall be decided by a private tribunal, is not *per se* a contract to oust the jurisdiction of the courts, but is valid and enforceable. If, in breach of its terms, one of the parties commences legal proceedings against the other party, the latter may apply to the court for an order staying those proceedings.[4] Under the Arbitration Act 1996, section 9 the

---

[1] *Thompson v Charnock* (1799) 8 Term Rep 139. An agreement to oust the jurisdiction of the courts must be distinguished from the case where the parties do not intend that their legal relations shall be affected by their agreement (pp 148 ff, above). Parties are at liberty to declare that they do not wish to make a legally binding contract, but only a 'gentleman's agreement'. But having decided to make and having in fact made a binding contract, they are not allowed to exclude it from the supervision of the courts.

[2] *Lee v Showmen's Guild of Great Britain* [1952] 2 QB 329 at 342, [1952] 1 All ER 1175 at 1181.

[3] [1954] 2 All ER 553, [1954] 1 WLR 1005. *Re Davstone Estates Ltd's Leases, Manprop v O'Dell* [1969] 2 Ch 378, [1969] 2 All ER 849; *Re Tuck's Settlement Trusts, Public Trustee v Tuck* [1978] Ch 49, [1978] 1 All ER 1047; *Johnson v Moreton* [1978] 3 All ER 37, [1978] 3 WLR 538. Cf *Jones v Sherwood Computer Services plc* [1992] 1 WLR 277, Berg 109 LQR 35.

[4] Arbitration Act 1996, s 9.

court is directed to grant a stay 'unless satisfied that the arbitration agreement is null and void, inoperative, or incapable of being performed'.[5]

In *Scott v Avery*,[6] the House of Lords held that though it is lawful to make the award of an arbitrator on a question of law a condition precedent to the institution of legal proceedings, it is contrary to public policy to agree that the submission of such a question to the Court shall be prohibited. The Arbitration Act 1979 introduced for the first time a general right of appeal from an Arbitrator to the High Court on a point of law,[7] replacing the complex provisions for stating a special case.[8] The position is now governed by the Arbitration Act 1996, section 69, which largely reflects the way in which the 1979 Act was interpreted by the courts. The parties may agree either that there shall or shall not be appeals on questions of law. In the absence of such agreement the party wishing to appeal must apply for leave to the court and stringent conditions for leave are contained in the Act. If, as they are now entitled to do under the Arbitration Act 1996, the parties agree that there shall be no appeals on questions of law, the Court will have only a very limited supervisory jurisdiction.

Another example of this principle is an agreement by a wife not to apply to the court for maintenance. It is clear that there is a public interest against such promises since if the husband does not maintain his wife, her support may become a charge on public funds[9] but where such a promise by the wife is given in exchange for a promise by the husband to pay maintenance, it may appear unmeritorious to allow the husband to escape performance of his promise. After producing much litigation[10] such situations are now governed by legislation.[11] An agreement may also be invalid[12] in so far as it attempts to exclude mandatory rules of law. So for instance a perfectly valid agreement between two companies as to how accounts between them are to be

---

[5] This provision replaces the position under the previous legislation where the court had a discretion. A term in the arbitration agreement that no application for a stay of proceedings shall be made is void: *Czarnikow v Roth, Schmidt & Co* [1922] 2 KB 478.

[6] (1856) 5 HL Cas 811. *Czarnikow v Roth, Schmidt & Co* [1922] 2 KB 478.

[7] Arbitration Act 1979, s 1.

[8] Under Arbitration Act 1950, s 21(1).

[9] *Hyman v Hyman* [1929] AC 601. *Sutton v Sutton* [1984] Ch 184, [1984] 1 All ER 168.

[10] See eg *Bennett v Bennett* [1952] 1 KB 249, [1952] 1 All ER 413; *Brooks v Burns Philp Trustee Co* [1969] ALR 321.

[11] Matrimonial Causes Act 1973, s 34. And see *Minton v Minton* [1979] AC 593, [1979] 1 All ER 79; *Jessel v Jessel* [1979] 3 All ER 645, [1979] 1 WLR 1148.

[12] Does a clause providing that disputes under a contract are to be litigated in a foreign forum infringe the principle? This question has been much discussed in the United States. See Nadelman 21 Am J Comp L 124; Denning 2 J Maritime Law and Commerce 17; Mendelssohn ibid 661; Delaume 4 ibid 275. *Bremen v Zapata* 407 US 1 (1972), [1972] 2 Lloyd's Rep 315; *Carvalho v Hull Blyth (Angola) Ltd* [1979] 3 All ER 280, [1979] 1 WLR 1228. In general the problem has not been approached in this way in English law. For signatories it is now substantially governed by the Brussels Convention enacted into English law by the Civil Jurisdiction and Judgments Act 1992. For other countries see *The Eleftheria* [1969] 2 All ER 641, [1970] P94.

settled may become inoperative if one goes into liquidation because it runs contrary to the provisions of the insolvency legislation.[13]

B Contracts prejudicial to the status of marriage

The status of marriage is a matter of public interest in all civilised countries and it is important that nothing should be allowed to impair the sanctity of its solemn obligations or to weaken the loyalty that one spouse owes to the other. The general view of English law is that any contract is void which unduly restricts or hampers the freedom of persons to marry whom they will, or which after marriage tends to encourage in one or both of the parties an immoral mode of life incompatible with their mutual obligations.

Marriage ought to be free, and therefore a contract which restrains a person from marrying anybody, or from marrying anybody except a particular person without imposing a similar and reciprocal restriction on that person, is void as being contrary to the social welfare of the state.[14] Thus in *Lowe v Peers*[15] a contract made by a man under seal to the following effect was held to be contrary to public policy:

> I do hereby promise Mrs Catherine Lowe, that I will not marry with any person besides herself: if I do, I agree to pay the said Catherine Lowe £1,000 within three months next after I shall marry anybody else.

Again, it is in the interests of society that reckless or unsuitable marriages should be prevented, but this desirable state of affairs is not likely to be attained if third parties are free to reap financial profit by bringing about matrimonial unions. It has therefore been ruled that what is called a marriage brokage contract, ie a contact by which A undertakes in consideration of a money payment to procure a marriage for B, is void.[16] This is so whether the contract is to procure B's marriage with one particular person or with one out of a whole class of persons.[17]

Considerations of public policy, which, as we have just seen, apply to contracts made prior to marriage, also affect those made after marriage. The difficulty is to state the governing principle with precision, and we probably cannot venture further than this: that any contract which during cohabitation tends to encourage infidelity in one or both of the spouses or to provide an inducement for immoral conduct is void as being contrary to public policy. It is sometimes claimed that any contract whatsoever,

---

[13] *British Eagle International Airlines Ltd v Compagnie Nationale Air France* [1975] 2 All ER 390, [1975] 1 WLR 758. Similarly an agreement between master and servant to release the master from a statutory duty to provide safe working conditions is invalid: *Baddeley v Earl Granville* (1887) 19 QBD 423. But cf *Imperial Chemical Industries v Shatwell* [1965] AC 656, [1964] 2 All ER 999. See Dias [1966] CLJ 75.

[14] Story *Equity Jurisprudence* s 274.

[15] (1768) 4 Burr 2225. See also *Re Michelham's Will Trusts* [1964] Ch 550, [1963] 2 All ER 188.

[16] *Hermann v Charlesworth* [1905] 2 KB 123. See Powell 1953 Current Legal Problems 254.

[17] *Hermann v Charlesworth*, above.

that tends to induce a course of conduct inconsistent with the maintenance of the marriage tie, is void, but the authorities show that this is to state the rule too widely. Two lines of decisions illustrate the subject: those relating to separation agreements and those concerned with a promise made by a married person to marry a third person at some future time.

It has been established for over a hundred years that a contract providing for immediate separation of the spouses is valid and enforceable if followed by immediate separation, notwithstanding that this breaks the *consortium vitae* and is therefore to that extent inconsistent with the primary and fundamental obligation of the marriage tie.[18] On the other hand, a contract for a possible future separation, eg a promise by a husband that he will make provision for his wife if she should ever live apart from him, is contrary to public policy and void as being opposed to elementary consider-ations of morality.[19] The distinction between the two classes of agreement is obvious. Once the melancholy fact is apparent that the parties cannot live together in amity, it is desirable that the separation which has become inevitable should be concluded upon reasonable terms; but a promise for the benefit of one of the parties in the event of a possible future separation, if it does not put a premium on immorality, at least weakens the resolve of the promisee to maintain with loyalty and fidelity the obliga-tions of the marriage tie.

> If a separation has actually occurred or become inevitable, the law allows the matter to be dealt with according to realities and not according to a fiction. But the law will not permit an agreement which contemplates the future possibility of so undesirable a state of affairs.[20]

The one exception to the rule that a contract for future separation is void occurs where parties, who have been separated already, make a reconciliation agreement and resume cohabitation. In this case the agreement is valid although it may make provision for a renewed separation.[21]

The second lie of cases is concerned with a contract by A, who is already married to B, to marry X at some future date. In *Spiers v Hunt*[22] and *Wilson v Carnley*,[23] Phillimore J, in the former, and the Court of Appeal in the latter, case, held that a promise of marriage made by a man, who to the knowledge of the promisee was at the time married to another woman, was void on grounds of public policy, and that it could not be enforced after the death of the wife. In *Fender v St John-Mildmay*[24] the House of Lords held, by a majority, that these decisions did not extend to a promise of

---

[18] *Wilson v Wilson* (1848) 1 HL Cas 538; subsequent proceedings (1854) 5 HL Cas 40.

[19] *H v W* (1857) 3 K & J 382; *Brodie v Brodie* [1917] P 271.

[20] *Fender v St John-Mildmay* [1938] AC 1 at 44, [1937] 3 All ER 402 at 429, per Lord Wright.

[21] *Harrison v Harrison* [1910] 1 KB 35. See also *Re Johnson's Will Trusts, National Provincial Bank v Jeffrey* [1967] Ch 387, [1967] 1 All ER 553; *Re Hepplewhite Will Trusts* [1977] CLY 2710.

[22] [1908] 1 KB 720.

[23] [1908] 1 KB 729; *Siveyer v Allison* [1935] 2 KB 403.

[24] [1938] AC 1, [1937] 3 All ER 402. See especially the judgment of Lord Atkin.

marriage made by a married man whose marriage was so moribund that it had already been the subject of a decree nisi of divorce.[25] The practical situation in these cases can no longer be the subject of litigation since the abolition of actions for breach of promise of marriage[26] but they are still of interest as illustrating the public policy in respect of marriage.

C Contracts in restraint of trade[27]

A contract in restraint of trade is one by which a party restricts his future liberty to carry on his trade, business or profession in such manner and with such persons as he chooses. A contract of this class is prima facie void, but it becomes binding upon proof that the restriction is justifiable in the circumstances as being reasonable from the point of view of the parties themselves and also of the community.

Such has long been the legal effect of two familiar types of contract. First, one by which an employee agrees that after leaving his present employment he will not compete against his employer, either by setting up business on his own account or by entering the service of a rival trader. Secondly, an agreement by the vendor of the goodwill of a business not to carry on a similar business in competition with the purchaser.

This doctrine of restraint of trade is based upon public policy, and its application has been peculiarly influenced by changing views of what is desirable in the public interest.[28] This is inevitable. 'Public policy is not a constant', and it necessarily alters as economic conditions alter.[29] In Elizabethan days all restraints of trade, whether general or partial, were regarded as totally void because of their tendency to create monopolies. This view, however, did not prevail, for it was gradually realised that a restriction of trading activities was in certain circumstances justifiable in the interests both of the public and of the parties themselves. It was clear, for instance, that the purchaser of a business was at the mercy of the vendor, if the latter were free to carry on his former trade in the same place; and that a master was equally at the mercy of his

[25] This reasoning could be argued to cover the case of a marriage factually dead but not yet the subject of legal proceedings. See Furmston 16 U of Toronto LJ 267 at 300–302. Cf *Dobersek v Petrizza* [1968] NZLR 211.

[26] By the Law Reform (Miscellaneous Provisions) Act 1970. Under the previous law a woman who accepted a proposal of marriage from a married man in ignorance of his status could enforce the contract. *Shaw v Shaw* [1954] 2 QB 429, [1954] 2 All ER 638. This was a valuable remedy where, as in that case, the parties went through a ceremony of marriage and lived together for years. The action for breach of contract would provide a substitute for the succession rights which the 'wife' would have had if the 'marriage' has been valid. As to the present law, see s 6 of the 1970 Act; Thomson 87 LQR 158; Gower 87 LQR 314.

[27] Heydon *The Restraint of Trade Doctrine*. Trebilcock *The Common Law of Restraint of Trade*. Smith 15 Oxford JLS 565.

[28] *Attwood v Lamont* [1920] 3 KB 571 at 581, per Younger LJ. See Holdsworth *History of English Law* vol 8, pp 56–62.

[29] *Vancouver Malt and Sake Brewing Co Ltd v Vancouver Breweries Ltd* [1934] AC 181 at 189, per Lord Macmillan.

servants and apprentices if they were free to exploit to their own gain the knowledge that they had acquired of his personal customers or his trade secrets. Moreover, the evil was not limited to one side, for if all contracts against future competition were to be regarded as unlawful, the aim of employers, it was feared, might be to reduce the number of their servants to a minimum and so to increase unemployment. The law was therefore relaxed, though only gradually, and in 1711 in *Mitchel v Reynolds*,[30] a case which is the foundation of the modern law, Lord Macclesfield stated what he understood to be the current position. He said:

> Wherever a sufficient consideration appears to make it a proper and useful contract, and such as cannot be set aside without injury to a fair contractor, it ought to be maintained; but with this constant diversity—namely where the restraint is general not to exercise a trade throughout the kingdom, and where it is limited to a particular place; for the former of these must be void, being of no benefit to either party and only oppressive.[31]

The true significance of this passage, no doubt, was that everything must turn upon whether the contract was reasonable and fair. Lord Macclesfield, in speaking of the 'diversity', presumably did not intend to create a rigid distinction between a general and a limited restraint, the former void, the latter valid if reasonable. He was merely illustrating what, in the conditions of transport and communications prevailing in 1711, obviously could not be reasonable. 'What does it signify', he said in a later passage, 'to a tradesman in London what another does in Newcastle?' But no doubt he would have been the first to admit that, as conditions changed and communications improved, any rigid demarcation between general and limited restraints would be inconsistent with commercial realities. Indeed a time was to come when it might signify a great deal to the purchaser of a business in London what the vendor did in Newcastle. A long line of authority, however, interpreting Lord Macclesfield's words literally, established, and maintained until the close of the nineteenth century, that a contract, whether made between a master and servant or between a vendor and purchaser of a business which imposed a general restraint, was necessarily and without exception void; but that a partial restraint was prima facie valid, and if reasonable was enforceable. In summing up these authorities, Bowen LJ said:

> Partial restraints, or, in other words, restraints which involve only a limit of places at which, or persons with whom, or of modes in which, the trade is to be carried on, are valid when made for a good consideration, and where they do not extend further than is necessary for the reasonable protection of the covenantee.[32]

The first inroad on this rule came in 1894 in the *Nordenfelt* case,[33] when Nordenfelt, a manufacturer of quick-firing guns and other implements of war, sold his business to a company for £287,500 and entered into a contract restraining his future activities.

---

[30] (1711) 1 P Wms 181.   [31] Ibid at 182.

[32] *Maxim Nordenfelt Guns and Ammunition Co v Nordenfelt* [1893] 1 Ch 630 at 662.

[33] *Nordenfelt v Maxim Nordenfelt Guns and Ammunition Co* [1894] AC 535 especially at 536.

Two years later the company was amalgamated with another company which agreed to employ Nordenfelt as managing director at a salary of £2,000 a year. The deed of employment continued, indeed amplified, the contract in restraint of trade made by him two years earlier. He covenanted that he would

> not during the term of twenty-five years . . . if the company so long continued to carry on business, engage except on behalf of the company either directly or indirectly in the trade or business of a manufacturer of guns gun mountings or carriages, gunpowder explosives or ammunition, or *in any business competing or liable to compete in any way with that for the time being carried on by the company.*

This restraint was general in the most absolute sense, since the business of the company extended to all parts of the world. Nevertheless, the House of Lords held that, except for the part which has been italicised above, it was in the particular circumstances valid. The actual decision marked a break with the past. It came to this—that a contract in general restraint of trade, made between a vendor and purchaser of a business, was not necessarily void, but only prima facie void, and that it was valid if it was reasonable in the interests of the parties and in the interests of the public. It was reasonable in the interests of the parties to restrain Nordenfelt from trading in guns, gun mountings or carriages, gunpowder explosives or ammunition, since the business that he had sold for a large sum of money consisted in the manufacture of those very things. This part of the covenant was also reasonable in the interests of the public, since it secured to England the business and inventions of a foreigner and thus increased the trade of the country. On the other hand, to restrain Nordenfelt from engaging in 'any business competing or liable to compete in any way with that for the time being carried on by the company' was unreasonable, since it was wider than was reasonably necessary to protect the proprietary interest that the company had bought. That part of the covenant must therefore be severed from the rest and declared void.

So much then for the actual decision. But the case is equally important for the further break with tradition made by Lord Macnaghten, when he denied that general and partial restraints fell into distinct categories. A partial restraint, in his opinion, was not prima facie valid. It was on the same footing as a general restraint, ie prima facie void, but valid if reasonable. The relevant part of his speech is this:

> All interference with individual liberty of action in trading, and all restraints of trade of themselves, if there is nothing more, are contrary to public policy, and therefore void. That is the general rule. But there are exceptions: restraints of trade . . . may be justified by the special circumstances of a particular case. It is a sufficient justification, and indeed it is the only justification, if the restriction is reasonable—reasonable, that is, in reference to the interests of the parties concerned and reasonable in reference to the interests of the public, so framed and so guarded as to afford adequate protection to the party in whose favour it is imposed, while at the same time it is in no way injurious to the public.[34]

---

[34] Ibid at 565.

In a later passage he summarised the law in these words:

> My Lords . . . I think the only true test in all cases, whether of partial or general restraint, is the test proposed by Tindal CJ: What is a reasonable restraint with reference to the particular case?[35]

Lord Macnaghten's view, so far as it related to partial restraints, did not meet with the approval of all the Law Lords, and indeed it was irrelevant, since the issue in the *Nordenfelt* case was confined to the validity of a general restraint. Until 1913 his view was not adopted by the lower courts, which consistently acted on the assumption that partial restraints were prima facie valid,[36] but in that year the House of Lords in *Mason v Provident Clothing and Supply Co Ltd*,[37] held that Lord Macnaghten's proposition was a correct statement of the modern law. The House of Lords in this case developed the law in two respects:

First, it held that all covenants in restraint of trade, partial as well as general, are prima facie void and that they cannot be enforced unless the test of reasonableness as propounded by Lord Macnaghten is satisfied.

Secondly, it made a sharp distinction, stressed as long ago as 1869 by James LJ,[38] between contracts of service and contracts for the sale of a business. It confirmed that a restraint may be imposed more readily and more widely upon the vendor of a business in the interests of the purchaser, than upon a servant in the interests of the master. In the former case, not only are the parties dealing at arm's length, but the purchaser has paid the full market value for the acquisition of a proprietary interest, and it is obvious that this will lose much of its value if the vendor is free to continue his trade with his old customers. Indeed public policy demands that the covenantor should be allowed to restrict his future activities, for otherwise he will find it impossible to sell to the best advantage what he has created by his skill and labour.[39] Different considerations affect a contract of service. For one thing the parties are not in an equally strong bargaining position, and the servant will often find it difficult to resist the imposition of terms favourable to the master and unfavourable to himself.[40]

---

[35] Ibid at 574. The words of Tindal CJ appear in *Horner v Graves* (1831) 7 Bing 735.

[36] *Attwood v Lamont* [1920] 3 KB 571 at 585–586, per Younger LJ: the whole judgment is worthy of the closest attention.

[37] [1913] AC 724.

[38] *Leather Cloth Co v Lorsont* (1869) LR 9 Eq 345. An agreement between professional partners is for this purpose equated to the sale of a business: *Whitehill v Bradford* [1952] Ch 236, [1952] 1 All ER 115. And see *Oswald Hickson Collier & Co v Carter-Ruck* [1984] AC 720n, [1984] 2 All ER 15; *Bridge v Deacons* [1984] AC 705, [1984] 2 All ER 19; *Kerr v Morris* [1987] Ch 90, [1986] 3 All ER 217.

[39] *Mason v Provident Clothing and Supply Co Ltd* [1913] AC 724 at 734, per Lord Haldane; *Ronbar Enterprises Ltd v Green* [1954] 2 All ER 266, [1954] 1 WLR 815, per Jenkins LJ at 820 and 270, respectively. If no provision is made upon the sale of goodwill for the prevention of competition, the vendor may set up a rival business, but he may not canvass his former customers: *Trego v Hunt* [1896] AC 7.

[40] *Leather Cloth Co v Lorsont* (1869) LR 9 Eq 345 at 354. This might appear less true with the development of powerful trade unions but most restraints affect 'white-collar' workers, who are much less unionised.

He may even find his freedom to request higher wages seriously impeded, for should he be unsuccessful his choice of fresh employment will be considerably narrowed if the restraint is binding.[41] Again, the master cannot as a rule show any proprietary interest of a permanent nature that requires protection, since the servant's skill and knowledge, even though acquired in the service, as not bought for his life, but only for the duration of the employment.[42] The possibility that the servant may be a competitor in the future is not a danger against which the master is entitled to safeguard himself. On the contrary, it accords with public policy that a servant shall not be at liberty to deprive himself or the state of his labour, skill or talent.[43] Decisive effect was given to these considerations in *Herbert Morris Ltd v Saxelby*,[44] where the House of Lords held that a covenant which restrains a servant from competition is always void as being unreasonable, unless there is some exceptional proprietary interest owned by the master that requires protection. In the course of his speech Lord Parker said:

> The reason, and the only reason, for upholding such a restraint on the part of an employee is that the employer has some proprietary right, whether in the nature of trade connection or in the nature of trade secrets, for the protection of which such a restraint is—having regard to the duties of the employee—reasonably necessary. Such a restraint has, so far as I know, never been upheld, if directed only to the prevention of competition or against the use of the personal skill and knowledge acquired by the employee in his employer's business.[45]

The most recent landmark in the history of the subject is the decision of the House of Lords in *Esso Petroleum Co Ltd v Harper's Garage (Stourport) Ltd*.[46] This is of general importance on several counts. The speeches show how the issues that arise in a contested case should be segregated; they show that the broad generalisations which figure so frequently in the reports are misleading guides; they reaffirm the true role of public policy in this context; and they contain much of value upon the categories of contract that attract the doctrine of restraint of trade.

In the first place, their Lordships stress the importance of segregating the two independent questions that require an answer where the doctrine is invoked. The first is whether the contract under review is so restrictive of the promisor's liberty to trade with others that it must be treated as prima facie void. If such is the finding of the court, the second question is whether the restrictive clause can be justified as being reasonable. If so the contract is valid.

To neglect this segregation is to court confusion, for the facts relevant to the second question are not necessarily relevant to the first. If, for instance, the first is under investigation, it is a matter of indifference that the contract is contained in a

---

[41] *M and S Drapers (a firm) v Reynolds* [1956] 3 All ER 814 at 820, [1957] 1 WLR 9 at 18, per Denning LJ.

[42] *Attwood v Lamont* [1920] 3 KB 571 at 589.

[43] *Leather Cloth Co v Lorsont* (1869) LR 9 Eq 345 at 353, per James LJ.   [44] [1916] 1 AC 688.

[45] Ibid at 710.   [46] [1968] AC 269, [1967] 1 All ER 699. Heydon 85 LQR 229.

mortgage; but in estimating the reasonableness of the restriction, the harshness or moderation of the mortgage terms may be the decisive element.[47] Where a judge combines the two questions, it is often impossible to discern to which of the two issues his remarks are directed.

It is in connection with the first question that some confusion has been caused by judicial generalisations. The reports abound with statements of the most sweeping nature, such as that of Lord Macnaghten quoted above,[48] in which he dismissed as contrary to public policy 'all interferences with individual liberty of action in trading and all restraints of trade themselves, if there is nothing more'. But, as was pointed out in the *Esso* case, such statements are not to be taken literally.[49] They were not intended to indicate that 'any contract which in whatever way restraints a man's liberty to trade was (either historically under the common law or at the time of which they were speaking) prima facie unenforceable and must be shown to be reasonable'.[50] Moreover, the changing face of commerce must always be borne in mind.[51] Restrictions which in an earlier age were classified as restraints of trade may, in the different circumstances of today, have become 'part of the accepted pattern or structure of trade' as encouraging rather than limiting trade.[52]

Where, then, is the line to be drawn between restrictions that require justification and those that are innocuous? What at any rate is clear beyond doubt is that two categories of contract are prima facie void as being in restraint of trade: those which restrict competition by an employee against his employer or by the vendor of a business against the purchaser.

On the other hand, it may be said with reasonable confidence that certain restrictive agreements have now 'passed into the accepted and normal currency of commercial or contractual or conveyancing relations',[53] and are therefore no longer suspect. If, for instance, a manufacturer agrees that X shall be the sole agent for the sale of his output, the scope of his liberty of disposition is no doubt fettered, but the object of the arrangement is to increase his trade, and it has become a normal incident of commercial practice.[54] Again, it has been established for well over a hundred years that an agreement by the lessee of a public house that he will sell no beer on the

---

[47] Ibid, at 326 and 725, respectively, per Lord Pearce,.

[48] P 519, above.

[49] [1968] AC 269, [1967] 1 All ER 699, at 293–295 and at 705, respectively, per Lord Reid; at 307 and 713, respectively, per Lord Morris of Borth-y-Gest.

[50] Ibid, per Lord Wilberforce at 333 and 730, respectively. Strictly speaking, the word 'unenforceable' used in this passage should be replaced by 'void'.

[51] Ibid, at 324 and 724, respectively, per Lord Pearce.

[52] Ibid, at 335 and 731, respectively, per Lord Wilberforce.

[53] Ibid at 332–333 and 729, respectively, per Lord Wilberforce; see also at 327 and 724, respectively, per Lord Pearce.

[54] Ibid at 328–329 and 726, respectively, per Lord Pearce; at 336 and 731, respectively, per Lord Wilberforce. See *Servais v Prince's Hall Restaurant Ltd* (1904) 20 TLR 574.

premises except that brewed by his lessor is outside the doctrine of restraint of trade.[55] The same reasoning applies to the negative covenants, so familiar in practice, by which a lessee or purchaser of land agrees to surrender his common law right to use the premises for trading purposes. These have long been an accepted, indeed an essential, feature of conveyancing practice and for that reason are excluded from the doctrine of restraint of trade.[56] So much is reasonably clear. Two categories of contract are subject to the doctrine of restraint; certain other categories are exempt. Where a contract which falls within none of these categories places some degree of restriction upon a party's trading activities, the court may feel obliged to consider whether in the light of its terms and of the attendant circumstances it must be construed as prima facie void. This may be an enquiry of some delicacy, for it involves the adjustment of two freedoms, both based on public policy—the one the freedom to contract, the other the freedom to trade[57]—or, as Lord Shaw once put it, 'the right to bargain and the right to work'.[58] The perplexing problem is to identify the type of restrictive contract that requires the intervention of the court. Is there any rigid test that serves to distinguish the impeachable from the unimpeachable restriction? It may be answered at once that such a simple solution is unattainable. Any attempt to classify the categories of contract that are prima facie void is hazardous in the extreme. There is no accurate rubric under which they can be brought. 'The classification must remain fluid and the categories can never be closed.'[59]

The manner in which the courts approach the problem is illustrated by the decision of the House of Lords in the *Esso* case,[60] where the respondent company had tied its two garages to the appellant company under what is called the '*solus* system'.[61]

---

[55] *Esso Petroleum Co Ltd v Harper's Garage (Stourport) Ltd* [1968] AC 269 at 325, [1967] 1 All ER at 725, per Lord Pearce; per Lord Wilberforce at 333–334 and 730–731, respectively. 'Tied houses' became common while partial restraints were thought prima facie valid. Such agreements may, however, fall foul of statutory competition law. See above pp 424 ff.

[56] Ibid at 334–335, and 731, respectively, per Lord Wilberforce. The reason for this exclusion given by the other Law Lords was that the covenantor surrenders no freedom that he formerly possessed, since prior to the contract he had no right to trade on the land. This however, would not explain the exclusion where the owner of two properties sells one and covenants not to trade on the other that he retains. This reason was relied on however in *Cleveland Petroleum Co Ltd v Dartstone Ltd* [1969] 1 All ER 201, [1969] 1 WLR 116.

[57] *Esso Petroleum Co Ltd v Harper's Garage (Stourport) Ltd* [1968] AC 269 at 306, [1967] 1 All ER 699 at 712, per Lord Morris of Borth-y-Gest.

[58] *Mason v Provident Clothing and Supply Co Ltd* [1913] AC 724 at 738.

[59] *Esso Petroleum Co Ltd v Harper's Garage (Stourport) Ltd* [1968] AC 269 at 337, [1967] 1 All ER 699 at 732, per Lord Wilberforce.

[60] [1968] AC 269, [1967] 1 All ER 699.

[61] A *solus* agreement normally contains a 'tying covenant' by which the garage owner agrees, in return for a rebate on the price, to sell only the supplier's brand of petrol; a 'compulsory trading covenant', which obliges him to keep the garage open at reasonable hours and to provide the public with an efficient service; and a 'continuity covenant' which requires him, if he sells his business, to procure the acceptance of the agreement by the purchaser. As a further incentive, the supplier frequently makes a loan to the garage owner on favourable terms: see generally Whiteman 29 MLR 507; Graupner 18 ICLQ 879.

Separate contracts were entered into in respect of each garage, but each contained the following main provisions.

> The respondent company agreed to buy its total requirements of motor fuel from Esso; and to operate the garages in accord with the Esso co-operation plan under which it was obligatory to keep the garages open at all reasonable hours and not to sell them without ensuring that the purchaser entered into a similar sale agreement with Esso. The appellant agreed to allow a rebate of 1d a gallon on all fuels bought. The agreements were to operate for four years five months in the case of one of the garages, but for twenty-one years in respect of the other. In addition, the latter was mortgaged to Esso in return for an advance of £7,000 which was to be repaid by instalments lasting for twenty-one years and not at any earlier date. In other words, the mortgage was not redeemable before the end of that period.

It was held unanimously that both agreements fell within the category of contracts in restraint of trade. They were not mere contracts of exclusion as in the case of a sole agency, for they restricted the manner in which the respondent company was to carry on its trade during a fixed period that could not be terminated before it had run its full course. Nor could it be said that the solus system had become a normal and established incident of the motor trade, since it was of far too recent an origin. Moreover, there was no substance in the appellant's main argument that the restrictions against trading were imposed not upon the respondent company personally, but upon its use of the land, and that therefore, as in the case where a tenant covenants not to use the demised land for the purposes of trade, they were excluded from the doctrine of restraint of trade. Lord Wilberforce stigmatised this argument as artificial and unreal,[62] while Lord Pearce said that the practical effect of the contract was to create a personal restraint since it imposed a positive obligation upon the respondent to carry on the business in the manner prescribed in the cooperation plan.[63] The further argument that the restriction in respect of the second garage, since it was contained in a mortgage, was exempt from the doctrine of restraint was dismissed as unsound in principle.

Thus, both contracts were prima facie void and required to be justified according to the test of reasonableness.[64]

An attempt will now be made to summarise the main rules applicable to contracts in restraint of trade, especially those that relate to the test of reasonableness.

The basic rule is that, if the contract is so restrictive of the promisor's liberty to trade as to require review by the court, it is prima facie void and cannot become binding unless it is reasonable in the interest of both parties and also in the interest of the public.

[62] Ibid at 338 and 733, respectively.   [63] Ibid at 327 and 726, respectively.
[64] The decision on this aspect of the case is discussed below.

The view that the interest of the public should be consulted was current in the nineteenth century, but for many years the courts have usually concentrated their attention on the interests of the parties. In the *Esso* case, however, three of the Law Lords deprecated this dismemberment of the principle of public policy on which the doctrine of restraint of trade is based. In every case 'there is one broad question: Is it in the interests of the community that this restraint should be held to be reasonable and enforceable?[65] This is a revival of the view expressed by the Court of Exchequer as long ago as 1843: 'The test appears to be whether the contract be prejudicial or not to the public interest, for it is on grounds of public policy alone that these contracts are supported or avoided.'[66]

The concept of public interest admits of no precise definition, and it is not surprising that at times it has been allowed a latitude which it is difficult to defend. An instance of this in the context of restraint of trade is the decision of the Court of Appeal in *Wyatt v Kreglinger and Fernau*,[67] where the facts were as follows:

> In June 1923, the defendants wrote to the plaintiff, who had been in their service for many years, intimating that upon his retirement they proposed to give him an annual pension of £200 subject to the condition that he did not compete against them in the wool trade. The plaintiff's reply was lost, but he retired in the following September and received the pension until June 1932, when the defendants refused to make further payments. The plaintiff sued them for breach of contract. The defendants denied that any contract existed, and also pleaded that if a contract did exist it was void as being in restraint of trade.

The Court of Appeal gave judgment for the defendants, but there was no unanimity with regard to the *ratio decidendi*. Scrutton LJ held that the defendants had not bound themselves contractually but had merely made a gratuitous promise. The other two Lords Justices inclined to a contrary view on this point, but all three held that if the contract existed it was void, since it imposed a restraint that was too wide. It also appeared to them that the contract was injurious to the interests of the public, for to restrain the plaintiff from engaging in the wool trade was to deprive the community of services from which it might derive advantage. This is a somewhat extravagant suggestion. It is a little difficult to appreciate what injury was caused to the public by the

---

[65] Ibid at 324 and 724, respectively, per Lord Pearce. See also at 319 and 720, respectively, per Lord Hodson; at 340–341 and 733–735, respectively, per Lord Wilberforce; and see *Herbert Morris v Saxelby* [1916] 1 AC 688 at 716, per Lord Shaw; *Bull v Pitney-Bowes Ltd* [1966] 3 All ER 384, [1967] 1 WLR 273 at 282, per Thesiger J.

[66] *Mallan v May* (1843) 11 M & W 653 at 665, per Parke B, delivering the judgment of the court. The onus of proving that the restraint is reasonable in the interests of the parties lies upon the party who seeks to enforce the agreement; whether it is reasonable in the public interest lies upon the party so alleging. As to these rules, see the *Esso* case at 319 and 323–324 and 720–721, 724, respectively.

[67] [1933] 1 KB 793; followed by Thesiger J in *Bull v Pitney-Bowes Ltd* [1966] 3 All ER 384, [1967] 1 WLR 273; p 531, below.

retirement of a man who, in common with a very considerable number of his fellow citizens, occupied but a comparatively humble position in the trade. Reason and justice would seem to prescribe that an agreement, reasonable between the parties, should not be upset for some fancied and problematical injury to the public welfare.

In applying the test of public policy, the first task of the court is to construe the contract in the light of the circumstances existing at the time when it was made in order to determine the nature and extent of the restraint contemplated by the parties. The decisive factor is not the mere wording of the contract, but the object that the parties had in view. In one case, for instance, a contract with a milk roundsman contained the following clause:

> The Employee expressly agrees not at any time during the period of one year after the determination of his employment, . . . either on his own account or as representative or agent of any person or company, to serve or sell milk or dairy produce to . . . any person or company who at any time during the last six months of his employment shall have been a customer of the Employer and served by the Employee in the course of his employment.[68]

The expression 'dairy produce' manifestly includes butter and cheese and therefore the agreement, literally construed, would preclude the roundsman from entering the employment of a grocer who dealt in those commodities. The Court of Appeal, however, held that so stringent a restraint was not contemplated by the parties. The clear object of the contract was to protect the employers *qua* purveyors of milk which was the only commodity in which they dealt. Since this was the rational construction of the contract, it was held that the restraint was valid.

Once the intention of the parties had been disclosed, the validity of the contract falls to be determined. This is a question of law. Evidence is indeed admissible to prove the special circumstances which are alleged to justify the restriction. The promisee may, for instance, produce evidence to show what is customary in the particular trade, what particular dangers require precautions, what steps are necessary in order to protect him against competition by the promisor, and what is usual among businessmen as to the terms of employment.[69] But evidence that a witness considers the restraint to be reasonable is inadmissible, for that is the very question which the court alone can decide.[70]

The onus of proving such special circumstances as are alleged to justify a restraint fall upon the promisee. 'When once they are proved, it is a question of law for the decision of the judge whether they do or do not justify the restraint. There is no question of onus one way or the other.'[71]

---

[68] *Home Counties Dairies Ltd v Skilton* [1970] 1 All ER 1227, [1970] 1 WLR 526.

[69] *Haynes v Doman* [1899] 2 Ch 13 at 24, per Lindley MR.

[70] Ibid; *Leng & Co Ltd v Andrews* [1909] 1 Ch 763 at 770–771, per Fletcher Moulton LJ. And as to the admissibility of general economic evidence, see *Texaco Ltd v Mulberry Filling Station Ltd* [1972] 1 All ER 513, [1972] 1 WLR 814.

[71] *Herbert Morris Ltd v Saxelby* [1916] AC 688 at 707, per Lord Parker.

In considering the issue of justification, the court must scrutinise the restraint as at the date when the contract was made in the light of the circumstances then existing and also in the light of what at that date might possibly happen in the future. The temptation to consider what in fact has happened by the time of the trial must be resisted, for a contract containing a restraint alleged to be excessive must be either invalid *ab initio* or valid *ab initio*. There cannot come a moment at which it passes from the class of invalid into that of valid covenants.[72]

A restraint to be permissible must be no wider than is reasonably necessary to protect the relevant interest of the promisee.[73] The existence of some proprietary or other legitimate interest such as his right to work,[74] must first be proved, and then it must be shown to the satisfaction of the court that the restraint as regards its area, its period of operation and the activities against which it is directed, is not excessive.

We will now consider the question of reasonableness with reference to the different categories of contracts in restraint of trade. But, as we have seen, any attempt to classify these categories would be a hazardous, if not an impossible, undertaking. The doctrine of restraint is by no means static. Moreover it extends beyond the confines of contract. It has been extended, for instance, to the refusal of the Jockey Club to grant a training licence to a woman merely on the ground of her sex;[75] to the 'retain and transfer' system of the Football League Ltd, by which a player, 'retained' by his club at the end of his year's engagement, is debarred from joining another club unless he obtains the consent of that by which he has been retained,[76] to the rules adopted by the International Cricket Conference and the Test and County Cricket Board as to which players should be permitted to play test cricket and English first class county cricket respectively;[77] and to restrictions imposed by a professional body, such as the Pharmaceutical Society, upon the trading activities of its members.[78] In the present book it seems better to limit the discussion to contractual restrictions and to group these under four headings, namely (a) restraints accepted by an employee; (b) restraints accepted by the vendor of a business; (c) restraints arising

---

[72] *Gledhow Autoparts Ltd v Delaney* [1965] 3 All ER 288 at 295, [1965] 1 WLR 1366 at 1377, per Diplock LJ. See also *Putsman v Taylor* [1927] 1 KB 637 at 643, per Salter J. The contrary view was taken by Lord Denning MR in *Shell (UK) Ltd v Lostock Garage Ltd* [1977] 1 All ER 481, [1976] 1 WLR 1187 but this was supported only by a selective and out of context quotation from *Esso Petroleum Co Ltd v Harper's Garage (Stourport) Ltd* [1968] AC 269, [1967] 1 All ER 699 and was not concurred in by the other members of the Court of Appeal. See Russell 40 MLR 582 and *Watson v Prager* [1991] 3 All ER 487. The position may be different with the statutory regime. See above pp 424 ff.

[73] *E Underwood & Son Ltd v Barker* [1899] 1 Ch 300 at 305, per Lindley MR; *Herbert Morris Ltd v Saxelby* [1916] 1 AC 688 at 710, per Lord Parker.

[74] *Nagle v Feilden* [1966] 2 QB 633 at 646, per Lord Denning MR. 'A man's right to work at his trade or profession is just as important to him, perhaps more important than, his rights of property.'

[75] *Nagle v Feilden*, above.

[76] *Eastham v Newcastle United Football Club* [1964] Ch 413, [1963] 3 All ER 139.

[77] *Greig v Insole* [1978] 3 All ER 449, [1978] 1 WLR 302.

[78] *Pharmaceutical Society of Great Britain v Dickson* [1970] AC 403, [1968] 2 All ER 686.

from combinations for the regulation of trade relations; (d) restraints accepted by distributors of merchandise.

a Restraints accepted by employees

It has already been seen that a restraint imposed upon a servant is never reasonable, unless there is some proprietary interest owned by the master which requires protection. The only matters in respect to which he can be said to possess such an interest are his trade secrets, if any, and his business connection.[79] It is obvious that a restraint against competition is justifiable if its object is to prevent the exploitation of trade secrets learned by the servant in the course of his employment.[80] An instance of this occurred in *Forster & Sons Ltd v Suggett*:[81]

> The works manager of the plaintiffs, who were chiefly engaged in making glass and glass bottles, was instructed in certain confidential methods concerning, inter alia, the correct mixture of gas and air in the furnaces. He agreed that during the five years following the determination of his employment he would not carry on in the United Kingdom, or be interested in, glass bottle manufacture or any other business connected with glass-making as conducted by the plaintiffs.

It was held that the plaintiffs were entitled to protection in this respect, and that the restraint was reasonable. In such a case the employer must prove definitely that the servant has acquired substantial knowledge of some secret process or mode of manufacture used in the course of his business. Even the general knowledge, derived from secret information, which has taught an employee how best to solve particular problems as they arise may be a proper subject matter of protection.[82] But if, as was the case in *Herbert Morris Ltd v Saxelby*,[83] the so-called secret is nothing more than a special method of organisation adopted in the business, or if only part of the secret is known to the servant so that its successful exploitation by him is impossible, there can be no valid restraint.

An employer is also entitled to protect his trade connection, ie to prevent his customers from being enticed away from him by a servant who was formerly in his employ. Protection is required against the unfair invasion of his connection by a servant who has had the special opportunities of becoming acquainted with his clientele, and if the protection is no more than adequate for this purpose it is

---

[79] It was held in *Eastham v Newcastle United Football Club* [1964] Ch 413, [1963] 3 All ER 139, that the rules of the Football Association and the Football League relating to the retention and transfer of professional footballers were not justified by any interest capable of protection. Some protection will be granted to trade secrets and trade connection even if there is no express term, *Faccenda Chicken Ltd v Fowler* [1987] Ch 117, [1986] 1 All ER 617.

[80] *Hagg v Darley* (1878) 47 LJ Ch 567; *Caribonum Co Ltd v Le Couch* (1913) 109 LT 587; *Haynes v Doman* [1899] 2 Ch 13.

[81] (1918) 35 TLR 87.

[82] *Commercial Plastics Ltd v Vincent* [1965] 1 QB 623, [1964] 3 All ER 546.

[83] [1916] 1 AC 688.

permitted by the law.[84] The difficulty, however, is to specify the kind of business or the class of servant in respect to which this protection is legitimate. What servants acquire such an intimate knowledge of customers as to make the misuse of their knowledge a potential source of danger to their masters? The answer must depend upon the nature of the business and the nature of the employment entrusted to the servant. In one case Romer LJ proposed a test that would seem to be too wide. He said:

> It is, in my opinion, established law that where an employee is being offered employment which will probably result in his coming into direct contact with his employer's customers, or which will enable him to obtain knowledge of the names of his employer's customers, then the covenant against solicitation is reasonably necessary for the protection of the employer.[85]

This, however, is surely too sweeping, for most shop assistants come into direct contact with customers, and even where this is not so they frequently have access to lists of clients. In *Herbert Morris Ltd v Saxelby*, Lord Parker stressed that, before any restraint is justifiable, the servant must be one who will acquire, not merely knowledge of customers, but in addition influence over them.[86] It seems a reasonable and workable criterion. A restraint is not valid unless the nature of the employment is such that customers will either learn to rely upon the skill or judgement of the servant or will deal with him directly and personally to the virtual exclusion of the master, with the result that he will probably gain their custom if he sets up business on his own account.

Restraints against the invasion of trade connection have been upheld in the case of a solicitor's clerk,[87] a tailor's cutter-fitter,[88] a milk roundsman,[89] a stockbroker's clerk,[90] the manager of a brewery[91] and an estate agent's clerk.[92] On the other hand, they have been disallowed in the case of a grocer's assistant;[93] in the case of a bookmaker's 'manager who had no personal contact with his employer's clients, since the business was conducted mostly by telephone';[94] and in a case where the restriction against future competition, imposed upon the traveller of a firm supplying accessories to the lighting system of motor cars, extended to retailers in the prescribed area even though he might never visit them during his employment.[95]

---

[84] *Dewes v Fitch* [1920] 2 Ch 159 at 181–182, per Warrington LJ.

[85] *Gilford Motor Co v Horne* [1933] Ch 935 at 966.   [86] [1916] 1 AC 688 at 709.

[87] *Fitch v Dewes* [1921] 2 AC 158.

[88] *Nicoll v Beere* (1885) 53 LT 659; cf *Attwood v Lamont* [1920] 3 KB 571, p 544, below where the restraint might have been valid had it been less widely framed.

[89] *Cornwall v Hawkins* (1872) 41 LJ Ch 435.

[90] *Lyddon v Thomas* (1901) 17 TLR 450.

[91] *White, Tomkins and Courage v Wilson* (1907) 23 TLR 469.

[92] *Scorer v Seymour-Johns* [1966] 3 All ER 347, [1966] 1 WLR 1419, distinguishing *Bowler v Lovegrove* [1921] 1 Ch 642.

[93] *Pearks Ltd v Cullen* (1912) 28 TLR 371.

[94] *S W Strange Ltd v Mann* [1965] 1 All ER 1069, [1965] 1 WLR 629.

[95] *Gledhow Autoparts Ltd v Delaney* [1965] 3 All ER 288, [1965] 1 WLR 1366.

A restraint is permissible if it is designed to prevent a misuse of trade secrets or business connection, but it will be invalid if it affords any more than adequate protection to the covenantee. In deciding this question the court considers, inter alia, the nature and extent of the trade and of the servant's employment therein, but it pays special attention to the two factors of time and area.[96] 'As the time of restriction lengthens or the space of its operation grows, the weight of the onus on the convenantee to justify it grows too.'[97]

There are many instances of a restraint being invalidated by the excessive area of its sphere of intended operation. Thus contracts have been held void where an agent employed to canvass for orders in Islington was restricted from trading within twenty-five miles of London;[98] where a junior reporter of the *Sheffield Daily Telegraph* agreed that he would not be connected with any other newspaper business carried on within twenty miles of Sheffield;[99] where a traveller for a firm of brewers was restrained, without limit of area, from being concerned in the sale of ale or porter brewed at Burton;[100] where the manager of a butcher's shop at Cambridge agreed not to carry on a similar business within a radius of five miles from the shop;[101] and where an assistant to a dentist carrying on business in London agreed that he would not practise in any of the other towns in England or Scotland where the covenantee might happen to practise before the end of the covenantor's employment.[102] Nevertheless, everything depends upon the circumstances, and these may well justify a far wider restraint than those repudiated in the above examples. A restriction extending throughout the United Kingdom has been allowed,[103] and in one case the Eastern Hemisphere was regarded as a reasonable area.[104] It is not necessary for the covenantee to prove that the business, for the protection of which the restraint was imposed, has in fact been carried on in every part of the area specified in the contract.[105]

A restraint may be invalid on the ground that its duration is excessive.[106] The burden on the covenantee to prove the reasonableness of the covenant is increased by the absence of a time limit, but it by no means follows that a restraint for life is void. In *Fitch v Dewes*,[107] for instance, a contract was enforced by which a solicitor's

[96] *Badische Anilin und Soda Fabrik v Schott, Segner & Co* [1892] 3 Ch 447 at 451, per Chitty J. Where the covenant is in general terms, it may be permissible for the court to construe it as no wider than reasonable: *Littlewoods Organisation Ltd v Harris* [1978] 1 All ER 1026, [1977] 1 WLR 1472.

[97] *Attwood v Lamont* [1920] 3 KB 571 at 589, per Younger LJ.

[98] *Mason v Provident Clothing and Supply Co Ltd* [1913] AC 724.

[99] *Leng & Co Ltd v Andrews* [1909] 1 Ch 763.   [100] *Allsopp v Wheatcroft* (1872) LR 15 Eq 59.

[101] *Empire Meat Co Ltd v Patrick* [1939] 2 All ER 85.   [102] *Mallan v May* (1843) 11 M & W 653.

[103] *E Underwood & Con Ltd v Barker* [1899] 1 Ch 300.

[104] *Lamson Pneumatic Tube Co v Phillips* (1904) 91 LT 363 (pneumatic tube system for use in shops was invented in the Western hemisphere and practically unknown in the Eastern hemisphere).

[105] *Connors Bros Ltd v Connors* [1940] 4 All ER 179.

[106] *Eastes v Russ* [1914] 1 Ch 468 (a lifetime's restraint imposed upon an assistant to a pathologist); *Wyatt v Kreglinger and Fernau* [1933] 1 KB 793; *M and S Drapers (a firm) v Reynolds* [1956] 3 All ER 814, [1957] 1 WLR 9; *Stenhouse Australia Ltd v Phillips* [1974] AC 391, [1974] 1 All ER 117.

[107] [1921] 2 AC 158.

clerk at Tamworth agreed that, after leaving his employer, he would never practise within seven miles of Tamworth Town Hall.

There are, indeed, many cases in which restraints have been upheld notwithstanding that they have been unlimited as regards both area and time, but all decisions prior to *Mason's* case in 1913,[108] which as we have seen revolutionised the law by adopting Lord Macnaghten's test, should be viewed with suspicion. As Younger LJ remarked in 1920:

> Restrictive covenants imposed upon an employee which a few years ago would not have seemed open to question would now, I think, with equal certainty be treated as invalid.[109]

The courts are astute to prevent an employer from obtaining by indirect means a protection against competition that would not be available to him by an express contract with his employee. In *Bull v Pitney-Bowes Ltd*,[110] for instance:

> The plaintiff was employed by the defendants, manufacturers of postal franking machines, and it was a condition of his employment that he should become a member of a non-contributory pension scheme. Rule 16 of this scheme provided that a retired member should be liable to forfeit his pension rights if he engaged in any activity or occupation which was in competition with or detrimental to the interests of the defendants.
>
> After twenty-six years service the plaintiff voluntarily retired and joined another company carrying on a business similar to that of the defendants. On being warned that he might lose his pension unless he left his new employment, he sued for a declaration that rule 16 was an unreasonable restraint of trade and therefore void.

If the rule fell to be classified as a restraint of trade, it was manifestly void, since inter alia it was unlimited in duration and area of operation, but the defendants contended that it merely defined the beneficiaries of the pension fund. Thesiger J, following the earlier case of *Wyatt v Kreglinger and Fernau*,[111] rejected this contention. He held that the provisions of the pension fund, including rule 16, were part of the terms of the plaintiff's employment, and that on grounds of public policy this rule was to be treated as equivalent to a covenant in restraint of trade. It was contrary to public policy that the community should be deprived of the services of a man skilled in a particular trade or technique.[112] Another case which bears on this problem of indirect

---

[108] *Mason v Provident Clothing and Supply Co Ltd* [1913] AC 724.

[109] *Dewes v Fitch* [1920] 2 Ch 159 at 185.

[110] [1966] 3 All ER 384, [1967] 1 WLR 273.   [111] [1933] 1 KB 793; p 525, above.

[112] Thesiger J accepted the reasoning in *Wyatt v Kreglinger and Fernau*, but reached a contrary result. In *Wyatt's* case the plaintiff lost his pension, in *Bull's* case he won it. The reason is clear. In the former case, assuming that there was a contract at all, the covenant in restraint of trade was the only consideration for the promise to give him a pension; in *Bull's* case the covenant formed part of a general agreement for which, apart from the void covenant, there was sufficient consideration. It was held, therefore, that the covenant could and should be severed, with the result that the promise to give the pension was untainted and enforceable; as to severance, see pp 541 ff, below.

evasion is *Kores Manufacturing Co Ltd v Kolok Manufacturing Co Ltd*[113] where two companies, manufacturers of similar products, agreed that neither would employ any servant who had been employed by the other during the last five years. The defendants broke their promise, and in the resulting action the arguments and the decision turned solely upon whether the agreement was unreasonable as between the parties. The Court of Appeal held it to be unreasonable in this respect, since it imposed upon the parties a restraint grossly in excess of what was adequate to prevent a misuse of their trade secrets and confidential information.

But Lord Reid and Lord Hodson have since observed that it would have been more correct to have stigmatised the agreement as contrary to the public interest.[114] It is respectfully submitted that this is a just criticism. The agreement was clearly designed to prevent employees from moving from one firm to the other in search of higher wages, but had the defendants attempted to do this by taking covenants against competition from individual employees the attempt would have failed. It is against the interests of the state that a man should be allowed to contract out of his right to work for whom he will. It would surely make a mockery of public policy if this liberty could be effectively restricted by a contract between third parties.[115]

b Restraints accepted by the vendor of a business

Although this type of restraint is more readily upheld than one imposed upon a servant, it will not be enforced unless it is connected with some proprietary interest in need of protection.[116] This requirement has at least two repercussions in the present class of contract.

First, there must be a genuine, not merely a colourable, sale of a business by the covenantor to the covenantee. This essential is well illustrated by *Vancouver Malt and Sake Brewing Co Ltd v Vancouver Breweries Ltd*[117] where the facts were these:

> The appellants held a brewer's licence in respect of their premises under which they were at liberty to brew beer. In fact, however, they brewed only sake, a concoction much appreciated by Japanese. The respondents held a similar licence and did in fact brew beer. The appellants purported to sell the goodwill of their brewer's licence, except so far as sake was concerned, and agreed not to manufacture beer for fifteen years.

Since the appellants were not in fact brewers of beer, the contract transferred to the respondents no proprietary interests in respect of which any restraint was

---

[113] [1959] Ch 108, [1958] 2 All ER 65.

[114] *Esso Petroleum Co Ltd v Harper's Garage (Stourport) Ltd* [1968] AC 269 at 300 and 319. This was the view taken by Lloyd Jacob J in the court of first instance in *Kores Manufacturing Co Ltd v Kolok Manufacturing Co* [1957] 3 All ER 158, [1957] 1 WLR 1012.

[115] The question of indirect evasion was mentioned by the Court of Appeal in the *Kores* case but was left open.

[116] P 527, above.   [117] [1934] AC 181.

justifiable. The covenant was a naked covenant not to brew beer, and as such it was void.

Secondly, it is only the actual business sold by the covenantor that is entitled to protection. In *British Reinforced Concrete Engineering Co Ltd v Schelff*,[118] for instance:

> The plaintiffs carried on a large business for the manufacture and sale of 'BRC' road reinforcements; the defendant carried on a small business for the sale of 'Loop' road reinforcements. The defendant sold his business to the plaintiffs and agreed not to compete with them in the manufacture or sale of road reinforcements.

The covenant was void. All that the defendant transferred was the business of selling the reinforcements called 'Loop'. It was, therefore, only with regards to that particular variety that it was justifiable to curb his future activities.

An express covenant by a vendor not to carry on a business similar to that which he has sold may, therefore, be valid, but only if it is no wider than is necessary for the adequate protection of the proprietary interest acquired by the purchaser. In considering this question, the court, as in the case of an employee's contract, pays special attention to the two factors of time and area. If there is no limit of time[119] or no reasonable limit of area[120] a restraint may be invalidated. Nevertheless, everything depends upon the circumstances, and a covenant which extends over the whole of the United Kingdom[121] or throughout the Dominion of Canada[122] or over the whole world,[123] or which restricts the covenantor for the remainder of his life,[124] may be valid in appropriate circumstances.

c Restraints arising from combinations for the regulation of trade relations

It frequently happens that manufacturers or traders form an association with the object of restricting the output or maintaining the selling price of certain commodities. At common law, a combination of this nature may be void as being in excessive restraint of trade. Whether it is so or not is determined according to the principles described above. The restriction is prima facie void and it cannot be enforced unless it is reasonable between the parties and consistent with the interests of the public.[125]

In applying these principles, however, the courts have in the past borne in mind the difference of environment in the various types of contract in restraint of trade. While they have looked jealously at a restraint imposed upon a servant, they have been

---

[118] [1921] 2 Ch 563.   [119] *Pellow v Ivey* (1933) 49 TLR 422.
[120] *Goldsoll v Goldman* [1915] 1 Ch 292.   [121] *Leather Cloth Co v Lorsont* (1869) LR 9 Eq 345.
[122] *Connors Bros Ltd v Connors* [1940] 4 All ER 179.
[123] *Nordenfelt v Maxim Nordenfelt Guns and Ammunition Co* [1894] AC 535, pp 518–520, above.
[124] *Elves v Crofts* (1850) 10 CB 241.
[125] *McEllistrim v Ballymacelligott Co-operative Agricultural and Dairy Society* [1919] AC 548 at 562, per Lord Birkenhead.

unsympathetic to a trader who, having voluntarily entered into a restrictive arrangement with other traders, attempts to escape from his obligation by the plea that he has imposed an unreasonable burden upon himself.[126] In commercial agreements of this kind, the parties themselves are the best judges of their own interests.[127] This disfavour, indeed distaste, for a plea that sounds peculiarly ill in the mouth of a man of business who has negotiated on an equal footing with the other members of the combination is well illustrated by *English Hop Growers v Dering*,[128] where the defendant had agreed to deliver to the plaintiff association, of which he was a member, all hops grown on his land in 1926: short shrift was given by the court to his contention that this restriction upon his power of disposal was unreasonable. Growers were faced with ruin owing to excessive stocks of hops accumulated during government control in the 1914–1918 war, and the association had been formed in order to ensure that in any year when there was a surplus the inevitable loss to members should be reduced to a minimum and should be equitably distributed among them. In the words of Scrutton LJ:

> I see nothing unreasonable in hop growers combining to secure a steady and profitable price, by eliminating competition amongst themselves, and putting the marketing in the hands of one agent, with full power to fix prices and hold up supplies, the benefit and loss being divided amongst the members.[129]

Everything, however, depends upon the circumstances, and a different decision was reached by the House of Lords in *McEllistrim v Ballymacelligott Co-operative Agricultural and Dairy Society*.[130]

> The respondent society manufactured cheese and butter from milk supplied by its members. The rules of the society provided that no member should sell milk to any other person without the consent of a committee; that no member should be entitled to withdraw from the society unless his shares were transferred or cancelled; and that the consent of the committee, which might be refused without giving reasons, should be essential to the effectiveness of such a transfer or cancellation.

It is not surprising that this arrangement was held to be unreasonable between the parties. The society, no doubt, was entitled to such a degree of protection as would ensure stability in the supply of milk. It was not entitled to impose a life-long embargo upon the trading freedom of its members. The obligation of a member to allocate all

---

[126] *English Hop Growers v Dering* [1928] 2 KB 174 at 181, per Scrutton LJ.
[127] *North-Western Salt Co Ltd v Electrolytic Alkali Co Ltd* [1914] AC 461 at 471, per Lord Haldane.
[128] [1928] 2 KB 174. See also *Birtley and District Co-operative Society Ltd v Windy Nook and District Industrial Co-operative Society Ltd (No 2)* [1960] 2 QB 1, [1959] 1 All ER 623.
[129] [1928] 2 KB 174 at 181, [1928] All ER 396 at 400.
[130] [1919] AC 548.

his milk to the society was to endure for his life, unless he was fortunate enough to obtain the sanction of the committee to a transfer of his shares. Therefore, as Lord Birkenhead remarked, a member, if he joined the society young enough and lived long enough, would be precluded for a period of sixty years or more from selling his milk in the free market.[131] The arrangement was an attempt to eliminate competition altogether and was void.

d Restrictions accepted by distributors of merchandise

It not infrequently happens that a manufacturer or a wholesaler refuses to make merchandise available for distribution to the public unless the distributor accepts certain conditions that restrict his liberty of trading. The object may be, for instance, to prevent him from selling similar goods supplied by competitors of the manufacturer. Such was the main purpose of the *solus* agreements that were discussed in *Esso Petroleum Co Ltd v Harper's Garage (Stourport) Ltd.*[132]

The primary question that arose in this case was whether the agreements were caught by the doctrine of restraint of trade. Nothing need be added to the account already given of this aspect of the dispute.[133] But, having decided that the doctrine applied to the facts, the House of Lords then considered the second question, namely, whether the restrictions were nevertheless justifiable and enforceable on the ground that they were reasonable and not in conflict with the requirements of public policy. On this aspect of the case, it was held that there was nothing unreasonable in the adoption by the parties of the *solus* system. They both benefited. The Esso firm were able to organise a more efficient and economical system of distribution; the distributor not only gained a rebate on the wholesale price of petrol, but if short of funds he could rely on the financial backing of a powerful corporation. Nevertheless, tying agreements of this nature, though reasonable in general, will become unreasonable if made to endure for an excessive period. In the instant circumstances, four-and-a-half years was reasonable, twenty-one years was unreasonable. Therefore the first contract was valid, the second was void.[134]

The majority of their Lordships emphasised that, since a restraint of trade implies that the covenantor agrees to surrender some freedom which otherwise he would enjoy, a distinction must be drawn between a covenantor who is already in possession of the garage site when he enters into a *solus* agreement with an oil company, and one who obtains possession from the company after the agreement has been made. In the latter case, the fact that he surrenders no freedom previously enjoyed by him must

---

131 Ibid at 564.
132 [1968] AC 269, [1967] 1 All ER 69. For the facts, see p 523, above.
133 Pp 523–525, above.
134 Distinguishing *Petrofina (Great Britain) Ltd v Martin* [1966] Ch 146, [1966] 1 All ER 126. In *Alec Lobb (Garages) Ltd v Total Oil (GB) Ltd* [1985] 1 All ER 303 the Court of Appeal upheld a restraint for 21 years as reasonable in all the circumstances.

have a significant bearing upon the question whether the restraint is reasonable.[135] In the later case of *Cleveland Petroleum Co Ltd v Dartstone Ltd*,[136] the Court of Appeal stressed the merit of this distinction and laid down the rule that where a person takes possession of premises under a *solus* agreement, not having been in possession previously, the restrictions placed upon his trading activities are prima facie binding upon him. But the presumption in favour of their validity will be rebutted, it would seem, if the inference from the relevant circumstances is that their enforcement will manifestly be detrimental to the interests of the public. If this were not so, it would be possible to avoid a rule of public policy by a mere conveyancing device. That the question is one of substance and not of form is clearly shown by the decision of the Privy Council in *Amoco Australia Pty Ltd v Rocca Bros Motor Engineering Co Pty Ltd*.[137]

An analogy to the restriction placed upon the distributor in these cases is furnished by that type of exclusive agreement by which a trader promises to take all the goods of a particular kind required in his business from one supplier. Such was the case in *Servais Bouchard v Prince's Hall Restaurant Ltd*[138] where the plaintiff was given the exclusive right for an indefinite period of supplying burgundy to a restaurant keeper. In the Court of Appeal two views were expressed upon the question whether this agreement was subject to the doctrine of restraint of trade. The majority view, which would seem to be preferable, was that it was prima facie void and therefore in need of justification; but Henn Collins MR considered that it was not caught by the doctrine. In the result, however, it was unanimously held that in the instant circumstances the restraint was justifiable as being reasonable.

Similar considerations apply to a contract for exclusive services. So in *A Schroeder Music Publishing Co Ltd v Macaulay*.[139]

> The plaintiff, a young and unknown song writer, entered into a contract with the defendants, a music publishing company, on their standard terms. Under the contract the plaintiff assigned the world copyright in any musical composition produced by him solely or jointly. The defendants did not undertake to exploit all or any of the compositions though they agreed to pay royalties on those in fact exploited. The agreement was to run for five years but to be automatically extended for a further five years if the royalties reached a total of £5,000. The defendants

---

[135] *Esso Petroleum Co Ltd v Harper's Garage (Stourport) Ltd* [1968] AC 269 at 298 (Lord Reid); at 309 (Lord Morris of Borth-y-Gest); at 316–317 (Lord Hodson); at 325 (Lord Pearce). Lord Pearce, indeed, citing the analogy of the tie between a publican and brewer expressed the view that if a man takes a lease of land subject to a tie, thereby obtaining favourable terms, he cannot repudiate the tie and retain the benefits. The doctrine of restraint of trade is altogether excluded.

[136] [1969] 1 All ER 201, [1969] 1 WLR 116.

[137] [1975] AC 561, [1975] 1 All ER 968 and see also *Alec Lobb (Garages) Ltd v Total Oil (GB) Ltd* [1985] 1 All ER 303, [1985] 1 WLR 173, CA.

[138] (1904) 20 TLR 574.

[139] [1974] 3 All ER 616, [1974] 1 WLR 1308. See also *Clifford Davis Management Ltd v WEA Records Ltd* [1975] 1 All ER 237, [1975] 1 WLR 61.

could terminate the agreement at any time by giving a month's notice, but there was no similar provision in favour of the plaintiff.

The House of Lords had no difficulty in holding that such an agreement was within the ambit of restraint of trade and that this particular agreement was unreasonable since the terms combined a total commitment by the plaintiff with a striking lack of obligation on the defendant.

These rules of the common law which have brought within the doctrine of restraint of trade restrictions, designed by manufacturers or distributors of goods to stifle competition, have lost much of their value. Their practical importance has been greatly reduced as a result of legislative changes effected since the Second World War. These changes are discussed in Chapter 10.

2 THE LEGAL CONSEQUENCES

A The contract is void in so far as it contravenes public policy

Contracts that tend to oust the jurisdiction of the courts or to prejudice the status of marriage and contracts in restraint of trade, though contrary to public policy, are by no means totally void. Suppose, for instance, that as part of a contract of employment a servant enters into a contract in restraint of trade which is in fact excessively wide and therefore void. Is it to be said that this invalidity affects the whole contract and precludes the servant from suing for wrongful dismissal or the master from recovering damages if the servant leaves without due notice? It is clear that the law does not go to these lengths.[140] The truth of this was recognised as far back as 1837 by Lord Abinger in *Wallis v Day*.[141] In that case the plaintiff had sold his business of a carrier to the defendant and had agreed, in return for a weekly salary of £2 3s 10d, to serve the defendant as assistant for life. He further agreed that, except as such assistant, he would not for the rest of his life exercise the trade of a carrier. In an action brought by the plaintiff to recover eighteen weeks' arrears of salary, the defendant demurred on the ground that the agreement, being in restraint of trade, was void and that no part of it was enforceable. It became unnecessary to decide this point, since the court held the restraint to be reasonable, but Lord Abinger dealt with the demurrer as follows:

> The defendant demurred, on the ground that this covenant, being in restraint of trade, was illegal, and that therefore the whole contract was void. I cannot however accede to that conclusion. If a party enters into several covenants, one of which cannot be enforced against

---

[140] *Bennett v Bennett* [1952] 1 KB 249 at 260, [1952] 1 All ER 413 at 421; see also Salmond and Williams *The Law of Contract* p 375.

[141] (1837) 2 M & W 273.

him, he is not therefore released from performing the others. And in the present case, the defendants might have maintained an action against the plaintiff for not rendering them the services he covenanted to perform, there being nothing illegal in that part of the contract.[142]

The same reasoning was adopted in a later case,[143] where pensions were payable under a trust which, in one of its clauses, imposed an excessive restraint upon the pensioners. Eve J directed that the trust might lawfully be carried out, since it was not invalidated merely because the restraint might be declared void in future litigation. It was impossible, he said, to regard the trust as destroyed by the invalidity of one of its clauses. Any doubt that might still have survived was finally dispelled in two modern cases where the Court of Appeal held that the invalidity of a promise which is contrary to public policy does not nullify the whole contract, but that the valid promises, if severable, remain fully enforceable.[144]

In short, the invalidity of the class of contract now being considered goes no further than is necessary to satisfy the requirements of public policy. Unless the offending clause is in question in the actual litigation, it has no effect upon the validity of the contract.

B Money paid or property transferred by one party to the other is recoverable

Suppose that the vendor of a business agrees not to compete with the purchaser and that as security for this undertaking he deposits a sum of money with the purchaser. If this restraint against competition is held to be excessive and void, is the vendor precluded from recovering the deposit? It would seem on principle that the right of recovery is unaffected. The contract is not improper in itself, and it would be extravagant to suggest that the whole transaction is so objectionable as to be caught by the maxim *ex turpi causa non oritur actio*. The decisions are too few to be conclusive one way or the other, but there is authority for the view that equity at least does not always regard an infringement of public policy as a bar to relief.[145] Thus Lord Eldon went so far as to say:

> It is settled, that if a transaction be objectionable on grounds of public policy, the parties to it may be relieved; the relief not being given for their sake, but for the sake of the public.[146]

It may be that this statement is too wide in view of the more expanded meaning that has been given to the term 'public policy' since Lord Eldon's day, or it may be that relief will be granted only where one party has been less guilty than the other,[147] but at

---

[142] Ibid at 280–281.   [143] *Re Prudential Assurance Co's Trust Deed* [1934] Ch 338.
[144] *Bennett v Bennett* [1952] 1 KB 249, [1952] 1 All ER 413; *Goodinson v Goodinson* [1954] 2 QB 118, [1954] 2 All ER 255. As to when the promises may be severed, see pp 541 ff, below.
[145] Ashburner *Principles of Equity* (2nd edn) p 471.
[146] *Vauxhall Bridge Co v Earl Spencer* (1821) Jac 64 at 67.
[147] *Reynell v Sprye* (1851) 1 De GM & G 656 at 678–679, per Knight Bruce LJ.

any rate it is well established that money paid under a marriage brokage contract is recoverable both at common law and in equity. This was decided in *Hermann v Charlesworth*,[148] where the facts were as follows:

> Charlesworth agreed that he would introduce gentlemen to Miss Hermann with a view to matrimony, in consideration of an immediate payment of £52 and a payment of £250 on the day of the marriage. He introduced her to several gentlemen and corresponded with others on her behalf, but his efforts were fruitless. Miss Hermann sued for the return of the £52 and was successful.

Her right at common law rested on the principle that money deposited to abide the result of an event is recoverable if the event does not happen. No marriage had taken place and there had been a total failure of consideration. But quite apart from this she was entitled to exploit the wider form of relief granted by equity. Sir Richard Henn Collins, citing the old case of *Goldsmith v Bruning*[149] amongst other authorities, showed that equity did not apply the rigid test of total failure of consideration, but so disliked contracts of this type that it was prepared to grant relief even after the marriage had been solemnised.

It is difficult to believe that the court would nowadays apply a more stringent test than this to a contract in restraint of trade. If money paid under a marriage brokage contract is recoverable, on what sensible ground can recovery of payments made under a contract in restraint of trade be refused?

C Subsequent transactions are not necessarily void

It has already been seen that if a contract as formed is illegal at common law, then any transaction which is founded on and springs from it is void.[150] This is not the case with the contracts under discussion. They are not illegal nor, indeed, are they void *in toto*. It follows that subsequent contracts are void only so far as they are related to that part of the original contract that is itself void. Suppose, for instance, that the vendor of a business agrees, in terms which are unreasonably wide, not to compete with the purchaser, and that after committing a breach of this void undertaking he executes a bond agreeing to pay £1,000 to the purchaser by way of reparation. It goes without saying that no action will lie on the bond. It is impossible to divorce the apparently valid promise of payment from the void restraint. If, on the other hand, the title to part of the premises conveyed with the business turned out to be defective, and the vendor agreed to compensate the purchaser with the payment of £1,000, there would be no obstacle to the recovery of this sum.

---

[148] [1905] 2 KB 123.
[149] (1700) 1 Eq Cas Abr 89, pl 4.
[150] Pp 503–505, above. *Fisher v Bridges* (1853) 3 E & B 642.

D The contract, if subject to a foreign law by which it is valid, is enforceable in England

We have seen that a foreign contract which contravenes what is regarded in England as an essential moral interest is not enforceable by action in this country, notwithstanding that it is valid by its proper law.[151] Such is the case where the principle of morality infringed by the contract is in the English view of so compelling a nature that it must be maintained at all costs and in all circumstances. In other words, certain of the specific rules derived from the doctrine of public policy are of universal, not merely domestic, application. It would be an exaggeration, however, to assert that the three types of contract now being considered offend any principle of so commanding a nature. The reason why these particular contracts are frowned upon by the law is not that they are essentially reprehensible, but that they conflict with the accepted standards of English life. If, for instance, the employee of a Parisian tradesman were to be sued in England for breach of an undertaking never to enter a similar employment anywhere in France, it would be an affectation of superior virtue for the English court to invoke the doctrine of public policy and to dismiss the action, always assuming, of course, that such an undertaking is valid by French law. The position might no doubt be different in the exceptional case where a French contract imposed an unreasonable restraint on competition *in England*.

After certain indeterminate decisions,[152] this view has now prevailed, and it has been held in *Addison v Brown*[153] that a foreign contract of the present class is unaffected by the English doctrine.

> An American citizen, domiciled in California, agreed to pay his wife a weekly sum by way of maintenance, and it was further agreed that neither party should apply to the Californian court for a variation of the agreement and that if in subsequent divorce proceedings the court should provide for maintenance 'the provisions hereof shall control notwithstanding the terms of any such judgment'. Some years later the Californian court granted a decree of divorce at the instance of the husband and incorporated the agreement as part of the divorce.

To an action brought by the wife in England for the recovery of arrears of maintenance, it was objected that her claim was not sustainable, since the agreement was designed to oust the jurisdiction of the Californian court and was therefore contrary to the English doctrine of public policy. The objection failed. It is not the function of the doctrine to dictate to a foreign law whether an agreement of this kind shall be enforceable.

---

[151] Pp 505–506, above.

[152] *Rousillon v Rousillon* (1880) 14 ChD 351; *Hope v Hope* (1857) 8 De GM & G 731. These are inconclusive because, certainly in the first case and probably in the second, the proper law was English.

[153] [1954] 2 All ER 213, [1954] 1 WLR 779. Compare *Bennett v Bennett* [1952] 1 KB 249, [1952] 1 All ER 413.

E Lawful promises may be severable and enforceable[154]

Severance means the rejection from a contract of objectionable promises or the objectionable elements of a particular promise, and the retention of those promises or of those parts of a particular promise that are valid.

It should be noticed at once that this is not allowed in the case of the contracts discussed in the previous chapter and which are illegal at common law as being contrary to public policy.

> If one of the promises is to do an act which is either in itself a criminal offence or *contra bonos mores*, the court will regard the whole contract as void.[155]

On principle the same is true of contracts prohibited by statute, and there is clear authority to that effect;[156] but in at least one case, *Kearney v Whitehaven Colliery Co*[157] the principle seems to have been ignored.

On the other hand, severance may be allowed if the contract is one that is void at common law on grounds of public policy or if it is void by statute, provided in this latter case that the statute, when properly construed, admits the possibility.[158] Most, but by no means all, of the relevant decisions have been concerned with agreements in restraint of trade.

The doctrine of severance in the case of a void contract is used with two meanings to serve two purposes. First, it may be invoked to cut out altogether an objectionable promise from a contract leaving the rest of the contract valid and enforceable, as, for example, where a promise is void as being designed to oust the jurisdiction of the court. In such a case the offending promise is eliminated from the contract. Secondly, severance may operate to cut down an objectionable promise in extent, but not to cut it out of the contract altogether, as, for example, where an agreement in restraint of trade which is void as being unreasonably wide is converted into a valid promise by

---

[154] The history of this branch of the law has been long and tortuous and many of the older decisions and judicial generalisations are no longer acceptable. Its development is fully traced by Marsh 64 LQR 230, 347, 69 LQR 111.

[155] *Bennett v Bennett* [1952] 1 KB 249 at 253–254; *Goodinson v Goodinson* [1954] 2 QB 118 at 120–121. See eg *Lound v Grimwade* (1888) 39 ChD 605; *Alexander v Rayson* [1936] 1 KB 169; *Napier v National Business Agency Ltd* [1951] 2 All ER 264; *Kuenigl v Donnersmarck* [1955] 1 QB 515 at 537. In *Fielding and Platt Ltd v Selim Najjar Ltd* [1969] 2 All ER 150 at 153, [1969] 1 WLR 357 at 362, Lord Denning MR suggested that an illegal term might be severed from a contract leaving the rest intact. But his statement was clearly an obiter dictum, and it is respectfully submitted that it was made *per incuriam*. The contract before the court was lawful, not illegal, though one party without the knowledge of the other had exploited it illegally. Therefore the innocent could enforce it, and no question of severance arose.

[156] *Hopkins v Prescott* (1847) 4 CB 578; *Ritchie v Smith* (1848) 6 CB 462.

[157] [1893] 1 QB 700.

[158] See eg the Race Relations Act 1968, s 23; ss 86, 88 and 89 of Rent Act 1968; *Ailion v Spiekermann* [1976] Ch 158, [1976] 1 All ER 497.

the elimination of its unreasonable features. In such a case, the promise remains in the contract shorn of its offending parts and so reduced in extent.

To distinguish these two ways in which the doctrine of severance may operate it is not mere pedantry, for the test of severability is not the same in each case. Whether an entire promise may be eliminated from a contract is tested by the rule laid down in *Goodinson v Goodinson*;[159] whether a particular promise may be reduced in extent is governed by the different principle of divisibility laid down in a series of decisions culminating in *Attwood v Lamont*.[160]

i Elimination of a promise

Whether an entire promise may be eliminated from a contract depends upon whether it forms the whole or only part of the consideration. If it is substantially the only return given for the promise of the other party, severance is ruled out and the contract fails *in toto*. If, on the other hand, it goes only to part of the consideration—if it is merely subsidiary to the main purpose of the contract—severance is permissible. This distinction was laid down and applied by the Court of Appeal in *Goodinson v Goodinson*.[161]

> A contract made between husband and wife, who had already separated provided, according to the interpretation put upon it by the court, that the husband would pay his wife a weekly sum by way of maintenance in consideration that she would indemnify him against all debts incurred by her, would not pledge his credit and would not take any matrimonial proceedings against him in respect of maintenance.

The last promise thus made by the wife was void since its object was to oust the jurisdiction of the courts, but it was held that this did not vitiate the rest of the contract. It was not the only, and in the view of the court not the main, consideration furnished by the wife. She had also promised to indemnify the husband against her debts and not to pledge his credit. With the exception of the objectionable promise, therefore, the contract stood and the wife was entitled to recover arrears of maintenance.[162]

ii Reduction of a promise

The second question is whether the scope of an individual promise may be reduced without eliminating it *in toto*.

---

[159] See n 161, below.   [160] P 544, below.

[161] [1954] 2 QB 118, [1954] 2 All ER 255. See also *Brooks v Burns Philp Trustee Co Ltd* [1969] ALR 321 and *Stenhouse Australia Ltd v Phillips* [1974] AC 391, [1974] 1 All ER 117. *Carney v Herbert* [1985] AC 301, [1985] 1 All ER 438. *Marshall v NM Financial Management* [1995] 4 All ER 785.

[162] The Matrimonial Causes Act 1973, s 7, now provides that the court may approve any agreement made between husband and wife prior to a divorce suit. This provision, however, in no way affects the rule that any agreement whose object is to oust the jurisdiction of the court is void: *Wright v Wright* [1970] 3 All ER 209 at 213, [1970] 1 WLR 1219 at 1223, per Sir Gordon Willmer. See *Hyman v Hyman* [1929] AC 601. See also Matrimonial Causes Act 1973, s 34.

The predominant principle here is that the court will not rewrite the promise as expressed by the parties. It will not add or alter words and thus frame a promise that the promisor might well have made, but did not make,[163] for that would be to destroy the 'main purport and substance' of what has been agreed.[164] The parties themselves must have sown the seeds of severability in the sense that it is possible to construe the promise drafted by them as divisible into a number of separate and independent parts. If this is the correct construction, then one or more of the parts may be struck out and yet leave a promise that is substantially the same in character as that framed by the parties, though it will be diminished in extent by the reduction of its sphere of operation.[165]

In a modern case, it was argued that a clause in a lease was void as purporting to oust the jurisdiction of the court on question of law.[166] Ungoed Thomas J held that the contract, when properly construed, did not have this object in view. Had such been its purpose, it would have been void. But the learned judge also considered what the situation would have been had he found that the clause did purport to exclude the court's jurisdiction. Might it then have been severed from the contract as a whole? Its severability would have been prima facie possible, since there was no question of illegality and the offending words were subsidiary to the main purpose of the contract. The stumbling-block, however, would have been that the clause had not been so drafted as to enable these words to be deleted without altering the general character of the contract. The removal of the objectionable clause would have required the contract to be remodelled; and this was not within the province of the court.

The possibility of reducing the scope of promise without eliminating it *in toto* has often arisen in cases of restraint of trade. If a promise not to compete against an employer or against the purchaser of a business is void as being unreasonably wide, the promisee may argue that it may and should be reduced to reasonable dimensions and thus be rendered enforceable.

A clear example of a promise that, according to the language used by the parties, was divisible in the above sense was *Price v Green*[167] where the seller of a perfumery business, apparently carried on in London, agreed with the purchaser that he would not carry on a similar business 'within the cities of London or Westminster or within the distance of 600 miles from the same respectively'. The promise was held to be valid so far as it related to London and Westminster, but void as to the distance of 600 miles. The substantial character of the promise remained unimpaired, despite the loss of one of its parts. Again, in *Nordenfelt v Maxim Nordenfelt Guns and*

163 *Putsman v Taylor* [1927] 1 KB 637 at 639–640.
164 *Mason v Provident Clothing and Supply Co Ltd* [1913] AC 724 at 745, per Lord Moulton.
165 *Attwood v Lamont* [1920] 3 KB 571.
166 *Re Davstone Estates Ltd's Leases, Manprop Ltd v O'Dell* [1969] 2 Ch 378, [1969] 2 All ER 849.
167 (1847) 16 M & W 346. See also *Scorer v Seymour-Johns* [1966] 3 All ER 347, [1966] 1 WLR 1419 (restraint imposed on employee); *Macfarlane v Kent* [1965] 2 All ER 376, [1965] 1 WLR 1019 (restraint imposed on expelled partner); *Bull v Pitney-Bowes* [1966] 3 All ER 384, [1967] 1 WLR 273.

Ammunition Co,[168] as we have already seen, the House of Lords allowed the severance of a covenant against competition that was clearly divisible into two parts, one reasonable the other not.

On the other hand, where the promise is indivisible, where it cannot be construed as falling into distinct parts, severance is ruled out, for to attempt it would inevitably result in an agreement different in nature from that made by the parties. In *Baker v Hedgecock,*[169] for instance:

> A foreman cutter entered the service of the plaintiff, a tailor carrying on business at 61 High Holborn, and agreed that for a period of two years after leaving the employment he would not carry on, either on his own account or otherwise, *any business whatsoever* within a distance of one mile from 61 High Holborn. After his dismissal he set up as a tailor within 100 yards of that address.

The plaintiff admitted that the agreement, since it extended to any business whatsoever, was so wide as to be unreasonable, but he asked the court 'to treat the covenant as divisible, and to enforce it to the extent to which it is reasonable, while declining to enforce such part of it as is unreasonable'.[170] In refusing this request, Chitty J illustrated the fallacy of the plaintiff's argument in these words:

> Thus if the covenant were, eg, not to carry on a business in any part of the whole world, the Court would be asked to uphold it by construing it as a covenant not to carry on the business within, say, a limit of two miles, which would in effect be making a new covenant, not that to which the parties agreed. In *Price v Green* there were in fact two covenants, or one covenant which was capable of being construed divisibly.[171]

A comparison of the two leading cases of *Attwood v Lamont* and *Goldsoll v Goldman* may illustrate the nice problems of discrimination that may arise in this branch of the law. In *Attwood v Lamont:*[172]

> A carried on business as a draper tailor and general outfitter in a shop at Kidderminster which was organised in several different departments each with a manager. X, who was head cutter and manager of the tailoring department but who had nothing to do with the other departments, agreed that he would not at any time either on his own account or on behalf of anybody else carry on the trades of a tailor, dressmaker, general draper, milliner, hatter, haberdasher, gentlemen's, ladies' or children's outfitter at any place within ten miles of Kidderminster.

---

[168] Pp 518–520, above. See also *Nicholls v Stretton* (1847) 10 QB 346, *Goldsoll v Goldman* [1915] 1 Ch 292; *Putsman v Taylor* [1927] 1 KB 637.

[169] (1888) 39 ChD 520.

[170] Ibid at 521, per counsel.

[171] Ibid at 522–523, see also *Continental Tyre and Rubber (Great Britain) Co Ltd v Heath* (1913) 29 TLR 308.

[172] [1920] 3 KB 571.

The question was whether any part of the agreement could be enforced. It would have been legitimate to restrain the improper use by X of the knowledge of customers acquired by him in his capacity as manager of the tailoring department. But the restraint as drafted, since it affected trade in other departments where he would not meet customers, admittedly gave A more than adequate protection. It was argued, however, that the agreement ought to be severed and limited to the business of a tailor.

The divisional court allowed this severance. It took the view that the agreement constituted 'a series of distinct obligations in separate and clearly defined divisions',[173] and that it was possible to run a blue pencil through all the trades except that of tailoring without altering the main 'purport and substance'[174] of what the parties had written. The Court of Appeal unanimously reversed this decision. It took the view that the parties had made a single indivisible agreement the substantial object of which was to protect the entire business carried on by the employer. Younger LJ summarised this view as follows:

> The learned judges of the divisional court, I think, took the view that such severance always was permissible when it could be effectively accomplished by the action of a blue pencil. I do not agree. The doctrine of severance has not, I think, gone further than to make it permissible in a case where the covenant is not really a single covenant but is in effect a combination of several distinct covenants. In that case and where the severance can be carried out without the addition or alteration of a word, it is permissible. But in that case only.
>
> Now, here, I think, there is in truth but one covenant for the protection of the respondent's entire business, and not several covenants for the protection of his several businesses. The respondent is, on the evidence, not carrying on several businesses but one business, and, in any opinion this covenant must stand or fall in its unaltered form.[175]

In *Goldsoll v Goldman*:[176]

> The defendant, who carried on a business in London for the sale of imitation jewellery, sold his business to the plaintiff and agreed that for a period of two years he would not, either solely or jointly, deal in real or imitation jewellery in any part of the United Kingdom or in France, USA, Russia or Spain, or within twenty-five miles of Potsdammerstrasse, Berlin, or St Stefans Kirche, Vienna.

The extension of the restraint to the whole of the United Kingdom was reasonable, for the plaintiff, who had for a considerable time carried on a similar business in London, gained most of his customers from advertisements in the illustrated papers which circulated throughout the country. It was held that the contract could and must be severed in two respects: first, the area outside the United Kingdom must be removed from it; secondly, the prohibition against dealing in real jewellery must also be removed.

---

[173] [1920] 2 KB 146 at 159.   [174] Ibid at 156.   [175] [1920] 3 KB at 593.
[176] [1915] 1 Ch 292.

The question is whether this decision can be reconciled with that in *Attwood v Lamont*. The crux of the matter seems to be whether in each of these cases the contract as framed by the parties was divisible into a number of separate promises, for if so, and only if so, the elimination of one or more of the objectionable promises would still leave the substantial character of the contract unchanged. It may perhaps fairly be said that this basic element of divisibility, while present in *Goldsoll v Goldman*, was absent in *Attwood v Lamont*, for in the latter case the enumeration of the various trades was only a laborious description of the entire business carried on by the employer. Since the contract was essentially indivisible, it had to stand or fall as originally drafted.

It has been thought, however, that the reconciliation of these two decisions is to be found in the fact that the one concerned a service contract, the other a contract for a sale of a business, for it is now generally accepted that the latter merits a less rigorous treatment than the former. It is only common justice that the purchaser shall be able to reap the benefit of what he has bought, and therefore the courts are more astute than they would be in the case of a service contract to construe an agreement by the seller not to compete as a combination of several distinct promises. This distinction was viewed with apparent approval by the Court of Appeal in *Ronbar Enterprises Ltd v Green*[177] (a case of vendor and purchaser) but it was disapproved in *T Lucas & Co Ltd v Mitchell*[178] (a case of master and servant).

---

[177] [1954] 2 All ER 266, [1954] 1 WLR 815, where the court merely expunged two words from what appears to have been an indivisible covenant. See also Lord Moulton in *Mason v Provident Clothing and Supply Co Ltd* [1913] AC 724 at 745.
[178] [1974] Ch 129, [1972] 3 All ER 689.

13 CAPACITY OF PARTIES

SUMMARY

1 MINORS[1]

A The effect of contracts made by minors

Contracts made by minors, ie persons under eighteen years of age,[2] are governed by the rules of common law as altered by the Minors' Contracts Act 1987.[3]

The general rule at common law was that a contract made by an infant was voidable at his option. The word 'voidable', however, was used in two different senses. Certain contracts were voidable in the sense that they were valid and binding upon him unless he repudiated them before, or within a reasonable time after, the attainment of his majority. Other contracts were voidable in a different sense, ie they were not binding upon the infant unless ratified by him when he reached 21 years of age.

Two types of transactions, namely beneficial contracts of service and contracts for necessaries, were treated as exceptional. The former were regarded as valid. The latter imposed liability upon the infant, though whether this was of a contractual nature or not was a matter of controversy.

It will be convenient to discuss the different types of transactions in the following order:

1   Contracts for necessaries.

2   Beneficial contracts of service.

3   Voidable contracts.

4   Other contracts.

1 Contracts for necessaries

It has been recognised from the earliest times that an infant is obliged to pay for necessaries that have been supplied to him. The word *necessaries* is not confined to articles necessary to the support of life, but includes articles and services fit to maintain the particular person in the station of life in which he moves.[4] So far as concerns

---

[1] Until 1969 minors were more usually called infants in the legislation and cases. See Family Law Reform Act 1969, s 12.

[2] Family Law Reform Act 1969, s 1. At common law, the age of majority was twenty-one. The Act provides that persons over eighteen but under twenty-one years of age on 1 January 1970, shall be regarded as having attained full age on that day. For a comparative survey of the law, see Hartwig 15 ICLQ 780; Thomas 1972 Acta Juridica 151; Valero 27 ICLQ 215. The Act of 1969 was based on the report of the Committee on the Age of Majority (Cmnd 3342). For reform proposals in other common law jurisdictions see Harland *The Law of Minors in Relation to Contracts and Property*, Pearce 44 ALJ 269; Percy 53 Can Bar Rev 1.

[3] Between 1874 and 1987 the law was bedevilled by the Infants' Relief Act 1874, a singularly badly drafted statute. Proposals for reform were made by the Committee on the Age of Majority but not enacted. The 1987 Act arose from proposals made by the Law Commission (Law Com No 134).

[4] *Peters v Fleming* (1840) 6 M & W 42 at 46–47, per Parke B.

goods it has been statutorily defined as meaning 'goods suitable to the condition in life of the minor and to his actual requirements at the time of the sale and delivery'.[5] Perhaps the best statement of the law, at least as applied to nineteenth-century conditions, is that given by Alderson B.

> Things necessary are those without which an individual cannot reasonably exist. In the first place, food, raiment, lodging and the like. About these there is no doubt. Again, as the proper cultivation of the mind is as expedient as the support of the body, instruction in art or trade, or intellectual, moral and religious information may be a necessary also. Again, as man lives in society, the assistance and attendance of others may be a necessary to his well-being. Hence attendance may be the subject of an infant's contract. Then the classes being established, the subject matter and extent of the contract may vary according to the state and condition of the infant himself. His clothes may be fine or coarse according to his rank; his education may vary according to the station he is to fill; and the medicines will depend on the illness with which he is afflicted, and the extent of his probable means when of full age. So again, the nature and extent of the attendance will depend on his position in society . . . But in all these cases it must first be made out that the class itself is one in which the things furnished are essential to the existence and reasonable advantage and comfort of the infant contractor. Thus, articles of *mere* luxury are always excluded,[6] though luxurious articles of utility are in some cases allowed.[7]

Necessaries for the members of a married minor's family are on the same footing as necessaries for himself, and it is well established that he is liable on a contract for the burial of his wife or children.[8]

To render a minor liable for necessaries it must be proved, not only that the goods are suitable to his station in life, but also that they are suitable to his actual requirements at the time of their delivery. If he is already sufficiently provided with goods of the kind in question, then, even though this fact is not known to the plaintiff, the price is irrecoverable.[9]

Thus in a case in 1908, where a Savile Row tailor sought to recover £122 19s 6d for clothes (including eleven fancy waistcoats at two guineas each), supplied to an infant undergraduate at Cambridge, it was held that the action must fail, since the evidence

---

[5] Sale of Goods Act 1979, s 3(3). Winfield 58 LQR 82.

[6] 'Suppose the son of the richest man in the kingdom to have been supplied with diamonds and racehorses, the judge ought to tell the jury that such articles cannot possibly be necessaries': *Wharton v Mackenzie* (1844) 5 QB 606 at 612, per Coleridge J. In that case it was held that fruits, ices and confectionery supplied to an Oxford undergraduate for private dinner parties could not without further explanation be treated as necessaries.

[7] *Chapple v Cooper* (1844) 13 M & W 252 at 258. It would appear that in the affluent and permissive society of today many articles that would have ranked as luxurious in the learned baron's time would now be regarded as 'things essential to the existence and reasonable advantage and comfort of the infant contractor'.

[8] *Chapple v Cooper*, above.

[9] *Barnes & Co v Toye* (1884) 13 QBD 410; *Nash v Inman* [1908] 2 KB 1.

showed that the defendant was already amply supplied with clothing suitable to his position.[10]

Whether articles are necessaries is a question of mixed law and fact.[11] The preliminary question of law for the court is whether in the circumstances the article is capable of being a necessary. The onus of establishing this lies on the plaintiff, who must prove that the goods are of a description reasonably suitable to a person in the station in life of the minor defendant. If he fails, the court rules that there is no evidence on which it can properly find for him, and judgment is declared in favour of the defendant.

Thus in one case it was held that a pair of jewelled solitaires worth £25 and an antique goblet worth fifteen guineas could not possibly be regarded as necessaries for an infant possessing an income of £500 a year.[12] There was no case to be submitted to the jury.

If, however, the court decides that the articles are clearly capable of being necessaries, as, for instance, clothes or food, it is a question of fact whether they are necessaries in the particular circumstances. The actual requirements of the minor must be assessed, and it must be decided whether he was adequately supplied with articles of the kind in question at the time of their delivery.[13] Again, if the article is one which may or may not be necessary, such as a watch, an exceptionally expensive coat or a pair of binoculars, it must be decided whether it is so in fact having regard inter alia to the social standing, profession and duties of the minor.

So in *Peters v Fleming*[14] the court decided that prima facie it was not unreasonable for a minor undergraduate to have a watch and consequently a watch-chain, but they left it to the jury to find whether the gold chain supplied to him on credit was of a kind reasonably suitable for his requirements.

In addition to food, clothing and lodging, the following amongst other things, have been held to be necessaries: uniforms for a member of one of the fighting forces;[15] means of conveyance required by a minor for the exercise of his calling;[16] and legal advice.[17]

A contract for the supply even of goods or services that are clearly suitable to the requirements of a minor is void if it contains terms that are harsh and onerous to him.[18] In one case, for instance, a contract by which an infant hired a car for the transport of his luggage was held to be void, since it stipulated that he should be absolutely liable for injury to the car whether caused by his neglect or not.[19] In other words, a contract for necessaries will not be binding unless it is substantially for the benefit of the minor. This rule, however, is not confined to the supply of necessaries. It

---

[10] *Nash v Inman* [1908] 2 KB 1. [11] *Ryder v Wombwell* (1868) LR 4 Exch 32 at 38.
[12] *Ryder v Wombwell*, above. [13] *Nash v Inman* [1908] 2 KB 1.
[14] (1840) 6 M & W 42. [15] *Coates v Wilson* (1804) 5 Esp 152.
[16] *Barber v Vincent* (1680) Freem KB 531 (horse); *Clyde Cycle Co v Hargreaves* (1898) 78 LT 296.
[17] *Helps v Clayton* (1864) 17 CBNS 553.
[18] *Roberts v Gray* [1913] 1 KB 520 at 528. [19] *Fawcett v Smethurst* (1914) 84 LJKB 473.

is only a facet of the wider principle that no contract is binding upon a minor if it is prejudicial to his interests, even one which is normally valid.[20]

What is the basis of minor's liability?

A question that is by no means of purely academic interest is what is the basis of a minor's liability for necessaries? Two conflicting theories have been advocated.

First, he is liable *ex contractu* just as a contracting party of full capacity is liable. 'The plaintiff', said Buckley LJ, 'when he sues the defendant for goods supplied during infancy, is suing him in contract on the footing that the contract was such as the infant, notwithstanding infancy, could make.'[21] Secondly, the minor is liable *re*, not *consensu*. In other words his liability is based, not on contract, but on quasi-contract. He is bound, not because he has agreed, but because he has been supplied.[22]

> The old course of pleading was a count for goods sold and delivered, a plea of infancy, and a replication that the goods were necessaries; and then the plaintiff did not necessarily recover the price alleged, he recovered a reasonable price for the necessaries. That does not imply a consensual contract.[23]

The question whether a minor is liable on an executory contract for necessaries depends upon which of these two theories is correct. If his obligation arises *re* and is non-existent in the absence of delivery, he clearly cannot be liable for goods not actually supplied, and presumably his refusal of them when tendered is justifiable. A learned writer on the subject failed to find a single case where liability has been established in the absence of delivery,[24] and it is probably safe to assume that in the case of goods the second theory is correct and that an executory contract is unenforceable.

A further point must be noted. Even if the goods have been actually supplied there is an express enactment that he shall pay a reasonable, not necessarily the contract, price;[25] and those judges who have advocated the contractual basis of a minor's liability have said that he is still liable only for a reasonable sum.[26] This is a curious admission, for if the basis of liability is truly contractual, it is odd that the minor should not be bound by the price that he has agreed to pay, whether reasonable or not.

It is more difficult to determine the basis of liability where the subject matter is not goods, as for instance in a contract for the hire of lodgings or for education. A case in point is *Roberts v Gray*[27] where the facts were these:

---

[20] See, eg *Shears v Mendeloff* (1914) 30 TLR 342 (appointment of a manager by an infant boxer); *Chaplin v Leslie Frewin (Publishers) Ltd* [1966] Ch 71 at 88. See also beneficial contracts of service, p 552, below.

[21] *Nash v Inman* [1908] 2 KB 1 at 12.

[22] *Re J* [1909] 1 Ch 574 at 577, per Fletcher-Moulton LJ; *Nash v Inman*, above at 8, per Fletcher-Moulton LJ.

[23] *Pontypridd Union v Drew* [1927] 1 KB 214 at 220, per Scrutton LJ.   [24] Miles 43 LQR 389.

[25] Sale of Goods Act 1979, s 3.   [26] See eg *Nash v Inman* [1908] 2 KB 1 at 12.

[27] [1913] 1 KB 520.

The defendant, an infant, who desired to become a professional billiard player, made a contract with Roberts, a leading professional, by which the parties agreed to accompany each other on a world tour and to play matches together in the principal countries. Roberts expended much time and trouble and incurred certain liabilities in the course of making the necessary preparations. A dispute arose between the parties and before the tour began Gray repudiated the contract.

Roberts sued for breach of contract and was awarded £1,500 by the court of first instance. The Court of Appeal, in affirming this decision, treated the contract as being one for necessaries. The doctrine of necessaries, said Cozens-Hardy MR, applies not merely to bread and cheese and clothes, but also to education, a word which in this connection extends to any form of instruction that is suitable for the particular infant. It had been argued, however, that though the defendant would have been liable to pay on a *quantum meruit* for services rendered had he actually received the plaintiff's instruction, yet, since he had repudiated the contract while it was still to a large extent executory, he was immune from liability. The court would have none of this. Hamilton LJ said:

> I am unable to appreciate why a contract which is in itself binding, because it is a contract for necessaries not qualified by unreasonable terms, can cease to be binding merely because it is executory . . . If the contract is binding at all, it must be binding for all such remedies as are appropriate to the breach of it.[28]

Unless this decision can be discounted on the ground that the contract had been partly executed, it would seem to create a difficult distinction between goods and other types of necessaries such as instruction. In the first case the minor is not liable unless he has actually received the goods, in the second the fact that no instruction has yet been imparted does not release him from his obligation. Perhaps the solution lies in separating the contract for education from the category of necessaries. It is true that Coke included it in the category and that his words have been echoed by modern judges. But there is another and independent type of valid contract, namely the beneficial contract of service, which is wide enough, and certainly more appropriate, to include education and other forms of instruction. As we shall see in the following section such a contract is binding even though it has not been completely executed. It is significant that all the authorities relied upon by the court in *Roberts v Gray* concerned beneficial contracts of service.

2 Beneficial contracts of service

It has been held from a very early date that an infant may bind himself by a contract of apprenticeship or of service, since it is to his advantage that he should acquire the

---

[28] Ibid at 530. Yet in *Walter v Everard* [1891] 2 QB 369 at 374, Lord Esher said: 'The person who sues the infant on his covenant must show that he did in fact supply him with the necessary education.'

means of earning his livelihood. Such a contract, however, when construed as a whole, must be substantially for his advantage, if he is not to be free to repudiate it.[29] Prima facie it is valid, but in the event of a dispute it is the province of the court[30] to decide whether the agreement when carefully examined in all its terms was, at the time when it was entered into,[31] for his benefit. The mere fact that one or more of the stipulations are prejudicial to him is not decisive, for some terms not directly beneficial to the servant must be expected in all service agreements. The court must look at the whole contract, must weigh the onerous against the beneficial terms, and then decide whether the balance is in favour of the minor.

> It must be shewn that the contract which he entered into with the plaintiff company was not merely a contract under which he improved himself in his business, under which he got a salary which I assume to have been adequate and reasonable, but it must be shewn by the plaintiffs that it was a contract which contained clauses, and only clauses, that are usual and customary in an employment of this nature.[32]

Two cases may be contrasted.

In *De Francesco v Barnum*:[33] A girl, fourteen years old, bound herself by an apprenticeship deed to the plaintiff for seven years to be taught stage dancing. She agreed inter alia that she would not marry during the apprenticeship, and would not accept professional engagements without the plaintiff's permission. The plaintiff did not bind himself to provide the infant with engagements or to maintain her while unemployed, and the pay that he agreed to give in the event of her employment was the reverse of generous. It was 9d per night and 6d for each matinee. He was entitled to engage her in performances abroad, and in this event was bound to pay her 5s a week with board and lodging. He could terminate the contract if, after a fair trial, the infant was found unfit for stage dancing.

It was held by Fry J that the provisions of the deed were unreasonable and unenforceable. The learned judge came to the conclusion that the child was at the absolute disposal of the plaintiff. She was to receive no pay and no maintenance except when employed, there was no correlative obligation on the plaintiff to find employment for her, and it was left to him to terminate the contract and thus to destroy her chances of success.

In *Clements v London and North Western Rly Co*:[34]

---

[29] *De Francesco v Barnum* (1890) 45 ChD 430; *Clements v London and North Western Rly Co* [1894] 2 QB 482.

[30] *Flower v London and North Western Rly Co* [1894] 2 QB 65.

[31] *Chaplin v Leslie Frewin (Publishers) Ltd* [1966] Ch 71 at 95, [1965] 3 All ER 764, per Danckwerts LJ; *Mackinlay v Bathurst* (1919) 36 TLR 31 at 33.

[32] *Sir WC Leng & Co Ltd v Andrews* [1909] 1 Ch 763 at 769, per Cozens Hardy MR.

[33] (1890) 45 ChD 430.

[34] [1894] 2 QB 482; followed in *Slade v Metrodent Ltd* [1953] 2 QB 112, [1953] 2 All ER 336 (infant held bound by an arbitration clause contained in an apprenticeship deed).

An infant, upon entering the service of a railway company as a porter, agreed to join the company's own insurance scheme and to relinquish his right of suing for personal injury under the Employers' Liability Act 1880. The scheme was more favourable to him than the Act since it covered more accidents for which compensation was payable, though on the other hand it fixed a lower scale of compensation.

It was held that the agreement as a whole was manifestly to the advantage of the infant and was binding.

Benefit to the minor, as we see then, is the keynote to the validity of this type of contract. At the same time there is no general principle that any agreement is binding upon a minor merely because it is for his benefit.[35] For instance, it has been established for over 200 years that a trading contract is not binding upon him however much it may be for his benefit.[36] So in *Cowern v Nield*[37] it was held that an infant hay and straw dealer was not liable to repay the price of a consignment of hay that he failed to deliver, and in a later case that a haulage contractor aged twenty was not liable for instalments due under a hire-purchase agreement by which a lorry had been hired to him for use in his business.[38] The essential fact to appreciate is that, for a beneficial agreement to be valid, it must either be a service or apprenticeship contract properly so called or at least analogous to such a contract.[39] In recent years, however, the courts have taken a progressively wider view of what is a contract of service. So in *Doyle v White City Stadium Ltd*,[40] for instance, it was held that a contract between an infant boxer and the British Boxing Board of Control, under which the infant received a licence to box that enabled him to gain proficiency in his profession, was so closely connected with a contract of service as to be binding.

3 Voidable contracts

We now have to deal with contracts that are voidable in the sense that they are valid and binding upon a minor unless he repudiates them during infancy or within a reasonable time after the attainment of his majority. They are confined to contracts by which the infant acquires an interest in some subject matter of a permanent nature, ie a subject matter to which continuous or recurring obligations are incident. The

---

[35] *Martin v Gale* (1876) 4 ChD 428 at 431, per Jessel MR; *Clements v London and North Western Rly Co*, above, at 565, per Kay LJ; *Doyle v White City Stadium Ltd* [1935] 1 KB 110 at 131, per Slesser LJ.
[36] *Whywall v Champion* (1738) 2 Stra 1083. The remark of McNair J in *Slade v Metrodent Ltd* [1953] 2 QB 112 at 115, [1953] 2 All ER 336 at 337, is presumably confined to the case of a service contract.
[37] [1912] 2 KB 419.
[38] *Mercantile Union Guarantee Corpn Ltd v Ball* [1937] 2 KB 498, [1937] 3 All ER 1.
[39] *Cowern v Nield* [1912] 2 KB 419 at 422.
[40] [1935] 1 KB 110; applied in *Chaplin v Leslie Frewin (Publishers) Ltd* [1966] Ch 71; p 559, below, where the Court of Appeal extended the analogy to a contract by a publisher to publish the autobiography of an infant. Similarly a contract by an infant 'pop group' to appoint a manager is valid if beneficial: *Denmark Productions Ltd v Boscobel Productions Ltd* [1967] CLY 1999 (decided on other grounds [1969] 1 QB 699, [1968] 3 All ER 513). See also *IRC v Mills* [1975] AC 38, [1974] 1 All ER 722.

principle is that if a minor undertakes such a contractual obligation, it 'remains until he thinks proper to put an end to it'.[41]

The most obvious example is a contract made by a minor for a lease. A minor is precluded by legislation from acquiring a legal estate in land,[42] but a lease which purports to convey to him a term of years absolute gives him an equitable interest for the agreed period.[43] This is voidable at his option, but while in possession he is subject to the liabilities imposed by the contract and may for instance be successfully sued for the non-payment of rent.[44] The same principle applies to the acquisition of shares. A minor purchaser of shares acquires an interest in a subject matter of a permanent nature carrying with it certain obligations that he is bound to discharge until he repudiates the transaction.[45] Thus a plea of infancy will not relieve him from liability to pay a call, ie a demand to pay to the company what is still due on the shares, if it is made before repudiation,[46] but as soon as he repudiates, or as it is often termed 'rescinds', the transaction, the interest acquired by him is at an end, and with it his liability for future calls.

Much the same principle applies to a partnership. A minor partner in a firm is not liable for partnership debts contracted during his infancy,[47] though he has no right to prevent their discharge out of the common assets. On reaching his majority he may repudiate the partnership contract altogether, but if he fails to do so and thus holds himself out as a continuing partner, he remains responsible for all debts contracted since he came of age.[48]

A contract of the class that we are now considering, in order to become permanently binding upon a minor, does not require ratification by him when he attains his majority. It remains binding upon him unless he repudiates it within a reasonable time after he comes of age.[49]

If he chooses to be inactive, his opportunity passes away; if he chooses to be active the law comes to his assistance.[50]

What is a reasonable time depends of course upon the particular circumstances of each case. In *Edwards v Carter*,[51] for instance:

A marriage settlement was executed by which the father of the intended husband agreed to pay £1,500 a year to the trustees, who were to pay it to the husband for

[41] *Goode v Harrison* (1821) 5 B & Ald 147 at 169, per Best J.
[42] Law of Property Act 1925, s 1(6); Settled Land Act 1925, s 27(1).
[43] *Davies v Beynon-Harris* (1931) 47 TLR 424; Settled Land Act 1925, s 27(2).
[44] *Davies v Beynon-Harris*, above.
[45] *North Western Rly Co v McMichael* (1850) 5 Exch 114 at 123 and 124.
[46] *Cork and Bandon Rly Co v Cazenove* (1847) 10 QB 935.
[47] *Lovell and Christmas v Beauchamp* [1894] AC 607 at 611.
[48] *Goode v Harrison* (1821) 5 B & Ald 147.
[49] *Carter v Silber* [1892] 2 Ch 278 at 284, per Lindley LJ.
[50] *Edwards v Carter* [1893] AC 360 at 366, per Lord Watson.   [51] Above.

life and then to the wife and issue of the marriage. The intended husband, an infant at the time of the settlement, executed a deed binding him to vest in the trustees all property that he might acquire under the will of his father. A month later he came of age and three-and-a-half years later he became entitled to an interest under his father's will. More than a year after his father's death, ie about four-and-a-half years after he came of age, he repudiated his agreement.

It was argued that the repudiation was in time, since the infant, when he signed the agreement, did not realise the extent of his obligation, and could not decide upon his best course of action until he knew the extent of his interest under the will. It was held however, that his repudiation was too late and was ineffective.

Effect of repudiation

It is clear that a minor who repudiates a voidable contract is no longer liable to honour future obligations. What is not authoritatively settled, however, is whether he is freed from those that have accrued due at the time of his repudiation. If, for example, he repudiates a lease of land, is he none the less liable for rent *already* due? This is a question upon which there are conflicting dicta and no direct authority in modern times.[52] Two views have been advanced.

The first is that repudiation is the equivalent of rescission, which, as we have already seen, is retrospective in its operation. It 'terminates the contract, puts the parties in *status quo ante* and restores things, as between them, to the position in which they stood before the contract was entered into'.[53] In *North Western Rly Co v McMichael*,[54] for instance, an action was brought against an infant to recover a call on certain railway shares that he had bought. The defendant merely pleaded that he had never ratified the purchase and had not received any benefit from it. Parke B, however, who delivered the judgment of the court, stated what the position would have been had repudiation been pleaded and substantiated.

> Our opinion is that an infant is not absolutely bound, but is in the same situation as an infant acquiring real estate or any other permanent interest: he is not deprived of the right which the law gives every infant of waiving and disagreeing to a purchase which he has made; and if he waives it the estate acquired by the purchaser is at an end and with it his liability to pay calls, though the avoidance may not have taken place till the call was due.[55]

The court relied upon a case decided in 1613 which is reported under a variety of names in different reports.[56] In this case, it was indeed affirmed that a voidable lease would be rendered void if disclaimed by an infant; and that if the disclaimer had been made *before* the rent fell due, the tenant's liability in this respect would be cancelled.

---

[52] Hudson 35 Can Bar Rev 1213.
[53] *Abram Steamship Co v Westville Steamship Co* [1923] AC 773 at 781, per Lord Atkinson.
[54] (1850) 5 Exch 114.
[55] Ibid at 125; (italics supplied).
[56] *Ketsey's Case* (1613) Cro Jac 320; *Keteley's Case* 1 Brownlow 120; *Kirton v Eliott* Roll Abr 731.

No mention was made of rent already due.[57] Yet Younger LJ once said that an infant shareholder 'is no longer liable to pay the instalments [due under a call] which she has not paid'.[58]

The principle stated by Parke B, however, that the repudiation of his contract by an infant has a retrospective effect, has not been universally accepted. Thus, an Irish judge has reached the opposite conclusion. This was in *Blake v Concannon*,[59] where an infant tenant, after occupying the premises for nearly a year, quitted possession and on attaining full age repudiated the tenancy. Nevertheless, he was held liable for half a year's rent which had accrued due while he was in possession. His liability was based upon his use and occupation of the land.[60] In *Steinberg v Scala (Leeds) Ltd*,[61] there is a dictum of Warrington LJ that an infant shareholder who rescinds his purchase is relieved of liability for future calls, no mention being made of calls already due. Moreover, the views of textbook writers are not unanimous on the question, though their general conclusion is that liability for an accrued debt survives a repudiation of the contract.[62]

In view of this disarray of opinions it would be misleading to say that the authorities have reached a definite conclusion upon the matter. It is submitted, however, that it is preferable to accept the logic of the retrospective principle as explained by Parke B in *McMichael's* case.

An entirely different question in the present context is whether a minor, on repudiation of a contract, can recover money which he has paid or property which he has delivered to the other party. The rule here is that if, for instance, he has paid money to the defendant, he cannot recover it at common law as being money had and received unless he can show that he has suffered a total failure of consideration.

To succeed, he must prove that he has received no part of what he was promised. This he was able to do in *Corpe v Overton*.[63]

An infant agreed to enter into a partnership with the defendant in three months' time and to pay him £1,000 when the partnership deed was executed. He also made an immediate payment of £100 as security for the fulfilment of his promise. He rescinded the contract as soon as he came of age and sued for the recovery of the £100.

---

[57] See *Re Jones, ex p Jones* (1881) 18 ChD 109 at 117, per Jessel MR,
[58] *Steinberg v Scala (Leeds) Ltd* [1923] 2 Ch 452 at 463.
[59] (1870) IR 4 CL 323.
[60] The citation of this case in an English action provoked Jessel MR to say: 'That is founded on an implied contract. How can a court imply a contract against a person who is incapable of contracting?': *Re Jones, ex p Jones* (1881) 18 ChD 109 at 118.
[61] [1923] 2 Ch 452 at 461.
[62] Those who take this view include *Sutton and Shannon on Contracts* (8th edn) p 220; Salmond and Winfield *Principles of the Law of Contracts* p 461. The opposite view is expressed by Salmond and Williams *Principles of the Law of Contracts* p 300.
[63] (1833) 10 Bing 252.

The money was held to be recoverable since there had been a total failure of consideration. The money had been deposited by the plaintiff to secure the due performance of the partnership contract, but at the time when the contract was effectively rescinded he had received no consideration for what he had paid.[64]

In *Holmes v Blogg*,[65] however, the test of total failure of consideration was not satisfied. An infant paid a sum of money to a lessor as part of the consideration for a lease of premises in which he and a partner proposed to carry on their trade. He occupied the premises for twelve weeks, but the day after he came of age he dissolved the partnership, repudiated the lease and left the premises. He failed in his attempt to recover what he had paid. There was no total failure of consideration, since he had received the very thing he had been promised and for which he had made the payment.

To the same effect in *Steinberg v Scala (Leeds) Ltd*.[66]

The plaintiff, an infant, applied for shares in a company and paid the amounts due on allotment and on the first call. She neither received any dividends nor attended any meetings of the company, and the shares appear always to have stood at a discount. Eighteen months after allotment, while still an infant, she rescinded the contract and claimed to recover what she had paid.

Her claim failed. The company, by allotting the shares, had done all that it had bargained to do by way of consideration for her payment.

Some of the expressions used by the judges in the relevant cases on this matter appear at first sight to make the right of recovery turn upon whether or not the infant has derived *any* substantial benefit from the contract. This is misleading. In the words of Younger LJ: 'The question is not: Has the infant derived any real advantage? But the question is: Has the consideration wholly failed?'[67] Thus in *Steinberg*'s case, since the infant had obtained the very consideration for which she had bargained, it was irrelevant that what she had obtained might be valueless.

Cases such as *Edwards v Carter*[68] show that a disposition by a minor of any form of property, whether realty or personalty, is not finally and conclusively binding upon him. 'There is a total absolute disability in an infant that by no manner of conveyance can he dispose of his inheritance.'[69] He may either confirm or rescind it on the attainment of his majority. If he exercises his right of rescission, his disposition, hitherto valid until avoided, now becomes retrospectively void *ab initio*. In principle

---

[64] *Steinberg v Scala (Leeds) Ltd* [1923] 2 Ch 452 at 461, per Lord Sterndale MR.

[65] (1818) 8 Taunt 508.

[66] [1923] 2 Ch 452; overruling *Hamilton v Vaughan-Sherrin Electrical Engineering Co* [1894] 3 Ch 589.

[67] *Steinberg v Scala (Leeds) Ltd* [1923] 2 Ch 452 at 465.

[68] P 484, above.

[69] *Hearle v Greenbank* (1749) 3 Atk 695 at 712, per Lord Hardwicke. See also *Re D'Angibau, Andrews v Andrews* (1879) 15 ChD 228 at 241, per Cotton LJ; *Burnaby v Equitable Reversionary Interest Society* (1885) 28 ChD 416 at 424, per Pearson J.

this requires the restoration of the *status quo ante*—a giving back and a taking back on both sides—and it has long been understood that the infant is entitled to recover the property that he has transferred.

This general principle, which allows a minor to recover what he has transferred by a completed disposition, has been somewhat clouded by the decision of the Court of Appeal in *Chaplin v Leslie Frewin (Publishers) Ltd*[70] where the facts were as follows:

> The plaintiffs, an infant and his adult wife, entered into a contract with the defendants by which the latter agreed to publish the autobiography of the infant which was to be written by two journalists based on information furnished by the plaintiffs. The plaintiffs approved the final page proofs on 21 July, and the legal right to the copyright was assigned in writing to the defendants. Advance royalties of £600 were paid to the plaintiffs, who also knew that the defendants had contracted with third parties for the foreign publication of the work.
>
> On 26 August the plaintiffs repudiated the contract on the ground that the book contained libellous matter and attributed to the infant views that he did not hold. They commenced an action for an injunction restraining the publication of the book, and for an order restoring the copyright to them. They conceded that, as part of this equitable relief, they were obliged to repay the money they had received. Pending the trial of the action, they moved for an interlocutory injunction to prevent publication.

The Court of Appeal was unanimous in holding that the contract was analogous to a service contract, which, as has been seen,[71] is valid if it is substantially for the infant's benefit. The majority (Lord Denning MR dissenting) held that the test of substantial benefit was satisfied, since the contract, viewed at the time of its making, would enable the infant to make a start in life as an author. The contract was valid and there was no room for the grant of equitable relief.

This finding was sufficient to dispose of the case and it was unnecessary to consider whether the assignment of the copyright precluded its recovery by the infant. The court, however, canvassed the matter, and again there was a difference of opinion. Danckwerts and Winn LJJ held that, even had the contract been voidable, its rescission by the infant could not divest the copyright that had been vested in the publishers. It is submitted with respect that the opposite view expressed by Lord Denning MR is to be preferred.[72] The infant's claim was not at common law for money had and received, but a claim for equitable relief which, since he who seeks equity must do equity, would be granted only on the footing that any advantages already received by him would be returned to the publishers. The majority did not

---

[70] [1966] Ch 71, [1965] 3 All ER 764. See Mummery 82 LQR 471; Yale [1966] CLJ 17.
[71] P 552, above.
[72] [1966] Ch at 90, [1965] 3 All ER at 770.

examine the established principles relating to an infant's right of restitution, but were content to accept the authorities cited by counsel for the publishers, namely *Valentini v Canali*,[73] *Pearce v Brain*[74] and *Steinberg v Scala (Leeds) Ltd*.[75] The coupling of the first two of these cases with the last is a further instance of the confusion which surrounds the law of infancy. The first two were cases of void contracts, but in *Steinberg v Scala (Leeds) Ltd* the contract was voidable. It was assumed by counsel and the court that if the contract was not valid, it was voidable. It has been plausibly suggested however that the contract if not valid, was void,[76] but even if the *contract* were void, it would not necessarily follow that the *assignment* was void.

It is suggested that if this part of the decision in the *Chaplin* case is to be supported it must be based upon the impossibility of *restitutio in integrum*. The infant was prepared to restore the royalty payments, but he could not undo the contracts which to his knowledge the defendants had made with foreign publishers.[77]

4 Other contracts

It is clear that if the contract does not fall within one of the three above categories it does not bind the minor but this does not mean that the contract is without legal effect. In principle it appears that the contract is binding on the other party though it is not clear what consideration the infant is providing for the transaction. Before 1874 a minor (or an infant, as he was then called) could become bound if he ratified the contract when he achieved his majority. Ratification was made ineffective by section 2 of the Infants Relief Act 1874 but now that this Act has been repealed it would seem that ratification is once more possible.

In many cases contracts made by minors will be carried out. The practical importance of minors' contracts was greatly reduced when the age of majority was reduced from 21 to 18, since many more long term transactions are entered into by those in the 18 to 21 years age group. Nevertheless, today, even those under 18 dispose in aggregate of a very substantial amount of money and a few, such as entertainers or professional athletes, may command large fees even before they are 18. The general principle appears to be that once the transaction has been carried out, the minor cannot undo it unless the circumstances are such that an adult, having entered into the same transaction, could undo it, for example, because of total failure of consideration. So a minor cannot buy a compact disc on one Saturday and take it back the following Saturday asking for his or her money back. It would seem too that ownership in the compact disc would have passed to the minor according to the usual rules of passing of property under contracts of sale. This is implicitly assumed by section 3 of the Minors' Contracts Act 1987 which provides:

---

[73] (1889) 24 QBD 166. [74] [1929] 2 KB 310. [75] [1923] 2 Ch 452; p 557, above.

[76] Reynolds 10 JSPTL 294 at 295.

[77] Leave to appeal to the House of Lords was granted, but the action was settled. The infant withdrew his repudiation of the contract, and it was agreed that the book should be rewritten.

(1) Where—

    (a) a person ('the plaintiff') has after the commencement of this Act entered into a contract with another ('the defendant'), and

    (b) the contract is unenforceable against the defendant (or he repudiates it) because he was a minor when the contract was made, the court may, if it is just and equitable to do so, require the defendant to transfer to the plaintiff any property acquired by the defendant under the contract, or any property representing it.

(2) Nothing in this section shall be taken to prejudice any other remedy available to the plaintiff.

This section is aimed at the situation where the minor has acquired property on credit and refuses, as he is entitled to do, to pay for it. It gives the court a discretionary power to order restoration to the seller or the supplier. It clearly assumes however that property can pass. If property can pass to the minor under a credit sale, all the more so it would seem under a cash sale.

Where the person dealing with the minor realises that he is dealing with a minor, he may ask for a guarantee from an adult. This possibility gave rise to considerable technical difficulties in respect of loans between 1874 and 1987 because the loan was absolutely void under the Infants' Relief Act 1874 and it was believed that the guarantee might be equally void, though this was not clear and the difficulty could be overcome by formulating the transaction as one of indemnity rather than guarantee.[78] This possibility is now controlled by section 2 of the Minors' Contracts Act 1987 which provides:

(2) Where—

    (a) a guarantee is given in respect of an obligation of a party to a contract made after the commencement of this Act, and

    (b) the obligation is unenforceable against him (or he repudiates the contract) because he was a minor when the contract was made, the guarantee shall not for that reason alone be unenforceable against the guarantor.

B Delictual liability of minors

Although a minor is generally liable in tort, as, for instance, for defamation, trespass or conversion, he is not answerable for a tort directly connected with any contract upon which no action will lie against him. It is impossible indirectly to enforce such a contract by changing the form of action to one *ex delicto*.[79] Thus an action of deceit

---

[78] *Coutts & Co v Browne-Lecky* [1947] KB 104, [1946] 2 All ER 207; *Yeoman Credit Ltd v Latter* [1961] 2 All ER 294, [1961] 1 WLR 828; Furmston 24 MLR 648; Steyn 90 LQR 246.

[79] *Burnard v Haggis* (1863) 14 CBNS 45, per Byles J.

does not lie against a minor who, by falsely representing himself to be of full age, has fraudulently induced another to contract with him, for 'it was thought necessary to safeguard the weakness of infants at large, even though here and there a juvenile knave slipped through'.[80] A fraudulent representation did not estop a minor from relying upon the Infants' Relief Act.[81] Although perhaps this is to put a premium on knavery, it is clear that to enable a plaintiff to convert a breach of contract into a tort would destroy the protection that the law affords to minors.[82]

The only, but a real, difficulty is to determine in each case whether the tort is so directly connected with a contract as to render the minor immune even from delictual liability. It was held, for instance, in *Jennings v Rundall*[83] that if an infant hires a mare for riding and injures her by excessive and improper riding, he is not liable in tort for negligence; but in *Burnard v Haggis*[84] that if, contrary to the express instructions of the owner accepted by himself, he jumps and consequently injures her, he can be successfully sued in tort. At first sight it is not easy to appreciate the exact distinction between these two cases. In each of them the wrongful act of the infant arose out of and was connected with a contract in the sense that it could not have been committed had no contract been made. Why was the wrongful jumping in a different legal category from the wrongful riding? What is the test which determines whether the conduct of the infant is a tort independent of the contract and therefore actionable? The answer would appear to be that an infant is liable in tort only if the wrongful act that he has done is one of a kind not contemplated by the contract.[85] If he hires a horse for riding, the act contemplated by the contract is riding, and he cannot be liable however immoderately he may ride; but on the other hand, the hire of a horse only for riding does not contemplate the act of jumping. The same test serves to distinguish two more recent cases. In *Fawcett v Smethurst*[86] an infant hired a car for the specific purpose of fetching his luggage from Cairn Ryan Station, and when he got to the latter place he drove further away to Ballantrae. It was held that he was not liable in tort for an accident that occurred during the further drive. In the words of Atkin J:

> Nothing that was done on that further journey made the defendant an independent tortfeasor . . . The extended journey was of the same nature as the original one, and the defendant did no more than drive the car further than was intended.

[80] *R Leslie Ltd v Sheill* [1914] 3 KB 607 at 612, per Lord Sumner.
[81] *Levene v Brougham* (1909) 25 TLR 265.
[82] *Jennings v Rundall* (1799) 8 Term Rep 335 at 336, per Lord Kenyon.
[83] Above.
[84] (1863) 14 CBNS 45.
[85] This was the view of Pollock *Contracts* (12th edn), p 63. It was adopted by Kennedy LJ, in *R Leslie Ltd v Sheill* [1914] 3 KB 607 at 620, and confirmed by Atkin J in *Fawcett v Smethurst* (1914) 84 LJKB 473; and by the Court of Appeal in *Ballett v Mingay* [1943] KB 281, [1943] 1 All ER 143.
[86] (1914) 84 LJKB 473.

But in *Ballett v Mingay*,[87] an action of detinue succeeded against an infant for the return of certain articles which he had borrowed from the respondent and which he had without authority lent to a friend. Lord Greene MR said:

> From the evidence it seems that, properly construed, the terms of the bailment of these articles to the defendant did not permit him to part with their possession at all. If it was the bargain that he might part with them, it was for him to establish that fact and he has failed to do so. On that basis the action of the defendant in parting with the goods fell outside the contract altogether, and that fact brings this case within *Burnard v Haggis*.[88]

Whether the act that the infant has done must be taken to be within the contemplation of the parties may perhaps depend upon the nature of the subject matter. In *Ballett v Mingay* this consisted of an amplifier and a microphone, articles that a lender would naturally expect a borrower to retain in his own possession, but the decision might have been different had the infant parted temporarily with a bicycle that he had hired from the plaintiff.

In *Ballett v Mingay* the transaction involved a bailment and it has already been seen that a bailment does not necessarily involve a contract.[89] In the case of a gratuitous loan of a chattel, it is clear that the lender has a tortious action in the event of refusal to return or failure to exercise reasonable care[90] and it would seem that since there is no contractual action, one who lends gratuitously to an infant can sue in such circumstances. If this is correct, it is not clear why one who lends for reward should be in a worse position than one who lends gratuitously.[91] It should be noted that gratuitous[92] loans of money are in a different position since historically refusal to return sounded in debt, rather than detinue or conversion and was therefore treated as contractual.

C The equitable doctrine of restitution

We have just seen that at common law an infant is not liable in deceit if he induces another to contract with him by making some false representation, as for example that he has reached the age of majority. If, for instance, he obtains money or non-necessary goods from another by such a misrepresentation, he cannot be sued either on the express contract, or for money had and received, or, since the fraud is connected with the contract, in tort.[93] But since it should be obvious that 'infants are no more entitled than adults to gain benefits to themselves by fraud',[94] equity has developed a principle

---

[87] [1943] KB 281, [1943] 1 All ER 143.   [88] Ibid at 282–283 and 145, respectively.

[89] Pp 111–112, above; Palmer *Bailment* (2nd edn) pp 26–31.   [90] *Palmer* (2nd edn) pp 665–676.

[91] Clearly contractual stipulations, which seek to put the lender in a better position, are on a different footing.

[92] That is loans which contemplate simply the return of capital without payment of any interest.

[93] *R Leslie Ltd v Sheill* [1914] 3 KB 607 at 612–613, per Lord Sumner.

[94] *Nelson v Stocker* (1859) 4 De G & J 458, per Turner LJ at 464. Atiyah has suggested that an extended meaning should be given to the word 'fraud' in this context; 22 MLR 273.

which requires benefits to be disgorged, if they are still in the possession of the fraudulent infant.

The limits of this doctrine of restitution are somewhat ill-defined.[95] There are three types of case to which it may be relevant.

First, the infant obtains goods by fraud and remains in possession of them. Here there is no doubt that the doctrine applies and that an order for restitution will be made.[96] Secondly, the infant obtains goods by fraud but ceases to possess them. If the doctrine is limited to the restitution of the very goods obtained, it follows that it cannot be invoked in this case, for to make the infant liable to repay the value of the goods, or even to restore another article for which they have been exchanged, would in effect be to enforce a contract declared void by statute. The authorities would seem to establish that the doctrine is so limited. As A T Lawrence J said in *R Leslie Ltd v Sheill,*[97] 'if when the action is brought both the property and the proceeds are gone, I can see no ground upon which a Court of Equity could have founded its jurisdiction'. In the same case Lord Sumner stated the position as follows:

> I think that the whole current of decisions down to 1913, apart from dicta which are incon-
> clusive, went to shew that, when an infant obtained an advantage by falsely stating himself to
> be of full age, the equity required him to restore his ill-gotten gains, or to release the party
> deceived from obligations or acts in law induced by the fraud,[98] but scrupulously stopped
> short of enforcing against him a contractual obligation, entered into while he was an infant,
> even by means of a fraud—Restitution stopped where repayment began.[99]

The reason why Lord Sumner confined this review of the law to the discussions prior to 1913 was that in that year Lush J held, in *Stocks v Wilson,*[100] that an infant who had obtained goods by misrepresenting his age and had later sold them was accountable for the proceeds of sale. It is extremely difficult to reconcile this decision either with the principles laid down by the Court of Appeal in *R Leslie Ltd v Sheill* or with what was decided in that case.[101] Lush J relied chiefly upon a decision in 1858 where the Lords Justices held, though with reluctance, that a loan obtained by an infant who had

---

[95] In practice plaintiffs will often prefer to rely on s 3 of the Minors' Contracts Act 1987, set out at p 561, above, but the Act does not replace the equitable jurisdiction.

[96] *Clarke v Cobley* (1789) 2 Cox Eq Cas 173; *Lempière v Lange* (1879) 12 ChD 675.

[97] [1914] 3 KB 607 at 627.

[98] If, for example, an infant, by fraudulently misrepresenting his age, induces his trustees to pay a sum of money to him and thus to commit a breach of trust, he cannot after he is of full age compel them to rectify the breach by paying the money over again: *Cory v Gertcken* (1816) 2 Madd 40.

[99] [1914] 3 KB 607 at 618.

[100] [1913] 2 KB 235.

[101] But see Goff and Jones *The Law of Restitution* (3rd edn) pp 431–439. In *R Leslie Ltd v Sheill* the Court of Appeal refrained from expressing a definite opinion upon the decision of Lush J though Lord Sumner remarked that it was 'open to challenge': [1914] 3 KB at 619.

misrepresented his age was provable as a debt in his subsequent bankruptcy.[102] It is now admitted, however, that this decision merely expresses a rule of bankruptcy law, not a principle of general application relevant to such facts as arose in *Stocks v Wilson*.[103] Moreover, the question in the 1858 case was not whether the lender had a personal claim against the infant, but whether, in competition with other creditors, he could claim a share of the assets that had been surrendered to the trustee in bankruptcy.[104]

Thirdly, the infant obtains a loan of money by fraud. The contrast stressed by Lord Sumner between restitution and repayment necessarily excludes the doctrine in this case, for the very essence of a loan of money is that the borrower shall repay the equivalent amount, not that he shall restore the identical coins. Thus it was held in *Leslie Ltd v Sheill*[105] that an infant could not be compelled to restore a loan of £400 which he had obtained by a fraudulent misstatement of his age, for to do so would constitute in effect an enforcement of the contract, not an application of the doctrine of restitution. If, of course, the very coins or notes obtained by the infant were identifiable and if they were still in his possession, a highly improbable case, the doctrine could no doubt be invoked.

2 CORPORATIONS

The doctrine of *ultra vires*

It is essential, of course, that a contracting party should be a person recognised as such by the law. Persons in law, however, are not confined to individual men and women. If two or more persons form themselves into an association for the purpose of some concerted enterprise, as happens, for example, upon the formation of a club, a trade union, a partnership or a trading company, the association is in some cases regarded by the law as an independent person, ie as a legal entity called a 'corporation', separate from the men and women of whom it consists, but in other cases it is denied a separate personality and is called an unincorporated association. Whether an association falls into one class or the other depends upon whether it has been incorporated by the state.

> Independent juristic personality can only be conferred upon an association, according to English law, by some act on the part of the State, represented either by the Crown in the exercise of its prerogative rights, or by the sovereign power of Parliament.[106]

---

[102] *Re King, ex p Unity Joint Stock Mutual Banking Association* (1858) 3 De G & J 63.
[103] *R Leslie Ltd v Sheill* [1914] 3 KB 607 at 624, 628.   [104] Ibid at 616.
[105] Above.   [106] Stephen's *Commentaries* (21st edn) vol II, p 558. See also Pickering 31 MLR 481.

An unincorporated association, such as a club, is not a competent contracting party. If a contract is made on its behalf no individual member can be sued upon it except the person who actually made it and any other members who authorised him to do so.[107]

The main classification of corporations is into aggregate and sole. A corporation aggregate is a body of several persons united together into one society which, since it may be maintained by a constant succession of members, has the capacity of perpetual existence. Examples are the mayor and corporation of a city and a trading company incorporated under the Companies Act 1985. A corporation sole consists of a single person occupying a particular office and each and several of the persons in perpetuity who succeed him in that office, such as a bishop or the vicar of a parish.

> The law therefore has wisely ordained that the parson, *quatenus* parson, shall never die, by making him and his successors a corporation. By which means all the original rights of the parsonage are preserved entire to the successor; for the present incumbent and his predecessor who lived seven centuries ago are in law one and the same person; and what was given to the one was given to the other also.[108]

The consent of the Crown, thus necessary to the creation of a corporation, may either be express or implied. It is express in the case of chartered and statutory corporations. The Crown has a prerogative right to incorporate any number of persons by charter, and it is to this method that some of the older trading companies such as the Hudson's Bay Company and the P&O Steam Navigation Company, owe their existence. Incorporation by statute may take two forms. The members of an association, whether united for trade or for some other purpose, may form themselves into a corporation by obtaining a special Act of Parliament; or alternatively, if united for trading purposes and if not less than seven in number, they may comply with the general conditions laid down in the Companies Act 1985, and obtain registration as a limited liability company. The consent of the Crown to incorporation is implied in the case both of common law and of prescriptive corporations. An example of the former is an ecclesiastical corporation sole such as a bishop or a parson. A prescriptive corporation is a body of persons which has been treated as a corporation from time immemorial but which cannot produce a charter of incorporation. The existence of a charter is presumed by the law, and such a body enjoys the same rights as a chartered company.

The doctrine of *ultra vires* stated that a statutory corporation could exercise only those powers which are expressly or implicitly conferred by the statute itself. It did not apply to corporations created by charter. In the words of Bowen LJ:

---

[107] *Bradley Egg Farm Ltd v Clifford* [1943] 2 All ER 378. For a critique of the law, see Keeler 34 MLR 61.

[108] Blackstone's *Commentaries* vol I, p 470.

At common law a corporation created by the King's charter has prima facie the power to do with its property all such acts as an ordinary person can do, and to bind itself to such contracts as an ordinary person can bind himself to.[109]

A trading company, for instance, incorporated under the Companies Act is required to have articles of association (which regulate matters of internal administration), and also a memorandum of association. The memorandum is the charter which defines the statutory creature by stating the objects of its existence, the scope of its operations and the extent of its powers. A company so created should pursue only those objects set out in the memorandum. Its area of corporate activity is thereby restricted, so that if, for instance, it is authorised to run tramways, it should not run omnibuses. It may exercise and only exercise the powers set out in the memorandum and such powers as are reasonably incidental to or consequential upon the operations that it is authorised to perform. In the middle of the nineteenth century it was held the transactions which went outside the scope of the powers conferred by the memorandum was *ultra vires* and void.[110] The *locus classicus* was *Ashbury Railway Carriage Co v Riche*.[111]

> The objects of the appellant company, as stated in the memorandum of association, were 'to make, sell or lend on hire, railway carriages and waggons, and all kinds of railway plant, fittings, machinery and rolling stock; to carry on the business of mechanical engineers and general contractors; to purchase, lease and sell mines, minerals, land and buildings; to purchase and sell as merchants, timber, coal, metals and other materials, and to buy and sell any such materials on commission or as agents'.
>
> The directors agreed to assign to a Belgian company a concession which they had bought for the construction of a railway in Belgium.

It was held that this agreement, since it related to the construction of a railway, a subject matter not included in the memorandum, was *ultra vires*, and that not even the subsequent assent of the whole body of shareholders could make it binding. Therefore, an action brought by the Belgian company to recover damages for breach of the contract necessarily failed.

The *ultra vires* doctrine has long been criticised. Although in theory it operates to protect shareholders against use of the company's funds for unauthorised purposes, this protection is largely illusory because of the common practice of drafting the

---

[109] *Baroness Wenlock v River Dee Co* (1877) 36 ChD 674, note at 685. *Institution of Mechanical Engineers v Cane and Westminster Corpn* [1961] AC 696 at 724–725, [1960] 3 All ER 715 at 728–729, per Lord Denning; Hudson 28 Solicitor 7.

[110] *A-G v Great Eastern Rly Co* (1880) 5 App Cas 473 at 478. For a fuller account, see Gower *Modern Company Law* (6th edn) pp 201–221. Under ss 4, 5, 6 of Companies Act 1985 there is a limited power to change the objects. See Davies 90 LQR 79.

[111] (1875) LR 7 HL 653.

objects clause in very broad and general terms. On the other hand the doctrine can operate as a trap for those who do business with the company since it is quite unrealistic to expect them to read the memorandum of association to discover the company's authorised purposes. It is not surprising therefore that both the Cohen Committee in 1945[112] and the Jenkins Committee in 1962[113] recommended substantial amendment of the doctrine.

The European Communities Act 1972, section 9(1) made substantial changes in the doctrine.[114] Further changes were made in the Companies Act 1989 as a result of a DTI consultative document following a Report by Dr Prentice. Section 108 of the Companies Act 1989 inserts new sections 35, 35A and 35B into the Companies Act 1985. This provides that:

A company's capacity not limited by its memorandum

35 (1) The validity of an act done by a company shall not be called into question on the ground of lack of capacity by reason of anything in the company's memorandum.

(2) A member of a company may bring proceedings to restrain the doing of an act which but for subsection (1) would be beyond the company's capacity; but no such proceedings shall lie in respect of an act to be done in fulfilment of a legal obligation arising from a previous act of the company.

(3) It remains the duty of the directors to observe any limitations on their powers flowing from the company's memorandum; and action by the directors which but for subsection (1) would be beyond the company's capacity may also be ratified by the company by special resolution. A resolution ratifying such action shall not affect any liability incurred by the directors or any other person; relief from any such liability must be agreed to separately by special resolution.

(4) The operation of this section is restricted by section 30B(1) of the Charities Act 1960 and section 112(3) of the Companies Act 1989 in relation to companies which are charities; and section 322A below (invalidity of certain transactions to which directors or their associates are parties) has effect notwithstanding this section.

Power of directors to bind the company

35A (1) In favour of a person dealing with a company in good faith, the power of the board of directors to bind the company, or authorise others to do so, shall be deemed to be free of any limitation under the company's constitution.

(2) For this purpose—

(a) a person 'deals with' a company if he is a party to any transaction or other act to which the company is a party;

---

[112] Cmd 6659, para 12, Horrwitz 62 LQR 66.
[113] Cmnd 1249, paras 35/42.
[114] Prentice 89 LQR 518; Farrar and Powles 36 MLR 270.

(b) a person shall not be regarded as acting in bad faith by reason only of his knowing that an act is beyond the powers of the directors under the company's constitution; and

(c) a person shall be presumed to have acted in good faith unless the contrary is proved.

(3) The references above to limitations on the directors' powers under the company's constitution include limitations deriving—

(a) from a resolution of the company in general meeting or a meeting of any class of shareholders, or

(b) from any agreement between the members of the company or of any class of shareholders.

(4) Subsection (1) does not affect any right of a member of the company to bring proceedings to restrain the doing of an act which is beyond the powers of the directors; but no such proceedings shall lie in respect of an act to be done in fulfilment of a legal obligation arising from a previous act of the company.

(5) Nor does that subsection affect any liability incurred by the directors, or any other person, by reason of the directors exceeding their powers.

(6) The operation of this section is restricted by section 30B(1) of the Charities Act 1960 and section 112(3) of the Companies Act 1989 in relation to companies which are charities; and section 322A below (invalidity of certain transactions to which directors or their associates are parties) has effect notwithstanding this section.

No duty to enquire as to capacity of company or authority of directors

35B (1) A party to a transaction with a company is not bound to enquire as to whether it is permitted by the company's memorandum or as to any limitation on the powers of the board of directors to bind the company or authorise others to do so.

(2) In Schedule 21 to the Companies Act 1985 (effect of registration of companies not formed under that Act), in paragraph 6 (general application of provisions of Act), after sub-paragraph (5) insert—

'(6) Where by virtue of sub-paragraph (4) or (5) a company does not have power to alter a provision, it does not have power to ratify acts of the directors in contravention of the provision.'

(3) In Schedule 22 to the Companies Act 1985 (provisions applying to unregistered companies), in the entries relating to Part I, in the first column for 'section 35' substitute 'sections 35 to 35B'.

The effect of this is to make the *ultra vires* doctrine a rule relating to the internal management of the company. Third parties dealing with the company will no longer be under any obligation to check the company's capacity and there will be no question of a contract made by the company being invalid because it is outside the purpose of the company as defined in the memorandum. Nevertheless, as a matter of internal management, if the directors do things which they are not entitled to do under the memorandum, a shareholder if he acts in time may be able to restrain them by injunction and the company itself will in principle have an action against the directors for acting outside their powers.

3 PERSONS MENTALLY DISORDERED, AND DRUNKARDS

A Mental disorder[115]

The word 'lunatic' has been used since at least the sixteenth century to describe a person who becomes insane after birth, but it was discarded by the legislature in 1930 in favour of 'person of unsound mind',[116] a term that was not statutorily defined. This in turn has been replaced by 'person mentally disordered' or more shortly 'mental patient', and mental disorder is exhaustively defined.[117] This definition relates to the treatment and care of mental patients and to the administration of their property, but it does not affect the question of their contractual capacity. This remains subject to the rules formulated by the courts.

If a genuine consent were necessary to the formation of every agreement it would follow that a mental patient could not make a valid contract. Here as elsewhere, however, the necessity of interpreting conduct by its effect upon reasonable persons has forbidden so simple a proposition. The law on the subject has varied, but the modern rules are clear.

The first question in all cases is whether the party at the time of contracting was suffering from such a degree of mental disability that he was incapable of understanding the nature of the contract.[118] If so, the contract is not void but voidable at the mental patient's option, provided that his mental disability was known or ought to have been known by the other contracting party.[119] The burden of proving this knowledge lies upon the person mentally disordered.[120] If, however, the contract was made by him during a lucid interval, it is binding upon him notwithstanding that his disability was known to the other party.[121]

Again, it is immaterial that the mental disability is known to the other party, if necessaries are supplied to a person mentally disordered or to his wife, suitable to the position in life in which he moves, for in this case an implied obligation arises to pay

---

[115] Fridman 79 LQR 502 at 509–516. Hudson 35 Can Bar Rev 205, 37 Can Bar Rev 497, 25 Conv (NS) 319.

[116] Mental Treatment Act 1930.   [117] Mental Health Act 1983, s 1.

[118] *Boughton v Knight* (1873) LR 3 PD 64 at 72.

[119] *Molton v Camroux* (1848) 2 Exch 487; affd 4 Exch 17; *Imperial Loan Co v Stone* [1892] 1 QB 599. *York Glass Co Ltd v Jubb* (1925) 134 LT 36. *Hart v O'Connor* [1985] AC 1000, [1985] 2 All ER 880.

[120] *Molton v Camroux*, above.

[121] *Hall v Warren* (1804) 9 Ves 605. *Selby v Jackson* (1844) 6 Beav 192.

for them out of his property.[122] The obligation does not arise unless it was the intention of the person supplying the necessaries that he should be repaid. He must intend, not to play the role of a benefactor, but to constitute himself a creditor.[123]

As regards the supply of necessary goods, this obligation to pay is converted by the Sale of Goods Act 1979 into a statutory obligation to pay a reasonable price. Section 3(2) provides that:

> Where necessaries are sold and delivered to a person who by reason of mental incapacity or drunkenness is incompetent to contract, he must pay a reasonable price for them.

Jurisdiction to manage the property and affairs of a mental patient is now conferred by Part VII of the Mental Health Act 1983 upon 'the judge', ie certain nominated judges of the Chancery Division and also the master and deputy master of the Court of Protection. The jurisdiction is exercisable when the judge is satisfied that a person is incapable by reason of mental disability of managing his property and affairs,[124] and it is of the widest nature. It includes the power to make contracts for the benefit of the patient and also to carry out a contract already made by him.[125]

B Drunkenness

It is generally said, both by judges[126] and by textbook writers, that the contractual capacity of a drunken person is the same as that of one who is mentally afflicted, but the decisions are few and not too satisfactory. The effect of *Gore v Gibson*,[127] as qualified by *Matthews v Baxter*,[128] would seem to be that if A, when he contracts with B, is in such state of drunkenness as not to know what he is doing, and if this fact is appreciated by B, then the contract is voidable at the instance of A. It may, for instance, be ratified by him when he regains sobriety. It would appear, therefore, that a contract with a person so seriously afflicted must always be voidable, for unlike the case of insanity it is almost inconceivable that the extent of his intoxication can be unknown to the other party.

A drunken person to whom necessaries are sold and delivered is under the same liability to pay a reasonable price for them as is an infant or an insane person.[129]

---

122 *Re Rhodes* (1890) 44 ChD 94; *Read v Legard* (1851) 6 Exch 636.
123 *Re Rhodes*, above.
124 The former procedure under which after a formal inquiry ('inquisition'), a person could be declared to be of unsound mind ('lunatic so found'), and a person appointed (the 'committee') to manage his person and property has been abolished: Mental Health Act 1959, s 149(2).
125 Mental Health Act 1983, s 96(1)(h); cf *Baldwyn v Smith* [1900] 1 Ch 588.
126 *Molton v Camroux* (1848) 2 Exch 487.
127 (1845) 13 M & W 623.
128 (1873) LR 8 Exch 132.
129 Sale of Goods Act 1979, s 3.

14 PRIVITY OF CONTRACT

SUMMARY

1 THE DOCTRINE OF PRIVITY OF CONTRACT

In the middle of the nineteenth century the common law judges reached a decisive conclusion upon the scope of a contract. No one, they declared, may be entitled to or bound by the terms of a contract to which he is not an original party.[1]

The decisive case was *Tweddle v Atkinson* in 1861.[2]

---

[1] *Price v Easton* (1833) 4 B & Ad 433; *Tweddle v Atkinson* (1861) 1 B & s 393. For history, see Simpson *History* pp 475–485; *Dutton v Poole* (1677) 2 Lev 210; *Bourne v Mason* (1668) 1 Vent 6; EJP 70 LQR 467. See also the review of the history by Windeyer J in *Coulls v Bagot's Executor and Trustee Co Ltd* [1967] ALR 385 at 407–409. See Dowrick 19 MLR 374; Furmston 23 MLR 373; Simpson 15 ICLQ 835; Millner 16 ICLQ 446; Scammell 1955 Current Legal Problems 131; Andrews 8 LS 14; Wilson 11 Sydney LR 230. Kincaid [1989] CLJ 243; Adams and Brownsword 10 LS 12; Flannigan 103 LQR 564.

[2] (1861) 1 B & s 393.

In consideration of an intended marriage between the plaintiff and the daughter of William Guy, a contract was made between Guy and the plaintiff's father, whereby each promised to pay the plaintiff a sum of money. Guy failed to do so, and the plaintiff sued his executors.

The action was dismissed. Wightman J said:

> Some of the old decisions appear to support the proposition that a stranger to the consideration of a contract may maintain an action upon it, if he stands in such a near relationship to the party from whom the consideration proceeds, that he may be considered a party to the consideration . . . But there is no modern case in which the proposition has been supported. On the contrary, it is now established that no stranger to the consideration can take advantage of a contract, although made for his benefit.[3]

The learned judge, by basing his decision on the rule that consideration must move from the promisee, emphasised the English identification of contract and bargain. But it has already been observed that this rule is itself an insular reflection of the general assumption that contract, as a juristic concept, is the intimate if not the exclusive relationship between the parties who have made it.[4]

The doctrine of privity was reaffirmed by the House of Lords in 1915. In *Dunlop v Selfridge*:[5]

> The plaintiffs sold a number of their tyres to Dew & Co, described as 'motor accessory factors', on the terms that Dew & Co would not resell them below certain scheduled prices and that, in the event of a sale to trade customers, they would extract from the latter a similar undertaking. Dew & Co sold the tyres to Selfridge, who agreed to observe the restrictions and to pay to Messrs Dunlop the sum of £5 for each tyre sold in breach of this agreement. Selfridge in fact supplied tyres to two of their own customers below the listed price.

As between Dew and Selfridge this act was undoubtedly a breach of contract for which damages could have been recovered. But the action was brought, not by Dew, but by Messrs Dunlop, who sued to recover two sums of £5 each as liquidated damages and asked for an injunction to restrain further breaches of agreement. They were met by the objection that they were not parties to the contract and had furnished no consideration for the defendants' promise. The objection, indeed, was obvious, and plaintiffs' counsel, not daring to contest it, sought to evade its application by pleading that their clients were in the position of undisclosed principals. The House of Lords not unnaturally considered such a suggestion difficult to reconcile with the facts of the case, and gave judgment for the defendants.

It is important to see what *Tweddle v Atkinson* and *Dunlop v Selfridge* decided. In any legal system, and at any period in history, a contract will be primarily a matter

---

[3] Ibid at 397–398.
[4] P 102, above; and see *Price v Easton* (1833) 4 B & Ad 433.   [5] [1915] AC 847. p 102, above.

between the contracting parties. A contract will normally simply state the rights of the parties and have nothing to do with other people. However, it is undoubtedly the case that there will be a significant number of cases where the contract, if properly performed, will confer benefits on non parties. Suppose a contractor makes a contract with the Department of Transport to build a motorway from A to B; the completion of the motorway will be seen as a benefit by many drivers who plan to drive along it. If, in breach of contract, the contractor is late completing the motorway, this may well in a sense cause loss to those who would have used the motorway but in most instances they would not have the right to sue the contractor for late performance of his contract with the Department of Transport. The main reason for this is that the contractor and the Department of Transport, when they made the contract, did not intend to create any contractual rights in anyone else.

The main difference between English law as established in 1915 and many other systems was that the third party would not derive contractual rights even if the contracting parties clearly intended to confer benefits on the third party. It is clear that in *Tweddle v Atkinson* the whole purpose of the transaction was to confer enforceable rights on the husband and that in *Dunlop v Selfridge* one of the major purposes was to confer enforceable rights on Dunlop. What English law said was that even if the parties clearly intended by contract to confer a right on a third party, they could, in general, not succeed in doing so. It was this result that was unique and special to English law and which distinguished it from most other systems.

Substantial reform of the doctrine was proposed by the Law Revision Committee as long ago as 1937 in its Sixth Interim Report,[6] but this was not implemented. In *Woodar Investment Development Ltd v Wimpey Construction (UK) Ltd,*[7] Lord Scarman forcefully urged the desirability of the House of Lords reconsidering the rule and so did Steyn LJ in *Darlington Borough Council v Wiltshier.*[8] In *Trident General Insurance Co Ltd v McNiece Bros Pty Ltd,*[9] the majority of the majority in the High Court of Australia (Mason CJ, Wilson J and Toohey J) thought the time had come to reject the privity doctrine. Gaudron J came to the same result on reasoning based on unjust enrichment principles. Brennan J, Deane J and Dawson J thought the doctrine still law.[10] Cogent criticism of the doctrine is to be found in the decision of the Supreme Court of Canada in *London Drugs Ltd v Kuehne and Nagel International Ltd.*[11]

In 1991 the Law Commission produced a Consultative Paper which suggested radical change in the law. Although the proposal to change the law obtained widespread support, the technical questions of exactly how to bring the change about proved much more difficult than had been anticipated and it was not in fact until 1999 that the Contract (Rights of Third Parties) Act[12] became law.

---

[6] Para 50(a).   [7] [1980] 1 All ER 571 at 590, [1980] 1 WLR 277 at 300.
[8] [1995] 3 All ER 895 at 903.   [9] (1988) 80 ALR 574.   [10] Kincaid 2 JCL 160.
[11] [1993] 1 WWR 1; Waddams 109 LQR 349; Adams and Brownsword 56 MLR 722.
[12] Merkin (ed) *Privity of Contract* (London 2000); Andrews [2001] Cambridge LJ 353.

There is a theoretical question whether the Act should be regarded as abolishing the doctrine or merely as creating a large exception to it. On the whole, discussion of the Act seems to proceed on the basis that the Act is taken as a large exception to the doctrine of privity but this must depend on exactly what the doctrine of privity says. It is clear that both before and after the Act there will be many contracts which create rights and duties between the parties only but this can be regarded not as being the result of the doctrine of privity properly understood since the doctrine's principal thrust was that parties could not confer contractual rights on a third party even if they wanted to. Under the 1999 Act, the parties (or in practice sometimes one of them) may choose to confer rights on a third party. As we shall see, there is no doubt now that the parties enjoy the freedom to create rights in third parties and the problem is whether they have in fact done so. As we shall see, this turns on the technique used by the Act to answer this question.[13]

Finally, we should note that the doctrine of privity of contract means only that a non-party cannot bring *an action on the contract*.[14] This does not exclude the possibility that he may have some other cause of action. Thus if A buys a car from B and gives it to his wife, she will probably have no rights under the contract against B but she could have an action in tort if she suffered personal injuries because of B's negligent pre-delivery inspection.[15] Similarly if A threatens to break his contract with B unless B dismisses his servant C, C may be able to sue A in the tort of intimidation.[16]

It is also the case that if the parties think ahead and draft the contract carefully, it is often possible to structure the contract so as to sidestep the difficulties which the doctrine of privity causes.[17]

2 QUALIFICATIONS TO DOCTRINE

One exception to the doctrine, admitted in the first half of the eighteenth century, when the rule itself was obscure, has since maintained its ground. If A has made a contract with B, C may intervene and take A's place if he can show that A was acting

---

[13] See p 588, below.

[14] As to whether a contract can operate to afford a non-party a defence, see pp 214 ff, above.

[15] *Donoghue v Stevenson* [1932] AC 562, where the contrary theory was put to rest. This is not to say that the present complex of rules is satisfactory since the standards of liability in sale and negligence are very different and legally the wife's position would be much better if A gave her the money to buy the car herself. Jolowicz 32 MLR 1; Pasley 32 MLR 241; Legh-Jones [1969] CLJ 54.

[16] *Rookes v Barnard* [1964] AC 1129, [1964] 1 All ER 367; Hoffmann 81 LQR 116.

[17] So in the case of *Beswick v Beswick* [1968] AC 58, [1967] 2 All ER 1197, discussed p 581, below, the difficulties could have been avoided entirely if the uncle, before selling the business to his nephew, had first sold a share in it to his wife for £1 and they had then jointly sold the business to the nephew. See also *Law Debenture Trust Corpn plc v Ural Caspian Oil Corp Ltd* [1993] 2 All ER 355.

throughout as his agent, and it is irrelevant that B entered into the contract in ignorance of this fact. This right of intervention, known usually as the doctrine of the undisclosed principal, has, indeed, been attacked on the very ground that it offends the common law doctrine of privity. But criticism has been fruitless, and the undisclosed principal is a well-established character in the modern law of agency.[18]

The doctrine of privity also clashed with the needs and concepts of the law of property. A lease, for instance, is a contract, but it creates rights of property that cannot be kept within contractual bounds. If A lets land to B, the lease will contain mutual rights and duties—to pay the rent, to keep the premises in repair and many other obligations. As between the parties themselves there is privity of contract; but if either transfers his interest to a stranger, convenience demands that he in his turn shall take the benefit and the burden of the original covenants. The need was felt and a partial remedy devised as long ago as the sixteenth century, and the modern position is the result of the combined efforts of common law and statute.[19] Similar problems are raised when a freeholder sells his land and wishes to restrict its use not only by the purchaser but by anyone to whom it may be transferred.[20] Another illustration is offered by the modern case of *Smith and Snipes Hall Farm Ltd v River Douglas Catchment Board.*[21]

By a contract under seal made in 1938 the defendants agreed with eleven owners of land adjoining a certain stream to improve its banks and to 'maintain for all time the work when completed'. The landowners agreed to pay a proportion of the cost. In 1940 one of the landowners conveyed her land to Smith, the first plaintiff, and in 1944 Smith leased it to Snipes Hall Farm Ltd, the second plaintiff. In 1946, owing to the defendants' negligence, the banks burst and the land was flooded.

Both plaintiffs were strangers to the contract. But the Court of Appeal held that the covenants undertaken by the defendants affected the use and value of the land, that they were intended from the outset to benefit anyone to whom the land might be transferred and that the defendants were liable. Even in this area, however, the principle of privity of contract is not rendered irrelevant but rather greatly diminished in importance. If it is sought to enforce a covenant over land either by or against a non-party, the factual situation must be brought within one of the rules which common law, equity and statute have developed. These rules cover much but not all of the ground.

In *Dunlop v Selfridge*, the House of Lords drew the logical inference from the common law premises. But the result may be inconvenient or even unjust. Thus it is

---

[18] See pp 621 ff, below. The criticism will be found in Ames *Lectures in Legal History* pp 453–463. See also the statutory agency created by Consumer Credit Act 1974, s 56(2).

[19] *Spencer's Case* (1583) 5 Co Rep 16a. On the whole subject, see Cheshire and Burn *Modern Law of Real Property* (15th edn) pp 448–457.

[20] P 593, below, and Cheshire and Burn *Modern Law of Real Property* (15th edn) pp 614 ff.

[21] [1949] 2 KB 500, [1949] 2 All ER 179. This resulted from a combination of a common law exception and the extension of it by s 78(1) of Law of Property Act 1925. See Cheshire & Burn *Modern Law of Real Property* (15th edn) pp 609–614.

quite common for insurances to be taken out by one person on behalf of another—a husband for his wife, or a parent for his child. Yet, even if the policy expressly confers benefits on the third party, the latter has no claim at common law.[22] A result, so inconsistent with the needs of the modern world, would seem to invite the intervention of Parliament, and from time to time Acts have been passed to redress a particular grievance. Husband and wife have thus, in reversal of the common law rule, been enabled to take out life insurance policies in favour of each other or of their children; third parties have been allowed, in certain circumstances, to sue on marine or fire insurance policies, or on the policies covering road accidents required by the provisions of the Road Traffic Act 1972.[23]

By the rules governing negotiable instruments, moreover, it has long been established—first by the custom of the law merchant, then by judicial decision and finally by statute[24]—that a third party may sue on a bill of exchange or a cheque. The usages of trade and commerce have thus done something to modify the rigour of the common law doctrine. Nor is their force exhausted. It is still true that, if it is clear in any particular case that a commercial practice exists in favour of third party rights and that all concerned in the litigation have based their relations upon it, the court will do what it can to support and sanction it.[25]

Rule modified by equitable doctrine of constructive trust

Outside the law of property and the commercial world few, if any, exceptions were allowed at common law. Litigants have therefore invoked the assistance of equity. As early as 1753 Lord Hardwicke indicated the possibilities of the trust. He was prepared, in a case where A promised B to pay money to C, to regard B as trustee for C of the benefit of the contract.[26] In 1817 Sir William Grant affirmed the suggestion in the case of *Gregory and Parker v Williams*.[27]

> Parker owed money both to Gregory and to Williams. He agreed with Williams to assign to him the whole of his property, if Williams would pay the debt due to Gregory. The property was duly assigned, but Williams failed to implement his promise.

---

[22] See the remarks of Lord Esher, in *Cleaver v Mutual Reserve Fund Life Association* [1892] 1 QB 147 at 152.

[23] See s 11 of the Married Women's Property Act 1882 (extended to illegitimate children by Family Law Reform Act 1969, s 19); s 14(2) of the Marine Insurance Act 1906; s 47(1) of the Law of Property Act 1925; s 148(4) of the Road Traffic Act 1972. See also Third Parties (Rights Against Insurers) Act 1930; *P Samuel & Co v Dumas* [1923] 1 KB 592; affd [1924] AC 431; *Hepburn v A Tomlinson (Hauliers) Ltd* [1966] AC 451, [1966] 1 All ER 418.

[24] See Bills of Exchange Act 1882, s 29.

[25] *United Dominions Trust Ltd v Kirkwood* [1966] 2 QB 431 at 454–455, [1966] 1 All ER 968 at 980, per Lord Denning MR. This may provide a rationale for the enforcement of bankers' commercial credits, discussed p 77, above.

[26] *Tomlinson v Gill* (1756) Amb 330. See Corbin 46 LQR 12; Williams 7 MLR 123.

[27] (1817) 3 Mer 582.

Gregory and Parker filed a bill in equity to compel performance of the promise, and succeeded. Sir William Grant held that Parker must be regarded as trustee for Gregory, and that the latter 'derived an equitable right through the mediation of Parker's agreement'. After the Judicature Act 1873, the propriety of this device was affirmed and its use sanctioned in any division of the High Court. In the words of Lush LJ in *Lloyd's v Harper*:[28]

> I consider it to be an established rule of law that where a contract is made with A for the benefit of B, A can sue on the contract for the benefit of B and recover all that B could have recovered if the contract had been made with B himself.

Implicit in this statement is the conclusion that if A fails in his duty, B, the beneficiary under the implied trust, may successfully maintain an action to which A and the other contracting party are joint defendants.

One particular application of this equitable doctrine was recognised as effective by the House of Lords in *Walford's* case in 1919.[29]

> Walford, as broker, had negotiated a charterparty between the owners of the *SS Flore* and the Lubricating and Fuel Oils Co Ltd. By a clause in the charterparty the owners promised the charterers to raise no objection, and the action proceeded as if they had in fact been joined. The House of Lords affirmed judgment in Walford's favour. Lord Birkenhead cited the previous decisions and declared that 'in such cases charterers can sue as trustees on behalf of the broker'.

Such decisions indicate the possibilities of the trust in evading the rigidity of the common law rule. At first sight it appears to be an effective means of evasion. It is useful to recall Maitland's definition:

> Where a person has rights which he is bound to exercise on behalf of another or for the accomplishment of some particular purpose, he is said to have those rights in trust for another or for that purpose, and he is called a trustee.[30]

It is true that the subject matter of a trust is normally some tangible property, such as land or goods, or a definite sum of money, and that, if the conception is to be applied in the present context, it is necessary to speak of the 'trust of a promise'. But Maitland's definition is wide enough to include such a phrase, and, on the assumption that the judges are resolved to avoid the limitations of the common law, the machinery would seem to be simple and adequate. The third party may ask the contracting party

[28] (1880) 16 ChD 290 at 321. See also *Re Flavell, Murray v Flavell* (1883) 25 ChD 89; *Royal Exchange Assurance v Hope* [1928] Ch 179.
[29] *Les Affréteurs Réunis SA v Walford* [1919] AC 801.
[30] Maitland *Equity* p 44.

to sue as trustee, and, in the event of a refusal, may himself sue and join the 'trustee' as co-defendant.[31]

But, despite its promising appearance and the positive terms in which it has occasionally been acclaimed, the device has in practice proved a disappointing and unreliable instrument.

In *Re Schebsman, Official Receiver v Cargo Superintendents (London) Ltd and Schebsman:*[32]

> S was employed by two companies. By a contract made between him and them, one of the companies agreed in certain eventualities to pay £5,500 to his widow and daughter.

It was held that the contract did not create a trust in favour of the widow and daughter. Du Parcq LJ said:[33]

> It is true that, by the use possibly of unguarded language, a person may create a trust, as Monsieur Jourdain talked prose, without knowing it, but unless an intention to create a trust is clearly to be collected from the language used and the circumstances of the case, I think that the court ought not to be astute to discover indications of such an intention. I have little doubt that in the present case both parties (and certainly the debtor) intended to keep alive their common law right to vary consensually the terms of the obligation undertaken by the company, and if circumstances had changed in the debtor's life-time injustice might have been done by holding that a trust had been created and that those terms were accordingly unalterable.

A later example of the reluctance of the courts to discover a trust is offered by the case of *Green v Russell.*[34]

> The plaintiff's son, Alfred Green, was employed by the defendant's husband, Arthur Russell. Both son and husband died in a fire at their office. Mr Russell had made a contract with an insurance company in which he himself was described as 'the insured' and by which the company undertook to pay £1,000 if certain of Mr Russell's employees, including Mr Green, died as a result of bodily injuries. Nothing in the contract of employment between Mr Green and Mr Russell required such a policy to be taken out, nor did its terms confer any right or impose any obligation on Mr Green in respect of the policy. The insurance company paid

---

[31] It is strange that the device was not exploited by the plaintiffs in *Dunlop v Selfridge*, p 573, above. Lord Haldane had recognised its existence, and the facts in the case would seem to suggest the possibility of a trust at least as clearly as those in *Walford's* case. *Dunlop v Selfridge*, however, was fought and decided exclusively on common law principles.

[32] [1944] Ch 83, [1943] 2 All ER 768. See also *Gandy v Gandy* (1885) 30 ChD 57; *Vandepitte v Preferred Accident Insurance Corpn of New York* [1933] AC 70; *Re Stapleton-Bretherton, Weld-Blundell v Stapleton-Bretherton* [1941] Ch 482, [1941] 3 All ER 5; and *Re Miller's Agreement, Uniacke v A-G* [1947] Ch 615, [1947] 2 All ER 78.

[33] [1944] Ch 83 at 104, [1943] 2 All ER 768 at 779.

[34] [1959] 2 QB 226, [1959] 2 All ER 525. Furmston 23 MLR 373 at 377–385.

the £1,000 to Mrs Russell, as her husband's administratrix, and she paid it over to the plaintiff.

The plaintiff, as the son's administratrix, sued the defendant, as the husband's administratrix, under the Fatal Accidents Acts 1846 to 1908. The defendant admitted liability in principle but claimed that the £1,000 she had paid over to the plaintiff should be deducted from the damages. The issue turned on the wording of section 1 of the Act of 1908, that 'there shall not be taken into account any sum paid or payable on the death of the deceased under any contract of assurance or insurance'.[35]

At first sight these words were conclusive. The money had certainly been paid on the death of Mr Green under a contract of insurance. But the defendant argued that the words applied only to sums to which the deceased had either a legal or an equitable right and that no such right existed. There was none at common law since the deceased was a stranger to the insurance contract, and none in equity since no trust could be inferred in his favour. The Court of Appeal held that the words were clear in themselves and that there was no reason to restrict them on the grounds suggested. This conclusion disposed of the case. But the court agreed that, had it been necessary to decide the question, they would have ruled that the policy conferred no right on the deceased and therefore none on the plaintiff. 'An intention to provide benefits for someone else and to pay for them', said Romer LJ, 'does not in itself give rise to a trusteeship'; and he stressed the incompatibility of this status with the contractual liberty enjoyed by the insured to terminate the policy without the concurrence of his employees. 'There was nothing to prevent Mr Russell at any time, had he chosen to do so, from surrendering the policy and receiving back a proportionate part of the premium which he had paid.'[36]

At one time it looked as if the trust concept might provide a convenient equitable means to circumvent the common law rule. Over the last fifty years, however, without locking the door the courts have consistently failed to open it. A trust will not now be inferred simply because A and B make a contract with the intention of benefiting C; in the few cases where trusts have been discovered, there have been much stronger indicia.[37] A variety of reasons have combined to produce this result: a feeling that the trust was a 'cumbrous fiction':[38] an insistence that intention to create a trust be affirmatively proved and a concern lest the irrevocable nature of a trust should prevent the contracting parties from changing their minds.[39]

---

[35] S 1 of the 1908 Act has now been repealed and replaced by s 2(1) of the Fatal Accidents Act 1959: 'There shall not be taken into account any insurance money, benefit, pension or gratuity which has been or will or may be paid as a result of the death.'

[36] Ibid at 241 and 531, respectively.

[37] See *Re Webb, Barclays Bank Ltd v Webb* [1941] Ch 225, [1941] 1 All ER 321. *Re Foster Clark's Indenture Trusts, Loveland v Horsecroft* [1966] 1 All ER 43, [1966] 1 WLR 125.

[38] See per Lord Wright 55 LQR 189 at 208.

[39] Cf per Fullagar J, in *Wilson v Darling Island Stevedoring and Lighterage Co* (1956) 95 CLR 43 at 67. See also *Olsson v Dyson* (1969) 43 ALJR 77.

Section 56 of the Law of Property Act 1925
Since the retreat of equity a further attempt to cut if not to unloose the technical knots was made by a bold essay in statutory interpretation. By section 56(1) of the Law of Property Act 1925, it is declared that:

> A person may take an immediate or other interest in land or other property, or the benefit of any condition, right of entry, covenant or agreement over or respecting land or other property, although he may not be named as a party to the conveyance or other instrument.

This section replaced section 5 of the Real Property Act 1845, which itself abolished a common law rule that no person could take advantage of a covenant in a deed unless he was a party to that deed; but, in replacing it, it widened its terms, especially by adding the words 'or other property' and 'or agreement'. It must also be noticed that by section 205(1) of the Law of Property Act, 'unless the context otherwise requires . . . "Property" includes anything in action and any interest in real or personal property'. In a number of cases Lord Denning suggested that the section should be read as abrogating the doctrine of privity in the case of contracts in writing affecting property.[40] This view has now been rejected by the House of Lords in the case of *Beswick v Beswick*.[41]

> Peter Beswick was a coal merchant. In March 1962, he contracted to sell the business to his nephew John in consideration (1) that for the rest of Peter's life John should pay him £6 10s a week, (2) that if Peter's wife survived him John should pay her an annuity of £5 a week. John took over the business and paid Peter the agreed sum until Peter died in November 1963. He then paid Peter's widow £5 for one week and refused to pay any more. The widow brought an action against John in which she claimed £175 as arrears of the annuity and asked for specific performance of the contract. She sued (a) as administratrix of Peter's estate, (b) in her personal capacity.

The Court of Appeal held unanimously that she was entitled, as administratrix, to an order for specific performance. Lord Denning and Lord Justice Danckwerts also held that she could succeed in her personal capacity under section 56(1) of the Law of Property Act 1925.[42] The defendant appealed to the House of Lords. The House held that, as administratrix, the widow could obtain an order for specific performance which would enforce the provision in the contract for the benefit of

---

[40] *Smith and Snipes Hall Farm Ltd v River Douglas Catchment Board* [1949] 2 KB 500 at 517, [1949] 2 All ER 179 at 189; *Drive Yourself Hire Co (London) Ltd v Strutt* [1954] 1 QB 250 at 274, [1953] 2 All ER 1475 at 1483. Cf *Re Foster* (1938) 159 LT 279 at 282; *Re Miller's Agreement* [1947] Ch 615, [1947] 2 All ER 78; *Stromdale and Ball Ltd v Burden* [1952] Ch 223, [1952] 1 All ER 59. See Elliott 20 Conv (NS) 43, 114; Andrews 23 Conv (NS) 179; Furmston 23 MLR 373 at 380–385; Ellinger 26 MLR 396.

[41] [1968] AC 58, [1967] 2 All ER 1197. For the judgments in the Court of Appeal, see [1966] Ch 538, [1966] 3 All ER 1.

[42] Salmon LJ was not prepared to accept this interpretation of the section. All three members of the Court of Appeal agreed that no trust could be found in the plaintiff's favour.

herself;[43] but that in her personal capacity she could derive no right of action from the statute.

Their lordships admitted that, if section 56(1) was to be literally construed, its language was wide enough to support the conclusions of Lord Denning and Lord Justice Danckwerts. But they were reluctant to believe that the legislature, in an act devoted to real property, had inadvertently and irrelevantly revolutionised the law of contract. The avowed purpose of the Act of 1925, according to its title, was 'to consolidate the enactments relating to conveyancing and the law of property in England and Wales'. It must therefore be presumed that the legislature designed no drastic changes in such enactments; and this presumption was to be rebutted only by plain words. The words of section 56(1) were not plain. By section 205(1), moreover, it was provided that the definitions which it contained were to apply 'unless the context otherwise requires'. In so far as the Law of Property Act 1925 was an essay in consolidation, the context required the word 'property' to be restrictively construed, and it should not be allowed to spill over into contract. Whatever the force of this argument, the House of Lords has decisively rejected the attempt to use section 56(1) so as to enable third parties to sue upon a contract.[44]

3 ENFORCEMENT BY PROMISEE

At first sight the decision in *Beswick v Beswick* appears to be a sanguinary defeat for those who would hope to see the doctrine of privity curbed, if not abolished. It is noteworthy, however, that the nephew was compelled to perform his promise and this shows that at least in some cases a satisfactory result can be achieved if an action is brought not by a third party beneficiary but by the original promisee. This possibility is further illuminated by the decision in *Snelling v John G Snelling Ltd*.[45]

> The plaintiff and his two brothers were all directors of the defendant company. The company was financed by substantial loans from all three brothers. As part of an arrangement to borrow money from a finance company, the three brothers made a contract, to which the company was not a party, not to demand repayment of their loans during the currency of the loan from the finance company. The agreement further provided that if any of the brothers should voluntarily resign his

---

[43] On the order for specific performance see p 797, below.

[44] It is far from clear what the House of Lords decided that s 56(1) did mean. See Treitel 30 MLR 681. Fortunately this is now a problem for property lawyers and not for contract lawyers. See *Re Windle, (a bankrupt), ex p trustee of the bankrupt v Windle* [1975] 3 All ER 987, [1975] 1 WLR 1628. *Amsprop Trading Ltd v Harris Distribution Ltd* [1997] 2 All ER 990.

[45] [1973] QB 87, [1972] 1 All ER 79; Wilkie 36 MLR 214. See also *Gurtner v Circuit* [1968] 2 QB 587, [1968] 1 All ER 328.

directorship, he should forfeit the money owing on the loan. A few months later the plaintiff resigned his directorship and sued the company for repayment of his loan.

The plaintiff argued that as the company was not a party to the agreement with his brothers, that agreement did not affect his rights against the company. The brothers applied to be joined as co-defendants to the action and Ormrod J held that although the company was not entitled to rely directly on the agreement, the co-defendant brothers were entitled to a stay of proceedings and that indeed since all the parties were before the court and the reality of the situation was that the plaintiff's claim had failed, the action should be dismissed.

It seems therefore that what cannot be obtained directly by the third party can, in appropriate circumstances, be obtained on his behalf by the promisee by specific performance, stay of proceedings or (presumably) injunction. In many circumstances, however, the only satisfactory remedy is an action for damages. It was long believed that in an action for damages, the promisee could recover only for the damage he himself suffered (often only nominal) and not the damage suffered by the third party. This seems to have been assumed by the majority of the House of Lords, though not by Lord Pearce in *Beswick v Beswick*.

The principle that a plaintiff can only recover for his own loss is certainly subject to exceptions. So, for instance, a carrier of goods may insure the full value of the goods and recover it from an insurance company, even though he himself has but a limited interest in the goods.[46] Similarly, a consignor of goods for carriage by sea may, in certain circumstances, recover the full value of the goods if the contract is broken even though, by the date of breach, he is no longer owner of the goods so long as the original contract of carriage did not contemplate that the carrier would enter into fresh contracts of carriage with transferees of the goods.[47] It will be remembered, too, that Lush LJ stated the contrary in *Lloyd's v Harper*.[48] It has been widely thought that Lush LJ was talking only of situations of trust[49] but this was firmly denied by Lord Denning MR in *Jackson v Horizon Holidays Ltd*.[50]

The plaintiff made a contract with the defendant for a holiday for himself, his wife and two children in Ceylon. The holiday was a disaster and the defendants accepted that they were in breach of contract.

The Court of Appeal held that the plaintiff could recover damages not only for the discomfort and disappointment he suffered himself but also for that experienced by

---

[46] *Hepburn v A Tomlinson (Hauliers) Ltd* [1966] AC 451, [1966] 1 All ER 418.

[47] *The Albazero* [1977] AC 774, [1976] 3 All ER 129.   [48] (1880) 16 ChD 290, p 578, above.

[49] See eg per Windeyer J in *Coulls v Bagot's Executor and Trustee Co* [1967] ALR 385 at 409–411, though in his illuminating judgment Windeyer J did not agree that the promisee could get only nominal damages.

[50] [1975] 3 All ER 92, [1975] 1 WLR 1468.

his wife and children. This could, perhaps, have been put on the (relatively) narrow ground that the plaintiff was recovering for his own disappointment that his family's holiday was spoilt but Lord Denning MR stated clearly that the words of Lush LJ were of general application. Clearly, if this is the law the doctrine of privity will be substantially neutralised in any case where the promisee can be persuaded to sue.[51]

Lord Denning MR's statement was said to be incorrect by the House of Lords in *Woodar Investment Development Ltd v Wimpey Construction (UK) Ltd.*[52]

> The vendors agreed to sell 14 acres of land to the purchasers. The purchasers were to pay a price of £850,000 and on completion a further £150,000 to third parties, having no legal connection with the vendors. In circumstances considered more fully later in this book,[53] the vendors alleged that the purchasers had repudiated the contract and brought an action for damages. The purchasers argued that if they were liable to damages, such damages should only be nominal so far as non-payment to the third party was concerned.

This argument was upheld by the House of Lords.[54] Their Lordships thought that *Jackson v Horizon Holidays Ltd*[55] was probably correctly decided on its facts but that the reasons given by Lord Denning MR were clearly wrong and that Lush LJ's statement only applied where A stands in a fiduciary relationship to B.[56]

The notion that there is a general prohibition on a party recovering damages for breach of contract which reflect the loss of someone else cannot however survive three recent decisions, two of the House of Lords and the other of the Court of Appeal. The first decision of the House of Lords came in the two consolidated appeals in *Linden Gardens Trust v Lenesta Sludge Disposals* and *St Martin's Property v Sir Robert McAlpine*[57] In the *St Martin's* case:

> Two of the protagonists were similarly named companies which were part of the Kuwait financial empire in Great Britain and which we will call, for ease of exposition, St Martin's I and St Martin's II. St Martin's I entered into a building contract with the defendants, which was on standard Joint Contracts Tribunal 1963 terms which include prohibition on assignment without the consent of the defendant. It appears to have been decided for tax reasons that it would be more efficient if the transaction were transferred to St Martin's II and a purported but invalid assignment was made without seeking the consent of the defendant. In due

---

[51] Clearly if the promisee does recover substantial damages, the question will arise as to whether he must account to the beneficiary but any obligation to do so will not usually sound in contract.

[52] [1980] 1 All ER 571.

[53] See p 684, below.

[54] Since the House of Lords held by a majority that the purchasers had not repudiated, the reservations on this point are technically obiter but they are clearly carefully considered.

[55] [1975] 3 All ER 92, [1975] 1 WLR 1468.

[56] This would include situations where A is an agent of B.

[57] [1994] 1 AC 85, [1993] 3 All ER 417, see p 658, below.

course, the contract was completed and it was alleged that there were serious defects in the work.

Both St Martin's I and St Martin's II brought an action against the defendant. The defendant argued that St Martin's II could not sue because the assignment was invalid. This argument was accepted by the House of Lords. The defendant also argued that although there was a technical breach of contract with St Martin's I, St Martin's I could not recover substantial damages because the loss had in fact been suffered by St Martin's II. This argument was rejected by the House of Lords. Their Lordships did not say that their earlier decisions in *Woodar v Wimpey* and *The Albazero* were wrong but they did hold that they did not apply on the facts of the present case. Lord Browne-Wilkinson, who spoke for the majority, thought there was much to be said for:

> . . . drawing a distinction between those cases where the ownership of goods or property is relevant to prove that the plaintiff has suffered loss through the breach of a contract other than a contract to supply those goods or property and the measure of damages in a supply contract where the contractual obligation itself requires the provision of those goods and services . . . In my view the point merits exposure to academic consideration before it is decided by this House.[58]

He thought that in any event St Martin's I could recover in the present case because:

> . . . it could be foreseen that damage caused by a breach would cause loss to a later owner and not merely to the original contracting party . . . [I]t seems to me proper . . . to treat the parties as having entered into the contract on the footing that [St Martins I] would be entitled to enforce contractual rights for the benefit of those who suffered from defective performance.[59]

Lord Griffiths, who had delivered a separate speech on this point alone, would have gone further. The core of his judgment can be found in the following passage:[60]

> I cannot accept that in a contract of this nature, namely for work, labour and the supply of materials, the recovery of more than nominal damages for breach of contract is dependent upon the plaintiff having a proprietary interest in the subject matter of the contract at the date of breach. In everyday life contracts for work and labour are constantly being placed by those who have no proprietary interest in the subject matter of the contract. To take a common example, the matrimonial home is owned by the wife and the couple's remaining assets are owned by the husband and he is the sole earner. The house requires a new roof and the husband places a contract with a builder to carry out the work. The husband is not acting as agent for his wife, he makes the contract as principal because only he can pay for it. The builder fails to replace the roof properly and the husband has to call in and pay another builder

---

[58] Ibid at 112 and 435, respectively.   [59] Ibid at 114 and 437, respectively.
[60] Ibid at 96 and 421, respectively.

to complete the work. Is it to be said that the husband has suffered no damage because he does not own the property? Such a result would in my view be absurd and the answer is that the husband has suffered loss because he did not receive the bargain for which he had contracted with the first builder and the measure of the damages is the cost of securing the performance of that bargain by completing the roof repairs properly by the second builder. To put this simple example closer to the facts of this appeal—at the time the husband employs the builder he owns the house but just after the builder starts work the couple are advised to divide their assets so the husband transfers the house to his wife. This is no concern of the builder whose bargain is with the husband. If the roof turns out to be defective the husband can recover from the builder the cost of putting it right and thus obtain the benefit of the bargain that the builder had promised to deliver.

This case was followed and perhaps extended by the Court of Appeal in *Darlington Borough Council v Wiltshier*.[61] In this case, the plaintiff local authority, in order to side step (legitimately) government restrictions on borrowing, decided to carry out the construction of a recreational centre by a complex scheme. It was arranged that the finance company would pay for the erection of the building and be paid by the plaintiff. The finance company entered into the construction contract with the defendant contractors. It was always intended that the building, and any rights under the construction contract, would be assigned by the finance company to the plaintiffs. It was alleged that the building, when completed, had major defects. The plaintiff duly took an assignment of the building contract from the finance company and commenced an action against the contractor. It was accepted that the plaintiff could not be better off than the finance company and the question before the Court of Appeal, and the preliminary point, was which damages could have been recovered by the finance company. The contractor argued that the finance company could not have recovered substantial damages since it had suffered no loss. It was always intended that the building would be transferred to the plaintiffs and the plaintiffs had agreed to pay the finance company in full. The finance company was in no way responsible to the plaintiff for the condition of the building. The defendant argued that the *St Martin's* case could be distinguished since that was a case of a defective assignment whereas the present case was one of a valid assignment and, further, that in *St Martin's* there had been no contemplation that the building would be transferred to someone else at the time of the contract whereas, in the present case, it was always expected by all the parties that the building would end up belonging to the plaintiffs. The Court of Appeal did not regard these distinctions as of any significance and indeed, if anything, as strengthening the case of the plaintiff.

These questions were exhaustively reconsidered in *Panatown v McAlpine Construction Ltd*.[62] All of the members of the House of Lords thought the *Linden Gardens* case correctly decided but the House was divided as to how much further this line of reasoning should go.

---

[61] [1995] 3 All ER 895. [62] [2001] 1 AC 518, [2000] 4 All ER 97.

In 1989, the claimant had entered into a contract as employer with the defendant as main contractor to build an office building and a car park in Cambridge on the 1981 JCT Design & Build contract. Panatown was a member of the UNEX group of companies, of which UNEX Corp Ltd was the parent company. The site in Cambridge belonged to another member of the group, UNEX Investment Properties Ltd. The group had deliberately decided that Panatown should be the employer under the building contract and this was apparently based on perfectly proper tax considerations as to the incidence of VAT. After the building had been completed it was alleged that there were major flaws in the building work done by McAlpine and Panatown brought an action for damages. So far the facts are very similar to those in *Linden Gardens* except that there are no problems about assignment of the contract. However, at the time the contract was made, McAlpine had entered into a separate contract under a so-called duty of care deed with UNEX Investment Properties Ltd under which that company acquired a direct remedy against McAlpine in respect of any failure by McAlpine to exercise reasonable care and attention in respect of any matter within their responsibilities under the building contract. (It seems to be assumed in the case, though it is not anywhere fully explained, that UNEX Investment Properties Ltd's rights under the duty of care deed were in certain respects less extensive than Panatown's rights under the building contract, assuming that there were no problems about Panatown's rights under the contract).

All the members of the House of Lords assumed that the *Linden Gardens* case was correctly decided. However, the majority (Lord Clyde, Lord Jauncey and Lord Browne-Wilkinson) took the view that this case was fundamentally different. They explained the earlier case on what may be called the black-hole theory, that is that it was based on abhorrence of a result in which one party had a claim but had not suffered damage and another party had suffered damage but had no claim so that a contract breaker who had been guilty of a serious breach of contract could escape scot-free because no one had an effective action. This problem was not present in the *Panatown* case because the true owner of the building had a substantial remedy under the duty of care deed, even though this remedy might not be quite as attractive as allowing Panatown to sue under the building contract. Lord Goff and Lord Millett dissented. They took the view that the duty of care deed was essentially irrelevant since its commercial purpose was to provide a remedy to someone who bought the development from UNEX Investment Properties Ltd since the duty of care deed was expressly said to be transferrable. (It does seem to be clear that the development was always intended to be sold and not used by the UNEX Group as offices of its own.)

4 THE CONTRACTS (RIGHTS OF THIRD PARTIES) ACT 1999[63]

The Law Commission does not appear to have had much doubt that the privity doctrine was ripe for reform. Few of those consulted appear to have disagreed except for a group of lawyers in the construction industry who appear to have been very attached to the existing methods in the construction industry where subcontracting and sub-subcontracting is normal and where it has been clear in the past that an employer has no contract claim against subcontractors or sub-subcontractors nor they against him. This argument seems, with respect, to be misplaced since there is nothing in the Act which prevents the construction industry retaining this contractual model. The fundamental principle underlying the reform is that of party autonomy; the parties should be free to create a right by contract in other parties if they want to do so. There is no suggestion that they should be forced to do so.

The Law Commission had much more difficulty with deciding how the change should actually be brought about. One possibility, suggested by a similar body in Ontario, would have been to pass a very short statute saying that the doctrine was no more and leaving it to the courts to work out the consequences of this. This course was not without attractions but it would have been an uncharacteristic piece of legislation in this jurisdiction and, perhaps more important, would have left parties unclear what the position was probably for a rather long time.

The 1937 Law Revision Committee had proposed a simple statute which in effect required parties who wished to confer contractual rights on third parties to do so expressly. This would have produced a clear and simple result for all those who had access to competent lawyers though, as the cases show, many contracts are made without such access and, in general, in English contract law anything which can be done expressly can also be done impliedly.

This leads to the conclusion that the circumstances in which a third party will acquire enforceable contractual rights should be set out expressly and this is what the Act does. The solution is to be found in section 1(1) and (2) which provides:

(1) Subject to the provisions of this Act, a person who is not a party to a contract (a 'third party') may in his own right enforce a term of the contract if—

(a) the contract expressly provides that he may, or

(b) subject to subsection (2), the term purports to confer a benefit on him.

(2) Subsection (1)(b) does not apply if on a proper construction of the contract it appears that the parties did not intend the term to be enforceable by the third party.

---

[63] Phang 18 J Contract L 33; Chee Ho Tham 21 J Contract L 107; O'Meara 21 JCL 131.

The effect of this is that a third party may acquire contractual rights either if the contract expressly says so (section 1(1)(a)) or where the contract purports to confer a benefit on him unless as a matter of construction it appears that the parties did not intend the third party to get an enforceable right. Obviously, by far the clearest way for an intention not to confer a benefit to be demonstrated would be for the contract expressly to say so. Many standard printed forms have already acquired language clearly designed to produce this result and it appears that a competent contract draftsman should carefully consider either expressly saying that the third party is to acquire rights or that the third party is not to acquire rights.

It is clear, however, that the contract will not in practice always contain an express answer and difficult situations will arise where the arguments as to the parties' intention appear nicely balanced. We must remember that where the contract does not contain an express answer, the parties' intention is to be objectively deduced. Much may turn on the meaning given to the expression 'purport to confer a benefit'. As we have already said, there are many cases in which a third party will be better off if a contract is properly performed. It is thought, however, that something more than this is required in order to be able to say that the contract purports to confer a benefit.

The difficulties may be considered with relation to the leading decision of the House of Lords in *White v Jones*.[64] In this case, an intending testator wished to change his will and summoned his solicitor for the purpose of so doing. There was clear evidence that the purpose of the new will was to confer rights on his daughters. In what was treated as a breach of his contract with the testator, the solicitor took longer than he should have done to attend to his client's request and as a result the client died before the will could be revised. The House of Lords held by a majority of three to two that on these facts the disappointed beneficiaries could maintain a tort action against the solicitor on the basis that he owed them a duty of care to carry out his contract with their father with reasonable care, skill and despatch and that, if he had done so, they would have recovered under the will. At the time, it was clear that the beneficiaries could succeed only in a tort claim in English law because they were clearly not parties to any contract with the solicitor. It is clear, however, that in 2001 there was a contract between the testator and a solicitor and that if the contract had been properly performed, the beneficiaries would have been better off. Professor Andrew Burrows, who at the time was the responsible Law Commissioner, has taken the view that the Act clearly does not stretch to giving the beneficiaries a contract right against the solicitor. This may well be correct but it is worth noting that in the American version of the common law, successful actions have been brought against lawyers in this kind of situation, sometimes in tort and sometimes in contract.

The principal case to have arisen under the Act so far presented a relatively simple

[64] [1995] 2 AC 207, [1993] 3 All ER 481.

problem of application. In *Nisshin Shipping Co v Cleaves & Co Ltd*,[65] a contract between shipowners and charterers contained, as such contracts often do, a provision for the payment of commission to brokers who had negotiated the charterparty but were not parties to it.[66] Colman J had little difficulty in deciding that the brokers had an action under the 1999 Act. The contract conferred a benefit on the brokers and there was nothing in its wording to suggest an intention that the term should not be enforceable by the brokers.

Section 1(3) of the Act provides:

> The third party must be expressly identified in the contract by name, as a member of a class or as answering a particular description but need not be in existence when the contract is entered into.

If I make a contract with an insurance company which provides that on my death the insurance company should pay money to my grandchildren, this will sufficiently identify the third parties who are to benefit from the contract, whether or not the grandchildren were alive at the time the contract was made.

Section 1(6) provides:

> Where a term of a contract excludes or limits liability in relation to any matter references in this Act to the third party enforcing the term shall be construed as references to his availing himself of the exclusion or limitation.

This deals with the problem discussed above as to whether a non party can take advantage of an exemption or limitation clause in a contract of which he is not a party. It is now clear that this is possible though there will still be a question in any particular case as to whether a particular contract is intended to confer such an immunity on a particular party. So it is still possible to argue that on the facts of *Scruttons Ltd v Midland Silicones Ltd*[67] the defendant stevedores were not expressly identified in the bill of lading and were therefore not entitled to take advantage of it.

Variation and cancellation

It would be possible to take the view that the contracting parties, having created rights in the third party, were entitled to take those rights away. Alternatively, one might take the view that once the contract had been made, the rights of the third parties would be inviolate. The Act has not taken either of these extreme positions. Instead, it has taken an intermediate position which is set out in section 2:

---

[65] [2003] EWHC 2602; [2004] 1 All ER (Comm) 481

[66] These are of course essentially the facts of *Les Affréteurs Réunis SA v. Leopold Walford (London) Ltd* [1919] AC 801 discussed p 578, above. Brokers have been enforcing such agreements since *Robertson v Wait* [1853] 8 Exch 299 by actions in the name of the charterer.

[67] [1962] AC 446, [1962] 1 All ER 1. See p 215, above.

(1) Subject to the provisions of this section, where a third party has a right under section 1 to enforce a term of the contract, the parties to the contract may not without his consent cancel the contract, or vary it in such a way as to extinguish, or alter his entitlement under, that right, if—

(a) the third party has communicated his assent to the term to the promisor,

(b) the promisor is aware that the third party has relied on the term, or

(c) the promisor can reasonably be expected to have foreseen that the third party would rely on the term and the third party has in fact relied on it.

(2) The assent referred to in subsection (1)(a)—

(a) may be by words or conduct, and

(b) if sent to the promisor by post or other means, shall not be regarded as communicated to the promisor until received by him.

(3) Subsection (1) is subject to any express term of the contract under which—

(a) the contract may be cancelled or varied without the consent of the third party, or

(b) the consent of the third party is required in circumstances specified in the contract instead of those set out in subsection (1)(a) to (c).

(4) Where the consent of a third party is required under subsection (1) or (3), the court may, on the application of the parties to the contract, dispense with his consent if satisfied—

(a) that his consent cannot be obtained because his whereabouts cannot reasonably be ascertained, or

(b) that he is mentally incapable of giving his consent.

(5) The court may, on the application of the parties to a contract, dispense with any consent that may be required under subsection (1)(c) if satisfied that it cannot reasonably be ascertained whether or not the third party has in fact relied on the term.

(6) If the court dispenses with a third party's consent, it may impose such conditions as it thinks fit, including a condition requiring the payment of compensation to the third party.

(7) The jurisdiction conferred by subsections (4) to (6) is exercisable by both the High Court and a county court.

This sets out what may be regarded as the basic position but also clearly permits the parties to modify it and, in practice, it seems quite likely that the parties will want to do so. This has certainly been the position in continental systems where experience of third party rights is now extensive over many years. So one can easily imagine a contract for life insurance in which there would be power to change beneficiaries. It is likely that this power would be granted to the person who is paying the premiums since, in normal circumstances, the insurance company will have no interest in who actually receives the payments provided that it is clearly stated.

Defences

A and B may make a contract intended to confer rights on a third party T but after they have made the contract things may go wrong with the performance of the contract in a way which would make it unfair simply to allow T to enforce the contract. This is dealt with by section 3 which provides:

(1) Subsections (2) to (5) apply where, in reliance on section 1, proceedings for the enforcement of a term of a contract are brought by a third party.

(2) The promisor shall have available to him by way of defence or set-off any matter that;

(a) arises from or in connection with the contract and is relevant to the term, and

(b) would have been available to him by way of defence or set-off if the proceedings had been brought by the promisee.

(3) The promisor shall also have available to him by way of defence or set-off any matter if—

(a) an express term of the contract provides for it to be available to him in proceedings brought by the third party, and

(b) it would have been available to him by way of defence or set-off if the proceedings had been brought by the promisee.

(4) The promisor shall also have available to him—

(a) by way of defence or set-off any matter, and

(b) by way of counterclaim any matter not arising from the contract,

that would have been available to him by way of defence or set-off or, as the case may be, by way of counterclaim against the third party if the third party had been a party to the contract.

(5) Subsections (2) and (4) are subject to any express term of the contract as to the matters that are not to be available to the promisor by way of defence, set-off or counterclaim.

(6) Where in any proceedings brought against him a third party seeks in reliance on section 1 to enforce a term of a contract (including, in particular, a term purporting to exclude or limit liability), he may not do so if he could not have done so (whether by reason of any particular circumstances relating to him or otherwise) had he been a party to the contract.

It should be noted that this section is not limited to defences arising under the contract itself but is wide enough to deal also with matters of set-off, which may involve other contracts. Suppose A, a wine merchant, makes a contract with B, a business, under which it undertakes to deliver a case of wine to T. Clearly, A would normally be able to justify not having delivered the wine to T if it could show that B had not paid for the wine but A and B may have a contract which entitles A to set-off against T matters which arise from earlier transactions which he made with B.[68]

[68] The width of this possibility depends on the complexities of the law of set-off which are outside the scope of this book.

Existing exceptions

Section 7(1) provides:

> Section 1 does not affect any right or remedy of a third party that exists or is available apart from this Act.

This means that any of the exceptions to privity which were already established before 1999 continue in force.[69]

5 ATTEMPTS TO IMPOSE LIABILITIES UPON STRANGERS

It has long been an axiom of the common law that a contract between A and B cannot impose a liability upon C.

This rule, however, was found to be so inconvenient in the case of contracts concerning land that counter-measures had to be devised to meet it. It has already been seen that, where a lease was concerned, such measures originated at an early date in the common law itself and were subsequently extended by statute.[70] A second modification is due entirely to equity, and it did not emerge until 1848, when the case of *Tulk v Moxhay*[71] was decided. The problem in that case was this: will a restrictive covenant, voluntarily accepted by the purchaser of land as part of the contract of sale, bind persons who later acquire the land? The facts of the case itself afford a simple illustration.

> The plaintiff, the owner of several plots of land in Leicester Square, sold the garden in the centre to one Elms, who agreed not to build upon it but to preserve it in its existing condition. After a number of conveyances the garden was sold to the defendant Moxhay, who, though he knew of the restriction, proposed to build. The plaintiff, accepting his inability at common law to recover damages from one who was not a party to the contract, sought an injunction against the erection of the proposed buildings.

The injunction was granted. The decisive factor in the view of the court was the knowledge by the defendant of the existence of the covenant. A court of equity, being a court of conscience, could not permit him to disregard a contractual obligation affecting the land of which he had notice at the time of his purchase.

Thus was established the doctrine that a restrictive covenant, binding a purchaser not to perform certain acts of ownership upon the land bought, may be enforced, not

---

[69] This includes the matters discussed pp 575 ff, above.
[70] P 575, above.   [71] (1848) 2 Ph 774.

only against him as the contracting party, but also against third parties who later acquire the land. It is undesirable in a general book on contracts to specify the conditions upon which enforcement depends, but it is essential to observe that the liability of the third party soon ceased to be based exclusively on notice. There has been a radical development in the doctrine initiated by *Tulk v Moxhay*, and it has been established since the latter years of the nineteenth century that something more than mere notice by the third party of the existence of the covenant is necessary to render him liable. In particular, it is essential that the covenantee, ie the original vendor, should have retained other land in the neighbourhood for the benefit and protection of which the restrictive covenant was taken. If an owner sells only a portion of his property, the selling value of what he retains will often depreciate unless restrictions are placed upon the enjoyment of the part sold, and it is only where the covenantee has retained land capable of being benefited in this way that equity will enforce a restrictive covenant against a third party.[72]

The question now arises whether this equitable doctrine may be applied where the subject matter of the contract is property other than land.[73] The relevant cases and statutes suggest that there are two different situations which require, or at least have received, different treatment:[74]

(1) Attempts to enforce against third parties restrictions upon the use of goods.

(2) Attempts to enforce against third parties restrictions upon the price at which goods may be resold.

These situations will be considered separately.

A Restrictions upon use

It was a restriction upon use that the court enforced in the parent case of *Tulk v Moxhay*, and within a few years of this decision the propriety of a similar restriction was canvassed in the case of a ship. In *De Mattos v Gibson* in 1858:[75]

> A chartered a ship from X. During the currency of the charterparty X mortgaged the ship to B, who knew at the time that this charterparty existed. A alleged that B now threatened, as mortgagee, to sell the ship in disregard of his contract rights and he applied for an interlocutory injunction to restrain B from doing so.

The application was refused by Vice-Chancellor Wood, but allowed on appeal by Knight Bruce and Turner LJJ. Knight Bruce LJ observed:[76]

---

[72] See *Formby v Barker* [1903] 2 Ch 539, and *LCC v Allen* [1914] 3 KB 642.
[73] Gardner 98 LQR 279.
[74] This distinction was taken by Wade 44 LQR 51.
[75] 4 De G & J 276.   [76] Ibid at 282.

Reason and justice seem to prescribe that, at least as a general rule, where a man, by gift or purchase, acquires property from another, with knowledge of a previous contract, lawfully and for valuable consideration made by him with a third person, to use and employ the property for a particular purpose in a specified manner, the acquirer shall not, to the material damage of the third person, in opposition to the contract and inconsistently with it, use and employ the property in a manner not allowable to the giver or seller.

Turner LJ was careful not to be involved in so comprehensive a principle. He would not go further than to grant an interlocutory injunction 'until the hearing of the cause' because of the 'difficult and important questions to be tried at the hearing'. The case then went back to Wood V-C for the cause to be heard; and he ruled that, on the facts before him, no injunction should be granted. This ruling was upheld by the Lord Chancellor, Lord Chelmsford, and the plaintiff's application thus finally failed. Lord Chelmsford emphasised, however, that his decision was based on the finding that the defendant had not in fact interfered with the performance of the charterparty. Had he done so, an injunction might well have been granted.

Five years later, the same court was faced with similar facts in *Messageries Imperiales Co v Baines*.[77]

The plaintiff had chartered a ship from X. During the currency of the charter, X sold the ship to the defendant who knew at the time of the existence of the charter but declined to allow the ship to fulfil the charter obligations.

Wood V-C now felt constrained by the observations of his brothers in the superior courts and granted the injunction for which the plaintiff asked.

For the next fifty years the sweeping assertion of Knight Bruce LJ was cited from time to time but in 1914 the Court of Appeal refused to accept it as offering a catholic principle upon which it was safe to depend.

Notwithstanding what was said by Knight Bruce LJ in *De Mattos v Gibson*, it is not true as a general proposition that a purchaser of property with notice of a restrictive covenant affecting the property is bound by the covenant.[78]

However, in 1926 the case of the *Lord Strathcona Steamship Co v Dominion Coal Co* came before the Judicial Committee of the Privy Council.[79]

B, the owner of the steamer *Lord Strathcona*, chartered her to A on the terms that, for a period of years, A should be free to use her on the St Lawrence river for the summer season and should surrender her to B in November of each year. During the currency of the charterparty, but while the ship was in B's possession, B sold

---

[77] (1863) 7 LT 763.
[78] *LCC v Allen* [1914] 3 KB 642 at 658–59. See also *Barker v Stickney* [1919] 1 KB 121.
[79] [1926] AC 108.

and delivered her to C, who in turn resold her to D. D, though he knew of the charterparty, refused to deliver the ship to A for the summer season.

A obtained an injunction against D in the courts of Nova Scotia restraining him from using the ship in any way inconsistent with the charterparty, and D's appeal to the Privy Council was dismissed. The Privy Council quoted with approval the familiar words of Knight Bruce LJ. The advice of the Board has often been read as deciding in effect that the defendant in the case before them was caught by the rule in *Tulk v Moxhay* on the basis that he had bought a ship with notice that she was affected by a restrictive covenant in favour of the plaintiff and was therefore, in their view, in the same position as if he had bought an estate in land with notice of a similar restriction. It must be remembered, however, that in the years that had elapsed since the case of *De Mattos v Gibson* the rule in *Tulk v Moxhay* had been radically developed by the courts and had ceased to be based solely upon notice. A restrictive covenant imposed on land could no longer be enforced against later purchasers unless the original covenantee had retained a proprietary interest in other land for the benefit of which the covenant was taken. Where was the proprietary interest in the *Strathcona* case? The Privy Council recognised the necessity for its existence, but they could only assert that A enjoyed an interest in the ship for the period covered by the charterparty. But this interest was no more than that conferred by the very contract which A sought to enforce against the third party: it was certainly not the independent proprietary interest which equity requires in the case of restrictive covenants over land. Moreover, it is well established that a charterparty creates no right of property in a ship.[80]

Whether the decision in the *Strathcona* case should be accepted as valid and worthy to command the assent of English courts has been the subject of much debate.

In 1936 the Court of Appeal thought that it must in any event be confined 'to the very special case of a ship under a charter-party',[81] and the decision itself was challenged in *Port Line Ltd v Ben Line Steamers Ltd.*[82]

In March 1955, the plaintiffs chartered a ship from X the owner, for a period of 30 months. The ship was to remain in X's possession but to be at the complete disposal of the plaintiffs. In February 1956, X sold the ship to the defendants. The defendants at once chartered it back to X so that it never ceased to be in X's possession. The plaintiffs knew of the sale and acquiesced in it since the ship was to remain available under their own charter. The charter between X and the defendants contained a clause that 'if the ship is requisitioned, the charter shall thereupon cease'. No such clause existed in the plaintiffs' charter. The defendants,

---

[80] See Bailhache J in *Federated Coal and Shipping Co v R* [1922] 2 KB 42 at 46, and cases there cited. Except in the case of a charterparty by demise, *Baumwoll Manufacturer Von Carl Scheibler v Furness* [1893] AC 8.

[81] *Clore v Theatrical Properties Ltd* [1936] 3 All ER 483.

[82] [1958] 2 QB 146, [1958] 1 All ER 787.

when they bought the ship, knew of the existence of the plaintiff's charter but not of its terms. In August 1956, the Ministry of Transport requisitioned the ship and paid compensation to the defendants as owners. In November 1956, the requisition ended.

The plaintiffs now sued the defendants to obtain this compensation money and relied, inter alia, on the *Strathcona* case and the dictum in *De Mattos v Gibson*.

Diplock J gave judgment for the defendants. He thought, in the first place, that the *Strathcona* case was not good law.[83]

> The difficulty I have found in ascertaining its *ratio decidendi*, the impossibility which I find of reconciling the actual decision with well-established principles of law, the unsolved and, to me, insoluble problems which that decision raises combine to satisfy me that it was wrongly decided.

He stressed, in particular, the necessity, in the twentieth century, of finding some proprietary interest to support a claim based on *Tulk v Moxhay* and the absence of any such interest in the *Strathcona* case. In the second place, he was of opinion that, even assuming it possible to support the *Strathcona* case in principle, the facts before him did not fall within its scope. The defendants, when they bought the ship, had no actual knowledge of the plaintiffs' rights: though they knew that a charter existed, they did not know its terms. Nor were they in breach of any duty. It was not by their act but by the act of the Crown that the ship had been used inconsistently with the plaintiffs' charter. Finally, the only remedy possible under the doctrine of *Tulk v Moxhay* and therefore under the *Strathcona* case was the grant of an injunction. No damages or money compensation could be obtained.

However, in *Swiss Bank Corpn v Lloyds Bank Ltd*[84] Browne-Wilkinson J thought both *De Mattos v Gibson* and the *Strathcona* case correctly decided, though he found some of the reasoning in the latter case difficult to follow. He found two lines of reasoning which might be applicable in addition to the restrictive covenant argument which he thought generally not to the point. One approach is that a purchaser who takes expressly subject[85] to the terms of an earlier contract as to the use of the property may be held to be a constructive trustee.[86] He gave greater weight to a second approach which arises out of the tort of inducing breach of contract.[87] He considered

---

[83] Ibid at 168 and 797, respectively.

[84] [1979] Ch 548, [1979] 2 All ER 853; the judgment of Browne Wilkinson J was varied by the House of Lords [1982] AC 584, [1981] 2 All ER 449 but in such a way that that Court did not need to consider the correctness of his judgment on the present issues.

[85] That is, not only knowing of, but agreeing to be bound by, the earlier contract.

[86] He thought this certainly one of the grounds of decision in the *Strathcona* case, though he expressed no conclusion as to the correctness of this reason. It derives some support from cases such as *Binions v Evans* [1972] Ch 359, [1972] 2 All ER 70.

[87] See eg *Winfield and Jolowicz on Tort* (14th edn) pp 517–532.

that the granting of the injunction in *De Mattos v Gibson*[88] was 'the counterpart in equity of the tort of knowing interference with contractual rights'.[89]

It is perhaps unfortunate that discussion of the application of real property analogies to personal property has concentrated on restrictive covenants to the exclusion of other interests, perhaps more readily applicable to chattels. Thus it is clear that an option to purchase land creates an equitable interest in the land capable of being enforced against a purchaser of the land[90] and there is authority for the application of the same principle to options to purchase chattels[91] and choses in action, such as copyrights.[92]

A question, potentially of great practical importance, is whether a contract under which possession of a chattel is transferred for a fixed term creates property rights analogous to a lease.[93] Such contracts, eg for the rental of television sets or for hire or hire purchase[94] of motor vehicles, are extremely common and it is difficult to see any good reason why the owner of the goods should be able to convert the hirer's right to possession in to a right to damages by selling the goods over his head. Holdsworth saw the position with his usual clarity over fifty years ago when he said:[95]

> It is obvious that if A has let or pledged his chattel to B and has transferred its possession to B and if he then sells it to C, C can only take it subject to B's legal rights, and since they are legal rights whether C has notice of those rights or not.[96]

B Restrictions upon price

An attempt to enforce a price restriction against a third party was made in 1904 in the case of *Taddy v Sterious*.[97]

---

[88] (1858) 4 De G & J 276.

[89] [1979] Ch 548 at 575, [1979] 2 All ER 853 at 874. See also the decision of the Court of Appeal in *Sefton v Tophams* [1965] Ch 1140, [1965] 3 All ER 1 (reversed on other grounds [1967] 1 AC 50, [1966] 1 All ER 1039).

[90] See eg *London and South Western Rly Co v Gomm* (1882) 20 ChD 562.

[91] *Falcke v Gray* (1859) 4 Drew 651.

[92] *MacDonald v Eyles* [1921] 1 Ch 631. *Quaere* whether this depends on the contract being specifically enforceable.

[93] This was not the case in *The Strathcona* since the charterer does not ordinarily get possession of the chartered ship but merely a contractual right to control its use. In the special case of a charterparty by demise, the charterer does get possession and in the leading authority on such charterparties, *Baumvoll Manufacturer Von Carl Scheibler v Furness* [1893] AC 8, extensive use was made of analogies from the law of leases.

[94] A hire-purchase contract also contains an option to purchase, see p 178, above.

[95] 49 LQR 576 at 579; see also Gutteridge 51 LQR 91 at 98; Thornely 13 JSPTL 150 at 151; Lawson *The Law of Property* (2nd edn) pp 96–97.

[96] In practice C will very often have notice since A will not have possession.

[97] [1904] 1 Ch 354.

The plaintiffs, who were manufacturers of 'Myrtle Grove' tobacco, sought to prevent retailers from selling it below a minimum price. They attached to each packet a printed sheet, stating that the tobacco was sold 'on the express condition that retail dealers do not sell it below the prices above set forth' and adding that 'acceptance of the goods will be deemed a contract between the purchaser and Messrs Taddy & Co that he will observe these stipulations. In the case of a purchase by a retail dealer through a wholesale dealer, the latter shall be deemed to be the agent of Taddy & Co'. The plaintiffs sold tobacco under these conditions to Messrs Nutter, wholesale dealers, who resold it to the defendants, retail tobacconists. The defendants, though they had notice of the conditions, resold below the minimum price.

The plaintiffs sued in the Chancery Division for a declaration that the defendants were bound by the conditions. They put their case on two grounds. First, they maintained that the printed sheet constituted a contract between themselves and the defendants and that Messrs Nutter were their agents. The court dismissed this attempt to create a contract by ultimatum. There was in truth no contract between Taddy and Sterious, Messrs Nutter were not Taddy's agents, and no unilateral declaration, however peremptory, could alter the legal position. Secondly, the plaintiffs invited the court to extend to them the protection of the rule in *Tulk v Moxhay*. The invitation was summarily rejected. In the words of Swinfen Eady J:

> Conditions of this kind do not run with goods, and cannot be imposed upon them. Subsequent purchasers, therefore, do not take subject to any conditions which the court can enforce.

Another attempt to enforce a price restriction against a third party, made later in the same year, was met by the Court of Appeal with the same uncompromising refusal.[98]

The legal position remained unchanged for half a century, but then became the subject of somewhat irresolute legislation. By section 24 of the Restrictive Trade Practices Act 1956[99] agreements for the *collective* enforcement of stipulations as to resale prices were declared unlawful. But this declaration was balanced by a new sanction given by section 25(1) of that Act to the *individual* enforcement of such stipulations. The practical importance of this provision was greatly reduced, however, some eight years later when legislation was introduced to restrict *individual* minimum resale price maintenance.[100] Section 25(1) of the 1956 Act had provided that there goods were sold by a supplier subject to a condition as to the resale price of those goods, the condition was (with certain exceptions),[101] enforceable by the supplier

---

[98] *McGruther v Pitcher* [1904] 2 Ch 306.

[99] The provisions of this section were re-enacted by the consolidation legislation of 1976. See Resale Prices Act 1976, Part I, ss 1 to 4.

[100] Resale Prices Act 1964, s 1.

[101] Thus the condition was not enforceable in respect of the resale of any goods by a person acquiring those goods otherwise than for the purpose of resale in the course of business. Ibid, s 25(2)(a). See now Resale Prices Act 1976, s 26(3)(a).

against any person not party to the sale who subsequently acquired the goods with notice[102] of the condition as if he had been a party to the sale; but, with the introduction of the Resale Prices Act 1964 (in the light of which section 25(1) had thereafter to be read), there was little scope for its further implementation.

By section 1(1) of the Resale Prices Act 1964,[103] any term or condition of a contract for the sale of goods by a supplier to a dealer (or of any agreement between a supplier and a dealer relating to such a sale) was unlawful. It was, accordingly, unenforceable by the supplier, either against his own dealer or against a third party to the contract. The subsection was, however, subject to provisions for exemption by the Restrictive Practices Court of particular classes of goods.[104]

The whole of this question has now become one of competition law, an outline of which is to be found above.[105]

---

[102] For the meaning of 'notice' in a case on s 25(1) of the Restrictive Trade Practices Act 1956, see *Goodyear Tyre and Rubber Co Great Britain Ltd v Lancashire Batteries Ltd* [1958] 3 All ER 7, [1958] 1 WLR 655; Wedderburn [1958] CLJ 163.

[103] See now Resale Prices Act 1976, s 9(1).

[104] Provision for exemption by the court of particular clauses of goods was originally contained in s 5 of the Resale Prices Act 1964. See now Resale Prices Act 1976, s 14.

[105] See Ch 10, above.

15 PRIVITY OF CONTRACT UNDER THE LAW OF AGENCY

SUMMARY

1 THE PLACE OF AGENCY IN ENGLISH LAW

'Agency' is a comprehensive word which is used to describe the relationship that arises where one man is appointed to act as the representative of another. The act to be done may vary widely in nature. It may for example be the making of a contract, the institution of an action, the conveyance of land or, in the case of a power of attorney, the exercise of any proprietary right available to the employer himself. The following account, however, is solely concerned with the case where the agent purports to enter into a contract on behalf of his principal.

Regarded from this aspect, an agency agreement is one by which the agent is authorised to establish privity of contract between his employer, called the principal, and a third party.[1] It produces effects of two quite different kinds.

First, it creates an obligation between the principal and the agent, under which each acquires in regard to the other certain rights and liabilities. In this respect agency takes its place as one of the special contracts of English law, such as the contract for the sale of goods or for the hire of a chattel.

Secondly, when acted upon by the agent, it leads to the creation of privity of contract between the principal and the third party. A contract made with a third party by the agent in the exercise of his authority is enforceable both by and against the principal. Thus the English doctrine is that an agent may make a contract for his principal which has the same consequences as if the latter had made it himself. In other words the general rule is not only that the principal acquires rights and liabilities, but also that the agent drops out and ceases to be a party to the contract.

The question sometimes arises whether a man has acted as an agent or as an independent contractor in his own interest.[2] The latter is a person who is his own master in the sense that he is employed to bring about a given result in his own manner and not according to orders given to him from time to time by his employer. Thus a retailer A, who in response to an order from a customer B, buys goods from a wholesaler C and then resells them to B, is normally acting as an independent contractor. He is a middleman, not the agent of B.

But in other situations it may be a difficult matter to decide whether a person is acting as agent or as independent contractor. What, for example, is the position in the case of a hire-purchase transaction where a dealer sells goods to a finance company which then lets them out on hire to the hire purchaser? Is the dealer the agent of the finance company? Parliament has provided that he shall be deemed the agent of the company (a) as regards any representations concerning the goods made by him

---

[1] 'The essential characteristic of an agent is that he is invested with a legal power to alter his principal's legal relations with third parties; the principal is under a correlative liability to have his legal relations altered': Dowrick 17 MLR 36. Reynolds 94 LQR 225.

[2] Fridman 84 LQR 224.

in the course of negotiations with the hirer to induce or promote the agreement; (b) for the purpose of receiving notice that the offer to enter the agreement is withdrawn; (c) for the purpose of receiving notice that the agreement is rescinded.[3] But the question whether the dealer is to be regarded in general as the agent of the finance company remains unsettled. Two views have been expressed. On the one hand, Pearson LJ, in his judgment in *Financings Ltd v Stimson*[4] denied that any general rule could be laid down, and repeated the denial in *Mercantile Credit Co Ltd v Hamblin*:

> There is no rule of law that in a hire-purchase transaction the dealer never is, or always is, acting as agent for the finance company or as agent for the customer. In a typical hire-purchase transaction the dealer is a party in his own right, selling his car to the finance company, and he is acting primarily on his own behalf and not as general agent for either of the other two parties. There is no need to attribute to him an agency in order to account for his participation in the transaction. Nevertheless, the dealer is to some extent an intermediary between the customer and the finance company, and he may well have in a particular case some *ad hoc* agencies to do particular things on behalf of one or the other or it may be both of these two parties.[5]

On the other hand, Lord Denning and Lord Justice Donovan in *Financings Ltd v Stimson* considered the dealer in fact and in law to be the agent for many purposes of the finance company.[6]

In *Branwhite v Worcester Works Finance*[7] the House of Lords discussed the general position of the dealer. The discussion was not strictly necessary to the decision of the case, and divergent views were expressed. Lord Morris, Lord Guest and Lord Upjohn[8] approved the opinion given by Lord Justice Pearson in *Mercantile Credit Co Ltd v Hamblin*. Lord Wilberforce, with the concurrence of Lord Reid, supported the opposing opinion of Lord Denning and Lord Justice Donovan in *Financings Ltd v Stimson*, and set the question against the mercantile background of hire-purchase transactions.

> Such questions as arise of the vicarious responsibility of finance companies, for acts or defaults of dealers, cannot be resolved without reference to the general mercantile structure within which they arise: or if one prefers the expression, to mercantile reality. This has become well known and widely understood by the public, as well as by the commercial interests involved. So, far from thinking first of a purchase from the dealer, and then, separately, of obtaining finance from an outside source, the identity or even existence of the finance company or bank which is going to provide the money is a matter to [the customers] of indifference; they look to the dealer, or his representative, as the person who fixes the payment terms and makes all the

---

[3] Hire-Purchase Act 1964, ss 10 and 11; Hire-Purchase Act 1965, s 12(2) and (3) and see now Consumer Credit Act 1974, ss 56(1), (2), 57(3), 69(6), 102(1), 175.
[4] [1962] 3 All ER 386, [1962] 1 WLR 1184.
[5] [1965] 2 QB 242 at 269, [1964] 3 All ER 592 at 600–601.
[6] [1962] 3 All ER 386, [1962] 1 WLR 1184.   [7] [1969] 1 AC 552, [1968] 3 All ER 104.
[8] Ibid at 573, 574, 576 and 113 and 115, respectively.

necessary arrangements . . . If this is so, a general responsibility of the finance company for the acts, receipts and omissions of the dealer in relation to the proposed transaction of hire-purchase ought to flow from this structure of relationship and expectation, built up from accepted custom and methods of dealing; a general responsibility which requires to be displaced by evidence of particular circumstances rather than to be positively established in each individual case.[9]

Until a final choice between these views is authoritatively made by the House of Lords it is submitted that the presumption of agency favoured by Lord Denning, Lord Justice Donovan and Lord Wilberforce is, in the latter's words more consistent with 'mercantile reality' and is to be preferred.[10]

Alternatively, it may be clear that A is an agent but obscure for which of two parties he acts. Thus an agent employed by an insurance company to solicit business is undoubtedly an agent of the company for some purposes but it was held in *Newsholme Bros v Road Transport and General Insurance Co Ltd*[11] that where he helped the insured to complete the proposal form, he acted as agent for the insured. This means that the insured will be liable for misrepresentation or non-disclosure where he tells the agent the truth but the agent records his statement inaccurately on the form. Granted that the insured will normally regard communication to the agent as communication to the insurer and that the agent's commission is dependent on the proposal being acceptable to the insurer this has the makings of an unsatisfactory rule in practice. It is not surprising therefore that it has been rejected in Ghana,[12] reversed by legislation in Jamaica[13] and restrictively distinguished in England.[14]

The parties may of course agree that an intermediary is to act for both of them. This is in practice quite common. So, in a transaction involving both the buying and selling of a house and the lending of money by way of mortgage to the purchaser, it is often agreed that the same solicitor will act both for the purchaser and for the lender. If all goes well this will reduce the costs of the transaction but things do not always go well and there may be conflicts between the solicitor's duty to the purchaser and to the lender.

The most common problem appears to be whether the solicitor is bound to pass on to the lender information which he has discovered in pursuance of his duty to the purchaser. There is no general rule that he must pass on all such information.[15] The solicitor must carry out his express instructions from lender[16] and is under an implied

---

[9] Ibid at 586–587 and 121–122, respectively.   [10] Cf Hughes 27 MLR 395.

[11] [1929] 2 KB 356. This conclusion is often reinforced by clauses in the proposal form.

[12] *Mohamed Hijazi v New India Assurance Co Ltd* 1969 (1) African L Rev Comm 7.

[13] Insurance Act 1971, s 74(1).

[14] *Stone v Reliance Mutual Insurance Society Ltd* [1972] 1 Lloyd's Rep 469; Reynolds 88 LQR 462; followed with approval by Supreme Court of Canada in *Blanchette v CIS Ltd* (1973) 36 DLR (3d) 561.

[15] *Halifax Mortgage Services Ltd v Stepsky* [1996] 2 All ER 277

[16] *Bristol and West Building Society v May, May & Merriman* [1996] 2 All ER 801; *Bristol and West Building Society v Fancy & Jackson* [1997] 4 All ER 582.

obligation to do what a reasonably competent solicitor in the same position would do.[17]

Normally, in such a situation, the money which constitutes the loan will pass through the solicitor's hands on the way from the lender to the vendor (so that it is never in the hands of the borrower). In relation to this money, the solicitor is clearly a fiduciary. In *Bristol and West Building Society v Mothew*[18] the purchasers were seeking an advance of £59,000 to finance the purchase of a house for £73,000. It was a term of the loan that the borrowers would find all the £14,000 from their own resources and would not take out another loan. In fact, the borrowers had a loan of some £3,350 on a second mortgage on their existing house with Barclays Bank and arranged to transfer this to the new house. The solicitor knew of this loan but forgot to tell the lender, who argued that there had been a breach of fiduciary duty. The Court of Appeal held that although the solicitor had certainly been guilty of a negligent breach of contract, 'not every breach of duty by a fiduciary is a breach of fiduciary duty'.[19]

Of the two aspects of agency, only the second concerns a book purporting to deal with the general principles of contract law. We shall, therefore, consider the formation and termination of agency and also the position of third parties with whom the agent contracts, but shall omit all reference to the rights and liabilities of the principal and agent *inter se*.

2 FORMATION OF AGENCY

The relationship of principal and agent may arise in any one of five ways: by express appointment, by virtue of the doctrine of estoppel, by the subsequent ratification by the principal of a contract made on his behalf without any authorisation from him, by implication of law in cases where it is urgently necessary that one man should act on behalf of another, and by presumption of law in the case of cohabitation.

A Express appointment

Except in one case no formality, such as writing, is required for the valid appointment of an agent. An oral appointment is effective. This is so even though the contract which the agent is authorised to make is one that is required by law to be made in writing, such as a contract to buy or to take a lease of land. Thus if an agent appointed

---

[17] *Mortgage Express Ltd v Bowerman & Partners* [1996] 2 All ER 836; *National Home Loans Corpn plc v Giffen Couch & Archer* [1997] 3 All ER 808.

[18] [1996] 4 All ER 698.

[19] Ibid, at 711–712 per Millett LJ. The lender hoped to recover more of its loss in equity than it would have done at common law.

orally signs a contract in his own name for the purchase of land, the principal can give parol evidence to show the existence of the agency, and can then enforce the contract against either the agent or the vendor.[20]

The one exception is where the authority of the agent is to execute a deed on behalf of the principal, in which case the agency itself must be created by deed. The agent, in other words, must be given a power of attorney. Instances of transactions for which a deed is necessary are conveyances of land, leases exceeding three years, and the transfer of a share in a British ship. So if an agent is authorised to execute a conveyance of land to a purchaser, he must be appointed by deed, but this is not necessary if his authority is merely to enter into a contract for the sale of the land.

B Agency by estoppel

The subject of agency by estoppel may be introduced by a quotation from Lord Cranworth:

> No one can become the agent of another person except by the will of that person. His will may be manifested in writing, or orally or simply by placing another in a situation in which according to the ordinary rules of law, or perhaps it would be more correct to say, according to the ordinary usages of mankind, that other is understood to represent and act for the person who has so placed him . . . This proposition, however, is not at variance with the doctrine that where one has so acted as from his conduct to lead another to believe that he has appointed someone to act as his agent, and knows that that other person is about to act on that belief, then, unless he interposes, he will in general be estopped from disputing the agency, though in fact no agency really existed . . . Another proposition to be kept constantly in view is, that the burden of proof is on the person dealing with anyone as an agent, through whom he seeks to charge another as principal. He must show that the agency did exist, and that the agent had the authority he assumed to exercise, or otherwise that the principal is estopped from disputing it.[21]

While, therefore, a person cannot be bound as principal by a contract made without his authority, yet if the proved result of his conduct is that A appears to be his agent and makes a contract with a third person who relies on that appearance, he may be estopped from denying the existence of the authority. An apparent or ostensible agency is as effective as an agency deliberately created. Appearance and reality are one.

If, for instance, a member of a partnership retires without notifying the public, he will be bound by contracts made by the remaining partners with persons who had previously had dealings with the firm or who were aware of his membership, provided, of course, that they had no notice of his retirement.[22] A retiring member must give

---

[20] *Heard v Pilley* (1869) 4 Ch App 548.
[21] *Pole v Leask* (1862) 33 LJ Ch 155 at 161–162. See also *Spiro v Lintern* [1973] 3 All ER 319, [1973] 1 WLR 1002.
[22] *Scarf v Jardine* (1882) 7 App Cas 345 at 349, per Lord Selborne.

reasonable public notice of his retirement, or he will be guilty of conduct calculated to induce others to rely on his credit. Again, if p has been accustomed to accept and to pay for goods bought on his behalf by A from X, he may be liable for a purchase made in the customary manner, even though it is made by A fraudulently after he has left his employment.[23] In such a case A would appear to X to retain his former authority. Or suppose that a husband has for several years paid for articles of luxury bought by his wife at X's shop and then forbids her to pledge his credit any further in this manner; it cannot be doubted that, failing an express warning to X, he will be liable as principal if she makes similar contracts in the future.[24]

In all these cases a person who has no authority whatever to represent another is nevertheless regarded as an apparent agent. But, as we shall see later, the doctrine of estoppel, employed here to create the relationship of principal and agent, plays an even more important part where a regularly constituted agent exceeds his actual authority.[25]

C Ratification

If A, without any precedent authority whatsoever, purports to contract with X for and on behalf of P, and later p ratifies and adopts the contract, the relationship of principal and agent arises between p and A.

> In that case the principal is bound by the act whether it be for his detriment or advantage, and whether it is founded on a tort or a contract, and with all the consequences which follow from the same act done by his authority.[26]

If a principal ratifies part of a contract he is taken to have ratified it *in toto*. He cannot select such of its provision as may operate to his advantage.[27] The ratification relates back to the contract made by A, and both X and p are in exactly the same position as if p had been the original contracting party. *Omnis ratihabitio retrotrahitur ac priori mandato aequiparatur.*

> Suppose that on 1 May, X offers to buy land from A who in fact is manager and agent of the property on behalf of P. On 2 May, A accepts this offer on P's behalf though he has no actual or apparent authority to do so. On 4 May, X purports to revoke the offer; on 10 May, p ratifies the acceptance of A.

Here, the ratification relates back to the moment of acceptance. It follows, therefore, that X's attempted revocation is inoperative as being too late, and that p is entitled to

---

[23] *Summers v Solomon* (1857) 26 LJQB 301. This case was distinguished in *Hambro v Burnand* [1903] 2 KB 399.

[24] *Debenham v Mellon* (1880) 5 QBD 394 at 403.

[25] Pp 627 ff, below.

[26] *Wilson v Tumman* (1843) 6 Man & G 236 at 242.

[27] *Cornwal v Wilson* (1750) 1 Ves Sen 509; *Re Mawcon Ltd* [1969] 1 WLR 78 at 83, per Pennycuick J.

claim specific performance.[28] There can, however, be no ratification unless the offer has been unconditionally accepted, for, unless and until this is proved, no contract exists to be ratified. If A's acceptance on 2 May was not absolute, but was expressly made subject to ratification by P, there would be no complete contract until p ratified, and a revocation by X before that date would be effective.[29]

The prerequisites of ratification are as follows:

i Contract must be professedly made on behalf of the principal
First, the person who makes the contract must profess at the time of making it to be acting on behalf of, and intending to bind, the person who subsequently ratifies the contract.[30] Ordinarily, the person making the contract will be required to name his professed principal, but it has been said to be sufficient if the principal, though not named, is 'capable of being ascertained' at the time of the contract,[31] an expression which is presumably employed here to mean 'identifiable'. So understood, it would cover, for instance, the case of a person contracting 'on behalf of my brother'.[32] It is not, however, sufficient that the person contracting should merely indicate that he is acting as agent without more. He must name, or otherwise sufficiently identify, the person for whom he professes to act. A fortiori, if he makes no allusion to agency, but gives the appearance of contracting in his own right, the contract cannot later be adopted by another for whom in truth he intended to act. This primary requirement, that an agent should be obliged to advertise his intention, though now well established, is scarcely consistent with the earlier and equally well established doctrine of the undisclosed principal, under which a principal can enforce a contract made by an agent *with his authority* even though the existence of the agency was not disclosed

---

[28] *Bolton Partners v Lambert* (1889) 41 ChD 295. This case, though approved in *Lawson (Inspector of Taxes) v Hosemaster Ltd* [1966] 2 All ER 944, [1966] 1 WLR 1300, was severely criticised by Fry in his *Specific Performance*, note A. He regards the contract between X and p as being one made without consensus. The court said that it was made when A accepted, but at that moment p had not consented to such a contract being made on his behalf. It was a contract made at the will of a stranger and without the will of one of the contracting parties. There is force in this criticism, though it is coloured by contemporary preoccupation with the idea of consensus. It is true that the effect of the decision is to impose a liability upon X if p so wishes, while leaving p a free choice in the matter. The decision was also doubted by the Privy Council in *Fleming v Bank of New Zealand* [1900] AC 577 at 587. Cf *Presentaciones Musicales SA v Secunda* [1994] 2 All ER 737.

[29] *Watson v Davies* [1931] 1 Ch 455; *Warehousing and Forwarding Co of East Africa Ltd v Jafferali & Sons Ltd* [1964] AC 1, [1963] 3 All ER 571.

[30] *Keighley, Maxsted & Co v Durant* [1901] AC 240; *Imperial Bank of Canada v Begley* [1936] 2 All ER 367.

[31] *Watson v Swann* (1862) 11 CBNS 756 at 771, per Willes J; *Keighley, Maxsted & Co v Durant* [1901] AC 240 at 255; *Eastern Construction Co Ltd v National Trust Co Ltd and Schmidt* [1914] AC 197 at 213.

[32] 'It is not necessary that he should be named but there must be such a description of him as shall amount to a reasonable designation of the person intended to be bound by the contract': *Watson v Swann*, above, at 771, per Willes J.

to the other contracting party.[33] The doctrine of ratification may be anomalous, but it is difficult to appreciate why it should not apply to an agency which is not only unauthorised, but also undisclosed, if an undisclosed principal can avail himself of an authorised act. In *Keighley, Maxsted & Co v Durant*,[34] Lord James, in repudiating this suggestion, said:

> To establish that a man's thoughts unexpressed and unrecorded can form the basis of a contract so as to bind other persons and make them liable on a contract they never made with persons they never heard of seems a somewhat difficult task.

It is, however, a difficulty that has been readily surmounted by the law in its evolution of the doctrine of the undisclosed principal. In the *Keighley, Maxsted* case:

> A was authorised by p to buy wheat at 44s 3d a quarter on a joint account for himself and P. Wheat was unobtainable at this price, and therefore in excess of his authority he agreed to buy from X at 44s 6d a quarter. Though he intended to purchase on the joint account, A contracted in his own name and did not disclose the agency to X. The next day p ratified the purchase at the unauthorised price, but ultimately he and A failed to take delivery.

An action brought by X against p for breach of contract failed on the ground that the purchase had not been professedly made on his behalf. Apparently ignoring the doctrine of the undisclosed principal, Lord Macnaghten remarked that 'obligations are not to be created by, or founded upon, undisclosed intentions'.

ii Must be competent principal at time of contract
The second condition of ratification is that at the time when the contract was made the agent must have had a competent principal.[35] This condition is not satisfied, for instance, if he purported to act on behalf of an alien enemy.[36] Nor is it satisfied if he purported to contract on behalf of a principal who at the time of the contract lacked legal personality, for rights and obligations cannot attach to a non-existent person. This is important in the case of contracts made on behalf of a company projected but not yet formed.

> If, for instance, it is proposed to form a motor garage company provided that a certain plot of land can be obtained, and A, purporting to act on behalf of the projected company, makes a contract for the purchase of the land, the contract cannot be ratified by the company upon its formation.

As Erle CJ said in the leading case of *Kelner v Baxter*:[37]

[33] Pp 621–624, below.   [34] [1901] AC 240.
[35] *Kelner v Baxter* (1866) LR 2 CP 174; *Scott v Lord Ebury* (1867) LR 2 CP 255.
[36] *Boston Deep Sea Fishing and Ice Co Ltd v Farnham* [1957] 3 All ER 204, [1957] 1 WLR 1051.
[37] (1866) LR 2 CP at 183.

When the company came afterwards into existence it was a totally new creature, having rights and obligations from that time, but no rights or obligations by reason of anything which might have been done before.

The proper course to adopt in the case of such a potential company is to provide that if the company is not registered by a certain date the contract shall be null and void, but that if it is so registered there shall be a transfer to it of the contractual rights and liabilities.

Whether a person who contracts on behalf of a non-existent principal is himself liable depends upon the circumstances. The fact that the principal when he comes into existence is not liable does not necessarily mean that the agent is in all cases an effective party to the contract. As was said in an Australian case:

The fundamental question *in every case* must be what the parties intended or must be fairly understood to have intended.[38]

The agent may so conduct himself as to become a party, and if this is the common intention and if it does not contradict any written instrument, then, as in *Kelner v Baxter*, the contract is enforceable by and against him. But if there is nothing in the circumstances to show that he contracted personally, there is no rule which converts him automatically into a principal merely because at the time of the contract there was nobody else capable of being bound.[39] Thus in one case, a memorandum of a contract for the sale of goods by a company was signed by the sellers: 'Yours faithfully, Leopold Newborne (London) Ltd', after which was written the name Leopold Newborne. On it appearing that the company was incapable of being a contracting party since it had not been registered when the memorandum was completed, it was held that Leopold Newborne himself could not sue the buyers for non-acceptance of the goods, since there was nothing to show that he intended himself to be the seller. The only contracting party was the company, and all that Newborne intended to do by the addition of his own name was to authenticate the signature of the company.[40]

The position has been altered by section 9(2) of the European Communities Act 1972 (now Companies Act 1985, section 36(C)1 which provides:[41]

A contract which purports to be made by or on behalf of a company, at a time when the company has not been formed, has effect subject to any agreement to the contrary as one made with the person purporting to act for the company or as agent for it and he is personally liable on the contract accordingly.

It will be seen that this provision makes no change in the position of the company,

---

[38] *Summergreene v Parker* (1950) 80 CLR 304 at 323, per Fullager J. See also *Black v Smallwood* (1965) 39 ALJR 405. For a general discussion, see Baxt 30 MLR 328.

[39] *Hollman v Pullin* (1884) Cab & El 254; *Newborne v Sensolid (Great Britain) Ltd* [1954] 1 QB 45, [1953] 1 All ER 708.

[40] *Newborne v Sensolid (Great Britain) Ltd* above, criticised by Gross 87 LQR 367 at 382–385.

[41] See Prentice 89 LQR 518 at 530–533; Farrar and Powles 36 MLR 270 at 277.

which still cannot ratify the contract. It is clearly intended however to increase the number of cases where the agent is personally liable. How far it in fact does so depends on the meaning given to the words 'subject to any agreement to the contrary'. In *Phonogram Ltd v Lane*[42] the Court of Appeal held that an agreement to the contrary could not be inferred from the fact that the agents had signed 'for and on behalf of [the unformed company]'. In *Braymist Ltd v Wise Finance Co Ltd*[43], the Court of Appeal held that in appropriate circumstances the contract could be enforced by the agent.

iii Void contracts cannot be ratified

The third essential is that there should be an act capable of ratification. Any contract made by A professing to act on behalf of p is capable of ratification, even though A acted fraudulently and with intent to benefit himself alone,[44] provided, however, that it is a contract which p could validly have made. A contract that is void in its inception cannot be ratified. It would seem on principle that a forgery is incapable of ratification not because it is a legal nullity, as indeed it is, but because a forger does not profess to act as an agent. The question arose in *Brook v Hook*:[45]

> P's name was forged by A to a joint and several promissory note for £20 purporting to be made by p and A in favour of X. In order to save A, p later signed the following memorandum:
>
> I hold myself responsible for a bill dated November 7th for £20 bearing my signature and that of A.

What A had written in effect was: 'Here is P's signature written by himself.' He did not say or imply, 'I make this note as agent of P.' The majority of the court, therefore, repudiated the suggestion that p was liable as having ratified the contract of 7 November, for as Kelly CB observed in an interlocutory remark: 'The defendant could not ratify an act which did not profess to be done for him or on his account.'[46]

D Agency of necessity

There is a limited class of case in which, on the ground of urgent necessity, one person may be bound by a contract made by another on his behalf but without his authority. This doctrine, which the courts are reluctant to extend,[47] probably applies only where there is already some existing contractual relationship between the principal and the person who acts on his behalf, as there is for instance between the owner and the master of a ship. It is extremely doubtful whether a person can be bound by the act of

---

[42] [1982] QB 938, [1981] 3 All ER 182.   [43] [2002] 2 All ER 333
[44] *Re Tiedemann and Ledermann Frères* [1899] 2 QB 66.   [45] (1871) LR 6 Exch 89.
[46] See also per Lord Blackburn in *M'Kenzie v British Linen Co* (1881) 6 App Cas 82 at 99.
[47] *Munro v Willmott* [1949] 1 KB 295, [1948] 2 All ER 983.

a complete stranger.[48] It is well settled, however, that the master of a ship is entitled, in cases of accident and emergency, to enter into a contract which will bind the owners of the cargo, notwithstanding that it transcends his express authority, if it is *bona fide* made in the best interests of the owners concerned.[49] The same power is possessed by a land carrier in respect of perishable goods.[50]

A person who seeks to bind a principal on these grounds bears the onus of proving that the course adopted by the carrier was reasonably necessary in the circumstances, and also that it was practically impossible to communicate with the cargo owners.

E Presumed agency in the case of cohabitation

Marriage does not give the wife any innate power to bind her husband by contracts with third persons, but where she is living with him there is a presumption, though no more, that she is entitled to pledge his credit for necessaries which are suitable to his style of living and which fall within the domestic department usually confided to the care of the wife.[51]

> There is a presumption that she has such authority in the sense that a tradesman supplying her with necessaries upon her husband's credit and suing him, makes out a prima facie case against him, upon proof of that fact and of the cohabitation. But this is a mere presumption of fact founded upon the supposition that wives cohabiting with their husbands ordinarily have authority to manage in their own way certain departments of the household expenditure, and to pledge their husband's credit in respect of matters coming within those departments.[52]

The presumption applies equally in the case of a woman living with a man as his mistress.[53]

Necessaries for this purpose have been authoritatively defined as 'things that are really necessary and suitable to the style in which the husband chooses to live, in so far as the articles fall fairly within the domestic department which is ordinarily confided to the management of the wife'.[54] It is the ostensible not the justifiable mode of living that sets the standard, and if a husband chooses to live beyond his means his liability

---

[48] *Jebara v Ottoman Bank* [1927] 2 KB 254 at 271, per Scrutton LJ.

[49] *The Argos* (1873) LR 5 PC 134; *Notara v Henderson* (1872) LR 7 QB 225.

[50] *Sims v Midland Rly Co* [1913] 1 KB 103 at 112; *Sachs v Miklos* [1948] 2 KB 23 at 35, [1948] 1 All ER 67 at 68. The wife's agency of necessity was abolished by Matrimonial Proceedings and Property Act 1970, s 41. It is thought that the repeal of this section by Matrimonial Causes Act 1973, Sch 3 has not revived the doctrine. O'Neill 36 MLR 638 at 642, 37 MLR 360; Cartwright Sharp 37 MLR 240, 480.

[51] *Debenham v Mellon* (1880) 6 App Cas 24 at 36; *Miss Gray Ltd v Earl of Cathcart* (1922) 38 TLR 562.

[52] *Debenham v Mellon* (1880) 5 QBD 394 at 402, per Thesiger LJ.

[53] *Ryan v Sams* (1848) 12 QB 460.

[54] *Phillipson v Hayter* (1870) LR 6 CP 38 at 42, per Willes J.

may be correspondingly increased.[55] Necessaries include clothing, both for the wife and her children, articles of household equipment, food, medicines and medical attendance, and the hiring of servants. The liability of the husband, however, is always subject to the proviso that the goods are suitable and reasonable not only in kind but also in quantity. An action cannot be maintained against him in respect of extravagant orders.[56]

The tradesman bears the burden of proving affirmatively to the satisfaction of the court that the goods supplied to the wife are necessaries.[57] If he is unable to do this, as for instance where the goods consist of jewels[58] or articles of luxury such as a gold pencil case or a guitar,[59] his only action lies against the wife, unless he can show an express or implied assent by the husband to the contract.

> If a tradesman is about to trust a married woman for what are not necessaries, and to an extent beyond what her situation in life requires, he ought in common prudence to enquire of the husband if she has his consent for the order she is giving.[60]

It was held in 1870 that a judge may withdraw a case from a jury if he considers that there is no reasonable evidence upon which they could classify the goods as necessaries.[61]

Even where the goods, however, are undoubtedly necessaries the husband is only presumptively liable, and he may rebut the presumption and so escape liability. The presumption is rebutted if he proves that he expressly warned the tradesman not to supply goods on credit; that his wife was already supplied with sufficient articles of that kind[62] or with a sufficient allowance with which to purchase them;[63] or that he had expressly forbidden her to pledge his credit.[64] The reason why an express prohibition not communicated to the tradesman is a sufficient rebuttal is that the right of a wife to bind her husband rests solely upon the law of agency and, as we have seen, no one can occupy the position of a principal against his will. At the same time it is important to observe that if the husband has held his wife out in the past to the plaintiff so as to invest her with apparent authority under the doctrine of estoppel, a mere private prohibition addressed solely to her will not relieve him from liability in respect of her future purchases of a similar nature. In such a case it is his duty to convey an express warning to the tradesman.

---

[55] *Waithman v Wakefield* (1807) 1 Camp 120.
[56] *Lane v Ironmonger* (1844) 13 M & W 368.   [57] *Phillipson v Hayter* (1870) LR 6 CP 38 at 42.
[58] *Montague v Benedict* (1825) 3 B & C 631.   [59] *Phillipson v Hayter*, above.
[60] *Montague v Benedict* (1825) 3 B & C 631 at 636, per Bayley J.
[61] *Phillipson v Hayter* (1870) LR 6 CP 38 at 40.   [62] *Seaton v Benedict* (1828) 5 Bing 28.
[63] *Morel Bros & Co Ltd v Earl of Westmoreland* [1904] AC 11.
[64] *Jolly v Rees* (1864) 15 CBNS 628.

3 POSITION OF PRINCIPAL AND AGENT WITH REGARD TO THIRD PARTIES

The question to be considered here is whether the principal or the agent is capable of suing, or of being sued, by the third party with whom the agent has completed the contract. The position of the agent with regard to such a third party varies according to the circumstances. Presuming that the agent is authorised to make the contract, there are three possible cases.

First, the agent may not only disclose to the third party the fact that he is a mere agent, but may also name his principal.

Secondly, he may disclose the fact of the agency but withhold the name of the principal.

Thirdly, he may conceal both facts, in which case the third party will believe, contrary to the truth, that the agent is himself the principal and that nobody else is interested in the contract.

In considering the question whether the principal or the agent is a competent party to litigation the courts have gradually evolved certain general rules which vary with each of these three cases. The prima facie rule is, for instance, that if the contract is made for a named principal, then the principal *alone* can sue or be sued. It is important, however, to recognise at once that these rules are of a purely general character—mere rebuttable presumptions that are capable of being displaced by proof that the parties intended otherwise. Too much force must not be attributed to them, for at bottom the question whether the agent or the principal is competent to sue or to be sued is one of construction dependent inter alia upon the form of the contract between the agent and the third party. In short, the intention of the parties, so far as it appears from the circumstances, is decisive, but if no clear intention is evidenced then the question is determined by certain general principles that have been laid down to meet the three different cases.

Our discussion of the matter is based upon the following classification:

A   The agent has authority and is known to be an agent, and his principal is (1) named, (2) not named.

B   The agent has authority in fact but he does not disclose the existence of the agency.

A The agent has authority and is known to be an agent

1 His principal is named

The general rule in this case is traditionally stated as follows:

The contract is the contract of the principal, not that of the agent, and prima facie at common law the only person who can sue is the principal and the only person who can be sued is the principal.[65]

Normally the agent possesses neither rights[66] nor liabilities[67] with regard to third parties. This general rule, however, though constantly repeated, is, as we have said, far from inflexible. It may be excluded by the express intention of the parties. In the words of Wright J:

> Also, and this is very important, in all cases the parties can by their express contract provide that the agent shall be the person liable either concurrently with or to the exclusion of the principal, or that the agent shall be the party to sue either concurrently with or to the exclusion of the principal.[68]

Thus, an agent may sue or be sued upon a written contract in which he states: 'I for my own self contract', though of course, the principal also remains liable and entitled.[69]

So too cases have arisen where a seller, when asked by an agent to supply goods to a named principal, refuses to do so unless the agent assumes sole liability for payment. In such a case, of course, the agent makes himself liable if he accepts the condition, and the seller cannot afterwards charge the principal. The judges have sometimes explained the position by saying that the seller is held to an election made at a time when he was free to choose between the one party and the other.[70]

Further, the intention to make the agent a party may be inferred as well as expressed, and it is purely a question of construction in each case, dependent upon the form and terms of the particular contract and upon the surrounding circumstances, whether such an intention is disclosed.

> The intention for which the court looks is an objective intention of both parties, based on what two businessmen making a contract of that nature, in those terms and those surrounding circumstances must be taken to have intended.[71]

The tenor of the decisions is that if a man signs a contract in his own name without any qualification, something very strong indeed on the face of the contract is needed to exclude his personal liability;[72] but if his signature is qualified by such expressions

---

65 *Montgomerie v United Kingdom Steamship Association* [1891] 1 QB 370 at 372, per Wright J.
66 *Fairlie v Fenton* (1870) LR 5 Exch 169.
67 *Paquin v Beauclerk* [1906] AC 148.
68 *Montgomerie v United Kingdom Steamship Association* [1891] 1 QB 370 at 372.
69 *Fisher v Marsh* (1865) 6 B & s 411 at 415, per Blackburn J.
70 *Calder v Dobell* (1871) LR 6 CP 486 at 494, citing *Addison v Gandassequi* (1812) 4 Taunt 574; *Paterson v Gandassequi* (1812) 15 East 62.
71 *The Swan* [1968] 1 Lloyd's Rep 5 at 12, per Brandon J.
72 *Cooke v Wilson* (1856) 1 CBNS 153 at 162, per Cresswell J. *Gadd v Houghton* (1876) 1 Ex D 357 at 360.

as 'on account of', 'for and on behalf of' or 'as agent', his personal liability is certainly negatived.[73]

To infer the intention of parties is seldom a simple matter, but in this particular context the chief sources of enlightenment are, first, the description of the parties in the body of the contract and, secondly, the signature of the agent.

If in *both* places the agent is referred to as agent, it is almost impossible to regard him as a contracting party; but if in neither place is there any mention of the agency, it is almost impossible to deny that he is a contracting party.

If he is described as agent in one part of the contract only, whether in the body or in the signature, it is presumed that he is not a contracting party, but the presumption may be rebutted from the context.

2 His principal is not named

Does the mere non-disclosure of the name of the principal vary the position of the parties? Once more the general rule is that the agent drops out, but once more whether he does so or not depends essentially upon the intention of the parties. It is still a question of construction, dependent inter alia upon the form of the contract or the nature of the agent's business, whether they intended that the agent should possess rights and liabilities. Where, however, the name of the principal has not been disclosed an intention that the agent shall be a contracting party will more readily be inferred. Obviously, where there has been no such disclosure, greater significance is to be attached to the rule already cited that, if a man signs a contract in his own name, there must be something very strong on the face of the contract to deprive him of rights and liabilities. But the contract is construed according to its natural meaning and, if it clearly shows that the agent must have been understood to have contracted merely as an agent, then, despite the fact that the principal for whom he acted has not been named, effect is given to the natural meaning of the words, and he drops out of the transaction.

The position may be illustrated by the case of *Southwell v Bowditch*.[74]

A broker issued a contract note couched in these terms:

Messrs Southwell. I have this day sold by your order to my principals, etc. 1 per cent brokerage.

(Signed) W A Bowditch.

---

[73] *Gadd v Houghton*, above; *Universal Steam Navigation Co Ltd v James McKenvie & Co* [1923] AC 492; *Lester v Balfour Williamson Merchant Shippers Ltd* [1953] 2 QB 168, [1953] 1 All ER 1146. It is a little difficult to reconcile *The Swan* [1968] 1 Lloyd's Rep 5, with these authorities; see Legh-Jones 32 MLR 327; *contra* Reynolds 85 LQR 92.

[74] (1876) 1 CPD 374. For a parallel situation in an oral contract, see *N and J Vlassopulos Ltd v Ney Shipping Ltd, The Santa Carina* [1977] 1 Lloyd's Rep 478.

It will be observed that the defendant, though referring to principals, signed this contract in his own name without any additional words to show that he signed in the capacity of agent, but nevertheless it was held that he was not personally liable for the price of the goods sold. In the course of his judgment Jessel MR said:

There is nothing whatever on the contract to show that the defendant intended to act otherwise than as broker. No doubt it does not absolutely follow from the defendant appearing on the contract to be a broker that he is not liable as principal. There are two ways in which he might so be made liable: first, intention on the face of the contract making the agent liable as well as the principal; secondly, usage.

Special cases Whether the principal has been named or not, there are three exceptional cases in each of which the position of the agent is determined by special rules. These are where the agent executes a deed in his own name; where he puts his name to a negotiable instrument; and where there is some relevant trade usage. We will take these cases separately.[75]

i Contracts under seal

If an agent makes a contract *under seal* on behalf of another it has long been established that he is personally liable and entitled under it, and that the principal has neither rights nor obligations.[76] That is what is called a 'technical rule', ie to quote the words of Martin B, a rule 'which is established by authority and precedent, which does not depend upon reasoning or argument, but is a fixed established rule to be acted upon, and only discussed as regards its application'.[77]

It formerly produced this inconvenient result, that a man who gave a power of attorney to another in order, for instance, that his affairs might be administered during his absence or illness, could neither sue nor be sued upon contracts made under its authority if they were made by deed. This particular inconvenience has, however, been removed by legislation.[78]

The technical rule, however, is subject to this limitation, that if the agent enters into a sealed contract as *trustee* for the principal, whether the trust is disclosed on the face of the contract or not, and he refuses to enforce it against the other party, then the principal, *qua* beneficiary, may himself enforce any proprietary right to which he is entitled by bringing an action against the third party and the agent.[79] It would seem to follow that in such a case the principal is equally liable to be sued by the third party.

---

[75] Some of these cases may occur when the agent is acting for an undisclosed principal, but as this is not likely to happen in practice, it seems more convenient to deal with them here. It was formerly thought that a fourth exceptional case is where an agent contracts on behalf of a foreign principal; p 619, below.

[76] *Re International Contract Co, Pickering's Claim* (1871) 6 Ch App 525; *Schack v Anthony* (1813) 1 M & s 573.

[77] *Chesterfield Colliery Co v Hawkins* (1865) 3 H & C 677 at 691–692.

[78] Law of Property Act 1925, s 123.

[79] *Harmer v Armstrong* [1934] Ch 65. In such a case the rights and liabilities of the parties are governed by the doctrine discussed, pp 576 ff, above.

ii Negotiable instruments

An agent contracts no personal liability under a negotiable instrument in the issue of which he is implicated unless he adds his name as a party to it; but if he does appear as a party then his liability depends upon whether he signs as acceptor or in some other capacity such as drawer or endorser.

Where he appears as acceptor the crucial question is whether the bill is drawn on him or not. If it is drawn on him in his own name, his acceptance renders him personally liable even though he adds words to his signature describing himself as agent. To escape liability he must add words indicating that he is acting in a purely ministerial capacity.[80] In one case, for instance, Charles, the agent of a company, wrote the following across the face of a bill which had been drawn on him, not on the company:

> Accepted for the company. W Charles. Purser.

It was held that he was personally liable.[81]

If, however, the bill is not drawn on the agent, his acceptance, even though unqualified, does not render him liable.[82] Thus, for instance, if a bill is drawn on a company, the directors incur no personal liability if they write the following on the instrument:

> Accepted. X and Y, Directors of the company.

Where an agent draws or endorses a negotiable instrument the position is as follows. If he signs his name without any qualification he is personally liable.[83] If he adds a qualification there are two classes of cases. A qualification which clearly indicates that he is contracting as agent for another, as, for example, where he writes: 'For and on behalf of Jones, as agent', relieves him of personal liability;[84] but an ambiguous qualification, which leaves it doubtful whether he is acting in a purely representative capacity or not, renders him liable. The endorsement, for instance, 'X and Y, Directors', will render X and Y liable, for the word 'Directors' does not necessarily show that they were acting as agents, but may equally well have been used to explain why their names appeared on the bill at all.[85]

iii Trade usage

The position of an agent as a contracting party may be determined by a trade usage. In one case, for instance, X and Y, who were brokers in the Colonial fruit trade, signed the following contract:

> We have this day sold for your account to our principal, etc.
>
> (Signed) X and Y, Brokers.

---

[80] Bills of Exchange Act 1882, s 26.   [81] *Mare v Charles* (1856) 5 E & B 978.
[82] *Stacey & Co Ltd v Wallis* (1912) 106 LT 544.   [83] *The Elmville* [1904] p 319.
[84] *Elliott v Bax-Ironside* [1925] 2 KB 301 at 307, per Scrutton LJ.
[85] *Rew v Pettet* (1834) 1 Ad & El 196; *Elliott v Bax-Ironside*, above.

The principal, whose name was disclosed before delivery, refused to accept the whole of the goods, and an action of non-acceptance succeeded against the agent on proof of a custom in the fruit trade that a broker was personally liable if the name of the principal was not inserted in the written contract.[86] A custom, however, is disregarded if it is inconsistent with the contract.[87]

Foreign principal One of the trade usages established by the law merchant was that a person who contracted as agent for a foreign principal was to be regarded as having contracted as principal to the exclusion of the foreigner. In 1873, Blackburn J said:

> Where a foreigner has instructed English merchants to act for him, I take it that the usage of trade, established for many years, has been that it is understood that the foreign constituent has not authorised the merchants to pledge his credit to the contract, to establish privity between him and the home supplier. On the other hand, the home supplier, knowing that to be the usage, unless there is something in the bargain shewing the intention to be otherwise, does not trust the foreigner, and so does not make the foreigner responsible to him, and does not make himself responsible to the foreigner.[88]

The law merchant, however, is not immutable, and with the vast increase in international trade this particular usage has steadily waned in importance and has now disappeared. As long ago as 1917, its continued existence was doubted by such an experienced judge as Bray J,[89] and its final extinction has now been confirmed.[90] In every case, foreign element or no foreign element, the question whether the agent becomes a party to the contract or whether privity of contract has been created between his principal and the third party must be determined in the light of the intention of the parties as disclosed by the terms of the contract and the surrounding circumstances. The nationality or domicile of the principal is merely one of those circumstances, and even so it is only of minimal importance. The statement of Lord Blackburn no longer represents the law.[91] A case in which the intention of the parties was disclosed by the terms of the contract itself was *Miller, Gibb & Co v Smith and Tyrer Ltd*,[92] where the facts were these:

A firm called Smith & Tyrer Ltd executed the following instrument on behalf of a foreign principal:

[86] *Fleet v Murton* (1871) LR 7 QB 126.

[87] *Barrow and Bros v Dyster, Nalder & Co* (1884) 13 QBD 635.

[88] *Elbinger Act. für Fabrication von Eisenbahn Materiel v Claye* (1873) LR 8 QB 313 at 317; and see the authorities there cited.

[89] *Miller, Gibb & Co v Smith and Tyrer Ltd* [1917] 2 KB 141; see also *H O Brandt v H N Morris & Co* [1917] 2 KB 784 at 797.

[90] *Teheran-Europe Co Ltd v s T Belton (Tractors) Ltd* [1968] 2 QB 53; affd [1968] 2 QB 545, [1968] 2 All ER 886. See Hudson 29 MLR 353.

[91] *Holt and Moseley (London) Ltd v Cunningham Partners* (1949) 83 Ll L Rep 141 at 145; *Rusholme, Bolton and Roberts, Hadfield Ltd v s G Read & Co (London) Ltd* [1955] 1 All ER 180, [1955] 1 WLR 146, 150, where the foreign principal was undisclosed; *Teheran-Europe Co Ltd v s T Belton (Tractors) Ltd*, above.

[92] [1917] 2 KB 141.

Contract by which our principals sell through the agency of Smith & Tyrer Ltd, wood brokers, Liverpool, and Messrs Miller, Gibb & Co, of Liverpool, buy, etc.

> (Signed) By authority of our principals
> Smith & Tyrer Ltd,
> Chas H Tyrer, managing director, as agents.

The Court of Appeal had no difficulty in holding that the intention was to exclude the personal liability of the agents.

> It seems to me difficult for the parties to have used clearer words to show that the principals were to be liable and the agents were not to be liable . . . The agents were not professing to contract at all, the principals were; and the agents state expressly that they have authority from their principals to sign the contract.[93]

Indeed, to have denied that the agents had acted in a purely representative capacity would have flatly contradicted the tenor of the instrument.

Where agent is in fact principal It remains to consider a peculiar situation that may arise where a man, though purporting to be an agent, is in fact himself the principal. Here there is no doubt that he is personally liable.[94] This seems to be common sense. As Scrutton LJ once remarked 'I am sure it is justice. It is probably the law for that reason.'[95]

Moreover the agent in such a case can himself enforce the contract, provided that the supposed principal has not been named and also that the terms of the contract show that the identity of the party is not material. This was decided in *Schmaltz v Avery*,[96] where the facts were these:

> A charterparty was executed between X, the owner of the ship, and A, which expressly stated that A was acting as agent of the freighters. It contained these words: 'This charterparty, being concluded on behalf of another party, it is agreed that all responsibility on the part of A shall cease as soon as the cargo is shipped.' Actually A was himself the freighter, and he later brought an action against X.

It was argued that the action would not lie, since X had relied for the fulfilment of the contract upon the undisclosed freighters with whom he believed himself to be dealing. This argument failed and the action was allowed. It was obvious, in accordance with the doctrine of the undisclosed principal, that the freighters, if they had actually existed, could have enforced the contract. The only question was whether one person can fill the characters both of principal and agent, or rather, whether he can repudiate that of agent and assume that of principal. It is no doubt true that the identity of the other party is often a matter of vital importance, but in this case the court was of

---

[93] Ibid at 163, per Bray J.
[94] *Jenkins v Hutchinson* (1849) 13 QB 744 at 752, per Lord Denman.
[95] *Gardiner v Heading* [1928] 2 KB 284.
[96] (1851) 16 QB 655; followed in *Harper v Vigers Bros* [1909] 2 KB 549.

opinion that as the name of the freighter had never been demanded it was impossible to presume that X would not have made the contract had he known A to be the principal.

A person who has contracted as agent cannot, however, assume the character of principal if the name of his supposed principal has been given.[97]

B The agent has authority in fact but he does not disclose the existence of the agency

Where an agent, having authority to contract on behalf of another, makes the contract in his own name, concealing the fact that he is a mere representative, the doctrine of the undisclosed principal comes into play. By this doctrine either the agent, or the principal when discovered, may be sued; and either the agent or the principal may sue the other party to the contract.

There is nothing remarkable in this doctrine so far as it concerns the agent. The existence of an enforceable contract between him and the third party is scarcely deniable, for he purports to act on his own behalf and the other party is content with this apparent state of affairs. At any rate it is well settled that the contract is enforceable either by[98] or against[99] the agent. The primary liability that rests upon him as being a party to the contract is not destroyed by the fact that the principal also may be added as a party.[100] Parol evidence is admissible to introduce a new party, ie the principal, but is never admissible for the purpose of discharging an apparent party, ie the agent.

What is more curious about the doctrine is that the principal should be allowed to intervene, for at first sight it seems inconsistent with elementary principles that a person should be allowed to enforce a contract that he has not in fact made. On the other hand this right of intervention is in many cases both just and convenient. If, for instance, the agent of an undisclosed seller were to go bankrupt after delivery of the goods but before the payment of the price, the money, unless it were demandable by the seller direct from the buyer, would go to swell the assets divisible among the general creditors of the agent. Considerations of this nature ultimately produced the rule, though without any manifest enthusiasm on the part of the business community, that a principal may disclose his existence and may himself maintain an action against the person with whom his agent contracted.[101] Thus, for example, if two or more arrange that one of themselves shall buy goods in his own name on their joint behalf, they may jointly or severally sue the vendor in the event of a breach of contract.[102]

---

[97] *Fairlie v Fenton* (1870) LR 5 Exch 169. Where there is undoubtedly a contract which calls for acts to be done by the agent of one party, it may be, as a matter of construction that those acts cannot be done by the principal himself: *Finchbourne Ltd v Rodrigues* [1976] 3 All ER 581.

[98] *Sims v Bond* (1833) 5 B & Ad 389.   [99] *Saxon v Blake* (1861) 29 Beav 438.

[100] *Higgins v Senior* (1841) 8 M & W 834.

[101] *Schrimshire v Alderton* (1743) 2 Stra 1182.   [102] *Skinner v Stocks* (1821) 4 B & Ald 437.

These rights possessed by the agent and by the principal against the third party are independent rights, except that the rights of the agent are subordinate to those of the principal.[103] If, for example, an action for breach of contract brought by the agent against the third party is dismissed, this does not preclude a similar action by the principal. It cannot be said that the agent sued on behalf of his principal and that therefore the latter is estopped from taking further proceedings.

The right of action possessed by the undisclosed principal is, however, subject to two limitations:

First, the authority of the agent to act for the principal must have existed at the time of the contract.[104]

Secondly, if the contract, expressly or by implication, shows that it is to be confined in its operation to the parties themselves, the possibility of agency is negatived and no one else can intervene as principal.[105] Whether this is the intention of the parties is a matter of construction. Thus it has been held that for an agent to describe himself as 'owner'[106] or 'proprietor'[107] of the subject matter of the contract precludes the principal, whether disclosed or not, from suing or being sued. In such a case the other party contracts upon the basis that the person with whom he is dealing is sole owner of the subject matter, and as Lord Haldane once said:

> Where it is a term of the contract that he should contract as owner of that property, you cannot show that another person is the real owner.[108]

On the other hand, the description of a person as 'charterer'[109] or 'tenant'[110] or 'landlord'[111] no more negatives the existence of agency than would the description 'contracting party'.

As a corollary to the right of intervention by an undisclosed principal it is well established that when discovered he may be sued upon the contract made by his agent.[112] Nevertheless, the third party must elect which of these two inconsistent rights he will enforce, for the contract cannot be enforced against both the principal and the agent.

---

[103] *Pople v Evans* [1969] 2 Ch 255, [1968] 2 All ER 743.

[104] *Keighley, Maxsted & Co v Durant* [1901] AC 240 at 251, per Lord James of Hereford. See the remarks of Diplock LJ in *Garnac Grain Co In v H M F Faure and Fairclough Ltd and Bunge Corpn* [1966] 1 QB 650 at 648, [1965] 3 All ER 273 at 286. See pp 607–611, above.

[105] See two notes by PAL in 61 LQR 130–133; 62 LQR 20–22. See also Goodhart and Hamson 4 CLJ 320 at 352–353. Cf *Siu Yin Kwan v Eastern Insurance Co Ltd* [1994] 1 All ER 213. Rolls-Royce Power Engineering plc v Ricardo Consulting Engineers Ltd [2003] EWHC 2871 (TCC); [2004] 2 All ER (Comm) 129.

[106] *Humble v Hunter* (1848) 12 QB 310 at 317.

[107] *Formby Bros v Formby* (1910) 102 LT 116.

[108] *Fred Drughorn Ltd v Rederiaktiebolaget Transatlantic* [1919] AC 203 at 207.   [109] Ibid.

[110] *Danziger v Thompson* [1944] KB 654, [1944] 2 All ER 151.

[111] *Epps v Rothnie* [1945] KB 562, [1946] 1 All ER 146.

[112] *Thomson v Davenport* (1829) 9 B & C 78.

If a man is entitled to one of two inconsistent rights it is fitting that where with full knowledge he has done an unequivocal act showing that he has chosen the one he cannot afterwards pursue the other, which after the first choice is by reason of the inconsistency no longer his to choose.[113]

Whether the conduct of the third party shows an unequivocal election to resort to the agent alone or to the principal alone is a question of fact that must be decided in the light of all the relevant circumstances. For instance, the initiation by him of proceedings against one of the two parties is strong evidence of a final election. Yet it is not necessarily conclusive, for further evidence may show that the right of action against the other party had not been abandoned.[114] This was the decision reached by the Court of Appeal in *Clarkson Booker Ltd v Andjel*.[115] The plaintiffs supplied air tickets to the value of £728 7s 6d to the defendant, a travel agent, with whom, on several occasions in the past, they had dealt as principal. Later, p & Co, also operating as travel agents, disclosed that the defendant had in fact acted solely as their agent.

> The plaintiffs wrote separate letters to the defendant and to p & Co threatening proceedings if payment were not made. After waiting for some five weeks they issued a writ against p & Co, but on learning two months later that the company was insolvent they proceeded no further with the action. They then issued a writ against the defendant and judgment was given in their favour in the court of first instance. The defendant appealed on the ground that the plaintiffs, by serving the earlier writ on p & Co had elected to exonerate him personally from liability.

It was held that no such election had been made. The threat to proceed against the defendant had never been withdrawn; his position had not been prejudiced by the action against p & Co; and above all it was to him alone that in the past the plaintiffs had always looked for payment.

Had the plaintiffs obtained judgment against p & Co they would, indeed, have been precluded from suing the defendant, not because they had made a final election, but because the law does not countenance the co-existence of two judgments in respect of the same debt or cause of action.[116] There shall not be more than one judgment on one entire debt.[117] If, for instance, the third party obtains judgment against a defendant who is in fact an agent, he cannot sue the principal, even though at the time of the action against the defendant he was ignorant of the principal's

---

[113] *United Australia Ltd v Barclays Bank Ltd* [1941] AC 1 at 30, per Lord Atkin.

[114] *Clarkson Booker Ltd v Andjel* [1964] 2 QB 775, [1964] 3 All ER 260. For a critique of the doctrine of election, see Reynolds 86 LQR 318.

[115] [1964] 2 QB 775, [1964] 3 All ER 260.

[116] *Kendall v Hamilton* (1879) 4 App Cas 504 at 515, per Lord Cairns.

[117] *Hammond v Schofield* [1891] 1 QB 453 at 457, per Vaughan Williams J; *Moore v Flanagan* [1920] 1 KB 919 at 925–926.

existence and even though the judgment remains unsatisfied.[118] He must first get that judgment set aside and then sue the principal.[119]

The juridical basis of the doctrine of the undisclosed principal has aroused considerable controversy.[120] The anomalous feature of the doctrine is that it allows 'one person to sue another on a contract not really made with the person suing'.[121] This patently ignores the common law requirement of privity of contract, and the view of Lord Lindley—that 'the contract is in truth, although not in form, that of the undisclosed principal himself'—has found few supporters.[122]

If, therefore, we look no further than the common law, the rule that the undisclosed principal can sue or be sued must find its justification in business convenience, though this will not warrant the conclusion that privity of contract exists between him and the third party. However, it has been suggested by high authority that the doctrine can be rationalised as avoiding circuity of action if the aid of equity is invoked. 'For the principal could in equity compel the agent to lend his name in an action to enforce the contract against the contractor, and would at common law be liable to indemnify the agent in respect of the performance of the obligations assumed by the agent under the contract.'[123]

C The effect of a payment to the agent

It may happen that either the principal or the third party settles with the agent, who, however, by reason of bankruptcy or fraud, fails to pass the money on to the creditor. The question then arises whether the payer is liable to pay over again. There are two separate cases.

First, the principal, having instructed his agent to buy goods, pays the purchase price to the agent, who fails to pay the seller.

Secondly, the principal instructs his agent to sell goods; the agent sells to a buyer and receives payment from him, but does not pay the principal.

In the first case, the general rule is that the principal remains liable to the seller, provided at least that the agent was known by the seller to be acting as an agent.[124] The seller, however, may be estopped by his conduct from taking advantage of this rule. If his conduct unequivocally showed that he looked to the agent alone for payment and thereby induced the principal, after the debt became due, to settle with

---

[118] *Kendall v Hamilton* (1879) 4 App Cas 504 at 514.

[119] *Partington v Hawthorne* (1888) 52 JP 807.

[120] 3 LQR 359; Ames *Lectures on Legal History* pp 453–463: Goodhart and Hamson 4 CLJ 320; Higgins 28 MLR 167.

[121] Pollock 3 LQR 359.

[122] *Keighley Maxsted & Co v Durant* [1901] AC 240 at 261. The fallacy of the view has been exposed by Goodhart and Hamson 4 CLJ 320.

[123] *Freeman and Lockyer v Buckhurst Park Properties (Magnal) Ltd* [1964] 2 QB 480 at 503, per Diplock LJ.

[124] *Irvine v Watson* (1879) 5 QBD 102; affd 5 QBD 414.

the agent, resort cannot afterwards be had to the principal.[125] To gain this immunity the principal must show that he was reasonably misled by the seller's conduct into settling with the agent. If, for instance, the seller takes security from the agent and gives him a receipt for the purchase price, the principal will be discharged if he settles with the agent on the faith of the receipt.[126] The whole subject was reviewed in *Irvine v Watson*,[127] where the facts were these:

> P employed A, a broker, to buy oil for him. A bought from S, telling him that he was buying for a principal but not disclosing the name. The terms of the sale were that payment should be made 'by cash on or before delivery', but, despite this, S delivered the oil without receiving payment. P, unaware that s had not been paid, in good faith paid A. A became insolvent, whereupon S sued P. It was proved that it was not the invariable custom in the oil trade to insist upon pre-payment even where the terms were cash on or before delivery.

It was argued on behalf of P that, since he knew that the contract provided for payment in cash on or before delivery, he was justified in presuming that s would not have made delivery without receipt of the money. This argument did not prevail. The clause in the contract providing for cash on or before delivery was not sufficient to raise an estoppel, since S had a perfect right to deliver without requiring pre-payment. Had the invariable custom been to exact pre-payment, the conclusion might well have been different.

The question remains whether the rule is different if the seller is unaware of the agency and deals with the agent as sole principal. If the person who is in fact principal *bona fide* settles with the agent, does he remain liable for the price? It was decided in *Heald v Kenworthy*[128] that even here the general rule applies and that failing estoppel the principal may be compelled to make a second payment. In that case:

> An undisclosed principal, who had authorised an agent to buy goods on his behalf, was sued for the price by the seller. He pleaded that within a reasonable time after the sale and not unduly early he had *bona fide* paid his agent in full.

It was held on demurrer that this plea was bad. The general rule was stated as follows in the head note:

> Where a principal authorises his agent to pledge his credit, and the latter makes a purchase on his behalf and thereby creates a debt, the principal is not discharged by payment to the agent if the money is not paid over to the seller, unless the latter by his conduct makes it unjust that the principal should be sued, eg, where the seller by his words or conduct induces the principal to believe that a settlement has been come to between the seller and the agent, in consequence of which the principal pays the amount of the debt to the agent.

---

[125] *Macfarlane v Giannacopula* (1858) 3 H & N 860.
[126] *Wyatt v Marquis of Hertford* (1802) 3 East 147.
[127] (1879) 5 QBD 102; affd 5 QBD 414.   [128] (1855) 10 Exch 739.

This rule, however, was somewhat rudely disturbed sixteen years later by the decision in *Armstrong v Stokes*.[129] In that case:

> P & Co employed A & Co, commission merchants, who acted sometimes for themselves and sometimes as agents, to buy goods on their behalf. A & Co bought from S, with whom they had often had dealings in the past. s did not inquire whether A & Co were on this occasion acting for principals. p & Co in accordance with their usual custom paid A & Co in full on the next settling day, but the money did not reach S.

An action brought by s against p & Co failed. The court considered that, as p & Co had paid A & Co at a time when s still gave exclusive credit to A & Co, s could not afterwards claim from p & Co. On the surface, therefore, *Armstrong v Stokes* is a flat reversal of *Heald v Kenworthy*. Which decision represents the modern law? Was the later distinguished from the earlier decision by some form of estoppel? On the whole it is safer to follow *Heald v Kenworthy*. *Armstrong v Stokes* was severely criticised by the Court of Appeal in *Irvine v Watson*, where its reconsideration at some later date was foreshadowed,[130] and the better opinion is that it turned in some measure upon the fact that A & Co were not normal agents but commission merchants.

The second case in which the effect of a settlement with an agent requires consideration is where the agent, having sold his principal's goods, receives payment from the buyer but does not pay the money over to his principal. Whether the buyer is in these circumstances liable to pay over again depends entirely upon whether the agent is authorised to receive the purchase money. If he possesses this authority, the buyer is discharged from further liability; if not, the liability remains. The general rule is that an agent authorised to sell is not authorised to receive payment.[131] The buyer, therefore, who seeks to avoid a double payment, must prove that the authority existed in fact. If the principal has expressly authorised the agent to accept payment, the matter is of course clear; but failing this the buyer must prove either that what he did was the usual and well-recognised practice in that particular type of agency, or that the agent had ostensible authority to receive the money.[132]

The right to set-off one debt against another raises a similar problem. If an agent authorised to sell goods owes a personal debt to the buyer, can the latter set this off against the purchase price that is due to the principal? The answer is that he enjoys this right only if he has been led to believe by the conduct of the principal that the agent is himself the owner of the goods sold. The law has been summarised by Martin B in the following words:

---

[129] (1872) LR 7 QB 598.

[130] (1880) 5 QBD 414 at 421. For a reappraisal of the decision, see Higgins 28 MLR 167 at 175–178.

[131] *Drakeford v Piercy* (1866) 7 B & s 515; *Butwick v Grant* [1924] 2 KB 483. So an estate agent does not normally have apparent authority to receive a deposit on behalf of the vendor of a house. *Sorrell v Finch* [1977] AC 728, [1976] 2 All ER 371; Reynolds 92 LQR 484.

[132] *Butwick v Grant*, above.

Where a principal permits an agent to sell as apparent principal and afterwards intervenes, the buyer is entitled to be placed in the same situation at the time of disclosure of the real principal as if the agent had been the real contracting party, and is entitled to the same defence, whether it be by common law or by statute, payment or set-off, as he was entitled to at that time against the agent, the apparent principal.[133]

The question generally arises when the principal has entrusted the agent with possession of the goods.[134] In this case the buyer is entitled to a set-off if he proves that the agent sold the goods in his own name as if they were his own, that he himself *bona fide* believed the agent to be the principal in the transaction, and that before he was undeceived in this respect the set-off had accrued.[135]

It is clear, therefore, that no right of set-off exists if the buyer knows the agent to be an agent though ignorant of the principal's identity, or if he knows that the agent sometimes deals as agent, sometimes on his own account, but does not trouble to ascertain the capacity in which he is acting in the present transaction.[136]

4 UNAUTHORISED ACTS OF THE AGENT

A The position of the principal

It is obvious that the principal is bound by every contract or disposition of property made by the agent with his authority. The reverse is equally obvious. If a man acts as agent without any authority whatsoever, or if an agent exceeds his authority, the principal (apart from ratification), is not liable at all in the first case and in the second is not liable for the excess. Thus, if the managing committee of a club has no authority to buy goods on credit, an order given for wine by one of the members does not bind his colleagues. The same rule applies where an agent is adjudicated bankrupt after having disposed of his principal's goods contrary to instructions. In this case the principal is not reduced to proving in the bankruptcy equally with the other creditors, but can recover the whole price if the agent has wrongfully sold goods, and can recover in full money or property which may have passed to the trustee in bankruptcy.[137] A similar rule applied at common law to a wrongful disposition by an agent of goods which had been entrusted to him by a principal.[138] This rule, however, and the maxim

---

[133] *Isberg v Bowden* (1853) 8 Exch 852 at 859.
[134] *George v Clagett* (1797) 7 Term Rep 359.
[135] *Montagu v Forwood* [1893] 2 QB 350 applied *Lloyds and Scottish Finance Ltd v Williamson* [1965] 1 All ER 641, [1965] 1 WLR 404.
[136] *Cooke & Sons v Eshelby* (1887) 12 App Cas 271.
[137] *Taylor v Plumer* (1815) 3 M & s 562; *Re Strachan, ex p Cooke* (1876) 4 ChD 123.
[138] *Cole v North Western Bank* (1875) LR 10 CP 354 at 362, per Blackburn J.

upon which it was based—*nemo dat quod non habet*—has been largely modified by subsequent legislation.[139]

Nevertheless, to say that a principal is liable only for what has been done within the authority of his agent leaves open the critical question: What is the meaning of 'authority' in the eyes of the law? The meaning is not self-evident, for what has not in fact been authorised may none the less be regarded by the law as authorised. The position with regard to this matter has been restated and clarified by two modern decisions of the Court of Appeal.[140] These show that a distinction must be drawn between the agent's *actual* authority on the one hand, and his *apparent* or *ostensible* authority on the other.

> An 'actual' authority is a legal relationship between principal and agent created by a consensual agreement to which they alone are parties. Its scope is to be ascertained by applying ordinary principles of construction of contracts, including any proper implications from the express words used, the usages of the trade or the course of business between the parties.[141]

Thus actual authority may be express or implied.

> It is *express* when it is given by express words, such as when a board of directors pass a resolution which authorises two of their number to sign cheques. It is *implied* when it is inferred from the conduct of the parties and the circumstances of the case, such as where the board of directors appoint one of their number to be managing director. They thereby impliedly authorise him to do all such things as fall within the usual scope of that office.[142]

If the agent enters into a contract with a third party within the scope of his actual authority the result is to create contractual obligations between the principal and the third party. It is irrelevant that the latter was unaware of the existence of the authority, and irrelevant even that the agent acted with improper motives with a desire solely to promote his own interests.[143]

On the other hand, 'ostensible or apparent authority is the authority of the agent as it *appears to others*'.[144] Its operation has been described as follows by Diplock LJ.

> An 'apparent' or 'ostensible' authority . . . is a legal relationship between the principal and the contractor created by a representation, made by the principal to the contractor, intended to be and in fact acted upon by the contractor, that the agent has authority to enter on behalf of the principal into a contract of a kind within the scope of the 'apparent' authority, so as to

---

[139] Pp 630 ff, below.

[140] *Freeman and Lockyer v Buckhurst Park Properties (Magnal) Ltd* [1964] 2 QB 480, [1964] 1 All ER 630, especially the judgment of Diplock LJ; *Hely-Hutchinson v Brayhead Ltd* [1968] 1 QB 549, [1967] 3 All ER 98.

[141] *Freeman and Lockyer v Buckhurst Park Properties (Magnal) Ltd* [1964] 2 QB 480 at 502, [1964] 1 All ER 630 at 644, per Diplock LJ.

[142] *Hely-Hutchinson v Brayhead Ltd* [1968] 1 QB 549 at 583, [1967] 3 All ER 98 at 102.

[143] *Hambro v Burnand* [1904] 2 KB 10.

[144] *Hely-Hutchinson v Brayhead Ltd* [1968] 1 QB 549, per Lord Denning at 583.

render the principal liable to perform any obligations imposed upon him by such contract . . . The representation, when acted upon by the contractor by entering into a contract with the agent, operates as an estoppel, preventing the principal from asserting that he is not bound by the contract. It is irrelevant whether the agent had actual authority to enter into the contract.[145]

Implied and apparent authority are not mutually exclusive. 'Generally they co-exist and coincide, but either may exist without the other and their respective scopes may be different.'[146] But normally the third party will rely upon the apparent authority of the agent, since all that he will know of the actual authority, whether express or implied, will be what he hears from the principal or agent, and that may or may not be true.

The 'representation' that creates an apparent authority generally arises from some conduct on the part of the principal, as for instance where he holds the agent out as entitled to act for him in a business capacity.[147]

By so doing the principal represents to anyone who becomes aware that the agent is so acting that the agent has authority to enter on behalf of the principal into contracts with other persons of the kind which an agent so acting in the conduct of the principal's business has usually 'actual' authority to enter into.[148]

On the other hand an agent himself cannot normally enlarge the scope of his apparent authority.[149] It is impossible to classify precisely and exhaustively the circumstances in which a principal is thus liable on the basis of apparent authority, but the position may be clarified by examples.[150]

Thus, an agent who is employed to conduct a certain business transaction is deemed to possess authority to do everything usually incidental to a business transaction of that type.[151] In *Dingle v Hare*,[152] for instance, an agent with authority to sell

[145] *Freeman and Lockyer v Buckhurst Park Properties (Magnal) Ltd* [1964] 2 QB 480 at 503, [1964] 1 All ER 630 at 644.

[146] Ibid. The relationship between implied and ostensible authority is well illustrated by *Waugh v MB Clifford & Sons Ltd* [1982] Ch 374, [1982] 1 All ER 1095. See also *Owners of the Borvigilant v Owners of the Romina G* [2002] EWHC 1759; [2003] 1 All ER (Comm) 129, [2003] 2 All ER (Comm) 736.

[147] For a discussion of the wide scope of the ostensible authority possessed by the secretary of a company, see *Panorama Developments (Guildford) Ltd v Fidelis Furnishing Fabrics Ltd* [1971] 2 QB 711, [1971] 3 All ER 16. For a deduction of ostensible authority from previous transactions see *Pharmed Medicare Private Ltd v Univar Ltd* [2003] EWCA Civ 1569, [2003] 1 All ER (Comm) 321.

[148] *Freeman and Lockyer v Buckhurst Park Properties (Magnal) Ltd* [1964] 2 QB 480 at 503–504, [1964] 1 All ER 630 at 644. The usage with regard to the epithets appropriate to qualify 'authority' is not completely consistent either among judges or commentators; eg 'implied' is sometimes used to mean 'apparent'.

[149] *Armagas Ltd v Mundogas SA, The Ocean Frost* [1986] AC 717, [1986] 2 All ER 385 cf *First Energy (UK) Ltd v Hungarian International Bank* [1993] 2 Lloyd's Rep 194.

[150] For an illuminating account of which free use has been made in these pages, see Ewart *Estoppel* pp 488 ff.

[151] *Sutton v Tatham* (1839) 10 Ad & El 27 at 30, per Littledale J. [152] (1859) 7 CBNS 145.

artificial manure warranted to the buyer that it contained 30 per cent phosphate of lime. Upon proof that it was usual to give a warranty of this nature in the artificial manure trade, it was held that the principal was liable for its breach, although he had not authorised the agent to enter into such an undertaking. Byles J said:

> But when the Jury found that it was usual to sell these artificial manures with a warranty, the nice distinction as to the extent of the agent's authority became quite immaterial. An agent to sell has a general authority to do all that is usual and necessary in the course of such employment.

Again, an agent employed as manager of a certain class of business, to the conduct of which the drawing of bills of exchange is normally incidental, is implicitly authorised to draw upon his principal.[153] If it is the usual practice of hotel managers to purchase cigars, then purchases of this nature made by a manager will bind his principal.[154]

So, an agent employed to act at a definite place, such as a market, has apparent authority to do what persons transacting business at that place usually do. In the words of Alderson B:

> A person who deals in a particular market must be taken to deal according to the custom of that market, and he who directs another to make a contract at a particular place must be taken as intending that the contract may be made according to the usage of that place.[155]

The Factors Act 1889, which repealed a series of Acts passed in 1823, 1842 and 1877, amplified further the doctrine of apparent authority. The object of these statutes was to determine the effect of unauthorised dispositions of goods made by factors and other similar agents in favour of third persons acting *bona fide*. A principal, for instance, delivers goods to a factor with instructions that they are not to be disposed of but are to be retained pending further directions. The factor, however, in breach of his authority, sells or pledges the goods to a third party who acts *bona fide* and for value. Is the principal to be allowed to rely upon the maxim *nemo dat quod not habet*, and to succeed in an action of trover against the third party? The common law doctrine of ostensible ownership, analogous to the doctrine of ostensible agency, could indeed have settled this problem without any aid from the legislature, for it was designed to meet just such a case as that proposed above.

> The doctrine is that if the owner of goods acts in such a way as to induce the belief in a third party that the ownership is vested in X, and if in *bona fide* reliance upon this belief the third party enters into some transaction with X under which he acquires the goods for value, the owner is estopped from disputing the validity of the transaction.

---

[153] *Edmunds v Bushell and Jones* (1865) LR 1 QB 97.
[154] *Watteau v Fenwick* [1893] 1 QB 346. See Hornby [1961] CLJ 239. See also *IRC v UFITEC Group Ltd* [1977] 3 All ER 924; *St Margaret's Trust v Byrne* [1976] CLY 1342.
[155] *Bayliffe v Butterworth* (1847) 1 Exch 425 at 429.

In such circumstances the apparent ownership is in the eye of the law equivalent to real ownership. Since a factor is a mercantile agent whose ordinary course of business is to dispose of the goods of which he is in possession, it is obvious that to put him in possession must induce the belief in the business community that he enjoys the powers of disposition usually exercised by this type of agent. The courts, indeed, recognised this fact to a large extent, for they held that if a factor *sold* the goods of which he was in possession his principal was estopped from denying his authority to sell. They refused, however, to make other forms of disposition equally binding upon the principal. Although the well-established custom was for factors who had received goods for disposal to advance money to the owner and then to pledge the goods in order to keep themselves in funds, the courts persistently held that a pledge, as distinct from a sale, did not raise an estoppel against the owner so as to confer a good title on an innocent pledgee. Lord Ellenborough said:

> It was a hard doctrine when the pawnee was told that the pledger of goods had no authority to pledge them, being a mere factor for sale; and yet since the case of *Paterson v Tash*[156] that doctrine has never been overturned.[157]

The Factors Act, however, now affords adequate protection to persons who *bona fide* enter into transactions with mercantile agents as defined by the Act.[158] Section 2(1) provides as follows:

> Where a mercantile agent is, with the consent of the owner, in possession of goods or of the documents of title to goods, any sale, pledge or other disposition of the goods, made by him when acting in the ordinary course of business of a mercantile agent, shall, subject to the provisions of this Act, be as valid as if he were expressly authorised by the owner of the goods to make the same; provided that the person taking under the disposition acts in good faith, and has not at the time of the disposition notice that the person making the disposition has no authority to make the same.

This provision is extended by a later section to the case where a buyer, having obtained goods with the consent of the seller, later transfers their possession to a person who receives them in good faith under a sale, pledge or other disposition. In this event, the buyer in making the disposition is placed in the same position by the Act as if he were a mercantile agent in possession of the goods with the consent of the owner. It is irrelevant that such is not his true description.[159]

Finally, it must be stressed that once 'an agent is clothed with ostensible authority, no private instructions prevent his acts within the scope of that authority from

---

[156] (1743) 2 Stra 1178. [157] *Pickering v Busk* (1812) 15 East 38 at 44.

[158] The statutory definition is: 'A mercantile agent having in the customary course of his business as such agent authority either to sell goods, or to consign goods for the purpose of sale, or to buy goods, or to raise money on the security of goods.' See Factors Act 1889, s 1(1).

[159] Ibid, s 9; substantially reproduced in s 25(2) of the Sale of Goods Act 1893; *Newtons of Wembley Ltd v Williams* [1965] 1 QB 560, [1964] 3 All ER 532.

binding his principal'.[160] Limitation is in fact imposed upon the powers of the agent and ignored by him and will not exonerate the principal from liability, unless, of course, their existence is known to the third party to the transaction[161] or the third party has not relied upon the ostensible authority of the agent.[162]

B The position of the agent

If a man contracts as agent without any authority in that behalf, the question arises whether he acquires either benefits or liabilities under the transaction.

With regard to benefits, the rule is that if a man contracts as agent for a *named* principal who has given no authority and who does not later ratify the contract, the self-styled agent acquires no rights whatsoever, since the solvency of the supposed principal may have induced the third party to enter into the transaction.[163] Thus, a purchaser at an auction sale signed a memorandum as agent for a named principal, and later sued in his own name to recover the deposit. He attempted to give evidence proving that he was the principal in the transaction, but the evidence was held to be inadmissible.[164]

On the other hand, if a man without any precedent authority contracts as agent but does not disclose the name of his supposed principal, it has been held in *Schmaltz v Avery*[165] that he is entitled to maintain an action in his own name on the contract.

The position with regard to the liability of an unauthorised agent is clear. It varies according to the state of his belief.

If he knows that he possesses no authority to act as agent, but nevertheless makes a representation to the contrary and in consequence causes loss to the party with whom he contracts, he may be sued in tort for the deceit.[166]

If, on the other hand, he mistakenly though innocently believes that he possesses authority, he cannot be liable in tort for deceit. Nor can he be made liable upon the contract which he purported to make on behalf of the principal, since this was not his contract, nor was it regarded as such by the third party. Thus in *Smouth v Ilbery*:[167]

> A wife, acting as the authorised agent of her husband, continually bought goods from the plaintiff, an English tradesman. The plaintiff knew that the husband was in China. The husband died without the knowledge of the parties, and the plaintiff sued the wife to recover the price of goods supplied to her after her authority had been revoked by the death of the principal.

---

[160] *National Bolivian Navigation Co v Wilson* (1880) 5 App Cas 176 at 209, per Lord Blackburn.
[161] *Watteau v Fenwick* [1893] 1 QB 346.
[162] *Nationwide Building Society v Lewis* [1998] 3 All ER 143.
[163] *Bickerton v Burrell* (1816) 5 M & s 383; *Fairlie v Fenton* (1870) LR 5 Exch 169.
[164] *Bickerton v Burrell,* above.
[165] (1851) 20 LJQB 228, followed in *Harper & Co v Vigers Bros* [1909] 2 KB 549.
[166] *Polhill v Walter* (1832) 3 B & Ad 114.
[167] (1842) 10 M & W 1.

The plaintiff sued on the contract of sale but failed, for it was clear that both in fact and in intention it was the husband, not the wife, who was the buyer.

A contractual basis upon which the agent himself can be held liable was, however, ultimately established in *Collen v Wright*.[168] In that case:

A, describing himself as the agent of P, agreed in writing to lease to the plaintiff a farm which belonged to P. Both the plaintiff and A believed that A had the authority of p to make the lease, but this in fact was not the case. The plaintiff, having failed in a suit for specific performance against P, later sued to recover as damages from A's executors the costs that he had incurred in the suit.

The action succeeded. The court inferred from the circumstances a separate and independent contract by which A promised that he possessed the authority of p and in consideration of this promise the plaintiff agreed to take a lease of the farm. Willes J, in delivering the judgment of the majority of the Exchequer Chamber, said:

The obligation arising in such a case is well expressed by saying that a person, professing to contract as agent for another, impliedly, if not expressly, undertakes to, or promises the person who enters into such contract, upon the faith of the professed agent being duly authorised, that the authority which he professes to have done in point of fact exist. The fact of entering into the transaction with the professed agent, as such, is good consideration for the promise.

The decision, in other words, is an early example—perhaps the forerunner—of the so-called 'collateral contract'[169] which has been discussed in an earlier chapter,[170] though it has frequently been regarded as having established a particular doctrine called 'implied warranty of authority'. This is a misleading description of the reasoning in the case. The court did not imply a term of warranty in an already existing contract. It constructed a new and independent contract based upon the exchange of promises; on the one side that the authority existed and on the other that a lease would be taken.

The doctrine thus propounded in *Collen v Wright* was at once accepted by the profession and it has since been given wide currency. It is not confined to contracts, but extends to every business transaction into which a third party is induced to enter by a representation that the person with whom he is dealing has authority from some other person.[171] As Bramwell LJ put it in a later case:

If a person requests and, by asserting that he is clothed with the necessary authority induces another to enter into a negotiation with himself and into a transaction with the person whose

---

[168] (1857) 8 E & B 647 at 657. See Fifoot *English Law and its Background* pp 174–177.
[169] See Wedderburn [1959] CLJ 68.
[170] Pp 81 ff, above.
[171] *Firbank's Executors v Humphreys* (1886) 18 QBD 54; *Starkey v Bank of England* [1903] AC 114; *V/O Rasnoimport v Guthrie & Co Ltd* [1966] 1 Lloyd's Rep 1. *Penn v Bristol and West Building Society* [1997] 3 All ER 470.

authority he represents that he has, in that case there is a contract by him that he has the authority of the person with whom he requests the other to enter into the transaction.[172]

The result is the same if an authority that has been expressly conferred is ended by some event, such as the death or the lunacy of the principal, which supervenes without the knowledge of the agent. This occurred, for instance, in *Yonge v Toynbee*,[173] where the facts were these:

> P instructed A, a solicitor, to defend an action on his behalf, but he became insane before the action was begun. In ignorance of P's insanity A entered an appearance, delivered a defence and took other steps in connection with the litigation. When the plaintiff learned of P's condition he got the proceedings struck out and then sued to recover his costs from A, who, he contended, had defended the action without authority.

This contention was upheld. Although the solicitor's authority had automatically terminated with the insanity of the principal, his conduct tacitly guaranteed its continued existence. 'I can see no difference of principle', said Buckley LJ, 'between the case where the authority never existed at all and the case in which the authority has once existed and has ceased to exist.'[174]

5 TERMINATION OF AGENCY

Agency is determinable either by act of the parties or by operation of law. It is determined by act of the parties if there is a mutual agreement to that effect; or if the authority of the agent is renounced by him or revoked by the principal. Determination by operation of law occurs by the happening of some event which renders the agency unlawful and also by the death, insanity or bankruptcy of one of the parties. We will consider these methods *seriatim*.

A Termination by act of the parties

An agent who renounces his authority or a principal who revokes the authority may find that he has rendered himself liable for breach of contract. In deciding whether a breach has been committed, much will depend upon whether or not the actual relationship between the parties is akin to that which exists between an employer and an employee.

---

[172] *Dickson v Reuter's Telegram Co* (1877) 3 CPD 1 at 5.
[173] [1910] 1 KB 215.
[174] Ibid at 226. For consideration of damages recoverable for breach of warranty of authority, see *Nimmo v Habton Farms* [2003] EWCA Civ 68, [2003] 1 All ER 1136.

If the result of their agreement is to create an immediate and continuing *nexus* between them, as for example where the agent has promised to devote his time and energy on behalf of the principal in return for reward, their relationship bears a close analogy to that between an employer and employee. The agent has agreed to serve the principal; the principal has agreed to accept and to pay for that service. It is clear, therefore, that any unilateral termination of the relationship by either party will be wrongful unless it is in accordance with the contract. If there is an express term dealing with the matter, *cadit quaestio*. If not, all depends upon the construction of the contract. In the case of every contract, whether it be one of agency or not, the common intention of the parties with regard to the power of termination must be ascertained in the light of all the admissible evidence.

> An agreement which is silent about determination will not be determinable unless the facts of the case, such as the subject matter of the agreement, the nature of the contract or the circumstances in which the agreement was made, support a finding that the parties intended that it should be determinable.[175]

Thus in *Martin-Baker Aircraft Co v Canadian Flight Equipment*:[176]

> A was appointed sole selling agent on the North American Continent of all the products of P & Co. He agreed to use his best endeavours to promote sales in that territory, to act as general marketing consultant for P & Co and not to become interested in the sale of competitive products. His remuneration was to be a commission at the rate of 17½/% on orders obtained by him.

P & Co desired to determine the relationship, but A contended that it was terminable only by mutual consent. There could be no doubt that the mutual promises constituted a contract binding upon both parties. There was express provision for the summary termination of the relationship in two particular events, but no similar provision to meet other circumstances. McNair J construed the contract as being closely analogous to one between master and servant and therefore as one that could not rationally be regarded as establishing a permanent bond between the parties. One party alone could not, indeed, terminate it summarily, but he could terminate it by serving reasonable notice on the other, that is to say in the instant case, twelve months' notice.

The presence or absence of a power of termination is a question which raises formidable difficulties throughout the law of contract—difficulties endemic in the application of rules of construction. Such rules are not docile servants and are the more intractable where unaccompanied by some initial presumption. Buckley J in *Re Spenborough UDC's Agreement*[177] denied the existence of any presumption either in

---

[175] *Re Spenborough UDC's Agreement* [1968] Ch 139 at 147, [1967] 1 All ER 959 at 962, per Buckley LJ.

[176] [1955] 2 QB 556.   [177] [1968] Ch 139 at 147.

favour of or against terminability. He was, indeed, confronted with inconsistent dicta in two House of Lords cases[178] and he may well have felt reluctant to choose between them. Neither of them was, in fact, concerned with problems of agency or employment, and in these two types of contract at least the possibility of termination is tolerably well settled.[179]

In many cases of agency, the relationship between the parties, unlike that between employer and servant, imposes no binding obligation upon either party. This is so, for instance, where an owner puts the sale of his property into the hands of an estate agent on commission terms. Here, the agent is not bound to do anything. Nor, at the outset, is the principal bound to do anything, for his only promise is to pay commission if and when the agent has brought about the intended result.[180] Only then does a contractual *nexus* arise between the parties. This is another example of a promise that ripens into a contract upon the performance of a specified act, as in the case where a reward is offered for the supply of information. We have seen that the revocability of such offers is the subject of debate but it is clear that the property owner may revoke his mandate before his obligation to pay matures, ie at any time before the authorised act is performed by the agent.[181] Thus a commission agreement is a speculative contract under which the agent must take the risk that the prospective purchaser whom he has introduced may not be accepted as such by his principal.[182]

The general principles that govern the contract between the principal and agent in such a case were stated by Lord Russell of Killowen in *Luxor (Eastbourne) Ltd v Cooper*:

> (1) Commission contracts are subject to no peculiar rules or principles of their own; the law which governs them is the law which governs all contracts and all questions of agency. (2) No general rule can be laid down by which the rights of the agent or the liability of the principal under commission contracts are to be determined. In each case these must depend upon the exact terms of the contract in question, and upon the true construction of those terms. And (3) contracts by which owners of property, desiring to dispose of it, put it in the hands of agents on commission terms, are not (in default of specific provisions) contracts of employment in the ordinary meaning of those words. No obligation is imposed on the agent to do anything.[183]

The second and, in the present context, the most important observation of Lord Russell is in effect that the principal's liability for the payment of commission depends

---

[178] *Llanelly Rly and Dock Co v London and North Western Rly Co* (1875) LR 7 HL 550; *Winter Garden Theatre (London) Ltd v Millennium Productions Ltd* [1948] AC 173, [1947] 2 All ER 331.

[179] The question of terminability in the law of contract as a whole is discussed by Carnegie 85 LQR 392. He argues cogently in favour of a general presumption of terminability in all contracts of unspecified duration.

[180] *Luxor (Eastbourne) Ltd v Cooper* [1941] AC 108 at 124, 141, 153, [1941] 1 All ER 33 at 45, 55, 63. Murdoch 91 LQR 357.

[181] *Motion v Michaud* (1892) 8 TLR 253; affd 8 TLR at 447. See pp 75–77, above.

[182] See Ash *Willing to Purchase* p 3.   [183] [1941] AC 108 at 124, [1941] 1 All ER 33 at 43.

on whether, on the proper interpretation of the contract between him and the agent, the event has happened upon which the commission is to be paid.[184] The agent is not entitled to claim payment for work as such, but only for an event, ie the event required by his contract with the principal. Moreover, there is no implied condition that the principal will do nothing to prevent the agent from earning his commission. The effect, therefore, of this ruling is that the principal may terminate the contract at any time before the agent has accomplished what he undertook to do. This was decided in the *Luxor* case[185] itself, where the facts were these:

> P authorised A to negotiate for the sale of certain properties and promised to pay him a commission of £10,000 'on completion of the sale' if a price of £175,000 were procured. A obtained an offer to purchase at this price and the offer was accepted by P. Both the offer and acceptance, however, were made 'subject to contract', a formula which, as we have seen, postpones the creation of a binding contract.[186] P availed himself of this rule and refused to proceed further with the transaction.

A was unable to recover £10,000 by way of commission, since there had been no *completion of the sale*, the stipulated event that was to convert P's promise into an obligation. The action was brought, therefore, to recover damages for breach of an implied term alleged to be contained in the agency contract. It was argued that P had implicitly promised that he 'would do nothing to prevent the satisfactory completion of the transaction so as to deprive the [agent] of the agreed commission'.

This attempt to invoke the doctrine of *The Moorcock*[187] failed. The contract did not lack business efficacy merely because it left p free to ignore or disown what A had done. The chances are that an agent of this type will reap substantial profit for comparatively little effort, and the possibility that he may lose the fruits of his labour at the caprice of the principal is a business risk that in practice is recognised and accepted. Moreover, it would be almost impossible to frame an implied term that would fairly and reasonably provide for the varying contingencies that may complicate such an agency, as for example the habit of entrusting the sale of a house to several agents each acting on a commission basis.

Thus the guiding rule in every case is 'that before you find the commission payable you must be satisfied that the condition on which it is payable has been satisfied'.[188] The intention of the parties as to the exact meaning of the condition must be ascertained by construing the actual words by which it is defined in the contract. Broadly speaking the intention which as a matter of probability the court should impute to the parties is that if no sale in fact results from the agent's efforts no commission shall be

---

[184] *Ackroyd & Sons v Hasan* [1960] 2 QB 144 at 154, per Upjohn LJ.

[185] [1941] AC 108, [1941] 1 All ER 33.

[186] P 76, above.   [187] (1889) 14 PD 64; pp 157–162, above.

[188] *A L Wilkinson Ltd v Brown* [1966] 1 All ER 509 at 510, [1966] 1 WLR 194 at 197, per Harman LJ; *Jacques v Lloyd D George & Partners Ltd* [1968] 1 WLR 625 at 630, per Lord Denning MR.

payable. This is the normal expectation of the vendor. Where the condition is described in general or ambiguous terms, such is the intention that the courts have usually attributed to the parties.[189] Examples of descriptive words that have led to this construction are where the agent has agreed to introduce 'a purchaser';[190] 'a person willing and able to purchase';[191] 'a person ready, able and willing to purchase';[192] 'a person prepared to enter into a contract to purchase'.[193]

Nevertheless, if the condition upon which commission is payable is defined in clear and unambiguous terms, effect will be given to it even though for some reason or other the sale turns out to be abortive.[194] Thus in *Midgley Estates Ltd v Hand*,[195] the bargain was that commission should be payable as soon as a purchaser introduced by the agent 'shall have signed a legally binding contract within a period of three months from this date'. The agents satisfied this condition and were held to be entitled to their commission notwithstanding the ultimate failure of the sale owing to the financial collapse of the purchaser.

Where a sale fails owing to the default of the principal, commission is payable if the default is wilful, but not if it is due merely to his inability to prove his title to the *res vendita*.[196]

One clear case in which an authority cannot be unilaterally revoked by the principal is where it is coupled with an interest held by the agent. If, for instance, a borrower, in consideration of a loan, authorises the lender to receive the rents of Blackacre by way of security, the authority remains irrevocable until repayment of the loan in full has been effected.

> Where an agreement is entered into on a sufficient consideration, [or by deed] whereby an authority is given for the purpose of securing some benefit to the donee of the authority, such an authority is irrevocable. This is what is usually meant by an authority coupled with an interest, and which is commonly said to be irrevocable.[197]

---

[189] *Midgley Estates Ltd v Hand* [1952] 2 QB 432 at 435–436, [1952] 1 All ER 1394 at 1396, per Jenkins LJ.

[190] *Jones v Lowe* [1945] KB 73, [1945] 1 All ER 194.

[191] *Dellafiora v Lester* [1962] 3 All ER 393, [1962] 1 WLR 1208.

[192] *Dennis Reed Ltd v Goody* [1950] 2 KB 277, [1950] 1 All ER 919. But cf *Christie Owen and Davies Ltd v Rapacioli* [1974] QB 781, [1974] 2 All ER 311.

[193] *Ackroyd & Sons v Hasan* [1960] 2 QB 144, [1960] 2 All ER 254; *A L Wilkinson Ltd v Brown* [1966] 1 All ER 509, [1966] 1 WLR 194. In the former of these cases, Winn J in the court of first instance, [1959] 1 WLR 706 at 711, insisted that any such phrase as 'introduce a person who is prepared to enter into a contract' must always be construed as 'a person who *does* enter into a contract'. This view was not favoured by the Court of Appeal, but it has been vigorously defended by Peter Ash in *Willing to Purchase* pp 91 ff.

[194] *Midgley Estates Ltd v Hand* [1952] 2 QB 432 at 436.

[195] [1952] 2 QB 432; applied in *Sheggia v Gradwell* [1963] 3 All ER 114, [1963] 1 WLR 1049, Lord Denning dissenting. This surprising decision was criticised by Salmon LJ in *Wilkinson Ltd v Brown* [1966] 1 All ER 509 at 515, [1966] 1 WLR 194 at 202–203.

[196] *Blake & Co v Sohn* [1969] 3 All ER 123, [1969] 1 WLR 1412.

[197] *Smart v Sandars* (1848) 5 CB 895 at 917, per Wilde CJ.

This doctrine applies, however, only where the authority is created in order to protect the interest of the agent; it does not extend to a case where the authority has been given for some other reason and the interest of the agent arises later. This was the issue in *Smart v Sandars*,[198] where the facts were as follows:

> Goods were consigned by the principal to a factor for the purpose of being sold. The factor later advanced £3,000 to the principal. The principal then counter-manded his instructions to sell the goods, but nevertheless they were sold by the factor.

In the action that was subsequently brought against him, the factor argued that the authority to sell which he had undoubtedly been given had become irrevocable, since in his capacity as lender he had acquired an interest in the proceeds of sale. This argument did not prevail. The authority arose prior to, and independently of, the creation of the interests, and therefore it was not irrevocable under the general doctrine, but could become so only if an express agreement to that effect were made. Had a contract of loan been concluded between the parties by which the factor had been put into possession of the goods with authority to sell them and to repay himself out of the proceeds, the authority would have been irrevocable.

The solution to problems of this kind will often now be different because of the Commercial Agents Regulations 1993. This gives effect to the European Directive on Commercial Agents and introduce a whole new notion into English law, which is that where the agent has participated in the building up of the business, the agent has a quasi property interest in the business which should be protected. It follows that in the area covered by the Directive, broadly, in situations where A has power to buy and sell on P's behalf, A is entitled to be compensated for invasions of this quasi-property interest. The interest is protected even against express terms in the agency contract. The details are complex but the regulations represent a major change in English agency law.[199] They are largely based on Continental systems, particularly German law.

Such, then, is the position where the principal revokes the authority of the agent. The fact that similar rules apply in the reverse case where the agent renounces his employment scarcely needs elaboration. If the revocation is in breach of contract, the principal may successfully institute an action for damages.[200]

---

[198] (1848) 5 CB 895.

[199] *Page v Combined Shipping and Transport Co Ltd* [1997] 3 All ER 656; *Moore v Piretta Pta Ltd* [1999] 1 All ER 174. *Mercantile International Group plc v Chuan Soon Huat Industrial Group Ltd* [2002] EWCA Civ 288, [2002] 1 All ER Comm 788; *Light v Ty Europe Ltd* [2003] EWHC 174 (QB), [2003] 1 All ER (Comm) 568.

[200] *Hochster v De La Tour* (1853) 2 E & B 678.

B Termination by operation of law

A contract of agency is automatically determined by the occurrence of some event which renders the continuance of the relationship unlawful, as for example, where the principal becomes an alien enemy owing to the outbreak of war.[201]

The death of the principal determines the agency and relieves his estate from liability upon contracts made by the agent after his death, even though made in the honest belief that he was still alive.[202] On the other hand, the agent is liable in such a case under the doctrine of the independent or 'collateral' contract.[203] In the case of a power of attorney, however, it has been enacted that if the attorney makes any payment or does any act in good faith in pursuance of the power, he shall not thereby incur liability by reason that without his knowledge the principal has died, or become bankrupt or has revoked the power.[204]

The death of the agent likewise determines the agency.[205]

A difficult question arises where an agent makes a contract with a third party after his principal has become insane. There are only two relevant authorities: *Drew v Nunn*[206] and *Yonge v Toynbee*.[207] In *Drew v Nunn*:

> The defendant, when sane, gave his wife authority to act for him and held her out to the plaintiff, a tradesman, as clothed with that authority. He became insane and was confined in an asylum. During this period, his wife bought goods on credit from the plaintiff who was unaware that the defendant had become mentally deranged. The defendant recovered his reason and resisted an action to recover the price of the goods supplied to his wife.

Two questions required an answer.

First, does insanity terminate the authority of the agent? This received an affirmative answer from Brett LJ and Bramwell LJ, though Cotton LJ felt some doubt. Since the husband could no longer act for himself, his wife could no longer act for him. The effect of this ruling is that the insanity of the principal renders the contract *between the principal and agent* void, so that for instance no commission is payable on transactions later effected by the agent.

The second question then arose: What is the effect where the principal, having held out another as his agent, becomes insane and a third person deals with the agent without notice of the insanity? The court held that the principal remains liable for what the agent has done in his capacity as agent. Having held him out in that capacity, he has made a representation upon which third parties are entitled to act and to continue to act if they have no notice of the insanity. In the words of Bramwell LJ:

---

[201] *Stevenson v Aktiengesellschaft für Cartonnagen-Industrie* [1918] AC 239.
[202] *Blades v Free* (1829) 9 B & C 167.   [203] *Yonge v Toynbee* [1910] 1 KB 215; p 634, above.
[204] Law of Property Act 1925, s 124(1).   [205] *Friend v Young* [1897] 2 Ch 421.
[206] (1879) 4 QBD 661.   [207] [1910] 1 KB 215.

Insanity is not a privilege, it is a misfortune, which must not be allowed to injure innocent persons: it would be productive of mischievous consequences, if insanity annulled every representation made by a person afflicted with it without any notice being given of his malady.[208]

It is submitted that the decision accords with common sense and with the view that a distinction must be drawn between the *authority* and the *power* of the agents, ie between his authority to act for the principal and his power to put his principal in a contractual relationship with third parties. The latter may continue after the former has ceased.[209]

But though the rule laid down in *Drew v Nunn* may be regarded as satisfactory, it has been confused by the decision of the Court of Appeal in *Yonge v Toynbee*.[210] The facts in this case, which have already been given,[211] were broadly similar to those in *Drew v Nunn*, except that the agent was ignorant of his principal's insanity when he contracted with the third party. The court applied the rule in *Collen v Wright*[212] and held that the agent was personally liable as having impliedly warranted the existence of his authority. The application of this rule would seem to be in conflict with the decision in *Drew v Nunn* that in similar circumstances the agent is still empowered to create a contractual relationship between his principal and a third party. If an agent has indeed this power, the principal could not possibly have been held liable, since a person under a disability may not defend any proceedings except by his guardian *ad litem*.[213] Secondly, and this carried great weight with Swinfen Eady J, the agent was a solicitor, an officer of the court upon whom the judiciary and other parties to litigation place great reliance. Much confusion would ensue 'if a solicitor were not to be under any liability to the opposite party for continuing to act without authority in cases where he originally possessed one'.[214]

An agency is terminated by an act of bankruptcy committed by the principal, if he is later adjudicated bankrupt upon a petition presented within three months after the commission of the act. In other words the adjudication relates back to the act of bankruptcy, provided that it is followed within three months by a successful petition. Despite this general rule, however, every act done or contract made by the agent before the receiving order is valid in favour of a third person dealing with him for value and without notice of an act of bankruptcy,[215] and is also valid in favour of the agent in the sense that he is freed from personal liability if, at the time of acting, he had no notice of an available act of bankruptcy.[216]

---

208 *Drew v Nunn* (1879) 4 QBD 661 at 668.

209 Powell *The Law of Agency* (2nd edn) pp 5–6 and 389–391. See Higgins 1 Tasmanian L Rev 569, where the distinction is examined in a most helpful article.

210 [1910] 1 KB 215. 211 P 634, above. 212 P 633, above.

213 RSC Ord 80, r 2(1); replacing Ord 16B, r 2(1).

214 *Yonge v Toynbee* [1910] 1 KB 215 at 233, per Swinfen Eady J. This reasoning did not impress Buckley LJ, ibid at 228–229.

215 Bankruptcy Act 1914, s 45. *Re Douglas, ex p Snowball* (1872) 7 Ch App 534.

216 *Elliott v Turquand* (1881) 7 App Cas 79.

16 THE VOLUNTARY ASSIGNMENT OF CONTRACTUAL RIGHTS AND LIABILITIES

SUMMARY

1 THE ASSIGNMENT OF CONTRACTUAL RIGHTS [1]

We now come to consider whether the right created by a contract can be expressly assigned by its owner to a third party. If A has sold goods of the value of £10 to B, can he assign to C the right to receive the £10? It is important to appreciate at the outset the significance of the word 'assignment'. What we have to ascertain is whether C, by virtue merely of the assignment, without the collaboration of the assignor and without

---

[1] See Bailey 47 LQR 516, 48 LQR 248 and 547. Ong Chin-Aun 18 J Contract L 107.

the consent of the debtor, can enforce payment of the debt to himself. In short, can an assignee bring an action on his own initiative against a recalcitrant debtor? Does an assignment bind the debtor as well as the assignor?

This topic is generally described as the assignment of choses in action.

'Chose in action' is a known legal expression used to describe all personal rights of property which can only be claimed or enforced by action, and not by taking physical possession.[2]

It is a term that comprises a large number of proprietary rights, such as debts, shares, negotiable instruments, rights under a trust, legacies, policies of insurance, bills of lading, patents, copyrights and rights of action arising out of tort or breach of contract. Many of these have been made assignable by statute, as, for instance, policies of life or marine insurance,[3] negotiable instruments,[4] copyrights,[5] bills of lading[6] and shares in companies.[7] Our concern, however, is to show that apart from such statutory provisions a chose in action is also assignable in equity. We shall deal principally with ordinary contractual rights.

A The assignability of contractual rights

At common law a chose in action, such as a right arising under a contract, could not be assigned so as to entitle the assignee to sue for its recovery in his own name. The assignment gave the assignee a right against the assignor personally, but not an independent right of action against the debtor. An action for recovery had to be brought by or in the name of the assignor, and this depended upon the willingness of the assignor to lend his name to the proceedings. The assignee could enforce payment by taking a power of attorney authorising him to sue on behalf of the assignor, but in this case he recovered the debt not as assignee, but as directly representing the person of the assignor.[8] The common law rule was subject to two exceptions, for from the earliest times it was recognised that the Crown might make or take an assignment of choses in action; and with the growth of the doctrine of negotiability rights under bills of exchange and promissory notes became freely assignable.[9]

The notion that a contractual right is incapable of transfer represents an archaic and inconvenient view, and it is therefore not remarkable that it was soon repudiated by

---

[2] *Torkington v Magee* [1902] 2 KB 427 at 430, per Channell J. A good modern discussion of the relevant principles can be found in *Pacific Brands Sport & Leisure Pty Ltd v Underworks Pty Ltd* [2006] FCAFC 40.

[3] Policies of Assurance Act 1867, s 1. Marine Insurance Act 1906, s 50(2).

[4] Bills of Exchange Act 1882; pp 661 ff, below.

[5] Copyright, Designs and Patents Act 1988, s 90(3). Assignment must be written.

[6] Bills of Lading Act 1855, s 1.

[7] Companies Act 1985, s 182. Assignment must be made in the manner prescribed by the articles of the particular company.

[8] *Master v Miller* (1791) 4 Term Rep 320 at 340.

[9] Holden *The History of Negotiable Instruments in English Law.*

equity. As early as the beginning of the seventeenth century the Court of Chancery recognised and enforced the assignment of choses in action generally.

> At common law such a debt was looked upon as a strictly personal obligation, and an assignment of it was regarded as a mere assignment of a right to bring an action at law against the debtor . . . But the Courts of Equity took a different view . . . They admitted the title of an assignee of a debt, regarding it as a piece of property, an asset capable of being dealt with like any other asset, and treating the necessity of an action at law to get it in as a mere incident.[10]

An equitable assignment could not of course transfer the right of action at law, but it conferred upon the assignee the right to invoke the aid of equity. Equity considers that as done which ought to be done, and, since the parties have agreed that the common law right under the contract is the property of the assignee, the assignor must allow an action at law to be brought in his own name so as to make the transaction effectual.

> An assignment . . . operates in equity by way of agreement, binding the conscience of the assignor, and so binding the property from the moment when the contract becomes capable of being performed.[11]

No particular form is required to constitute a valid equitable assignment. The transaction upon which the assignee relies need not even purport to be an assignment nor use the language of an assignment. If the intention of the assignor clearly is that the contractual right shall become the property of the assignee, then equity requires him to do all that is necessary to implement his intention. The only essential and the only difficulty is to ascertain that such is the intention. Lord MacNaghten, speaking of an equitable assignment, said:

> It may be addressed to the debtor. It may be couched in the language of command. It may be a courteous request. It may assume the form of mere permission. The language is immaterial if the meaning is plain.[12]

Where there is a contract between the owner of a chose in action and another person which shows a clear intention that such person is to have the benefit of the chose, there is without more a sufficient assignment in the eye of equity. It follows, therefore, that to perfect the title *as between assignor and assignee* no notice to the debtor is necessary.[13] The object of notice, as we shall see later, is to prevent the

---

[10] *Fitzroy v Cave* [1905] 2 KB 364 at 372, per Cozens-Hardy LJ.

[11] *Tailby v Official Receiver* (1888) 13 App Cas 523 at 546, per Lord MacNaghten. See Nash 32 Australian LJ 34.

[12] *Brandt's Sons & Co v Dunlop Rubber Co* [1905] AC 454 at 462. *Re Wale* [1956] 3 All ER 280 at 283, [1956] 1 WLR 1346 at 1350; *Letts v IRC* [1956] 3 All ER 588 at 592, [1957] 1 WLR 201 at 212–214. Cf *Hobbs v Marlowe* [1978] AC 16, [1977] 2 All ER 241. In principle, it would seem that the assignor need not inform the assignee of what he has done. The decisive factor is the assignor's intention, see *Comptroller of Stamps (Victoria) v Howard-Smith* (1936) 54 CLR 614 at 622.

[13] *Gorringe v Irwell India Rubber Works* (1886) 34 ChD 128.

debtor from paying the assignor, and also to give the assignee priority over other assignees.[14]

Our next inquiry is to ascertain the exact effect of an equitable assignment as regards the assignee's right of action against the debtor. Can an equitable assignee always sue the debtor by bringing an action in his own name? The answer to this question depends, first, upon the nature of the right assigned, ie whether it is a legal or an equitable chose in action; secondly, upon the nature of the assignment, ie whether it is absolute or non-absolute.

A legal chose in action is a right that can be enforced by an action at law, as, for example, a debt due under a contract. An equitable chose in action is a right that was enforceable before the Judicature Act 1873 only by a suit in equity. It is a right connected with some form of property, such as trust property, over which Chancery formerly had exclusive jurisdiction, and it is exemplified by a legacy or by an interest in a trust fund.

An absolute assignment is one by which the entire interest of the assignor in the chose in action is for the time being transferred unconditionally to the assignee and placed completely under his control. To be absolute it is not necessary, however, that the assignment should take the form of an out and out transfer which deprives the assignor for ever of all further interest in the subject matter. Thus, it is now well settled that a mortgage in the ordinary form, ie an assignment of a chose in action as security for advances, with a proviso for redemption and reassignment upon repayment of the loan, is an absolute assignment.[15] In such a case the whole right of the mortgagor in the subject matter passes for the time being to the mortgagee, and the fact that there is an express or implied right to reassignment upon redemption does not destroy the absolute character of the transfer. In *Hughes v Pump House Hotel Co*:[16]

> A building contractor executed a written instrument by which, in consideration of his bankers allowing him an overdraft, and by way of security to them for all money due or falling due in the future under his account, he assigned to them all moneys due or to become due to him under his building contracts. He also empowered the bankers to settle all accounts in connection with the buildings and to give receipts for money paid for work done by him.

It was held that the written instrument, since it unconditionally assigned for the time being all moneys due or to become due under the building contracts, constituted an absolute assignment.

From absolute assignments must be distinguished, firstly, conditional assignments; secondly, assignments by way of charge; and thirdly, assignments of part of a debt.

---

[14] P 653, below.
[15] *Tancred v Delagoa Bay and East Africa Rly Co* (1889) 23 QBD 239; *Hughes v Pump House Hotel Co* [1902] 2 KB 190.
[16] [1902] 2 KB 190.

A conditional assignment is one which is to become operative or to cease to be operative upon the happening of an uncertain event. An example of this occurred in *Durham Bros v Robertson*[17] where:

> A firm of builders executed the following document in favour of the plaintiffs: 'Re Building Contract, South Lambeth Road. In consideration of money advanced from time to time we hereby charge the sum of £1,080, which will become due to us from John Robertson on the completion of the above buildings, as security for the advances, and we hereby assign our interest in the above-mentioned sum *until the money with added interest be repaid to you.*'

It was held that this was merely a conditional assignment. At first sight, perhaps, it appears difficult to reconcile this decision with that given in *Hughes v Pump House Hotel Co*,[18] but if the position of the respective debtors is considered, the difference between the two cases becomes apparent. In the present case the whole sum due from Robertson was not assigned to the plaintiffs, but only so much of it as would suffice to repay the money actually advanced together with interest. The document stated in effect that when that amount was paid, which was an uncertain event, the interest of the assignee was automatically to cease. Thus the debtor, Robertson, became directly concerned with the state of accounts between the assignor and assignee, for he would not be justified under the document in making a payment to the latter after the money actually lent with interest had been repaid. In *Hughes v Pump House Hotel Co*, on the other hand, the debt was in terms transferred completely to the assignee. There was no limitation of the amount for which the assignment should be effective, there was to be no automatic reverter to the assignor upon repayment of the loan, and therefore the debtors, until they received notice of redemption and actual reassignment, would be entitled to make payments to the assignee without reference to the state of accounts between him and the assignor.

The distinction, then, is this: Where a reassignment is necessary, as it is in the case of an assignment by way of mortgage, 'notice of the reassignment will be given to the original debtor, and he will thus know with certainty in whom the legal right to sue him is vested. On the other hand, where the assignment is conditional, the original debtor is left uncertain as to the person to whom the legal right is transferred.'[19]

An assignment by way of charge is one which merely entitles the assignee to payment out of a particular fund and which, unlike the case of a mortgage, does not transfer the fund to him.[20] Thus in *Jones v Humphreys*:[21]

---

[17] [1898] 1 QB 765.   [18] [1902] 2 KB 190.

[19] Ashburner *Principles of Equity* (2nd edn) p 238.

[20] *Tancred v Delagoa Bay and East Africa Rly Co* (1889) 23 QBD 239 at 242, per Denman J; *Burlinson v Hall* (1884) 12 QBD 347 at 350.

[21] [1902] 1 KB 10. Where there is no intention to assign a debt to X, he may in certain circumstances be able to maintain an action for money had and received against the debtor; *Shamia v Joory* [1958] 1 QB 448, [1958] 1 All ER 111.

A schoolmaster assigned to a money-lender so much of his salary as should be necessary to repay a sum of £ which he had already borrowed and any further sums which he might borrow.

It was held that this was not an absolute assignment of the salary, but a mere security which entitled the money-lender to have recourse to the salary according to the state of the schoolmaster's indebtedness.

After considerable conflict of judicial opinion it is now settled that the assignment of a definite part of a debt is not an absolute assignment.[22] To be absolute an assignment must transfer the chose in action in its entirety.

Effect of equitable assignment
We are now in a position to state the effect of an equitable assignment upon the right of recovery vested in the assignee. The effect may be stated in three rules.

(a) Absolute assignment of equitable chose: assignee may sue in his own name An absolute assignment of an *equitable* chose in action entitles the assignee to bring an action in his own name against the debtor.[23] If, for instance, A assigns to B the whole of his beneficial interest in a legacy, B can sue the executor in his own name. The common law prohibition of assignments has, of course, never applied to a chose that was within the exclusive jurisdiction of equity, and since the absolute character of the transfer makes it unnecessary to examine the state of accounts between the parties, there is no reason why the assignor should be a party to the action.

(b) Non-absolute assignment of equitable chose: assignor must be party to an action The non-absolute assignment of an *equitable* chose in action does not entitle the assignee to sue in his own name, but requires him to join the assignor as a party. This joinder of the assignor is necessary on practical grounds, for in every case where an assignment is not absolute, as, for instance, where it is conditional or by way of charge, the state of accounts between the parties is the critical factor. The debtor occupies the position of a stakeholder who is willing to pay the person rightfully entitled, but as neither he nor the court knows what the exact rights of the parties are it is essential that the assignor should be a party to the action in order that his interest may be bound. Again, if an assignment affects part only of the assignor's interest, the court cannot adjudicate finally without the presence of both parties.

> The absence of such parties might result in the debtor being subjected to future actions in respect of the same debt, and moreover might result in conflicting decisions being arrived at concerning such debt.[24]

---

[22] *Re Steel Wing Co Ltd* [1921] 1 Ch 349; *Williams v Atlantic Assurance Co* [1933] 1 KB 81; *Walter and Sullivan Ltd v J Murphy & Sons Ltd* [1955] 2 QB 584, [1955] 1 All ER 843. The title to the part assigned, however, passes to the assignee in equity. Cf *Ramsey v Hartley* [1977] 2 All ER 673, [1977] 1 WLR 686.

[23] *Cator v Croydon Canal Co* (1843) 4 Y & C Ex 593 at 593–594.

[24] *Re Steel Wing Co* [1921] 1 Ch 349 at 357, per P O Lawrence J.

By the same reasoning the assignor cannot recover the amount remaining due to him from the debtor without joining the assignee as a party to the action.[25]

(c) Assignment of legal chose: assignor must be a party to an action An assignment, whether absolute or not, of a *legal* chose in action does not entitle the assignee to sue in his own name, but requires him to join the assignor as a party to any action he may bring for the recovery of the right assigned. The reason for this is due to the different views taken by common law and equity. A legal chose is one that would be recoverable only in a common law court, and since the rule at law was that a contractual right was incapable of assignment, it followed that the court could not allow an assignee to sue in his own name. The solution was for the assignor to sue personally or to join in the action brought by the assignee, and the Court of Chancery would compel him to collaborate in this fashion in order to complete the equitable title that he had transferred. This would necessitate the institution of a suit in Chancery as a preliminary to the common law action.[26] Such, however, is no longer the case, and the practice has long been for the assignee to join a contumacious assignor as co-defendant with the debtor.[27] The assignor cannot sue in his own name alone.[28]

These equitable rules with regard to the assignment of choses in action were adequate except in one respect. Where the assignment related to a legal chose in action the machinery of recovery was unnecessarily complicated, since the assignee might be compelled to initiate Chancery proceedings before he was qualified to sue at law. There is no reason in nature why the assignee of an ordinary debt should, as regards his right of recovery, be in any different position from the assignee of a purely equitable right such as a share in a trust fund; yet owing solely to a conflict between law and equity he was compelled in the former case to sue in collaboration with the assignor, while in the latter he could sue alone. This was an anachronism which called for abolition when the Judicature Act 1873 amalgamated the superior courts of law and equity into the Supreme Court of Judicature. The main purpose of this legislation 'was to enable a suitor to obtain by one proceeding in one court the same ultimate result as he would previously have obtained either by having selected the right court, as to which there frequently was a difficulty, or after having been to two courts in succession, which in some cases he had to do under the old system'.[29] In pursuance of this policy, section 25(6) of the Act introduced a statutory form of assignment which enabled the assignee of a legal chose in action to sue in his own name, subject to certain conditions. This provision has now been replaced by the Law of Property Act 1925,[30] in a section which runs as follows:

---

[25] *Walter and Sullivan Ltd v J Murphy & Sons Ltd* [1955] 2 QB 584, [1955] 1 All ER 843.
[26] *Wood v Griffith* (1818) 1 Swan 43 at 55–56, per Lord Eldon.
[27] *Bowden's Patents Syndicate Ltd v Herbert Smith & Co* [1904] 2 Ch 86 at 91, per Warrington J.
[28] *Three Rivers District Council v Bank of England* [1995] 4 All ER 312.
[29] *Torkington v Magee* [1902] 2 KB 427 at 430, per Channell J.
[30] S 136.

Any absolute assignment by writing under the hand of the assignor (not purporting to be by way of charge only) of any debt or other legal thing in action, of which express notice in writing has been given to the debtor, trustee or other person from whom the assignor would have been entitled to claim such debt or thing in action, is effectual in law (subject to equities having priority over the right of the assignee) to pass and transfer from the date of such notice:

(a) the legal right to such debt or thing in action;

(b) all legal and other remedies for the same; and

(c) the power to give a good discharge for the same without the concurrence of the assignor.

The phrase in the statute 'debt or other legal thing in action' is misleading. It might be supposed that it bore the same meaning as before the Judicature Act 1873, and that it was confined to such *choses in action* as were recoverable only in a common law court. It has, however, been interpreted judicially to mean 'all rights the assignment of which a court of law or equity would before the Act have considered *lawful*', and it therefore includes equitable as well as legal *choses in action*.[31]

Essentials of statutory assignment
There are three conditions that must be satisfied if an assignment is to derive validity from the statute:

it must be absolute;
it must be written; and
written notice must be given to the debtor.

If there is a failure to comply with either of the last two conditions, or if compliance with the first is impossible, as, for instance, where the assignment is conditional or by way of charge, the transaction is not void. It is void as a statutory assignment but it still stands as a perfectly good equitable assignment. This means that the assignee of the legal chose in action cannot take advantage of the new machinery set up by the Act and bring an action in his own name, but must fall back upon the rules governing equitable assignments and join the assignor as a party. It is still the law that an assignee of a legal chose in action, who for some reason or other cannot prove a good statutory assignment, must make the assignor either a co-plaintiff or a co-defendant to any action that he brings.[32]

The statute has not altered the law in substance. It is merely machinery. It does not confer a right of action which did not exist before, but enables the right of action that

---

[31] *King v Victoria Insurance Co Ltd* [1896] AC 250 at 254; *Re Pain, Gustavson v Haviland* [1919] 1 Ch 38 at 44–45.

[32] *Performing Right Society Ltd v London Theatre of Varieties Ltd* [1924] AC 1 at 14, 20, 30–31.

has always existed to be pursued in a less roundabout fashion.[33] It 'has not made contracts assignable which were not assignable in equity before, but it has enabled assigns of assignable contracts to sue upon them in their own names without joining the assignor'.[34] Again it 'does not forbid or destroy equitable assignments or impair their efficacy in the slightest degree'.[35]

An assignment, whether of a legal or an equitable chose in action, which satisfies the requirements of the statute, transfers the title by virtue of the statute itself and requires no consideration.[36] A question, however, that has been much canvassed is whether a non-statutory, ie an equitable assignment, is effective as between assignor and assignee if made for no consideration.[37] Is a gift of the chose in action valid and irrevocable? The answer depends upon a distinction, fundamental throughout equity, between a completed and an incomplete assignment.

The equitable assignment of a chose, *if completed*, even though it is unsupported by consideration, is just as effective and just as irrevocable as the gift of personal chattels perfected by delivery of possession.[38] It is, indeed, almost superfluous to say that 'a person *sui juris*, acting freely, fairly and with sufficient knowledge, has it in his power to make, in a binding and effectual manner, a voluntary gift of any part of his property, whether capable or incapable of manual delivery, whether in possession or reversion'.[39]

On the other hand it is equally clear that a gratuitous agreement to assign a chose in action, like a gratuitous promise to give any form of property, is *nudum pactum* unless made under seal, and creates no obligation either legal or equitable.

> The rule in equity comes to this; that so long as a transaction rests in expression of intention only, and something remains to be done by the donor to give complete effect to his intention, it remains uncompleted, and a Court of Equity will not enforce what the donor is under no obligation to fulfil. But when the transaction is completed, and the donor has created a trust in favour of the object of his bounty, equity will interfere to enforce it.[40]

---

[33] *Re Westerton, Public Trustee v Gray* [1919] 2 Ch 104 at 112–113. In Australia it has been held that since the introduction of a statutory form of assignment, all assignments must follow the statutory form. Thus the statutory rules displace the equitable rules though an imperfect assignment may in some cases take effect as a contract to assign. *Olsson v Dyson* (1969) 120 CLR 365. This is not an illogical view but it clearly does not represent English law, which treats the statutory rules as supplementing and not supplanting those of equity.

[34] *Tolhurst v Associated Portland Cement Manufacturers (1900) Ltd* [1903] AC 414 at 424, per Lord Lindley.

[35] *Brandt's Sons & Co v Dunlop Rubber Co* [1905] AC 454 at 461, per Lord MacNaghten.

[36] *Re Westerton, Public Trustee v Gray* [1919] 2 Ch 104 at 112–113.

[37] Marshall *The Assignment of Choses in Action* ch 4; Megarry 59 LQR 58, 208; Holland 59 LQR 129; Hall [1959] CLJ 99.

[38] *Spellman v Spellman* [1961] 2 All ER 498 at 501, [1961] 1 WLR 921 at 925, per Danckwerts J; Diamond 24 MLR 789.

[39] *Kekewich v Manning* (1851) 1 De GM & G 176 at 188, per Knight Bruce LJ. *Re McArdle* [1951] Ch 669 at 674, [1951] 1 All ER 905 at 908.

[40] *Harding v Harding* (1886) 17 QBD 442 at 444, per Wills J.

Thus the question in each case is whether the transaction upon which the voluntary assignee relies constitutes a perfect and complete assignment or not, and this in turn depends upon the meaning of a completed assignment. The general principle of law is that a gift is complete as soon as everything has been done by the donor that, according to the nature of the subject matter, is necessary to pass a good title to the donee. A good title is vested in the donee if he has been placed in such a position that he is free to pursue the appropriate proprietary remedy on his own initiative, without the necessity of seeking the further collaboration of the donor. Whether the donee has been put in this position depends upon the nature of the *res donata*. If, for instance, A delivers a chattel to B with the intention of passing the ownership, he has done all that the law requires for the transfer of the property in the chattel, and it is clear that B has obtained a title which he can protect by an action of trover. But if the donative intention has not been fulfilled by delivery of the chattel or alternatively by the creation of a trust in favour of the donee, the gift remains incomplete and the intended donee is remediless. He cannot compel the donor to fulfil the promise to give. The promise is *nudum pactum* at common law for want of consideration, and it is a well-established principle of equity that the court will not perfect an imperfect gift—will not constrain a donor to take the requisite steps for the transfer of ownership.[41]

Applying these principles to the gift by way of equitable assignment of an existing *chose in action*, all that is necessary is to ascertain whether the donee is in a position to pursue the appropriate remedy against the debtor without the necessity of any further act on the part of the assignor. If so, the gift is complete and its efficacy remains undisturbed by the absence of consideration.[42] Whether the donee is in this position depends upon the nature of the equitable assignment.

An equitable assignment is one that does not satisfy the requirements of the Law of Property Act.[43] It may fail in this respect for two different reasons.

First, it may be defective in form because not made in writing.[44] Secondly, it may not be absolute.

To take the first defect, it is now clear that a mere failure to observe the statutory form is immaterial in the present context. it does not prevent the assignment from being perfect and complete in the eyes of equity. An absolute assignment of an existing *chose in action*, whether legal or equitable, is complete as soon as the assignor has finally and unequivocally indicated that it is henceforth to belong to the assignee. Nothing more is necessary.

---

[41] *Ellison v Ellison* (1802) 6 Ves 656. *Milroy v Lord* (1862) 4 De GF & J 264 at 274, per Turner LJ.

[42] *Re McArdle* [1951] Ch 669 at 677, [1951] 1 All ER 905 at 909–910.

[43] P 649, above.

[44] The statutory requirement of written notice to the debtor is irrelevant in the present context, for notice is not necessary to perfect the assignment between the assignor and assignee: *Holt v Heatherfield Trust Ltd* [1942] 2 KB 1 at 4–5, [1942] 1 All ER 404 at 407, though it is necessary for other reasons.

This has always been true of the equitable *chose in action*, since this was a species of property formerly within the exclusive jurisdiction of Chancery and therefore free from the restrictions of the common law. It was not, however, formerly true of the legal *chose in action*. This was recoverable only by an action at law and, since common law did not recognise the assignment of contractual rights, the assignee, though admitted by equity to have acquired a good title, was inevitably obliged to sue in the name of the assignor. To this extent, the collaboration of the assignor was necessary to perfect the transaction. But when the existing practice was admitted of allowing the assignee to satisfy the requirement of joinder of parties by merely adding the assignor as a defendant,[45] nothing remained to be done by the assignor to complete the transaction. At the present day, therefore, the absolute assignment of a legal or equitable *chose in action*, though not in the statutory form, is effective despite the want of consideration.[46]

The second class of equitable assignment is one which is not of an absolute character, though it may be in writing as required by the statute. In this case the assignment is not yet complete, for something still remains to be done to complete the title of the assignee. If it is conditional, as when its efficacy depends upon the consent of a third party, it remains incomplete until the condition is satisfied;[47] if it is by way of charge, as in *Jones v Humphreys*,[48] nothing definite is due until the state of accounts between the assignor and assignee has been finally settled and divulged to the debtor. Since the assignment is unsupported by consideration and since the assignee is not yet entitled to demand payment from the debtor, there is no escape from the rule that equity will not perfect an imperfect gift.

Another possible defect, distinct in nature, is that the assignment may relate to future property, such as a share of money that may fall in on the death intestate of a person now living, or the damages that may be recovered in a pending action. In

[45] *E M Bowden's Patents Syndicate Ltd v Herbert Smith & Co* [1904] 2 Ch 86 at 91.

[46] *Harding v Harding* (1886) 17 QBD 442; *Re Patrick, Bills v Tatham* [1891] 1 Ch 82; *Re Griffin, Griffin v Griffin* [1899] 1 Ch 408; *Holt v Heatherfield Trust Ltd* [1942] 2 KB 1, [1942] 1 All ER 404; *Re McArdle* [1951] Ch 669, [1951] 1 All ER 905. The dictum of Parker J in *Glegg v Bromley* [1912] 3 KB 474 at 491, that: 'If there be no consideration there can be no equitable assignment', must be confined to the assignment of a *future* debt, with which alone the case was concerned, see per Lush LJ in *German v Yates* (1915) 32 TLR 52. *Re McArdle*, the facts of which have been given at p 83, above, is in one respect a difficult case. The so-called assignment was written and therefore it satisfied the statute as regards form. On the assumption, however, that the document was what it purported to be, ie an agreement to transfer a specific sum of £488 in consideration of the promisee carrying out certain future improvements, the Court of Appeal was apparently prepared to treat it as a valid equitable assignment of the £488 (at 677, 910, respectively). This seems a curious approach to what would have been a normal and valid contract. Why should the promisee do more than sue for breach? If the document had in terms assigned the £488 in consideration of improvements already executed, it would indeed have been necessary to plead an assignment, for the past nature of the consideration would have prevented any claim in contract. But it would have been a statutory assignment.

[47] *Re Fry, Chase National Executors and Trustees Corpn v Fry* [1946] Ch 312, [1946] 2 All ER 106.

[48] P 646, above.

such a case what purports to be an assignment is nothing more than an agreement to assign, under which even in equity nothing is capable of passing until the subject matter comes into present existence. The agreement binds the conscience of the assignor, and, if supported by consideration, it binds the subject matter when it comes into existence.[49] Until this event occurs, however, the agreement cannot be converted into a completed assignment, for there is nothing definite capable of forming the subject matter of a transfer.[50] It followed, therefore, that the donee of a future chose in action is remediless. He cannot allege a completed assignment, and he cannot enforce a gratuitous promise.

B Rules that govern assignments, whether statutory or equitable

1 Notice

Written notice to the debtor or other person from whom the right assigned is due is necessary to complete the title of one who claims to be a statutory assignee under the Law of Property Act. It becomes effective at the date on which it is received by or on behalf of the debtor.[51] The written notice is an essential part of the statutory transfer of the title to the debt and therefore it is ineffective unless strictly accurate—accurate, for instance, as regards the date of the assignment and *semble* as regards the amount due from the debtor.[52]

On the other hand, notice is not necessary to perfect an equitable assignment. Even without notice to the debtor the title of the assignee is complete, not only against the assignor personally,[53] but also against persons who stand in the same position as the assignor, as, for instance, his trustee in bankruptcy, a judgment creditor or a person claiming under a later assignment made without consideration.[54]

Nevertheless, there are at least two reasons why failure to give notice may seriously prejudice the title of an equitable assignee.

Firstly, an assignee is bound by any payments which the debtor may make to the assignor in ignorance of the assignment.[55]

Secondly, it is established by the rule in *Dearle v Hall*[56] that an assignee must give notice to the debtor in order to secure his title against other assignees. An assignee

---

[49] *Re Trytel, ex p the Trustee of the Property of the Bankrupt v Performing Rights Society Ltd and Soundtrac Film Co Ltd* [1952] 2 TLR 32.

[50] *Tailby v Official Receiver* (1888) 13 App Cas 523 at 546, per Lord MacNaghten; *Glegg v Bromley* [1912] 3 KB 474 at 489.

[51] *Holt v Heatherfield Trust Ltd* [1942] 2 KB 1 at 5–6, [1942] 1 All ER 404 at 407–408.

[52] *W F Harrison & Co Ltd v Burke* [1956] 2 All ER 169, [1956] 1 WLR 419.

[53] *Gorringe v Irwell India Rubber Works* (1886) 34 ChD 128.

[54] *Re Trytel, ex p the Trustee of the Property of the Bankrupt v Performing Right Society Ltd and Soundtrac Film Co Ltd* [1952] 2 TLR 32. See Kloss 39 Conv (NS) 261.

[55] *Stocks v Dobson* (1853) 4 De GM & G 11. See also *Warner Bros Records Inc v Rollgreen Ltd* [1976] QB 430, [1975] 2 All ER 105.

[56] (1828) 3 Russ 1.

who, at the time when he completes the transaction, has no notice of an earlier assignment and who himself gives notice of the transaction to the debtor, gains priority over an earlier assignee who has failed to give a like notice. The fact that he has discovered the existence of the prior assignment at the time when he gives notice is immaterial, provided that he had no actual or constructive knowledge of it when his own assignment was completed.[57]

The form of the notice depends upon the nature of the right assigned. If what is assigned is an equitable interest in land or in personalty then notice is required by statute to be in writing,[58] but in other cases no formality is required. The one essential in all cases is that the notice should be clear and unambiguous. It must expressly or implicitly record the fact of assignment, and must plainly indicate to the debtor that by virtue of the assignment the assignee is entitled to receive the money.[59] If it merely indicates that on grounds of convenience payment should be made to a third party as agent of the creditor, the debtor is not liable if he pays the creditor direct.[60]

2 An assignee takes subject to equities

An assignee, whether statutory or not, takes subject to all equities that have matured at the time of notice to the debtor. This means that the debtor may plead against the assignee all defences that he could have pleaded against the assignor at the time when he received notice of the assignment.

> The authorities upon this subject, as to liabilities, show that if a man does take an assignment of a chose in action he must take his chance as to the exact position in which the party giving it stands.[61]

A simple illustration is afforded by *Roxburghe v Cox*:[62]

> Lord Charles Ker, an army officer, assigned to the Duke of Roxburghe the money that would accrue to him from the sale of his commission. This money, amounting to £3,000, was paid on 6 December to the credit of his account with his bankers, Messrs Cox. On that date his account was overdrawn to the extent of £647. On 19 December the Duke gave notice of the assignment to Messrs Cox.

It was held that Messrs Cox could set-off the debt of £647 against the right of the Duke to the sum of £3,000. In the course of his judgment, James LJ said:

> Now an assignment of a chose in action takes subject to all rights of set-off and other defences which were available against the assignor, subject only to this exception, that after notice of an assignment of a chose in action the debtor cannot by payment or otherwise do anything to

---

[57] *Mutual Life Assurance Society v Langley* (1886) 32 ChD 460.

[58] Law of Property Act 1925, s 137(3). See *Van Lynn Developments Ltd v Pelias Construction Co Ltd* [1969] 1 QB 607, [1968] 3 All ER 823.

[59] *James Talcott Ltd v John Lewis & Co Ltd and North American Dress Co Ltd* [1940] 3 All ER 592.

[60] Ibid at 596.

[61] *Mangles v Dixon* (1852) 3 HL Cas 702 at 735, per Lord St Leonards.

[62] (1881) 17 ChD 520.

take away or diminish the rights of the assignee as they stood at the time of the notice. That is the sole exception. Therefore the question is, Was this right of set-off existing at the time when the notice was given by the Duke of Roxburghe? Under the old law the proper course for the Duke to take would have been, not to come into a Court of Equity, but to use the name of Lord Charles Ker at law . . . In that case set-off could have been pleaded as against the assignor, and in the present mode of procedure that defence is equally available.[63]

Even unliquidated damages may by way of counterclaim be set-off by the debtor against the assignee, provided that they flow out of and are inseparably connected with the contract which has created the subject matter of the assignment.[64] Thus if a builder assigns to the plaintiff money that will be due from the defendant upon completion of a building, the defendant may set-off against the claim of the plaintiff any damage caused to him by the delay or by the defective work of the builder.[65] But nothing in the nature of a personal claim against the assignor can be used to defeat the assignee.[66]

The question was recently considered by Templeman J in *Business Computers Ltd v Anglo-African Leasing Ltd*[67] who said:

> The result of the relevant authorities is that a debt which accrues due before notice of an assignment is received, whether or not it is payable before that date, or a debt which arises out of the same contract as that which gives rise to the assigned debt, or is closely connected with that contract, may be set off against the assignee. But a debt which is neither accrued nor connected may not be set off even though it arises from a contract made before the assignment.[68]

In *Pan Ocean Shipping Ltd v Creditcorp Ltd, The Trident Beauty,*[69] the appellants were time-charterers under a time charterparty which provided for the hire to be payable 15 days in advance. The charterparty had the usual hire clauses which meant that the hire was repayable where the ship was, for various reasons, not available for the charterers' use. Under the charterparty there was a contractual scheme by which such repayable sums would normally be deducted from the next due payment.

The owners had irrevocably assigned the right to receive advance payments of hire to the respondents. Notice of this assignment had been given to the time-charterers and the time-charterers had made the payment of hire direct to the respondents. The time-charterers now claimed that they were entitled to recover these sums from the respondents. All the judges who considered the case agreed that the advance hire could have been recovered by the charterers from the owners. There is an important explanation in the House of Lords by Lord Goff as to why this right of recovery is contractual rather than restitutionary in the circumstances of the case.[70] The

---

[63] Ibid at 526.
[64] *Newfoundland Government v Newfoundland Rly Co* (1888) 13 App Cas 199 at 213.
[65] *Young v Kitchin* (1878) 3 Ex D 127.   [66] *Stoddart v Union Trust Ltd* [1912] 1 KB 181.
[67] [1977] 2 All ER 741.   [68] Ibid at 748.   [69] [1994] 1 All ER 470, [1994] 1 WLR 161.
[70] Ibid at 475 and 166, respectively.

charterers had not, however, claimed recovery from the owners, apparently because the owners were not worth suing. They claimed recovery from the respondents. The House of Lords agreed with the Court of Appeal that there was no right to recover in the circumstances. The debt which the owners had assigned to the respondents in the present case was payable at the time when it was paid. The assignment did not impose on the respondents any contingent duty to repay the money and there was no reason why the charterers should have a right to recover from two people because the owners had chosen, as part of their own financial arrangements, to assign the sum to the respondents.

3 Rights incapable of assignment

The rights that are incapable of assignment include pensions and salaries payable out of national funds to public officers, and alimony granted to a wife, but the most important examples are a bare right of litigation and rights under contracts that involve personal skill or confidence.

It used to be said that any assignment is void if it savours of maintenance, ie if it amounts to assistance given to one of the parties to an action by a person who has no legitimate interest in that action. This was the stated basis of the rule that a 'bare right of action' is unassignable.[71]

This rule involved the drawing of a somewhat arid distinction between a bare right of litigation and one which was attached to a property interest.[72] This difficulty has been removed by the decision of the House of Lords in *Trendtex Trading Corpn v Credit Suisse*[73] where it was held that the assignment was valid if the assigner had a genuine commercial interest in taking the assignment. For this purpose the court should look at the totality of the transaction.[74]

It may be added that there is nothing objectionable in the assignment of the fruits of litigation, which for this purpose are on all fours with other forms of property. In *Glegg v Bromley*[75] for instance, a wife mortgaged to her husband whatever damages she might recover in her pending action against X. This was an assignment of future property under which nothing would pass to the husband unless and until the property came into existence upon the successful conclusion of the action. Therefore, no question of maintenance could ever arise.

---

[71] Marshall *The Assignment of Choses in Action* pp 49–65.

[72] *Prosser v Edmonds* (1835) 1 Y & C Ex 481; *Defries v Milne* [1913] 1 Ch 98.

[73] [1982] AC 679, [1981] 3 All ER 520.

[74] For further discussion of maintenance and champerty see above, pp 482 ff. And see the further consideration of the question in *Brownton Ltd v Edward Moore Inbucon Ltd* [1985] 3 All ER 499 and *Camdex International Ltd v Bank of Zambia* [1996] 3 All ER 431. In *Norglen Ltd (in liquidation) v Reeds Rains Prudential Ltd* [1998] 1 All ER 218, a company assigned a cause of action to an individual in circumstances where the individual would be eligible for legal aid when the company would not and where the company might have been required to give security for costs when the individual would not. This motivation was held by the House of Lords not to make the assignment contrary to public policy.

[75] [1912] 3 KB 474.

If A purports to assign the benefit of a contract which he has made with B, it is essential to consider whether the position of B, the person liable, will be prejudicially affected. No man can be compelled to perform something different from that which he stipulated for, and any assignment that will put him in this position is void.[76] If, for instance, the contract between A and B involves personal skill or confidence, each party can insist upon personal performance by the other, for otherwise he would not receive that to which he is entitled. Thus an agreement by an author to write a book for a publisher is a personal contract, the benefit of which cannot be assigned by the publisher without the consent of the author.[77] In fact, the rule would seem to be that assignment 'is confined to those cases where it can make no difference to the person on whom the obligation lies to which of two persons he is to discharge it'.[78] In *Kemp v Baerselman*[79] for instance:

> The defendant, a provision merchant, agreed to supply the plaintiff, a cake manufacturer, with all the eggs that he should require for manufacturing purposes for one year, there being a stipulation that if supplies were maintained the plaintiff would not buy eggs elsewhere. At the time of the contract the plaintiff had three places of business, but four months later he transferred his business to the National Bakery Company, to which he purported to assign the benefit of his contract with the defendant.

It was held that the contract was intended to be a personal one, and that it could not be assigned against the will of the defendant. The eggs were to be supplied as the plaintiff, whose needs throughout the year could be estimated at the time of the contract, should require; and again, the plaintiff was not to purchase eggs elsewhere. This last provision would cease to benefit the defendant, and would, indeed, become meaningless, if the contract were assigned to another person.[80]

What is the position if the contract sought to be assigned itself prohibits assignment? Such prohibitions are common, for example, in contracts of hire purchase and in building and engineering contracts.[81] Much must depend on the precise wording of

---

[76] *Tolhurst v Associated Portland Cement Manufacturers (1900) Ltd* [1902] 2 KB 660 at 670.

[77] *Stevens v Benning* (1854) 1 K & J 168; affd 6 De GM & G 223; *Reade v Bentley* (1857) 3 K & J 271; *Griffiths v Tower Publishing Co* [1897] 1 Ch 21.

[78] *Tolhurst v Associated Portland Cement Manufacturers (1900) Ltd* [1902] 2 KB 660 at 668, per Collins MR.

[79] [1906] 2 KB 604.

[80] *Tolhurst v Associated Portland Cement Manufacturers (1900) Ltd* [1900] KB 660, which at first sight seems difficult to reconcile with the general rule, was decided on the ground that the terms of the contract, when properly construed, provided for assignment; see *Nokes v Doncaster Amalgamated Collieries Ltd* [1940] AC 1014 at 1020, [1940] 3 All ER 549 at 552, per Lord Simon.

[81] See Guest *The Law of Hire Purchase* para 700; Atiyah 5 Business L Rev 24; *Re Turcan* (1888) 40 ChD 5; *United Dominions Trust v Parkway Motors Ltd* [1955] 2 All ER 557, [1955] 1 WLR 719; *Spellman v Spellman* [1961] 2 All ER 498, [1961] 1 WLR 921; Diamond 24 MLR 789; *Wickham Holdings Ltd v Brooke House Motors Ltd* [1967] 1 All ER 117, [1967] 1 WLR 295; Diamond 30 MLR 322.

the prohibition but it is thought that only very clear words will make the assignment ineffective between assignor and assignee. There is clear authority, however, that such a prohibition renders an assignment ineffective against the debtor.[82]

In *Linden Gardens Trust Ltd v Lenesta Sludge Disposals Ltd*[83] the plaintiffs were leaseholders of premises in Jermyn Street, London. They had acquired their leasehold interests by assignment. Before the assignment, the assignors made a contract with the defendants for the carrying out of alteration work on the JCT 63 Form which contains a clause providing that 'The Employer shall not without the written consent of the contractor assign this contract'. The first defendants were nominated sub-contractors for the removal of blue asbestos who had entered into a collateral contract with the plaintiffs. The third defendants were contractors whose scope of works also included the removal of blue asbestos. The plaintiffs wished to complain of the work done by the defendants for the removal of blue asbestos. In this case all the building work had been completed before the assignment of the lease to the plaintiffs. (In fact the assignment took place in stages as different floors of the building were transferred at different times.) Apparently completion took place in March 1980: the first discovery of significant remaining quantities of blue asbestos was in January 1985 when an agreement for remedial work with the third defendants was made. The first assignment of part of the building took place on 1 April 1985 and the original lessees issued a writ against the first defendants in July 1985. In January 1987 and 1988 further blue asbestos was found in the premises.

In this case there had not only been an assignment of the lease but an assignment of the original lessee's causes of action against the contractors or sub-contractors.

The Court of Appeal held that the clause in the JCT contracts prohibited the assignment of the benefit of the contract but did not prohibit the assigning of benefits arising under the contract. Accordingly, the contractual clause did not interfere with the general law about the assignment of rights of action. It was clear that all the relevant breaches of contract had taken place at a time when the assignor was the owner of the property. It was therefore perfectly permissible for the assignor to assign the rights of action which had accrued during his period as lessee to the new lessee when the lease was assigned. It did not matter that the assignor no longer had a proprietary interest in the property at the time when he made the assignment nor that at that time nobody knew the full extent of the claim.

The House of Lords rejected the reasoning of the majority of the Court of Appeal. Lord Browne-Wilkinson, delivering the only speech on this point said:[84]

---

[82] *Helstan Securities Ltd v Hertfordshire County Council* [1978] 3 All ER 262; Goode 42 MLR 553; Munday [1979] CLJ 50 Kloss 43 Conv (NS) 133.

[83] [1994] 1 AC 85, [1993] 3 All ER 417, Furmston, 23 University of Western Australia Law Review, 251.

[84] Ibid at 105 and 429, respectively.

I accept that it is at least hypothetically possible that there might be a case in which the contractual prohibitory term is so expressed as to render invalid the assignment of rights to future performance but not so as to render invalid assignments of the fruits of performance . . . In the context of a complicated building contract, I find it impossible to construe cl 17 as prohibiting only the assignment of rights to future performance, leaving each party free to assign the fruits of the contract. The reason for including the contractual prohibition viewed from the contractor's point of view must be that the contractor wishes to ensure that he deals, and deals only, with the particular employer with whom he has chosen to enter into a contract. Building contracts are pregnant with disputes: some employers are much more reasonable than others in dealing with such disputes.

The House of Lords also considered and rejected an argument, which has not been addressed to the lower courts, that it was contrary to policy to allow prohibitions or restraints on the ability to assign contractual rights. The argument drawn from analogy with real property rights was that the right of ownership was so important that it should not be tethered by restraints on the ability to transfer ownership. It was held that the relationship between the contracting parties was such that not only may each party legitimately insist on the personal performance of the other party, but each party may legitimately wish to be obliged to perform its duties only to the other party. Construction contracts are a good example of the practical application of this policy since, in many construction contracts, there will be claims on both sides. So a contractor's claim for payment may be qualified by an employer's claim in respect of defective work or late completion. An employer may wish to restrict the contractor from assigning the right to be paid because of a wish to dispose in a single proceeding of the contractor's claims and its own claims. Conversely, the contractor may wish to restrict the employer from assigning because the operation of the contract in practice depends heavily on the behaviour of the parties and some employers are easier to co-operate with than others.

In *Don King Promotions Inc v Warren*[85] a contract was made between the plaintiff company, which was the corporate vehicle of a leading American boxing promoter and the defendant who was a leading English promoter. The purpose of the contract was to create a partnership for the promotion and management of boxing in Europe. In pursuance of the contract, Warren purported to assign to the partnership all his existing promotion and management contracts with boxers. These assignments were ineffective as assignments because many of the contracts contained prohibitions on assignment and in any case the relationship between a boxer and his manager is of a personal nature not permitting of assignment. Nevertheless, the Court of Appeal held that the ineffective assignments should be treated as declarations of trust because it

---

[85] [1999] 2 All ER 218. See also *Foamcrete (UK) Ltd v Thrust Engineering Ltd*, Court of Appeal 21/12/2000 (2001) 6 Finance & Credit Law 1.

was clear that the intention of the contract was that the management contracts should be held for the benefit of the partnership and treating the partners as trustees was the effective way to produce this result.

C Novation distinguished from assignment

The assignment of a debt as described in the preceding pages, which operates as an effective transfer without the consent or the collaboration of the debtor, is distinguishable from novation, a transaction to which the debtor must be a party.

Novation is a transaction by which, with the consent of all the parties concerned, a new contract is substituted for one that has already been made. The new contract may be between the original parties, eg where a written agreement is later incorporated in a deed; or between different parties, eg where a new person is substituted for the original debtor or creditor.[86] It is this last form, the substitution of one creditor for another, that concerns us at the moment. The effectiveness of such a substitution was concisely illustrated by Buller J.

> Suppose A owes B £100, and B owes C £100, and the three meet, and it is agreed between them that A shall pay C the £100; B's debt is extinguished, and C may recover the sum against A.[87]
>
> In this case a contract is made between A, B and C, by which the original liability of A to B is discharged in consideration of his promise to perform the same obligation in favour of C, the other party to the new contract. A transaction of this nature, however, is not effective as a novation unless an intention is clearly shown that the debt due from A to B is to be extinguished. Otherwise the novation fails for want of consideration.[88]

Thus novation, unlike assignment, does not involve the transfer of any property at all, for it comprises, (a) the annulment of one debt and then (b) the creation of a substituted debt in its place.[89]

In modern practice it is not unusual to plan the contractual arrangements on the basis that a novation will take place. So an employer who plans to engage a contractor on a Design and Build contract, under which the design of the building is to be the responsibility of the contractor, might himself engage an architect to design the building on the understanding that there would be a novation under which the architect would be transferred to the contractor. The main attraction of this would be that it would usually save time because engaging the architect is quicker than engaging the contractor.

---

[86] *Scarf v Jardine* (1882) 7 App Cas 345 at 351, per Lord Selborne.
[87] *Tatlock v Harris* (1789) 3 Term Rep 174 at 180.
[88] *Liversidge v Broadbent* (1859) 4 H & N 603.
[89] *Re United Railways of Havana and Regla Warehouses Ltd* [1960] Ch 52 at 84, 86; affd [1961] AC 1007, [1960] 2 All ER 332, HL.

D Negotiability distinguished from assignability

A negotiable instrument is like cash in the sense that the property in it is acquired by one who takes it *bona fide* and for value. Just as the true owner cannot recover stolen money once it has been honestly taken by a tradesman in return for goods, so also the *bona fide* holder for value obtains a good title to a negotiable instrument even though the title of the previous holder is defective. This is one of the cases in which the maxim *nemo dat quod non habet* has no application. One who delivers either cash or a negotiable instrument can pass a better title than he himself possesses. The law on negotiability has passed through three historical stages. It began as a body of custom among merchants; it was later incorporated by the courts into the common law; it was then consolidated by the Bills of Exchange Act 1882.

For an instrument to be negotiable, two things must concur:

(1) it must be one which is transferable by delivery by virtue either of statute or of the law merchant.

(2) it must be in such a state that nothing more than its delivery is required to transfer the right which it contains to a transferee.

We may illustrate these attributes from the case of a cheque. According to the usage of bankers as recognised by the courts, it has long been established that the mere delivery of a cheque is capable of transferring to the deliveree the right to demand the amount for which it is drawn. Whether delivery, without more, will transfer this right depends, however, upon the state of the cheque. If a cheque for £100 is made payable to 'Edward Coke *or bearer*' it is negotiable in the fullest sense of the term, for by its very terms its mere delivery to William Blackstone entitles the latter to demand £100 from the bank. The position, however, is different if the cheque is made payable to 'Edward Coke *or order*'. The words 'Edward Coke *or order*' means that the bank will pay any person to whom Coke, by a declaration of his intention on the back of the instrument, orders payment to be made. Before this intention has been declared, however, the cheque is not a negotiable instrument, for delivery alone does not entitle the deliveree to demand payment. An order, called an *endorsement*, must be added by the payee Coke. If he merely signs his own name on the back, he is said to endorse the cheque *in blank*, and the result is that the bank will pay any person who tenders the instrument and demands payment. In other words, the effect of an endorsement in blank is to render the cheque payable to bearer and thus to confer upon the holder for the time being a good title.[90] Coke, however, may *specially endorse* the cheque, ie in addition to signing his own name he may write on the back 'Thomas Littleton *or order*'. The effect of this is that the bank will pay Littleton or any person designated

---

[90] S 2 of the Cheques Act 1957, however, has now removed the necessity for an endorsement in blank where a cheque payable to order is cashed at the payee's own bank or credited to his account there.

by him, so that if he merely signs his own name the cheque once more becomes negotiable. The law has been summed up by Blackburn J in the following words:[91]

> It may therefore be laid down as a safe rule that where an instrument is by the custom of trade transferable, like cash, by delivery, and is also capable of being sued upon by the person holding in *pro tempore*, then it is entitled to the name of a negotiable instrument . . . The person who, by a genuine indorsement, or, where it is payable to bearer, by a delivery, becomes a holder, may sue in his own name on the contract, and if he is a *bona fide* holder for value, he has a good title notwithstanding any defect of title in the party (whether indorser or deliverer) from whom he took it.

In modern practice, most cheques are not negotiable since they usually bear crossings and such words as 'not negotiable' and 'account payee only'. Such cheques can still be transferred but they are not negotiable because the transferee will get no greater rights than the transferor had.[92]

An instrument does not possess the benefit of negotiability merely because it contains an undertaking by one of the parties to pay a definite sum of money to any holder for the time being. To rank as negotiable it must be recognised as such either by statute or by the law merchant. Cheques, bills of exchange and promissory notes are now negotiable by virtue of the Bills of Exchange Act 1882, but there are certain other instruments which still derive their negotiability from the law merchant. This part of the law is of comparatively recent origin.

> It is neither more nor less than the usages of merchants and traders in the different departments of trade, ratified by the decisions of courts of law, which, upon such usages being proved before them, have adopted them as settled law with a view to the interests of trade and the public convenience; the court proceeding herein on the well-known principle of law that, with reference to transactions in the different departments of trade, courts of law, in giving effect to the contracts and dealings of the parties, will assume that the latter have dealt with one another on the footing of any custom or usage prevailing generally in the particular department. By this process, what before was usage only, unsanctioned by legal decision, has become engrafted upon, or incorporated into, the common law, and may thus be said to form part of it.[93]

A custom of the mercantile world by which a certain document is treated as negotiable, if proved to be of a sufficiently general nature, may be adopted by the courts, and it is by this process that the list of negotiable instruments has gradually been increased. In determining whether a custom has become so well established as to be recognisable by the courts, the length of time for which it has prevailed is of great importance; but in the modern world a still more important factor is the number of transactions of

---

[91] *Crouch v Credit Foncier of England* (1873) LR 8 QB 374 at 381–382, adopting a passage in *Smith's Leading Cases* (13th edn) pp 533–534.

[92] *Universal Guarantee Pty Ltd v National Bank of Australasia Ltd* [1965] 2 All ER 98, [1965] 1 WLR 691.

[93] *Goodwin v Robarts* (1875) LR 10 Exch 337 at 346, per Cockburn CJ.

which it has formed the basis, and, if its adoption by merchants is frequent and widespread, the fact that it is of very recent origin does not prevent its judicial recognition.[94] Among the instruments which owe their negotiability to the usage of merchants are Exchequer Bills, certain bonds issued by foreign governments or by English or foreign companies, and debentures payable to bearer.

The transfer of a negotiable instrument differs from the assignment of a contractual right in three important respects.

First, since one of the characteristics of a negotiable instrument is that the person liable for payment, as for instance, the acceptor of a bill of exchange or the banker in the case of a cheque, is under a duty to pay the holder for the time being, it follows that upon a transfer of the instrument there is no necessity that he should be notified by the new holder of the change of ownership.

Secondly, unlike the assignee of a contractual right, the transferee of a negotiable instrument does not take subject to equities. A holder for value who takes an instrument without notice of any defect in the title of the person who negotiated it to him acquires a perfect title. Thus in *Miller v Race*:[95]

> On 11 December 1756, the mail coach from London to Chipping Norton was robbed and a bank note that had been posted by a London debtor to his creditor in the country was stolen. The next day the note was cashed by the plaintiff, who took it in the usual course of his business and without any notice that it had been stolen. It was held that the plaintiff was entitled to recover payment from the Bank of England.

Thirdly, the rule that consideration must move from the promisee, which as we have seen applies to contracts in general,[96] does not apply to a negotiable instrument, for the holder can sue for payment without proof that he himself gave value. The only essential is that consideration should have been given at some time in the history of the instrument. The Bills of Exchange Act provides that:

> Where value has *at any time* been given for a bill the holder is deemed to be a holder for value as regards the acceptor and all parties to the bill who became parties prior to such time, ie prior to the time at which value was given.[97]

If, for instance, A accepts what is called an *accommodation bill* in favour of B, ie makes himself liable to pay (say) £100 to B or to B's order without receiving consideration, he is not liable without more to pay this amount to B; but if B negotiates the bill to C in payment for goods received, C acquires a right of action against A and B; and further, if C makes a gift of the bill to D the latter has a similar right of action against A and B.

---

[94] *Edelstein v Schuler* [1902] 2 KB 144 at 154, per Bingham J.
[95] (1758) 1 Burr 452.   [96] Pp 101–104, above.   [97] S 27(2).

As regards consideration, there is another respect in which negotiable instruments are free from a general principle of contract law. The general rule requires proof by a plaintiff to an action for breach of contract that he has given consideration, but in the case of a negotiable instrument the consideration is presumed to have been given. The burden is on the defendant to prove that none has been given.[98]

Moreover, the holder is presumed to have taken the instrument in good faith and without notice of any illegality or other defect in the title of the person who negotiated it to him. There is this difference, however, between a plea of no consideration and a plea of illegality, that, once it has been shown that the instrument is vitiated by illegality as between previous parties, the burden of proving that he himself took in good faith passes to the holder.[99]

2 THE ASSIGNMENT OF CONTRACTUAL LIABILITIES[100]

The question that arises here is whether B can assign the obligation that rests upon him by virtue of his contract with A to a third person, C, so that the contractual liability is effectively transferred from him to C. Can he substitute somebody else for himself as obligor? English law has unhesitatingly answered this question in the negative. In the words of Collins MR:

> It is, I think, quite clear that neither at law nor in equity could the burden of a contract be shifted off the shoulders of a contractor on to those of another without the consent of the contractee. A debtor cannot relieve himself of his liability to his creditor by assigning the burden of the obligation to somebody else; this can only be brought about by the consent of all three, and involves the release of the original debtor.[101]

Novation, therefore, is the only method by which the original obligor can be effectively replaced by another. A, B and C must make a new contract by which in consideration of A releasing B from his obligation, C agrees that he will assume responsibility for its performance. This transaction is frequently required upon the retirement of one of the partners of a firm. B, the retiring partner, remains liable at law for partnership debts contracted while he was a member of the firm; but if a particular creditor, A, expressly agrees with him and with the remaining members to accept the sole liability of the latter for past debts in place of the liability of the firm as previously

---

98 *Mills v Barker* (1836) 1 M & W 425.
99 See pp 419–420, above, where the subject is illustrated by reference to wagering contracts.
100 Furmston 13 J Contract Law 42; Hunter 13 J Contract Law 51.
101 *Tolhurst v Associated Portland Cement Manufacturers (1900) Ltd* [1902] 2 KB 660 at 668.

constituted, the right of action against B is extinguished. As is said in the headnote to *Lyth v Ault and Wood*:[102]

> The acceptance by a creditor of the sole and separate liability of one of two or more joint debtors is a good consideration for an agreement to discharge all the other debtors from liability.

An agreement by a creditor, A, to accept the liability of C in substitution for that of his former debtor, B, need not be express. Acceptance may be inferred from his conduct. Whether this inference is justifiable depends, of course, upon the circumstances. Thus, if a trader knows that a certain partner has retired, but nevertheless continues to deal with the newly constituted firm, the inference, in the absence of further rebutting circumstances, is that he regards the existing partners as solely liable.[103]

Except by novation, then, it is impossible for a debtor, B, to make a contract with C, by which he extinguishes his existing obligation to A and assigns it to C. The assignment may well be binding between himself and C, but it cannot *per se* deprive A of his right to proceed against B as being the contracting party. On the other hand, there are many cases in which vicarious performance is permissible in the sense that the promisee, A, cannot object that the work has been done by a third person, provided always, of course, that it has been done in accordance with the terms of the contract.

> Much work is contracted for, which it is known can only be executed by means of sub-contracts; much is contracted for as to which it is indifferent to the party for whom it is to be done, whether it is done by the immediate party to the contract, or by someone on his behalf.[104]

If, for instance, B, who has contracted to deliver goods to A or to do work for A, arranges that C shall perform this obligation, then A is bound to accept C's act as complete performance, if in fact it fulfils all that B has agreed to do.[105] A cannot disregard the performance merely because it is not the act of B personally. *Qui facit per alium facit per se.*

The essential fact to appreciate, however, in this case of delegated performance is that the debtor, B, who has assigned his liability to C, is not relieved from his obligation to ensure due performance of his contract with A. B still remains liable to A, and C cannot be sued by A in contract for non-performance or for defective performance.[106] The legal effect of the delegation is that A cannot repudiate a

---

[102] (1852) 7 Exch 669.
[103] *Hart v Alexander* (1837) 2 M & W 484; *Bilborough v Holmes* (1876) 5 ChD 255.
[104] *British Waggon Co Ltd v Lea* (1880) 5 QBD 149 at 154, *per curiam*.
[105] *British Waggon Co Ltd v Lea* (1880) 5 QBD 149; *Tolhurst v Associated Portland Cement Manufacturers (1900) Ltd* [1903] AC 414 at 417, per Lord MacNaghten.
[106] *Schmaling v Thomlinson* (1815) 6 Taunt 147. In certain cases there might be a tortious action, for example, where C's negligence causes personal injury or property damage to A.

performance which satisfies the terms of the contract merely because it has not been completed by the original contracting party, B. In other words, the so-called assignment of an obligation is not an assignment in the true sense of the term, since it does not result in the substitution of one debtor for another. In the case of rights one creditor may be substituted for another, but the principle with regard to obligations is that they cannot be 'shifted off the shoulders of a contractor on to those of another without the consent of the contractee'.[107]

It is not, however, permissible in all cases to delegate the task of performance to another person. Each case depends upon its own particular circumstances. In the words of Lord Greene:

> Whether or not in any given contract performance can properly be carried out by the employment of a sub-contractor, must depend on the proper inference to be drawn from the contract itself, the subject matter of it and other material surrounding circumstances.[108]

For instance, a contract of carriage may normally be sub-contracted by the carrier, but this will not avail the contractor if the subject matter of the load is an easy and a frequent target for lorry thieves.[109]

Moreover, it is clear that delegation is not permissible if personal performance by B, the promisor, is the essence of the contract. If it can be proved that A relied upon performance by B and by B only, the inability or unwillingness of B to perform his obligation discharges A from all liability, even though performance has been completed by a third person in exact accordance with the agreed terms.[110] Vicarious performance of a personal contract is not performance in the eye of the law. It neither discharges the debtor nor binds the creditor. If it can be shown that A has contracted with B because he reposes confidence in him, as for example where he relies upon his individual skill, competency, judgement, taste or other personal qualification,[111] or if it is clear that he has some private reason for contracting with B and with B only,[112] then the inference is that the contract is one of a personal nature which does not admit of vicarious performance. Thus, it has been held that the personal skill and care of the warehouseman is of the essence of a contract for the storage of furniture, and that if he employs a sub-contractor he does so at his own risk.[113] A case which goes perhaps to the verge of the law is *Robson and Sharpe v Drummond*,[114] where the facts were these:

---

[107] *Tolhurst v Associated Portland Cement Manufacturers (1900) Ltd* [1902] 2 KB 660 at 668, per Collins MR.

[108] *Davies v Collins* [1945] 1 All ER 247 at 250.

[109] *Garnham, Harris and Elton Ltd v Alfred W Ellis (Transport) Ltd* [1967] 2 All ER 940, [1967] 1 WLR 940 (copper wire).

[110] *British Waggon Co Ltd v Lea* (1880) 5 QBD 149 at 153.

[111] *Robson and Sharpe v Drummond* (1831) 2 B & Ad 303.

[112] *Boulton v Jones* (1857) 2 H & N 564, p 258, above.

[113] *Edwards v Newland & Co (E Burchett Ltd Third Party)* [1950] 2 KB 534, [1950] 1 All ER 1072.

[114] (1831) 2 B & Ad 303.

B agreed to build a carriage and to hire it out to A for five years for a yearly payment of 75 guineas. B was to keep the carriage in repair, to paint it once within the five years and to supply new wheels when required. More than two years later B retired from business and he purported to assign to his successor, C, all his interest in the contract with A.

It was held that the contract was personal and that A was entitled to reject the performance offered by C. Although Parke J expressed his unhesitating opinion that A was entitled to the benefit of the judgment and taste of B himself throughout the five years, it might perhaps have been objected that, as the carriage had been designed and built by B to the satisfaction of A, the only detail which in any sense depended upon these personal qualifications was the painting. In a later case the Court of Appeal refused to apply the principle of this decision to a contract by which B had agreed to hire out railway wagons to A and to keep them in repair for seven years.[115]

In *Southway Group Ltd v Wolff*,[116]

In January 1989, Southway owned and occupied a property in North London (Hendon) which consisted of a warehouse and a small amount of adjoining land. In January 1989 it contracted to sell the property for £1.2 million to a company called Brandgrange Ltd. Brandgrange was a shell company wholly owned by Initiative Co-Partnership Ltd, a company itself owned as to 49 per cent by a Mr Ormonde, and as to 51 per cent by Initiative Developments Ltd, a company owned by Mr Obermeister and his wife. Mr Obermeister was an architect and Mr Ormonde was a property developer with particular expertise in devising and financing development schemes, obtaining property rights for development and obtaining planning permission for development. Under the contract of sale, completion was to be on 30 April 1990, or earlier on 27 days' written notice to Southway, such notice not to be given earlier than 5 December 1989. Notice, which was treated as being good, was given on 17 November 1989 to complete on 5 March 1990.

By a contract dated 21 December 1989, Brandgrange agreed to sell the property to the defendants who were mother and son and the trustees of the Wolff Charity Trust. This second contract contained an undertaking by the vendor to carry out re-development works to the property, the content and scope of these works being described in a specification attached to the contract which was skeletal in the extreme.

Brandgrange failed to complete on 5 March 1990 and on the same day Southway served notice to complete in accordance with clause 22 of the National Conditions

---

[115] *British Waggon Co Ltd v Lea* (1880) 5 QBD 149.
[116] [1991] 28 Con LR 109. *Pacific Brands Sport & Leisure Pty Ltd v Underworks Pty Ltd* [2006] FCAFC 40 is another example of a contract held on careful construction to call for personal performance and not to be assignable.

of Sale. On 21 March 1990 Southway and Brandgrange entered into a deed of assignment, by which the notice of 5 March 1990 was withdrawn and a new completion date of 17 April 1990 was fixed, time being expressed to be of the essence.

This deed of assignment contained provisions by which Brandgrange assigned to Southway the benefits of the re-sale contract to the Trustees and Southway gave notice of that assignment to the Trustees.

Brandgrange failed to complete on 17 April 1990. On 19 April 1990 Southway accepted this failure as repudiation and terminated the contract. Southway then decided that it would carry out itself or through its own contractors the works which had been set out in the contract of 21 December 1989 between Brandgrange and the Trustees. The Trustees indicated to Southway that, 'If you proceed without my approval, you do so at your own risk'. Southway therefore sought declarations that if it carried out work which complied with the specification within the time provided by the contract and tendered a valid transfer of the building, it would be entitled to the purchase price under the contract between Brandgrange and the Trustees. The Trustees argued that the essence of the re-sale contract was the confidence which the Trustees placed in particular in Mr Ormonde and that they were not bound to accept the performance of the refurbishment contract by any-one else. In other words, the Trustees argued that the contract was one which called for personal and not vicarious performance.

This argument was accepted by the Court of Appeal. The Court held that in the present circumstances, where the content of the contract was extremely vague (verging according to some members of the Court on the contract being void for uncertainty), it was clear that personal performance was essential. It was not that the Trustees expected Mr Ormonde to do the building work himself, but they expected that the development and refurbishment of the building would be done in a style which involved close and daily co-operation, and it was inconceivable that the Trustees would have entered into an agreement of this kind with someone with whom they did not have personal contact.

17 THE INVOLUNTARY ASSIGNMENT OF CONTRACTUAL RIGHTS AND LIABILITIES

The automatic assignment by operation of law of contractual rights and liabilities may occur upon the death or bankruptcy of one of the contracting parties.

The general rule of common law, that the maxim *actio personalis moritur cum persona* does not apply to an action for breach of contract, has been confirmed by statute. This provides that on the death of a contracting party 'all causes of action subsisting against or vested in him shall survive against or, as the case may be, for the benefit of, his estate'.[1] If the deceased made a contract with X, his personal representatives, whether executors or administrators, may recover damages for its breach, or may themselves perform what remains to be done and then recover the contract price.[2]

Conversely, they may be sued by X in their representative capacity for a breach of the contract, whether committed before or after the death of the deceased, though they are liable only to the extent of the assets in their hands.[3]

This rule that the right of action survives does not apply where personal considerations are the foundation of the contract. This is the position, for instance, where the contracting parties are master and servant,[4] or racehorse owner and jockey.[5] Thus, if a servant dies his executors are not faced with the alternative of performing the services or of paying damages; if the master dies, the servant is discharged of his obligation to serve.[6]

---

[1] Law Reform (Miscellaneous Provisions) Act, 1934, s 1(1). For discussion of the effect of death, see North 116 NLJ 1364.

[2] *Marshall v Broadhurst* (1831) 1 Cr & J 403.

[3] *Wentworth v Cock* (1839) 10 Ad & El 42; *Cooper v Jarman* (1866) LR 3 Eq 98; *Ahmed Angullia bin Hadjee Mohammed Salleh Angullia v Estate and Trust Agencies (1927) Ltd* [1938] AC 624, [1938] 3 All ER 106.

[4] *Farrow v Wilson* (1869) LR 4 CP 744.

[5] *Graves v Cohen* (1929) 46 TLR 121.   [6] *Farrow v Wilson*, above.

The object of bankruptcy proceedings is to collect all the property of the bankrupt and to divide it rateably among his creditors The rule, therefore, is that any right of action for breach of contract possessed by him which relates to his property and which, if enforced, will swell his assets, passes to his trustee in bankruptcy.[7] Instances are a contract by a third person to deliver goods or to pay money to the bankrupt. On the other hand, the right to sue for an injury to the character, feelings or reputation of a bankrupt, though arising from a breach of contract, does not vest in the trustee.[8]

> The right of action does not pass where the damages are to be estimated by immediate reference to pain felt by the bankrupt in respect to his body, mind or character, and without immediate reference to his rights of property.[9]

For instance, in *Wilson v United Counties Bank*,[10] a trader entrusted the financial side of his business to a bank during his absence on military duty in the European war of 1914. He was subsequently adjudicated bankrupt owing to the negligent manner in which this contractual duty was performed, and, in an action which he and the trustee brought against the bank, damages of £45,000 were awarded for the loss to his estate and of £7,500 for the injury to his credit and reputation. It was held that of these two sums the £7,500 belonged personally to the bankrupt as representing compensation for damage to his reputation, while the £45,000 went to the trustee for the benefit of the creditors.

If a bankrupt has made a contract for personal services, the question whether his right to sue for its breach remains with him or passes to his trustee depends upon the date of breach. If the breach occurs before the commencement of the bankruptcy, the right of action passes to the trustee; if it occurs after this date the right of action remains with the bankrupt, subject to the power of the trustee to intervene and to retain out of the sum covered what is not required for the maintenance of the bankrupt and his family. Thus the person entitled to recover damages against an employer for the wrongful dismissal of the bankrupt varies according as the dismissal occurs before or after the bankruptcy.[11]

---

[7] *Beckham v Drake* (1849) 2 HL Cas 579 at 627; *Jenning's Trustee v King* [1952] Ch 899, [1952] 2 All ER 608.

[8] *Rose v Buckett* [1901] 2 KB 449.

[9] *Beckham v Drake*, n 7, at 604, per Erle J.

[10] [1920] AC 102.

[11] *Drake v Beckham* (1843) 11 M & W 315 (before bankruptcy); *Bailey v Thurston & Co Ltd* [1903] 1 KB 137 (after bankruptcy).

18 PERFORMANCE AND BREACH[1]

SUMMARY

---

[1] Carter *Breach of Contract*; Birds, Bradgate and Villiers, *Termination of Contracts*.

1 INTRODUCTION

This chapter and the two succeeding chapters deal principally with the problem of discharge, that is, the ways in which the parties, or one of them, may be freed from their obligations. In previous editions of this work the subject matter of this chapter has been contained in two chapters entitled, respectively, 'Discharge by performance' and 'Discharge by breach'. It is easy to see that if one party completely and perfectly performs what he has promised to do, his obligations are at an end. However, important and difficult questions arise as to the effect of something less than perfect performance. From the viewpoint of the performer, this is a problem in performance but to the other party it will appear as a problem in breach, since usually[2] a less than perfect performance will be a breach. It seems more convenient, therefore, to consider the problems together, since to a considerable extent one is the mirror image of the other.

---

[2] See p 674, below.

2 THE ORDER OF PERFORMANCE

In a bilateral contract, where both parties have obligations to perform, questions may arise as to who is to perform first. This is primarily a question of construction of the contract, assisted by presumptions as to the normal rule for contracts of a particular kind. Often, it will not be a case of one party performing all his obligations first but rather of some obligations of one side having to be performed before related obligations of the other side. So in a contract of employment, the employer's obligation to pay wages will normally be dependent on the servant's having completed a period of employment but his obligation to provide a safe system of work will arise from the start of the employment.

It is often helpful to analyse this problem by using the language of conditions.[3] In a contract between A and B, we may discover at least three possibilities, viz: first, an undertaking by A is a condition precedent to an undertaking by B; secondly, undertakings by A and B may be concurrent conditions; or, finally, some undertakings by A and B may be independent. We may illustrate the first two possibilities by considering the obligations of buyer and seller as to delivery of the goods and payment of the price. Under the provisions of the Sale of Goods Act 1979, the obligations of the seller to deliver and of the buyer to pay the price are said to be prima facie concurrent,[4] but in many cases the contract varies this rule. In many commercial contracts, the seller agrees to grant the buyer normal trade terms, for example, payment within thirty days of delivery of invoice. It is clear that in such a case the seller must deliver first and cannot demand payment on delivery.[5] Conversely, in international sales, buyers often agree to pay by opening a banker's commercial credit, and here it is clear that the seller need take no steps until the buyer has arranged for the opening of a credit in conformity with the contract.[6] Where the buyer's and seller's obligations are concurrent, this means in practice that the ability of either party to complain of the other's non-performance depends on his own ability to show that he was ready, willing and able to perform.[7]

It is quite common for some of the obligations of the parties to be quite independent of performance of obligations by the other party. We have already mentioned the employer's duty to provide a safe system of work; an example on the other side would be the servant's duty of fidelity to the master.[8] In the case of such independent

---

[3] See pp 192 ff, above.   [4] S 28.

[5] This is a very important rule in practice where there have been a series of contracts and the buyer is late in paying in respect of an earlier delivery. See eg *Total Oil (Great Britain) Ltd v Thompson Garages (Biggin Hill) Ltd* [1971] 3 All ER 1226 discussed at pp 697 ff, below.

[6] See eg *W J Alan & Co Ltd v El Nasr Export and Import Co* [1972] 2 QB 189, [1972] 2 All ER 127.

[7] As to tendering performance, see p 705, below.

[8] *Hivac Ltd v Park Royal Scientific Instruments Ltd* [1946] Ch 169.

covenants, the covenantor cannot argue that his obligation is postponed until the covenantee has performed some other obligations.

3 EXCUSES FOR NON-PERFORMANCE

It was stated above[9] that usually failure to perform will amount to breach. This is true, but it is important to recognise that in certain circumstances failure to perform is excusable.

A Agreement

The parties may have made some agreement or arrangement after the contract was concluded, which permits one party not to perform or to perform in a different way. This will be examined in detail in the next chapter.

B Impossibility of performance and frustration

Sometimes events take place after the contract has been made, which make performance impossible or commercially sterile. In a limited number of cases, this may have the effect of bringing the contract to an end. This possibility is considered more fully in Chapter 20.

C Impossibility of performance falling short of discharging frustration

In some cases, unforeseeable events, although not bringing the contract to an end, may provide an excuse for non-performance. So in most modern contracts of employment, an employee who did not go to work because he had influenza would not be in breach of contract, although the illness would not be sufficiently serious to frustrate the contract.[10]

D Contractual excuses for non-performance

Outside the relatively narrow scope of the last two headings, the common law has been slow to infer that unforeseen developments should relieve a party from prompt and perfect performance. This attitude is commonly justified on the ground that the

---

[9] P 672, above.

[10] It should be noted that whether he would be in breach and whether he would be entitled to sick pay, are two distinct questions. See Stannard 46 MLR 738.

parties should make express provision themselves,[11] and this invitation is very often accepted. So, for instance, all the standard forms of building and engineering contract contain provisions which may entitle the contractor to extra time for performance where he has been delayed by such matters as exceptionally adverse weather conditions or labour disputes. The effectiveness of these clauses may involve consideration of the law as to exemption clauses though it is thought that many of them should be regarded as defining liability rather than excluding it.[12]

E Limitation

In principle, when one party has failed to perform on time, the other party can sue and at this moment the appropriate limitation period will begin to run. At the end of this period the action will normally no longer be maintainable. This matter is discussed more fully later.[13]

4 CAN A PARTY WHO DOES NOT PERFORM PERFECTLY CLAIM PAYMENT OR PERFORMANCE FROM THE OTHER PARTY?

There is no doubt that there are a number of cases where it has been stated that a party who does not perform perfectly is not so entitled. This is vividly illustrated by the old case of *Cutter v Powell*.[14]

> The defendant agreed to pay Cutter thirty guineas provided that he proceeded, continued and did his duty as second mate in a vessel sailing from Jamaica to Liverpool. The voyage began on 2 August and Cutter died on 20 September when the ship was nineteen days short of Liverpool.

An action by Cutter's widow to recover a proportion of the agreed sum failed, for by the terms of the contract the deceased was obliged to perform a given duty before he could demand payment.

In this case, of course, Mr Cutter did not break the contract by dying in mid-Atlantic[15] but his right to payment was held to depend on completion of the voyage and the same principle was held to apply in the case of breach in *Sumpter v Hedges*.[16]

---

[11] See p 721, below. [12] See pp 202 ff, above. [13] See pp 806–815, below.
[14] (1795) 6 Term Rep 320; see also *Sinclair v Bowles* (1829) 9 B & C 92; *Vigers v Cook* [1919] 2 KB 475; Stoljar 34 Can Bar Rev 288.
[15] In modern terms the contract was frustrated, see Ch 20, below.   [16] [1898] 1 QB 673.

In that case the plaintiff, who had agreed to erect upon the defendant's land two houses and stables for £565, did part of the work to the value of about £333 and then abandoned the contract. The defendant himself completed the buildings. It was held that the plaintiff could not recover the value of the work done.

A modern example of this principle is *Bolton v Mahadeva*.[17]

> The plaintiff contracted to install a central heating system in the defendant's house for the sum of £800. He installed the system but it only worked very ineffectively and the defendant refused to pay for it. The Court of Appeal held the plaintiff could recover nothing.

It will be seen that in each of these cases, the defendant made an uncovenanted profit, since he obtained part of what the plaintiff had promised to perform without having to pay anything. It is not surprising therefore that these results have been criticised nor that attempts have been made to mitigate or avoid them.[18]

A The doctrine of substantial performance

The courts, in their desire to do justice between contracting parties, have developed what is called the doctrine of substantial performance, which in effect has somewhat relaxed the requirement of exact and precise performance of entire contracts.[19] According to this doctrine, which dates back to Lord Mansfield's judgment in *Boone v Eyre* in 1779,[20] if there has been a substantial though not an exact and literal performance by the promisor, the promisee cannot treat himself as discharged. Despite a minute and trifling variation from the exact terms by which he is bound, the promisor is permitted to sue on the contract, though he is of course liable in damages for his partial non-performance. According to this doctrine, the question whether entire performance is a condition precedent to any payment is always a question of construction.[21] Thus in *Cutter v Powell*[22] the court construed the contract to mean that the sailor was to get nothing unless he served as mate during the whole voyage. Again, in a contract to erect buildings or to do work on another's land for a lump sum, the contractor can recover nothing if he abandons operations when only part of the work is completed, since his breach has gone to the root of the contract. But if, for example, the contractor has completed the erection of the buildings, there has been substantial performance and the other party cannot refuse all payment merely because the work is

[17] [1972] 2 All ER 1322, [1972] 1 WLR 1009.
[18] In 1983 the Law Commission proposed (Law Com No 121) legislation to change them but the dissenting report of Brian Davenport QC appears to have obtained wider support.
[19] See Williams 57 LQR 373, 490; Corbin 28 Yale LJ 739; Morison 28 LQR 398, 29 LQR 61; Ballantine 5 Minnesota L Rev 329.
[20] (1779) 1 Hy Bl 273, n.
[21] *Hoenig v Isaacs* [1952] 2 All ER 176.   [22] P 675, above.

not in exact accordance with the contract,[23] any more than the employer in *Cutter v Powell* could have repudiated all liability if on one or two occasions the sailor had failed in his duty as mate.[24]

In such circumstances the present rule is that 'so long as there is substantial performance the contractor is entitled to the stipulated price, subject only to a cross-action or counter-claim for the omissions or defects in execution'.[25] If this were not the case and if exact performance in the literal sense were always required, a tradesman who had contracted to decorate a house according to certain specifications for a lump sum might find himself in an intolerable position. If, for instance, he had put two coats of paint in one room instead of three as agreed, the owner would be entitled to take the benefit of all that had been done throughout the house without paying one penny for the work.[26]

In a sense the substantial performance doctrine can be regarded as a qualification of the rule, rather than as an exception to it, and it will be noticed that in the cases of *Cutter v Powell, Sumpter v Hedges* and *Bolton v Mahadeva* there was in fact a failure of substantial performance. A significant key to understanding here is again the distinction between individual undertakings and the whole *corpus* of undertakings which a party makes. It will be very unusual for a party to have to perform exactly every undertaking he has made but much less uncommon for exact compliance with one requirement to be necessary. Clearly the distinctions between conditions and warranties, discussed earlier in this book,[27] can be of substantial significance here.

B Acceptance of partial performance by the promisee

Although a promisor has only partially fulfilled his obligations under the contract, it may be possible to infer from the circumstances a fresh agreement by the parties that payment shall be made for the work already done or for the goods in fact supplied. Where this inference is justifiable the plaintiff sues on a *quantum meruit* to recover remuneration proportionate to the benefit conferred upon the defendant, but an essential of success is an implicit promise of payment by the defendant.

Thus it has been held that if a ship freighted to Hamburg is prevented by restraints of princes from arriving, and the consignees accept the cargo at another port to which

---

[23] *H Dakin & Co Ltd v Lee* [1916] 1 KB 566, approved and followed in *Hoenig v Isaacs* [1952] 2 All ER 176, despite the dicta in *Eshelby v Federated European Bank Ltd* [1932] 1 KB 423.

[24] *Hoenig v Isaacs*, above, per Somervell LJ.

[25] Smith LC (13th edn) at 19, approved in *Hoenig v Isaacs*, above. See also *Broom v Davis* (1794) cited 7 East 480n; *Bolton v Mahadeva* [1972] 2 All ER 1322, [1972] 1 WLR 1009. Cf Beck 38 MLR 413.

[26] *Mondel v Steel* (1841) 8 M & W 858 at 870, per Parke B; *H Dakin & Co Ltd v Lee* [1916] 1 KB 566 at 579, per Cozens Hardy MR.

[27] See above pp 192 ff.

they have directed it to be delivered, they are liable upon an implied contract to pay freight *pro rata itineris.*[28]

An implicit promise to pay connotes a benefit received by the promisor, but the receipt of the benefits is not in itself enough to raise the implication. No promise can be inferred unless it is open to the beneficiary either to accept or to reject the benefit of the work.[29] This option exists where partial performance takes the form of short delivery under a contract for the sale of goods. If less than the agreed quantity of goods is delivered, and the buyer, instead of exercising his right of rejection, elects to accept them, he must pay for them at the contract rate.[30]

This principle could not be applied in *Cutter v Powell* since it was not possible for the owners to return the mate's services after his death, nor in *Sumpter v Hedges*, and *Bolton v Mahadeva* since the work had been incorporated in the defendant's property and could not be unscrambled. This was clearly explained by Collins LJ in *Sumpter v Hedges.*[31]

> There are cases in which, though the plaintiff has abandoned the performance of a contract, it is possible for him to raise the inference of a new contract to pay for the work on a *quantum meruit* from the defendant's having taken the benefit of that work, but, in order that that may be done, the circumstances must be such as to give an option to the defendant to take or not to take the benefit of the work done . . . Where, as in the case of work done on land, the circumstances are such as to give the defendant no option whether he will take the benefit of the work or not, then one must look to other facts than the mere taking the benefit in order to ground the inference of a new contract. In this case I see no other facts on which such an inference can be founded. The mere fact that a defendant is in possession of what he cannot help keeping, or even has done work upon it, affords no ground for such an inference. He is not bound to keep unfinished a building which in an incomplete state would be a nuisance on his land.

C Prevention of performance by the promisee

If a party to an entire contract performs part of the work that he has undertaken and is then prevented by the fault of the other party from proceeding further, the law does not allow him to be deprived of the fruits of his labour. He is entitled, of course, to recover damages for breach of contract, but alternatively he can recover reasonable remuneration on a *quantum meruit* for what he has done. The leading authority for this obvious rule is *Planché v Colburn.*[32,33]

---

[28] *Christy v Row* (1808) 1 Taunt 300. But the acceptance must be such as to raise the fair inference that the further carriage of the cargo is dispensed with: *St Enoch Shipping Co Ltd v Phosphate Mining Co* [1916] 2 KB 624 at 628.

[29] *Munro v Butt* (1858) 8 E & B 738.   [30] Sale of Goods Act 1979, s 30(1).

[31] [1898] 1 QB 673 at 676.   [32] (1831) 8 Bing 14.

[33] Perhaps, also on the facts of this case, the plaintiff could actually have insisted on going on to complete performance. See *White and Carter (Councils) Ltd v McGregor* [1962] AC 413, [1961] 3 All ER 1178, discussed p 782, below.

D Divisible covenants[34]

Another avenue of escape is presented by the distinction between entire and divisible contracts. A contract may be described as divisible in several senses. In contracts of employment, it is usual to provide for payment at weekly or monthly intervals and this has the effect of ousting the principle in *Cutter v Powell* at least for every completed week or month.[35] Similarly in building contracts, it is usual to provide for payment at intervals, usually against an architect's certificate, and this avoids to a substantial extent the result in *Sumpter v Hedges*.[36]

In its technical connotation, the term divisible, means, however, rather that situation where one party's performance is made independent of the other's. In this sense, as we have already seen, it is more accurate to talk of divisible covenants rather than divisible contracts, since in relation to any particular contract, there may be some obligations which are dependent and others which are independent of the other party's.[37]

5 CAN AN INNOCENT PARTY WHO HAS PAID IN ADVANCE RECOVER HIS PAYMENT IN THE EVENT OF A FAILURE OF PERFECT PERFORMANCE?

Suppose that in *Bolton v Mahadeva*[38] the defendant had paid for the work in advance, could he have recovered his payment? It is clear that he could not, since the test for recovery in such cases is total failure of consideration. We may note immediately the striking difference in result that is caused. The defendant would have been limited to an action for damages, which would presumably have provided about £200,[39] and therefore was £600 better off because he was paying on completion rather than in advance. The result is particularly striking in a case such as *Cutter v Powell*[40] where the

---

[34] Notes to *Pordage v Cole* (1669) 1 Wm Saund 319; Williams 57 LQR 373, 490.

[35] One justification for the actual result in *Cutter v Powell* is that the rate for the voyage was substantially in excess of what would have been earned on a daily, monthly, or weekly, basis, so that the contract had an aleatory element.

[36] Such modification is practically essential granted that *Sumpter v Hedges* would apply where the builder stopped work because of financial difficulties, which are endemic in the building industry.

[37] See *General Bill Posting Co Ltd v Atkinson* [1909] AC 118; *Taylor v Webb* [1937] 2 KB 283, [1937] 1 All ER 590; *Appleby v Myers* (1867) LR 2 CP 651 at 660–661; *Roberts v Havelock* (1832) 3 B & Ad 404; *Menetone v Athawes* (1764) 3 Burr 1592; *Heywood v Wellers* [1976] QB 446, [1976] 1 All ER 300.

[38] [1972] 2 All ER 1322, [1972] 1 WLR 1009; p 676, above.

[39] The cost of making the work good.

[40] (1795) 6 Term Rep 320; p 675, above.

employer would have had no action for damages, since there was no breach of contract.[41]

6 CAN THE INNOCENT PARTY TERMINATE THE CONTRACT?

This question is connected with but distinct from the question discussed in sections 2 and 4 above. So if, for instance, A charters a ship from B for a voyage charterparty to carry frozen meat from Auckland to Liverpool, it is clear that A is under no obligation to load the meat if on arrival at the docks he finds that the ship's refrigeration is not working,[42] but it does not follow that he is entitled to bring the contract to an end. This will depend on whether the law permits B time to repair the refrigerators and whether, if so, he is able to make use of it.

In the case of sale of goods, some very strict doctrines have been developed as to the buyer's right to reject goods which do not conform to the contract. The strictness of the law in this respect is well illustrated by the duty of the seller to make delivery of the goods in exact accordance with the terms of the contract. Thus, if he delivers more goods than have been ordered, the buyer may reject the whole consignment and cannot be required to select the correct quantity out of the bulk delivered.[43] Again, if less than the correct quantity is delivered, the buyer may reject the goods.[44] If the seller delivers the goods ordered accompanied by goods of a different description not ordered, the buyer may accept those which are in accordance with the contract and reject the rest, or he may reject the whole consignment.[45] In one case, for instance:

A agreed to sell to B tinned fruits and to deliver them in cases each containing thirty tins. He tendered the correct quantity ordered, but about half the cases contained only twenty-four tins.

It was held that the buyer was entitled to reject the whole consignment.[46]

These rules are analogous to those discussed in section 4 since they turn on the classification of these obligations of the seller as conditions, but in this case there is no question of the buyer being able to keep the goods and not pay for them.

---

[41] But see Law Reform (Frustrated Contracts) Act 1943, discussed pp 741 ff, below.
[42] *Stanton v Richardson* (1872) LR 7 CP 421; affd LR 9 CP 390.
[43] Sale of Goods Act 1979, s 30(2); *Cunliffe v Harrison* (1851) 6 Exch 903.
[44] Sale of Goods Act 1979, s 30(1).
[45] Ibid, s 30(3); *Levy v Green* (1857) 8 E & B 575. The provision of s 30 of Sale of Goods Act 1979 are amended by the Sale and Supply of Goods Act 1994, s 4.
[46] *Re Moore & Co and Landauer & Co* [1921] 2 KB 519. In *Reardon Smith Line Ltd v Hansen-Tangen* [1976] 3 All ER 570, [1976] 1 WLR 989 there are clear hints that these cases may be due for review by the House of Lords.

In what circumstances does a breach entitle the innocent party to terminate the contract?[47]

A breach of contract, no matter what form it may take, always entitles the innocent party to maintain an action for damages, but the rule established by a long line of authorities is that the right of a party to treat a contract as discharged arises only in two types of case.

(1) Where the party in default has repudiated the contract before performance is due or before it has been fully performed.

(2) Where the party in default has committed what in modern judicial parlance is called a *fundamental* breach. A breach is of this nature if, having regard to the contract as a whole, the promise that has been violated is of major as distinct from minor importance.

We will deal separately with these two causes of discharge.

A Repudiation

Repudiation in the present sense occurs where a party intimates by words or conduct that he does not intend to honour his obligations when they fall due in the future.[48] In the words of Lord Blackburn:

> Where there is a contract to be performed in the future, if one of the parties has said to the other in effect 'if you go on and perform your side of the contract I will not perform mine', that in effect, amounts to saying 'I will not perform the contract'. In that case the other party may say, 'you have given me distinct notice that you will not perform the contract. I will not wait until you have broken it,[49] but I will treat you as having put an end to the contract, and if necessary I will sue you for damages, but at all events I will not go on with the contract.'[50]

Repudiation may be either explicit or implicit. An example of the former type is afforded by *Hochster v De la Tour*,[51] where the defendant agreed in April to employ the plaintiff as his courier during a foreign tour commencing on 1 June. On 11 May he wrote that he had changed his mind and therefore would not require a courier. The plaintiff sued for damages before 1 June and succeeded.

---

[47] Devlin [1966] CLJ 192; Treitel 30 MLR 139. See the valuable papers by Mr Justice McGarvie and Mrs Dwyer on Discharge of Contracts (Leo Cussen Institute for continuing legal education, 1980).

[48] This is the most usual sense in which the word is used by the judges and it is retained in the present account, though admittedly it is ambiguous and has been adopted in other contexts; see *Heyman v Darwins Ltd* [1942] AC 356 at 378, 398, [1942] 1 All ER 337 at 350, 360.

[49] Since the repudiation itself is an immediate breach of the contract, Lord Blackburn clearly meant that the innocent party need not wait until performance falls due.

[50] *Mersey Steel and Iron Co v Naylor Benzon & Co* (1884) 9 App Cas 434.

[51] (1853) 2 E & B 678.

A repudiation is implicit where the reasonable inference from the defendant's conduct is that he no longer intends to perform his side of the contract. Thus, 'if a man contracts to sell and deliver specific goods on a future day, and before the day he sells and delivers them to another, he is immediately liable to an action at the suit of the person with whom he first contracted'.[52] So also, if A conveys a house to C which he had previously agreed to devise to B, A will be taken to have repudiated the contract.[53] The leading authority on this type of case is *Frost v Knight*[54] where the defendant, having agreed to marry the plaintiff upon the death of his father, broke off the engagement during the latter's lifetime. The plaintiff immediately sued for damages and was successful. This particular situation can no longer recur, since actions for breach of promise of marriage have now been abolished,[55] but the principles laid down in *Frost v Knight* are still of general application.

The result, then, of a repudiation, whether explicit or implicit, is that the innocent party acquires an immediate cause of action. But he need not enforce it. He can either stay his hand and wait until the day for performance arrives or treat the contract as discharged and take immediate proceedings.

A breach of contract caused by the repudiation of obligation not yet ripe for performance is called an *anticipatory breach*.[56] The word anticipatory is perhaps a little misleading, for at first sight it seems illogical to admit that a contract can be capable of breach before the time for its performance has arrived. Kelly CB, for instance, denied this possibility when *Frost v Knight* was argued before the Court of Exchequer. 'If it can be called a breach at all, it is a promissory or prospective breach only; a possible breach, which may never occur, and not an actual breach'.[57] This, however, is an untenable view. On appeal to the Exchequer Chamber, Cockburn CJ demonstrated that the defendant, in retracting his promise to marry the plaintiff, violated not a future, but an existing obligation.

> The promisee has an inchoate right to the performance of the bargain, which becomes complete when the time for performance has arrived. In the meantime he has a right to have the contract kept open as a subsisting and effective contract.[58] On the facts of *Frost v Knight* this would have meant that the plaintiff would have to wait until the death of the defendant's father to see if perchance he was available for performance, meanwhile declining all offers of marriage!

---

[52] Ibid at 688, per Lord Campbell.

[53] *Synge v Synge* [1894] 1 QB 466; *Lovelock v Franklyn* (1846) 8 QB 371.

[54] (1872) LR 7 Exch 111. See also *Short v Stone* (1846) 8 QB 358 (A married C having already promised to marry B).

[55] Law Reform (Miscellaneous Provisions) Act 1970, s 1(1), which came into force on 1 January 1971. See Cretney 33 MLR 534.

[56] Dawson [1981] CLJ 83, Carter 47 MLR 422.

[57] *Frost v Knight* (1870) LR 5 Exch 322 at 326–327.

[58] *Frost v Knight* (1872) LR 7 Exch 111 at 114.

Thus, the promisee, while awaiting performance, is entitled to assume that the promisor will himself remain ready, willing and able to perform his side of the contract at the agreed date. Any conduct by him which destroys this assumption 'is a breach of a presently binding promise, not an anticipatory breach of an act to be done in the future'.[59]

It is not all anticipatory breaches which will entitle the other party to treat the contract as at an end.

> If one party to a contract states expressly or by implication to the other party in advance that he will not be able to perform a particular primary obligation on his part under the contract when the time for performance arrives, the question whether the other party may elect to treat the statement as a repudiation depends on whether the threatened non-performance would have the effect of depriving the other party of substantially the whole benefit which it was the intention of the parties that he should obtain from the primary obligation of the parties under the contract.[60]

The proof of repudiation

Whether a breach of contract amounts to a repudiation is 'a serious matter not to be lightly found or inferred'.[61] What has to be established is that the defaulting party has made his intention clear beyond reasonable doubt no longer to perform his side of the bargain. Proof of such an intention requires an investigation inter alia of the nature of the contract, the attendant circumstances and motives which prompted the breach. In the words of Lord Selborne:

> You must look at the actual circumstances of the case in order to see whether the one party to the contract is relieved from its future performance by the conduct of the other; you must examine what that conduct is so as to see whether it amounts to a renunciation, to an absolute refusal to perform the contract . . . and whether the other party may accept it as a reason for not performing his part.[62]

A refusal to proceed with the contract must not be regarded in isolation, for it may be that the party *bona fide*, albeit erroneously, concluded that he was justified in staying his hand. 'A mere honest misapprehension, especially if open to correction, will not justify a charge of repudiation.'[63] If, for instance, his refusal to proceed is based upon a misconstruction of the agreement, it does not represent an absolute refusal to fulfil his

[59] *Bradley v Newsom Sons & Co* [1919] AC 16 at 53–54, per Lord Wrenbury. See Lloyd 37 MLR 121.

[60] Per Lord Diplock in *Afovos Shipping Co Sa v Pagnan* [1983] 1 All ER 449 at 455.

[61] *Ross Smyth & Co Ltd v Bailey, Son & Co* [1940] 3 All ER 60 at 71, per Lord Wright.

[62] *Mersey Steel and Iron Co v Naylor Benzon & Co* (1884) 9 App Cas 434 at 438–439; *James Shaffer Ltd v Findlay, Durham and Brodie* [1953] 1 WLR 106; *Peter Dumenil & Co Ltd v James Ruddin Ltd* [1953] 2 All ER 294, [1953] 1 WLR 815.

[63] *Ross Smyth & Co Ltd v Bailey, Son & Co* [1940] 3 All ER 60 at 72, per Lord Wright.

obligations, provided that he shows his readiness to perform the contract according to its true tenor. He has merely put its true tenor in issue.[64]

The House of Lords has been presented with this problem in two contrasting cases. In the first, *Federal Commerce and Navigation Co Ltd v Molena Alpha Inc*[65] disputes arose between shipowners and time-charterers over the latter's deduction of counter-claims from their periodic payments of hire. The owners, acting on legal advice, instructed the master not to issue freight pre-paid bills of lading, and to require the bills of lading to be endorsed with the charterparty terms and informed the charterers of these instructions. It was accepted that the owners believed that they were entitled to take these steps and that they were exceptionally coercive to the charterers, who would not be able to operate the ships if they were unable to obtain freight pre-paid bills of lading. The charterers claimed that the owners had wrongfully repudiated the contract and this view was upheld by the House of Lords. Little weight was attached to the owners' belief that they were entitled to act in this way, when weighed against the disastrous impact of the threatened conduct on the charterers' business.

At first sight, this decision is not easy to reconcile with that in the second case, *Woodar Investment Development Ltd v Wimpey Construction (UK) Ltd.*[66]

> The plaintiffs agreed to sell fourteen acres of land to the defendants, completion to be two months after the granting of outline planning permission or 21 February 1980, whichever was the earlier. The market having turned against them, the defendants claimed to exercise a right to rescind granted by the contract, but exercisable only in circumstances which did not exist. It was accepted that although their motive was to escape from an unprofitable transaction, the defendants honestly believed that they were entitled so to act. The plaintiffs claimed that the defendants' conduct amounted to a repudiatory breach.

The House of Lords held (Lords Salmon and Russell dissenting) that it did not.

There is clearly force in the minority view that the two cases are identical. In both cases, one party honestly took a view of the contract's meaning, which had no real merit and substance and relying on it, indicated a determination to depart from the contract in a fundamental way. It is however possible to detect a significant difference. In the *Woodar* case, there was no call for the plaintiffs to take immediate action and they could, for instance, have taken out a construction summons to test the correctness of their view of the contract's meaning. Again, the time for completion was some way off. It would seem clear that if Wimpeys had actually refused to complete on this ground, that would have been a repudiatory breach. In the *Federal Commerce* case, although the breach was probably anticipatory, the gap between

---

[64] *Sweet and Maxwell Ltd v Universal News Services Ltd* [1964] 2 QB 699, [1964] 3 All ER 30 esp per Buckley J at 737 and 45, respectively.

[65] [1979] AC 757, [1979] 1 All ER 307; Carter [1979] CLJ 270.

[66] [1980] 1 All ER 571, [1980] 1 WLR 277; Nicol and Rawlings 43 MLR 696; Carter [1980] CLJ 256.

repudiation and performance was fairly short and the pressure on the charterers correspondingly great.

The question of repudiation often arises where, in the case of a contract for the sale of goods to be delivered by instalments which are to be separately paid for, either the seller makes short deliveries or the buyer neglects to pay for one or more of the instalments. A default of either kind does not necessarily amount to a discharge. It depends in each case, as the Sale of Goods Act 1979 provides, upon the terms of the contract and the particular circumstances whether the breach is repudiation of the whole contract or merely a ground for the recovery of damages.[67]

There have been many decisions upon instalments contracts, several of which are difficult to reconcile; but the leading authority is *Mersey Steel and Iron Co v Naylor Benzon & Co*,[68] where the facts were these:

> The respondents sold to the appellants 5,000 tons of steel, to be delivered at the rate of 1,000 tons monthly, commencing in January, and payment to be made within three days after receipt of shipping documents. In January the sellers delivered about half the correct quantity, and in February made a further delivery, but shortly before payment for these deliveries became due, a petition was presented for winding-up their company. Thereupon the buyers, acting *bona fide* under the erroneous legal advice that pending the petition they could not safely pay the price due without the leave of the court, refused to make any payment unless this leave was obtained. The sellers then declared that they would treat this refusal to pay as discharging them from all further obligation.

It was held that it was impossible to ascribe to the conduct of the buyers the character of a repudiation of the contract.

> It is just the reverse; the purchasers were desirous of fulfilling the contract; they were advised that there was a difficulty in the way, and they expressed anxiety that that difficulty should be as soon as possible removed by means which were suggested to them, and which they pointed out to the solicitors of the company.[69]

It will often be difficult in a contract for delivery by instalments to decide whether a particular breach defeats the whole object of the contract so as to amount to a complete repudiation of his obligations by the party in default. It has been indicated, however, by the Court of Appeal that the chief considerations are 'first, the ratio quantitatively which the breach bears to the contract as a whole, and secondly, the degree of probability or improbability that such a breach will be repeated'.[70] It has also been recognised that the further the parties have proceeded in the performance of the

---

[67] S 31(2); *Decro-Wall International SA v Practitioners in Marketing Ltd* [1971] 2 All ER 216, [1971] 1 WLR 361.

[68] (1884) 9 App Cas 434.   [69] Ibid at 441, per Lord Selborne.

[70] *Maple Flock Co Ltd v Universal Furniture Products (Wembley) Ltd* [1934] 1 KB 148 at 157.

contract the more difficult it is to infer that a breach represents a complete repudiation of liability.[71]

The summary dismissal of an employee, founded upon his alleged repudiation of the contract, affords a further illustration of the warning that repudiation of the contract is a serious matter not lightly to be inferred. So drastic a step by the employer will not be justified unless the conduct of the employee has disclosed a deliberate intention to disregard the essential requirements of a contract of service.[72]

B Fundamental breach

The second class of case in which a party is entitled to treat himself as discharged from further liability is where his co-contractor, without expressly or implicitly repudiating his obligations, commits a fundamental breach of the contract. Of what nature, then, must a breach be before it is to be called 'fundamental'? There are two alternative tests that may provide the answer. The court may find the decisive element either in the importance that the parties would seem to have attached to the term which has been broken or to the seriousness of the consequences that have in fact resulted from the breach. We have already discussed this question at length[73] and suggested that although the tests are often stated as alternatives, they in fact both have a part to play.

If one applies the first test the governing principle is that everything depends upon the construction of the contract in question. The court has to decide whether, at the time when the contract was made, the parties must be taken to have regarded the promise which has been violated as of major or of minor importance. In the words of Bowen LJ:

> There is no way of deciding that question except by looking at the contract in the light of the surrounding circumstances, and then making up one's mind whether the intention of the parties, as gathered from the instrument itself, will best be carried out by treating the promise as a warranty sounding only in damages, or as a condition precedent by the failure to perform which the other party is relieved of his liability.[74]

Whether one looks to promise or breach one of the difficulties has been to formulate with any approach to precision the degree of importance that a promise or breach must possess to warrant the discharge of the contract. A variety of phrases has been used in an endeavour to meet this need. It has been said, for instance, that no breach will discharge the innocent party from further liability unless it goes to the whole root

---

[71] *Cornwall v Henson* [1900] 2 Ch 298 at 304, per Collins LJ.

[72] Contrast, for instance, *Laws v London Chronicle (Indicator Newspapers) Ltd* [1959] 2 All ER 285, [1959] 1 WLR 698 (dismissal not justified), with *Pepper v Webb* [1969] 2 All ER 216, [1969] 1 WLR 514 (dismissal justified); see Grime 32 MLR 575. See also *Cantor Fitzgerald International v Callaghan* [1999] 2 All ER 411.

[73] Pp 192 ff, above. *Bunge Corpn v Tradax Export SA* [1981] 2 All ER 513, [1981] 1 WLR 711.

[74] *Bentsen v Taylor, Sons & Co (No 2)* [1893] 2 QB 274 at 281.

of the contract, not merely to part of it,[75] or unless it goes so much to the root of the contract that it makes further performance impossible[76] or unless it affects the very substance of the contract.[77] Sachs LJ, 'at the risk of being dubbed old-fashioned', has recently stated his preference for the expression 'goes to the root of the contract', which has been the favourite of the judges for at least 150 years.

> That leaves the question whether the breach does go to the root as a matter of degree for the court to decide on the facts of the particular case in the same way as it has to decide which terms are warranties and which are conditions.[78]

To speak of 'the root of the contract' is, no doubt, to rely on a metaphor; and Lord Sumner once said that 'like most metaphors it is not nearly so clear as it seems'.[79] It does not solve the problem, but rather restates it in picturesque language. Yet a picture is not without value; and the phrase may help judges to crystallise the impression made on their minds by the facts of a particular case. In the Australian case of *Tramways Advertising Pty Ltd v Luna Park (NSW) Ltd*,[80] Jordan CJ said:

> The test of essentiality is whether it appears from the general nature of the contract considered as a whole, or from some particular term or terms, that the promise is of such importance to the promisee that he would not have entered into the contract unless he had been assured of a strict or substantial performance of the promise, as the case may be, and that this ought to have been apparent to the promisor.

Illustrations of cases in which the question of fundamental breach has been raised will be found at an earlier stage in this book.[81] But it may be useful to call attention to the early case of *Ellen v Topp*,[82] where the facts were these:

> An infant was placed by his father as apprentice to learn the trade of a master who was described in the contract as an 'auctioneer, appraiser and corn factor'. After about half the contractual period had elapsed the master abandoned his trade as a corn factor, whereupon the apprentice absented himself on the ground that this abandonment relieved him from further liability.

The master sued for breach of contract and argued that this retirement from the actual practice of one of the three trades did not discharge the contract, since he was still able to teach the apprentice the theory of a corn factor's business. It was held, however,

---

[75] *Davidson v Gwynne* (1810) 12 East 381 at 389, per Lord Ellenborough.

[76] *Hong Kong Fir Shipping Co Ltd v Kawasaki Kaisen Kaisha Ltd* [1962] 2 QB 26 at 64, [1962] 1 All ER 474 at 484 per Upjohn LJ.

[77] *Wallis, Son and Wells v Pratt and Haynes* [1910] 2 KB 1003 at 1012, per Fletcher Moulton LJ.

[78] *Decro-Wall International SA v Practitioners in Marketing Ltd* [1971] 2 All ER 216 at 227, [1971] 1 WLR 361 at 374.

[79] *Bank Line Ltd v A Capel & Co* [1919] AC 435 at 459.

[80] (1938) 38 SRNSW 632 at 641. Though the decision of the learned Chief Justice was reversed (1938) 61 CLR 286, his test of essentiality was unanimously approved by the High Court of Australia in the later case of *Associated Newspapers Ltd v Bancks* (1951) 83 CLR 322.

[81] Pp 225 ff, above.   [82] (1851) 6 Exch 424.

that the apprentice was discharged from further liability. The object of the contract, as clearly shown by its terms, was that the infant should serve the master after the manner of an apprentice in the three trades specified; but, as the court explained, service of this nature imports that the master shall actually carry on the trade which the apprentice is to learn, for otherwise 'the one is teaching and the other learning the trade, not as master and apprentice, but as instructor and pupil'. In the present case, therefore, the master had wilfully made it impossible for the essential object or the substantial benefit of the contract to be attained.

7 WHAT IS THE EFFECT OF A REPUDIATION OR A FUNDAMENTAL BREACH?[83]

It must be observed that, even if one of the parties wrongfully repudiates all further liability or has been guilty of a fundamental breach, the contract will not automatically come to an end. Since its termination is the converse of its creation, principle demands that it should not be recognised unless this is what both parties intend. The familiar test of offer and acceptance serves to determine their common intention. Where A and B are parties to an executory contract and A indicates that he is no longer able or willing to perform his outstanding obligations, he in effect makes an offer to B that the contract shall be discharged.

Therefore B is presented with an option. He may either refuse or accept the offer.[84] More precisely, he may either affirm the contract by treating it as still in force, or on the other hand he may treat it as finally and conclusively discharged. The consequences vary according to the choice that he prefers.

A The innocent party treats the contract as still in force

If the innocent party chooses the first option and, with full knowledge of the facts, makes it clear by words or acts, or even by silence,[85] that he refuses to accept the breach as a discharge of the contract, the effect is that the *status quo ante* is preserved intact. The contract 'remains in being for the future on both sides. Each [party] has a right to sue for damages for *past or future breaches*'.[86] Thus, for instance, a seller of goods who refuses to treat a fundamental breach as a discharge of the contract remains

[83] McGarvie 53 Aust LJ 687; Shea 42 MLR 623; Dawson 96 LQR 239; Hetherington 96 LQR 403; Nicholls 3 JCL 132, 163; Priestley 3 JCL 218; Mason 3 JCL 232.

[84] *Denmark Productions Ltd v Boscobel Productions Ltd* [1969] 1 QB 699 at 731, [1968] 3 All ER 513 at 527, per Winn LJ.

[85] Ibid at 732 and 527–528, respectively.

[86] *Harbutt's Plasticine Ltd v Wayne Tank and Pump Co Ltd* [1970] 1 QB 447 at 464–465, [1970] 1 All ER 225 at 233, per Lord Denning MR.

liable for delivery of possession to the defaulting buyer, while the latter remains correspondingly liable to accept delivery and to pay the contractual price.[87]

The significance of the rule that the contract continues in existence is well illustrated by the case where a party has repudiated his obligations.

> In that case he[88] keeps the contract alive for the benefit of the other party as well as his own; he remains subject to all his own obligations and liabilities under it, and enables the other party not only to complete the contract, if so advised, notwithstanding his previous repudiation of it, but also to take advantage of any supervening circumstance which would justify him in declining to complete it.[89]

The case of *Avery v Bowden* illustrates the way in which supervening circumstances may operate to relieve the party in default from all liability.[90]

> The defendant chartered the plaintiff's ship at a Russian port and agreed to load her with a cargo within forty-five days. Before this period had elapsed he repeatedly advised the plaintiff to go away as it would be impossible to provide him with a cargo. The plaintiff, however, remained at the port in the hope that the defendant would fulfil his promise, but the refusal to load was maintained, and then, before the forty-five days had elapsed, the Crimean war broke out between England and Russia.

On the assumption that the refusal to load amounted to a complete repudiation of liability by the defendant, the plaintiff might have treated the contract as discharged; but his decision to ignore this repudiation resulted, as events turned out, in the defendant being provided with a good defence to an action for breach. He would have committed an illegal act if he had loaded a cargo at a hostile port after the declaration of war. Similarly, in *Fercometal SARL v Mediterranean Shipping Co, SA The Simona*[91] the contract was a charterparty which called for a ship to go to Durban and carry a cargo of steel coils to Bilbao. The charterparty contained a cancellation clause under which the charterer could cancel if the vessel was not ready to load on or before 9 July. On 2 July the ship owners asked if they might have an extension of the cancellation date because they wished to load another cargo first. The charterers responded to this by purporting to cancel the charterparty. This they were clearly not entitled to do since there is clear authority that one cannot exercise the cancellation clause in advance, even if it is very likely or morally certain that the ship will not be ready to load in time. So the purported cancellation by the charterers was undoubtedly a

---

[87] *R V Ward Ltd v Bignall* [1967] 1 QB 534, [1967] 2 All ER 449. The position that arises if, instead of merely continuing to tender performance, the innocent party fully completes his side of the contract in defiance of a repudiation, thereby increasing the loss flowing from the breach, was considered by the House of Lords in *White and Carter (Councils) Ltd v McGregor* [1962] AC 413, [1961] 3 All ER 1178; discussed at pp 782 ff, below.

[88] Ie the innocent party.

[89] *Frost v Knight* (1872) LR 7 Exch 111 at 112, per Cockburn CJ; see also *Johnstone v Milling* (1886) 16 QBD 460 at 467, per Lord Esher.

[90] (1855) 5 E & B 714.   [91] [1989] AC 788, [1988] 2 All ER 742.

repudiation of the contract. However, the ship owners chose to carry on with the contract and in fact the ship arrived in Durban on 8 July and gave notice of readiness to load on that day. In fact, the ship was not ready to load, on either 8 July or 9 July. The charterers had loaded the cargo on another ship and the ship owners brought an action for dead freight. The House of Lords held that the ship owners' action failed. By refusing to accept the charterers' repudiation and trying to carry on with performance, the ship owners had given the charterers a second chance to cancel, which they were entitled to take, as the ship was not in fact ready to load on the contract date. Having kept the contract alive, the ship owners had kept all of it alive, including the charterers' right to cancel if the ship was not ready to load in time.

On the other hand, a refusal to treat a breach of contract as a discharge may operate to the disadvantage of the defendant.

Supposing that, in the case of a contract for the sale of goods to be delivered in May, the seller announced in February that he will not make delivery, but the buyer refuses to accept this repudiation and ultimately sues for breach at the contractual date for performance. The measure of damages will depend upon the market price of the goods, not at the date of the repudiation but at the time appointed for performance. If, therefore, the market price of the goods is higher in May than it was in February the amount payable by the seller as damages will be correspondingly higher.[92]

It is obvious that a party who elects to disregard a repudiation by his co-contractor cannot recover damages at law for breach of contract: if the contract is still in being it has not yet been broken. As Asquith LJ remarked in one case: 'An unaccepted repudiation is a thing writ in water and of no value to anybody; it affords no legal rights of any sort or kind.'[93] But this is not true where the equitable remedy of specific performance is sought. If the circumstances justify it, equity is prepared to protect the innocent party even though he cannot plead the breach of contract upon which the common law remedy of damages depends. In one case, for instance:

> By a written contract signed on 19 February, the vendor agreed to sell a plot of land to the purchaser, completion to be on 19 August. A few minutes later the vendor repudiated the contract. The purchaser elected to affirm the contract and on 2 August, some six weeks before the agreed date for completion, he sued for a decree of specific performance. The court granted the decree.[94]

This did not mean that the purchaser could call for the land to be conveyed to him before 19 August, but that on that date he would be at liberty, without taking out a new writ, to apply for a consequential direction requiring the vendor to execute a conveyance.

---

[92] *Roper v Johnson* (1873) LR 8 CP 167; *Michael v Hart* [1902] 1 KB 482; *Tai Hing Cotton Mill Ltd v Kamsing Knitting Factory* [1979] AC 91, [1978] 1 All ER 515; *Lusograin Commercio Internacional De Cereas Ltd v Bunge AG* [1986] 2 Lloyd's Rep 654.

[93] *Howard v Pickford Tool Co* [1951] 1 KB 417 at 421.

[94] *Hasham v Zenab* [1960] AC 316; REM 76 LQR 200.

In principle an election by the innocent party to treat the contract as still in force depends on the innocent party knowing of his rights. However an innocent party, who has not in fact made an election, may behave in such a way that the court will hold that he is estopped from denying that he has made an election.[95]

B The innocent party treats the contract as at an end

A party who treats a contract as discharged is often said to *rescind* the contract. To describe the legal position in such a manner, however, must inevitably mislead and confuse the unwary. In its primary and more correct sense, as we have already seen,[96] rescission means the retrospective cancellation of a contract *ab initio*, as for instance where one of the parties has been guilty of fraudulent misrepresentation. In such a case the contract is destroyed as if it had never existed, but its discharge by breach never impinges upon rights and obligations that have already matured. It would be better therefore in this context to talk of *termination* or *discharge* rather than of *rescission*.[97]

This has recently been the subject of a full and authoritative statement by the House of Lords in *Johnson v Agnew*.[98]

By a contract in writing the vendors agreed to sell a house and some grazing land to the purchaser. The properties were separately mortgaged and the purchase price agreed was sufficient to pay off these mortgages and also a bank loan which the vendors had secured to buy another property. The purchaser failed to complete on the agreed completion date, and a fortnight later the vendors issued a notice making time of the essence,[99] and fixing 21 January 1974 as the final completion date. The purchaser failed to complete on this day and it is clear that the vendors were thereupon entitled to bring the contract to an end. They chose instead to sue for specific performance, which was obtained on 27 June 1974. Before the order was entered, however, both the mortgagees of the house and the mortgagees of the

---

[95] *Cerealmangimi SpA v Alfred C Toepfer, The Eurometal* [1981] 3 All ER 533 (where the innocent party appears to have known of all the relevant facts but not that they entitled him to terminate); *Société Italo-Belge pour le Commerce et l'Industrie SA v Palm and Vegetable Oils, The Post Chaser* [1982] 1 All ER 19. Clearly the guilty party could not allege waiver where he had no reason to believe that the innocent party knew of his rights. As to position where the innocent party has the means of knowing his rights see *Bremer Handelgesellschaft MbH v Vanden Avenue-Izegem PVBA* [1978] 2 Lloyd's Rep 109 and *Bremer Handelgesellschaft MbH v C Mackprang Jr* [1979] 1 Lloyd's Rep 221; *Procter & Gamble Philippine Manufacturing Corpn v Peter Cremer GmbH & Co, The Manila* [1988] 3 All ER 843.

[96] P 352, above.

[97] See Albery 91 LQR 337, discussing *Horsler v Zorro* [1975] Ch 302, [1975] 1 All ER 584. In his instructive article in 53 Aust LJ 687 Mr Justice McGarvie criticises the use of the word *termination* in the ninth edition of this work and prefers the term discharge. It may perhaps be answered that though it is clear that *rescission* is the wrong word, what is the right word is unclear.

[98] [1980] AC 367, [1979] 1 All ER 883, Woodman 42 MLR 696.

[99] See p 702, below.

grazing land had exercised their rights to possession and had sold the properties.[100] The vendors thereupon applied to the court for leave to proceed by way of an action for damages.

The House of Lords held that by choosing to sue for specific performance the vendors had not made a final election and that it was open to the Court to allow the vendors to sue for damages if it appeared equitable to do so Lord Wilberforce said:[101]

> It is important to dissipate a fertile source of confusion and to make clear that although sometimes the vendor is referred to . . . as 'rescinding' the contract, this so-called 'rescission' is quite different from rescission *ab initio*, such as may arise for example, in cases of mistake, fraud or lack of consent. In those cases the contract is treated in law as never having come into existence . . . In the case of an accepted repudiatory breach the contract has come into existence but has been put an end to, or discharged. Whatever contrary indications may be disinterred from old authorities, it is now quite clear, under the general law of contract, that acceptance of a repudiatory breach does not bring about 'rescission *ab initio*'.[102]

If the innocent party elects to treat the contract as discharged, he must make his decision known to the party in default. Once he has done this, his election is final and cannot be retracted.[103] The effect is to terminate the contract for the future as from the moment when the acceptance is communicated to the party in default. The breach does not operate retrospectively. The previous existence of the contract is still relevant with regard to the past acts and defaults of the parties. Thus the party in default is liable in damages both for any earlier breaches and also for the breach that has led to the discharge of the contract, but he is excused from further performance.[104] But this does not mean, in the case of an anticipatory breach, that the obligations which would

---

[100] For substantially less than the purchasers had agreed to pay.

[101] Ibid at 392–393 and 889, respectively.

[102] See also *Buckland v Farmer and Moody* [1978] 3 All ER 929, [1979] 1 WLR 221 and *Photo Production Ltd v Securicor Transport Ltd* [1980] AC 827, [1980] 1 All ER 556.

[103] *Scarf v Jardine* (1882) 7 App Cas 345 at 361, per Lord Blackburn. Such is the general principle wherever there is a choice between two remedies. The election must be made without unreasonable delay; *Allen v Robles* [1969] 3 All ER 154, [1969] 1 WLR 1193. As to whether the innocent party can extend the time for decision by reserving his position, see *Antaios Cia Naviera SA v Salen Rederierna AB, The Antaios* [1983] 3 All ER 777, [1983] 1 WLR 1362 (affirmed on other grounds [1985] AC 191, [1984] 3 All ER 229). Difficult questions may arise as to whether or not the innocent party has in fact elected to treat the contract as discharged. See *Vitol SA v Norelf Ltd, The Santa Clara* [1994] 4 All ER 109; reversed by the Court of Appeal [1995] 3 All ER 971; reversed in turn by the House of Lords [1996] 3 All ER 193. Note that at the end of the day, the House of Lords held the question whether the innocent party had elected to terminate the contract was a question of fact within the exclusive jurisdiction of the arbitrator.

[104] *Mussen v Van Diemen's Land Co* [1938] Ch 253 at 260, [1938] 1 All ER 210 at 216, per Farwell J; *Boston Deep Sea Fishing and Ice Co v Ansell* (1888) 39 ChD 339 at 365, per Bowen LJ; *Fibrosa Spolka Akcyjna v Fairburn Lawson Combe Barbour Ltd* [1943] AC 32 at 65, per Lord Wright; *R V Ward Ltd v Bignall* [1967] 1 QB 534 at 548, [1967] 2 All ER 449 at 455, per Diplock LJ.

have matured after the election are to be completely disregarded. They may still be relevant to the assessment of damages. This is exemplified by *Moschi v Lep Air Services Ltd*[105] on the following facts:

> The defendant company agreed to pay £40,000 to the plaintiffs in seven weekly instalments. X, the managing director of the defendants, personally guaranteed the payment, of this debt. At the end of three weeks, the payments were so seriously in arrear as to amount to a repudiation of the contract by the defendants. On 22 December, the plaintiffs accepted this repudiation and then sued the guarantor, X, for the recovery of £40,000, less what had already been paid.

One of the defences raised by the guarantor was that he was not liable in respect of instalments falling due after 22 December. This defence was rejected by the House of Lords.[106]

This decision is in line with the earlier decision of the Court of Appeal in the case of *The Mihalis Angelos*.[107]

> By clause 11 of a charterparty, the owners stated that their ship was 'expected ready to load at Haiphong under this charter about July 1st, 1965'. Clause 11 provided that, if the ship was not ready to load on or before 20 July 1965, the charterers should have the option of cancelling the contract. On 17 July, the charterers repudiated the contract and the owners accepted the repudiation. The majority of the Court of Appeal held that the option to cancel the contract was not exercisable before 20 July even though on the 17th it was certain that the ship would not arrive before 20 July. The charterers were thus guilty of an 'anticipatory breach'.[108]

One question that arose was whether the owners could recover substantial damages in respect of the wrongful repudiation on the ground that its acceptance by them had put an end to the contract, together with the right of cancellation. The arbitrators took the view that though the contract was terminated in the sense that its performance was no longer binding upon the owners, yet 'it (or its ghost)' survived for the purpose of measuring the damages. The Court of Appeal accepted this view and granted the owners only nominal damages. In the case of an anticipatory breach, the innocent party is entitled to recover the true value of the contractual rights which he has lost. If these 'were capable by the terms of the contract of being rendered either less valuable

---

[105] [1973] AC 331, [1972] 2 All ER 393.

[106] See also *Hyundai Heavy Industries Co Ltd v Papadopoulos* [1980] 2 All ER 29, [1980] 1 WLR 1129 and *Super Chem Products Ltd v American Life and General Insurance Co Ltd* [2004] UK PC2, [2004] 2 All ER 358.

[107] [1971] 1 QB 164, [1970] 3 All ER 125.

[108] Or, rather, they would have been if owners had not themselves been in breach of condition; see pp 198 ff, above.

or valueless in certain events, and if it can be shown that those events were, at the date of acceptance of repudiation, predestined to happen, then in my view the damages which he can recover are not more than the true value, if any, of the rights which he has lost, having regard to those predestined events'.[109] So, since the charterers would certainly have lawfully cancelled on 20 July, the owners have suffered no loss.

8 THE EFFECT OF DISCHARGING THE CONTRACT FOR A BAD REASON, WHEN A GOOD REASON ALSO EXISTS

The discharge of a contract, based upon a reason that is in fact inadequate, may nevertheless 'be supported if there are at the time facts in existence which would have provided a good reason'.[110] For instance, a seller of goods deliverable by instalments makes a short delivery, whereupon the buyer claims that the contract is discharged. This, however, may be unwarranted, since an intention on the part of the seller to repudiate his obligations is not inferable from the circumstances that led to the short delivery. If it is then discovered that the goods already delivered do not comply with their contractual description, this fundamental breach suffices to justify the discharge of the contract.[111]

It would seem that this principle requires some qualification in the light of the decision of the Court of Appeal in *Panchaud Frères SA v Establissements General Grain Co.*[112]

The plaintiff contracted to sell to the defendant 5,300 metric tons Brazilian yellow maize cif Antwerp, shipment to be June/July 1965. The bill of landing was dated 31 July 1965, but amongst the other shipping documents was a certificate of quality which stated that the goods were loaded 10 August to 12 August 1965. This would have entitled the defendant to reject the shipping documents but they were received without objection (presumably, though this is not explicitly stated in

---

[109] [1971] 1 QB 164 at 210, [1970] 3 All ER 125 at 142, per Megaw LJ.

[110] *Universal Cargo Carriers Corpn v Citati* [1957] 2 QB 401 at 447, [1957] 2 All ER 70 at 89, per Devlin J.

[111] Cf *Denmark Productions Ltd v Bosobel Productions Ltd* [1969] 1 QB 699 at 722, per Salmon LJ; at 732, per Winn LJ; *The Mihalis Angelos* [1971] 1 QB 164 at 195–196, 200 and 204. This principle has often been applied in actions by servants for wrongful dismissal but it does not apply to the statutory action for unfair dismissal. *W Devis & Sons Ltd v Atkins* [1977] AC 931, [1977] 2 All ER 321.

[112] [1970] 1 Lloyd's Rep 53; see also *Carvill v Irish Industrial Bank Ltd* [1968] IR 325; *Cyril Leonards & Co v Simo Securities Trust Ltd* [1971] 3 All ER 1313, [1972] 1 WLR 80; Denning *The Discipline of Law* pp 210–214.

the report, because the inconsistency was not detected). When the ship arrived the defendant rejected the goods on another ground ultimately held insufficient and only three years later sought to justify rejection on the ground that the goods had been shipped out of time.

The Court of Appeal held that it was too late for the defendant to rely on this ground since in the words of Winn LJ:[113]

> There may be an inchoate doctrine stemming from the manifest convenience of consistency in pragmatic affairs, negativing any liberty to blow hot and cold in commercial conduct.[114]

9 SOME POSSIBLE SPECIAL CASES

We must now consider some cases where it has sometimes been thought that these rules do not apply in the ordinary way.

A Wrongful dismissal of servants

It is often said that the wrongful dismissal of a servant employed under a contract of personal services provides an exception to the rule that a party may elect to keep a repudiated contract alive and that despite the unjustifiable repudiation of his obligations by the employer, the employee, though ready and willing to serve for the agreed period, has no option but to treat the contract as discharged.[115] On the other hand it has been doubted whether this is correct.[116] It is true that as a rule specific performance will not be ordered of a contract of personal service[117] and that since a servant cannot ordinarily perform his contract of employment if his master wrongfully excludes him from the workplace, in practice he must sue either for damages for breach of contract, in which case he must do what he reasonably can to mitigate his

---

113 [1970] 1 Lloyd's Rep at 59.

114 See also *The Vladimir Ilich* [1975] 1 Lloyd's Rep 322. A helpful discussion of what *Panchaud Freres* decided can be found in *Glencore Grain Rotterdam BV v Lebanese Organisation for International Commerce* [1997] 4 All ER 514; Carter 14 JCL 239.

115 See eg *Denmark Productions Ltd v Boscobel Productions Ltd* [1969] 1 QB 699, [1968] 3 All ER 513 at 524, per Salmon LJ; at 737 and 533, respectively, per Harman LJ; *contra*, at 731–732 and 528, respectively, per Winn LJ. See Freedland 32 MLR 314.

116 See eg *Decro-Wall International SA v Practitioners in Marketing Ltd* [1971] 2 All ER 216, [1971] 1 WLR 361 at 370, per Salmon LJ, and at 229 and 376, respectively, per Sachs LJ.

117 The rule that a servant cannot obtain specific performance is deducted from the undoubtedly sensible rule that the master cannot get specific performance. This may have made excellent sense in the eighteenth century but in a modern industrial context it no longer appears inevitable. Historically the law would appear to be moving slowly but perceptibly toward a remedy by way of reinstatement. See Williams 38 MLR 292.

loss by obtaining other employment,[118] or on a *quantum meruit* for the value of the work that he has already done.[119] In *Hill v C A Parsons & Co Ltd*[120] the Court of Appeal granted a declaration that the contract of service still subsisted.

The decision in *Thomas Marshall (Exports) Ltd v Guinle*[121] took the view that contracts of service are not an exceptional case and are subject to the general rule that repudiation does not terminate the contract until accepted.

> The defendant had been engaged as managing director of the plaintiff company under a ten-year service agreement. After six years he purported to resign and began to compete with the plaintiff through companies he had formed himself. Such competition was in clear breach of express terms of the service agreement but the defendant argued that the service agreement was no longer in force because of his wrongful repudiation.

After an elaborate examination of the authorities which he found 'in a far from satisfactory state',[122] Megarry V-C rejected this argument and granted an injunction restraining the defendant from such competition.

The same view was taken by the majority of the Court of Appeal (Shaw LJ dissenting) in *Gunton v London Borough of Richmond upon Thames*.[123] In this case the plaintiff was employed by the defendant Council under a contract which could be terminated either by a month's notice or by disciplinary procedures. He was dismissed by the giving of a month's notice after the carrying out of disciplinary procedures which contained technical irregularities. It was agreed that this dismissal was in breach of contract in that once the disciplinary procedures were invoked the plaintiff was entitled to one month's notice to run from the completion of correctly conducted contractual disciplinary procedures. The plaintiff sought a declaration that the letter of dismissal was ineffective lawfully to terminate his employment. Though they doubted whether it would make much practical difference, the majority of the court held that the plaintiff was so entitled. Shaw LJ thought this conclusion 'has no reality in relation to a contract of service where the repudiation takes the form of an express and direct termination of the contract in contravention of its terms'.[124] But it may be noted that an employee may have good reasons for wanting to keep the contract technically alive, for example, in order to complete a qualifying period of service for pension rights or for statutory entitlement to redundancy rights, maternity leave, etc.

---

[118] Pp 779 ff, below.
[119] *Planché v Colburn* (1831) 5 C & P 58.
[120] [1972] Ch 305, [1971] 3 All ER 1345.
[121] [1979] Ch 227, [1978] 3 All ER 193; Benedictus 95 LQR 14; Thomson 42 MLR 91.
[122] Ibid at 239 and 202, respectively.
[123] [1980] 3 All ER 577, [1981] Ch 448; Thomson 97 LQR 8.
[124] Ibid at 582 and 459, respectively.

B Leases

In *Total Oil (Great Britain) Ltd v Thompson Garages (Biggin Hill) Ltd*[125] the Court of Appeal held that the general rule did not apply to a contract contained in a lease. The facts were as follows:

> A lease of a garage for fourteen years, granted by the plaintiffs, an oil company, to the defendants, contained a tying covenant by which the defendants agreed to sell only motor fuel supplied by the plaintiffs. Payment for each load supplied was to be cash on delivery. On two occasions, the cheques given by the defendants were not honoured, whereupon the plaintiffs refused to supply more fuel unless they first received a banker's draft for each load ordered prior to its dispatch from their depot. This alteration of an essential term amounted to a repudiation of the contract, and the defendants accepted it as a discharge from liability to observe the tying covenant.

In the present action an injunction was sought restraining the defendants from selling fuel other than that supplied by the plaintiffs. The Court of Appeal held that the plaintiffs were entitled to this relief.

There was no obvious authority upon which the court could rely. Lord Denning MR, however, stressed that the tying covenant was inseparable from the lease. Together, they formed one composite legal transaction. He then invoked the doctrine of frustration, and recalled that in *Cricklewood Property and Investment Trust Ltd v Leighton's Investment Trust Ltd*[126] two of the Law Lords were of opinion that frustration does not bring a lease to an end.[127] He then said: 'Nor, I think, does repudiation and acceptance.'[128] Edmund Davies LJ and Stephenson LJ agreed with his reasoning.

Thus the lease and its covenants still stood, and so long as the plaintiffs remained in breach of their obligations they could not enforce the tying covenant. But in the opinion of the court, they had a *locus poenitentiae*, and since they had now agreed to resume the practice of cash on delivery, they were entitled to the injunction which they claimed.

In so far as this decision rests on the non-applicability of the doctrine of frustration to leases, it would appear to have been overtaken by the more recent decision of the House of Lords in *National Carriers Ltd v Panalpina (Northern) Ltd*[129] that the doctrine can apply to leases.

It is noteworthy that in this case the tenant did not purport to terminate the lease and the decision might perhaps be supported on the ground that he could not elect to terminate part of the transaction but must choose between terminating the lease and

---

[125] [1972] 1 QB 318, [1971] 3 All ER 1226.   [126] [1945] AC 221. See p 736, below.
[127] Lord Russell of Killowen and Lord Goddard.
[128] [1972] 1 QB 318 at 324, [1971] 3 All ER 1226 at 1229.
[129] [1981] AC 675, [1981] 1 All ER 161; see p 737, below.

keeping the whole transaction alive. Obviously this would be an unattractive choice to the tenant but the distinction is important in the converse case of repudiation by a tenant to which the Court of Appeal's reasoning is equally applicable.

It is interesting to note that different reasoning was adopted by the Supreme Court of Canada in *Highway Properties Ltd v Kelly, Douglas & Co Ltd.*[130]

> The plaintiff was the developer of a shopping centre and let premises in the centre to the defendant for fifteen years for use as a supermarket. The defendant covenanted to open for business within thirty days of completion 'and to carry on its business on the said premises continuously'. This covenant was of great importance to the plaintiff since the viability of such shopping centres as a whole depends on a number of major shops acting as magnets for customers. The willingness of other shopkeepers to take tenancies of the smaller units is often dependent on the presence of such major stores within the complex. The defendant opened for business but after five months abandoned the premises and removed its stock. The plaintiff elected to retake possession of the premises with a view to re-letting. Eventually the premises were re-let in a partitioned form to three new tenants at a lower rent but the value of business at the shopping centre fell off with the closing of the supermarket and many other tenants left their premises.

The defendant argued that the plaintiff's remedies were determined by the law of land rather than the law of contract and that while it would have been open to the plaintiffs to leave the premises vacant and sue the defendant for rent, they had by terminating the lease brought their right to rent to an end. The defendant further argued that the plaintiffs could not recover damages under the ordinary principles of the law of contract for consequential loss. This argument was rejected. Laskin J, speaking for the court said:[131]

> It is . . . untenable to persist in denying resort to the full armoury of remedies ordinarily available to redress repudiation of covenants, merely because the covenants may be associated with an estate in land.

C Partnerships

In *Hurst v Bryk*[132] Mr Hurst was a solicitor who was a partner in a firm called Malkin Janner which did business in Covent Garden. Relationships between the partners became so bad that it became clear that the partnership would have to come to an end. Unfortunately, the process of winding up the partnership itself ran into difficulties. On 4 October 1990 all of the partners except Mr Hurst entered into an agreement to

---

[130] (1971) 17 DLR (3d) 710.
[131] Ibid at 721. This reasoning was cited with approval in *National Carriers Ltd v Panalpina (Northern) Ltd* [1981] AC 675, [1981] 1 All ER 161, [1981] 2 WLR 45 where the *Total Oil* case was not cited.
[132] [2000] 2 All ER 193.

dissolve the partnership on 31 October 1990. Mr Hurst took the view that the partnership could only be terminated at such short notice by unanimous agreement and that since he did not agree the agreement of 4 October 1990 amounted to a repudiatory breach of the partnership agreement by the other partners which he was entitled to treat as terminating the partnership. This view was upheld by the trial judge and the Court of Appeal and accepted before the House of Lords.

The live issue before the House of Lords was the effect of an accepted repudiation on the obligations of the partners. It had been assumed before the lower courts that this was governed by the principles of general contract law discussed in the preceding section. Lord Millett in a speech with which the other members of the House concurred doubted whether this was so since this was certainly not expressly stated in the Partnership Act 1890 or reflected in the previous case law.[133]

The importance of this lay in whether Mr Hurst was relieved from an onerous obligation which the partnership had assumed by taking a lease of office accommodation at the top of the market which could not be economically assigned or sublet. Lord Millett held that by whatever means the partnership came to an end it did not free Mr Hurst from his obligation to the landlord nor from his obligation to contribute to the accruing liabilities to the firm. It was possible that Mr Hurst might have a claim to damages against his partners but he had not argued his case in this way. Such a claim would have involved showing that the damages flowed from the wrongful decision of the other partners to terminate the partnership prematurely.

10 CONTRACTUAL PROVISIONS FOR TERMINATION[134]

We have so far considered the application of basic rules, which apply in the absence of contrary agreement. In practice the parties often do make provisions which substantially alter the impact of these ordinary rules. So in commercial contracts for the sale of goods, it is not unusual to find non-rejection clauses, under which the buyer is not to reject non-conforming goods but to look only to his remedy in damages.[135]

It is common in many kinds of contract to find provisions which extend one party's right of termination outside the areas of repudiation and fundamental breach. We may divide such provisions into two sub-groups.

---

[133] There is a discretionary power to decree a dissolution under s 35(b) of the Act where one party 'wilfully or persistently commits a breach of the partnership agreement'.

[134] Carter 3 JCL 90; Cornwell 3 JCL 126.

[135] Such a clause is probably a species (relatively harmless) of exemption clause. See pp 202 ff, above.

A Termination for 'minor' breach

The common law rules can operate indulgently to some classes of contract-breakers, especially, slow payers. In practice, those who make a habit of paying slowly seldom make repudiatory statements. More commonly their delays are accompanied by pro-testations of good will and a wide range of more or less plausible excuses. Creditors often find it prudent therefore to insert contractual counter-measures. This is particu-larly so in contracts which call for a series of periodic payments where it is common to have an 'acceleration clause', making all the payments due on failure of timely payments of any or a 'withdrawal clause', enabling one party to bring the contract to an end if the other party does not pay promptly. So in *Mardorf Peach & Co Ltd v Attica Sea Carriers Corpn of Liberia, The Laconia*[136] the plaintiff shipowners had time chartered a ship to the defendants. The charterparty provided for payment of hire 'in cash semi-monthly in advance' into a named bank account and also provided that failing 'punctual and regular payment of the hire' the owners should be entitled to withdraw the vessel. The seventh and final instalment was due on Sunday April 12 1970, when the banks were, of course, closed. The hire was paid over the counter of the owners' bank for the credit of their account on Monday afternoon. The House of Lords upheld the owners' claim to be entitled to withdraw the vessel for failure of punctual payment.[137] The House did not consider that in a commercial contract using a well-known standard form, there was any need to develop doctrines limiting the strict application of such contractual provisions.[138]

B Termination 'without cause'

It is not unusual for contracts to contain provisions entitling one party to terminate without the other party having done anything wrong. At first sight this seems strange, but there are many situations where it makes excellent sense. For instance, the com-mon law says that if a contract is made on Monday and cancelled on Tuesday before any work has been done, the contractor is entitled to his loss of profit on the trans-action. This does not correspond with many businessmen's expectations. Contracts

---

[136] [1977] AC 850, [1977] 1 All ER 545.

[137] The owners might, of course, have waived their right but they had taken prompt steps to return the money and their bank had no authority to accept late payment.

[138] See also *China National Foreign Trade Transportation Corpn v Eulogia Shipping Co SA of Panama, The Mihalis Xilas* [1979] 2 All ER 1044, [1979] 1 WLR 1018 where the same principle was applied in case of underpayment and *Awilco, A/S v Fulvia SpA di Navigazione, The Chikuma* [1981] 1 All ER 652, [1981] 1 WLR 314 where the money was paid into the owners' bank on the due date but in a form which would have led to the owners suffering an interest penalty if they had withdrawn it on that day. It is now common for such withdrawal clauses to be qualified by anti-technicality clauses requiring a short period of notice and thereby giving the charterer a second chance to pay, See *Afovos Shipping Co SA v Pagnan* [1983] 1 All ER 449, [1983] 1 WLR 195; *Italmare Shipping Co v Ocean Tanker Co Inc (No 2)* [1982] 3 All ER 273. As to whether any relief is possible against the consequences of this rule see pp 795 ff, below.

often contain provisions permitting cancellation without charge where the contract is wholly executory. Even where work has been done, it is not unusual to find provisions for cancellation in return for payment of compensation.[139] The most common examples are in the field of government contracts, where the need to be able to cancel weapon projects, or motorway schemes makes such provisions easily understandable.

The most obvious example, however, is in long-term contracts of indefinite duration, such as contracts of employment. Here it is common to make express provision for termination by notice and usually easy to infer that the contract is terminable by notice, even in the absence of express provision.[140] In this context a difficult case is *Staffordshire Area Health Authority v South Staffordshire Waterworks Co.*[141]

> In 1908 the predecessors in title of the plaintiffs owned a hospital which took its water from its own well. Under a private Act of 1909, the defendants were empowered to pump water from a well a mile away, subject to providing the hospital with any water which it needed, if the supply from the hospital's well was reduced. The rate was to be that which it would have cost the hospital to get the water from their own well and disputes were to be subject to arbitration. By 1918 there was a deficiency which was supplied by the defendants and in 1927 the hospital decided to abandon their well. In 1929 a contract was then concluded under which 'at all times hereafter' the hospital was to receive 5,000 gallons of water a day free and all the additional water it required at the rate of 7d (2.9p) per thousand gallons. By 1975 the normal rate was 45p per 1,000 gallons and the Water Company claimed to be entitled to terminate the agreement by giving six months' notice.

The Court of Appeal upheld this argument though for different reasons. Lord Denning MR invoked the doctrine of frustration and his judgment will be considered later.[142] Goff and Cumming-Bruce LJJ held that despite the words 'at all times hereafter' the contract was terminable by reasonable notice. This decision is not lacking in boldness, when it is remembered that the original agreement was to provide water substantially below the market rate, and that it represented a compromise of the respective rights of the parties under the previous statutory provision. It is difficult to believe that any court in 1930 or 1940 would have held the agreement terminable by reasonable notice and not easy to explain when it had achieved this condition.

---

[139] These provisions often cover only cost of work done plus a profit element and do not cover profit on work that has not been done.

[140] See p 636, above; Carnegie 85 LQR 392.

[141] [1978] 3 All ER 769, [1978] 1 WLR 1387. See also *Tower Hamlets London Borough Council v British Gas Corpn* [1984] CLY 393.

[142] See p 731, below.

11 STIPULATIONS AS TO TIME [143]

Many contracts contain express provision as to the time by which performance is to be completed. In most if not all, others, it would be reasonable to infer that performance was to be within a reasonable time. What is the effect of late performance? This obviously presents problems similar to other failures in performance—in some cases a day late will be a disaster; in others, a month's delay will do no harm.

The treatment of the question has not however been identical, partly because of differences of terminology and partly because equity has played a much more active role than in relation to other problems of performance and breach. The problem has traditionally been put by asking whether time is of the essence of the contract.

The principle at common law was that, in the absence of a contrary intention, time was essential, even though it has not been expressly made so by the parties. Performance, therefore, must be completed upon the precise date specified, otherwise the contract might be brought to an end.[144] A good illustration is afforded by the rule that, unless a contrary intention is clearly shown, a time fixed for delivery in a contract for the sale of goods must be exactly observed.[145]

On the other hand courts of equity, which have had to consider the matter in connection with suits for specific performance, have always taken a less rigid view.[146] Their view was that time was not necessarily essential, and if they could do so without injustice they would decree specific performance notwithstanding the failure of the plaintiff to observe the time fixed for completion.[147] This was especially so in the case of contracts for the sale of land. But the maxim that in equity the time fixed for completion is not of the essence of the contract does not mean that stipulations as to time may always be disregarded. Lord Parker made this clear in a well-known passage:

> But this maxim never had any application to cases in which the stipulation as to time could not be disregarded without injustice to the parties, when, for example, the parties, for reasons best known to themselves, had stipulated that the time fixed should be essential, or where there was something in the nature of the property or the surrounding circumstances which would render it inequitable to treat it as a non-essential term of the contract. It should be observed, too, that it was only for the purposes of granting specific performance that equity in this class of case interfered with the remedy at law. A vendor who . . . had by his conduct lost the

---

[143] Stoljar 71 LQR 527.   [144] *Parkin v Thorold* (1852) 16 Beav 59.

[145] *Bowes v Shand* (1877) 2 App Cas 455 (sale of rice); *Reuter Hufeland & Co v Sala & Co* (1879) 4 CPD 239 (sale of pepper); *Sharp v Christmas* (1892) 8 TLR 687 (sale of potatoes); *Hartley v Hymans* [1920] 3 KB 475 at 484.

[146] 71 LQR 556.

[147] *Stickney v Keeble* [1915] AC 386 at 415, per Lord Parker; *Williams v Greatrex* [1956] 3 All ER 705, [1957] 1 WLR 31.

right to specific performance had no equity to restrain proceedings at law based on the non-observance of the stipulation as to time.[148]

In short, time is of the essence of the contract if such is the real intention of the parties and an intention to this effect may be expressly stated or may be inferred from the nature of the contract or from its attendant circumstances. By way of summary it may be said that time is essential firstly, if the parties expressly stipulate in the contract that it shall be so,[149] secondly, if in a case where one party has been guilty of undue delay, he is notified by the other that unless performance is completed within a reasonable time the contract will be regarded as at an end;[150] and lastly, if the nature of the surrounding circumstances or of the subject matter makes it imperative that the agreed date should be precisely observed. Under this last head it has been held that a date fixed for completion is essential if contained in a contract for the sale of property which fluctuates in value with the passage of time, such as a public house,[151] business premises,[152] a reversionary interest[153] or shares of a speculative nature liable to considerable fluctuation in value.[154]

The topic was exhaustively reconsidered by the House of Lords in *United Scientific Holdings Ltd v Burnley Borough Council*[155] where it was forcefully stated that it was no longer appropriate to analyse the problem in terms of what the rules of common law and equity were before 1873.[156]

The landlords had granted the tenants a 99-year lease of premises from 31 August 1962. The rent was fixed for the first ten years and there was provision for periodic rent reviews thereafter and machinery was laid down in the lease, which contemplated that the landlord would take steps to activate the machinery in the tenth year of each ten-year period if he wished to raise the rent. The landlord took no steps until 12 October 1972, ie after the end of the first ten years had been completed. The tenant argued that time was of the essence and that as the landlord had not acted in time, he had lost the chance to increase the rent. This argument had succeeded in several Court of Appeal decisions over the previous few years, but it was decisively rejected by the House of Lords, who held that the nature

---

[148] *Stickney v Keeble* [1915] AC 386 at 416.

[149] *Hudson v Temple* (1860) 29 Beav 536.

[150] *Stickney v Keeble* [1915] AC 386; *Parkin v Thorold* (1852) 16 Beav 59; *Hartley v Hymans* [1920] 3 KB 475 at 595–596; *Charles Rickards Ltd v Oppenheim* [1950] 1 KB 616, [1950] 1 All ER 420; *Ajit v Sammy* [1967] 1 AC 255.

[151] *Lock v Bell* [1931] 1 Ch 35.   [152] *Harold Wood Brick Co v Ferris* [1935] 2 KB 198.

[153] *Newman v Rogers* (1793) 4 Bro CC 391.

[154] *Hare v Nicoll* [1966] 2 QB 130, [1966] 1 All ER 285.

[155] [1978] AC 904, [1977] 2 All ER 62 and see *Bunge Corpn v Tradax SA* [1981] 2 All ER 513, [1981] 1 WLR 711.

[156] It does not follow, of course, that it is possible to explain the modern law without reference to its history.

of the contract was such that there was a presumption that time was not of the essence.[157]

The Law of Property Act 1925[158] re-enacting section 25 of the Judicature Act 1873, provides as follows:

> Stipulations in a contract, as to time or otherwise, which according to rules of equity are not deemed to be or to have become of the essence of the contract, are also construed and have effect at law in accordance with the same rules.

It has been suggested that this provision means that, if, say, in the contract for the sale of land, time is not of the essence in equity, then late completion would not give rise to damages at common law. This view was decisively rejected in *Raineri v Miles*[159] where the House of Lords held (Viscount Dilhorne dissenting) that it meant that in such a case late performance does not give rise to a right to terminate but does give rise to a right to damages.

Where time is not of the essence late performance will be a ground for termination where it causes 'frustrating delay'.[160]

A very important practical problem arises where time is not originally of the essence and one party is guilty of delay. The innocent party appears to have two options at this point. He can either wait until the delay is so long as to be a frustrating delay, as set out in the previous paragraph, or he can seek to give a notice making time of the essence. If he gives the notice then it will only be necessary to give a reasonable time for further chance of performance rather than wait the longer period which will be needed for a frustrating delay. There is a certain untidiness here and it is not entirely clear why the innocent party is given these two rather different remedies. A second problem is at what stage the innocent party can give the notice calling on the other party to perform within a further reasonable time. In *British and Commonwealth Holdings plc v Quadrex Holdings Inc*[161] the Court of Appeal assumed that the guilty party must not merely be late but be unreasonably late before the notice can be given. However, in practice, a very short period indeed was treated as satisfying this requirement on the facts of the particular case which was one involving trading in the shares of a volatile private company where normally time would have been of the essence except that the parties had not provided expressly for any completion date. In *Behzadi v Shaftsbury Hotels Ltd*[162] the Court of Appeal held that the innocent party could serve a notice making time of the essence as soon as there was any delay. It seems to follow

---

[157] It will be noted that the landlord did not break the contract by not applying in time for an increase but the tenant's argument was that his obligation to pay the increased rent was conditional on the landlord acting in time.

[158] S 41.

[159] [1981] AC 1050, [1980] 2 All ER 145.

[160] *Universal Cargo Carriers Corpn v Citati* [1957] 2 QB 401, [1957] 2 All ER 70. Many difficulties surround this rule. Stannard 46 MLR 738.

[161] [1989] QB 842, [1989] 3 All ER 492.   [162] [1991] 2 All ER 477.

from this that where time is not initially of the essence the alert and well-advised innocent party can greatly accelerate his possibility of terminating the contract by giving a very prompt notice calling on the guilty party to perform within a reasonable time.

12 TENDER OF PERFORMANCE

If A, one party to a contract, cannot complete performance without the concurrence of the other party B, it is obvious that an offer by him to perform and a rejection of that offer by B entitles him to a discharge from further liability. His readiness to perform has been nullified solely by the conduct of the other party. The rule, therefore, is that a tender of performance is equivalent to performance. In *Startup v Macdonald*:[163]

> The plaintiffs agreed to sell ten tons of oil to the defendant and to deliver it to him 'within the last fourteen days of March', payment in cash to be made at the expiration of that time. Delivery was tendered at 8.30 pm on 31 March, a Saturday, but the defendant refused to accept or to pay for the goods owing to the lateness of the hour.

It was held that the tender of the oil was in the circumstances equivalent to performance and that the plaintiffs were entitled to recover damages for non-acceptance. The law is stated with such lucidity by Rolfe B, that the following passage from his judgment deserves emphasis:

> In every contract by which a party binds himself to deliver goods or pay money to another, he in fact engages to do an act which he cannot completely perform without the concurrence of the party to whom the delivery or the payment is to be made. Without acceptance on the part of him who is to receive, the act of him who is to deliver or to pay can amount only to a tender. But the law considers a party who has entered into a contract to deliver goods or pay money to another as having, substantially, performed it if he has tendered the goods or the money . . . provided only that the tender has been made under such circumstances that the party to whom it has been made has had a reasonable opportunity of examining the goods, or the money, tendered, in order to ascertain that the thing tendered really was what it purported to be. Indeed, without such an opportunity an offer to deliver or pay does not amount to a tender. Now to apply this principle to the present case. The contract was to deliver the oil before the end of March. The plaintiffs did in pursuance of that contract tender the oil to the defendant at a time which, according to the express finding of the jury, left him full opportunity to examine, weigh and receive it before the end of March. If he had then accepted it . . . the

---

[163] (1843) 6 Man & G 593.

contract would have been literally performed; and the neglect of the defendant to perform his part of the contract . . . cannot in my opinion in any manner affect the rights of the plaintiffs . . . They fulfilled all they had contracted to do.[164]

The effect, however, of a tender varies according as the subject matter is goods or money.

If A actually produces goods of the correct quantity and quality to B, the rejection of his offer entirely discharges him from further liability and entitles him to recover damages for breach of contract.[165]

If A produces to B the exact amount of money that he is contractually bound to pay, it is true that he need make no further tender, but nevertheless his obligation to pay the debt remains. If he is sued for breach he merely pays the money into court, whereupon the costs of the action must be borne by B.[166]

In order to constitute a valid tender of money, 'there must be an actual production of the money, or a dispensation of such production'[167] and also payment must be offered in what is called 'legal tender', ie in the current coin of the realm or in Bank of England notes according to the rules established by law. These rules prescribe that Bank of England notes are good tender for any amount;[168] gold coins for any amount; coins of cupro-nickel or silver exceeding ten new pence in value for any amount up to ten pounds; coins of cupro-nickel or silver of not more than ten new pence in value up to five pounds only; coins of bronze for any amount up to twenty new pence only.[169] The debtor must not ask for change but must tender the precise amount due, unless he is content to leave the surplus with the creditor.[170]

---

[164] Ibid at 610–611.   [165] *Startup v Macdonald*, above.

[166] *Griffiths v School Board of Ystradyfodwg* (1890) 24 QBD 307.

[167] *Finch v Brook* (1834) 1 Bing NC 253 at 256, per Tindal J; *Farquharson v Pearl Assurance Co* [1937] 3 All ER 124.

[168] Currency and Bank Notes Act 1954, s 1.

[169] Coinage Act 1971, s 2.   [170] *Robinson v Cook* (1815) 6 Taunt 336.

19 DISCHARGE BY AGREEMENT [1]

What has been created by agreement may be extinguished by agreement. An agreement by the parties to an existing contract to extinguish the rights and obligations that have been created is itself a binding contract, provided that it is either made under seal or supported by consideration.

Consideration raises no difficulty if the contract to be extinguished is still executory, for in such a case each party agrees to release his rights under the contract in consideration of a similar release by the other. The discharge in such a case is bilateral, for each party surrenders something of value. The position is different where the contract to be extinguished, which we will call in future the original contract, is wholly executed on one side, as for instance where a seller has delivered the goods but the buyer has not paid the price. Here the seller has performed his part, and if he were merely to agree that the original contract should be discharged, ie that the buyer should be released from his obligation of payment, he would receive nothing of value in exchange. The buyer would have neither suffered a detriment himself nor have conferred an advantage upon the seller, but would be in the position of a donee. This, in other words, is a unilateral discharge, and it is ineffective unless it is made under seal or unless some valuable consideration is given by the buyer. Unilateral discharge in return for consideration is often called accord and satisfaction. The accord is the agreement for the discharge of the original contract; the satisfaction is the consideration conferred upon the party who has performed his obligations.

[1] The process of discharging or modifying the contract by agreement presents many problems both as to stating the law and as to deciding what it should be. For a valuable analysis see Aivazian, Trebilcock and Penny 22 Osgoode Hall LJ 173. See also Carter 13 JCL 185; Waddams 13 JCL 199; Hunter 13 JCL 205; Furmston 13 JCL 210.

Discharge by deed, which is equally effective in both cases, requires no discussion, but we will now deal separately with bilateral and unilateral discharge effected by a simple contract.

Of course this discussion assumes that the parties are agreed.[2] In most cases this will be clear but difficult cases may arise where it is argued that the contract has been implicitly abandoned by conduct. This point has arisen in a number of recent cases where it has been argued that the parties have tacitly abandoned an agreement to arbitrate by prolonged inaction. In the leading case *Paal Wilson & Co A/S v Partenreederei Hannah Blumenthal, The Hannah Blumenthal*[3] this possibility was recognised by the House of Lords. In delivering the principal speech Lord Brandon identified two ways in which implicit abandonment might be shown:

> The first way is by showing that the conduct of each party, as evinced to the other party and acted on by him, leads necessarily to the inference of an implied agreement between them to abandon the contract. The second method is by showing that the conduct of B, as evinced towards A, has been such as to lead A reasonably to believe that B has abandoned the contract, even though it has not in fact been B's intention to do so, and that A has significantly altered his position in reliance on that belief.[4]

In most of the cases the parties have done nothing more than appoint an arbitrator and then allow the matter to rest for several years. In the case of litigation the defendant would be able to apply to the court to have the action struck out for want of prosecution but the House of Lords held in *Bremer Vulkan Schiffbau und Maschinenfabrik v South India Shipping Corpn*[5] that neither the arbitrator nor the court had inherent jurisdiction to terminate an arbitration for want of prosecution. In *André et Cie SA v Machine Transocean Ltd, The Splendid Sun*[6] an arbitration agreement was held to have been implicitly abandoned by inaction and this decision was approved in the *Hannah Blumenthal*. On the other hand other courts in cases not

---

[2] See *Bank of Credit and Commerce International SA v Ali* [2001] UKHL 8, [2001] 1 All ER 961 discussed above, pp 109 ff.

[3] [1983] 1 AC 854, [1983] 1 All ER 34.

[4] Ibid at 914 and 47, respectively.

[5] [1981] AC 909, 962, [1981] 1 All ER 289. This was based on a doctrine accepted by the majority that in an arbitration both parties are under reciprocal obligations to keep the process moving so that it is the fault of both parties if the arbitration grinds to a halt. It seems clear that as a matter of arbitral law this decision was unfortunate and it is not surprising therefore that many ways have been sought to get round it of which mutual abandonment is but one. See the Freshfields Arbitration Lecture for 1989, 'The Problem of Delay in Arbitration', by Lord Justice Bingham, reproduced in 'Arbitration' August 1990 164. The departmental advisory committee on English arbitration law chaired by Lord Justice Mustill produced a report recommending that the arbitrator should be given by statute power to strike out the claim where there has been delay to such an extent that a fair hearing of the dispute is no longer possible, and this was done by s 102 of the Courts and Legal Services Act 1990, which introduced a new s 13A into the Arbitration Act 1950 and came into force on 1 January 1992. For fuller discussion, see Furmston, Norisada and Poole, *Contract Formation and Letters of Intent* pp 38–49.

[6] [1981] QB 694, [1981] 2 All ER 993.

easily distinguishable on the facts have refused to hold that mutual inaction amounts to abandonment.[7] It is clear that there are difficulties in analysing inaction by one side as an offer and inaction by the other side as an acceptance. On the other hand, if the parties appoint arbitrators and then do nothing for five, ten, fifteen, twenty years, there must come a point at which the only inference can be that the parties have abandoned the arbitration. The correct question must be not can the facts be slotted into the mechanical concepts of offer and acceptance but has each party led the other party reasonably to believe that the arbitration has been abandoned? Even this question will not be easy to answer but it seems clear that the answer will sometimes be in the affirmative.

1 BILATERAL DISCHARGE

This form of discharge is available to the parties whether their contract is either wholly or partially executory. In the case of a contract for the sale of goods, for instance, it is available not only where there has been no payment and no delivery, but also where there has been partial though not complete delivery of the goods. It is immaterial that the contract is contained in a deed. There was, indeed, a technical rule at common law that a contract under seal could not be dissolved, either wholly or partially, except by another contract under seal;[8] but courts of equity took an opposite view and held that a simple contract which extinguished or varied the deed was a good defence to an action on the deed. This has become the rule in all courts since 1873, for the Judicature Act of that year provided that 'in all matters in which there is any conflict or variance between the rules of equity and the rules of the common law with reference to the same matter, the rules of equity shall prevail'.[9] Thus in *Berry v Berry*:[10]

> A husband covenanted in a deed of separation to pay his wife £18 a month. Eight years later, by a written contract not under seal, he agreed to pay her £9 a month and 30 per cent of his earnings if they exceeded £350 a year.

It was held that this simple contract was a good defence to an action brought by the wife to recover the sum fixed by the deed of separation.

---

[7] *Allied Marine Transport Ltd v Vale do Rio, Doce Navegacao SA, The Leonidas D* [1985] 2 All ER 796, [1985] 1 WLR 925; *Food Corpn of India v Antclizo Shipping Corpn, The Antclizo* [1988] 2 All ER 513, [1988] 1 WLR 630 was taken on appeal to the House of Lords in the hope of resolving the issue but the House of Lords held that it could not review the concurrent findings of the trial judge and the Court of Appeal that the particular arbitration agreement has not been abandoned. See also *Pearl Mill Co Ltd v Ivy Tannery Co Ltd* [1919] 1 KB 78, [1918–1919] All ER Rep 702.

[8] *West v Blakeway* (1841) 2 Man & G 729.

[9] Re-enacted in the Judicature Act 1925, s 44.

[10] [1929] 2 KB 316.

Form of discharge where executory contract unenforceable unless evidenced in writing

A problem, however, that requires discussion arises where the executory contract is one which is rendered unenforceable by action unless supported by adequate written evidence as prescribed by statute.[11] In such a case the question is whether the discharging contract must also conform to the statutory requirement. If, for example, a contract for the sale of land contains the written evidence required by the Law of Property Act 1925,[12] must an agreement to discharge it also comply with the Act? It was laid down by the House of Lords in the leading case of *Morris v Baron & Co*[13] that the solution of this problem depends upon the extent to which the parties intended to alter their existing contractual relations. Their intention in this respect must be collected from the terms of the discharging contract. There are three possibilities.[14]

i Partial discharge

First, the intention revealed by the second agreement may be merely to vary or modify the terms of the prior contract without altering them in substance. It has long been established that such a partial discharge is ineffective unless it is contained in a contract that also provides the written evidence required by the relevant statute. An oral variation leaves the written contract intact and enforceable. What the parties are taken to intend is not that the first contract shall be extinguished, but that it shall continue as varied. Yet effect cannot be given to their intention, since there is no written evidence of the contract as now varied. A statute such as the Statute of Frauds or the Law of Property Act 1925 requires that the whole, not part, of the contract, shall be evidenced by writing.[15]

ii Discharge simpliciter

Secondly, the parties may intend to extinguish the original contract in its entirety and to put an end to their contractual relations. In this case the original contract is rescinded even though the discharging contract is not evidenced as required in the case of the original contract. Thus, an oral agreement to abrogate a written contract for sale of land is effective.[16] The requirements of the Law of Property Act are directed to the creation of an enforceable contract, not to its extinction.

---

[11] Examples of such statutes are the Statute of Frauds, s 4 (contract of guarantee); Law of Property Act 1925, s 40(1) (contract for the sale or other disposition of land); this statute is now repealed but the illustration is retained since it figures in many of the leading cases; see *United Dominions Corpn (Jamaica) Ltd v Shoucair* [1969] 1 AC 340, [1968] 2 All ER 904.

[12] S 40(1).   [13] [1918] AC 1.   [14] Stoljar 35 Can Bar Rev 485.

[15] *Morris v Baron & Co* [1918] AC 1 at 31; *British and Beningtons Ltd v N W Cachar Tea Co* [1923] AC 48 at 62, in both cases per Lord Atkinson.

[16] *Goman v Salisbury* (1684) 1 Vern 240; *Morris v Baron & Co*, above, at 18, per Lord Haldane; at 26, per Lord Dunedin.

iii Original contract extinguished but replaced by fresh agreement

Thirdly, the intention of the parties may be to extinguish the former written contract, but to substitute for it a new and self-contained agreement. The result of such a bargain is that the prior written contract is rescinded, but the substituted agreement, if made orally, is unenforceable for want of written evidence.[17]

A difficult question of construction that may arise in this context is to discover what the parties intended to accomplish by their later oral agreement. Did they intend to extinguish the original contract altogether and to substitute a new contract in its place, or did they intend merely to vary the original contract? If the first of these hypotheses is correct, then the later contract effectively extinguishes the original contract but is itself unenforceable. If, on the other hand, the object of the parties was to modify their existing rights and obligations, the later contract is entirely destitute of effect. In order to decide this question the terms of the oral agreement must be examined; and if it is found that they are so far inconsistent with the original contract as to destroy its substance, though perhaps the shadow remains, the inference is that the parties intended to abrogate their former contract by the substitution of a new and self-contained agreement.

> A written contract may be rescinded by parol either expressly or by the parties entering into a parol contract entirely inconsistent with the written one, or, if not entirely inconsistent with it, inconsistent with it to an extent that goes to the very root of it.[18]

To justify the conclusion in favour of abrogation, however, the inconsistency must relate to something fundamental.

> What is of course essential is that there should have been made manifest the intention in any event of a complete extinction of the first and formal contract, and not merely the desire of an alteration, however sweeping, in terms which still leave it subsisting.[19]

The manner in which the courts deal with this problem may be illustrated by two contrasting cases.

In *Morris v Baron & Co*,[20] the facts were as follows:

> Morris agreed to sell goods to Baron & Co. He delivered only part of the goods, valued at £888 4s, and six months later began proceedings to recover this sum. The company counter-claimed for £934 17s 3d as damages for non-delivery of the whole of the goods. Before this action came to trial, the parties compromised the dispute. They made an oral contract under which the action was to be withdrawn; the company was to have another three months within which to pay the sum due under the contract; it was to have the option either to accept or to refuse

---

[17] *Morris v Baron & Co* [1918] AC 1.
[18] *British and Beningtons Ltd v N W Cachar Tea Co* [1923] AC 48 at 62, Per Lord Atkinson.
[19] *Morris v Baron & Co* [1918] AC 1 at 19, per Lord Haldane.   [20] [1918] AC 1.

the undelivered goods; it was to be allowed £30 to meet the expenses incurred owing to the failure of Morris to make complete delivery.

Ten months later, the £888 4s was still unpaid and Morris brought a second action to recover this sum. The company admitted liability, but again counter-claimed for damages in respect of the undelivered goods. The action failed for two reasons.

First, Morris could not claim under the original contract. It had been extinguished. Its terms were so fundamentally inconsistent with the provisions of the compromise as to justify the inference that the parties intended to replace it by an entirely new contract.[21]

Secondly, neither Morris nor Baron & Co could base any claim on the compromise, which itself amounted to a contract for the sale of goods.[22] Since it was made orally, it was unenforceable under section 4 of the Sale of Goods Act 1893, which still applied to such a contract at the time when *Morris v Baron & Co* was decided.[23] It operated to extinguish the original contract, but it could not be actively enforced.

On the other hand, *United Dominions Corpn (Jamaica) Ltd v Shoucair*[24] was a case in which the facts disclosed an intention to retain, not to abrogate, the original contract:

> A loan, secured by a mortgage and carrying interest at 9 per cent, was made in Jamaica by the appellants to the respondent. Owing to a rise in the local bank rate, the respondent at the request of the appellants agreed in writing to alter the rate of interest to 11 per cent. This written agreement was unenforceable since it did not comply with the Jamaican Moneylenders Act which corresponds to section 6 of the English Act of 1927. The Jamaican Act does not apply to loans bearing interest at 9 per cent or less and therefore it did not affect the mortgage. The appellants, realising that they could not enforce the agreement of variation, sued for the recovery of interest at 9 per cent due under the mortgage.

The Privy Council gave judgment for the appellants. The parties intended by their written agreement to keep the mortgage alive, but to amend its provision relating to the rate of interest. But the mortgage remained intact, since it could not be affected by an amendment that infringed the statute. 'If the new agreement reveals an intention to rescind the old, the old goes; and if it does not, the old remains in force and unamended.'[25]

The cases discussed above all arose in the context of statutory requirements for written evidence of contracts which have now disappeared but the doctrine of consideration can generate very similar problems.

---

[21] See especially Lord Atkinson at 33.

[22] Ibid at 10, per Lord Finlay; at 29, per Lord Dunedin; at 34, per Lord Atkinson; at 36, per Lord Parmoor.

[23] P 262, above. The repeal of this section of the Sale of Goods Act has greatly reduced the area of this question of construction.

[24] [1969] 1 AC 340, [1968] 2 All ER 904.   [25] Ibid at 348 and 907, respectively.

Suppose A and B have made a contract that A will sell his car to B for £5,000. Suppose later two alternative scenarios:

(1) A and B agree that the contract shall be abandoned. Five minutes later A and B agree that A will sell his car to B for £4,900.

(2) A and B agree to change the contract so that A sells the car to B for £4,900.

Conventional theory appears to say that there is no consideration problem in (1) but that there is (or may be) in (2).[26]

Waiver of a contractual term by one party at the request of the other

Such, then, is the law where the variation is made for the mutual advantage of both parties. A different and a slightly more complex situation may arise where the alteration of the contractual terms is designed to suit the convenience of one only of the parties. One party may accede, perhaps reluctantly, to the request of the other, and promise that he will not insist upon performance according to the strict letter of the contract. This is an indulgence that is a common feature of commercial life. In the case of a contract for the sale of goods, for instance, approval may be given to the request either of the seller or the buyer that the date of delivery be postponed for a short time. An arrangement of this kind for a substituted mode of performance is generally described as either a waiver or a forbearance by the party who grants the indulgence.[27]

The efficacy of such a waiver is open to the technical objection that it is unsupported by consideration. If, for instance, the seller agrees at the request of the buyer to postpone delivery until 1 July, but ultimately refuses to deliver on the latter date, it is arguable that according to strict doctrine he has a complete answer to an action for breach of contract. The buyer is theoretically in a difficult position. He was not ready and willing to accept delivery at the contract date, so that he himself is guilty of a breach; and he gave no consideration for the promise by the seller to extend the time for delivery. If a similar concession is made orally in the case of a guarantee, there is the further difficulty that the requirements of the Statute of Frauds have not been satisfied. The natural instinct of judges, however, is to uphold reasonable arrangements for the relaxation of contractual terms and to refuse to be unduly distracted by strict doctrine. Even at common law they have been at pains to implement the intention of the parties; but in the efforts to do this they have not only ignored the question of consideration, but have propounded a supposed distinction between variation and

---

[26] Much useful analysis relevant to this problem can be found in the judgment of Tuckey LJ in *Compagnie Noga D'Importation et D'Exportation SA v Abacha* [2003] EWCA Civ 1100, [2003] 2 All ER (Comm) 915.

[27] For a fuller discussion of this subject, see Cheshire and Fifoot 63 LQR 283 at 289–301; Dugdale and Yates 39 MLR 680; Adams 36 Conv (NS) 245; Reiter 27 U Toronto LJ 439.

waiver which has no substance and which has merely served to confuse matters. There is support for two common law propositions.

First, a waiver cannot be repudiated by the party for whose benefit it has been granted, so that if A abstains at B's request from insisting upon performance according to the exact terms of the contract, B is compelled to treat this indulgence as effective. Thus, if in the case of a written contract for the sale of goods to be delivered on 1 June the seller at the request of the buyer extends the time for acceptance until 1 July, the buyer, if he defaults on the latter date, cannot escape liability by averring that the seller did not deliver according to the original contract and that the parol variation is ineffective.[28]

Secondly, there is considerable authority for the rule that even the party who grants the indulgence cannot go back on his agreement.[29] Thus, in the example just given, the seller is not allowed to withhold delivery on 1 July on the ground that the buyer himself committed a breach by failure to accept the goods at the contract date.

These common law decisions, though dictated by a laudable desire to sustain reasonable arrangements between businessmen, affect to make everything turn upon a supposed distinction between the variation and the waiver of a contractual term. If the subject matter of the arrangement is a written contract falling under the Statute of Frauds or the Law of Property Act, it is said that a variation must be evidenced by writing, but that a waiver may be parol. Yet the enigma is to formulate some test by which to distinguish the one from the other. The search will be in vain. When we are told, for instance, that an agreed alteration of the date at which delivery is due constitutes a variation, but that a forbearance by one party at the request of the other to call for delivery until a month later than the contract date is a waiver,[30] it becomes apparent that the dichotomy is visionary and one from which reason recoils. The truth is that every alteration of the kind with which we are concerned is a variation of the contract, but that it is called a waiver when the court is willing to give effect to the intention of the parties. The unfortunate result is the virtual impossibility of anticipating what view the court will take.

In this state of confusion it is not unnatural that recourse should be had to equity. The equitable doctrine has been stated in these words by Bowen LJ:

> If persons who have contractual rights against others induce by their conduct those against whom they have such rights to believe that such rights will either not be enforced or will be kept in suspense or abeyance for some particular time, those persons will not be allowed by a

---

[28] *Hickman v Haynes* (1875) LR 10 CP 598; *Ogle v Earl of Vane* (1868) LR 3 QB 272; *Levey & Co v Goldberg* [1922] 1 KB 688.

[29] *Leather-Cloth Co v Hieronimus* (1875) LR 10 QB 140; *Tyers v Rosedale and Ferryhill Iron Co* (1875) LR 10 Exch 195; *Panoutsos v Raymond Hadley Corpn of New York* [1917] 2 KB 473; *Hartley v Hymans* [1920] 3 KB 475.

[30] See eg *Besseler, Waechter, Glover & Co v South Derwent Coal Co Ltd* [1938] 1 KB 408 at 416, [1937] 4 All ER 552 at 556.

court of equity to enforce the rights until such time has elapsed, without at all events placing the parties in the same position as they were in before.[31]

In short, a voluntary concession granted by one party, upon the faith of which the other may have shaped his conduct, remains effective until it is made clear by notice or otherwise that it is to be withdrawn and the strict position under the contract restored. The concession raises an equity against the party who consented to it. If, for instance, in the case of a written contract for the sale of goods the buyer at the request of the sellers orally consents to the postponement of delivery, he cannot peremptorily hold the sellers to the original contract. No repudiation of his waiver will be effective except a clear intimation to them that he proposes to resume his strict rights. Normally he will do this by giving express notice of his intention, but this method is not essential and anything will suffice which makes it abundantly clear that the concession is withdrawn. Within a reasonable time thereafter the original position will be restored. The rights of the seller under such a waiver have been stated by Denning LJ:

> If the defendant, as he did, led the plaintiffs to believe that he would not insist on the stipulation as to time, and that, if they carried out the work, he would accept it, and they did it, he could not afterwards set up the stipulation as to the time against them. Whether it be called waiver or forbearance on his part, or an agreed variation or substituted performance, does not matter. It is a kind of estoppel. By his conduct he evinced an intention to affect their legal relations. He made, in effect, a promise not to insist on his strict legal rights. That promise was intended to be acted on, and was in fact acted on. He cannot afterwards go back on it.[32]

The operation of this doctrine of waiver is well illustrated by *Charles Rickards Ltd v Oppenheim*[33] where the facts were as follows:

> Early in 1947 the defendant ordered from the plaintiffs a Rolls Royce chassis, and in July the plaintiffs agreed that a body should be built for it within 'six or at most seven months'. The body was not completed seven months later, but the defendant agreed to wait another three months. At the end of this extended period the body was still not built. The defendant then gave a final notice that if the work were not finished within a further period of four weeks he would cancel the order. The body was not finished within this period and the defendant cancelled the order. The completed body was tendered to the defendant three months later, but he refused to accept it.

This was a case where the time of delivery was of the essence of the contract. The defendant's agreement, however, that delivery should be postponed for three months constituted a waiver of his right in this respect, and if the body had been completed

---

[31] *Birmingham and District Land Co v London and North Western Rly Co* (1888) 40 ChD 268 at 286.
[32] *Charles Richards Ltd v Oppenheim* [1950] 1 KB 616 at 623, [1950] 1 All ER 420 at 423.
[33] [1950] 1 KB 616, [1950] 1 All ER 420.

within the extended time he would have been estopped from denying that the contract had been performed. But by granting a further and final indulgence of four weeks' delay he had given reasonable notice that time was once more to be of the essence of the matter, and, since the car was not ready within this final period, the plaintiffs were in breach of their contract. The Court of Appeal, therefore, gave judgment for the defendant.

Again, if the rent book relating to premises, let originally on a weekly tenancy, contains the words 'one month's notice each party', but this is later crossed out and replaced by a statement, initialled by the landlord, which runs 'one month's notice from tenant; two years' notice from landlord', the new promise made by the landlord is without consideration. But if the tenant acts on the faith of the promise by remaining in possession and continuing to pay rent he is entitled to receive two years' notice.[34]

These cases clearly have much in common with the doctrine of promissory estoppel which we have already considered at length.[35] Indeed on one view they are examples of it. On the other hand there is authority for the view that though on many sets of facts, waiver and estoppel produce the same result, yet the doctrines remain distinct. An instructive case is *Brikom Investments Ltd v Carr*.[36]

> The landlords of four blocks of flats offered to sell 99-year leases to their sitting tenants. The leases contained undertakings by the landlords to maintain the structure of the buildings and by the tenants to contribute to the cost. At the time of the negotiations, the roofs were in need of repair and the landlords made oral representations to the tenants' association and individual tenants that they would repair the roofs at their own expense and in some cases confirmed this in writing before the leases were signed. Subsequently the landlords effected the repairs and claimed contributions from the defendants, who included both original lessees and assignees therefrom.

The Court of Appeal held for the lessees for a variety of reasons. As regards the original lessees, it was held that there was a binding collateral contract where the tenants had entered into leases in reliance on the landlord's promise to repair.[37] Alternatively Lord Denning MR thought that the doctrine of promissory estoppel applied whereas Roskill and Cumming-Bruce LJJ thought that the case was one of waiver. All three judges agreed, however, that these respective doctrines operated to protect not only the original lessees but also their assignees.

---

[34] *Wallis v Semark* [1951] 2 TLR 222. For an earlier authority to the same effect, see *Bruner v Moore* [1904] 1 Ch 305.

[35] Pp 125 ff, above.

[36] [1979] QB 467, [1979] 2 All ER 753. See also *Glencore Grain Ltd v Flacker Shipping Ltd, The Happy Day* [2002] EWCA Civ 1068, [2002] 2 All ER (Comm) 896.

[37] Cf *City and Westminster Properties (1934) Ltd v Mudd* [1959] Ch 129, [1958] 2 All ER 733.

It must be confessed that the topic of waiver is not a clear one and awaits an authoritative modern statement. One of the difficulties is that the doctrine has many facets and is applied in many different situations. Two important distinctions may usefully be kept in mind. The first is between remedies and rights. Certain remedies need to be exercised promptly and it may be relatively easy to infer their waiver.[38] An example is the innocent party's right to terminate for repudiation or fundamental breach.[39] A second distinction turns on whether the waiver comes before or after the departure from the strict terms of the contract. If the waiver precedes the departure, it may have played a part in causing it and justice may more readily be held to demand that there be no retraction.

2 UNILATERAL DISCHARGE

A contract, which has been performed by A but has not been performed by the other party B, may be the subject of unilateral discharge. In the majority of cases B has committed a breach of the contract in the sense that he is not ready and willing to perform his obligation, as for instance where he is unable to pay for goods that have been delivered to him under a contract of sale. In such a case A may agree to release B from his obligation. A release given by deed is effective. A release expressed in an agreement not under seal, however, as we have already seen, is *nudum pactum* unless A receives some valuable consideration in return for the right that he abandons.[40] Since B has received all that he is entitled to receive under the contract, he cannot aver, as he can in the case of bilateral discharge, that by the mere acceptance of the release he furnishes consideration to A.

The agreement, if supported by the necessary consideration, is called accord and satisfaction. This has been judicially defined as follows:

> Accord and satisfaction is the purchase of a release from an obligation, whether arising under contract or tort, by means of any valuable consideration, not being the actual performance of the obligation itself. The accord is the agreement by which the obligation is discharged. The satisfaction is the consideration which makes the agreement operative.[41]

If, for instance, £50 is due for goods sold and delivered, a promise by the seller to accept a cash payment of £45 in discharge of the buyer's obligation is not a good accord and satisfaction, since the buyer is relieved of a liability to pay £5 without

---

[38] See eg *Aquis Estates Ltd Minton* [1975] 3 All ER 1043, [1975] 1 WLR 1452.
[39] And see discussion at pp 680 ff, above.
[40] Pp 125 ff, above.
[41] *British Russian Gazette Ltd v Associated Newspapers Ltd* [1933] 2 KB 616 at 643–644; the definition was adopted from *Salmond and Winfield on Contracts* p 328.

giving or promising anything in return.[42] A promise by the buyer, however, to confer upon the seller some independent benefit, actual or contingent, may constitute sufficient consideration for the acceptance of the smaller sum.[43] Thus in 1602 it was said that 'the gift of a horse, hawk or a robe' would suffice, since it would not have been accepted by the creditor had it not been more beneficial to him than the money.[44] This reasoning even persuaded the divisional court in *Goddard v O'Brien*[45] to hold that the payment of a smaller sum by cheque instead of in cash was an independent benefit sufficient to rank as consideration; but the Court of Appeal has now refused to follow this decision.[46] Yet, the general rule remains that the acceptance by a creditor of something different from that to which he is entitled may discharge the debtor from liability.

Thus a promise by the debtor to pay a smaller sum at a date earlier than that on which it is contractually due,[47] or to pay a larger sum at a later date, is a good accord and satisfaction if accepted by the creditor. Again, if A claims from B a sum that is not finally determined, as for example where he demands £50 on a *quantum meruit* for services rendered or demands £50 by way of damages for libel, his promise to release B in consideration of the payment of a lesser sum than that claimed is a good accord and satisfaction. In other words the payment of a lesser sum is satisfaction if the sum claimed is unliquidated, but not if it is liquidated.[48]

The essential fact is, then, that an accord without satisfaction is ineffective. This statement, however, is ambiguous. Is the discharge effective as soon as the debtor has promised to give the satisfaction, or only when the promise has been implemented? In other words, is it sufficient if the consideration is executory? The correct answer is given by Scrutton LJ in these words:

> Formerly it was necessary that the consideration should be executed: 'I release you from your obligation in consideration of £50 now paid by you to me.' Later it was conceded that the consideration might be executory: 'I release you from your obligation in consideration of your promise to pay me £50 and give me a letter of withdrawal.' The consideration on each side might be an executory promise, the two mutual promises making an agreement enforceable in law, a contract. Comyns puts it in his Digest, and the passage was approved by Parke B in *Good v Cheesman*[49] and by the Court of King's Bench in *Cartwright v Cooke*.[50] 'An accord, with mutual promises to perform, is good, though the thing be not performed at the time of action; for the party has a remedy to compel the performance,' that is to say, a cross-action on the contract of accord.[51]

---

[42] *Foakes v Beer* (1884) 9 App Cas 605; p 621, above.   [43] Ibid at 613, per Lord Selborne.
[44] *Pinnel's Case* (1602) 5 Co Rep 117a.   [45] (1882) 9 QBD 37.
[46] *D & C Builders Ltd v Rees* [1966] 2 QB 617, [1965] 3 All ER 837, p 125, above.
[47] Co Litt 212b.
[48] *Wilkinson v Byers* (1834) 1 Ad & El 106. See also *Ferguson v Davies* [1997] 1 All ER 315 discussed above, p 91.
[49] (1831) 2 B & Ad 328 at 335.   [50] (1832) 3 B & Ad 701 at 703.
[51] *British Russian Gazette Ltd v Associated Newspapers Ltd* [1933] 2 KB 616 at 644.

The modern rule is, then, that if what the creditor has accepted in satisfaction is merely his debtor's promise to give consideration, and not the performance of that promise, the original cause of action is discharged from the date when the agreement is made.[52]

This, however, raises a question of construction in each case, for it has to be decided as a fact whether it was the making of the promise itself or the performance of the promise that the creditor consented to take by way of satisfaction.

> Suppose for instance, that a buyer is unable to pay £50 which is due for goods delivered and that the seller agrees to discharge him from obligation of immediate payment in consideration of receiving a bill of exchange from a third party, X, for £55 payable four months hence.

If the seller were to sue for the £50 before receipt of the bill of exchange, the question would arise whether he had committed a breach of the agreement. This would depend upon whether the agreement constituted a good accord and satisfaction, and this in turn would depend upon the true bargain between the parties. Did they mean that the discharge should be complete when X promised to give the bill or only when he actually gave it?

The question of construction that arises in such a case is well illustrated by *British Russian Gazette Ltd v Associated Newspapers Ltd,*[53] where the facts relevant to the present matter were as follows:

> Mr Talbot agreed to compromise two actions of libel, which had been commenced by him and by the *British Russian Gazette*, in respect of certain articles in the *Daily Mail*. His promise was expressed in a letter couched in these terms: 'I accept the sum of one thousand guineas on account of costs and expenses in full discharge and settlement of my claims . . . and I will forthwith instruct my solicitors to serve notice of discontinuance; or to take other steps . . . to end the proceedings now pending.' Before payment of the thousand guineas had been made, Talbot disregarded this compromise and proceeded with the action.

If this letter meant that Talbot agreed to discharge the defendants from their obligation in consideration of their promise to make the payment, his continuance of the libel action constituted a breach of a good accord and satisfaction. His argument, of course, was that there was no binding discharge until actual payment, but this did not prevail with the Court of Appeal. It was held that the letter recorded an agreement in which the consideration was a promise for a promise: 'In consideration of your

---

[52] *Morris v Baron & Co* [1918] AC 1 at 35, per Lord Atkinson; *Elton Cop Dyeing Co v Broadbent & Son Ltd* (1919) 89 LJKB 186; *British Russian Gazette Ltd v Associated Newspapers Ltd* [1933] 2 KB 616.

[53] [1933] 2 KB 616.

promise to pay me a thousand guineas, I promise to discontinue proceedings.' The defendants were, therefore, entitled to enforce the accord by way of counter-claim.

There is one exception to the rule that a unilateral discharge requires consideration. It is enacted that if the holder of a bill of exchange or of a promissory note either unconditionally renounces his rights in writing or delivers the instrument to the person liable, the effect is to discharge the obligation of the acceptor or promisor even though no consideration is received.[54]

---

[54] Bills of Exchange Act 1882, ss 62 and 89.

20 DISCHARGE UNDER THE DOCTRINE OF FRUSTRATION[1]

1 NATURE AND RATIONALE OF THE DOCTRINE

After the parties have made their agreement, unforeseen contingencies may occur which prevent the attainment of the purpose that they had in mind. The question is whether this discharges them from further liability.

In the seventeenth century the judges in *Paradine v Jane*[2] laid down what is sometimes called the rule as to absolute contracts. It amounts to this: When *the law* casts a duty upon a man which, through no fault of his, he is unable to perform, he is excused for non-performance; but if he binds himself *by contract* absolutely to do a thing, he cannot escape liability for damages for proof that as events turned out performance is futile or even impossible. The alleged justification for this somewhat harsh principle is that a party to a contract can always guard against unforeseen contingencies by express stipulation; but if he voluntarily undertakes an absolute and unconditional obligation he cannot complain merely because events turn out to his disadvantage. It

---

[1] Treitel *Frustration and force majeure*; McKendrick (ed) *Force majeure and frustration* (2nd edn); Phang 21 Anglo-American LR 278.

[2] (1647) Aleyn 26. Simpson 91 LQR 247 at 269–273.

has accordingly been held, for instance, that if a builder agrees to construct a house by a certain date and fails to do so because a strike occurs[3] or because the soil contains a latent defect which suspends operations[4] he is none the less liable. Again, if a ship-owner agrees that he will load his ship with guano at a certain place in West Africa, he is liable in damages notwithstanding that no guano is obtainable.[5]

In practice parties very often insert in their contracts provisions designed to deal with unforeseen difficulties. Such *force majeure* or hardship clauses are particularly common where the contract is of a kind where the parties can foresee that such problems are likely to occur but cannot foresee their nature or extent as in building or engineering contracts. Such clauses often present problems of construction and application,[6] the details of which, however, fall outside the scope of this book.

Nevertheless, starting with the case of *Taylor v Caldwell*[7] in 1863, a substantive and particular doctrine has gradually been evolved by the courts which mitigates the rigour of the rule in *Paradine v Jane* by providing that if the further fulfilment of the contract is brought to an abrupt stop by some irresistible and extraneous cause for which neither party is responsible, the contract shall terminate forthwith and the parties be discharged.[8]

The most obvious cause which brings this doctrine into operation, and the one which provided the issue in the parent case of *Taylor v Caldwell,* is the physical destruction of the subject matter of the contract before performance falls due. Another, equally obvious, is a subsequent change in the law which renders performance illegal. A less obvious cause, but nevertheless one that has occasioned a multitude of decisions, is what is called the 'frustration of the common venture'. Owing to an event that has supervened since the making of the contract, the parties are frustrated in the sense that the substantial object that they had in view is no longer attainable. Literal performance may still be possible, but nevertheless it will not fulfil the original and common design of the parties. What the courts have held in such a case is that, if some catastrophic event occurs for which neither party is responsible and if the result of that event is to destroy the very basis of the contract, so that the venture to which the parties now find themselves committed is radically different from that originally contemplated, then the contract is forthwith discharged.[9] Mere hardship or

---

[3] *Budgett & Co v Binnington & Co* [1891] 1 QB 35.

[4] *Bottoms v York Corpn* (1892) 2 Hudson's BC (4th edn) 208.

[5] *Hills v Sughrue* (1846) 15 M & W 253.

[6] See eg *Superior Overseas Development Corpn and Phillips Petroleum (UK) Co Ltd v British Gas Corpn* [1982] 1 Lloyd's Rep 262.

[7] (1863) 3 B & S 826.

[8] *Denny, Mott and Dickson Ltd v James B Fraser & Co Ltd* [1944] AC 265 at 272, 274, [1944] 1 All ER 678 at 681, 683.

[9] *Sir Lindsay Parkinson & Co Ltd v Works and Public Buildings Comrs* [1949] 2 KB 632 at 665, [1950] 1 All ER 208 at 227, per Asquith LJ; *Cricklewood Property and Investment Trust Ltd v Leighton's Investment Trust Ltd* [1945] AC 221 at 228, [1945] 1 All ER 252 at 255, per Lord Simon; *Davis Contractors Ltd v Fareham UDC* [1956] AC 696 at 728–729, per Lord Radcliffe.

inconvenience to one of the parties is not sufficient to justify discharge. 'There must be as well such a change in the significance of the obligation that the thing undertaken would, if performed, be a different thing from that contracted for.'[10] Two simple illustrations may be given of circumstances which have been held sufficiently catastrophic to change the significance of the obligation.

> In *Krell v Henry*,[11] the plaintiff agreed to let a room to the defendant for the day upon which Edward VII was to be crowned. Both parties understood that the purpose of the letting was to view the coronation procession, but this did not appear in the agreement itself. The procession was postponed owing to the illness of the king.

The Court of Appeal took the view that the procession was the foundation of the contract and that the effect of its cancellation was to discharge the parties from the further performance of their obligations. It was no longer possible to achieve the substantial purpose of the contract. A similar result was reached in *Tatem Ltd v Gamboa*.[12] In that case:

> In June 1937, at the height of the Spanish Civil War, a ship was chartered by the plaintiffs to the Republican Government for a period of thirty days from 1 July, for the express purpose of evacuating civilians from the North Spanish ports to French Bay ports. The hire was at the rate of £250 a day until actual redelivery of the ship. This rate was about three times that prevailing in the market for equivalent ships not trading with Spanish ports. After one successful voyage, the ship was seized by Nationalists on 14 July and detained in Bilbao until 7 September, when she was released and ultimately redelivered to the plaintiffs on 11 September. The hire had been paid in advance up to 31 July, but the Republican Government refused to pay for the period from 1 August to 11 September, on the ground that the common venture of the parties had been frustrated by the seizure of the ship.

Goddard J held that the seizure had destroyed the foundation of the contract and that the Republican Government was not liable. He said:

> If the foundation of the contract goes, either by the destruction of the subject-matter or by reason of such long interruption or delay that the performance is really in effect that of a

---

[10] *Davis Contractors Ltd v Fareham UDC*, [1956] AC 696 at 728–729, per Lord Radcliffe. But Parliament can by statute give the courts power to vary agreements because of changed circumstances as it has done in the case of maintenance agreements: Matrimonial Causes Act 1973, s 35.

[11] [1903] 2 KB 740. The decision has not escaped judicial criticism; see *Larrinaga & Co v Société Franco-Americaine des Phosphates de Medulla* (1922) 29 Com Cas 1 at 7, per Lord Finlay; *Maritime National Fish Ltd v Ocean Trawlers Ltd* [1935] AC 524 at 529, per Lord Wright.

[12] [1939] 1 KB 132, [1938] 3 All ER 135.

different contract, and the parties have not provided what in that event is to happen, the performance of the contract is to be regarded as frustrated.[13]

Theories as to the basis of the doctrine

The precise legal theory upon which this doctrine of frustration is based has aroused much controversy. No fewer than five theories have been advanced at one time or another;[14] but the essential question is whether the courts strive to give effect to the supposed intention of the parties or whether they act independently and impose the solution that seems reasonable and just.

The former method was preferred by Blackburn J in *Taylor v Caldwell*[15] in 1863, when he made the first breach in the long-established rule as to absolute contracts. In that case, A had agreed to give B the use of a music hall on certain specified days for the purpose of holding concerts. The hall was accidentally destroyed by fire six days before the contract date, and B claimed damages for breach of the agreement. Blackburn J held the contract to be discharged, but he found it necessary to walk with circumspection in order to reconcile reason and justice with the established rule as to absolute contracts. His reasoning was that a contract is not to be construed as absolute if the parties must from the beginning have known that its fulfilment depended upon the continued existence of some particular thing, and therefore must have realised that this continuing existence was the foundation of the bargain. In such a case, he said, the contract 'is subject to an implied condition that the parties shall be excused in case, before breach, performance becomes impossible from the perishing of the thing without default of the contractor'.[16] In short, he attributed a conventional character to an obviously reasonable, if not inevitable, solution. Thus arose the theory of the implied term. No express term for the discharge of the contract was made by the parties, but had they anticipated and considered the catastrophic event that in fact happened, they would have said, 'if that happens it is all over between us'.[17] In implying such a term it has been said that 'the law is only doing what the parties really (though subconsciously) meant to do themselves'.[18]

This theory, though it still has its unrepentant adherents,[19] has been heavily

---

[13] Ibid at 139 and 144, respectively.

[14] McNair and Watts *Legal Effects of War* (4th edn) pp 156 ff; and see his articles in 35 LQR 84, 56 LQR 173. See *National Carriers Ltd v Panalpina (Northern) Ltd* [1981] AC 675, [1981] 1 All ER 161, esp at 165–166 and 686–687 respectively, per Lord Hailsham of St Marylebone LC.

[15] (1863) 3 B & S 826.

[16] Ibid at 883–884.

[17] *F A Tamplin Steamship Co Ltd v Anglo-Mexican Petroleum Products Co Ltd* [1916] 2 AC 397 at 404, per Lord Loreburn.

[18] *Hirji Mulji v Cheong Yue Steamship Co Ltd* [1926] AC 497 at 504.

[19] *Port Line Ltd v Ben Line Steamers Ltd* [1958] 2 QB 146 at 162, per Diplock J; and see *British Movietonews Ltd v London and District Cinemas Ltd* [1952] AC 166 at 183, per Lord Simon; and at 187, per Lord Simonds); and see *Joseph Constantine Steamship Line Ltd v Imperial Smelting Corpn Ltd* [1942] AC 154 at 163, per Lord Simon.

attacked in recent years and has substantially been replaced by the more realistic view that the court imposes upon the parties the just and reasonable solution that the new situation demands. Perhaps the most careful analysis of this theory has been made by Lord Wright, and the following two passages from his speech in a leading case illustrate his view that the doctrine of frustration has been invented by the courts in order to supplement the defects of the actual contract. In the first passage he said:

> Where, as generally happens, and actually happened in the present case, one party claims that there has been frustration and the other party contests it, the court decides the issue and decides it *ex post facto* on the actual circumstances of the case. The data for decision are, on the one hand the terms and construction of the contract, read in the light of the then existing circumstances, and on the other hand the events which have occurred. It is the court which has to decide what is the true position between the parties.[20]

The second passage is as follows:

> The event is something which happens in the world of fact, and has to be found as a fact by the judge. Its effect on the contract depends on the meaning of the contract, which is matter of law. Whether there is frustration or not in any case depends on the view taken of the event and of its relation to the express contract by 'informed and experienced minds'.[21]

It is perhaps fair to say that this is now the more generally accepted view. To attempt to guess the arrangements that the parties would have made at the time of the contract, had they contemplated the event that has now unexpectedly happened, is to attempt the impossible. Instead, the courts refuse to apply the doctrine of frustration unless they consider that to hold the parties to further performance would, in the light of the changed circumstances, alter the fundamental nature of the contract.[22] In an illuminating passage, Lord Radcliffe has said:

> By this time it might seem that the parties themselves have become so far disembodied spirits that their actual persons should be allowed to rest in peace. In their place there rises the figure of the fair and reasonable man. And the spokesman of the fair and reasonable man, who represents after all no more than the anthropomorphic conception of justice, is and must be the court itself. So perhaps it would be simpler to say at the outset that frustration occurs whenever the law recognises that without default of either party a contractual obligation has become incapable of being performed because the circumstances in which performance is called for would render it a thing radically different from that which

---

[20] *Denny, Mott and Dickson Ltd v James Fraser & Co Ltd* [1944] AC 265 at 274–275, [1944] 1 All ER 678 at 683. In an extra-judicial utterance Lord Wright was more outspoken. 'The truth is', he said, 'that the court or jury as a judge of fact decides the question in accordance with what seems to be just and reasonable in its eyes. The judge finds in himself the criterion of what is reasonable. The court is in this sense making a contract for the parties, though it is almost blasphemy to say so': *Legal Essays and Addresses* p 259.

[21] Ibid at 276 and 684, respectively.

[22] *Tsakiroglou & Co Ltd v Noblee and Thorl GmbH* [1962] AC 93 at 115, per Lord Simonds.

was undertaken by the contract. *Non haec in foedera veni.*[23] It was not this that I promised to do.[24]

There has been much discussion as to whether frustration presents a question of fact or law. One answer suggested by Devlin J[25] is that:

> While the application of the doctrine of frustration is a matter of law; the assessment of a period of delay sufficient to constitute frustration is a question of fact.

More recently the House of Lords has held[26] that if an arbitrator correctly directs himself on the applicable general principles, his decision will only be open to review if it is one that no reasonable arbitrator could reach.

It would appear that there are in fact three questions. First, what are the general rules about the doctrine of frustration. This is clearly a question of law. Secondly, what are the primary facts. This is equally clearly a question of fact. Thirdly, how is the first to be applied to the second. This is a question of degree or judgement which does not fall naturally as a matter of abstract logic into either category and the practical question is the extent to which the trier of fact's views are open to challenge.[27]

2 OPERATION OF THE DOCTRINE

It is not possible to tabulate or to classify the circumstances to which the doctrine of frustration applies, but we will illustrate its operation by a reference to a few of the cases in which it has been invoked.[28]

Upon proof that the continuing availability of a physical thing or a given person is essential to the attainment of the fundamental object which the parties had in view, the contract is discharged if, owing to some extraneous cause such thing or person is

---

[23] In a letter to *The Times*, 20 December 1980, Sir John Megaw points out that these words are drawn from the *Aeneid* Book 4, lines 338 and 339, where they form part of Aeneas' shabby excuses for his planned desertion of Queen Dido!

[24] *Davis Contractors Ltd v Fareham UDC* [1956] AC 696 at 728–729, see also at 719–720, per Lord Reid. *Ocean Tramp Tankers Corpn V/O Sovfracht, The Eugenia* [1964] 2 QB 226 at 238–239, [1964] 1 All ER 161 at 166, per Lord Denning. In *National Carriers Ltd v Panalpina (Northern) Ltd* [1981] AC 675, [1981] 1 All ER 161 Lord Radcliffe's statement was treated as the preferred view by Lord Hailsham of St Marylebone LC and Lord Roskill.

[25] *Universal Cargo Carriers Corpn v Citati* [1957] 2 QB 401 at 435, [1957] 2 All ER 70 at 83.

[26] *Pioneer Shipping Ltd v BTP Tioxide Ltd, The Nema* [1982] AC 724, [1981] 2 All ER 1030; disapproving *The Angelia* [1973] 2 All ER 144, [1973] 1 WLR 210.

[27] See *Jackson v Union Marine Insurance Co Ltd* (1874) LR 10 CP 125; *Tsakiroglou & Co Ltd v Noblee and Thorl GmbH* [1962] AC 93, [1961] 2 All ER 179; *National Carriers Ltd v Panalpina (Northern) Ltd* [1981] AC 675, [1981] 1 All ER 161.

[28] For a more detailed statement, see McNair and Watts *Legal Effects of War* (4th edn) pp 177 ff; Webber *Effect of War on Contracts* (2nd edn) pp 394 ff.

no longer available. *Taylor v Caldwell*[29] sufficiently illustrates the case of a physical thing, but the rule laid down in that decision applies with equal force if it is a fundamental requirement that a person should remain available. Thus, a contract to perform services which can be rendered only by the promisor personally necessarily contemplates that his state of health, which at present is sufficiently good for the fulfilment of his obligations, will continue substantially unchanged, and if this ceases to be so owing to his death or illness, the court decrees that both parties shall be discharged from further liability.[30] A similar decree may be made if in time of war one of the parties is interned[31] or is called-up for military service,[32] provided that the interruption in performance is likely to be so long as to defeat the purpose of the contract. Contracts liable to discharge on this ground include an agreement to act as the agent of a music hall artiste,[33] to perform at a concert,[34] not to remove a child from school without a term's notice,[35] and a contract of apprenticeship.[36]

Another cause of frustration is the non-occurrence of some event which must reasonably be regarded as the basis of the contract. This is well illustrated by the coronation cases, especially by *Krell v Henry*,[37] but it is not necessary to expand the account already given of that decision.[38] It should be observed, however, that discharge will not be decreed if the event cannot reasonably be regarded as the real basis of the contract. The same judges who decided *Krell v Henry* had already refused in *Herne Bay Steamboat Co v Hutton*[39] to regard a somewhat similar contract as frustrated. In that case an agreement was made that the plaintiff's ship should be 'at the disposal of' the defendant on 28 June to take passengers from Herne Bay 'for the purpose of viewing the naval review and for a day's cruise round the fleet'. The review was later cancelled, but the fleet remained at Spithead on 28 June. It was held that the contract was not discharged. The case is not easy to distinguish from *Krell v Henry*, but perhaps the explanation is that the holding of the review was not the sole

[29] (1863) 3 B & s 826. Compare *Baily v De Crespigny* (1869) LR 4 QB 180; (a covenant by a lessor not to allow the erection of any building upon a paddock fronting the demised premises was discharged when a railway company compulsorily acquired and built a station on the paddock).

[30] *Boast v Firth* (1868) LR 4 CP 1. *Condor v Barron Knights Ltd* [1966] 1 WLR 87. Obviously, not every illness will bring the contract to an end. To draw the line it will be necessary to consider the extent of the illness and the nature and terms of the contract: *Marshall v Harland and Wolff Ltd* [1972] 2 All ER 715, [1972] 1 WLR 899; *Hebden v Forsey & Son* [1973] ICR 607; *Hart v A R Marshall & Sons (Bulwell) Ltd* [1978] 2 All ER 413, [1977] 1 WLR 1067.

[31] *Unger v Preston Corpn* [1942] 1 All ER 200.

[32] *Morgan v Manser* [1948] 1 KB 184, [1947] 2 All ER 666; *Marshall v Glanvill* [1917] 2 KB 87. Similarly if one of the parties is imprisoned; *Hare v Murphy Bros* [1974] 3 All ER 940, [1974] ICR 603. But see *Chakki v United Yeast Co Ltd* [1982] 2 All ER 446.

[33] *Morgan v Manser*, above.

[34] *Robinson v Davison* (1871) LR 6 Exch 269; *Poussard v Spiers and Pond* (1876) 1 QBD 410.

[35] *Simeon v Watson* (1877) 46 LJQB 679.

[36] *Boast v Firth* (1868) LR 4 CP 1, Cf *Mount v Oldham Corpn* [1973] QB 309, [1973] 1 All ER 26.

[37] [1903] 2 KB 740.   [38] P 723, above.   [39] [1903] 2 KB 683.

adventure contemplated. The cruise round the fleet, which formed an equally basic object of the contract, was still capable of attainment.

So fine a distinction reflects a difficulty that frequently occurs when the doctrine of frustration falls to be applied to a contract that is not in fact incapable of performance. The doctrine is certainly applicable if the object which is the foundation of the contract becomes unobtainable, but the judges are equally insistent that the motive of the parties is not a proper subject of inquiry. That the distinction, however, between motive and object is not always clear is apparent from the *Herne Bay* case.

> Suppose, for example, that a car is hired in Oxford to go to Epsom on a future date which in fact is known by both parties to be Derby day. If the Derby is subsequently abandoned, the question whether the contract is discharged or not depends upon whether the court regards the race as the foundation of the contract, or merely as the motive which induced the contract. Must the case be equated with *Krell v Henry* or with *Herne Bay Steamboat Co v Hutton*?

A common cause of frustration, especially in time of war, is interference by the government in the activities of one or both of the parties. For example, the acts contemplated by the contract may be prohibited for an indefinite duration, the labour or materials necessary for performance may be requisitioned, or premises upon which work is to be done may be temporarily seized for public use. In such cases the contract is discharged if to maintain it would be to impose upon the parties a contract fundamentally different from that which they made. A well-known example is *Metropolitan Water Board v Dick Kerr & Co.*[40] In that case:

> By a contract made in July 1914, the respondents agreed with the appellants to construct a reservoir within six years, subject to a proviso that the time should be extended if delay were caused by difficulties, impediments or obstructions howsoever occasioned. In February 1916, the Minister of Munitions ordered the respondents to cease work and to disperse and sell the plant.

It was held that the provision for extension of time did not cover such a substantial interference with the performance of the work as this, and that the contract was completely discharged. The interruption was likely to be so long that the contract, if resumed, would be radically different from that originally made.

Whether the outbreak of war or an interference by the government discharges a contract depends upon the actual circumstances of each case.[41] The principle itself is

---

[40] [1918] AC 119.

[41] In *Finelvet AG v Vinava Shipping Co Ltd* [1983] 2 All ER 658 a time chartered ship was trapped in the Shatt-Al-Arab as a result of the Iran–Iraq war. The arbitrator held that the charterparty was frustrated not on 22 September 1980 when war broke out (since many informed commentators expected a speedy victory for Iraq) but on 24 November 1980, by which time informed opinion expected a protracted war. Mustill J held that the arbitrator had made no error of law in reaching this conclusion. See also *The Evia* [1983] 1 AC 736, [1982] 3 All ER 350; *The Wenjiang (No 2)* [1983] 1 Lloyd's Rep 400.

constant, but the difficulty of its application remains. Discharge must be decreed only if the result of what has happened is that, if the contract were to be resumed after the return of peace or the removal of the interference, the parties would find themselves dealing with each other under conditions completely different from those that obtained when they made their agreement. The contract must be regarded as a whole and the question answered whether its purpose as gathered from its terms has been defeated.[42] The answer often turns upon the probable duration of the interference. Businessmen must not be left in indefinite suspense and as Lord Wright has said:

> If there is a reasonable probability from the nature of the interruption that it will be of indefinite duration, they ought to be free to turn their assets, their plant and equipment and their business operations into activities which are open to them, and to be free from commitments which are struck with sterility for an uncertain future period.[43]

The question whether the interruption will be of indefinite duration, rendering further performance of the contract impracticable, must be considered by the court in the light of the circumstances existing at the moment when it occurred. What view would a reasonable man have formed at that moment, without regard to the fuller information available to the court at the time of the trial? Would the reasonable inference have been that the interruption was indefinite in duration or merely transient?[44] The view that the effect of the interruption must be determined at its inception is clearly the orthodox one and it fits in with the rule, discussed below,[45] that frustration when it occurs operates automatically. However, the rule poses very considerable practical difficulties with some types of interruption. An illness may clear up quickly or it may linger on for months, a strike may be settled in a few days or continue for many weeks; a war may last for six days or thirty years. In such cases it appears permissible to wait for a short period to see how things turn out.[46]

That individual views may vary as to whether an interference is calculated to defeat the purpose of a contract is well illustrated by two cases. In *F A Tamplin Steamship Co Ltd v Anglo-Mexican Petroleum Products Co Ltd*[47] there was a sharp conflict of judicial opinion in the House of Lords. The facts were these:

> A tanker was chartered for five years from December 1912 to December 1917, to be used by the charterers for the carriage of oil. In February 1915, she was requisitioned by the government and used as a troopship. The charterers were willing to pay the agreed freight to the owners, but the latter, desirous of receiving

---

[42] *Denny, Mott and Dickson, Ltd v James B Fraser & Co Ltd* [1944] AC 265 at 273, [1944] 1 All ER 678 at 682; per Lord Macmillan.

[43] [1944] AC 265 at 278, [1944] 1 All ER 678 at 685, per Lord Wright.

[44] *Atlantic Maritime Co Inc v Gibbon* [1954] 1 QB 88, [1953] 2 All ER 1086.

[45] See p 737, below.

[46] *Pioneer Shipping Ltd BTP Tioxide Ltd, The Nema* [1981] 2 All ER 1030 at 1047 per Lord Roskill. See also *Chakki v United Yeast Co Ltd* [1982] 2 All ER 446 and cases cited in n 41 p 728, above.

[47] [1916] 2 AC 397.

the much larger sum paid by the government, contended that the requisition had frustrated the commercial object of the venture and had therefore put an end to the contract.

The House of Lords by a bare majority rejected this contention. Of the majority Lord Parker took the view that there was nothing concrete capable of frustration, since the parties never contemplated a definite adventure. The owners were not concerned in the charterers doing any specific thing except paying freight as it fell due. Lord Loreburn, though admitting that the parties contemplated a continuing state of peace and did not envisage loss of control over the ship, denied that the interruption was of such a character as to make it unreasonable to keep the contract alive. Judging the situation as at the date of the requisition, there might be many months during which the ship would be available for commercial purposes before the five years expired in December 1917.[48] On the other hand, Lords Haldane and Atkinson took the opposite view. Lord Haldane was of opinion that the entire basis of the contract so far as concerned its performance at any calculable date in the future was swept away. Lord Atkinson regarded the requisition as constituting such a substantial invasion of the freedom of both parties that the foundation of the contract had disappeared.

In the second case—*Tsakiroglou & Co Ltd v Noblee, and Thorl GmbH*[49]—the House of Lords had to consider the effect of the closing of the Suez Canal in 1956, an event which had already provoked a diversity of judicial opinion.

On 4 October 1956, sellers agreed to sell to buyers Sudanese groundnuts for shipment cif Hamburg, and to ship them during November/December 1956.[50] On 7 October, they booked space in one of four vessels scheduled to call at Port Sudan in these two months. On 2 November, the Suez Canal was closed to traffic. The seller failed to make the shipment and, when sued for damages, claimed that the contract had been frustrated.

The nature and extent of the contractual obligations were clear. The seller under a cif contract must prepare an invoice of the goods, ship goods of the right description at the port of shipment, procure a contract of affreightment providing for delivery at the agreed destination, effect an adequate insurance of the cargo and send the shipping documents, ie the invoice, bill of lading and insurance policy, to the buyers.

So much being clear, the sole question to be decided was whether shipment via the Cape of Good Hope would constitute a fundamental alteration in the contractual obligations of the sellers. Would such a mode of performance be radically different from what they had agreed to perform?

---

[48] Ibid at 405.

[49] [1962] AC 93, [1961] 2 All ER 179.

[50] A cif contract is one under which the agreed price covers the cost of the goods, the premium for their insurance and the freight for their carriage. The buyer's obligation is to pay the price upon the delivery of the shipping documents, not upon the delivery of the goods.

The House of Lords unanimously repudiated the suggestion. The freight and perhaps the insurance would be more expensive, but extra expense does not *per se* justify a finding of frustration; the voyage to Hamburg would take four weeks longer than by the canal, but no delivery date was fixed by the contract. Since no particular route had been agreed to, the sellers were bound to choose one that was practicable in the circumstances. The argument, that every cif contract contains an implied term requiring the sellers to send the goods by the usual and customary route, found no favour with their Lordships, for even if such be the rule, what is usual must be estimated at the time when the obligation is performed, not when the contract is made.[51]

In many cases of government interference the discharge of the contract may equally be justified on the ground that further performance has been made illegal. 'It is plain', said Lord Macmillan, 'that a contract to do what it has become illegal to do cannot be legally enforceable. There cannot be default in not doing what the law forbids to be done.'[52] Thus, a contract for the sale of goods to be shipped from abroad to an English port is terminated as to the future if supervening legislation prohibits the importation of goods of that description.[53] The result is the same if the goods are to be shipped to a foreign port, and while the contract is still executory war breaks out with the country of destination.[54] To continue the contract would involve trading with the enemy.[55]

Lord Denning MR reached an interesting and controversial decision in *Staffordshire Area Health Authority v South Staffordshire Waterworks Co*[56] the facts of which have already been stated.[57] In this case Lord Denning MR held that the contract had been frustrated by inflation 'outside the realm of their speculations altogether, or of any reasonable person sitting in their chairs'.[58] With respect, however, this view, which was

---

[51] As to the effect of closure of the Suez Canal on voyage charterparties, see the differing views in *Société Franco-Tunisienne D'Armement v Sidermar SPA* [1961] 2 QB 278, [1960] 2 All ER 529; *Ocean Tramp Tankers Corpn v V/O Soufracht, The Eugenia* [1964] 2 QB 226, [1964] 1 All ER 161; *Palmco Shipping Inc v Continental Ore Corpn* [1970] 2 Lloyd's Rep 21. Charterparties usually now contain a 'Suez Canal clause' which purports to determine the rights of the parties if the ship proceeds *via* the Cape instead of through the canal. The obscurity of the clause, however, has raised difficulties; see, for example, *Achille Lauro Fugioacchino & Co v Total Societa Italiana per Azioni* [1969] 2 Lloyd's Rep 65.

[52] *Denny, Mott and Dickson Ltd v James B Fraser & Co Ltd* [1944] AC 265 at 272, [1944] 1 All ER 678 at 681.

[53] *Denny Mott and Dickson Ltd v James B Fraser and Co Ltd*, above.

[54] *Zinc Corpn Ltd v Hirsch* [1916] 1 KB 541.

[55] It is clear law that a purchaser who cannot complete a contract because he has no money, cannot invoke the doctrine of frustration. *Universal Corpn v Five Ways Properties Ltd* [1979] 1 All ER 552.

[56] [1978] 3 All ER 769, [1978] 1 WLR 1387.

[57] P 703, above.

[58] Ibid at 777, and 1395, respectively. It is clear law that frustration brings the contract to an end automatically (see p 737, below) but in this case Lord Denning MR held that the effect of inflation was to render the contract terminable by reasonable notice. Presumably this is because this was all that the Water Authority were claiming but it relieved him from the onerous task of deciding when the inflation rate became sufficiently great to frustrate the contract. Cf *Wates Ltd v Greater London Council* (1983) 25 BLR 1.

not concurred in by the other members of the Court is either wrong or involves a massive change in the law as previously understood. There are thousands, if not millions, of contracts potentially within the scope of this principle, for example, long leases for 99 years or more at fixed ground rents or long-term policies of life insurance. Furthermore, the facts of the case would not appear to satisfy Lord Denning MR's own test since in 1929 hyper-inflation was a well-known phenomenon which had recently devastated the economies of several European countries.

Two further factors which affect the operation of the doctrine of frustration require particular notice.

Effect when parties expressly provide for the frustrating event

The first is relevant where a contingency for which the parties have expressly provided occurs in fact, but assumes a more fundamental and serious form than perhaps they contemplated. The question of construction that arises here is whether the express provision is intended to be a complete and exclusive solution of the matter in the sense that its object is to govern any form, fundamental or not, that the contingency may take. Unless it is intended to be of this all embracing character, it will not prevent the discharge of the obligation if in the result the effect of the contingency is to frustrate the essential object of the contract. The leading case is *Jackson v Union Marine Insurance Co Ltd.*[59]

> A ship was chartered in November 1871, to proceed with all possible despatch, *dangers and accidents of navigation excepted*, from Liverpool to Newport and there to load a cargo of iron rails for carriage to San Francisco. She sailed on 2 January, but on the 3rd ran aground in Carnarvon Bay. She was got off by 18 February and was taken to Liverpool where she was still under repair in August. On 15 February the charterers repudiated the contract.

The question was whether the charterers were liable for not loading the ship, or whether the time likely to be required for repairs was so long as to excuse their failure to do so. The question put to the jury, which they answered in the affirmative, was 'whether such time was so long as to put an end in a commercial sense to the commercial speculation entered upon by the shipowner and the charterers'. On this finding it was held that the adventure contemplated by the parties was frustrated and the contract discharged. A voyage to San Francisco carried out after the repair of the ship would have been a totally different adventure from that originally envisaged. The express exception, read literally, no doubt covered the accident that had happened, and it would have precluded the charterers from recovering damages in respect of the

---

[59] (1874) LR 10 CP 125; and see *Bank Line Ltd v A Capel & Co* [1919] AC 435; see also the remarks of Diplock J on the *Jackson* case in *Tsakiroglou & Co Ltd v Noblee and Thorl GmbH* [1960] 2 QB 318 at 330–331, [1959] 1 All ER 45 at 50; see also *Metropolitan Water Board v Dick Kerr & Co* [1918] AC 119.

delay; but it was not intended to cover an accident causing injury of so extensive a nature.

In a later case, a contract was made in 1913 by which shipowners undertook to provide charterers with certain vessels in each of the years 1914 to 1918, and it was agreed that if war broke out shipments might at the option of either party be suspended until the end of hostilities. After the start of the war, Rowlatt J held that the contract was discharged, not merely suspended. The suspension clause was not intended by the parties to cover a war of such a catastrophic nature and with such dislocating effects as in fact occurred.[60]

Party cannot rely upon self-induced frustration[61]

A second relevant factor is whether one of the parties has himself been responsible for the frustrating event. 'Reliance', said Lord Sumner, 'cannot be placed on a self-induced frustration.'[62] The point arose in a neat form in *Maritime National Fish Ltd v Ocean Trawlers Ltd*[63] where:

> The appellants chartered from the respondents a steam trawler which was useless for fishing unless it was fitted with an otter trawl. To the knowledge of both parties it was a statutory offence to use an otter trawl except under licence from the Canadian Minister of Fisheries. Later, the appellants, who had four other ships of their own, applied for five licences, but were granted only three. In naming the ships to which these licences should apply they excluded the trawler chartered from the respondents.

The appellants contended that they were not liable for the hire due under the charter-party, since performance had been frustrated by the refusal of the Minister to grant the full number of licences. The Privy Council, however, refused to regard this fact as sufficient to bring the case within the doctrine, for 'the essence of frustration is that it should not be due to the act or election of the party', and here it was the appellants themselves who had chosen to defeat the common object of the adventure. In this case it was arguable that in any event the refusal of the minister to grant licences was not a frustrating event since both parties knew that a licence was needed and the appellants might well have been thought to have taken their chance on whether or not they would get a licence. It also looks as if the decision to licence their own trawlers was self serving. Neither of these factors was present in *J Lauritzen AS v Wijsmuller BV, The Super Servant Two.*[64]

---

[60] *Pacific Phosphate Co Ltd v Empire Transport Co Ltd* (1920) 36 TLR 750.

[61] Swanton 2 JCL 206.

[62] *Bank Line Ltd v A Capel & Co* [1919] AC 435 at 452. The requirement was emphatically restated and applied by the House of Lords in *Paal Wilson & Co A/S v Partenreederei Hannah Blumenthal, The Hannah Blumenthal* [1983] 1 AC 854, [1983] 1 All ER 34.

[63] [1935] AC 524. *See also Mertens v Home Freeholds Co* [1921] 2 KB 526.

[64] [1990] 1 Lloyd's Rep 1.

In this case the defendants agreed to carry the plaintiffs' drilling rig from Japan to a delivery location off Rotterdam using what was described in the contract as the 'transportation unit'. This was a highly specialised form of ocean transport and required a special kind of vessel. The defendants in fact had two such vessels, The Super Servant One and The Super Servant Two. Under the contract the transportation unit was defined as meaning either Super Servant One or Super Servant Two, that is the defendants were given the option of using either vessel.

The rig was to be delivered between 20 June 1981 and 20 August 1981. On 29 January 1981 Super Servant Two sank. The defendants had in fact intended to use Super Servant Two to perform this contract though they had made no election which was binding on them to do so. They had entered into contracts with other parties which they could only perform using Super Servant One. It was agreed that if the contract had, from the start, contemplated the use of Super Servant Two and Super Servant Two only, the sinking of Super Servant Two would have frustrated the contract. The defendants argued that since their decision to use Super Servant One on other contracts was reasonable they were entitled to be discharged.

There was powerful support for this view since Treitel has argued[65] that

> where a party has entered into a number of contracts, supervening events may deprive him of the power of performing them all, without depriving him of the power of performing some of them . . . It is submitted that frustration should not be excluded by a party's 'election' where his only choice was which of two contracts to frustrate.

The Court of Appeal rejected this reasoning principally on the grounds that where frustration operates it operates automatically on the happening of the frustrating event. It was clear that the contract was not frustrated by the sinking of Super Servant Two since the defendants might have chosen to perform this contract and not perform some other contract. The contract would therefore have been frustrated, if at all, by the defendants' decision as to which contract to perform.

On the other hand, the phrase 'self-induced frustration' does not imply that every degree of fault will preclude a party from claiming to be discharged.

> The possible varieties [of fault] are infinite, and can range from the criminality of the scuttler who opens the sea-cocks and sinks his ship, to the thoughtlessness of the prima donna who sits in a draught and loses her voice. I wish to guard against the supposition that every destruction of *corpus* for which a contractor can be said, to some extent or in some sense, to be responsible, necessarily involves that the resultant frustration is self-induced within the meaning of the phrase.[66]

---

[65] Treitel, *The Law of Contract* (7th edn), pp 700–701 cf (10th edn), pp 845–846.
[66] *Joseph Constantine Steamship Line Ltd v Imperial Smelting Corpn Ltd* [1942] AC 154 at 179, [1941] 2 All ER 165 at 175, per Lord Russell of Killowen.

This rule, that a party cannot claim to be discharged by a frustrating event for which he is himself responsible, does not require him to prove affirmatively that the event occurred without his fault. The onus of proving that the frustration was self-induced rests upon the party raising this allegation.[67] For instance:

> On the day before a chartered ship was due to load her cargo an explosion of such violence occurred in her auxiliary boiler that the performance of the charterparty became impossible. The cause of the explosion could not be definitely ascertained, but only one of three possible reasons would have imputed negligence to the shipowners.

It was held by the House of Lords that, since the charterers were unable to prove that the explosion was caused by the fault of the owners, the defence of frustration succeeded and the contract was discharged.[68] It should perhaps be noted that in many cases a self-induced frustrating event will be a breach of contract but this will not necessarily be so. In *Maritime National Fish Ltd v Ocean Trawlers Ltd,*[69] the applicants were not contractually bound to licence the chartered trawler but could not excuse failure to pay hire by relying on the absence of a licence.

Controversy whether doctrine of frustration applies to a lease

It has been a controversial question whether the doctrine of frustration can be applied to a lease of land. If, for instance, land which has been let for building purposes for 99 years is, within five years from the beginning of the tenancy, completely submerged in the sea or zoned as a permanent open space, can it be said that the fundamental purpose of the contract has been frustrated and that the term itself must automatically cease?[70]

It is, indeed, well settled by a number of decisions that if, during the continuance of the lease, the premises are requisitioned by the government[71] or destroyed by fire[72] or by enemy action,[73] the tenant remains liable on his covenants to pay rent and to repair the property. But these decisions, which assume that individual covenants by a landlord or tenant are absolute, do not preclude the possibility that an event may be regarded as frustrating the fundamental purpose of the contract and therefore as terminating the lease altogether. For many years the view was taken in the lower courts, that leases are outside the doctrine of frustration. This is based on the argument that a lease creates not merely a contract, but also an estate. Thus in *London and Northern Estates Co v Schlesinger,*[74] it was held that the lease of a flat was not

---

67 Ibid at 179 and 175, respectively, per Lord Russell of Killowen.   68 Ibid.
69 P 733, above. See also *Hare v Murphy Bros* [1974] 3 All ER 940, [1974] ICR 603.
70 Yahuda 21 MLR 637.
71 *Whitehall Court Ltd v Ettlinger* [1920] 1 KB 680.
72 *Matthey v Curling* [1922] 2 AC 180. Atiyah *Accidents, Compensation and the Law* p 318, points out that it is normal practice for landlords to insure against such loss.
73 See *Redmond v Dainton* [1920] 2 KB 256.
74 [1916] 1 KB 20.

terminated by the fact that the tenant had become an alien enemy and was therefore prohibited from residing on the premises. Lush J said:

> It is not correct to speak of this tenancy agreement as a contract and nothing more. A term of years was created by it and vested in the appellant, and I can see no reason for saying that, because this order disqualified him from personally residing in the flat, it affected the chattel interest which was vested in him by virtue of the agreement.[75]

Conflicting opinions were expressed in *Cricklewood Property and Investment Trust Ltd v Leighton's Investment Trust Ltd.*[76]

> In May 1936, a building lease was made to the lessees for a term of 99 years. Before any buildings had been erected the war of 1939 broke out and restrictions imposed by the government made it impossible for the lessees to erect the shops that they had covenanted to erect. In an action brought against them for the recovery of rent they pleaded that the lease was frustrated.

It was held unanimously by the House of Lords that the doctrine of frustration, even if it were capable of application to a lease, did not apply in the instant circumstances. The compulsory suspension of building did not strike at the root of the transaction, for when it was imposed the lease still had more then ninety years to run, and therefore the interruption in performance was likely to last only for a small fraction of the term.

Lord Russell and Lord Goddard LCJ expressed the opinion that the doctrine of frustration cannot apply to a demise of real property while Lord Simon and Lord Wright took the opposite view. Lord Porter expressed no opinion on the question.

In the ninth edition of this work it was submitted however that if the question should come before the House of Lords, the view that a lease is capable of being frustrated should be preferred. It is no doubt true that in many cases the object of the parties is *in fact* to transfer an estate but it surely goes too far to say that this is so as a *matter of law*. In many cases the parties may contemplate that the risk of unforeseen disasters will pass to the lessee on the execution of the lease just as surely as if he had taken a conveyance of the fee simple but this will not always be so. If the lease is for a specific purpose which becomes impossible of achievement, there may be a strong case for holding the lease frustrated. Similar arguments may apply if the lease is of short duration and here it is relevant to observe that a contractual licence to use land is certainly capable of frustration,[77] and that the distinction between leases and licences is notoriously hard to draw.[78] These views derive considerable support from the

---

[75] Ibid at 24. This statement was approved by the Court of Appeal in *Whitehall Court Ltd v Ettlinger* [1920] 1 KB 680 at 686, 687, which decision was approved by Lord Atkinson in *Matthey v Curling* [1922] 2 AC 180 at 237.

[76] [1945] AC 221, [1945] 1 All ER 252.

[77] *Taylor v Caldwell* (1863) 3 B & s 826; *Krell v Henry* [1903] 2 KB 740.

[78] Cheshire and Burn *Modern Real Property* (15th edn) pp 585 ff.

decision of the Supreme Court of Canada in *Highway Properties Ltd v Kelly, Douglas & Co*,[79] that for the purpose of applying the rules about breach 'it is no longer sensible to pretend that a commercial lease . . . is simply a conveyance and not also a contract'.[80]

This is in fact the position that was adopted by the House of Lords in the decision in *National Carriers Ltd v Panalpina (Northern) Ltd*.[81] The facts of this case need not be recounted since the House of Lords were unanimously of the view that there was no arguable case of frustration on the merits but they clearly held (Lord Russell *dubitante*) that the doctrine of frustration could apply to a lease. The decisive argument was the essential unity of the law of contract and the belief that no type of contract should as a *matter of law* be excluded from the doctrine. On the other hand it was agreed that it would be relatively rare for the doctrine to be applied in practice. The difference was neatly put as being between 'never' and 'hardly ever'.

This reasoning must of necessity carry with it the cases of an agreement for a lease[82] and a contract for the sale of freehold land.[83] Both must be capable of frustration, though the nature of the contracts may well be such as to fix on one party or the other the risk of many disasters. For instance in a straightforward contract of house purchase, it is normally understood that the risk of the house being destroyed by fire passes at the moment of exchange of contracts and prudent purchasers insure on this basis.

3 EFFECT OF THE DOCTRINE

Presuming that a contract is frustrated by the operation of the doctrine, it is now necessary to examine the legal consequences. The first point to appreciate is the moment at which the discharge becomes operative. The rule established at common law is that the occurrence of the frustrating event 'brings the contract to an end forthwith, without more and automatically'.[84] Lord Wright said:

> In my opinion the contract is automatically terminated as to the future, because at that date its further performance becomes impossible in fact in circumstances which involve no liability for damages for the failure on either party.[85]

---

[79] (1971) 17 DLR (3d) 710. See p 698, above.   [80] Ibid at 721, per Laskin J.

[81] [1981] 1 All ER 161.

[82] See *Rom Securities Ltd v Rogers (Holdings) Ltd* (1967) 205 Estates Gazette 427.

[83] See *Hillingdon Estates Co v Stonefield Estates Ltd* [1952] Ch 627, [1952] 1 All ER 853. As to options to purchase land see *Denny, Mott and Dickson Ltd v James B Fraser & Co Ltd* [1944] AC 265, [1944] 1 All ER 678.

[84] *Hirji Mulji v Cheong Yue Steamship Co* [1926] AC 497 at 505, per Lord Sumner.

[85] *Fibrosa Spolka Akcyjna v Fairbairn Lawson Combe Barbour Ltd* [1943] AC 32 at 70, [1942] 2 All ER 122 at 140. But see the criticism of Williams *Law Reform (Frustrated Contracts) Act 1943* pp 41–42.

It is worth noting that it is not a logical necessity that impossibility of performance should operate to discharge a contract. In many Continental systems it is viewed rather as a defence[86] and English law might have accommodated it in the same way. In most cases only one party's performance is impossible—the other's obligation consisting in payment. In such a situation the party who could not perform might plead impossibility of performance and the other total failure of consideration.[87] English law has not taken this path in general and this has concealed the undoubted existence of cases where impossibility does excuse but does not discharge. Thus we have seen[88] that a prolonged illness may frustrate a contract of personal service while a shorter and less serious illness will not do so. The shorter illness however while not bringing the contract to an end, will usually excuse absence from work. Similarly a statute may operate to provide a defence for non-performance of the contract without discharging it.[89]

The contract is terminated as to the future only. Unlike one vitiated by mistake, it is not void *ab initio*. It starts life as a valid contract, but comes to an abrupt and automatic end the moment that the common adventure is frustrated. From this premise the common law drew inferences which, though sometimes harsh, were not illogical. The rule adopted by the judges until 1943 may thus be stated:

> Each party must fulfil his contractual obligations so far as they have fallen due before the frustrating event, but he is excused from performing those that fall due later.[90]

In *Krell v Henry*,[91] for instance, it was held that the plaintiff could not recover the agreed rent from the defendant, since it did not fall due until the last minute of 24 June, and before this moment had arrived the abandonment of the procession had been announced. In *Jackson v Union Marine Insurance Co*[92] the grounding of the ship under charter terminated the contract, with the result that the owners were not bound to provide an alternative vessel, nor were the charterers bound to pay freight.

This common law principle, since it meant that any loss arising from the termination of the contract must lie where it had fallen, might well cause hardship to one or other of the parties, as is shown by *Chandler v Webster*.[93] In that case:

> X agreed to let a room in Pall Mall to Y for the purpose of viewing the coronation procession of 1902. The price was £141 15s payable immediately. Y paid £100, but he still owed the balance when the contract was discharged on 24 June owing to the

---

[86] See Nicholas 48 Tulane L Rev 946 at 954–966.

[87] See Lord Porter in *Joseph Constantine Steamship Line Ltd v Imperial Smelting Corpn Ltd* [1942] AC 154 at 203; Weir [1970] CLJ 189; for a similar analysis of initial impossibility, see Stoljar *Mistake and Misrepresentation* ch 3.

[88] P 636, above.   [89] See eg Remuneration, Charges and Grants Act 1975, s 1.

[90] See the *Fibrosa* case [1943] AC 32 at 58, [1942] 2 All ER 122 at 134.

[91] [1903] 2 KB 740; p 723, above.

[92] (1874) LR 10 CP 125; p 732, above.   [93] [1904] 1 KB 493.

abandonment of the procession. It was held, not only that Y had no right to recover the sum of £100, but also that he remained liable for the balance of £41 15s.

If attention is confined to the contract the decision is logical enough. The obligation to pay the £141 had matured before the moment of frustration. The plaintiff's counsel, however, argued that he was entitled to disregard the contract and to recover in quasi-contract the £100 actually paid, on the ground of a total failure of consideration.[94] But the Court of Appeal held that, as the doctrine of frustration does not avoid a contract *ab initio* but ends it only from the moment of frustration, it was inadmissible to predicate a *total* failure of consideration. The quasi-contractual remedy was therefore inapplicable. In the words of Collins MR:

> If the effect were that the contract were wiped out altogether, no doubt the result would be that money paid under it would have to be repaid as on a failure of consideration. But that is not the effect of the doctrine [of frustration]; it only releases a party from further performance of the contract. Therefore the doctrine of failure of consideration does not apply.[95]

If, as in *Chandler v Webster*, the money was due before the date of frustration, the loss lay upon the debtor; but it was borne by the creditor if, as in *Krell v Henry*, the obligation to pay did not mature until after the discharge of the contract.

It is not surprising, therefore, that the decision in *Chandler v Webster* should have caused general dissatisfaction. But, despite judicial criticism,[96] it was not until 1942 that the House of Lords succeeded, in the *Fibrosa* case,[97] in avoiding the consequences of the rule that the contract remained in full force up to the moment of frustration. The facts of the case were as follows:

> The respondents, an English company, agreed in July 1939, to sell and to deliver within three or four months certain machinery to a Polish company in Gdynia. The contract price was £4,800, of which £1,600 was payable in advance. Great Britain declared war on Germany on 3 September, and on 23 September the Germans occupied Gdynia. The contract was therefore frustrated. On 7 September the London agent of the Polish company requested the return of £1,000 which had been paid in July to the respondents. The request was refused on the ground that 'considerable work' had already been done on the machinery.

It was, of course, clear that when the money was paid it was due under an existing contract, so that it could not be recovered by an action based upon the contract. The

---

[94] There are certain circumstances where the law, in its dislike of unjust enrichment, allows a person to sustain an action for money had and received, and by this restitutionary remedy to recover a payment for which he has received nothing.

[95] [1904] 1 KB 493 at 499.

[96] See the various criticisms summarised by Lord Wright in the *Fibrosa* case [1943] AC 32 at 71, [1942] 2 All ER 122 at 140.

[97] *Fibrosa Spolka Akcyjna v Fairbairn Lawson Combe Barbour Ltd* [1943] AC 32, [1942] 2 All ER 122.

House of Lords held, however, that it was recoverable in quasi-contract **or, as we would now say, restitution**. They set themselves, with sufficient success, to defeat the assumption upon which the Court of Appeal in *Chandler v Webster* had proceeded, namely, that there could be no total failure of consideration unless the contract was void *ab initio*. Lord Simon surmounted the difficulty by distinguishing the meaning of consideration, as used in this quasi-contractual sense, from that normally given to it in contract. He said:

> In English law, an enforceable contract may be formed by an exchange of a promise for a promise, or by the exchange of a promise for an act—I am excluding contracts under seal—and thus, in the law relating to the formation of contract, the promise to do a thing may often be the consideration but when one is considering the law of failure of consideration and of the quasi-contractual right to recover money on that ground, it is, generally speaking, not the promise which is referred to as the consideration, but the performance of the promise. The money was paid to secure performance and, if performance fails the inducement which brought about the payment is not fulfilled.[98]

Others of their Lordships, such as Lord Atkin and Lord Macmillan, were content to repudiate *Chandler v Webster* as devoid of authority. The result at least was to overrule that decision and to enable the Polish company to succeed in quasi-contract.

The rule established by the *Fibrosa* case has thus diminished the injustice of the former law, but since it operates only in the event of a total failure of consideration, it does not remove every hardship. On the one hand, it does not permit the recovery of an advance payment if the consideration has only partly failed, ie if the payer has received some benefit, though perhaps a slender one, for his money.[99] On the other hand, the payee, in his turn, may suffer an injustice. Thus, while he may be compelled to repay the money on the ground that the payer has received no benefit, he may himself, in the partial performance of the contract, have incurred expenses for which he has no redress. In the words of Lord Simon:

> He may have incurred expenses in connexion with the partial carrying out of the contract which are equivalent, or more than equivalent, to the money which he prudently stipulated should be prepaid, but which he now has to return for reasons which are no fault of his. He may have to repay the money, though he has executed almost the whole of the contractual work, which will be left on his hands. These results follow from the fact that the English common law does not undertake to apportion a prepaid sum in such circumstance—contrast the provision, now contained in section 40 of the Partnership Act 1890 for apportioning a premium if a partnership is prematurely dissolved.[100]

---

[98] Ibid at 48 and 129. This reasoning, which is now only of historical interest because of the Act of 1943, below, has not escaped criticism: see Gow 3 ICLQ 303 at 311–312.

[99] *Fibrosa Spolka Akcynja v Fairbairn Lawson Combe Barbour Ltd* [1943] AC 32 at 54–55, [1942] 2 All ER 122 at 131, 132, per Lord Atkin; at 56 and 133, per Lord Russell.

[100] Ibid at 49 and 129, respectively.

The *Fibrosa* case, therefore, while it removed the worst consequences of the decision in *Chandler v Webster*, left other difficulties untouched. A further attempt to clarify the law has, however, been made by the Law Reform (Frustrated Contracts) Act 1943, which gives general effect to the recommendations of the Law Revision Committee.[101]

Law Reform (Frustrated Contracts) Act 1943

The preliminary fact to observe is that the Act is confined to a case where 'a contract governed by English law has *become impossible of performance or been otherwise frustrated*, and the parties thereto have for that reason been discharged from the further performance of the contract'.[102] In other words, the statutory provisions do not apply where a contract is discharged by breach or for any reason other than impossibility or frustration.

In general it may be said that the Act makes two fundamental changes in the law. First, it amplifies the decision in the *Fibrosa* case by permitting the recovery of money prepaid, even though at the date of frustration there has been no total failure of consideration. Secondly, it allows a party who has done something in performance of the contract prior to the frustrating event to claim compensation for any benefit thereby conferred upon the other. In this respect it modifies the common law rule laid down, for instance, in *Cutter v Powell*.[103] We will now consider the Act under these two general headings.

A The right to recover money paid

Section 1(2) enacts as follows:

> All sums paid or payable to any party in pursuance of the contract before the time when the parties were so discharged (in this Act referred to as 'the time of discharge') shall, in the case of sums so paid, be recoverable from him as money received by him for the use of the party by whom the sums were paid, and, in the case of sums so payable, cease to be so payable.

This confirms the reversal by the *Fibrosa* case of *Chandler v Webster*.[104] On 1 May, A agrees to hire a room from B for the purpose of viewing a procession on 26 June, and by the terms of the contract he is required to pay the agreed price on 7 May. On 23 June, the procession is abandoned, and therefore the contract is discharged at common law. If A has already fulfilled his obligation to pay the price, he has a statutory right of recovery; if he has not done so, he is statutorily free from liability.

The subsection then proceeds to offset this relief to the party on whom the contractual duty of payment rests by giving a limited protection to the payee in so far, but only in so far, as he has incurred expense in the course of fulfilling the contract. This protection is expressed in the following proviso:

[101] 7th Interim Report (Cmd 6009 (1939))
[102] S 1(1). For a full account of the Act, see Williams *Law Reform (Frustrated Contracts) Act.*
[103] (1795) 6 Term Reports 320; p 675, above.   [104] [1904] 1 KB 493; p 738, above.

Provided that, if the party to whom the sums were so paid or so payable incurred expenses before the time of discharge in or for the purpose of the performance of the contract, the court may, if it considers it just to do so having regard to all the circumstances of the case, allow him to retain or, as the case may be, to recover the whole or any part of the sums so paid or payable, not being an amount in excess of the expenses so incurred.

The extent of the protection thus afforded to the payee may become clearer if the proviso is sub-divided. It then becomes apparent that:

(a) If the party to whom the sums have been paid has incurred expenses before the time of discharge in, or for the purpose of, the performance of the contract, the court may in its discretion allow him to *retain* the whole or any part of such sums, not being an amount in excess of the expenses incurred.

(b) If the party to whom the sums were *payable* has incurred expenses before the time of discharge in, or for the purpose of, the performance of the contract, the court may in its discretion allow him to *recover* the whole or any part of such sums, not being an amount in excess of the expenses incurred.[105]

It will thus be noticed that a party can receive no allowance for his expenditure unless it was incurred before the occurrence of the frustrating event.

This discretionary power of the court to make an allowance for expenses was beyond the power of the House of Lords in the *Fibrosa* case. But if the facts of that case were to recur and if, for example, machinery of a special nature, not realisable in the open market, had been substantially completed by the English company under the contract, the court would be able to order the repayment to the Polish company of a proportion only of the prepaid amount.

In *Gamerco SA v ICM/Fair Warning (Agency) Ltd*[106] the plaintiffs had agreed to promote a rock concert to be held at a stadium in Madrid on 4 July 1992. The plaintiffs had paid $412,000 on account and had contracted to pay a further $362,500. Both parties had incurred expenses, the plaintiffs of about $450,000 and the defendants of about $50,000.

There were safety concerns about the stadium because of the use of high alumina cement in its construction. On 1 July 1992 the relevant government body withdrew the permit for the use of the stadium and the parties became aware of this on 2 July 1992. It was not possible to find another stadium.

Garland J held that the contract was frustrated.[107] He held that section 1(2) gave the Court a very wide discretion as to the defendants' expenses. In the circumstances it was established that neither party derived any benefit from the expenses they

---

[105] S 1(2), proviso.   [106] [1995] 1 WLR 1226. Carter and Tolhurst 10 JCL 264.

[107] The contract was frustrated by the withdrawal of permission. The condition of the stadium would not have been a frustrating event since it was the same as at the time of the contract. If relevant, it would have been to an argument that the contract was void for common mistake. Cf *Griffiths v Brymer* (1903) 19 TLR 434.

had incurred or had conferred any benefit on the other party. Garland J ordered the defendants to repay the $412,000 that had been paid in advance and made no deduction from this sum in respect of the defendants' expenses.

B The right to recover compensation for partial performance

It will be recalled that, in accordance with the doctrine of strict performance established at common law in such cases as *Cutter v Powell*, a man who fails to complete *in toto* his obligation under an entire contract can often recover nothing for what he may have done, even though the non-completion is due to an extraneous cause which, through no fault of his own, frustrates the common adventure or even renders further performance altogether impossible.[108] An outstanding example of the injustice that this doctrine may cause is afforded by *Appleby v Myers*.[109]

> The plaintiffs, in consideration of a promise to pay £459, agreed to erect machinery on the defendant's premises, and to keep it in order for two years from the date of completion. When the erection was nearly complete an accidental fire entirely destroyed the premises together with all that they contained.

An action brought to recover £419 for work done and materials supplied failed. Under the doctrine of frustration the effect of the destruction of the subject matter of the contract was that both parties were excused from the further performance of their obligations. The plaintiffs were not bound to erect new machinery; the defendant was not bound to pay for what had been done, since his obligation to pay had not matured at the time when the contract was discharged.

An attempt to deal with difficulties of this nature, however, has now been made by the Act. Section 1(3) enacts that:

> Where any party to the contract has, by reason of anything done by any other party thereto in, or for the purpose of, the performance of the contract, obtained a valuable benefit (other than a payment of money . . .) before the time of discharge, there shall be recoverable from him by the said other party such sum (if any) not exceeding the value of the said benefit to the party obtaining it as the court considers just having regard to all the circumstances of the case . . .

In estimating the amount of the sum to be recovered, the court must consider all the circumstances of the case, especially any expenses that the benefited party may have incurred in the performance of the contract before the time of discharge, and also whether the circumstances causing the frustration have affected the value of the benefit.[110]

The Act goes a long way towards removing the injustice of the common law rule. If, for instance, a builder agrees for a lump sum to erect a warehouse, and when he has completed a part of the work further construction is prohibited by the government

---

[108] P 675, above.　　　[109] (1867) LR 2 CP 651.　　　[110] S 1(3)(a) and (b).

owing to the outbreak of war, he may in the discretion of the court be awarded a sum commensurate with the value of the benefit conferred upon the other contracting party. It is not clear, however, whether this particular subsection does full justice, for it is only where 'a valuable benefit' has been 'obtained' by the other party that the court is empowered to give relief. If, for instance, the facts of *Appleby v Myers* were to recur, it could be argued that, since the completed work had been totally destroyed, no benefit would have been conferred on the defendant. The loss, for which neither party was to blame, would fall entirely on the builder and this view has been taken in a Newfoundland case.[111] On the other hand it has been suggested,[112] that, by a liberal interpretation of the subsection, a 'valuable benefit' might be said to have been 'obtained' by the owner by the mere fact that the work has been done on his land in accordance with the contract, even though it may be destroyed before it has brought him any sensible advantage.

This view can be reinforced by two further arguments, one technical, the other substantial. The technical argument is that the Act talks of obtaining a benefit '*before the time of discharge*'. This suggests that the time to ask the question benefit *vel non* is the moment before the frustrating event. At this moment the position of the customer is the same whether in the next moment the contract is to be frustrated by a government ban on building or the destruction of the premises. The substantial argument is that it is inconceivable in modern circumstances that such a contract could be undertaken without either the builder or the customer carrying insurance against fire and a just allocation of the loss must necessarily take this into account. A wide construction of 'benefit' would enable the court to do this. In this respect it should be noted that the 'benefit' is not an entitlement but simply a ceiling on liability.

Section 1 (3) was considered in a most elaborate and helpful judgment by Robert Goff J in *BP Exploration Co (Libya) Ltd v Hunt (No 2)*.[113] Both the facts and the legal arguments in this case are exceptionally complex and must be oversimplified for present purposes.

> The defendant, a wealthy Texan, owned an oil concession in Libya. It was likely but by no means certain that it contained oil, and uncertain where, if at all, the oil would turn out to be located. Vast sums would be involved in locating the oil and bringing it on stream but equally the potential profits were enormous. Hunt therefore entered into a contract with the plaintiffs under which the parties were to share the field, if it existed, but the plaintiffs were to take the risks. In essence, the plaintiffs were to bear the cost of exploration and exploitation and then to pay themselves back out of Hunt's share of the oil. The exploration was exceptionally

---

[111] *Parsons Bros Ltd v Shea* (1965) 53 DLR (2d) 86.

[112] Webber *Effect of War on Contracts* (2nd edn) p 687; *Glanville Williams* pp 48–51.

[113] [1982] 1 All ER 925, [1979] 1 WLR 783; Baker [1979] CLJ 266. See Goff and Jones *The Law of Restitution* (3rd edn) pp 486 ff.

successful; a very large field was discovered; oil wells were erected and pipeline laid, but the contract was then frustrated when the Libyan Government cancelled the concession.

At this stage BP had paid about $10 m to Hunt, had spent about $87 m on exploration etc and had recovered about $62 m. They brought a claim under section 1 (3). A central question was what valuable benefit had been conferred on Hunt. Robert Goff J held that the benefit did not consist in the services of exploration since the act of looking for the oil did not of itself confer benefit on Hunt, nor in the oil which was already his, under the terms of the concession, but in the increased value of the concession produced by discovering the oil. However, he thought that the injunction to take account of 'the effect, in relation to the said benefit, of the circumstances giving rise to the frustration' meant that the value had therefore to be assessed after the frustrating event, so that it would consist of the value of the oil already removed and of any claim for compensation against the Libyan Government. (It would seem to follow from this that *Appleby v Myers* should still be decided the same way today.) This calculation produced 'a valuable benefit' of about $85 m but the plaintiffs only recovered $35 m ($10 m + $87 m − $62 m), this being in effect their 'loss', taking into account that the parties own contractual provisions had allocated a substantial share of the risk to the plaintiffs. It will be seen that because of the precise timetable of events the amount which the judge considered the 'just sum' was less than the 'valuable benefit'. His construction of 'valuable benefit' did not therefore limit his ability to award the whole of the 'just sum'. Clearly if the contract has been frustrated by earlier expropriation this would not have been the case.

The judgment of Robert Goff J was affirmed by the Court of Appeal and the House of Lords[114] but the appeals were on progressively narrower grounds and left the Judge's analysis of section 1(3) substantially untouched.[115]

General provisions of the Act

It should be noted that the Act binds the Crown; that it applies to contracts whenever made, provided that the time of discharge occurs on or after 1 July 1943; and that it may be excluded by the parties in the sense that if their contract contains a provision to meet the event of frustration, the provision applies to the exclusion of the Act.[116]

Contracts excluded from the Act

The Act does not apply to the following classes of contract.[117]

---

[114] [1983] 2 AC 352, [1982] 1 All ER 925.

[115] In the House of Lords the defendant sought to rely on s 2(3) and argued that because under the contract the plaintiffs had taken the risk that there would be no oil, they had also taken the risk of expropriation. This argument was not successful.

[116] S 2(1), (2), and (3).   [117] S 2(5).

(a) A contract for the carriage of goods by sea or a charterparty (except a time charterparty or a charterparty by way of demise). Two important common law rules governing these excepted contracts therefore remain in force.

The first is that, if the contract provides that the freight shall not become payable until the conclusion of the voyage, the shipowner is entitled to no remuneration if he is prevented from reaching the stipulated port of discharge by some frustrating event. If, for example, the agreed port is Hamburg and the shipowner puts into Antwerp owing to the outbreak of war with Germany, he cannot recover freight unless the shipper voluntarily accepts delivery at Antwerp.[118] The second rule is that freight paid in advance is regarded as a payment at the risk of the shipper and is not recoverable, either in whole or in part, if, owing to the frustration of the contract or to any other cause, the goods are not delivered.[119] It is customary, however, to insure against the risks engendered by these two rules.

(b) A contract of insurance. The doctrine of frustration is not normally applicable to a contract of insurance, for the customary understanding in this type of business and indeed the rule of law, is that, once the premium is paid and the risk assumed by the insurer, 'there shall be no apportionment or return of premium afterwards',[120] even though the subject matter of the risk may vanish before the period of cover has elapsed.[121] 'If I insure against sickness on January 1st and die on February 1st, my executors cannot get back 11/12th of the premium.'[122] So too, if a house which has been insured against fire is requisitioned by a government department before expiry of the policy, the assured is not entitled to recover any part of the premium.

(c) The Act excepts from its provisions:

> Any contract to which section 7 of the Sale of Goods Act 1893 applies, or any other contract for the sale or for the sale and delivery of specific goods, where the contract is frustrated by reason of the fact that the goods have perished.[123]

This subsection is clumsily drafted and is difficult to understand, but its effect appears to be as follows.[124]

It excludes two classes of contract.

(1) 'Any contract to which section 7 of the Sale of Goods Act 1893 applies.' Section 7 now of the Sale of Goods Act 1979 provided that:

---

[118] *St Enoch Shipping Co v Phosphate Mining Co* [1916] 2 KB 624.

[119] *Byrne v Schiller* (1871) LR 6 Exch 319. Of course, if the goods are lost owing to the shipowner's default the freight already paid is included in the damages.

[120] *Tyrie v Fletcher* (1777) 2 Cowp 666 at 668, per Lord Mansfield.

[121] *Webber* p 693.

[122] Speech by the Attorney-General on the Committee stage of the Bill, 1943, cited *Webber* p 679, n 4.

[123] S 2(5)(c).   [124] For a full discussion, see *Williams* pp 81–90.

> Where there is an agreement to sell specific goods and subsequently the goods, without any fault on the part of the seller or buyer, perish before the risk passes to the buyer, the agreement is thereby avoided.

It will be observed that for this section to operate, four elements must be present:

(i)   There must be an agreement to sell, not a sale. By section 2 of the Sale of Goods Act, the concept of 'contract of sale' is sub-divided into a 'sale' and an 'agreement to sell'. If the property in the goods is transferred to the buyer under the contract, there is a 'sale'; if the property is not immediately transferred by virtue of the contract, there is an 'agreement to sell'.

(ii) The risk must not have passed to the buyer. The general rule for the passing of the risk is stated in section 20 of the Sale of Goods Act.

> Unless otherwise agreed, the goods remain at the seller's risk until the property therein is transferred to the buyer, but when the property therein is transferred to the buyer, the goods are at the buyer's risk whether delivery has been made or not.

In other words, risk prima facie follows the property. In the case of an agreement to sell, therefore, since the property remains with the seller, so also does the risk, and this is what normally happens. The parties, however, may 'agree otherwise' and may thus arrange that while the seller remains the owner of the goods, the risk shall pass to the buyer.[125] If such is the arrangement, section 7 of the Sale of Goods Act does not apply.

(iii) The goods must be specific. By section 62 of the Sale of Goods Act, 'specific goods means goods identified and agreed upon at the time a contract of sale is made'. It is clear, therefore, that a contract for the sale of unascertained or generic goods cannot satisfy this definition, as where A agrees to sell to B 'a dozen bottles of 1919 port' or '500 quarters of wheat'. A will fulfil his contract by delivering any dozen of such bottles or any 500 quarters of wheat, and it is obvious that, as the subject matter of such contract has no individuality, it cannot perish. It seems, moreover, that goods will still be unascertained even if the source from which they are to come is specifically defined, provided that the actual goods to be delivered are not yet identified.[126] If, for example, A agrees to sell 'a dozen bottles of the 1919 port now in my cellar', the goods are not specific in the statutory sense. No particular dozen bottles have yet been set aside and earmarked for the contract. To this case also section 7 of the Sale of Goods Act is inapplicable.

---

[125]   The separation of property and risk may also be the result of a trade custom. Thus in *Bevington and Morris v Dale & Co Ltd* (1902) 7 Com Cas 112, A agreed to sell furs to B 'on approval'. The furs were delivered to B and then stolen from him. By the Sale of Goods Act; s 18, sub-s (4), the property had not yet passed to B and therefore by the normal operation of s 20, the risk would still be with A. But A proved a custom of the fur trade that goods were at the risk of persons ordering them 'on approval' and B was therefore held liable for the invoice price.

[126]   *Howell v Coupland* (1876) 1 QBD 258. *Aliter* if the contract is for all the port in my cellar: *Sainsbury Ltd v Street* [1972] 3 All ER 1127, [1972] 1 WLR 834.

(iv) The goods must have perished. The word 'perish' includes cases not only where the goods have been physically destroyed, but also where they are so damaged that they no longer answer to the description under which they were sold, as, for instance, where dates, carried on a ship which sinks but is later raised, are irretrievably contaminated with sewage.[127] But, unless the goods have perished within this extended meaning of the word, section 7 does not apply. If the contract is frustrated by some other event, as where the goods are requisitioned by the government after the agreement has been made, the section is excluded.[128]

If the above four elements are all present, section 7 declares that the contract is 'avoided'. The result is that the seller cannot be sued by the buyer for breach of contract in failing to make delivery; though, as the risk remains with the seller, it is he who bears the loss of the goods.

(2) The second class of contract excluded from the Law Reform (Frustrated Contracts) Act 1943 is:

> Any other contract for the sale or for the sale and delivery of specific goods, where the contract is frustrated by reason of the fact that the goods have perished.

The problem here is to discover what type of contract is covered by these words and is not caught by section 7 of the Sale of Goods Act. In each case the goods must be 'specific' and in each case the cause of the frustration must be their perishing. The difference must therefore lie in the absence of the first or the second of the two elements discussed above. If there is a 'sale' or if, though there is only an agreement to sell, the risk, by custom or by the terms of the particular agreement, is to pass immediately to the buyer, the Act of 1943 does not apply. In these cases the risk is with the buyer and if, due to some catastrophe not due to the seller's fault, the goods perish before delivery, it is the buyer who must bear the loss.

From this summary it will be seen that, in the first type of contract of sale excluded from the Act of 1943, the risk has not passed to the buyer, while in the second type it has so passed. It thus seems that all contracts for the sale of specific goods are kept outside the operation of that Act, whether the risk has passed or not, provided only that the cause of frustration is the perishing of the goods. But if the goods are not specific or if the frustration is due to some other reason, such as requisitioning, the Act of 1943 applies.

These statutory provisions are a little bewildering, and it is difficult to see why an arbitrary distinction should have been made between different contracts for the sale of goods or, indeed, why it was thought necessary to exclude any such contract from the operation of the Act in a case where the doctrine of frustration is relevant. There seems no reason why the statutory provisions for the apportionment of loss should not have been permitted in the case of any contract for the sale of goods.

---

[127] *Asfar & Co v Blundell* [1896] 1 QB 123.
[128] *Re Shipton, Anderson & Co and Harrison Bros & Co* [1915] 3 KB 676.

21 REMEDIES FOR BREACH OF CONTRACT[1]

1 INTRODUCTION

This chapter is concerned with the practical steps which an innocent party may take if the other party breaks the contract. It should be noted, however, that in the law of

---

[1] Lawson *Remedies of English Law*; Beale *Remedies for Breach of Contract*; Treitel *Remedies for Breach of Contract*; Burrows *Remedies for Tort and Breach of Contract*; Harris *Remedies in Contract and Tort*; Bishop 14 Journal of Legal Studies 299, Harris and Veljanovski, 5 Law and Policy Quarterly 97.

contract, unlike some other branches of the law, rights and remedies are inextricably intertwined. So we have already seen,[2] that if a party is induced to enter into a contract by the other party's misrepresentation, he can *rescind* and similarly[3] that serious failure by one party to perform may entitle the other to *withhold his own performance* and/or to *terminate* the contract. Rescission, withholding one's performance and termination are all in one sense rights[4] but equally they are often the most effective way of remedying the breach.

We may make some other preliminary points. It is common, even for lawyers, to talk of 'enforcing the contract'. In fact English law does not usually enforce the contract in the sense of compelling the parties to carry out their primary obligations. At common law the only case is where the guilty party's outstanding obligation is to pay a fixed sum of money; in equity there exist the remedies of specific performance and injunction but these, as we shall see, are only exceptionally granted. In practice, the injured party's remedy is most commonly an action for damages to compensate him for the breach of contract.

As the previous paragraph has already revealed, this is an area of the law of contract which has been much influenced by the division between common law and equity. The common law courts early decided that they would not order contracts to be specifically performed. This was probably because common law judgments were enforced by distraint on the defendant's goods which ultimately produced a money sum. Orders of the Court of Chancery were enforced by committal for contempt and the Court of Chancery came to order specific performance but only in cases where it regarded the common law remedy of damages as inadequate. During the nineteenth century there was legislation which enabled common law courts to order specific performance and the Court of Chancery to award damages[5] and since the Judicature Acts of 1873–75 all remedies have been available in all divisions of the High Court. Nevertheless the distinction between common law remedies and equitable remedies bears very clearly the impress of their historical origins.

It is important finally to notice that the parties enjoy a wide freedom not only to provide for their primary rights but also to plan their own remedies. In contracts of any sophistication it is very common for the parties to insert provisions which either add to or subtract from the remedies that the general law would otherwise provide. Even in relatively simple contracts it may make excellent sense to contract for a remedy which will avoid the need to go to court. So those who sell package holidays normally require deposits at the time of the booking and payment in full before the holiday starts. This is because experience has shown that some customers will not turn up. Although a customer who does not turn up would break the contract by failing to

---

[2] P 352, above.   [3] P 682, above.

[4] See the illuminating distinction drawn by Lord Diplock between primary and secondary rights for example, in *Photo Production Ltd v Securicor Transport Ltd* [1980] AC 827, [1980] 1 All ER 556.

[5] Mercantile Law Amendment Act 1856, Chancery Amendment Act 1858.

pay in full it would usually not be cost effective to sue such customers. Taking a deposit in advance avoids this problem.

2 DAMAGES[6]

A Remoteness of damage and measure of damages

The extent to which a plaintiff is entitled to demand damages for breach of contract was not fully considered by the courts until *Hadley v Baxendale* in 1854.[7] The principle laid down in that case has since been repeatedly affirmed. In the ultimate analysis a claim for damages raises two distinct questions. These emerge from the fundamental principle that the remoteness of the damage for which compensation is claimed must be distinguished from the monetary assessment of that compensation.[8]

The first is: for what *kind* of damage is the plaintiff entitled to recover compensation? Damage of the most catastrophic and unusual nature may ensue from breach, but on practical grounds the law takes the view that a line must he drawn somewhere and that certain kinds or types of loss, though admittedly caused as a direct result of the defendant's conduct, shall not qualify for compensation. As Lord Wright said in a case of tort:

> The law cannot take account of everything that follows a wrongful act; it regards some subsequent matters as outside the scope of its selection, because 'it were infinite for the law to judge the cause of causes', or consequences of consequences . . . In the varied web of affairs the law must abstract some consequences as relevant, not perhaps on grounds of pure logic, but simply for practical reasons.[9]

To this end *Hadley v Baxendale*[10] defined the kind of damage that is the appropriate subject of compensation, and excluded all other kinds as being too remote. The decision was concerned solely with what is correctly called *remoteness of damage*, and it will conduce to clarity if this expression is reserved for cases where the defendant denies liability for certain of the consequences that have flowed from his breach.

The second question, which must be kept quite distinct from the first, concerns the principles upon which damage must be evaluated or quantified in terms of money. This may appropriately be called the question of the *measure of damages*. The principle adopted by the courts in many cases dating back to at least 1848 is that of

---

[6] *McGregor on Damages* (14th edn, 1980); Ogus *The Law of Damages* (1973), Street *Principles of the Law of Damages* (1962). Cooke [1978] CLJ 288.

[7] (1854) 9 Exch 341, Danzig (1975) 4 JLS 249.

[8] *Chaplin v Hicks* [1911] 2 KB 786 at 797, per Farwell LJ; *Boys v Chaplin* [1968] 1 QB 1 at 41, [1968] 1 All ER 283 at 299, per Diplock LJ.

[9] *Liesbosch Dredger v Edison SS* [1933] AC 449 at 460.   [10] (1854) 9 Exch 341; p 756, below.

restitutio in integrum. If the plaintiff has suffered damage that is not too remote, he must, so far as money can do it, be restored to the position he would have been in had that particular damage not occurred.[11]

Historically it has been treated as clear in principle that what is to be recovered by way of damages is the loss which the plaintiff has suffered, and not the profit which the defendant has made. In *Surrey County Council v Bredero Homes*, the plaintiffs were Surrey County Council and Mole Valley District Council who were the respective freehold owners of two parcels of land totalling 12.33 acres in an area which had originally been acquired for road purposes. By 1980 the land was no longer required for those purposes and the councils acting together decided to offer the entire site for development as a housing estate. In due course, by a written contract dated 28 November 1980, the councils agreed to sell the entire site to the defendant for £1.52m, subject to the defendant obtaining planning permission for the development of the site in accordance with the councils' development brief and the scheme for the development of the site. The defendant duly obtained planning permission and by transfers dated 22 January 1981 the councils transferred the land to it. Under clause 2 of each transfer the defendant covenanted with each council that it would carry out the development of the housing estate in accordance with the terms of the planning permission and the approved scheme. Later, the defendant obtained a fresh planning permission permitting more houses to be built on the site than that specified in the approved scheme. Although this was clearly not a breach of the public law controls over land through the planning mechanism, it was a clear breach of the defendant's contractual obligations to the two councils. However, although the councils knew about the new planning permission, they took no legal steps to restrain the revised development. On the face of it the councils, if they had acted promptly, could have obtained an inunction to restrain such development and could have obtained further payments from the defendant in order to get the injunction released.

However, the plaintiffs did none of these things but simply waited until the development was complete and then argued that they were entitled to recover as damages for breach of contract the extra profits which the defendant had made by more intensive development of the site arising from their admitted breach of contract.[12] The Court of Appeal held that the plaintiffs could only recover nominal damages.[13]

---

[11] *Robinson v Harman* (1848) 1 Exch 850; *Wertheim v Chicoutimi Pulp Co* [1911] AC 301 at 307; *The Edison* [1932] p 52 at 62–63, per Scrutton LJ; *B Sunley & Co Ltd v Cunard White Star Ltd* [1940] 1 KB 740 at 745, [1940] 2 All ER 97 at 100, per curiam. The distinction between remoteness of damage and measure of damages was applied in *J D'Almeida Araujo Lda v Sir Frederick Becker & Co Ltd* [1953] 2 QB 329, [1953] 2 All ER 288. This was an action brought in England for breach of a contract governed by Portuguese law.

[12] [1993] 1 WLR 1362. Birks 109 LQR 518.

[13] Cf *Wrotham Park Estate Co. v Parkside Homes Ltd* [1974] 1 WLR 798. A difficult case is *White Arrow Express Ltd v Lamey's Distribution Ltd. The Times* 21 July 1995 where the defendants charged extra for a deluxe service but provided only a basic service. However the plaintiffs failure to recover substantial damages may be explained as turning on inadequate pleading, Beale 112 LQR 205.

The House of Lords held, however, in *A-G v Blake*[14] that it was not always the case that a claimant was limited to his own loss. Blake was for many years employed by the British Secret Intelligence Service and had signed a contract of employment which contained a provision for lifelong confidentiality. Unknown to the SIS Blake was also employed by the KGB. In 1961 this was discovered and he was charged, convicted and sentenced to 42 years imprisonment. In 1965 he escaped and has since been in Moscow. He made a contract with the publisher, Jonathan Cape Ltd, to publish his autobiography. Under the contract he was entitled to £150,000 and at the time of the case had received £60,000. The Government, which had not known of the book contract until the book appeared, was anxious to stop him receiving the balance of the advance and even to obtain it for itself.

The case is complex because it was argued on different grounds at each judicial level and on both public and private law grounds. Although the House of Lords thought nearly all the arguments adopted in favour of the Crown in the Court of Appeal unsustainable, it nevertheless held (by a majority, Lord Hobhouse dissenting) for the Crown.

The Crown could show little if any loss since although Blake had clearly broken his confidentiality agreement, the information revealed was all very old and mostly in the public domain. On the other hand, Blake had been very handsomely paid.[15] Lord Nicholls, delivering the principal speech, deplored the use of the expression 'restitutionary damages' and preferred to talk of 'requiring a defendant to account to the plaintiff for the benefits he had received from his breach of contract'. Lord Nicholls stated that this remedy would be exceptional and that no fixed rules could be prescribed.

It may be tempting to see *A-G v Blake* as limited to the treatment of spies but this is not the way the common law develops. Counsel are bound to invoke it and it is likely that substantial damages will as a result be awarded in some cases where previously only nominal damages would have been granted. The decision of the Court of Appeal in *Experience Hendrix LLC v PPX Enterprises Inc*[16] supports this view. Under a compromise agreement the first defendants were entitled to license various masters of recordings listed in a schedule. In breach of contract various other masters were licensed. There was clearly profit to the defendants but apparently no loss to the plaintiffs. The Court of Appeal refused to award an account of profits but gave damages to be calculated on the basis of a reasonable payment for the use of the material.

Another important qualification to the principle that a claimant can only recover damages to reflect his own loss occurs in cases where a claimant has recovered damages

---

[14] [2000] 4 All ER 385. Connington 17 J Contract L 212; Phang and Pey-Woan Lee 17 J Contract L 240, 19 J Contract Law 1, Jaffey 20 J Contract L 57.

[15] Presumably, Blake's profit was not the full £150,000 since there must have been costs involved in the production of the book, for example, the cost of getting it typed. This question was not seriously discussed.

[16] [2003] EWCA Civ 323, [2003] 1 All ER (Comm) 830

which have been suffered by a third party as a result of the breach of contract. These are discussed in the chapter on privity of contract.[17]

The question of what exactly it is that the plaintiff has lost is often a subtle one and for this purpose it is useful to use the terminology popularised by a famous American article[18] and distinguish between *expectation* loss and *reliance* loss. Expectation loss is the loss of that which the plaintiff would have received if the contract had been properly performed. Of course in a sense the plaintiff has not lost this because he never had it but he expected to have it and the reports are full of statements that the plaintiff is entitled to be put into the position he would have been in if the contract had been performed.[19]

The most obvious expectation loss is the profit the plaintiff would have made on the contract. But the contract may he so speculative that it is unclear what, if any, profit it would have made. This does not mean that the plaintiff has suffered no loss since he may have relied upon the defendant honouring his contract and incurred expenditure which was wasted as a result. So, for instance, in *Anglia Television Ltd v Reed*[20] the plaintiffs engaged the defendant, an American actor, to appear in a film which they were making for television. At the last moment he repudiated the contract and, as the plaintiff could not find a replacement, they abandoned the project. The plaintiffs, no doubt wisely, did not claim the profit they would have made on the film. It is impossible to tell in advance whether an unmade film will he a success or a failure. Instead the plaintiffs claimed and were awarded the money they had spent in preparation such as hiring other actors, engaging a script writer, looking for suitable locations and so on.[21]

In principle, it seems that the plaintiff has a free choice whether to quantify his loss on an expectation or a reliance basis.[22] However it is open to a defendant to show that the plaintiff made a bad bargain so that there was no loss on an expectation basis and that the wasted expenditure would have been incurred whether the contract was broken or not.[23] It seems that the onus is on the defendant affirmatively to show this.[24] In *Commonwealth of Australia v Amann Aviation Pty Ltd*:[25]

---

[17] pp 572–600.

[18] Fuller and Purdue 46 Yale L J 52. Friedman 111 LQR 628

[19] See eg *Robinson v Harman* (1848) 1 Exch 850.

[20] [1972] 1 QB 60, [1971] 3 All ER 690.

[21] The decision has been criticised on the grounds that the Court of Appeal awarded expenditure incurred before the contract. Ogus 35 MLR 423. This might perhaps be justified on the ground that if the contract had not been broken the film would have been sufficiently successful to cover all these setting up costs. For further discussion see *Ogus* chs 8,9; Stoljar 91 LQR 68 and Owen 4 Oxford JLS 393.

[22] *Anglia Television Ltd v Reed* [1972] 1 QB 60, [1971] 3 All ER 690, per Lord Denning MR; *CCC Films (London) Ltd v Impact Quadrant Films Ltd* [1985] QB 16, [1984] 3 All ER 298.

[23] *C & P Haulage v Middleton* [1983] 3 All ER 94, [1983] 1 WLR 1461.

[24] *CCC Films (London) Ltd v Impact Quadrant Films Ltd* [1985] QB 16, [1984] 3 All ER 298.

[25] [1991] 174 CLR 64, Treitel 108 LQR 226.

Amann secured a contract to provide surveillance of the North coastline of Australia for three years. The contract was wrongfully terminated by the Commonwealth of Australia before the three-year period had run. Amann had spent much money, particularly in acquiring suitable aircraft to perform the contract. The resale value of the aircraft was substantially less than their cost since they had been especially adapted to perform this contract, and there was no other ready market for such specially adapted airplanes.

The Commonwealth of Australia argued that Amann would not have recovered all their reliance loss if the contract had run its full three years. However, the High Court of Australia held that at the end of the three years although Amann would not have been certain to secure a renewal of the contract, that they would having acquired so much relevant equipment had an excellent chance of being the most competitive bidder. Taking loss of this chance into account, the Commonwealth of Australia could not demonstrate that the contract was in fact unprofitable and therefore Amann recovered its reliance loss.

The amount of money adjudged to be due to the plaintiff has usually been assessed as at the time when the contract was broken. Traditionally this 'breach-date' rule has meant that any change in the value of sterling after the date when the cause of action accrued must be ignored.[26] But the House of Lords has now mitigated the effect of this rule in an era of fluctuating currencies by holding that in appropriate circumstances judgments may be given in a foreign currency.[27]

In *Wroth v Tyler*[28] Megarry J held that if the plaintiff is claiming not damages at common law but damages in lieu of specific performance under the Chancery Amendment Act 1858 (Lord Cairns' Act) damages will be assessed as at the date of judgment. In *Malhotra v Choudhury*[29] this was treated as correct by the Court of Appeal but in *Johnson v Agnew*[30] Lord Wilberforce was clear that the same principles must govern damages at common law and under Lord Cairns' Act. He left open the question whether the cases (of contracts for the sale of land) were correctly decided on the basis that the 'breach-date' rule did not apply.

It seems clear that the breach-date rule is simply a starting point. In appropriate cases the court will take account of events after the breach.[31]

---

[26] *Re United Railways of Havana and Regla Warehouses Ltd* [1961] 1 AC 1007, [1960] 2 All ER 332; *The Teh Hu* [1970] p 106, [1969] 3 All ER 8.

[27] *Miliangos v George Frank (Textiles) Ltd* [1976] AC 443, [1975] 3 All ER 801.

[28] [1974] Ch 30, [1973] 1 All ER 897. As to Lord Cairns' Act, see Jolowicz [1975] CLJ 224; Pettit [1979] CLJ 369.

[29] [1980] Ch 52, [1979] 1 All ER 186. See for further discussion Burgess 34 ICLQ 317; Hayton [1979] CLJ 35.

[30] [1980] AC 367, [1979] 1 All ER 883.

[31] *Golden Strait Corporation v Nippon Yusen Kubishika Kaisha* [2005] 1 All ER (Comm) 467, [2006] 1 All ER (Comm) 235.

The evaluation of the damage, however, must be based solely upon the legal obligations of the defendant. 'A defendant is not liable in damages for not doing that which he is not bound to do.'[32] An employee, for instance, who has been wrongfully dismissed, is admittedly entitled to recover what he would have received had his employment run its full course; but if his contractual salary was increasable by any bonus that the employer at his discretion might from time award, the assessment of damages must ignore undeclared bonuses, even though it is highly probable that they would have been declared had the employment continued.[33]

> The law is concerned with legal obligations only, and the law of contract only with legal obligations created by mutual agreement between contractors—not with the expectations, however reasonable, of one contractor that the other will do something that he has assumed no legal obligation to do.[34]

This principle also means that if the contract provides for the defendant to have an option as to performance, damages should be calculated on the basis that the defendant would have exercised this option in the way which would minimise his liability. So if the contract is for 1000 tons of coffee, 10% more or less at the seller's option, a defaulting seller can argue that he would have chosen only to deliver 900 tons.[35]

The rule that governs remoteness of damage was stated as follows by Alderson B in delivering the judgment of the Court of Exchequer in *Hadley v Baxendale*:

> Where two parties have made a contract which one of them has broken, the damages which the other party ought to receive in respect of such breach of contract should be such as may fairly and reasonably be considered either arising naturally, ie, according to the usual course of things, from such breach of contract itself, or such as may reasonably be supposed to have been in the contemplation of both parties, at the time they made the contract, as the probable result of the breach of it.[36]

The facts of the case were as follows:

> The mill of the plaintiffs at Gloucester was brought to a standstill by a broken crank shaft and it became necessary to send the shaft to the makers at Greenwich as a pattern for a new one. The defendant, a common carrier, promised to deliver it at Greenwich on the following day. Owing to his neglect, it was unduly delayed in transit, with the result that the mill remained idle for longer than it would have

---

[32] *Abrahams v Herbert Reiach Ltd* [1922] 1 KB 477 at 482, per Scrutton LJ.

[33] *Lavarack v Woods of Colchester Ltd* [1967] 2 QB 278, [1966] 3 All ER 683.

[34] Ibid at 292, per Diplock LJ.

[35] But he cannot argue that he would have exercised the option in a way which would itself have been a breach; *Paula Lee Ltd v Robert Zehil & Co Ltd* [1983] 2 All ER 390.

[36] (1854) 9 Exch 341 at 354.

done had there been no breach of the contract of carriage. The plaintiffs, therefore, claimed to recover damages for the loss of profit caused by the delay.

The evidence of the parties was conflicting, but the Court of Exchequer considered the case on the footing that the only information given to the carrier was 'that the article to be carried was the broken shaft of a mill and that the plaintiffs were the millers of that mill'.[37]

It was obvious that the failure of the carrier to perform the contract punctually was the direct cause of the stoppage of the mill for an unnecessarily long time, and, if the plaintiffs were entitled to an indemnity against all the consequences of the breach, they should have been awarded damages for the loss of profit. At the trial the jury did indeed allow the claim, but on appeal the court ordered a new trial. Alderson B demonstrated that, in accordance with the principle that he had just expressed, there were only two possible grounds upon which the plaintiffs could sustain their claim. Firstly, that in the usual course of things the work of the mill would cease altogether for the want of the shaft. This, he said, would not be the normal occurrence, for, to take only one reasonable possibility, the plaintiffs might well have had a spare shaft in reserve. Secondly, that the special circumstances were so fully disclosed that the inevitable loss of profit was made apparent to the defendant. This, however, was not the case, since the only communication proved was that the article to be carried was the shaft of a mill and that the plaintiffs were the owners of the mill. The jury, therefore, should not have taken the loss of profit into consideration in their assessment of damages.

The words 'either' and 'or', used in the formulation of the rule as explained by Alderson B, shows that it contains two branches. The first deals with the normal damage that occurs in the usual course of things; the second with abnormal damage that arises because of special or exceptional circumstances. The defendant is taken to have contemplated both kinds of damage, but where it is abnormal only if he knew of the special circumstances at the time of the contract.

In *Victoria Laundry (Windsor) Ltd v Newman Industries Ltd*[38] the test of remoteness of liability laid down by Alderson B was reformulated by Asquith LJ in what is generally regarded as a classic exposition of the developed law. In the course of delivering the judgment of the court, he summarised the substance of the test in the following three propositions.

In cases of breach of contract, the aggrieved party is only entitled to recover such part of the loss actually resulting as was at the time of the contract reasonably foreseeable as liable to result from the breach.

---

[37] Ibid at 355, per Alderson B. In *Victoria Laundry (Windsor) Ltd v Newman Industries Ltd* [1949] 2 KB 528 at 537, [1949] 1 All ER 997 at 1001, the Court of Appeal pointed out that the headnote to *Hadley v Baxendale* is definitely misleading in its statement that the carrier was told of the stopping of the mill and the necessity for the immediate delivery of the shaft.

[38] [1949] 2 KB 528, [1949] 1 All ER 997.

What was at that time reasonably so foreseeable depends on the knowledge then possessed by the parties or, at all events, by the party who later commits the breach.

For this purpose, knowledge 'possessed' is of two kinds; one imputed, the other actual. Everyone, as a reasonable person, is taken to know the 'ordinary course of things' and consequently what loss is liable to result from a breach of contract in that ordinary course. This is the subject-matter of the 'first rule' in *Hadley v Baxendale.* But to this knowledge, which a contract-breaker is assumed to possess whether he actually possesses it or not, there may have to be added in a particular case knowledge which he actually possesses of special circumstances outside the 'ordinary course of things', of such a kind that a breach in those special circumstances would be liable to cause more loss. Such a case attracts the operation of the 'second rule' so as to make additional loss also recoverable.[39]

The case concerned a claim made by a buyer for the recovery of the business profits that he had lost owing to the delayed delivery of a chattel essential to the furtherance of his trade, a type of question that not infrequently comes before the courts. The facts were these:

> The plaintiffs, launderers and dyers, decided to extend their business. For this purpose and for the purpose of obtaining certain dyeing contracts of an exceptionally profitable character, they required a larger boiler. The defendants, an engineering firm, contracted to sell and deliver to the plaintiffs on 5 June a certain boiler of the required capacity. This, however, was damaged in the course of removal and was not delivered until the following 8 November. The defendants were aware of the nature of the plaintiffs' business and they were informed in more than one letter before the conclusion of the contract that the plaintiffs were 'most anxious' to put the boiler into use 'in the shortest possible space of time'.

In an action for breach of contract, the plaintiffs claimed (a) damages for the loss of profit, assessed by them at £16 a week, that they would have earned through the extension of their business but for the delay in delivery of the boiler, and (b) damages, assessed at £262 a week, for the loss of the exceptional profits that they would similarly have earned on the 'highly lucrative' dyeing contracts. In the opinion of the Court of Appeal, the defendants, with their engineering experience and with the knowledge of the facts possessed by them, could not reasonably contend that the likelihood of some loss of business was beyond their prevision. They were, indeed, ignorant that the plaintiffs had in prospect the 'highly lucrative' dyeing contracts and so could not be liable specifically for the 'highly lucrative' profits that the plaintiffs had hoped to make. Even so, however, the plaintiffs were not precluded from recovering a general, if conjectural, sum which might represent the *normal* profit to be expected from the completion of the dyeing contracts. The case, therefore, was remitted to an Official

---

[39] Ibid at 539 and 1002, respectively . . .

Referee to ascertain the damage that might reasonably he expected to result from the failure to extend the business and the inability to execute normal dyeing contracts.

In *The Heron II*,[40] however, the House of Lords differed from the judgment of Asquith LJ, with regard to the criterion by which to determine the remoteness of damage arising from a breach of contract. They stated that the question is not, as Asquith LJ said, whether the damage should have been foreseen by the defendant, but whether the probability of its occurrence should have been within the reasonable contemplation of both parties at the time when the contract was made, having regard to their knowledge at that time. The law of contract and of tort differ in this respect. A tortfeasor is liable for any damage which is of such a kind as should have been foreseen by a reasonable man, however unlikely its occurrence might have been.[41] Of these two criteria, that of reasonable foresight is the more stringent. A tortfeasor is generally a stranger to the injured person, and it falls to the law to define both the persons to whom he owes a duty of care and also the extent of that duty. The intention of the parties is irrelevant.

> But in contract the parties have only to consider the consequences of a breach to the other; it is fair that the assessment of damages should depend upon their assumed common knowledge and contemplation and not on a foreseeable but most unlikely consequence.[42]

It has been held, however, that if the kind of damage caused by a breach of contract is within the reasonable contemplation of the parties at the time when the contract was made and is therefore not too remote, it is immaterial that its results are far more serious than could have been reasonably contemplated.[43]

The criterion of reasonable contemplation, as it may shortly be described, applies to both branches of the rule in *Hadley v Baxendale*. The difference in this respect between the two is that in the case of the first branch the 'horizon of contemplation' is confined to loss which arises naturally in the usual course of things and which is therefore presumed to have been within the contemplation of the parties. The second branch, by reason of the special knowledge possessed by the defendant, extends the horizon of contemplation to loss that does not arise in the usual course of things.[44]

---

40 [1969] 1 AC 350. Pickering 31 MLR 203.

41 *The Wagon Mound* [1961] AC 388, [1961] 1 All ER 404.

42 *The Heron II* [1969] 1 AC 350 at 422, [1967] 3 All ER 686 at 716, per Lord Upjohn; see also at 413 and 711, respectively, per Lord Pearce. There is a group of cases where the plaintiff can formulate his claim either in contract or in tort. If the test of remoteness is different, then the result may be different depending on whether the claim is formulated in contract or tort. The House of Lords did not discuss this situation in the *Heron II*. See Hamson [1969] CLJ 15.

43 *Vacwell Engineering Co Ltd v BDH Chemicals Ltd* [1971] 1 QB 111n, [1970] 3 All ER 553. *Wroth v Tyler* [1974] Ch 30, [1973] 1 All ER 897. *Brown v KMR Services Ltd* [1995] 4 All ER 598. But everything here turns on the classification of 'kind of damage'. So in the *Victoria Laundry* case profits and exceptional profits were treated as different kinds.

44 *The Heron II* [1969] 1 AC 350 at 415–416, [1967] 3 All ER at 712, per Lord Pearce.

A further question arises when the courts seek to apply the criterion of reasonable contemplation. What is the degree of probability required and how is it to be defined, if indeed it is capable of exact definition? In the *Victoria Laundry* case, Asquith LJ said:

> In order to make the contract-breaker liable under [*Hadley v Baxendale*] it is not necessary that he should have actually asked himself what loss is liable to result from a breach. It suffices that, if he had considered the question, he would as a reasonable man have concluded that the loss in question was liable to result . . . Nor . . . to make a particular loss recoverable, need it be proved that upon a given state of knowledge the defendant could, as a reasonable man, foresee that a breach must necessarily result in that loss. It is enough if he could foresee it was likely so to result. It is indeed enough . . . if the loss (or some factor without which it would not have occurred) is a 'serious possibility' or a 'real danger'. For short, we have used the word 'liable' to result. Possibly the colloquialism 'on the cards' indicates the shade of meaning with some approach to accuracy.[45]

In *The Heron II*, the House of Lords indulged in a punctilious, and at times involved, analysis of these phrases used by the learned Lord Justice. Their Lordships all deprecated the phrase 'on the cards'. Thus Lord Pearce discarded it as a useful test. 'I suspect', he said, 'that it owes its attraction, like many other colloquialisms, to the fact that one may utter it without having the trouble of really thinking out with precision what one means oneself or what others understand by it, a spurious attraction which in general makes colloquialism unsuitable for definition, though it is often useful as shorthand for a collection of definable ideas.[46] But, while their Lordships unanimously rejected the use of this phrase, they could not agree upon a suitable substitute. Lord Reid distrusted the expression 'liable to result'. 'Liable', he said, 'is a very vague word, but I think that one would usually say that when a person foresees a very improbable result he foresees that it is liable to happen.'[47] His Lordship preferred 'not unlikely', or 'quite likely' to happen. Lord Hodson, on the other hand, disapproved of 'likely to result' and preferred 'liable to result', the phrase which Asquith LJ had suggested. 'If the word "likelihood" is used it may convey the impression that the chances are all in favour of the thing happening, an idea which I would reject.'[48] Lord Upjohn was content to adopt the phrases 'a real danger' or 'a serious possibility'.[49] If, indeed, a single phrase must he chosen 'liable to result' seems to have secured the most general assent.

It is questionable whether this exercise in semantics is of any great value. Lord Morris of Borth-y-Gest showed little enthusiasm for it,[50] and when the case was before the Court of Appeal, Sellers LJ remarked that 'the phrases and words of *Hadley v Baxendale* have been hallowed by long usage and gain little advantage from the para-

[45] [1949] 2 KB 528 at 540, [1949] 1 All ER 997.
[46] [1969] 1 AC at 415, [1967] 3 All ER at 711.
[47] Ibid at 389 and 694, respectively.   [48] Ibid at 410–411 and 708, respectively.
[49] Ibid at 425 and 717, respectively.   [50] Ibid at 399 and 699, respectively.

phrases or substitutes. The ideas and factors conveyed by the words are clear enough.'[51] As Lord Upjohn said in the House of Lords, 'the assessment of damages is not an exact science';[52] and it may be added that the search for such an elusive quantity as a person's assumed contemplation can scarcely be governed by any particular formula.

During the twenty years that elapsed between the *Victoria Laundry* case and *The Heron II*, the judgment of Asquith LJ remained unchallenged. Devlin J considered that it had liberated judges of first instance from the bondage of the earlier authorities.[53] In a later case in the House of Lords, Lord Guest, Lord Upjohn and Lord Pearson all cited it with approval.[54] Moreover it has emerged virtually unscathed from its ordeal in *The Heron II* except with regard to the test of liability.[55]

That the difficulties in this field have not been laid to rest by *The Heron II* is shown by *H Parsons (Livestock) Ltd v Uttley Ingham & Co Ltd.*[56]

> The plaintiffs owned an intensive pig farm on which they had a top grade herd. In order to feed the pigs, they needed facilities for the storage of large quantities of pig-nuts and for this purpose they entered into a contract with the defendants for the supply and erection of a bulk-storage hopper. The defendants knew the purpose for which the hopper was being supplied and it was a term of the contract that it should be 'fitted with ventilated top'. In breach of this undertaking, the ventilator, which had been sealed in transit was left closed on installation. As a result of this some of the nuts went mouldy.

There was no difficulty, of course, in seeing that the defendants would be liable for the damage to the nuts but the plaintiffs continued to feed the nuts to the pigs believing this to be safe. In fact as a result of eating the mouldy nuts, the pigs developed a rare intestinal disease and 254 died. The plaintiffs sued for the loss of the pigs. Swanwick J held that it was not within the contemplation of the parties at the time of the contract that the pigs would contract this disease.

In the Court of Appeal it was observed that if the defendants had manufactured a hopper with a defective ventilator and sold it to a retailer who had in turn sold it to the plaintiffs, their action would have been in tort and the test of remoteness would have been foreseeability. All the members of the Court of Appeal thought 'it absurd that the test for remoteness of damage should, in principle, differ according to the legal classification of the cause of action'.[57] But they avoided this result in differing ways.

---

51 [1966] 2 QB 695 at 722. 52 [1969] 1 AC at 425, [1967] 3 All ER at 715.

53 *Heskell v Continental Express Ltd* [1950] 1 All ER 1033 at 1048.

54 *East Ham Corpn v Bernard Sunley & Sons Ltd* [1966] AC 406, [1965] 3 All ER 619.

55 *Aruna Mills Ltd v Dhanrajmal Gobindram* [1968] QB 655 at 668, [1968] 1 All ER 113 at 119.

56 [1978] QB 791, [1978] 1 All ER 525; Hadjihambis 41 MLR 483.

57 Ibid at 806 and 525–535, respectively.

Lord Denning MR thought that as *Hadley v Baxendale*, the *Victoria Laundry* case and the *Heron II* all dealt with loss of profits, they could be regarded as laying down a principle applicable only where breach of contract led to economic loss and that where it led to physical loss, the same test as in tort, foreseeability, should apply. Scarman LJ (with whom Orr LJ agreed) rejected this distinction, but found it possible to find for the plaintiffs on the ground that it was within the party's contemplation that the pigs would have upset stomachs as a result of eating mouldy nuts and that what happened was simply a more extensive example of a contemplatable loss. Both approaches present difficulties. Not only does Lord Denning MR's view have no explicit support in the authorities, but the distinction between economic and physical loss is itself difficult to apply. Scarman LJ's view places a heavy burden on the distinction between type and extent of loss. None of the judgments explain why, if any illness to the pigs were contemplatable, the plaintiffs were not at fault in continuing to feed the nuts to the pigs.

The two branches of *Hadley v Baxendale* do not represent two separate rules, and it may sometimes be difficult to identify which is applicable. Loss of profits arising from the breach of a trading contract, at least made between experienced parties, will more frequently than might be expected fall under the first branch; for each party 'must he taken to understand the ordinary practices and exigencies of the other's trade or business'.[58] This is well illustrated by the actual facts of *The Heron II*.[59]

> The appellant, a shipowner, agreed to carry a cargo of sugar belonging to the respondents from Constanza to Basrah. He knew that there was a sugar market at Basrah and that the respondents were sugar merchants, but did not know that they intended to sell the cargo immediately on its arrival, at the market rate, and that if the ship were nine days late, the price might have dropped during that period. Owing to the appellant's default, the voyage was delayed by at least nine days, and the sugar fetched a lower price than it would have done had it arrived on time.

The consequential loss fell to be borne by the appellant under the first branch of the rule, for though he had no knowledge of special circumstances he could and should at the very least have contemplated that if the ship arrived nine days late the respondents would suffer some financial loss.

Again, if the parties are in the fruit trade between England and Spain and one of them agrees to carry a consignment of oranges to London, he is presumed to know that owing to seasonal fluctuations, the prices available at Covent Garden may largely depend upon the arrival of the goods within the stipulated time.[60]

The first question, then, is—What loss arises in the usual course of things from the breach of a contract where there is nothing exceptional known to the defendant? It is

---

[58] *Monarch ss Co Ltd v Karlshamns Oljefabriker (A/B)* [1949] AC 196 at 224, [1949] 1 All ER 1 at 14, per Lord Wright.

[59] [1969] 1 AC 350, [1967] 3 All ER 686.

[60] *Ardennes (Cargo Owners) v Ardennes (Owners)* [1951] 1 KB 55, [1950] 2 All ER 517.

impossible, of course, to answer the question in general, for just as contracts vary infinitely in character so also do the types of loss that their non-performance normally causes. The nature of the damage that ensues 'in the usual course of things' from a breach obviously varies with the circumstances of each contract. It is proposed, therefore, to illustrate the nature of the subject from the particular case of the sale of goods.

What the buyer is deprived of in the usual course of things by a non-delivery is the value of the goods at the time and place of delivery, less the price payable by him under the contract. If the seller, for instance, has promised to deliver a hundred tons of coal of a specified quality at £20 a ton upon 1 January at Oxford and fails to do so, the injury to the buyer is that he lacks possession of a hundred tons of coal for which he would have paid £2,000. This loss of value, if the seller has no actual or constructive knowledge of further exceptional circumstances, is the only *natural* result of the breach, the only kind of damage that ensues *in the usual course of things*. Every other kind of loss, though actually and directly suffered by the buyer, is in the eye of the law abnormal, not within the reasonable contemplation of the seller in ordinary circumstances, and therefore too remote. Thus, to take one common example, a subcontract loss is usually too remote, ie a buyer, who has agreed before delivery to resell the goods to a third person at a price higher than the contract price, loses the profit that he would have made on the resale had delivery been made to him; but nevertheless the loss is too remote, since it is not the natural and normal result of a failure to deliver sold goods.[61] In order to recover for this exceptional loss he must prove that at the time of the contract the seller knew of special circumstances that signalised the probable resale of the goods.[62]

To turn now to the measure of damages, we must recall that the principle here is to effect a *restitutio in integrum* so far as the actionable damage is concerned. The actionable damage, namely, that which occurs in the usual course of things, is, as we have seen, the loss of the value of the goods at the time and place of delivery, diminished by the price. The buyer, therefore, must be placed in the position that he would have occupied had he received a hundred tons of coal of the specified quality in Oxford on 1 January after paying for it at the rate of £20 a ton. All that is required to put him in this position is sufficient money to enable him to buy similar coal in the open market.

The market value is taken because it is presumed to he the true value of the goods to the purchaser. In the case of non-delivery, where the purchaser does not get the goods he purchased, it is assumed that these would be worth to him, if he had

[61] *Williams Bros v Agius* [1914] AC 510.
[62] *Hall v Pim* [1927] All ER Rep 227, as explained in *Finlay & Co v NV Kwik Hoo Tong* [1929] 1 KB 400 at 411–412, 417–418; *Patrick v Russo-British Grain Export Co* [1927] 2 KB 535; *Brading v F McNeill & Co Ltd* [1946] Ch 145; *Household Machines Ltd v Cosmos Exporters Ltd* [1947] KB 217, [1946] 2 All ER 622. *Seven Seas Properties Ltd v Al-Essa* (M2) [1993] 3 All ER 577.

them, what they would fetch in the open market; and that, if he wanted to get others in their stead, he could obtain them in that market at that price.[63]

The actual sum payable by way of damages for the actionable damage depends, therefore, upon the difference between the market and the contract prices upon the day appointed for delivery. If, for instance, the market price is higher by two pounds a ton than that fixed by the contract the buyer is entitled to two hundred pounds, but if it is less than the contract price he will receive only nominal damages. Thus section 51 of the Sale of Goods Act 1893, in dealing with damages for non-delivery, provides as follows:

> Where there is an available market for the goods in question the measure of damages is prima facie to be ascertained by the difference between the contract price and the market or current price of the goods at the time or times when they ought to have been delivered, or, if no time was fixed, then at the time of refusal to deliver.[64]

A difficulty in estimating what sum suffices for the purchase of similar goods arises where there is no available market. In this case the value of the goods must be otherwise ascertained. If, for instance, the buyer has agreed to resell the goods, it is generally accepted that their resale price may be taken as representing their value, and the seller will be required to pay the difference between the sale and resale prices even though he had no notice of the sub-contract.[65]

A slightly different analysis is required in the reverse case where it is the buyer who breaks the contract. The loss resulting from such a breach must inevitably vary with the particular circumstances and especially with the character of the seller and the local demand for goods of the kind in question.

If the seller is not a dealer, if, for example, he is a householder who has agreed to sell an antique table to the defendant, his loss is the deprivation of the purchase price upon a certain date, less the value of the table that he still unwillingly possesses. He will be indemnified against this loss, therefore, if he is able to sell the table to another person and if he recovers from the defendant the difference between the price thus received and the price fixed by the first contract should the latter be the higher. Section 50 of the Sale of Goods Act,[66] indeed, provides that the indemnity shall prima facie he measured on this basis.

> Where there is an available market for the goods in question the measure of damages is prima facie to be ascertained by the difference between the contract price and the market or current price at the time or times when the goods ought to have been accepted, or, if no time was fixed for acceptance, then at the time of refusal to accept.

---

[63] *Wertheim v Chicoutimi Pulp Co* [1911] AC 301 at 307.   [64] S 51(3).

[65] *Stroud v Austin & Co* (1883) Cab & El 119; *Patrick v Russo-British Grain Export Co* [1927] 2 KB 535; *France v Gaudet* (1871) LR 6 QB 199. See also *Kwei Tek Chao v British Traders and Shippers Ltd* [1954] 2 QB 459 at 489, [1954] 1 All ER 779 at 797, per Devlin J.

[66] S 50 (3).

Where, however, the plaintiff seller is a dealer in the particular goods sold, the position may be different. In such a case, what ensues from the breach in the usual course of things is that the plaintiff loses the profit that he would have made had the sale to that particular buyer been completed, and he is entitled to be recompensed for that loss. It is no answer to say that he has sold, or may readily sell, the goods to another person, for even if he has been successful the fact remains that he has profited from one sale instead of from two. This was the position in *W L Thompson Ltd v Robinson (Gunmakers) Ltd*,[67] where the facts were as follows:

> The defendants refused to accept delivery of a Vanguard motor car which they had agreed to buy from the plaintiffs, dealers in new and secondhand cars, carrying on business in the East Riding of Yorkshire. The price, from which no dealer was allowed to depart, was that fixed by the manufacturers. The plaintiffs mitigated their loss by persuading their supplier to take the car back. The defendants, while admitting their breach of contract, invoked section 50 of the Sale of Goods Act and contended that they were liable only for nominal damages, since the plaintiffs could have sold the car to another customer or could, as they had in fact done, return it to their supplier.

On this hypothesis, the plaintiffs had suffered only trivial loss. Upjohn J, however, rejected the contention. Section 50 provides only a prima facie rule, and it is inapplicable where the difference between the contract and the market price does not indemnify the plaintiff for the loss which is normally caused and has in fact been caused to him by the breach in question. What the plaintiffs had lost was the profit on that particular bargain. In the words of the learned judge:

> Apart altogether from authority and statute it would seem to me on the facts which I have to consider to be quite plain that the plaintiffs' loss in this case is the loss of their bargain. They have sold one 'Vanguard' less than they otherwise would. The plaintiffs, as the defendants must have known, are in business as dealers in motorcars and make their profit in buying and selling motor-cars, and what they have lost is their profit on the sale of this 'Vanguard'.[68]

Judgment was, therefore, given for the plaintiffs for £61 1s 9d.

The learned judge also considered the meaning of the statutory phrase 'available market', upon which there is little authority. Does it mean something in the nature of an established market, such as the Liverpool Cotton Exchange or the Baltic Exchange? Such had been the opinion of James LJ in *Dunkirk Colliery Co v Lever.*[69]

---

[67] [1955] Ch 177, [1955] 1 All ER 154. The same principle applies in the case of a contract to hire goods. *Inter-office Telephones Ltd v Robert Freeman Co Ltd* [1958] 1 QB 190. Apparently it does not apply to sales by dealers of secondhand cars: *Lazenby Garages Ltd v Wright* [1976] 2 All ER 770, [1976] 1 WLR 459.

[68] [1955] Ch 177 at 183, [1955] 1 All ER 154 at 157.

[69] (1878) 9 ChD 20 at 24.

Though in view of the circumstances the question was academic in the instant case, Upjohn J favoured a more extended definition of the expression. In his view, an available market exists if the situation in the particular trade in the areas is such that the goods can freely and readily be resold in the event of the purchaser's default.[70] If, as in the later case of *Charter v Sullivan*,[71] Vanguard cars could have been sold as quickly as they came into stock, only nominal damages would have been recoverable, for in those circumstances the defendants' default would have been a matter of indifference to the plaintiffs. On the contrary, the position in the East Riding was that the supply of those particular cars exceeded the demand and thus the loss of that sale was injurious.[72] It is respectfully submitted, however, that the view of Upjohn J is to be preferred where the seller is a dealer or a manufacturer, for even though he resells the article he will none the less have lost his profit on the abortive sale.[73]

Instead of failing to deliver, the seller may deliver defective goods. Section 53(3) of the Sale of Goods Act 1979 provides:

> "In the case of breach of warranty of quality such loss is prima facie the difference between the value of the goods at the time of delivery to the buyer and the value they would have had if they had fulfilled the warranty."

In *Bence Graphics International Ltd v Fasson UK Ltd*[74] the defendants were suppliers of cast vinyl film and supplied film to the value of £564,328 to the plaintiffs. The plaintiffs, to the defendants' knowledge, intended to use the film to manufacture decals which were used in the shipping industry to identify bulk containers. It was a term of the contract that the film would last in good legible condition for five years. In fact the film was defective and degraded prematurely. The plaintiffs argued that the film was worthless at the time of delivery and that they should get their money back. This view appeared to be supported by an earlier Court of Appeal decision in *Slater v*

---

[70] This was the view adopted in the case of a defaulting seller by the High Court of Australia fifty years earlier in *Francis v Lyon* (1907) 4 CLR 1023 at 1036, per Griffith CJ: 'I understand the term "available market" to mean that the circumstances, including conditions of time and place, are such that a purchaser having the purchase money in his hands can, there and then, if he so desires, buy other goods of the same quality.' As to the position where there is an available market for goods of the kind but selling all the contract goods at once would swamp the market, see *Shearson Lehman Hutton Inc v Maclaine Watson & Co Ltd (no 2)* [1990] 3 All ER 723 [1990] 1 Lloyd's Rep 441.

[71] [1957] 2 QB 117, [1957] 1 All ER 809.

[72] [1955] Ch at 187, [1955] 1 All ER at 159. Another view as to the meaning of 'available market' was taken in *Charter v Sullivan* [1957] 2 QB 117 at 125–126, per Jenkins LJ. See *McGregor on Damages* (15th edn) paras 741–743, 837–838.

[73] See *Cameron v Campbell and Worthington Ltd* [1930] SASR 402. So far as the reasoning in *Thompson v Robinson* turns on the dealer being bound by a price maintenance scheme, the decision may now be suspect. But the general principle that a dealer-seller may be compensated for loss of a bargain is not dependent on the existence of binding price maintenance schemes. For an interesting general discussion of the extent to which a buyer can recover in respect of defective goods when it has not paid damages to the sub-buyer see *Total Liban SA v Vitol Energy SA* [2000] 1 All ER 267.

[74] [1997] 1 All ER 979. See Treitel 113 LQR 188 for vigorous criticism of this decision.

Hoyle and Smith Ltd[75] and was accepted by the trial judge and by Thorpe LJ but the majority of the Court of Appeal disagreed. They attached decisive weight to the fact that nearly all the film had been sub sold but that very few customers had pursued claims. In their view, therefore, the buyers had in practice suffered little loss and an inquiry should be directed as to how much.[76]

It now remains to consider the case where, owing to special circumstances known at the time of the contract to the party ultimately in default, the breach causes losses outside the natural course of events. The position then is that the horizon of contemplation attributable to him is expanded. He is taken to have contemplated the kind of loss that was liable to arise in the usual course of things from a breach, having regard to the special circumstances of which he had actual or constructive knowledge. Thus the extent of his liability varies with the extent of his knowledge. In the *Victoria Laundry* case,[77] for instance, the defendants knew that the boiler was required by a laundry and dyeing firm not as a spare part, but for immediate use in the running of its business. They should have contemplated, therefore, that some loss of business profits would ensue in the normal course of events if delivery of the boiler were unduly delayed. But the loss flowing from the inability of the firm to fulfil the lucrative dyeing contracts was too remote, since the very existence of those contracts was unknown to the defendants.

Thus the crux of the matter is whether the special circumstances were within the actual or constructive knowledge of the defaulting party at the time of the contract. This may be illustrated by two relevant cases.

In *Pilkington v Wood*[78] the facts were these:

In April 1950, the plaintiff, desiring to live near his place of business in Surrey, bought a house in Hampshire for £6,000, having been advised by the defendant, his solicitor, that the title was good. He raised the purchase money by a bank overdraft and went into occupation. In December 1951, he decided to sell the house as he now wished to reside in Lancashire, where he was about to obtain employment. A purchaser was found who was willing to pay £7,500 for the house and for certain additional land recently acquired by the plaintiff, but it was then discovered that the property was not saleable at that price, since the title was bad.

The defendant, having admitted that he had been negligent in his investigation of the title, was clearly liable to pay by way of damages the difference between the market value in April of the house with a good title and its market value at that date with the

---

75 [1920] 2 KB 11.
76 There was still time for sub buyers to come forward with claims. For a case where a plaintiff did recover in full even though someone else had repaired all his loss see *Gardner v Marsh & Parsons* [1997] 3 All ER 871.
77 [1949] 2 KB 528, [1949] 1 All ER 997; p 758 above.
78 [1953] Ch 770, [1953] 2 All ER 810.

defective title, a difference which the learned judge estimated at £2,000.[79] It was claimed, however, that additional damages were payable by reason of the following facts.

The plaintiff gave evidence that his inability to sell the Hampshire house had precluded him from raising the money required for the purchase of a residence in Lancashire. He had been forced, therefore, to reside in a Lancashire hotel during the week and each weekend to visit his wife who had continued to occupy the Hampshire house. In the light of these and other exceptional circumstances, he claimed compensation in respect inter alia of the following heads of damage:

(a) The cost of the valuation of the Hampshire house.

(b) Interest on his bank overdraft.

(c) Expenses resulting from the mode of living forced upon him after he had obtained work in Lancashire, namely £175 for hotel expenses, £250 for car journeys between Hampshire and Lancashire, £50 for nightly telephone calls to his wife.

Harman J held that none of these items was admissible, since at the time of the contract with the solicitor none could be described as likely to result from a breach. The first two items derived from the plaintiff's own impecuniosity, a misfortune which, though common enough, was not within the actual or constructive knowledge of the defendant. To attribute to him foresight of the third item would imply a degree of prescience possessed by few. In the words of the learned judge:

> The change of place of the plaintiff's employment was not one of the chances that could have been known to either of them. It was the voluntary act of the plaintiff, not a result of any contract existing when the bargain was made. The plaintiff chose a new job in Lancashire; he might as well have selected one more remote in Kamschatka or less remote in Hampshire. The defendant cannot he responsible for the expense. The plaintiff might have bought or rented accommodation suitable to his new employment, and there is no evidence that the defendant knew that his financial position might render this impracticable. Still less can the defendant be called upon to pay for the telephone calls, a luxury no doubt exemplary, yet uxorious.[80]

---

[79] The plaintiff had not obtained what he had contracted and paid for, ie a house with a good title. Distinguish *Ford v White Co* [1964] 2 All ER 775, [1964] 1 WLR 885, where he obtained at the market value precisely what he had contracted for, ie, land subject to a restriction against building upon part of it. Therefore, although he had a right of action against his solicitor who had wrongly advised him that no restriction existed, all that he was entitled to recover was the difference between the market value of the land and the price actually paid. Since there was no such difference, no damages were recoverable. See also *Perry v Sidney Phillips & Son (a firm)* [1982] 3 All ER 705 [1982] 1 WLR 1297 where the measure of damages against a negligent surveyor were considered. Cf *County Personnel (Employment Agency) Ltd v Alan R Pulver & Co* [1987] 1 All ER 289, [1987] 1 WLR 916.

[80] [1953] Ch 770 at 780, [1953] 2 All ER 810 at 815. The law as to foreseeability of the claimant's impecuniosity has probably moved on since 1953. See *Lagden v O'Connor* [2004] UKHL 64, [2004] 1 All ER 277.

The second authority is *Diamond v Campbell Jones.*[81]

> In July 1956, the defendants contracted to sell leasehold premises in Mayfair to the plaintiff for £6,000. The defendants wrongfully repudiated the contract. The only question raised was that of damages.

The plaintiff claimed the profit that he would have made if he had converted the ground floor into offices and the four upper floors into maisonettes. The defendants, while they acknowledged that such a conversion was a possible use of the premises, denied that they knew or should have known that the plaintiff had bought with this intention. The plaintiff, indeed, admitted that the conversion was 'only one of alternative possible methods of turning the bargain to account'. Buckley J held that he could recover only the difference between the purchase price and the market value at the date of the breach of contract.

> Special circumstances are necessary to justify imputing to a vendor of land a knowledge that the purchaser intends to use it in any particular manner. In my judgment neither the fact that [the house] was ripe for conversion, nor indeed the fact that everybody recognised this, was sufficient ground for imputing to the vendors knowledge that the purchaser was a person whose business it was to carry out such conversions or that he intended, or was even likely, to convert the house himself for profit.[82]

We have seen that in cases of frequent occurrence, such as a contract for the sale of goods, certain rules relating to the measure or assessment of damages have gradually been evolved, as for instance the rule that a defaulting seller must pay to the buyer the difference between the market and the contract price of the goods. But in general there is no specific rule upon the matter, and it is left to the good sense of the court to assess as best it can what it considers to be an adequate recompense for the loss suffered by the plaintiff. The assessment may well be a matter of great difficulty, indeed in some cases one of guesswork; but the fact that it cannot be made with mathematical accuracy is no reason for depriving the plaintiff of compensation. A case in point is *Chaplin v Hicks*[83] where the facts were these:

> The defendant, an actor and theatrical manager, agreed with the plaintiff that if she would attend a meeting at which he proposed to interview forty-nine other actresses, he would select twelve out of the fifty and would give remunerative employment to each of these successful candidates. He broke his contract with the plaintiff by failing to give her a reasonable opportunity to attend the interview.

---

[81] [1961] Ch 22, [1960] 1 All ER 583. See also *Cottrill v Steyning and Littlehampton Building Society* [1966] 2 All ER 295, [1966] 1 WLR 753 and *Cochrane (Decorators) Ltd v Sarabandi* (1983) 133 NLJ 558.

[82] Ibid at 36 and 591, respectively.

[83] [1911] 2 KB 786; distinguished *Sykes v Midland Bank Executor and Trustee Co Ltd* [1971] 1 QB 113 at 129, per Salmon LJ. See also *Hall v Meyrick* [1957] 2 QB 455, in the lower court. The decision of the House of Lords in *Jackson v Royal Bank of Scotland* [2005] 2 All ER 71 is probably best analysed as turning on evaluation of chances.

In an action for breach of contract, he contended that only nominal damages were payable, since the plaintiff would have had only a chance of one in four of being successful, a chance moreover which depended among other imponderables upon his own volition. Nevertheless, it was held by the Court of Appeal that the award of £100, given by the jury, must stand. Fletcher Moulton LJ said:

> Where by contract a man has a right to belong to a limited class of competitors, he is possessed of something of value, and it is the duty of the jury to estimate the pecuniary value of that advantage if it is taken from him.[84]

At one time it was believed that there was a general rule that one could not recover damages for non-pecuniary losses in actions for breach of contract. It is now clear that there is no such general rule. So a plaintiff who books a holiday with a tour operator may recover for loss of enjoyment if the holiday is spoilt by a breach of contract.[85] The same principle was applied to an employee who suffered distress through the employer's breach of contract[86] (but this was later said to be wrong),[87] or to a client who suffers distress arising out of her solicitor's incompetent handling of an injunction designed to prevent molestation;[88] or to a client whose solicitor negligently fails to take effective steps to prevent her former husband taking their children to Tunisia.[89] In these cases distress was precisely the result to be expected from breach of the contract. It seems that damages cannot be recovered for distress arising from breach of an ordinary commercial contract.[90]

The leading case is now the decision of the House of Lords in *Farley v Skinner*.[91] The claimant was considering buying a house in Sussex, not far from Gatwick airport. He engaged the defendant to conduct a survey and specifically asked him to advise on aircraft noise. The defendant negligently gave a reassuring answer. In fact in certain conditions, particularly early in the morning, the house was below a stacking point for Gatwick. The claimant did not discover this until he had spent over £100,000 on improving the house. The trial judge held that the claimant had paid no more for the house than would a reasonable purchaser who had known of the aircraft noise but awarded him £10,000 for his distress at discovering the aircraft noise.

The House of Lords, though clearly thinking that £10,000 was at the top end of the acceptable range, unanimously agreed.

---

[84] *Chaplin v Hicks* [1911] 2 KB at 796. *Allied Maples Group v Simmons & Simmons* [1995] 4 All ER 907. *Maden v Clifford Coppock and Carter* [2005] 2 All ER 43.

[85] See *Jarvis v Swans Tours Ltd* [1973] QB 233, [1973] 1 All ER 71; *Jackson v Horizon Holidays Ltd* [1975] 3 All ER 92, [1975] 1 WLR 1468. *Baltic Shipping Co v Dillon* [1993] 176 CLR 344.

[86] *Cox v Phillips Industries Ltd* [1976] 3 All ER 161, [1976] ICR 138

[87] *Bliss v SE Thames Regional Health Authority* [1987] ICR 700

[88] *Heywood v Wellers* [1976] QB 446, [1976] 1 All ER 300.

[89] *Hamilton Jones v David & Snape* [2003] EWHC 3147 (Ch) [2004] 1 All ER 657.

[90] *Hayes v James and Charles Dodd (a firm)* [1990] 2 All ER 815, [1988] BTLC 38. *Watts v Morrow* [1991] 4 All ER 937. Rose 55 Can Bar Rev 333; Jackson 26 ICLQ 502. MacDonald 7 JCL 134.

[91] [2001] UKHL 49, [2001] 4 All ER 801.

A separate but perhaps overlapping principle was thought to have been laid down by the House of Lords in *Addis v Gramophone Co Ltd*.[92] In this case the plaintiff was wrongfully dismissed from an important post in India in humiliating circumstances, which could hardly have failed adversely to affect his future employment prospects. It was held that his damages were limited to the wages that would have been earned during the period of notice that should have been given. The headnote, based upon the speech of Lord Loreburn (with which a majority of the House did not perhaps clearly agree) purported to lay down a rule that a wrongfully dismissed servant could not recover damages for the manner of his dismissal, for his injured feelings or for the loss that he may suffer because it is more difficult for him to obtain fresh employment. Of these, the manner of dismissal and injured feelings may be regarded as non-pecuniary loss but the effect on future employment prospects is clearly financial.

Addis v Gramophone has attracted criticism since it was decided.[93] In the last few years it has been considered in a number of important House of Lords decisions. In *Malik v Bank of Credit and Commerce International*,[94] the facts of which have already been set out,[95] the House of Lords held that, in principle, a plaintiff could recover damages for the loss of reputation and for the financial loss which flowed from it—so called 'stigma damages'.[96]

Malik was not a case of wrongful dismissal but of breach of the implied term of trust and confidence but the matter came before the House of Lords again in a dismissal context in *Johnson v Unisys Ltd*.[97] In this case the claimant had successfully alleged unfair dismissal before an industrial tribunal on the ground that his employer had not given him a fair opportunity to defend himself and had not followed its own disciplinary procedure. He had been awarded the then statutory maximum. He then began an action for breach of the implied term of trust and confidence, claiming that his future employment prospects had been irretrievably damaged.

The House of Lords held that the claim failed. The majority view was that though employment law had been the subject matter of major developments through implied terms, it would not be appropriate to have a further common law development in the field of dismissal where Parliament had introduced a statutory system of unfair dismissal which was not based on contract. Lord Steyn concurred in this result because he thought that on the particular facts the claimant would have insuperable remoteness difficulties but in all other respects his analysis was very different and he considered that in principle on such facts an employee had a reasonable cause of action based on the implied obligation of trust and confidence. He took the view that if the headnote of *Addis's* case correctly stated the ratio decidendi the time had arrived to depart from it and indeed that the House of Lords had done so in *Malik's* case.

---

[92] [1909] AC 488.　　[93] Pollock 26 LQR 1　　[94] [1997] 3 All ER 1.
[95] See above p 184.
[96] In practice making out such claims has proved very difficult. See [1999] 4 All ER 85.
[97] [2001] 2 All ER 801.

In the later decision in *Eastwood v Magnox Electric plc*[98] the House of Lords held that the reasoning in *Johnson v Unisys* did not apply to unfair suspension as opposed to unfair dismissal, so that breaches of the implied terms of trust and confidence leading to suspension were actionable at common law. Of course, as Lord Steyn pointed out in his concurring speech, it is inelegant for an employer to be better off because he has unfairly dismissed as opposed to unfairly suspended an employee.

In some cases the results of the defendants breach of contract is not that the plaintiff has been deprived of the chance of making a profit, but that the plaintiff has been caused to make a loss. The same general principles apply but again the process of calculation may prove very difficult. This was the situation in a large group of cases arising out of negligent valuations of commercial properties in London.[99] The detailed facts of these cases varies widely but the general pattern was that the plaintiffs had lent large sums of money to purchase commercial properties in London relying on valuations which were held to have been negligently given by the defendants. As a result the plaintiffs paid more than the properties were worth rather than the 90 per cent of the properties value which they were prepared to lend. It is perhaps fair to say that the loans took place at a time when both the lender, the borrowers, and the valuers assumed that property prices would continue indefinitely to rise steeply upwards. In due course, the borrowers defaulted and the lenders found that they could not recover the full value of the loans, partly because of excessive valuations given by the defendants, partly because of a dramatic collapse in the property market. The central question in the cases was whether the plaintiffs could recover all of their loss made against the transaction or were limited to the loss which directly arose out of the negligent valuation. The Court of Appeal argued that as the plaintiffs would not have entered into the transaction at all but for the negligent valuation, they should recover the whole of their loss. The House of Lords disagreed. The valuers were liable not for the foreseeable consequences of a loan being granted, but for the foreseeable consequences of the valuation being negligent. This still left open the possibility of proving on the facts of some of the cases the lender would have had adequate security if the valuation had been carefully carried out.[100]

In other cases it may be entirely clear what the actual loss is that the plaintiff has suffered, and the problem may be to choose the correct method of valuing it. This was the case in *Ruxley Electronics v Forsyth*[101] concerning damages for breach of a building contract. In this case, the plaintiff contractors had agreed to build a swimming pool for the defendant. (By a separate contract, an allied company had agreed to build a

---

[98] [2004] UKHL 35, [2004] 3 All ER 991. See *also Dunnachie v Kingston-upon-Hull City Council* [2004] UKHL 36 [2004] 3 All ER 1011.

[99] *Banque Bruxelles Lambert v Eagle Star* [1995] 2 All ER 769 (Court of Appeal). *South Australia Asset Management Corporation v York Montague Ltd* [1997] AC 191; [1996] 3 All ER 365.

[100] For a quite different kind of loss flowing from careless valuation see *Swing Castle Ltd v Alistair Gibson* [1991] 2 All ER 353.

[101] [1995] 3 All ER 268. Poole 59 MLR 272. Friedmann 111 LQR 628.

structure in which the swimming pool was housed. No questions about this contract arose before the House of Lords.) It was a term of the swimming pool contract that the swimming pool should be 7ft 6 in deep at the deep end so that Mr Forsyth could safely dive into the pool. In fact the pool, as built, was only 6ft 9 in deep and at the natural dive point not more than 6ft. However, the trial judge held that the pool was perfectly safe for diving; that the shortfall in depth made no difference to the value of the pool; that it could cost some £21,000 to cure the defect since all that could be done was to break out the bottom of the pool and dig deeper. He further held that it was extremely unlikely that Mr Forsyth would spend such damages on rebuilding the pool and that it would not have been reasonable of him to do so. On these findings, he held that the appropriate measure of damages was the difference in value between the pool as it was and the pool as it should have been if the contract was properly performed but made an award of £2,500 to Mr Forsyth for loss of amenity. (The effect of this finding was a judgment for the plaintiffs because there was substantially more than £2,500 outstanding on the price of the pool.)

The Court of Appeal, by a majority, reversed the trial judge and awarded Mr Forsyth the full cost of cure. The House of Lords unanimously reversed the Court of Appeal and upheld the trial judge's decision.

There are many earlier cases in which the courts have held that the measure of damages for a defectively carried out building contract is sometimes the difference in value and sometimes the cost of cure.[102] In deciding which measure to adopt, the courts have often referred to the question of whether cure would be reasonable in all the circumstances and also to whether the injured party would be likely to carry out the cure. The House of Lords attached much more importance to reasonableness than to intention. They regarded intention as primarily a matter going to reasonableness. In other words, in the cases where the courts have not believed that cure would be carried out, this has always been because in the circumstances it would not be reasonable to carry it out.

At one level, the judgments are simply an affirmation of orthodox doctrine. Nevertheless, there are some important signs for development and change in the future. Particularly significant is Lord Mustill's acceptance that the damages award in a case of this kind should reflect the consumer surplus, that is the special benefit which the promisee expects to receive from performance. It is noteworthy also that he stated at the bottom there are not two tests for quantification of damages but only one, that is what is the loss which the injured party has suffered. This is particularly important in a case of the present kind where the injured party has received a defective but nevertheless substantially useful performance. The decision of the House of Lords reflects a strong intuitive feeling that if Mr Forsyth had received £21,000 and kept the pool as it was, he would have been overcompensated. On the other hand, if he had

---

[102] See especially the decision of the House of Lords in *East Ham B C v Bernard Sunley* [1965] 3 All ER 619 and of the New York Court of Appeals in *Jacobs & Youngs v Kent* (1921) 230 NY 239.

simply received nothing, he might reasonably have felt that he was undercompensated. So one way to approach the question is to ask what figure between £0 and £21,000 would together with the usable pool leave him in, as near as money could do it, the same position as he should have been in. This is substantially what happened in the case, though it should be noted there was no argument before the House of Lords by either side as to whether £2,500 or some other figure was the correct one. Nevertheless several judgments expressly approved the trial judge's holding on this point.

B Some special problems

1 Effect of tax liability on damages

It is clear, therefore, that no court may avoid the task of assessing damages on the ground of its difficulty. But, as *Chaplin v Hicks* shows, the inquiry may well be speculative. The obligations thus imposed were increased by the decision of the House of Lords in *British Transport Commission v Gourley*[103] that, in the course of assessment, account may have to be taken of the plaintiff's liability for taxation. In measuring the damages for the loss of income or profits, the court must deduct an amount equivalent to the sum that he would have paid by way of income tax had he continued to receive such yearly income. As the object of damages is to compensate the plaintiff, not to punish the defendant, it might indeed seem logical to award the plaintiff, not a gross sum, but a net sum, reached after the deduction of his own liabilities to the Inland Revenue. *Gourley's* case itself was a decision in the law of tort; but, as the function of damages in contract is similarly compensatory and not retributive, the principle upon which it rested is no less applicable to contract. It has, in fact, been so applied: in *Beach v Reed Corrugated Cases Ltd*,[104] to a claim for wrongful dismissal, and in *Re Houghton Main Colliery Co*,[105] to breach of contract in general. The principle, however, operates only if the damages awarded to the plaintiff will not, in his hands, be liable to taxation. Otherwise the plaintiff would in effect pay tax twice over and would not receive just compensation for the breach of contract or tort committed by the defendant.

> It is impossible to maintain that there can be derived from *Gourley's* case any principle requiring taxation to be taken into account in assessing damages where both the lost earnings or profits and the damages are taxable.[106]

---

[103] [1956] AC 185, [1955] 3 All ER 796.

[104] [1956] 2 All ER 652, [1956] 1 WLR 807. See also *Shindler v Northern Raincoat Co Ltd* [1960] 2 All ER 239 at 250, [1960] 1 WLR 1038 at 1050.

[105] [1956] 3 All ER 300, [1956] 1 WLR 1219. The authorities were reviewed by the Court of Appeal in *Parsons v BNM Laboratories Ltd* [1964] 1 QB 95, [1963] 2 All ER 658.

[106] Per Pearson LJ in *Parsons v BNM Laboratories Ltd* [1964] 1 QB 95 at 136, [1963] 2 All ER 658 at 679.

The logic of the principle may be impeccable, but the difficulties involved in its application are formidable. Thus in *Beach v Reed Corrugated Cases Ltd*, the plaintiff, had he not been wrongly dismissed, would have received as salary over the next ten years the sum of £48,000. But he had a large private fortune which, to estimate his tax liability, had to be taken into account. In the result, and admittedly as a pure conjecture, Pilcher J reduced the damages to £18,000. So, too, in *Re Houghton Main Colliery Co*:

> The company was under contract to pay two employees pensions at monthly rates of £160 and £75 respectively. The company went into voluntary liquidation. This was, as against the two employees, a breach of contract, since it prevented the company from continuing to pay the pensions. For the purposes of the liquidation the two pension rights were capitalised at £14,000 and £10,000 respectively.

These two sums had therefore to be treated as damages caused by the breach of contract; and, in deference to the decision of the House of Lords, Wynn-Parry J ruled that they must be subject to deduction for income tax. How to assess this deduction was a more difficult question. The learned judge proposed to adjourn the case in the hope that the parties' accountants could reach an agreed figure. He offered them 'guidance' thus the damages were not to be taken as falling within a single fiscal year but were to be spread over a number of years. If unhappily the accountants were unable to agree, the case would have to come back to him, and he would then have to reach a decision as best he could. The truth is that in such cases the assessment of the amount to be deducted is a matter of guesswork rather than of calculation.[107]

Here as elsewhere, therefore, logic produces practical difficulties. Its results, moreover, may be ludicrous. In some circumstances it may well be cheaper to break a contract than to keep it; and, if an exact rather than a conjectural estimate were required of the tax liability involved, a preliminary case on this particular question might itself have to be fought up to the House of Lords. The whole question was reviewed in 1958 by the Law Reform Committee,[108] but, as its members were divided among themselves upon the solution, no recommendations were made. In the one case of wrongful dismissal, however, the Finance Act 1960 modified the principle of *Gourley's* case by providing that any excess over £5,000 of the sum awarded to the plaintiff as damages for loss of employment shall be taxable in his hands and thus be payable without reduction by the defendant.[109] The figure under the Income and Corporation Taxes Act 1988 ss 148 and 188(4) as amended by Finance Act 1988 s74 is currently

107 See eg the remarks of Lord Reid in *Taylor v O'Connor* [1971] AC 115 at 129.
108 Law Reform Committee, 7th Report (Effect of Tax Liability on Damages), Cmnd 501.
109 S 38; *Bold v Brough, Nicholson and Hall Ltd* [1964] 3 All ER 849, [1964] 1 WLR 201; applying *Parsons v BNM Laboratories Ltd*, above. The matter was also considered in *Shore v Downs Surgical plc* [1984] 1 All ER 7, but unfortunately *Parsons v BNM Laboratories* does not appear to have been cited to the court in this case.

£30,000.[110] Whatever the difficulties or indeed the absurdities which attend its application, it is clear that—subject to this statutory exception—the principle laid down in *Gourley's* case is now established in English law. So much was assumed by the House of Lords both in *Parry v Cleaver*[111] and in *Taylor v O'Connor*.[112] It is interesting to notice that the Supreme Court of Canada has rejected the reasoning of the decision.[113]

The decision in *Gourley's* case rests upon the basic principle that the plaintiff should recover no more than his real loss. Taxation is simply one of the more spectacular ways in which this principle may be brought into play. There are many cases in which a defendant has argued that the plaintiff's loss is less than at first sight appears because he has received some compensating benefit; plaintiffs have often replied that the benefit is 'collateral' and should be ignored. This label does not help to draw the line.[114] The one clear case is where the plaintiff is insured; he can recover in full even though he has been fully indemnified by his insurer.[115]

Most of the litigated cases have in fact involved tort claims but the principles are equally applicable in contract. A good example is *Westwood v Secretary of State for Employment*.[116]

In this case the claimant's employers became insolvent, which resulted in his employment being terminated without the twelve weeks notice to which he was entitled under section 49(1)(c) of the Employment Protection (Consolidation) Act 1978. Under section 122(1), (3)(b) of that Act the employer's liability was transferred to the Secretary of State to be met out of the redundancy funds. For purposes of analysis it was taken that the claim should be treated in exactly the same way as a contract action for damages. After losing his job the claimant had been unemployed and had claimed unemployment benefit. The House of Lords had no difficulty in holding that unemployment benefit had reduced the plaintiff's loss and therefore went to reduce the amount of the award. However the facts presented a secondary and more difficult question. The claimant had received unemployment benefit for twelve months and earnings related supplement for six months, the maximum periods provided for by the scheme. After this he had claimed supplementary benefit which was

---

[110] The primary object of these sections was to discourage what has come to he known as the 'golden handshake'; *Parsons v BNM Laboratories Ltd* [1964] 1 QB 95 at 137, per Harman LJ.

[111] [1970] AC 1, [1969] 1 All ER 555.

[112] [1971] AC 115, [1970] 1 All ER 365.

[113] *Ontario v Jennings* (1966) 57 DLR (2d) 644; Samuels 30 MLR 83. For the position in Australia, see the fifth Australian edition of Cheshire and Fifoot *The Law of Contract* p 664.

[114] *Parry v Cleaver* [1970] AC 1, [1969] 1 All ER 555.

[115] *Bradburn v Great Western Rly Co* (1874) LR 10 Exch 1. This rule was settled before more sophisticated analysis had penetrated this area. It can perhaps be justified on the ground that the prudence of the plaintiff in insuring should not inure to the benefit of the defendant. In most, though not all, cases there will not be double recovery because the insurer, having indemnified the plaintiff, will be subrogated to the fruits of his action.

[116] [1985] AC 20, [1984] 1 All ER 874.

paid at a lower rate. In total he was unemployed for more than fifteen months. The House of Lords held that the combined effect of these events was that it was the lower rate of supplementary benefit which should be used to calculate the claimant's exact loss. This was because if the plaintiff had received the period of notice to which he was entitled he would have still (granted that the total period of unemployment was over fifteen months) have received unemployment benefit and earnings related benefit for the maximum period. In effect the employer's breach accelerated the time at which supplementary benefit was payable.

2 Failure to pay money

The common law said that if the defendant's breach consisted of a failure to pay money the plaintiff's loss consisted only of that sum.[117] This is clearly not an application of the ordinary rules of remoteness since there will be cases when the defendant can readily contemplate that his failure to pay his money on time will prevent the plaintiff from completing a profitable transaction[118]. Further a secondary rule states that debts do not as a rule carry interest.[119] This rule appears very hard on creditors, particularly with modern rates of interest and inflation which have accentuated the historic inability of even solvent debtors to pay on time. The Law Commission indeed recommended the effective abolition of the rule in a report in 1978[120] but the government did not at the time accept this recommendation.[121]

In *President of India v La Pintada Cia Navegacion SA (No 2)*[122] all the members of the House of Lords thought the rule unsatisfactory, and urged Parliament to reverse it. They refused however to do so themselves on the ground that Parliament's deliberate failure to implement the Law Commission's proposals[123] made it inappropriate for the courts to do so. The no interest rule is however subject to a number of exceptions:

(a) The parties are, of course, free to agree expressly for the payment of interest. It has always been common for lenders of money to stipulate for interest. It is now increasingly common for suppliers of goods and services to protect themselves against late payment in this way.

---

[117] *William v Reynolds* (1865) 6 B & s 495. Cf *Wallis v Smith* (1882) 21 Ch D 243. See Ogus, pp 304–307. *Hopkins v Norcross Plc* [1993] 1 All ER 565.

[118] Cf *Trans Trust SPRL v Danubian Trading Co Ltd* [1952] 2 QB 297, [1952] 1 All ER 970, where a buyer failed to open a credit and thereby prevented the seller from buying the goods.

[119] *London Chatham and Dover Rly Co v South Eastern Rly Co* [1893] AC 429. This second rule is very important in practice since in many cases a plaintiff might mitigate the effect of the first rule by borrowing at interest.

[120] Law Commission no 88, Cmnd 7229.

[121] See 429 HL official Report (5th series) cols 165–174 (6 April 1982).

[122] [1985] 1 Ac 104, [1984] 2 All ER 773. Cf *Tehno-Impex v Gebr van Weelde Scheepoaastkantoor BV* [1981] QB 648, [1981] 2 All ER 669. See also *President of India v Lips Maritime corps, The Lips* [1988] AC 395, [1987] 3 All ER 110.

[123] Evidenced by the Administration of Justice Act 1982, s 15, which had increased the courts' discretionary powers.

(b) In at least one case the court has decided that the parties have implicitly agreed on the payment of interest.[124]

(c) The court has a discretionary power to award interest where the claim is pursued to judgment. Under the Law Reform (Miscellaneous Provisions) Act 1934, section 3, this power depended on a capital sum being owed at the date of the judgment. This was unsatisfactory, since the debtor might pay in full at the trial having had the use of the plaintiff's money for years. This weakness has been reduced but not removed by the Administration of Justice Act 1982, section 15, which provides that the court can award interest provided money was owing at the time the proceedings were instituted.[125]

(d) The rule is substantially qualified by the decision of the Court of Appeal in *Wadsworth v Lydall*,[126] which was endorsed by the House of Lords in the *La Pintada* case.

A purchaser of land had agreed to pay £10,000 by a fixed date, knowing that the vendor intended to use the money to make a down payment on another piece of land. In fact the purchaser only paid £7,200 and the vendor had to borrow the other £2,800 to pay interest on the loan.

It was held that the vendor could recover the interest as part of his damages under the second branch of the rule in Hadley v Baxendale. This decision seems to open the door to heavy qualification of both the rules discussed in this section since in a commercial context a debtor will very often know that if he pays late, his creditor will lose this opportunity to make profitable use of the money or will have to bear interest charges on an increased overdraft.

(e) The Late Payment of Commercial Debts (Interest) Act 1998 introduces a statutory right to interest in respect of late payment of commercial debts.

3 Inability to make title to land

Another old rule, reaffirmed by the House of Lords in 1874[127] stated that if a vendor of land is unable, without any fault on his part, to show a good title the purchaser's damages were limited to the money wasted in investigating tide. This rule was criticised by most, though not all, critics[128] and has now been abolished by the Law of Property (Miscellaneous Provisions) Act 1989.

---

[124] *Minter v Welsh Health Technical Services Organisation* (1980) 13 BLR 1.

[125] In some cases careful analysis will be necessary to decide the date at which interest should start to run. See *Nykredit Mortgage Bank plc v Edward Erdman Group Ltd* (No 2) [1998] 1 All ER 305; *IM Properties plc v Cape and Dalgleish* [1998] 3 All ER 203.

[126] [1981] 2 All ER 401, [1981] 1 WLR 598. See also *Bacon v Cooper (Metals) Ltd* [1982] 1 All ER 397.

[127] *Bain v Fothergill* (1874) LR 7HL 158.

[128] Sydenham 41 Conv 341; Emery 42 Conv 338; Thompson [1982] Conv 191; Harpum [1982] Conv 435.

C Mitigation [129]

The rules given above are subject to this limitation, that the law does not allow a plaintiff to recover damages to compensate him for loss which would not have been suffered if he had taken reasonable steps to mitigate his loss.[130] Whether the plaintiff has failed to take a reasonable opportunity of mitigation is a question of fact dependent upon the particular circumstances of each case and the burden of proving such failure rests upon the defendant.[131] It has thus been held that the master of a ship, upon the failure of the charterer to provide a cargo in accordance with the contract, should normally accept cargo from other persons at the best freight obtainable.[132] The wrongful dismissal of a servant has often raised this question of mitigation. In *Brace v Calder*,[133] for instance:

> The defendants, a partnership consisting of four members, agreed to employ the plaintiff as manager of a branch of the business for two years. Five months later the partnership was dissolved by the retirement of two of the members, and the business was transferred to the other two, who offered to employ the plaintiff on the same terms as before. He rejected the offer.

The dissolution of the partnership constituted in law a wrongful dismissal of the plaintiff, and in his action for breach of contract he sought to recover the salary that he would have received had he served for the whole period of two years. It was held, however, that he was entitled only to nominal damages, since it was unreasonable to have rejected the offer of continued employment.

A particularly instructive case is that of *Payzu Ltd v Saunders*,[134] where the plaintiff had been the victim of a wrongful repudiation by the defendant.

> Under a contract to deliver goods by instalments, payment to be made within one month of each delivery, less 2½ per cent discount, the buyers failed to make punctual payment for the first instalment. The seller treated this as sufficient to repudiate the contract, but offered to continue deliveries at the contract price if the buyers would pay cash at the time of each order. This offer was rejected. The price of the goods having risen, the buyers sued for breach of contract.

---

[129] Feldman and Libling 96 LQR 270; Duncan Wallace 96 LQR 101; Bridge 105 LQR 398.

[130] *British Westinghouse Electric and Manufacturing Co v Underground Electric Rly Co of London* [1912] AC 673 at 689, per Lord Haldane. It is wrong to express this rule by stating that the plaintiff is under a duty to mitigate his loss: *Sotiros Shipping Inc v Sameiet, The Solholt* [1983] 1 Lloyd's Rep 605.

[131] *Payzu Ltd v Saunders* [1919] 2 KB 581.

[132] *Harries v Edmonds* (1845) 1 Car & Kir 686.

[133] [1895] 2 QB 253. See also *Shindler v Northern Raincoat Co Ltd* [1960] 2 All ER 239, [1960] 1 WLR 1038; and *Yetton v Eastwoods Froy Ltd* [1966] 3 All ER 353, [1967] 1 WLR 104, examples of a reasonable refusal to accept alternative employment. The question arose in a more unusual form in *Lavarack v Woods of Colchester Ltd* [1967] 1 QB 278, [1966] 3 All ER 683.

[134] [1919] 2 KB 581.

It was held in the first place that the seller was liable in damages, since the circumstances did not warrant his repudiation of the contract. On the other hand, it was held that the buyers should have mitigated their loss by accepting the seller's offer, and that the damages recoverable were not to be measured by the difference between the contract and market price, but by the loss that would have been suffered had the offer been accepted. 'In commercial contracts', said Scrutton LJ, 'it is generally reasonable to accept an offer from the party in default'.[135]

But the burden which lies on the defendant of proving that the plaintiff has failed in his duty of mitigation is by no means a light one, for this is a case where a party already in breach of contract demands positive action from one who is often innocent of blame. This may be illustrated from *Pilkington v Wood*, the facts of which have already been given.[136] It was there argued by the defendant's solicitor that the plaintiff, the purchaser of the Hampshire house, should have mitigated his loss by taking proceedings against the vendor for having conveyed a defective title. The proposed action, however, would have involved complicated litigation upon a somewhat difficult provision in the Law of Property Act 1925, and it was far from clear that it would have succeeded. Harman J therefore held that the purchaser was under no duty to embark upon such a hazardous venture, merely 'to protect his solicitor from the consequences of his own carelessness'.

An illustration of a different kind is afforded by *James Finlay & Co v N V Kwik Hoo Tong HM*.[137]

> Sugar, which under a contract of sale ought to have been shipped in September, was not in fact shipped by the sellers until October. They nevertheless tendered a bill of lading which stated, though not fraudulently, that the shipment had been made in September. This was a breach of contract, since it is well settled that on a sale of goods a condition as to the time of shipment is vital and is of the essence of the contract'.[138] The buyers, being unaware of the late shipment, resold the goods to X & Co, merchants in Bombay, under a contract containing a clause that 'the bill of lading shall be conclusive evidence of the date of shipment'. X and Co discovered that the sugar had not been shipped in September, and therefore refused to take delivery.

The buyers were, of course, entitled to recover damages from the original sellers, but it was contended that they should have forced the sub-contract on X & Co by relying upon the conclusive evidence clause in the bill of lading. This contention was rejected. The Court of Appeal took the view that for the buyers to have insisted upon payment

---

[135] Ibid at 589. In *Sotiros Shipping Inc v Saneiet Solholt, The Solholt* [1983] 1 Lloyd's Rep 605 the Court of Appeal upheld, as available on the evidence a finding of the judge that the plaintiffs should have sought to mitigate by offering to perform the contract on its original terms and such an offer would have been accepted by the contract breaker.

[136] [1953] Ch 770, [1953] 2 All ER 810, p 767, above.

[137] [1929] 1 KB 400.   [138] Ibid at 407, per Scrutton LJ.

by X & Co of the agreed price after their discovery that the goods were not in accordance with the contract, having been shipped in the wrong month, 'would violate the standard of morality which should attach to an English firm of standing and would in fact ruin their credit in India'.[139]

In relation to the computation of damages, mitigation is substantially an aspect of remoteness, since it is within the contemplation of the parties that the plaintiff will take reasonable steps to mitigate his loss. This interrelationship was emphasised by Oliver J in *Radford v De Froberville*.[140]

> The plaintiff owned a house which stood in a large garden. The house was divided into flats, which were let to tenants, who had rights in common to use the garden. The plaintiff obtained planning permission to build a house on a plot of land in the garden and sold the plot to the defendant. The defendant contracted to develop the plot and to build a brick wall of stated height and thickness on the plot as a boundary between the plot and the area retained by the plaintiff. The defendant failed to build the wall or develop the plot and sold the plot to a third party, who covenanted to perform the covenants in the transfer from the plaintiff to the defendant but failed to do so.

The plaintiff brought an action for damages and the judgment of Oliver J was directed to the specific issue of the defendant's failure to build the wall. The defendant argued that the appropriate test was the difference in value between the land with the wall built and the land without. Since the evidence was that the absence of the wall made no difference to the rentable value of the flats, this would have led to a nominal award. Alternatively it was argued that the plaintiff should mitigate his loss by building the cheapest reasonable boundary, that is, a prefabricated fence.

Oliver J rejected these contentions. The first might have been appropriate if the plaintiff had no intention of building a wall but the plaintiff's evidence was that he intended to build a wall on his side of the boundary as nearly as possible identical with that which the defendant had contracted to build. On that footing the plaintiff was suffering a genuine loss[141] and the cost of rebuilding was the proper measure of that loss. Furthermore in the circumstances it was reasonable for the plaintiff not to have built the wall before judgment, so that damages should be based on the cost of

---

[139] Ibid at 410, per Scrutton LJ. Similarly in *London and South of England Building Society v Stone* [1983] 3 All ER 105, [1983] 1 WLR 1242, the majority of the Court of Appeal thought that a building society which had advanced money on a worthless house as a result of the defendant's negligent valuation acted reasonably in not seeking to shift this loss to the mortgagor.

[140] [1978] 1 All ER 33, [1977] 1 WLR 1262. In *Ruxley Electronics v Forsyth* (discussed, p 623 above) the result would have been exactly the same if Mr Forsyth had carried out the alterations to the swimming pool before the case. It would have been a question whether it was reasonable to do this and the question of reasonableness must receive the same answer whether it was posed before or after the work was done.

[141] Cf *Tito v Waddell (No 2)* [1977] Ch 106, [1977] 3 All ER 129.

building the wall at the date of the hearing.[142] Of course at the time when the contract is broken it is not always clear what to do for the best. A plaintiff will not be treated as behaving unreasonably when he chooses one of the possible reasonable alternatives only to find out later that the other one would have been cheaper.[143]

The problem of mitigation is presented in a special light in the case of the so-called 'anticipatory breach'. It has already been seen that, if a defendant repudiates in May a contract for the delivery of goods in July, the plaintiff has an option.[144] On the one hand, he may accept the repudiation and sue at once for breach of contract: he will then be under the ordinary duty to mitigate.[145] On the other hand, he may refuse the repudiation, hold the defendant to the contract and await the date of performance. If he prefers this course, the contract remains alive and no question of damages or of mitigation has yet arisen.

> It cannot be said that there is any duty on the part of the plaintiff to mitigate his damages before there has been any breach which he has accepted as a breach.[146]

The reasoning is logical; but the result may be grotesque. In *White and Carter (Councils) Ltd v McGregor*.[147]

> The business of the appellants was to supply litter bins to local councils throughout Great Britain. They were not paid by the councils, but by traders who hired advertising space on the bins. On 26 June 1957, the respondent agreed to hire space for three years beginning on the date when the first advertisement was exhibited. Later in the same day the respondent wrote to cancel the contract. The appellants refused to accept the repudiation. Up to this moment they had taken no steps to carry out the contract. But they now prepared advertisement plates, attached them to the bins and continued to display them for the next three years. They made no attempt to minimise their loss by procuring other advertisers to take the respondent's place. In due course they sued the respondent for the full contract price.

The House of Lords, by a majority of three to two, held that they were entitled to succeed.

The implications of the decision were exposed by Lord Keith.

---

[142] See also *Dodd Properties (Kent) Ltd v Canterbury City Council* [1980] 1 All ER 928, [1980] 2 WLR 433.

[143] *Gebruder Metalmann GmbH & Co KG v NBR (London) Ltd* [1984] 1 Lloyd's Rep 614.

[144] See p 682, above.

[145] *Roth & Co v Taysen, Townsend & Co* (1895) 1 Com Cas 240; affd (1896) 12 TLR 211.

[146] *Shindler v Northern Raincoat Co Ltd* [1960] 1 WLR 1038 at 1048. See *Brown v Muller* (1872) LR 7 Exch 319; *Tredegar Iron and Coal Co Ltd v Hawthorn Bros & Co* (1902) 18 TLR 716.

[147] [1962] AC 413, [1961] 3 All ER 1178; distinguished, *Hounslow London Borough Council v Twickenham Garden Developments Ltd* [1971] Ch 233 at 251–254. The decision in *White and Carter (Council) Ltd v McGregor* is criticised by Goodhart in 78 LQR 263, and defended by Nienaber in [1962] CLJ 213.

If it is right it would seem that a man who has contracted to go to Hong Kong at his own expense and make a report, in return for remuneration of £10,000, and who, before the date fixed for the Start of the journey and perhaps before he has incurred any expense, is informed by the other contracting party that he has cancelled or repudiates the contract, is entitled to set off for Hong Kong and produce his report in order to claim in debt the stipulated sum.[148]

The result, as Lord Keith described it, is 'startling', and invites some method of avoiding it which will not offend accepted principle. The means may be found, it is suggested, as soon as it is realised that the mitigation rule is not a rule *sui generis*, functioning in isolation, but an example of the wider if vaguer doctrine of causation. Alike in contract and in tort a plaintiff may claim compensation only for the loss caused by the defendant's wrongful act: any loss created by his own unreasonable conduct he must bear himself. In a case in 1955, Hodson LJ had to consider the question

whether the damages flow from the breach in accordance with the ordinary law of damages for breach of contract. Were they the natural and probable consequences of the breach? If not, they are too remote . . . The question is one of causation. If the master, by acting as he did, either caused the damage by acting unreasonably in the circumstances in which he was placed, or failed to mitigate the damage, the [defendants] would be relieved, accordingly from the liability which would otherwise have fallen upon them.[149]

The appellants in *White and Carter (Councils) Ltd v McGregor*, as they had refused the repudiation, were entitled to remain inactive and await the date of performance. But they were not content to be passive. They embarked upon a course of conduct which cost money, served no useful purpose and was, as they knew, unwanted by the respondent. They had chosen, in other words, to inflate their loss; and, while under no duty to mitigate, they were surely bound not to aggravate the damage. In the words of Hodson LJ, quoted above, they had 'acted unreasonably in the circumstances in which they had been placed', and the respondent should have been 'relieved from the liability which would otherwise have fallen on him'. Their expense was self-imposed and was not caused by the breach of contract.

In his speech in *White and Carter (Councils) Ltd v McGregor* Lord Reid said that the rule might not apply if the plaintiff 'has no legitimate interest, financial or otherwise, in performing the contract rather than claiming damages.' This qualification seems to have been accepted as correct by the Court of Appeal in *Attica Sea Carriers v Ferrostaal*

---

[148] [1962] AC at 442, [1961] 3 All ER at 1190. One apparent implication of the decision is that it enables a plaintiff to obtain the advantages of a decree of specific performance in circumstances that would not normally attract the remedy, a possibility anticipated in the Australian case of *Automatic Fire Sprinklers Pty Ltd v Watson* (1946) 72 CLR 435 at 451.

[149] *Compania Naveira Maropan SA v Bowaters Lloyd, Pulp and Paper Mills Ltd* [1955] 2 QB 68 at 98–99, [1955] 2 All ER 241 at 251–252. For a parallel case in tort, see *Pacific Concord, Georgidore (Owners) v Pacific Concord (Owners)* [1961] 1 All ER 106, [1961] 1 WLR 873.

Poseidon Bulk Reederei GmbH, The Puerto Buitrago[150] and by Kerr J in *The Odenfeld.*[151] It was certainly so treated by Lloyd J in *Clea Shipping Corpn v Bulk Oil International Ltd, the Alaskan Trader (No 2).*[152]

> In October 1979 the owners chartered a vessel to the charterers for about 24 months. After the vessel had been in service for about a year it required extensive repairs. The charterers said that they had no further use for the ship but the shippers nevertheless spent £800,000 repairing it.[153] In April 1981 the owners told the charterers the ship was now available but the charterers refused to give the master any instructions. This was certainly a repudiatory breach but the owners kept the ship fully crewed in the Piraeus for the rest of the charter period awaiting instruction. The charterers having paid the hire now sought to recover it. The arbitrator held that the owners had no legitimate reason not to accept the charterers' repudiation. Lloyd J held that the arbitrator had stated the right test and that it could not be said that no reasonable arbitrator could have reached the same result and therefore rejected the appeal.

The marked self-restraint which modern courts show in regard to arbitral awards makes it difficult to evaluate this decision. Much would seem to turn on the reasons for the behaviour which are unclear. It can be assumed that the ship could not be relet at a profit and it may be that it could not be relet at all. But in that case most of the hire could have been recovered as damages since the only step which could have been taken to reduce the loss would have been to lay off the crew.

D Contributory negligence

The problem of mitigation arises where the defendant breaks the contract and it is alleged that the plaintiff did not respond reasonably and therefore suffered more loss than he need. The defendant may allege that the plaintiff behaved unreasonably before or contemporaneously with the breach of contract. Such arguments arise very frequently in tort actions under the rubric 'contributory negligence'. Until 1945, contributory negligence was a complete defence to tort actions, subject to the last opportunity rule. Since 1945 the effect of the Law Reform (Contributory Negligence) Act 1945 has been to reduce the plaintiff's damages.

The position of contributory negligence in relation to contract actions is not wholly clear. One problem is that liability in contract is usually strict. If the defendant has not been at fault, his negligence cannot be compared with that of the plaintiff. Of course the defendant may have been careless even though his liability was independent of

---

[150] [1976] 1 Lloyds Rep 250.   [151] [1978] 2 Lloyds Rep 357.
[152] [1984] 1 All ER 129. See also *Ministry of Sound (Ireland) Ltd v World On Line Ltd* [2003] EWHC 2178 (Ch), [2003] 2 All ER (Comm) 823.
[153] In a time charterparty there is usually an off-hire clause under which while the ship is being repaired the charterers are not paying for the use of the ship and time stops running.

fault and there is a substantial number of cases where the defendant has simply contracted to take care. In many of these cases the plaintiff has alternative causes of action in contract and tort and contributory negligence would be available as a defence to the tort action.

One may distinguish at least the following situations:

(1) Defendant's liability is strict. Defendant is not negligent, plaintiff is.

(2) Defendant's liability is strict but both defendant and plaintiff are in fact negligent.

(3) Defendant's liability depends on proof of negligence. Both defendant and plaintiff are negligent. Plaintiff sues in tort.

(4) Defendant's liability depends on proof of negligence. Both defendant and plaintiff are negligent. Plaintiff sues in contract.

In case (3) it seems clear that the 1945 Act applies.[154] In case (1) contributory negligence if available would be a complete defence. Courts tend to reach this result by the similar, though conceptually distinct, route, of treating the plaintiff's carelessness as the sole cause of his loss.[155]

The most difficult cases are (2) and (4). These appear to turn on the construction of section 1(1) of the 1945 Act which provides: 'Where any person suffers damage as the result partly of his own fault and partly of the fault of any other person or persons . . .' and section 4 which provides that ' "fault" means negligence, breach of statutory duty or other act or omission which gives rise to a liability in tort *or would, apart from this Act, give rise to the defence of contributory negligence.*'[156]

After a number of first instance decisions[157] which took different views as to the answer, the question came before the Court of Appeal in *Forsikringsaktieselskapet Vesta v Butcher*[158] where approval was given to an analysis by Hobhouse J at first instance in the same case. There it was held that contributory negligence could be raised 'where the defendant's liability in contract is the same as his liability in the tort of negligence independently of the existence of any contract.'[159] This decision was followed by the

---

[154] *Sayers v Harlow UDC* [1958] 2 All ER 342, [1958] 1 WLR 623.

[155] *Quinn v Burch Bros (Builders) Ltd* [1966] 2 QB 370, [1965] 3 All ER 801; *Lexmead (Basingstoke) Ltd v Lewis* [1982] AC 225, [1980] 1 All ER 978. Where the gist of the claim against the defendant is that he is dishonest, courts have refused to allow the plea that the plaintiff was contributorily negligent in failing to notice this. *Alliance and Leicester Building Society v Edgestop Ltd* [1994] 2 All ER 38. *Corporacion Nacional del Cobre de Chile v Sogemin Metals Ltd* [1997] 2 All ER 917.

[156] Italics supplied.

[157] *Basildon District Council v JE Lesser (Properties) Ltd* [1985] QB 839, [1985] 1 All ER 20; *Marintrans AB v Comet Shipping Co Ltd, The Shinjitsu Mara No 5* [1985] 3 All ER 442, [1985] 1 WLR 1270.

[158] [1988] 2 All ER 43, [1988] 3 WLR 565. The case subsequently went on appeal to the House of Lords but not on this point [1989] AC 852, [1989] 1 All ER 402.

[159] See Glanville Williams Joint *Torts and Contributory Negligence* (1951) pp 216–222. Swanton 55 ALJ 278; Law Commission Working Paper 114 (1990).

Court of Appeal in *Platform Home Loans Ltd v Oyston Shipways*.[160] On appeal the House of Lords effectively took the correctness of this view for granted and concentrated on the interaction of contributory negligence and the damages rules.[161] In *Barclays Bank v Fairclough*[162] the Court of Appeal held that contributory negligence was not available where the contractual duty which was broken was strict.

E Liquidated damages and penalties [163]

The parties to a contract may agree beforehand what sum shall be payable by way of damages in the event of breach, as, for example, where a builder agrees that he will pay £50 a day for every day that the building remains unfinished after the contractual date for completion. A sum fixed in this manner falls into one of two classes.

First, it may be a genuine pre-estimate of the loss that will be caused to one party if the contract is broken by the other. In this case it is called liquidated damages and it constitutes the amount, no more and no less, that the plaintiff is entitled to recover in the event of breach without being required to prove actual damage.[164]

Secondly, it may be in the nature of a threat held over the other party *in terrorem*—a security to the promisee that the contract will be performed.[165] A sum of this nature is called a penalty, and it has long been subject to equitable jurisdiction. Courts of equity have taken the view that, the promisee is sufficiently compensated by being indemnified for his actual loss, and that he acts unconscionably if he demands a sum which, though certainly fixed by agreement, may well be disproportionate to the injury.[166] Where the agreed sum, though a penalty, is in fact less than the damage actually suffered, it appears that the plaintiff can recover his actual loss.[167]

It is always, therefore, a question of importance whether a conventional sum is liquidated damages or a penalty. This is a question of construction 'to be decided upon the terms and inherent circumstances of each particular contract, judged of as at the time of making the contract, not as at the time of the breach'.[168] What has to be ascertained is whether it can reasonably be inferred that the parties intended to form a genuine pre-estimate of the damage likely to ensue from a breach.

---

[160] [1998] 4 All ER 252.   [161] [1999] 1 All ER 833.   [162] [1995] 1 All ER 289.

[163] Kaplan 50 Southern California L Rev 1055; Milner 42 MLR 508.

[164] *Wallis v Smith* (1882) 21 ChD 243 at 267, per Cotton LJ.

[165] Lord Radcliffe has expressed scepticism at the assumption that a penalty is based on the idea that it is a threat *in terrorem* of the other party: *Bridge v Campbell Discount Co Ltd* [1962] AC 600 at 622, [1962] 1 All ER 385 at 395.

[166] Story *Equity Jurisprudence* s 1316.

[167] *Public Works Comr v Hills* [1906] AC 368 at 375. *Wall v Rederiaktiebolaget Luggude* [1915] 3 KB 66, approved *Watts, Watts & Co Ltd v Mitsui & Co Ltd* [1917] AC 227. See *Cellulose Acetate Silk Co Ltd v Widnes Foundry (1925) Ltd* [1933] AC 20 at 26. Hudson 90 LQR 31; Gordon 90 LQR 296; Hudson 91 LQR 25.

[168] *Dunlop Pneumatic Tyre Co Ltd v New Garage and Motor Co Ltd* [1915] AC 79 at 86–87; *Lombank Ltd v Excell* [1963] 3 All ER 486.

The distinction between penalties and liquidated damages depends on the intention of the parties to be gathered from the whole of the contract. If the intention is to secure performance of the contract by the imposition of a fine or penalty, then the sum specified is a penalty; but if, on the other hand, the intention is to assess the damages for breach of the contract, it is liquidated damages.[169]

The onus of showing that the specified sum is a penalty lies upon the party who is sued for its recovery.[170]

The fact that the parties may have used the expression 'penalty' or 'liquidated damages' does not conclude the matter, and the court must still decide whether the sum fixed is a genuine forecast of the probable loss.[171] The expressions used must not, however, be disregarded, and if for instance, the sum is made payable as a penalty the onus of disproving that this is its correct character lies on the party who claims that it was intended to be liquidated damages.[172]

Rules for guidance of court Certain rules for the guidance of the judge have been laid down by the courts and these were usefully summarised by Lord Dunedin in *Dunlop Pneumatic Tyre Co Ltd v New Garage and Motor Co Ltd*.[173] They are as follows:

(a) The conventional sum is a penalty if it is extravagant and unconscionable in amount in comparison with the greatest loss that could possibly follow from the breach.[174]

(b) If the obligation of the promisor under the contract is to pay a certain sum of money, and it is agreed that if he fails to do so he shall pay a larger sum, this larger sum is a penalty.[175] The reason is that, since the damage arising from breach is capable of exact definition, the fixing of a larger sum cannot be a pre-estimate of the probable damage.

(c) Subject to the preceding rules, it is a canon of construction that, if there is only one event upon which the conventional sum is to be paid, the sum is liquidated damages.[176] This was held to be the case, for instance, where it was provided in a contract for the construction of sewerage works that, if the operations were

---

[169] *Law v Redditch Local Board* [1892] 1 QB 127 at 132, per Lopes J.

[170] *Robophone Facilities Ltd v Blank* [1966] 1 WLR 1428 at 1447.

[171] *Dunlop Pneumatic Tyre Co v New Garage and Motor Co* [1915] AC 79 at 86, per Lord Dunedin.

[172] *Wilson v Love* [1896] 1 QB 626 at 630, per Lord Esher.

[173] [1915] 1 AC 79 at 86 ff.

[174] *Clydebank Engineering and Shipbuilding Co v Yzquierdo-y-Castaneda, Don Jose Ramos* [1905] AC 6, especially at 10.

[175] *Kemble v Farren* (1829) 6 Bing 141. This would not be true of a provision for the payment of interest in the event of late payment unless the rate of interest stipulated was not a reasonable pre-estimate of the payee's loss. *Jeancharm Ltd v Barnet Football Club Ltd* (2004) 92 Con LR 26.

[176] *Law v Redditch Local Board* [1892] 1 QB 127.

not complete by 30 April, the contractor should pay £100 and £5 for every seven days during which the work was unfinished after that date.[177]

(d) If a single lump sum is made payable upon the occurrence of one or more or all of several events, some of which may occasion serious and others mere trifling damage, there is a presumption (but no more) that it is a penalty.[178] This presumption, however, is weakened if it is practically impossible to prove the exact monetary loss that will accrue from a breach of the various stipulations. The sum fixed by the parties in such a case, if reasonable in amount, will be allowed as liquidated damages.[179] Two cases will illustrate the distinction. In the *Dunlop Pneumatic Tyre Co* case:

The Dunlop Company supplied tyres to the defendants under an agreement, headed 'Price Maintenance Agreement', by which the defendants bound themselves not to tamper with the marks on the goods, not to sell below the listed prices, not to supply persons who were on a suspended list, not to exhibit or export without consent, and to pay £5 by way of liquidated damages for every tyre, tube or cover sold or offered in breach of the agreement.

It was held that the sum of £5 was liquidated damages. A fine of £5 for selling, for example, a single tube below the list price might seem disproportionate to the harm caused; but the news of the undercutting would soon spread and the resultant damage to Dunlop's selling organisation would be impossible to estimate. It was, therefore, reasonable to quantify the damage at a fixed but not extravagant figure.

The Court of Appeal reached the opposite conclusion in the somewhat similar case of *Ford Motor Co v Armstrong*[180] where the facts were these:

The defendant, a retailer, in consideration of receiving supplies from the Ford Company, agreed not to sell any car or parts below the listed price, not to sell Ford cars to other motor dealers, and not to exhibit any car supplied by the company without their permission. He also agreed that for every breach of this agreement he would pay £250 as being 'the agreed damage which the manufacturer will sustain'.

In the view of the majority of the court the £250 was a penalty. It was not only substantial but was arbitrary and fixed *in terrorem*, for, since it was made payable for various breaches differing in kind, its very size prevented it from being a reasonable pre-estimate of the probable damage.[181]

---

[177] Ibid.
[178] *Lord Elphinstone v Monkland Iron and Coal Co* (1886) 11 App Cas 332 at 342, per Lord Watson. *Inter-office Telephones Ltd v Robert Freeman Co Ltd* [1958] 1 QB 190 at 194.
[179] *Dunlop Pneumatic Tyre Co v New Garage and Motor Co* [1915] AC 79 at 95–96, per Lord Atkinson. There are many cases where it is difficult to pre-estimate the loss and where over ingenious speculation after the event should not be encouraged *Phillips Hong Kong Ltd v AG of Hong Kong* [1993] 61 BLR 41.
[180] (1915) 31 TLR 267.
[181] See also *Alder v Moore* [1961] 2 QB 57, [1961] 1 All ER 1. Goodhart 77 LQR 300; Goff 24 MLR 637.

The necessity of deciding between liquidated damages and penalty may clearly involve the courts in nice distinctions; and the problem has arisen in an acute form on the construction of a hire-purchase contract, in this as in other respects a fertile mother of actions. The difficulties are illustrated by the decision of the House of Lords in *Bridge v Campbell Discount Co Ltd*.[182]

> The appellant made a hire-purchase contract with the respondents for a second-hand car. The total hire-purchase price was £482, of which £105 was due at once and the balance by 36 monthly instalments. The appellant met the initial payment and the first instalment, and then, after writing to the respondents that he would not be able to pay any more, he returned the car to the dealers. Clause 9 of the contract provided that 'if the hiring be terminated for any reason before the vehicle becomes the property of the hirer, the hirer shall . . . pay to the owners . . . by way of agreed compensation for depreciation of the vehicle such further sum as may be necessary to make the rentals paid and payable hereunder equal to two-thirds of the hire-purchase price'. The respondents sued on this clause for £206, being two-thirds of the price less the initial payment and the first instalment.

The county court judge held that the clause, despite its wording, imposed a penalty and dismissed the action. The Court of Appeal reversed this decision. They were of opinion that, on the true construction of the facts, the hirer had not broken his contract but had merely exercised his right to terminate it. As there had been no breach, no question of penalty arose and the hirer must pay the sum stipulated in the event of termination. The House of Lords, by a majority of four to one, restored the judgment of the county court. They held that the hirer had in fact broken his contract, that they must therefore decide whether the clause offered a genuine pre-estimate of damages or imposed a penalty, and that it was a penalty. Lord Morton said:[183]

> I find it impossible to regard the sum stipulated in clause 9 as a genuine pre-estimate of the loss which would be suffered by the respondents in the events specified in the same clause . . . This was a second-hand car when the appellant took it over on hire-purchase. The depreciation in its value would naturally become greater the longer it remained in the appellant's hands. Yet the sum to be paid under clause 9(6), is largest when, as in the present case, the car is returned after it has been in the hirer's possession for a very short time, and gets progressively smaller as time goes on.

In Lord Radcliffe's words, 'it is a sliding scale of compensation, but a scale that slides in the wrong direction'. The decision of the House of Lords that the hirer had broken his contract side-stepped the difficult question of whether the Court of Appeal was

---

[182] [1962] AC 600, [1962] 1 All ER 385.
[183] Ibid at 616 and 391, respectively; applied, *EP Finance Co Ltd v Dooley* [1964] 1 All ER 527, [1963] 1 WLR 1313; *United Dominions Trust (Commercial) v Ennis* [1968] 1 QB 54, [1967] 2 All ER 345.

correct in holding that if there were no breach, there could be no penalty.[184] This decision looks odd since it means that a well instructed hirer would be better off to break the contract than to exercise his contractual right to terminate. On the other hand the rule is entirely consistent with the general rule of English law that the value of the contractual undertakings is a matter for the parties. In the most recent case of *Export Credits Guarantee Department v Universal Oil Products Co*[185] the House of Lords has in fact held that the penalty rules only apply where the money is payable on an event which is a breach of contract as between the plaintiff and defendant.[186]

In his helpful judgment in *Alfred McAlpine Capital Projects Ltd v Tilebox Ltd*[187] Jackson J pointed out that in contracts between businesses there are not many decisions holding that the agreed sum was a penalty. He stressed that although the judgments talk about 'genuine pre-estimates' the important question is not so much how the figure is arrived at but whether it is reasonable in regard to likely loss. A figure does not have to be right to be reasonable.

Defaults under hire purchase and similar contracts have given rise to a second set of problems. In such contracts it is universal to provide that if the debtor does not pay each instalment promptly the creditor will have a right to bring the contract to an end. The consequential provisions as to how much the debtor shall pay after the creditor has terminated for such a breach are clearly, as we have seen, subject to the penalty doctrine. Suppose the creditor decides instead to sue for unliquidated damages? In *Financings Ltd v Baldock*[188] the Court of Appeal held that in such a case the creditor could not recover as unliquidated damages compensation for the loss of the later instalments because he had lost those not because of the breach but because of his election to exercise his contractual power to terminate the contract. However it appears that this decision may be side-stepped by skilful draftsmanship. In *Lombard North Central plc v Butterworth*[189] the contract was in very much the standard form except that it provided that 'punctual payment of each instalment was of the essence of the agreement'. The Court of Appeal held that the effect of this clause was that any failure to pay an instalment punctually was a breach which went to the root of the contract giving rise to a right to terminate at common law not simply to a right to terminate under the contractual power. It followed that the creditor was therefore entitled to compensation for loss of the future instalments (making due allowance for

---

184 See Wedderburn [1961] CLJ 156; Fridman 24 MLR 507, 26 MLR 198. As to the effect of *Campbell Discount Co Ltd v Bridge* upon the decision of the Court of Appeal in *Phonographic Equipment (1958) Ltd v Muslu* [1961] 3 All ER 626, [1961] 1 WLR 1379, see *Lombank Ltd v Excell* [1964] 1 QB 415, [1963] 3 All ER 486, CA. This latter case overrules the decision of Winn J in *Lombank Ltd v Cook* [1962] 3 All ER 491, [1962] 1 WLR 1133.

185 [1983] 2 All ER 205, [1983] 1 WLR 339.

186 This was held on a preliminary point of law. The case is puzzling since it appears that the sum agreed to be paid, though very large, was exactly the same as the plaintiff's loss and therefore not penal.

187 (2005) 104 Con LR 39. See also *State of Tasmania v Leighton Contractors Pty Ltd* [2005] TASSC 133.

188 [1963] 2 QB 104, [1963] 1 All ER 443.   189 [1987] QB 527, [1987] 1 All ER 267.

accelerated payment and so on) since now the loss flowed from the fundamental breach by the debtor and not from the creditor's election to terminate. This decision seems entirely logical but it shows how much difference careful pre-planning and draftsmanship can make.

An interesting application of the penalty rules in an unusual context was provided by *Jobson v Johnson.*[190]

> The defendant agreed to buy 62,566 shares in a football club for a total purchase price £351,688. The price was payable by an initial payment of £40,000 and six instalments of £51,948 payable half yearly. There was a further provision that if the defendant defaulted on the payment of the second or any subsequent instalments he should transfer the shares back to the vendors for £40,000. That was clearly not a genuine pre-estimate of the vendor's loss since it did not represent the true value of the shares and the same sum was payable however many instalments the purchaser had paid before he defaulted. In due course, having paid some of the instalments the purchaser did default and the plaintiff who was the assignee of the seller sued for specific performance. The defendant entered a defence claiming that the re-transfer arrangement was penal and also seeking relief against forfeiture if it was enforceable.

At the trial the application for relief against forfeiture was struck out because of the defendant's failure to comply with a mandatory instruction of the trial judge which had not substantially related to the question at issue. The trial judge then held that although the re-transfer clause was penal it could be enforced since non-enforcement of penalties was part of the court's equitable jurisdiction to relieve against forfeiture. The Court of Appeal disagreed with this latter point and held that the jurisdiction to strike down penalties and the jurisdiction to relieve against forfeiture were distinct though obviously related.

So it was clear that the Court of Appeal would not simply order the specific performance of the agreement to re-transfer for £40,000. On the other hand the purchaser had got the shares and had not paid for them according to the terms of the contract. So there must be some remedy. Clearly, the plaintiff was entitled to sue for the balance of the purchase price but it is clear from the report that both the plaintiff and the defendant regarded the shares, by the time of the trial, as worth more than the purchase price. The Court of Appeal was divided as to what to do in this position. The majority view was that the plaintiff should be offered the choice either for sale of the shares by the court and payment of all the unpaid money out of the proceeds or of an enquiry as to his actual loss with the view of giving specific performance if the present value of the shares did not exceed by more than £40,000 the present aggregate of the unpaid instalments and the present amount charged on the shares under a charging order obtained by Chartered Standard Bank. Kerr LJ

[190] [1989] 1 All ER 621, [1989] 1 WLR 1026.

thought that neither of these alternatives was fair to the plaintiff and that he should be offered the opportunity of having specific performance of the agreement to re-transfer the shares subject to his repaying to the defendant all the money he had received under the contract (perhaps with interest). Granted that the real dispute was about who was to have the shares and that the defendant was certainly in breach, there seems much force in the argument that this is the fairer solution. It is clear here that the plaintiff suffered in the result from formulating the contract in too ambitious a way. It would certainly have been possible to draft the contract in such a way that the defendant would have been under a specifically enforceable obligation to re-transfer the shares if he had not also sought to attach too low a price to the re-conveyance.

F Deposits, part payments and forfeitures [191]

Since the discharge of a contract has no retrospective effect, it can be argued that the party in default cannot recover property which, in fulfilment of his contractual obligations, he may have transferred to the innocent party prior to the discharge.

> The contract remains alive for the purpose of vindicating rights already acquired under it on either side.[192]

This suggestion, however, requires modification where money is paid in advance. Whether it is recoverable by the contract breaker if the contract is discharged by reason of his breach depends upon the construction of the contract. The object that the parties had in view must be ascertained.[193]

If their intention was that the money should be deposited as an earnest or guarantee for the due performance of the payer's obligations, the rule at common law is that it is forfeited to the payee upon the discharge of the contract for the default of the payer, notwithstanding that it would have gone in part payment of the price had the contract been completed.[194] 'The payer cannot insist on abandoning the contract and yet recover the deposit, because that would be to enable him to take advantage of his own wrong.'[195]

The position is different where there is simply an advance payment. In *Dies v British and International Mining and Finance Corpn Ltd*,[196] Stable J held[197] that if a

[191] Beatson 97 LQR 389; Tolhurst and Carter 20 J Contract L 74.
[192] *Hirji Mulji v Cheon Yue ss Co Ltd* [1926] AC 497 at 510, per Lord Sumner.
[193] *Mayson v Clouet* [1924] AC 980 at 985.
[194] *Howe v Smith* (1884) 27 ChD 89. If the full amount of the deposit has not been paid at the time of discharge it can be recovered by way of damages: *Damon v Hapag-Lloyd International SA* [1985] 1 All ER 475.
[195] *Howe v Smith* (1884) 27 ChD at 98, per Bowen LJ.
[196] [1939] 1 KB 724; and see *Stockloser v Johnson* [1954] 1 QB 476 at 490, [1954] 1 All ER 630, per Denning LJ.
[197] Cf *Fitt v Cassanett* (1842) 4 Man & G 898, where the money, though described in the headnote as a 'deposit', was in fact paid on account of the full price.

contract for the sale of goods is discharged owing to the buyer's default, the seller must return any part of the price that has been pre-paid.

> In my judgment there would be a manifest defect in the law if, where a buyer had paid for the goods but was unable to accept delivery, the vendor could retain the goods and the money quite irrespective of whether the money so retained bore any relation to the amount of the damage, if any, sustained as a result of the breach. The seller is already amply protected, since he can recover such damage as he has sustained.[198]

It appears that in deciding whether money has been paid as a deposit or as a part payment great weight is to be attached to the label attached to the payment by the parties.[199] This account appears to need revision in the light of the decision of the House of Lords in *Hyundai Heavy Industries Co Ltd v Papadopoulos*.[200] This case involved a guarantee of a shipbuilding contract.

> The plaintiffs were South Korean shipbuilders who entered into contracts to build ships for various customers. The contracts provided for a series of stage payments during the building of the ships and the defendants guaranteed the contracts. There were failures to pay the stage payments; the plaintiffs terminated the contracts and sued the defendant on the guarantees.

The plaintiff succeeded in the House of Lords where the reasoning depended in part on the wording of the guarantees. The majority of the House of Lords, however, clearly held that on these facts the buyers would be liable for the instalments which were due but unpaid at the date of termination and that the guarantors were accordingly liable equally. Lord Edmund-Davies said:[201]

> It has to be said, at the outset, that the assertion that the builders' exercise of their undoubted right to cancel the ship contract terminated it for all purposes and, in particular, rendered the second instalment no longer exigible is an irrational assumption unsupported by any direct authority. It is true on cancellation the builders acquired a right to recover damages for such injury flowing from the buyers' default as, in due course and on proper accounts being taken and a balance struck, the builders could establish. But there is no warrant for saying that such right was acquired in substitution for their accrued right to recover the due but unpaid second instalment. On the contrary . . . there are sound commercial reasons for holding that a vested and indubitable right to prompt payment on a specified date of a specified sum, expressly provided for in the contract, should not be supplanted by or merged in or substituted by a right to recover at some future date such indefinite sum by way of damages as, on balance and on proof, might be awarded to the builders.

What is the relationship between this decision and the decision in the *Dies* case? There are a number of possible answers. One is that *Dies* was wrong. Another is that *Dies* is a

---

[198] [1939] 1 KB 724 at 744.   [199] *Howe v Smith* (1884) 27 Ch D 89.
[200] [1980] 2 All ER 29, [1980] 1 WLR 1129.   [201] Ibid at 39 and 1141, respectively.

rule which applies only to contracts of sale and not to a shipbuilding contract. Although a shipbuilding contract obviously involves a transfer of the ownership of the ship at the end of the contract it obviously involves a great deal of work before and the payment structure is typically related to the progress of the work. Another way of putting the same distinction, or a very similar one, would be to say that in *Dies* there was a total failure of consideration since the buyer had received nothing whereas in *Hyundai* there was no total failure of consideration since the defendants had had the benefit of all the work which had been done before the date of termination.[202]

The practical effect of the rules about deposits is quite the reverse of the rules as to the penalties since deposits are often greater than the loss which would have been contemplated at the time of the contract. The difference is particularly marked if the payee is entitled to recover an unpaid deposit.[203] It is difficult to see any adequate policy reason for this difference, which seems to be the result of the two groups of rules developing in isolation from each other. The decision of the Privy Council in *Workers Trust and Merchant Bank Ltd v Dojap Investments Ltd*[204] recognises the inelegance and goes some way to mitigate it without expunging it from the law.

> The appellant bank acting as a mortgagee sold certain premises in Jamaica at auction to the respondent for $11,500,000. Clause 4 of the contract provided for payment of the deposit of 25 per cent and a deposit of $2,875,000 was duly paid. The contract required the balance to be paid within 14 days of the date of the auction. For various reasons which do not require to be gone into in detail, the purchase did not pay the balance on the 14th day though it tendered the full sum on the 21st day. The appellant claimed to be entitled to keep the whole of the deposit.

The Privy Council held that, although the deposit rule was not in general subject to the penalty rule, this was only the case where the amount of the deposit was reasonable. It held, further, that long usage had established that 10 per cent was reasonable and any deposit in excess of 10 per cent appeared to be a penalty unless special circumstances could be shown which justified taking a deposit at a higher level. The Board further held that although if the appellant had taken a 10 per cent deposit he would have been entitled to keep that sum, since the sum it had taken was not a deposit at all but a penalty the appellant could not keep any part of it and must repay the deposit in

---

[202] For another case involving a similar shipbuilding contract but with bizarre facts see *Stocznia Gdanska SA v Latvian Shipping Co* [1998] 1 All ER 883 and *Stocznia Gdanska SA v Latvian Shipping Co (No 3)* [2002] EWCA Civ 889, [2002] 2 All ER (Comm) 768.

[203] See the facts of *Damon Cia Naviera SA v Hapag-Lloyd International SA* [1985] 1 All ER 475, [1985] 1 WLR 435. But see *Luong Dinh Luu v Sovereign Developments Pty Ltd* (2006) (as yet unreported), where a contract for the sale of land provided for a 10% deposit but the seller accepted a payment of about 1%. The New South Wales Court of Appeal held that a contractual provision for the payment of the balance was penal. The vice in the provision seems to be that the sum was payable on the purchaser's default.

[204] [1993] 2 All ER 370

full. It was accepted that there was no logic to approving the figure of 10 per cent and the figure could only be justified by long usage both in England and Jamaica.

Under section 49 (2) of the Law of Property Act 1925 the court has a wide discretion to order the return of deposits paid under a contract for the sale of land.[205]

When, however, money has been paid as a deposit, equity is prepared within limits to grant relief against the forfeiture. Nevertheless, the circumstances in which and the extent to which the relief will be given are by no means clear.

> Suppose, for instance, that a buyer of goods agrees to pay the price by periodic instalments and further agrees that, if he defaults in any one payment, instalments already paid shall be forfeited to the seller and possession of the goods surrendered. If, after payment of a large percentage of the price, the contract is discharged because of the buyer's default, will relief be granted to him against the forfeiture of the instalments already paid?

It is clear at least that equity, where warranted by the circumstances, will relieve the buyer to the extent of giving him further time within which to complete the contract. In other words, the forfeiture will be suspended, provided that the buyer expresses himself ready and willing to pay the balance of the price within the extended time fixed by the court.[206] In *Union Eagle Ltd v Golden Achievment Ltd*[207] the parties had entered into a written contract for the appellant to buy a flat in Hong Kong from the respondent for $HK 4.2 million. The purchaser paid a 10 per cent deposit. The contract provided that completion was to take place before 5.00 pm on 30 September 1991, that time was to be of the essence of the contract in every respect and that if the purchaser failed to perform any of the terms, the deposit was to be absolutely forfeited. A messenger carrying cheques for the balance of the account arrived 10 minutes late at the office of the vendor's solicitor. The solicitor on behalf of the vendor refused to accept the cheque and purported to terminate the contract. The purchaser sued for specific performance arguing that it was entitled to relief. The Privy Council found for the vendor on the basis that the provision that time was of the essence was decisive.

It should be noted that in this case the purchaser was seeking specific performance and not return of the deposit. It seems clear that, at least under English law, the Court would have jurisdiction on these facts to order return of the deposit. It is clear that the decision of the Privy Council adopts a different approach from that taken in the important Australian cases of *Legione v Hateley*[208] and *Stern v McCarthur*.[209] Some have also thought it difficult to reconcile with the decision of the Court of Appeal in *Re Dagenham (Thames) Dock Company*.[210]

---

[205] *County and Metropolitan Homes Surrey Ltd v Topclaim Ltd* [1997] 1 All ER 254.

[206] *Re Dagenham (Thames) Dock Co, ex p Hulse* (1873) 8 Ch App 1022; *Kilmer v British Columbia Orchard Lands Ltd* [1913] AC 319.

[207] [1997] 2 All ER 215.   [208] (1983) 152 CLR 406.   [209] (1988) 165 CLR 489.

[210] (1873) LR 8 Ch App 1022. For further discussion see Abedian and Furmston 12 JCL 189.

What is doubtful is whether equity will intervene and give relief otherwise than by extending the time allowed for payment. The question was canvassed in *Stockloser v Johnson.*[211] On the facts of the case the Court of Appeal agreed that intervention was not warranted, but its members differed as to the principle upon which such relief might be granted. Romer LJ concluded that 'in the absence of some special circumstances such as fraud, sharp practice or other unconscionable conduct of the vendor' no intervention by the court is permissible after the contract has been rescinded, except to allow an extension of time for payment.[212] Somervell and Denning LJJ thought that the province of equity is not so circumscribed and that it may permit more general relief whenever the forfeiture clause is of a penal nature—where, that is, the sum forfeited is wholly disproportionate to the damage suffered—provided that in the circumstances it is unconscionable for the money to be retained.

For each of these views persuasive arguments may be advanced. On the one hand, precedent would clearly seem to favour the more restricted view;[213] and it may well be thought that to upset agreements contracted freely and with open eyes save on urgent grounds would defeat reasonable expectations and obstruct the course of business. As Lord Radcliffe observed in another case unconscionable" must not be taken to be a panacea for adjusting any contract between competent persons when it shows a rough edge to one side or the other'.[214] On the other hand, the inexorable maxim of Lord Nottingham, cited by Romer LJ,[215] that 'Chancery mends no man's bargain', does scant justice to the modern law. The twentieth century has refused to be sterilised by the dead hand of the seventeenth. The courts have in fact 'mended bargains' through the doctrines of undue influence, of 'clogs on the equity of redemption', of equitable mistake. They have allowed contracts to be severed, at least in certain types of illegality, and have wholly discharged them on the ground of frustration. Which of the two judicial views advanced in *Stockloser v Johnson* will ultimately prevail must therefore await further elucidation.[216]

In two more recent decisions the House of Lords has taken a narrow view of the scope of the jurisdiction to give relief against forfeiture. In *Scandinavian Trading Tanker Co v Flota Petrolera Ecuatoriana, The Scaptrade*[217] it denied that there was any

---

[211] [1954] 1 QB 476, [1954] 1 All ER 630. See also in the Court of Appeal *Campbell Discount Co v Bridge* [1961] 1 QB 445, [1961] 2 All ER 97.

[212] [1954] 1 QB 476 at 501, [1954] 1 All ER 630 at 644.

[213] *Hill v Barclay* (1811) 18 Ves 56; *Bracebridge Buckley* (1816) 2 Price 200; *Barrow v Isaacs* [1891] 1 QB 417; *Sparks v Liverpool Waterworks Co* (1807) 13 Ves 428; *Wallingford v Mutual Society* (1880) 5 App Cas 685; *Protector Endowment Loan and Annuity Co v Grice* (1880) 5 QBD 592. See generally, Story *Equity Jurisdiction* ss 1319–1326.

[214] *Bridge v Campbell Discount Co Ltd* [1962] AC 600 at 626, [1962] 1 All ER 385 at 397.

[215] *Stockloser v Johnson* [1954] 1 QB 476 at 495, [1954] 1 All ER 630 at 640.

[216] *Galbraith v Mitchenall Estates Ltd* [1965] 2 QB 473, [1964] 2 All ER 653 favours Romer LJ while *Starside Properties Ltd v Mustapha* [1974] 2 All ER 567, [1974] 1 WLR 816 inclines in the opposite direction.

[217] [1983] 2 AC 694, [1983] 2 All ER 763.

such jurisdiction in relation to termination of time charterparties for non-payment of hire.[218] The principal reason given by Lord Diplock delivering the leading speech was that to give equitable relief would be tantamount to ordering specific performance and the jurisdiction should therefore be limited to contracts, especially contracts for the sale of land, where specific performance was an available remedy. In *Sport International Bussum Bv v Inter-Footwear Ltd*[219] it refused to intervene where one party had failed to comply with the terms of the consent order made to settle litigation about the licensing of trade marks and registered designs. On the other hand the Court of Appeal in *BICC plc v Burndy Corpn*[220] has even more recently held that there is no reason why the jurisdiction should not extend to proprietary or possessory interests in chattels.

3 SPECIFIC PERFORMANCE[221]

A decree of specific performance is a decree issued by the court which constrains a contracting party to do that which he has promised to do. It is a form of relief that is purely equitable in origin and is one of the earliest examples of the maxim that equity acts *in personam.*

It originated in the realisation that there are many cases in which the remedy available at common law is not adequate. The normal remedy for breach of contract is the recovery of damages at common law. In most cases this affords adequate reparation, as, for example, where the contract is for the sale of goods easily procurable elsewhere, or for the delivery of stocks or shares for which there is a free market; but in many instances, and especially where a vendor refuses to convey the land sold, a mere award of damages would defeat the just and reasonable expectations of the plaintiff. The fundamental rule, therefore is that specific performance will not be decreed if there is an adequate remedy at law.[222] The purpose of such a decree is to ensure that justice is done. 'The court gives specific performance instead of damages, only when it can by that means do more perfect and complete justice.'[223] In one case, for instance,

---

[218] Although in time charterparties, the time charterer normally pays in advance, termination for the late payment of the next advance payment will not usually leave the time charterer having paid for services he has not had. In practice it usually allows the owner to relet (often to the same charterer) at a higher rate because of movements in the freight market.

[219] [1984] 2 All ER 321, [1984] 1 WLR 776.

[220] [1985] Ch 232, [1985] 1 All ER 417. See also *Nutting v Baldwin* [1995] 2 All ER 321; *On Demand Information plc v Michael Gerson (Finance) plc* [2002] 2 All ER 949.

[221] Kronman 45 U Chicago LR 351; Schwartz 89 Yale LJ 271.

[222] *Cud v Rutter* (1720) 1 P Wms 570 (where specific performance of an agreement to transfer £1,000 South-Sea Stock was refused).

[223] *Wilson v Northampton and Banbury Junction Rly Co* (1874) 9 Ch App 279 at 284, per Lord Selborne.

where the court refused specific performance of the defendant's promise to make good a gravel pit which he had quarried, the Master of the Rolls explained the position as follows:

> This court does not profess to decree a specific performance of contracts of every description. It is only where the legal remedy is inadequate or defective that it becomes necessary for courts of equity to interfere . . . In the present case complete justice can be done at law. The matter in controversy is nothing more than the sum it will cost to put the ground in the condition in which by the covenant it ought to be.[224]

The contrary conclusion was reached in *Beswick v Beswick*,[225] the facts of which have already been given.[226] In that case the plaintiff was not only the administratrix of her late husband's estate but also the person to whom the annuity had been made payable by the contract between the husband and the defendant. Being a stranger to that contract, her only course was to claim payment of the annuity by suing in her representative, not in her personal, capacity. The defendant argued that *qua* adminis-tratrix her only right was to recover compensation for such loss as the estate had in fact suffered. Therefore, so the argument ran, since the non-payment of the annuity after the husband's death caused no loss to his estate, the only remedy available either to the plaintiff or to the estate was the recovery of nominal damages. This argument was rejected by the House of Lords. To accept it would be repugnant to the concept of justice.[227] A decree of specific performance would clearly have been available to the husband had the agreement made the annuity payable in his lifetime, and it followed that this remedy was equally available to his personal representatives under the instant contract.

Where a contract contains interdependent undertakings, a plaintiff cannot obtain an order for specific performance if he is in breach of his own obligations or if he fails to show that he is ready and willing to perform his outstanding obligations in the future.[228]

Specific performance a discretionary remedy
The exercise of the equitable jurisdiction to grant specific performance is not a matter of right in the person seeking relief, but of discretion in the court.[229] This does not mean that the decision is left to the uncontrolled caprice of the individual judge, but that a decree which would normally be justified by the principles governing the

---

[224] *Flint v Brandon* (1803) 8 Ves 159.

[225] [1968] AC 58, [1967] 2 All ER 1197. See, on the present aspect of the decision, Treitel 30 MLR 690.

[226] P 581, above.

[227] Lord Pearce alone thought that the damages would be substantial, but whether nominal or substantial he agreed that the agreement was specifically enforceable: ibid at 88 and 1212, respectively.

[228] See, for instance, *Australian Hardwoods Pty Ltd v Railways Comr* [1961] 1 All ER 737, [1961] 1 WLR 425.

[229] *Lamare v Dixon* (1873) LR 6 HL 414 at 423, per Lord Chelmsford.

subject may be withheld, if to grant it in the particular circumstances of the case will defeat the ends of justice. Lord Parker said:

> Indeed, the dominant principle has always been that equity will only grant specific performance it' under all the circumstances, it is just and equitable so to do.[230]

Thus the plaintiff will be left to his remedy at law if a decree of specific performance would inflict a hardship on the defendant, as for example where the enforcement of a restrictive covenant would be a burdensome futility owing to a change in the neighbourhood brought about by the plaintiff himself;[231] or where the defendant will be unable to enter the land that he has agreed to buy unless he is fortunate enough to obtain a licence from adjoining owners;[232] or where the plaintiff attempts to take advantage of an obvious mistake made by the defendant.[233]

In *Co-op Insurance Society Ltd v Argyll Stores (Holdings) Ltd*[234] the plaintiffs were the developers of a shopping centre and they had secured the defendants, a leading supermarket chain, as tenants of one of the major stores in the centre. In such developments the presence of such a tenant is very important to other tenants who look to the supermarket as a magnet for shoppers. The defendants had not only taken a 35-year lease but had expressly covenanted that they would operate the leased land as a supermarket. After 15 years they decided that the supermarket was no longer viable and left without notice.

This was clearly a breach of contract and in principle the plaintiffs were entitled to damages which reflected the impact on the whole development of the defendant's departure but the calculation of these damages would necessarily be a difficult exercise involving peering into an uncertain future. The plaintiffs chose instead to sue for specific performance and were successful before the Court of Appeal (by a majority).

This decision would possibly have presaged a significant widening of the scope of specific performance but it was unanimously reversed by the House of Lords. The House considered in particular that it would be wrong to order specific performance where the effect would be to compel the defendant to carry on business at a loss.

The principle of mutuality

Mutuality is often said to be a condition of specific performance. This statement really involves two assertions, which may be called positive and negative mutuality. The first is exemplified by the vendor of land who can obtain specific performance even though

---

230 *Stickney v Keeble* [1915] AC 386 at 419. A good illustration of the judicial exercise of discretion may be found in *Verrall v Great Yarmouth Borough Council* [1981] QB 202, [1980] 1 All ER 839.

231 *Duke of Bedford v British Museum Trustees* (1822) 2 My & K 552.

232 *Denne v Light* (1857) 8 De GM & G 774. Usually the hardship has been one that existed at the time of the contract but in *Patel v Ali* [1984] Ch 283, [1984] 1 All ER 978 Goulding J took into account a number of disasters which had overtaken the plaintiff after the contract had been made. It should be noted that the court was given assurances that money was available to meet the common law claim for damages. Cf *Roberts v O'Neill* [1983] IR 47.

233 Pp 277–280, above.   234 [1998] AC 1; [1997] 3 All ER 297.

damages would usually be an adequate remedy because the purchaser is entitled to specific performance and it is thought unfair to deny to the vendor what is granted to the purchaser. Negative mutuality involves denial of specific performance to a plaintiff because it would not be available to the defendant. Thus, an infant cannot maintain an action for specific performance, since it is not maintainable against him.[235] Again, if the defendant agrees to form a company for the purpose of working the plaintiff's patent, and the plaintiff agrees that he will devote the whole of his time to the interests of the company, there can be no specific performance at the instance of the plaintiff for, as we shall see,[236] he himself cannot be compelled to render personal services to another.[237]

It has been doubted whether mutuality amounts to a rule.[238] Certainly it is subject to several exceptions. If, for instance, the defendant has signed the memorandum required by section 40 of the Law of Property Act 1925,[239] in order to render a contract to sell land actionable against 'the party to be charged', it is specifically enforceable at the instance of the plaintiff, though he himself has signed nothing.[240] Again, a vendor who has agreed to sell a larger interest in land than in fact he is entitled to, cannot enforce the contract; but the purchaser can compel him to convey at a reduced price such interest as he has.[241] In *Price v Strange*[242] the Court of Appeal held that want of mutuality went not to the jurisdiction to order specific performance but to the exercise of discretion whether so to order and that questions of mutuality were to be considered as at the date of the trial rather than the date of the contract.

The remedy of injunction

Another way in which the performance of a contract *in specie* may be enforced is by the grant of an injunction. An injunction is either prohibitory or mandatory. So far as concerns the law of contract, a prohibitory injunction is granted only in the case of a negative promise. If, for instance, the defendant has broken his agreement not to ring the church bell at five o'clock each morning[243] or not to sell beer other than that brewed by the plaintiff,[244] the court will order him to refrain from doing what he has expressly promised not to do. This is equivalent to 'the specific performance by the court of that negative bargain which the parties have made'.[245]

---

[235] *Flight v Bolland* (1828) 4 Russ 298; *Lumley v Ravenscroft* [1895] 1 QB 683.

[236] P 801, below.

[237] *Stocker v Wedderburn* (1857) 3 K & J 393.

[238] Particularly in the United States. See Ames *Lectures on Legal History* p. 370; Cardozo *Growth of the Law* pp 14–16; Stone 16 Col L Rev 443; *Epstein v Gluckin* 233 NY 490 (1922). See also *O'Regan v White* [1919] 2 IR 392. Cf Fry *Specific Performance* (6th edn) pp 219–228.

[239] Pp 273–274, above.

[240] *Morgan v Holford* (1852) 1 Sm & G 101 at 116.   [241] *Horrocks v Rigby* (1878) 9 ChD 180.

[242] [1978] Ch 337, [1977] 3 All ER 371. See also *Sutton v Sutton* [1984] Ch 184, [1984] 1 All ER 168.

[243] *Martin v Nutkin* (1724) 2 p Wms 266.

[244] *Clegg v Hands* (1890) 44 Ch D 503.

[245] *Doherty v Allman* (1878) 3 App Cas 709 at 720, per Lord Cairns.

A mandatory injunction, on the other hand, is restorative in its effect, not merely preventive. It directs the defendant to take positive steps to undo what he has already done in breach of the contract. Thus he may be compelled to demolish or modify a building which he has erected[246] or to remove a road which he has constructed[247] if what he has done is not in accordance with the terms of the contract. It has been stressed by Buckley J, however, that such a drastic remedy must not be granted unless in the circumstances it will produce a fair result. The advantage that will accrue to the plaintiff must be balanced against the detriment likely to be suffered by the defendant.

> A plaintiff should not, of course, be deprived of relief to which he is justly entitled merely because it will be disadvantageous to the defendant. On the other hand he should not be permitted to insist on a form of relief which will confer no appreciable benefit on himself and will be materially detrimental to the defendant.[248]

In accordance with the general principle that equity does nothing in vain, there are two particular types of contract of which specific performance will not be granted. These are contracts for personal service, and those in which performance cannot be ensured without the constant superintendence of the court.

Since it is undesirable, and indeed in most cases impossible, to compel an unwilling party to maintain continuous personal relations with another, it is well established that a contract for personal services is not specifically enforceable at the suit of either party. Jessel MR said:

> The courts have never dreamt of enforcing agreements strictly personal in their nature, whether they are agreements of hiring and service, being the common relation of master and servant, or whether they are agreements for the purpose of pleasure, or for the purpose of scientific pursuits, or for the purpose of charity or philanthropy.[249]

This denial of relief has been extended to contracts of agency,[250] of partnership,[251] and of apprenticeship.[252] In all such cases the plaintiff must pursue his remedy at law.

---

[246] *Lord Manners v Johnson* (1875) 1 ChD 673; *Jackson v Normanby Brick Co* [1899] 1 Ch 438.

[247] *Charrington v Simons & Co Ltd* [1970] 2 All ER 257, [1970] 1 WLR 725.

[248] *Charrington v Simons & Co Ltd* [1970] 1 WLR 725 at 730.

[249] *Rigby v Connol* (1880) 14 ChD 482 at 487; *Francis v Municipal Councillors of Kuala Lumpur* [1962] 3 All ER 633, [1962] 1 WLR 1411. Distinguish *Vine v National Dock Labour Board* [1957] AC 488, [1956] 3 All ER 939, where the plaintiff obtained a declaration that his name had been wrongfully removed from the register of dockers. See Ganz 30 MLR 288. This rule has often been associated with the suggested rule that wrongful dismissal automatically terminates a contract of employment: See pp 695–696 above. See especially *Hill v C A Parsons & Co Ltd* [1972] Ch 305, [1971] 3 All ER 1345; Bridge 88 LQR 391; Hall [1972A] CLJ 47.

[250] *Chinnock v Sainsbury* (1860) 30 LJ Ch 409.

[251] *Scott v Rayment* (1868) LR 7 Eq 112.   [252] *Webb v England* (1860) 29 Beav 44.

The only possible relief other than damages that can be granted to the plaintiff in such a case is an injunction, ie an order which forbids the defendant to perform a like personal service for other persons. If for instance, as in *Lumley v Wagner*,[253] the defendant has agreed that she will sing at the plaintiff's theatre in London for three months from 1 April and will not sing elsewhere during that period, it is obvious that an injunction prohibiting a breach of the negative part of the agreement may tempt the defendant to fulfil the positive part. The question is whether the courts will coerce the defendant in this oblique manner. They are confronted with a dilemma, for they must not decree specific performance of a contract for personal services, and they must not encourage a deliberate breach of contract by refusing an injunction in a case which is normally subject to this form of relief.

Since the decision of Lord St Leonards in *Lumley v Wagner* it is well settled that the courts have jurisdiction to forbid the infringement of a negative stipulation, even though it is accessory to a positive covenant for the performance of personal services. The inability of the plaintiff to prove that he will suffer damage if the stipulation is broken is not a bar to the grant of an injunction.[254] Thus injunctions have been issued in the case of agreements not to sing elsewhere than at the plaintiff's theatre;[255] not, during the period of employment, to engage in any business similar to that carried on by the employer;[256] and not, during the period of employment, to act as a film artist for any motion picture company other than the employer's.[257]

Nevertheless the courts invariably refuse the issue of an injunction if it will inevitably result in the enforcement *in specie* of a contract not otherwise specifically enforceable.[258]

If, for instance, A agrees to give the whole of his time to the service of B and not to serve anybody else *in any capacity whatever*, an injunction will not be granted, for its inevitable result would be to compel A to work for B or otherwise to starve. It is one thing to tempt him to perform the contract, another to subject him to irresistible compulsion. As Lindley LJ said in a leading case:

> What injunction can he granted in this particular case which will not be, in substance and effect, a decree for specific performance of this agreement? It appears to me the difficulty of the plaintiffs is this, that they cannot suggest anything which, when examined, does not amount

---

[253] (1852) 1 De G M & G 604.

[254] *Marco Productions Ltd v Pagola* [1945] KB 111, [1945] 1 All ER 155.

[255] *Lumley v Wagner* (1852) 1 De G M & G 604.

[256] *William Robinson & Co Ltd v Heuer* [1898] 2 Ch 451.

[257] *Warner Bros Pictures Inc v Nelson* [1937] 1 KB 209, [1936] 3 All ER 160; *Marco Productions Ltd v Pagola* [1945] KB 111, [1946] 1 All ER 155; *Warren v Mendy* [1989] 3 All ER 103, [1989] 1 WLR 853; *Provident Financial Group plc v Hayward* [1989] 3 All ER 28 [1989] ICR 160.

[258] *Whitwood Chemical Co v Hardman* [1891] 2 Ch 416; *Ehrman v Bartholomew* [1898] 1 Ch 671. As to the limits of this proposition see *Lauritzencool AB v Lady Navigation Inc* [2005] 2 All ER (Comm) 183.

to this, that the man must either be idle, or specifically perform the agreement into which he has entered.[259]

On the other hand, if A agrees to serve B as a film actress, and not to act for another film company, an injunction will be granted forbidding her to break the negative stipulation. In this case she is not faced with the alternative of starvation or of service with B, since there are many other ways in which she may earn a living.[260]

The distinction which the judges have drawn in these cases borders upon sophistry, and suggests that, while bound to follow *Lumley v Wagner* when it forms a precise precedent, they are ready to adopt any possible argument to avoid it.[261] Thus they have insisted that in no circumstances will an injunction be granted unless the defendant has entered into an independent negative stipulation by which he expressly precludes himself from acting inconsistently with his positive contract.[262] There is no doubt, for instance, that an agreement by the defendant 'to give the whole of his time' to the plaintiff's business, which is positive in form, imports the negative stipulation that he will not give any of his time to others; but the courts have so far refused to say that 'because a person has agreed to do a particular thing, he is therefore to be restrained from doing everything else which is inconsistent with it'.[263]

It is often said that specific performance will not be decreed if constant supervision is required to ensure obedience by the defendant. However, this is probably no more than a statement of the way in which the court ought as a rule to exercise its discretion. There has been a significant change in the way in which discretion is exercised in this kind of case. In *Ryan v Mutual Tontine Westminster Chambers Association*:[264]

> The lessor of a flat in a block of buildings agreed that he would appoint a resident porter who should perform certain duties for the benefit of the tenants, such as the cleansing of the common passages and stairs, the delivery of letters and the acceptance of articles for safe custody. He appointed a porter who was by avocation a cook and who absented himself for several hours each day in order to act as *chef* at a neighbouring club. During his absence his duties were performed by various boys and charwomen not resident on the premises.

It was held that, though the lessor had committed a breach of contract, the only remedy was an action for damages.

---

[259] *Whitwood Chemical Co v Hardman* [1891] 2 Ch 416 at 427. An injunction was refused on this ground in *Page One Records Ltd v Britton* [1967] 3 All ER 822, [1968] 1 WLR 157. The court, however, has a discretion and may sever a covenant which, as it stands, is too wide: *Rely-a-Bell Burglar and Fire Alarm Co v Eisler* [1926] Ch 609.

[260] *Warner Bros Pictures Inc v Nelson* [1937] 1 KB 209, [1936] 3 All ER 160.

[261] See the remarks of Jessel MR in *Fothergill v Rowland* (1873) LR 17 Eq 132 at 140–141.

[262] *Mortimer v Beckett* [1920] 1 Ch 571.

[263] *Whitwood Chemical Co v Hardman* [1891] 2 Ch 416 at 426, per Lindley LJ.

[264] [1893] 1 Ch 116.

Very similar facts occurred in *Posner v Scott-Lewis*[265] where the plaintiffs were tenants in a block of residential flats in London of which the defendants were the landlords. One of the landlord's covenants in the leases was 'to employ (so far as in the lessor's power lies) a resident porter for the following purposes . . .' The defendant's affidavits alleged that they were not in breach of the covenants since they employed a non-resident porter who carried out all the duties which the resident porter was required by the covenant to do. Mervyn Davies J had little difficulty in dismissing this argument since it was a central part of the obligation to provide a resident porter that he would be present continuously. He also had no hesitation in awarding specific performance of the obligation. It was clear that damages would not be an adequate remedy since no sum of money would enable the tenants to go on the market and buy a resident porter. There was no sufficient difficulty in defining what had to be done that the defendant would be in any serious risk of committal for contempt because he did not understand his obligations. Furthermore, the balance of hardship between the parties lay heavily in favour of the plaintiffs since a block of flats without a resident porter was quite different from a block of flats with a resident porter.

Again the court will not as a rule enforce specific performance of a contract to erect or repair buildings, for not only is it unable to superintend the execution of the work, but also in most cases damages afford an adequate remedy. The one exception to this rule occurs where the defendant has purchased or taken a lease of land from the plaintiff and has agreed to erect a building upon it. In this case the plaintiff will succeed in an action for specific performance if the following conditions are satisfied.[266]

First, the particulars of the work must be so clearly specified that the court can ascertain without difficulty exactly what it is that requires performance.

Secondly, the interest of the plaintiff in the performance of the work must be of such a substantial nature that he will not be adequately compensated for breach of the contract by damages.[267]

Thirdly, the defendant must, under the contract, be in possession of the land on which the work is to be done.[268]

A plaintiff who failed in a suit in equity for specific performance was originally driven to sue for damages at common law, and it was not until 1858 that the power to award damages as an alternative form of relief was conferred upon the Court of Chancery. In that year Lord Cairns's Act[269] provided that in all cases in which the court had jurisdiction to grant an injunction or an order for specific performance it should be entitled to award damages to the party injured either in addition to or in substitu-

---

[265] [1987] Ch 25, [1986] 3 All ER 513.
[266] *Wolverhampton Corpn v Emmons* [1901] 1 KB 515.
[267] *Molyneux v Richard* [1906] 1 Ch 34 at 43–46.
[268] *Carpenters Estates Ltd v Davies* [1940] Ch 160, [1940] 1 All ER 13.
[269] 21 and 22 Vict c 27. Jolowicz [1975] CLJ 224; Pettit [1977] CLJ 369.

tion for such injunction or specific performance.[270] A plaintiff, therefore, could not claim damages under this Act unless he first proved that he was entitled to specific performance. The present Chancery Division, however, unlike its predecessor the Court of Chancery, is in better case, for the Judicature Act 1873[271] provided that the High Court of Justice and the Court of Appeal shall grant all such remedies whatsoever as the parties may appear to be entitled to in respect of any legal or equitable claim, so that, as far as possible, all matters in controversy may be finally determined. Nowadays, therefore, a plaintiff 'may come into court and say, "if you think I am not entitled to specific performance of the whole or any part of the agreement, then give me damages" '.[272]

Analogous to the specific performance of contracts is the specific delivery of goods. At common law the delivery or restitution of an article cannot be enforced. The remedy in tort for the wrongful withholding of a chattel is the recovery of damages, and the remedy against a vendor for non-delivery of the goods sold is an action for damages.

Equity, however, has long possessed jurisdiction to order the delivery of specific chattels whether the cause of complaint is a breach of contract or not, but it has never been prepared to grant this relief unless the article is of such exceptional value and importance that damages would clearly be an inadequate remedy.[273] Thus specific delivery has been ordered of the famous Pusey horn,[274] an ancient altar piece,[275] and a valuable painting.[276]

The common law rule, however, was modified by the Mercantile Law Amendment Act 1856, which provided that in actions for breach of contract to deliver specific goods the court at its discretion might make an order for the delivery of the goods without giving the defendant an option to pay damages.[277] This enactment has been repealed and replaced by the following section of the Sale of Goods Act 1979:[278]

> In any action for breach of contract to deliver specific or ascertained goods the court may, if it thinks fit ... direct that the contract shall be performed specifically, without giving the defendant the option of retaining the goods on payment of damages.

---

[270] The Act was repealed by the Statute Law Revision and Civil Procedure Act 1883, but its effect was preserved by a general section (s 5) in the repealing Act.

[271] Now the Judicature Act 1925, s 43.

[272] *Elmore v Pirrie* (1887) 57 LT 333, per Kay J; but there are still differences between the common law claim for damages and claims under Lord Cairns' Act. See *Oakacre Ltd v Claire Cleaners (Holdings) Ltd* [1982] Ch 197, [1981] 3 All ER 667.

[273] Story *Equity* s 709; White and Tudor *Leading Cases in Equity* vol II, pp 404–409.

[274] *Pusey v Pusey* (1684) 1 Vern 273.   [275] *Duke of Somerset v Cookson* (1735) 3 p Wms 390.

[276] *Lowther v Lowther* (1806) 13 Ves 95. In *Dougan v Ley* (1946) 71 CLR 142, the High Court of Australia, after concluding that this equitable principle applies to chattels of exceptional value in the business sense, ordered the specific performance of a contract to sell a vehicle which was already licensed as a taxi-cab. The exceptional value derived by the buyer from the contract and reflected in the price lay in the fact that the number of licences issued by the local authority was strictly limited.

[277] 19 and 20 Vict c 97, s 2.   [278] S 52.

The power given by this section is exercisable whether the property has passed to the buyer or not,[279] always provided that the goods are specific or ascertained.[280] It is, however, a discretionary power and will not be exercised if the chattel is an ordinary article of commerce of no special value or interest, such as a piano[281] or a set of ordinary chairs,[282] where damages will be adequate compensation for the plaintiff. The power given by section 52 is not an exhaustive statement of the law of specific performance in relation to sale of goods. The court retains an inherent jurisdiction to order specific performance of a contract for the sale of unascertained goods where damages would be an insufficient remedy.[283]

4 EXTINCTION OF REMEDIES

A right of action for breach of contract may be expressly released either by a release under seal or by accord and satisfaction, or it may be extinguished by the effluxion of time in accordance with the provisions of the Limitation Act 1980. The first two methods have already been described.[284]

The statutory time limits
The Limitation Act 1980 contains three provisions that impose a time limit within which an action for a breach of a contract must be brought.

i Action founded on simple contract
First, an action founded on simple contract or on tort shall not be brought after the expiration of six years from the date on which the cause of action accrued.[285]

The expression 'cause of action' means the factual situation stated by the plaintiff which, if substantiated, entitles him to a remedy against the defendant.[286] If, when

---

[279] *Jones v Tankerville* [1909] 2 Ch 440 at 445, per Parker J.

[280] 'Specific' means 'goods identified and agreed upon at the time a contract of sale is made'; Sale of Goods Act, s 62 (1). 'Ascertained' probably means 'identified in accordance with the agreement *after* the time a contract of sale is made': *Re Wait* [1927] 1 Ch 606 at 630, per Atkin LJ.

[281] *Whiteley v Hilt* [1918] 2 KB 808 at 819.

[282] *Cohen v Roche* [1927] 1 KB 169. The chattels dismissed by the learned judge McCardie J as 'ordinary articles of commerce of no special value or interest' were in fact eight genuine Hepplewhite chairs which had been sold to the plaintiff in 1925 for £60. Berryman [1984] Conv 130. As to specific performance of contracts for the sale of ships see *CN Marine Inc v Stena Lime AB* [1982] 2 Lloyd's Rep 336 and *Eximenco Handels AG v Partrederiet Oro Chief* [1983] 2 Lloyd's Rep 509.

[283] *Sky Petroleum Ltd v VIP Petroleum Ltd* [1974] 1 All ER 954, [1974] 1 WLR 576; Treitel [1966] JBL 211.

[284] Pp 709–713, above.

[285] S 5. The basic period is three years if damages are claimed for personal injuries caused by negligence, nuisance or breach of duty, whether the duty arises contractually or not: s 11. By s 33, this period may be extended. s 6 prescribes a special accrual date for certain loans of an indefinite duration.

[286] *Letang v Cooper* [1965] 1 QB 232, [1964] 2 All ER 929.

analysed, it discloses a breach of contract, it accrues when that breach occurs, from which moment time begins to run against the plaintiff. The fact that actual damage is not suffered by him until some date later than the breach does not extend the time within which he must sue. If, on the other hand, the factual situation discloses the commission of the tort of negligence, which is not actionable unless actual damage is proved, the cause of action does not accrue until the damage is in fact sustained. When, therefore, the defendant has acted negligently in the performance of a contract, the plaintiff may be able to formulate a claim both in contract and in tort and to take advantage of the fact that the limitation period starts to run at a later date in tort. This was applied by Oliver J in *Midland Bank Trust Co Ltd v Hett, Stubbs and Kemp*,[287] the facts of which have already been discussed.[288] In this case Oliver J also held that the defendant had committed a continuing series of breaches of contract, which had the effect of extending the contract period as well.[289] In a similar way it has been held that if a defendant has by one clause of a contract agreed to indemnify the plaintiff against the consequences of breaches of other terms, the limitation period for the indemnity will not start until those consequences have been suffered.[290]

The principle that the limitation period starts when the plaintiff can bring a cause of action has given rise to many difficulties where the plaintiff does not know (and indeed often could not possibly know) at that moment that he has a cause of action. This problem first came to prominence in 1963 in *Carttledge v E Jopling & Sons Ltd*[291] where the House of Lords held that the plaintiff's course of action in relation to negligently caused pneumoconiosis started to run from the time when he had the disease even though at that stage it was not detectable by existing medical knowledge. The result was that the plaintiff's cause of action was barred by limitation before he could have discovered its existence. In relation to personal injuries this particular problem has been addressed by statute but the general problem has continued and was revealed again in relation to professional negligence giving rise to defective construction work in *Pirelli General Cable Works Ltd v Oscar Faber & Partners*.[292] The problem has now been addressed by the Latent Damage Act 1986 which introduces a subsidiary limitation period under which where the cause of action was not discoverable at the time it arose the plaintiff may sue within three years from the date of which it could have been discovered. This is done by inserting a new section 14A into

---

287 [1979] Ch 384, [1978] 3 All ER 571; not following *Bagot & Stevens Scanlan & Co Ltd* [1966] 1 QB 197, [1964] 3 All ER 577. See also *UBAF Ltd v European American Banking Corpn* [1984] QB 713, [1984] 2 All ER 226. When a plaintiff has suffered damage for the purpose of a tort action is often a difficult question, see, for example, *Dew Moore & Co Ltd v Ferrier* [1988] 1 All ER 400, [1988] 1 WLR 267.

288 P 345, above. This reasoning was expressly approved by the House of Lords in *Henderson v Merrett* [1994] 3 All ER 506 [1994] 3 WLR 761.

289 On continuing duties, see also *Scally v Southern Health and Social Services Board* [1992] 1 AC 294, [1991] 4 All ER 563.

290 *R & H Green & Silley Weir Ltd v British Railways Board* [1985] 1 All ER 237; *Telfair Shipping Corpn v Inersea Carriers SA* [1985] 1 All ER 243.

291 [1963] AC 758, [1963] 1 All ER 341.   292 [1983] 2 AC 1, [1983] 1 All ER 65.

the Limitation Act 1980. This refers to 'any action for damages for negligence where facts relevant to the cause of action were not known at the date of the accrual of the cause of action.' Unfortunately, it appears that this section does not apply where the plaintiff is suing in contract alleging that the defendant has been in breach of the contractual obligation to act with reasonable care.[293]

ii Action upon a specialty
Secondly, an action upon a contract under seal cannot be brought after the expiration of twelve years after the date on which the cause of action accrued.[294]

iii Action for an account
Thirdly, an action for an account shall not be brought after the expiration of any time limit which is applicable to the claim which is the basis of the duty to account.[295]

Effect of defendant's fraud
As a general rule the fact that the plaintiff fails to discover the existence of his cause of action until the expiration of the statutory period does not prevent the operation of the statute. This rule, however, works a hardship where his ignorance has been caused by the fraud of the defendant. The plaintiff may be the victim of fraud in two respects. First, his action may be based upon the fraud of the defendant. In these circumstances an action of deceit is available to him, but he may remain ignorant of the fact until time has run against him.[296]

Secondly, his cause of action, whatever its nature, may have been fraudulently concealed by the defendant, as for example, by the deliberate destruction of evidence. Common law and equity took different views on these situations.

In both cases equity took the view that time did not begin to run against the plaintiff until he had discovered or ought to have discovered the fraud. At common law, on the other hand, the defendant's fraud did not prevent time from running. After the Judicature Act 1873, the equitable doctrine prevailed when the cause of action had been fraudulently concealed, but it remained doubtful whether it applied to a common law action of deceit when the plaintiff was ignorant of the deceit.[297]

A similar difficulty existed prior to the statute in the case of money paid or property transferred under a mistake of fact. If the plaintiff claimed purely equitable relief, as for example where a trustee claimed the repayment of money mistakenly paid to a *cestui que trust*, time did not begin to run against the plaintiff until he had discovered or ought to have discovered the mistake,[298] but in an action at common law time began to run from the date of payment or transfer.[299]

---

[293] *Iron Trade Mutual Insurance Co Ltd v J K Buckenham Ltd* [1990] 1 All ER 808.
[294] S 8 (1). The period was formerly 20 years. *Aiken v Stewart Wrightson* [1995] 3 All ER 449.
[295] S 23.   [296] *Beaman v ARTS Ltd* [1949] 1 KB 550 at 558, [1949] 1 All ER 465.
[297] Preston and Newsom *Limitation of Actions* (2nd edn) pp 228–229.
[298] *Brooksbank v Smith* (1836) 2 Y & C (Ex) 58.   [299] *Baker v Courage & Co* [1910] 1 KB 56.

The 1939 Act, however, removed these difficulties and simplified the law by extending the equitable principles to all actions to which the statutory periods apply. Section 32 of the Limitation Act 1980 provides as follows:

(1) Subject to subsection (3) below, where in the case of any action for which a period of limitation is prescribed by this Act, either—

    (a) the action is based upon the fraud of the defendant; or

    (b) any fact relevant to the plaintiff's right of action has been deliberately concealed from him by the defendant; or

    (c) the action is for relief from the consequences of a mistake;

    the period of limitation shall not begin to run until the plaintiff has discovered the fraud, concealment or mistake (as the case may be) or could with reasonable diligence have discovered it.

(2) For the purposes of subsection (1) above, deliberate commission of a breach of duty in circumstances in which it is unlikely to be discovered for some time amounts to deliberate concealment of the facts involved in that breach of duty.

(3) Nothing in this section shall enable any action—

    (a) to recover, or recover the value of, any property; or

    (b) to enforce any charge against, or set aside any transaction affecting, any property;

    to be brought against the purchaser of the property or any person claiming through him in any case where the property has been purchased for valuable consideration by an innocent third party since the fraud or concealment or (as the case may be) the transaction in which the mistake was made took place.

(4) A purchaser is an innocent third party for the purposes of this section—

    (a) in the case of fraud or concealment of any fact relevant to the plaintiff's right of action, if he was not a party to the fraud or (as the case may be) to the concealment of that fact and did not at the time of the purchase know or have reason to believe that the fraud or concealment had taken place; and

    (b) in the case of mistake, if he did not at the time of the purchase know or have reason to believe that the mistake had been made.

Although this section involves some changes in terminology from its predecessors[300] and makes clear some things which litigation had revealed to be unclear,[301] its effect is substantially unchanged.

The operation of this section is well illustrated by *Applegate v Moss.*[302]

---

[300] Particularly the disappearance of 'concealed fraud'.

[301] See eg *Eddis v Chichester Constable* [1969] 2 Ch 345, [1969] 2 All ER 912.

[302] [1971] 1 QB 406, [1971] 1 All ER 747. See also *King v Victor Parsons & Co* [1973] 1 All ER 206, [1973] 1 WLR 29.

By a contract made in February 1957, the defendant agreed to build two houses for the plaintiffs and to support them on a raft foundation reinforced with a steel network of a specified type. He employed a Mr Piper, an independent contractor, to do the work. The plaintiffs went into occupation of the houses when they were completed towards the end of 1957. In 1965, it was observed that, owing to the defective manner in which the foundations had been constructed, the houses were irreparable and unsafe for habitation. There was no raft, the reinforcement was grossly inferior to that specified and wide cracks had appeared beneath the houses.

The plaintiffs claimed damages for breach of contract. Despite the fact that their action was brought more than six years after the breach of contract they succeeded on the ground that there had been concealment within the meaning of section 26 of the Limitation Act 1939. 'The builder put in rubbishy foundations and then covered them up.'[303]

The meaning of 'reasonable diligence' was considered by Webster J in *Peco Arts Inc v Hazlitt Gallery Ltd*,[304] where he held that it meant 'the doing of that which an ordinarily prudent [purchaser] would do having regard to all the circumstances, including the circumstances of the purchase'.

In *Sheldon v RHM Outhwaite*,[305] the House of Lords reversed by a majority of 3 to 2 a decision of the Court of Appeal by 2 to 1, which itself allowed an appeal from the original decision of Saville J. This impressive display of judicial disharmony was caused by attempts to construe s.32(1)(b) of the Limitation Action 1980. The one thing on which all were universally agreed was that this provision was badly drafted and obscure and that all of its possible meanings were odd.

The problem was what the position was where the deliberate concealment from the plaintiff did not start until after the limitation period had begun to run. Two views were canvassed. One was that if the concealment took place after the time it started, it had no effect. This was the view of the majority of the Court of Appeal and the minority of the House of Lords. The other view was that, in the event of concealment, time did not start to run until the discovery by the plaintiff of the cause of action. Of course, the result of this would in an extreme case be that if there were concealment in the last few days of the first six year limitation period, there would then be a second six year limitation period running from discovery. Of course, this result seems absurd. On the face of it, the sensible rule would be for the limitation period to stop on the date of concealment but to start again when the truth is discovered by the plaintiff so that the periods before and after the concealment could be added together. No-one, however, thought that this construction was possible on the wording of the section.

In *Cave v Robinson Jarvis & Rolf*[306] the House of Lords held that a solicitor who had

---

[303] Ibid at 413 and 750, respectively, per Lord Denning MR.
[304] [1983] 3 All ER 193, [1983] 1 WLR 1315.   [305] [1995] 2 All ER 558.
[306] [2002] UKHL 18 [2002] 2 All ER 641. Cf *Williams v Fanshaw Porter & Hazlehurst* [2004] EWCA Civ 157 [2004] 2 All ER 616.

made an allegedly careless mistake of which he was unaware could not be said to have concealed it.

Extension of time in case of disability

Special provisions are made to meet the case of a plaintiff who is an infant or of unsound mind at the time when his cause of action accrues. Such a person may sue despite the disability, but is not prejudiced if he fails to do so, for it is enacted that the action may be brought at any time within six years from the removal of the disability or from his death, whichever event first occurs, notwithstanding that the period of limitation from the accrual of the cause of action has expired.[307]

It must be observed that there is no extension of time unless the disability exists when the cause of action accrues. When time has once begun to run it is not stopped by the subsequent occurrence of some disability, as for example where the plaintiff becomes insane soon after the accrual of the cause of action.[308] Again, if a person under a disability is succeeded by another person in like case there is no further extension of time by reason of the disability of the second person.[309]

Where the same person is affected by successive disabilities, as for example where a plaintiff who is an infant at the accrual of the cause of action later becomes insane, the question whether there is a further extension of time depends upon whether there is an interval between the disabilities. Successive disabilities, unless they are separated by an interval, exclude the operation of the statute. If, for instance, the plaintiff is an infant when his cause of action accrues but becomes insane before he reaches his majority, time does not begin to run until the insanity is determined; but if he is sane at eighteen time begins to run against him and is not stopped by his later insanity, however soon this may occur.[310]

There was one case prior to 1940 in which the disability of the defendant prevented time from running, namely, where at the time of the accrual of the cause of action he was beyond the seas. In this case a statute of Anne provided that time should not begin to run in his favour until he returned from beyond the seas.[311] This statute has now, however, been repealed.[312]

Effect of acknowledgement or part payment

In the particular case of a claim to a debt or other liquidated sum, it has long been recognised that time which has started to run against the creditor may be stopped and made to start afresh by an acknowledgment of liability, or by a part payment made by

---

[307] Ss 22 and 31 (2). In this context a person of unsound mind means a person who, by reason of mental disorder within the meaning of the Mental Health Act 1959, is incapable of managing and administering his affairs: *Kirby v Leather* [1965] 2 QB 367, [1965] 2 All ER 441. The Criminal Justice Act 1948 removed as from 18 April 1949, the former disability of a convict sentenced to death or to penal servitude. As to the effect of dilatory conduct of an action started on behalf of a person under disability, see *Tolley v Morris* [1979] 2 All ER 561, [1979] 1 WLR 592.
[308] S 28(1).   [309] S 28(2).   [310] *Borrows v Ellison* (1871) LR 6 Exch 128.
[311] 4 & 5 Anne c 3, s 19.   [312] Limitation Act 1939, Sch.

the debtor. This was so even though the acknowledgment or payment was not given until after the expiration of the full statutory period. But this particular possibility is now excluded by the Limitation Act 1980.[313] The law on the matter, however, was far from uniform before 1940. There were express statutory provisions that determined the effect of an acknowledgment in the case of actions relating to land, but the only enactment that concerned contracts was the Civil Procedure Act 1833,[314] which applied to specialty debts alone. It provided that if a written acknowledgment was signed by the party liable upon a contract under seal or by his agent, the creditor could sustain an action at any time within the next twenty years. There was no direct statutory provision that an acknowledgment of a simple contract debt should be effective, but a doctrine on the matter was gradually evolved by the courts. This judge-made rule was that any acknowledgment which amounted to an express or to an implied promise to pay took the case out of the statute and made time begin afresh. The existence of this doctrine, once it had been judicially established, was recognised by two statutes, one of which required that the acknowledgment should be in writing and signed by the person chargeable,[315] while the other made the signature of his agent sufficient.[316] There was frequently, however, the greatest difficulty in deciding whether a particular acknowledgment amounted to a promise to pay, for if it failed to satisfy this test it was totally ineffective.[317] There is no necessity any longer to discuss the somewhat subtle distinctions that formerly obscured the subject, for simple contract debts have now been put upon the same footing as specialty debts. The Act of 1980 provides as follows:

> Where any right of action has accrued to recover any debt or other liquidated pecuniary claim . . . and the person liable or accountable therefore acknowledges the claim or makes any payment in respect thereof, the right shall be deemed to have accrued on and not before the date of the acknowledgment or the last payment.[318]

Such an acknowledgment does not create a new cause of action.

> The subsection does not change the nature of the right; it provides that in the specific circumstances of an acknowledgment or payment the right shall be given a notional birthday and on that day, like the phoenix of fable, it rises again in renewed youth—and also like the phoenix it is still itself.[319]

The acknowledgment must be in writing and must be signed by the person making it.[320] It must admit legal liability to pay the sum claimed by the creditor. So a statement by the debtor that he only owes a smaller sum, because for example, he has a

---

[313] S 29 (7).   [314] S 5.

[315] Statute of Frauds Amendment Act 1828 (Lord Tenterden's Act), s 1.

[316] Mercantile Law Amendment Act 1856, s 13.

[317] See eg *Spencer v Hemmerde* [1922] 2 AC 507.   [318] S 29 (5).

[319] *Busch v Stevens* [1963] 1 QB 1 at 6, [1962] 1 All ER 413 at 415, per Lawton J.   [320] S 30(1).

set-off, is only an acknowledgment as to that smaller sum.[321] Similarly a later payment by the debtor of that sum would not be a part payment.[322] An acknowledgment or a payment may be made by the agent of the person liable, and it must be made to the person, or to the agent of the person, who is the claimant of the debt.[323] The Privy Council has suggested that an acknowledgment is not effective unless it is an admission of a present debt subsisting at the date of signature and that it is not enough to admit that the debt existed in the past. On this basis, the entry of a debt in the annual balance sheet of a company does not operate as an acknowledgment, since it is usually completed some considerable time before it is signed at the annual general meeting.[324] More recently however this suggestion was rejected by Brightman J in *Re Gee & Co (Woolwich) Ltd*.[325] Provided that the present existence of the debt is admitted, the precise amount of what is due need not be stated. It is sufficient if this is ascertainable by extrinsic evidence.[326]

The effect of an acknowledgment or a part payment by one of a number of persons liable for a liquidated debt is determined by the statute. An acknowledgment binds the person acknowledging and his successors only,[327] not his co-debtors; but a part payment binds all the co-debtors.[328]

An acknowledgment is not effective unless it relates to a debt or other liquidated sum.[329] Thus if A is entitled to recover unliquidated damages for breach of a contract by B, an acknowledgment by B of his liability does not revive the cause of action.[330]

If the statutory period expires before action is brought, the plaintiff's *right* is not extinguished. He is merely deprived of his two remedies of action and set-off. The statute is procedural not substantive.[331] A statute-barred debt is still payable despite the fact that its payment cannot be enforced by action, and if there is any other method by which the creditor can obtain satisfaction it is at his disposal. Thus if a debtor pays money on account of debts, some of which are statute-barred and some not, and does not expressly indicate that the payment is made in respect of those which are still actionable, the creditor may appropriate the money to those that are statute-barred.[332] Again if a party is entitled to a lien on goods for a general balance,

---

[321] *Surrendra Overseas Ltd v Government of Sri Lanka* [1977] 2 All ER 481, [1977] 1 WLR 565.
[322] Ibid.
[323] S 30 (2).   [324] *Consolidated Agencies Ltd v Bertram Ltd* [1965] AC 470, [1964] 3 All ER 282.
[325] [1975] Ch 52, [1974] 1 All ER 1149. But only if the creditor can show that he has received copies of the balance sheet. *Re Compania de Electricdad de la Provincia de Buenos Aires* [1980] Ch 146, [1978] 3 All ER 668, see also *Re Overmark Smith Warden Ltd* [1982] 3 All ER 513, [182] 1 WLR 1195.
[326] *Dungate v Dungate* [1965] 3 All ER 818, [1965] 1 WLR 1477, explaining *Good v Parry* [1963] 2 QB 418, [1963] 2 All ER 59.
[327] S 31 (6).   [328] S 31 (7).   [329] *Whitehead v Howard* (1820) 2 Brod & Bing 372.
[330] *Boydell v Drummond* (1808) 2 Camp 157 at 162.
[331] *Rodriguez v Parker* [1967] 1 QB 116, [1966] 2 All ER 349.
[332] Law Revision Committee, 5th Interim Report, p 32; *Mills v Fowkes* (1839) 5 Bing NC 455.

and he gets possession of the goods of his debtor, he may hold them until his whole demand is satisfied notwithstanding that it is barred by the Limitation Act.[333]

Effect of lapse of time on equitable claims;

It is expressly enacted that the statutory provisions shall not apply to any claim for specific performance of a contract or for an injunction or for other equitable relief.[334] The object of this section is to preserve those principles applicable to claims for relief that, prior to the Judicature Act 1873, could be entertained only by courts of equity. The attitude of equity with regard to Statutes of Limitation and to a failure to pursue a remedy with expedition may, so far as contracts are concerned, be summarised in two propositions.

First, in the case of equitable claims that formerly fell within its concurrent jurisdiction, equity acts on the analogy of the current Limitation Act. In the words of Lord Westbury:

> Where the remedy in equity is correspondent to the remedy at law, and the latter is subject to a limit in point of time by the Statute of Limitations, a court of equity acts by analogy to the statute, and imposes on the remedy it affords the same limitation. This is the meaning of the common phrase that a court of equity acts by analogy to the Statute of Limitations, the meaning being that, where the suit in equity corresponds with an action at law which is included in the words of the statute, a court of equity adopts the enactment of the statute as its own rule of procedure.[335]

Hence the Limitation Act 1980, after enacting that its provisions shall not apply to a claim for equitable relief, says 'except in so far as any provision thereof may be applied by the court by analogy . . .'.[336] Any proceedings in equity to recover a simple contract debt are subject to this doctrine of analogy. Thus an action brought in the Chancery Division by one *cestui que trust* against another *cestui que trust* to recover money paid by the trustee to the latter under a mistake of fact is in the nature of a common law action for money had and received, and, by analogy to the Limitation Act, the claim will be barred after the lapse of six years.[337]

The second proposition is that in the exercise of its exclusive jurisdiction—in the case of purely equitable claims—equity, in accordance with the maxim *vigilantibus et non dormientibus lex succurrit,* refuses to grant relief to stale claims. A plaintiff who has been dilatory in the prosecution of his equitable claim and has acquiesced in the wrong done to him is said to be guilty of *laches* and is barred from relief, although his claim is not affected by any statute of limitation.

No exact rule can be laid down as to when laches will or will not bar a claim. It is a question that depends in each case upon the degree of diligence that might reasonably

---

[333] *Spears v Hartly* (1800) 3 Esp 81.
[334] S 36 (1).   [335] *Knox v Gye* (1872) LR 5 HL 656 at 674.   [336] S 36 (1).
[337] *Re Robinson, McLaren v Public Trustee* [1911] 1 Ch 502.

have been expected from the plaintiff, but the two important factors to be considered are acquiescence on the part of the plaintiff and the length of the delay.

> The doctrine of laches in courts of equity is not an arbitrary or a technical doctrine. Where it would be *practically unjust* to give a remedy, either because the party has by his conduct done that which might fairly be regarded as an equivalent to a waiver of it, or where by his conduct and neglect he has, though perhaps not waiving that remedy, put the other party in a situation in which it would not be reasonable to place him if the remedy were afterwards to be asserted, in either of these cases lapse of time and delay are most material.[338]

In the case of contracts the doctrine is well illustrated by an action for specific performance or for the rescission of a contract on the ground of misrepresentation. Those who seek specific performance of contracts must be unusually vigilant and active in asserting their rights, especially where the subject matter of the contract is one that fluctuates in value from day to day. Thus, in the leading case of *Pollard v Clayton*:[339]

> The defendants agreed to raise and sell at a fixed price per ton to the plaintiffs all the coal contained in a particular mine. After performing this contract in part the defendants refused to deliver any more coal, but instead sold it to other persons, and when objection was taken to their default they referred the plaintiffs to their solicitors. The plaintiffs waited for eleven months after this before filing a bill for specific performance.

It was held that the delay which occurred after the plaintiffs had become aware of the breach of contract was a complete bar to their equitable claim.

The effect of lapse of time upon the right to sue for rescission of a contract has already been considered.[340]

This doctrine of laches is preserved by the Limitation Act 1980, in a section which provides that:

> Nothing in this Act shall affect any equitable jurisdiction to refuse relief on the ground of acquiescence or otherwise.[341]

---

[338] *Lindsay Petroleum Co v Hurd* (1874) LR 5 PC 221 at 239, per Lord Selborne. See also *Shaw v Applegate* [1978] 1 All ER 123, [1977] 1 WLR 970.

[339] (1855) 1 K & J 462.   [340] P 357, above.   [341] S 36 (2).

INDEX